SIXTH EDITION

ORGANIZATIONAL BEHAVIOR

CONCEPTS, CONTROVERSIES, AND APPLICATIONS

STEPHEN P. ROBBINS

San Diego State University

PRENTICE HALL INTERNATIONAL, INC.

Printed in the United States of America
10 9 8 7 6 5 4 3 2 1

ISBN 0-13-639048-X

Prentice-Hall International (UK) Limited, *London*
Prentice-Hall of Australia Pty. Limited, *Sydney*
Prentice-Hall Canada Inc., *Toronto*
Prentice-Hall Hispanoamericana, S.A., *Mexico*
Prentice-Hall of India Private Limited, *New Delhi*
Prentice-Hall of Japan, Inc., *Tokyo*
Simon &Sdhuster Asia Pte. Ltd., *Singapore*
Editora Prentice-Hall do Brasil, Ltda., *Rio de Janeiro*
Prentice Hall Englewood Cliffs, New Jersey

To Joyce Rothschild,
for bringing a macro perspective
to my micro world

THE NEW YORK TIMES / PRENTICE HALL CONTEMPORARY VIEW PROGRAM

THE NEW YORK TIMES and PRENTICE HALL are sponsoring A CONTEMPORARY VIEW: a program designed to enhance student access to current information of relevance in the classroom.

Through this program, the core subject matter provided in the text is supplemented by a collection of time-sensitive articles from one of the world's most distinguished newspapers, THE NEW YORK TIMES. These articles demonstrate the vital, ongoing connection between what is learned in the classroom and what is happening in the world around us.

To enjoy the wealth of information of THE NEW YORK TIMES daily, a reduced subscription rate is available in deliverable areas. For information, call toll-free: 1–800–631–1222.

PRENTICE HALL and THE NEW YORK TIMES are proud to co-sponsor A CONTEMPORARY VIEW. We hope it will make the reading of both textbooks and newspapers a more dynamic, involving process.

OVERVIEW

CONTENTS

PART III   THE GROUP

9   *Foundations of Group Behavior   283*

PART IV   THE ORGANIZATION SYSTEM

14 *Foundations of Organization Structure* *485*

15   *Organization Design   513*

16   *Human Resources Policies and Practices   559*

PART V   ORGANIZATIONAL DYNAMICS

TO THE STUDENT

When the first edition of this text came to life in the late 1970s, I was determined to write a book that would help students understand the behavior of people at work and make the learning process enjoyable. Maybe I was a bit naive in thinking I could create a textbook as lively and riveting as a good novel. Well, I have to admit that this book hasn't replaced Stephen King or Tom Clancy on very many people's leisure-time reading lists, but five editions and more than a quarter of a million copies later, I have received a sizable number of unsolicited letters from "satisfied customers" telling me how much they enjoyed it and commenting on the relevance of its contents.

In the following pages, I'll tell you a bit about the book and why I think you'll find it interesting and relevant. Let me begin by explaining why this book's 19 chapters are organized the way they are.

ORGANIZATION OF THE TEXT

If a textbook is to be an effective learning device, it has to be more than merely fifteen or twenty topics, each called a "chapter," randomly shuffled together. It needs integration. It must provide some logical framework that can guide readers through its maze of topics.

I was particularly sensitive to this need for integration when I began planning the first edition. What I came up with at that time was a building block model of OB. This model describes OB as focusing on three levels—the individual, the group, and the organization system—with each level adding increased complexity. This model has stood the test of time. It has proven to be an effective structure for overviewing the field of organizational behavior and for helping students to integrate concepts. In Chapter 2, the building block model is introduced, as well as the key topics that make up OB and the interrelationships between them. This model, then, becomes the framework upon which the rest of the text is built. Specifically, Parts II, III, and IV focus on the individual, the group, and the organization system, respectively.

KEEPING YOUR INTEREST

OB is a serious and intellectually rigorous discipline. That, however, should not preclude a textbook on the subject from being interesting. What have I done in this book to help sustain your interest? Two things! First, I have worked very hard to create a lively writing style. Second, I've made sure that I've included a healthy dose of provocative topics and issues.

Writing Style

You can almost take for granted today that any textbook will be well-written. By that I mean that explanations will be clear, concise, and logical. But I don't think that's enough. I wanted this book to be more. So I concentrated on developing detailed and focused explanations, using lots of examples, and creating a conversational writing style.

In order to cover a large number of concepts, many textbook authors end up creating cursory "laundry lists." Their books are more like 700-page outlines. You'll find that I take the time to carefully explain every concept so that it can be readily grasped. Ideas are developed, explained, and linked. The result is that this text teaches rather than outlines.

The best content, of course, means little if a book can't hold your attention. Years ago I decided to mold my writing style to the way people talk. I use contractions. I ask questions, which I then answer. And I use other techniques to create an informal, lively style. Some of my friends tell me that when they read my books, they hear me talking. I take that a compliment since that's my goal.

Provocative Issues

The second thing that I've done to make this book interesting is to emphasize stimulating and thought-provoking ideas.

One of the best things about OB is that there is no shortage of provocative issues. Let me give you a sampling. The following statements, each of which is discussed in this book, are essentially true, although they run counter to what many people intuitively think:

Happier workers are not necessarily more productive workers.

Voluntary employee turnover is often functional for an organization.

Interviews are generally poor selection devices.

Organizations engage in brainwashing-like practices to shape new hires into good employees.

The "average" employee rates his or her performance at about the seventy-fifth percentile.

Much of what is often described as poor communication in organizations is purposeful.

Bureaucracy is the best structural form for many organizations.

A strong corporate culture can be a significant liability for an organization.

Money doesn't motivate most employees today.

Conflict can enhance group performance.

I think you'll find that this book offers enough surprises and provocative ideas to stimulate your continued interest in reading further.

MAKING OB RELEVANT

As a group, today's students are increasingly seeking relevance in their course work. You want realism, applications, and useful knowledge. I've sought to make the concepts in this book relevant by means of several features.

First, there are lots of examples. Wherever possible, I use examples to illustrate concepts. Some of these come from the corporate world—IBM, General Motors, Walt Disney, Sony, and the like. But I've also found that, since we've all shared the college experience, the classroom and campus often offer excellent illustrations of concepts with which we can readily identify.

Second, I've updated this books' content to address current issues. In North America, for instance, managers are finding themselves overseeing an increasingly diverse work force. These same managers are also facing a coming labor shortage. And, of course, all employees are having to cope with an increasing number of ethical issues on their jobs. These are examples of important issues of the 1990s, and I address a number of them here. On a more macro level, you'd have had to have been in a cave for the past couple of years to have missed the globalization trend in business. The global economy is effectively breaking down traditional national boundaries. Chapter 3 introduces the idea of viewing OB in a global context. Each of the following chapters then reinforces this viewpoint by applying OB concepts in diverse cultural settings.

Third, each chapter ends with a case incident and two exercises that give you an opportunity to apply the knowledge you've gained from that chapter. About half of the exercises are of the self-assessment variety. You'll get the chance, for instance, to test how flexible you are in adjusting your leadership style, to learn what motivates you, to determine how power-oriented you are, and to find out how well you adapt to change. The other half of the exercises are group-oriented and allow you to experience with some of your classmates a number of OB concepts firsthand.

ACKNOWLEDGMENTS

Textbooks are a team project. While my name is on the cover of this book, literally hundreds of people have contributed to this text and its previous editions.

A number of colleagues have been kind enough to review the previous edition, make suggestions for improvement, and review all or parts of this revision. This book is a whole lot better because of insights and suggestions provided by:

Dominic A. Aquila, Rochester Institute of Technology

Jesse W. Bakor, Husson College

Frank J. Barrett, Naval Postgraduate School

John H. Boyd, Baylor University

Ellis G. Buchanan, University of Texas at San Antonio

Vernon E. Buck, University of Washington

Robert Callahan, Seattle University

Donald E. Conlon, University of Delaware

Edward J. Conlon, University of Iowa

John A. Dopp, San Francisco State University

Dennis Duchon, University of Texas at San Antonio

Nancy Eushe, University of California at Berkeley

Richard H. Fabris, Jersey City State College

Alexander Farkash, Canisius College

William E. Fulmer, Clarion University of Pennsylvania

Terry Gaston, Southern Oregon State College

Cherlyn Granrose, Temple University

Peggy Heath, University of Washington

I.E. Jernigan, University of North Carolina at Charlotte

Bruce H. Johnson, Gustavus Adolphus College

Kathleen Kane, University of San Francisco

Edward J. Kelleher, San Jose State University

Mary C. Kernan, University of Delaware

John P. Lazarus, University of San Francisco

Rodney G. Lim, Tulane University

Morton Litwack, California State University at Hayward

Sharon A. Lobel, Seattle University

Michael B. London, University of Bridgeport

Mark Mallinger, Pepperdine University at Malibu

Stephen H. Miller, California State University at Hayward

Kathleen L. Mosier, University of California at Berkeley

Marvin M. Okones, University of San Francisco

Christine Pearson, University of Southern California

Trond Peterson, University of California at Berkeley

Soo Hoon Phan, University of Washington

Peter P. Poole, Lehigh University

Paul Preston, University of Texas

Mark Seabright, Santa Clara University

James Shaw, University of San Francisco

Janice Stringer, Bradley University

Greg Uhlig, University of Texas at Austin

Kathleen M. Utecht, Central Michigan University

John W. Wells, Seattle University

Charles K. Woodruff, Winthrop College

My students have also been a rich source of ideas over the years. Many have been quick to tell me which concepts they found difficult to understand or thought needed better examples. This revision includes dozens of their ideas. As with the comments made by colleagues, this is certainly a better book because of the feedback my students have provided me.

I extend special thanks to my colleague at San Diego State University, Mark Butler. Mark has done another superb job in writing the Annotated Instructor's Edition of this book and has been a valuable source of feedback as the revision progressed. As in the past, I also want to thank Dean Allan Bailey and department chairs Penny Wright and F. Neil Brady for providing the supportive climate that allows me to effectively blend my writing activities and my teaching responsibilities.

Regardless of how good the manuscript is that I turn in, it's only a tall pile of paper until my friends at Prentice Hall swing into action. Then P-H's crack team of editors, production personnel, designers, marketing specialists, and sales representatives turn that pile of paper into a bound textbook and see to it that it gets into faculty and students' hands. My thanks on this project go to Alison Reeves, Garret White, Sandy Steiner, Diane Pierano,

Frank Lyman, Belen Poltorak, Carolyn Del Corso, John Nestor, Suzanne Behnke, Shari Toron, Meg Van Arsdale, and Jeff Grossman.

Finally, I want to acknowledge my gratitude to the hundreds of members of the Organizational Behavior Teaching Society who share their thoughtful and creative teaching ideas at the Society's annual conference and through publication in the *Organizational Behavior Teaching Review*. The people in this group demonstrate amazing commitment to their teaching. Additionally, they are not afraid to experiment, to take risks, and to share both their classroom successes and failures with their colleagues. A number of ideas in this revision, especially the exercises, came from members of this group.

Oh yes. One last point. I'm always looking for suggestions on how I can improve this book. If you have some ideas and would like to share them with me, please drop me a line. My address is: Department of Management; College of Business Administration; San Diego State University; San Diego, CA 92182.

Stephen P. Robbins
Del Mar, California

WHAT IS ORGANIZATIONAL BEHAVIOR?

LEARNING OBJECTIVES

After studying this chapter, you should be able to:

1. Define organizational behavior (OB)

2. Describe what managers do

3. Explain the value of the systematic study of OB

4. Summarize the importance of cultural diversity to OB

5. List and describe three different perspectives for classifying ethical positions

6. Identify the contributions made by major behavioral science disciplines to OB

7. Describe why managers require a knowledge of OB

8. Explain the need for a contingency approach to the study of OB

It's not what we don't know that gives us trouble, it's what we know that ain't so.

                                                                W. ROGERS

Meet David Kwok. A 1987 graduate of the University of California at Los Angeles, with a major in cognitive science, David works for a company called The Princeton Review that prepares students to take college and graduate school admission tests. Although he is only twenty-six years old, David directs fifty to sixty instructors at Princeton Review's Los Angeles office.

"My academic training in artificial intelligence didn't really prepare me for my biggest job challenge—understanding and motivating people," says David. "For instance, nothing at UCLA really emphasized how to get people psyched up. For me, people are the unknown part of the equation that determines how effective I am in my job. Other tasks, like scheduling or customer relations, give me very few headaches. What I've learned is that when things go wrong, it's almost always a people problem. I've worked hard to make our teaching staff feel like a small family and to learn techniques for getting them motivated. But it's been on-the-job training for me. I didn't learn any of this in school."

David Kwok has learned what most managers learn very quickly: A large part of the success in any management job is developing good interpersonal or people skills. Lawrence Weinbach, chief executive at the accounting firm of Arthur Andersen & Co., puts it this way: "Pure technical knowledge is only going to get you to a point. Beyond that, interpersonal skills become critical."[1] As the following items attest, this recognition of the importance of developing managers' interpersonal skills seems to be spreading:

The former president of Ford Motor Co. notes, "I have seen more careers flame out because people were unable to work effectively with peers than [for] any other reason. I have rarely seen someone stop his rise and level off or even go down and said to myself that it's because he didn't have intelligence, or didn't have the knowledge. It's almost always because he could not work effectively with people."[2]

A study of 191 top executives at six Fortune 500 companies sought an answer to the question: Why do managers fail? The single biggest reason for failure, according to these executives, is poor interpersonal skills.[3] The Center for Creative Leadership in Greensboro, North Carolina, estimates that half of all managers and thirty percent of all senior managers have some type of difficulty with people.[4] ■

*I*n the 1990s, we've come to understand that technical skills are necessary, but insufficient, for succeeding in management. In today's increasingly competitive and demanding workplace, managers can't succeed on their technical skills alone. They've also got to have good people skills. This book has been written to help both managers and potential managers develop those people skills.

WHAT MANAGERS DO

Managers Individuals who achieve goals through other people.

Organization A consciously coordinated social unit, composed of two or more people, that functions on a relatively continuous basis to achieve a common goal or set of goals.

Let's begin by briefly defining the terms *manager* and the place where managers work—the *organization*. Then let's look at the manager's job; specifically, what do managers do?

Managers get things done through other people. They make decisions, allocate resources, and direct the activities of others to attain goals. Managers do their work in an **organization.** This is a consciously coordinated social unit, composed of two or more people, that functions on a relatively continuous basis to achieve a common goal or set of goals. Based on this definition, manufacturing and service firms are organizations and so are schools, hospitals, churches, military units, retail stores, police departments, and local, state, and federal government agencies. The people who oversee the activities of others and who are responsible for attaining goals in these organizations are their managers (although they're sometimes called *administrators,* especially in not-for-profit organizations).

Management Functions

In the early part of this century, a French industrialist by the name of Henri Fayol wrote that all managers perform five management functions: they plan, organize, command, coordinate, and control.[5] Today, we've condensed these down to four: planning, organizing, leading, and controlling.

If you don't know where you're going, any road will get you there. Since organizations exist to achieve goals, someone has to define these goals and the means by which they can be achieved. Management is that someone. The **planning** function encompasses defining an organization's goals, establishing an overall strategy for achieving these goals, and developing a comprehensive hierarchy of plans to integrate and coordinate activities.

Planning Includes defining goals, establishing strategy, and developing plans to coordinate activities.

Organizing Determining what tasks are to be done, who is to do them, how the tasks are to be grouped, who reports to whom, and where decisions are to be made.

Leading Includes motivating subordinates, directing others, selecting the most effective communication channels, and resolving conflicts.

Controlling Monitoring activities to ensure they are being accomplished as planned and correcting any significant deviations.

Managers are also responsible for designing an organization's structure. We call this function **organizing.** It includes the determination of what tasks are to be done, who is to do them, how the tasks are to be grouped, who reports to whom, and where decisions are to be made.

Every organization contains people, and it is management's job to direct and coordinate these people. This is the **leading** function. When managers motivate subordinates, direct the activities of others, select the most effective communication channel, or resolve conflicts among members, they are engaging in leading.

The final function managers perform is **controlling.** After the goals are set; the plans formulated; the structural arrangements delineated; and the people hired, trained, and motivated, there is still the possibility that something may go amiss. To ensure that things are going as they should, management must monitor the organization's performance. Actual performance must be compared with the previously set goals. If there are any significant deviations, it is management's job to get the organization back on track. This monitoring, comparing, and potential correcting is what is meant by the controlling function.

So, using the functional approach, the answer to the question, what do managers do? is that they plan, organize, lead, and control.

TABLE 1-1 Mintzberg's Managerial Roles

Role	Description	Examples
Interpersonal		
Figurehead	Symbolic head; required to perform a number of routine duties of a legal or social nature	Ceremonies, status requests, solicitations
Leader	Responsible for the motivation and direction of subordinates	Virtually all managerial activities involving subordinates
Liaison	Maintains a network of outside contacts who provide favors and information	Acknowledgment of mail, external board work
Informational		
Monitor	Receives wide variety of information; serves as nerve center of internal and external information of the organization	Handling all mail and contacts categorized as concerned primarily with receiving information
Disseminator	Transmits information received from outsiders or from other subordinates to members of the organization	Forwarding mail into organization for informational purposes; verbal contacts involving information flow to subordinates such as review sessions
Spokesperson	Transmits information to outsiders on organization's plans, policies, actions, and results; serves as expert on organization's industry	Board meetings; handling contacts involving transmission of information to outsiders
Decisional		
Entrepreneur	Searches organization and its environment for opportunities and initiates projects to bring about change	Strategy and review sessions involving initiation or design of improvement projects
Disturbance handler	Responsible for corrective action when organization faces important, unexpected disturbances	Strategy and review sessions involving disturbances and crises
Resource allocator	Making or approving significant organizational decisions	Scheduling; requests for authorization; budgeting; the programming of subordinates' work
Negotiator	Responsible for representing the organization at major negotiations	Contract negotiation

Source: Adapted from *The Nature of Managerial Work* by H. Mintzberg. Copyright © 1973 by H. Mintzberg. Reprinted by permission of Harper Collins Publishers.

Management Roles

In the late 1960s, a graduate student at MIT, Henry Mintzberg, undertook a careful study of five executives to determine what these managers did on their jobs. Based on his observations of these managers, Mintzberg concluded that managers perform ten different, highly interrelated roles, or sets of behaviors attributable to their jobs.[6] As shown in Table 1-1, these ten roles can be grouped as being primarily concerned with interpersonal relationships, the transfer of information, and decision making.

Interpersonal Roles Roles that include figurehead, leadership, and liaison activities.

INTERPERSONAL ROLES   All managers are required to perform duties that are ceremonial and symbolic in nature. When the president of a college hands out diplomas at commencement or a factory supervisor gives a group of high school students a tour of the plant, he or she is acting in a *figurehead* role. All managers have a *leadership* role. This role includes hiring, training, motivating, and disciplining employees. The third role within the interpersonal grouping is the *liaison* role. Mintzberg described this activity as contacting outsiders who provide the manager with information. These may be individuals or groups inside or outside the organization. The sales manager who obtains information from the personnel manager in his or her own company has an internal liaison relationship. When that sales manager has contacts with other sales executives through a marketing trade association, he or she has an outside liaison relationship.

Informational Roles Roles that include monitoring, disseminating, and spokesperson activities.

INFORMATIONAL ROLES   All managers will, to some degree, receive and collect information from organizations and institutions outside their own. Typically, this is done through reading magazines and talking with others to learn of changes in the public's tastes, what competitors may be planning, and the like. Mintzberg called this the *monitor* role. Managers also act as a conduit to transmit information to organizational members. This is the *disseminator* role. Managers additionally perform a *spokesperson* role when they represent the organization to outsiders.

Decisional Roles Roles that include those of entrepreneur, disturbance handler, resource allocator, and negotiator.

DECISIONAL ROLES   Finally, Mintzberg identified four roles that revolve around the making of choices. In the *entrepreneur* role, managers initiate and oversee new projects that will improve their organization's performance. As *disturbance handlers*, managers take corrective action in response to previously unforeseen problems. As *resource allocators*, managers are responsible for allocating human, physical, and monetary resources. Lastly, managers perform a *negotiator* role, in which they discuss and bargain with other units to gain advantages for their own unit.

Management Skills

Still another way of considering what managers do is to look at the skills or competencies they need to successfully achieve their goals. Robert Katz has identified three essential management skills: technical, human, and conceptual.[7]

Technical Skills The ability to apply specialized knowledge or expertise.

TECHNICAL SKILLS   **Technical skills** encompass the ability to apply specialized knowledge or expertise. When you think of the skills held by professionals such as civil engineers, tax accountants, or oral surgeons, you typically focus on their technical skills. Through extensive formal education, they have learned the special knowledge and practices of their field. Of course, professionals don't have a monopoly on technical skills and these skills don't have to be learned in schools or formal training programs. All jobs require some specialized expertise and many people develop their technical skills on the job.

HUMAN SKILLS The ability to work with, understand, and motivate other people, both individually and in groups, describes **human skills.** Many people are technically proficient but interpersonally incompetent. They might, for example, be poor listeners, unable to understand the needs of others, or have difficulty managing conflicts. Since managers get things done through other people, they must have good human skills to communicate, motivate, and delegate.

CONCEPTUAL SKILLS Managers must have the mental ability to analyze and diagnose complex situations. These are **conceptual skills.** Decision making, for instance, requires managers to spot problems, identify alternatives that can correct them, evaluate these alternatives, and select the best one. Managers can be technically and interpersonally competent, yet still fail because of an inability to rationally process and interpret information.

Effective vs. Successful Managerial Activities

Fred Luthans and his associates looked at the issue of what managers do from a somewhat different perspective.[8] They asked the question: Do managers who move up most quickly in an organization do the same activities and with the same emphasis as those managers who do the best job? You would tend to think that those managers who were the most effective in their jobs would also be the ones who were promoted fastest. But that's not what appears to happen.

Luthans and his associates studied more than 450 managers. What they found was that these managers all engaged in four managerial activities:

1. *Traditional management:* Decision making, planning, and controlling
2. *Communication:* Exchanging routine information and processing paperwork
3. *Human resource management:* Motivating, disciplining, managing conflict, staffing, and training
4. *Networking:* Socializing, politicking, and interacting with outsiders

The "average" manager studied spent thirty-two percent of his or her time in traditional management activities, twenty-nine percent communicating, twenty percent in human resource management activities, and nineteen percent networking. However, the amount of time and effort that different managers spent on these four activities varied a great deal. Specifically, as shown in Table 1–2, managers who were *successful* (defined in terms of the speed of promotion within their organization) had a very different emphasis than managers who were *effective* (defined in terms of the quantity and quality of their performance and the satisfaction and commitment of their subordinates). Networking made the biggest relative contribution to manager success, while human resource management activities made the least relative contribution. Among effective managers, communication made the largest relative contribution and networking the least.

This study adds important insights to our knowledge of what managers do. On average, managers spend approximately twenty to thirty percent of their time on each of the four activities: traditional management, communication, human resource management, and networking. However, successful managers don't give the same emphasis to each of these activities as do effective managers. In fact, their emphases are almost the opposite. This chal-

TABLE 1-2   Allocation of Activities by Time

Activity	Average Managers	Successful Managers	Effective Managers
Traditional management	32%	13%	19%
Communication	29	28	44
Human resource management	20	11	26
Networking	19	48	11

Source: Based on F. Luthans, R. M. Hodgetts, and S. A. Rosenkrantz, *Real Managers* (Cambridge, MA: Ballinger Publishing, 1988).

lenges the historical assumption that promotions are based on performance, vividly illustrating the importance that social and political skills play in getting ahead in organizations.

A Review of the Manager's Job

One common thread runs through the functions, roles, skills, and activities approaches to management: each recognizes the paramount importance of managing people. Whether it is called "the leading function," "interpersonal roles," "human skills," or "human resource management and networking activities," it is clear that managers need to develop their people skills.

ENTER ORGANIZATIONAL BEHAVIOR

Organizational Behavior (OB)
A field of study that investigates the impact that individuals, groups, and structure have on behavior within organizations, for the purpose of applying such knowledge toward improving an organization's effectiveness.

We've made the case for the importance of people skills. But neither this book nor the discipline upon which it rests is called *People Skills*. The term that is widely used to describe the discipline is called *Organizational Behavior*.

Organizational behavior (frequently abbreviated as OB) is *a field of study that investigates the impact that individuals, groups, and structure have on behavior within organizations, for the purpose of applying such knowledge toward improving an organization's effectiveness*. That's a lot of words, so let's break it down.

Organizational behavior is a field of study. This means that it is a distinct area of expertise with a common body of knowledge. What does it study? It studies three determinants of behavior in organizations: individuals, groups, and structure. Additionally, OB applies the knowledge gained about individuals, groups, and the effect of structure on behavior in order to make organizations work more effectively.

To sum up our definition, OB is concerned with the study of what people do in an organization and how that behavior affects the performance of the organization. And because OB is specifically concerned with employment-related situations, you should not be surprised to find that it emphasizes behavior as related to jobs, work, absenteeism, employment turnover, productivity, human performance, and management.

There is increasing agreement as to the components or topics that constitute the subject area of OB. While there is still considerable debate as to the relative importance of each, there appears to be general agreement that OB includes the core topics of motivation, leader behavior and power, interpersonal communication, group structure and process, learning, attitude development and perception, change processes, conflict, job design, and work stress.[9]

People Skills: A Primary Deficiency of Today's Business School Graduates

A recent study prepared by the major accrediting body of collegiate business schools reported that a primary deficiency of business school graduates is not their inability to write, perform analytical studies, or make decisions. It's their people or interpersonal skills.[10]

Schools of business are preparing tomorrow's managers. But managers fail more often because they lack solid interpersonal skills than because of inadequate technical competencies. Successful managers must be able to lead, motivate, communicate, work as part of a team, resolve conflicts, and engage in similar interpersonal activities. Unfortunately, until very recently, courses in organizational behavior, interpersonal processes, human relations, and applied psychology have taken a back seat to those in finance, accounting, and quantitative techniques. However, now that this weakness in the preparation of business students has been identified, actions are being planned to correct the problem. Colleges will be expanding their courses in the applied behavioral sciences, and making more of these courses required. Business, too, will respond by ensuring that current managers, and those with management potential, receive training to improve their interpersonal skills. Some companies will send employees to workshops offered by universities and training firms. Others will offer in-house programs for employees.

REPLACING INTUITION WITH SYSTEMATIC STUDY

Each of us is a student of behavior. Since our earliest years, we have watched the actions of others and have attempted to interpret what we see. Whether or not you have explicitly thought about it before, you have been "reading" people almost all your life. You watch what others do and try to explain to yourself why they have engaged in their behavior. Additionally, you've attempted to predict what they might do under different sets of conditions.

Generalizations About Behavior

You have already developed some generalizations that you find helpful in explaining and predicting what people do and will do. But how did you arrive at these generalizations? You did so by observing, sensing, asking, listening, and reading. That is, your understanding comes either directly from your own experience with things in the environment, or secondhand, through the experience of others.

How accurate are the generalizations that you hold? Some may represent extremely sophisticated appraisals of behavior and may prove highly effective in explaining and predicting the behavior of others. However, most of us also carry with us a number of beliefs that frequently fail to explain why people do what they do.[11] To illustrate, consider the following statements about work-related behavior:

1. Happy workers are productive workers.
2. All individuals are most productive when their boss is friendly, trusting, and approachable.
3. Interviews are effective selection devices for separating job applicants who would be high-performing employees from those who would be low performers.
4. Everyone wants a challenging job.
5. You have to scare people a little to get them to do their jobs.
6. Everyone is motivated by money.
7. Most people are much more concerned with the size of their own salaries than with others'.
8. The most effective work groups are devoid of conflict.

How many of these statements do you think are true? For the most part, they are all false, and we shall touch on each later in this text. But whether these statements are true or false is not really important at this time. What is important is to be aware that many of the views you hold concerning human behavior are based on intuition rather than fact. As a result, a systematic approach to the study of behavior can improve your explanatory and predictive abilities.

Consistency vs. Individual Differences

Casual or commonsense approaches to obtaining knowledge about human behavior are inadequate. In reading this text, you will discover that a systematic approach will uncover important facts and relationships, and provide a base from which more accurate predictions of behavior can be made.

Underlying this systematic approach is the belief that behavior is not random. It is caused and directed toward some end that the individual believes, rightly or wrongly, is in his or her best interest.

> Behavior generally is predictable if we know how the person perceived the situation and what is important to him or her. While people's behavior may not appear to be rational to an outsider, there is reason to believe it usually is *intended* to be rational and it is seen as rational by them. An observer often sees behavior as nonrational because the observer does not have access to the same information or does not perceive the environment in the same way.[12]

Certainly there are differences between individuals. Placed in similar situations, all people do not act alike. However, there are certain fundamental consistencies underlying the behavior of all individuals that can be identified and then modified to reflect individual differences.

These fundamental consistencies are very important. Why? Because they allow predictability. When you get into your car, you make some definite and usually highly accurate predictions about how other people will behave. In North America, for instance, you would predict that other drivers will stop at stop signs and red lights, drive on the right side of the road, pass on your left, and not cross the solid double line on mountain roads. Notice that your predictions about the behavior of people behind the wheels of their cars are almost always correct. Obviously, the rules of driving make predictions about driving behavior fairly easy.

Systematic Study Looking at relationships, attempting to attribute causes and effects, and drawing conclusions based on scientific evidence.

Intuition A feeling not necessarily supported by research.

What may be less obvious is that there are rules (written and unwritten) in almost every setting. Therefore, it can be argued that is possible to predict behavior (undoubtedly, not always with one hundred percent accuracy) in supermarkets, classrooms, doctors' offices, elevators, and in most structured situations. To illustrate further, do you turn around and face the doors when you get into an elevator? Almost everyone does, yet did you ever read that you're supposed to do this? Probably not! Just as I make predictions about automobile drivers (where there are definite rules of the road), I can make predictions about the behavior of people in elevators (where there are few written rules). In a class of sixty students, if you wanted to ask a question of the instructor, I would predict that you would raise your hand. Why don't you clap, stand up, raise your leg, cough, or yell "Hey, over here!"? The reason is that you have learned that raising your hand is appropriate behavior in school. These examples support a major contention in this text: Behavior is generally predictable, and the **systematic study** of behavior is a means to making reasonably accurate predictions.

When we use the phrase "systematic study," we mean looking at relationships, attempting to attribute causes and effects, and basing our conclusions on scientific evidence; that is, on data gathered under controlled conditions and measured and interpreted in a reasonably rigorous manner.

Systematic study replaces **intuition** or those "gut feelings" about "why I do what I do" and "what makes others tick." Of course, a systematic approach does not mean that those things you have come to believe in an unsystematic way are necessarily incorrect. Some of the conclusions we make in this text, based on reasonably substantive research findings, will only support what you always knew was true. But you will also be exposed to research evidence that runs counter to what you may have thought was common sense. In fact, one of the challenges to teaching a subject like organizational behavior is to overcome the notion, held by many, that "it's *all* common sense."[13] You will find that many of the so-called commonsense views you hold about human behavior are, on closer examination, wrong. Moreover, what one person considers "common sense" frequently runs counter to another's version of "common sense." Are leaders born or made? What is it that motivates people at work nowadays? You probably have answers to such questions, and individuals who have not reviewed the research are likely to differ on their answers. The point is that one of the objectives of this text is to encourage you to move away from your intuitive views of behavior toward a systematic analysis, in the belief that such analysis will improve your accuracy in explaining and predicting behavior.

CHALLENGES AND OPPORTUNITIES FOR OB IN THE 1990s

Understanding organizational behavior has never been more important for managers. A quick look at a few of the dramatic changes now taking place in organizations supports this claim. For instance, the typical employee is getting older; there are more and more women and nonwhites in the workplace; corporate restructuring and cost cutting are severing the bonds of loyalty that historically tied many employees to their employers; and global competition is requiring employees to become more flexible and to learn to cope with rapid change and innovation.

In short, there are a lot of challenges and opportunities for OB in the 1990s. In this section, we'll review a half-dozen of the more critical issues confronting managers for which OB offers solutions—or at least some meaningful insights toward solutions.

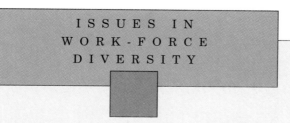

Diversity: The Key to Getting and Keeping the Best Employees

Diversity provides management with the opportunity to bring to its organization people with skills, experiences, and outlooks that, in the past, were frequently excluded or subutilized. A few examples can clarify this point.

Leigh Compton and her mother have several things in common. Both graduated in the top one-percent of their Chicago-area high school graduating classes. Both also then went to the University of Illinois and received degrees in biology. But when Leigh's mother graduated in 1962, she saw few opportunities for female scientists in Corporate America.

So instead of going on to graduate school, as she preferred, she took a job as a high school science teacher and business lost a valuable resource. Leigh, graduating in 1985, saw no such barriers. She went on to earn her masters and Ph.D. at Northwestern and is now a successful project manager at Genentech.

Jack O'Malley spent 42 years as a tool and die designer. He retired in 1989 with a nice pension. Yet, within six months, he was bored to death. Even though he was 67 years old, he was hired as a full-time designer by a small firm in St. Louis. Said the firm's owner, "It's almost impossible for us to find experienced tool designers like Jack. They're few and far between. Our diversity-recruitment program has specifically targeted seniors. They've got a wealth of experience and they come highly motivated."

Jim Kordosky has ten years experience repairing expensive imported cars. He wants to work but, as a widower with three young children, his family responsibilities make a full-time job impossible. Because his employer, the German Auto Clinic, has adjusted its policies to allow employees to choose permanently reduced work days, Jim is able to balance his family and work responsibilities.

Tina Thompson suffers from Downs Syndrome, yet holds a full-time job. She was hired by McDonald's, a company with one of the most progressive value-in-diversity programs. Tina's shift manager describes her as one of the hardest working and most conscientious employees she has ever had.

Skilled, experienced, and enthusiastic employees are a scarce resource. Those organizations with the best reputations for managing diversity will win the competition to hire and keep those individuals who are different.

Work-Force Diversity

Work-Force Diversity The increasing heterogeneity of organizations with the inclusion of different groups.

Arguably, the most important and broad-based challenge for U.S. organizations in the 1990s will be adapting to people who are different. **Work-force diversity** means that organizations are becoming obviously more heterogeneous in terms of gender, race, and ethnicity. But the term encompasses *anyone* who varies from the "norm." That means that it also includes the physically handicapped, gays and lesbians, the elderly, and even people who are significantly overweight.

We used to take a "melting pot" approach to differences in organizations, assuming that people who were different would somehow automatically want to assimilate. But we now recognize that employees don't set aside their cultural values and lifestyle preferences when they come to work. The challenge for organizations, therefore, is to make themselves more accommodating to diverse groups of people by addressing their different lifestyles,

In the 1990s, progressive organizations are responding to work-force diversity in many ways. For example, many are providing flexible work schedules, child and elder day care, parental leaves, language training, mentoring programs, and workshops to help employees understand differences and appreciate the value of diversity.

family needs, and work styles. The "melting pot" assumption is being replaced by one that recognizes and values differences.[14]

Haven't organizations always included members of diverse groups? Yes, but they were such a small percentage of the work force that no one paid much attention to them. Moreover, it was assumed that these minorities would seek to blend in and assimilate. The bulk of the pre-1980s work force were male Caucasians working full time to support a nonemployed wife and school-aged children. Now such employees are the true minority! Currently, forty-five percent of the U.S. labor force are women. Minorities and immigrants make up twenty-two percent.[15] As a case in point, Hewlett-Packard's work force is nineteen percent minorities and forty percent women.[16] A Digital Equipment Corp. plant in Boston provides a partial preview of the future. The factory's 350 employees include men and women from forty-four countries who speak nineteen languages. When plant management issues written announcements, they are printed in English, Chinese, French, Spanish, Portuguese, Vietnamese, and Haitian Creole.

As Figure 1–1 illustrates, new-worker growth in the United States through the rest of this decade will be occurring most rapidly among women and Hispanics. Almost two-thirds of all new entrants into the work force will be women. And by the year 2000, white non-Hispanic males will make up only thirty-nine percent of the total work force.

Work-force diversity has important implications for management practice. Managers will need to shift their philosophy from treating everyone alike to recognizing differences and responding to those differences in ways that will ensure employee retention and greater productivity—while, at the

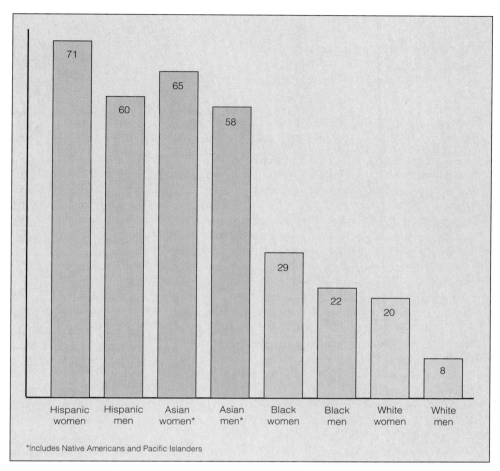

Hispanic women: 71
Hispanic men: 60
Asian women*: 65
Asian men*: 58
Black women: 29
Black men: 22
White women: 20
White men: 8

*Includes Native Americans and Pacific Islanders

FIGURE 1–1   Composition of the New-Worker Pool   Source: S. Pedigo, "Diversity in the Workforce: Riding the Tide of Change," *The Wyatt Communicator*, The Wyatt Company, Winter 1991, p. 9

same time, not discriminating. Diversity, if positively managed, can increase creativity and innovation in organizations as well as improve decision making by providing different perspectives on problems.[17] When diversity is not managed properly, there is potential for higher turnover, more difficult communication, and more interpersonal conflicts. In many of the following chapters, you'll find boxes where we address some of these challenges specifically.

Declining Loyalty

Corporate employees used to believe that their employers would reward their loyalty and good work with job security, generous benefits, and pay increases. But beginning in the mid-1980s, in response to global competition, unfriendly takeovers, leveraged buyouts, and the like, corporations began to discard traditional policies on job security, seniority, and compensation. They sought to become "lean and mean" by closing factories, moving operations overseas, selling off or closing down less profitable businesses, and eliminating entire levels of management.

These changes have resulted in a sharp decline in employee loyalty.[18] In one recent survey of workers, for instance, fifty-seven percent said companies are less loyal to employees today than they were a decade ago.[19] And as

Dealing with Ethical Issues in Organizational Behavior

Members of organizations often confront ethical dilemmas. A few examples to illustrate this point: Is it unethical to "pad" an expense account? How about using the company telephone for personal long-distance calls or using company postage on personal mail? Is it wrong to use insider information for personal financial gain? Should someone follow orders that he or she doesn't personally agree with? Is it wrong for a manager to show favoritism in selection decisions or disciplinary practices? Is it unethical to "play politics" in an organization?

Ethics refers to "the rules or principles that define right and wrong conduct."[20] Ethical questions like those stated in the previous paragraph have no "right" answers. These questions fall into a gray area where individuals must make judgments based on some ethical standards. Throughout this book, you'll be presented with ethical issues related to organizational behavior. To help you deal with these issues, here are three different ethical positions that can provide guidance in evaluating your own ethical standards.[21]

The first is the utilitarian view of ethics, in which decisions are made solely on the basis of their outcomes or consequences. The goal of utilitarianism is to provide the greatest good for the greatest number. This view tends to dominate business decision making. It is consistent with goals like efficiency, productivity, and high profits. By maximizing profits, for instance, a business executive can argue that he or she is securing the greatest good for the greatest number.

Another ethical perspective is the rights view of ethics. This calls upon individuals to make decisions consistent with fundamental liberties and privileges as set forth in documents like the Bill of Rights. The rights view of ethics is concerned with respecting and protecting the basic rights of individuals, such as the right to privacy, to free speech, and to due process. For instance, this position would protect employees who report unethical or illegal practices by their organization to the press or government agencies on the grounds of their right to free speech.

A third perspective is the justice view of ethics. This requires individuals to impose and enforce rules fairly and impartially so there is an equitable distribution of benefits and costs. Union members typically favor this view. It justifies paying people the same wage for a given job, regardless of performance differences, and it uses seniority as the criterion in making layoff decisions.

Each of these perspectives has advantages and liabilities. The utilitarian view promotes efficiency and productivity, but it can result in ignoring the rights of some individuals, particularly those with minority representation in the organization. The rights perspective protects individuals from injury and is consistent with freedom and privacy, but it can create an overly legalistic work environment that hinders productivity and efficiency. The justice perspective protects the interests of the underrepresented and less powerful, but it can encourage a sense of entitlement that reduces risk-taking, innovation, and productivity.

In each of the following chapters, you'll find theme boxes that address ethical issues in OB. The three ethical views presented here—utilitarian, rights, and justice—provide a frame of reference for analyzing these issues.

corporations have shown less commitment to employees, employees have shown less commitment to them.

An important OB challenge will be for managers to devise ways to motivate workers who feel less committed to their employers, while maintaining the organization's global competitiveness.

Labor Shortages

The work force grew in the 1960s and 1970s as a direct result of Baby Boomers (the huge number of people born between 1945 and 1964) entering the labor market. However, fertility rates began dropping world-wide in the late 1960s, resulting in what is called the Baby Bust. Forgetting for a moment the effects of short-term economic recessions, the long-term demographic reality means that most advanced industrialized countries—including Germany, Japan, Italy, Sweden, the United Kingdom, Canada, and the United States—will face a severe and ongoing shortage of workers through the early part of the next century.[22] Because of this trend, middle-aged and older workers will make up a rising share of the total labor supply.

Again, except in economic downturns, the labor market trend during the next fifteen to twenty years will strongly favor sellers of labor, especially professionals and people with technical skills. And a seller's market means that organizations will need to rethink their policies regarding recruiting, training, compensation, and employee benefits. When there are more jobs available than there are people to fill them, organizations will have to have progressive human resource policies and their managers will need good people skills in order to get and keep the best-qualified workers.

Many companies are already responding to labor shortages by hiring retirees. Chuck Fletcher once supervised 175 people at TWA as a manager of food and beverage service. Bothered by pressure, he retired at age 57. Builders Emporium hired him and he's now head of the plumbing and electrical department at one of its Southern California stores.

Skill Deficiencies

Compounding the problem of a labor shortage is the fact that a significant proportion of people looking for work don't have the skills that organizations need. Many immigrants, for instance, are deficient in English, while too many U.S. high school graduates can't read well enough to qualify for entry-level jobs.

As most developed countries move from a manufacturing-based economy to one based on knowledge, make cutbacks in the managerial ranks, and decentralize decision making, workers are having to take greater responsibility for their jobs. They have to make more decisions on their own. They have to read complex operating manuals and blueprints, work computers, perform statistical quality control, make judgments in response to client requests, and the like. Unfortunately, the United States does not have enough workers with the reading, mathematical, verbal, and specialized skills that employers need. As one expert noted, "Three-fourths of new workforce entrants will be qualified for only 40 percent of the new jobs created between 1985 and 2000.[23]

Some organizations have responded by de-skilling jobs—that is, making them less complex and more routine. Some fast-food restaurants, for example, put pictures of food items on cash register keys to minimize employee mistakes. But even these de-skilling efforts can't overcome the problem of workers who can't consistently make accurate change from a five-dollar bill. The implications are obvious: Employers must train and reeducate their less-skilled employees, and managers must become more responsive to the needs of their skilled employees to keep them from going to work for a competitor.

The Bi-Modal Work Force

Twenty or thirty years ago, the U.S. produced plenty of unskilled jobs in the steel, automobile, rubber, and other manufacturing industries that paid solid middle-class wages. A young man in Pittsburgh, for instance, could graduate from high school and immediately get a relatively high-paying and secure job in a local steel plant. That job would allow him to buy a home, finance a car or two, support a family, and enjoy other lifestyle choices that come with a middle-class income. But that's ancient history.[24] A good percentage of those manufacturing jobs in First World industrialized countries are gone forever—either replaced by automated equipment, reconstituted into jobs requiring considerably higher technical skills, or taken by people in other countries who will do the same work for a fraction of the wages Americans received. What we have now can best be described as a bi-modal work force—a division between those who perform low-skilled service jobs for near-minimum wages and those who perform high-skilled jobs that provide the passport to a middle-class or upper-middle-class lifestyle.

Figure 1–2 illustrates this bi-modal phenomenon. It has been created by the massive decline of blue-collar manufacturing jobs that pay $20,000 to $30,000 a year in current dollars.

Most organizations have employee policies that are successful in keeping and motivating high-paid skilled workers. They don't, however, have policies that work very well at motivating the low-skilled, low-paid service workers represented in the left curve of Figure 1–2.

Working for wages of $4.50 to $7.00 an hour, today's low-skilled employees can't possibly move into the middle class. Moreover, their promotion opportunities are limited. This leads to a major challenge for managers: How do you motivate people who are making very low wages and have little opportunity to significantly increase their pay, either in their current jobs or through promotions? Can effective leadership fill the void? Can these employees' jobs be redesigned to make them more challenging? Or should management target these kinds of jobs for elimination? These are questions on which OB may offer some guidance.

Stimulating Innovation and Change

Whatever happened to W. T. Grant, Gimbel's, and Eastern Airlines? All these giants went bust! Why have other giants like General Motors, CBS,

FIGURE 1–2   The Bi-Modal Work-Force

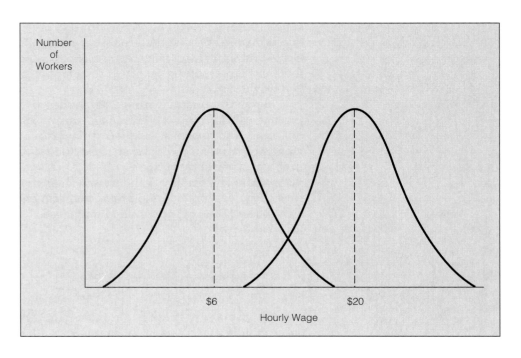

and AT&T implemented huge cost-cutting programs and eliminated thousands of jobs? To *avoid* going bust!

Today's successful organizations must foster innovation and master the art of change or they will become candidates for extinction. Victory will go to those organizations that maintain their flexibility, continually improve their quality, and beat their competition to the marketplace with a constant stream of innovative products and services. Domino's single-handedly brought on the demise of thousands of small pizza parlors whose managers thought they could continue doing what they had been doing for years. Compaq succeeded by creating more powerful personal computers for the same or less money than IBM or Apple, and by getting their products to market faster than the bigger competitors.

An organization's employees can be the impetus for innovation and change, or they can be a major stumbling block. The challenge for managers is to stimulate employee creativity and tolerance for change. The field of organizational behavior provides a wealth of ideas and techniques to aid in realizing these goals.

CONTRIBUTING DISCIPLINES TO THE OB FIELD

Organizational behavior is an applied behavioral science that is built upon contributions from a number of behavioral disciplines. The predominant areas are psychology, sociology, social psychology, anthropology, and political science.[25] As we shall learn, psychology's contributions have been mainly at the individual or micro level of analysis, while the other four disciplines have contributed to our understanding of macro concepts such as group processes and organization. Figure 1–3 overviews the major contributions to the study of organizational behavior.

Psychology

Psychology is the science that seeks to measure, explain, and sometimes change the behavior of humans and other animals. Psychologists concern themselves with studying and attempting to understand *individual* behavior. Those who have contributed and continue to add to the knowledge of OB are learning theorists, personality theorists, counseling psychologists, and, most important, industrial and organizational psychologists.

Early industrial/organizational psychologists concerned themselves with problems of fatigue, boredom, and other factors relevant to working conditions that could impede efficient work performance. More recently, their contributions have been expanded to include learning, perception, personality, training, leadership effectiveness, needs and motivational forces, job satisfaction, decision-making processes, performance appraisals, attitude measurement, employee selection techniques, job design, and work stress.

Sociology

Whereas psychologists focus their attention on the individual, sociologists study the social system in which individuals fill their roles; that is, sociology studies people in relation to their fellow human beings. Specifically, sociologists have made their greatest contribution to OB through their study of group behavior in organizations, particularly formal and complex organiza-

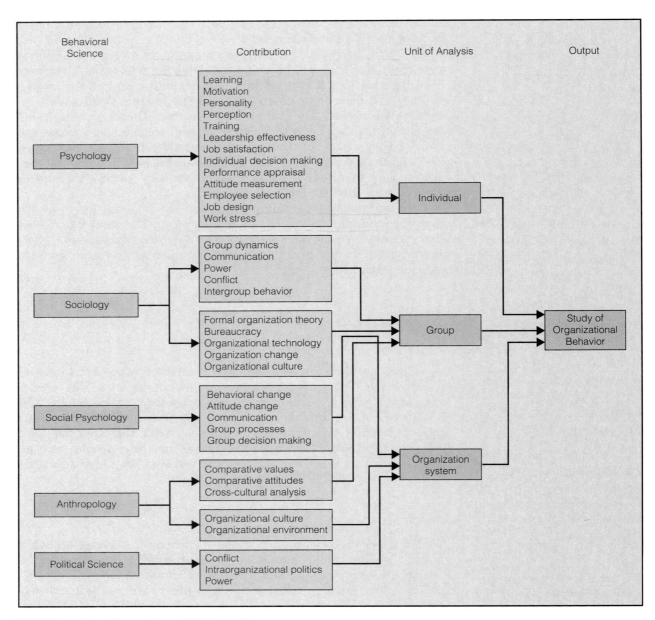

FIGURE 1–3   Toward an OB Discipline

tions. Some of the areas within OB that have received valuable input from sociologists are group dynamics, organizational culture, formal organization theory and structure, organizational technology, bureaucracy, communications, power, conflict, and intergroup behavior.

Social Psychology

Social psychology is an area within psychology, but blends concepts from both psychology and sociology. It focuses on the influence of people on one another. One of the major areas receiving considerable investigation from social psychologists has been *change*—how to implement it and how to

FIGURE 1-4

*"I'm a social scientist, Michael. That means I can't explain
electricity or anything like that, but if you ever want to know
about people I'm your man."*

Drawing by Handelsman; © 1986 The New Yorker Magazine, Inc.

reduce barriers to its acceptance. Additionally, we find social psychologists making significant contributions in the areas of measuring, understanding, and changing attitudes; communication patterns; the ways in which group activities can satisfy individual needs; and group decision-making processes.

Anthropology

Anthropologists study societies to learn about human beings and their activities. Their work on cultures and environments, for instance, has helped us understand differences in fundamental values, attitudes, and behavior between people in different countries and within different organizations. Much of our current understanding of organizational culture, organizational environments, and differences between national cultures is the result of the work of anthropologists or those using their methodologies.

Political Science

Although frequently overlooked, the contributions of political scientists are significant to the understanding of behavior in organizations. Political scientists study the behavior of individuals and groups within a political environment. Specific topics of concern here include structuring of conflict, allocation of power, and how people manipulate power for individual self-interest.

Twenty-five years ago, little of what political scientists were studying was of interest to students of organizational behavior. But times have changed. We have become increasingly aware that organizations are political entities; if we are to be able to accurately explain and predict the behavior of people in organizations, we need to bring a political perspective to our analysis.

Lucy Suchman, an anthropologist working for Xerox's Palo Alto Research Center, studies workers at her local airport to see how they keep track of people, airplanes, suitcases and cargo without letting each takeoff and landing touch off chaos. Xerox plans to use her observations, along with other company anthropologists studying a variety of work groups, to fine-tune its methods of handling documents, improve its instruction manuals, train its repair teams, and help it design user-friendly equipment.
Terrence McCarthy/NYT Pictures

Viewing a Common Event Through Dissimilar Eyes

The diversity of training, interests, and perspective among members of the various behavioral disciplines has contributed to divergent approaches to the study of many OB topics. To illustrate, take the issue of conflict within organizations. If an industrial psychologist and an organizational sociologist look at the same conflict situation, they rarely see it in the same way. Psychologists tend to see the cause of most conflicts as lying in the motives and personalities of the parties involved. In contrast, sociologists tend to see the source of the conflict as the roles and structure that define the relationships between the parties.

As a result, the psychologist's solution to conflict focuses on changing people, whereas the sociologist's solution is more likely to emphasize restructuring relationships.

This illustration dramatizes two important points that you should keep in mind as you read this text: The field of OB has clearly been broadened by the diverse insights brought to it by psychologists, sociologists, social psychologists, anthropologists, and political scientists. However, each discipline molds issues of interest to fit into the perspective with which that discipline views the world.

THERE ARE FEW ABSOLUTES IN OB

Contingency Variables
Situational factors that moderate the relations between two variables and improve a prediction's validity.

There are few, if any, simple and universal principles that explain organizational behavior. There are laws in the physical sciences—chemistry, astronomy, physics—that are consistent and apply in a wide range of situations. They allow scientists to generalize about the pull of gravity or to confidently send astronauts into space to repair satellites. But as one noted behavioral researcher aptly concluded, "God gave all the *easy* problems to the physicists." Human beings are very complex. They are not alike, which limits the ability to make simple, accurate, and sweeping generalizations. Two people often act very differently in the same situation, and the same person's behavior changes in different situations. For instance, not everyone is motivated by money, and you behave differently at church on Sunday than you did at the beer party the night before.

That doesn't mean, of course, that we can't offer reasonably accurate explanations of human behavior or make valid predictions. It does mean, however, that OB concepts must reflect situational or contingency conditions. We can say that x leads to y, but only under conditions specified in z (the **contingency variables**). The science of OB was developed by using general concepts and then altering their application to the particular situation. So, for example, OB scholars would avoid stating that effective leaders should always seek the ideas of their subordinates before making a decision. Rather, we shall find that in some situations a participative style is clearly superior, but in other situations, an autocratic decision style is more effective. In other words, the effectiveness of a particular leadership style is *contingent* upon the situation in which it is utilized.

As you proceed through this text, you'll encounter a wealth of research-based theories about how people behave in organizations. But don't expect to find a lot of straightforward cause–effect relationships. There aren't many! Organizational behavior theories mirror the subject matter with which they deal. People are complex and complicated, and so too must be the theories developed to explain their actions.

Consistent with the contingency philosophy, you'll find point–counterpoint debates at the conclusion of each chapter. These debates are included to reinforce the fact that within the OB field there are many issues over which there is significant disagreement. By directly addressing some of the more controversial issues using the point–counterpoint format, you get the opportunity to explore different points of view, discover how diverse perspectives complement and oppose each other, and gain insight into some of the debates currently taking place within the OB field.[26]

So at the end of one chapter, you'll find the argument that leadership plays an important role in an organization's attaining its goals, followed by the argument that there is little evidence to support this claim. Similarly, at the end of other chapters, you'll read both sides of the debate on whether money is a motivator, clear communication is always desirable, bureaucracies have become obsolete, and other controversial issues. These arguments are meant to demonstrate that OB, like many disciplines, has disagreements over specific findings, methods, and theories. Some of the point–counterpoint arguments are more provocative than others, but each makes some valid points that you should find thought-provoking. The key is to be able to decipher under what conditions each argument may be right or wrong.

FOR DISCUSSION

1. Contrast an intuitive approach to studying behavior with a systematic approach. Is intuition always inaccurate?

2. "Behavior generally is predictable." Do you agree or disagree? Explain.

3. Contrast the research comparing *effective* managers with *successful* managers. What are the implications from this research for practicing managers?

4. Define *organizational behavior*. How does this compare with *management*?

5. What is an *organization*? Is the family unit an organization? Explain.

6. How might cultural diversity improve the performance of an organization?

7. What is meant by the phrase *bi-modal work force?* What are its implications for managers?

8. In what areas has *psychology* contributed to OB? *Sociology? Social psychology? Anthropology? Political science?* What other academic disciplines may have contributed to OB?

9. "The best way to view OB is through a contingency approach." Build an argument to support this statement.

10. "Since behavior is generally predictable, there is no need to formally study OB." Why is this statement wrong?

11. Why do you think the subject of OB might be criticized as being "only common sense," when one would rarely hear such a criticism of a course in physics or statistics?

12. Can the behavioral sciences such as psychology, sociology, and organizational behavior ever reach the precision of predictability that exists in the physical sciences? Support your position.

POINT

OB Is a Social Science

OB has grown out of at least two older fields in business schools: human relations and management. It also includes significant ideas from psychology and sociology, although other social sciences such as economics, anthropology, and political science have certainly contributed to OB's development. In the past twenty-five years, OB has received substantial inputs from a younger generation of scholars who have received their training in business schools either under the label of Organizational Behavior itself or under some related term. If one were required to select the single discipline that has most influenced the content of OB and its research methodologies, however, there is little disagreement over the answer: psychology. In second place, and closing slowly on the leader, is sociology.

Any study of the OB field would be generally acknowledged as incomplete without a discussion of the following ten topics: attitudes, job satisfaction, personality, perception, motivation, learning, job design, leadership, communication, and group dynamics. With the exception of the last two, the major work on each of these topics has been done by individuals whose primary training has been in psychology. The study of communication and groups has belonged to the social psychologist and the sociologist. The interest in the past twenty years in power and conflict in organizations has also generally been furthered by individuals with sociological training. But the topics of power, con-

flict, and other interests of sociologists—including organizational culture and structure—have suffered in contrast to the previously mentioned psychologically based concepts by failing to achieve unanimous legitimacy among OB scholars.

Using contributions from researchers in psychology, sociology, and other social sciences, we have made substantial progress in our search to explain and predict the behavior of people at work. We have, for example, identified a number of factors that contribute to employees voluntarily quitting their jobs. More important, we have also developed models that show how these factors interact. Does this imply that we now have a science of OB that can consistently and perfectly predict behavior? No! We have made substantial progress, but our knowledge is far from complete. There are many questions that remain unanswered. There is also considerable research that is inconsistent and, in some cases, even contradictory. Unfortunately, understanding human behavior is not as simple as understanding, say, polio. The latter led to a vaccine that effectively eliminated polio in North America. Further research on polio is not necessary. Human behavior, in contrast, will never be fully understood. Research will continue, leading us to replace old theories with new ones. We have come a long way in our understanding of human behavior, but we still have considerable distance to cover.

Behavior Is Genetically Determined

Harvard zoologist Edward O. Wilson has, for more than two decades, been developing his argument that social behavior is substantially based on biology. He claims that the study of human behavior is not the sole province of social scientists. Human beings are not born a blank slate, as social scientists claim, with their behavior being totally a response to their environment. Wilson views a large part of human behavior—why we organize ourselves as we do, act as we do, and perhaps even think as we do—as a result of a gene-culture coevolution. Genetic make-up helps to guide and create culture, and culture, in turn, operates directly on the genes. Wilson believes that the future of understanding and changing behavior may lie in sociobiology—the study of the biological basis of social behavior.

Sociobiology began innocently enough as an attempt to understand the social behavior of animals, particularly insects. Wilson focused on their population structure, castes, and communication, together with all the physiology underlying the social adaptations. For instance, he found that the incest taboo, which prohibits sexual relations between close relatives, has been strengthened in the animal world by natural selection. In some animal social systems, males are programmed to leave home and find a new colony or herd when they reach puberty. And in a specialized form of programmed learning known as "imprinting," many young animals, birds as well as mammals, memorize the appearance, voice, or odor of their siblings and parents and use the resulting image to make later mating decisions. They will go to great lengths in adulthood to avoid mating with a sibling with whom they have been raised.

Of course, it is one thing to talk about insects and another to talk about human beings. Not surprisingly, it's been Wilson's extension of sociobio-

logical concepts to humans that has generated the most discussion and criticism. He is suggesting some interesting ideas—such as the possibility of social engineering—that touch the deepest level of human motivation and moral reasoning. By selectively controlling the genetic make-up of our society, we could significantly increase SAT scores, produce employees with high internal motivation, and eradicate racial divisiveness and wars.

Is this such a preposterous notion? Not really. Scientists at the National Institute of Health recently initiated a $3 billion project that seeks to map the chromosomes and decipher the complete instructions for making a human being by the year 2005. Encoded in an infant's forty-six chromosomes are instructions that affect not only structure, size, coloring, and other physical attributes, but also intelligence, susceptibility to disease, life span, and some aspects of behavior. The ultimate goal of the NIH project is to read and understand those instructions. This project may well lead to scientists being able to read the entire genetic message—perhaps even to alter it.

Keep in mind that Wilson and his followers are not proposing that sociobiology will replace the social sciences. Rather, they see disciplines such as psychology and sociology in some future time—probably one hundred or more years from now—being encompassed by the physical sciences. The study of topics like stress, perception, learning, and creativity would then be analyzed in physiological terms. Stress would be evaluated in terms of the neurophysiological perturbations and their relaxation times. Perception would be translated into brain circuitry. Learning and creativity would be defined as the alteration of specific portions of the cognitive machinery regulated by input from the motive centers.

What Do You Know About Human Behavior?

Much of what we "know" about the world is based on intuition. We have opinions, biases, hunches, and misinformation that we use both in making statements about others and in deciding what we do. The following twenty questions are designed to provide you with some feedback regarding what you "know" about human behavior. Read each statement and mark T (true) or F (false).

True or False?

_____ 1. People who graduate in the upper third of their college class tend to make more money during their careers than do average students.

_____ 2. Exceptionally intelligent people tend to be physically weak and frail.

_____ 3. Most great athletes are of below-average intelligence.

_____ 4. All people in America are born equal in capacity for achievement.

_____ 5. On the average, women are slightly more intelligent than men.

_____ 6. People are definitely either introverted or extroverted.

_____ 7. After you learn something, you forget more of it in the next few hours than in the next several days.

_____ 8. In small doses, alcohol facilitates learning.

_____ 9. Women are more intuitive than men.

_____ 10. Smokers take more sick days per year than do nonsmokers.

_____ 11. Forty-year-old people are more intelligent than twenty-year-olds.

_____ 12. If you have to reprimand someone for a misdeed, it is best to do so immediately after the mistake occurs.

_____ 13. People who do poorly in academic work are superior in mechanical ability.

_____ 14. High-achieving people are high risk-takers.

_____ 15. Highly cohesive groups are also highly productive.

_____ 16. When people are frustrated, they frequently become aggressive.

_____ 17. Experiences as an infant tend to determine behavior in later life.

_____ 18. Successful top managers have a greater need for money than for power.

_____ 19. Most people who work for the federal government are low risk-takers.

_____ 20. Most managers are highly democratic in the way that they supervise their people.

Turn to page 713 for scoring directions and key.

Source: Adapted from *Organizational Behavior: Theory and Practice* by S. Altman, E. Valenzi, and R. M. Hodgetts,© 1985 by Harcourt Brace Jovanovich, Inc. Reprinted by permission of the publisher.

Work-Force Diversity Exercise[*]

PURPOSE   To learn about the different needs of a diverse work force.

TIME REQUIRED   Approximately forty minutes.

PARTICIPANTS AND ROLES   Divide the class into six groups of approximately equal size. Each group is assigned one of the following roles:

Nancy is twenty-eight years old. She is a divorced mother of three children, aged three, five, and seven. She is the department head. She earns $33,000 a year on her job and receives another $3600 a year in child support from her ex-husband.

Ethel is a seventy-two-year-old widow. She works twenty-five hours a week to supplement her $7000-a-year pension. Based on her hourly wage of $7.50, she earns $9375 a year.

John is a thirty-four-year-old black male born in Trinidad, but now a U.S. resident. He is married and the father of two small children. John attends college at night and is within a year of earning his bachelor's degree. His salary is $22,000 a year. His wife is an attorney and earns approximately $40,000 a year.

Lu is a twenty-six-year-old physically impaired male Asian-American. He is single and has a master's degree in education. Lu is paralyzed and confined to a wheelchair as a result of an auto accident. He earns $27,000 a year.

Maria is a single twenty-two-year-old Hispanic. Born and raised in Mexico, she came to the U.S. only three months ago. Maria's English needs considerable improvement. She earns $17,000 a year.

Mike is a sixteen-year-old white male high school sophomore who works fifteen hours a week after school. He earns $6.25 an hour, or approximately $4700 a year.

The members of each group are to assume the character consistent with their assigned role.

BACKGROUND   Our six participants work for a company that has recently installed a flexible benefits program. Instead of the traditional "one benefit package fits all," the company is allocating an additional twenty-five percent of each employee's annual pay to be used for discretionary benefits. Those benefits and their annual cost are listed below.

Supplementary health care for employee:
   Plan A (No deductible and pays 90%) = $3000
   Plan B ($200 deductible and pays 80%) = $2000
   Plan C ($1000 deductible and pays 70%) = $500

Supplementary health care for dependents (same deductibles and percentages as above):
   Plan A = $2000

[*]Special thanks to Prof. Penny Wright for her suggestions during the development of this exercise.

Plan B = $1500

Plan C = $500

Supplementary dental plan = $500

Life insurance:

Plan A ($25,000 coverage) = $500

Plan B ($50,000 coverage) = $1000

Plan C ($100,000 coverage) = $2000

Plan D ($250,000 coverage) = $3000

Mental health plan = $500

Prepaid legal assistance = $300

Vacation = 2% of annual pay for each week, up to 6 weeks a year

Pension at retirement equal to approximately 50% of final annual earnings = $1500

4-day workweek during the three summer months (available only to full-time employees) = 4% of annual pay

Day-care services (after company contribution) = $2000 for all of an employee's children

Company-provided transportation to and from work = $750

College tuition reimbursement = $1000

Language class tuition reimbursement = $500

THE TASK

1. Each group has fifteen minutes to develop a flexible benefits package that consumes twenty-five percent (and no more!) of their character's pay.

2. After completing step 1, each group appoints a spokesperson who describes to the entire class the benefits package they have arrived at for their character.

3. The entire class then discusses the results. How have the needs, concerns, and problems of each participant influenced his or her decision? What do these results suggest for trying to motivate a diverse work force?

C A S E I N C I D E N T 1

Rosenbluth Travel, Inc.

Rosenbluth Travel, Inc., isn't like your typical travel agency. First of all, it's huge. It employs 2350 people in 340 offices in the United States, England, and Asia. It is growing very quickly—adding about forty new offices a year—but what makes this agency unique is the way its president and chief executive officer, Hal F. Rosenbluth, runs it. Rosenbluth believes he has a responsibility to make work a pleasant and happy experience, so he has things like the Happiness Barometer Group. This is made up of eighteen employees, randomly selected from various offices, who provide feedback on how people

Source: Based on "Many Happy Returns," *INC.,* October 1990, pp. 31-44; and "First Impressions," *INC.,* December 1991, p. 157.

are feeling about their jobs. And when was the last time you heard of a firm that puts its employees ahead of its customers? Rosenbluth does!

The travel business, according to Rosenbluth, is stressful: "It's like being an air traffic controller, one call after another." As a result, turnover in the industry tends to be high—sometimes up to forty-five or fifty percent a year. Yet Rosenbluth's turnover is only six percent. His hiring and training programs help explain why.

Job candidates are carefully screened to find people who will fit into the agency. Rosenbluth wants team players and people with an upbeat attitude. Entry-level candidates undergo three to four hours of interviewing. For senior positions, Rosenbluth personally gets to know each applicant. For instance, he invited a sales executive candidate and his wife to go on a vacation with Rosenbluth and his wife. "On the third day of a vacation, things start to come out."

Once hired, the new employee becomes acclimated to the agency real quick. Instead of filling out forms on the first day, the new employee takes a role in skits meant to convey that Rosenbluth wants his people to laugh and have fun. But the skits are also learning experiences. New employees may be asked to play out an experience they've had with negative service, for example. Then the experience is analyzed to learn how the episode could be turned into great service. All new employees go through two to eight weeks of training, partly to allow managers to assess whether they will fit into Rosenbluth's high-energy team-focused environment. People who need the individual limelight are released.

One of Rosenbluth's more unusual qualities is putting the employee ahead of the customer. On rare occasions, he has even gone so far as to help a corporate client find another travel agency. He notes that usually these are firms that mistreat their own people, so they mistreat his employees on the phone. "I think it's terrible to ask one of our [employees] to talk with someone who's rude to them every fifteen minutes."

Questions

1. Would you want to work for Rosenbluth Travel? Why or why not?
2. If Rosenbluth's approach to managing people is so effective, why do you think so many organizations try hard to create a *serious* work climate?
3. Do you think happy workers are more productive?

FOR FURTHER READING

COATES, J. F., J. JARRAT, AND J. B. MAHAFFIE *Future Work* (San Francisco: Jossey–Bass, 1990). This book discusses seven critical forces reshaping work and the work force in North America.

COX, T., JR., "The Multicultural Organization," *Academy of Management Executive*, May 1991, pp. 34–47. This article describes the "multicultural" organization and how it differs from organizations of the past.

FREEMAN, R. E., "Ethics in the Workplace: Recent Scholarship," in C. L. Cooper and I. T. Robertson (eds.), *International Review of Industrial and Organizational Psychology*, Vol. 5 (Chichester: John Wiley, 1990), pp. 149–67. Identifies some of the main themes in the business ethics literature and illustrates the pervasiveness of ethical/moral issues in organizational life.

ILGEN, D. R., and H. J. KLEIN, "Organizational Behavior," in M. R. Rosenzweig and L. W. Porter (eds.), *Annual Review of Psychology*, Vol. 40 (Palo Alto, CA: Annual Reviews, Inc., 1989), pp. 327–51. Reviews recent contributions to OB using a cognitive perspective.

KRAUT, A. I., P. R. PEDIGO, D. D. MCKENNA, and M. D. DUNNETTE, "The Role of the Manager: What's Really Important in Different Management Jobs," *Academy of Management Executive*, November 1989, pp. 286–93. The authors found that managers who understand the differences as well as the similarities in managerial jobs across levels and functions gain certain advantages over those who don't.

PETTIT, J. D., JR., B. C. VAUGHT, and R. L. TREWATHA, "Interpersonal Skill Training: A Prerequisite for Success," *Business*, April–June 1990, pp. 8– 14. By teaching individuals how to improve their interpersonal skills, employee development programs will have a better chance of enhancing the performance of organizational members as well as the organization itself.

NOTES

[1] D. Milbank, "Managers Are Sent to 'Charm Schools' to Discover How to Polish Up Their Acts," *The Wall Street Journal*, December 14, 1990, p. B1.

[2] J. Flint, "We Need Manufacturing People at the Top: An Interview with Don Petersen," *Forbes*, August 20, 1990, p. 58.

[3] C. Hymowitz, "Five Main Reasons Why Managers Fail," *The Wall Street Journal*, May 2, 1988, p. 25.

[4] Milbank, "Managers Are Sent to 'Charm Schools' to Discover How to Polish Up Their Acts."

[5] H. Fayol, *Industrial and General Administration* (Paris: Dunod, 1916).

[6] H. Mintzberg, *The Nature of Managerial Work* (New York: Harper & Row, 1973).

[7] R. L. Katz, "Skills of an Effective Administrator," *Harvard Business Review*, September-October 1974, pp. 90-102.

[8] F. Luthans, "Successful vs. Effective Real Managers," *Academy of Management Executive*, May 1988, pp. 127-32; and F. Luthans, R. M. Hodgetts, and S. A. Rosenkrantz, *Real Managers* (Cambridge, MA: Ballinger Publishing, 1988).

[9] See, for instance, J. E. Garcia and K. S. Keleman, "What Is Organizational Behavior Anyhow?", paper presented at the Organizational Behavior Teaching Conference, Columbia, MO, June 1989.

[10] L. W. Porter and L. E. McKibbin, *Future of Management Education and Development: Drift or Thrust into the 21st Century?* (New York: McGraw-Hill, 1988).

[11] See, for instance, A. Kohn, "You Know What They Say..." *Psychology Today*, April 1988, pp. 36-41.

[12] E. E. Lawler III and J. G. Rhode, *Information and Control in Organizations* (Pacific Palisades, CA: Goodyear, 1976), p. 22.

[13] R. Weinberg and W. Nord, "Coping with 'It's All Common Sense'," *Exchange*, Vol. VII, No. 2 (1982), pp. 29-33; R. P. Vecchio, "Some Popular (But Misguided) Criticisms of the Organizational Sciences," *Organizational Behavior Teaching Review*, Vol. 10, No. 1 (1986-87), pp. 28-34; and M. L. Lynn, "Organizational Behavior and Common Sense: Philosophical Implications for Teaching and Thinking," paper presented at the 14th Annual Organizational Behavior Teaching Conference, Waltham, MA, May 1987.

[14]See, for instance, R. R. Thomas, Jr., "From Affirmative Action to Affirming Diversity," *Harvard Business Review,* March-April 1990, pp. 107-17; B. Mandrell and S. Kohler-Gray, "Management Development That Values Diversity," *Personnel,* March 1990, pp. 41-47; and J. Dreyfuss, "Get Ready for the New Work Force," *Fortune*, April 23, 1990, pp. 165-81.

[15]See S. Pedigo, "Diversity in the Workforce: Riding the Tide of Change," *The Wyatt Communicator,* Winter 1991, pp. 4-11.

[16]Dreyfuss, "Get Ready for the New Work Force," p. 168.

[17]See, for instance, P. L. McLeod and S. A. Lobel, "The Effects of Ethnic Diversity on Idea Generation in Small Groups," paper presented at the Annual Academy of Management Conference, Las Vegas, August 1992.

[18]J. Traub, "Loyalty: A Spasm of Layoffs and Downsizing in the 1980s Obliterated What Was Left of Corporate Loyalty," *Business Month,* October 1990, pp. 85-87.

[19]Reported in J. Castro, "Where Did the Gung-Ho Go?", *Time,* September 11, 1989, p. 53.

[20]K. Davis and W. C. Frederick, *Business and Society: Management, Public Policy, Ethics,* 5th ed. (New York: McGraw-Hill, 1984), p. 76.

[21]G. F. Cavanagh, D. J. Moberg, and M. Valasquez, "The Ethics of Organizational Politics," *Academy of Management Journal,* June 1981, pp. 363-74.

[22]L. S. Richman, "The Coming World Labor Shortage," *Fortune,* April 9, 1990, pp. 70-77; and A. Bernstein, "Do More Babies Mean Fewer Working Women?", *Business Week,* August 5, 1991, pp. 49-50.

[23]J. C. Szabo, "Finding the Right Workers," *Nation's Business,* February 1991, p. 19.

[24]S. Dentzer, "The Vanishing Dream," *U.S. News & World Report,* April 22, 1991, pp. 39-43.

[25]See, for example, M. J. Driver, "Cognitive Psychology: An Interactionist View;" R. H. Hall, "Organizational Behavior: A Sociological Perspective;" and C. Hardy, "The Contribution of Political Science to Organizational Behavior," all in J. W. Lorsch (ed.), *Handbook of Organizational Behavior* (Englewood Cliffs, NJ: Prentice Hall, 1987), pp. 62-108.

[26]D. Tjosvold, "Controversy for Learning Organizational Behavior," *Organizational Behavior Teaching Review,* Vol. XI, No. 3 (1986-87), pp. 51-59; and L. F. Moore, D. C. Limerick, and P. J. Frost, "Debating the Issue: Increasing Understanding of the 'Close Calls' in Organizational Decision Making," *Organizational Behavior Teaching Review,* Vol. XIV, No. 1 (1989-90), pp. 37-43.

TOWARD EXPLAINING AND PREDICTING BEHAVIOR

LEARNING OBJECTIVES

After studying this chapter, you should be able to:

1. Describe the purpose of research
2. Summarize the criteria used to evaluate research
3. Identify the research designs most used by OB researchers
4. List the individual advantages of laboratory and field settings
5. Define the three levels of analysis in OB
6. Describe the four key dependent variables in OB

Get your facts first, and then you can distort them as much as you please.

M. TWAIN

*T*here's an old adage that "there's nothing wrong with employee turnover, as long as the right employees are turning over." But what if the people you most want to keep are the ones leaving? What can management do? That was the dilemma faced by Kenn Ricci, president of Corporate Wings, Inc., an air-charter firm based in Cleveland, Ohio.[1]

When Corporate Wings was founded in 1978, it had no trouble hiring pilots. The war in Vietnam was over and the airlines were fully staffed, so there was a pilot surplus. Corporate Wings could hire experienced pilots and pay them substandard wages—starting at about $24,000 a year. Of course, as openings occurred at the major airlines, Ricci accepted the fact that his pilots would desert his firm for their higher wages and greater prestige and stability. Pilots stuck around Corporate Wings for about fourteen months and then left. As Ricci put it, "We were programmed for turnover."

This revolving-door policy worked fine for several years. Then regular customers began to complain about flying with new people all the time. In late 1986, two of the company's biggest clients severed their ties with Corporate Wings. Between October 1986 and March 1987, the company lost about a third of its business, almost all directly due to the high turnover among its pilots. Ricci realized that it was time to change the way his firm handled its pilots. He needed to continue to attract good people, but he also had to do something to keep them.

Ricci knew he couldn't pay his pilots the $100,000-plus yearly salaries that they could earn with the commercial airlines and still keep his firm profitable. What he decided to do was to create a two-tiered personnel system similar to that found in law firms. Ricci created a new rank called senior flight captain, reserved for only thirty percent of the company's pilots. Attaining this position was the equivalent of making partner in a law firm, and it was allocated only to the best of the company's pilots. Senior flight captains made fifteen to twenty percent more than the company's other senior pilots and these top-tiered jobs were secure as long as pilots maintained safety, health, and personal-conduct standards. They also got more health and life insurance, more paid vacation time, deferred compensation payable at retirement, and a greater say in scheduling their flying assignments.

After its first year of operation, the program seemed to be working. Corporate Wings had been losing about six or seven pilots a year but lost only two during the first twelve months of the program. Additionally, Ricci was pleased to find that the caliber of applicants for pilot positions had significantly improved. ■

*T*he Corporate Wings story illustrates a widespread concern of managers: How do you keep turnover down? In this chapter, we'll show you that employee turnover is one of four primary concerns that OB addresses, and we'll give you an overview of the factors that influence an employee's decision to leave an organization. Later in the chapter, we'll present a model that demonstrates how topics within OB fit together and how they can help you to predict outcomes such as employee turnover.

First, however, we want to briefly discuss the research upon which this book is built. This text will introduce hundreds of research studies in support of a number of behavioral theories. But theories are only as good as the research presented to support them. How do you, as a consumer of OB theories, evaluate the individual research studies presented in this text? We'll begin to answer that in the next section.

So this chapter addresses two concerns: research methodology and the structuring of the topics within OB into an integrative whole. These two concerns may, at first glance, seem somewhat unrelated. However, by the time you get to the end of this chapter, it should become obvious that these two issues form the foundation for building an integrative framework for explaining and predicting behavior.

RESEARCH IN ORGANIZATIONAL BEHAVIOR

A few years back, a friend was all excited because he had read about the findings from a research study that finally, once and for all, resolved the question of what it takes to make it to the top in a large corporation. I doubted there was any simple answer to this question but, not wanting to dampen his enthusiasm, I asked him to tell me what he had read. The answer, according to my friend, was: *participation in college athletics.* To say I was skeptical of his claim is a gross understatement, so I asked him to tell me more.

The study encompassed 1,700 successful senior executives at the 500 largest U.S. corporations. The researchers found that half of these executives had played varsity-level college sports.[2] My friend, who happens to be good with statistics, informed me that since fewer than two percent of all college students participate in intercollegiate athletics, the probability of this finding occurring by mere chance is less than one in 10 million! He concluded his analysis by telling me that, based on this research, I should encourage my management students to get into shape and to make one of the varsity teams.

My friend was somewhat perturbed when I suggested that his conclusions were likely to be flawed. These executives were all males who attended college in the 1940s and 1950s. Would his advice be meaningful to females in the 1990s? These executives also weren't your typical college students. For the most part, they had attended elite private colleges like Princeton and Lehigh, where a large proportion of the student body participates in intercollegiate sports. And these "jocks" hadn't necessarily played football or basketball; many had participated in golf, tennis, baseball, cross-country running, crew, rugby, and similar minor sports. Moreover, maybe the researchers had confused the direction of causality. That is, maybe individuals with the motivation and ability to make it to the top of a large corporation are drawn to competitive activities like college athletics.

My friend was guilty of misusing research data. Of course, he is not alone. We are all continually bombarded with reports of experiments that link certain substances to cancer in mice and surveys that show changing attitudes toward sex among college students, for example. Many of these studies are carefully designed, with great caution taken to note the implications and limitations of the findings. But some studies are poorly designed, making their conclusions at best suspect, and at worst meaningless.

Rather than attempting to make you a researcher, the purpose of this section is to increase your awareness as a consumer of behavioral research. A knowledge of research methods will allow you to appreciate more fully the care in data collection that underlies the information and conclusions presented in this text. Moreover, an understanding of research methods will make you a more skilled evaluator of those OB studies you will encounter in business and professional journals. So an appreciation of behavioral research is important because (1) it is the foundation upon which the theories in this text are built, and (2) it will benefit you in future years when you read reports of research and attempt to assess their value.

Purpose of Research

Research *The systematic gathering of information.*

Research is concerned with the systematic gathering of information. Its purpose is to help us in our search for the truth. While we will never find ultimate truth—in our case, that would be to know precisely how any person would behave in any organizational context—ongoing research adds to our body of OB knowledge by supporting some theories, contradicting others, and suggesting new theories to replace those that fail to gain support.

Research Terminology

Researchers have their own vocabulary for communicating among themselves and with outsiders. The following briefly defines some of the more popular terms you're likely to encounter in behavioral science studies.[3]

Variable *Any general characteristic that can be measured and that changes in either amplitude, intensity, or both.*

VARIABLE   A.**variable** is any general characteristic that can be measured and that changes in either amplitude, intensity, or both. Some examples of OB variables you'll find in this text are job satisfaction, employee productivity, work stress, ability, personality, and group norms.

Hypothesis *A tentative explanation of the relationship between two or more variables.*

HYPOTHESIS   A tentative explanation of the relationship between two or more variables is called a **hypothesis.** My friend's statement that participation in college athletics leads to a top executive position in a large corporation is an example of a hypothesis. Until confirmed by empirical research, a hypothesis remains only a *tentative* explanation.

Dependent Variable A response that is affected by an independent variable.

DEPENDENT VARIABLE A **dependent variable** is a response that is affected by an independent variable. In terms of the hypothesis, it is the variable that the researcher is interested in explaining. Referring back to the previous example, the dependent variable in my friend's hypothesis was executive succession. In organizational behavior research, the most popular dependent variables are productivity, absenteeism, turnover, job satisfaction, and organizational commitment.[4]

Independent Variable The presumed cause of some change in the dependent variable.

INDEPENDENT VARIABLE An **independent variable** is the presumed cause of some change in the dependent variable. Participating in varsity athletics was the independent variable in my friend's hypothesis. Popular independent variables studied by OB researchers include intelligence, personality, job satisfaction, experience, motivation, reinforcement patterns, leadership style, reward allocations, selection methods, and organization design. We have said that job satisfaction is frequently used by OB researchers as both a dependent and an independent variable. This is not an error. It merely reflects that the label given to a variable depends on its place in the hypothesis. In the statement "Increases in job satisfaction lead to reduced turnover," job satisfaction is an independent variable. However, in the statement "Increases in money lead to higher job satisfaction," job satisfaction becomes a dependent variable.

Moderating Variable Abates the effect of the independent variable on the dependent variable; also known as *contingency variable*.

MODERATING VARIABLE A **moderating variable** abates the effect of the independent variable on the dependent variable. It might also be thought of as the contingency variable: If X (independent variable), then Y (dependent variable) will occur, but only under conditions Z (moderating variable). To translate this into a real-life example, we might say that if we increase the amount of direct supervision in the work area (X), then there will be a change in worker productivity (Y), but this effect will be moderated by the complexity of the tasks being performed (Z).

Causality The implication that the independent variable causes change in the dependent variable.

CAUSALITY A hypothesis, by definition, implies a relationship. That is, it implies a presumed cause and effect. This direction of cause and effect is called **causality.** Changes in the independent variable are assumed to *cause* changes in the dependent variable. However, in behavioral research, it is possible to make an incorrect assumption of causality when relationships are found. For example, as we'll show in a later chapter, early behavioral scientists found a relationship between employee satisfaction and productivity. They concluded that a happy worker was a productive worker. Follow-up research has supported the relationship, but disconfirmed the direction of the arrow. The evidence more correctly suggests that high productivity leads to satisfaction rather than the other way around.

Correlation Coefficient Indicates the strength of a relationship between two or more variables.

CORRELATION COEFFICIENT It is one thing to know that there is a relationship between two or more variables. It is another to know the *strength* of that relationship. The term **correlation coefficient** is used to indicate that strength, and is expressed as a number between–1.00 (a perfect negative relationship) to +1.00 (a perfect positive correlation).

When two variables vary directly with one another, the correlation will be expressed as a positive number. When they vary inversely—that is, one increases as the other decreases—the correlation will be expressed as a negative number. If the two variables vary independently of each other, we say that the correlation between them is zero.

For example, a researcher might survey a group of employees to determine the satisfaction of each with his or her job. Then, using company absenteeism reports, the researcher could correlate the job satisfaction scores against individual attendance records to determine whether employees who are more satisfied with their jobs have better attendance records than their counterparts who indicated lower job satisfaction. Let's suppose the researcher found a correlation coefficient between satisfaction and attendance of +0.50. Would that be a strong association? There is, unfortunately, no precise numerical cutoff separating strong and weak relationships. A standard statistical test would need to be applied to determine whether or not the relationship was a significant one.

A final point needs to be made before we move on: A correlation coefficient measures only the strength of association between two variables. A high value does *not* imply causality. The length of women's skirts and stock market prices, for instance, have long been noted to be highly correlated, but one should be careful not to infer that a causal relationship between the two exists. In this instance, the high correlation is more happenstance than predictive.

THEORY   The final term we'll introduce in this section is **theory.** Theory describes a set of systematically interrelated concepts or hypotheses that purport to explain and predict phenomena. In OB, theories are also frequently referred to as *models.* We'll use the two terms interchangeably.

There are no shortages of theories in OB. For instance, we have theories to describe what motivates people, the most effective leadership styles, the best way to resolve conflicts, and how people acquire power. In some cases, we have half-a-dozen or more separate theories that purport to explain and predict a given phenomenon. In such cases, is one right and the others wrong? No! They tend to reflect science at work—researchers testing previous theories, modifying them, and, when appropriate, proposing new models that may prove to have higher explanatory and predictive powers. Multiple theories attempting to explain common phenomena merely attest that OB is an active discipline, still growing and evolving.

As we proceed through this text, we'll introduce and describe a great many theories. We'll also review the research evidence underlying them. In this way, you'll be able to see the present state of the field and assess which theories, at least at the current time, provide the best explanations of OB phenomena.

Evaluating Research

As a potential consumer of behavioral research, you should follow the dictum of *caveat emptor*—let the buyer beware! In evaluating any research study, you need to ask three questions.[5]

Is it valid? Is the study actually measuring what it claims to be measuring? Many psychological tests have been discarded by employers in recent years because they have not been found to be valid measures of the applicants' ability to successfully do a given job. But the **validity** issue is relevant to all research studies. So, if you find a study that links cohesive work groups with higher productivity, you want to know how each of these variables were measured and whether they are actually measuring what they are supposed to be measuring.

Is it reliable? **Reliability** refers to consistency of measurement. If you were to have your height measured every day with a wooden yardstick, you would get highly reliable results. On the other hand, if you were measured each day by an elastic tape measure, there would probably be considerable disparity between your height measurements from one day to the next. Your height, of course, does not change from day to day. The variability is due to the unreliability of the measuring device. So if a company asked a group of its employees to complete a reliable job satisfaction questionnaire, and then repeat the questionnaire six months later, we would expect the results to be very similar—provided nothing changed in the interim that might significantly affect employee satisfaction.

Is it generalizable? Are the results of the research study **generalizable** to groups of individuals other than those who participated in the original study? Be aware, for example, of the limitations that might exist in research that uses college students as subjects. Are the findings in such studies generalizable to full-time employees in real jobs? Similarly, how generalizable to the overall work population are the results from a study that assesses job stress among ten nuclear power plant engineers in the hamlet of Mahone Bay, Nova Scotia?

Research Design

Doing research is an exercise in trade-offs. Richness of information typically comes with reduced generalizability. The more a researcher seeks to control for confounding variables, the less realistic his or her results are likely to be. High precision, generalizability, and control almost always translate into higher costs. When researchers make choices about whom they'll study, where their research will be done, the methods they'll use to collect data, and so on, they must make some concessions. Good research designs are not perfect, but they do carefully reflect the questions being addressed. Keep these facts in mind as we review the strengths and weaknesses of five popular research designs: case studies, field surveys, laboratory experiments, field experiments, and aggregate quantitative reviews.

CASE STUDY   You pick up a copy of Lee Iacocca's autobiography. In it he describes how he moved up the management ladder at Ford Motor Co., eventually became president, was fired, took over as head of Chrysler Corp., and, in one of the most dramatic turnarounds in U.S. corporate history, took Chrysler from the brink of bankruptcy to billions in profits. Or you're in a business class and the instructor distributes a fifty-page handout covering two companies: Apple Computer and Control Data Corporation. The handout details the two firms' histories, describes their product lines, production facilities, management philosophies, and marketing strategies, and includes copies of their recent balance sheets and income statements. The instructor asks the class members to read the handout, analyze the data, and determine why Apple has been more successful in recent years than CDC.

Lee Iacocca's autobiography and the Apple and CDC handouts are **case studies.** Drawn from real-life situations, case studies present an in-depth analysis of one setting. They are thorough descriptions, rich in details about an individual, a group, or an organization. The primary source of information in case studies is obtained through observation, occasionally backed up by interviews and a review of records and documents.

Case studies have their drawbacks. They're open to the perceptual bias and subjective interpretations of the observer. The reader of a case is captive to what the observer/case writer chooses to include and exclude. Cases also trade off generalizability for depth of information and richness of detail. Since it's always dangerous to generalize from a sample of one, case studies make it difficult to prove or reject a hypothesis. On the other hand, you can't ignore the in-depth analysis that cases often provide. They are an excellent

Generalizability The degree to which results of a research study are applicable to groups of individuals other than those who participate in the original study.

Case Study An in-depth analysis of one setting.

device for initial exploratory research and for evaluating real-life problems in organizations.

FIELD SURVEY   A questionnaire made up of approximately a dozen items sought to examine the content of supervisory training programs in billion-dollar corporations. Copies of the questionnaire, with a cover letter explaining the nature of the study, were mailed to the corporate training officers at 250 corporations randomly selected from the Fortune 500 list; 155 officers responded to it. The results of this survey found, among other things, that the most common training topic was providing performance evaluation feedback to employees (ninety-two percent of the surveyed companies selected this topic as the most common aspect of their program). This was closely followed by developing effective delegation skills (ninety percent) and listening skills (eighty-three percent).[6]

Field Survey   Questionnaire or interview responses are collected from a sample, analyzed, and then inferences are made from the representative sample about the larger population.

The preceding study illustrates a typical **field survey.** A sample of respondents (in this case, 250 corporate training officers) was selected to represent a larger group that was under examination (corporate training officers in Fortune 500 firms). The respondents were then surveyed using a questionnaire or interviewed to collect data on particular characteristics (the content of supervisory training programs) of interest to the researcher. The standardization of response items allows for data to be easily quantified, analyzed, and summarized, and for the researcher to make inferences from the representative sample about the larger population.

The field survey provides economies for doing research. It's less costly to sample a population than to obtain data from every member of that population. Moreover, as the supervisory training program example illustrates, field surveys provide an efficient way to find out how people feel about issues or how they say they behave. These data can then be easily quantified. But the field survey has a number of potential weaknesses. First, mailed questionnaires rarely obtain one hundred percent returns. Low response rates call into question whether conclusions based on respondents' answers are generalizable to nonrespondents. Second, the format is better at tapping respondents' attitudes and perceptions than behaviors. Third,

Some of the most widely recognized field surveys are done by the Gallup Polls. Using a carefully selected sample of less than 1500 people, they are able to obtain extremely accurate estimates of the attitudes held by millions of people on many diverse issues.

Bohdan Hyrnewych/Stock, Boston

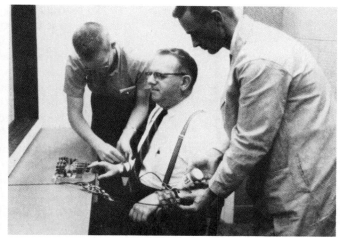
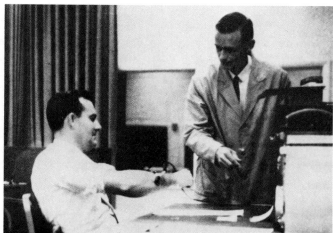

How far would you go in following orders? That was the question proposed by Yale social psychologist, Stanley Milgram. His research results—which indicated that a majority of subjects would follow commands that they found personally objectionable—created much discussion among behavioral scientists who were greatly surprised by Milgram's findings. Copyright 1956 by Stanley Milgram.

From the film Obedience, distributed by the New York University Film Library.

responses can suffer from social desirability; that is, people saying what they think the researcher wants to hear. Fourth, since field surveys are designed to focus on specific issues, they're a relatively poor means of acquiring depth of information. Finally, the quality of the generalizations is largely a factor of the population chosen. Responses from executives at Fortune 500 firms, for instance, tell us nothing about small- or medium-sized firms or not-for-profit organizations. In summary, even a well-designed field survey trades off depth of information for breadth, generalizability, and economic efficiencies.

Laboratory Experiment In an artificial environment, the researcher manipulates an independent variable under controlled conditions, and then concludes that any change in the dependent variable is due to the manipulation or change imposed on the independent variable.

LABORATORY EXPERIMENT The following study is a classic example of the **laboratory experiment:** A researcher, Stanley Milgram, wondered how far individuals would go in following commands. If subjects were placed in the role of a teacher in a learning experiment and told by an experimenter to administer a shock to a learner each time that learner made a mistake, would the subjects follow the commands of the experimenter? Would their willingness to comply decrease as the intensity of the shock was increased?

To test these hypotheses, Milgram hired a set of subjects. Each was led to believe that the experiment was to investigate the effect of punishment on memory. Their job was to act as teachers and administer punishment whenever the learner made a mistake on the learning test.

Punishment was administered by an electric shock. The subject sat in front of a shock generator with thirty levels of shock—beginning at zero and progressing in 15-volt increments to a high of 450 volts. The demarcations of these positions ranged from "Slight Shock" at 15 volts to "Danger: Severe Shock" at 450 volts. To increase the realism of the experiment, the subjects received a sample shock of 45 volts and saw the learner—a pleasant, mild-mannered man about fifty years old—strapped into an "electric chair" in an adjacent room. Of course, the learner was an actor, and the electric shocks were phony, but the subjects didn't know this.

Taking his seat in front of the shock generator, the subject was directed to begin at the lowest shock level and to increase the shock intensity to the next level each time the learner made a mistake or failed to respond.

When the test began, the shock intensity rose rapidly because the learner made many errors. The subject got verbal feedback from the learner: At 75 volts, the learner began to grunt and moan; at 150 volts, he demanded to be released from the experiment; at 180 volts, he cried out that he could no longer stand the pain; and at 300 volts, he insisted that he be let out, yelled about his heart condition, screamed, and then failed to respond to further questions.

Most subjects protested and, fearful they might kill the learner if the increased shocks were to bring on a heart attack, insisted they could not go on with their job. Hesitations or protests by the subject were met by the experimenter's statement, "You have no choice, you must go on! Your job is to punish the learner's mistakes." Of course, the subjects did have a choice. All they had to do was stand up and walk out.

The majority of the subjects dissented. But dissension isn't synonymous with disobedience. Sixty-two percent of the subjects increased the shock level to the maximum of 450 volts. The average level of shock administered by the remaining thirty-eight percent was nearly 370 volts.[7]

In a laboratory experiment such as that conducted by Milgram, an artificial environment is created by the researcher. Then the researcher manipulates an independent variable under controlled conditions. Finally, since all other things are held equal, the researcher is able to conclude that any change in the dependent variable is due to the manipulation or change imposed on the independent variable. Note that, because of the controlled conditions, the researcher is able to imply causation between the independent and dependent variables.

The laboratory experiment trades off realism and generalizability for precision and control. It provides a high degree of control over variables and precise measurement of those variables. But findings from laboratory studies are often difficult to generalize to the real world of work. This is because the artificial laboratory rarely duplicates the intricacies and nuances of real organizations. Additionally, many laboratory experiments deal with phenomena that cannot be reproduced or applied to real-life situations.

Field Experiment A controlled experiment conducted in a real organization.

FIELD EXPERIMENT The following is an example of a **field experiment:** The management of a large company is interested in determining the impact that a four-day workweek would have on employee absenteeism. To be more specific, they want to know if employees working four ten-hour days have lower absence rates than similar employees working the traditional five-day week of eight hours each day. Because the company is large, it has a

Is OB the "Science of the College Sophomore"?

A major determinant of the generalizability of any laboratory experiment is the characteristics of the study's subjects. If the subjects are all male managers, between the ages of forty-five and sixty, working in large corporations like General Motors and IBM, conclusions based on the study's findings need to be limited to reflect this.

This recognition of limiting generalizability to reflect characteristics of the subjects would not be a problem in OB if laboratory experiments tended to include all sizes, shapes, and kinds of subjects. After all, organizations come in all types, and so do their employees. But it has long been observed that the behavioral studies that compose a large part of the OB research literature rely heavily upon college students as experimental subjects.[8] Generations of college students have toiled in university laboratories solving problems they didn't create, working at "jobs" that only hours before they knew nothing about, selecting applicants for hire in nonexistent organizations, and the like. The results of these experiments then find their way into the behavioral literature and form the basis for current theories as well as suggestions for improved practices. For instance, approximately seventy-five percent of published research in social psychology has involved college students.

Why has this occurred? The best answer is:

Convenience. College students are a readily available resource to faculty researchers and a low-cost alternative to investigating full-time employees in work organizations.

Does this wide use of college students invalidate OB theories? This question is not easily answered. On one hand, clearly college students are not representative of the general work population. This is especially true where subjects are young undergraduates with little or no substantive work experience. On the other hand, for many research objectives, students are not unlike nonstudents. For example, studies dealing with perception, attitude change, learning processes, or communication are likely to be as generalizable with college students as with any other population. Additionally, any research population can be argued to be atypical. Homogeneously defined groups of subjects—be they college-educated white-collar professionals, employees in high-tech industries, or college students—require the researcher to qualify his or her findings. And since no group can fully represent the complete diversity of employees in all types of organizations in all countries of the world, all studies will have some limitations to their generalizability. The key is understanding who the subjects are in a study and the limitations this imposes on the study's findings.

number of manufacturing plants that employ essentially similar work forces. Two of these are chosen for the experiment, both located in the greater Cleveland area. Obviously, it would not be appropriate to compare two similar-sized plants if one is in rural Mississippi and the other is in downtown Boston, because factors such as transportation and weather, might be more likely to explain any differences found than changes in the number of days worked per week.

In one plant, the experiment was put into place—workers began the four-day week. At the other plant, which became the control group, no changes were made in the employees' five-day week. Absence data was gathered from the company's records at both locations for a period of eighteen months. This extended time period lessened the possibility that any results would be distorted by the mere novelty of changes being implemented in the

Ethics in Research

Researchers are not always tactful or candid with subjects when they do their studies. For instance, questions in field surveys may be perceived as embarrassing by respondents or as an invasion of privacy. Also, researchers in laboratory studies have been known to deceive participants as to the true purpose of their experiment "because they felt deception was necessary to get honest responses."[9]

The "learning experiments" conducted by Stanley Milgram were widely criticized by psychologists on ethical grounds. He lied to subjects, telling them his study was investigating learning, when, in fact, he was concerned with obedience. The shock machine he used was a fake. Even the "learner" was an accomplice of Milgram's who had been trained to act as if he were hurt and in pain.

Professional associations like the American Psychological Association, the American Sociological Association, and the Academy of Management have published formal guidelines for the conduct of research. Yet the ethical debate continues. On one side are those who argue that strict ethical controls can damage the scientific validity of an experiment and cripple future research. Deception, for example, is often necessary to avoid contaminating results. Moreover, proponents of minimizing ethical controls note that few subjects have been appreciably harmed by deceptive experiments. Even in Milgram's highly manipulative experiment, only 1.3 percent of the subjects reported negative feelings about their experience. The other side of this debate focuses on the rights of participants. Those favoring strict ethical controls argue that no procedure should ever be emotionally or physically distressing to subjects, and that, as professionals, researchers are obliged to be completely honest with their subjects and to protect the subjects' privacy at all costs.

Now, let's take a look at a sampling of ethical questions relating to research. Do you think Milgram's experiment was unethical? Would you judge it unethical for a company to anonymously survey its employees with mail questionnaires on their intentions to quit their present job? Would your answer be any different if the company coded the survey responses to identify those who didn't reply so they could send them follow-up questionnaires? Would it be unethical for management to hide a video camera on the production floor to study group interaction patterns (with the goal of using the data to design more effective work teams) without first telling employees that they were subjects of research? What do *you* think?

experimental plant. After eighteen months, management found that absenteeism had dropped by forty percent at the experimental plant, and by only six percent in the control plant. Because of the design of this study, management believed that the larger drop in absences at the experimental plant was due to the introduction of the compressed workweek.

The field experiment is similar to the laboratory experiment, except it is conducted in a real organization. The natural setting is more realistic than the laboratory setting, and this enhances validity but hinders control. Additionally, unless control groups are maintained, there can be a loss of control if extraneous forces intervene—for example, an employee strike, a major layoff, or a corporate restructuring. Maybe the greatest concern with field studies has to do with organizational selection bias. Not all organizations are going to allow outside researchers to come in and study their employees and operations. This is especially true of organizations that have serious problems. Therefore, since most published studies in OB are done by outside researchers, the selection bias might work toward publication of studies conducted almost exclusively at successful and well-managed organizations.

Our general conclusion is that, of the four research designs we've discussed, the field experiment typically provides the most valid and generalizable findings and, except for its high cost, trades off the least to get the most.

AGGREGATE QUANTITATIVE REVIEWS   What relationship, if any, is there between the sex of employees and occupational stress? There have been a number of individual field surveys and qualitative reviews of these surveys that have sought to throw light on this question. Unfortunately, these various studies produced conflicting results.

To try to reconcile these conflicts, researchers at Michigan State University identified all published correlations between sex and stress in work-related contexts.[10] After discarding reports that had inadequate information, nonquantitative data, and failed to include both men and women in their sample, the researchers narrowed their set to fifteen studies that included data on 9439 individuals. Using an aggregating technique called meta-analysis, the researchers were able to integrate the studies quantitatively and conclude that there are no differences in experienced stress between men and women in a work setting.

Meta-analysis A statistical technique that quantitatively integrates and synthesizes a number of independent studies to determine if they consistently produced similar results.

The sex–stress review done by the Michigan State researchers illustrates the use of **meta-analysis,** a quantitative form of literature review that enables researchers to look at validity findings from a comprehensive set of individual studies, and then apply a formula to them to determine if they consistently produced similar results.[11] If results prove to be consistent, it allows researchers to conclude more confidently that validity is generalizable. Meta-analysis is a means for overcoming the potentially imprecise interpretations of qualitative reviews. Additionally, the technique enables researchers to identify potential moderating variables between an independent and a dependent variable.

In the past decade, there has been a surge in the popularity of this research method. Why? It appears to offer a more objective means for doing traditional literature reviews. While the use of meta-analysis requires researchers to make a number of judgment calls, which can introduce a considerable amount of subjectivity into the process, there is no arguing that meta-analysis reviews have now become widespread in the OB literature. In coming chapters, we'll frequently mention comprehensive reviews of research on a given issue. When those reviews use aggregate studies based on the quantitative techniques of meta-analysis, we'll use the term *meta-analysis.* Now you'll have some idea of what we mean by that term.

Summary

The subject of organizational behavior is composed of a large number of theories that are research-based. Research studies, when cumulatively integrated, become theories; and theories are proposed and followed by research studies designed to validate them. The concepts that make up OB, therefore, are only as valid as the research that supports them.

As you review the topics and issues introduced in this text, keep in mind that they are—for the most part—largely research-derived. They represent the result of systematic information gathering rather than merely hunch, intuition, or opinion. But this does not mean that we have all the

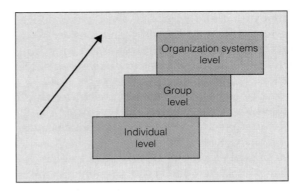

FIGURE 2-1   Basic OB Model, Stage I

answers to OB issues. Many require far more corroborating evidence. The generalizability of others is limited by the research methods used. As we proceed through the topics in this text and as the research is reviewed, every effort will be made to point out limitations to the findings that relate to the quality or quantity of supporting research.

DEVELOPING AN OB MODEL

The second part of this chapter presents a general model that defines the field of OB, stakes out its parameters, and identifies its primary dependent and independent variables. The end result will be a "coming attraction" of the topics making up the remainder of this book.

An Overview

Model   Abstraction of reality; simplified representation of some real-world phenomenon.

A **model** is an abstraction of reality; a simplified representation of some real-world phenomenon. A mannequin in a retail store is a model. So, too, is the accountant's formula: Assets = Liabilities + Owners' Equity. Figure 2–1 presents the skeleton on which we will construct our OB model. It proposes that there are three levels of analysis in OB, and that as we move from the individual level to the organization systems level, we add systematically to our understanding of behavior in organizations. The three basic levels are analogous to building blocks—each level is constructed upon the previous level. Group concepts grow out of the foundation laid in the individual section; we overlay structural constraints on the individual and group in order to arrive at organizational behavior.

The Dependent Variables

What are the primary dependent variables in OB? Scholars tend to emphasize productivity, absenteeism, turnover, and job satisfaction. Because of their wide acceptance, we shall use these four as the critical determinants of an organization's human resources effectiveness. However, there is nothing magical about these variables. They merely show that OB research has strongly reflected managerial interests over those of individuals or of society as a whole. Of course, in years to come, new dependent variables may be added to, or may replace, those that currently dominate the OB field. For instance, one author has argued for the growing importance of job stress, individual dissent, and innovation as dependent variables.[12] In defense of innovation, he argues, "As a greater percentage of work becomes highly skilled and professionalized, the criteria of performance will likely become more ambiguous and subject to change. Therefore, questions of [employee] productivity may become translated into inquiries about working smarter rather than harder....Where there is rapid change or competition is fierce, innovation may be the organization's most important outcome variable."[13] The fact remains, however, that productivity, absenteeism, turnover, and job satisfaction currently dominate the field. So let's review these terms to ensure that we understand what they mean and why they have achieved the distinction of being OB's primary dependent variables.

Productivity A performance measure including effectiveness and efficiency.

Effectiveness Achievement of goals.

Efficiency The ratio of effective output to the input required to achieve it.

PRODUCTIVITY   An organization is productive if it achieves its goals, and does so by transferring inputs to outputs at the lowest cost. As such, **productivity** implies a concern for both **effectiveness** and **efficiency**.

A hospital, for example, is *effective* when it successfully meets the needs of its clientele. It is *efficient* when it can do this at a low cost. If a hospital manages to achieve higher output from its present staff by reducing the average number of days a patient is confined to a bed or by increasing the number of staff—-patient contacts per day, we say that the hospital has gained productive efficiency. Similarly, a school may be effective when a certain percentage of students achieve a specified score on standardized achievement tests. The school can improve its efficiency if these higher test scores can be secured by a smaller teaching and support staff. A business firm is effective when it attains its sales or market share goals, but its productivity also depends on achieving these goals efficiently. Measures of such efficiency may include return on investment, profit per dollar of sales, and output per hour of labor.

We can also look at productivity from the perspective of the individual employee. Take the cases of Mike and Al, who are both long-distance truckers. If Mike is supposed to haul his fully loaded rig from New York to its destination in Los Angeles in seventy-five hours or less, he is effective if he makes the three-thousand-mile trip within this time period. But measures of productivity must take into account the costs incurred in reaching the goal. That's where efficiency comes in. Let's assume that Mike made the New York to Los Angeles run in sixty-eight hours and averaged seven miles per gallon. Al, on the other hand, made the trip in sixty-eight hours also, but averaged nine miles per gallon (rigs and loads are identical). Both Mike and Al were effective—they accomplished their goal—but Al was more efficient than Mike because his rig consumed less gas and, therefore, he achieved his goal at a lower cost.

In summary, one of OB's major concerns is productivity. We want to know what factors will influence the effectiveness and efficiency of individuals, of groups, and of the overall organization.

Absenteeism Failure to report to work.

ABSENTEEISM   The annual cost of **absenteeism** has been estimated at over $40 billion for U.S. organizations and $12 billion for Canadian firms.[14] At the job level, a one-day absence by a clerical worker can cost an employer up to $100 in reduced efficiency and increased supervisory workload.[15] These figures indicate the importance to an organization of keeping absenteeism low.

It is obviously difficult for an organization to operate smoothly and to attain its objectives if employees fail to report to their jobs. The work flow is disrupted, and often important decisions must be delayed. In organizations that rely heavily upon assembly-line technology, absenteeism can be considerably more than a disruption—it can result in a drastic reduction in quality

High Turnover Among Minorities and Women

Monsanto's chemical subsidiary has prided itself on aggressively hiring minorities and women since the 1970s.[16] For instance, in one recent year, seventeen percent of nonunion new hires were minorities and twenty-nine percent were women. But the company has found it hard to keep these people. In that same year, the percentages of minorities and women who quit were twenty percent and twenty-six percent, respectively. Corning Glass reports similar problems.[17] Over a recent eight-year period, turnover among women in professional jobs was double that of men, and the rates for blacks were two-and-one-half times those for whites.

Unfortunately, these two companies' experiences are not unusual. The evidence clearly indicates that minorities and women have significantly higher turnover rates than white males. For example, one study reported that the overall turnover rate for blacks in the United States' work force is forty percent higher than for whites.[18] Another study cites the turnover rate among women in management as twice that of men.[19] The primary reason for these higher turnover rates is the perception by minorities and women that there is a lack of opportunity for them in their organizations. Sadly, far too often this perception is accurate. Minorities and women frequently do face limited promotion opportunities, especially into the very top levels of management.

Two researchers have analyzed the cost savings that can result from lowering these unusually high turnover rates.[20] They assumed an organization of ten thousand employees that has a work force that is thirty-five percent women and minorities and sixty-five percent white men. They further assumed that this organization's annual turnover rate for white males is ten percent and the rate for women and minorities mirrors the national average of about twice the rate for white males, hence, in this case, twenty percent. Given these assumptions, they concluded that the organization is losing 350 additional employees a year from the women and minority groups. If turnover costs average $20,000 per employee, and if half the turnover rate difference could be eliminated, the potential cost savings for this organization would be $3.5 million a year.

of output, and, in some cases, it can bring about a complete shutdown of the production facility. Examples abound of the problems that the major U.S. automobile manufacturers have with alarmingly large increases in absences on Mondays and Fridays, especially in summer months and at the onset of the hunting and fishing seasons. Certainly, levels of absenteeism beyond the normal range have a direct impact on an organization's effectiveness and efficiency.

Are *all* absences bad? Probably not! While most absences impact negatively on the organization, we can conceive of situations where the organization may benefit by an employee voluntarily choosing not to come to work. For instance, fatigue or excess stress can significantly decrease an employee's productivity. In jobs where an employee needs to be alert—surgeons and airline pilots are obvious examples—it may well be better for the organization if the employee does not report to work rather than show up and perform poorly. The cost of an accident in such jobs could be prohibitive. Even in managerial jobs, where mistakes are less spectacular, performance may be improved when incumbents absent themselves from work rather than make a poor decision under stress. But these examples are clearly atypical. For the most part, we can assume that organizations benefit when employee absenteeism is reduced.

Turnover Voluntary and involuntary permanent withdrawal from the organization.

TURNOVER A high rate of **turnover** in an organization means increased recruiting, selection, and training costs. It can also mean a disruption in the efficient running of an organization when knowledgeable and experienced personnel leave and replacements must be found and prepared to assume positions of responsibility. All organizations, of course, have some turnover. If the right people are leaving the organization—the marginal and submarginal employees—turnover can be positive. It may create the opportunity to replace an underperforming individual with someone with higher skills or motivation, open up increased opportunities for promotions, and add new and fresh ideas to the organization.[21] But turnover often means the loss of people the organization doesn't want to lose. For instance, one study covering nine hundred employees who had resigned their jobs found that ninety-two percent earned performance ratings of "satisfactory" or better from their superiors.[22] So when turnover is excessive, or when it involves valuable performers, it can be a disruptive factor, hindering the organization's effectiveness.

Job Satisfaction A general attitude toward one's job; the difference between the amount of rewards workers receive and the amount they believe they should receive.

JOB SATISFACTION The final dependent variable we will look at is **job satisfaction,** which we'll define simply, at this point, as the difference between the amount of rewards workers receive and the amount they believe they should receive. (We'll expand considerably on this definition in Chapter 6.) Unlike the previous three variables, job satisfaction represents an attitude rather than a behavior. Why, then, has it become a primary dependent variable? For two reasons: its demonstrated relationship to performance factors and the value preferences held by many OB researchers.

The belief that satisfied employees are more productive than dissatisfied employees has been a basic tenet among managers for years. While much evidence questions this assumed causal relationship, it can be argued that advanced societies should be concerned not only with the quantity of life—that is, concerns such as higher productivity and material acquisitions—but also with its quality. Those researchers with strong humanistic values argue that satisfaction is a legitimate objective of an organization. Not only is satisfaction negatively related to absenteeism and turnover, but, they argue, organizations have a responsibility to provide employees with jobs that are challenging and intrinsically rewarding. Therefore, although job satisfaction represents an attitude rather than a behavior, OB researchers typically consider it an important dependent variable.

The Independent Variables

What are the major determinants of productivity, absenteeism, turnover, and job satisfaction? Our answer to that question brings us to the independent variables. Consistent with our belief that organizational behavior can best be understood when viewed essentially as a set of increasingly complex building blocks, the base or first level of our model lies in understanding individual behavior.

INDIVIDUAL-LEVEL VARIABLES It has been said that "managers, unlike parents, must work with used, not new, human beings—human beings whom others have gotten to first."[23] When individuals enter an organization, they're a bit like used cars. Each is different. Some are "low-mileage"—they have been treated carefully and have had only limited expo-

Organizational behavior addresses three levels of analysis. It looks at individual-level variables (top right), group-level variables (top), and organization system-level variables (bottom right). Right and top, Hewlett Packard; bottom right , Andrea Brizzi/ The Stock Market.

sure to the realities of the elements. Others are "well-worn," having experienced a number of rough roads. This metaphor indicates that people enter organizations with certain characteristics that will influence their behavior at work. The more obvious of these are personal or biographical characteristics such as age, sex, and marital status; personality characteristics; values and attitudes; and basic ability levels. These characteristics are essentially intact when an individual enters the work force, and, for the most part, there is little management can do to alter them. Yet, they have a very real impact on employee behavior. Therefore, each of these factors—biographical characteristics, personality, values and attitudes, and ability—will be discussed as independent variables in Chapters 4 and 6.

There are four other individual-level variables that have been shown to affect employee behavior: perception, individual decision making, learning, and motivation. These topics will be introduced and discussed in Chapters 4, 5, 7, and 8.

Figure 2–2 diagrams the individual level in our OB model. Note the dotted line around biographical characteristics, personality, values and attitudes, and ability. This is to dramatize that these variables, for the most

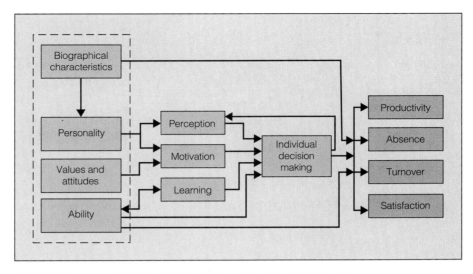

FIGURE 2-2   The Individual Level in the OB Model

part, are already in place when an employee joins an organization. The individual variables shown in Figure 2–2 are the subject matter of Chapters 4 through 8.

GROUP-LEVEL VARIABLES   The behavior of people in groups is more than the sum total of each individual acting in his or her own way. The complexity of our model is increased when we acknowledge that people's behavior when they are in groups is different from their behavior when they are alone. Therefore, the next step in the development of an understanding of OB is the study of group behavior.

Chapter 9 lays the foundation for an understanding of the dynamics of group behavior. This chapter discusses how individuals in groups are influenced by the patterns of behavior they are expected to exhibit, what the group considers to be acceptable standards of behavior, and the degree to

FIGURE 2-3   The Group Level in the OB Model

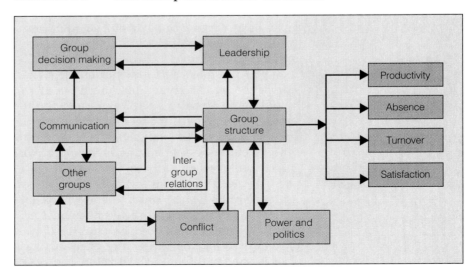

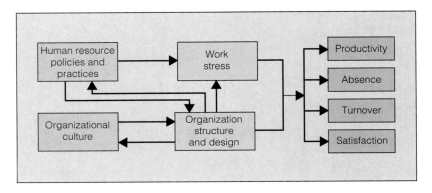

FIGURE 2-4   The Organization System Level in the OB Model

which group members are attracted to each other. Chapters 10 through 13 demonstrate how communication patterns, group decision-making processes, leadership styles, power and politics, intergroup relations, and levels of conflict affect group behavior. Figure 2–3 describes how these concepts interact and form the group level in our OB model.

ORGANIZATION SYSTEM-LEVEL VARIABLES   Organizational behavior reaches its highest level of sophistication when we add formal structure to our previous knowledge of individual and group behavior. Just as groups are more than the sum of their individual members, so are organizations more than the sum of their member groups. The structural design of the formal organization, the organization's human resource policies and practices (that is, selection processes, training programs, performance appraisal methods), levels of work stress, and internal culture all have an impact on the dependent variables.

Figure 2–4 describes the organization system–level variables in our model. These are discussed in detail in Chapters 14 through 18.

Toward a Contingency OB Model

Our final model is shown in Figure 2–5. It shows the four key dependent variables and a large number of independent variables that research suggests have varying impacts on them. Of course, the model does not do justice to the complexity of the OB subject matter, but it should prove valuable in helping to explain and predict behavior.

For the most part, our model does not explicitly identify the vast number of moderating variables because of the tremendous complexity that would be involved in such a diagram. Rather, throughout this text we shall introduce important moderating variables that will improve the explanatory linkage between the independent and dependent variables in our OB model. One exception is the specific inclusion of *national culture* as a variable that affects all levels of analysis.

We need to look at OB from a global perspective. Why? Because organizations are no longer constrained by national borders, because organizational behavior is different in different countries, and because these differences affect all our independent variables. The next chapter presents several frameworks for analyzing differences between countries. The global perspective is then reinforced throughout the rest of this book in OB in a Global

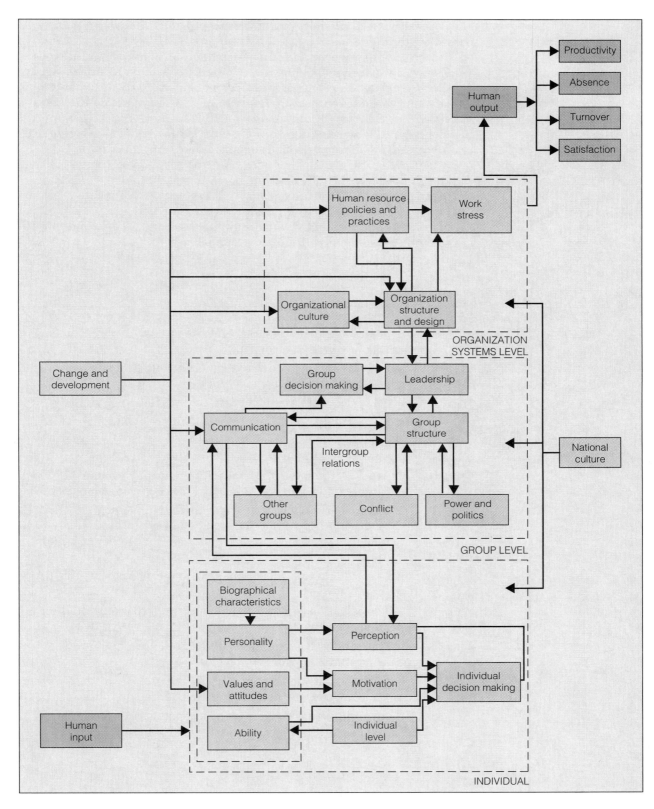

FIGURE 2-5   Basic OB Model, Stage II

Context boxes that show you how concepts and practices must be modified to reflect differences across national cultures.

Note that we've added the concepts of change and development to Figure 2–5, acknowledging the dynamics of behavior and recognizing that there are ways for change agents or managers to modify many of the independent variables if they are having a negative impact on the key dependent variables. Specifically, in Chapter 19 we'll discuss the change process and techniques for changing employee attitudes, improving communication processes, modifying organization structures, and the like.

Finally, Figure 2–5 includes linkages between the three levels of analysis. For instance, organization structure is linked to leadership. This is meant to convey that authority and leadership are related—management exerts its influence on group behavior through leadership. Similarly, communication is the means by which individuals transmit information; thus, it is the link between individual and group behavior.

FOR DISCUSSION

1. Why should students of OB spend time to develop an elementary understanding of research design?

2. What factors might reduce the generalizability of a research study?

3. What are the advantages and disadvantages of a (a) case study, (b) field survey, (c) laboratory experiment, and (d) field experiment?

4. What is reliability? Validity? What is the relevance of each to research?

5. Define *independent, dependent,* and *moderating variables.* Explain their relationship.

6. It is well-documented that married men and women live longer than their unmarried counterparts. Does marriage *cause* longer life? Explain.

7. Statistics clearly show that college graduates earn substantially more money during their working lives than do individuals who have not attended college. Does the college experience *cause* higher earnings? Explain.

8. What are the three levels of analysis in our OB model? Are they related? If so, how?

9. If job satisfaction is not a behavior, why is it considered an important dependent variable?

10. What are "effectiveness" and "efficiency," and how are they related to organizational behavior?

11. What are the four dependent variables in the OB model? Why have they been chosen over, for instance, percent return on investment?

12. Why are individual-, group-, and organization system–level behaviors described as successively more complex?

Employee Turnover Is Dysfunctional to an Organization

This text presents employee turnover as one of the four primary dependent variables in OB. This is consistent with the widespread conviction among executives, personnel managers, and researchers in OB that turnover has negative consequences for organizational performance.

When an employee quits and has to be replaced, an organization incurs both obvious and hidden costs. The following breakdown itemizes the turnover costs that experts calculate are incurred when a middle-level manager earning $39,000 a year has to be replaced. Keep in mind that these costs are not atypical.

■ Inefficiencies as the new employee learns the job (it usually takes about 13.5 months for a new employee to reach 100 percent efficiency)...$18,600
Additional time lost by supervisors and peers while the new employee gets up to speed...$11,700

■ Lost efficiency of departing employee in those weeks or months just prior to his or her leaving...$2,200

■ Additional time lost by supervisors and peers just prior to the departing employee's leaving...$800

■ Productivity lost while the position is vacant...$19,000

■ Out-of-pocket processing costs, including search fees and expenses, orientation, training, and travel costs for recruiters and candidates...$2,400

■ Cost of processing incoming and departing employees, including relocation costs...$3,400

■ Total costs $58,100

The evidence indicates that the ratio of turnover costs to annual salary is between 1.2 and 2.0, with the average at about 1.5. The range reflects differences in position level, organizational function, the extent to which agency search and outplacement services are used, and relocation costs. What this means is that the loss of even a $15,000-a-year clerk can cost an organization $18,000 or more.

Given both the obvious and hidden costs associated with turnover, any management team that is concerned with maintaining effectiveness and efficiency will want to hold employee turnover to a minimum.

Based on J. D. Phillips, "The Price Tag on Turnover," *Personnel Journal,* December 1990, pp. 58–61.

Employee Turnover Can Be Functional

All turnover is not bad for an organization. Discussions on the subject tend to stress the costs side of the ledger. But turnover also provides benefits to the organization. In fact, healthy levels of employee turnover may be a virtual windfall—in hard dollar terms—for the organization.

To consider all turnover negatively overstates its impact. Why? Well, first we need to look only at voluntary turnover. Involuntary turnover—where management initiates the departure—is functional, if we assume the decision is for a cause. Second, there are people who voluntarily leave the organization and in so doing benefit it. They may have been poor or, at best, marginal performers. But because of institutionalized employment security (labor unions, appeal boards, etc.), sympathetic bosses, the desire to maintain group morale, or similar factors, these people are not terminated. Finally, all voluntary quits are not controllable by management. That is, there are situations in which no reasonable action by management could have prevented it. It's a waste of organizational resources to try to reduce this element of turnover. In summary, any discussion of turnover should be concerned only with voluntary quits, and from that number we need to subtract all functional turnover plus the portion that, while dysfunctional, is unavoidable.

Now let's turn to a neglected issue: Turnover has a positive "dollar and cents" impact on the organization. In support of this position, we need to recognize that turnover may be reduced, but at a cost that exceeds its benefits, and new hires are not as costly to maintain in terms of salary and benefits as are more senior employees.

A number of jobs have characteristically high levels of turnover—for instance, waitresses and bank clerks—that could be significantly reduced by merely raising their wage rates. But management has chosen not to pay the wages that would be necessary to keep these people. In cost-effectiveness terms, management's strategy has been to trade off higher turnover for lower labor costs.

An overlooked fact in organizations is that there are a number of jobs where wage rates increase with time, but there is no comparable increase in productivity. For instance, at one public utility, entry-level employees receive $7.82 per hour and then move through the wage progression to $15.45 in their fifth year. The job remains the same, but the hourly wage cost nearly doubles. While employee productivity will increase over this five-year period, the increase is more likely to be in the ten-to-twenty-percent range. Additionally, given that benefit costs tend to be a percentage of direct labor costs, these too go up significantly as employee seniority increases. The result: Recent hires cost the organization less.

There are relatively large economies to be realized by employee turnover. To the extent that turnover is not excessive—that is, its costs do not exceed its benefits—a large amount of money might be saved each year by reasonable levels of turnover. Vigorous programs by organizations to reduce the incidence of employee turnover may be thoroughly shortsighted. This caveat may be particularly appropriate for organizations in which training requirements are minimal and experience may not lead to appreciably higher levels of performance.

Based on D. R. Dalton, W. D. Todor, and D. M. Krackhardt, "Turnover Overstated: The Functional Taxonomy," *Academy of Management Review,* January 1982, pp. 117–23; Dalton and Todor, "Turnover: A Lucrative Hard Dollar Phenomenon," *Academy of Management Review,* April 1982, pp. 212–18; and J. R. Hollenbeck and C. R. Williams, "Turnover Functionality versus Turnover Frequency: A Note on Work Attitudes and Organizational Effectiveness," *Journal of Applied Psychology,* November 1986, pp. 606–11.

The Memory Test

Who has the better memory—men or women? There is no better way to answer this question than by undertaking a research study. And that is precisely what a college professor recently did. The following paragraphs describe that professor's research design.

The professor made up two sets of five-by-eight-inch flashcards. Set No. 1 contained fifteen cards with unfamiliar three-letter combinations printed on them in three-inch letters with a thin black marker. Set No. 2 contained ten cards with familiar three-letter combinations printed in four-inch letters with a thick red marker.

Set No. 1				Set No. 2	
DLS	UQW	KBA		IBM	AAA
KHX	VBC	MWM		NBC	CBS
MWW	DXS	CTD		ABC	FOX
MDP	HWT	CRN		MTV	TWA
KVL	NCE	EDB		TNT	FBI

The professor divided the class into two groups according to gender. He ran the men's trial first, using Set No. 1. He presented each card at two-second intervals, but did not read them out loud and would not let the students write anything down. After the first run-through, the professor shuffled the cards and then showed them a second time. Immediately following the men's trial, he ran the women's trial using Set No. 2. He presented the cards at five-second intervals and read the cards aloud. Without shuffling them, he went through the cards a second time with the women. They, too, were not allowed to write anything down.

Immediately after the women's trial, the students were asked to write down as many of the cards as they could recall in a ninety-second period. The professor then reread both lists of cards and had the students count the number of cards they correctly recalled. On the chalkboard, he constructed a frequency table of number of cards recalled by gender. The average number remembered by the men was three, while the average number remembered by the women was seven. The professor concluded that his experiment demonstrated clearly that women have better memories than men.

The quality of any research conclusion is only as good as the design of the research. What flaws can you find in this research design? Break into groups of three to five students each. Take ten minutes to list specific flaws in this research design that taint the conclusions. After each group has developed its list, all the groups will discuss any flaws that they have uncovered.

Source: Based on K. M. York, "An Experiment: Teaching Experimental Design," *Organizational Behavior Teaching Review,* Vol. 13, No. 2 (1988–89), pp. 107–10.

Gender and Diversity

Each class member should independently write up answers to the following questions:

1. In what ways, if any, do you think men and women differ?
2. In what ways, if any, do you think these differences affect their behavior at work?
3. What, if anything, have your family, friends, teachers, coaches, or other significant people in your life encouraged you to do or discouraged you from doing because of your gender?
4. Have you felt subtle or not-so-subtle barriers or constraints because of your gender regarding self-expression, relationships with the same/other sex, career plans, or sports participation? If so, elaborate.

The class should be divided into two groups by gender and each group should select a leader. Large classes may require creating more groups, but each should be single-sex. Members of each group should share their answers to the four questions with their group and each group's leader should summarize that group's insights.

The group leaders should then come to the front of the class and briefly share their groups' findings, after which the issue should be explored in an open class discussion.

Source: This exercise was influenced by E. Avery, M. Crary, D. Spelman, and B. Walker, "Teaching a Managing Diversity Course: Unresolved Issues and Dilemmas," paper presented at the 1991 Organizational Behavior Teaching Conference, Bellingham, WA.

Evaluating *In Search of Excellence*

Tom Peters and Robert Waterman's *In Search of Excellence* (Harper & Row, 1982), with sales in excess of 5 million copies, has become one of the largest selling and most often quoted books in the popular management literature. The book describes what the authors found to be distinct cultural traits that led to excellence in a company. Based on their research, they proposed that there are eight cultural characteristics (the independent variables) that predict companies' excellence as defined in terms of financial performance and innovation (the dependent variables).

The authors made no mention of how their original population of firms was chosen. Nevertheless, they identified seventy-five firms that appeared, on the surface, to be excellent companies. Most or all of the European firms were eliminated, which brought the sample down to sixty-two. These firms were then screened on the basis of seven criteria. Six criteria were measures of financial performance: compound asset growth, compound equity growth, ratio of market value to book value, average return on total capital, average return on equity, and average return on sales. If a firm was in the top half of its industry on at least four of these six financial criteria for each year over a twenty-year period, the authors considered it an excellent company and kept it in the research set. The seventh selection criterion was innovation. An informal group of businesspeople, consultants, members of the press, and business academics was used to judge the innovativeness of the companies that survived the financial test. This was a subjective assessment.

The result was a set of forty-three "excellent" firms that became the primary focus of Peters and Waterman's study. Some of the companies that were described as excellent were Avon, Boeing, Walt Disney Co., Dow Chemical, IBM, Johnson & Johnson, K Mart, 3M, Marriott, Procter & Gamble, Texas Instruments, and Wang Labs. A few of the firms that didn't "make the cut" were General Electric, General Foods, Lockheed, Polaroid, and Xerox. The authors conducted extensive interviews in twenty-one of the firms, and briefer interviews in the remaining twenty-two. The structure and substance of the interviews are not clearly revealed in the book.

The major conclusion of *In Search of Excellence* is that there is a strong link between culture and business performance. More specifically, excellent companies share eight common cultural characteristics: (1) a bias for action; (2) keeping close to the customer; (3) autonomy and entrepreneurship; (4) productivity through people; (5) hands-on, value driven; (6) sticking to what the organization knows; (7) a simple form and lean staff; and (8) maintaining simultaneous loose-tight properties. It should be noted, however, that Peters and Waterman do not tell us if all forty-three firms had all eight characteristics or whether some had only six or seven.

Questions

1. What flaws can you find in the research upon which this book is based?
2. How generalizable do you think this study's findings are?
3. How do you explain the tremendous popularity of this book, given its questionable research base?

FOR FURTHER READING

BACHARACH, S. B., "Organizational Theories: Some Criteria for Evaluation," *Academy of M* nd rules and a vocabulary to facilitate focused discussion about the structure of organization and management theories.

BRIEF, A. P., and J. M. DUKERICH, "Theory in Organizational Behavior: Can It Be Useful?" in L. L. Cummings and B. M. Staw (eds.), *Research in Organizational Behavior*, Vol. 13. Greenwich, CT: JAI Press, 1991, pp. 327–52. Argues that theory in organizational behavior may have practical value, even though it may not be useful in a narrow sense.

DIPBOYE, R. L., "Laboratory vs. Field Research in Industrial and Organizational Psychology," in C. L. Cooper and I. T. Robertson, eds, *International Review of Industrial and Organizational Psychology*, Vol. 5 (West Sussex, UK: John Wiley & Sons, 1990), pp. 1–34. Reviews two approaches to research from an applied psychology perspective.

EISENHARDT, K. M., "Building Theories from Case Study Research," *Academy of Management Review*, October 1989, pp. 532–50. Provides a framework for building theories from case study research and puts theory building from case studies into the larger context of social science research.

LEONARD-BARTON, D., "A Dual Methodology for Case Studies: Synergistic Use of a Longitudinal Single Site with Replicated Multiple Sites," *Organization Science*, Vol. 1, No. 3, 1990, pp. 248–66. Describes two different approaches to case studies and notes how the strengths of each compensate for some particular weakness in the other.

NAUGHTON, T. J., "Levels of Analysis and Organizational Behavior: A Suggested Cognitive Framework for Educational Use," *Organizational Behavior Teaching Review*, Vol. XII, No. 2, 1987–88. Proposes a general cognitive framework that views organizational problems and solutions in terms of multiple levels of analysis.

NOTES

[1]Based on B. G. Posner, "To Have and To Hold," *INC.*, October 1988, pp. 130–32.

[2]J. A. Byrne, "Executive Sweat," *Forbes*, May 20, 1985, pp. 198–200.

[3]This discussion is based on material presented in E. Stone, *Research Methods in Organizational Behavior* (Santa Monica, CA: Goodyear, 1978).

[4]B. M. Staw and G. R. Oldham, "Reconsidering Our Dependent Variables: A Critique and Empirical Study," *Academy of Management Journal*, December 1978, pp. 539–59; and B. M. Staw, "Organizational Behavior: A Review and Reformulation of the Field's Outcome Variables," in M. R. Rosenzweig and L. W. Porter (eds.), *Annual Review of Psychology*, Vol. 35 (Palo Alto, CA: Annual Reviews, 1984), pp. 627–66.

[5]R. S. Blackburn, "Experimental Design in Organizational Settings," in J. W. Lorsch (ed.), *Handbook of Organizational Behavior* (Englewood Cliffs, NJ: Prentice Hall, 1987), pp. 127–28.

[6]G. G. Alpander, "Supervisory Training Programmes in Major U.S. Corporations," *Journal of Management Development*, Vol. 5, No. 5, 1986, pp. 3–22.

[7]S. Milgram, *Obedience to Authority* (New York: Harper & Row, 1974). For a critique of this research, see T. Blass, "Understanding Behavior in the Milgram Obedience Experiment: The Role of Personality, Situations, and Their Interactions," *Journal of Personality and Social Psychology*, March 1991, pp. 398–413.

[8]This box is based on M. E. Gordon, L. A. Slade, and N. Schmitt, "The 'Science of the Sophomore' Revisited: From Conjecture to Empiricism," *Academy of Management Review*, January 1986, pp. 191–207; J. Greenberg, "The College Sophomore as Guinea Pig: Setting the Record Straight," *Academy of Management Review*, January 1987, pp. 157–59; and E. A. Locke (ed.), *Generalizing from Laboratory to Field Settings: Research Findings from Industrial–Organizational Psychology, Organizational Behavior, and Human Resource Management* (Lexington, MA: Lexington Books, 1986).

[9]For more on ethical issues in research, see T. L. Beauchamp, R. R. Faden, R. J. Wallace, Jr., and L. Walters (eds.), *Ethical Issues in Social Science Research* (Baltimore, MD: Johns Hopkins University Press, 1982); and D. Baumrind, "Research Using Intentional Deception," *American Psychologist*, February 1985, pp. 165–74.

[10]J. J. Martocchio and A. M. O'Leary, "Sex Differences in Occupational Stress: A Meta-Analytic Review," *Journal of Applied Psychology*, June 1989, pp. 495–501.

[11]See, for example, R. A. Guzzo, S. E. Jackson, and R. A. Katzell, "Meta-Analysis Analysis," in L. L. Cummings and B. M. Staw (eds.), *Research in Organizational Behavior*, Vol. 9 (Greenwich, CT: JAI Press, 1987), pp. 407–42; and A. L. Beaman, "An Empirical Comparison of Meta-Analytic and Traditional Reviews," *Personality and Social Psychology Bulletin*, June 1991, pp. 252–57.

[12]B. M. Staw, "Organizational Behavior: A Review and Reformulation."

[13]Ibid., pp. 655–56.

[14]S. R. Rhodes and R. M. Steers, *Managing Employee Absenteeism* (Reading, MA: Addison-Wesley, 1990).

[15]Cited in "Expensive Absenteeism," *The Wall Street Journal*, July 29, 1986, p. 1.

[16]J. E. Ellis, "Monsanto's New Challenge: Keeping Minority Workers," *Business Week*, July 8, 1991, pp. 60–61.

[17]C. Hymowitz, "One Firm's Bid to Keep Blacks, Women," *The Wall Street Journal*, February 16, 1989, p. B1.

[18]B. R. Bergmann and W. R. Krause, "Evaluating and Forecasting Progress in Racial Integration of Employment," *Industrial and Labor Relations Review*, April 1968, pp. 399–409.

[19]F. Schwartz, "Management Women and the New Facts of Life," *Harvard Business Review*, January–February 1989, pp. 65–76.

[20]T. H. Cox and S. Blake, "Managing Cultural Diversity: Implications for Organizational Competitiveness," *Academy of Management Executive*, August 1991, p. 48.

[21]See, for example, D. R. Dalton and W. D. Todor, "Functional Turnover: An Empirical Assessment," *Journal of Applied Psychology*, December 1981, pp. 716–21; and G. M. McEvoy and W. F. Cascio, "Do Good or Poor Performers Leave? A Meta-Analysis of the Relationship Between Performance and Turnover," *Academy of Management Journal*, December 1987, pp. 744–62.

[22]Cited in "You Often Lose the Ones You Love," *Industry Week*, November 21, 1988, p. 5.

[23]H. J. Leavitt, *Managerial Psychology*, rev. ed. (Chicago: University of Chicago Press, 1964), p. 3.

C H A P T E R

T H R E E

ORGANIZATIONAL BEHAVIOR IN A GLOBAL CONTEXT

CHAPTER OUTLINE

Welcome to the Global Village

Facing the International Challenge

The Relevant Question: Are National Cultures Becoming More Homogeneous?

Assessing Differences Between Countries

The Reality of Culture Shock

Keeping OB in a Global Context

Summary

LEARNING OBJECTIVES

After studying this chapter, you should be able to:

1. Define a multinational corporation

2. Describe the effects of regional cooperative arrangements on managing global enterprises

3 Contrast *parochialism* and *ethnocentrism*

4. Explain how American cultural values permeate the organizational behavior literature

5. List the six basic dimensions along which cultures vary in Kluckhohn and Strodtbeck's framework

6. Describe Hofstede's four cultural dimensions

7. Explain the four stages that individuals go through in adjusting to a foreign country

*I*t opened in the spring of 1992, and it cost more than $4.2 billion. While the corporation that developed it has an impressive record of doing projects very similar to it, this new project may be the most visible and expensive flop in the company's history. The project we're talking about is Euro Disneyland and the corporation that developed it is the Walt Disney Co.[1]

Disney, of course, is the king of theme parks. Its U.S. parks in California and Florida are unparalleled successes. Why should Euro Disneyland, twenty miles east of Paris, be any different? Consider a few of the challenges that Euro Disneyland presents that the Disney Co. never had to face in California or Florida:

- Unlike Americans, the French have had little previous exposure to theme parks. Just the idea of having to pay to merely walk inside the gate of any park is totally alien to them.

- The French reserve one day and only one day of the week—Sunday—for family outings. The notion of going out with the family on a Saturday or a weekday isn't something they're used to.

- The French do their vacationing en masse. In August, businesses and schools close down and everyone goes on vacation. Demand at the theme park is unlikely, therefore, to be ongoing, as it is in the United States.

- The French have a traditional aversion to meeting strangers. Being welcomed by strangers with buoyant smiles and a lighthearted greeting is not appreciated.

- In the United States, fifty percent of Disney visitors eat fast food at the parks. But most French people don't snack. Moreover, they don't select their "lunchtime" arbitrarily, as Americans do. The French insist on eating their lunch at exactly 12:30.

- The French are impatient. They are not comfortable waiting in long lines. Americans seem to accept waiting thirty minutes or more for the most popular rides at Disneyland and Disney World.

- The French adore their dogs. They take them everywhere—inside resorts and even fine restaurants. Dogs, however, have always been banned from Disney parks.
- The practice of having Disney employees wear badges with only their first names on them is fine in the United States, where informality is well accepted. But this is not the French way of doing business.
- French workers don't like to obey orders. They are not likely to take kindly to management's demands that they obey a dress code and not smoke, chew gum, or converse with their co-workers. ■

*T*he French are obviously different from Americans, so managing a successful theme park in France will require adopting practices different from those followed in the United States. This Euro Disneyland example is meant to illustrate a problem that managers are increasingly likely to face in the 1990s and beyond: What changes, if any, do you need to make in your management style when managing in a different country?

WELCOME TO THE GLOBAL VILLAGE

A number of respected observers of world affairs have been arguing for more than a decade that our world has become a global village. Transportation and communication capabilities—for example, supersonic jets, international

FIGURE 3-1

"Tonights's program 'America, America' is being brought to you by a grant from the Sony and Nissan corporations."

Source: *Wall Street Journal*, September 5, 1990. With permission, Cartoon Features Syndicate.

telephone and computer networks, and world-wide news broadcasts via satellite—make it easier to talk with or visit people on other continents than it was for our ancestors of a century ago to do the same with friends in a neighboring village. Distance and national borders are rapidly disappearing as a major barrier to business transactions. With the advent of the global village, identifying the "home country" of a company and its product has become a lot more difficult. For instance, Honda is supposedly a Japanese firm, but it builds its Accords in Ohio. Ford, which has its headquarters in Detroit, builds its Mercury Tracers in Mexico. "All-American" firms like Exxon, Coca-Cola, and IBM get more than half of their revenues from operations outside the United States; while other "All-American" firms such as CBS Records, General Tire, and Pillsbury are actually foreign-owned.

The reality of the global village can be demonstrated by looking at the growing impact of multinational corporations and the rise of regional cooperative arrangements between countries.

Multinational Corporations

Multinational Corporations
Companies that maintain significant operations in two or more countries simultaneously.

Most of the firms currently listed in the Fortune 500 are **multinational corporations**—companies that maintain significant operations in two or more countries simultaneously.

While international businesses have been around for centuries, multinationals are a relatively recent phenomenon. They are a natural outcome of the global economy. Multinationals use their world-wide operations to develop global strategies. Rather than confining themselves to their domestic borders, they scan the world for competitive advantages. The result? Manufacturing, assembly, sales, and other functions are being strategically located to give firms advantages in the marketplace. A photocopying machine, for instance, might be designed in Toronto, have its microprocessing chips made in Taiwan, its physical case manufactured in Japan, be assembled in South Korea, and then be sold out of warehouses located in Melbourne, London, and Los Angeles.

Coca–Cola's products are as well known in Bangkok or Madrid as in Atlanta, Georgia.
Ralf-Finn Hestoft / Picture Group

How big are multinationals? It's hard to overstate their size and influence. In a list in which nations are ranked by gross national product and industrial firms by total sales, thirty-seven of the first one hundred names on the list would be industrial corporations.[2] Exxon's sales, as a case in point, exceed the GNPs of such countries as Indonesia, Nigeria, Argentina, and Denmark.

Managers of multinationals confront a wealth of challenges. They face diverse political systems, laws, and customs. But these differences create both problems and opportunities. It's obviously more difficult to manage an operation that spans fifteen thousand miles and whose employees speak five different languages than one located under a single roof where a common language is spoken. Differences create opportunities, and that has been the primary motivation for corporations to expand their worldwide operations.

RegionalCooperative Arrangements

National boundaries are also being blurred by the creation of regional cooperative arrangements. The most notable of these, so far, is the European Community, made up of twelve West European countries. But the United States and Mexico have established border zones to stimulate low-cost manufacturing, the United States and Canada have negotiated an agreement to reduce trade barriers, and the recent reunification of Germany signals the beginning of inter-nation cooperative arrangements among East European countries.

THE EUROPEAN COMMUNITY   On December 31, 1992, the United States of Europe was created. There are 335 million people in the twelve nations—France, Denmark, Belgium, Greece, Ireland, Italy, Luxembourg, the Netherlands, Portugal, Spain, the United Kingdom, and Germany—that make up the European Community. Before 1992, they had border controls, border taxes, border subsidies, nationalistic policies, and protected industries. Now they are a single market. Gone are national barriers to travel, employment, investment, and trade. In their place are a free flow of money, workers, goods, and services. A driver hauling cargo from Amsterdam to Lisbon is now able to clear four border crossings and five countries merely by showing a single piece of paper. In 1991, that same driver needed two pounds of documents.

The primary motivation for these twelve nations to unite was the desire to strengthen their position against the industrial might of the United States and Japan. When they were separate countries creating barriers against one another, their industries were unable to develop the economies of scale enjoyed by the United States and Japan. The new European Community, however, allows European firms to tap into what has become the world's single richest market. This reduction in trade barriers also encourages non–West European companies to invest in these countries to take advantage of new opportunities. Finally, European multinationals have new clout in attacking American, Japanese, and other world-wide markets.

Maquiladoras Domestic Mexican firms that manufacture or assemble products for a company of another nation, which are then sent back to the foreign company for sale and distribution.

MAQUILADORAS   **Maquiladoras** are domestic Mexican firms that manufacture or assemble products for a company of another nation, which are then sent back to the foreign company for sale and distribution.[3] The key to the success of maquiladoras is that they allow non-Mexican firms to take advantage of Mexico's low labor costs with minimal trade restrictions. More than fourteen

Mexican workers assemble
Whirlpool appliances in this
maquiladora in Reynosa, Mexico.
The plant is just over the border
from McAllen, Texas.
Bob Daemmrich / The Image Works

hundred foreign companies—including General Motors, GE, Zenith, Honeywell, Hitachi, and Sanyo—are currently doing business with maquiladoras along the Mexican side of the border from Texas to California.

The maquiladoras concept was devised by the Mexican and U.S. governments in 1965 to help develop both sides of the impoverished border region. But it was the massive devaluation of the peso that occurred in 1982 that initiated a virtual explosion of maquiladoras. Since 1982, the number of these plants has nearly tripled. They're in Cuidad Juaréz, Nogales, Tijuana, Mexicali, and similar northern Mexican cities. One estimate indicates that these cross-border plants could employ as many as three million workers by the year 2000.

Mexican wages are equal to, or even lower than, wages in many Asian countries. With a Mexican minimum wage of around 40 cents an hour at current exchange rates, companies producing for North American markets no longer have to go to the Far East to find low-cost labor.

U.S.–CANADA ALLIANCE   Another set of national barriers is coming down between the United States and Canada. These two countries are already the world's largest trading partners—they do at least $150 billion worth of business a year with each other. The recent signing of the United States–Canadian Free Trade Agreement means increased competition for firms and expanded opportunities in each country.

The Free Trade Agreement phases out tariffs on most goods traded between the two countries. It is also triggering a wave of consolidations as Canadian companies merge among themselves or with American companies to form single giant firms.

The U.S.–Canada alliance is likely to soon be expanded to include Mexico—establishing a unified North American free trade zone stretching from the Yukon to the Yucatån.[4] When this occurs, it will create a market with 360 million consumers; shift a number of low-paying jobs to Mexico from the United States, Canada, and the Far East; and generate high-skilled and better-paying jobs in the United States and Canada as a result of the growth in exports.

THE NEW EASTERN EUROPE   In early 1989, Romania, Poland, Hungary, and East Germany were communist countries whose peoples were confined behind an Iron Curtain. East Germans, for instance, literally put their lives on the line when they sneaked into West Germany. Eighteen months later, East Germany and West Germany were reunified and vendors were selling the Berlin Wall in two-inch-square pieces to tourists. U.S.–Soviet relations are now better than they have been in nearly fifty years; the concern over a world war between these superpowers has almost completely faded; and entrepreneurs are creating new businesses to serve the needs of the East European masses.

A free Eastern Europe creates almost unlimited opportunities for multinationals. It offers new markets with huge growth potentials. It also creates a new supply of high-skilled, low-cost labor. More than any other incident in recent times, the fall of communism in Eastern Europe signaled the arrival of a truly global economy.

FACING THE INTERNATIONAL CHALLENGE

A global economy presents challenges to managers that they never had to confront when their operations were constrained within national borders.

Managing across national borders provides new challenges. For instance, Malaysia's ethnic mix shows up in this Hewlett-Packard microchip factory.   Munshi Ahmed.

National Culture   The primary values and practices that characterize a particular country.

They face different legal and political systems. They confront different economic climates and tax policies. But they also must deal with varying **national cultures**—the primary values and practices that characterize particular countries—many of which are nothing like those in which they have spent their entire lives.

If this were an economics text, we would carefully dissect the economic implications for managers of a global economy. But this book is about organizational behavior and understanding people at work. Therefore, let's look at why managers, especially those born and raised in the United States, often find managing people in foreign lands so difficult.

American Biases

Parochialism   A narrow view of the world; an inability to recognize differences between people.

Americans have been singled out as suffering particularly from **parochialism;** that is, they view the world solely through their own eyes and perspective.[5] People with a parochial perspective do not recognize that other people have different ways of living and working. We see this most explicitly in Americans' knowledge of foreign languages. While it is not uncommon for Europeans to speak three or four languages, Americans are almost entirely monolingual. The reasons probably reflect the huge domestic market in the United States, the geographical separation of the United States from Europe and Asia, and the reality that English has become the international business language in many parts of the world.

Ethnocentric Views   The belief that one's cultural values and customs are superior to all others.

Americans have also been frequently criticized for holding **ethnocentric views.**[6] They believe that their cultural values and customs are superior to all others. This may offer another explanation for why Americans don't learn foreign languages. Many think their language is superior and that it's the rest of the world's responsibility to learn English.

There is no shortage of stories illustrating the problems created when American managers failed to understand cultural differences. Consider the following examples:

An American manager recently transferred to Saudi Arabia successfully obtained a million-dollar contract from a Saudi manufacturer. The manufacturer's representative had arrived at the meeting several hours late, but the American executive considered it unimportant. The American was certainly surprised and frustrated to learn later that the Saudi had no intention of honoring the contract. He had signed it only to be polite after showing up late for the appointment.

An American executive operating in Peru was viewed by Peruvian managers as cold and unworthy of trust because, in face-to-face discussions, the American kept backing up. He did not understand that in Peru, the custom is to stand quite close to the person with whom you are speaking.

An American manager in Japan offended a high-ranking Japanese executive by failing to give him the respect his position deserved. The American was introduced to the Japanese executive in the latter's office. The American assumed that the executive was a low-level manager and paid him little attention because of the small and sparsely furnished office he occupied. The American didn't realize that the offices of top Japanese executives do not flaunt the status symbols of their American counterparts.[7]

U.S. parochialism and enthnocentrism may not have been debilitating in the post–World War II period, when the United States accounted for seventy-five percent of the world's gross national product. But it is a "life-threatening disease" today, when U.S. firms produce only about twenty-two percent of the world's GNP.[8] The point is that the world is not dominated by U.S. economic power any more, and unless U.S. managers conquer their parochialism and ethnocentrism, they will not be able to take full advantage of the new global opportunities.

Foreigners in America

Don't assume that Americans are alone in blundering on foreign soil. Cultural ignorance goes two ways. Foreign owners now control more than twelve percent of all American manufacturing assets and employ over three million American workers. In one recent year alone, foreign investors acquired nearly four hundred American businesses, worth a total of $60 billion.[9] However, these foreign owners are facing the same challenges and making many of the same mistakes that American executives have long made overseas.[10]

Americans, for instance, are used to stability. When new owners with different management styles take over a U.S. company, American workers often feel threatened by high uncertainty, yet this is often ignored by foreign managers. Some foreign owners, especially those from relatively homogeneous cultures, have the outmoded, stereotypical attitudes toward women and minorities that build ill-will. Many American employees complain that they feel left out of the established personal networks in traditional European and Asian corporations that acquire American firms. Japanese managers, as a case in point, work ten- to twelve-hour days and then socialize until midnight. A lot of important business is done at these social gatherings, but American managers are excluded, and this exclusion creates feelings of hurt and distrust. The Japanese way of dealing with people also confounds Americans. Communication, for example, is often more difficult. Americans value directness. They tend to say exactly what they mean. The Japanese are more subtle and see this directness as rude and abrasive. The

Cultural Relativism in Ethics

It is hard enough for people to develop an ethical framework to guide them in their day-to-day decision making. When they go to another country with very different cultural traditions, the ethical framework they have come to rely on may no longer be appropriate. *Cultural relativism* recognizes that people's notions of right and wrong derive from their country's societal values.[11]

Discrimination, racism, and bribery are good examples of practices that appear to be culturally relative. Several Middle Eastern and Asian countries overtly discriminate against women. While North American executives aren't likely to think twice about promoting a woman to a middle-management position if she is the best-qualified candidate, their executive counterparts in Saudi Arabia or Japan would be likely to promote a less-qualified male. Similarly, managers who were born and raised in a different country found it very hard in the 1980s to ignore the ethical implications of South African apartheid for such activities as hiring, job assignments, work group composition, and promotion decisions. But the ethical issue that has probably received the greatest amount of attention in the international context is bribery.[12] For instance, a cash payoff to a government official that would be considered unethical in Canada may be accepted practice in Mexico, Costa Rica, or an emerging African nation.

Deeply rooted cultural traditions have tended to create country-specific ethical standards. When national borders were real barriers to trade and communication, cultural relativism created few ethical problems because interactions were essentially intranational. Today, however, the global context of business indicates the need for a standardized set of moral values. When companies operate in dozens of different countries with a multicultural work force, the lack of universal ethical standards creates major dilemmas for managers. Do they apply the ethical standards of their home country, the standards used by people from the country where their organization headquarters is based, or the standards of the host country?

Is it reasonable to expect the world to adopt a standard set of moral values? Can all organizations agree on a set of standards that overrides national traditions and is based on the needs of the global community? What do *you* think?

Japanese emphasis on group consensus is another practice that doesn't fit well in the United States. Americans, used to making decisions fast, get frustrated by what they interpret as unnecessary delays.[13]

THE RELEVANT QUESTION: ARE NATIONAL CULTURES BECOMING MORE HOMOGENEOUS?

It can be argued that the creation of a true global village is making the concern over cultural differences irrelevant. Today, when Cable News Network is watched in over 140 countries, Levi's are as popular in Moscow as in Dallas, and a significant portion of students in American graduate business programs are foreigners who expect to return to their homelands to prac-

Work-Force Diversity Is a World-Wide Issue

The issue of work-force diversity is not unique to the United States. Canada, for example, must blend English- and French-speaking employees. South African organizations are integrating blacks into management ranks. The Japanese have to deal with an increasing number of women moving into managerial and professional positions. And no sooner had the Berlin Wall fallen than German firms had to begin the task of merging employees from East and West.

Work-force diversity is likely to be most severely tested in Western Europe.[14] Eight million legal immigrants and an estimated two million illegal immigrants live in the twelve nations of the European Community. A particularly large increase in Muslim and African immigration in recent years has been changing the religious and racial composition of these countries.

Unfortunately, Europeans are discovering that they are not as tolerant of foreign cultures as they once thought they were. In France, for instance, one study showed that seventy-one percent of French citizens said their country had too many Arabs, forty-five percent thought it had too many blacks, and ninety-four percent acknowledged that racism is "widespread." Similarly, a study in the United Kingdom revealed that seventy-nine percent of blacks, sixty-seven percent of whites, and fifty-six percent of Asians regarded the nation as "very racist" or "fairly racist."

This growing intolerance in Western Europe of people from different cultures has serious long-term implications for management. The birth rates in most West European countries are flat. Even with increasing immigration from East Europe, over the next thirty years they are likely to experience a serious labor shortage. Meanwhile, the populations of Arabic and African nations are increasing rapidly. If enough workers for West European industries and services are to be found in the coming years, managers in Western European firms must raise the threshold of racial tolerance.

tice management, it may be naive to think that cultural differences are very important. If they are, they are so only in the near term. In the long run, the global village will become a single homogeneous culture—that is, a world melting pot in which cross-cultural differences will all but disappear.

Is this argument correct? Are national cultures becoming more homogeneous? At one level, they are.[15] Research demonstrates that organization strategies, structures, and technologies are becoming more alike. However, there are still differences among people within organizations in different cultures.[16] In other words, national culture continues to be a powerful force in explaining a large proportion of organizational behavior. In further support of this viewpoint, research comparing employees in forty countries concluded that national culture explained approximately fifty percent of the differences in these employees' attitudes and behavior.[17]

If people were becoming more homogeneous, we could take a culture-free approach to organizational behavior. But such an approach does not appear to be justified at present, for the following reasons: (1) There are differences in OB across national cultures. (2) These differences explain a large proportion of the variance in attitudes and behaviors. (3) And for now at least, and probably for a number of years to come, these differences are not decreasing at any significant rate. On the last point we might speculate that, despite the tremendous increase in cross-cultural communication, there continue to be unique country-specific traditions and customs that shape the attitudes and behaviors of the people in those countries.

ASSESSING DIFFERENCES BETWEEN COUNTRIES

American children are taught early the values of individuality and uniqueness. In contrast, Japanese children are taught to be "team players," to work within the group, and to conform. A significant part of American students' education is to learn to think, to analyze, and to question. Their Japanese counterparts are rewarded for recounting facts. These different socialization practices reflect different cultures and, not surprisingly, result in different types of employees. The average American worker is more competitive and self-focused than is the Japanese worker. Predictions of employee behavior based on samples of American workers are likely to be off-target when they are applied to a population of employees—like the Japanese—who perform better in standardized tasks, as part of a work team, with group-based decisions and rewards.

It's relatively easy to get a reading of the Japanese culture—dozens of books and hundreds of articles have been written on the subject. But how do you gain an understanding of Venezuela's or Denmark's national culture? A popular notion is that you should talk with people from those countries. Evidence suggests, however, that this rarely works.[18] Why? Because people born and raised in a country are fully programmed in the ways of its culture by the time they're adults. They understand how things are done and can work comfortably within their country's unwritten norms, but they *can't* explain their culture to someone else. It is pervasive, but it is hidden. Most people are unaware of just how their culture has shaped them. Culture is to people as water is to fish. It's there all the time but the fish are oblivious to it. So one of the frustrations of moving into a different culture is that the "natives" are often the least capable of explaining its unique characteristics to an outsider.

To illustrate the difficulty of accurately describing the unique qualities of one's own culture, if you're an American, raised in the United States, ask yourself: What are Americans like? Think about it for a moment and then see how many of the points in Table 3–1 you identified correctly.

TABLE 3–1   What Are Americans Like?

Americans are very *informal*. They don't tend to treat people differently even when there are great differences in age or social standing.

Americans are *direct*. They don't talk around things. To some foreigners, this may appear as abrupt or even rude behavior.

Americans are *competitive*. Some foreigners may find Americans assertive or overbearing.

Americans are *achievers*. They like to keep score, whether at work or at play. They emphasize accomplishments.

Americans are *independent* and *individualistic*. They place a high value on freedom and believe that individuals can shape and control their own destinies.

Americans are *questioners*. They ask a lot of questions, even of someone they have just met. Many of these questions may seem pointless ("How ya doing?") or personal ("What kind of work do you do?").

Americans dislike *silence*. They would rather talk about the weather than deal with silence in a conversation.

Americans value *punctuality*. They keep appointment calendars and live according to schedules and clocks.

Americans value *cleanliness*. They often seem obsessed with bathing, eliminating body odors, and wearing clean clothes.

Source: Based on M. Ernest (ed.), *Predeparture Orientation Handbook: For Foreign Students and Scholars Planning to Study in the United States* (Washington, DC: U.S. Information Agency, Bureau of Cultural Affairs, 1984), pp. 103–5; A. Bennett, "American Culture Is Often a Puzzle for Foreign Managers in the U.S.," *The Wall Street Journal,* February 12, 1986, p. 29; "Don't Think Our Way's the Only Way," *The Pryor Report,* February 1988, p. 9; and B. J. Wattenberg, "The Attitudes Behind American Exceptionalism," *U.S. News & World Report,* August 7, 1989, p. 25.

Aren't Canadians Just Like Their Neighbors to the South?

Most Americans don't see much difference between themselves and Canadians. Yet many Canadians resent the assumption by Americans that they're just like their southern neighbors.[19] For example, in a recent survey, seventy-nine percent of Canadians polled stated that they consider themselves to be different from Americans. However, there was no consensus among those respondents as to what exactly makes Canadians unique.

Studies indicate that Canadians *perceive* themselves as more collective, traditional, and readier to accept government authority with passivity than Americans. Canadians see Americans as more aggressive, individualistic, and violent. In contrast, Canadians see themselves as more concerned about the environment and the poor than their southerly neighbors. They also see themselves as more honest and fair.

But perceptions can be erroneous. For instance, a number of Canadian companies, run by Canadians, are highly fierce competitors in the American market. These include Bombardier Inc., Labatt Ltd., Seagrams, and Cineplex Odeon Corporation. Many of the executives at these firms are as (or more) aggressive than their American counterparts.

On close examination of the research, the most meaningful conclusion that can be drawn is that Canada is a more regionalized nation than the United States and that English-speaking Canadians (anglophones) and Americans seem to be more alike in their styles of communication and influence than anglophones and French-speaking Canadians (franco-phones). Research evidence indicates, for instance, that francophones take a more competitive approach to negotiations than do either Americans or anglophone Canadians.

Canadians are different from Americans, but the differences are nebulous rather than substantive. In fact, the differences between French-speaking and English-speaking Canadians are probably more significant than the difference between English-speaking Canadians and Americans.

Although foreign culture is difficult to fathom from what its "natives" tell you, there is an expanding body of research that can tell us how cultures vary and what the key differences are between, say, the United States and Venezuela. Let's look at the two best known of these research frameworks.

The Kluckhohn-Strodtbeck Framework

One of the most widely referenced approaches for analyzing variations among cultures is the Kluckhohn-Strodtbeck framework.[20] It identifies six basic cultural dimensions: relationship to the environment, time orientation, nature of people, activity orientation, focus of responsibility, and conception of space. In this section, we'll review each of these dimensions.

RELATIONSHIP TO THE ENVIRONMENT Are people *subjugated* to their environment, in *harmony* with it, or able to *dominate* it? In many Middle Eastern countries, people see life as essentially preordained. When something happens, they tend to see it as "God's will." In contrast, Americans and Canadians believe they can control nature. They're willing

Two facts suggest that Canadians are more egalitarian than Americans. First, Canadians are far more supportive of unions. In the U.S., only 16 percent of workers belong to labor unions compared to 37 percent in Canada. Second, the pay differences between top management and supervisors is much greater in the U.S. CEOs in the U.S. earn approximately nine times more than first-line supervisors. In Canada, it's only five times.

tospend billions of dollars each year on cancer research, for instance, because they think that cancer's cause can be identified, a cure found, and the disease eventually eradicated.

In between these two extreme positions is a more moderate view that seeks harmony with nature. In many Far Eastern countries, for example, people's way of dealing with the environment is to work around it.

You should expect these different perspectives toward the environment to influence organizational practices. Take the setting of goals as an example. In a subjugation society, goal setting is not likely to be very popular. Why set goals if you believe people can't do much toward achieving them? In a harmony society, goals are likely to be used, but deviations are expected and penalties for failing to reach the goals are likely to be minimal. In a domination society, goals are widely applied, people are expected to achieve them, and the penalties for failure tend to be quite high.

TIME ORIENTATION   Does the culture focus on the *past, present,* or *future?* Societies differ in the value they place on time. For instance, Western cultures perceive time as a scarce resource. "Time is money" and must be used efficiently. Americans focus on the present and the near-future. You see evidence of this in the short-term orientation of performance appraisals. In the typical North American organization, people are evaluated every six months or once a year. The Japanese, in contrast, take a longer-term view and this is reflected in their performance appraisal methods. Japanese workers are often given ten years or more to prove their worth.

Some cultures take still another approach to time: They focus on the past. Italians, for instance, follow their traditions and seek to preserve their historical practices.

Knowledge of different cultures' time orientations can provide you with insights into the importance of deadlines, whether long-term planning is widely practiced, the length of job assignments, and what constitutes lateness. It can explain, for instance, why Americans are obsessed with making and keeping appointments. It also suggests why not every society is as likely to be enamored of timesaving devices—such as day planners, overnight mail delivery, car phones, and fax machines—as North Americans are.

NATURE OF PEOPLE   Does a culture view people as *good, evil,* or some *mix* of these two? In many Third World countries, people see themselves as basically honest and trustworthy. People in the former Soviet Union, on the other hand, take a rather evil view of human nature. North Americans tend to be somewhere in between. They see people as basically good, but are cautious so as not to be taken advantage of.

You can readily see how a culture's view of the nature of people might influence the dominant leadership style of its managers. A more autocratic style is likely to rule in countries that focus on the evil aspects of people. Participation or even a laissez-faire style should prevail in countries that emphasize trusting values. In mixed cultures, leadership is likely to emphasize participation but provide close controls that can quickly identify deviations.

ACTIVITY ORIENTATION   Some cultures emphasize *doing* or action. They stress accomplishments. Some cultures emphasize *being* or living for the moment. They stress experiencing life and seeking immediate gratification of desires. Still other cultures focus on *controlling*. They stress restraining desires by detaching oneself from objects.

North Americans live in doing-oriented societies. They work hard and expect to be rewarded with promotions, raises, and other forms of recognition for their accomplishments. Mexico, in contrast, is being-oriented. The afternoon siesta is consistent with the slower pace and enjoying-the-moment orientation of the culture. The French have a controlling orientation and put emphasis on rationality and logic.

An understanding of a culture's activity orientation can give you insights into how its people approach work and leisure, how they make decisions, and the criteria they use for allocating rewards. For instance, in cultures with a dominant being orientation, decisions are likely to be emotional. In contrast, doing and controlling cultures are likely to emphasize pragmatism and rationality, respectively, in decision making.

FOCUS OF RESPONSIBILITY   Cultures can be classified according to where responsibility lies for the welfare of others. Americans, for instance, are highly *individualistic*. They use personal characteristics and achievements to define themselves. They believe that a person's responsibility is to take care of himself or herself. Countries like Malaysia and Israel focus more on the *group*. In an Israeli kibbutz, for example, people share chores and rewards. Emphasis is on group harmony, unity, and loyalty. The British and French follow another orientation by relying on *hierarchical* relationships. Groups in these countries are hierarchically ranked and a group's position remains essentially stable over time. Hierarchical societies tend to be aristocratic.

This dimension of culture has implications for the design of jobs, approaches to decision making, communication patterns, reward systems, and selection practices in organizations. For instance, selection in individualistic societies emphasizes personal accomplishments. In group societies, working well with others is likely to be of primary importance. In hierarchical societies, selection decisions are made on the basis of a candidate's social ranking. This dimension helps to explain the popularity in the United States of the resumé, which lists personal achievements, and the negative judgment of "nepotism" (hiring one's relatives).[21]

CONCEPTION OF SPACE   The final dimension in the Kluckhohn-Strodtbeck framework relates to ownership of space. Some cultures are very open and conduct business in *public*. At the other extreme are cultures that place a great deal of emphasis on keeping things *private*. Many societies *mix* the two and fall somewhere in between.

Japanese organizations reflect the public nature of their society. There are, for instance, few private offices. Managers and operative employees work in the same room and there are no partitions separating their desks. North American firms also reflect their cultural values. They use offices and privacy to reflect status. Important meetings are held behind closed doors. Space is frequently given over for the exclusive use of specific individuals. In societies that have a mixed orientation, there is a blend of the private and public. For instance, there might be a large office where walls are only five or six feet high, thus creating "limited privacy." These differences in the conception of space have obvious implications for organizational concerns such as job design and communication.

SUMMARY   Table 3–2 summarizes the six cultural dimensions in the Kluckhohn-Strodtbeck framework and the possible variations for each. As a point of reference, the jagged line in the table identifies where the United States tends to fall along these dimensions.

TABLE 3–2   Variations in Value Dimensions

Value Dimension	Variations		
Relationship to the environment	Domination	Harmony	Subjugation
Time orientation	Past	Present	Future
Nature of people	Good	Mixed	Evil
Activity orientation	Being	Controlling	Doing
Focus of responsibility	Individualistic	Group	Hierarchical
Conception of space	Private	Mixed	Public

Note: The jagged line identifies where the United States tends to fall along these dimensions.

The Hofstede Framework

A more comprehensive analysis of cultural diversity has been done by Geert Hofstede.[22] In contrast to most of the previous organizational studies, which either included a limited number of countries or analyzed different companies in different countries, Hofstede surveyed over 116,000 employees in forty countries who all worked for a single multinational corporation. This database eliminated any differences that might be attributable to varying practices and policies in different companies. So any variations that he found between countries could reliably be attributed to national culture.

What did Hofstede find? His huge database confirmed that national culture had a major impact on employees' work-related values and attitudes. More important, Hofstede found that managers and employees vary on four dimensions of national culture: (1) individualism versus collectivism; (2) power distance; (3) uncertainty avoidance; and (4) quantity versus quality of life. (Actually, Hofstede called this fourth dimension masculinity versus femininity, but we've changed his terms because of their strong sexist connotation.)

Individualism A national culture attribute describing a loosely knit social framework in which people emphasize only the care of themselves and their immediate family.

Collectivism A national culture attribute that describes a tight social framework in which people expect others in groups of which they are a part to look after them and protect them.

INDIVIDUALISM VS. COLLECTIVISM   **Individualism** refers to a loosely knit social framework in which people are chiefly supposed to look after their own interests and those of their immediate family. This is made possible because of the large amount of freedom that such a society allows individuals. Its opposite is **collectivism,** which is characterized by a tight social framework in which people expect others in groups to which they belong (such as an organization) to look after them and protect them when they are in trouble. In exchange for this security, they feel they owe absolute loyalty to the group.

Hofstede found that the degree of individualism in a country is closely related to that country's wealth. Rich countries like the United States, Great Britain, and the Netherlands are very individualistic. Poor countries like Colombia and Pakistan are very collectivist.

Power Distance A national culture attribute describing the extent to which a society accepts that power in institutions and organizations is distributed unequally.

POWER DISTANCE   People naturally vary in their physical and intellectual abilities. This, in turn, creates differences in wealth and power. How does a society deal with these inequalities? Hofstede used the term **power distance** as a measure of the extent to which a society accepts the fact that power in institutions and organizations is distributed unequally. A high-power-distance society accepts wide differences in power in organizations. Employees show a great deal of respect for those in authority. Titles, rank, and status carry a lot of weight. When negotiating in high-power-distance countries, companies find it helps to send representatives with titles at least as high as those with whom they're bargaining. Countries high in power distance include the Philippines, Venezuela, and India. In contrast, a low-power-distance society plays down inequalities as much as possible. Superiors still have authority, but employees are not fearful or in awe of the boss. Denmark, Israel, and Austria are examples of countries with low-power-distance scores.

UNCERTAINTY AVOIDANCE   We live in a world of uncertainty. The future is largely unknown and always will be. Societies respond to this uncertainty in different ways. Some socialize their members into accepting it with equanimity. People in such societies are more or less comfortable with risks. They're also relatively tolerant of behavior and opinions that differ from their own because they don't feel threatened by them. Hofstede describes such societies as having low **uncertainty avoidance;** that is, people feel relatively secure. Countries that fall into this category include Singapore, Hong Kong, and Denmark.

A society high in uncertainty avoidance is characterized by a high level of anxiety among its people, which manifests itself in nervousness, stress, and aggressiveness. Because people feel threatened by uncertainty and ambiguity in these societies, mechanisms are created to provide security and reduce risk. Organizations are likely to have more formal rules, there will be less tolerance for deviant ideas and behaviors, and members will strive to believe in absolute truths. Not surprisingly, in organizations in countries with high uncertainty avoidance, employees demonstrate relatively low job mobility and lifetime employment is a widely practiced policy. Countries in this category include Japan, Portugal, and Greece.

QUANTITY VS. QUALITY OF LIFE   The fourth dimension, like individualism and collectivism, represents a dichotomy. Some cultures emphasize the **quantity of life** and value things like assertiveness and the acquisition of money and material things. Other cultures emphasize the **quality of life,** the importance of relationships, and show sensitivity and concern for the welfare of others.

Hofstede found that Japan and Austria scored high on the quantity dimension. In contrast, Norway, Sweden, Denmark, and Finland scored high on the quality dimension.

THE UNITED STATES AND OTHER COUNTRIES ON HOFSTEDE'S DIMENSIONS   Comparing the forty countries on the four dimensions, Hofstede found U.S. culture to rank as follows:

- Individualism – collectivism = Highest among all countries on individualism
- Power distance = Below average

Uncertainty Avoidance A national culture attribute describing the extent to which a society feels threatened by uncertain and ambiguous situations and tries to avoid them.

Quantity of Life A national culture attribute describing the extent to which societal values are characterized by assertiveness and materialism.

Quality of Life A national culture attribute that emphasizes relationships and concern for others.

TABLE 3–3   Examples of Hofstede's Cultural Dimensions

Country	Individualism–Collectivism	Power Distance	Uncertainty Avoidance	Quantity of Life*
Australia	Individual	Small	Moderate	Strong
Canada	Individual	Small	Low	Moderate
England	Individual	Small	Moderate	Strong
France	Individual	Large	High	Weak
Greece	Collective	Large	High	Moderate
Italy	Individual	Moderate	High	Strong
Japan	Collective	Moderate	High	Strong
Mexico	Collective	Large	High	Strong
Singapore	Collective	Large	Low	Moderate
Sweden	Individual	Small	Low	Weak
United States	Individual	Small	Low	Strong
Venezuela	Collective	Large	High	Strong

*A weak quantity-of-life score is equivalent to a high quality-of-life score.

Source: Based on G. Hofstede, "Motivation, Leadership, and Organization: Do American Theories Apply Abroad?", *Organizational Dynamics,* Summer 1980, pp. 42–63.

A person's rank and position in his or her company is very important in Japan. It allows executives to know how much deference to show others. As a result, the exchange of business cards is a widely-followed custom and the cards always clearly state a person's title.
Dennis Brack/Black Star

- Uncertainty avoidance = Well below average
- Quantity – quality = Well above average on quantity

These results are not inconsistent with the world image of the United States. The below-average score on power distance aligns with what one might expect in a country with a representative type of government with democratic ideals. In this category, the United States would rate below nations with a small ruling class and a large, powerless set of subjects, and above those nations with very strong commitments to egalitarian values. The well-below-average ranking on uncertainty avoidance is also consistent with a representative type of government having democratic ideals. Americans perceive themselves as being relatively free from threats of uncertainty. The individualistic ethic is one of the most frequently used stereotypes to describe Americans, and, based on Hofstede's research, the stereotype seems well founded. The United States was ranked as the single most individualistic country in his entire set. Finally, the well-above-average score on quantity of life is also no surprise. Capitalism—which values aggressiveness and materialism—is consistent with Hofstede's quantity characteristics.

We haven't the space here to review the results Hofstede obtained for all forty countries, although a dozen examples are presented in Table 3–3. Since our concern is essentially with identifying similarities and differences among cultures, let's briefly identify those countries that are most and least like the United States on the four dimensions.

The United States is strongly individualistic but low on power distance. This same pattern was exhibited by England, Australia, Sweden, the Netherlands, and New Zealand. Those least similar to the United States on these dimensions were Venezuela, Colombia, Pakistan, Singapore, and the Philippines.

The United States scored low on uncertainty avoidance and high on quantity of life. The same pattern was shown by Ireland, the Philippines, New Zealand, India, and South Africa. Those least similar to the United States on these dimensions were Chile, Yugoslavia, and Portugal.

What's It Really Like Working in Japan?

No foreign country has received more attention in the last decade from students of management than Japan. Japanese organizations are routinely described as models of efficiency, and Japanese workers are depicted as loyal and hard-working partners in the production process. But is this the way it really is? Research tells us that Japanese workers *are* loyal and hardworking,[23] yet theirs is a life many North Americans might not opt for.

For example, Japanese employees put in very long hours. It is not uncommon for them to spend several hours a day commuting to and from work. After work, employees regularly go out drinking and socializing together. The end result is that—including commuting and socializing time—the typical Japanese worker is away from home sixty to seventy hours a week.

In addition to long hours, loyalty and dedication to the organization are a must in Japan, not an option. Japanese organizations have a strong seniority system with strict adherence to order, rank, and authority. For the most part,

new recruits have their salaries fixed for the first six years. Only after they have demonstrated a capacity for hard work and respect for their boss—which typically takes a dozen years—can employees begin to move up the ranks. And then promotions tend to be in small, incremental steps. Japanese organizations tend to have more steps in the career ladder than their American counterparts, but the steps are smaller. Inequality in status and rewards between top management and production rank-and-file in Japan is also typically much less than in the United States.

Yes, the Japanese are loyal and hardworking. Surprisingly, however, research shows that Japanese workers are no more committed to their organizations than are American workers. Maybe even more surprising is the finding that American employees appear to be much more satisfied with their jobs than the Japanese are. In fact, surveys contrasting Japanese and Western work attitudes regularly find that work satisfaction is lowest among the Japanese.

THE REALITY OF CULTURE SHOCK

Culture Shock Confusion, disorientation, and emotional upheaval caused by being immersed in a new culture.

Any move from one country to another will create a certain amount of confusion, disorientation, and emotional upheaval. We call this **culture shock.** The transfer of an executive from the United States to Canada, for example, would require about as little adjustment as one could possibly make. Why? Because the United States and Canada look very much alike in terms of Hofstede's four cultural dimensions. Even so, there would be some culture shock. The executive would still have to adjust to differences that would include the form of representative government (Canadians have a parliamentary system, much like the one in Great Britain), language (Canada is a bilingual—English- and French-speaking—country), and even holidays (the Canadian Thanksgiving is in early October). However, culture shock will obviously be more severe when individuals move to cultures that are most unlike their old environment.

The adjustment to a foreign country has been found to follow a U-shaped curve that contains four distinct stages.[24] This is shown in Figure 3–2.

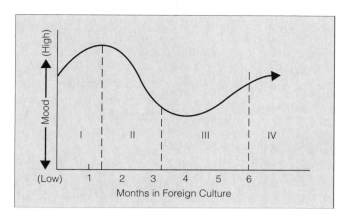

FIGURE 3–2 Culture Shock Cycle

The initial stage, I, is one of novelty. The newcomer is excited and optimistic. His or her mood is high. For the temporary visitor to a foreign country, this stage is all that is experienced. A person who spends a week or two on vacation in a strange land considers cultural differences to be interesting, even educational. However, the employee who makes a permanent, or relatively permanent, move experiences euphoria and then disillusionment. In this stage, II, the "quaint" quickly becomes "obsolete," and the "traditional," "inefficient." The opportunity to learn a new language turns into the reality of struggling to communicate. After a few months, the newcomer hits bottom. At this stage, III, any and all of the culture's differences have become blatantly clear. The newcomer's basic interpretation system, which worked fine at home, now no longer functions. He or she is bombarded by millions of sights, sounds, and other cues that are uninterpretable. Frustration and confusion are highest and mood lowest in Stage III. Finally, the newcomer begins to adapt, and the negative responses related to culture shock dissipate. In this stage, IV, the newcomer has learned what is important and what can be ignored about the new culture.

What are the implications of this model? There are at least two. First, if you're a newcomer in a foreign land or you are managing a newcomer, expect culture shock. It's not abnormal. To some degree, everyone goes through it. Second, culture shock follows a relatively predictable pattern. Expect early euphoria, followed by depression and frustration. However, after about four to six months, most people adjust to their new culture. What was previously different and strange becomes understandable.

KEEPING OB IN A GLOBAL CONTEXT

Most of the concepts that currently make up the body of knowledge we call *organizational behavior* have been developed by Americans using American subjects within domestic contexts. A comprehensive study, for instance, of more than eleven thousand articles published in twenty-four management and organizational behavior journals over a ten-year period revealed that approximately eighty percent of the studies were done in the United States and had been conducted by Americans.[25] What this means is that not all the concepts that you'll read about in future chapters are universally applicable to managing people around the world.

As you review concepts in this book, ask yourself: *Is this concept culture-bound?* If it was developed and tested in the United States, for instance, do you think it is generalizable to Mexico, or France, or India? If not, *why not?*

The more that a country's culture deviates from that of the United States, as depicted by the jagged line in Table 3–2 or the United States' ratings on Hofstede's four cultural dimensions, the more you need to be on guard to consider how cultural differences might modify the application of OB concepts.

Throughout the remainder of this book, you'll find a number of "OB in a Global Context" boxes. They are an explicit attempt to help you see how concepts might be modified for different national cultures.

SUMMARY

An understanding of differences between cultures should be particularly valuable for people who were born and raised in non–Anglo countries, those who plan on living and working in another country, and those who work with or manage people whose cultural backgrounds are different from their own.

If you fall into one of these groups, how do you use the information provided in this book? First, find out where the person or people whose behavior you're trying to understand comes from. Second, evaluate that country, using one or both of the cultural-differences frameworks presented in this chapter. Third, compare the national culture in question against the data for the United States and identify relevant differences. This is necessary because most of the research in OB has been conducted on Americans in the U.S.. Finally, modify those concepts about to be introduced here that explain and predict employee behavior to reflect these differences. The "OB in a Global Context" boxes, placed strategically throughout the book, will help you in this effort.

■ FOR DISCUSSION

1. What is the argument in support of the proposition that the world has become a global village?
2. What is the *European Community*? Why was it created?
3. What are *maquiladoras*? What advantages do they provide management?
4. How does American parochialism hinder U.S. companies' effectiveness in international business?
5. Is the variance between national cultures increasing, decreasing, or staying about the same?
6. Why is a country's national culture so hard to identify and understand?
7. What are Americans like?
8. Describe the United States in terms of Americans' relationship to the environment, time orientation, activity orientation, and conception of space.
9. Describe American culture in terms of Hofstede's four major criteria.

10. How could you use Hofstede's research if you were an American manager transferred to Mexico?

11. In which countries are employees *most* like those in the United States? *Least* like those in the United States?

12. What is *culture shock*? How could you use the four-stage culture-shock model to better understand employee behavior?

Cross-Cultural Training Doesn't Work

Academics seem to take it as a truism that the expanding global marketplace has serious implications for management practice. As a result, they have become strong advocates for the necessity of cross-cultural training. But most corporations don't provide cross-cultural training for employees. Studies indicate, for instance, that only thirty percent of American managers who are sent on foreign assignments scheduled to last from one to five years receive any cross-cultural training before their departure.

Why don't most organizations provide their managers with cross-cultural training? We propose two possible explanations. One is that top managers believe that "managing is managing," so *where* it is done is irrelevant. The other explanation is that top management doesn't believe that cross-cultural training is effective.

Contrary to the evidence presented in this chapter, many senior managers continue to believe that managerial skills are perfectly transferable across cultures. A good manager in New York or Los Angeles, for instance, should be equally effective in Paris or Hong Kong. In organizations where this belief dominates, you won't find any concern with cross-cultural training. Moreover, there is likely to be little effort made to select candidates for foreign assignments based on their ability to fit into, or adapt to, a specific culture. Selection decisions for overseas postings in these organizations are primarily made using a single criterion: the person's domestic track record.

It's probably fair to say that most senior managers today recognize that cultural differences *do* affect managerial performance. But their organizations still don't provide cross-cultural training because these managers doubt the effectiveness of this training. They argue that people can't learn to manage in a foreign culture after only a few weeks or months of training. An understanding of a country's culture is something one assimilates over many years based on input from many sources. It is not something that lends itself to short-term learning, no matter how intensive a training program might be.

Given the previous arguments, it would be surprising to find organizations offering cross-cultural training. We submit that top executives of organizations typically take one of three approaches in dealing with the selection of managerial personnel for staff foreign assignments. One approach is to ignore cultural differences. They don't worry about them, and make their selection decisions based solely on individuals' previous managerial records. Another approach is to hire nationals to manage foreign operations. Since cross-cultural training isn't effective, when a firm such as IBM needs an executive to fill a key post in Italy, it might be best served by hiring an Italian. This solution has become even easier for North American firms in recent years as the number of foreigners in American and Canadian business schools has increased. For instance, there are now literally thousands of Italians, Arabs, Germans, Japanese, and other foreign nationals who have graduate business degrees from American universities, understand American business practices, and have returned to their homelands. The third solution to the problem is to either hire nationals or intensively train people to be expert advisors to management. AT&T, as a case in point, sent one executive and his family to Singapore for a lengthy stay to soak up the atmosphere and learn about the Singaporian way of doing business. He then returned to New York as the resident expert on Singapore. When problems involving that country arise, he is called upon to provide insight.

The evidence in this argument is drawn from J. S. Black and M. Mendenhall, "Cross-Cultural Training Effectiveness: A Review and a Theoretical Framework for Future Research," *Academy of Management Review,* January 1990, pp. 113–36; and A. Kupfer, "How to Be a Global Manager," *Fortune,* March 14, 1988, p. 52.

Cross-Cultural Training Is Effective

Yes, it's true that most corporations don't provide cross-cultural training. And that's a mistake! Clearly, the ability to adapt to the cultural differences in a foreign assignment is important to managerial success. Moreover, contrary to what many managers believe, cross-cultural training is very effective. Let's elaborate on this second point.

A comprehensive review of studies that specifically looked at the effectiveness of cross-cultural training shows overwhelming evidence that this training fosters the development of cross-cultural skills and leads to higher performance. Training has been shown to improve an individual's relationships with host nationals, to allow that person to adjust more rapidly to a new culture, and to improve his or her work performance.

While these results are impressive, they don't say anything about the type of training the employee received. Does that make a difference?

There are a variety of training techniques available to prepare people for foreign work assignments. They range from documentary programs that merely expose people to a new culture through written materials on the country's sociopolitical history, geography, economics, and cultural institutions, to intense interpersonal-experience training, where individuals participate in role-playing exercises, simulated social settings, and similar experiences to "feel" the differences in a new culture.

A recent research study looked at the effectiveness of these two approaches on a group of American managers. These managers, who worked for an electronic products firm, were sent on assignment to Seoul, South Korea. Twenty of them received no training, twenty got only the documentary program, and twenty received only interpersonal-experience training. The training activities were all completed in a three-day period. All participants, no matter which group they were in, received some language training, briefings covering company operations in South Korea, and a cursory three-page background description of the country.

The results of this study confirmed the earlier evidence that cross-cultural training works. Specifically, the study found that managers who received either form of training were better performers and perceived less need to adjust to the new culture than those who received no such training. Additionally, neither method proved superior to the other.

The evidence in this argument is drawn from J. S. Black and M. Mendenhall, "Cross-Cultural Training Effectiveness: A Review and a Theoretical Framework for Future Research," *Academy of Management Review,* January 1990, pp. 113–36; and P. C. Earley, "Intercultural Training for Managers: A Comparison of Documentary and Interpersonal Methods," *Academy of Management Journal,* December 1987, pp. 685–98.

Learning About Cross-Cultural Differences Through Analyzing Prejudice

Prejudice is defined as an unfounded generalization about a group of people. Whether we like to admit it or not, we *all* have prejudices. For example, the following are groups of people that students have indicated feeling some prejudice toward: fraternity and sorority members, athletes on scholarship, college professors, surfers, people with heavy accents, the homeless, shy individuals, and people with assertive personalities.

1. Select a prejudice that *you* hold.
2. Individually, take approximately fifteen minutes and analyze this prejudice:
   a. Why did you develop it?
   b. What functions, if any, does it currently serve?
   c. Do you want to keep it? Explain your answer.
   d. How could you go about removing it from your world-view?
3. As a total class exercise, discuss how people can go about reducing prejudices that they hold toward those from different cultures.

Source: This exercise is based on an assignment described in M. Mendenhall, "A Painless Approach to Integrating 'International' into OB, HRM, and Management Courses," *Organizational Behavior and Teaching Review*, Vol. XIII, No. 3 (1988–89), p. 29.

Culture Shock: Welcome to Japan

OBJECTIVE To compare two countries' cultures and to become more familiar with the concept of culture shock.

TIME Approximately forty minutes.

Japan is different from the United States. The following facts highlight a few of the differences:

1. Birth control pills are illegal; abortion is legal.
2. There is a ninety-five percent conviction rate for those arrested for major crimes.
3. Japan has one-twentieth the crime rate of the United States.
4. Superiors resign if their subordinates engage in wrongdoing.
5. The Shinto religion has about eighty-thousand gods.

6. Dependency is a sign of health; independence is considered a kind of sickness.

7. Most prime ministers and company presidents are in their sixties and seventies.

8. Bosses often introduce their subordinates to prospective marriage partners.

9. All titles in Japanese companies mean the same thing across companies.

10. Japanese people literally do not know what words to use in a conversation until the hierarchical relationship between the speakers is clarified.

11. Compulsory retirement is often at the age of fifty-five.

12. Japanese people have the longest life expectancy in the world. For women, it is close to eighty years.

13. Taken together, the budgets of Japanese companies for after-work entertainment exceed the nation's defense budget.

14. Most Japanese can't stand American food.

15. Fifteen-hour workdays are common.

16. There are four thousand characters in the average Japanese person's alphabet.

17. Japan is a country of 120 million people on a landmass the size of California.

18. Land in Tokyo sometimes sells for several thousand dollars a square foot.

19. It is not unusual for an employee who works in Tokyo to spend five hours a day commuting to and from work.

20. In large Japanese companies, there are over a million employee suggestions a year for improvement of operations.

21. Japan has more than ten times as many industrial robots in operation as the United States has.

PROCEDURES

1. After reviewing this list, do you see any major patterns or themes that differentiate Japanese from American culture? If so, what are they?

2. Of the twenty-one "facts," which three shocked you the most? That is, which did you find the most unusual?

3. For each of the facts you found most shocking, why did you think them strange?

4. Form groups of three to five students each and compare your individual assessments. Prepare to discuss with the whole class:

   a. Themes differentiating the two cultures.

   b. What difficulties Americans might have adjusting to living and working in Japan.

   c. What challenges an American might have managing a group of Japanese employees.

Source: This exercise is based on B. Van Buskirk, "Five Classroom Exercises for Sensitizing Students to Aspects of Japanese Culture and Business Practice," *Journal of Management Education,* February 1991, pp. 98–100.

General Electric in Hungary

Tungsram was, by Hungarian standards, a large and successful manufacturer of light bulbs. In 1989, it held seven percent of the European market and had annual sales of $300 million. Yet it was hard to see it as a well-run company. For instance, its technologically dated assembly lines broke one out of every four bulbs. Its accounting and control practices looked more like those described in a novel by Charles Dickens than the practices found at most modern North American companies.

Tungsram was founded in 1896. In the early part of this century, the company pioneered the use of tungsten filament, the key element in modern light bulbs, and was on the cutting edge of high technology of the day. But after World War II, many of Hungary's best scientists fled the country when the communists took control. Over the next four decades, innovation at Tungsram and other Hungarian companies was trampled in the manic drive to meet the production quotas set out in the government's central plan.

Nevertheless, in January 1990, General Electric bought a controlling interest in Tungsram. GE's motivation? Access to the growing markets in Western and Eastern Europe. The task of converting a formerly state-run enterprise to capitalism is proving a real challenge for GE.

Managers at Tungsram have had no real experience making decisions. Karoly Vigh, for instance, has been with Tungsram for over thirty years and rose to a top management position. Yet he was discouraged from making decisions on his own. Compliance, not initiative, was rewarded by the old regime. After GE took over, Vigh was made technical director in the previously neglected environmental division. As he had always done, Vigh waited for instructions from the central planners. But none came. Tentatively, he began making some decisions, but, again as a result of his long experience working in a socialist enterprise, he wanted to tell his boss everything he was doing and get his boss's opinion on everything. What Vigh found out was that his American-trained boss didn't want to baby-sit him. He was told, "If I have to make all the decisions for you, one of us isn't necessary." Vigh's response: Amazement! "So much freedom, so much responsibility. We're not used to this."

One of the more challenging tasks facing GE is overhauling Tungsram's quaint record-keeping system. The introduction of an integrated data communication network capable of linking all of Tungsram's operations locally and throughout Europe has been delayed for a couple of years by a Hungarian phone system that makes calling the United States often easier than calling the other side of Budapest. And computers can only accomplish so much in Hungary. For instance, they can automate the payroll, but human hands are still needed to stuff envelopes with cash because personal banking services are rare.

David Gadra, one of GE's American managers transferred to Hungary, describes his frustration in trying to introduce sophisticated information systems into Tungsram. "Every morning I gather my managers together to see what can be learned from the problems of the previous twenty-four hours. What I often get is an eloquent, detailed description of what went

Source: Based on R. Thurow, "Seeing the Light," *The Wall Street Journal,* September 20, 1991, pp. R1–R2.

wrong and what the current situation is, but an absolute silence about a plan to go forward to solve it. Day in and day out, you go back to the fundamentals. You keep reinforcing, reinforcing. As in athletics, you keep raising the bar of expectations. Some days you go out and see you can't even match yesterday. So you go back again to the fundamentals."

Questions

1. Does this case suggest that North American business practices are globally transferable? Discuss.

2. How do you think Hungary's culture compares with that of the United States? Be as specific as possible.

3. Contrast the problems of motivating employees in a GE plant in Cleveland, Ohio, with those encountered in a Tungsram plant in Budapest.

FOR FURTHER READING

ADLER, N. J., *International Dimensions of Organizational Behavior,* 2nd ed. (Boston: Kent Publishing, 1991). An excellent resource that discusses the impact of culture on organizations, managing cultural diversity, and managing international transitions.

BLACK, J. S., M. MENDENHALL, and G. ODDOU, "Toward a Comprehensive Model of International Adjustment: An Integration of Multiple Theoretical Perspectives," *Academy of Management Review,* April 1991, pp. 291–317. Integrates theoretical and empirical work of both the international and domestic adjustment literatures.

JOHNSTON, W. B., "Global Work Force 2000: The New World Labor Market," *Harvard Business Review,* March–April 1991, pp. 115–27. The world's work force is becoming increasingly mobile and so are employers, who increasingly reach across borders to find the skills they need.

OHMAE, K., "Managing in a Borderless World," *Harvard Business Review,* May–June 1989, pp. 152–61. This article argues that the economy is now so globalized that the national identity of companies no longer matters.

PHATAK, A. V., *International Dimensions of Management,* 2nd ed. (Boston: Kent Publishing, 1989). Reviews the cultural environment of international management and how it impacts on the management activities of planning, organizing, staffing, and controlling.

SHAW, J. B., "A Cognitive Categorization Model for the Study of Intercultural Management," *Academy of Management Review,* October 1990, pp. 626–45. Presents a model of intercultural management that focuses on the interaction between an expatriate manager and a host-country subordinate.

NOTES

[1] See R. Tempest, "No Magic in These Kingdoms," *Los Angeles Times,* October 21, 1989, p. A1; and B. Rudolph, "Monsieur Mickey," *Time,* March 25, 1991, pp. 48–49.

[2] World Bank, *World Development Report: 1986* (Washington, DC: 1986); and "International i0," *Business Week,* April 1992.

[3] See J. Darling, "Mexico Is Learning a New Word for Wealth," *Los Angeles Times,* May 1, 1990, p. H4; and M. Satchell, "Poisoning the Border," *U.S. News & World Report,* May 6, 1991, pp. 33–41.

[4] A. R. Dowd, "Viva Free Trade with Mexico!", *Fortune,* June 17, 1991, pp. 97–100.

[5] N. J. Adler, *International Dimensions of Organizational Behavior,* 2nd ed. (Boston: Kent Publishing, 1991), p. 11.

[6] R. Knotts, "Cross-Cultural Management: Transformations and Adaptations," *Business Horizons,* January–February 1989, p. 32.

[7] See D. A. Ricks, M. Y. C. Fu, and J. S. Arpas, *International Business Blunders* (Columbus, OH: Grid, 1974); A. Bennett, "American Culture Is Often a Puzzle for Foreign Managers in the U.S.," *The Wall Street Journal,* February 12, 1986; and C. F. Valentine, "Blunders Abroad," *Nation's Business,* March 1989, p. 54.

[8] Reported in N. A. Boyacigiller and N. J. Adler, "The Parochial Dinosaur: Organizational Science in a Global Context," *Academy of Management Review,* April 1991, pp. 264–65.

[9] W. McWhirter, "I Came, I Saw, I Blundered," *Time,* October 9, 1989, p. 72.

[10] Ibid, pp. 72–77.

[11] Ibid.

[12] T. Donaldson, *The Ethics of International Business* (New York: Oxford Press, 1989), pp. 14–19.

[13] See H. W. Lane and D. G. Simpson, "Bribery in International Business: Whose Problem Is It?" in H. W. Lane and J. J. DiStefano (eds.), *International Management Behavior: From Policy to Practice* (Scarborough, Ontario: Nelson Canada, 1988), pp. 236–47.

[14] Lane and DiStefano, *International Management Behavior,* pp. 4–5.

[15] J. Child, "Culture, Contingency and Capitalism in the Cross-National Study of Organizations," in L. L. Cummings and B. M. Staw (eds.), *Research in Organizational Behavior,* Vol. 3 (Greenwich, CT: JAI Press, 1981), pp. 303–56.

[16] Ibid.

[17]G. Hofstede, *Culture's Consequences: International Differences in Work Related Values* (Beverly Hills, CA: Sage Publications, 1980).

[18]The following is based on M. Hornblower and R. T. Zintl, "Racism," *Time,* August 12, 1991, pp. 36–38.

[19]F. Kluckhohn and F. L. Strodtbeck, *Variations in Value Orientations* (Evanston, IL: Row, Peterson, 1961).

[20]This box is based on K. Freed, "Canadians New Pride in Own Identity," *Los Angeles Times,* January 22, 1986, p. 1; M. McDonald, "Pride and Patriotism," *Maclean's,* July 7, 1986, pp. 10–13; N. J. Adler and J. L. Graham, "Business Negotiations: Canadians Are Not Just Like Americans," *Canadian Journal of Administrative Sciences,* September 1987, pp. 211–38; A. Phillips, "Defining Identity," *Maclean's,* January 4, 1988, pp. 44–45; D. Baer, E. Grabb, and W. A. Johnston, "The Values of Canadians and Americans: A Critical Analysis and Reassessment," *Social Forces,* March 1990, pp. 693–713; and F. Livsey, "Employee Compensation and Benefits: Canada vs. U.S.," *Business Quarterly,* Spring 1990, pp. 20–26.

[21]Boyacigiller and Adler, "The Parochial Dinosaur," p. 274.

[22]Hofstede, *Culture's Consequences;* and G. Hofstede, "The Cultural Relativity of Organizational Practices and Theories," *Journal of International Business Studies,* Fall 1983, pp. 75–89.

[23]See J. R. Lincoln, "Employee Work Attitudes and Management Practice in the U.S. and Japan: Evidence From a Large Comparative Survey," *California Management Review,* Fall 1989, pp. 89–106; B. D. Cooney, "Japan and America: Culture Counts," *Training and Development Journal,* August 1989, pp. 58–61; and J. R. Lincoln and A. L. Kalleberg, *Culture, Control and Commitment: A Study of Work Organization and Work Attitudes in the United States and Japan* (New York: Cambridge University Press, 1990).

[24]This section is based on the work of J. T. Gullahorn and J. E. Gullahorn, "An Extension of the U-Curve Hypothesis," *Journal of Social Sciences,* January 1963, pp. 34–47.

[25]N. J. Adler, "Cross-Cultural Management Research: The Ostrich and the Trend," *Academy of Management Review,* April 1983, pp. 226–32.

FOUNDATIONS OF INDIVIDUAL BEHAVIOR

CHAPTER OUTLINE	LEARNING OBJECTIVES
Biographical Characteristics	After studying this chapter, you should be able to:
Ability	1. Define the key biographical characteristics
Personality	2. Identify two types of ability
Learning	3. Explain the factors that determine an individual's personality
Implications for Performance and Satisfaction	4. Describe the impact of job typology on the personality–job performance relationship
	5. Summarize how learning theories provide insights into changing behavior
	6. Distinguish between the four schedules of reinforcement
	7. Clarify the role of punishment in learning

His detractors often refer to him as "Neutron Jack."[1] Since becoming chief executive of General Electric in 1981, John ("Jack") F. Welch, Jr., has totally restructured GE, including the elimination of well over 100,000 jobs through layoffs, attrition, and the sale of businesses. Although he is widely regarded as one of the world's toughest managers, you can't argue with his success.

Jack Welch joined GE right out of graduate school and quickly rose through the ranks. His appointment to the CEO job when he was only forty-five, made him the youngest chief executive in the company's history. Since taking the top spot, he has bought companies worth $19 billion, notably RCA and the investment banking firm Kidder Peabody, and sold operations worth $10 billion. He has refocused GE's product lines, trimmed corporate staff by forty percent, and turned America's largest diversified corporation into a growth machine. Between 1981 and 1991, GE's annual revenues went from under $25 billion to more than $60 billion. Its return on equity and earnings per share far outpaced most Fortune 500 firms.

What makes Jack Welch the kind of executive he is? Here are some clues. He was an only child whose main source of inspiration was his dominant mother. "She always felt I could do anything. It was my mother who trained me, taught me the facts of life. She wanted me to be independent. Control your own destiny—she always had that idea. Saw reality. No mincing words. Whenever I got out of line she would whack me one. But always positive. Always constructive. Always uplifting." Jack Welch's philosophy of business was also strongly influenced by his mother's values: Face reality, even when doing so is uncomfortable, and communicate candidly, even when doing so may sting. His mother believed that these values were the necessary means to achieve what was to her the all-important end: control of one's destiny. As she regularly told her son, "If you don't control your destiny, someone else will control it for you." ■

Jack Welch's determination to control his own life is a personality characteristic that he developed at an early age. His mother instilled in him the idea that assertive behavior was acceptable, even desirable. And she shaped his behavior through encouragement and physical punishment.

Jack Welch is not unique. *All* our behavior is somewhat shaped by our personalities and the learning experiences we've encountered. In this chapter, we'll look at four individual-level variables—biographical characteristics, ability, personality, and learning—and consider their effect on employee performance and satisfaction.

BIOGRAPHICAL CHARACTERISTICS

As discussed in Chapter 2, this text is essentially concerned with finding and analyzing those variables that have an impact on employee productivity, absence, turnover, and satisfaction. The list of these variables—as shown in Figure 2-5 on page 51—is long and contains a number of complicated concepts. Many of these concepts—motivation level, say, or power relations or organizational culture—are hard to assess. It might be valuable, then, to begin by looking at factors that are easily definable and readily available, data that can be obtained, for the most part, simply from information available in an employee's personnel file. What factors would these be? Obvious characteristics would be an employee's age, gender, marital status, number of dependents, and length of service with an organization. Fortunately, there is a sizable amount of research that has specifically analyzed many of these **biographical characteristics**.

Biographical Characteristics
Personal characteristics—such as age, gender, and marital status—that are objective and easily obtained from personnel records.

Age

The relationship between age and job performance is likely to be an issue of increasing importance during the next decade. Why? There are at least three reasons. First, there is a widespread belief that job performance declines with increasing age. Regardless of whether it's true or not, a lot of people believe it and act on it. Second is the reality that the work force is aging. For instance, between the years 1985 and 2000, the number of workers between the ages of forty-five and sixty-five will grow by forty-one percent.[2] The third reason is recent American legislation that, for all intents and purposes, outlaws mandatory retirement. Most workers today no longer have to retire at the age of seventy.

Now let's take a look at the evidence. What effect does age actually have on turnover, absenteeism, productivity, and satisfaction?

The older you get, the less likely you are to quit your job. That is the overwhelming conclusion based on studies of the age-turnover relationship.[3] Of course, this conclusion should not be too surprising. As workers get older, they have fewer alternative job opportunities. In addition, older workers are less likely to resign because their longer tenure tends to provide them with higher wage rates, longer paid vacations, and more attractive pension benefits.

With the work force aging, more attention is being given to the effect of age on employee attitudes and behavior. In general, we find that older workers are more stable and, contrary to popular belief, experience no significant difference in productivity from their younger co-workers.   Keven Horan/Picture Group

It's tempting to assume that age is also inversely related to absenteeism. After all, if older workers are less likely to quit, wouldn't they also demonstrate higher stability by coming to work more regularly? Not necessarily! Most studies *do* show an inverse relationship, but closer examination finds that the age–absence relationship is partially a function of whether the absence is avoidable or unavoidable.[4] Generally, older employees have lower rates of avoidable absence than do younger employees. However, they have higher rates of unavoidable absence. This is probably due to the poorer health associated with aging and the longer recovery period that older workers need when injured.

How does age affect productivity? There is a widespread belief that productivity declines with age. It is often assumed that an individual's skills—particularly speed, agility, strength, and coordination—decay over time, and that prolonged job boredom and lack of intellectual stimulation all contribute to reduced productivity. The evidence, however, contradicts these beliefs and assumptions. A recent meta-analysis of the literature found that age and job performance were unrelated.[5] Moreover, this seems to be true for all types of jobs, professional and nonprofessional. The natural conclusion is that the demands of most jobs, even those with heavy manual labor requirements, are not extreme enough for any declines in physical skills due to age to have an impact on productivity; or if there is some decay due to age, it is offset by gains due to experience.

Our final concern is the relationship between age and job satisfaction. On this issue, the evidence is mixed. Most studies indicate a positive association between age and satisfaction, at least up to age sixty.[6] Other studies, however, have found a U-shaped relationship.[7] Several explanations could clear up these results, the most plausible being that these studies are inter-mixing professional and nonprofessional employees. When the two types are separated, satisfaction tends to continually increase among professionals as they age, whereas it falls among nonprofessionals during middle age and then rises again in the later years.

Gender

Few issues initiate more debates, myths, and unsupported opinions than whether females perform as well on jobs as males do. In this section, we review the research on this issue.

The evidence suggests that the best place to begin is with the recognition that there are few, if any, important differences between males and females that will affect their job performance. There are, for instance, no consistent male-female differences in problem-solving ability, analytical skills, competitive drive, motivation, sociability, or learning ability.[8] While psychological studies have found that women are more willing to conform to authority, and that men are more aggressive and more likely than women to have expectations of success, these differences are minor. Given the significant changes that have taken place in the last twenty years in terms of increasing female participation rates in the work force and rethinking what constitutes male and female roles, you should operate on the assumption that there is no significant difference in job productivity between males and females. Similarly, there is no evidence indicating that an employee's gender affects job satisfaction.[9]

But what about absence and turnover rates? Are females less stable employees than males? First, on the question of turnover, the evidence is mixed.[10] Some have found females to have higher turnover rates, while others have found no difference. There doesn't appear to be enough information from which to draw meaningful conclusions. The research on absence, however, is a different story. The evidence consistently indicates that women have higher rates of absenteeism than men do.[11] The most logical explanation for this finding is that our society has historically placed home and family responsibilities on the female. When a child is ill or someone needs to stay home to await the plumber, it has been the woman who has traditionally taken time off from work. However, this research is undoubtedly time-bound.[12] The historical role of the woman in child caring and as secondary breadwinner has definitely changed in the past decade; and a large proportion of men nowadays are as interested in day care and the problems associated with child care in general as are women.

Marital Status

There are not enough studies to draw any conclusions about the effect of marital status on productivity. But consistent research indicates that married employees have fewer absences, undergo less turnover, and are more satisfied with their jobs than their unmarried coworkers.[13]

Marriage imposes increased responsibilities that may make a steady job more valuable and important. Of course, the results represent correlational studies, so the causation issue is not clear. It may very well be that conscientious and satisfied employees are more likely to be married. Another offshoot of this issue is that research has not pursued other statuses besides single or married. Does being divorced have an impact on an employee's performance and satisfaction? What about couples who live together without being married? These are questions in need of investigation.

Both male & female employees are increasingly combining parent and job responsibilities.   Ed Bock/The Stock Market.

Number of Dependents

Again, we don't have enough information relating to employee productivity, but quite a bit of research has been done on the relationship between the number of dependents an employee has and absence, turnover, and job satisfaction.

There is very strong evidence that the number of children an employee has is positively correlated with absence, especially among females.[14] Similarly, the evidence seems to point to a positive relationship between number of dependents and job satisfaction.[15] In contrast, studies relating number of dependents and turnover produce a mixed bag of results.[16] Some indicate that children increase turnover, while others show that they result in lower turnover. At this point, the evidence regarding turnover is just too contradictory to permit us to draw conclusions.

Tenure

The last biographical characteristic we'll look at is tenure. With the exception of the issue of male–female differences, probably no issue is more subject to myths and speculations than the impact of seniority on job performance.

Extensive reviews of the seniority—productivity relationship have been conducted.[17] While past performance tends to be related to output in a new position, seniority by itself is not a good predictor of productivity. In other words, holding all other things equal, there is no reason to believe that people who have been on a job longer are more productive than are those with less seniority.

The research relating tenure to absence is quite straightforward. Studies consistently demonstrate seniority to be negatively related to absenteeism.[18] In fact, in terms of both absence frequency and total days lost at work, tenure is the single most important explanatory variable.[19]

As with absence, tenure is also a potent variable in explaining turnover. "Tenure has consistently been found to be negatively related to turnover and has been suggested as one of the single best predictors of turnover."[20] Moreover, consistent with research that suggests that past behavior is the best predictor of future behavior,[21] evidence indicates that tenure on an employee's previous job is a powerful predictor of that employee's future turnover.[22]

ABILITY

Ability An individual's capacity to perform the various tasks in a job.

Contrary to what we were taught in grade school, we *weren't* all created equal. Most of us are to the left of the median on some normally distributed ability curve. Regardless of how motivated you are, it is unlikely that you can act as well as Meryl Streep, run as fast as Carl Lewis, write horror stories as well as Stephen King, or sing as well as Whitney Houston. Of course, just because we aren't all equal in abilities does not imply that some individuals are humanly inferior to others. What we're acknowledging is that everyone has strengths and weaknesses in terms of ability that make him or her relatively superior or inferior to others in performing certain tasks or activities.[23] From management's standpoint, the issue isn't whether or not people differ in terms of their abilities. They do! The issue is knowing *how* people differ in abilities and *using* that knowledge to increase the likelihood that an employee will perform his or her job well.

What does **ability** mean? As we'll use the term, ability refers to an individual's capacity to perform the various tasks in a job. It is a current assessment of what one *can* do. An individual's overall abilities are essentially made up of two sets of skills: intellectual and physical.

Intellectual Abilities

Intellectual Ability That required to do mental activities

Intellectual abilities are those needed to perform mental activities. IQ tests, for example, are designed to ascertain one's intellectual abilities. So, too, are popular college admission tests like the SAT and ACT and graduate admission tests in business (GMAT), law (LSAT), and medicine (MCAT). Some of the more relevant dimensions making up intellectual abilities include number aptitude, verbal comprehension, perceptual speed, and inductive reasoning. Table 4–1 describes these dimensions.

Jobs differ in the demands they place on incumbents to use their intellectual abilities. Generally speaking, the higher an individual rises in an organization's hierarchy, the more general intelligence and verbal abilities will be necessary to perform the job successfully. A high IQ is not a prerequisite for all jobs. In fact, for many jobs—where employee behavior is highly routine and there are little or no opportunities to exercise discretion—a high IQ may be unrelated to performance. On the other hand, a careful review of the evidence demonstrates that tests that assess verbal, numerical, spatial,

TABLE 4–1   Dimensions of Intellectual Ability

Dimension	Description	Job Example
Number aptitude	Ability to do speedy and accurate arithmetic	Accountant: Computing the sales tax on a set of items
Verbal comprehension	Ability to understand what is read or heard and the relationship of words to each other	Plant Manager: Following corporate policies
Perceptual speed	Ability to identify visual similarities and differences quickly and accurately	Fire Investigator: Identifying clues to support a charge of arson
Inductive reasoning	Ability to identify a logical sequence in a problem and then solve the problem	Market Researcher: Forecasting demand for a product in the next time period

and perceptual abilities are valid predictors of job proficiency across all levels of jobs.[24] So tests that measure specific dimensions of intelligence have been found to be strong predictors of job performance.

The major dilemma faced by employers who use mental ability tests for selection, promotion, training, and similar personnel decisions is that they may have a negative impact on racial and ethnic groups.[25] The evidence indicates that some minority groups score, on the average, as much as one standard deviation lower than whites on verbal, numerical, and spatial ability tests. The negative impact from these tests can be eliminated either by avoiding these types of tests or by seeking racial and ethnic balance by hiring and promoting on the basis of ability within each ethnic group separately. The latter suggestion, incidentally, underlies legal efforts by the courts to eliminate employment discrimination through the use of targets and goals.

Physical Abilities

Physical Ability   That required to do tasks demanding stamina, dexterity, strength, and similar skills.

To the same degree that intellectual abilities play a larger role in performance as individuals move up the organizational hierarchy, specific **physical abilities** gain importance for successfully doing less skilled and more standardized jobs in the lower part of the organization. Jobs in which success demands stamina, manual dexterity, leg strength, or similar talents require management to identify an employee's physical capabilities.

Research on the requirements needed in hundreds of jobs has identified nine basic abilities involved in the performance of physical tasks.[26] These are described in Table 4–2. Individuals differ in the extent to which they have each of these abilities. Not surprisingly, there is also little relationship between them: A high score on one is no assurance of a high score on others. High employee performance is likely to be achieved when management has ascertained the extent to which a job requires each of the nine abilities and then ensures that employees in that job have those abilities.

The Ability–Job Fit

Our concern is with explaining and predicting the behavior of people at work. In this section, we have demonstrated that jobs make differing demands on people and that people differ in the abilities they possess. Employee performance, therefore, is enhanced when there is a high ability-job fit.

TABLE 4–2   Nine Basic Physical Abilities

Strength Factors

1. Dynamic strength	Ability to exert muscular force repeatedly or continuously over time
2. Trunk strength	Ability to exert muscular strength using the trunk (particularly abdominal) muscles
3. Static strength	Ability to exert force against external objects
4. Explosive strength	Ability to expend a maximum of energy in one or a series of explosive acts

Flexibility Factors

5. Extent flexibility	Ability to move the trunk and back muscles as far as possible
6. Dynamic flexibility	Ability to make rapid, repeated flexing movements

Other Factors

7. Body coordination	Ability to coordinate the simultaneous actions of different parts of the body
8. Balance	Ability to maintain equilibrium despite forces pulling off balance
9. Stamina	Ability to continue maximum effort requiring prolonged effort over time

Source: Reprinted from the June 1979 issue of *Personnel Administrator*, copyright 1979, The American Society for Personnel Administration; 606 North Washington Street; Alexandria, Virginia 22314, pp. 82–92..

The specific intellectual or physical abilities required for adequate job performance depend on the ability requirements of the job. Directing attention at only the employee's abilities or the ability requirements of the job ignores that employee performance depends on the interaction of the two.

What predictions can we make when the fit is poor? As alluded to previously, if employees lack the required abilities, they are likely to fail. If you're hired as a word processor and you can't meet the job's basic keyboard typing requirements, your performance is going to be poor irrespective of your positive attitude or your high level of motivation. When the ability–job fit is out of sync because the employee has abilities that far exceed the requirements of the job, our predictions would be very different. Job performance is likely to be adequate, but there will be organizational inefficiencies and possible declines in employee satisfaction. Given that pay tends to reflect the highest skill level that employees possess, if an employee's abilities far exceed those necessary to do the job, management will be paying more than it needs to. Abilities significantly above those required can also reduce the employee's job satisfaction when the employee's desire to use his or her abilities is particularly strong and is frustrated by the limitations of the job.

PERSONALITY

Why are some people quiet and passive, while others are loud and aggressive? Are certain personality types better adapted for certain job types? What do we know from theories of personality that can help us to explain and predict the behavior of individuals in organizations? In this section, we will attempt to answer such questions.

What Is Personality?

When we talk of personality, we do not mean that a person has charm, a positive attitude toward life, a smiling face, or is a finalist for "Happiest and Friendliest" in this year's Miss America contest. When psychologists talk of personality, they mean a dynamic concept describing the growth and development of a person's whole psychological system. Rather than looking at parts of the person, personality looks at some aggregate whole that is greater than the sum of the parts.

The most frequently used definition of personality was produced by Gordon Allport more than fifty years ago. He said personality is "the dynamic organization within the individual of those psychophysical systems that determine his unique adjustments to his environment."[27] For our purposes, you should think of **personality** as the sum total of ways in which an individual reacts and interacts with others. This is most often described in terms of measurable personality traits that a person exhibits.

Personality The sum total of ways in which an individual reacts and interacts with others.

Personality Determinants

An early argument in personality research was whether an individual's personality was the result of heredity or environment. Was the personality predetermined at birth, or was it the result of the individual's interaction with his or her environment? Clearly, there is no simple black-and-white answer. Personality appears to be a result of both influences. Additionally, there has recently been an increased interest in a third factor—the situation. Thus, an adult's personality is now generally considered to be made up of both hereditary and environmental factors, moderated by situational conditions.

HEREDITY   Heredity refers to those factors that were determined at conception. Physical stature, facial attractiveness, sex, temperament, muscle composition and reflexes, energy level, and biological rhythms are characteristics that are generally considered to be either completely or substantially influenced by who your parents were; that is, by their biological, physiological, and inherent psychological make-up. The heredity approach argues that the ultimate explanation of an individual's personality is the molecular structure of the genes, located in the chromosomes. "In fact, much of the early work in personality could be subsumed under the series: Heredity is transmitted through the genes; the genes determine the hormone balance; hormone balance determines physique; and physique shapes personality."[28]

The heredity argument can be used to explain why Veronica's nose looks like her father's or why her chin resembles her mother's. It may explain why Diane is a gifted athlete when both her parents were similarly gifted. More controversy would surround the conclusion, by those who advocate the heredity approach, that Michael is lethargic as a result of inheriting this characteristic from his parents.

If all personality characteristics were completely dictated by heredity, they would be fixed at birth and no amount of experience could alter them. If you were relaxed and easygoing as a child, for example, that would be the result of your genes, and it would not be possible for you to change these characteristics. While this approach may be appealing to the bigots of the world, it is an inadequate explanation of personality.

ENVIRONMENT   Among the factors that exert pressures on our personality formation are the culture in which we are raised, our early conditioning, the norms among our family, friends, and social groups, and other influences that we experience. The environment we are exposed to plays a critical role in shaping our personalities.

For example, culture establishes the norms, attitudes, and values that are passed along from one generation to the next and create consistencies over time. An ideology that is intensely fostered in one culture may have only moderate influence in another. For instance, North Americans have had the themes of industriousness, success, competition, independence, and the Protestant work ethic constantly instilled in them through books, the school system, family, and friends. North Americans, as a result, tend to be ambitious and aggressive relative to individuals raised in cultures that have emphasized getting along with others, cooperation, and the priority of family over work and career.

An interesting area of research linking environmental factors and personality has focused on the influence of birth order. It has been argued that sibling position is an important psychological variable "because it represents a microcosm of the significant social experiences of adolescence and adulthood."[29] Those who see birth order as a predictive variable propose that while personality differences between children are frequently attributed to heredity, the environment in which the children are raised is really the critical factor that creates the differences. And the environment that a firstborn child is exposed to is different from that of later-born children.

The research indicates that firstborns are more prone to schizophrenia, more susceptible to social pressure, and more dependent than the later-born.[30] The firstborn are also more likely to experience the world as more orderly, predictable, and rational than later-born children. Of course, there is much debate as to the differing characteristics of first-versus later-born children, but the evidence does indicate that firstborns are "more concerned with social acceptance and rejection, less likely to break the rules imposed by authority, more ambitious and hard-working, more cooperative, more prone to guilt and anxiety, and less openly aggressive."[31]

Careful consideration of the arguments favoring either heredity or environment as the primary determinant of personality forces the conclusion that both are important. Heredity sets the parameters or outer limits, but an individual's full potential will be determined by how well he or she adjusts to the demands and requirements of the environment.

SITUATION   A third factor, the situation, influences the effects of heredity and environment on personality. An individual's personality, while generally stable and consistent, does change in different situations. The different demands of different situations call forth different aspects of one's personality. We should not, therefore, look at personality patterns in isolation.

While it seems only logical to suppose that situations will influence an individual's personality, a neat classification scheme that would tell us the impact of various types of situations has so far eluded us. "Apparently we are not yet close to developing a system for clarifying situations so that they might be systematically studied."[32] However, we do know that certain situations are more relevant than others in influencing personality.

> What is of interest taxonomically is that situations seem to differ substantially in the constraints they impose on behavior, with some situations—e.g. church, an employment interview—constraining many behaviors and others—e.g. a picnic in a public park—constraining relatively few.[33]

Furthermore, although certain generalizations can be made about personality, there are significant individual differences. As we shall see,

New Evidence Emphasizes the Importance of Heredity

While no expert in personality psychology would argue today that heredity is the *sole* determinant of an individual's personality, the latest research makes a very strong argument for the importance of heredity.[34]

Researchers looking at this issue have studied more than one hundred sets of identical twins who were separated at birth and raised apart. If environment is the major determinant of personality characteristics, you'd expect the researchers to find few similarities between separated twins. That, however, is not what they discovered. They found that for almost every behavioral trait, "an important fraction of the variation among people turns out to be associated with genetic variation."[35] More specifically, they found that genetics accounts for about fifty percent of personality differences and about forty percent of job interest variations.

"We think of each pair of identical twins as one piece of music played by two different musicians," said the lead researcher. "The music can be played fantastically, or it may not run right. But you'll always be able to recognize the piece. That's because nature writes the score. Environment is responsible for the playing technique."[36]

the study of individual differences has come to receive greater emphasis in personality research, which originally sought out more general, universal patterns.

Personality Traits

Personality Traits Enduring characteristics that describe an individual's behavior.

The early work in the structure of personality revolved around attempts to identify and label enduring characteristics that describe an individual's behavior. Popular characteristics include shy, aggressive, submissive, lazy, ambitious, loyal, and timid. These characteristics, when they are exhibited in a large number of situations, are called **personality traits**.[37] The more consistent the characteristic and the more frequently it occurs in diverse situations, the more important that trait is in describing the individual.

Efforts to isolate traits have been hindered because there are so many of them. In one study, 17,953 individual traits were identified.[38] It is virtually impossible to predict behavior when such a large number of traits must be

FIGURE 4–1

Peanuts reprinted by permission of UFS, Inc.

TABLE 4–3   Sixteen Primary Traits

1. Reserved	vs.	Outgoing
2. Less intelligent	vs.	More intelligent
3. Affected by feelings	vs.	Emotionally stable
4. Submissive	vs.	Dominant
5. Serious	vs.	Happy-go-lucky
6. Expedient	vs.	Conscientious
7. Timid	vs.	Venturesome
8. Tough-minded	vs.	Sensitive
9. Trusting	vs.	Suspicious
10. Practical	vs.	Imaginative
11. Forthright	vs.	Shrewd
12. Self-assured	vs.	Apprehensive
13. Conservative	vs.	Experimenting
14. Group-dependent	vs.	Self-sufficient
15. Uncontrolled	vs.	Controlled
16. Relaxed	vs.	Tense

taken into account. As a result, attention has been directed toward reducing these thousands to a more manageable number.

One researcher isolated 171 traits but concluded that they were superficial and lacking in descriptive power.[39] What he sought was a reduced set of traits that would identify underlying patterns. The result was the identification of sixteen personality factors, which he called the *source* or *primary traits*. They are shown in Table 4-3. These sixteen traits have been found to be generally steady and constant sources of behavior, allowing prediction of an individual's behavior in specific situations by weighing the characteristics for their situational relevance.

Traits can additionally be grouped to form personality types. Instead of looking at specific characteristics, we can group those qualities that go together into a single category. For example, ambition and aggression tend to be highly correlated. Efforts to reduce the number of traits into common groups tend to isolate introversion–extroversion and something approximating high anxiety–low anxiety as the underlying interconnecting characteristics.[40] As depicted in Figure 4–2, these dimensions suggest four personality types.[41] For example, an individual with high anxiety and extroversion would be tense, excitable, unstable, warm, sociable, and dependent.

Should you put a lot of weight on personality traits as explanatory devices or predictors of employee behavior across a broad spectrum of situations? Probably not! This is because traits ignore situational contexts. They

FIGURE 4–2   Four-Type Thesis

	High anxety	Low axiety
Extrovert	Tense, excitable, unstable, warm, sociable, and dependent	Composed, confident, trustful, adaptable, warm, sociable, and dependent
Introvert	Tense, excitable, unstable, cold, and shy	Composed, confident, trustful, adaptable, calm, cold, and shy

The MBTI: Using Personality Tests to Improve Communication

The Myers-Briggs Type Indicator (MBTI) is a one-hundred-question personality test that asks people how they usually feel or act in particular situations.[42] It is one of the most widely used personality tests in the United States—in one recent year alone, some 20 million people took it. Organizations using the MBTI include Allied-Signal, Apple Computer, AT&T, Citicorp, Exxon, GE, Honeywell, and 3M Co., plus many hospitals, educational institutions, and even the U.S. Armed Forces.

The test labels people as extroverted or introverted (E or I), sensing or intuitive (S or N), thinking or feeling (T or F), and perceiving or judging (P or J). These are then combined into sixteen personality types. (These are different from the sixteen primary traits in Table 4-3.) To illustrate, let's take several examples. INTJ's are visionaries. They usually have original minds and great drive for their own ideas and purposes. They're characterized as skeptical, critical, independent, determined, and often stubborn. ESTJ's are organizers. They're practi-

cal, realistic, matter-of-fact, with a natural head for business or mechanics. They like to organize and run activities. The ENTP type is a conceptualizer. He or she is quick, ingenious, and good at many things. This person tends to be resourceful in solving challenging problems, but may neglect routine assignments.

Users of MBTI aren't using the test to screen job applicants. Rather, it is being used to improve employee self-awareness, and in management development programs to help executives understand how they come across to others who may see things differently. For instance, some users report that the results help explain behaviors of colleagues that have puzzled them for years. Proponents argue that when people are aware of their own and their co-workers' types, communication improves, and with it, productivity. Whether the use of MBTI actually improves employee productivity is problematic. But the growing popularity of MBTI in organizations can't be ignored.

are not contingency-oriented and, therefore, largely ignore the dynamic interchange that occurs between an individual's personality and his or her environment. As a result, personality traits tend to be most valuable as predictors with individuals who hold a trait at its extreme. We might be able to predict some common behaviors among *extreme* extroverts or individuals who are *highly* anxious. But since the majority of people are in the vast middle range on most trait characteristics, personality traits must be considered in their situational context.

Major Personality Attributes Influencing OB

A number of specific personality attributes have been isolated as having potential for predicting behavior in organizations. The first of these is related to where one perceives the locus of control in one's life. The others are achievement orientation, authoritarianism, Machiavellianism, self-esteem, self-monitoring, and propensity for risk-taking. In this section, we shall briefly introduce these attributes and summarize what we know about their ability to explain and predict employee behavior.

LOCUS OF CONTROL   Some people believe that they are masters of their own fate. Other people see themselves as pawns of fate, believing that what happens to them in their lives is due to luck or chance. The first type, those who believe that they control their destinies, have been labeled **internals**, whereas the latter, who see their lives as being controlled by outside forces, have been called **externals**.[43]

    A large amount of research comparing internals with externals has consistently shown that individuals who rate high in externality are less satisfied with their jobs, have higher absenteeism rates, are more alienated from the work setting, and are less involved on their jobs than are internals.[44]

    Why are externals more dissatisfied? The answer is probably because they perceive themselves as having little control over those organizational outcomes that are important to them. Internals, facing the same situation, attribute organizational outcomes to their own actions. If the situation is unattractive, they believe that they have no one else to blame but themselves. Also, the dissatisfied internal is more likely to quit a dissatisfying job.

    The impact of **locus of control** on absence is an interesting one. Internals believe that health is substantially under their own control through proper habits, so they take more responsibility for their health and have better health habits. This leads to lower incidences of sickness and, hence, lower absenteeism.[45]

    We shouldn't expect any clear relationship between locus of control and turnover. The reason is that there are opposing forces at work. "On the one hand, internals tend to take action and thus might be expected to quit jobs more readily. On the other hand, they tend to be more successful on the job and more satisfied, factors associated with less individual turnover."[46]

    The overall evidence indicates that internals generally perform better on their jobs, but that conclusion should be moderated to reflect differences in jobs. Internals search more actively for information before making a decision, are more motivated to achieve, and make a greater attempt to control their environment. Externals, however, are more compliant and willing to follow directions. Therefore, internals do well on sophisticated tasks—which includes most managerial and professional jobs—that require complex information processing and learning. Additionally, internals are more suited to jobs that require initiative and independence of action. In contrast, externals should do well on jobs that are well structured and routine and where success depends heavily on complying with the direction of others.

ACHIEVEMENT ORIENTATION   We have noted that internals are motivated to achieve. This achievement orientation has also been singled out as a personality characteristic that varies among employees and that can be used to predict certain behaviors.

    Research has centered around the need to achieve (**nAch**). People with a high need to achieve can be described as continually striving to do things better. They want to overcome obstacles, but they want to feel that their success (or failure) is due to their own actions. This means they like tasks of intermediate difficulty. If a task is very easy, it will lack challenge. High achievers receive no feeling of accomplishment from doing tasks that fail to challenge their abilities. Similarly, they avoid tasks that are so difficult that

Internals   Individuals who believe that they control what happens to them.

Externals   Individuals who believe that what happens to them is controlled by outside forces such as luck or chance.

Locus of Control   The degree to which people believe they are masters of their own fate.

nAch   Need to achieve or strive continually to do things better.

the probability of success is very low and where, even if they do succeed, it is more apt to be due to luck than to ability. Given the high achiever's propensity for tasks where the outcome can be attributed directly to his or her efforts, the high-*nAch* person looks for challenges having approximately a fifty–fifty chance of success.

What can we say about high achievers on the job? In jobs that provide intermediate difficulty, rapid performance feedback, and allow the employee control over his or her results, the high-*nAch* individual will perform well.[47] This implies that high achievers will do better in sales, professional sports, or in management than on an assembly line or in clerical tasks. That is, those individuals with a high *nAch* will not *always* outperform those who are low or intermediate in this characteristic. The tasks that high achievers undertake must provide the challenge, feedback, and responsibility they look for if the high-*nAch* personality is to be positively related to job performance.

AUTHORITARIANISM   There is evidence that there is such a thing as an authoritarian personality, but its relevance to job behavior is more speculation than fact. With that qualification, let us examine authoritarianism and consider how it might be related to employee performance.

Authoritarianism refers to a belief that there should be status and power differences among people in organizations.[48] The extremely high-authoritarian personality is intellectually rigid, judgmental of others, deferential to those above and exploitative of those below, distrustful, and resistant to change. Of course, few people are extreme authoritarians, so conclusions must be guarded. It seems reasonable to postulate, however, that possessing a high-authoritarian personality would be related negatively to performance where the job demands sensitivity to the feelings of others, tact, and the ability to adapt to complex and changing situations.[49] On the other hand, where jobs are highly structured and success depends on close conformance to rules and regulations, the high-authoritarian employee should perform quite well.

MACHIAVELLIANISM   Closely related to authoritarianism is the characteristic of **Machiavellianism** (Mach), named after Niccolo Machiavelli, who wrote in the sixteenth century on how to gain and manipulate power. An individual high in Machiavellianism is pragmatic, maintains emotional distance, and believes that ends can justify means. "If it works, use it" is consistent with a high-Mach perspective.

A considerable amount of research has been directed toward relating high- and low-Mach personalities to certain behavioral outcomes.[50] High-Machs manipulate more, win more, are persuaded less, and persuade others more than do low-Machs.[51] Yet these high-Mach outcomes are moderated by situational factors. It has been found that high-Machs flourish (1) when they interact face-to-face with others rather than indirectly; (2) when the situation has a minimum number of rules and regulations, thus allowing latitude for improvisation; and (3) where emotional involvement with details irrelevant to winning distracts low-Machs.[52]

Should we conclude that high-Machs make good employees? That answer depends on the type of job and whether you consider ethical implications in evaluating performance. In jobs that require bargaining skills (such as labor negotiation) or where there are substantial rewards for winning (as in commissioned sales), high-Machs will be productive. But if ends can't justify the means, if there are *absolute* standards of behavior, or if the three sit-

Authoritarianism The belief that there should be status and power differences among people in organizations.

Machiavellianism Degree to which an individual is pragmatic, maintains emotional distance, and believes that ends can justify means.

Dominant Personality Attributes Should Vary
Across National Cultures

There are certainly no common personality types for a given country. You can, for instance, find high and low risk-takers in almost any culture. Yet a country's culture should influence the dominant personality characteristics of its population. Let's build this case by looking at three personality attributes—locus of control, achievement orientation, and authoritarianism.

In Chapter 3, we introduced a "person's relationship to the environment" as a value dimension that separates national cultures. We noted that North Americans believe that they can dominate their environment, while people in other societies, such as Middle Eastern countries, believe that life is essentially preordained. Notice the close parallel to internal and external locus of control. We should expect a larger proportion of internals in the American and

Canadian work force than in the Saudi Arabian or Iranian work force.

The United States is well known for its emphasis on individualism and achievement. Managers in the United States, in contrast to, say, those in Third World nations, should expect to find more employees with a high–achievement focus.

Authoritarianism is closely related to the concept of power distance. In high power–distance societies, such as Mexico or Venezuela, there should be a large proportion of individuals with authoritarian personalities, especially among the ruling class. In contrast, since the United States rates below average on this dimension, we'd predict that authoritarian personalities would be less prevalent than in the high power-distance countries.

uational factors noted in the previous paragraph are not in evidence, our ability to predict a high-Mach's performance will be severely curtailed.

Self-esteem Individuals' degree of liking or disliking for themselves.

SELF-ESTEEM   People differ in the degree to which they like or dislike themselves. This trait is called **self-esteem**.[53]

The research on self-esteem (SE) offers some interesting insights into organizational behavior. For example, self-esteem is directly related to expectations for success. High-SEs believe that they possess more of the ability they need in order to succeed at work. Individuals with high SEs will take more risks in job selection and are more likely to choose unconventional jobs than people with low SEs.

The most generalizable finding on self-esteem is that low-SEs are more susceptible to external influence than are high-SEs. Low-SEs are dependent on the receipt of positive evaluations from others. As a result, they are more likely to seek approval from others and more prone to conform to the beliefs and behaviors of those they respect than are high-SEs. In managerial positions, low-SEs will tend to be concerned with pleasing others and, therefore, are less likely to take unpopular stands than are high-SEs.

Not surprisingly, self-esteem has also been found to be related to job satisfaction. A number of studies confirm that high-SEs are more satisfied with their jobs than low-SEs.

Self-monitoring A personality trait that measures an individual's ability to adjust his or her behavior to external situational factors.

SELF-MONITORING   Another personality trait that has recently received increased attention is called **self-monitoring.**[54] It refers to an individual's ability to adjust his or her behavior to external, situational factors.

Individuals high in self-monitoring show considerable adaptability in adjusting their behavior to external situational factors. They are highly sensitive to external cues and can behave differently in different situations. High self-monitors are capable of presenting striking contradictions between their public persona and their private self. Low self-monitors can't disguise themselves this way. They tend to display their true dispositions and attitudes in every situation; hence, there is high behavioral consistency between who they are and what they do.

The research on self-monitoring is in its infancy, so predictions must be guarded. However, preliminary evidence suggests that high self-monitors tend to pay closer attention to the behavior of others and are more capable of conforming than are low self-monitors.[55] We might also hypothesize that high self-monitors will be more successful in managerial positions where individuals are required to play multiple, and even contradicting, roles. The high self-monitor is capable of putting on different "faces" for different audiences.

RISK-TAKING   People differ in their willingness to take chances. This propensity to assume or avoid risk has been shown to have an impact on how long it takes managers to make a decision and how much information they require before making their choice. For instance, seventy-nine managers worked on simulated personnel exercises that required them to make hiring decisions.[56] High-risk-taking managers made more rapid decisions and used less information in making their choices than did the low-risk-taking managers. Interestingly, the decision accuracy was the same for both groups.

While it is generally correct to conclude that managers in organizations are risk-aversive,[57] there are still individual differences on this dimension.[58] As a result, it makes sense to recognize these differences and even to consider aligning risk-taking propensity with specific job demands. For instance, a high-risk-taking propensity may lead to more effective performance for a stock trader in a brokerage firm because this type of job demands rapid decision making. On the other hand, this personality characteristic might prove a major obstacle to accountants performing auditing activities. The latter job might be better filled by someone with a low-risk-taking propensity.

Matching Personalities and Jobs

In the previous discussion of personality attributes, our conclusions were often qualified to recognize that the requirements of the job moderated the relationship between possession of the personality characteristic and job performance. This concern with matching the job requirements with personality characteristics has recently received increased attention. It is best articulated in John Holland's personality-job fit theory.[59] The theory is based on the notion of fit between a person's personality characteristics and his or her occupational environment. Holland presents six personality types and proposes that satisfaction and the propensity to leave a job depend on the degree to which individuals successfully match their personalities to a congruent occupational environment.

Each one of the six personality types has a congruent occupational environment. Table 4—4 describes the six types and their personality characteristics, and gives examples of congruent occupations.

According to John Holland, social types tend to be friendly, cooperative, and understanding.   Howard Grey/Tony Stone Worldwide

Holland has developed a Vocational Preference Inventory questionnaire that contains 160 occupational titles. Respondents indicate which of these occupations they like or dislike, and these answers are used to form personality profiles. Utilizing this procedure, research strongly supports

TABLE 4–4   Holland's Typology of Personality and Congruent Occupations

Type	Personality Characteristics	Congruent Occupations
Realistic: Prefers physical activities that require skill, strength, and coordination	Shy, genuine, persistent, stable, conforming, practical	Mechanic, drill press operator, assembly-line worker, farmer
Investigative: Prefers activities that involve thinking, organizing, and understanding	Analytical, original, curious, independent	Biologist, economist, mathematician, news reporter
Social: Prefers activities that involve helping and developing others	Sociable, friendly, cooperative, understanding	Social worker, teacher, counselor, clinical psychologist
Conventional: Prefers rule-regulated, orderly, and unambiguous activities	Conforming, efficient, practical, unimaginative, inflexible	Accountant, corporate manager, bank teller, file clerk
Enterprising: Prefers verbal activities where there are opportunities to influence others and attain power	Self-confident, ambitious, energetic, domineering	Lawyer, real estate agent, public relations specialist, small-business manager
Artistic: Prefers ambiguous and unsystematic activities that allow creative expression	Imaginative, disorderly, idealistic, emotional, impractical	Painter, musician, writer, interior decorator

the hexagonal diagram in Figure 4–3.[60] This figure shows that the closer two fields or orientations are in the hexagon, the more compatible they are. Adjacent categories are quite similar, while those diagonally opposite are highly dissimilar.

What does all this mean? The theory argues that satisfaction is highest and turnover lowest where personality and occupation are in agreement. Social individuals should be in social jobs, conventional people in conventional jobs, and so forth. A realistic person in a realistic job is in a more congruent situation than is a realistic person in an investigative job. A realistic person in a social job is in the most incongruent situation possible. The key points of this model are that (1) there do appear to be intrinsic differences in personality among individuals, (2) there are different types of jobs, and (3) people in job environments congruent with their personality types should be more satisfied and less likely to voluntarily resign than should people in incongruent jobs.

LEARNING

The last topic we will introduce in this chapter is learning. It is included for the obvious reason that almost all complex behavior is learned. If we want to explain and predict behavior, we need to understand how people learn.

A Definition of Learning

Learning Any relatively permanent change in behavior that occurs as a result of experience.

What is **learning?** A psychologist's definition is considerably broader than the layperson's view that "it's what we did when we went to school." In actuality, each of us is continuously going "to school." Learning occurs all of the time. A generally accepted definition of learning is, therefore, *any relatively permanent change in behavior that occurs as a result of experience.* Ironically, we can say that changes in behavior indicate that learning has taken place and that learning is a change in behavior.

**FIGURE 4–3
Relationships Among
Occupational Personality
Types** *J.L Holland, Making Vocational Choices: A Theory of Vocational Personalities and Work Environments*, 2nd ed. (Englewood Cliffs, NJ: Prentice Hall, 1985). Used by permission. The model originally appeared in J. L. Holland et al., *An Empirical Occupational Classification Derived from a Theory of Personality and Intended for Practice and Research*, ACT Research Report No. 29 (Iowa City: The American College Testing Program, 1969).

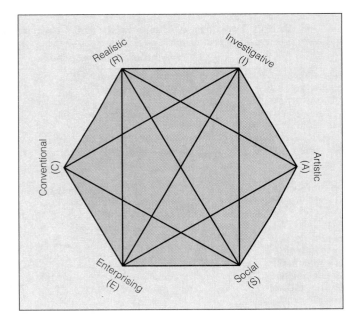

Obviously, the foregoing definition suggests that we shall never see someone "learning." We can see changes taking place, but not the learning itself. The concept is theoretical and, hence, not directly observable:

> You have seen people in the process of learning, you have seen people who behave in a particular way as a result of learning and some of you (in fact, I guess the majority of you) have "learned" at some time in your life. In other words, we infer that learning has taken place if an individual behaves, reacts, responds as a result of experience in a manner different from the way he formerly behaved.[61]

Our definition has several components that deserve clarification. First, learning involves change. This may be good or bad from an organizational point of view. People can learn unfavorable behaviors—to hold prejudices or to restrict their output, for example—as well as favorable behaviors. Second, the change must be relatively permanent. Temporary changes may be only reflexive and fail to represent any learning. Therefore, this requirement rules out behavioral changes caused by fatigue or temporary adaptations. Third, our definition is concerned with behavior. Learning takes place where there is a change in actions. A change in an individual's thought processes or attitudes, if accompanied by no change in behavior, would not be learning. Finally, some form of experience is necessary for learning. This may be acquired directly through observation or practice. Or it may result from an indirect experience, such as that acquired through reading. The crucial test still remains: Does this experience result in a relatively permanent change in behavior? If the answer is "Yes," we can say that learning has taken place.

Theories of Learning

How do we learn? Three theories have been offered to explain the process by which we acquire patterns of behavior. These are classical conditioning, operant conditioning, and social learning.

Classical Conditioning A type of conditioning where an individual responds to some stimulus that would not invariably produce such a response.

CLASSICAL CONDITIONING **Classical conditioning** grew out of experiments to teach dogs to salivate in response to the ringing of a bell, conducted at the turn of the century by a Russian physiologist, Ivan Pavlov.[62]

A simple surgical procedure allowed Pavlov to measure accurately the amount of saliva secreted by a dog. When Pavlov presented the dog with a piece of meat, the dog exhibited a noticeable increase in salivation. When Pavlov withheld the presentation of meat and merely rang a bell, the dog had no salivation. Then Pavlov proceeded to link the meat and the ringing of the bell. After repeatedly hearing the bell before getting the food, the dog began to salivate as soon as the bell rang. After a while, the dog would salivate merely at the sound of the bell, even if no food was offered. In effect, the dog had learned to respond—that is, to salivate—to the bell. Let's review this experiment to introduce the key concepts in classical conditioning.

The meat was an *unconditioned stimulus;* it invariably caused the dog to react in a specific way. The reaction that took place whenever the unconditioned stimulus occurred was called the *unconditioned response* (or the noticeable increase in salivation, in this case). The bell was an artificial stimulus, or what we call the *conditioned stimulus.* While it was originally neutral, after the bell was paired with the meat (an unconditioned stimulus), it eventually produced a response when presented alone. The last key concept is the *conditioned response.* This describes the behavior of the dog salivating in reaction to the bell alone.

Using these concepts, we can summarize classical conditioning. Essentially, learning a conditioned response involves building up an association between a conditioned stimulus and an unconditioned stimulus. Using the paired stimuli, one compelling and the other one neutral, the neutral one becomes a conditioned stimulus and, hence, takes on the properties of the unconditioned stimulus.

Classical conditioning can be used to explain why Christmas carols often bring back pleasant memories of childhood—the songs being associated with the festive Christmas spirit and initiating fond memories and feelings of euphoria. In an organizational setting, we can also see classical conditioning operating. For example, at one manufacturing plant, every time the top executives from the head office were scheduled to make a visit, the plant management would clean up the administrative offices and wash the windows. This went on for years. Eventually, employees would turn on their best behavior and look prim and proper whenever the windows were cleaned—even in those occasional instances when the cleaning was not paired with the visit from the top brass. People had learned to associate the cleaning of the windows with the visit from the head office.

Classical conditioning is passive. Something happens and we react in a specific way. It is elicited in response to a specific, identifiable event. As such it can explain simple reflexive behaviors. But most behavior—particularly the complex behavior of individuals in organizations—is emitted rather than elicited. It is voluntary rather than reflexive. For example, employees choose to arrive at work on time, ask their boss for help with problems, or "goof off" when no one is watching. The learning of these behaviors is better understood by looking at operant conditioning.

Operant Conditioning A type of conditioning in which desired voluntary behavior leads to a reward or prevents a punishment.

OPERANT CONDITIONING **Operant conditioning** argues that behavior is a function of its consequences. People learn to behave to get something they want or avoid something they don't want. Operant behavior means voluntary or learned behavior in contrast to reflexive or unlearned behavior. The tendency to repeat such behavior is influenced by the reinforcement or lack of reinforcement brought about by the consequences of the behavior. Reinforcement, therefore, strengthens a behavior and increases the likelihood that it will be repeated.

What Pavlov did for classical conditioning, the late Harvard psychologist B. F. Skinner did for operant conditioning. [63] Building on earlier work in the field, Skinner's research extensively expanded our knowledge of operant conditioning. Even his staunchest critics, who represent a sizable group, admit that his operant concepts work.

Behavior is assumed to be determined from without—that is, learned—rather than from within—reflexive or unlearned. Skinner argued that by creating pleasing consequences to follow specific forms of behavior, the frequency of that behavior will increase. People will most likely engage in desired behaviors if they are positively reinforced for doing so. Rewards, for example, are most effective if they immediately follow the desired response. Additionally, behavior that is not rewarded, or is punished, is less likely to be repeated.

You see illustrations of operant conditioning everywhere. For example, any situation in which it is either explicitly stated or implicitly suggested that reinforcements are contingent on some action on your part involves the use of operant learning. Your instructor says that if you want a high grade in the course you must supply correct answers on the test. A commissioned salesperson wanting to earn a sizable income finds that this is contingent on generating high sales in her territory. Of course, the linkage can also work to teach the individual to engage in behaviors that work against the best interests of the organization. Assume your boss tells you that if you will work overtime during the next three-week busy season, you will be compensated for it at the next performance appraisal. However, when performance appraisal time comes, you find that you are given no positive reinforcement for your overtime work. The next time your boss asks you to work overtime, what will you do? You will probably decline! Your behavior can be explained by operant conditioning: If a behavior fails to be positively reinforced, the probability that the behavior will be repeated declines.

SOCIAL LEARNING   Individuals can also learn by observing what happens to other people and just by being told about something, as well as by direct experiences. So, for example, much of what we have learned comes from watching models—parents, teachers, peers, motion picture and television performers, bosses, and so forth. This view that we can learn through both observation and direct experience has been called **social-learning theory.**[64]

While social-learning theory is an extension of operant conditioning—that is, it assumes that behavior is a function of consequences—it also acknowledges the existence of observational learning and the importance of perception in learning. People respond to how they perceive and define consequences, not to the objective consequences themselves.

The influence of models is central to the social-learning viewpoint. Four processes have been found to determine the influence that a model will have on an individual. As we'll show later in this chapter, the inclusion of the following processes when management sets up employee training programs will significantly improve the likelihood that the programs will be successful:

1. *Attentional processes.* People only learn from a model when they recognize and pay attention to its critical features. We tend to be most influenced by models that are attractive, repeatedly available, important to us, or similar to us in our estimation.

2. *Retention processes.* A model's influence will depend on how well the individual remembers the model's action after the model is no longer readily available.

3. *Motor reproduction processes.* After a person has seen a new behavior by observing the model, the watching must be converted to doing. This process then demonstrates that the individual can perform the modeled activities.

4. *Reinforcement processes.* Individuals will be motivated to exhibit the modeled behavior if positive incentives or rewards are provided. Behaviors that are reinforced will be given more attention, learned better, and performed more often.

Shaping: A Managerial Tool

Because learning takes place on the job as well as prior to it, managers will be concerned with how they can teach employees to behave in ways that most benefit the organization. When we attempt to mold individuals by guiding their learning in graduated steps, we are **shaping behavior.**

Consider the situation in which an employee's behavior is significantly different from that sought by management. If management only reinforced the individual when he or she showed desirable responses, there might be very little reinforcement taking place. In such a case, shaping offers a logical approach toward achieving the desired behavior.

Social Learning Theory
People can learn through both observation and direct experience.

Shaping Behavior
Systematically reinforcing each successive step that moves an individual closer to the desired response.

We *shape* behavior by systematically reinforcing each successive step that moves the individual closer to the desired response. If an employee who has chronically been a half-hour late for work comes in only twenty minutes late, we can reinforce this improvement. Reinforcement would increase as responses more closely approximate the desired behavior.

METHODS OF SHAPING BEHAVIOR   There are four ways in which to shape behavior: through positive reinforcement, negative reinforcement, punishment, and extinction.

When a response is followed with something pleasant, it is called *positive reinforcement*. This would describe, for instance, the boss who praises an employee for a job well done. When a response is followed by the termination or withdrawal of something unpleasant, it is called *negative reinforcement*. If your college instructor asks a question and you don't know the answer, looking through your lecture notes is likely to preclude your being called on. This is a negative reinforcement because you have learned that looking busily through your notes prevents the instructor from calling on you. *Punishment* is causing an unpleasant condition in an attempt to eliminate an undesirable behavior. Giving an employee a two-day suspension from work without pay for showing up drunk is an example of punishment. Eliminating any reinforcement that is maintaining a behavior is called *extinction*. When the behavior is not reinforced, it tends to gradually be extinguished. College instructors who wish to discourage students from asking questions in class can eliminate this behavior in their students by ignoring those who raise their hands to ask questions. Hand-raising will become extinct when it is invariably met with an absence of reinforcement.

Both positive and negative reinforcement result in learning. They strengthen a response and increase the probability of repetition. In the preceding illustrations, praise strengthens and increases the behavior of doing a good job because praise is desired. The behavior of "looking busy" is similarly strengthened and increased by its terminating the undesirable consequence of being called on by the teacher. Both punishment and extinction, however, weaken behavior and tend to decrease its subsequent frequency.

Reinforcement, whether it is positive or negative, has an impressive record as a shaping tool. Our interest, therefore, is in reinforcement rather than in punishment or extinction. A review of research findings on the impact of reinforcement upon behavior in organizations concluded that

1. Some type of reinforcement is necessary to produce a change in behavior.

2. Some types of rewards are more effective for use in organizations than others.

3. The speed with which learning takes place and the permanence of its effects will be determined by the timing of reinforcement.[65]

Point 3 is extremely important and deserves considerable elaboration.

SCHEDULES OF REINFORCEMENT   The two major types of reinforcement schedules are *continuous* and *intermittent*. A **continuous reinforcement** schedule reinforces the desired behavior each and every time it is demonstrated. For example, in the case of someone who has historically had trouble arriving at work on time, every time he is *not* tardy his manager might compliment him on his desirable behavior. In an intermittent schedule, on the other hand, not every instance of the desirable behavior is reinforced, but reinforcement is given often enough to make the behavior worth repeating. This latter schedule can be compared to the workings of a slot machine, which people will continue to play even when they know that it is

Continuous Reinforcement   A desired behavior is reinforced each and every time it is demonstrated.

adjusted to give a considerable return to the gambling house. The intermittent payoffs occur just often enough to reinforce the behavior of slipping in coins and pulling the handle. Evidence indicates that the intermittent or varied form of reinforcement tends to promote more resistance to extinction than does the continuous form.[66]

An **intermittent reinforcement** can be of a ratio or interval type. Ratio schedules depend upon how many responses the subject makes. The individual is reinforced after giving a certain number of specific types of behavior. Interval schedules depend upon how much time has passed since the last reinforcement. With interval schedules, the individual is reinforced on the first appropriate behavior after a particular time has elapsed. A reinforcement can also be classified as fixed or variable. Intermittent techniques for administering rewards can, therefore, be placed into four categories, as shown in Figure 4–4.

When rewards are spaced at uniform time intervals, the reinforcement schedule is of the **fixed-interval** type. The critical variable is time, and it is held constant. This is the predominant schedule for almost all salaried workers in North America. When you get your paycheck on a weekly, semimonthly, monthly, or other predetermined time basis, you are rewarded on a fixed-interval reinforcement schedule.

If rewards are distributed in time so that reinforcements are unpredictable, the schedule is of the **variable-interval** type. When an instructor advises her class that there will be a number of pop quizzes given during the term (the exact number of which is unknown to the students), and the quizzes will account for twenty percent of the term grade, she is using such a variable-interval schedule. Similarly, a series of randomly timed unannounced visits to a company office by the corporate audit staff is an example of a variable-interval schedule.

In a **fixed-ratio** schedule, after a fixed or constant number of responses are given, a reward is initiated. For example, a piece-rate incentive plan is a fixed-ratio schedule—the employee receives a reward based on the number of work pieces generated. If the piece rate for a zipper installer in a dressmaking factory is $5.00 a dozen, the reinforcement (money in this case) is fixed to the number of zippers sewn into garments. After every dozen is sewn in, the installer has earned another $5.00.

When the reward varies relative to the behavior of the individual, he or she is said to be reinforced on a **variable-ratio** schedule. Salespeople on commission are examples of individuals on such a reinforcement schedule. On some occasions, they may make a sale after only two calls on potential customers. On other occasions, they might need to make twenty or more calls to secure a sale. The reward, then, is variable in relation to the number of successful calls the salesperson makes. Figure 4–5 visually depicts the four categories of intermittent schedules.

Intermittent Reinforcement
A desired behavior is reinforced often enough to make the behavior worth repeating, but not every time it is demonstrated.

Fixed-Interval Schedule
Rewards are spaced at uniform time intervals.

Variable-Interval Schedule
Rewards are distributed in time so that reinforcements are unpredictable.

Fixed-Ratio Schedule
Rewards are initiated after a fixed or constant number of responses.

Variable-Ratio Schedule The reward varies relative to the behavior of the individual.

FIGURE 4–4   Schedules of Reinforcement

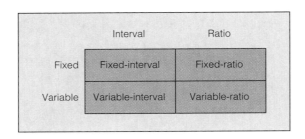

	Interval	Ratio
Fixed	Fixed-interval	Fixed-ratio
Variable	Variable-interval	Variable-ratio

REINFORCEMENT SCHEDULES AND BEHAVIOR   Continuous rein-forcement schedules can lead to early satiation, and under this schedule behavior tends to weaken rapidly when reinforcers are withheld. However, continuous reinforcers are appropriate for newly emitted, unstable, or low-frequency responses. In contrast, intermittent reinforcers preclude early satiation because they don't follow every response. They are appropriate for stable or high-frequency responses.

In general, variable schedules tend to lead to higher performance than fixed schedules. For example, as noted previously, most employees in organizations are paid on fixed-interval schedules. But such a schedule does not clearly link performance and rewards. The reward is given for time spent on the job rather than for a specific response (performance). In contrast, variable-interval schedules generate high rates of response and more stable and

FIGURE 4-5   Intermittent Schedules of Reinforcement

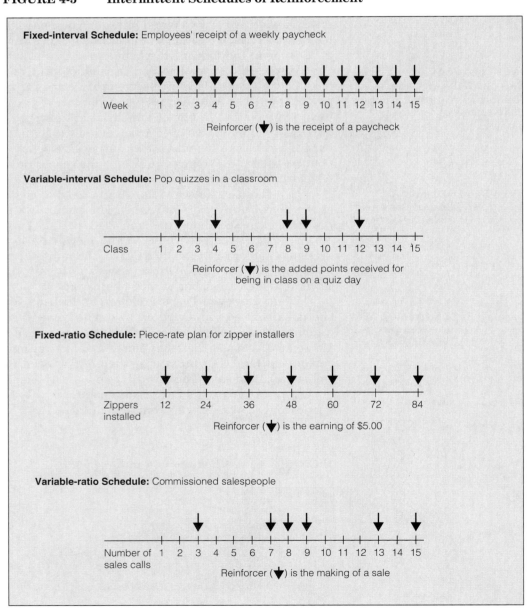

116   PART 2   THE INDIVIDUAL

Reinforcement and Ethical Behavior

An employee's ethical behavior is dependent on both his or her values and the ethical climate within the organization.[67] Good people can be encouraged to do bad things when their organization's reward system positively reinforces wrong behaviors. When an organization praises, promotes, gives large pay increases, and offers other desirable rewards to employees who lie, cheat, and misrepresent, its employees learn that unethical behaviors pay off.

Regardless of what management *says* is important, people in organizations pay attention to how actual rewards are handed out. This helps explain why some college faculty pay little attention to their students and teaching responsibilities. Despite the importance that all college administrators claim teaching carries, many colleges ignore good teaching and confer tenure, promotions, and other rewards on those who do research. Faculty who engage in research at the expense of their teaching are not bad people. They are merely people whose behavior has been shaped by their organization's reward system.

It has been noted that an organization's rewards can encourage employee practices that run counter to society's ethical norms.[68] For instance, North American norms encourage openness, honesty, and candor; yet organizations often reward those employees who resort to secrecy and lying to get their jobs done. Similarly, following the rules is part of North American culture, but many organizations give out promotions to those who achieve their goals by disregarding the rules.

In recent years, considerable national attention has been focused on the corruption in U.S. college sports programs. Athletes' high school grades are altered to allow them admission. Cash payments are made to star athletes by college boosters. Jobs are provided by boosters to parents of prized recruits. Athletes are discouraged by their coaches from taking the English, math, and science courses they need to graduate out of fear that poor grades in these courses will jeopardize their eligibility to play the sport they were recruited for. On what can these unethical (and sometimes illegal) practices be blamed? The pressure on coaches to win! College presidents want the revenues that come from filled arenas and appearances in postseason competitions, and these are only possible when teams win. So coaches who produce winning teams get rewarded with extended contracts and fat compensation packages. Coaches who lose games—no matter how successful they may be in "building character"—get fired!

Give an example of a situation where you observed unethical behavior that was encouraged or supported by the organization's reward system. What, if anything, could management have done to encourage ethical behavior in that situation?

consistent behavior because of a high correlation between performance and reward and because of the uncertainty involved—the employee tends to be more alert since there is a surprise factor.

Some Specific Organizational Applications

We have alluded to a number of situations where learning theory could be helpful to managers. In this section, we will briefly look at five specific applications: reducing absenteeism through the use of lotteries, substituting well pay for sick pay, disciplining problem employees, developing effective

Commissioned salespeople are reinforced on a variable-ratio schedule since the reward varies relative to the number of successful calls they make.
Chuck Keeler/Tony Stone Worldwide

employee training programs, and creating mentoring programs for new employees.

USING LOTTERIES TO REDUCE ABSENTEEISM   Management can design programs to reduce absenteeism utilizing learning theory. For example, New York Life Insurance Co. created a lottery that rewarded employees for attendance.[69] Each quarter the names of all those headquarters employees with no absences are placed in a drum. In a typical quarter, about four thousand of the company's seventy-five hundred employees have their names placed in the drum. The first ten names pulled earn a $200 bond, the next twenty earn a $100 bond, and seventy more receive a paid day off. At the end of the year, another lottery is held for those with twelve months of perfect attendance. Twelve prizes are awarded—two employees receive $1000 bonds and ten more earn five days off with pay.

This lottery follows a variable-ratio schedule. A good attendance record increases an employee's probability of winning, yet having perfect attendance is no assurance that an employee will be rewarded by winning one of the prizes. Consistent with the research on reinforcement schedules, this lottery resulted in lower absence rates. In its first ten months of operation, for instance, absenteeism was twenty-one percent lower than for the comparable period in the preceding year.

WELL PAY VS. SICK PAY   Most organizations provide their salaried employees with paid sick leave as part of the employee's fringe benefit program. But ironically, organizations with paid sick leave programs experience almost twice the absenteeism of organizations without such programs.[70] The reality is that sick leave reinforces the wrong behavior—absence from work. Organizations should have programs that encourage employees to be on the job by discouraging unnecessary absences. When employees receive ten paid sick days a year, it is the unusual employee who isn't sure to use them all up, regardless of whether or not he or she is sick.

This suggests that organizations should reward attendance, not absence. As a case in point, one Midwest organization implemented a well-pay program that paid a bonus to employees who had no absence for any given four-week period and then only paid for sick leave after the first eight hours of absence.[71] Evaluation of the well-pay program found that it produced increased savings to the organization, reduced absenteeism, increased productivity, and improved employee satisfaction.

EMPLOYEE DISCIPLINE   Every manager will, at some time, have to deal with an employee who drinks on the job, is insubordinate, steals company property, arrives consistently late for work, or engages in similar problem behaviors. Managers will respond with disciplinary actions such as oral reprimands, written warnings, and temporary suspensions. Research on discipline shows that the manager should act immediately to correct the problem, match the severity of the punishment to the severity of the "crime," and ensure that the employee sees the link between the punishment and the undesirable behavior.[72] But, our knowledge about punishment's effect on behavior indicates that the use of discipline carries costs. It may provide only a short-term solution and result in serious side effects.

Disciplining employees for undesirable behaviors only tells them what *not* to do. It doesn't tell them what alternative behaviors are preferred. The result is that this form of punishment frequently leads to only short-term suppression of the undesirable behavior rather than its elimination. Continued use of punishment, rather than positive reinforcement, also tends to produce a conditional fear of the manager. As the punishing agent, the manager becomes associated in the employee's mind with adverse consequences. Employees respond by "hiding" from their boss. Hence, the use of punishment can undermine manager-employee relations.

The popularity of discipline undoubtedly lies in its ability to produce fast results in the short run. Managers are reinforced for using discipline because it produces an immediate change in the employee's behavior. But over the long run, when used without positive reinforcement of desirable behaviors, it is likely to lead to employee frustration, fear of the manager, reoccurrences of the problem behaviors, and increases in absenteeism and turnover.

DEVELOPING TRAINING PROGRAMS   Most large organizations are actively involved with employee training. Can these organizations draw from our discussion of learning in order to improve the effectiveness of their training programs? Certainly.

Social-learning theory offers such a guide. It tells us that training should offer a model to grab the trainee's attention; provide motivational properties; help the trainee to file away what he or she has learned for later use; provide opportunities to practice new behaviors; offer positive rewards for accomplishments; and, if the training has taken place off the job, allow the trainee some opportunity to transfer what he or she has learned to the job.

CREATING MENTORING PROGRAMS   It's the unusual senior manager who, early in his or her career, didn't have an older, more experienced mentor higher up in the organization. This mentor took the protégé under his or her wing and provided advice and guidance on how to survive and get ahead in the organization. Mentoring, of course, is not limited to the managerial ranks. Union apprenticeship programs, for example, do the same thing by preparing individuals to move from unskilled apprentice status to that of skilled journeyman. A young electrician apprentice typically works under an

Learning theory helps managers in the design of training programs. For example, Motorola spends $50 million a year to train its employees. Learning theory helped develop the techniques this Motorola employee uses in programming robots.   David Walberg

experienced electrician for several years to develop the full range of skills necessary to effectively execute his or her job.

A successful mentoring program will be built on modeling concepts from social-learning theory. That is, a mentor's impact comes from more than merely what he or she explicitly tells a protégé. Mentors are role models. Protégés learn to convey the attitudes and behaviors that the organization wants by emulating the traits and actions of their mentors. They observe and then imitate. Top managers who are concerned with developing employees who will fit into the organization and with preparing young managerial talent for greater responsibilities should give careful attention to who takes on mentoring roles. The creating of formal mentoring programs— where young individuals are officially assigned a mentor—allows senior executives to manage the process and increases the likelihood that protégés will be molded the way top management desires.

IMPLICATIONS FOR PERFORMANCE AND SATISFACTION

Let's try to summarize what we've found in terms of what impact biographical characteristics, ability, personality, and learning have on an employee's performance and satisfaction.

Biographical Characteristics

Biographical characteristics are readily available to management. For the most part, they represent data that are contained in almost every employee's personnel file.

A review of the research allows some noteworthy conclusions. First, it is difficult to make accurate predictions about an employee's productivity based on biographical data. Perhaps the strongest statement we can make is that the belief that productivity declines with employee age is a myth. However, absence rates, turnover, and job satisfaction *are* influenced by several biographical characteristics.

Using Learning Concepts for Self-Management

Organizational applications of learning concepts are not restricted to managing the behavior of others. These concepts can also be used to allow individuals to manage their own behavior and, in so doing, reduce the need for managerial control. This is called **self-management**.[73]

Self-management requires an individual to deliberately manipulate stimuli, internal processes, and responses to achieve personal behavioral outcomes. The basic processes involve observing one's own behavior, comparing the behavior with a standard, and rewarding oneself if the behavior meets the standard.

So how might self-management be applied?

To illustrate, a group of state government blue-collar employees received eight hours of training in which they were taught self-management skills.[74] They were then shown how the skills could be used for improving job attendance. They were instructed on how to set specific goals for job attendance, both short-term and intermediate-term. They learned how to write a behavioral contract with themselves and identify self-chosen reinforcers. Finally, they learned the importance of self-monitoring their attendance behavior and administering incentives when they achieved their goals. The net result for these participants was a significant improvement in job attendance.

Self-management   Learning techniques that allow individuals to manage their own behavior so that less external management control is necessary.

The strongest evidence concerns an employee's age and seniority in the organization. Older workers are less likely to resign their jobs. Similarly, tenure is negatively related to both absence and turnover; that is, employees with longer service have better attendance records and are less likely to quit. Moreover, the longer an employee held his or her previous job, the less likely that employee is to quit his or her current job.

Investigation of two other variables—gender and marital status—also produced significant findings. Women demonstrate poorer attendance records than do men. However, this statistic is undoubtedly dated. It tends to reflect the historical role of women in our culture. As more women work and pursue long-term careers in organizations, any difference between males and females in terms of absenteeism will undoubtedly disappear. Finally, the evidence indicates that married employees show greater stability and higher satisfaction than do their single counterparts.

Ability

Ability directly influences an employee's level of performance and satisfaction through the ability–job fit. Given management's desire to get a compatible fit, what can be done?

First, an effective selection process will improve the fit. A job analysis will provide information about jobs currently being done and the abilities that individuals need to perform the jobs adequately. Applicants can then be tested, interviewed, and evaluated as to the degree to which they possess the necessary abilities. Second, promotion and transfer decisions affecting individuals already in the organization's employment should reflect the abilities of candidates. As with new employees, care should be taken to assess critical abilities that incumbents will need in the job and matching those requirements with the organization's human resources. Third, the fit can be improved by fine-tuning the job to better match an incumbent's abilities. Often modifications can be made in the job that, while not having a significant impact on the job's basic activities, better adapts it to the specific talents of a given employee. Examples of this are changing some of the equipment used and reorganizing tasks within a group of employees. A final alternative is to provide training for employees. This is applicable to both new workers and present job incumbents. For the latter, training can keep their abilities current or provide new skills as times and conditions change.

Personality

A review of the personality literature offers general guidelines that can lead to effective job performance.[75] As such, it can improve hiring, transfer, and promotion decisions. Because personality characteristics create the parameters for people's behavior, they give us a framework for predicting behavior. For example, individuals who are shy, introverted, and uncomfortable in social situations would probably be ill-suited as salespeople. Individuals who are submissive and conforming might not be effective as advertising "idea" people.

Can we predict which people will be high performers in sales, research, or assembly-line work based on their personality characteristics alone? The answer is no. But a knowledge of an individual's personality can aid in reducing mismatches, which, in turn, can lead to reduced turnover and higher job satisfaction.

We can look at certain personality characteristics that tend to be related to job success, test for these traits, and use these data to make selection more effective. A person who accepts rules, conformity, and dependence and rates high on authoritarianism is likely to feel more comfortable in, say, a structured assembly-line job, as an admittance clerk in a hospital, or as an administrator in a large public agency than as a researcher or an employee whose job requires a high degree of creativity. Such selection matching is likely to lead to lower turnover rates.

There is strong evidence linking personality traits and job satisfaction. Individuals who, as adolescents, possess generally positive personality characteristics—they're cheerful, likable, giving—tend to be content with their jobs later in life.[76] This suggests that satisfaction may lie more in the person than in the characteristics of the job or the work environment, and reaffirms the value of personality tests as possible potent predictors of an applicant's later job satisfaction.

Learning

Any observable change in behavior is, by definition, prima facie evidence that learning has taken place. What we want to do, of course, is ascertain if learning concepts provide us with any insights that would allow us to explain and predict behavior. The evidence suggests that conditioning and shaping offer important tools for explaining levels of productivity, absenteeism rates, lateness, and the quality of employees' work. These concepts also can be valuable for giving insight into how undesirable work behaviors can be modified.

Positive reinforcement is a powerful tool for modifying behavior. By identifying and rewarding performance-related behaviors, management increases the likelihood that they will be repeated.

Our knowledge about learning further suggests that reinforcement is a more effective tool than punishment. Punished behavior tends to be only temporarily suppressed rather than permanently changed, and the recipients of punishment tend to become resentful of the punisher. Although punishment eliminates undesired behavior more quickly than negative reinforcement does, its effect is only temporary and it may later produce unpleasant side effects such as lower morale and higher absenteeism or turnover. Managers, therefore, are advised to use reinforcement rather than punishment.

FOR DISCUSSION

1. Which biographical characteristics best predict *productivity? Absenteeism? Turnover? Satisfaction?*

2. Describe the specific steps you would take to ensure that an individual has the appropriate abilities to satisfactorily do a given job.

3. How does *heredity* influence personality? *Environment? The situation?*

4. What constrains the ability of personality traits to precisely predict behavior?

5. What behavioral predictions might you make if you knew that an employee had (a) an external locus of control? (b) a high *nAch?* (c) a low Mach score? (d) low self-esteem?

6. "The type of job an employee does moderates the relationship between personality and job productivity." Do you agree or disagree with this statement? Discuss.

7. One day your boss comes in and he's nervous, edgy, and argumentative. The next day he is calm and relaxed. Does this suggest that personality traits aren't consistent from day to day?

8. How might employees actually learn unethical behavior on their jobs?

9. Contrast classical conditioning, operant conditioning, and social learning.

10. "Managers should never use discipline with a problem employee." Do you agree or disagree? Discuss.

11. Learning theory can be used to *explain* behavior and to *control* behavior. Can you distinguish between the two objectives? Can you give any ethical or moral arguments why managers should not seek control over others' behavior? How valid do you think these arguments are?

12. What have you learned about "learning" that could help you to explain the behavior of students in a classroom if (a) the instructor gives only one test—a final examination at the end of the course? (b) the instructor gives four exams during the term, all of which are announced on the first day of class? (c) the student's grade is based on the results of numerous exams, none of which are announced by the instructor ahead of time?

The Value of Traits in Explaining Attitudes and Behavior

The essence of trait approaches in OB is that employees possess stable personality characteristics—such as dependency, anxiety, and sociability—that significantly influence their attitudes toward, and behavioral reactions to, organizational settings. People with particular traits tend to be relatively consistent in their attitudes and behavior over time and across situations.

Of course, trait theorists recognize that all traits are not equally powerful. *Cardinal traits* are so strong and generalized that they influence every act a person performs. For instance, a person who possesses dominance as a cardinal trait is domineering in virtually all of his or her actions. The evidence indicates that cardinal traits are relatively rare. More typical are *primary traits*. These are generally consistent influences on behavior, but they may not show up in all situations. So a person may be generally sociable but not display this primary trait in, say, large meetings. Finally, *secondary traits* are attributes that do not form a vital part of the personality but come into play only in particular situations. An otherwise assertive person may be submissive, for example, when confronted by his or her boss. For the most part, trait theories have focused on the power of primary traits to predict employee attitudes and behavior.

Trait theories do a fairly good job of meeting the average person's face-validity test. That is, they look like a reasonably accurate way to describe people. Think of friends, relatives, and acquaintances you've known for a number of years. Do they have traits that have remained essentially stable over time? Most of us would answer this question in the affirmative. If Cousin Anne was shy and nervous when we last saw her ten years ago, we'd be surprised to now find her outgoing and relaxed.

In an organizational context, researchers have found that a person's job satisfaction in one given year was a significant predictor of his or her job satisfaction five years later, even when changes in occupational status, pay, occupation, and employer were controlled for.* This led the researchers to conclude that individuals possess a predisposition toward happiness, which significantly affects their job satisfaction in all types of jobs and organizations.

A final point regarding the function of traits in organizations: Managers must have a strong belief in the power of traits to predict behavior. Otherwise, they would not bother testing and interviewing prospective employees. If they believed that situations determined behavior, they would hire people almost at random and structure the situation properly. But the employee selection process in many organizations throughout the industrialized world places a great deal of emphasis on how applicants perform in interviews and on tests. Pretend you are an interviewer and ask yourself: What am I looking for in job candidates? If you answered with terms like *conscientious, hardworking, ambitious, confident, independent,* and *dependable,* you're a trait theorist!

---

*B. M. Staw and J. Ross, "Stability in the Midst of Change: A Dispositional Approach to Job Attitudes," *Journal of Applied Psychology,* August 1985, pp. 469–80.

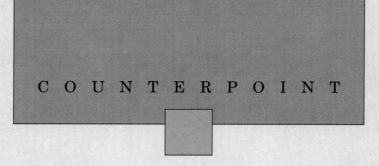

COUNTERPOINT

The Limited Power of Traits in Organizations

Few people would dispute the point that there are some stable individual attributes that affect experience in and reactions to the workplace. But trait theorists go beyond this generality and argue that individual behavior consistencies are widespread and account for much of the variance in behavior among people.

There are two important problems with using traits to explain a large proportion of behavior in organizations. First, a substantial amount of evidence shows that organizational settings are strong situations that have a large impact on employee attitudes and behavior. Second, a growing body of research indicates that individuals are highly adaptive and that personality traits change in response to organizational situations. Let's elaborate on each of these problems.

It has been well known for some time that the effects of traits are likely to be strongest in relatively weak situations and weakest in relatively strong situations. Organizational settings tend to be strong situations. Why? Because they have both formal structures with rules, regulations, policies, and reward systems that define acceptable behavior and punish deviant behaviors and informal norms that dictate appropriate behaviors. These formal and informal constraints lead employees to adopt attitudes and behaviors that are consistent with their organizational roles, thus minimizing the effects of personality traits.

By arguing that employees possess stable traits that lead to cross-situational consistency in their attitudes and behaviors, trait theorists are implying that individuals do not really adapt to different situations. But there is a growing body of evidence that an individual's traits are changed by the organizations that individual participates in. Thus, instead of remaining stable over time, an individual's personality is changed by all the organizations in which he or she has taken part. If the individual's personality changes as a result of exposure to organizational settings, in what sense can that individual be said to have traits that persistently and consistently affect his or her reactions to those very settings? Moreover, people demonstrate their situational flexibility when they change roles as they participate in different organizations. Employees often belong to many organizations. Bob is a corporate accountant during the day, presides over church meetings two nights a week, and coaches his daughter's soccer team on weekends. Most of us are like Bob; we belong to multiple organizations that often include very different kinds of members. We adapt to these different situations. Instead of being the prisoners of a rigid and stable personality framework as trait theorists propose, we regularly adjust our behavior and attitudes to reflect the requirements of various situations.

Based on A. Davis-Blake and J. Pfeffer, "Just a Mirage: The Search for Dispositional Effects in Organizational Research," *Academy of Management Review*, July 1989, pp. 385–400.

Who Controls Your Life?

Instructions: Read the following statements and indicate whether you agree more with choice A or choice B.

A	B	
1. Making a lot of money is largely a matter of getting the right breaks.	1. Promotions are earned through hard work and persistence.	___
2. I have noticed that there is usually a direct connection between how hard I study and the grades I get.	2. Many times the reactions of teachers seem haphazard to me.	___
3. The number of divorces indicates that more and more people are not trying to make their marriages work.	3. Marriage is largely a gamble.	___
4. It is silly to think that one can really change another person's basic attitudes.	4. When I am right I can convince others.	___
5. Getting promoted is really a matter of being a little luckier than the next person.	5. In our society a person's future earning power is dependent upon his or her ability.	___
6. If one knows how to deal with people they are really quite easily led.	6. I have little influence over the way other people behave.	___
7. The grades I make are the result of my own efforts; luck has little or nothing to do with it.	7. Sometimes I feel that I have little to do with the grades I get.	___
8. People like me can change the course of world affairs if we make ourselves heard.	8. It is only wishful thinking to believe that one can readily influence what happens in our society at large.	___
9. A great deal that happens to me is probably a matter of chance.	9. I am the master of my fate.	___
10. Getting along with people is a skill that must be practiced.	10. It is almost impossible to figure out how to please some people.	___

Turn to page 713 for scoring directions and key.

Source: Adapted from Julian B. Rotter, "External Control and Internal Control," *Psychology Today,* June 1971, p. 42. Copyright 1971 by the American Psychological Association. Adapted with permission.

How Self-Monitoring Are You?

Indicate the degree to which you think the following statements are true or false by circling the appropriate number; for example, if a statement is always true, you would circle the 5 next to that statement.

5 = Certainly, always true
4 = Generally true
3 = Somewhat true, but with exceptions
2 = Somewhat false, but with exceptions
1 = Generally false
0 = Certainly, always false

1. In social situations, I have the ability to alter my behavior if I feel that something else is called for.   5 4 3 2 1 0

2. I am often able to read people's true emotions correctly through their eyes.   5 4 3 2 1 0

3. I have the ability to control the way I come across to people, depending on the impression I wish to give them.   5 4 3 2 1 0

4. In conversations, I am sensitive to even the slightest change in the facial expression of the person I'm conversing with.   5 4 3 2 1 0

5. My powers of intuition are quite good when it comes to understanding others' emotions and motives.   5 4 3 2 1 0

6. I can usually tell when others consider a joke in bad taste, even though they may laugh convincingly.   5 4 3 2 1 0

7. When I feel that the image I am portraying isn't working, I can readily change it to something that does.   5 4 3 2 1 0

8. I can usually tell when I've said something inappropriate by reading the listener's eyes.   5 4 3 2 1 0

9. I have trouble changing my behavior to suit different people and different situations.   5 4 3 2 1 0

10. I have found that I can adjust my behavior to meet the requirements of any situation I find myself in.   5 4 3 2 1 0

11. If someone is lying to me, I usually know it at once from that person's manner of expression.   5 4 3 2 1 0

12. Even when it might be to my advantage, I have difficulty putting up a good front.   5 4 3 2 1 0

13. Once I know what the situation calls for, it's easy for me to regulate my actions accordingly.   5 4 3 2 1 0

Turn to page 714 for scoring directions and key.

Source: R. D. Lennox and R. N. Wolfe, "Revision of the Self-Monitoring Scale," *Journal of Personality and Social Psychology,* June 1984, p. 1361. Copyright 1984 by the American Psychological Association. Reprinted by permission.

CASE INCIDENT 4

Predicting Performance

Alix Maher is the new admissions director at a small, highly selective New England college. She has a bachelor's degree in education and a recent M.A. in Educational Administration. But she has no prior experience in college admissions.

Alix's predecessor, in conjunction with the college's admissions committee (made up of five faculty members), had given the following weights to student selection criteria: high school grades (forty percent); Scholastic Aptitude Test (SAT) scores (forty percent); extracurricular activities and achievements (ten percent); and the quality and creativity of a written theme submitted with the application (ten percent).

Alix has serious reservations about using SAT scores. In their defense, she recognizes that the quality of high schools varies greatly, so that the level of student performance that receives an "A" in American History at one school might earn only a "C" at a far more demanding school. And Alix is aware that the people who design the SATs, the Educational Testing Service, argue forcibly that these test scores are valid predictors of how well a person will do in college. Yet, Alix has several concerns:

1. The pressure of the SAT exam is very great and many students suffer from test anxiety. The results, therefore, may not be truly reflective of what a student knows.

2. There is evidence that coaching improves scores by between 40 and 150 points. Test scores, therefore, may adversely affect the chances of acceptance for students who cannot afford the $500 or $600 to take test-coaching courses.

3. Are SAT's really valid? Or do they discriminate against minorities, the poor, and those who have had limited access to cultural growth experiences?

As Alix ponders whether she wants to recommend changing the college's selection criteria and weights, she is reminded of a recent conversation she had with a friend who is an industrial psychologist with a Fortune 100 company. He told her that his company regularly uses intelligence tests to help select from among job applicants. For instance, after the company's recruiters interview graduating seniors on college campuses and identify possible hirees, they give the applicants a standardized intelligence test. Those who fail to score at least in the 80th percentile are eliminated from the applicant pool.

Alix thinks that if intelligence tests are used by billion-dollar corporations to screen job applicants, why shouldn't colleges use them? Moreover, since one of the objectives of a college should be to get its graduates placed in good jobs, maybe SAT scores should be given even higher weight than forty percent in the selection decision. After all, she wonders, if SATs tap intelligence and employers want intelligent job applicants, why not make college selection decisions predominantly on the basis of SAT scores? Or should her college replace the SAT with a pure intelligence test like the Wechsler Adult Intelligence Scale?

QUESTIONS

1. What do *you* think SATs measure: aptitude, innate ability, achievement potential, intelligence, ability to take tests, or something else?

2. If the best predictor of future behavior is past behavior, what should college admissions directors use to identify the most qualified applicants?

3. If you were Alix, what would you do? Why?

FOR FURTHER READING

ACKERMAN, P. L., and L. G. HUMPHREYS, "Individual Differences Theory in Industrial and Organizational Psychology," in M. D. Dunnette and L. M. Hough (eds.), *Handbook of Industrial and Organizational Psychology,* 2nd ed. Vol. 1. (Palo Alto, CA: Consulting Psychologists Press, 1990), pp.223-82.. Reviews literature on ability and its effects on performance.

CALDWELL, D. F., and C. A. O'REILLY III, "Measuring Person–Job Fit with a Profile–Comparison Process," *Journal of Applied Psychology,* December 1990, pp. 648–57. Illustrates the use of a congruence model for assessing person–job fit and relating fit to job performance and work attitudes.

DIGMAN, J. M., "Personality Structure: Emergence of the Five-Factor Model," in M. F. Rosenzweig and L. W. Porter (eds.), *Annual Review of Psychology,* Vol. 41 (Palo Alto, CA: Annual Reviews, 1990), pp. 417–40. Reviews the literature and concludes that there is a five–factor model of personality.

EDWARDS, J. R., "Person–Job Fit: A Conceptual Integration, Literature Review, and Methodological Critique," in C. L. Cooper and I. T. Robertson (eds.), *International Review of Industrial and Organizational Psychology,* Vol. 6 (Chichester, England: John Wiley, 1991), pp. 283–357. Provides a comprehensive review and assessment of the person–job fit concept.

KHAN, S. B., S. A. Alvi, N. SHAUKAT, M. A. HUSSAIN, and T. BAIG, "A Study of the Validity of Holland's Theory in a Non–Western Culture," *Journal of Vocational Behavior,* April 1990, pp. 132–46. These authors found Holland's six–factor personality–job fit theory to be applicable in non–Western cultures.

WEISS, H. M., "Learning Theory and Industrial and Organizational Psychology," in M. D. Dunnette and L. M. Hough (eds.), *Handbook of Industrial and Organizational Psychology,* 2nd ed. Vol. 1, (Palo Alto, CA: Consulting Psychologists Press, 1990), pp. 223–82. Discusses the role that learning concepts, theories, and findings play in developing full explanations of work behavior.

NOTES

[1]Based on S. P. Sherman, "Inside the Mind of Jack Welch," *Fortune,* March 27, 1989, pp. 38–50; T. A. Stewart, "GE Keeps Those Ideas Coming," *Fortune,* August 12, 1991, pp. 41–49; and A. J. Michels, "Now For Jack Welch's Second Act," *Fortune,* January 13, 1992, p. 12.

[2]Reported in W. B. Johnston, *Workforce 2000: Work and Workers for the 21st Century* (Indianapolis: Hudson Institute, 1987).

[3]L. W. Porter and R. Steers, "Organizational, Work and Personal Factors in Employee Turnover and Absenteeism," *Psychological Bulletin,* January 1973, pp. 151–76; W. H. Mobley, R. W. Griffeth, H. H. Hand, and B. M. Meglino, "Review and Conceptual Analysis of the Employee Turnover Process," *Psychological Bulletin,* May 1979, pp. 493–522; and S. R. Rhodes, "Age–Related Differences in Work Attitudes and Behavior: A Review and Conceptual Analysis," *Psychological Bulletin,* March 1983, pp. 328–67.

[4]Rhodes, "Age–Related Differences," pp. 347–49; and R. D. Hackett, "Age, Tenure, and Employee Absenteeism," *Human Relations,* July 1990, pp. 601–19.

[5]G. M. McEvoy and W. F. Cascio, "Cumulative Evidence of the Relationship Between Employee Age and Job Performance," *Journal of Applied Psychology,* February 1989, pp. 11–17.

[6]A. L. Kalleberg and K. A. Loscocco, "Aging, Values, and Rewards: Explaining Age Differences in Job Satisfaction," *American Sociological Review,* February 1983, pp. 78–90; and R. Lee and E. R. Wilbur, "Age, Education, Job Tenure, Salary, Job Characteristics, and Job Satisfaction: A Multivariate Analysis," *Human Relations,* August 1985, pp. 781–91.

[7]K. M. Kacmar and G. R. Ferris, "Theoretical and Methodological Considerations in the Age–Job Satisfaction Relationship," *Journal of Applied Psychology,* April 1989, pp. 201–07; and G. Zeitz, "Age and Work Satisfaction in a Government Agency: A Situational Perspective," *Human Relations,* May 1990, pp. 419–38.

[8]See, for example, E. Maccoby and C. Nagy Jacklin, *The Psychology of Sex Differences* (Stanford, CA: Stanford University Press, 1974); A. H. Eagly and L. L. Carli, "Sex Researchers and Sex–Typed Communications as Determinants of Sex Differences in Influenceability: A Meta–Analysis of Social Influence Studies," *Psychological Bulletin,* August 1981, pp. 1–20; J. S. Hyde, "How Large Are Cognitive Gender Differences?" *American Psychologist,* October 1981, pp. 892–901; and P. Chance, "Biology, Destiny, and All That," *Across the Board,* July–August 1988, pp. 19–23.

[9]R. P. Quinn, G. L. Staines, and M. R. McCullough, *Job Satisfaction: Is There a Trend?* (Washington, DC: U.S. Government Printing Office, Document 2900–00195, 1974).

[10]T. W. Mangione, "Turnover—Some Psychological and Demographic Correlates," in R. P. Quinn and T. W. Mangione (eds.), *The 1969–70 Survey of Working Conditions* (Ann Arbor: University of Michigan, Survey Research Center, 1973); and R. Marsh and H. Mannari, "Organizational Commitment and Turnover: A Predictive Study," *Administrative Science Quarterly,* March 1977, pp. 57–75.

[11]R. J. Flanagan, G. Strauss, and L. Ulman, "Worker Discontent and Work Place Behavior," *Industrial Relations,* May 1974, pp. 101–23; K. R. Garrison and P. M. Muchinsky, "Attitudinal and Biographical Predictors of Incidental Absenteeism," *Journal of Vocational Behavior,* April 1977, pp. 221–30; G. Johns, "Attitudinal and Nonattitudinal Predictors of Two Forms of Absence from Work," *Organizational Behavior and Human Performance,* December 1978, pp. 431–44; and R. T. Keller, "Predicting Absenteeism from Prior Absenteeism, Attitudinal Factors, and Nonattitudinal Factors," *Journal of Applied Psychology,* August 1983, pp. 536–40.

[12]See, for instance, M. Tait, M. Y. Padgett, and T. T. Baldwin, "Job and Life Satisfaction: A Reevaluation of the Strength of the Relationship and Gender Effects as a Function of the Date of the Study," *Journal of Applied Psychology,* June 1989, pp. 502–07.

[13]Garrison and Muchinsky, "Attitudinal and Biographical Predictors"; C. J. Watson, "An Evaluation and Some Aspects of the Steers and Rhodes Model of Employee Attendance," *Journal of Applied Psychology,* June 1981, pp. 385–89; Keller, "Predicting Absenteeism"; J. M. Federico, P. Federico, and G. W. Lundquist, "Predicting Women's Turnover as a Function of Extent of Met Salary Expectations and Biodemographic Data," *Personnel Psychology,* Winter 1976, pp. 559–66; Marsh and Mannari, "Organizational Commitment;" and D. R. Austrom, T. Baldwin, and G. J. Macy, "The Single Worker: An Empirical Exploration of Attitudes, Behavior, and Well–Being," *Canadian Journal of Administrative Sciences,* December 1988, pp. 22–29.

[14]Porter and Steers, "Organizational, Work, and Personal Factors"; N. Nicholson and P. M. Goodge, "The Influence of Social, Organizational and Biographical Factors on Female Absence," *Journal of Management Studies,* October 1976, pp. 234–54; P. M. Muchinsky, "Employee Absenteeism: A Review of the Literature," *Journal of Vocational Behavior,* June 1977, pp. 316–40; and R. M. Steers and S. R. Rhodes, "Major Influences on Employee Attendance: A Process Model," *Journal of Applied Psychology,* August 1978, pp. 391–407.

[15]Porter and Steers, "Organizational, Work, and Personal Factors"; Federico, Federico, and Lundquist, "Predicting Women's Turnover"; and Marsh and Mannari, "Organizational Commitment."

[16]A. S. Gechman and Y. Wiener, "Job Involvement and Satisfaction as Related to Mental Health and Personal Time Devoted to Work," *Journal of Applied Psychology,* August 1975, pp. 521–23.

[17]M. E. Gordon and W. J. Fitzgibbons, "Empirical Test of the Validity of Seniority as a Factor in Staffing Decisions," *Journal of Applied Psychology,* June 1982, pp. 311–19; M. E. Gordon and W. A. Johnson, "Seniority: A Review of Its Legal and Scientific Standing," *Personnel Psychology,* Summer 1982, pp. 255–80; and M. A. McDaniel, F. L. Schmidt, and J. E. Hunter, "Job Experience Correlates of Job Performance," *Journal of Applied Psychology,* May 1988, pp. 327–30.

[18]Garrison and Muchinsky, "Attitudinal and Biographical Predictors"; N. Nicholson, C. A. Brown, and J. K. Chadwick–Jones, "Absence from Work and Personal Characteristics," *Journal of Applied Psychology,* June 1977, pp. 319–27; and Keller, "Predicting Absenteeism."

[19]P. O. Popp and J. A. Belohlav, "Absenteeism in a Low Status Work Environment," *Academy of Management Journal,* September 1982, p. 681.

[20]H. J. Arnold and D. C. Feldman, "A Multivariate Analysis of the Determinants of Job Turnover," *Journal of Applied Psychology,* June 1982, p. 352.

[21]R. D. Gatewood and H. S. Feild, *Human Resource Selection* (Chicago: Dryden Press, 1987).

[22]J. A. Breaugh and D. L. Dossett, "The Effectiveness of Biodata for Predicting Turnover," paper presented at the National Academy of Management Conference, New Orleans, August 1987.

[23]L. E. Tyler, *Individual Differences: Abilities and Motivational Directions* (Englewood Cliffs, NJ: Prentice Hall, 1974).

[24]J. E. Hunter and R. F. Hunter, "Validity and Utility of Alternative Predictors of Job Performance," *Psychological Bulletin,* January 1984, pp. 72–98; J. E. Hunter, "Cognitive Ability, Cognitive Aptitudes, Job Knowledge, and Job Performance," *Journal of Vocational Behavior,* December 1986, pp. 340–62; and W. M. Coward and P. R. Sackett, "Linearity of Ability–Performance Relationships: A Reconfirmation," *Journal of Applied Psychology,* June 1990, pp. 297–300.

[25]Hunter and Hunter, "Validity and Utility," pp. 73–74.

[26]E. A. Fleishman, "Evaluating Physical Abilities Required by Jobs," *Personnel Administrator,* June 1979, pp. 82–92.

[27]G. W. Allport, *Personality: A Psychological Interpretation* (New York: Holt, Rinehart & Winston, 1937), p. 48.

[28]J. Kelly, *Organizational Behavior,* rev. ed. (Homewood, IL: Richard D. Irwin, 1974), p. 243.

[29]I. Janis, G. F. Mahl, J. Kagan, and R. P. Holt, *Personality: Dynamics, Development and Assessment* (New York: Harcourt, Brace & World, 1969), p. 555.

[30]J. R. Warren, "Birth Order and Social Behavior," *Psychological Bulletin,* January 1966, pp. 38–49.

[31]Janis et al., *Personality,* p. 552.

[32]L. Sechrest, "Personality," in M. R. Rosenzweig and L. W. Porter (eds.), *Annual Review of Psychology,* Vol. 27 (Palo Alto, CA: Annual Reviews, 1976), p. 10.

[33]Ibid.

[34]T. J. Bouchard, D. T. Lykken, M. McGue, N. L. Segal, and A. Tellegen, "Sources of Human Psychological Differences—The Minnesota Study of Twins Reared Apart," *Science,* October 12, 1990; pp. 223–38.

[35]T. H. Maugh II, "Study of Twins Emphasizes Importance of Heredity," *Los Angeles Times,* October 12, 1990, p. A1.

[36]Ibid., p. A40.

[37]See A. H. Buss, "Personality as Traits," *American Psychologist,* November 1989, pp. 1378–88.

[38]G. W. Allport and H. S. Odbert, "Trait Names, A Psycholexical Study," *Psychological Monographs,* No. 47 (1936).

[39]R. B. Cattell, "Personality Pinned Down," *Psychology Today,* July 1973, pp. 40–46.

[40]R. B. Cattell, *The Scientific Analysis of Personality* (Chicago: Aldine, 1965); and H. J. Eysenck, *The Structure of Human Personality* (London: Methuen, 1953).

[41]S. R. Maddi, *Personality Theories* (Homewood, IL: Dorsey, 1968).

[42]See A. J. Vaccaro, "Personality Clash," *Personnel Administrator,* September 1988, pp. 88–92; and R. R. McCrae and P. T. Costa, Jr., "Reinterpreting the Myers–Briggs Type Indicator from the Perspective of the Five–Factor Model of Personality," *Journal of Personality,* March 1989, pp. 17–40.

[43]J. B. Rotter, "Generalized Expectancies for Internal versus External Control of Reinforcement," *Psychological Monographs,* Vol. 80, no. 609 (1966).

[44]See P. E. Spector, "Behavior in Organizations as a Function of Employee's Locus of Control," *Psychological Bulletin,* May 1982, pp. 482–97; and G. J. Blau, "Locus of Control as a Potential Moderator of the Turnover Process," *Journal of Occupational Psychology,* Fall 1987, pp. 21–29.

[45]Keller, "Predicting Absenteeism."

[46]Spector, "Behavior in Organizations," p. 493.

[47]J. B. Miner, *Theories of Organizational Behavior* (Hinsdale, IL: Dryden Press, 1980), pp. 46–75.

[48]T. Adorno et al., *The Authoritarian Personality* (New York: Harper & Brothers, 1950).

[49]H. Gough, "Personality and Personality Assessment," in M. D. Dunnette (ed.), *Handbook of Industrial and Organizational Psychology* (Chicago: Rand McNally, 1976), p. 579.

[50]R. G. Vleeming, "Machiavellianism: A Preliminary Review," *Psychological Reports,* February 1979, pp. 295–310.

[51]R. Christie and F. L. Geis, *Studies in Machiavellianism* (New York: Academic Press, 1970), p. 312.

[52]Ibid.

[53]Based on J. Brockner, *Self–Esteem at Work* (Lexington, MA: Lexington Books, 1988), Chapters 1–4.

[54]See M. Snyder, *Public Appearances/Private Realities: The Psychology of Self–Monitoring* (New York: W. H. Freeman, 1987).

[55]Ibid.

[56]R. N. Taylor and M. D. Dunnette, "Influence of Dogmatism, Risk–Taking Propensity, and Intelligence on Decision–Making Strategies for a Sample of Industrial Managers," *Journal of Applied Psychology,* August 1974, pp. 420–23.

[57]I. L. Janis and L. Mann, *Decision Making: A Psychological Analysis of Conflict, Choice, and Commitment* (New York: Free Press, 1977).

[58]N. Kogan and M. A. Wallach, "Group Risk Taking as a Function of Members' Anxiety and Defensiveness," *Journal of Personality,* March 1967, pp. 50–63.

[59]J. L. Holland, *Making Vocational Choices: A Theory of Vocational Personalities and Work Environments,* 2nd ed. (Englewood Cliffs, NJ: Prentice Hall, 1985).

[60]See, for example, A. R. Spokane, "A Review of Research on Person–Environment Congruence in Holland's Theory of Careers," *Journal of Vocational Behavior,* June 1985, pp. 306–43; and D. Brown, "The Status of Holland's Theory of Career Choice," *Career Development Journal,* September 1987, pp. 13–23.

[61]W. McGehee, "Are We Using What We Know About Training?—Learning Theory and Training," *Personnel Psychology,* Spring 1958, p. 2.

[62]I. P. Pavlov, *The Work of the Digestive Glands,* trans. W. H. Thompson (London: Charles Griffin, 1902).

[63]B. F. Skinner, *Contingencies of Reinforcement* (East Norwalk, CT: Appleton–Century–Crofts, 1971).

[64]A. Bandura, *Social Learning Theory* (Englewood Cliffs, NJ: Prentice Hall, 1977).

[65]T. W. Costello and S. S. Zalkind, *Psychology in Administration* (Englewood Cliffs, NJ: Prentice Hall, 1963), p. 193.

[66]F. Luthans and R. Kreitner, *Organizational Behavior Modification and Beyond,* 2nd ed. (Glenview, IL: Scott, Foresman, 1985).

[67]L. K. Trevino, "Ethical Decision Making in Organizations: A Person–Situation Interactionist Model," *Academy of Management Review,* July 1986, pp. 601–17.

[68]E. Jansen and M. A. Von Glinow, "Ethical Ambivalence and Organizational Reward Systems," *Academy of Management Review,* October 1985, pp. 814–22.

[69]A. Halcrow, "Incentive! How Three Companies Cut Costs," *Personnel Journal,* February 1986, p. 12.

[70]D. Willings, "The Absentee Worker," *Personnel and Training Management,* December 1968, pp. 10–12.

[71]B. H. Harvey, J. F. Rogers, and J. A. Schultz, "Sick Pay vs. Well Pay: An Analysis of the Impact of Rewarding Employees for Being on the Job," *Public Personnel Management Journal,* Summer 1983, pp. 218–24.

[72]A. Belohlav, *The Art of Disciplining Your Employees* (Englewood Cliffs, NJ: Prentice Hall, 1985).

[73]See, for instance, C. C. Manz and H. P. Sims, "Self–Management as a Substitute for Leadership: A Social Learning Theory Perspective," *Academy of Management Review,* July 1980, pp. 361–67.

[74]G. P. Latham and C. A. Frayne, "Self–Management Training for Increasing Job Attendance: A Follow–Up and a Replication," *Journal of Applied Psychology,* June 1989, pp. 411–16.

[75]See, for instance, D. V. Day and S. B. Silverman, "Personality and Job Performance: Evidence of Incremental Validity," *Personnel Psychology,* Spring 1989, pp. 25–36.

[76]B. M. Staw, N. E. Bell, and J. A. Clausen, "The Dispositional Approach to Job Attitudes: A Lifetime Longitudinal Test," *Administrative Science Quarterly,* March 1986, pp. 56–77.

PERCEPTION AND INDIVIDUAL DECISION MAKING

LEARNING OBJECTIVES

After studying this chapter, you should be able to:

1. Distinguish between perception and reality in determining behavior

2. Explain how two people can see the same thing and interpret it differently

3. List the three determinants of attribution

4. Describe how shortcuts can assist in or distort our judgment of others

5. Explain how perception affects the decision-making process

6. Outline the six steps in the optimizing decision process

7. List the assumptions of the optimizing model

8. Explain how individuals satisfice

9. Describe the implicit favorite model of decision making

10. Identify the conditions in which individuals are most likely to use intuition in decision making

First umpire: "Some's balls and some's strikes and I calls 'em as they is."
Second umpire: "Some's balls and some's strikes and I calls 'em as I sees 'em."
Third umpire: "Some's balls and some's strikes but they ain't nothin' till I calls 'em."

H. CANTRIL

*P*ictured above is an executive for a large company. From the picture, can you tell if he is working or "goofing off"? Probably not! Yet this executive's boss makes judgments about him all the time. Whether the boss perceives him, in this instance, as "sitting around staring at a wall" or as "engaged in deep thinking" will depend on a number of factors. For example, how long has the boss known him? What's his past performance record? Has he engaged in this practice previously? How do other people in similar jobs behave? Answers to questions like these will go a long way toward shaping the boss's interpretation of the executive's behavior.

This example reminds us that we don't *see* reality. We *interpret* what we see and call it reality. You will probably complete an evaluation form on the course you're currently taking and the instructor who is teaching it. If the class is large enough, it's almost a sure bet that there will be some range of answers in evaluating your instructor. In some cases, an instructor will be rated "excellent" by some students and "unsatisfactory" by other students in the same class. The instructor's teaching behavior, of course, is a constant. Even though the students see the same instructor, they perceive his or her effectiveness differently. Apparently, perception is like beauty, in that it lies "in the eye of the beholder." ■

WHAT IS PERCEPTION AND WHY IS IT IMPORTANT?

Perception A process by which individuals organize and interpret their sensory impressions in order to give meaning to their environment.

Perception can be defined as a process by which individuals organize and interpret their sensory impressions in order to give meaning to their environment. However, as we have noted, what one perceives can be substantially different from objective reality. It need not be, but there is often disagreement. For example, it is possible that all employees in a firm may view it as a great place to work—favorable working conditions, interesting job assignments, good pay, an understanding and responsible management—but, as most of us know, it is very unusual to find such agreement.

Why is perception important in the study of OB? Simply because people's behavior is based on their perception of what reality is, not on reality itself. The world as it is perceived is the world that is behaviorally important.

FACTORS INFLUENCING PERCEPTION

How do we explain that individuals may look at the same thing, yet perceive it differently? A number of factors operate to shape and sometimes distort perception. These factors can reside in the *perceiver,* in the object or *target* being perceived, or in the context of the *situation* in which the perception is made.

The Perceiver

When an individual looks at a target and attempts to interpret what he or she sees, that interpretation is heavily influenced by personal characteristics of the individual perceiver. Have you ever bought a new car and then suddenly noticed a large number of cars like yours on the road? It's unlikely that the number of such cars suddenly expanded. Rather, your own purchase has influenced your perception so that you are now more likely to notice them. This is an example of how factors related to the perceiver influence what he or she perceives. Among the more relevant personal characteristics affecting perception are attitudes, motives, interests, past experience, and expectations.

Sandy likes small classes because she enjoys asking a lot of questions of her teachers. Scott, on the other hand, prefers large lectures. He rarely asks questions and likes the anonymity that goes with being lost in a sea of bodies. On the first day of classes this term, Sandy and Scott find themselves walking into the university auditorium for their introductory course in psychology. They both recognize that they will be among some eight hundred students in this class. But given the different attitudes held by Sandy and Scott, it shouldn't surprise you to find that they interpret what they see differently. Sandy sulks, while Scott's smile does little to hide his relief in being able to blend unnoticed into the large auditorium. They both see the same thing, but they interpret it differently. A major reason is that they hold divergent *attitudes* concerning large classes.

Unsatisfied needs or *motives* stimulate individuals and may exert a strong influence on their perceptions. This was dramatically demonstrated in research on hunger.[1] Individuals in the study had not eaten for varying numbers of hours. Some had eaten an hour earlier, while others had gone as long as sixteen hours without food. These subjects were shown blurred pictures, and the results indicated that the extent of hunger influenced the interpretation of the blurred pictures. Those who had not eaten for sixteen hours perceived the blurred images as pictures of food far more frequently than did those subjects who had eaten only a short time earlier.

This same phenomenon has application in an organizational context as well. It would not be surprising, for example, to find that a boss who is insecure perceives a subordinate's efforts to do an outstanding job as a threat to his or her own position. Personal insecurity can be transferred into the perception that others are out to "get my job," regardless of the intention of the subordinates. Likewise, people who are devious are prone to see others as also devious.

It should not surprise you that a plastic surgeon is more likely to notice an imperfect nose than a plumber is. The supervisor who has just been reprimanded by her boss for the high level of lateness among her staff is more likely to notice lateness by an employee tomorrow than she was last week. If you are preoccupied with a personal problem, you may find it hard to be attentive in class. These examples illustrate that the focus of our attention appears to be influenced by our *interests*. Because our individual interests differ considerably, what one person notices in a situation can differ from what others perceive.

Just as interests narrow one's focus, so do one's *past experiences*. You perceive those things to which you can relate. However, in many instances, your past experiences will act to nullify an object's interest.

Objects or events that have never been experienced before are more noticeable than those that have been experienced in the past. You are more likely to notice a machine that you have never seen before than a standard filing cabinet that is exactly like a hundred others you have previously seen. Similarly, you are more likely to notice the operations along an assembly line if this is the first time you have seen an assembly line. In the late 1960s and early 1970s, women and minorities in managerial positions were highly visible because, historically, these positions were the province of white males. Today, these groups are more widely represented in the managerial ranks, so we are less likely to take notice that a manager is female, African-American, Asian-American, or Latino.

Finally, *expectations* can distort your perceptions in that you will see what you expect to see. If you expect police officers to be authoritative, young people to be unambitious, personnel directors to "like people," or individuals holding public office to be "power hungry," you may perceive them this way regardless of their actual traits.

The Target

Characteristics in the target that is being observed can affect what is perceived. Loud people are more likely to be noticed in a group than are quiet ones. So, too, are extremely attractive or unattractive individuals. Motion, sounds, size, and other attributes of a target shape the way we see it.

Because targets are not looked at in isolation, the relationship of a target to its background influences perception, as does our tendency to group close things and similar things together.

What we see is dependent on how we separate a figure from its general background. For instance, what you see as you read this sentence is black letters on a white page. You do not see funny-shaped patches of black and white because you recognize these shapes and organize the black shapes against the white background. Figure 5–1 dramatizes this effect. The object

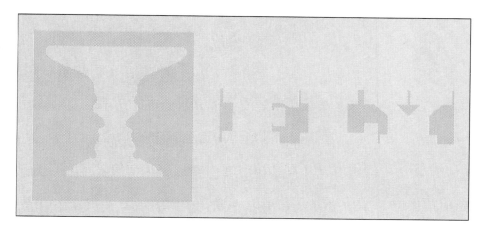

FIGURE 5–1   Figure-Ground Illustrations

on the left may at first look like a beige vase. However, if beige is taken as the background, we see two blue profiles. At first observation, the group of objects on the right appears to be some blue modular figures against a beige background. Closer inspection will reveal the word "FLY" once the background is defined as blue.

Objects that are close to each other will tend to be perceived together rather than separately. As a result of physical or time proximity, we often put together objects or events that are unrelated. Employees in a particular department are seen as a group. If in a department of four members two suddenly resign, we tend to assume that their departures were related when, in fact, they may be totally unrelated. Timing may also imply dependence when, for example, a new sales manager is assigned to a territory and, soon after, sales in that territory skyrocket. The assignment of the new sales manager and the increase in sales may not be related—the increase may be due to the introduction of a new product line or to one of many other reasons—but there is a tendency to perceive the two occurrences as related.

Would you put your money into these rowers' hands? They may look like a group of college students staying in shape but they're actually members of a Wall Street rowing club. Had they been in their business suits, you would have more likely perceived them as the professional money-managers that they are.   John S. Abbott

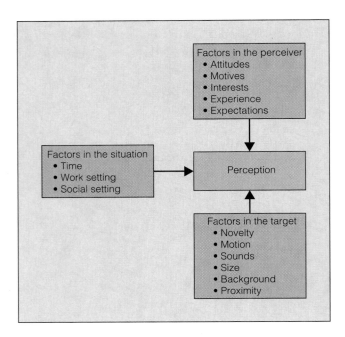

FIGURE 5-2   Factors that Influence Perception

Persons, objects, or events that are similar to each other also tend to be grouped together. The greater the similarity, the greater the probability that we will tend to perceive them as a common group. Women, blacks, or members of any other group that has clearly distinguishable characteristics in terms of features or color will tend to be perceived as alike in other, unrelated, characteristics as well.

The Situation

The context in which we see objects or events is important. Elements in the surrounding environment influence our perceptions.

I may not notice a twenty-five-year-old female in an evening gown and heavy makeup at a nightclub on Saturday night. Yet that same woman so attired for my Monday morning management class would certainly catch my attention (and that of the rest of the class). Neither the perceiver nor the target changed between Saturday night and Monday morning, but the situation is different. Similarly, you are more likely to notice your subordinates goofing off if your boss from head office happens to be in town. Again, the situation affects your perception. The time at which an object or event is seen can influence attention, as can location, light, heat, or any number of situational factors. Figure 5-2 summarizes the factors influencing perception.

PERSON PERCEPTION: MAKING JUDGMENTS ABOUT OTHERS

Now we turn to the most relevant application of perception concepts to OB. This is the issue of person perception.

Attribution Theory

Our perceptions of people differ from our perceptions of inanimate objects like desks, machines, or buildings because we make inferences about the actions of people that we don't make about inanimate objects. Nonliving objects are subject to the laws of nature, but they have no beliefs, motives, or intentions. People do. The result is that when we observe people, we attempt to develop explanations of why they behave in certain ways. Our perception and judgment of a person's actions, therefore, will be significantly influenced by the assumptions we make about the person's internal state.

Attribution Theory When individuals observe behavior, they attempt to determine whether it is internally or externally caused.

Attribution theory has been proposed to develop explanations of the ways in which we judge people differently, depending on what meaning we attribute to a given behavior.[2] Basically, the theory suggests that when we observe an individual's behavior, we attempt to determine whether it was internally or externally caused. That determination, however, depends largely on three factors: (1) distinctiveness, (2) consensus, and (3) consistency. First, let's clarify the differences between internal and external causation and then we will elaborate on each of the three determining factors.

Internally caused behaviors are those that are believed to be under the personal control of the individual. *Externally* caused behavior is seen as resulting from outside causes; that is, the person is seen as forced into the behavior by the situation. If one of your employees is late for work, you might attribute his lateness to his partying into the wee hours of the morning and then oversleeping. This would be an internal attribution. But if you attribute his arriving late to a major automobile accident that tied up traffic on the road that this employee regularly uses, then you would be making an external attribution.

Distinctiveness refers to whether an individual displays different behaviors in different situations. Is the employee who arrives late today also the source of complaints by co-workers for being a "goof-off"? What we want to know is if this behavior is unusual or not. If it is, the observer is likely to give the behavior an external attribution. If this action is not unusual, it will probably be judged as internal.

If everyone who is faced with a similar situation responds in the same way, we can say the behavior shows *consensus*. Our late employee's behavior would meet this criterion if all employees who took the same route to work were also late. From an attribution perspective, if consensus is high, you would be expected to give an external attribution to the employee's tardiness, whereas if other employees who took the same route made it into work on time, your conclusion as to causation would be internal.

Finally, an observer looks for *consistency* in a person's actions. Does the person respond the same way over time? Coming in ten minutes late for work is not perceived in the same way for the employee for whom it is an unusual case (she hasn't been late for several months), as for the employee for whom it is part of a routine pattern (she is regularly late two or three times a week). The more consistent the behavior, the more the observer is inclined to attribute it to internal causes.

Figure 5–3 summarizes the key elements in attribution theory. It would tell us, for instance, that if an employee—let's call her Ms. Smith—generally performs at about the same level on other related tasks as she does on her current task (low distinctiveness), if other employees frequently perform differently—better or worse—than Ms. Smith does on that current task (low consensus), and if Ms. Smith's performance on this current task is consistent over time (high consistency), her manager or anyone else who is judging Ms. Smith's work is likely to hold her primarily responsible for her task performance (internal attribution).

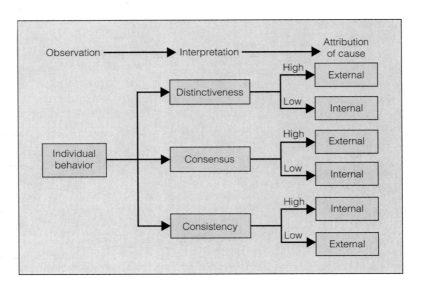

FIGURE 5–3   Attribution Theory

One of the more interesting findings from attribution theory is that there are errors or biases that distort attributions. For instance, there is substantial evidence that when we make judgments about the behavior of other people, we have a tendency to underestimate the influence of external factors and overestimate the influence of internal or personal factors.[3] This is called the **fundamental attribution error** and can explain why a sales manager is prone to attribute the poor performance of her sales agents to laziness rather than the innovative product line introduced by a competitor. There is also a tendency for individuals to attribute *their own* successes to internal factors like ability or effort while putting the blame for failure on external factors like luck. This is called the **self-serving bias** and suggests that feedback provided to employees in performance reviews will be predictably distorted by recipients depending on whether it is positive or negative.

Frequently Used Shortcuts in Judging Others

We use a number of shortcuts when we judge others. Perceiving and interpreting what others do is burdensome. As a result, individuals develop techniques for making the task more manageable. These techniques are frequently valuable—they allow us to make accurate perceptions rapidly and provide valid data for making predictions. However, they are not foolproof. They can and do get us into trouble. An understanding of these shortcuts can be helpful toward recognizing when they can result in significant distortions.

SELECTIVE PERCEPTION   Any characteristic that makes a person, object, or event stand out will increase the probability that it will be perceived. Why? Because it is impossible for us to assimilate everything we see—only certain stimuli can be taken in. This explains why, as we noted earlier, you're more likely to notice cars like your own or why some people may be reprimanded by their boss for doing something that when done by another employee goes unnoticed. Since we can't observe everything going

Fundamental Attribution Error   The tendency to underestimate the influence of external factors and overestimate the influence of internal factors when making judgments about the behavior of others

Self-serving Bias   The tendency for individuals to attribute their own successes to internal factors while putting the blame for failures on external factors.

Selective Perception People selectively interpret what they see based on their interests, background, experience, and attitudes.

on about us, we engage in **selective perception.** A classic example shows how vested interests can significantly influence what problems we see.

Dearborn and Simon[4] performed a perceptual study in which twenty-three business executives read a comprehensive case describing the organization and activities of a steel company. Six of the twenty-three executives were in the sales function, five in production, four in accounting, and eight in miscellaneous functions. Each manager was asked to write down the most important problem he found in the case. Eighty-three percent of the sales executives rated sales important, while only twenty-nine percent of the others did so. This, along with other results of the study, led the researchers to conclude that the participants perceived aspects of a situation that related specifically to the activities and goals of the unit to which they were attached. A group's perception of organizational activities is selectively altered to align with the vested interests they represent. In other words, where the stimuli are ambiguous, as in the steel company case, perception tends to be influenced more by an individual's base of interpretation (that is, attitudes, interests, and background) than by the stimulus itself.

But how does selectivity work as a shortcut in judging other people? Since we cannot assimilate all that we observe, we take in bits and pieces. But these bits and pieces are not chosen randomly; rather, they are selectively chosen according to our interests, background, experience, and attitudes. Selective perception allows us to "speed-read" others, but not without the risk of drawing an inaccurate picture. Because we see what we want to see, we can draw unwarranted conclusions from an ambiguous situation. If there is a rumor going around the office that your company's sales are down and that large layoffs may be coming, a routine visit by a senior executive from headquarters might be interpreted as the first step in management's identification of people to be fired, when in reality such an action may be the farthest thing from the mind of the senior executive.

Halo Effect Drawing a general impression about an individual based on a single characteristic.

HALO EFFECT   When we draw a general impression about an individual based on a single characteristic, such as intelligence, sociability, or appearance, a **halo effect** is operating. This phenomenon frequently occurs when students appraise their classroom instructor. Students may isolate a single trait such as enthusiasm and allow their entire evaluation to be tainted by how they judge the instructor on this one trait. Thus, an instructor may be quiet, assured, knowledgeable, and highly qualified, but if his style lacks zeal, he will be rated lower on a number of other characteristics.

The reality of the halo effect was confirmed in a classic study where subjects were given a list of traits like intelligent, skillful, practical, industrious, determined, and warm and asked to evaluate the person to whom these traits applied.[5] Based on these traits, the person was judged to be wise, humorous, popular, and imaginative. When the same list was modified to substitute cold for warm in the trait list, a completely different set of perceptions was obtained. Clearly, the subjects were allowing a single trait to influence their overall impression of the person being judged.

The propensity for the halo effect to operate is not random. Research suggests that it is likely to be most extreme when the traits to be perceived are ambiguous in behavioral terms, when the traits have moral overtones, and when the perceiver is judging traits with which he or she has had limited experience.[6]

CONTRAST EFFECTS   There's an old adage among entertainers who perform in variety shows: Never follow an act that has kids or animals in it. Why? The common belief is that audiences love children and animals so

"I do not hate you. You're projecting."

FIGURE 5–4

Drawing by William Steig; © 1987 The New Yorker Magazine, Inc.

much that you will look bad in comparison. In a similar vein, your author remembers when he was a college freshman having to give a presentation in a speech class. I was scheduled to speak third that morning. After both of the first two speakers stammered, stumbled, and forgot their lines, I suddenly got a rush of confidence because I figured that even though my talk might not go too well, I'd probably get a pretty good grade. I was counting on the instructor raising my evaluation after contrasting my speech to those that immediately preceded it.

These two examples demonstrate how **contrast effects** can distort perceptions. We don't evaluate a person in isolation. Our reaction to one person is often influenced by other persons we've recently encountered.

An illustration of how contrast effects operate is an interview situation in which one sees a pool of job applicants. Distortions in any given candidate's evaluation can occur as a result of his or her place in the interview schedule. The candidate is likely to receive a more favorable evaluation if preceded by mediocre applicants, and a less favorable evaluation if preceded by strong applicants.

PROJECTION It is easy to judge others if we assume they are similar to us. For instance, if you want challenge and responsibility in your job, you assume that others want the same. This tendency to attribute one's own characteristics to other people—which is called **projection**—can distort perceptions made about others.

People who engage in projection tend to perceive others according to what they themselves are like rather than according to what the person being observed is really like. When observing others who actually *are* like them, these observers are quite accurate—not because they are perceptive, but rather because they always judge people as being similar to themselves, so when they finally find someone who is, they are naturally correct. When managers engage in projection, they compromise their ability

Contrast Effects Evaluations of a person's characteristics that are affected by comparisons with other people recently encountered who rank higher or lower on the same characteristics.

Projection Attributing one's own characteristics to other people.

to respond to individual differences. They tend to see people as more homogeneous than they really are.

STEREOTYPING When we judge someone on the basis of our perception of the group to which he or she belongs, we are using the shortcut called **stereotyping**. F. Scott Fitzgerald engaged in stereotyping in his reported conversation with Ernest Hemingway when he said, "The very rich are different from you and me." Hemingway's reply, "Yes, they have more money," indicated that he refused to generalize characteristics about people based on their wealth.

Generalization, of course, is not without advantages. It makes assimilating easier since it permits us to maintain consistency. It is less difficult to deal with an unmanageable number of stimuli if we use stereotypes. But the problem occurs when we inaccurately stereotype. All accountants are *not* quiet and introspective just as all salespeople are *not* aggressive and outgoing.

In an organizational context, we frequently hear comments that represent stereotyped representation of certain groups: "Managers don't give a damn about their people, only getting the work out"; or "Union people expect something for nothing." Clearly, these judgments are stereotypes, but if people expect to perceive managers or union workers this way, that is what they will perceive, whether it is true or not of an individual manager or worker.

Obviously, one of the problems of stereotypes is that they are so widespread, despite the fact that they may not contain a shred of truth or may be irrelevant. Their being widespread may only mean that many people are making the same inaccurate perception based on a false premise about a group.

Specific Applications in Organizations

People in organizations are always judging each other. Managers must appraise their subordinates' performances. We evaluate how much effort our

Stereotyping Judging someone on the basis of one's perception of the group to which that person belongs.

Women in high-ranking positions often suffer from sex-role stereotypes. Studies indicate that male and female managers alike hold negative stereotypes about the ability of women to manage effectively. Research demonstrates that successful managers—whether male or female—tend to be perceived as having personality traits and skills associated with men.   Four by Five

Challenging Stereotypes of Older Workers and Women

Older workers have higher absentee rates because they're often sick. They're also slower, more accident prone, and tend to complain more than younger workers. And women! They show less initiative than men on the job; they're less committed; and they typically won't relocate, especially if they have children.

All of these stereotypes are wrong.[7] Yet as long as they prevail, they hurt women and older workers and they hurt the organizations that need their skills.

What terms come to mind when you think of workers over fifty-five? Incompetent? Old codgers? Past their prime? How about reliable, trained, and experienced? The latter set of terms better matches reality. The facts confirm that older workers almost inevitably display significantly lower absenteeism than younger workers, have about half the accident rate of their juniors, and consistently score higher in job satisfaction. Moreover, as we noted in the previous chapter, there is no evidence that age negatively affects job productivity.

The stereotype of women as uncommitted employees who won't stay with an organization or who won't relocate has also been found to be dead wrong. The primary reason female professionals resign their jobs is not home or child-rearing responsibilities. It's frustration with career progress. Seventy-three percent of women who quit large companies moved to another company, while only seven percent resigned to stay at home.

Negative ageist and gender stereotypes not only adversely affect older workers and women, but are also likely to be a major handicap for organizations in the future. The projected labor shortage in North America and much of Western Europe beginning about the year 2001 means that organizations will be desperately searching for skilled employees. Organizations that refuse to recognize that both older workers and women are a valuable labor resource will lose a large part of an increasingly smaller talent pool.

co-workers are putting into their jobs. When a new person joins a department, he or she is immediately "sized up" by the other department members. In many cases, these judgments have important consequences for the organization. Let us briefly look at a few of the more obvious applications.

EMPLOYMENT INTERVIEW   A major input into who is hired and who is rejected is the employment interview. It's fair to say that few people are hired without an interview. But the evidence indicates that interviewers make perceptual judgments that are often inaccurate. Additionally, inter-rater agreement among interviewers is often poor; that is, different interviewers see different things in the same candidate and thus arrive at different conclusions about the applicant.

Interviewers generally draw early impressions that become very quickly entrenched. If negative information is exposed early in the interview, it tends to be more heavily weighted than if that same information comes out later.[8] Studies indicate that most interviewers' decisions change very little after the first four or five minutes of the interview. As a result, information elicited early in the interview carries greater weight than does information elicited later, and a "good applicant" is probably characterized more by the absence of unfavorable characteristics than by the presence of favorable characteristics.

Importantly, who you think is a good candidate and who I think is one may differ markedly. Because interviews usually have so little consistent structure and interviewers vary in terms of what they are looking for in a candidate, judgments of the same candidate can vary widely. If the employment interview is an important input into the hiring decision—and it usually is—you should recognize that perceptual factors influence who is hired and eventually the quality of an organization's labor force.

PERFORMANCE EVALUATION Although the impact of performance evaluations on behavior will be discussed fully in Chapter 16, it should be pointed out here that an employee's performance appraisal is very much dependent on the perceptual process. An employee's future is closely tied to his or her appraisal—promotions, pay raises, and continuation of employment are among the most obvious outcomes. The performance appraisal represents an assessment of an employee's work. While this can be objective (for example, a salesperson is appraised on how many dollars of sales she generates in her territory), many jobs are evaluated in subjective terms. Subjective measures are easier to implement, they provide managers with greater discretion, and many jobs do not readily lend themselves to objective measures. Subjective measures are, by definition, judgmental. The evaluator forms a general impression of an employee's work. To the degree that managers use subjective measures in appraising employees, what the evaluator perceives to be "good" or "bad" employee characteristics/behaviors will significantly influence the appraisal outcome.

EMPLOYEE EFFORT An individual's future in an organization is usually not dependent on performance alone. In many organizations, the level of an employee's effort is given high importance. Just as teachers frequently consider how hard you try in a course as well as how you perform on examinations, so often do managers. And assessment of an individual's effort is a subjective judgment susceptible to perceptual distortions and bias. If it is true, as some claim, that "more workers are fired for poor attitudes and lack of discipline than for lack of ability,"[9] then appraisal of an employee's effort may be a primary influence on his or her future in the organization.

EMPLOYEE LOYALTY Another important judgment that managers make about employees is whether they are loyal to the organization. Few organizations appreciate employees, especially those in the managerial ranks, disparaging the firm. Further, in some organizations, if the word gets around that an employee is looking at other employment opportunities outside the firm, that employee may be labeled as disloyal and cut off from all future advancement opportunities. The issue is not whether organizations are right in demanding loyalty, but that many do, and that assessment of an employee's loyalty or commitment is highly judgmental. What is perceived as loyalty by one decision maker may be seen as excessive conformity by another. An employee who questions a top-management decision may be seen as disloyal by some, yet caring and concerned by others. When evaluating a person's attitude, as in loyalty assessment, we must recognize that we are involved with person perception.

THE LINK BETWEEN PERCEPTION
AND INDIVIDUAL DECISION MAKING

Individuals in organizations make decisions. That is, they make choices from among two or more alternatives. Top managers, for instance, determine their organization's goals, what products or services to offer, how best to organize corporate headquarters, or where to locate a new manufacturing plant. Middle- and lower-level managers determine production schedules, select new employees, and decide how pay raises are to be allocated. Of course, making decisions is not the sole province of managers. Nonmanagerial employees also make decisions that affect their jobs and the organizations they work for. The more obvious of these decisions might include whether to come to work or not on any given day, how much effort to put forward once at work, and whether to comply with a request made by the boss. Individual decision making, therefore, is an important part of organizational behavior. But how individuals in organizations make decisions, and the quality of their final choices, are largely influenced by their perceptions.

Decision making occurs as a reaction to a problem. There is a discrepancy between some *current* state of affairs and some *desired* state, requiring consideration of alternative courses of action. So if your car breaks down and you rely on it to get to school, you have a problem that requires a decision on your part. Unfortunately, most problems don't come neatly packaged with a label "problem" clearly displayed on them. One person's *problem* is another person's *satisfactory state of affairs*. One manager may view her division's two percent decline in quarterly sales to be a serious problem requiring immediate action on her part. In contrast, her counterpart in another division of the same company, who also had a two percent sales decrease, may consider that quite satisfactory. So the awareness that a problem exists and that a decision needs to be made is a perceptual issue.

Moreover, every decision requires interpretation and evaluation of information. Data is typically received from multiple sources and it needs to be screened, processed, and interpreted. What data, for instance, is relevant to the decision and what isn't? The perceptions of the decision maker will answer this question. Alternatives will be developed and the strengths and weaknesses of each will need to be evaluated. Again, because alternatives don't come with "red flags" identifying themselves as such or with their strengths and weaknesses clearly marked, the individual decision maker's perceptual process will have a large bearing on the final outcome.

THE OPTIMIZING DECISION–MAKING MODEL

Optimizing Model A decision-making model that describes how individuals should behave in order to maximize some outcome.

Let's begin by describing how individuals should behave in order to maximize some outcome. We will call this the **optimizing model** of decision making.[10]

Steps in the Optimizing Model

Table 5–1 outlines the six steps an individual should follow, either explicitly or implicitly, when making a decision.

STEP 1: ASCERTAIN THE NEED FOR A DECISION   The first step requires recognition that a decision needs to be made. The existence of a problem—or, as we stated previously, a disparity between some desired state and the actual condition—brings about this recognition. If you calcu-

TABLE 5–1   Steps in the Optimizing Decision-Making Model

1. Ascertain the need for a decision
2. Identify the decision criteria
3. Allocate weights to the criteria
4. Develop the alternatives
5. Evaluate the alternatives
6. Select the best alternative

late your monthly expenses and find that you're spending $50 more than you allocated in your budget, you have ascertained the need for a decision. There is a disparity between your desired expenditure level and what you're actually spending.

STEP 2: IDENTIFY THE DECISION CRITERIA   Once an individual has determined the need for a decision, the criteria that will be important in making the decision must be identified. For illustration purposes, let's consider the case of a high school senior confronting the problem of choosing a college. The concepts derived from this example may be generalized to any decision a person might confront.

For the sake of simplicity, let's assume that our high school senior has already chosen to attend college (versus other, noncollege options). We know that the need for a decision is precipitated by graduation. Once she has recognized this need for a decision, the student should begin to list the criteria or factors that will be relevant to her decision. For our example, let's assume she has identified the following criteria about the colleges she is considering attending: annual cost, availability of financial aid, admission requirements, status or reputation, size, geographic location, curricula offering, male-female ratio, quality of social life, and the physical attractiveness of the campus. These criteria represent what the decision maker thinks is relevant to her decision. Note that, in this step, what is *not* listed is as important as what *is*. For example, our high school senior did not consider factors such as where her friends were going to school, availability of part-time employment, and whether freshmen are required to reside on campus. To someone else making a college selection decision, the criteria used might be considerably different.

This second step is important because it identifies only those criteria that the decision maker considers relevant. If a criterion is omitted from this list, we treat it as irrelevant to the decision maker.

STEP 3: ALLOCATE WEIGHTS TO THE CRITERIA   The criteria listed in the previous step are not all equally important. It's necessary, therefore, to weight the factors listed in Step 2 in order to prioritize their importance in the decision. All the criteria are relevant, but some are more relevant than others.

How does the decision maker weight criteria? A simple approach would merely be to give *the* most important criteria a number—say ten—and then assign weights to the rest of the criteria against this standard. So the result of Steps 2 and 3 is to allow decision makers to use their personal preferences both to prioritize the relevant criteria and to indicate their relative degree of importance by assigning a weight to each. Table 5–2 lists the criteria and weights our high school senior is using in her college decision.

TABLE 5–2   Criteria and Weights in Selection of a College

Criteria	Weights
Availability of financial aid	10
School's reputation	10
Annual cost	8
Curricula offering	7
Geographic location	6
Admission requirements	5
Quality of social life	4
School size	3
Male-female ratio	2
Physical attractiveness of the campus	2

STEP 4: DEVELOP THE ALTERNATIVES   The fourth step requires the decision maker to list all the viable alternatives that could possibly succeed in resolving the problem. No attempt is made in this step to appraise the alternatives; only to list them. To return to our example, let us assume that our high schooler has identified eight potential colleges—Alpha, Beta, Delta, Gamma, Iota, Omega, Phi, and Sigma.

STEP 5: EVALUATE THE ALTERNATIVES   Once the alternatives have been identified, the decision maker must critically evaluate each one. The strengths and weaknesses of each alternative will become evident when they are compared against the criteria and weights established in Steps 2 and 3.

The evaluation of each alternative is done by appraising it against the weighted criteria. In our example, the high school senior would evaluate each college using every one of the criteria. To keep our example simple, we'll assume that a ten means that the college is rated as "most favorable" on that criterion. The results from evaluating the various alternative colleges are shown in Table 5–3.

Keep in mind that the ratings given the eight colleges shown in Table 5–3 are based on the assessment made by the decision maker. Some assessments can be made in a relatively objective fashion. If our decision maker prefers a small school, one with an enrollment of one thousand is obviously superior to one with ten thousand students. Similarly, if a high male-female ratio is sought, 3:1 is clearly higher than 1.2:1. But the assessment of criteria such as reputation, quality of social life, and the physical attractiveness of the campus reflects the decision maker's values. The point is that most decisions contain judgments. They are reflected in the criteria chosen in Step 2, the weights given to these criteria, and the evaluation of alternatives. This explains why two people faced with a similar problem—such as selecting a college—may look at two totally different sets of alternatives or even look at the same alternatives but rate them very differently.

Table 5–3 represents an evaluation of eight alternatives only against the decision criteria. It does not reflect the weighting done in Step 3. If one choice had scored ten on every criterion, there would be no need to consider the weights. Similarly, if the weights were all equal, you could evaluate each alternative merely by summing up the appropriate column in Table 5–3. For instance, Omega College would be highest, with a total score of eighty-four. But our high school senior needs to multiply each alternative against its weight. The result of this process is shown in Table 5–4. The summation of these scores represents an evaluation of each college against the previously established criteria and weights.

To optimize the college-choice decision, an individual needs to identify all the criteria that are relevant, weight those criteria, and then evaluate every alternative against these criteria. This process explains how two people can look at the same set of alternatives but make very different choices.

Claudia Parks/The Stock Market

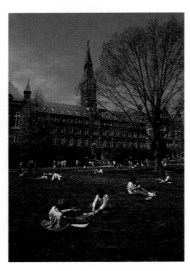

TABLE 5–3   Evaluation of Eight Alternatives Against the Decision Criteria*

| | Alternatives | | | | | | | |
Criteria	Alpha College	Beta College	Delta College	Gamma College	Iota College	Omega College	Phi College	Sigma College
Availability of financial aid	5	4	10	7	7	8	3	7
School's reputation	10	6	6	6	9	5	9	6
Annual cost (low cost preferred)	5	7	8	8	5	10	5	8
Curricula offering	6	10	8	9	8	8	9	8
Geographic location	6	7	10	10	6	9	10	7
Admission requirements (in terms of likelihood of acceptance)	7	10	10	10	8	10	8	10
Quality of social life	10	5	7	7	3	7	10	8
School size	10	7	7	7	9	7	9	4
Male–female ratio	2	2	8	8	8	10	2	8
Physical attractiveness of the campus	8	10	6	3	4	10	5	9

*The colleges that achieved the highest rating for a criterion are given ten points.

STEP 6: SELECT THE BEST ALTERNATIVE   The final step in the optimizing decision model is the selection of the best alternative from among those enumerated and evaluated. Since best is defined in terms of highest total score, the selection is quite simple. The decision maker merely chooses the alternative that generated the largest total score in Step 5. For our high school senior, that means Delta College. Based on the criteria identified, the weights given to the criteria, and the decision maker's evaluation of each college on each of the criteria, Delta College scored highest and thus becomes the best.

Assumptions of the Optimizing Model

The steps in the optimizing model contain a number of assumptions. It is important to understand these assumptions if we are to determine how accurately the optimizing model describes actual individual decision making.

TABLE 5–4   Evaluation of College Alternatives

| | Alternatives | | | | | | | |
Criteria (and weight)	Alpha College	Beta College	Delta College	Gamma College	Iota College	Omega College	Phi College	Sigma College
Availability of financial aid (10)	50	40	100	70	70	80	30	70
School's reputation (10)	100	60	60	60	90	50	90	60
Annual cost (8)	40	56	64	64	40	80	40	64
Curricula offering (7)	42	70	56	63	56	56	63	56
Geographic location (6)	36	42	60	60	36	54	60	42
Admission requirements (5)	35	50	50	50	40	50	40	50
Quality of social life (4)	40	20	28	28	12	28	40	32
School size (3)	30	21	21	21	27	21	27	12
Male–female ratio (2)	4	4	16	16	16	20	4	16
Physical attractiveness of the campus (2)	16	20	12	6	8	20	10	18
Totals	393	373	467	438	395	459	404	420

Rationality Choices that are consistent and value-maximizing.

The assumptions of the optimizing model are the same as those that underlie the concept of **rationality**. Rationality refers to choices that are consistent and value-maximizing. Rational decision making, therefore, implies that the decision maker can be fully objective and logical. The individual is assumed to have a clear goal, and all of the six steps in the optimizing model are assumed to lead toward the selection of the alternative that will maximize that goal. Let's take a closer look at the assumptions inherent in rationality and, hence, the optimizing model.

GOAL–ORIENTED The optimizing model assumes that there is no conflict over the goal. Whether the decision involves selecting a college to attend, determining whether or not to go to work today, or choosing the right applicant to fill a job vacancy, it is assumed that the decision maker has a single, well-defined goal that he or she is trying to maximize.

ALL OPTIONS ARE KNOWN It is assumed that the decision maker can identify *all* the relevant criteria and can list *all* viable alternatives. The optimizing model portrays the decision maker as fully comprehensive in his or her ability to assess criteria and alternatives.

PREFERENCES ARE CLEAR Rationality assumes that the criteria and alternatives can be assigned numerical values and ranked in a preferential order.

PREFERENCES ARE CONSTANT The same criteria and alternatives should be obtained every time because, in addition to the goal and preferences being clear, it is assumed that the specific decision criteria are constant and the weights assigned to them are stable over time.

FINAL CHOICE WILL MAXIMIZE THE OUTCOME The rational decision maker, following the optimizing model, will choose the alternative that rates highest. This most preferred solution will, based on Step 6 of the process, give the maximum benefits.

FIGURE 5–5   The Optimizing Model

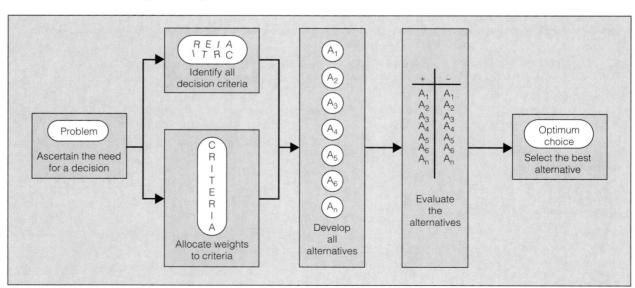

ETHICAL ISSUES
IN OB

Codes of Ethics and Decision Rules

An increasingly popular means of helping employees deal with ethical problems is for organizations to create a code of ethics. These codes formally state the organization's primary values and the ethical rules it expects its employees to follow. A recent survey included the following examples from corporate codes: Demonstrate courtesy, respect, honesty, and fairness; Bribes are prohibited; Maintain confidentiality of records; Do not use company property for personal benefit; Do not propagate false or misleading information.[11]

Another approach to improving ethical behavior is the use of decision rules. One author has proposed twelve questions to guide managers in handling the ethical dimensions of decision making:[12]

1. Have you defined the problem accurately?
2. How would you define the problem if you stood on the other side of the fence?
3. How did this situation occur in the first place?
4. To whom and to what do you give your loyalty as a person and as a member of the corporation?
5. What is your intention in making this decision?
6. How does this intention compare with the probable results?
7. Whom could your decision or action injure?
8. Can you discuss the problem with the affected parties before you make the decision?
9. Are you confident that your position will be as valid over a long period of time as it seems now?
10. Could you disclose without qualm your decision or action to your boss, your chief executive officer, the board of directors, your family, society as a whole?
11. What is the symbolic potential of your action if understood? If misunderstood?
12. Under what conditions would you allow exceptions to your stand?

Proponents of formal ethical codes and decision rules argue that they reduce ambiguity and can significantly raise ethical standards. Opponents see these devices as nothing more than public relations tools. What do *you* think?

Predictions from the Optimizing Model

Using the preceding assumptions, we would predict that the individual decision maker would have a clear and specific goal; a fully comprehensive set of criteria that determine the relevant factors in the decision; and a precise ranking of the criteria, which will be stable over time. We further assume that the decision maker will select the alternative that scores highest after all options have been evaluated. (See Figure 5–5).

In terms of the college selection decision introduced earlier, the optimizing model would predict that the high school student could identify every factor that might be important in her decision. Each of these factors would be weighted in terms of importance. All of the colleges that could possibly be viable options would be identified and evaluated against the criteria. Remember, because all alternatives are assumed to be considered, our decision maker might be looking at hundreds of colleges. Also, even if this activity took six months to complete, the criteria and weights would not vary over time. If the college's reputation was most important in September, it would still be so in March. Further, if Beta College was given a score of six on this criterion in September, six months later the assessment would be the same. Finally, since every factor that is important in the decision has been considered and given its proper weight, and since every alternative has been identified and evaluated against the criteria, the decision maker can be assured that the college that scores highest in the evaluation is the best choice. There are no regrets because all information has been obtained and evaluated in a logical and consistent manner.

ALTERNATIVE DECISION–MAKING MODELS

Do individuals actually make their decisions the way the optimizing model predicts? Sometimes. When decision makers are faced with a simple problem having few alternative courses of action, and when the cost of searching out and evaluating alternatives is low, the optimizing model provides a fairly accurate description of the decision process.[13] Buying a pair of shoes or a new personal computer might be examples of decisions where the optimizing model would apply. But many decisions, particularly important and difficult ones—the kind a person hasn't encountered before and for which there are no standardized or programmed rules to provide guidance—don't involve simple and well-structured problems. Rather, they're characterized by complexity, relatively high uncertainty (all the alternatives, for example, are unlikely to be known), and goals and preferences that are neither clear nor consistent. This category of decision would include choosing a spouse, considering whether to accept a new job offer in a different city, selecting among job applicants for a vacancy in your department, developing a marketing strategy for a new product, deciding where to build an additional manufacturing plant, and determining the proper time to take your small company public by selling stock in it. In this section, we'll review three alternatives to the optimizing model: the satisficing or bounded rationality model, the implicit favorite model, and the intuitive model.

The Satisficing Model

Satisficing Model A decision-making model where a decision maker chooses the first solution that is "good enough"; that is, satisfactory and sufficient.

The essence of the **satisficing model** is that, when faced with complex problems, decision makers respond by reducing the problems to a level at which they can be readily understood. This is because the information-processing capability of human beings makes it impossible to assimilate and understand all the information necessary to optimize. Since the capacity of the human mind for formulating and solving complex problems is far too small to meet all the requirements for full rationality, individuals operate within the confines of **bounded rationality**. They construct simplified models that extract the essential features from problems without capturing all their complexity.[14] Individuals can then behave rationally within the limits of the simple model.

Bounded Rationality Individuals make decisions by constructing simplified models that extract the essential features from problems without capturing all their complexity.

How does bounded rationality work for the typical individual? Once a problem is identified, the search for criteria and alternatives begins. But the list of criteria is likely to be far from exhaustive. The decision maker will identify a limited list made up of the more conspicuous choices. These are the choices that are easy to find and that tend to be highly visible. In most cases, they will represent familiar criteria and the tried-and-true solutions. Once this limited set of alternatives is identified, the decision maker will begin reviewing them. But the review will not be comprehensive. That is, not all the alternatives will be carefully evaluated. Instead, the decision maker will begin with alternatives that differ only in a relatively small

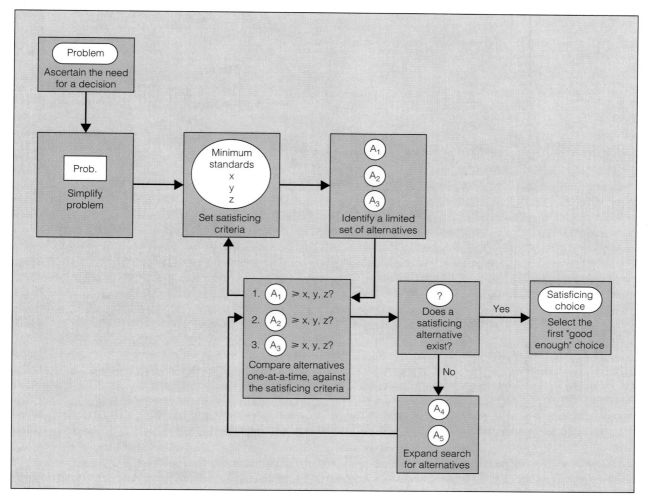

FIGURE 5-6   **The Satisficing Model**

degree from the choice currently in effect. Following along familiar and well-worn paths, the decision maker proceeds to review alternatives only until he or she identifies an alternative that satisfices—one that is satisfactory and sufficient. So the satisficer settles for the first solution that is "good enough," rather than continuing to search for the optimum. The first alternative to meet the "good enough" criterion ends the search, and the decision maker can then proceed toward implementing this acceptable course of action. This is illustrated in Figure 5-6.

One of the more interesting aspects of the satisficing model is that the order in which alternatives are considered is critical in determining which alternative is selected. If the decision maker were optimizing, all alternatives would eventually be listed in a hierarchy of preferred order. Since all the alternatives would be considered, the initial order in which they were evaluated would be irrelevant. Every potential solution would get a full and complete evaluation. But this is not the case with satisficing. Assuming that a problem has more than one potential solution, the satisficing choice will be the first acceptable one the decision maker encounters. Since decision makers use simple and limited models, they typically begin by identifying alternatives that are obvious, ones with which they are familiar, and those not too far from the status quo. Those solutions that depart least from the status quo

Many hiring decisions are made using the satisficing model because cost and time constraints make optimizing impossible.

Bob Daemmrich/Image Works

and meet the decision criteria are most likely to be selected. This may help to explain why many decisions that people make don't result in the selection of solutions radically different from those they have made before. A unique alternative may present an optimizing solution to the problem; however, it will rarely be chosen. An acceptable solution will be identified well before the decision maker is required to search very far beyond the status quo.

Using the satisficing model, how might we predict that the high school senior introduced earlier would make her college choice? Obviously, she will not consider all of the more than two thousand colleges in the United States or the multitude of others in foreign countries. Based on schools that she's heard about from friends and relatives, plus possibly a quick look through a guide to colleges, she will typically select a half-a-dozen or a dozen colleges to which she will send for catalogs, brochures, and applications. Based on a cursory appraisal of the materials she receives from the colleges, and using her rough decision criteria, she will look for a school that meets her minimal requirements. When she finds one, the decision search will be over. If none of the colleges in this initial set meet the "good enough" standards, she will expand her search to include more diverse colleges. But even following this extended search, the first college she uncovers that meets her minimal requirements will become the alternative of choice.

The Implicit Favorite Model

Implicit Favorite Model
A decision-making model where the decision maker implicitly selects a preferred alternative early in the decision process and biases the evaluation of all other choices.

Another model designed to deal with complex and nonroutine decisions is the **implicit favorite model**.[15] Like the satisficing model, it argues that individuals solve complex problems by simplifying the process. However, simplification in the implicit favorite model means not entering into the difficult "evaluation of alternatives" stage of decision making until one of the alternatives can be identified as an implicit "favorite." In other words, the decision maker is neither rational nor objective. Instead, early in the deci-

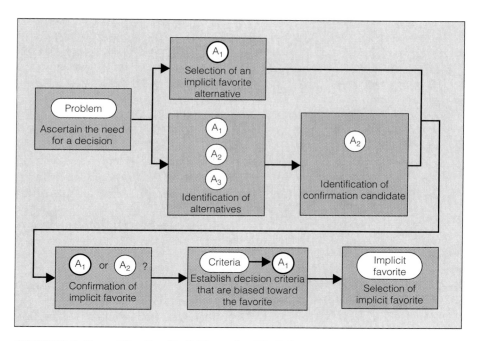

FIGURE 5–7   **The Implicit Favorite Model**

sion process, he or she implicitly selects a preferred alternative. Then the rest of the decision process is essentially a decision confirmation exercise, where the decision maker makes sure that his or her implicit favorite is indeed the "right" choice.

The implicit favorite model evolved from research on job decisions by graduate management students at the Massachusetts Institute of Technology. Clearly, these students knew and understood the optimizing model. They had spent several years repeatedly using it for solving problems and analyzing cases in accounting, finance, management, marketing, and quantitative methods courses. Moreover, the job choice decision was an important one. If there was a decision where the optimizing model should be used, and a group experienced in using it, this should be it. But the researcher found that the optimizing model was not followed. Rather, the implicit favorite model provided an accurate description of the actual decision process.

The implicit favorite model is outlined in Figure 5–7. Once a problem is identified, the decision maker implicitly identifies an early favorite alternative. But the decision maker doesn't end the search at this point. In fact, the decision maker is often unaware that he or she has already identified an implicit favorite and that the rest of the process is really an exercise in prejudice. So more alternatives will be generated. This is important, for it gives the appearance of objectivity. Then the confirmation process begins. The alternative set will be reduced to two—the choice candidate and a confirmation candidate. If the choice candidate is the only viable option, the decision maker will try to obtain another acceptable alternative to become the confirmation candidate, so he or she will have something to compare against. At this point, the decision maker establishes the decision criteria and weights. A great deal of perceptual and interpretational distortion is taking place, with the selection of criteria and their weight being "shaped" to ensure victory for the favored choice. And, of course, that's exactly what transpires. The evaluation demonstrates unequivocally the superiority of the choice candidate over the confirmation candidate.

If the implicit favorite model is at work, the search for new alternatives ends well before the decision maker is willing to admit having made his or her decision. In the job search with MIT students, the researcher found that he was able to accurately predict eighty-seven percent of the career jobs taken two to eight weeks before the students would admit that they had reached a decision.[16] This points to a decision process that is influenced a lot more by intuitive feelings than by rational objectivity.

Using the implicit favorite model, let's look at how our high school senior might go about choosing which college to attend. Early on in the process, she will find that one of the colleges seems intuitively right for her. However, she may not reveal this to others, nor be aware of it herself. She'll review catalogs and brochures on a number of schools, but eventually reduce the set to two. One of these two, of course, will be her implied favorite. She'll then focus in on the relevant factors in her decision. Which college has the best reputation? Where will she have the better social life? Which campus is more attractive? Her evaluation of criteria such as these are subjective judgments. Her assessment, though, won't be fair and impartial. Rather, she'll distort her judgments to align with her intuitive preference. Since "the race is fixed," the winner is a foregone conclusion. Our high school student won't necessarily choose the optimum alternative, nor can we say that her choice will satisfice. Remember, she distorted her evaluations to get the results she wanted, so there is no guarantee that her final selection will reflect the assumptions of bounded rationality. What we can say is that, if she follows the implicit favorite model, she'll choose the college that was her early preference, regardless of any relevant facts that may have surfaced later in the decision process.

The Intuitive Model

Joe Garcia has just committed his corporation to spend in excess of $40 million to build a new plant in Atlanta to manufacture electronic components for satellite-communication equipment. A vice president of operations for his firm, Joe had before him a comprehensive analysis of five possible plant locations developed by a site location consulting firm he had hired. This report ranked the Atlanta location third among the five alternatives. After carefully reading the report and its conclusions, Joe decided against the consultant's recommendation. When asked to explain his decision, Joe said, "I looked the report over very carefully. But in spite of its recommendation, I felt that the numbers didn't tell the whole story. *Intuitively*, I just sensed that Atlanta would prove to be the best bet over the long run."

Intuitive decision making, like that used by Joe Garcia, has recently come out of the closet and into some respectability. Experts no longer automatically assume that using intuition to make decisions is irrational or ineffective.[17] There is growing recognition that rational analysis has been overemphasized and that, in certain instances, relying on intuition can improve decision making.

What do we mean by intuitive decision making? There are a number of ways to conceptualize intuition.[18] For instance, some consider it a form of extra-sensory power or sixth sense, and some believe it is a personality trait that a limited number of people are born with. For our purposes, we'll define **intuitive decision making** as an unconscious process created out of distilled experience. It doesn't necessarily operate independently of rational analysis; rather, the two complement each other.

Intuitive Decision Making An unconscious process created out of distilled experience.

Research on chess playing provides an excellent example of how intuition works.[19] Novice chess players and grandmasters were shown an actual, but unfamiliar, chess game with about twenty-five pieces on the board. After five or ten seconds, the pieces were removed and each was asked to reconstruct the pieces by position. On average, the grandmaster could put twenty-three or twenty-four pieces in their correct squares, while the novice was able to replace only six. Then the exercise was changed. This time the pieces were placed randomly on the board. Again, the novice got only about six correct, but so did the grandmaster! The second exercise demonstrated that the grandmaster didn't have any better memory than the novice. What he did have was the ability, based on the experience of having played thousands of chess games, to recognize patterns and clusters of pieces that occur on chessboards in the course of games. Studies further show that chess professionals can play fifty or more games simultaneously, where decisions often must be made in only seconds, and exhibit only a moderately lower level of skill than when playing one game under tournament conditions, where decisions take half an hour or longer. The expert's experience allows him or her to recognize a situation and draw upon previously learned information associated with that situation to quickly arrive at a decision choice. The result is that the intuitive decision maker can decide rapidly with what appears to be very limited information.

When are people most likely to use intuitive decision making? Eight conditions have been identified: (1) when a high level of uncertainty exists; (2) when there is little precedent to draw on; (3) when variables are less scientifically predictable; (4) when "facts" are limited; (5) when facts don't clearly point the way to go; (6) when analytical data are of little use; (7) when there are several plausible alternative solutions to choose from, with good arguments for each; and (8) when time is limited and there is pressure to come up with the right decision.[20]

Is there a standard model that people follow when using intuition? Individuals seem to follow one of two approaches. They apply intuition to either the front end or the back end of the decision-making process.[21]

When intuition is used at the front end, the decision maker tries to avoid systematically analyzing the problem, but instead gives intuition a free rein. The idea is to try to generate unusual possibilities and new options that might not normally emerge from an analysis of past data or traditional ways of doing things. A back-end approach to using intuition relies on rational analysis to identify and allocate weights to decision criteria, as well as to develop and evaluate alternatives. Once this is done, the decision maker stops the analytical process in order to "sleep on the decision" for a day or two before making the final choice.

Although intuitive decision making has gained in respectability since the early 1980s, don't expect people who use it—especially in North America, Great Britain, and other cultures where rational analysis is the approved way of making decisions—to acknowledge they are doing so. People with strong intuitive abilities don't usually tell their colleagues how they reached their conclusions. Since rational analysis is considered more socially desirable, intuitive ability is often disguised or hidden. As one top executive commented, "Sometimes one must dress up a gut decision in 'data clothes' to make it acceptable or palatable, but this fine-tuning is usually after the fact of the decision."[22]

IMPLICATIONS FOR PERFORMANCE AND SATISFACTION

Perception

Individuals behave in a given manner based not on the way their external environment actually is but, rather, on what they see or believe it to be. Because individuals act on their interpretations of reality rather than on

Decision Making in Different Cultures

Who makes a decision, when it is made, and the importance placed on rationality vary in organizations around the world.[23]

Our knowledge of power–distance differences, for example, tells us that in high power–distance cultures, such as India, only very senior-level managers make decisions. But in low power–distance cultures, such as Sweden, low-ranking employees expect to make most of their own decisions about day-to-day operations. Our knowledge that cultures vary in terms of time orientation helps us understand why managers in Egypt will make decisions at a much slower and more deliberate pace than their American counterparts. Even the assumption of rationality is culturally biased. A North American manager might make an important decision intuitively, but he or she knows that it is important to appear to proceed in a rational fashion. This explains why, in the implicit favorite model, the decision maker develops a confirmation candidate. It reassures the decision maker that he or she is seeking to be rational and objective by reviewing alternative options. In countries such as Iran, where rationality is not deified, efforts to appear rational are not necessary.

We can also assess cultural influences in terms of the six steps in the optimizing decision model. To illustrate, let's look at just two of those steps: ascertaining the need for a decision and developing alternatives.

Based on a society's activity orientation, some cultures emphasize solving problems, while others focus on accepting situations as they are. The United States falls in the former category, while Thailand and Indonesia are examples of cultures that fall into the latter. Because problem-solving managers believe they can and should change situations to their own benefit, American managers might identify a problem long before their Thai or Indonesian counterparts would choose to recognize it as such. We can also use differences in time orientation to project the type of alternatives that decision makers might develop. Because Italians value the past and traditions, managers in that culture will tend to rely on tried-and-proven alternatives to problems. In contrast, the United States and Australia are more aggressive and now-oriented; managers in these countries are more likely to propose unique and creative solutions to their problems.

reality itself, it is clear that perception must be a critical determinant of our dependent variables.

An organization may spend millions of dollars to create a pleasant work environment for its employees. However, in spite of these expenditures, if an employee believes that his or her job is lousy, that employee will behave accordingly. It is the employee's perception of a situation that becomes the basis on which he or she behaves. The employee who perceives his or her supervisor as a hurdle reducer and an aid to help him or her do a better job and the employee who sees the same supervisor as "big brother, closely monitoring every motion, to ensure that I keep working," will differ in their behavioral responses to their supervisor. The difference has nothing to do with the reality of the supervisor's actions; the difference in employee behavior is due to different perceptions.

The evidence suggests that what individuals *perceive* from their work situation will influence their productivity more than will the situation itself.

Whether a job is actually interesting or challenging is irrelevant. Whether a manager successfully plans and organizes the work of his or her subordinates and actually helps them to structure their work more efficiently and effectively is far less important than how subordinates perceive his or her efforts. Similarly, issues like fair pay for work performed, the validity of performance appraisals, and the adequacy of working conditions are not judged by employees in a way that assures common perceptions, nor can we be assured that individuals will interpret conditions about their jobs in a favorable light. Therefore, to be able to influence productivity, it is necessary to assess how workers perceive their jobs.

A sales manager may argue that "John should be selling far more of our products in his territory. His territory is a gold mine. It has unlimited potential." But when John is interviewed, we find that he believes he is getting as much as possible out of his territory. Whether the salesman is right or wrong is irrelevant. He *perceives his view to be right*. If the manager hopes to improve sales in John's territory, he or she must first understand John's perspective and then succeed in changing John's perceptions.

As with productivity, absenteeism, turnover, and job satisfaction are reactions to the individual's perceptions. Dissatisfaction with working conditions or the belief that there is a lack of promotion opportunities in the organization are judgments based on attempts to make some meaning out of one's job. The employee's conclusion that a job is good or bad is an interpretation. Managers must spend time understanding how each individual interprets reality and, where there is a significant difference between what is seen and what exists, try to eliminate the distortions. Failure to deal with the differences when individuals perceive the job in negative terms will result in increased absenteeism and turnover and lower job satisfaction.

Individual Decision Making

Individuals think and reason before they act. It is because of this that an understanding of how people make decisions can be helpful for explaining and predicting their behavior.

Under some decision situations, people follow the optimizing model. But for most people, and most nonroutine decisions, this is probably more the exception than the rule. Few important decisions are simple or unambiguous enough for the optimizing model's assumptions to apply. So we find individuals looking for solutions that satisfice rather than optimize, injecting biases and prejudices into the decision process, and relying on intuition.

The alternative decision models we presented can help us explain and predict behaviors that would appear irrational or arbitrary if viewed under optimizing assumptions. Let's look at a couple of examples.

Employment interviews are complex decision activities. The interviewer finds himself or herself inundated with information. Research indicates that interviewers respond by simplifying the process.[24] Most interviewers' decisions change very little after the first four or five minutes of the interview. In a half-hour interview, the decision maker tends to make a decision about the suitability of the candidate in the first few minutes and then uses the rest of the interview time to select information that supports the early decision. In so doing, interviewers reduce the probability of identifying the highest-performing candidate. They bias their decision toward individuals who make favorable first impressions.

Evaluating an employee's performance is a complex activity. Decision makers simplify the process by focusing on visible and easy-to-measure criteria.[25] This may explain why factors such as neatness, promptness, enthusiasm, and a positive attitude are often related to good evaluations. It also explains why quantity measures typically override quality measures. The former category is easier to appraise. This effort at satisficing encourages individuals to take on visible problems rather than important ones.

FOR DISCUSSION

1. Define perception.
2. "That you and I agree on what we see suggests we have similar backgrounds and experiences." Do you agree or disagree? Discuss.
3. What is attribution theory? What are its implications for explaining organizational behavior?
4. What factors do you think might create the fundamental attribution error?
5. How might perceptual factors be involved when an employee receives a poor performance appraisal?
6. How does selectivity affect perception? Give an example of how selectivity can create perceptual distortion.
7. What is stereotyping? Give an example of how stereotyping can create perceptual distortion.
8. Give some positive results of using shortcuts when judging others.
9. What is the optimizing decision-making model? Under what conditions is it applicable?
10. Explain the satisficing model. How widely applicable do you think this model is?
11. Contrast the implicit favorite model to the satisficing model.
12. "For the most part, individual decision making in organizations is an irrational process." Do you agree or disagree? Discuss.

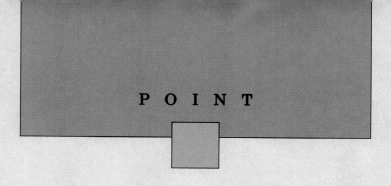

When Hiring Employees: Emphasize the Positive

Hiring new employees requires managers to become salespeople. They have to emphasize the positive, even if it means failing to mention the negative aspects in the job. While there is a real risk of setting unrealistic expectations about the organization and about the specific job, that's a risk managers have to take. As in dealing with any salesperson, it is the job applicant's responsibility to follow the dictum *caveat emptor*—let the buyer beware!

Why should managers emphasize the positive when discussing a job with a prospective candidate? They have no choice! First, there is a dwindling supply of qualified applicants; and second, this approach is necessary to meet the competition.

Recessions can cloud long-term trends. Although there appeared to be an ample supply of qualified job candidates for most employers in the early 1990s, this was due to an economic recession. The longer-term prognosis for the decade is a reduced supply of qualified applicants. In contrast to a generation ago, when there was a rising number of young workers entering the labor force, the 1990s are a different time. In the late 1960s, the Baby Boom turned into the Baby Bust. Since the early 1970s, birth rates have dropped significantly. For instance, an average of only 1.3 million people will enter the U.S. labor force every year throughout the 1990s compared to 3 million a year during the 1970s. This slower-growing population will create a labor shortage that is likely to last throughout the late-1990s; this shortage is compounded by a widening gap between the skills workers have and the skills employers need. In the 1990s labor market, managers must *sell* jobs to a limited pool of applicants. This means presenting the job and the organization in the most favorable light possible.

Another reason management is forced to emphasize the positive with job candidates is that that is what the competition is doing. Other employers also face a limited applicant pool. As a result, to get people to join their organizations, they are forced to put a positive "spin" on their descriptions of their organizations and the jobs they seek to fill. In this competitive environment, any employer who presents jobs realistically to applicants—that is, openly provides the negative aspects of a job along with the positive—risks losing most or all of his or her most desirable candidates.

Some of the facts in this argument are from L. S. Richman, "The Coming World Labor Shortage," *Fortune*, April 9, 1990, pp. 70–77.

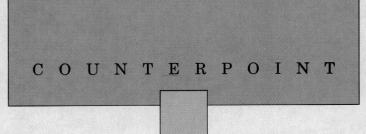

COUNTERPOINT

When Hiring Employees: Balance the Positive with the Negative

Regardless of the changing labor market, managers who treat the recruiting and hiring of candidates as if the applicants must be *sold* on the job and exposed to only positive aspects set themselves up to have a work force that is dissatisfied and prone to high turnover.

Every applicant acquires, during the selection process, a set of expectations about the organization and about the specific job he or she hopes to be offered. When the information an applicant receives is excessively inflated, a number of things happen that have potentially negative effects on the organization. First, mismatched applicants who would probably become dissatisfied with the job and soon quit are less likely to select themselves out of the search process. Second, the absence of negative information builds unrealistic expectations. If hired, the new employee is likely to become quickly disappointed. And inaccurate perceptions lead to premature resignations. Third, new hires are prone to become disillusioned and less committed to the organization when they come face-to-face with the negatives in the job. Employees who feel they were tricked or misled during the hiring process are unlikely to be satisfied workers.

To increase job satisfaction among employees and reduce turnover, applicants should be given a realistic job preview, with both unfavorable and favorable information, before an offer is made. For example, in addition to positive comments, the candidate might be told that there are limited opportunities to talk with co-workers during work hours, or that erratic fluctuations in work load create considerable stress on employees during rush periods.

Research indicates that applicants who have been given a realistic job preview hold lower and more realistic expectations about the job they'll be doing and are better prepared for coping with the job and its frustrating elements. The result is fewer unexpected resignations by new employees. In a tight labor market, retaining people is as critical as hiring them in the first place. Presenting only the positive aspects of a job to a recruit may initially entice him or her to join the organization, but it may be a marriage that both parties will quickly regret.

Information in this argument comes from J. A. Breaugh, "Realistic Job Previews: A Critical Appraisal and Future Research Directions," *Academy of Management Review*, October 1983, pp. 612–19; S. L. Premack and J. P. Wanous, "A Meta-Analysis of Realistic Job Preview Experiments," *Journal of Applied Psychology*, November 1985, pp. 706–20; B. M. Meglino, A. S. DeNisi, S. A. Youngblood, and K. J. Williams, "Effects of Realistic Job Previews: A Comparison Using an Enhancement and a Reduction Preview," *Journal of Applied Psychology*, May 1988, pp. 259–66; and R. J. Vandenberg and V. Scarpello, "The Matching Model: An Examination of the Processes Underlying Realistic Job Previews," *Journal of Applied Psychology*, February 1990, pp. 60–67.

Knowing Oneself

This exercise is intended to identify specific situations involving anxiety-laden associations that consciously or unconsciously affect an individual's self-perception. Examples of anxiety-laden associations are feelings of personal inadequacy; doubts about social relations with peers or members of the opposite sex; periods of loneliness or states of depression; feelings of anxiety with regard to past embarrassing situations (for example, with family or "losing face" before friends); anxieties about your body and its various functions, about your appearance, or perhaps about your future.

The purpose of this exercise is twofold: (1) To create an awareness of such associations within each exercise respondent. By confronting such difficulties and learning to replace anxiety-laden associations with substitute constructs, they can be "unlearned" or overcome. (2) To develop an understanding of how anxieties influence self-perception.

These descriptions will be used to demonstrate the commonality of such feelings and as a basis for future classroom discussion.

All respondents are *guaranteed* strict anonymity.

DIRECTIONS In your own words, describe *in detail* two anxiety-laden associations you experience or have experienced and describe how they affected your self-perception.

Source: A. G. Bedeian, "Knowing Oneself: An Exercise in Perceptual Accuracy," *Organizational Behavior Teaching Review*, Vol. XI, No. 4, 1986–87, pp. 137–39. With permission.

Decision–Making Style Questionnaire

Part I

Circle the response that comes closest to how you usually feel or act. There are no right or wrong responses to any of these items.

1. I am more careful about
   a. people's feelings
   b. their rights

2. I usually get on better with
   a. imaginative people
   b. realistic people

3. It is a higher compliment to be called
   a. a person of real feeling
   b. a consistently reasonable person

4. In doing something with other people, it appeals more to me
   a. to do it in the accepted way
   b. to invent a way of my own

5. I get more annoyed at
   a. fancy theories
   b. people who do not like theories

6. It is higher praise to call someone
   a. a person of vision
   b. a person of common sense

7. I more often let
   a. my heart rule my head
   b. my head rule my heart

8. I think it is a worse fault
   a. to show too much warmth
   b. to be unsympathetic

9. If I were a teacher, I would rather teach
   a. courses involving theory
   b. fact courses

Part II

Which word in the following pairs appeals to you more? Circle *a* or *b*.

10. a. Compassion
   b. Foresight

11. a. Justice
   b. Mercy

12. a. Production
   b. Design

13. a. Gentle
   b. Firm

14. a. Uncritical
   b. Critical

15. a. Literal
   b. Figurative

16. a. Imaginative
   b. Matter-of-fact

Turn to page 714 for scoring directions and key.

Source: Adapted from the Myers-Briggs Type indicator and a scale developed by D. Hellriegel, J. Slocum, and R.W. Woodman, *Organizational Behavior*, 3rd ed. (St. Paul, MN: West Publishing, 1983), pp. 127–41; and reproduced in J. M. Ivancevich and M. T. Matteson, *Organizational Behavior and Management*, 2nd ed. (Homewood, IL.: BPI/Irwin, 1990), pp. 538–39.

"I Don't Make Decisions"

I met Ted Kelly for the first time at a cocktail party. He was the plant manager at a large chemical refinery in town. About ten minutes into our conversation, I asked him about his leadership style.

Ted: "I don't make decisions at my plant."

Author: "You use democratic leadership?"

Ted: "No, I said I don't make decisions! My subordinates are paid to make decisions. No point in my doing their jobs."

I didn't really believe what I was hearing. I guess Ted sensed that, so he invited me to visit his plant. I asked him when I could come over. "Any time you like, except Mondays between 1 and 3 P.M."

The middle of the next week, I popped in on Ted unannounced. He had no secretary. He was lying on his sofa, half asleep. My arrival seemed to jar him awake. He offered me a seat.

Our conversation began by my inquiring exactly what he did every day. "You're looking at it. I sleep a lot. Oh yeah, I read the four or five memos I get from head office every week." I couldn't believe what I was hearing. Here was a fifty-year-old, obviously successful executive telling me he doesn't do anything. He could tell that I wasn't buying his story.

"If you don't believe what I'm saying, check with my subordinates," he told me. He said he had six department managers working for him. I asked him to choose one I could talk with.

"No, I can't do that. Remember, I don't make decisions. Here—these are the names and numbers of my department managers. You call them."

I did just that. I picked Peter Chandler, who headed up quality control. I dialed his number. I told him that I wanted to talk to him about his boss's leadership style. He said, "Come on over. I've got nothing to do anyway."

When I arrived at Pete's office, he was staring out the window. We sat down and he began to laugh. "I'll bet Ted's been telling you about how he doesn't make decisions." I concurred. "It's all true," he injected. "I've been here for almost three years and I've never seen him make a decision."

I couldn't figure out how this could be. "How many people do you have working here?" I asked.

Peter: "About two hundred."

Author: "How does this plant's operating efficiency stack up against the others?"

Peter: "Oh, we're number one out of the eighteen refineries. This is the oldest refinery in the company, too. Our equipment may be outdated, but we're as efficient as they come."

Author: "What does Ted Kelly do?"

Peter: "Beats me. He attends the staff meetings on Monday afternoon from 1 to 3, but other than that, I don't know."

Author: "I get it. He makes all the decisions at that once-a-week staff meeting?"

Peter: "No. Each department head tells what key decisions he has made last week. We then critique each other. Ted says nothing. The only thing he does at those meetings is listen and pass on any happenings up at headquarters."

I wanted to learn more, so I went back to Ted's office. I found him clipping his fingernails. What followed was a long conversation in which I learned the following facts:

The two-hour weekly staff meeting is presided over by one of the department heads. They choose among themselves who will be their leader. It's a permanent position. Any problem that has come up during the week, if it can't be handled by a manager, will first be considered by several of the managers together. Only if the problem is still unresolved will it be taken to the leader. All issues are resolved at that level. They are never taken to Ted Kelly's level.

The performance record at Kelly's plant is well known in the company. Three of the last four new plant managers have come out of Kelly's plant. When recommending candidates for a plant management vacancy, Ted always selects the department head who presides over the staff meetings, so there is a great deal of competition to lead the meetings. Additionally, because of Kelly's plant record for breeding management talent, whenever there is a vacancy for a department manager at Kelly's plant, the best people in the company apply for it.

Questions

1. Why does Ted Kelly's decision-making style work?
2. Is Ted Kelly abrogating his decision-making responsibilities? Explain.
3. Would you like to work for Ted Kelly? Why?
4. Would you want Ted Kelly working for you? Why?

Source: Based on A. E. Carlisle, "MacGregor," *Organizational Dynamics*, Summer 1976, pp. 50–62.

FOR FURTHER READING

BAZERMAN, M. H., *Judgment in Managerial Decision Making*, 2nd ed. (New York: John Wiley & Sons, 1990). Reviews the judgmental aspects of decision making, including biases in the human thinking process.

DUGAN, K. W., "Ability and Effort Attributions: Do They Affect How Managers Communicate Performance Feedback Information?", *Academy of Management Journal*, March 1989, pp. 87–114. When providing feedback on poor performance, managers follow a script. Managers' initial attributions of effort or ability influence both how they define their roles within the script and the flow of interaction.

FALKENBERG, L., "Improving the Accuracy of Stereotypes Within the Workplace," *Journal of Management*, March 1990, pp. 107–18. Describes a model of stereotyping and identifies the factors involved in developing more accurate stereotypes.

JANIS, I. L., *Crucial Decisions: Leadership in Policymaking and Crisis Management* (New York: Free Press, 1989). This book identifies common problems in making decisions and presents a model of vigilant problem solving that should result in higher-quality decision processes.

KAUFMAN, B. E., "A New Theory of Satisficing," *The Journal of Behavioral Economics*, Spring 1990, pp. 35–51. Presents a new satisficing model that integrates psychological concepts and processes into economic theory.

LANGLEY, A., "In Search of Rationality: The Purposes Behind the Use of Formal Analysis in Organizations," *Administrative Science Quarterly*, December 1989, pp. 598–631. Describes the results of a study that examines how formal analysis is actually used in practice in three different organizations.

NOTES

[1] D. C. McClelland and J. W. Atkinson, "The Projective Expression of Needs: The Effect of Different Intensities of the Hunger Drive on Perception," Journal of Psychology, Vol. 25 (1948), pp. 205–22.

[2] H. H. Kelley, "Attribution in Social Interaction," in E. Jones et al. (eds.), *Attribution: Perceiving the Causes of Behavior* (Morristown, NJ: General Learning Press, 1972).

[3] See L. Ross, "The Intuitive Psychologist and His Shortcomings," in L. Berkowitz (ed.), *Advances in Experimental Social Psychology*, Vol. 10 (Orlando, FL.: Academic Press, 1977), pp. 174–220; and A. G. Miller and T. Lawson, "The Effect of an Informational Option on the Fundamental Attribution Error," *Personality and Social Psychology Bulletin*, June 1989, pp. 194–204.

[4] D. C. Dearborn and H. A. Simon, "Selective Perception: A Note on the Departmental Identification of Executives," *Sociometry*, June 1958, pp. 140–44. Some of the conclusions in this classic study have recently been challenged in J. P. Walsh, "Selectivity and Selective Perception: An Investigation of Managers' Belief Structures and Information Processing," *Academy of Management Journal*, December 1988, pp. 873–96.

[5] S. E. Asch, "Forming Impressions of Personality," *Journal of Abnormal and Social Psychology*, July 1946, pp. 258–90.

[6] J. S. Bruner and R. Tagiuri, "The Perception of People," in E. Lindzey (ed.), *Handbook of Social Psychology* (Reading, MA: Addison-Wesley, 1954), p. 641.

[7] This box is based on W. Kiechel III, "How to Manage Older Workers," *Fortune*, November 15, 1990, pp. 183–86; and S. B. Garland, "How to Keep Women Managers on the Corporate Ladder," *Business Week*, September 2, 1991, p. 64.

[8] See, for example, E. C. Webster, *Decision Making in the Employment Interview* (Montreal: McGill University, Industrial Relations Center, 1964).

[9] D. Kipnis, *The Powerholders* (Chicago: University of Chicago Press, 1976).

[10] For a comprehensive review of the optimizing model and its assumptions, see E. F. Harrison, *The Managerial Decision-Making Process*, 2nd ed. (Boston: Houghton Mifflin, 1981), pp. 53–57 and 81–93.

[11] F. R. David, "An Empirical Study of Codes of Ethics: A Strategic Perspective," paper presented at the 48th Annual Academy of Management Conference, Anaheim, CA, August 1988.

[12] L. L. Nash, "Ethics Without the Sermon," *Harvard Business Review*, November-December 1981, p. 81.

[13]D. L. Rados, "Selection and Evaluation of Alternatives in Repetitive Decision Making," *Administrative Science Quarterly*, June 1972, pp. 196–206.

[14]See H. A. Simon, *Administrative Behavior*, 3rd ed. (New York: Free Press, 1976); and J. Forester, "Bounded Rationality and the Politics of Muddling Through," *Public Administration Review*, January-February 1984, pp. 23–31.

[15]See P. O. Soelberg, "Unprogrammed Decision Making," *Industrial Management Review*, Spring 1967, pp. 19–29; and D. J. Power and R. J. Aldag, "Soelberg's Job Search and Choice Model: A Clarification, Review, and Critique," *Academy of Management Review*, January 1985, pp. 48–58.

[16]Soelberg, "Unprogrammed Decision Making."

[17]W. H. Agor, "The Logic of Intuition: How Top Executives Make Important Decisions," *Organizational Dynamics*, Winter 1986, p. 5; W. H. Agor (ed.), *Intuition in Organizations* (Newbury Park, CA: Sage Publications, 1989); and O. Behling and N. L. Eckel, "Making Sense Out of Intuition," *Academy of Management Executive*, February 1991, pp. 46–47.

[18]Behling and Eckel, "Making Sense Out of Intuition," pp. 46–54.

[19]As described in H. A. Simon, "Making Management Decisions: The Role of Intuition and Emotion," *Academy of Management Executive*, February 1987, pp. 59–60.

[20]Agor, "The Logic of Intuition," p. 9.

[21]Ibid., pp. 12–13.

[22]Agor, "The Logic of Intuition," p. 15.

[23]Some of the ideas in this box are based on N. J. Adler, *International Dimensions of Organizational Behavior*, 2nd ed. (Boston: Kent Publishing, 1991), pp. 160–68.

[24]E. C. Mayfield in N. Schmitt's "Social and Situational Determinants of Interview Decisions: Implications for Employment Interviews," *Personnel Psychology*, Spring 1976, p. 81.

[25]G. P. Huber, *Managerial Decision Making* (Glenview, IL: Scott, Foresman, 1980), p. 215.

VALUES, ATTITUDES, AND JOB SATISFACTION

LEARNING OBJECTIVES

After studying this chapter, you should be able to:

1. Explain the source of an individual's value system

2. List the dominant values in today's work force

3. Describe the three primary job-related attitudes

4. Summarize the relationship between attitudes and behavior

5. Identify the role consistency plays in attitudes

6. Clarify how individuals reconcile inconsistencies

7. Explain what determines job satisfaction

8. State the relationship between job satisfaction and behavior

9. Describe the current level of job satisfaction among Americans in the workplace

10. Identify four employee responses to dissatisfaction

When you prevent me from doing anything I want to do, that is persecution; but when I prevent you from doing anything you want to do, that is law, order and morals.

G. B. SHAW

*I*t was 1983, and Keith Dunn opened his first McGuffey's restaurant in Asheville, North Carolina.[1] He started the business out of frustration over all the abuse *he* had suffered personally while working at big restaurant chains such as TGI Friday's and Bennigan's. His restaurant would be different. He was going to be authentically employee-oriented.

Dunn's Asheville restaurant was an immediate success. He soon opened another in a nearby city. It too started fast. Faithful to his original intentions, Dunn sought to make his employees feel appreciated. He gave them a free drink and a meal at the end of every shift, let them give away appetizers and desserts, and provided them with health and dental insurance plus a week of paid vacation each year.

Dunn was convinced that he had created a people-oriented business and a highly satisfied group of employees. He was aware that sales had plateaued and then declined a bit at each of his restaurants a few months after each opened, but he had all kinds of external rationalizations to explain this occurrence.

In 1986, Dunn was feeling a bit wary. He needed a shot of confidence. He knew how his 230 employees felt about him, but he wanted to hear it from them. That's why he decided to send them an attitude survey. He wanted to see their satisfaction in writing. One day he gathered up the anonymous questionnaires, sat down in his small office with one of his partners by his side, and began to open the envelopes. His eyes zoomed directly to the question where employees were asked to rate the owners' performance on a scale of one to ten. He couldn't believe what he was reading: "Zero," "Zero," "Two," "Zero," "One"…The written comments, too, said similar things: "Your nose is in the air"; "You never say hello"; "You're never around." How could his employees be so ungrateful, Dunn wondered. Why weren't they as thrilled as he was with the chain's growth and expansion? Out of curiosity, Dunn called in an assistant and asked him a favor. Can you calculate our annual turnover rate? Came the reply: "220 percent, sir."

Dunn realized that he had lost sight of the original reason why he had started McGuffey's. He had gotten more involved with impressing his bankers than in listening to his employees. He didn't know his employees' real needs and concerns. They felt ignored, resentful, and abandoned. In response, the restrooms weren't getting scrubbed as thoroughly, the food wasn't arriving quite piping hot, the servers weren't smiling as often. And sales were declining!

Dunn got the message. He began to listen to his employees and make the changes *they* felt were important. For example, employees now participate much more in decision making. They're helping to design new restaurants as well as their compensation programs. Today, McGuffey's is again a fun place to work at. Turnover is below sixty percent—roughly one-quarter the industry average. Sales and profits are at record levels. And the employees don't hate Keith Dunn anymore. ■

*P*eople at work have opinions, and you don't have to undertake a formal attitude survey to get at them. They're voiced all the time: "Managers should never socialize with their employees." "A little conflict in this place is good—it keeps everyone on their toes." "I don't think there's any justification for the president of this company making a million dollars a year." "To me, the best boss is one who just leaves me alone!"

Importantly, these opinions—which we call values and attitudes—are not meaningless. As Keith Dunn found out, they are often related to behavior. In this chapter, we will discuss values and attitudes and then look closely at the topic of job satisfaction.

VALUES

Is capital punishment right or wrong? How about racial quotas in hiring—are they right or wrong? If a person likes power, is that good or bad? The answers to these questions are value laden. Some might argue, for example, that capital punishment is right because it is an appropriate retribution for crimes like murder and treason. However, others might argue, just as strongly, that no government has the right to take anyone's life.

Values Basic convictions that a specific mode of conduct or end-state of existence is personally or socially preferable to an opposite or converse mode of conduct or end-state of existence.

Values represent basic convictions that "a specific mode of conduct or end-state of existence is personally or socially preferable to an opposite or converse mode of conduct or end-state of existence."[2] They contain a judgmental element in that they carry an individual's ideas as to what is right, good, or desirable. Values have both content and intensity attributes. The content attribute says that a mode of conduct or end-state of existence is *important*. The intensity attribute specifies *how important* it is. When we rank an individual's values in terms of their intensity, we obtain that person's **value system.** All of us have a hierarchy of values that forms our value system. This system is identified by the relative importance we assign to such values as freedom, pleasure, self-respect, honesty, obedience, and equality.

Value System A ranking of individual values according to their relative importance.

Importance of Values

Values are important to the study of organizational behavior because they lay the foundation for the understanding of attitudes and motivation and because they influence our perceptions. Individuals enter an organization with preconceived notions of what "ought" and what "ought not" to be. Of course, these notions are not value-free. On the contrary, they contain interpretations of right and wrong. Further, they imply that certain behaviors or outcomes are preferred over others. As a result, values cloud objectivity and rationality.

Values generally influence attitudes and behavior.[3] Suppose that you enter an organization with the view that allocating pay on the basis of performance is right, whereas allocating pay on the basis of seniority is wrong or inferior. How are you going to react if you find that the organization you have just joined rewards seniority and not performance? You're likely to be disappointed—and this can lead to job dissatisfaction and the decision not to exert a high level of effort since "it's probably not going to lead to more money, anyway." Would your attitudes and behavior be different if your values aligned with the organization's pay policies? Most likely.

Sources of Our Value Systems

When we were children, why did many of our mothers tell us "you should always clean your dinner plate"? Why is it that, at least historically in North America, achievement has been considered good and being lazy has been considered bad? The answer is that, in our culture, certain values have developed over time and are continuously reinforced. Achievement, peace, cooperation, equity, and democracy are societal values that are considered desirable in North America. These values are not fixed, but when they change, they do so very slowly.

The values we hold are essentially established in our early years—from parents, teachers, friends, and others. Your early ideas of what is right and wrong were probably formulated from the views expressed by your parents. Think back to your early views on such topics as education, sex, and politics. For the most part, they were the same as those expressed by your parents. As you grew up, and were exposed to other value systems, you may have altered a number of your values. For example, in high school, if you desired to be a member of a social club whose values included the conviction that "every person should carry a gun," there is a good probability that you changed your value system to align with that of the members of the club, even if it meant rejecting your parents' value that "only gang members carry guns, and gang members are bad."

Interestingly, values are relatively stable and enduring.[4] This has been explained as a result of the way in which they are originally learned.[5] As children, we are told that a certain behavior or outcome is *always* desirable or *always* undesirable. There are no gray areas. You were told, for example, that you should be honest and responsible. You were never taught to be just a little bit honest or a little bit responsible. It is this absolute or "black-or-white" learning of values that more or less assures their stability and endurance.

The process of questioning our values, of course, may result in a change. We may decide that these underlying convictions are no longer acceptable. More often, our questioning merely acts to reinforce those values we hold.

TABLE 6–1   Ranking of Values by Importance Among Three Groups

Ministers	Purchasing Executives	Scientists in Industry
1. Religious	1. Economic	1. Theoretical
2. Social	2. Theoretical	2. Political
3. Aesthetic	3. Political	3. Economic
4. Political	4. Religious	4. Aesthetic
5. Theoretical	5. Aesthetic	5. Religious
6. Economic	6. Social	6. Social

Source: R. Tagiuri, "Purchasing Executive: General Manager or Specialist?" *Journal of Purchasing,* August 1967, pp. 16–21.

Types of Values

Can we classify values? The answer is: Yes! In this section, we'll review three approaches to developing value typologies.

ALLPORT AND ASSOCIATES   One of the earliest efforts to categorize values was made by Allport and his associates.[6] They identified six types of values:

1. *Theoretical:* Places high importance on the discovery of truth through a critical and rational approach
2. *Economic:* Emphasizes the useful and practical
3. *Aesthetic:* Places the highest value on form and harmony
4. *Social:* Assigns the highest value to the love of people
5. *Political:* Places emphasis on acquisition of power and influence
6. *Religious:* Is concerned with the unity of experience and understanding of the cosmos as a whole

Allport and his associates developed a questionnaire that described a number of different situations and asked respondents to preference-rank a fixed set of answers. Based on their replies, the researchers were able to rank respondents in terms of the importance they gave to each of the six types of values and to identify a value system for each respondent.

Using this approach, it was found that people in different occupations placed different importance on the six value types. For instance, Table 6–1 shows responses from ministers, purchasing agents, and industrial scientists. As you might expect, religious leaders consider religious values most important and economic values least important. Economic values, on the other hand, are of highest importance to purchasing executives.

ROKEACH VALUE SURVEY   Milton Rokeach created the Rokeach Value Survey (RVS).[7] The RVS consists of two sets of values, with each set containing eighteen individual value items. One set, called **terminal values**, refers to desirable *end-states* of existence. These are the goals that a person would like to achieve during his or her lifetime. The other set, called **instrumental values**, refers to preferable *modes of behavior*, or means of achieving the terminal values. Table 6–2 gives common examples for each of these sets.

Several studies confirm that the RVS values vary among groups.[8] As with Allport's findings, people in the same occupations or categories (e.g., corporate managers, union members, parents, students) tend to hold similar values. For instance, one study comparing corporate executives, members of the steelworkers' union, and members of a community activist group found a

Terminal Values   Desirable end-states of existence; the goals that a person would like to achieve during his or her lifetime.

Instrumental Values   Preferable modes of behavior or means of achieving one's terminal values.

TABLE 6–2   Terminal and Instrumental Values in Rokeach Value Survey

Terminal Values	Instrumental Values
A comfortable life (a prosperous life)	Ambitious (hard-working, aspiring)
An exciting life (a stimulating, active life)	Broadminded (open–minded)
A sense of accomplishment (lasting contribution)	Capable (competent, effective)
A world at peace (free of war and conflict)	Cheerful (lighthearted, joyful)
A world of beauty (beauty of nature and the arts)	Clean (neat, tidy)
Equality (brotherhood, equal opportunity for all)	Courageous (standing up for your beliefs)
Family security (taking care of loved ones)	Forgiving (willing to pardon others)
Freedom (independence, free choice)	Helpful (working for the welfare of others)
Happiness (contentedness)	Honest (sincere, truthful)
Inner harmony (freedom from inner conflict)	Imaginative (daring, creative)
Mature love (sexual and spiritual intimacy)	Independent (self-reliant, self-sufficient)
National security (protection from attack)	Intellectual (intelligent, reflective)
Pleasure (an enjoyable, leisurely life)	Logical (consistent, rational)
Salvation (saved, eternal life)	Loving (affectionate, tender)
Self-respect (self-esteem)	Obedient (dutiful, respectful)
Social recognition (respect, admiration)	Polite (courteous, well-mannered)
True friendship (close companionship)	Responsible (dependable, reliable)
Wisdom (a mature understanding of life)	Self-controlled (restrained, self-disciplined)

Source: M. Rokeach, *The Nature of Human Values* (New York: The Free Press, 1973).

good deal of overlap among the three groups,[9] but also some very significant differences. (See Table 6–3.) The activists had value preferences that were quite different from those of the other two groups. They ranked equality as their most important terminal value; executives and union members ranked this value 14 and 13, respectively. Activists ranked "helpful" as their second-highest instrumental value. The other two groups both ranked it 14. These differences are important, since executives, union members, and activists all have a vested interest in what corporations do. "When corporations and critical stakeholder groups such as these [other] two come together in negotiations or contend with one another over economic and social policies, they are likely to begin with these built-in differences in personal value preferences... Reaching agreement on any specific issue or policy where these personal values are importantly implicated might prove to be quite difficult."[10]

CONTEMPORARY WORK COHORTS   Your author has integrated a number of recent analyses of work values into a four-stage model that attempts to capture the unique values of different cohorts or generations in the U.S. work force.[11] (No assumption is made that this framework would universally apply

TABLE 6–3   Mean Value Rankings of Executives, Union Members, and Activists (Top 5 Only)

Executives		Union Members		Activists	
Terminal	Instrumental	Terminal	Instrumental	Terminal	Instrumental
1. Self-respect	1. Honest	1. Family security	1. Responsible	1. Equality	1. Honest
2. Family security	2. Responsible	2. Freedom	2. Honest	2. A world at peace	2. Helpful
3. Freedom	3. Capable	3. Happiness	3. Courageous	3. Family security	3. Courageous
4. A sense of accomplishment	4. Ambitious	4. Self-respect	4. Independent	4. Self-respect	4. Responsible
5. Happiness	5. Independent	5. Mature love	5. Capable	5. Freedom	5. Capable

Source: Based on W. C. Frederick and J. Weber, "The Values of Corporate Managers and Their Critics: An Empirical Description and Normative Implications," in W. C. Frederick and L. E. Preston (eds.), *Business Ethics: Research Issues and Empirical Studies* (Greenwich, CT: JAI Press, 1990), pp. 123-44.

TABLE 6–4   Dominant Values in Today's Work Force

	Stage	Entered the Work Force	Approximate Current Age	Dominant Work Values
I.	Protestant work ethic	1940s –1950s	50–70	Hard work, conservative; loyalty to the organization
II.	Existential	1960s –Mid-1970s	40–50	Quality of life, nonconforming, seeks autonomy; loyalty to self
III.	Pragmatic	Mid-1970s–Mid-1980s	30–40	Success, achievement, ambition, hard work; loyalty to career
IV.	Symmetry	Mid-1980s–Present	Under 30	Flexibility, job satisfaction, leisure time; loyalty to relationships

across all cultures.)[12] Table 6–4 proposes that employees can be segmented by the era in which they entered the work force. Because most people start work between the ages of eighteen and twenty-three, the eras also correlate closely with the chronological age of employees.

Workers who grew up during the Great Depression and World War II entered the work force in the 1940s and 1950s believing in the Protestant work ethic. Once hired, they tended to be loyal to their employer. In terms of the terminal values on the RVS, these employees are likely to place the greatest importance on a comfortable life and family security.

Employees who entered the work force during the 1960s through the mid-1970s brought with them a large measure of the "hippie ethic" and existential philosophy. They are more concerned with the quality of their lives than with the amount of money and possessions they can accumulate. Their desire for autonomy has directed their loyalty toward themselves rather than toward the organization that employs them. In terms of the RVS, freedom and equality rate high.

Work values can be seen in characters from past television shows. Ward Cleaver, the father on "Leave it to Beaver," represented the era when Protestant Work Ethics' values dominated. The elder Keatons from "Family Ties" espoused existential values, while their son, Alex, typified pragmatism. Although the show's name doesn't fit, "Thirtysomething's" Michael and Hope reflected the symmetry values of today's younger worker.   Left, Photofest; center, Photofest; right, Neal Peters Collection

Values, Loyalty, and Ethical Behavior

Did a decline in business ethics set in sometime in the late 1970s? The issue is debatable.[13] Nevertheless, a lot of people think so. If there has been a decline in ethical standards, perhaps we should look to our four-stage model of work cohort values (see Table 6–4) for a possible explanation.

Through the mid-1970s, the managerial ranks were dominated by Protestant-work-ethic-types (Stage I) whose loyalties were to their employer. When faced with ethical dilemmas, their decisions were made in terms of what was best for their organization. Beginning in the mid-to-late 1970s, individuals with existential values began to rise into the upper levels of management. They were soon followed by pragmatic-types. By the late 1980s, a large portion of middle and top management positions in business organizations were held by people from Stages II and III.

The loyalty of existentials and pragmatics are to self and careers, respectively. Their focus is inward and their primary concern is with "looking out for No. 1." Such self-centered values would be consistent with a decline in ethical standards. Could this help explain the alleged decline in business ethics beginning in the late 1970s?

The potential good news in this analysis is that recent entrants to the work force, and tomorrow's managers, appear to be less self-centered. Since their loyalty is to relationships, they are more likely to consider the ethical implications of their actions on others around them. The result? We might look forward to an uplifting of ethical standards in business over the next decade or two merely as a result of changing values within the managerial ranks.

Individuals who entered the work force from the mid-1970s through the mid-1980s reflect the society's return to more traditional values, but with far greater emphasis on achievement and material success. Born towards the end of the Baby Boom period, these workers are pragmatists who believe that ends can justify means. They see the organizations that employ them merely as vehicles for their careers. Terminal values like a sense of accomplishment and social recognition rank high with them.

Our final category encompasses the "twentysomething" generation. They value flexibility, life options, and the achievement of job satisfaction. Family and relationships are very important to this cohort. Money is important as an indicator of career performance, but they are willing to trade off salary increases, titles, security, and promotions for increased leisure time and expanded lifestyle options. In search of symmetry in their lives, these more recent entrants into the work force are less willing to make personal sacrifices for the sake of their employer than previous generations were. On the RVS, they rate high on true friendship, happiness, and pleasure.

An understanding that individuals' values differ but tend to reflect the societal values of the period in which they grew up can be a valuable aid in explaining and predicting behavior. Employees in their thirties and fifties, for instance, are more likely to be conservative and accepting of authority than their existential co-workers in their forties. And workers under thirty are more likely than the other groups to balk at having to work weekends and more prone to leave a job in mid-career to pursue another that provides more leisure time.

ATTITUDES

Attitudes   Evaluative statements or judgments concerning objects, people, or events.

Attitudes are evaluative statements—either favorable or unfavorable—concerning objects, people, or events. They reflect how one feels about something. When I say "I like my job," I am expressing my attitude about work.

Attitudes are not the same as values, but the two are interrelated. You can see this by looking at the three components of an attitude: cognition, affect, and behavior.[14]

Cognitive Component   The opinion or belief segment of an attitude.

Affective Component   The emotional or feeling segment of an attitude.

Behavioral Component   An intention to behave in a certain way toward someone or something.

The belief that "discrimination is wrong" is a value statement. Such an opinion is the **cognitive component** of an attitude. It sets the stage for the more critical part of an attitude—its **affective component.** Affect is the emotional or feeling segment of an attitude and is reflected in the statement "I don't like Jon because he discriminates against minorities." Finally, and we'll discuss this issue at considerable length later in this section, affect can lead to behavioral outcomes. The **behavioral component** of an attitude refers to an intention to behave in a certain way toward someone or something. So, to continue our example, I might choose to avoid Jon because of my feeling about him.

Viewing attitudes as made up of three components—cognition, affect, and behavior—is helpful toward understanding their complexity and the potential relationship between attitudes and behavior. But for clarity's sake, keep in mind that the term *attitude* essentially refers to the affect part of the three components.

Sources of Attitudes

Attitudes, like values, are acquired from parents, teachers, and peer group members. In our early years, we begin modeling our attitudes after those we admire, respect, or maybe even fear. We observe the way family and friends behave, and we shape our attitudes and behavior to align with theirs. People imitate the attitudes of popular individuals or those they admire and respect. If the "right thing" is to favor eating at McDonald's, you are likely to hold that attitude.

In contrast to values, your attitudes are less stable. Advertising messages, for example, attempt to alter your attitudes toward a certain product or service: If the people at Ford can get you to hold a favorable feeling toward their cars, that attitude may lead to a desirable behavior (for them)—your purchase of a Ford product.

In organizations, attitudes are important because they affect job behavior. If workers believe, for example, that supervisors, auditors, bosses, and time and motion engineers are all in conspiracy to make employees work harder for the same or less money, then it makes sense to try to understand how these attitudes were formed, their relationship to actual job behavior, and how they can be made more favorable.

Types of Attitudes

A person can have thousands of attitudes, but OB focuses our attention on a very limited number of job-related attitudes. These job-related attitudes tap positive or negative evaluations that employees hold about aspects of their work environment. Most of the research in OB has been concerned with three attitudes: job satisfaction, job involvement, and organizational commitment.[15]

JOB SATISFACTION   The term *job satisfaction* refers to an individual's general attitude toward his or her job. A person with a high level of job satisfaction holds positive attitudes toward the job, while a person who is dissatisfied with his or her job holds negative attitudes about the job. When people speak of employee attitudes, more often than not they mean job satisfaction. In fact, the two are frequently used interchangeably. Because of the high importance OB researchers have given to job satisfaction, we'll review this attitude in considerable detail later in this chapter.

Job Involvement The degree to which a person identifies with his or her job, actively participates in it, and considers his or her performance important to self-worth.

JOB INVOLVEMENT The term **job involvement** is a more recent addition to the OB literature.[16] While there isn't complete agreement over what the term means, a workable definition states that job involvement measures the degree to which a person identifies psychologically with his or her job and considers his or her perceived performance level important to self-worth.[17] Employees with a high level of job involvement strongly identify with and really care about the kind of work they do.

High levels of job involvement have been found to be related to fewer absences and lower resignation rates.[18] However, it seems to more consistently predict turnover than absenteeism, accounting for as much as sixteen percent of the variance in the former.[19]

Organizational Commitment An individual's orientation toward the organization in terms of loyalty, identification, and involvement.

ORGANIZATIONAL COMMITMENT The third job attitude we shall discuss is **organizational commitment.** It's defined as a state in which an employee identifies with a particular organization and its goals, and wishes to maintain membership in the organization.[20] So, high *job involvement* means identifying with one's specific job, while high *organizational commitment* means identifying with one's employing organization.

As with job involvement, the research evidence demonstrates negative relationships between organizational commitment and both absenteeism and turnover.[21] In fact, studies demonstrate that an individual's level of organizational commitment is a better indicator of turnover than the far more frequently used job satisfaction predictor, explaining as much as thirty-four percent of the variance.[22] Organizational commitment is probably a better predictor because it is a more global and enduring response to the organization as a whole than is job satisfaction.[23] An employee may be dissatisfied with his or her particular job and consider it a temporary condition, yet not be dissatisfied with the organization as a whole. But when dissatisfaction spreads to the organization itself, individuals are more likely to consider resigning.

Attitudes and Consistency

Did you ever notice how people change what they say so it doesn't contradict what they do? Perhaps a friend of yours has consistently argued that American cars are poorly built and that he'd never own anything but a foreign import. But his dad gives him a late-model American-made car, and suddenly they're not so bad. Or, when going through sorority rush, a new freshman believes that sororities are good and that pledging a sorority is important. If she fails to make a sorority, however, she may say, "I recognized that sorority life isn't all it's cracked up to be, anyway!"

Research has generally concluded that people seek consistency among their attitudes and between their attitudes and their behavior. This means that individuals seek to reconcile divergent attitudes and align their attitudes and behavior so they appear rational and consistent. When there is an inconsistency, forces are initiated to return the individual to an equilibrium state where attitudes and behavior are again consistent. This can be done by altering either the attitudes or the behavior or by developing a rationalization for the discrepancy.

For example, a recruiter for the ABC Company, whose job it is to visit college campuses, identify qualified job candidates, and sell them on the advantages of ABC as a place to work, would be in conflict if he personally believes the ABC Company has poor working conditions and few opportunities for new college graduates. This recruiter could, over time, find his attitudes toward the ABC Company becoming more positive. He may, in effect, brainwash himself by continually articulating the merits of working for ABC. Another alternative would be for the recruiter to become overtly negative about ABC and the opportunities within the firm for prospective candidates. The original enthusiasm that the recruiter may have shown would dwindle, probably to be replaced by open cynicism toward the company. Finally, the recruiter might acknowledge that ABC is an undesirable place to work, but think that, as a professional recruiter, his obligation is to present the positive side of working for the company. He might further rationalize that no place is perfect to work at; therefore, his job is not to present both sides of the issue, but rather to present a rosy picture of the company.

Cognitive Dissonance Theory

Can we additionally assume from this consistency principle that an individual's behavior can always be predicted if we know his or her attitude on a subject? If Mr. Jones views the company's pay level as too low, will a substantial increase in his pay change his behavior; that is, make him work harder? The answer to this question is, unfortunately, more complex than merely a "Yes" or "No."

Cognitive Dissonance Any incompatibility between two or more attitudes or between behavior and attitudes.

Leon Festinger, in the late 1950s, proposed the theory of **cognitive dissonance**.[24] This theory sought to explain the linkage between attitudes and behavior. Dissonance means an inconsistency. Cognitive dissonance refers to any incompatibility that an individual might perceive between two or more of his or her attitudes, or between his or her behavior and attitudes. Festinger argued that any form of inconsistency is uncomfortable and that individuals will attempt to reduce the dissonance and, hence, the discomfort. Therefore, individuals will seek a stable state where there is a minimum of dissonance.

Of course, no individual can completely avoid dissonance. You know that cheating on your income tax is wrong, but you "fudge" the numbers a bit every year, and hope you're not audited. Or you tell your children to brush after every meal, but *you* don't. So how do people cope? Festinger would propose that the desire to reduce dissonance would be determined by the importance of the elements creating the dissonance, the degree of influence the individual believes he or she has over the elements, and the rewards that may be involved in dissonance.

If the elements creating the dissonance are relatively unimportant, the pressure to correct this imbalance will be low. However, say that a corporate manager—Mrs. Smith—believes strongly that no company should pollute the air or water. Unfortunately, Mrs. Smith, because of the requirements of her job, is placed in the position of having to make decisions that would trade off her company's profitability against her attitudes on pollution. She knows that dumping the company's sewage into the local river (which we shall assume is legal) is in the best economic interest of her firm. What will she do? Clearly, Mrs. Smith is experiencing a high degree of cognitive dissonance. Because of the importance of the elements in this example, we cannot expect Mrs. Smith to ignore the inconsistency. There are several paths that she can follow to deal with her dilemma. She can change her behavior (stop polluting the river). Or she can reduce dissonance by concluding that the dis-

Employees can cope with more dissonance at work than they can at home because organizations give them pay, titles, authority, impressive offices, attractive benefit plans, and similar rewards. These act to reduce the tension inherent in the dissonance.   Rob Kinmonth

sonant behavior is not so important after all ("I've got to make a living, and in my role as a corporate decision maker, I often have to place the good of my company above that of the environment or society"). A third alternative would be for Mrs. Smith to change her attitude ("There is nothing wrong in polluting the river"). Still another choice would be to seek out more consonant elements to outweigh the dissonant ones ("The benefits to society from our manufacturing our products more than offset the cost to society of the resulting water pollution").

The degree of influence that individuals believe they have over the elements will have an impact on how they will react to the dissonance. If they perceive the dissonance to be an uncontrollable result—something over which they have no choice—they are less likely to be receptive to attitude change. If, for example, the dissonance-producing behavior is required as a result of the boss's directive, the pressure to reduce dissonance would be less than if the behavior was performed voluntarily. While dissonance exists, it can be rationalized and justified.

Rewards also influence the degree to which individuals are motivated to reduce dissonance. High rewards accompanying high dissonance tends to reduce the tension inherent in the dissonance. The rewards act to reduce dissonance by increasing the consistency side of the individual's balance sheet.

These moderating factors suggest that just because individuals experience dissonance they will not necessarily move directly toward consistency; that is, toward reduction of this dissonance. If the issues underlying the dissonance are of minimal importance, if an individual perceives that the dissonance is externally imposed and is substantially uncontrollable by him or her, or if rewards are significant enough to offset the dissonance, the individual will not be under great tension to reduce the dissonance.

When Consistency Is Dysfunctional

Cognitive dissonance theory argues that an individual's motivation to change his or her attitudes is based on the desire to appear consistent to himself or herself. Put in terms of the optimizing model presented in the previous chapter, individuals seek to appear rational.

But this desire for consistency isn't always a positive attribute in decision makers because consistency can lead to inflexibility. If conditions change so that previous solutions no longer work, but the decision maker digs in his or her heels and refuses to acknowledge this fact, then this search for consistency can be counterproductive for the organization.

The desire to reduce dissonance has been shown to be dysfunctional when it leads to an *escalation of commitment;* that is, an increased commitment to a previous decision in spite of negative information. This is the proverbial situation where one "throws good money after bad."

It has been well documented that individuals escalate commitment to a failing course of action when they view themselves as responsible for the failure.[25] Congruent with cognitive dissonance theory, they want to demonstrate that the initial decision was not wrong.

Maybe the most frequently cited example of the escalation of commitment phenomenon was President Lyndon Johnson's decisions regarding the Vietnam War. Despite continued information that bombing North Vietnam was not bringing the war any closer to conclusion, his solution was to increase the tonnage of bombs dropped. Of course, escalation of commitment doesn't apply only to presidential decisions. Many business firms have suffered large losses because managers were determined to prove their original decisions were right by continuing to commit resources to what was a lost cause from the beginning.

What are the organizational implications of the theory of cognitive dissonance? It can help to predict the propensity to engage in attitude and behavioral change. If individuals are required, for example, by the demands of their job to say or do things that contradict their personal attitude, they will tend to modify their attitude in order to make it compatible with the cognition of what they have said or done. Additionally, the greater the dissonance—after it has been moderated by importance, choice, and reward factors—the greater the pressures to reduce it.

Measuring the A–B Relationship

We have maintained throughout this chapter that attitudes affect behavior. The early research work on attitudes assumed that they were causally related to behavior; that is, the attitudes that people hold determine what they do. Common sense, too, suggests a relationship. Is it not logical that people watch television programs that they say they like or that employees try to avoid assignments they find distasteful?

However, in the late 1960s, this assumed relationship between attitudes and behavior (A–B) was challenged by a review of the research.[26] Based on an evaluation of a number of studies that investigated the A–B relationship, the reviewer concluded that attitudes were unrelated to behavior or, at best, only slightly related.[27] More recent research has demonstrated that the A–B relationship can be improved by taking moderating contingency variables into consideration.

MODERATING VARIABLES   One thing that improves our chances of finding significant A–B relationships is the use of both specific attitudes and specific behaviors.[28] It is one thing to talk about a person's attitude toward "preserving the environment" and another to speak of his or her attitude toward recycling. The more specific the attitude we are measuring, and the more specific we are in identifying a related behavior, the greater the probability that we can show a relationship between A and B. If you ask people today whether they are concerned about preserving the environment, most will probably say "Yes." That doesn't mean, however, that they separate out recyclable items from their garbage. The correlation between a question that asks about concern-for-protecting-the-environment and recycling may be only +.20 or so. But as you make the question more specific—by asking, for example, about the degree of personal obligation one feels to separate recyclable items—the A–B relationship is likely to reach +.50 or higher.

Another moderator is social constraints on behavior. Discrepancies between attitudes and behavior may occur because the social pressures on the individual to behave in a certain way may hold exceptional power.[29] Group pressures, for instance, may explain why an employee who holds strong anti-union attitudes attends pro-union organizing meetings.

Still another moderating variable is experience with the attitude in question.[30] The A–B relationship is likely to be much stronger if the attitude being evaluated refers to something with which the individual has experience. For instance, most of us will respond to a questionnaire on almost any issue. But is my attitude toward starving fish in the Amazon any indication of whether I'd donate to a fund to save these fish? Probably not! Getting the views of college students with no work experience on job factors that are important in determining whether they would stay put in a job is an example of an attitude response that is unlikely to predict much in terms of actual turnover behavior.

SELF-PERCEPTION THEORY   While most A–B studies yield positive results[31]—that attitudes do influence behavior—the relationship tends to be weak before adjustments are made for moderating variables. But requiring specificity, an absence of social constraints, and experience in order to get a meaningful correlation imposes severe limitations on making generalizations about the A–B relationship. This has prompted some researchers to take another direction—to look at whether behavior influences attitudes. This view, called **self-perception theory,** has generated some encouraging findings. Let's briefly review the theory.[32]

When asked about an attitude toward some object, individuals recall their behavior relevant to that object and then infer their attitude from their past behavior. So if an employee were asked about her feelings about being a payroll clerk at Exxon, she would likely think, "I've had this same job at Exxon as a payroll clerk for ten years, so I must like it!" Self-perception theory, therefore, argues that attitudes are used, after the fact, to make sense out of an action that has already occurred rather than as devices that precede and guide action.

Self-perception theory has been well supported.[33] While the traditional attitude-behavior relationship is generally positive, it is also weak. In contrast, the behavior-attitude relationship is quite strong. So what can we con-

Self-Perception Theory
Attitudes are used, after the fact, to make sense out of an action that has already occurred.

clude? It seems that we are very good at finding reasons for what we do, but not so good at doing what we find reasons for.[34]

An Application: Attitude Surveys

The preceding review should not discourage us from using attitudes to predict behavior. In an organizational context, most of the attitudes management would seek to inquire about would be ones with which employees have some experience. If the attitudes in question are specifically stated, management should obtain information that can be valuable in guiding their decisions relative to these employees. But how does management get information about employee attitudes? The most popular method is through the use of **attitude surveys**.[35]

Attitude Surveys Eliciting responses from employees through questionnaires about how they feel about their jobs, work groups, supervisors, and/or the organization.

Table 6–5 illustrates what an attitude survey might look like. Typically, attitude surveys present the employee with a set of statements or questions. Ideally, the items are tailored to obtain the specific information that management desires. An attitude score is achieved by summing up responses to individual questionnaire items. These scores can then be averaged for job groups, departments, divisions, or the organization as a whole.

As Keith Dunn of McGuffey's found in the opening case at the beginning of this chapter, results from attitude surveys frequently surprise management. Consistent with our discussion of perceptions in the previous chapter, the policies and practices that management views as objective and fair may be seen as inequitable by employees in general or by certain groups of employees. That these distorted perceptions have led to negative attitudes about the job and organization should be important to management. This is because employee behaviors are based on perceptions, not reality. Remember, the employee who quits because she believes she is underpaid—when, in fact, management has objective data to support that her salary is highly competitive—is just as gone as if she had actually been underpaid. The use of regular attitude surveys can alert management to potential problems and employees' intentions early so that action can be taken to prevent repercussions.[36]

TABLE 6–5   Sample Attitude Survey

Please answer each of the following statements using the following rating scale:

5 = Strongly agree
4 = Agree
3 = Undecided
2 = Disagree
1 = Strongly disagree

Statement	Rating
1. This company is a pretty good place to work.	___
2. I can get ahead in this company if I make the effort.	___
3. This company's wage rates are competitive with those of other companies.	___
4. Employee promotion decisions are handled fairly.	___
5. I understand the various fringe benefits the company offers.	___
6. My job makes the best use of my abilities.	___
7. My work load is challenging but not burdensome.	___
8. I have trust and confidence in my boss.	___
9. I feel free to tell my boss what I think.	___
10. I know what my boss expects of me.	___

We have already discussed job satisfaction briefly—earlier in this chapter as well as in Chapter 2. In this section, we want to dissect the concept more carefully. How do we measure job satisfaction? Are most workers today satisfied with their jobs? What determines job satisfaction? What is its effect on employee productivity, absenteeism, and turnover rates? We'll answer each of these questions in this section.

Measuring Job Satisfaction

We've previously defined job satisfaction as an individual's general attitude toward his or her job. This definition is clearly a very broad one.[37] Yet this is inherent in the concept. Remember, a person's job is more than just the obvious activities of shuffling papers, waiting on customers, or driving a truck. Jobs require interaction with co-workers and bosses, following organizational rules and policies, meeting performance standards, living with working conditions that are often less than ideal, and the like.[38] This means that an employee's assessment of how satisfied or dissatisfied he or she is with his or her job is a complex summation of a number of discrete job elements. How, then, do we measure the concept?

The two most widely used approaches are a single global rating and a summation score made up of a number of job facets. The single global rating method is nothing more than asking individuals to respond to one question, such as "All things considered, how satisfied are you with your job?" Respondents then reply by circling a number between one and five that corresponds with answers from "Highly Satisfied" to "Highly Dissatisfied." The other approach—a summation of job facets—is more sophisticated. It identifies key elements in a job and asks for the employee's feelings about each. Typical factors that would be included are the nature of the work, supervision, present pay, promotion opportunities, and relations with co-workers.[39] These factors are rated on a standardized scale and then added up to create an overall job satisfaction score.

Is one of the foregoing approaches superior to the other? Intuitively, it would seem that summing up responses to a number of job factors would achieve a more accurate evaluation of job satisfaction. The research, however, doesn't support this intuition.[40] This is one of those rare instances in which simplicity wins out over complexity. Comparisons of one-question global ratings with the more lengthy summation-of-job-factors method indicate that the former is more valid. The best explanation for this outcome is that the concept of job satisfaction is inherently so broad that the single question actually becomes a more inclusive measure.

Job Satisfaction as a Dependent Variable

We now turn to considering job satisfaction as a dependent variable. That is, we seek an answer to the question: *What* work-related variables determine job satisfaction? An extensive review of the literature indicates that the more important factors conducive to job satisfaction are mentally challenging work, equitable rewards, supportive working conditions, and supportive colleagues.[41]

MENTALLY CHALLENGING WORK   Employees tend to prefer jobs that give them opportunities to use their skills and abilities and offer a variety of tasks, freedom, and feedback on how well they are doing. These characteristics make work mentally challenging. Jobs that have too little challenge create boredom, but too much challenge creates frustration and feelings of failure. Under conditions of moderate challenge, most employees will experience pleasure and satisfaction.

EQUITABLE REWARDS Employees want pay systems and promotion policies that they perceive as being just, unambiguous, and in line with their expectations. When pay is seen as fair based on job demands, individual skill level, and community pay standards, satisfaction is likely to result. Of course, not everyone seeks money. Many people willingly accept less money to work in a preferred location or in a less demanding job or to have greater discretion in the work they do and the hours they work. But the key in linking pay to satisfaction is not the absolute amount one is paid; rather, it is the perception of fairness. Similarly, employees seek fair promotion policies and practices. Promotions provide opportunities for personal growth, more responsibilities, and increased social status. Individuals who perceive that promotion decisions are made in a fair and just manner, therefore, are likely to experience satisfaction from their jobs.

SUPPORTIVE WORKING CONDITIONS Employees are concerned with their work environment for both personal comfort and facilitating doing a good job. Studies demonstrate that employees prefer physical surroundings that are not dangerous or uncomfortable. Temperature, light, noise, and other environmental factors should not be at either extreme—for example, having too much heat or too little light. Additionally, most employees prefer working relatively close to home, in clean and relatively modern facilities, and with adequate tools and equipment.

SUPPORTIVE COLLEAGUES People get more out of work than merely money or tangible achievements. For most employees, work also fills the need for social interaction. Not surprisingly, therefore, having friendly and supportive co-workers leads to increased job satisfaction. The behavior of one's boss also is a major determinant of satisfaction. Studies generally find

Supportive colleagues increase job satisfaction. Work meets many needs of people, one of which is the need for social interaction.   Nubar Alexanian/ Stock, Boston

Job Satisfaction in the Workplace Today

Are American workers satisfied with their jobs? The answer to this question, based on numerous studies, is a resounding "Yes!" Moreover, the numbers are surprisingly constant over time. Let's take a closer look at what we know.

Regardless of what studies you choose to look at, when employees are asked if they are satisfied with their jobs, the results tend to be very similar: Between seventy and eighty percent of American workers report they are satisfied with their jobs.[42] Older workers report the highest satisfaction (ninety-two percent for those age sixty-five and over), but even young people—under age twenty-five—report high levels of satisfaction (seventy-three percent).[43]

While there was some concern in the late 1970s that satisfaction was declining across almost all occupational groups,[44] recent reinterpretations of these data and additional longitudinal studies indicate that job satisfaction levels have held steady for decades—through economic recessions as well as prosperous times.[45]

How does one explain these results? Taken literally, we can say that whatever it is that people want from their jobs, they seem to be getting it and have been for quite some time, at least if we believe what people say in job satisfaction surveys. But if we dig a little deeper, we might question this literal interpretation. For instance, based on our knowledge of cognitive dissonance theory, we might expect employees to resolve inconsistencies between dissatisfaction with their jobs and their staying with those jobs by not reporting the dissatisfaction. Also, when employees are asked whether they would again choose the same work or whether they would want their children to follow in their footsteps, typically less than half answer in the affirmative.[46] So maybe employees aren't as satisfied with their jobs as the numbers would suggest.

An interesting explanation has also been proposed for the stability of job satisfaction findings over time. Satisfaction may lie more in the employee's personality than in the job.[47] Analysis of satisfaction data for a selected sample of individuals over a fifty-year period found that individual results were consistently stable over time, even when these people changed the employer for whom they worked and their occupation. It may well be that many of the work-related variables that we think *cause* job satisfaction aren't that important. Rather, most individuals' disposition toward life—positive or negative—is established by adolescence, holds over time, carries over into their disposition toward work, and—at least among Americans—is generally upbeat.

that employee satisfaction is increased when the immediate supervisor is understanding and friendly, offers praise for good performance, listens to employees' opinions, and shows a personal interest in them.

DON'T FORGET THE PERSONALITY – JOB FIT!   In Chapter 4, we presented Holland's personality-job fit theory. As you remember, one of Holland's conclusions was that high agreement between an employee's personality and occupation results in a more satisfied individual. His logic was essentially this: People with personality types congruent with their chosen vocations should find that they have the right talents and abilities to meet the demands of their jobs; are thus more likely to be successful on those jobs; and, because of this success, have a greater probability of achieving high satisfaction from their work. Studies to replicate Holland's conclusions have been almost universally supportive.[48] It's important, therefore, to add this to our list of factors that determine job satisfaction.

Job Satisfaction as an Independent Variable

Managers' interest in job satisfaction tends to center on its effect on employee performance. Researchers have recognized this interest, so we find a large number of studies that have been designed to assess the impact of job satisfaction on employee productivity, absenteeism, and turnover. Let's look at the current state of our knowledge.

SATISFACTION AND PRODUCTIVITY   A number of reviews were done in the 1950s and 1960s, covering dozens of studies that sought to establish the relationship between satisfaction and productivity.[49] These reviews could find no consistent relationship. In the 1990s, though the studies are far from unambiguous, we can make some sense out of the evidence.

The early views on the satisfaction-performance relationship can be essentially summarized in the statement "a happy worker is a productive worker." Much of the paternalism shown by managers in the 1930s, 1940s, and 1950s—forming company bowling teams and credit unions, having company picnics, providing counseling services for employees, training supervisors to be sensitive to the concerns of subordinates—was done to make workers happy. But belief in the happy worker thesis was based more on wishful thinking than hard evidence. A careful review of the research indicates that if there is a positive relationship between satisfaction and productivity, the correlations are consistently low—in the vicinity of 0.14.[50] However, introduction of moderating variables has improved the relationship.[51] For example, the relationship is stronger when the employee's behavior is not constrained or controlled by outside factors. An employee's productivity on machine-paced jobs, for instance, is going to be much more influenced by the speed of the machine than his or her level of satisfaction. Similarly, a stockbroker's productivity is largely constrained by the general movement of the stock market. When the market is moving up and volume is high, both satisfied and dissatisfied brokers are going to ring up lots of commissions. Conversely, when the market is in the doldrums, the level of broker satisfaction is not likely to mean much. Job level also seems to be

One of the greatest myths held by managers is that the happier a worker is, the more he or she will produce. Research tells us that positive emotions don't cause productivity. It is more likely that high productivity leads to satisfaction. Management may have to do specific things to increase productivity, and separate things to improve satisfaction, and the things may not be all that related.   Left, Roy Morsch/The Stock Market; right, John Coletti/Stock, Boston

an important moderating variable. The satisfaction-performance correlations are stronger for higher-level employees. Thus, we might expect the relationship to be more relevant for individuals in professional, supervisory, and managerial positions.

Another point of concern in the satisfaction-productivity issue is the direction of the causal arrow. Most of the studies on the relationship used research designs that could not prove cause and effect. Studies that have controlled for this possibility indicate that the more valid conclusion is that productivity leads to satisfaction rather than the other way around.[52] If you do a good job, you intrinsically feel good about it. Additionally, assuming that the organization rewards productivity, your higher productivity should increase verbal recognition, your pay level, and probabilities for promotion. These rewards, in turn, increase your level of satisfaction with the job.

SATISFACTION AND ABSENTEEISM   We find a consistent negative relationship between satisfaction and absenteeism, but the correlation is moderate—usually less than 0.40.[53] While it certainly makes sense that dissatisfied employees are more likely to miss work, other factors have an impact on the relationship and reduce the correlation coefficient. For example, remember our discussion of sick pay versus well pay in Chapter 4. Organizations that provide liberal sick leave benefits are encouraging all their employees—including those who are highly satisfied—to take days off. Assuming that you have a reasonable number of varied interests, you can find work satisfying and yet still take off work to enjoy a three-day weekend, tan yourself on a warm summer day, or watch the World Series on television if those days come free with no penalties. Also, as with productivity, outside factors can act to reduce the correlation.

An excellent illustration of how satisfaction directly leads to attendance, where there is a minimum impact from other factors, is a study done at Sears, Roebuck.[54] Satisfaction data were available on employees at Sears' two headquarters in Chicago and New York. Additionally, it is important to note that Sears' policy was not to permit employees to be absent from work for avoidable reasons without penalty. The occurrence of a freak April 2 snowstorm in Chicago created the opportunity to compare employee attendance at the Chicago office with attendance in New York, where the weather was quite nice. The interesting dimension in this study is that the snowstorm gave the Chicago employees a built-in excuse not to come to work. The storm crippled the city's transportation, and individuals knew they could miss work this day with no penalty. This natural experiment permitted the comparison of attendance records for satisfied and dissatisfied employees at two locations—one where you were expected to be at work (with normal pressures for attendance) and the other where you were free to choose with no penalty involved. If satisfaction leads to attendance, where there is an absence of outside factors, the more satisfied employees should have come to work in Chicago, while dissatisfied employees should have stayed home. The study found that, on this April 2 day, absenteeism rates in New York (the control group) were just as high for satisfied groups of workers as for dissatisfied groups. But in Chicago, the workers with high satisfaction scores had much higher attendance than did those with lower satisfaction levels. These findings are exactly what we would have expected if satisfaction is negatively correlated with absenteeism.

SATISFACTION AND TURNOVER   Satisfaction is also negatively related to turnover, but the correlation is stronger than what we found for absenteeism.[55] Yet, again, other factors such as labor market conditions,

A Cross-Cultural Look at Values and Job Satisfaction

A country's national culture shapes the values of its citizens. As noted earlier in this chapter, American culture reinforces values such as achievement, equity, and democracy. You should not, however, assume these values to be universally held.

On the assumption that today's students become tomorrow's managers, two Canadian researchers developed a comparative study of job values of business students in France and English Canada.[56] Their findings support the theory that the different cultural values have shaped the values held by students in each country. For instance, English Canadians placed a higher value on competition, achievement, independence, and pragmatism than did their French counterparts. The French students, on the other hand, placed a greater value on spiritual and society-oriented outcomes.

Another study on values, this one comparing American and Japanese managers, confirmed the value-divergence thesis and upheld many of the stereotypes about Americans and Japanese.[57] American managers placed greater importance on ambition, competence, and independence. The Japanese managers placed more value on self-respect, helpfulness, and forgiveness.

The level of job satisfaction also appears to vary from country to country. This is clearly dramatized by data from Japanese workers. You'll remember that seventy to eighty percent of American workers described themselves as satisfied with their jobs. A survey of Japanese workers found a dismal fourteen percent of their younger workers to be satisfied.[58] Is there any explanation for such a low rate? The answer seems to have to do with Japanese organizations' widespread practice of assigning employees and managers to jobs without regard for their interests. In contrast, most American firms take considerable care in identifying differences among new employees' personalities and preferences, and then use this information in making placement decisions.

expectations about alternative job opportunities, and length of tenure with the organization are important constraints on the actual decision to leave one's current job.[59]

Evidence indicates that an important moderating variable on the satisfaction-turnover relationship is the employee's level of performance.[60] Specifically, level of satisfaction is less important in predicting turnover for superior performers. Why? The organization typically makes considerable efforts to keep these people. They get pay raises, praise, recognition, increased promotional opportunities, and so forth. Just the opposite tends to apply to poor performers. Few attempts are made by the organization to retain them. There may even be subtle pressures to encourage them to quit. We would expect, therefore, that job satisfaction is more important in influencing poor performers to stay than superior performers. Regardless of level of satisfaction, the latter are more likely to remain with the organization because the receipt of recognition, praise, and other rewards gives them more reasons for staying.

How Employees Can Express Dissatisfaction

One final point before we leave the issue of job satisfaction: Employee dissatisfaction can be expressed in a number of ways.[61] For example, rather

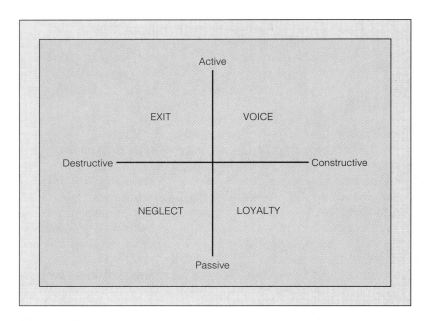

FIGURE 6–1   Responses to Job Dissatisfaction
Source: C. Rusbult and D. Lowery, "When Bureaucrats Get the Blues," Journal of Applied Social Psychology, Vol. 15, No. 1, 1985, p. 83. With permission.

than quit, employees can complain, be insubordinate, steal organizational property, or shirk a part of their work responsibilities. Figure 6–1 offers four responses that differ from one another along two dimensions: constructiveness/destructiveness and activity/passivity. They are defined as follows:[62]

Exit Dissatisfaction expressed through behavior directed toward leaving the organization.

Voice Dissatisfaction expressed through active and constructive attempts to improve conditions.

Loyalty Dissatisfaction expressed by passively waiting for conditions to improve.

Neglect Dissatisfaction expressed through allowing conditions to worsen.

> **Exit:** Behavior directed toward leaving the organization. Includes looking for a new position as well as resigning.
>
> **Voice:** Actively and constructively attempting to improve conditions. Includes suggesting improvements, discussing problems with superiors, and some forms of union activity.
>
> **Loyalty:** Passively but optimistically waiting for conditions to improve. Includes speaking up for the organization in the face of external criticism and trusting the organization and its management to "do the right thing."
>
> **Neglect:** Passively allowing conditions to worsen. Includes chronic absenteeism or lateness, reduced effort, and increased error rate.

Exit and neglect behaviors encompass our performance variables—productivity, absenteeism, and turnover. But this model expands employee response to include voice and loyalty—constructive behaviors that allow individuals to tolerate unpleasant situations or to revive satisfactory working conditions. It helps us to understand situations, such as those sometimes found among unionized workers, where low job satisfaction is coupled with low turnover.[63] Union members often express dissatisfaction through the grievance procedure or through formal contract negotiations. These voice mechanisms allow the union members to continue in their jobs while convincing themselves that they are acting to improve the situation.

Dissatisfaction and Whistleblowing

Whistleblowing refers to disclosing illegal, immoral, or illegitimate practices to authorities inside and/or outside the organization. Most cases described in the media involve someone who informs an outsider—a newspaper reporter, a government official, a public pressure group—about an assumed injustice, irresponsible action, or violation of law engaged in by an organization or by an employee of an organization. For instance, several engineers at Morton Thiokol complained, wrote memos, and "blew the whistle" to draw attention to design flaws in the O-rings that went into the space shuttle *Challenger*. Their cries were ignored and the result was the tragic loss of seven astronauts. When an MIT scientist exposed false research data in a scientific article co-authored by a Nobel laureate, she was fired from her job. These examples of whistleblowing illustrate that it is an active, but risky and controversial, response to dissatisfaction.

What makes whistleblowing risky and controversial?[64] First, there are the possible negative repercussions for the whistleblower, who is often punished for tarnishing the organization's reputation or embarrassing some key people in the organization. That punishment can be as extreme as being fired and blackballed, making it almost impossible for the whistleblower to find another job in the industry. Second, there is the question of the whistleblower's motives. Is he or she acting altruistically—that is, strictly to benefit others without regard to repercussions or retaliation? Or does the whistleblower intend to gain personal rewards? Our conclusion is that any would-be whistleblowers would be wise to balance the possible advantages against the possible disadvantages both to themselves and to others.

Do you think whistleblowing reflects disloyalty to the organization? Would you ever blow the whistle if you were aware of an illegal or unethical practice by your employer? What kind of actions would you consider worth blowing the whistle over?

IMPLICATIONS FOR PERFORMANCE AND SATISFACTION

Why is it important to know an individual's values? Although they don't have a direct impact on behavior, values strongly influence a person's attitudes. So knowledge of an individual's value system can provide insight into his or her attitudes.

Given that people's values differ, managers can use the Rokeach Value Survey to assess potential employees and determine if their values align with the dominant values of the organization. An employee's performance and satisfaction are likely to be higher if his or her values fit well with the organization. For instance, the person who places high importance on imagination, independence, and freedom is likely to be poorly matched with an organization that seeks conformity from its employees. Managers are more likely to appreciate, evaluate positively, and allocate rewards to employees who "fit in," and employees are more likely to be satisfied if they perceive that they do fit. This argues for management to strive during the selection of new employees to find job candidates who not only have the ability, experience, and motivation to perform, but also a value system that is compatible with the organization's.

Managers should be interested in their employees' attitudes because attitudes give warnings of potential problems and because they influence behavior. Satisfied and committed employees, for instance, have lower rates of turnover and absenteeism. Given that managers want to keep resignations and absences down—especially among their more productive employees— they will want to do those things that will generate positive job attitudes.

Managers should also be aware that employees will try to reduce cognitive dissonance. More important, dissonance can be managed. If employees are required to engage in activities that appear inconsistent to them or that are at odds with their attitudes, the pressures to reduce the resulting dissonance are lessened when the employee perceives that the dissonance is externally imposed and is beyond his or her control or if the rewards are significant enough to offset the dissonance.

■ *FOR DISCUSSION*

1. Contrast the Protestant work ethic, existential, pragmatic, and symmetry typologies with the terminal values identified in the Rokeach Value Survey.
2. "Thirty-five years ago, young employees we hired were ambitious, conscientious, hard-working, and honest. Today's young workers don't have the same values." Do you agree or disagree with this manager's comments? Support your position.
3. Do you think there might be any positive and significant relationship between the possession of certain personal values and successful career progression in organizations like Merrill Lynch, the AFL-CIO, and the city of Cleveland's police department? Discuss.
4. Contrast the cognitive and affective components of an attitude.
5. What is cognitive dissonance and how is it related to attitudes?
6. What is self-perception theory? Does it increase our ability to predict behavior?
7. What contingency factors can improve the statistical relationship between attitudes and behavior?
8. Why does job satisfaction receive so much attention by OB researchers? Do you think this interest is shared by practicing managers?
9. What determines job satisfaction?
10. What is the relationship between job satisfaction and productivity?
11. What is the relationship between job satisfaction and *absenteeism*? *Turnover*? Which is the stronger relationship?
12. Contrast exit, voice, loyalty, and neglect as employee responses to job dissatisfaction.

The Importance of High Job Satisfaction

The importance of job satisfaction is obvious. Managers should be concerned with the level of job satisfaction in their organizations for at least three reasons: (1) there is clear evidence that dissatisfied employees skip work more often and are more likely to resign; (2) it has been demonstrated that satisfied employees have better health and live longer; and (3) satisfaction on the job carries over to the employee's life outside the job.

We reviewed the evidence between satisfaction and withdrawal behaviors in this chapter. That evidence was fairly clear. Satisfied employees have lower rates of both turnover and absenteeism. If we consider the two withdrawal behaviors separately, however, we can be more confident about the influence of satisfaction on turnover. Specifically, satisfaction is strongly and consistently negatively related to an employee's decision to leave the organization. Although satisfaction and absence are also negatively related, conclusions regarding the relationship should be more guarded.

An often-overlooked dimension of job satisfaction is its relationship to employee health. Several studies have shown that employees who are dissatisfied with their jobs are prone to health setbacks ranging from headaches to heart disease. Some research even indicates that job satisfaction is a better predictor of length of life than is physical condition or tobacco use. These studies suggest that dissatisfaction is not solely a psychological phenomenon. The stress that results from dissatisfaction apparently increases one's susceptibility to heart attacks and the like. For managers, this means that even if satisfaction didn't lead to less voluntary turnover and absence, the goal of a satisfied work force might be justifiable because it would reduce medical costs and the premature loss of valued employees by way of heart disease or strokes.

Our final point in support of job satisfaction's importance is the spin-off effect that job satisfaction has for society as a whole. When employees are happy with their jobs, it improves their lives off the job. In contrast, the dissatisfied employee carries that negative attitude home. In wealthy countries such as the United States, doesn't management have a responsibility to provide jobs from which employees can receive high satisfaction? Some benefits of job satisfaction accrue to every citizen in our society. Satisfied employees are more likely to be satisfied citizens. These people will hold a more positive attitude toward life in general and make for a society of more psychologically healthy people.

The evidence is impressive. Job satisfaction is important. For management, a satisfied work force translates into higher productivity due to fewer disruptions caused by absenteeism or good employees quitting, as well as into lower medical and life insurance costs. Additionally, there are benefits for society in general. Satisfaction on the job carries over to the employee's off-the-job hours. So the goal of high job satisfaction for employees can be defended in terms of both dollars and cents and social responsibility.

Job Satisfaction Has Been Overemphasized

Few issues have been more blown out of proportion than the importance of job satisfaction at work. Let's look closely at the evidence.

There is no consistent relationship indicating that satisfaction leads to productivity. And, after all, isn't productivity the name of the game? Organizations are not altruistic institutions. Management's obligation is to use efficiently the resources that it has available. It has no obligation to create a satisfied work force if the costs exceed the benefits. As one executive put it, "I don't care if my people are happy or not! Do they produce?"

It would be naive to assume that satisfaction alone would have a major impact on employee behavior. As a case in point, consider the issue of turnover. Certainly there are a number of other factors that have an equal or greater impact on whether an employee decides to remain with an organization or take a job somewhere else—length of time on the job, financial situation, and availability of other jobs, to name the most obvious. If I'm fifty-five years old, have been with my company twenty-five years, perceive few other opportunities in the job market, and have no other source of income besides my job, does my unhappiness have much impact on my decision to stay with the organization? No!

Did you ever notice who seems to be most concerned with improving employee job satisfaction? It's usually college professors and researchers! They've chosen careers that provide them with considerable freedom and opportunities for personal growth. They place a very high value on job satisfaction. The problem is that they impose their values on others. Because job satisfaction is important to them, they suppose that it's important to everyone. To a lot of people, a job is merely the means to get the money they need to do the things they desire during their nonworking hours. Assuming you work forty hours a week and sleep eight hours a night, you still have seventy hours or more a week to achieve fulfillment and satisfaction in off-the-job activities. So the importance of job satisfaction may be oversold when you recognize that there are other sources—outside the job—where the dissatisfied employee can find satisfaction.

A final point against overemphasizing job satisfaction: Consider the issue in a contingency framework. Even if satisfaction were significantly related to performance, it is unlikely that the relationship would hold consistently across all segments of the work force. In fact, evidence demonstrates that people differ in terms of the importance that work plays in their lives. To some, the job is their central life interest. But for the majority of people, their primary interests are off the job. Non-job-oriented people tend not to be emotionally involved with their work. This relative indifference allows them to accept frustrating conditions at work more willingly. Importantly, the majority of the work force probably falls into this non-job-oriented category. So while job satisfaction might be important to lawyers, surgeons, and other professionals, it may be irrelevant to the average worker because he or she is generally apathetic about the job's frustrating elements.

Prioritizing Your Values

Rank the following values from 1 to 10. Place a 1 next to the value that is most important to you, a 2 next to the second most important, and so forth. There are no right or wrong answers, so be completely honest in your responses.

_____ A prosperous life

_____ Security for loved ones

_____ A sense of accomplishment

_____ A world free from conflict and war

_____ Equal opportunity for all

_____ Personal freedom and independence

_____ An enjoyable, leisurely life

_____ Inner peace and harmony

_____ Respect and admiration from others

_____ Close friendships

After completing your ranking, form into groups of five or six class members and discuss:

1. What *similarities,* if any, did you find among group members' rankings? Differences?
2. What degree of fit did members find between their rankings and their value type as identified in Table 6–4?
3. What might each person's rankings suggest in terms of the kind of job he or she might find satisfying?
4. What do differences in rankings mean, if anything, in terms of motivating different class members?

Work Attitude Exercise

OBJECTIVE To compare attitudes about the work force.

TIME Approximately thirty minutes.

PROCEDURE Answer the following five questions:

1. *Generally,* American workers (pick one)

___ a. are highly motivated and hardworking

___ b. try to give a fair day's effort

___ c. will put forth effort if you make it worthwhile

___ d. try to get by with a low level of effort

___ e. are lazy and/or poorly motivated

2. The people *I have worked with* (pick one)

___ a. are highly motivated and hardworking

___ b. try to give a fair day's effort

___ c. will put forth effort if you make it worthwhile

___ d. try to get by with a low level of effort

___ e. are lazy and/or poorly motivated

3. *Compared to foreign workers,* American workers are (pick one)

___ a. more productive

___ b. equally productive

___ c. less productive

4. *Over the past twenty years,* American workers have (pick one)

___ a. improved in overall quality of job performance

___ b. remained about the same in quality of job performance

___ c. deteriorated in overall quality of job performance

5. If you have a low opinion of the U.S. work force, give the one step (or action) that could be taken that would lead to the most improvement.

Your instructor will aggregate the class results for questions 1 through 4 by a show of hands. Responses for question 5 will be listed on the chalkboard

Your instructor will provide data from other student attitude responses to these questions, then lead the class in discussing the implications or accuracy of these attitudes.

Source: Based on D. R. Brown, "Dealing with Student Conceptions and Misconceptions About Worker Attitudes and Productivity," *Journal of Management Education,* May 1991, pp. 259–64.

CASE INCIDENT 6

How Workers' Attitudes Shape Productivity and Quality at Two GM Plants

This is the story of two General Motors auto plants. One is in Michigan and produces GM's luxury models using the latest in manufacturing technology. The other is in Oklahoma, manufactures plain-vanilla family cars, and is burdened with 1960s-vintage technology. In addition to the differences in the cars they make and the technology they use, these plants have very different quality records. One produces the highest-ranking Big Three model on the list of the ten most trouble-free cars compiled by J. D. Power & Associates, while the other is rated in the lowest quarter among all GM plants on overall product quality. The surprise in this story is that it's the outdated plant in Oklahoma that is GM's high-quality producer.

The Oklahoma City plant employs fifty-three hundred workers. The cars it produces—the Pontiac 6000, the Buick Century, and the Oldsmobile Cutlass Ciera—are nine-year-old relics of GM's look-alike fiasco of the mid-

1980s. But what makes this plant special is its management and its work force. Jack Evans, the plant manager, is determined to make his plant as competitive as the plants of his Japanese rivals. His employees are enthusiastically adopting the Japanese "lean production" process, which emphasizes doing more with less. For instance, the plant has introduced just-in-time manufacturing methods to cut inventory costs. This alone has cut its inventory by thirty-seven percent in four years and taken twenty percent off the time needed to fill a dealer's order. Evans has also introduced an extensive set of training classes, which, unlike those at other GM plants, are taught by union personnel rather than management. Evans has successfully convinced his employees that it's in their best interest to cut costs, work harder, and accept changes. Quality cars mean higher sales, which translate into more worker overtime and better job security.

The other plant is in Orion Township, Michigan. This seven-year-old factory uses fifty-six hundred employees and some 170 robots to build Cadillac Fleetwoods and Oldsmobile Ninety-Eights. On some days, the cars have more than three times the company goal of two defects per car, according to GM's own measurements. And while the Oklahoma City plant is characterized by labor-management cooperation, the Orion Township facility is an ongoing battleground. Police have had to be called several times in recent years to handle fights among workers. Employees quarrel over anything and everything, especially efforts to improve quality. Union members openly acknowledge their distrust of GM management. In trying to get Orion up to speed, GM keeps changing management. The plant has had four plant managers in its seven years, compared with only one at Oklahoma City during the same period. Union officials at Orion question the value of developing a working relationship with a manager who will likely soon be heading out the revolving door.

The contrast between the two plants' work forces largely stems from their initial composition. Orion's workers were assembled from the more senior employees at several dozen other GM plants in Michigan. They brought with them a history of long, painful layoffs in the early 1980s, when GM was closing and consolidating factories. Most believed that GM wouldn't close this brand-new facility no matter what they did. The Oklahoma City factory hired most of its workers locally. They came in untainted by past GM practices. They also received wages and benefits that, by Oklahoma standards, were extremely high.

Questions

1. How can employees working at two similar-sized plants in the same company have such different attitudes?

2. Why doesn't cognitive dissonance result in improved attitudes of the workers in Orion Township?

3. Using Figure 6–1, describe how employees at Orion Township seem to be expressing their dissatisfaction.

4. If you were a GM consultant, what recommendations would you make to improve quality and productivity at Orion Township?

Source: Based on G.A. Patterson, "Two GM Auto Plants Illustrate Major Role of Workers' Attitudes," *The Wall Street Journal*, August 29, 1991, pp. A1–A2.

FOR FURTHER READING

LEE, J. A., "Changes in Managerial Values, 1965–86," *Business Horizons,* July-August 1988, pp. 29–37. A twenty-one-year study of management values found that they did not change dramatically over time.

MAWHINNEY, T. C., "Job Satisfaction as a Management Tool and Responsibility," *Journal of Organizational Behavior Management,* Winter 1989, pp. 187–91. Calls for defining job satisfaction in objective, operant terms.

MEINDL, J. R., R. G. HUNT, and W. LEE, "Individualism-Collectivism and Work Values: Data from the United States, China, Taiwan, Korea, and Hong Kong," in G. R. Ferris and K. M. Rowland (eds.), *Research in Personnel and Human Resource Management* (Greenwich, CT: JAI Press, 1989), pp. 59–71. Researchers found relatively small differences in the value patterning of various work goals between the United States and the group of nations defined by Taiwan, Hong Kong, and Korea; whereas relatively large differences surfaced between China and the group of nations defined by the United States and others.

NORD, W. R., A. P. BRIEF, J. M. ATIEH, and E. M. DOHERTY, "Work Values and the Conduct of Organizational Behavior," in B. M. Staw and L. L. Cummings (eds.), *Research in Organizational Behavior,* Vol. 10 (Greenwich, CT: JAI Press, 1988), pp. 1–42. Reviews and critiques perspectives on work values, then presents a framework for classifying and analyzing conceptions of work values.

ORGAN, D. W., "A Restatement of the Satisfaction-Performance Hypothesis," *Journal of Management,* December 1988, pp. 547–57. Argues that satisfaction more generally correlates with organizational pro-social or citizenship-type behaviors than with traditional productivity variables.

RICE, R. W., D. B. MCFARLIN, and D. E. BENNETT, "Standards of Comparison and Job Satisfaction," *Journal of Applied Psychology,* November 1989, pp. 591–98. Found support for discrepancy theory as a conceptual basis for job satisfaction.

NOTES

[1]This is based on J. Hyatt, "The Odyssey of an 'Excellent' Man," INC., February 1989, pp. 63–69.

[2]M. Rokeach, *The Nature of Human Values* (New York: Free Press, 1973), p. 5.

[3]See, for instance, J. H. Barnett and M. J. Karson, "Personal Values and Business Decisions: An Exploratory Investigation," *Journal of Business Ethics,* July 1987, pp. 371–82.

[4]M. Rokeach and S. J. Ball-Rokeach, "Stability and Change in American Value Priorities, 1968–1981," *American Psychologist,* May 1989, pp. 775–84.

[5]M. Rokeach, *The Nature of Human Values,* p. 6.

[6]G.W. Allport, P.E. Vernon, and G. Lindzey, *Study of Values* (Boston: Houghton Mifflin, 1951).

[7]Rokeach, *The Nature of Human Values.*

[8]J. M. Munson and B. Z. Posner, "The Factorial Validity of a Modified Rokeach Value Survey for Four Diverse Samples," *Educational and Psychological Measurement,* Winter 1980, pp. 1073–79; and W. C. Frederick and J. Weber, "The Values of Corporate Managers and Their Critics: An Empirical Description and Normative Implications," in W. C. Frederick and L. E. Preston (eds.), *Business Ethics: Research Issues and Empirical Studies* (Greenwich, CN: JAI Press, 1990), pp. 123–44.

[9]Frederick and Weber, "The Values of Corporate Managers and Their Critics."

[10]Ibid., p. 132.

[11]See, for example, R. J. Aldag and A. P. Brief, "Some Correlates of Work Values," *Journal of Applied Psychology,* December 1975, pp. 757–60; D. J. Cherrington, S. J. Condie, and J. L. England, "Age and Work Values," *Academy of Management Journal,* September 1979, pp. 617–23; T. Carson, "Fast-Track Kids," *Business Week,* November 10, 1986, pp. 90–92; J. A. Raelin, "The '60s Kids in the Corporation: More Than Just 'Daydream Believers,'" *Academy of Management Executive,* February 1987, pp. 21–30; D. M. Gross and S. Scott, "Proceeding with Caution," *Time,* July 16, 1990, pp. 56–62; and A. Deutschman, "What 25-Year-Olds Want," *Fortune,* August 27, 1990.

[12]As noted to your author by R. Volkema and R. L. Neal, Jr., of American University, this model may also be limited in its application to minority populations and recent immigrants to North America.

[13]R. E. Hattwick, Y. Kathawala, M. Monipullil, and L. Wall, "On the Alleged Decline in Business Ethics," *Journal of Behavioral Economics,* Summer 1989, pp. 129–43.

[14]S. J. Breckler, "Empirical Validation of Affect, Behavior, and Cognition as Distinct Components of Attitude," *Journal of Personality and Social Psychology,* May 1984, pp. 1191–1205.

[15]P. P. Brooke Jr., D. W. Russell, and J. L. Price, "Discriminant Validation of Measures of Job Satisfaction, Job Involvement, and Organizational Commitment," *Journal of Applied Psychology,* May 1988, pp. 139–45.

[16]See, for example, S. Rabinowitz and D. T. Hall, "Organizational Research in Job Involvement," *Psychological Bulletin,* March 1977, pp. 265–88; G. J. Blau, "A Multiple Study Investigation of the Dimensionality of Job Involvement," *Journal of Vocational Behavior,* August 1985, pp. 19–36; and N. A. Jans, "Organizational Factors and Work Involvement," *Organizational Behavior and Human Decision Processes,* June 1985, pp. 382–96.

[17]Based on G. J. Blau and K. R. Boal, "Conceptualizing How Job Involvement and Organizational Commitment Affect Turnover and Absenteeism," *Academy of Management Review,* April 1987, p. 290.

[18]G. J. Blau, "Job Involvement and Organizational Commitment as Interactive Predictors of Tardiness and Absenteeism," *Journal of Management,* Winter 1986, pp. 577–84; and K. Boal and R. Cidambi, "Attitudinal Correlates of Turnover and Absenteeism: A Meta Analysis," paper presented at the meeting of the American Psychological Association, Toronto, Canada, 1984.

[19]G. Farris, "A Predictive Study of Turnover," *Personnel Psychology,* Summer 1971, pp. 311–28.

[20]Blau and Boal, "Conceptualizing," p. 290.

[21]See, for instance, P. W. Hom, R. Katerberg, and C. L. Hulin, "Comparative Examination of Three Approaches to the Prediction of Turnover," *Journal of Applied Psychology,* June 1979, pp. 280–90; H. Angle and J. Perry, "Organizational Commitment: Individual and Organizational Influence," *Work and Occupations,* May 1983, pp. 123–46; and J. L. Pierce and R. B. Dunham, "Organizational Commitment: Pre-Employment Propensity and Initial Work Experiences," *Journal of Management,* Spring 1987, pp. 163–78.

[22]Hom, Katerberg, and Hulin, "Comparative Examination"; and R. T. Mowday, L. W. Porter, and R. M. Steers, *Employee Organization Linkages: The Psychology of Commitment, Absenteeism, and Turnover* (New York: Academic Press, 1982).

[23]L. W. Porter, R. M. Steers, R. T. Mowday, and P. V. Boulian, "Organizational Commitment, Job Satisfaction, and Turnover Among Psychiatric Technicians," *Journal of Applied Psychology,* October 1974, pp. 603–09.

[24]L. Festinger, *A Theory of Cognitive Dissonance* (Stanford, CA: Stanford University Press, 1957).

[25]B. M. Staw, "The Escalation of Commitment to a Course of Action," *Academy of Management Review,* October 1981, pp. 577–87.

[26]A. W. Wicker, "Attitude versus Action: The Relationship of Verbal and Overt Behavioral Responses to Attitude Objects," *Journal of Social Issues,* Autumn 1969, pp. 41–78.

[27]Ibid., p. 65.

[28]T. A. Heberlein and J. S. Black, "Attitudinal Specificity and the Prediction of Behavior in a Field Setting," *Journal of Personality and Social Psychology,* April 1976, pp. 474–79.

[29]H. Schuman and M. P. Johnson, "Attitudes and Behavior," in A. Inkeles (ed.), *Annual Review of Sociology,* (Palo Alto, CA: Annual Reviews, 1976), pp. 161–207.

[30]R. H. Fazio and M. P. Zanna, "Direct Experience and Attitude-Behavior Consistency," in L. Berkowitz (ed.), *Advances in Experimental Social Psychology* (New York: Academic Press, 1981), pp. 161–202.

[31]L. R. Kahle and H. J. Berman, "Attitudes Cause Behaviors: A Cross-Lagged Panel Analysis," *Journal of Personality and Social Psychology,* March 1979, pp. 315–21; and C. L. Kleinke, "Two Models for Conceptualizing the Attitude-Behavior Relationship," *Human Relations,* April 1984, pp. 333–50.

[32]D. J. Bem, "Self-Perception Theory," in L. Berkowitz (ed.), *Advances in Experimental Social Psychology,* Vol. 6 (New York: Academic Press, 1972), pp. 1–62.

[33]See, for example, C. A. Kiesler, R. E. Nisbett, and M. P. Zanna, "On Inferring One's Belief from One's Behavior," *Journal of Personality and Social Psychology,* April 1969, pp. 321–27.

[34]R. Abelson, "Are Attitudes Necessary?" in B. T. King and E. McGinnies (eds.), *Attitudes, Conflicts, and Social Change* (New York: Academic Press, 1972), p. 25.

[35]See, for example, G. E. Lyne, "How to Measure Employee Attitudes," *Training and Development Journal,* December 1989, pp. 40–43.

[36]G. Gallup, "Employee Research: From Nice to Know to Need to Know," *Personnel Journal,* August 1988, pp. 42–43.

[37]For problems with the concept of job satisfaction, see R. Hodson, "Workplace Behaviors," *Work and Occupations,* August 1991, pp. 271–90.

[38]The Wyatt Company's 1989 national WorkAmerica study identified twelve dimensions of satisfaction: work organization, working conditions, communications, job performances and

performance review, co-workers, supervision, company management, pay, benefits, career development and training, job content and satisfaction, and company image and change.

[39]See J. L. Price and C. W. Mueller, *Handbook of Organizational Measurement* (Marshfield, MA: Pitman Publishing, 1986), pp. 223–27.

[40]V. Scarpello and J. P. Campbell, "Job Satisfaction: Are All the Parts There?" *Personnel Psychology,* Autumn 1983, pp. 577–600.

[41]E. A. Locke, "The Nature and Causes of Job Satisfaction," in M. D. Dunnette (ed.), *Handbook of Industrial and Organizational Psychology* (Chicago: Rand McNally, 1976), pp. 1319–28.

[42]See, for instance, studies cited in A. F. Chelte, J. Wright, and C. Tausky, "Did Job Satisfaction Really Drop During the 1970s?" *Monthly Labor Review,* November 1982, pp. 33–36; "Job Satisfaction High in America, Says Conference Board Study," *Monthly Labor Review,* February 1985, p. 52; and C. Hartman and S. Pearlstein, "The Joy of Working," *INC.,* November 1987, pp. 61–66. See also "Wyatt WorkAmerica," published by The Wyatt Company, 1990.

[43]"Job Satisfaction High in America," p. 52.

[44]G. L. Staines and R. P. Quinn, "American Workers Evaluate the Quality of Their Jobs," *Monthly Labor Review,* January 1979, pp. 3–12.

[45]Chelte, Wright, Tausky, "Did Job Satisfaction Really Drop?"; and B. M. Staw, N. E. Bell, and J. A. Clausen, "The Dispositional Approach to Job Attitudes: A Lifetime Longitudinal Test," *Administrative Science Quarterly,* March 1986, pp. 56–77.

[46]R. L. Kahn, "The Meaning of Work: Interpretation and Proposals of Measurement," in A. Campbell and P. E. Converse (eds.), *The Human Meaning of Social Change* (New York: Russell Sage Foundation, 1972).

[47]Staw, Bell, and Clausen, "The Dispositional Approach to Job Attitudes;" and R. D. Arvey, T. J. Bouchard, Jr., N. L. Segal, and L. M. Abraham, "Job Satisfaction: Environmental and Genetic Components," *Journal of Applied Psychology,* April 1989, pp. 187–92. These conclusions, however, have been challenged in B. Gerhart, "How Important Are Dispositional Factors as Determinants of Job Satisfaction? Implications for Job Design and Other Personnel Programs," *Journal of Applied Psychology,* August 1987, pp. 366–73; A. Davis-Blake and J. Pfeffer, "Just a Mirage: The Search for Dispositional Effects in Organizational Research," *Academy of Management Review,* July 1989, pp. 385–400; and R. D. Arvey, G. W. Carter, and D. K. Buerkley, "Job Satisfaction: Dispositional and Situational Influences," in C. L. Cooper and I. T. Robertson (eds.), *International Review of Industrial and Organizational Psychology,* Vol. 6 (Chichester, England: John Wiley, 1991), pp. 359–83.

[48]See, for example, D. C. Feldman and H. J. Arnold, "Personality Types and Career Patterns: Some Empirical Evidence on Holland's Model," *Canadian Journal of Administrative Science,* June 1985, pp. 192–210.

[49]A. H. Brayfield and W. H. Crockett, "Employee Attitudes and Employee Performance," *Psychological Bulletin,* September 1955, pp. 396–428; F. Herzberg, B. Mausner, R. O. Peterson, and D. F. Capwell, *Job Attitudes: Review of Research and Opinion* (Pittsburgh: Psychological Service of Pittsburgh, 1957); V. H. Vroom, *Work and Motivation* (New York: John Wiley, 1964); G. P. Fournet, M. K. Distefano, Jr., and M. W. Pryer, "Job Satisfaction: Issues and Problems," *Personnel Psychology,* Summer 1966, pp. 165–83.

[50]Vroom, *Work and Motivation;* and M. T. Iaffaldano and P. M. Muchinsky, "Job Satisfaction and Job Performance: A Meta-Analysis," *Psychological Bulletin,* March 1985, pp. 251–73.

[51]See, for example, J. B. Herman, "Are Situational Contingencies Limiting Job Attitude – Job Performance Relationship?", *Organizational Behavior and Human Performance,* October 1973, pp. 208–24; and M. M. Petty, G. W. McGee, and J. W. Cavender, "A Meta-Analysis of the Relationship Between Individual Job Satisfaction and Individual Performance," *Academy of Management Review,* October 1984, pp. 712–21.

[52]C. N. Greene, "The Satisfaction–Performance Controversy," *Business Horizons,* February 1972, pp. 31–41; E. E. Lawler III, *Motivation in Organizations* (Monterey, CA: Brooks/Cole, 1973); and Petty, McGee, and Cavender, "A Meta-Analysis of the Relationship Between Individual Job Satisfaction and Individual Performance."

[53]Locke, "The Nature and Causes of Job Satisfaction," p. 1331; S. L. McShane, "Job Satisfaction and Absenteeism: A Meta-Analytic Re-Examination," *Canadian Journal of Administrative Science,* June 1984, pp. 61–77; R. D. Hackett and R. M. Guion, "A Reevaluation of the Absenteeism-Job Satisfaction Relationship," *Organizational Behavior and Human Decision Processes,* June 1985, pp. 340–81; K. D. Scott and G. S. Taylor, "An Examination of Conflicting Findings on the Relationship Between Job Satisfaction and Absenteeism: A Meta-Analysis," *Academy of Management Journal,* September 1985, pp. 599–612; and R. D. Hackett, "Work Attitudes and Employee Absenteeism: A Synthesis of the Literature," paper presented at 1988 National Academy of Management Conference, Anaheim, CA., August 1988.

[54]F. J. Smith, "Work Attitudes as Predictors of Attendance on a Specific Day," *Journal of Applied Psychology,* February 1977, pp. 16–19.

[55]Brayfield and Crockett, "Employee Attitudes"; Vroom, *Work and Motivation;* J. Price, *The Study of Turnover* (Ames: Iowa State University Press, 1977); and W. H. Mobley, R. W.

Griffeth, H. H. Hand, and B. M. Meglino, "Review and Conceptual Analysis of the Employee Turnover Process," *Psychological Bulletin,* May 1979, pp. 493–522.

[56]S. A. Ahmed and J. Jabes, "A Comparative Study of Job Values of Business Students in France and English Canada," *Canadian Journal of Administrative Sciences,* June 1988, pp. 51–59.

[57]A. Howard, K. Shudo, and M. Umeshima, "Motivation and Values Among Japanese and American Managers," *Personnel Psychology,* Winter 1983, pp. 886–98.

[58]Cited in L. Smith, "Cracks in the Japanese Work Ethic," *Fortune,* May 14, 1984, pp. 162–68. See also "Office Woes East and West," *Fortune,* November 4, 1991, p. 14.

[59]See, for example, C. L. Hulin, M. Roznowski, and D. Hachiya, "Alternative Opportunities and Withdrawal Decisions: Empirical and Theoretical Discrepancies and an Integration," *Psychological Bulletin,* July 1985, pp. 233–50; and J. M. Carsten and P. E. Spector, "Unemployment, Job Satisfaction, and Employee Turnover: A Meta-Analytic Test of the Muchinsky Model," *Journal of Applied Psychology,* August 1987, pp. 374–81.

[60]D. G. Spencer and R. M. Steers, "Performance as a Moderator of the Job Satisfaction-Turnover Relationship," *Journal of Applied Psychology,* August 1981, pp. 511–14.

[61]S. M. Puffer, "Prosocial Behavior, Noncompliant Behavior, and Work Performance Among Commission Salespeople," *Journal of Applied Psychology,* November 1987, pp. 615–21; and J. Hogan and R. Hogan, "How to Measure Employee Reliability," *Journal of Applied Psychology,* May 1989, pp. 273–79.

[62]See D. Farrell, "Exit, Voice, Loyalty, and Neglect as Responses to Job Dissatisfaction: A Multidimensional Scaling Study," *Academy of Management Journal,* December 1983, pp. 596–606; C. E. Rusbult, D. Farrell, G. Rogers, and A. G. Mainous III, "Impact of Exchange Variables on Exit, Voice, Loyalty, and Neglect: An Integrative Model of Responses to Declining Job Satisfaction," *Academy of Management Journal,* September 1988, pp. 599–627; M. J. Withey and W. H. Cooper, "Predicting Exit, Voice, Loyalty, and Neglect," *Administrative Science Quarterly,* December 1989, pp. 521–39; and D. Farrell, C. Rusbult, Y-H Lin, and P. Bernthall, "Impact of Job Satisfaction, Investment Size, and Quality of Alternatives on Exit, Voice, Loyalty, and Neglect Responses to Job Dissatisfaction: A Cross-Legged Panel Study," in L. R. Jauch and J. L. Wall (eds.), *Proceedings of the 50th Annual Academy of Management Conference,* San Francisco, 1990, pp. 211–15.

[63]Freeman, "Job Satisfaction as an Economic Variable."

[64]See J. B. Dozier and M. P. Miceli, "Potential Predictors of Whistle-Blowing: A Prosocial Behavior Perspective," *Academy of Management Review,* October 1985, pp. 823–36.

BASIC MOTIVATION CONCEPTS

LEARNING OBJECTIVES

After studying this chapter, you should be able to:

1. Outline the motivation process

2. Describe Maslow's need hierarchy

3. Contrast Theory X and Theory Y

4. Differentiate motivators from hygiene factors

5. List the characteristics that high achievers prefer in a job

6. Explain the job characteristics model

7. Summarize the types of goals that increase performance

8. State the impact of underrewarding employees

9. Clarify the key relationships in expectancy theory

*L*incoln Electric is a Cleveland-based firm that employs about twenty-four hundred people and generates ninety percent of its sales from manufacturing arc-welding equipment and supplies. Founded in 1895, the company's legendary profit-sharing incentive system and resultant productivity record are the envy of the manufacturing world.[1]

Factory workers at Lincoln receive piece-rate wages with no guaranteed minimum hourly pay. After working for the firm for two years, employees begin to participate in the year-end bonus plan. Determined by a formula that considers the company's gross profits, the employees' base piece rate, and merit rating, it may be the most lucrative bonus system for factory workers in American manufacturing. The *average* size of the bonus over the past fifty-five years has been 95.5 percent of base wages!

The company has a guaranteed-employment policy, which it put in place in 1958. Since that time, it has not laid off a single worker. In return for job security, however, employees agree to several things. During slow times, they will accept reduced work periods. They also agree to accept work transfers, even to lower-paid jobs, if that is necessary to maintain a minimum of thirty hours of work per week.

You'd think the Lincoln Electric system would attract quality people, and it does. For instance, the company recently hired four Harvard M.B.A.s to fill future management slots. But, consistent with company tradition, they started out, like everyone else, doing piecework on the assembly line.

Lincoln Electric's profit-sharing incentive system has provided positive benefits for the company as well as for its employees. One company executive estimates that Lincoln's overall productivity is about double that of its domestic competitors. The company has earned a profit every year since the depths of the 1930s Depression and has never missed a quarterly dividend. And Lincoln has one of the lowest employee turnover rates in United States industry. ■

Lincoln Electric has successfully integrated employment security, financial incentives, job flexibility, and high productivity standards into a system that motivates its employees. Most organizations haven't been so successful. This may explain why the concept of motivation is probably the most researched and discussed topic in the organizational sciences.

A cursory look at most organizations quickly suggests that some people work harder than others. Who among us, for instance, hasn't seen an individual with outstanding abilities outperformed by someone with obviously inferior talents? Why do some people appear to be "highly motivated," while others are not? We'll try to answer this latter question in this and the following chapter.

WHAT IS MOTIVATION?

Motivation The willingness to exert high levels of effort toward organizational goals, conditioned by the effort's ability to satisfy some individual need.

Maybe the place to begin is to say what motivation isn't. Many people incorrectly view motivation as a personal trait—that is, some have it and others don't. In practice, some managers label employees who seem to lack motivation as lazy. Such a label assumes that an individual is always lazy or is lacking in motivation. Our knowledge of motivation tells us that this just isn't true. What we know is that motivation is the result of the interaction of the individual and the situation. Certainly, individuals diifer in their basic motivational drive. But the same employee who is quickly bored when pulling the lever on his drill press may pull the lever on a slot machine in Las Vegas for hours on end without the slightest hint of boredom. You may read a complete novel at one sitting, yet find it difficult to stay with a textbook for more than twenty minutes. It's not necessarily you—it's the situation. So as we analyze the concept of motivation, keep in mind that level of motivation varies both between individuals and within individuals at different times.

We'll define **motivation** as the willingness to exert high levels of effort toward organizational goals, conditioned by the effort's ability to satisfy some individual need. While general motivation is concerned with effort toward *any* goal, we'll narrow the focus to *organizational* goals in order to reflect our singular interest in work-related behavior. The three key elements in our definition are effort, organizational goals, and needs.

The effort element is a measure of intensity. When someone is motivated, he or she tries hard. But high levels of effort are unlikely to lead to favorable job performance outcomes unless the effort is channeled in a direction that benefits the organization.[2] Therefore, we must consider the quality of the effort as well as its intensity. Effort that is directed toward, and consistent with, the organization's goals is the kind of effort that we should be seeking. Finally, we will treat motivation as a need-satisfying process. This is depicted in Figure 7–1.

Need Some internal state that makes certain outcomes appear attractive.

A **need,** in our terminology, means some internal state that makes certain outcomes appear attractive. An unsatisfied need creates tension that stimulates drives within the individual. These drives generate a search behavior to find particular goals that, if attained, will satisfy the need and lead to the reduction of tension.

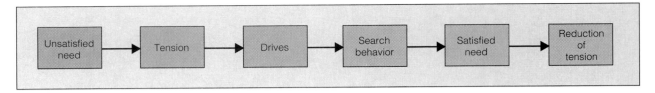

FIGURE 7–1   The Motivation Process

So we can say that motivated employees are in a state of tension. To relieve this tension, they exert effort. The greater the tension, the higher the effort level. If this effort successfully leads to the satisfaction of the need, tension is reduced. But since we are interested in work behavior, this tension-reduction effort must also be directed toward organizational goals. Therefore, inherent in our definition of motivation is the requirement that the individual's needs be compatible and consistent with the organization's goals. Where this does not occur, we can have individuals exerting high levels of effort that actually run counter to the interests of the organization. This, incidentally, is not so unusual. For example, some employees regularly spend a lot of time talking with friends at work in order to satisfy their social needs. There is a high level of effort, only it's being unproductively directed.

EARLY THEORIES OF MOTIVATION

The 1950s were a fruitful period in the development of motivation concepts. Three specific theories were formulated during this period, which, though heavily attacked and now questionable in terms of validity, are probably the best known explanations for employee motivation. These are the hierarchy of needs theory, Theories X and Y, and the motivation-hygiene theory. As you'll see later in this chapter, we have since developed more valid explanations of motivation, but you should know these early theories for at least two reasons: (1) they represent a foundation from which contemporary theories have grown, and (2) practicing managers regularly use these theories and their terminology in explaining employee motivation.

Hierarchy of Needs Theory

Hierarchy of Needs Theory
There is a hierarchy of five needs—physiological, safety, social, esteem, and self-actualization—and as each need is sequentially satisfied, the next need becomes dominant.

It's probably safe to say that the most well-known theory of motivation is Abraham Maslow's **hierarchy of needs.**[3] He hypothesized that within every human being there exists a hierarchy of five needs. These needs are:

1. *Physiological:* Includes hunger, thirst, shelter, sex, and other bodily needs
2. *Safety:* Includes security and protection from physical and emotional harm
3. *Social:* Includes affection, belongingness, acceptance, and friendship
4. *Esteem:* Includes internal esteem factors such as self-respect, autonomy, and achievement; and external esteem factors such as status, recognition, and attention

Self-actualization   The drive to become what one is capable of becoming.

5. ***Self-actualization:*** The drive to become what one is capable of becoming; includes growth, achieving one's potential, and self-fulfillment

As each of these needs becomes substantially satisfied, the next need becomes dominant. In terms of Figure 7–2, the individual moves up the

FIGURE 7–2   Maslow's Hierarchy of Needs   Source: By permission of the Modular Project of Organizational Behavior and Instructional Communications Centre. McGill University, Montreal, Canada

Lower-order Needs   Needs that are satisfied externally; physiological and safety needs.

Higher-order Needs   Needs that are satisfied internally; social, esteem, and self-actualization needs.

steps of the hierarchy. From the standpoint of motivation, the theory would say that although no need is ever fully gratified, a substantially satisfied need no longer motivates. So if you want to motivate someone, according to Maslow, you need to understand what level of the hierarchy that person is currently on and focus on satisfying those needs at or above that level.

Maslow separated the five needs into higher and lower orders. Physiological and safety needs were described as **lower-order** and social, esteem, and self-actualization as **higher-order** needs. The differentiation between the two orders was made on the premise that higher-order needs are satisfied internally (within the person), whereas lower-order needs are predominantly satisfied externally (by such things as money wages, union contracts, and tenure). In fact, the natural conclusion to be drawn from Maslow's classification is that in times of economic plenty, almost all permanently employed workers have their lower-order needs substantially met.

Maslow's need theory has received wide recognition, particularly among practicing managers. This can be attributed to the theory's intuitive logic and ease of understanding. Unfortunately, however, research does not generally validate the theory. Maslow provided no empirical substantiation, and several studies that sought to validate the theory found no support for it.[4]

Old theories, especially ones that are intuitively logical, apparently die hard. One researcher reviewed the evidence and concluded that "although of great societal popularity, need hierarchy as a theory continues to receive little empirical support."[5] Further, the researcher stated that the "available research should certainly generate a reluctance to accept unconditionally the implication of Maslow's hierarchy."[6] Another review came to the same conclusion.[7] Little support was found for the prediction that need structures are organized along the dimensions proposed by Maslow, that unsatisfied needs motivate, or that a satisfied need activates movement to a new need level.

Today, almost all permanently employed workers have their lower-order needs met. Retail clerks in Los Angeles, for example, earn more than $9 an hour and have attractive health and security benefits provided by their employer.
Lawrence Migdale/Stock, Boston

Theory X and Theory Y

Theory X The assumption that employees dislike work, are lazy, dislike responsibility, and must be coerced to perform.

Theory Y The assumption that employees like work, are creative, seek responsibility, and can exercise self-direction.

Douglas McGregor proposed two distinct views of human beings: one basically negative, labeled **Theory X,** and the other basically positive, labeled **Theory Y.**[8] After viewing the way in which managers dealt with employees, McGregor concluded that a manager's view of the nature of human beings is based on a certain grouping of assumptions and that he or she tends to mold his or her behavior toward subordinates according to these assumptions.

Under Theory X, the four assumptions held by managers are:

1. Employees inherently dislike work and, whenever possible, will attempt to avoid it.
2. Since employees dislike work, they must be coerced, controlled, or threatened with punishment to achieve goals.
3. Employees will avoid responsibilities and seek formal direction whenever possible.
4. Most workers place security above all other factors associated with work and will display little ambition.

In contrast to these negative views about the nature of human beings, McGregor listed the four positive assumptions that he called Theory Y:

1. Employees can view work as being as natural as rest or play.
2. People will exercise self-direction and self-control if they are committed to the objectives.
3. The average person can learn to accept, even seek, responsibility.
4. The ability to make innovative decisions is widely dispersed throughout the population and is not necessarily the sole province of those in management positions.

What are the motivational implications if you accept McGregor's analysis? The answer is best expressed in the framework presented by Maslow. Theory X assumes that lower-order needs dominate individuals. Theory Y assumes that higher-order needs dominate individuals. McGregor himself held to the belief that Theory Y assumptions were more valid than Theory X. Therefore, he proposed such ideas as participation in decision making, responsible and challenging jobs, and good group relations as approaches that would maximize an employee's job motivation.

Unfortunately, there is no evidence to confirm that either set of assumptions is valid or that accepting Theory Y assumptions and altering one's actions accordingly will lead to more motivated workers. As will become evident later in this chapter, either Theory X or Theory Y assumptions may be appropriate in a particular situation.

Motivation-Hygiene Theory

Motivation-Hygiene Theory
Intrinsic factors are related to job satisfaction, while extrinsic factors are associated with dissatisfaction.

The **motivation-hygiene theory** was proposed by psychologist Frederick Herzberg.[9] In the belief that an individual's relation to his or her work is a basic one and that his or her attitude toward this work can very well determine the individual's success or failure, Herzberg investigated the question, "What do people want from their jobs?" He asked people to describe, in detail, situations when they felt exceptionally *good* and *bad* about their jobs. These responses were tabulated and categorized. Factors affecting job attitudes as reported in twelve investigations conducted by Herzberg are illustrated in Figure 7–3.

FIGURE 7–3   Comparison of Satisfiers and Dissatisfiers   Reprinted by permission of *Harvard Business Review*. An exhibit from *One More Time: How Do You Motivate Employees?* by Frederick Herzberg, September/October 1987. Copyright © 1987 by the President and Fellows of Harvard College; all rights reserved.

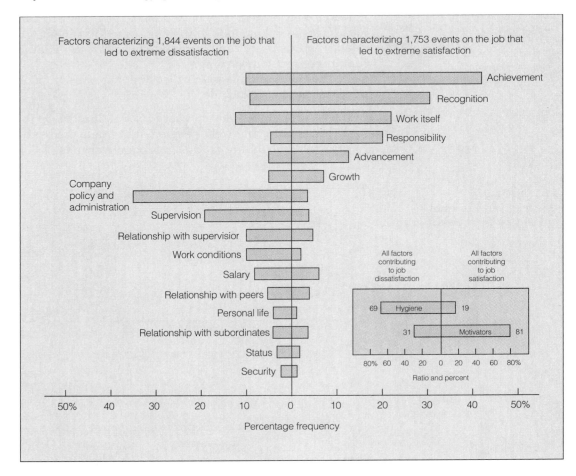

From the categorized responses, Herzberg concluded that the replies people gave when they felt good about their jobs were significantly different from the replies given when they felt bad. As seen in Figure 7–3, certain characteristics tend to be consistently related to job satisfaction (factors on the right side of the figure), and others to job dissatisfaction (the left side of the figure). Intrinsic factors, such as achievement, recognition, the work itself, responsibility, advancement, and growth, seem to be related to job satisfaction. When those questioned felt good about their work, they tended to attribute these characteristics to themselves. On the other hand, when they were dissatisfied, they tended to cite extrinsic factors, such as company policy and administration, supervision, interpersonal relations, and working conditions.

The data suggest, says Herzberg, that the opposite of satisfaction is not dissatisfaction, as was traditionally believed. Removing dissatisfying characteristics from a job does not necessarily make the job satisfying. As illustrated in Figure 7–4, Herzberg proposes that his findings indicate the existence of a dual continuum: The opposite of "Satisfaction" is "No Satisfaction," and the opposite of "Dissatisfaction" is "No Dissatisfaction."

According to Herzberg, the factors leading to job satisfaction are separate and distinct from those that lead to job dissatisfaction. Therefore, managers who seek to eliminate factors that create job dissatisfaction can bring about peace, but not necessarily motivation. They will be placating their work force rather than motivating them. As a result, such characteristics as company policy and administration, supervision, interpersonal relations, working conditions, and salary have been characterized by Herzberg as **hygiene factors.** When they are adequate, people will not be dissatisfied; however, neither will they be satisfied. If we want to motivate people on their jobs, Herzberg suggests emphasizing achievement, recognition, the work itself, responsibility, and growth. These are the characteristics that people find intrinsically rewarding.

The motivation-hygiene theory is not without its detractors. The criticisms of the theory include the following:

1. The procedure that Herzberg used is limited by its methodology. When things are going well, people tend to take credit themselves. Contrarily, they blame failure on the external environment.

Hygiene Factors Those factors—such as company policy and administration, supervision, and salary—that, when adequate in a job, placate workers. When these factors are adequate, people will not be dissatisfied.

FIGURE 7–4
Contrasting Views of Satisfaction-Dissatisfaction

TRADITIONAL VIEW

Satisfaction   Dissatisfaction

HERZBERG'S VIEW (Motivators)

Satisfaction   No Satisfaction

(Hygiene Factors)

Dissatisfaction   No Dissatisfaction

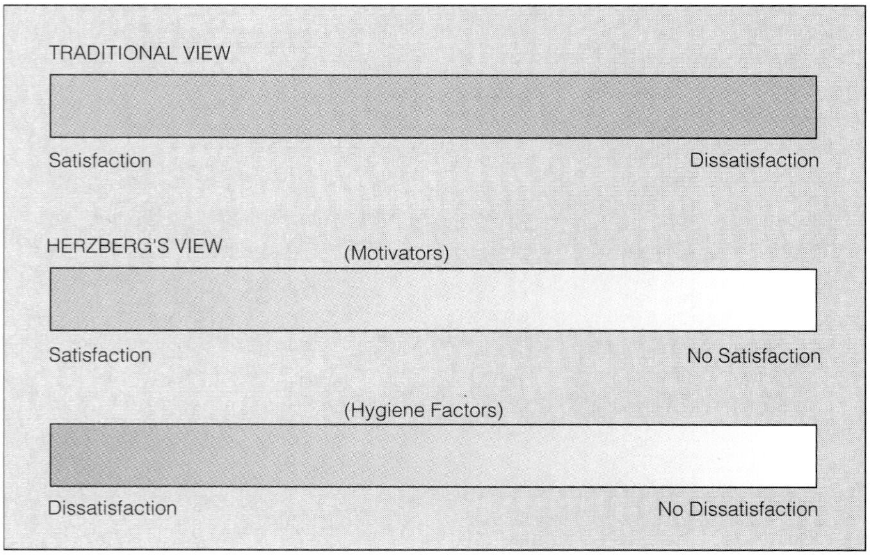

2. The reliability of Herzberg's methodology is questioned. Since raters have to make interpretations, it is possible that they may contaminate the findings by interpreting one response in one manner while treating another similar response differently.

3. The theory, to the degree that it is valid, provides an explanation of job satisfaction. It is not really a theory of motivation.

4. No overall measure of satisfaction was utilized. In other words, a person may dislike part of his or her job, yet still think the job is acceptable.

5. The theory is inconsistent with previous research. The motivation-hygiene theory ignores situational variables.

6. Herzberg assumes that there is a relationship between satisfaction and productivity. But the research methodology he used looked only at satisfaction, not at productivity. To make such research relevant, one must assume a high relationship between satisfaction and productivity.[10]

Regardless of criticisms, Herzberg's theory has been widely read and few managers are unfamiliar with his recommendations. The increased popularity since the mid-1960s of vertically expanding jobs to allow workers greater responsibility in planning and controlling their work can probably be largely attributed to Herzberg's findings and recommendations.

CONTEMPORARY THEORIES OF MOTIVATION

The previous theories are well known but, unfortunately, have not held up well under close examination. However, all is not lost.[11] There are a number of contemporary theories that have one thing in common—each has a reasonable degree of valid supporting documentation. Of course, this doesn't mean that the theories we are about to introduce are unquestionably "right." We call them "contemporary theories" not because they necessarily were developed recently, but because they represent the current "state of the art" in explaining employee motivation.

ERG Theory

ERG Theory There are three groups of core needs: existence, relatedness, and growth.

Clayton Alderfer of Yale University has reworked Maslow's need hierarchy to align it more closely with the empirical research. His revised need hierarchy is labeled **ERG theory**.[12]

Alderfer argues that there are three groups of core needs—existence, relatedness, and growth—hence the label: ERG theory. The existence group is concerned with providing our basic material existence requirements. They include the items that Maslow considered physiological and safety needs. The second group of needs are those of relatedness—the desire we have for maintaining important interpersonal relationships. These social and status desires require interaction with others if they are to be satisfied, and they align with Maslow's social need and the external component of Maslow's esteem classification. Finally, Alderfer isolates growth needs—an intrinsic desire for personal development. These include the intrinsic component from Maslow's esteem category and the characteristics included under self-actualization.

Besides substituting three needs for five, how does Alderfer's ERG theory differ from Maslow's? In contrast to the hierarchy of needs theory, the ERG theory demonstrates that (1) more than one need may be operative at the same time, and (2) if the gratification of a higher-level need is stifled, the desire to satisfy a lower-level need increases.

Maslow's need hierarchy is a rigid steplike progression. ERG theory does not assume that there exists a rigid hierarchy where a lower need must be substantially gratified before one can move on. A person can, for instance, be working on growth even though existence or relatedness needs are unsatisfied; or all three need categories could be operating at the same time.

ERG theory also contains a frustration-regression dimension. Maslow, you'll remember, argued that an individual would stay at a certain need level until that need was satisfied. ERG theory counters by noting that when a higher-order need level is frustrated, the individual's desire to increase a lower-level need takes place. Inability to satisfy a need for social interaction, for instance, might increase the desire for more money or better working conditions. So frustration can lead to a regression to a lower need.

In summary, ERG theory argues, like Maslow, that satisfied lower-order needs lead to the desire to satisfy higher-order needs; but multiple needs can be operating as motivators at the same time, and frustration in attempting to satisfy a higher-level need can result in regression to a lower-level need.

ERG theory is more consistent with our knowledge of individual differences among people. Variables such as education, family background, and cultural environment can alter the importance or driving force that a group of needs holds for a particular individual. The evidence demonstrating that people in other cultures rank the need categories differently—for instance, natives of Spain and Japan place social needs before their physiological requirements[13]—would be consistent with the ERG theory. Several studies have supported the ERG theory,[14] but there is also evidence that it doesn't work in some organizations.[15] Overall, however, ERG theory represents a more valid version of the need hierarchy.

McClelland's Theory of Needs

You've got one beanbag and there are five targets set up in front of you. Each one is progressively farther away and, hence, more difficult to hit. Target A is a cinch. It sits almost within arm's reach of you. If you hit it, you get $2. Target B is a bit farther out, but about eighty percent of the people who try can hit it. It pays $4. Target C pays $8, and about half the people who try can hit it. Very few people can hit Target D, but the payoff is $16 if you do. Finally, Target E pays $32, but it's almost impossible to achieve. Which target would you try for? If you selected C, you're likely to be a high achiever. Why? Read on.

In Chapter 4, we introduced the need to achieve as a personality characteristic. It is also one of three needs proposed by David McClelland and his associates as being important in organizational settings for understanding motivation.[16] **McClelland's theory of needs** focuses on three needs: achievement, power, and affiliation. They are defined as follows:

- **Need for achievement:** The drive to excel, to achieve in relation to a set of standards, to strive to succeed
- **Need for power:** The need to make others behave in a way that they would not have behaved otherwise
- **Need for affiliation:** The desire for friendly and close interpersonal relationships

McClelland's Theory of Needs Achievement, power, and affiliation are three important needs that help to understand motivation.

Achievement Need The drive to excel, to achieve in relation to a set of standards, to strive to succeed.

Power Need The desire to make others behave in a way that they would not otherwise have behaved in.

Affiliation Need The desire for friendly and close interpersonal relationships.

High achievers, like this salesperson at Schering-Plough, do well in sales positions because such jobs provide employees with freedom, personal responsibility for outcomes, immediate feedback on their performance, and the opportunity to take on moderate risks. Rhoda Baer

As described previously, some people who have a compelling drive to succeed are striving for personal achievement rather than the rewards of success per se. They have a desire to do something better or more efficiently than it has been done before. This drive is the achievement need (*nAch*). From research into the achievement need, McClelland found that high achievers differentiate themselves from others by their desire to do things better.[17] They seek situations where they can attain personal responsibility for finding solutions to problems, where they can receive rapid feedback on their performance so they can tell easily whether they are improving or not, and where they can set moderately challenging goals. High achievers are not gamblers; they dislike succeeding by chance. They prefer the challenge of working at a problem and accepting the personal responsibility for success or failure rather than leaving the outcome to chance or the actions of others. Importantly, they avoid what they perceive to be very easy or very difficult tasks.

Again as noted in Chapter 4, high achievers perform best when they perceive their probability of success as being 0.5, that is, where they estimate that they have a fifty-fifty chance of success. They dislike gambling with high odds because they get no achievement satisfaction from happenstance success. Similarly, they dislike low odds (high probability of success) because then there is no challenge to their skills. They like to set goals that require stretching themselves a little. When there is an approximately equal chance of success or failure, there is the optimum opportunity to experience feelings of accomplishment and satisfaction from their efforts.

The need for power (*nPow*) is the desire to have impact, to be influential, and to control others. Individuals high in *nPow* enjoy being "in charge," strive for influence over others, prefer to be placed into competitive and status-oriented situations, and tend to be more concerned with prestige and gaining influence over others than with effective performance.

The third need isolated by McClelland is affiliation (*nAff*). This need has received the least attention from researchers. Affiliation can be viewed as a Dale Carnegie-type of need—the desire to be liked and accepted by oth-

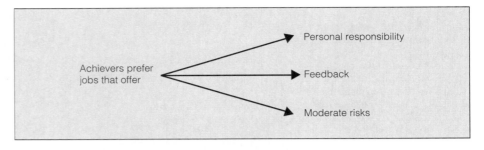

FIGURE 7–5   Matching Achievers and Jobs

ers. Individuals with a high affiliation motive strive for friendship, prefer cooperative situations rather than competitive ones, and desire relationships involving a high degree of mutual understanding.

Relying on an extensive amount of research, some reasonably well-supported predictions can be made based on the relationship between achievement need and job performance. Although less research has been done on power and affiliation needs, there are consistent findings here, too.

First, as shown in Figure 7–5, individuals with a high need to achieve prefer job situations with personal responsibility, feedback, and an intermediate degree of risk. When these characteristics are prevalent, high achievers will be strongly motivated. The evidence consistently demonstrates, for instance, that high achievers are successful in entrepreneurial activities such as running their own businesses and managing a self-contained unit within a large organization.[18]

Second, a high need to achieve does not necessarily lead to being a good manager, especially in large organizations. People with a high achievement need are interested in how well they do personally and not in influencing others to do well. High-*nAch* salespeople do not necessarily make good sales managers, and the good general manager in a large organization does not typically have a high need to achieve.[19]

Third, the needs for affiliation and power tend to be closely related to managerial success. The best managers are high in their need for power and low in their need for affiliation.[20] In fact, a high power motive may be a requirement for managerial effectiveness.[21] Of course, what is the cause and what is the effect is arguable. It has been suggested that a high power need may occur simply as a function of one's level in a hierarchical organization.[22] The latter argument proposes that the higher the level an individual rises to in the organization, the greater is the incumbent's power motive. As a result, powerful positions would be the stimulus to a high power motive.

Lastly, employees have been successfully trained to stimulate their achievement need. If the job calls for a high achiever, management can select a person with a high *nAch* or develop its own candidate through achievement training.[23]

Cognitive Evaluation Theory

Cognitive Evaluation Theory
Allocating extrinsic rewards for behavior that had been previously intrinsically rewarded tends to decrease the overall level of motivation.

In the late 1960s, one researcher proposed that the introduction of extrinsic rewards, such as pay, for work effort that had been previously intrinsically rewarding due to the pleasure associated with the content of the work itself would tend to decrease the overall level of motivation.[24] This proposal—which has come to be called the **cognitive evaluation theory**—has been extensively researched, and a large number of studies have been supportive.[25] As we'll show, the major implications for this theory relate to the way in which people are paid in organizations.

Historically, motivation theorists have generally assumed that intrinsic motivations such as achievement, responsibility, and competence are independent of extrinsic motivators like high pay, promotions, good supervisor relations, and pleasant working conditions. That is, the stimulation of one would not affect the other. But the cognitive evaluation theory suggests otherwise. It argues that when extrinsic rewards are used by organizations as payoffs for superior performance, the intrinsic rewards, which are derived from individuals doing what they like, are reduced. In other words, when extrinsic rewards are given to someone for performing an interesting task, it causes intrinsic interest in the task itself to decline.

Why would such an outcome occur? The popular explanation is that the individual experiences a loss of control over his or her own behavior so that the previous intrinsic motivation diminishes. Further, the elimination of extrinsic rewards can produce a shift—from an external to an internal explanation—in an individual's perception of causation of why he or she works on a task. If you're reading a novel a week because your English literature instructor requires you to, you can attribute your reading behavior to an external source. However, after the course is over, if you find yourself continuing to read a novel a week, your natural inclination is to say, "I must enjoy reading novels, because I'm still reading one a week!"

If the cognitive evaluation theory is valid, it should have major implications for managerial practices. It has been a truism among compensation specialists for years that if pay or other extrinsic rewards are to be effective motivators, they should be made contingent on an individual's performance. But, cognitive evaluation theorists would argue, this will only tend to decrease the internal satisfaction that the individual receives from doing the job. We have substituted an external stimulus for an internal stimulus. In fact, if cognitive evaluation theory is correct, it would make sense to make an individual's pay *non*contingent on performance in order to avoid decreasing intrinsic motivation.

We noted earlier that the cognitive evaluation theory has been supported in a number of studies. Yet it has also met with attacks, specifically on the methodology used in these studies[26] and in the interpretation of the findings.[27] But where does this theory stand today? Can we say that when organizations use extrinsic motivators like pay and promotions to stimulate workers' performance they do so at the expense of reducing intrinsic interest and motivation in the work being done? The answer is not a simple "Yes" or "No."

While further research is needed to clarify some of the current ambiguity, the evidence does lead us to conclude that the interdependence of extrinsic and intrinsic rewards is a real phenomenon.[28] But its impact on employee motivation at work, in contrast to motivation in general, may be considerably less than originally thought. First, many of the studies testing the theory were done with students, not paid organizational employees. The researchers would observe what happens to a student's behavior when a reward that had been allocated is stopped. This is interesting, but it does not represent the typical work situation. In the real world, when extrinsic rewards are stopped, it usually means the individual is no longer part of the organization. Second, evidence indicates that very high intrinsic motivation levels are strongly resistant to the detrimental impacts of extrinsic rewards.[29] Even when a job is inherently interesting, there still exists a powerful norm for extrinsic payment.[30] At the other extreme, on dull tasks extrinsic rewards appear to increase intrinsic motivation.[31] Therefore, the theory may have limited applicability to work organizations because most low-level jobs are not inherently satisfying enough to foster high intrinsic interest and many managerial and professional positions offer intrinsic rewards. Cognitive evaluation theory may be relevant to that set of organizational jobs that falls in between—those that are neither extremely dull nor extremely interesting.

Task Characteristics Theories

"Every day was the same thing," Frank Greer began. "Put the right passenger seat into Jeeps as they came down the assembly line, pop in four bolts locking the seat frame to the car body, then tighten the bolts with my electric wrench. Thirty cars and 120 bolts an hour, eight hours a day. I didn't care that they were paying me $17 an hour, I was going crazy. I did it for almost a year and a half. Finally, I just said to my wife that this isn't going to be the way I'm going to spend the rest of my life. My brain was turning to Jello on that job. So I quit. Now I work in a print shop and I make less than $12 an hour. But let me tell you, the work I do is really interesting. It challenges me! I look forward every morning to going to work again."

Frank Greer is acknowledging two facts we all know: (1) jobs are different and (2) some are more interesting and challenging than others. These facts have not gone unnoticed by OB researchers. They have responded by developing a number of **task characteristics theories** that seek to identify task characteristics of jobs, how these characteristics are combined to form different jobs, and the relationship of these task characteristics to employee motivation, satisfaction, and performance.

Task Characteristics Theories
Seek to identify task characteristics of jobs, how these characteristics are combined to form different jobs, and their relationship to employee motivation, satisfaction, and performance.

There are at least seven different task characteristics theories.[32] Fortunately, there is a significant amount of overlap between them.[33] For instance, Herzberg's motivation-hygiene theory and the research on the achievement need are essentially task characteristics theories. You'll remember that Herzberg argued that jobs that provided opportunities for achievement, recognition, responsibility, and the like would increase employee satisfaction. Similarly, McClelland demonstrated that high achievers performed best in jobs that offered personal responsibility, feedback, and moderate risks.

In this section, we'll review the three most important task characteristics theories—requisite task attributes theory, the job characteristics model, and the social information-processing model.

REQUISITE TASK ATTRIBUTES THEORY The task characteristics approach began with the pioneering work of Turner and Lawrence in the mid-1960s.[34] They developed a research study to assess the effect of different kinds of jobs on employee satisfaction and absenteeism. They predicted that employees would prefer jobs that were complex and challenging; that is, such jobs would increase satisfaction and result in lower absence rates. They defined job complexity in terms of six task characteristics: (1) variety; (2) autonomy; (3) responsibility; (4) knowledge and skill; (5) required social interaction; and (6) optional social interaction. The higher a job scored on these characteristics, according to Turner and Lawrence, the more complex it was.

Their findings confirmed their absenteeism prediction. Employees in high-complexity tasks had better attendance records. But they found no general correlation between task complexity and satisfaction—until they broke their data down by the background of employees. When individual differences in the form of urban-versus-rural background were taken into account, employees from urban settings were shown to be more satisfied with low-complexity jobs. Employees with rural backgrounds reported higher satisfaction in high-complexity jobs. Turner and Lawrence concluded that workers in larger communities had a variety of nonwork interests and thus were less involved and motivated by their work. In contrast, workers from smaller towns had fewer nonwork interests and were more receptive to the complex tasks of their jobs.

Turner and Lawrence's requisite task attributes theory was important for at least three reasons. First, they demonstrated that employees did respond differently to different types of jobs. Second, they provided a preliminary set of task attributes by which jobs could be assessed. And third, they focused attention on the need to consider the influence of individual differences on employees' reaction to jobs.

THE JOB CHARACTERISTICS MODEL   Turner and Lawrence's requisite task attributes theory laid the foundation for what is today the dominant framework for defining task characteristics and understanding their relationship to employee motivation. That is Hackman and Oldham's **job characteristics model** (JCM).[35]

According to the JCM, any job can be described in terms of five core job dimensions, defined as follows:

1. **Skill variety:** The degree to which the job requires a variety of different activities so the worker can use a number of different skills and talent
2. **Task identity:** The degree to which the job requires completion of a whole and identifiable piece of work
3. **Task significance:** The degree to which the job has a substantial impact on the lives or work of other people
4. **Autonomy:** The degree to which the job provides substantial freedom, independence, and discretion to the individual in scheduling the work and in determining the procedures to be used in carrying it out
5. **Feedback:** The degree to which carrying out the work activities required by the job results in the individual obtaining direct and clear information about the effectiveness of his or her performance

Table 7–1 offers examples of job activities that rate high and low for each characteristic.

Figure 7–6 presents the model. Notice how the first three dimensions—skill variety, task identity, and task significance—combine to create meaningful work. That is, if these three characteristics exist in a job, we can predict that the incumbent will view the job as being important, valuable, and worthwhile. Notice, too, that jobs that possess autonomy give the job incumbent a feeling of personal responsibility for the results and that, if a job provides feedback, the employee will know how effectively he or she is performing. From a motivational standpoint, the model says that internal rewards are obtained by an individual when he *learns* (knowledge of results) that he *personally* (experienced responsibility) has performed well on a task that he *cares* about (experienced meaningfulness).[36] The more that these three psychological states are present, the greater will be the employee's motivation, performance, and satisfaction, and the lower his or her absenteeism and likelihood of leaving the organization. As Figure 7–6 shows, the links between the job dimensions and the outcomes are moderated or adjusted by the strength of the individual's growth need; that is, by the employee's desire for self-esteem and self-actualization. This means that individuals with a high growth need are more likely to experience the psychological states

Job Characteristics Model Identifies five job characteristics and their relationship to personal and work outcomes.

Skill Variety The degree to which the job requires a variety of different activities.

Task Identity The degree to which the job requires completion of a whole and identifiable piece of work.

Task Significance The degree to which the job has a substantial impact on the lives or work of other people.

Autonomy The degree to which the job provides substantial freedom and discretion to the individual in scheduling the work and in determining the procedures to be used in carrying it out.

Feedback The degree to which carrying out the work activities required by a job results in the individual obtaining direct and clear information about the effectiveness of his or her performance.

TABLE 7–1   Examples of High and Low Job Characteristics

Skill Variety

High variety	The owner-operator of a garage who does electrical repair, rebuilds engines, does body work, and interacts with customers
Low variety	A body shop worker who sprays paint eight hours a day

Task Identity

High identity	A cabinet maker who designs a piece of furniture, selects the wood, builds the object, and finishes it to perfection
Low identity	A worker in a furniture factory who operates a lathe solely to make table legs

Task Significance

High significance	Nursing the sick in a hospital intensive care unit
Low significance	Sweeping hospital floors

Autonomy

High autonomy	A telephone installer who schedules his or her own work for the day, makes visits without supervision, and decides on the most effective techniques for a particular installation
Low autonomy	A telephone operator who must handle calls as they come according to a routine, highly specified procedure

Feedback

High feedback	An electronics factory worker who assembles a radio and then tests it to determine if it operates properly
Low feedback	An electronics factory worker who assembles a radio and then routes it to a quality control inspector who tests it for proper operation and makes needed adjustments

Source: G. Johns, *Organizational Behavior: Understanding Life at Work*, 3rd ed. (New York: Harper Collins, 1992), p.216. With permission.

when their jobs are enriched than are their counterparts with a low growth need. Moreover, they will respond more positively to the psychological states when they are present than will low-growth-need individuals.

The core dimensions can be combined into a single predictive index, called the **motivating potential score** (MPS). Its computation is shown in Figure 7–7.

Motivating Potential Score
A predictive index suggesting the motivation potential in a job.

Jobs that are high on motivating potential must be high on at least one of the three factors that lead to experienced meaningfulness, and they must be high on both autonomy and feedback. If jobs score high on motivating potential, the model predicts that motivation, performance, and satisfaction will be positively affected, while the likelihood of absence and turnover will be lessened.

The job characteristics model has been well researched. Most of the evidence supports the general framework of the theory—that is, there is a multiple set of job characteristics and these characteristics impact behavioral outcomes.[37] But there is still considerable debate around the five specific core dimensions in the JCM, the multiplicative properties of the MPS, and whether other moderating variables may not be as good or better than growth-need strength.

There is some question whether task identity adds to the model's predictive ability,[38] and there is evidence suggesting that skill variety may be redundant with autonomy.[39] Further, a number of studies have found that by adding all the variables in the MPS, rather than adding some and multiplying by others, the MPS becomes a better predictor of work outcomes.[40] Finally, while the strength of an individual's growth needs has been found to be a meaningful moderating variable in many studies,[41] other variables—such as the presence or absence of social cues, perceived equity with comparison groups, and propensity to assimilate work experience[42]—have also been found to moderate the job characteristics-outcome relationship. Given the current state of research on moderating variables, one should be cau-

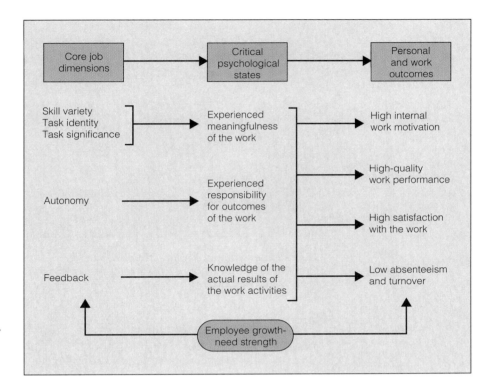

FIGURE 7–6   The Job Characteristics Model

Source: J. R. Hackman, "Work Design," in *Improving Life at Work*, eds. J. R. Hackman and J. L. Suttle (Glenview, IL: Scott, Foresman and Company, 1977), p. 129.

tious in unequivocally accepting growth-need strength as originally included in the JCM.

Where does this leave us? Given the current state of evidence, we can make the following statements with relative confidence: (1) People who work on jobs with high-core job dimensions are generally more motivated, satisfied, and productive than are those who do not. (2) Job dimensions operate through the psychological states in influencing personal and work outcome variables rather than influencing them directly.[43]

SOCIAL INFORMATION-PROCESSING MODEL   At the beginning of this section on task characteristics theories, do you remember Frank Greer complaining about his former job on the Jeep assembly line? Would it surprise you to know that one of Frank's best friends, Russ Wright, is still working at Jeep, doing the same job that Frank did, and that Russ thinks his job is perfectly fine? Probably not! Why? Because, consistent with our discussion of perception in Chapter 5, we recognize that people can look at the same job and evaluate it differently. The fact that people respond to their jobs *as they perceive them* rather than to the *objective* jobs themselves is the central the-

FIGURE 7–7   Computing a Motivating Potential Score

$$\text{Motivating Potential Score (MPS)} = \left[\frac{\text{Skill variety} + \text{Task identity} + \text{Task significance}}{3} \right] \times \text{Autonomy} \times \text{Feedback}$$

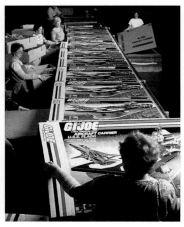

A Lenox craftsman applies finishing touches to fine china. An employee assembling and packaging toys at a Hasbro plant. The job at Lenox scores higher in motivating potential than does the Hasbro job. Why?   Left, John S. Abbott; right, David Walberg.

Social Information-Processing Model Employees adopt attitudes and behaviors in response to the social cues provided by others with whom they have contact.

sis in our third task characteristics theory. It's called the **social information-processing (SIP) model.**[44]

The SIP model argues that employees adopt attitudes and behaviors in response to the social cues provided by others with whom they have contact. These others can be co-workers, supervisors, friends, family members, or customers. For instance, Gary Ling got a summer job working in a British Columbia sawmill. Since jobs were scarce and this one paid particularly well, Gary arrived on his first day of work highly motivated. Two weeks later, however, his motivation was quite low. What happened was that his co-workers consistently bad-mouthed their jobs. They said the work was boring, that having to clock in and out proved management didn't trust them, and that supervisors never listened to their opinions. The objective characteristics of Gary's job had not changed in the two-week period; rather, Gary had reconstructed reality based on messages he had gotten from others.

A number of studies confirm the validity of the SIP model.[45] For instance, it has been shown that employee motivation and satisfaction can be manipulated by such subtle actions as a co-worker or boss commenting on the existence or absence of job features like difficulty, challenge, and autonomy. So managers should give as much (or more) attention to employees' perceptions of their jobs as to the actual characteristics of those jobs. They might spend more time telling employees how interesting and important their jobs are. And managers should also not be surprised that newly hired employees and people transferred or promoted to a new position are more likely to be receptive to social information than are those with greater seniority.

Goal-Setting Theory

Gene Broadwater, coach of the Hamilton High School cross-country team, gave his squad these last words before they approached the line for the league championship race: "Each one of you is physically ready. Now, get out there and do your best. No one can ever ask more of you than that."

You've heard the phrase a number of times yourself: "Just do your best. That's all anyone can ask for." But what does "do your best" mean? Do we ever know if we've achieved that vague goal? Would the cross-country runners have recorded faster times if Coach Broadwater had given each a spe-

Should Every Employee Have a Meaningful Job?

Organizational humanists have been widely critical of the mechanistic or "scientific management" approach to job design.[46] They claim that standardized tasks, repetitive job cycles, and narrow skill development are morally wrong. They argue that every employee is entitled to a meaningful job—that is, one that allows an individual dignity, creative freedom, and opportunities for self-development.

Do employers have a moral obligation to create meaningful jobs? Is it inadequate to merely provide employees with a safe workplace, healthful working conditions, reasonable pay, and adequate benefits? Are executives at General Motors and McDonald's unethical in requiring their workers to perform simple and standardized jobs tasks over and over again? Organizational humanists argue that employers in rich and developed nations can afford to provide their employees with interesting and challenging jobs—and,

should do so because it makes for satisfied and more productive workers.

Those who support the scientific management approach defend routine and programmed jobs on at least three counts. First, many jobs are difficult, if not impossible, to make "meaningful." The economic costs to employers would be prohibitive. Second, not *every* employee wants a meaningful job. A lot of people prefer jobs that make little or no intellectual demands on them. Such people can and do satisfy their higher-order needs *off* the job. Finally, individuals are amazingly adaptable. Through whatever happens to them—financial setbacks, health problems, personal tragedies—people survive and make do. Employees have an enormous capacity to adapt to, and accept, jobs that are routine and dull.

Do employers have a moral obligation to provide every employee with a meaningful job? What do *you* think?

Goal-setting Theory The theory that specific and difficult goals lead to higher performance.

cific goal to shoot for? Might you have done better in your high school English class if your parents had said, "You should strive for eighty-five percent or higher on all your work in English" rather than telling you to "do your best"? The research on **goal setting** addresses these issues, and the findings, as you will see, are impressive in terms of the impact specific and challenging goals have on performance.

In the late 1960s, Edwin Locke proposed that intentions to work toward a goal are a major source of work motivation.[47] That is, goals tell an employee what needs to be done and how much effort will need to be expended.[48] The evidence strongly supports the value of goals. More to the point, we can say that specific goals increase performance; that difficult goals, when accepted, result in higher performance than do easy goals; and that feedback leads to higher performance than does nonfeedback.[49]

Specific hard goals produce a higher level of output than does a generalized goal of "do your best." The specificity of the goal itself acts as an internal stimulus. For instance, when a trucker commits to making eighteen round-trip hauls between Baltimore and Washington, D.C., each week, this intention gives him a specific objective to reach for. We can say that, all things being equal, the trucker with a specific goal will outperform his counterpart operating with no goals or the generalized goal of "do your best."

If factors like ability and acceptance of the goals are held constant, we can also state that the more difficult the goal, the higher the level of performance. However, it's logical to assume that easier goals are more likely to be accepted. But once an employee accepts a hard task, he or she will exert a high level of effort until it is achieved, lowered, or abandoned.

People will do better when they get feedback on how well they are progressing toward their goals, because feedback helps to identify discrepancies between what they have done and what they want to do; that is, feedback acts to guide behavior. But all feedback is not equally potent. Self-generated feedback—where the employee is able to monitor his or her own progress—has been shown to be a more powerful motivator than externally generated feedback.[50]

If employees have the opportunity to participate in the setting of their own goals, will they try harder? The evidence is mixed regarding the superiority of participative over assigned goals.[51] In some cases, participatively set goals elicited superior performance, while in other cases, individuals performed best when assigned goals by their boss. But a major advantage of participation may be in increasing acceptance of the goal itself as a desirable one to work toward.[52] As we noted, resistance is greater when goals are difficult. If people participate in goal setting, they are more likely to accept even a difficult goal than if they are arbitrarily assigned it by their boss. The reason is that individuals are more committed to choices in which they have a part. Thus, although participative goals may have no superiority over assigned goals when acceptance is taken as a given, participation does increase the probability that more difficult goals will be agreed to and acted upon.

Are there any contingencies in goal-setting theory or can we take it as a universal truth that difficult and specific goals will *always* lead to higher performance? In addition to feedback, two other factors have been found to influence the goals-performance relationship. These are goal commitment and adequate self-efficacy. Goal-setting theory presupposes that an individual is *committed* to the goal; that is, is determined not to lower or abandon the goal. This is most likely to occur when goals are made public, when the individual has an internal locus of control, and when the goals are self-set rather than assigned.[53] **Self-efficacy** refers to an individual's belief that he or she is capable of performing a task.[54] The higher your self-efficacy, the more confidence you have in your ability to succeed in a task. So, in difficult situations, we find that people with low self-efficacy are more likely to lessen their effort or give up altogether, while those with high self-efficacy will try harder to master the challenge.[55] In addition, individuals high in self-efficacy seem to respond to negative feedback with increased effort and motivation, whereas those low in self-efficacy are likely to lessen their effort when given negative feedback.[56]

Our overall conclusion is that intentions—as articulated in terms of hard and specific goals—are a potent motivating force. They can lead to higher performance. However, there is no evidence that such goals are associated with increased job satisfaction.[57]

Reinforcement Theory

A counterpoint to goal-setting theory is **reinforcement theory.** The former is a cognitive approach, proposing that an individual's purposes direct his or her action. In reinforcement theory, we have a behavioristic approach, which argues that reinforcement conditions behavior. The two are clearly at odds philosophically. Reinforcement theorists see behavior as being environmen-

Self-efficacy The individual's belief that he or she is capable of performing a task.

Reinforcement Theory Behavior is a function of its consequences.

tally caused. You need not be concerned, they would argue, with internal cognitive events; what controls behavior are reinforcers—any consequence that, when immediately following a response, increases the probability that the behavior will be repeated.

Reinforcement theory ignores the inner state of the individual and concentrates solely on what happens to a person when he or she takes some action. Because it does not concern itself with what initiates behavior, it is not, strictly speaking, a theory of motivation. But it does provide a powerful means of analysis of what controls behavior, and it is for this reason that it is typically considered in discussions of motivation.[58]

We discussed the reinforcement process in detail in Chapter 4. We showed how using reinforcers to condition behavior gives us considerable insight into how people learn. Yet we cannot ignore the fact that reinforcement has a wide following as a motivational device. In its pure form, however, reinforcement theory ignores feelings, attitudes, expectations, and other cognitive variables that are known to impact behavior. In fact, some researchers look at the same experiments that reinforcement theorists use to support their position and interpret the findings in a cognitive framework.[59]

Reinforcement is undoubtedly an important influence on behavior, but few scholars are prepared to argue that it is the *only* influence. The behaviors you engage in at work and the amount of effort you allocate to each task are affected by the consequences that follow from your behavior. If you are consistently reprimanded for outproducing your colleagues, you will likely reduce your productivity. But your lower productivity may also be explained in terms of goals, inequity, or expectancies.

Equity Theory

Jane Pearson graduated last year from the State University with a degree in accounting. After interviews with a number of organizations on campus, she accepted a position with one of the nation's largest public accounting firms and was assigned to their Boston office. Jane was very pleased with the offer she received: challenging work with a prestigious firm, an excellent opportunity to gain important experience, and the highest salary any accounting major at State was offered last year—$2600 a month. But Jane was the top student in her class; she was ambitious and articulate and fully expected to receive a commensurate salary.

Twelve months have passed since Jane joined her employer. The work has proved to be as challenging and satisfying as she had hoped. Her employer is extremely pleased with her performance; in fact, she recently received a $200-a-month raise. However, Jane's motivational level has dropped dramatically in the past few weeks. Why? Her employer has just hired a fresh college graduate out of State University, who lacks the one-year experience Jane has gained, for $2850 a month—$50 more than Jane now makes! It would be an understatement to describe Jane in any other terms than livid. Jane is even talking about looking for another job.

Jane's situation illustrates the role that equity plays in motivation. Employees make comparisons of their job inputs and outcomes relative to those of others. We perceive what we get from a job situation (outcomes) in relation to what we put into it (inputs), and then we compare our outcome-input ratio with the outcome-input ratio of relevant others. This is shown in Table 7–2. If we perceive our ratio to be equal to that of the relevant others with whom we compare ourselves, a state of equity is said to exist. We perceive our situation as fair—that justice prevails. When we see the ratio as

TABLE 7–2   Equity Theory

Ratio Comparisons	Perception
$\dfrac{O}{I_A} < \dfrac{O}{I_B}$	Inequity due to being underrewarded
$\dfrac{O}{I_A} = \dfrac{O}{I_B}$	Equity
$\dfrac{O}{I_A} > \dfrac{O}{I_B}$	Inequity due to being overrewarded

Where $\dfrac{O}{I_A}$ represents the employee and $\dfrac{O}{I_B}$ represents relevant others

unequal, we experience equity tension. J. Stacy Adams has proposed that this negative tension state provides the motivation to do something to correct it.[60]

The referent that an employee selects adds to the complexity of **equity theory.** Evidence indicates that the referent chosen is an important variable in equity theory.[61] There are four referent comparisons that an employee can use:

1. *Self-inside:* An employee's experiences in a different position inside his or her current organization
2. *Self-outside:* An employee's experiences in a situation or position outside his or her current organization
3. *Other-inside:* Another individual or group of individuals inside the employee's organization
4. *Other-outside:* Another individual or group of individuals outside the employee's organization

So employees might compare themselves to friends, neighbors, co-workers, colleagues in other organizations, or past jobs they themselves have had. Which referent an employee chooses will be influenced by the information the employee holds about referents as well as by the attractiveness of the referent. This has led to focusing on three moderating variables—the employee's salary level, amount of education, and length of tenure.[62] Employees with higher salaries and more education tend to be more cosmopolitan and have better information; thus, they're more likely to make comparisons with outsiders. Employees with short tenure in their current organization tend to have little information about others inside the organization, so they rely on their own personal experiences. On the other hand, employees with long tenure rely more heavily on co-workers for comparisons.

Based on equity theory, when employees perceive an inequity they can be predicted to make one of six choices:[63]

1. Change their inputs (for example, don't exert as much effort)
2. Change their outcomes (for example, individuals paid on a piece-rate basis can increase their pay by producing a higher quantity of units of lower quality)
3. Distort perceptions of self (for example, "I used to think I worked at a moderate pace but now I realize that I work a lot harder than everyone else.")

Equity Theory Individuals compare their job inputs and outcomes with those of others and then respond so as to eliminate any inequities.

Most chief executives of public corporations are equity sensitive, especially since their compensation is widely publicized in business periodicals. In 1990, Stephen Wolf, CEO of UAL (the parent of United Airlines), earned $18.3 million. CEOs at other airlines like American and Delta undoubtedly compare their companies' performance to UAL and then contrast their total pay and benefits package to Wolf's.

David Strick/Onyx

4. Distort perceptions of others (for example, "Mike's job isn't as desirable as I previously thought it was.")

5. Choose a different referent (for example, "I may not make as much as my brother-in-law, but I'm doing a lot better than my Dad did when he was my age.")

6. Leave the field (for example, quit the job)

Equity theory recognizes that individuals are concerned not only with the absolute amount of rewards they receive for their efforts, but also with the relationship of this amount to what others receive. They make judgments as to the relationship between their inputs and outcomes and the inputs and outcomes of others. Based on one's inputs, such as effort, experience, education, and competence, one compares outcomes such as salary levels, raises, recognition, and other factors. When people perceive an imbalance in their outcome–input ratio relative to others, tension is created. This tension provides the basis for motivation, as people strive for what they perceive as equity and fairness.

Specifically, the theory establishes four propositions relating to inequitable pay:

1. *Given payment by time, overrewarded employees will produce more than will equitably paid employees.* Hourly and salaried employees will generate high quantity or quality of production in order to increase the input side of the ratio and bring about equity.

2. *Given payment by quantity of production, overrewarded employees will produce fewer, but higher-quality, units than will equitably paid employees.* Individuals paid on a piece-rate basis will increase their effort to achieve equity, which can result in greater quality or quantity. However, increases in quantity will only increase inequity since every unit produced results in further overpayment. Therefore, effort is directed toward increasing quality rather than increasing quantity.

3. *Given payment by time, underrewarded employees will produce less or poorer quality of output.* Effort will be decreased, which will bring about lower productivity or poorer-quality output than equitably paid subjects.

4. *Given payment by quantity of production, underrewarded employees will produce a large number of low-quality units in comparison with equitably paid employees.* Employees on piece-rate pay plans can bring about equity because trading off quality of output for quantity will result in an increase in rewards with little or no increase in contributions.

These propositions have generally been supported, with a few minor qualifications.[64] First, inequities created by overpayment do not seem to have a very significant impact on behavior in most work situations. Apparently, people have a great deal more tolerance of overpayment inequities than of underpayment inequities, or are better able to rationalize them. Second, not all people are equity-sensitive. For example, there is a small part of the working population who actually prefer that their outcome–input ratio be less than the referent comparison. Predictions from equity theory are not likely to be very accurate with these "benevolent types."

It's also important to note that while most research on equity theory has focused on pay, employees seem to look for equity in the distribution of other organizational rewards. For instance, it's been shown that the use of high-status job titles as well as large and lavishly furnished offices may function as outcomes for some employees in their equity equation.[65]

Most Professional Athletes Seem Very Equity Sensitive

No early season in professional sports would be complete without some athletes "holding out" for more money. And are these athletes impoverished? Hardly! They are people making half-million or million-dollar-a-year salaries. Do they argue that they can't make ends meet on their current pay? Not very often! Their arguments are almost always couched in terms of equity.

Take the case of Oakland A's baseball star Rickey Henderson. In November 1989, he negotiated a four-year, $12 million contract that made him one of the two highest-paid players in baseball. He proved his worth the following year by being named his league's most valuable player. But in 1990, baseball salaries skyrocketed. By March 1991, Henderson's $3 million a year tied him with five others for 36th place in the salary rankings.

Was Henderson upset? You bet he was! So upset, in fact, that he didn't show up for the A's 1991 spring training camp. His agent explained Henderson's frustration in equity terms: "It depends on the A's and their feeling of fairness toward him. If they can give him something, he can give them something in return."

Even though you and I might be euphoric over the opportunity to work six months a year for a couple of hundred thousand dollars a month—exclusive of earnings from endorsements and other promotional activities—professional athletes like Rickey Henderson are rarely concerned with the absolute dollars they receive. What they are doing is comparing themselves to other athletes who play similar positions and who have comparable or less impressive accomplishments. When they see a pay discrepancy, they seek equity. And when the managements of these professional franchises fail to correct these inequities, they frequently find themselves with disgruntled and demotivated athletes.

In conclusion, equity theory demonstrates that, for most employees, motivation is influenced significantly by relative rewards as well as by absolute rewards. But some key issues are still unclear.[66] For instance, how do employees handle conflicting equity signals, such as when unions point to other employee groups who are substantially *better off,* while management argues how much things have *improved?* How do employees define inputs and outcomes? How do they combine and weigh their inputs and outcomes to arrive at totals? When and how do the factors change over time? Yet, regardless of these problems, equity theory continues to offer us some important insights into employee motivation.

EXPECTANCY THEORY

Expectancy Theory The strength of a tendency to act in a certain way depends on the strength of an expectation that an act will be followed by a given outcome and on the attractiveness of that outcome to the individual.

Currently, one of the most widely accepted explanations of motivation is Victor Vroom's **expectancy theory.**[67] Although it has its critics,[68] most of the research evidence is supportive of the theory.[69]

Essentially, the expectancy theory argues that the strength of a tendency to act in a certain way depends on the strength of an expectation that the act will be followed by a given outcome and on the attractiveness of that outcome to the individual. It includes three variables or relationships.[70]

1. *Attractiveness:* The importance that the individual places on the potential outcome or reward that can be achieved on the job. This considers the unsatisfied needs of the individual.

2. *Performance–reward linkage:* The degree to which the individual believes that performing at a particular level will lead to the attainment of a desired outcome.

3. *Effort–performance linkage:* The probability perceived by the individual that exerting a given amount of effort will lead to performance.

While this may sound pretty complex, it really is not that difficult to visualize. Whether one has the desire to produce at any given time depends on one's particular goals and one's perception of the relative worth of performance as a path to the attainment of these goals.

Figure 7-8 is a considerable simplification of expectancy theory, but it expresses its major contentions. The strength of a person's motivation to perform (effort) depends on how strongly he or she believes that he or she can achieve attempted tasks. If the person achieves this goal (performance), will he or she be adequately rewarded and, if rewarded by the organization, will the reward satisfy the person's individual goals? Let us consider the four steps inherent in the theory.

First, what perceived outcomes does the job offer the employee? Outcomes may be positive: pay, security, companionship, trust, fringe benefits, a chance to use talent or skills, congenial relationships. On the other hand, employees may view the outcomes as negative: fatigue, boredom, frustration, anxiety, harsh supervision, threat of dismissal. Importantly, reality is not relevant here; the critical issue is what the individual employee *perceives* the outcome to be, regardless of whether or not his or her perceptions are accurate.

Second, how attractive do employees consider these outcomes? Are they valued positively, negatively, or neutrally? This obviously is an internal issue to the individual and considers his or her personal values, personality, and needs. The individual who finds a particular outcome attractive—that is, positively valued—would prefer attaining it to not attaining it. Others may find it negative and, therefore, prefer not attaining it to attaining it. Still others may be neutral.

Third, what kind of behavior must the employee produce in order to achieve these outcomes? The outcomes are not likely to have any effect on the individual employee's performance unless the employee knows, clearly and unambiguously, what he or she must do in order to achieve them. For example, what is "doing well" in terms of performance appraisal? What are the criteria the employee's performance will be judged on?

Fourth and last, how does the employee view his or her chances of doing what is asked? After the employee has considered his or her own competencies and ability to control those variables that will determine success, what probability does he or she place on successful attainment?

FIGURE 7–8   Simplified Expectancy Model

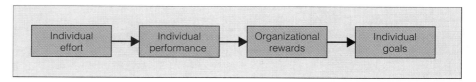

The key to expectancy theory, therefore, is the understanding of an individual's goals and the linkage between effort and performance, between performance and rewards, and, finally, between the rewards and individual goal satisfaction. As a contingency model, expectancy theory recognizes that there is no universal principle for explaining everyone's motivations. Additionally, just because we understand what needs a person seeks to satisfy does not ensure that the individual himself perceives high performance as necessarily leading to the satisfaction of these needs.

Let us summarize some of the issues expectancy theory has brought forward. First, it emphasizes payoffs or rewards. As a result, we have to believe that the rewards the organization is offering align with what the employee wants. It is a theory based on self-interest, wherein each individual seeks to maximize his or her expected satisfaction: "Expectancy theory is a form of calculative, psychological *hedonism* in which the ultimate motive of every human act is asserted to be the maximization of pleasure and/or the minimization of pain.[71] Second, we have to be concerned with the attractiveness of rewards, which requires an understanding and knowledge of what value the individual puts on organizational payoffs. We want to reward the individual with those things he or she values positively. Third, expectancy theory emphasizes expected behaviors. Does the person know what is expected and how he or she will be appraised? Finally, the theory is concerned with expectations. What is realistic or rational is irrelevant. It is an individual's own expectations of performance, reward, and goal satisfaction outcomes that will determine his or her level of effort, not the objective outcomes themselves.

Does the expectancy theory work? Attempts to validate the theory have been complicated by methodological, criterion, and measurement problems. As a result, many published studies that purport to support or negate the theory must be viewed with caution. Importantly, most studies have failed to replicate the methodology as it was originally proposed. For example, the theory proposes to explain different levels of effort from the same person under different circumstances, but almost all replication studies have looked at different people. Correcting for this flaw has greatly improved support for the validity of the expectancy theory.[72] Some critics suggest that the theory has only limited use, arguing that it tends to be more valid for predicting in situations where effort–performance and performance–reward linkages are clearly perceived by the individual.[73] Since few individuals perceive a high correlation between performance and rewards in their jobs, the theory tends to be idealistic. If organizations actually rewarded individuals for performance rather than according to such criteria as seniority, effort, skill level, and job difficulty, then the theory's validity might be considerably greater. However, rather than invalidating expectancy theory, this criticism can be used in support of the theory, for it explains why a large segment of the work force exerts a minimal level of effort in carrying out their job responsibilities.

Expectancy theory can be used to better understand student motivation. It would say that studying and preparation for a class (effort) is conditioned by its resulting in answering questions on exams correctly (performance), which will produce a high grade (reward), which will lead to the security, prestige, and other benefits that accrue from obtaining a desired job or getting into a good graduate school (individual goal). Among other things, for students to exert a high level of effort, they must believe that increased preparation is related to grades, that the tests fairly measure what they know, and they must value high grades.
Four By Five

Don't Forget Ability and Opportunity

Robin and Chris both graduated from college a couple of years ago with their degrees in elementary education. They each took jobs as first-grade teachers, but in different school districts. Robin immediately confronted a number of obstacles on the job: a large class (forty-two students), a small and dingy classroom, and inadequate supplies. Chris's situation couldn't have been more different. He had only fifteen students in his class, plus a teaching aide

Different Strokes for Different Folks

What motivates me doesn't necessarily motivate you. Expectancy theory recognizes this by proposing that rewards be tailored to the individual. But can we generalize about what different subgroups of employees might place greater importance upon? A study of one thousand employees asked them to rank-order ten work-related factors.[74] Their answers were then tabulated by subgroups on the basis of sex, age, income level, job type, and organization level. The results are shown in Table 7–3.

While the results suggest that there is a great deal of similarity in preferences, especially between men and women, there are a few important differences. For instance, younger workers, those with low incomes, and those in lower, nonsupervisory positions are most concerned with money. Job security also is significantly less important to older workers and to those higher in the organization. If nothing else, these results challenge those who simplistically assume that *everybody* considers factors such as good pay and promotion in the organization to be a high priority.

TABLE 7–3   What Workers Want, Ranked by Subgroups

	Sex		Age				Income Level				Job Type				Organization Level		
	Men	Women	Under 30	31–40	41–50	Over 50	Under $12,000	$12,000–$18,000	$18,001–$25,000	Over $25,000	Blue-Collar Unskilled	Blue-Collar Skilled	White-Collar Unskilled	White-Collar Skilled	Lower Nonsupervisory	Middle Nonsupervisory	Higher Nonsupervisory
Interesting work	2	2	4	2	3	1	5	2	1	1	2	1	1	2	3	1	1
Full appreciation of work done	1	1	5	3	2	2	4	3	3	2	1	6	3	1	4	2	2
Feeling of being in on things	3	3	6	4	1	3	6	1	2	4	5	2	5	4	5	3	3
Job security	5	4	2	1	4	7	2	4	4	3	4	3	7	5	2	4	6
Good wages	4	5	1	5	5	8	1	5	6	8	3	4	6	6	1	6	8
Promotion and growth in organization	6	6	3	6	8	9	3	6	5	7	6	5	4	3	6	5	5
Good working conditions	7	7	7	7	7	4	8	7	7	6	9	7	2	7	7	7	4
Personal loyalty to employees	8	8	9	9	6	5	7	8	8	5	8	9	9	8	8	8	7
Tactful discipline	9	9	8	10	9	10	10	9	9	10	7	10	10	9	9	9	10
Sympathetic help with personal problems	10	10	10	8	10	6	9	10	10	9	10	8	8	10	10	10	9

*Ranked from 1 (highest) to 10 (lowest).

Source: Reprinted from *Business Horizons*, September–October 1987. Copyright 1987 by the Foundation for the School of Business at Indiana University. Used with permission. K. A. Kovach, "What Motivates Employees? Workers and Supervisors Give Different Answers," *Business Horizons*, September–October 1987, p. 61.

for fifteen hours each week, a modern and well-lighted room, a well-stocked supply cabinet, the unlimited use of a personal computer for class planning, and a highly supportive principal. Not surprisingly, at the end of their first school year, Chris had been considerably more effective as a teacher than had Robin.

The preceding episode illustrates an obvious but often overlooked fact. Success on a job is facilitated or hindered by the existence or absence of support resources.

A popular, although arguably simplistic, way of thinking about employee performance is as a function of the interaction of ability and motivation; that is, performance = $f(A \times M)$. If either is inadequate, performance will be negatively affected. This helps to explain, for instance, the hardworking athlete or student with modest abilities who consistently outperforms his or her more gifted, but lazy, rival. So, as we noted in Chapter 4, an individual's intelligence and skills (subsumed under the label "ability") must be considered in addition to motivation if we are to be able to accurately explain and predict employee performance. But a piece of the puzzle is still missing. We need to add **opportunity to perform** to our equation—performance = $f(A \times M \times O)$.[75] Even though an individual may be willing and able, there may be obstacles that constrain performance. This is shown in Figure 7–9.

When you attempt to assess why an employee may not be performing to the level that you believe he or she is capable of, take a look at the work environment to see if it's supportive. Does the employee have adequate tools, equipment, materials, and supplies; does the employee have favorable working conditions, helpful co-workers, supportive rules and procedures to work under, adequate time to do a good job, and the like? If not, performance will suffer.

Opportunity to Perform
High levels of performance are partially a function of an absence of obstacles that constrain the employee.

INTEGRATING CONTEMPORARY THEORIES OF MOTIVATION

We've looked at a lot of motivation theories in this chapter. The fact that a number of these theories have been supported only complicates the matter. How simple it would have been if, after presenting half-a-dozen theories, only one was found valid. But these theories are not all in competition with one another! Because one is valid doesn't automatically make the others invalid. In fact, many of the theories presented in this chapter are comple-

FIGURE 7–9
Performance Dimensions
Adapted from M. Blumberg and C. D. Pringle, "The Missing Opportunity in Organizational Research: Some Implications for a Theory of Work Performance," *Academy of Management Review*, October 1982, p. 565.

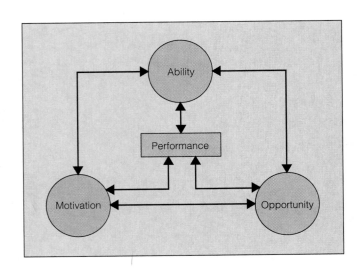

mentary. So the challenge is now to tie these theories together to help you understand their interrelationships.

Figure 7–10 presents a model that integrates much of what we know about motivation. Its basic foundation is the simplified expectancy model shown in Figure 7–8. Let's work through Figure 7–10.

We begin by explicitly recognizing that opportunities can aid or hinder individual effort. The individual effort box also has another arrow leading into it. This arrow flows out of the individual's goals. Consistent with goal-setting theory, this goals–effort loop is meant to remind us that goals direct behavior.

Expectancy theory predicts that an employee will exert a high level of effort if he or she perceives that there is a strong relationship between effort and performance, performance and rewards, and rewards and satisfaction of personal goals. Each of these relationships, in turn, is influenced by certain factors. For effort to lead to good performance, the individual must have the requisite ability to perform, and the performance evaluation system that measures the individual's performance must be perceived as being fair and objective. The performance–reward relationship will be strong if the individual perceives that it is performance (rather than seniority, personal favorites, or other criteria) that is rewarded. If cognitive evaluation theory were fully valid in the actual workplace, we would predict here that basing rewards on performance should decrease the individual's intrinsic motivation. The final link in expectancy theory is the rewards–goals relationship. ERG theory would come into play at this point. Motivation would be high to the degree that the rewards an individual received for his or her high performance satisfied the dominant needs consistent with his or her individual goals.

A closer look at Figure 7–10 will also reveal that the model considers the achievement need and reinforcement and equity theories. The high achiever is not motivated by the organization's assessment of his or her per-

FIGURE 7–10   Integrating Contemporary Theories of Motivation

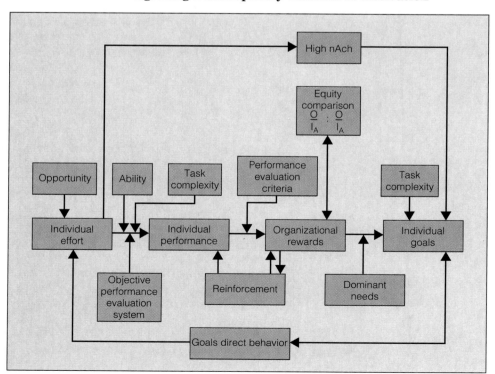

Motivation Theories Are Culture-Bound

Most current motivation theories were developed in the United States by Americans and about Americans.[76] Maybe the most blatant pro-American characteristics inherent in these theories is the strong emphasis on what we defined in Chapter 3 as individualism and quantity-of-life. For instance, both goal-setting and expectancy theories emphasize goal accomplishment as well as rational and individual thought. Let's take a look at how this bias has affected a few of the motivation theories introduced in this chapter.

Maslow's need hierarchy argues that people start at the physiological level and then move progressively up the hierarchy in this order: physiological, safety, social, esteem, and self-actualization. This hierarchy, if it has any application at all, aligns with American culture. In countries like Japan, Greece, and Mexico, where uncertainty avoidance characteristics are strong, security needs would be on top of the need hierarchy. Countries that score high on quality-of-life characteristics—Denmark, Sweden, Norway, the Netherlands, and Finland—would have social needs on top.[77] We would predict, for instance, that group work will motivate employees more when the country's culture scores high on the quality criterion.

Another motivation concept that clearly has an American bias is the achievement need. The view that a high achievement need acts as an internal motivator presupposes two cultural characteristics—a willingness to accept a moderate degree of risk (which excludes countries with strong uncertainty avoidance characteristics) and a concern with performance (which applies almost singularly to countries with strong quantity-of-life characteristics). This combination is found in Anglo-American countries like the United States, Canada, and Great Britain.[78] On the other hand, these characteristics are relatively absent in countries such as Chile and Portugal.

Goal setting certainly is also culture-bound. It is well adapted to the United States because its key components align reasonably well with American culture. It assumes that subordinates will be reasonably independent (not too high a score on power distance), that managers and subordinates will seek challenging goals (low in uncertainty avoidance), and that performance is considered important by both (high in quantity of life). Goal setting's recommendations are not likely to increase motivation in countries such as Portugal and Chile, where the opposite conditions exist.

formance or organizational rewards; hence, the jump from effort to individual goals for those with a high *nAch*. Remember, high achievers are internally driven as long as the jobs they are doing provide them with personal responsibility, feedback, and moderate risks. So they are not concerned with the effort–performance, performance–rewards, or rewards–goal linkages.

Reinforcement theory enters our model by recognizing that the organization's rewards reinforce the individual's performance. If management has designed a reward system that is seen by employees as "paying off" for good performance, the rewards will reinforce and encourage continued good performance. Rewards also play the key part in equity theory. Individuals will compare the rewards (outcomes) they receive from the inputs they make with the outcome–input ratio of relevant others ($O/I_A{:}O/I_B$), and inequities may influence the effort expended.

Finally, task characteristics influence motivation at two places in Figure 7–10. First, jobs that score high in motivating potential are likely to lead to higher actual job performance. So jobs that have high complexity increase the linkage between effort and performance. Second, jobs that score high in motivating potential increase an employee's control over key elements in his or her work. Therefore, jobs that offer autonomy, feedback, and similar complex task characteristics help to satisfy the individual goals of those employees who desire greater control over their work. Of course, consistent with the social information-processing model, the perception that task characteristics are complex is probably more important in influencing an employee's motivation than the objective task characteristics themselves. The key, then, is to provide employees with cues that suggest that their jobs score high on factors such as skill variety, task identity, autonomy, and feedback.

IMPLICATIONS FOR PERFORMANCE AND SATISFACTION

The theories we've discussed in this chapter do not all address our four dependent variables. Some, for instance, are directed at explaining turnover, while others emphasize productivity. The theories also differ in their predictive strength. In this section, we'll (1) review the key motivation theories to determine their relevance in explaining our dependent variables, and (2) assess the predictive power of each.[79]

NEED THEORIES   We introduced four theories that focused on needs. These were Maslow's hierarchy, motivation-hygiene, ERG, and McClelland's needs theories. The strongest of these is probably the last, particularly regarding the relationship between achievement and productivity. If the other three have any value at all, that value relates to explaining and predicting job satisfaction.

TASK CHARACTERISTICS THEORIES   The job characteristics model addresses all four dependent variables. Based on the evidence, we should expect that individuals with a high growth need—which probably includes an increasingly larger proportion of the work force today than in past generations because of increasing educational levels and technical job requirements—will be both high performers and satisfied when their jobs offer skill variety, task identity and significance, autonomy, and feedback.

GOAL-SETTING THEORY   There is little dispute that clear and difficult goals lead to higher levels of employee productivity. This evidence leads us to conclude that goal-setting theory provides one of the more powerful explanations of this dependent variable. The theory, however, does not address absenteeism, turnover, or satisfaction.

REINFORCEMENT THEORY   This theory has an impressive record for predicting factors like quality and quantity of work, persistence of effort, absenteeism, tardiness, and accident rates. It does not offer much insight into employee satisfaction or the decision to quit.

EQUITY THEORY   Equity theory deals with all four dependent variables. However, it is strongest when predicting absence and turnover behaviors and weak when predicting differences in employee productivity.

EXPECTANCY THEORY   Our final theory focused on performance variables. It has proved to offer a relatively powerful explanation of employee

TABLE 7–4   Power of Motivation Theories[a]

			Theories			
Variable	Need	Task Characteristics	Goal Setting	Reinforcement	Equity	Expectancy
Productivity	3[b]	3[c]	5	3	3	4[d]
Absenteeism		3		4	4	4
Turnover		3			4	5
Satisfaction	2	4			2	

[a]Theories are rated on a scale of 1 to 5, 5 being highest.
[b]Applies to individuals with a high need to achieve.
[c]Applies to individuals with a high need for growth.
[d]Limited value in jobs where employees have little discretionary choice.

Source: Based on F. J. Landy and W. S. Becker, "Motivation Theory Reconsidered," in L. L. Cummings and B. M. Staw (eds.), *Research in Organizational Behavior,* Vol. 9 (Greenwich, CT: JAI Press, 1987), p. 33.

productivity, absenteeism, and turnover. But expectancy theory assumes that employees have few constraints on their decision discretion. It makes many of the same assumptions that the optimizing model makes about individual decision making (see Chapter 5). This acts to restrict its applicability.

For major decisions, like accepting or resigning from a job, expectancy theory works well, because people don't rush into decisions of this nature. They're more prone to take the time to carefully consider the costs and benefits of all the alternatives. But expectancy theory is *not* a very good explanation for more typical types of work behavior, especially for individuals in lower-level jobs, because such jobs come with considerable limitations imposed by work methods, supervisors, and company policies. We would conclude, therefore, that expectancy theory's power in explaining employee productivity increases where the jobs being performed are more complex and higher in the organization (where discretion is greater).

SUMMARY

Table 7–4 summarizes what we know about the power of the more well-known motivation theories to explain and predict our four dependent variables. While based on a wealth of research, it also includes some subjective judgments. However, it does provide a reasonable guide through the motivation theory maze.

FOR DISCUSSION

1. Define motivation. Describe the motivation process.
2. What are the implications of Theories X and Y for motivation practices?
3. Compare and contrast Maslow's hierarchy of needs theory with (a) Alderfer's ERG theory and (b) Herzberg's motivation-hygiene theory.
4. Describe the three needs isolated by McClelland. How are they related to worker behavior?

5. "The cognitive evaluation theory is contradictory to reinforcement and expectancy theories." Do you agree or disagree? Explain.

6. According to the job characteristics model, how does a job score high in motivating potential?

7. "Goal setting is part of both reinforcement and expectancy theories." Do you agree or disagree? Explain.

8. What is the social information-processing model? What are its implications for motivating people at work?

9. Analyze the application of Maslow's and Herzberg's theories to an African or Caribbean nation where more than a quarter of the population is unemployed.

10. Can an individual be *too* motivated, so that his or her performance declines as a result of excessive effort? Discuss.

11. Explain the formula: Performance = $f(A \times M \times O)$ and give an example.

12. Identify three activities you *really enjoy* (for example, playing tennis, reading a novel, going shopping). Next, identify three activities you *really dislike* (for example, going to the dentist, cleaning the house, staying on a restricted calorie diet). Using the expectancy model, analyze each of your answers to assess why some activities stimulate your effort while others don't.

P O I N T

Money Motivates!

The importance of money as a motivator has been consistently downgraded by most behavioral scientists. They prefer to point out the value of challenging jobs, goals, participation in decision making, feedback, cohesive work groups, and other nonmonetary factors as stimulants to employee motivation. We will argue otherwise here—that money is *the* crucial incentive to work motivation. As a medium of exchange, it is the vehicle by which employees can purchase the numerous need-satisfying things they desire. Further, money also performs the function of a scorecard, by which employees assess the value that the organization places on their services and by which employees can compare their value to others.

Money's value as a medium of exchange is obvious. People may not work *only* for money, but take the money away and how many people would come to work? For the vast majority of the work force, a regular paycheck is absolutely necessary in order to meet their basic physiological and safety needs.

As equity theory suggests, money has symbolic value in addition to its exchange value. We use pay as the primary outcome against which we compare our inputs to determine if we are being treated equitably. That an organization pays one executive $80,000 a year and another $95,000 means more than the latter's earning $15,000 a year more. It is a message, from the organization to both employees, of how much it values the contribution of each.

In addition to equity theory, both reinforcement and expectancy theories attest to the value of money as a motivator. In the former, if pay is contingent on performance, it will encourage workers to high levels of effort. Consistent with expectancy theory, money will motivate to the extent that it is seen as being able to satisfy an individual's personal goals and is perceived as being dependent upon performance criteria.

The best case for money as a motivator is a review of studies done by Edwin Locke of the University of Maryland.* Locke looked at four methods of motivating employee performance: money, goal setting, participation in decision making, and redesigning jobs to give workers more challenge and responsibility. He found that the average improvement from money was thirty percent; goal setting increased performance sixteen percent; participation improved performance by less than one percent; and job redesign positively impacted performance by an average of seventeen percent. Moreover, every study Locke reviewed that used money as a method of motivation resulted in some improvement in employee performance. Such evidence demonstrates that money may not be the *only* motivator, but it is difficult to argue that it *doesn't* motivate!

*E. A. Locke et al., "The Relative Effectiveness of Four Methods of Motivating Employee Performance," in *Changes in Working Life,* eds. K. D. Duncan, M. M. Gruneberg, and D. Wallis (London: John Wiley, Ltd., 1980), pp. 363–83.

Money Doesn't Motivate Most Employees Today!

Money can motivate *some* people under *some* conditions. So the issue isn't really whether or not money *can* motivate. The answer to that is: It can! The more relevant question is: Does money motivate most employees in the work force today to higher performance? The answer to this question, we'll argue, is "No."

For money to motivate an individual's performance, certain conditions must be met. First, money must be important to the individual. Second, money must be perceived by the individual as being a direct reward for performance. Third, the marginal amount of money offered for the performance must be perceived by the individual as being significant. Finally, management must have the discretion to reward high performers with more money. Let's take a look at each of these conditions.

Money is not important to all employees. High achievers, for instance, are intrinsically motivated. Money should have little impact on these people. Similarly, money is relevant to those individuals with strong lower-order needs; but for most of the work force, their lower-order needs are substantially satisfied.

Money would motivate if employees perceived a strong linkage between performance and rewards in organizations. Unfortunately, pay increases are far more often determined by community pay standards, the national cost-of-living index, and the organization's current and future financial prospects than by each employee's level of performance.

For money to motivate, the marginal difference in pay increases between a high performer and an average performer must be significant. In practice, it rarely is. For instance, a high-performing employee who currently is earning $30,000 a year is given a $200-a-month raise. After taxes, that amounts to about $35 a week. But this employee's $30,000-a-year co-worker, who is an average performer, is rarely passed over at raise time. Instead of getting an eight percent raise, he is likely to get half of that. The net difference in their weekly paychecks is probably less than $20. How much motivation is there in knowing that if you work really hard you're going to end up with $20 a week more than someone who is doing just enough to get by? For a large number of people, not much!

Our last point relates to the degree of discretion that managers have in being able to reward high performers. Where unions exist, that discretion is almost zero. Pay is determined through collective bargaining and is allocated by job title and seniority, not level of performance. In nonunionized environments, the organization's compensation policies will constrain managerial discretion. Each job typically has a pay grade. So a Systems Analyst III can earn between $3525 and $4140 a month. No matter how good a job that analyst does, her boss cannot pay her more than $4140 a month. Similarly, no matter how poorly someone does in that job, he will earn at least $3525 a month. In most organizations, managers have a very small area of discretion within which they can reward their higher-performing employees. So money might be theoretically capable of motivating employees to higher levels of performance, but most managers aren't given enough flexibility to do much about it.

What Motivates You?

For each of the following fifteen statements, circle the number that most closely agrees with how you feel. Consider your answers in the context of your current job or past work experience.

	STRONGLY DISAGREE				STRONGLY AGREE
1. I try very hard to improve on my past performance at work.	1	2	3	4	5
2. I enjoy competition and winning.	1	2	3	4	5
3. I often find myself talking to those around me about nonwork matters.	1	2	3	4	5
4. I enjoy a difficult challenge.	1	2	3	4	5
5. I enjoy being in charge.	1	2	3	4	5
6. I want to be liked by others.	1	2	3	4	5
7. I want to know how I am progressing as I complete tasks.	1	2	3	4	5
8. I confront people who do things I disagree with.	1	2	3	4	5
9. I tend to build close relationships with co-workers.	1	2	3	4	5
10. I enjoy setting and achieving realistic goals.	1	2	3	4	5
11. I enjoy influencing other people to get my way.	1	2	3	4	5
12. I enjoy belonging to groups and organizations.	1	2	3	4	5
13. I enjoy the satisfaction of completing a difficult task.	1	2	3	4	5
14. I often work to gain more control over the events around me.	1	2	3	4	5
15. I enjoy working with others more than working alone.	1	2	3	4	5

Turn to page 714 for scoring directions and key.

Source: Based on R. Steers and D. Braunstein, "A Behaviorally Based Measure of Manifest Needs in Work Settings," *Journal of Vocational Behavior,* October 1976, p. 254; and R. N. Lussier, *Human Relations in Organizations: A Skill Building Approach* (Homewood, IL: Richard D. Irwin, 1990), p. 120.

How Equity-Sensitive Are You?

The following questions ask what you'd like your relationship to be with any organization for which you might work. For each question, divide ten points between the two answers (A and B) by giving the most points to the answer that is most like you and the fewest points to the answer that is least like you. You can, if you like, give the same number of points to both answers. And you can use zeros if you'd like. Just be sure to use all ten points on each question. Place your points in the blank next to each letter.

ANY ORGANIZATION I MIGHT WORK FOR:

1. It would be more important for me to:
   — A. Get from the organization
   — B. Give to the organization

2. It would be more important for me to:

   ___ A. Help others

   ___ B. Watch out for my own good

3. I would be more concerned about:

   ___ A. What I receive from the organization

   ___ B. What I contribute to the organization

4. The hard work I would do should:

   ___ A. Benefit the organization

   ___ B. Benefit me

5. My personal philosophy in dealing with the organization would be:

   ___ A. If you don't look out for yourself, nobody else will

   ___ B. It's better to give than to receive

Turn to page 715 for scoring direction and key.

Source: Courtesy of Prof. Edward W. Miles, Georgia State University, and Dean Richard C. Huseman, University of Central Florida. With permission.

C A S E   I N C I D E N T   7

Frank Pacetta Inspires Love and Fear

When Frank Pacetta took over the Cleveland area office for Xerox in 1987, it was in a shambles. Turnover was high, morale was low, customers were defecting, and the office's overall performance was ranked near the bottom at Xerox. "When Xerox came out with its 'Leadership Through Quality' literature," one customer said, "we read it and laughed."

They aren't laughing anymore. The thirty-three-year-old Pacetta called his staff together on his first day as district manager and vowed that the Cleveland district would finish the year number one in the region. It had finished last the previous year. The staff thought he was nuts. But in Pacetta's first year, the district soared to number one among the twelve regional offices and number four among all sixty-five Xerox districts. During the next three years, he increased operating profits forty-three percent.

How was Pacetta able to turn around the Cleveland office when others couldn't? Essentially, he plied his staff with sales incentives and pep talks, while weeding out employees who couldn't meet his pumped-up sales targets.

Pacetta established a new ethos. He arrived at 7 a.m., an hour earlier than his predecessor, and expected others to do the same. He created a fraternity atmosphere in the office, with parties and pep rallies and recognition for birthdays and anniversaries. He showered his people with plaques and praise for jobs well done. He wanted them to know that he sincerely cared about them and their work.

Pacetta's greatest motivational tools are money and prizes. His top entry-level salespeople can earn an additional $35,000 in commissions over and above their $25,000 base salary. In 1990, his top sales manager made

$93,000 and two account managers made just over $100,000. Pacetta has also created elaborate sales contests, with some winners getting cash of $2000 or $3000, and others getting videocassette recorders and microwave ovens. And, of course, Cleveland employees participate in company-wide incentives, such as a vacation trip each year for top sales reps.

The competitive atmosphere that Pacetta has created in the Cleveland office seems to overshadow the fact that some prizes have little real value. Rather, their value is symbolic. For instance, each month the district's eight sales managers vote for the best and worst manager of the previous month. The winner gets to park in a garage—all others use a lot—and the loser gets a troll-like doll on a rope hung in his or her office. Said one sales manager, "No one wants that doll!"

While Pacetta is quick to encourage and reward his high performers, he has little tolerance for slackers. In his first four years in Cleveland, about seventy percent of his fifty-seven-member staff quit, moved to another district, or were fired. "If someone is just going through the motions, I have no trouble pulling the trigger," Pacetta says.

Questions

1. What motivation concepts does Frank Pacetta seem to be using?
2. Pacetta's motivational approach has worked in Xerox's Cleveland office. Under what conditions do you think his approach would fail? Explain.
3. Would you like to work for Frank Pacetta? Why or why not?

Source: Based on J. S. Hirsch, "To One Xerox Man, Selling Photocopiers Is a Gambler's Game," *The Wall Street Journal*, September 24, 1991, pp. A1 and A9.

FOR FURTHER READING

GREENBERG, J. "Employee Theft as a Reaction to Underpayment Inequity: The Hidden Cost of Pay Cuts," *Journal of Applied Psychology,* October 1990, pp. 561–68. In manufacturing plants where pay was temporarily cut by fifteen percent, it was found that employee theft rates increased significantly. This is explained in equity terms in this article.

HARDER, J. W., "Equity Theory versus Expectancy Theory: The Case of Major League Baseball Free Agents," *Journal of Applied Psychology,* June 1991, pp. 458–64. Proposes a synthesis of these two theories and applies it to the performance of baseball players.

KANFER, R., "Motivation Theory and Industrial and Organizational Psychology," in M. D. Dunnette and L. M. Hough (eds.), *Handbook of Industrial and Organizational Psychology,* 2nd ed. Vol. 1 (Palo Alto, CA: Consulting Psychologists Press, 1990), pp. 75–170. Reviews and evaluates contemporary developments in motivation theory.

KATZELL, R. A., and D. E. THOMPSON, "Work Motivation: Theory and Practice," *American Psychologist,* February 1990, pp. 144–53. Reviews major theories of motivation and extracts seven key strategies for improving work motivation.

STEERS, R. M., and L. W. PORTER, *Motivation and Work Behavior,* 5th ed. (New York: McGraw-Hill, 1991). Reprints some of the major articles in the study of work motivation.

WOOD, R. E., and E. A. LOCKE, "Goal Setting and Strategy Effects on Complex Tasks," in B. M. Staw and L. L. Cummings (eds.), *Research in Organizational Behavior,* Vol. 12 (Greenwich, CT: JAI Press, 1990), pp. 73–109. Presents a model showing the relationships between goals, task strategies, and work performance.

NOTES

[1]Based on "Why This 'Obsolete' Company Is a 'Great Place to Work'," *International Management,* April 1986, pp. 46–51; and S. J. Modic, "Fine-Tuning a Classic," *Industry Week,* March 6, 1989, pp. 15–18.

[2]R. Katerberg and G. J. Blau, "An Examination of Level and Direction of Effort and Job Performance," *Academy of Management Journal,* June 1983, pp. 249–57.

[3]A. Maslow, *Motivation and Personality* (New York: Harper & Row, 1954).

[4]See, for example, E. E. Lawler III and J. L. Suttle, "A Causal Correlation Test of the Need Hierarchy Concept," *Organizational Behavior and Human Performance,* April 1972, pp. 265–87; D. T. Hall and K. E. Nougaim, "An Examination of Maslow's Need Hierarchy in an Organizational Setting," *Organizational Behavior and Human Performance,* February 1968, pp. 12–35; and J. Rauschenberger, N. Schmitt, and J. E. Hunter, "A Test of the Need Hierarchy Concept by a Markov Model of Change in Need Strength," *Administrative Science Quarterly,* December 1980, pp. 654–70.

[5]A. K. Korman, J. H. Greenhaus, and I. J. Badin, "Personnel Attitudes and Motivation," in M. R. Rosenzweig and L. W. Porter (eds.), *Annual Review of Psychology* (Palo Alto, CA: Annual Reviews, 1977), p. 178.

[6]Ibid., p. 179.

[7]M. A. Wahba and L. G. Bridwell, "Maslow Reconsidered: A Review of Research on the Need Hierarchy Theory," *Organizational Behavior and Human Performance,* April 1976, pp. 212–40.

[8]D. McGregor, *The Human Side of Enterprise* (New York: McGraw-Hill, 1960). For an updated analysis of Theory X and Theory Y constructs, see R. J. Summers and S. F. Cronshaw, "A Study of McGregor's Theory X, Theory Y and the Influence of Theory X, Theory Y Assumptions on Causal Attributions for Instances of Worker Poor Performance," in S. L. McShane (ed.), *Organizational Behavior,* ASAC 1988 Conference Proceedings, Vol. 9, Part 5. Halifax, Nova Scotia, 1988, pp. 115–23.

[9]F. Herzberg, B. Mausner, and B. Snyderman, *The Motivation to Work* (New York: John Wiley, 1959).

[10]R. J. House and L. A. Wigdor, "Herzberg's Dual-Factor Theory of Job Satisfaction and Motivations: A Review of the Evidence and Criticism," *Personnel Psychology,* Winter 1967, pp. 369–89; D. P. Schwab and L. L. Cummings, "Theories of Performance and Satisfaction: A Review," *Industrial Relations,* October 1970, pp. 403–30; and R. J. Caston

and R. Braito, "A Specification Issue in Job Satisfaction Research," *Sociological Perspectives,* April 1985, pp. 175–97.

[11]D. Guest, "What's New in Motivation," *Personnel Management,* May 1984, pp. 20–23.

[12]C. P. Alderfer, "An Empirical Test of a New Theory of Human Needs," *Organizational Behavior and Human Performance,* May 1969, pp. 142–75.

[13]M. Haire, E. E. Ghiselli, and L. W. Porter, "Cultural Patterns in the Role of the Manager," *Industrial Relations,* February 1963, pp. 95–117.

[14]C. P. Schneider and C. P. Alderfer, "Three Studies of Measures of Need Satisfaction in Organizations," *Administrative Science Quarterly,* December 1973, pp. 489–505.

[15]J. P. Wanous and A. Zwany, "A Cross-Sectional Test of Need Hierarchy Theory," *Organizational Behavior and Human Performance,* May 1977, pp. 78–97.

[16]D. C. McClelland, *The Achieving Society* (New York: Van Nostrand Reinhold, 1961); J. W. Atkinson and J. O. Raynor, *Motivation and Achievement* (Washington, D.C.: Winston, 1974); D. C. McClelland, *Power: The Inner Experience* (New York: Irvington, 1975); and M. J. Stahl, *Managerial and Technical Motivation: Assessing Needs for Achievement, Power, and Affiliation* (New York: Praeger, 1986).

[17]McClelland, *The Achieving Society.*

[18]D. C. McClelland and D. G. Winter, *Motivating Economic Achievement* (New York: Free Press, 1969).

[19]McClelland, *Power;* McClelland and D. H. Burnham, "Power Is the Great Motivator," *Harvard Business Review,* March–April 1976, pp. 100–10; and R. E. Boyatzis, "The Need for Close Relationships and the Manager's Job," in D. A. Kolb, I. M. Rubin, and J. M. McIntyre, *Organizational Psychology: Readings on Human Behavior in Organizations,* 4th ed. (Englewood Cliffs, NJ: Prentice Hall, 1984), pp. 81–86.

[20]Ibid.

[21]J. B. Miner, *Studies in Management Education* (New York: Springer, 1965).

[22]D. Kipnis, "The Powerholder," in J. T. Tedeschi (ed.), *Perspectives in Social Power* (Chicago: Aldine, 1974), pp. 82–123.

[23]D. Miron and D. C. McClelland, "The Impact of Achievement Motivation Training on Small Businesses," *California Management Review,* Summer 1979, pp. 13–28.

[24]R. de Charms, *Personal Causation: The Internal Affective Determinants of Behavior* (New York: Academic Press, 1968).

[25]E. L. Deci, *Intrinsic Motivation* (New York: Plenum, 1975); R. D. Pritchard, K. M. Campbell, and D. J. Campbell, "Effects of Extrinsic Financial Rewards on Intrinsic Motivation," *Journal of Applied Psychology,* February 1977, pp. 9–15; E. L. Deci, G. Betly, J. Kahle, L. Abrams, and J. Porac, "When Trying to Win: Competition and Intrinsic Motivation," *Personality and Social Psychology Bulletin,* March 1981, pp. 79–83; and P. C. Jordan, "Effects of an Extrinsic Reward on Intrinsic Motivation: A Field Experiment," *Academy of Management Journal,* June 1986, pp. 405–12.

[26]W. E. Scott, "The Effects of Extrinsic Rewards on 'Intrinsic Motivation': A Critique," *Organizational Behavior and Human Performance,* February 1976, pp. 117–19; B. J. Calder and B. M. Staw, "Interaction of Intrinsic and Extrinsic Motivation: Some Methodological Notes," *Journal of Personality and Social Psychology,* January 1975, pp. 76–80; and K. B. Boal and L. L. Cummings, "Cognitive Evaluation Theory: An Experimental Test of Processes and Outcomes," *Organizational Behavior and Human Performance,* December 1981, pp. 289–310.

[27]G. R. Salancik, "Interaction Effects of Performance and Money on Self-Perception of Intrinsic Motivation," *Organizational Behavior and Human Performance,* June 1975, pp. 339–51; and F. Luthans, M. Martinko, and T. Kess, "An Analysis of the Impact of Contingency Monetary Rewards on Intrinsic Motivation," *Proceedings of the Nineteenth Annual Midwest Academy of Management,* St. Louis, 1976, pp. 209–21.

[28]J.B. Miner, *Theories of Organizational Behavior,* (Hinsdale, IL: Dryden Press, 1980), p. 157.

[29]H. J. Arnold, "Effects of Performance Feedback and Extrinsic Reward upon High Intrinsic Motivation," *Organizational Behavior and Human Performance,* December 1976, pp. 275–88.

[30]B. M. Staw, "Motivation in Organizations: Toward Synthesis and Redirection," in B. M. Staw and G. R. Salancik (eds.), *New Directions in Organizational Behavior* (Chicago: St. Clair, 1977), p. 76.

[31]B. J. Calder and B. M. Staw, "Self-Perception of Intrinsic and Extrinsic Motivation," *Journal of Personality and Social Psychology,* April 1975, pp. 599–605.

[32]R. M. Steers and R. T. Mowday, "The Motivational Properties of Tasks," *Academy of Management Review,* October 1977, pp. 645–58.

[33]D. G. Gardner and L. L. Cummings, "Activation Theory and Job Design: Review and Reconceptualization," in B. M. Staw and L. L. Cummings (eds.), *Research in Organizational Behavior,* Vol. 10 (Greenwich, CT: JAI Press, 1988), p. 100.

[34]A. N. Turner and P. R. Lawrence, *Industrial Jobs and the Worker* (Boston: Harvard University Press, 1965).

[35]J. R. Hackman and G. R. Oldham, "Motivation Through the Design of Work: Test of a

Theory," *Organizational Behavior and Human Performance,* August 1976, pp. 250–79.

[36]J. R. Hackman, "Work Design," in J. R. Hackman and J. L. Suttle (eds.), *Improving Life at Work* (Santa Monica, CA: Goodyear, 1977), p. 129.

[37]See "Job Characteristics Theory of Work Redesign," in J. B. Miner, *Theories of Organizational Behavior* (Hinsdale, IL: Dryden Press, 1980), pp. 231–66; B. T. Loher, R. A. Noe, N. L. Moeller, and M. P. Fitzgerald, "A Meta-Analysis of the Relation of Job Characteristics to Job Satisfaction," *Journal of Applied Psychology,* May 1985, pp. 280–89; W. H. Glick, G. D. Jenkins, Jr., and N. Gupta, "Method versus Substance: How Strong Are Underlying Relationships Between Job Characteristics and Attitudinal Outcomes?," *Academy of Management Journal,* September 1986, pp. 441–64; Y. Fried and G. R. Ferris, "The Validity of the Job Characteristics Model: A Review and Meta-Analysis," *Personnel Psychology,* Summer 1987, pp. 287–322; and S. J. Zaccaro and E. F. Stone, "Incremental Validity of an Empirically Based Measure of Job Characteristics," *Journal of Applied Psychology,* May 1988, pp. 245–52.

[38]See R. B. Dunham, "Measurement and Dimensionality of Job Characteristics," *Journal of Applied Psychology,* August 1976, pp. 404–09; J. L. Pierce and R. B. Dunham, "Task Design: A Literature Review," *Academy of Management Review,* January 1976, pp. 83–97; and D. M. Rousseau, "Technological Differences in Job Characteristics, Employee Satisfaction, and Motivation: A Synthesis of Job Design Research and Sociotechnical Systems Theory," *Organizational Behavior and Human Performance,* October 1977, pp. 18–42.

[39]Ibid.; and Y. Fried and G. R. Ferris, "The Dimensionality of Job Characteristics: Some Neglected Issues," *Journal of Applied Psychology,* August 1986, pp. 419–26.

[40]See, for instance, Fried and Ferris, "The Dimensionality of Job Characteristics;" and M. G. Evans and D. A. Ondrack, "The Motivational Potential of Jobs: Is a Multiplicative Model Really Necessary?," in S. L. McShane (ed.), *Organizational Behavior,* ASAC Conference Proceedings, Vol. 9, Part 5, Halifax, Nova Scotia, 1988, pp. 31–39.

[41]See, for instance, P. E. Spector, "Higher-Order Need Strength as a Moderator of the Job Scope-Employee Outcome Relationship: A Meta-Analysis," *Journal of Occupational Psychology,* June 1985, pp. 119–27; G. B. Graen, T. A. Scandura, and M. R. Graen, "A Field Experimental Test of the Moderating Effects of Growth Need Strength on Productivity," *Journal of Applied Psychology,* August 1986, pp. 484–91; and Fried and Ferris, "The Validity of the Job Characteristics Model."

[42]C. A. O'Reilly and D. F. Caldwell, "Informational Influence as a Determinant of Perceived Task Characteristics and Job Satisfaction," *Journal of Applied Psychology,* April 1979, pp. 157–65; R. V. Montagno, "The Effects of Comparison Others and Prior Experience on Responses to Task Design," *Academy of Management Journal,* June 1985, pp. 491–98; and P. C. Bottger and I. K-H. Chew, "The Job Characteristics Model and Growth Satisfaction: Main Effects of Assimilation of Work Experience and Context Satisfaction," *Human Relations,* June 1986, pp. 575–94.

[43]Hackman, "Work Design," pp. 132–33.

[44]G. R. Salancik and J. Pfeffer, "A Social Information Processing Approach to Job Attitudes and Task Design," *Administrative Science Quarterly,* June 1978, pp. 224–53; J. G. Thomas and R. W. Griffin, "The Power of Social Information in the Workplace," *Organizational Dynamics,* Autumn 1989, pp. 63–75; and M. D. Zalesny and J. K. Ford, "Extending the Social Information Processing Perspective: New Links to Attitudes, Behaviors, and Perceptions," *Organizational Behavior and Human Decision Processes,* December 1990, pp. 205–46.

[45]See, for instance, J. Thomas and R. W. Griffin, "The Social Information Processing Model of Task Design: A Review of the Literature," *Academy of Management Journal,* October 1983, pp. 672–82.

[46]This argument is developed in G. Strauss, "The Personality-versus-Organization Theory," in L. R. Sayles (ed.), *Individualism and Big Business* (New York: McGraw-Hill, 1963), pp. 67–79; and J. R. Hackman, "The Design of Work in the 1980s," *Organizational Dynamics,* Summer 1978, pp. 3–17.

[47]E. A. Locke, "Toward a Theory of Task Motivation and Incentives," *Organizational Behavior and Human Performance,* May 1968, pp. 157–89.

[48]P. C. Earley, P. Wojnaroski, and W. Prest, "Task Planning and Energy Expended: Exploration of How Goals Influence Performance," *Journal of Applied Psychology,* February 1987, pp. 107–14.

[49]G. P. Latham and G. A. Yukl, "A Review of Research on the Application of Goal Setting in Organizations," *Academy of Management Journal,* December 1975, pp. 824–45; E. A. Locke, K. N. Shaw, L. M. Saari, and G. P. Latham, "Goal Setting and Task Performance," *Psychological Bulletin,* January 1981, pp. 125–52; A. J. Mento, R. P. Steel, and R. J. Karren, "A Meta-Analytic Study of the Effects of Goal Setting on Task Performance: 1966–1984," *Organizational Behavior and Human Decision Processes,* February 1987, pp. 52–83; M. E. Tubbs "Goal Setting: A Meta-Analytic Examination of the Empirical Evidence," *Journal of Applied Psychology,* August 1986, pp. 474–83; P. C. Earley, G. B. Northcraft, C. Lee, and T. R. Lituchy, "Impact of Process and Outcome Feedback on the Relation of Goal Setting to Task Performance," *Academy of Management Journal,* March 1990, pp. 87–105; and E. A. Locke and G. P. Latham, *A Theory of Goal Setting and Task Performance* (Englewood Cliffs, NJ: Prentice Hall, 1990).

[50]J. M. Ivancevich and J. T. McMahon, "The Effects of Goal Setting, External Feedback, and Self-Generated Feedback on Outcome Variables: A Field Experiment," *Academy of*

Management Journal, June 1982, pp. 359–72.

⁵¹See, for example, G. P. Latham, M. Erez, E. A. Locke, "Resolving Scientific Disputes by the Joint Design of Crucial Experiments by the Antagonists: Application to the Erez-Latham Dispute Regarding Participation in Goal Setting," *Journal of Applied Psychology,* November 1988, pp. 753–72.

⁵²M. Erez, P. C. Earley, and C. L. Hulin, "The Impact of Participation on Goal Acceptance and Performance: A Two-Step Model," *Academy of Management Journal,* March 1985, pp. 50–66.

⁵³J. R. Hollenbeck, C. R. Williams, and H. J. Klein, "An Empirical Examination of the Antecedents of Commitment to Difficult Goals," *Journal of Applied Psychology,* February 1989, pp. 18–23.

⁵⁴A. Bandura, "Self-Efficacy: Toward a Unifying Theory of Behavioral Change," *Psychological Review,* May 1977, pp. 191–215; and M. E. Gist, "Self-Efficacy: Implications for Organizational Behavior and Human Resource Management," *Academy of Management Review,* July 1987, pp. 472–85.

⁵⁵E. A. Locke, E. Frederick, C. Lee, and P. Bobko, "Effect of Self-Efficacy, Goals, and Task Strategies on Task Performance," *Journal of Applied Psychology,* May 1984, pp. 241–51.

⁵⁶A. Bandura and D. Cervone, "Differential Engagement in Self-Reactive Influences in Cognitively-Based Motivation," *Organizational Behavior and Human Decision Processes,* August 1986, pp. 92–113.

⁵⁷See J. C. Anderson and C. A. O'Reilly, "Effects of an Organizational Control System on Managerial Satisfaction and Performance," *Human Relations,* June 1981, pp. 491–501; and J. P. Meyer, B. Schacht-Cole, and I. R. Gellatly, "An Examination of the Cognitive Mechanisms by Which Assigned Goals Affect Task Performance and Reactions to Performance," *Journal of Applied Social Psychology,* Vol. 18, No. 5, 1988, pp. 390–408.

⁵⁸R. M. Steers and L. W. Porter, *Motivation and Work Behavior,* 2nd ed. (New York: McGraw-Hill, 1979), p. 13.

⁵⁹E. A. Locke, "Latham vs. Komaki: A Tale of Two Paradigms," *Journal of Applied Psychology,* February 1980, pp. 16–23.

⁶⁰J. S. Adams, "Inequity in Social Exchanges," in L. Berkowitz (ed.), *Advances in Experimental Social Psychology* (New York: Academic Press, 1965), pp. 267–300.

⁶¹P. S. Goodman, "An Examination of Referents Used in the Evaluation of Pay," *Organizational Behavior and Human Performance,* October 1974, pp. 170–95; S. Ronen, "Equity Perception in Multiple Comparisons: A Field Study," *Human Relations,* April 1986, pp. 333–46; R. W. Scholl, E. A. Cooper, and J. F. McKenna, "Referent Selection in Determining Equity Perception: Differential Effects on Behavioral and Attitudinal Outcomes," *Personnel Psychology,* Spring 1987, pp. 113–27; and T. P. Summers and A. S. DeNisi, "In Search of Adams' Other: Reexamination of Referents Used in the Evaluation of Pay," *Human Relations,* June 1990, pp. 497–511.

⁶²Goodman, "An Examination of Referents"; and G. R. Oldham, C. T. Kulik, L. P. Stepina, and M. L. Ambrose, "Relations Between Situational Factors and the Comparative Referents Used by Employees," *Academy of Management Journal,* September 1986, pp. 599–608.

⁶³See, for example, E. Walster, G. W. Walster, and W. G. Scott, *Equity: Theory and Research* (Boston: Allyn & Bacon, 1978); and J. Greenberg, "Cognitive Reevaluation of Outcomes in Response to Underpayment Inequity," *Academy of Management Journal,* March 1989, pp. 174–84.

⁶⁴P.S. Goodman and A. Friedman, "An Examination of Adams' Theory of Inequity," *Administrative Science Quarterly,* September 1971, pp. 271–88; R. P. Vecchio, "An Individual-Differences Interpretation of the Conflicting Predictions Generated by Equity Theory and Expectancy Theory," *Journal of Applied Psychology,* August 1981, pp. 470–81; J. Greenberg, "Approaching Equity and Avoiding Inequity in Groups and Organizations," in J. Greenberg and R. L. Cohen (eds.), *Equity and Justice in Social Behavior* (New York: Academic Press, 1982), pp. 389–435; R. T. Mowday, "Equity Theory Predictions of Behavior in Organizations," in R. M. Steers and L. W. Porter (eds.), *Motivation and Work Behavior,* 4th ed. (New York: McGraw-Hill, 1987), pp. 89–110; and E. W. Miles, J. D. Hatfield, and R. C. Huseman, "The Equity Sensitive Construct: Potential Implications for Worker Performance," *Journal of Management,* December 1989, pp. 581–88.

⁶⁵J. Greenberg and S. Ornstein, "High Status Job Title as Compensation for Underpayment: A Test of Equity Theory," *Journal of Applied Psychology,* May 1983, pp. 285–97; and J. Greenberg, "Equity and Workplace Status: A Field Experiment," *Journal of Applied Psychology,* November 1988, pp. 606–13.

⁶⁶P. S. Goodman, "Social Comparison Process in Organizations," in B. M. Staw and G. R. Salancik (eds.), *New Directions in Organizational Behavior* (Chicago: St. Clair, 1977), pp. 97–132.

⁶⁷V. H. Vroom, *Work and Motivation* (New York: John Wiley, 1964).

⁶⁸See, for example, H. G. Heneman III and D. P. Schwab, "Evaluation of Research on Expectancy Theory Prediction of Employee Performance," *Psychological Bulletin,* July 1972, pp. 1–9; T. R. Mitchell, "Expectancy Models of Job Satisfaction, Occupational Preference and Effort: A Theoretical, Methodological and Empirical Appraisal," *Psychological Bulletin,* November

1974, pp. 1053–77; and L. Reinharth and M. A. Wahba, "Expectancy Theory as a Predictor of Work Motivation, Effort Expenditure, and Job Performance," *Academy of Management Journal,* September 1975, pp. 502–37.

[69]See, for example, L. W. Porter and E. E. Lawler III, *Managerial Attitudes and Performance* (Homewood, IL: Richard D. Irwin, 1968); D. F. Parker and L. Dyer, "Expectancy Theory as a Within-Person Behavioral Choice Model: An Empirical Test of Some Conceptual and Methodological Refinements," *Organizational Behavior and Human Performance,* October 1976, pp. 97–117; and H. J. Arnold, "A Test of the Multiplicative Hypothesis of Expectancy-Valence Theories of Work Motivation," *Academy of Management Journal,* April 1981, pp. 128–41.

[70]Vroom refers to these three variables as *valence, instrumentality,* and *expectancy,* respectively.

[71]E. A. Locke, "Personnel Attitudes and Motivation," in M. R. Rosenzweig and L. W. Porter (eds.), *Annual Review of Psychology,* (Palo Alto, CA: Annual Reviews, 1975), p. 459.

[72]P. M. Muchinsky, "A Comparison of Within- and Across-Subjects Analyses of the Expectancy-Valence Model for Predicting Effort," *Academy of Management Journal,* March 1977, pp. 154–58.

[73]R. J. House, H. J. Shapiro, and M. A. Wahba, "Expectancy Theory as a Predictor of Work Behavior and Attitudes: A Re-evaluation of Empirical Evidence," *Decision Sciences,* January 1974, pp. 481–506.

[74]K. A. Kovach, "What Motivates Employees? Workers and Supervisors Give Different Answers," *Business Horizons,* September-October 1987, pp. 58–65.

[75]L. H. Peters, E. J. O'Connor, and C. J. Rudolf, "The Behavioral and Affective Consequences of Performance-Relevant Situational Variables," *Organizational Behavior and Human Performance,* February 1980, pp. 79–96; M. Blumberg and C. D. Pringle, "The Missing Opportunity in Organizational Research: Some Implications for a Theory of Work Performance," *Academy of Management Review,* October 1982, pp. 560–69; and D. A. Waldman and W. D. Spangler, "Putting Together the Pieces: A Closer Look at the Determinants of Job Performance," *Human Performance,* Vol. 2, 1989, pp. 29–59.

[76]N. J. Adler, *International Dimensions of Organizational Behavior,* 2nd ed. (Boston: PWS-Kent Publishing, 1991), p. 152.

[77]G. Hofstede, "Motivation, Leadership, and Organization: Do American Theories Apply Abroad?, *Organizational Dynamics,* Summer 1980, p. 55.

[78]Ibid.

[79]This section is based on F. J. Landy and W. S. Becker, "Motivation Theory Reconsidered," in L. L. Cummings and B. M. Staw (eds.), *Research in Organizational Behavior,* Vol. 9 (Greenwich, CT: JAI Press, 1987), pp. 24–35.

MOTIVATION: FROM CONCEPTS TO APPLICATIONS

LEARNING OBJECTIVES

After studying this chapter, you should be able to:

1. Identify the four ingredients common to MBO programs

2. Outline the typical five-step problem-solving model in OB Mod

3. Explain why managers might want to use participative decision making

4. Describe the link between performance-based compensation and expectancy theory

5. Explain how flexible benefits turn benefits into motivators

6. Describe the influence of comparable worth on female employees

7. Describe how flextime schedules work

8. Explain how managers can enrich jobs

*Set me anything to do as a task, and it is inconceivable the desire
I have to do something else.*

G. B. SHAW

*F*ew people have ever heard of United Electric Controls Co.[1] It's a sixty-year-old family-run business in Watertown, Massachusetts, that employs 350 people. The company makes industrial temperature and pressure controls.

UECC fell on rough times in the mid–1980s. In 1987, despite annual sales of $28 million, the company had its worst loss ever. In a desperate attempt to turn things around, management introduced new quality control methods and inventory control systems. But its big breakthrough came when it started a participative management program that allowed it to tap into a valued, but neglected, company resource: its employees.

Like many companies, UECC had long provided suggestion boxes for employee ideas. But also like many companies, UECC's suggestion system discouraged the generation of ideas from below by creating intimidating and drawn-out procedures. For instance, between 1968 and 1988, only twenty or so ideas had been suggested—about one a year. The new system that management has put in place now aggressively encourages and rewards employee participation. Cash awards of $100 are paid for every usable idea. In 1989, employees submitted five hundred suggestions. In 1990, the number of suggestions hit a thousand, of which about two-thirds were implemented. The new work climate at United Electric has unleashed employee creativity and motivated ninety percent of its employees to contribute ideas on how to improve the firm's operations. An idea by Harry Moumdjian (pictured above) provides an illustration of how UECC's participative management program has influenced its employees.

Harry Moumdjian has been building and rebuilding diaphragm assemblies for UECC since 1975. When the company appealed for new ideas, he knew he wanted to find a way to cut down on the number of faulty assemblies that came back from the inspection department. "They always found leaks," he says.

Harry made his supervisor an offer. Let me do the testing, he said, and I'll give you a one-hundred-percent leak-free guarantee. "When they said to put ideas on paper, I did." With the help of the model shop, Harry set about building an aquarium big enough to hold one of his diaphragm assemblies. To test an assembly, he figured, he could simply run an air hose through it, then stand back and watch for air bubbles. After a few modifications, the aquarium worked just as he had said it would. Harry can now tell quickly and exactly where a leak is coming from and fix it before the assembly goes to the inspection department.

Today, United Electric is making money again. No small part of that achievement can be attributed to management's drawing on concepts such as the motivation-hygiene theory, the expectancy theory, and the job characteristics model to create a workplace where employees are motivated and able to utilize all their talents more fully. ■

*I*n this chapter, we want to focus on how to apply motivation concepts. We want to link theories to practice. For it's one thing to be able to regurgitate motivation theories. It's often another to see how, as a manager, you could use them.

In the following pages, we'll review a number of techniques and programs that have gained varying degrees of acceptance in practice. For example, there will be discussions on popular programs such as management by objectives, performance-based compensation, and flexible work hours. Specific attention will be given to showing how these programs build on one or more of the motivation theories we covered previously.

MANAGEMENT BY OBJECTIVES

Goal-setting theory has an impressive base of research support. But as a manager, how do you make goal setting operational? The best answer to that question is: Install a management by objectives (MBO) program.

What Is MBO?

Management by Objectives (MBO) A program that encompasses specific goals, participatively set, for an explicit time period, with feedback on goal progress.

Management by objectives emphasizes participatively set goals that are tangible, verifiable, and measurable. It's not a new idea. In fact, it was originally proposed by Peter Drucker more than thirty-five years ago as a means of using goals to motivate people rather than to control them.[2] Today, no introduction to basic management concepts would be complete without a discussion of MBO.

MBO's appeal undoubtedly lies in its emphasis on converting overall organizational objectives into specific objectives for organizational units and individual members. MBO operationalizes the concept of objectives by devising a process by which objectives cascade down through the organization. As depicted in Figure 8–1, the organization's overall objectives are translated into specific objectives for each succeeding level (that is, divisional, departmental, individual) in the organization. But because lower-unit managers jointly participate in setting their own goals, MBO works from the "bottom up" as well as from the "top down." The result is a hierarchy of objectives that links objectives at one level to those at the next level. And for the individual employee, MBO provides specific personal performance objectives. Each person, therefore, has an identified specific contribution to make to his or her unit's performance. If all the individuals achieve their goals, then their unit's goals will be attained and the organization's overall objectives become a reality.

There are four ingredients common to MBO programs. These are goal specificity, participative decision making, an explicit time period, and performance feedback.[3]

The objectives in MBO should be concise statements of expected accomplishments. It's not adequate, for example, to merely state a desire to cut costs, improve service, or increase quality. Such desires have to be converted into tangible objectives that can be measured and evaluated. To cut departmental costs *by seven percent,* to improve service by ensuring that all telephone orders are processed *within twenty-four hours of receipt,* or to increase quality by keeping returns to *less than one percent of sales* are examples of specific objectives.

The objectives in MBO are not unilaterally set by the boss and then assigned to subordinates. MBO replaces imposed goals with participatively determined goals. The superior and subordinate jointly choose the goals and agree on how they will be measured.

Each objective has a specific time period in which it is to be completed. Typically the time period is three months, six months, or a year. So managers and subordinates not only have specific objectives, but also stipulated time periods in which to accomplish them.

The final ingredient in an MBO program is feedback on performance. MBO seeks to give continuous feedback on progress toward goals. Ideally, this is accomplished by giving ongoing feedback to individuals so they can monitor and correct their own actions. This is supplemented by periodic managerial evaluations, when progress is reviewed. This applies at the top of the organization as well as at the bottom. The vice president of sales, for instance, has objectives for overall sales and for each of his or her major products. He or she will monitor ongoing sales reports to determine progress toward the sales division's objectives. Similarly, district sales managers have objectives, as does each salesperson in the field. Feedback in terms of sales and performance data is provided to let these people know how they are doing. Formal appraisal meetings also take place at which superiors and subordinates can review progress toward goals and further feedback can be provided.

FIGURE 8–1   Cascading of Objectives

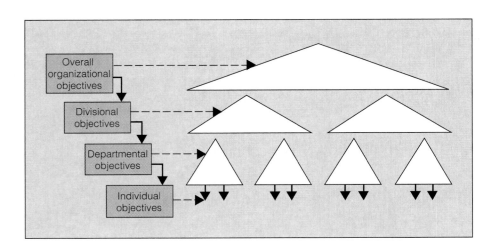

Linking MBO and Goal-Setting Theory

Goal-setting theory demonstrates that hard goals result in a higher level of individual performance than do easy goals, that specific hard goals result in higher levels of performance than do no goals at all or the generalized goal of "do your best," and that feedback on one's performance leads to higher performance. Compare these findings with MBO.

MBO directly advocates specific goals and feedback. MBO implies, rather than explicitly states, that goals must be perceived as feasible. Consistent with goal setting, MBO would be most effective when the goals are difficult enough to require the person to do some stretching.

The only area of possible disagreement between MBO and goal-setting theory relates to the issue of participation—MBO strongly advocates it, while goal setting demonstrates that assigning goals to subordinates frequently works just as well. The major benefit to using participation, however, is that it appears to induce individuals to establish more difficult goals.

MBO in Practice

How widely used is MBO? Reviews of studies that have sought to answer this question suggest that it's a popular technique. Among large organizations—in business and in the public sector—probably half currently have a formal MBO program or had one at some time.[4]

MBO's popularity should not be construed to mean that it always works. There are a number of documented cases where MBO has been implemented but failed to meet management's expectations.[5] A close look at these cases, however, indicates that the problems rarely lie with MBO's basic components. Rather, the culprits tend to be factors such as unrealistic expectations regarding results, lack of top-management commitment, and an inability or unwillingness by management to allocate rewards based on goal accomplishment. Nevertheless, MBO provides managers with the vehicle for implementing goal-setting theory.

BEHAVIOR MODIFICATION

OB Mod A program where managers identify performance-related employee behaviors and then implement an intervention strategy to strengthen desirable behaviors and weaken undesirable behaviors.

There is a now-classic study that took place a number of years ago with freight packers at Emery Air Freight (now part of Federal Express).[6] Emery's management wanted packers to use freight containers for shipments whenever possible because of specific economic savings. When packers were queried as to the percentage of shipments containerized, the standard reply was ninety percent. An analysis by Emery found, however, that the container utilization rate was only forty-five percent. In order to encourage employees to use containers, management established a program of feedback and positive reinforcements. Each packer was instructed to keep a checklist of his or her daily packings, both containerized and noncontainerized. At the end of each day, the packer computed his or her container utilization rate. Almost unbelievably, container utilization jumped to more than ninety percent on the first day of the program and held to that level. Emery reported that this simple program of feedback and positive reinforcements saved the company $2 million over a three-year period.

This program at Emery Air Freight illustrates the use of behavior modification, or what has become more popularly called **OB Mod.**[7] It represents the application of reinforcement theory to individuals in the work setting.

What Is OB Mod?

The typical OB Mod program, as shown in Figure 8–2, follows a five-step problem-solving model: (1) identification of performance-related behaviors; (2) measurement of the behaviors; (3) identification of behavioral contingencies; (4) development and implementation of an intervention strategy; and (5) evaluation of performance improvement.[8]

Everything an employee does on his or her job is not equally important in terms of performance outcomes. The first step in OB Mod, therefore, is to identify the critical behaviors that make a significant impact on the employee's job performance. These are those five to ten percent of behaviors that may account for up to seventy or eighty percent of each employee's performance. Using containers whenever possible by freight packers at Emery Air Freight is an example of a critical behavior.

The second step requires the manager to develop some baseline performance data. This is obtained by determining the number of times the identified behavior is occurring under present conditions. In our freight packing example at Emery, this would have revealed that forty-five percent of all shipments were containerized.

The third step is to perform a functional analysis to identify the behavioral contingencies or consequences of performance. This tells the manager the antecedent cues that emit the behavior and the consequences that are currently maintaining it. At Emery Air Freight, social norms and the greater difficulty in packing containers were the antecedent cues. This encouraged the practice of packing items separately. Moreover, the consequences for continuing this behavior, prior to the OB Mod intervention, were social acceptance and escaping more demanding work.

Once the functional analysis is complete, the manager is ready to develop and implement an intervention strategy to strengthen desirable performance behaviors and weaken undesirable behaviors. The appropriate strategy will entail changing some element of the performance-reward linkage—structure, processes, technology, groups, or the task—with the goal of making high-level performance more rewarding. In the Emery example, the work technology was altered to require the keeping of a checklist. The checklist plus the computation, at the end of the day, of a container utilization rate acted to reinforce the desirable behavior of using containers.

The final step in OB Mod is to evaluate performance improvement. In the Emery intervention, the immediate improvement in the container utilization rate demonstrated that behavioral change took place. That it rose to ninety percent and held at that level further indicates that learning took place. That is, the employees underwent a relatively permanent change in behavior.

Linking OB Mod and Reinforcement Theory

Reinforcement theory relies on positive reinforcement, shaping, and recognizing the impact of different schedules of reinforcement on behavior. OB Mod uses these concepts to provide managers with a powerful and proven means for changing employee behavior.

OB Mod in Practice

OB Mod has been used by a number of organizations to improve employee productivity and to reduce errors, absenteeism, tardiness, and accident rates.[9] Organizations like General Electric, Weyerhauser, the city of Detroit,

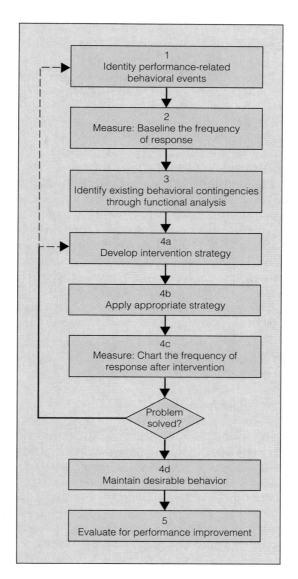

FIGURE 8–2   Steps in OB Mod

Source: Adapted by permission of the publisher from "The Management of Behavioral Contingencies," by F. Luthans and R. Kreitner, *Personnel*, July–August 1974 by AMACOM, a division of the American Management Association, p. 13. All rights reserved.

Dayton-Hudson Stores, and Xerox report impressive results using OB Mod.[10] For instance, in 1987, frustrated by customer complaints, Xerox's top management changed the basis for its executive bonus plan from traditional quotas to long-term customer satisfaction.[11] The company surveys forty thousand customers world-wide every month to determine the percentage who are satisfied with Xerox products and service. At the start of each year, top management looks at the previous year's results and develops a goal. In 1990, the target was ninety percent satisfaction, up from eighty-six percent at the start of 1989. By 1992, Xerox aimed to hit one hundred percent.

Seattle Pacific Supply Co., an apartment supply firm with only eleven employees, has used OB Mod to significantly improve employee performance.[12] Every day that the company books $5500 in sales, all employees receive an extra half-hour's pay. If daily sales hit $15,000, everyone gets another six hours' wages. The previous year's sales provide the basis for Pacific's bonus targets. Paid out once a month, the bonuses accrue daily and in a typical month amount to an extra twenty hours' salary for each employee. Since 1986, when Pacific scrapped its monthly incentive program in favor of this daily performance appraisal, company sales have increased more than fifty percent, turnover has dropped to almost zero, and daily sales targets have been hit four out of five days a week.

OB Mod has also proven effective in sports organizations. Researchers, for instance, helped a midwestern university hockey team win more games by significantly increasing the number of legal body blocks or hits by team members.[13] These legal hits are crucial for winning collegiate games because they give the offense more total time with the puck, more shots on goal, and, usually, more goals. Over a two-year period, using OB Mod techniques, the team's mean hit rate increased 141 percent and its win-loss-tie record went from 13-21-2 to 23-15-2.

The philosophy behind OB Mod additionally appears to be affecting many managers in the way they relate to their employees—in the kind and quantity of feedback they give, the content of performance appraisals, and the type and allocation of organizational rewards.

Despite the positive results that OB Mod has demonstrated, it is not without its critics.[14] Is it a technique for manipulating people? Does it decrease an employee's freedom? If so, is such action on the part of managers unethical? And do nonmonetary reinforcers like feedback, praise, and recognition get stale after a while? Will employees begin to see these as ways for management to increase productivity without providing commensurate increases in their pay? There are no easy answers to questions such as these.

PARTICIPATIVE MANAGEMENT

At a General Electric lighting plant in Ohio, work teams perform many tasks and assume many of the responsibilities once handled by their supervisors. When the plant was faced with a recent decline in the demand for the tubes it produces, the workers decided first to slow production and eventually to lay themselves off. The Boeing Co. is building a new plant in Auburn, Washington. Groups of employees, representing twelve different technical specialties, are actively participating in the decisions on the new equipment that will go onto the plant's production floor. Marketing people at USAA, a large insurance company, meet in a conference room for an hour every week to discuss ways in which they can improve the quality of their work and increase productivity. Management has listened and implemented many of their suggestions.[15]

What Is Participative Management?

Participative Management
A process where subordinates share a significant degree of decision-making power with their immediate superiors.

The preceding are examples of **participative management.** The common thread through these examples is joint decision making. That is, subordinates actually share a significant degree of decision-making power with their immediate superiors. But in actual practice, participative management is an umbrella term that encompasses such varied activities as goal setting, problem solving, direct involvement in work decisions, inclusion in consultation committees, representation on policy-making bodies, and selecting new co-workers.[16]

Participative management has, at times, been promoted as a panacea for poor morale and low productivity. One author has even argued that participative management is an ethical imperative.[17] But participative management is not appropriate for every organization or every work unit. For it to work, there must be adequate time to participate, the issues in which employees get involved must be relevant to their interests, employees must have the ability (intelligence, technical knowledge, communication skills) to participate, and the organization's culture must support employee involvement.[18]

Why would management want to share its decision-making power with subordinates? There are a number of good reasons. As jobs have become more complex, managers often don't know everything their employees do. So participation allows those who know the most to contribute. The result can be better decisions. The interdependence in tasks that employees often do today also requires consultation with people in other departments and work units. This increases the need for committees and group meetings to resolve issues that affect them jointly. Participation additionally increases commitment to decisions. People are less likely to undermine a decision at the time of its implementation if they shared in making that decision. Finally, participation provides intrinsic rewards for employees. It can make their jobs more interesting and meaningful. This has become an increasing concern of younger and more highly educated workers.

Dozens of studies have been conducted on the participation–performance relationship. The findings, however, are mixed.[19] When the research is looked at carefully, it appears that participation typically has only a modest influence on variables such as employee productivity, motivation, and job satisfaction. Of course, that doesn't mean that the use of participative management can't be beneficial under the right conditions. What it says, however, is that the use of participation is no sure means for improving employee performance.

Quality Circles

Quality Circle A work group of employees who meet regularly to discuss their quality problems, investigate causes, recommend solutions, and take corrective actions.

Currently, the most widely discussed form of participative management is the **quality circle.**[20] Originally begun in the United States and exported to Japan in the 1950s, the quality circle has been imported back to the United States. As it developed in Japan, the quality circle concept is frequently mentioned as one of the techniques that Japanese firms utilize that has allowed them to make high-quality products at low costs.

What is a quality circle? It's a work group of eight to ten employees and supervisors who have a shared area of responsibility. They meet regularly—typically once a week, on company time and on company premises—to discuss their quality problems, investigate causes of the problems, recommend solutions, and take corrective actions. They take over the responsibility for solving quality problems, and they generate and evaluate their own feedback. But management typically retains control over the final decision regarding implementation of recommended solutions. Of course, it is not presumed that employees inherently have this ability to analyze and solve quality problems. Therefore, part of the quality circle concept includes teaching participating employees group communication skills, various quality strategies, and measurement and problem analysis techniques. Figure 8–3 describes a typical quality circle process.

Quality circles draw on employees to identify and solve quality problems in their work area. Chuck Keeler/Tony Stone Worldwide

Linking Participation and Motivation Theories

Participative management draws on a number of the motivation theories discussed in the previous chapter. For instance, Theory Y is consistent with participative management, while Theory X aligns with the more traditional autocratic style of managing people. In terms of motivation-hygiene theory,

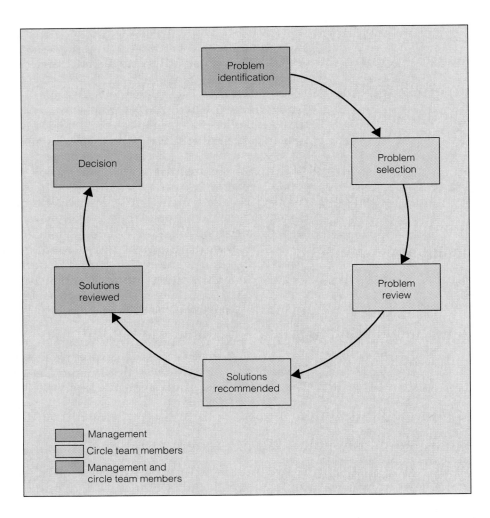

FIGURE 8–3   How a Typical Quality Circle Operates

participative management could provide employees with intrinsic motivation by increasing opportunities for growth, responsibility, and involvement in the work itself. Similarly, the process of making and implementing a decision, and then seeing it work out, can help satisfy an employee's needs for responsibility, achievement, recognition, growth, and enhanced self-esteem. So participative management is compatible with ERG theory and efforts to stimulate the achievement need.

Participative Management in Practice

Germany, France, Holland, and the Scandinavian countries have firmly established the principle of industrial democracy in Europe, and other nations, including Japan, Israel, and Yugoslavia, have traditionally practiced some form of participative decision making for decades.[21] But participation has been much slower to gain ground in American organizations. The resistance, surprisingly, doesn't come from operative employees, but rather from management—upper, middle, and lower.[22] Having "played the game" and achieved positions of authority, they are often resistant to sharing decision-making power. In addition, much of what is called "participative management" in American organizations is really "pseudo-participation." Managers go through the motions of seeking out employees' ideas on problems and including them in the decision-making process, but managers still retain almost complete control over the final choice.[23]

What about quality circles? How popular are they in practice? The names of U.S. companies presently using quality circles reads like a Who's Who of Corporate America: Hewlett-Packard, Digital Equipment, Westinghouse, General Electric, Texas Instruments, Inland Steel, Xerox, Eastman Kodak, Polaroid, Procter & Gamble, Control Data, General Motors, Ford, IBM, Martin Marietta, Motorola, American Airlines, TRW.[24] General Electric, for instance, has more than a thousand of the circles at plants across the United States.[25] But the success of quality circles has been far from overwhelming. Although the rigor of studies investigating the effectiveness of quality circles is quite uneven, the best evidence suggests that this technique does little to improve long-term attitudes, although it does positively affect product and service quality, efficiency, and cost reduction.[26] Because the results have not been consistently impressive, some organizations have dropped their quality circles. Yet, in defense of the concept, much of the disappointment can undoubtedly be attributed to improper introduction of the technique, inadequate support for the circle concept, and/or unrealistic expectations by management in terms of productivity improvement.

PERFORMANCE-BASED COMPENSATION

John F. Akers is chairman of IBM. His company had a bad year in 1991, suffering a loss of $2.8 billion. But Akers "suffered" along with the stockholders. Because his compensation is partly linked to company performance, his annual salary and bonus fell to less than $1.6 million from $2.6 million.[27]

Pay for performance is not reserved just for senior managers. Operative employees also can participate in such programs. Store employees at sixty Great Atlantic & Pacific Tea Co. (A&P) supermarkets in the Philadelphia area have taken a twenty-five percent pay cut in exchange for a cash bonus based on their store's sales. The program is given credit for having significantly increased labor productivity in these stores, while at the same time boosting employee overall wages.[28]

What Is Performance-Based Compensation?

Performance-Based Compensation Paying employees on the basis of some performance measure.

Piece-rate pay plans, wage incentive plans, profit-sharing, and lump-sum bonuses are all forms of **performance-based compensation.** What differentiates these forms of pay from more traditional plans is that instead of paying a person for *time* on the job, their pay is adjusted to reflect some performance measure. That might be individual productivity, work group or departmental productivity, unit profitability, or the overall organization's profit performance. Two of the more widely used of the performance-based compensation plans are piece-rate wages for production workers and annual performance bonuses based on corporate profits for senior executives.

Piece-Rate Pay Plans Workers are paid a fixed sum for each unit of production completed.

In **piece-rate pay plans,** workers are paid a fixed sum for each unit of production completed. When an employee gets no base salary and is paid only for what he or she produces, this is a pure piece-rate plan. People who work ball parks selling peanuts and soda pop frequently are paid this way. They might get to keep twenty-five cents for every bag of peanuts they sell. If they sell two hundred bags during a game, they make $50. If they sell only forty bags, their take is a mere $10. The harder they work and the more peanuts they sell, the more they earn. Many organizations use a modified piece-rate plan, where employees earn a base hourly wage plus a piece-rate differential. So a legal typist might be paid $6 an hour plus twenty cents per

The Ethics of CEO Compensation

The chief executive officers of America's largest companies earn, on average, 160 times as much as the typical blue-collar worker.[29] Some say this represents a classic economic response to a situation in which the demand is great for high-quality top-executive talent and the supply is low. Other arguments in favor of paying CEOs $1 million a year or more are: the need to compensate people for the tremendous responsibilities and stress that go with such jobs, the motivating potential that seven- and eight-figure annual incomes provide to both the CEOs and those who might aspire to the position, and the CEO's influence on the company's bottom line.

Critics describe the astronomical pay packages given to American CEO's as "rampant greed." They note, for instance, that during the 1980s, CEO compensation jumped by 212 percent, while factory workers saw their pay increase by just 53 percent. During the same decade, the average earnings per share of the Standard & Poor's 500 companies grew by only 78 percent. In 1990, the average chief executive's salary and bonus *rose* by 3.5 percent to $1,214,000, yet profits *dropped* 7 percent. Moreover, in the year 1990, all twenty of the highest-paid U.S. CEO's earned in excess of $5.8 million.

Executive pay is considerably higher in the United States than in most other countries. American CEOs typically make two or three times as much as their counterparts in Canada and Europe. In Japan, CEOs earn only seventeen times the pay of an ordinary worker. For example, in 1990, the top three U.S. auto-company chiefs were paid a total of $7.3 million. By contrast, the combined income for the heads of Japan's top-three automakers in that same year was $1.8 million. Critics of executive pay practices in the United States argue that CEOs choose board members whom they can count on to support ever-increasing pay for top management. If board members fail to "play along," they risk losing their positions, their fees, and the prestige and power inherent in board membership.

Does the blame for the problem lie with CEOs or with the shareholders and boards that knowingly allow the practice? Should we fault a Stephen Wolf, chairman of UAL Corp., for collecting $18,301,000 in salary, bonuses, and stock-based incentive plans in 1990 while, during that same year, his company's profits dropped seventy-one percent?

Are American CEO's greedy? Are these CEO's acting unethically?

page. Such modified plans provide a floor under an employee's earnings, while still offering a productivity incentive.

For years, senior corporate executives received regular increases in their pay, regardless of their company's success or failure. More top executives than ever are now finding their compensation linked directly to corporate performance. When things go well for a firm, it is assumed that management had a large part in that outcome, so they should share in the good times. For example, Charles Lazarus, chairman of Toys 'R' Us Inc., earns a base salary of $315,000 a year. Because his contract provides him an annual performance bonus of one percent of all pretax profits over $18 million, and because the company's 1990 income was a healthy $326 million, Lazarus pocketed over $3 million in performance pay that year.[30] Of course, in a bad year, executives may get no bonus at all.

Linking Performance-Based Compensation and Expectancy Theory

Performance-based compensation is probably most compatible with expectancy theory predictions. Specifically, individuals should perceive a strong relationship between their performance and the rewards they receive if motivation is to be maximized. If rewards are allocated completely on non-performance factors—such as seniority or job title—then employees are likely to reduce their effort.

The evidence supports the importance of this linkage, especially for operative employees working under piece-rate systems. For example, one study of four hundred manufacturing firms found that those companies with wage incentive plans achieved forty-three to sixty-four percent greater productivity than those without such plans.[31]

Performance-Based Compensation in Practice

"Pay-for-performance" is a concept that is rapidly replacing the annual cost-of-living raise. One reason, as cited above, is its motivational power—but don't ignore the cost implications. Bonuses and other incentive rewards avoid the fixed expense of permanent salary boosts.

Corporate America seems to have gotten this message. In 1991, thirty-five percent of the Fortune 500 companies had some form of pay-for-performance program—up from only seven percent ten years earlier.[32] Table 8–1, based on a national survey of 435 U.S. companies, demonstrates which programs are most popular.

Among firms that haven't introduced performance-based compensation programs, common concerns tend to surface.[33] Managers fret over what should constitute *performance* and how it should be measured. They have to

**TABLE 8–1   Pay-for-Performance in Practice
(Based on a Survey of 435 U.S. Companies)**

Program	Percentage of Companies That Use the Program
Individual incentive	35*
Payment is directly related to the meeting of individual goals	
Lump-sum payment	32
A one-time reward based on individual performance	
Exceptional stock options	29
Grants of stock or stock options to nonmanagement employees	
Profit sharing	19
A uniform payment given to all or most employees based on corporate earnings	
Gainsharing	13
Rewards, shared equally by employees, for productivity and efficiency gains in a unit or organization	
Small-group incentive	12
A one-time award to all members of a group for achievement of predetermined goals	
*Percentage totals more than 100 since some companies use more than one plan.	

Source: Based on E. C. Baig, "The Great Earnings Gamble," *U.S. News & World Report,* September 17, 1990, p. 68.

overcome the historical attachment to cost-of-living adjustments and the belief that they have an obligation to keep all employees' pay in step with inflation. Other barriers include salary scales keyed to what the competition is paying, traditional compensation systems that rely heavily on specific pay grades and relatively narrow pay ranges, and performance appraisal practices that produce inflated evaluations and expectations of full rewards. Of course, from the employees' standpoint, the major concern is a potential drop in earnings. Pay-for-performance means employees have to share in the risks as well as the rewards of their employer's business. So, for example, workers at a Monsanto plant in Idaho that mines and refines phosphorus earned more than $1800 each in performance bonuses in 1989, but only $255 in 1990, when the facility had to shut two of its three furnaces for extended maintenance and the economy stumbled into recession.[34]

FLEXIBLE BENEFITS

Mike Evans and Jane Murphy both work for PepsiCo, but they have very different needs in terms of fringe benefits. Mike is married, has three young children, and a wife who is at home full-time. Jane, too, is married, but her husband has a high-paying job with the federal government, and they have no children. Mike is concerned about having a good medical plan and enough life insurance to support his family if he weren't around. In contrast, Jane's husband already has her medical needs covered on his plan, and life insurance is a low priority for both her and her husband. Rather, she is more interested in extra vacation time and long-term financial benefits like a tax-deferred savings plan.

What Are Flexible Benefits?

Flexible Benefits Employees tailor their benefit program to meet their personal needs by picking and choosing from a menu of benefit options.

Flexible benefits allow employees to pick and choose from among a menu of benefit options. The idea is to allow each employee to choose a benefit package that is individually tailored to his or her own needs and situation. It replaces the traditional "one-benefit-plan-fits-all" programs that have dominated organizations for fifty years.[35]

The average organization provides fringe benefits worth approximately forty percent of an employee's salary. But traditional benefit programs were designed for the typical employee of the 1950s—a male with a wife and two children at home. Less than ten percent of employees now fit this stereotype. Twenty-five percent of today's employees are single and a third are part of two-income families without any children. As such, these traditional programs don't tend to meet the needs of today's more diverse work force. Flexible benefits, however, do meet these diverse needs. An organization sets up a flexible spending account for each employee, usually based on some percentage of his or her salary, and then a price tag is put on each benefit. Options might include inexpensive medical plans with high deductibles; expensive medical plans with low or no deductibles; hearing, dental, and eye coverage; vacation options; extended disability; a variety of savings and pension plans; life insurance; college tuition reimbursement plans; and extended vacation time. Employees then select benefit options until they have spent the dollar amount in their account.

Linking Flexible Benefits and Expectancy Theory

Giving all employees the same benefits assumes all employees have the same needs. Of course, we know this assumption is false. So flexible benefits turn the benefits' expenditure into a motivator.

Executive Pay Around the World

United States executives have historically earned considerably more than their peers in other countries. But the increasing globalization of business and the need to attract scarce managerial talent are resulting in a narrowing of the gap.[36] For instance, after adjusting to reflect net purchasing power, a typical European executive now earns seventy-five percent as much as a United States counterpart—up from seventy percent in 1985. Of course, the range is extremely broad. A chief operating officer in the United States averages $212,600 a year. That compares with $152,000 in Switzerland, $125,600 in France, $101,700 in the United Kingdom, and $43,700 in Portugal.

But don't expect the gap to narrow much more. Why? Because most European attitudes, values, tax systems, and customs are very different from those in the United States. For instance, nonmonetary rewards—from luxury company cars to better job security—still motivate many European managers as much as cold cash. And the huge salaries earned by American executives are seen as wildly exorbitant in many European countries. A couple of examples illustrate this point.

In 1986, banker Christopher Heath's performance-based pay package resulted in his earning £2.5 million—making him Britain's highest paid executive that year. The outraged British press hounded him so much that his employer had to hire guards for his home. As a point of comparison, the head of Citicorp recently made $1.8 million in one year and almost no one even gave a second look. The reason? Hundreds of American executives earn more than that.

As chief executive of Chrysler, Lee Iacocca made over $25 million between 1987 and 1989. His counterpart at Peugeot in France, Jacques Calvet, made a little more than $340,000, yet it infuriated Peugeot workers. A third-of-a-million annual income doesn't jibe with the strong socialistic values of French workers.

If you want to make a lot of money as a manager, you're more likely to do so in the United States. Just ask Robert Horton of British Petroleum. In 1988, he was transferred from the United States, where he headed up the company's American operations, back to Britain. The transfer included a promotion to the parent's governing board. To bring Horton's salary back into line with United Kingdom standards, he was *rewarded* with a pay *cut* of sixty percent!

Consistent with expectancy theory's thesis that organizational rewards should be linked to each individual employee's goals, flexible benefits individualize rewards by allowing each employee to choose the compensation package that best satisfies his or her current needs. That flexible benefits can turn the traditional homogeneous benefit program into a motivator was demonstrated at one company: Eighty percent of the organization's employees changed their benefit packages when a flexible plan was put into effect.[37]

Flexible Benefits in Practice

In 1991, about thirty-eight percent of large companies had flexible benefits programs.[38] Flexible benefits are even becoming routinely available in companies with fewer than fifty employees.[39] Clearly, flexible benefits is an idea whose time has come.

Now, let's look at the benefits and drawbacks. For employees, flexibility is attractive because they can tailor their benefits and levels of coverage to their own needs. The major drawback, from the employee's standpoint, is that the costs of individual benefits often go up, so fewer total benefits can be purchased.[40] For example, low-risk employees keep the cost of medical plans low for everyone. As they are allowed to drop out, the high-risk population occupies a larger segment and the cost of medical benefits go up. From the organization's standpoint, the good news is that flexible benefits often produce savings. Many organizations use the introduction of flexible benefits to raise deductibles and premiums. Moreover, once in place, costly increases in things like health insurance premiums often have to be substantially absorbed by the employee. The bad news for the organization is that these plans are more cumbersome for management to oversee and administering the programs is often expensive.

COMPARABLE WORTH

Is it fair that two people do jobs that are equally demanding, require the same amount of education and training, and have similar responsibilities, yet one receives significantly less pay than the other? Probably not! But such situations are actually not that uncommon, with women being the ones earning the lesser amounts. What's the source of this inequity? Some economists would argue that it merely reflects the market forces of supply and demand. Another interpretation—and one gaining an increasing audience—is that these differences are the result of gender-based wage discrimination.

It is not unusual for female-dominated jobs (i.e., elementary school teacher, nurse, librarian) to pay less than male-dominated jobs (i.e., truck driver, lumberjack, chef), even though they are of equal or greater comparable value. This inequity has stimulated considerable interest in the concept of *comparable worth*.

Flexible benefits are being adopted by small firms as well as large. ChromatoChem, Inc., a biotechnology firm in Missoula, Montana, recently introduced flexible benefits, although the company's entire work-force is pictured here (all six of them!)   Photo from *Nation's Bus.*, July 1991, p. 16).

What Is Comparable Worth?

Comparable Worth A doctrine that holds that jobs equal in value to an organization should be equally compensated, whether or not the work content of those jobs is similar.

Comparable worth is a doctrine that holds that jobs equal in value to an organization should be equally compensated, whether or not the work content of those jobs is similar.[41] That is, if the positions of secretary and draftsman (historically viewed as female and male jobs, respectively) require similar skills and make comparable demands on employees, they should pay the same, regardless of external market factors. Specifically, comparable worth argues that jobs should be evaluated and scored on four criteria—skill, effort, responsibility, and working conditions. The criteria should be weighted and given points, with the points then used to value and compare jobs.

Comparable worth is a controversial idea. It assumes that totally dissimilar jobs can be accurately compared, that pay rates based on supply and demand factors in the job market are frequently inequitable and discriminatory, and that job classes can be identified and objectively rated.

Comparable Worth and Equity Theory

Comparable worth expands the notion of "equal pay for equal work" to include jobs that are dissimilar but of comparable value. As such, it is a direct application of equity theory.

As long as women in traditionally lower-paid, female-dominated jobs compare themselves solely to other women in female-dominated jobs, they are unlikely to perceive gender-based pay inequities. But when other referents are chosen, inequities often become quickly evident. This is because "women's" jobs have been historically devalued. Take the following case. You went to a university for six years, earned a masters of library science degree, and over the past four years have taken on increased responsibilities as a reference librarian for a public library in the city of Seattle. Your current pay is $2460 a month. Your younger brother also works for the city of Seattle, but as a driver on a sanitation truck. He's a high school graduate with no college education and has also held his job for four years. He makes $2625 a month. If you were that librarian, wouldn't you be likely to compare your pay to your brother's and to conclude that you were being underpaid?

To the degree that job classes reflect historical gender discrimination and create pay inequities, comparable worth provides a potential remedy. For women in these discriminated job classes, the application of the comparable worth concept should reduce inequities and increase work motivation.

Nurse & police officer are examples of traditionally gender-sterotyped jobs. The concept of comparable worth has evolved as an attempt to correct pay inequities whose source lies in gender-based discrimination.   Left, Pete Saloutos/The Stock Market, right, Roy Morsch/The Stock Market

Comparable Worth in Practice

Women earn, on average, about 70 cents for each dollar that men earn. Part of this difference can be explained in market terms. For instance, the average number of years of professional job preparation is 4.2 for males and 0.4 for females. Males also have, on average, 12.6 years of job seniority compared to only 2.4 for females.[42] Yet even after objective differences are accounted for, a good portion of the variance remains. It is this variance that comparable worth is addressing.

In the United States, the comparable worth issue has been almost exclusively related to jobs in the public sector. Twenty states have specifically enacted legislation or adopted policies aggressively implementing comparable worth standards in the state civil service. A number of other states are currently examining their work forces for gender-based pay equities.[43] In the private sector, the most important and visible activity is currently taking place in Ontario, Canada.

The province of Ontario (which has a population of over 9 million) passed the Pay Equity Act in 1987. It defined male and female job classes, established criteria by which they were to be valued, and mandated equality of pay between classes of comparable worth in both the public and the private sectors. Because of the projected cost to Canadian employers, the law provided a multiyear phase-in period (1990–94).

The impact of this legislation cannot be underestimated. For instance, retailer T. Eaton Co. has fifteen thousand employees in 580 jobs within Ontario. Evaluating and comparing these jobs required four full-time employees and cost the company several million dollars a year in salary adjustments.[44] A regional distributor in Canada pays its "pickers"—mostly men—about $30,000 a year for filling orders by picking warehouse stock from bins. Female typists in nearby offices do jobs that are equally demanding but pay only $18,000. Their salaries will be increased to at least $30,000.[45]

Ontario may be merely the first of many provinces in Canada to adopt a private-sector comparable worth law. At this writing, for instance, the neighboring province of Manitoba is preparing similar legislation.

Business firms in the United States and other industrialized nations will be closely watching what happens in Ontario. We should also expect U.S. business executives to organize and lobby hard against comparable worth legislation. Their arguments will likely focus on the importance of allowing market forces to determine pay levels. Advocates of comparable worth will counter with statistics showing that cultural forces and societal pay systems have created gender-based discrimination in certain job classes and argue that only legislation can provide a near-term solution to the problem.

ALTERNATIVE WORK SCHEDULES

Susan Ross is your classic "morning person." She rises each day at 5 A.M. sharp, full of energy. On the other hand, as she puts it, "I'm usually ready for bed right after the 7 P.M. news."

Susan's work schedule as a claims processor at Hartford Insurance is flexible. It allows her some degree of freedom as to when she comes to work and when she leaves. Her office opens at 6 A.M. and closes at 7 P.M. It's up to her how she schedules her eight-hour day within this thirteen-hour period. Because Susan is a morning person and also has a seven-year-old son who gets out of school at 3 P.M. every day, she opts to work from 6 A.M. to 3 P.M. "My work hours are perfect. I'm at the job when I'm mentally most alert, and I can be home to take care of Sean after he gets out of school."

What Are Alternative Work Schedules?

Most people work an eight-hour day, five days a week.[46] They start at a fixed time and leave at a fixed time. But a number of organizations have introduced alternative work schedule options, such as the compressed workweek, flextime, and job sharing, as a way to improve employee motivation and to better utilize human resources.

Compressed Workweek A four-day week, with employees working ten hours a day.

COMPRESSED WORKWEEK   The most popular form of **compressed workweek** is four ten-hour days. The 4–40 program was conceived to allow workers more leisure time and shopping time, and to permit them to travel to and from work at nonrush-hour times. Supporters suggest that such a program can increase employee enthusiasm, morale, and commitment to the organization; increase productivity and reduce costs; reduce machine downtime in manufacturing; reduce overtime, turnover, and absenteeism; and make it easier for the organization to recruit employees.

Proponents argue that the compressed workweek may positively affect productivity in situations in which the work process requires significant start-up and shutdown periods.[47] When start-up and shutdown times are a major factor, productivity standards take these periods into consideration in determining the time required to generate a given output. Consequently, in such cases, the compressed workweek will increase productivity even though worker performance is not affected, simply because the improved work scheduling reduces nonproductive time.

The evidence on 4–40 program performance is generally positive.[48] While some employees complain of fatigue near the end of the day, and about the difficulty of coordinating their jobs with their personal lives—the latter a problem especially for working mothers—most like the 4–40 program. In one study, for instance, when employees were asked whether they wanted to continue their 4–40 program, which had been in place for six months, or go back to a traditional five-day week, seventy-eight percent wanted to keep the shorter workweek.[49]

FLEXTIME   The compressed workweek doesn't increase employee discretion. Management still sets the work hours. Flextime, however, is a scheduling option that allows employees, within specific parameters, to decide when to go to work. Susan Ross's work schedule at Hartford Insurance is an example of flextime. But what specifically is flextime?

Flextime Employees work during a common core time period each day but have discretion in forming their total workday from a flexible set of hours outside the core.

Flextime is short for flexible work hours. It allows employees some discretion over when they arrive and leave work. Employees have to work a specific number of hours a week, but they are free to vary the hours of work within certain limits. As shown in Figure 8–4, each day consists of a common core, usually six hours, with a flexibility band surrounding the core. For example, exclusive of a one-hour lunch break, the core may be 9:00 A.M. to 3:00 P.M., with the office actually opening at 6:00 A.M. and closing at 6:00 P.M. All employees are required to be at their jobs during the common core period, but they are allowed to accumulate their other two hours before and/or after the core time. Some flextime programs allow extra hours to be accumulated and turned into a free day off each month.

The benefits claimed for flextime are numerous. They include reduced absenteeism, increased productivity, reduced overtime expenses, a lessening

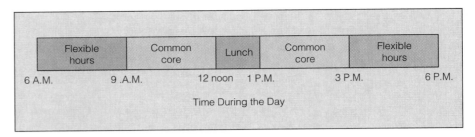

Flexible hours	Common core	Lunch	Common core	Flexible hours

6 A.M.   9 A.M.   12 noon   1 P.M.   3 P.M.   6 P.M.

Time During the Day

FIGURE 8–4   **Example of a Flextime Schedule**

Joan Girardi (left) and Stephanie Kahn are job sharers at American Express. They enroll college students as cardholders. Kahn covers the job Monday, Tuesday, and Thursday; while Girardi is on Tuesday, Wednesday, and Friday. Each supervises two of their team's four professionals.
Peter Gregoire

Job Sharing The practice of having two or more people split a forty-hour-a-week job.

in hostility toward management, reduced traffic congestion around work sites, elimination of tardiness, and increased autonomy and responsibility for employees that may increase employee job satisfaction.[50] But beyond the claims, what's flextime's record?

Most of the performance evidence stacks up favorably. Flextime tends to reduce absenteeism and frequently improves worker productivity,[51] probably for several reasons. Employees can schedule their work hours to align with personal demands, thus reducing tardiness and absences, and employees can adjust their work activities to those hours in which they are individually more productive.

Flextime's major drawback is that it's not applicable to every job. It works well with clerical tasks where an employee's interaction with people outside his or her department is limited. It is not a viable option for receptionists, sales personnel in retail stores, or similar jobs where comprehensive service demands that people be at their work stations at predetermined times.

JOB SHARING   A recent work-scheduling innovation is **job sharing.** It allows two or more individuals to split a traditional forty-hour-a-week job. So, for example, one person might perform the job from 8 A.M. to noon, while another performs the same job from 1 P.M. to 5 P.M.; or the two could work full, but alternate, days. From management's standpoint, job sharing allows the organization to draw upon the talents of more than one individual in a given job. It also opens up the opportunity to acquire skilled workers—for instance, women with school-age children and retirees—who might not be available on a full-time basis. From the employee's viewpoint, job sharing increases flexibility. As such, it can increase motivation and satisfaction for those to whom a forty-hour-a-week job is just not practical.

Linking Alternative Work Schedules and Motivation Theories

Not everyone prefers the traditional fixed eight-hour day. The larger blocks of leisure time created by the compressed workweek, for example, may be very appealing to the employee with a boat, a weekend house in the country, or a long daily commute. Employees with young children or other responsibilities that make high demands on their time find that scheduling alternatives like flextime and job sharing allow them more freedom to balance their work and personal commitments.[52]

In terms of motivation theories, alternative work schedules respond to the diverse needs of the work force. Flextime, for example, increases employee autonomy and responsibility. Therefore, it is consistent with the underlying concepts in motivation-hygiene theory.

Telecommuting: The Ultimate Flextime?

It might be close to the ideal job for many people. No commuting, flexible hours, freedom to dress as you please, and little or no interruptions from colleagues. It's called **telecommuting,** and refers to employees who do their work at home on a computer that is linked to their office.[53] Currently, over six million people work at home doing things like taking orders over the phone, filling out reports and other forms, and processing or analyzing information. Forecasters predict that 10 to 20 million people could be telecommuting by the year 2000.

Whether the forecasts prove accurate will depend on some questions for which we do not yet have the answers. Will people balk at losing the regular social contact that a formal office provides? Will employees who do their work at home be at a disadvantage in office politics? Might they be less likely to be considered for salary increases and promotions? Is being out of sight equivalent to being out of mind? Will non–work-related distractions like children, neighbors, and the close proximity of the refrigerator significantly reduce productivity? Will nontelecommuters in the organization feel discriminated against? When we can answer such questions, the future of telecommuting will become far more clear.

Telecommuting Employees do their work at home on a computer that is linked to their office.

Alternative Work Schedules in Practice

One of the underlying themes in organizations during the 1990s will be *flexibility*. Those alternative work schedule options that increase flexibility seem to be rapidly gaining in popularity. Thus, the compressed workweek is losing out to more flexible approaches such as flextime, job sharing, and telecommuting.[54]

Thirty-one percent of American businesses now offer flexible time schedules. This is about twice as many as a decade ago.[55] And large companies such as Du Pont, American Express, IBM, Levi Strauss, and PepsiCo are expanding their work schedule options—particularly to include job sharing, part-time work, and working at home—in order to attract and retain top-caliber people who either temporarily or permanently don't want to work in a traditional five-day, forty-hour-a-week job.[56]

JOB REDESIGN

When you think about how mass-produced automobiles are made, what images come to mind? Do you think of cars moving along an assembly line, with workers bolting on fenders and hooking on doors? That may be the way most cars are mass-produced, but not at Volvo's new manufacturing plant in Uddevalla, Sweden.[57]

Uddevalla produces the new Volvo 940 luxury model using teams. Each team is made up of eight to ten workers. The teams work in one area and each assembles about three cars per shift. Each team largely manages itself, handling scheduling, quality control, hiring, and other duties normally performed by supervisors. The teams, in fact, have no first-line supervisors.

Each team appoints a spokesperson, who reports to one of six plant managers, who in turn reports to the president of the entire complex.

Volvo's management believes the team concept provides several pluses for workers. It can reduce the tedium of the conventional assembly line where work cycles are only one or two minutes long, it encourages workers to increase their range of skills, and gives employees more control over their jobs. At Uddevalla, work team members are trained to handle a number of assembly jobs, so they work an average of three hours before having to repeat the same task.

Job Design The way that tasks are combined to form complete jobs.

Job design is concerned with the way that tasks are combined to form complete jobs. Job redesign focuses on changing jobs. The Volvo example illustrates how management can increase motivation by redesigning jobs around self-managed work teams. In this section, we will briefly look at this approach, plus three others, for improving motivation through job redesign.

Job Rotation

Job Rotation The periodic shifting of a worker from one task to another.

One way to deal with the routineness of work is to use **job rotation.** When an activity is no longer challenging, the employee is rotated to another job, at the same level, that has similar skill requirements. For example, G.S.I. Transcomm Data Systems Inc. in Pittsburgh uses job rotation to keep its staff of 110 people from getting bored.[58] Between 1988 and 1990, nearly twenty percent of Transcomm's employees made lateral job switches. Management believes the job rotation program has been a major contributor to cutting employee turnover from twenty-five percent to less than seven percent a year.

The strengths of job rotation are that it cuts injuries and reduces boredom through diversifying the employee's activities. Of course, it can also have indirect benefits for the organization since employees with a wider range of skills give management more flexibility in scheduling work, adapting to changes, and filling vacancies. On the other hand, job rotation is not without its drawbacks. Training costs are increased, and productivity is reduced by moving a worker into a new position just when his or her efficiency at the prior job was creating organizational economies. Job rotation also creates disruptions. Members of the work group have to adjust to the new employee. The supervisor may also have to spend more time answering questions and monitoring the work of the recently rotated employee. Finally, job rotation can demotivate intelligent and ambitious trainees who seek specific responsibilities in their chosen specialty.

The "production line" at Volvo's Uddevalla plant doesn't look like most of our stereotypes of an automobile assembly line where workers do the same narrow task over-and-over again. At Uddevalla, cars are built by self-managed teams, where workers do a variety of tasks. Courtesy Volvo Cars of North America

Job Enlargement

Job Enlargement The horizontal expansion of jobs.

More than thirty years ago, the idea of expanding jobs horizontally, or what we call **job enlargement,** grew in popularity. Increasing the number and variety of tasks that an individual performed resulted in jobs with more diversity. Instead of only sorting the incoming mail by department, for instance, a mail sorter's job could be enlarged to include physically delivering the mail to the various departments or running outgoing letters through the postage meter.

Efforts at job enlargement met with less than enthusiastic results. As one employee who experienced such a redesign on his job remarked, "Before I had one lousy job. Now, through enlargement, I have three!" However, there have been some successful applications of job enlargement. For example, U.S. Shoe Co. created modular work areas to replace production lines in over half of their factories. In these work areas, workers perform two or three shoe-making steps instead of only one, as in traditional production lines. The result has been footwear produced more efficiently and with greater attention to quality.

So, while job enlargement attacked the lack of diversity in overspecialized jobs, it did little to instill challenge or meaningfulness to a worker's activities. Job enrichment was introduced to deal with the shortcomings of enlargement.

Job Enrichment

Job Enrichment The vertical expansion of jobs.

Job enrichment refers to the vertical expansion of jobs. It increases the degree to which the worker controls the planning, execution, and evaluation of his or her work. An enriched job organizes tasks so as to allow the worker to do a complete activity, increases the employee's freedom and independence, increases responsibility, and provides feedback, so an individual will be able to assess and correct his or her own performance.

How does management enrich an employee's job? The following suggestions, based on the job characteristics model discussed in Chapter 7, specify the types of changes in jobs that are most likely to lead to improving their motivating potential. (See Figure 8–5.)

1. *Combine tasks.* Managers should seek to take existing and fractionalized tasks and put them back together to form a new and larger module of work. This increases skill variety and task identity.

FIGURE 8–5 Guidelines for Enriching a Job
Source: *From Improving Life at Work* by J.R. Hackman and J.L. Suttle Copyright © 1977 by Scott, Foresman and Company. Reprinted by permission.

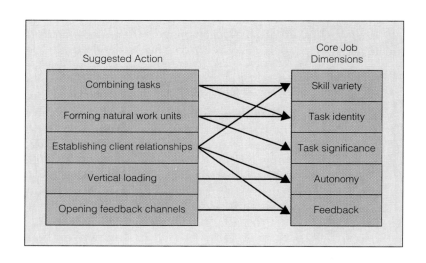

2. *Create natural work units.* The creation of natural work units means that the tasks an employee does form an identifiable and meaningful whole. This increases employee "ownership" of the work and improves the likelihood that employees will view their work as meaningful and important rather than as irrelevant and boring.

3. *Establish client relationships.* The client is the user of the product or service that the employee works on. Wherever possible, managers should try to establish direct relationships between workers and their clients. This increases skill variety, autonomy, and feedback for the employee.

4. *Expand jobs vertically.* Vertical expansion gives employees responsibilities and control that were formerly reserved to management. It seeks to partially close the gap between the "doing" and the "controlling" aspects of the job, and it increases employee autonomy.

5. *Open feedback channels.* By increasing feedback, employees not only learn how well they are performing their jobs, but also whether their performance is improving, deteriorating, or remaining at a constant level. Ideally, this feedback about performance should be received directly as the employee does the job, rather than from management on an occasional basis.[59]

Citibank used the previous suggestions to design a job enrichment program for its back office personnel who processed all the firm's financial transactions.[60] These jobs had been split up so that each person performed a single, routine task over and over again. Employees had become dissatisfied with these mundane jobs, and this dissatisfaction showed in their work. Severe backlogs had developed, and error rates were unacceptably high. Citibank's management redesigned the work around customer types. Tasks were combined and individual employees were given complete processing and customer-service responsibility for a small group of customers in a defined product area. In the newly designed jobs, employees dealt directly with customers and handled entire transactions from the time they came into the bank until they left. As predicted by the job characteristics model, this enrichment program improved the quality of work as well as employee motivation and satisfaction.

The Citibank example shouldn't be taken as a blanket endorsement of job enrichment. The overall evidence generally shows that job enrichment reduces absenteeism and turnover costs, but on the critical issue of productivity, the evidence is inconclusive.[61] In some situations, job enrichment has increased productivity; in others, it has decreased it. However, even when productivity goes down, there does seem to be consistently more conscientious use of resources and a higher quality of product or service.

Self-Managed Work Teams

Self-Managed Work Teams
Groups that are free to determine how the goals assigned to them are to be accomplished and how tasks are to be allocated.

Self-managed work teams represent job enrichment at the group level. As illustrated in the Volvo example at the beginning of this section on job redesign, work groups are given a high degree of self-determination in the management of their day-to-day work. Typically, this includes collective control over the pace of work, determination of work assignments, organization of breaks, and collective choice of inspection procedures. Fully autonomous work teams even select their own members and have the members evaluate each other's performance. As a result, supervisory positions take on decreased importance and may even be eliminated. Self-managed work

These ten employees make up one of the 30 self-managed work teams at Lake Superior Paper Industries. They hire, promote, and fire their own team members, as well as manage every aspect of the papermaking process, from loading logs to producing paper pulp.   Ed Kashi

teams draw from the job characteristics model. They have three features: (1) employees with functionally interrelated tasks who collectively are responsible for end products; (2) individuals who have a variety of skills so they may undertake all or a large proportion of the group's tasks; and (3) feedback and evaluation in terms of the performance of the whole group.[62]

The first major experiment with these self-managed teams in the United States was undertaken in the early 1970s by General Foods at a new pet food plant it built in Kansas.[63] Today, about one in five U.S. employers use self-managed teams. By the end of the decade, experts predict that 40 to 50 percent of all U.S. workers could be managing themselves through such teams.[64] General Motors is using teams in its joint venture with Toyota in California to make Chevrolet Novas and Toyota Corollas. Factory workers are divided into small teams that define their own jobs and monitor the quality of their output. The groups even conduct their own daily quality audits, a chore that once was relegated to a separate group of inspectors. They also have "stop-line" cords that allow them to shut down the line if they encounter a problem. GM is now attempting to transfer what it has learned from its joint venture with Toyota to other of its car and truck assembly plants.

Self-managed work teams will expand in popularity during the 1990s because they are consistent with current trends in organizations toward decentralization, team work, flexibility, and humanizing work. But a word of caution needs to be offered here. Research on the effectiveness of self-managed work teams is not uniformly positive.[65] For example, individuals on these teams *do* report higher levels of job satisfaction. However, counter to conventional wisdom and predictions based on the job characteristics model, employees on self-managed work teams seem to have higher absenteeism and turnover rates than do employees working in traditional work structures. The specific reasons for these findings are unclear, which implies a need for additional research.

IMPLICATIONS FOR PERFORMANCE AND SATISFACTION

There are a number of techniques and programs for applying motivation theories. In this chapter, we reviewed eight of them: management by objectives, OB Mod, participative management, performance-based compensation, flexible benefits, comparable worth, alternative work schedules, and job redesign. While it is always dangerous to synthesize a large number of complex ideas into a few simple guidelines, the following suggestions distill what we know about applying motivation theories toward improving employee performance and satisfaction.

RECOGNIZE INDIVIDUAL DIFFERENCES   Employees have different needs. Don't treat them all alike. Moreover, spend the time necessary to understand what's important to each employee. This will allow you to individualize rewards, schedule work, and design jobs to align with individual needs.

USE GOALS AND FEEDBACK   Employees should have hard, specific goals, as well as feedback on how well they are faring in pursuit of those goals.

ALLOW EMPLOYEES TO PARTICIPATE IN DECISIONS THAT AFFECT THEM   Employees can contribute to a number of decisions that affect them: setting work goals, choosing their own fringe benefit packages, select-

Motivating the Diversified Work Force

To maximize motivation among today's diversified work force, management needs to think *flexibility*. The following examples illustrate the importance of designing work schedules, benefits, and the physical work setting to respond to employees' varied needs.

Ann works for DuPont. As a mother of two pre-school children, she finds that the company's family-friendly benefits—day care, flextime, job sharing, flexible benefits, and personal leaves of absence—increase her commitment to her job and to DuPont.

Mark also works for DuPont. He is among the company's 2000 or so employees who work part-time. This DuPont option allows Mark to gain valuable experience and meet his financial obligations, while at the same time allowing him to pursue his graduate studies in chemistry.

Jack is 72 years old. Unfortunately, his Social Security check provides an inadequate income. So Jack works full-time at a local plant nursery. One of the firm's hardest working and enthusiastic employees, he regularly praises management for providing him with flexible work hours and an excellent health plan that supplements Medicare.

Rick is a production supervisor at Boeing. He is also a disabled Vietnam veteran, confined to a wheelchair. One of the reasons Rick chose Boeing to work for is that he appreciates the fact that the company doesn't condescend to the disabled or give him unusually favorable treatment. Boeing wants to attract and keep the best-qualified workers so it has reviewed the design of its jobs to eliminate barriers that might hinder the performance of employees with physical or mental disabilities.

ing preferred work schedules, and the like. This can increase employee productivity, commitment to work goals, motivation, and job satisfaction.

LINK REWARDS TO PERFORMANCE   Rewards should be contingent on performance. Importantly, employees must perceive a clear linkage. Regardless of how closely rewards are actually correlated to performance criteria, if individuals perceive this correlation to be low, the result will be low performance, a decrease in job satisfaction, and an increase in turnover and absenteeism statistics.

CHECK THE SYSTEM FOR EQUITY   Rewards should also be perceived by employees as equating with the inputs they bring to the job. At a simplistic level, this should mean that experience, abilities, effort, and other obvious inputs should explain differences in performance and, hence, pay, job assignments and other obvious rewards.

◼ *FOR DISCUSSION*

1. Relate goal-setting theory to the MBO process. How are they similar? Different?

2. How might a college instructor use OB Mod to improve learning in the classroom?

3. Do you think participative management is likely to be more effective in certain types of organizations? With certain types of employees? Discuss.

4. Identify five different criteria by which organizations can compensate employees. Based on your knowledge and experience, do you think performance is the criterion most used in practice? Discuss.

5. "Performance can't be measured, so pay-for-performance is a fantasy. Differences in performance are often caused by the system, which means the organization ends up rewarding the circumstances. It's the same thing as rewarding the weatherman for a pleasant day." Do you agree or disagree with this statement? Support your position.

6. What drawbacks, if any, do you see in implementing flexible benefits? (Consider this question from the perspective of both the organization and the employee.)

7. "The competitive marketplace acts as an efficient means of ensuring that pay equity is achieved." Do you agree or disagree with this statement? Support your position.

8. Does flextime have an impact on any of the five core dimensions in the job characteristics model? Discuss.

9. Would you want a full-time job telecommuting? How do you think most of your friends would feel about such a job? Do you think telecommuting has a future?

10. As a manager, what would you do to enrich an employee's job?

11. "Employees should have jobs that give them autonomy and diversity." Build an argument to support this statement. Then negate your argument.

12. Students often complain about doing group projects in a class. Why is that? Relate your answer to self-managed work teams. Would you want to be a member of one? Discuss.

The Case for Pay Secrecy

"Oh, and one last point," said the director of human resources to the new hiree. "We treat salary information as a private matter around here. What you make is your business and no one else's. We consider it grounds for termination if you tell anyone what you make."

This policy of pay secrecy is the norm in most organizations, though in the majority of cases, it's communicated informally. The message trickles down and new employees quickly learn from their boss and peers not to inquire about what other people make or to openly volunteer their own salary. However, in some companies, pay secrecy is a formal policy. For instance, at GM's Electronic Data Systems Corp. unit, new hirees sign a form acknowledging several policies, one of which states: Employees are allowed to disclose their salaries, but if such disclosure leads to disruption, they can be fired. It doesn't take a genius to predict that this policy effectively stifles discussion of pay at EDS.

For those raised in democratic societies, it may be tempting to surmise that there is something inherently wrong with pay secrecy. On the other hand, if it's wrong, why do the vast majority of successful corporations in democracies follow the practice? There are a number of logical reasons why organizations practice pay secrecy and why they are likely to continue to do so.

First, pay is privileged information to both the organization and the individual employee. Organizations hold many things privileged—manufacturing processes, product formulas, new-product research, marketing strategies—and U.S. courts have generally supported the argument that pay rightly belongs in this category. Salary information has been held to be confidential and the property of management. Employees who release such data can be discharged for willful misconduct. Moreover, most employees *want* their pay kept secret. Many people's egos are tied to their paycheck. They are as comfortable discussing their specific pay as they are providing details of their sex life to strangers. Employees have a right to privacy, and this includes ensuring that their pay is kept secret.

Second, pay secrecy lessens the opportunity for comparisons among employees and the exposure of *perceived* inequities. No pay system will ever be perceived as fair by everyone. One person's "merit" is another person's "favoritism." Knowledge of what other employees are making only highlights perceived inequities and causes disruptions.

Third, pay differences are often perfectly justified, yet only for subtle, complicated, or difficult-to-explain reasons. For instance, people doing similar jobs were hired under different market conditions. Or two managers have similar titles, although one supervises ten people while the other supervises twenty. Or one person earns more today than a co-worker because of responsibilities held or contributions made to the organization in a different job several years earlier.

Fourth, pay secrecy saves embarrassing underpaid and underperforming employees. By definition, half of an organization's work force is going to be below average. What kind of organization would be so cold and insensitive as to publicly expose those in the lower half of the performance distribution?

Finally, pay secrecy gives managers more freedom in administering pay because every pay differential doesn't have to be explained. A policy of openness encourages managers to minimize differences and allocate pay more evenly. Since employee performance in an organization tends to follow a normal distribution, only through pay secrecy can managers feel comfortable in giving large rewards to high performers and little or no rewards to low performers.

Based on J. Solomon, "Hush Money," *The Wall Street Journal*, April 18, 1990, pp. R22–R24; and K. Tracy, M. Renard, and G. Young, "Pay Secrecy: The Effects of Open and Secret Pay Policies on Satisfaction and Performance," in A. Head and W. P. Ferris (eds.), *Proceedings of the 28th Annual Meeting of the Eastern Academy of Management;* Hartford, CT, May 1991, pp. 248–51.

Let's Make Pay Information Open to All!

Open pay policies make good sense. They already exist for employees of most public institutions and for top executives in all publicly held corporations. A few private-sector companies have also seen the benefits that can accrue from making the pay of all employees public knowledge. For instance, the computer maker NeXT Inc. has lists of all its employees' salaries hanging in company offices for anyone to consult.

Why do open pay policies make good sense? We can articulate at least five reasons.

First, such pay policies open communication and build trust. As an executive at NeXT stated, "Anything less than openness doesn't establish the same level of trust." If the organization can be open about such a sensitive issue as pay, it makes employees believe that management can be trusted about other concerns that are not so sensitive. In addition, if an organization's pay system is fair and equitable, employees report greater satisfaction with pay and with pay differentials where pay is open.

Second, an employee's right to privacy needs to be balanced against his or her right to know. Laws to protect an employee's right to know have become more popular in recent years, especially in the area of hazardous working conditions. The case can be made that the right to a free flow of information includes the right to know what others in one's organization earn.

Third, pay secrecy is often supported by organizations not to prevent embarrassment of *employees,* but to prevent embarrassment of *management.* Pay openness threatens exposing system inequities caused by a poorly developed and administered pay system. An open pay system not only says to employees that management believes its pay policies are fair, but is itself a mechanism for increasing fairness. When true inequities creep into an open pay system, they are much more likely to be quickly identified and corrected than when they occur in pay-secrecy systems. Employees will provide the checks and balances on management.

Fourth, what management calls "freedom" in administering pay is really a euphemism for "control." Pay secrecy allows management to substitute favoritism for performance criteria in pay allocations. To the degree that we believe that organizations should reward good performance rather than good political skills, open pay policies take power and control away from managers. When pay levels and changes are public knowledge, organizational politics is less likely to surface.

Finally, and maybe most importantly, pay secrecy obscures the connection between pay and performance. Both equity and expectancy theories emphasize the desirability of linking rewards to performance. To maximize motivation, employees should know how the organization defines and measures performance, and the rewards attached to differing levels of performance. Unfortunately, when pay information is kept secret, employees make inaccurate perceptions. Even more unfortunately, those inaccuracies tend to work against increasing motivation. Specifically, research has found that people overestimate the pay of their peers and their subordinates and underestimate the pay of their superiors. So where pay is kept secret, actual differences tend to be discounted, which reduces the motivational benefits of linking pay to performance.

Based on E. E. Lawler III, "Secrecy About Management Compensation: Are There Hidden Costs?" *Organizational Behavior and Human Performance,* May 1967, pp. 182–89; J. Solomon, "Hush Money," *The Wall Street Journal,* April 18, 1990, pp. R22–R24; and K. Tracy, M. Renard, and G. Young, "Pay Secrecy: The Effects of Open and Secret Pay Policies on Satisfaction and Performance," in A. Head and W. P. Ferris (eds.), *Proceedings of the 28th Annual Meeting of the Eastern Academy of Management;* Hartford, CT, May 1991, pp. 248–51.

Improving Your Understanding of How to Motivate Others

This exercise is designed to help increase awareness of how and why one motivates others and to help focus on the needs of those we are attempting to motivate.

1. Begin by breaking the class into groups of five to seven each. Then each student should individually read and respond to the following:

    Situation 1: You are the owner and CEO of a moderate-sized corporation. Your objective is to motivate all your subordinates to the highest level possible.

    Task 1A: On a separate sheet of paper, list the factors you would use to motivate your employees. Avoid generalities—be as specific as possible.

    Task 1B: Rank-order the factors you listed in 1A above.

2. Now complete the following in the same manner.

    Situation 2: You are an employee of a moderate-sized corporation. The company CEO has asked all employees to help in developing an effective motivational system. The CEO has asked for your response to Task 2A and 2B.

    Task 2A: List the factors that would most effectively motivate you. Avoid generalities—be as specific as possible.

    Task 2B: Rank-order the factors you listed in 2A above.

3. After completing both 1 and 2 above, each group should do the following:

    a. Share the list of motivational factors 1A and ranking 1B with other members of their group.

    b. Share the list of motivational factors 2A and ranking 2B with other members of their group.

4. Group members should discuss the following:

    a. Are each individual's 1A and 2A lists more similar or more dissimilar? What does this mean?

    b. Does everyone's 1A and 2A list in your group contain basically the same items? What does this mean?

    c. Are the 1B and 2B lists in your group more similar or more dissimilar? What does this mean?

    d. What have you learned about how and why you motivate others as you do and how can you apply these data?

5. Each group should appoint a spokesperson to present its answers to 4a–d to the class.

Source: Adapted from B. E. Smith, "Why Don't They Respond: A Motivational Experience," *Organizational Behavior Teaching Review,* Vol. X, No. 2, 1985–86, pp. 98–100. With permission.

Goal-Setting Task

PURPOSE   This exercise will help you learn how to write tangible, verifiable, measurable, and relevant goals as might evolve from an MBO program.

TIME   Approximately 20 to 30 minutes.

INSTRUCTIONS
1. Break into groups of three to five.
2. Spend a few minutes discussing your class instructor's job. What does he or she do? What defines good performance? What behaviors will lead to good performance?
3. Each group is to develop a list of five goals that, although not established participatively with your instructor, you believe might be developed in an MBO program at your college. Try to select goals that seem most critical to the effective performance of your instructor's job.
4. Each group will select a leader who will share his or her group's goals with the entire class. For each group's goals, class discussion should focus on their: (a) specificity, (b) ease of measurement, (c) importance, and (d) motivational properties.

The Volvo Experiment: Where Happy Workers Aren't Productive Workers

In this chapter, Volvo's Uddevalla plant was briefly mentioned for its team-based approach to automobile production. It was noted that using teams raised employee's motivation by increasing their range of skills and giving them more control over their jobs. Well, it does. But not without some serious side effects. This case reassesses Volvo's experience at Uddevalla.

Volvo's Uddevalla car assembly plant opened in 1988. It was designed from scratch to be a replacement for the traditional assembly line. It has six assembly areas that can handle up to eight teams of eight to ten people. Each team builds four cars at the same time. No more than three people work on a car simultaneously. When running at capacity—one shift and forty-eight teams—the plant can produce forty thousand cars a year.

Volvo developed this novel plant mainly as a solution to the high absentee rates that prevail in Sweden. The company's goal was to get productivity and quality levels at Uddevalla to at least equal those of Volvo's two other Swedish assembly plants, but with absenteeism much lower than the twenty to thirty percent norm in Sweden. By way of comparison, the absenteeism rates at European assembly plants and at the North American assembly plants of American car makers are around twelve percent; they are a mere five percent at Japanese factories in Japan.

Three years after the plant opened, Volvo's management was rumored to be considering abandoning the team approach. Why? Conditions have changed in Sweden, the Uddevalla plant has failed to achieve its original productivity and absenteeism goals, and other Volvo plants and the competition have raised their productivity.

The Uddevalla concept was developed at a time when nearly all large Swedish employers were struggling to cope with the high absenteeism caused by national policies that made it easy for people to take time off from work. For instance, workers got at least ninety percent of their pay—and usually one hundred percent—for their first three days out of work. However, the Swedish government has since modified this policy, so that workers now receive only seventy-five percent of their pay when they stay home from work. This has lessened the absenteeism problem in the country.

While there is little debate about quality and worker satisfaction at Uddevalla—everyone seems to agree that the team approach has improved both—productivity and absenteeism rates have not responded the way management expected. Instead of making forty thousand cars a year, Uddevalla produces only twenty-two thousand. The number of labor-hours needed to assemble a car at Uddevalla is fifty, compared to twenty-five hours at Volvo's Belgium plant and less than twenty hours for Japanese car makers. And surprisingly, even the absence data are not impressive. Short-term absenteeism has not declined. It averaged 12.2 percent in 1990 and hit 14 percent in early 1991. When long-term leaves for caring for newborn children, military service, education, and long-term disability are taken into account, total absenteeism at Uddevalla is about twenty-two percent. And don't forget, the team approach is far more costly for management to install because workers have to be trained to do multiple jobs. At Uddevalla, a worker typically requires sixteen months of training before becoming capable of doing two or three of the seven groups of tasks needed to build a car. That compares with only about a month for most employees on North American auto assembly lines.

Finally, dramatic increases in productivity by its competitors means that all of Volvo's plants have to run faster just to stay even. Volvo's other two Swedish plants have responded to orders to improve their competitiveness dramatically. But being good by Swedish standards is not good enough. What really matters is how a factory stacks up against the world competition. By that standard, the Uddevalla plant is wanting. As noted, the Japanese can produce comparable cars using only forty percent of the labor.

Lennart Ericsson, president of the chapter of the Metal Workers Union that represents the blue-collar workers at Volvo's Uddevalla plant, says, "I am convinced that our way will be successful and competitive." He also says that the level of worker satisfaction is much higher than it would be if Uddevalla had a traditional assembly line. Volvo's president, Christer Zetterberg, says that it's premature to pronounce the Uddevalla approach a failure, but "we can never run factories long term which are not competitive." If it "doesn't come out as a viable concept from a productivity point of view, we will, of course, rebuild the factory."

Questions

1. Using the job characteristics model, explain how Uddevalla's team approach should increase motivation and productivity and lead to reduced absenteeism.

2. Why hasn't it worked out that way at Uddevalla?

3. What does this case suggest in terms of the universal effectiveness of self-managed teams?

Source: Based on S. Prokesch, "Edges Fray on Volvo's Brave New Humanistic World," *New York Times,* July 7, 1991, p. C5.

FOR FURTHER READING

CAMPION, M. A., "Interdisciplinary Approaches to Job Design: A Constructive Replication with Extension," *Journal of Applied Psychology,* August 1988, pp. 467–81. Describes four approaches to job design and their corresponding outcomes: motivational approach with satisfaction outcomes, mechanistic approach with efficiency outcomes, biological approach with comfort outcomes, and perceptual/motor approach with reliability outcomes.

EVANS, M. G., "Organizational Behavior: The Central Role of Motivation," *Journal of Management,* Summer 1986, pp. 203–22. Looks at individual behavior in terms of motivation theory, with emphasis on the antecedents of goals and goal acceptance, feedback, and attributions, and on the consequences of performance.

KATZELL, R. A., and D. E. THOMPSON, "Work Motivation: Theory and Practice," *American Psychologist,* February 1990, pp. 144–53. Reviews major theories of motivation and extracts seven key strategies for improving work motivation.

KENTON, S. B., "The Role of Communication in Managing Perceived Inequity," *Management Communication Quarterly,* May 1989, pp. 536–43. The many factors that influence the behavioral redress of inequity by an underrewarded person can be divided into four conceptual categories.

LEANA, C. R., E. A. LOCKE, and D. M. SCHWEIGER, "Fact and Fiction in Analyzing Research on Participative Decision Making: A Critique of Cotton, Vollrath, Froggatt, Lengnick-Hall, and Jennings," *Academy of Management Review,* January 1990, pp. 137–46. Challenges previous analyses of participative decision-making studies.

MILES, E. W., J. D. HATFIELD, and R. C. HUSEMAN, "The Equity Sensitive Construct: Potential Implications for Worker Performance," *Journal of Management,* December 1989, pp. 581–88. Argues that all employees are not equity-sensitive and proposes a classification scheme.

NOTES

[1]This section is based on J. Hyatt, "Ideas at Work," *INC.,* May 1991, pp. 59–66.

[2]P. F. Drucker, *The Practice of Management* (New York: Harper & Row, 1954).

[3]See, for instance, S. J. Carroll and H. L. Tosi, *Management by Objectives: Applications and Research* (New York, Macmillan, 1973); and R. Rodgers and J. E. Hunter, "Impact of Management by Objectives on Organizational Productivity," *Journal of Applied Psychology,* April 1991, pp. 322–36.

[4]See, for instance, F. Schuster and A. F. Kendall, "Management by Objectives, Where We Stand—A Survey of the *Fortune* 500," *Human Resource Management,* Spring 1974, pp. 8–11; F. Luthans, "Management by Objectives in the Public Sector: The Transference Problem," unpublished paper presented at the 35th Annual Academy of Management Conference, New Orleans, Louisiana, 1975; R. C. Ford, F. S. MacLaughlin, and J. Nixdorf, "Ten Questions About MBO," *California Management Review,* Winter 1980, p. 89; and C. H. Ford, "MBO: An Idea Whose Time Has Gone?", *Business Horizons,* December 1979, p. 49.

[5]Ford, "MBO: An Idea Whose Time Has Gone?"

[6]At Emery Air Freight: Positive Reinforcement Boosts Performance," *Organizational Dynamics,* Winter 1973, pp. 41–50.

[7]F. Luthans and R. Kreitner, *Organizational Behavior Modification and Beyond: An Operant and Social Learning Approach* (Glenview, IL: Scott, Foresman, 1985).

[8]F. Luthans and R. Kreitner, "The Management of Behavioral Contingencies," *Personnel,* July-August 1974, pp. 7–16.

[9]Luthans and Kreitner, *Organizational Behavior Modification and Beyond,* Chapter 8.

[10]See W. C. Hamner and E. P. Hamner, "Behavior Modification on the Bottom Line," *Organizational Dynamics,* Spring 1976, pp. 12–24; and "Productivity Gains from a Pat on the Back," *Business Week,* January 23, 1978, pp. 56–62.

[11]M. P. Heller, "Money Talks, Xerox Listens," *Business Month,* September 1990, pp. 91–92.

[12]"One Day at a Time," *INC.,* November 1990, p. 146.

[13]D. C. Anderson, C. R. Crowell, M. Doman, and G. S. Howard, "Performance Posting, Goal Setting, and Activity-Contingent Praise as Applied to a University Hockey Team,"

Journal of Applied Psychology, February 1988, pp. 87–95.

[14]See, for example, E. Locke, "The Myths of Behavior Mod in Organizations," *Academy of Management Review,* October 1977, pp. 543–53.

[15]B. Saporito, "The Revolt Against 'Working Smarter,'" *Fortune,* July 21, 1986, pp. 58–65; "Quality Circles: Rounding up Quality at USAA," *AIDE Magazine,* Fall 1983, p. 24; and L. Kuzela, "Boeing, Unions Plan New Plant," *Industry Week,* April 3, 1989, p. 27.

[16]J. L. Cotton, D. A. Vollrath, K. L. Froggatt, M. L. Lengnick-Hall, and K. R. Jennings, "Employee Participation: Diverse Forms and Different Outcomes," *Academy of Management Review,* January 1988, pp. 8–22.

[17]M. Sashkin, "Participative Management Is an Ethical Imperative," *Organizational Dynamics,* Spring 1984, pp. 5–22.

[18]R. Tannenbaum, I. R. Weschler, and F. Massarik, *Leadership and Organization: A Behavioral Science Approach* (New York: McGraw-Hill, 1961), pp. 88–100.

[19]E. Locke and D. Schweiger, "Participation in Decision Making: One More Look," in B. M. Staw (ed.), *Research in Organizational Behavior,* Vol. 1, Greenwich, CT: JAI Press, 1979; E. A. Locke, D. B. Feren, V. M. McCaleb, K. N. Shaw, and A. T. Denny, "The Relative Effectiveness of Four Methods of Motivating Employee Performance," in K. D. Duncan, M. M. Gruneberg, and D. Wallis (eds.), *Changes in Working Life* (London: Wiley, 1980), pp. 363–88; K. L. Miller and P. R. Monge, "Participation, Satisfaction, and Productivity: A Meta-Analytic Review," *Academy of Management Journal,* December 1986, pp. 727–53; J. A. Wagner III and R. Z. Gooding, "Effects of Societal Trends on Participation Research," *Administrative Science Quarterly,* June 1987, pp. 241–62; J. A. Wagner III and R. Z. Gooding, "Shared Influence and Organizational Behavior: A Meta-Analysis of Situational Variables Expected to Moderate Participation-Outcome Relationships," *Academy of Management Journal,* September 1987, pp. 524–41; D. I. Levine, "Participation, Productivity, and the Firm's Environment," *California Management Review,* Summer 1990, pp. 86–100; and J. W. Graham and A. Verma, "Predictors and Moderators of Employee Responses to Employee Participation Programs," *Human Relations,* June 1991, pp. 551–68.

[20]See, for example, G. W. Meyer and R. G. Stott, "Quality Circles: Panacea or Pandora's Box?", *Organizational Dynamics,* Spring 1985, pp. 34–50; M. L. Marks, P. H. Mirvis, E. J. Hackett, and J. F. Grady, Jr., "Employee Participation in a Quality Circle Program: Impact on Quality of Work Life, Productivity, and Absenteeism," *Journal of Applied Psychology,* February 1986, pp. 61–69; E. E. Lawler III and S. A. Mohrman, "Quality Circles: After the Honeymoon," *Organizational Dynamics,* Spring 1987, pp. 42–54; R. P. Steel and R. F. Lloyd, "Cognitive, Affective, and Behavioral Outcomes of Participation in Quality Circles: Conceptual and Empirical Findings," *Journal of Applied Behavioral Science,* Vol. 24, No. 1, 1988, pp. 1–17; T. R. Miller, "The Quality Circle Phenomenon: A Review and Appraisal," *SAM Advanced Management Journal,* Winter 1989, pp. 4–7; and E. E. Adams, Jr., "Quality Circle Performance," *Journal of Management,* March 1991, pp. 25–39.

[21]Halal and Brown, "Participative Management," p. 21.

[22]Saporito, "The Revolt Against 'Working Smarter,'" p. 59.

[23]Halal and Brown, "Participative Management," p. 20.

[24]Miller, "The Quality Circle Phenomenon," p. 5.

[25]J. Main, "The Trouble with Managing Japanese-Style," *Fortune,* April 2, 1984, p. 51.

[26]Adams, "Quality Circle Performance."

[27]P. B. Carroll, "IBM's Akers Expects 1991 Base Pay to be Cut 40% to Less Than $1.6 Million," *The Wall Street Journal,* February 24, 1992, p. A3.

[28]"How A&P Fattens Profits by Sharing Them," *Business Week,* December 22, 1986, p. 44.

[29]This box is based on J. Castro, "How's Your Pay?", *Time,* April 15, 1991, pp. 40–41; J. A. Byrne, "The Flap over Executive Pay," *Business Week,* May 6, 1991, pp. 90–96; and T. McCarroll, "Motown's Fat Cats," *Time,* January 20, 1992, pp. 34–35.

[30]"The Business Week 1000," *Business Week 1000 Special Issue,* 1991, pp. 104–05.

[31]M. Fein, "Work Measurement and Wage Incentives," *Industrial Engineering,* September 1973, pp. 49–51.

[32]Cited in J. Greenwald, "Workers: Risks and Rewards," *Time,* April 15, 1991, p. 42.

[33]Cited in "Pay for Performance," *The Wall Street Journal,* February 20, 1990, p. 1.

[34]Greenwald, "Workers: Risks and Rewards," pp. 42–43.

[35]See, for instance, "When You Want to Contain Costs and Let Employees Pick Their Benefits: Cafeteria Plans," *INC.,* December 1989, p. 142; "More Benefits Bend with Workers' Needs," *The Wall Street Journal,* January 9, 1990, p. B1; and R. Thompson, "Switching to Flexible Benefits," *Nation's Business,* July 1991, pp. 16–23.

[36]This box is based on J. S. Lublin, "The Continental Divide," *The Wall Street Journal,* April 18, 1990, p. R28–30.

[37]E. E. Lawler III, "Reward Systems," in Hackman and Suttle (eds.), *Improving Life at Work,* p. 182.

[38]Thompson, "Switching to Flexible Benefits," p. 17.

[39]"When You Want to Contain Costs and Let Employees Pick Their Benefits."

[40]H. Bernstein, "New Benefit Schemes Can Be Deceiving," *LA Times,* May 14, 1991, p. D3.

[41]D. Grider and M. Shurden, "The Gathering Storm of Comparable Worth," *Business Horizons,* July-August 1987, pp. 81–86.

[42]Cited in T. J. Patten, *Fair Play* (San Francisco: Jossey-Bass, 1988), p. 31.

[43]Ibid., pp. 74–81.

[44]Cited in K. A. Kovach and P. E. Millspaugh, "Comparable Worth: Canada Legislates Pay Equity," *Academy of Management Executive,* May 1990, p. 97.

[45]J. Solomon, "Pay Equity Gets a Tryout in Canada—And U.S. Firms Are Watching Closely," *The Wall Street Journal,* December 28, 1988, p. B1.

[46]S. J. Smith, "The Growing Diversity of Work Schedules," *Monthly Labor Review,* November 1986, pp. 7–13.

[47]E. J. Calvasina and W. R. Boxx, "Efficiency of Workers on the Four-Day Workweek," *Academy of Management Journal,* September 1975, pp. 604–10.

[48]See, for example, J. W. Seybolt and J. W. Waddoups, "The Impact of Alternative Work Schedules on Employee Attitudes: A Field Experiment," paper presented at the Western Academy of Management Meeting, Hollywood, CA, April 1987.

[49]J. C. Goodale and A. K. Aagaard, "Factors Relating to Varying Reactions to the 4-Day Work Week," *Journal of Applied Psychology,* February 1975, pp. 33–38.

[50]W. F. Glueck, "Changing Hours of Work: A Review and Analysis of the Research," *The Personnel Administrator,* March 1979, pp. 44–47.

[51]See, for example, D. A. Ralston and M. F. Flanagan, "The Effect of Flextime on Absenteeism and Turnover for Male and Female Employees," *Journal of Vocational Behavior,* April 1985, pp. 206–17; D. A. Ralston, W. P. Anthony, and D. J. Gustafson, "Employees May Love Flextime, but What Does It Do to the Organization's Productivity?," *Journal of Applied Psychology,* May 1985, pp. 272–79; J. B. McGuire and J. R. Liro, "Flexible Work Schedules, Work Attitudes, and Perceptions of Productivity," *Public Personnel Management,* Spring 1986, pp. 65–73; P. Bernstein, "The Ultimate in Flextime: From Sweden, by Way of Volvo," *Personnel,* June 1988, pp. 70–74; and D. R. Dalton and D. J. Mesch, "The Impact of Flexible Scheduling on Employee Attendance and Turnover," *Administrative Science Quarterly,* June 1990, pp. 370–87.

[52]R. B. Dunham, J. L. Pierce, and M. B. Castaneda, "Alternative Work Schedules: Two Field Quasi-Experiments," *Personnel Psychology,* Summer 1987, pp. 215–42.

[53]See, for example, C. Ansberry, "When Employees Work at Home, Management Problems Often Arise," *The Wall Street Journal,* April 20, 1987, p. 25; K. Christensen, "A Hard Day's Work in the Electronic Cottage," *Across the Board,* April 1987, pp. 17–22; C. A. Hamilton, "Telecommuting," *Personnel Journal,* April 1987, pp. 91–101; D. C. Bacon, "Look Who's Working at Home," *Nation's Business,* October 1989, pp. 20–31; and T. H. Willard, "Telecommuting: Some Myths and Hits," *Los Angeles Times,* April 17, 1991, p. D3.

[54]A. Deutschman, "Pioneers of the New Balance," *Fortune,* May 20, 1991, pp. 60–68; and C. Trost, "To Cut Costs and Keep the Best People, More Concerns Offer Flexible Work Plans," *The Wall Street Journal,* February 18, 1992, p. B1.

[55]E. G. Thomas, "Flextime Doubles in a Decade," *Management World,* April-May 1987, pp. 18–19; and "Flextime Pros and Cons," *Boardroom Reports,* March 1, 1989, p. 15.

[56]Deutschman, "Pioneers of the New Balance," p. 60.

[57]J. Kapstein, "Volvo's Radical New Plant: 'The Death of the Assembly Line'?", *Business Week,* August 28, 1989, pp. 92–93.

[58]B. G. Posner, "Role Changes," *INC.,* February 1990, pp. 95–98.

[59]J. R. Hackman, "Work Design," in J. R. Hackman and J. L. Suttle (eds.), *Improving Life at Work* (Santa Monica, CA: Goodyear, 1977), pp. 132–33.

[60]R. W. Walters, "The Citibank Project: Improving Productivity Through Work Design," in D. L. Kirkpatrick (ed.), *How to Manage Change Effectively* (San Francisco: Jossey-Bass, 1985), pp. 195–208.

[61]See, for example, J. R. Hackman and G. R. Oldham, *Work Redesign* (Reading, MA: Addison-Wesley, 1980); J. B. Miner, *Theories of Organizational Behavior* (Hinsdale, IL: Dryden Press, 1980), pp. 231–66; and R. W. Griffin, "Effects of Work Redesign on Employee Perceptions, Attitudes, and Behaviors: A Long-Term Investigation," *Academy of Management Journal,* June 1991, pp. 425–35.

[62]T. D. Wall, N. J. Kemp, P. R. Jackson, and C. W. Clegg, "Outcomes of Autonomous Workgroups: A Long-Term Field Experiment," *Academy of Management Journal,* June 1986, pp. 280–304.

[63]See R. E. Walton, "From Hawthorne to Topeka to Kalmar," in *Man and Work in Society,* E. L. Cass and F. G. Zimmer, (eds.), (New York: Van Nostrand Reinhold, 1975), pp. 118–21.

[64]J. S. Lublin, "Trying to Increase Worker Productivity, More Employers Alter Management Style," *The Wall Street Journal,* February 13, 1992, p. B1.

[65]See, for example, Wall, Kemp, Jackson, and Clegg, "Outcomes of Autonomous Workgroups"; and J. L. Cordery, W. S. Mueller, and L. M. Smith, "Attitudinal and Behavioral Effects of Autonomous Group Working: A Longitudinal Field Study," *Academy of Management Journal,* June 1991, pp. 464–76.

FOUNDATIONS OF GROUP BEHAVIOR

LEARNING OBJECTIVES

After studying this chapter, you should be able to:

1. Differentiate between formal and informal groups

2. Explain why people join groups

3. Compare two models of group development

4. Identify the key factors in explaining group behavior

5. Describe how role requirements change in different situations

6. Describe how norms exert influence on an individual's behavior

7. Explain the influence of group demography on member behavior

8. List the benefits and disadvantages of cohesive groups

One of the truly remarkable things about work groups is that they can make 2 + 2 = 5. Of course, they also have the capability of making 2 + 2 = 3.

S.P.R.

*T*he Boeing Co. has decided that the future of aircraft design lies with replacing the firm's historical military-style hierarchy with self-regulating, cross-discipline work teams.[1]

As a case in point, the development of Boeing's new 777 twinjets revolves around an internal collaboration of designers, production experts, customer-service personnel, and finance specialists. Grouped into small teams of eight or ten, they have been assigned to refine and mesh all aspects of the aircraft program right from the start. The intention is to have each team consider the aircraft as a whole and to act quickly on ideas, free from chain-of-command second-guessing.

Boeing's past practice was to develop a plane sequentially, starting at the tail and working forward to the nose. First, suggestions would come from the designers, then the production people, then customer-support personnel, and so on. In the process, refinements snowballed. Worse, development costs soared just before the plane went into production as last-minute fixes were made. The inefficiencies of this system resulted in reduced productivity and increased costs.

Today, Boeing is using teams on the 777 project to "front-load" development costs. That is, it is getting the "bugs" out of the aircraft before it ever goes into production. For instance, the novel folding wingtips on the new 777 had one significant shortcoming: Airlines that wanted a traditional continuous wing couldn't get one. The company initially said that the best it could offer was a wing with foldable tips locked in place. Under the old Boeing way, the airlines would have had to accept the accompanying weight penalty. That's because a bureaucratic chasm separated workers who designed parts from those who made them. However, working closely with shop experts, 777 engineers devised a way to build the continuous wing on the same tool used to make the foldable wing—without disrupting the production work flow.

Boeing's management believes that teams working intensely to hammer out designs well before the start of production will get the design right so there will be fewer fixes during production, which should lead to higher productivity and profits. ∎

This chapter introduces groups and teams. Two facts make this chapter critical for your understanding of organizational behavior. First, the behavior of individuals in groups is something more than the sum total of each acting in his or her own way. In other words, when individuals are in groups, they act differently than they do when they are alone. Second, work groups are a vital part of every organization. Examples are production teams, committees, task forces, staff groups, investigative commissions, boards of directors, cockpit crews, surgical teams, quality circles, and repair crews. This chapter defines groups, reviews the various reasons why people join them, describes how groups develop, and then presents a comprehensive model that will help you to explain work group behavior.

DEFINING AND CLASSIFYING GROUPS

Group Two or more individuals, interacting and interdependent, who have come together to achieve particular objectives.

Formal Group A designated work group defined by the organization's structure.

Informal Group A group that is neither formally structured nor organizationally determined; appears in response to the need for social contact.

Command Group A manager and his or her immediate subordinates.

Task Group Those working together to complete a job task.

Interest Group Those working together to attain a specific objective with which each is concerned.

Friendship Group Those brought together because they share one or more common characteristics.

A **group** is defined as two or more individuals, interacting and interdependent, who have come together to achieve particular objectives. Groups can be either formal or informal. By **formal groups,** we mean those defined by the organization's structure, with designated work assignments establishing tasks. In formal groups, the behaviors that one should engage in are stipulated by and directed toward organizational goals. The three members making up an airline flight crew are an example of a formal group. In contrast, **informal groups** are alliances that are neither formally structured nor organizationally determined. These groups are natural formations in the work environment that appear in response to the need for social contact.

It is possible to subclassify groups as command, task, interest, or friendship groups.[2] Command and task groups are dictated by the formal organization, whereas interest and friendship groups are informal alliances.

A **command group** is determined by the organization chart. It is composed of the subordinates who report directly to a given manager. An elementary school principal and her twelve teachers form a command group, as do the director of postal audits and his five inspectors.

Task Groups, also organizationally determined, represent those working together to complete a job task. However, a task group's boundaries are not limited to its immediate hierarchical superior. It can cross command relationships. For instance, if a college student is accused of a campus crime, it may require communication and coordination among the Dean of Academic Affairs, the Dean of Students, the Registrar, the Director of Security, and the student's advisor. Such a formation would constitute a task group. It should be noted that all command groups are also task groups, but because task groups can cut across the organization, the reverse need not be true.

People who may or may not be aligned into common command or task groups may affiliate to attain a specific objective with which each is concerned. This is an **interest group.** Employees who band together to have their vacation schedule altered, to support a peer who has been fired, or to seek increased fringe benefits represent the formation of a united body to further their common interest.

Groups often develop because the individual members have one or more common characteristics. We call these formations **friendship groups.** Social alliances, which frequently extend outside the work situation, can be based on similar age, support for "Big Red" Nebraska football, having attended the same college, or the holding of similar political views, to name just a few such characteristics.

Informal groups provide a very important service by satisfying their members' social needs. Because of interactions that result from the close proximity of work stations or task interactions, we find workers playing golf together, riding to and from work together, lunching together, and spending their breaks around the water cooler together. We must recognize that these types of interactions among individuals, even though informal, deeply affect their behavior and performance.

WHY DO PEOPLE JOIN GROUPS?

There is no single reason why individuals join groups. Since most people belong to a number of groups, it is obvious that different groups provide different benefits to their members. The most popular reasons for joining a group are related to our needs for security, status, self-esteem, affiliation, power, and goal achievement.

Security

"There's strength in numbers." By joining a group, we can reduce the insecurity of "standing alone"—we feel stronger, have fewer self-doubts, and are more resistant to threats. New employees are particularly vulnerable to a sense of isolation, and turn to the group for guidance and support. However, whether we are talking about new employees or those with years on the job, we can state that few individuals like to stand alone. We get reassurance from interacting with others and being part of a group. This often explains the appeal of unions—if management creates an environment in which employees feel insecure, they are likely to turn to unionization to reduce their feelings of insecurity.

In times when people feel alone or alienated, groups can meet security, status, esteem, and social needs. This may explain part of the attractiveness of sororities and fraternities on college campuses.
Bob Daemmrich/The Image Works

Status

"I'm a member of our company's running team. Last month, at the National Corporate Relays, we won the national championship. Didn't you see our picture in the company newsletter?" These comments demonstrate the role that a group can play in giving prestige. Inclusion in a group viewed as important by others provides recognition and status for its members.

Self-Esteem

"Before I was asked to pledge Phi Omega Chi, I felt like a nobody. Being in a fraternity makes me feel much more important." This quote demonstrates that groups can provide people with feelings of self-worth. That is, in addition to conveying status to those outside the group, membership can also give increased feelings of worth to the group members themselves. Our self-esteem is bolstered, for example, when we are accepted by a highly valued group. Being assigned to a task force whose purpose is to review and make recommendations for the location of the company's new corporate headquarters can fulfill one's needs for competence and growth, as well as for status.

Affiliation

"I'm independently wealthy, but I wouldn't give up my job. Why? Because I really like the people I work with!" This quote, from a $45,000-a-year purchasing agent who inherited several million dollars' worth of real estate, verifies that groups can fulfill our social needs. People enjoy the regular interaction that comes with group membership. For many people, these on-the-job interactions are their primary source for fulfilling their needs for affiliation. For almost all people, work groups significantly contribute to fulfilling their needs for friendships and social relations.

Power

"I tried for two years to get the plant management to increase the number of restrooms for women on the production floor to the same number as the men have. It was like talking to a wall. But I got about fifteen other women who were production employees together and we jointly presented our demands to management. The construction crews were in here adding restrooms for us within ten days!"

This episode demonstrates that one of the appealing aspects of groups is that they represent power. What often cannot be achieved individually becomes possible through group action. Of course, this power is not always sought to make demands on others. It may be desired merely as a countermeasure. In order to protect themselves from unreasonable demands by management, individuals may align with others.

Informal groups additionally provide opportunities for individuals to exercise power over others. For individuals who desire to influence others, groups can offer power without a formal position of authority in the organization. As a group leader, you may be able to make requests of group members and obtain compliance without any of the responsibilities that traditionally go with formal managerial positions. So, for people with a high power need, groups can be a vehicle for fulfillment.

Goal Achievement

"I'm part of a three-person team studying how we can cut our company's transportation costs. They've been going up at over thirty percent a year for several years now, so the corporate controller assigned representatives from cost accounting, shipping, and marketing to study the problem and make recommendations."

This task group was created to achieve a goal that would be considerably more difficult if pursued by a single person. There are times when it takes more than one person to accomplish a particular task—there is a need to pool talents, knowledge, or power in order to get a job completed. In such instances, management will rely on the use of a formal group.

STAGES OF GROUP DEVELOPMENT

For twenty years or more, we thought that most groups followed a specific sequence in their evolution and that we knew what that sequence was. But we were wrong. Recent research indicates that there is no standardized pattern of group development. In this section, we'll review the better-known five-stage model of group development, and then the recently discovered punctuated-equilibrium model.

The Five-Stage Model

From the mid-1960s, it was believed that groups passed through a standard sequence of five stages.[3] As shown in Figure 9–1, these five stages have been labeled *forming, storming, norming, performing,* and *adjourning.*

Forming The first stage in group development, characterized by much uncertainty.

The first stage, **forming,** is characterized by a great deal of uncertainty about the group's purpose, structure, and leadership. Members are "testing the waters" to determine what types of behavior are acceptable. This stage is complete when members have begun to think of themselves as part of a group.

Storming The second stage in group development, characterized by intragroup conflict.

The **storming** stage is one of intragroup conflict. Members accept the existence of the group, but there is resistance to the constraints that the group imposes on individuality. Further, there is conflict over who will control the group. When this stage is complete, there will be a relatively clear hierarchy of leadership within the group.

Norming The third stage in group development, characterized by close relationships and cohesiveness.

The third stage is one in which close relationships develop and the group demonstrates cohesiveness. There is now a strong sense of group identity and camaraderie. This **norming** stage is complete when the group structure solidifies and the group has assimilated a common set of expectations of what defines correct member behavior.

FIGURE 9–1   **Stages of Group Development**

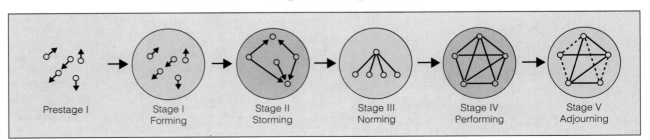

Prestage I | Stage I Forming | Stage II Storming | Stage III Norming | Stage IV Performing | Stage V Adjourning

Performing The fourth stage in group development, when the group is fully functional.

Adjourning The final stage in group development for temporary groups, characterized by concern with wrapping up activities rather than task performance.

The fourth stage is **performing.** The structure at this point is fully functional and accepted. Group energy has moved from getting to know and understand each other to performing the task at hand.

For permanent work groups, performing is the last stage in their development. However, for temporary committees, task forces, teams, and similar groups that have a limited task to perform, there is an **adjourning** stage. In this stage, the group prepares for its disbandment. High task performance is no longer the group's top priority. Instead, attention is directed toward wrapping up activities. Responses of group members vary in this stage. Some are upbeat, basking in the group's accomplishments. Others may be depressed over the loss of camaraderie and friendships gained during the work group's life.

Many interpreters of the five-stage model have assumed that a group becomes more effective as it progresses through the first four stages. While this assumption may be generally true, what makes a group effective is more complex than this model acknowledges. Under some conditions, high levels of conflict are conducive to high group performance. So we might expect to find situations where groups in Stage II outperform those in Stages III or IV. Similarly, groups do not always proceed clearly from one stage to the next. Sometimes, in fact, several stages go on simultaneously, as when groups are storming and performing at the same time. Groups even occasionally regress to previous stages. Therefore, even the strongest proponents of this model do not assume that all groups follow its five-stage process precisely or that Stage IV is always the most preferable.

The Punctuated-Equilibrium Model

Studies of more than a dozen field and laboratory task force groups confirmed that groups don't develop in a universal sequence of stages.[4] But the *timing* of when groups form and change the way they work is highly consistent. Specifically, it's been found that (1) the first meeting sets the group's direction; (2) the first phase of group activity is one of inertia; (3) a transition takes place at the end of the first phase, which occurs exactly when the group has used up half its allotted time; (4) the transition initiates major changes; (5) a second phase of inertia follows the transition; and (6) the group's last meeting is characterized by markedly accelerated activity. These findings are shown in Figure 9–2.

FIGURE 9–2   The Punctuated–Equilibrium Model

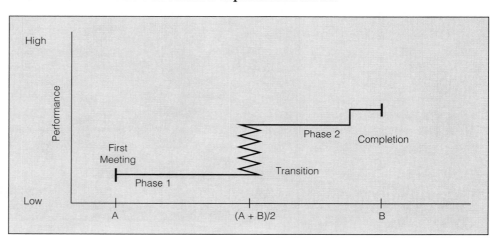

The first meeting sets the group's direction. A framework of behavioral patterns and assumptions through which the group will approach its project emerges in this first meeting. These lasting patterns can appear as early as the first few seconds of the group's life.

Once set, the group's direction becomes "written in stone" and is unlikely to be reexamined throughout the first half of the group's life. This is a period of inertia—that is, the group tends to stand still or become locked into a fixed course of action. Even if it gains new insights that challenge initial patterns and assumptions, the group is incapable of acting on these new insights in Phase 1.

One of the more interesting discoveries made in these studies was that each group experienced its transition at the same point in its calendar—precisely halfway between its first meeting and its official deadline—despite the fact that some groups spent as little as an hour on their project while others spent six months. It was as if the groups universally experienced a midlife crisis at this point. The midpoint appears to work like an alarm clock, heightening members' awareness that their time is limited and that they need to "get moving."

This transition ends Phase 1 and is characterized by a concentrated burst of changes, dropping of old patterns, and adoption of new perspectives. The transition sets a revised direction for Phase 2.

Phase 2 is a new equilibrium or period of inertia. In this phase, the group executes plans created during the transition period.

The group's last meeting is characterized by a final burst of activity to finish its work.

We can use this model to describe some of your experiences with student teams created for doing group term projects. At the first meeting, a basic timetable is established. Members size up one another. They agree they have nine weeks to do their project. The instructor's requirements are discussed and debated. From that point, the group meets regularly to carry

Conflict in a group is not necessarily bad. The storming stage can be merely a step in the group's development and signal the transition from passive inertia to new directions and high productivity.
Ron Rovtar/FPG

out its activities. About four or five weeks into the project, however, problems are confronted. Criticism begins to be taken seriously. Discussion becomes more open. The group reassesses where it's been and aggressively moves to make necessary changes. If the right changes are made, the next four or five weeks find the group developing a first-rate project. The group's last meeting, which will probably occur just before the project is due, lasts longer than the others. In it, all final issues are discussed and details resolved.

In summary, the punctuated-equilibrium model characterizes groups as exhibiting long periods of inertia interspersed with brief revolutionary changes triggered primarily by their members' awareness of time and deadlines. Or, to use the terminology of the five-stage group development model, the group begins by combining the forming and norming stages, then goes through a period of low performing, followed by storming, then a period of high performing, and, finally, adjourning.

TOWARD EXPLAINING WORK GROUP BEHAVIOR

Why are some group efforts more successful than others? The answer to that question is complex, but it includes variables such as the ability of the group's members, the size of the group, the level of conflict, and the internal pressures on members to conform to the group's norms. Figure 9–3 presents the major components that determine group performance and satisfaction.[5] It can help you sort out the key variables and their interrelationships.

Work groups don't exist in isolation. They are part of a larger organization. A research team in Dow's Plastic Products division, for instance, must live within the rules and policies dictated from the division's headquarters and Dow's corporate offices. So every work group is influenced by external conditions imposed from outside it. The work group itself has a distinct set of resources determined by its membership. This includes such things as intelligence and motivation of members. It also has an internal structure that defines member roles and norms. These factors—group member resources and structure—determine interaction patterns and other processes within the group. Finally, the group process–performance/satisfaction relationship is moderated by the type of task that the group is working on. In the following pages, we'll elaborate on each of the basic boxes identified in Figure 9–3.

FIGURE 9–3   Group Behavior Model

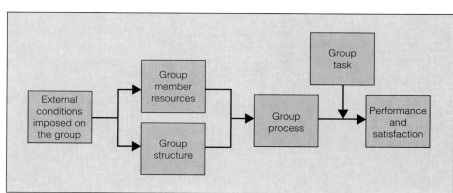

EXTERNAL CONDITIONS IMPOSED ON THE GROUP

To begin understanding the behavior of a work group, you need to view it as a subsystem embedded in a larger system.[6] That is, when we realize that groups are a subset of a larger organization system, we can extract part of the explanation of the group's behavior from an explanation of the organization to which it belongs.

Organization Strategy

An organization has a strategy that defines what business it is in or wants to be in, and the kind of organization it is or wants to be. It is set by top management, often in collaboration with lower-level managers. Strategy outlines the organization's goals and the means for attaining these goals. It might, for example, direct the organization toward reducing costs, improving quality, expanding market share, or shrinking the size of its overall operations. The strategy that an organization is pursuing, at any given time, will influence the power of various work groups, which, in turn, will determine the resources that the organization's top management is willing to allocate to it for performing its tasks. To illustrate, an organization that is retrenching through selling off or closing down major parts of its business is going to have work groups with a shrinking resource base, increased member anxiety, and the potential for heightened intragroup conflict.[7]

Authority Structures

Organizations have authority structures that define who reports to whom, who makes decisions, and what decisions individuals or groups are empowered to make. This structure typically determines where a given work group is placed in the organization's hierarchy, the formal leader of the group, and formal relationships between groups. So while a work group might be led by someone who emerges informally from within the group, the formally designated leader—appointed by management—has authority that others in the group don't have.

Formal Regulations

Organizations create rules, procedures, policies, and other forms of regulations to standardize employee behavior. Because McDonald's has standard operating procedures for taking orders, cooking hamburgers, and filling soda containers, the discretion of work group members to set independent standards of behavior is severely limited. The more formal regulations that the organization imposes on all its employees, the more the behavior of work group members will be consistent and predictable.

Organizational Resources

Some organizations are large and profitable, with an abundance of resources. Their employees, for instance, will have modern, high-quality tools and equipment to do their jobs. Other organizations aren't as fortunate. When organizations have limited resources, so do their work groups. What a group actually accomplishes is, to a large degree, determined by what it is capable of accomplishing. The presence or absence of resources such as money, time, raw materials, and equipment—which are allocated to the group by the organization—have a large bearing on the group's behavior.

Personnel Selection Process

Members of any work group are, first, members of the organization of which the group is a part. Members of a cost-reduction task force at Boeing first had to be hired as employees of the company. So the criteria that an organization uses in its selection process will determine the kinds of people that will be in its work groups.

The selection factor becomes even more critical if a large segment of the organization's employees are unionized. In such cases, the terms of the union's collective bargaining contract will play a key part in specifying who is hired as well as acceptable and unacceptable behaviors of work group members.

Performance Evaluation and Reward System

Another organization-wide variable that affects all employees is the performance evaluation and reward system.[8] Does the organization provide employees with challenging, specific performance objectives? Does the organization reward the accomplishment of individual or group objectives? Since work groups are part of the larger organizational system, group members' behavior will be influenced by how the organization evaluates performance and what behaviors are rewarded.

Organizational Culture

Every organization has an unwritten culture that defines for employees standards of acceptable and unacceptable behavior. After a few months, most employees understand their organization's culture. They know things like how to dress for work, whether rules are rigidly enforced, what kinds of questionable behaviors are sure to get them into trouble and which are likely to be overlooked, the importance of honesty and integrity, and the like. While many organizations have subcultures—often created around work groups— with an additional or modified set of standards, they still have a dominant culture that conveys to all employees those values the organization holds dearest. Members of work groups have to accept the standards implied in the organization's dominant culture if they are to remain in good standing.

Physical Work Setting

Finally, we propose that the physical work setting that is imposed on the group by external parties has an important bearing on work group behavior.[9] Architects, industrial engineers, and office designers make decisions regarding the size and physical layout of an employee's work space, the arrangement of equipment, illumination levels, and the need for acoustics to cut down on noise distractions. These create both barriers and opportunities for work group interaction. It's obviously a lot easier for employees to talk or "goof off" if their work stations are close together, there are no physical barriers between them, and their supervisor is in an enclosed office fifty yards away.

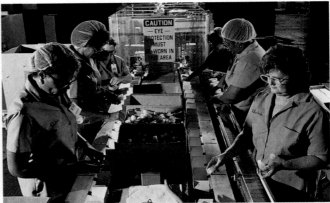

The physical work setting is a significant force facilitating or restricting group inter-action. The work layout in the photo on the left makes it very difficult for employees to communicate informally while they perform their work tasks. In contrast, the physical layout in the photo on the right creates abundant opportunities for informal group interactions.   Left: Craig Hammell/The Stock Market; Right: Steve Starr/Picture Group

GROUP MEMBER RESOURCES

A group's potential level of performance is, to a large extent, dependent on the resources that its members individually bring to the group. In this sec-tion, we want to look at two resources that have received the greatest amount of attention: abilities and personality characteristics.

Abilities

Part of a group's performance can be predicted by assessing the task-rele-vant and intellectual abilities of its individual members. Sure, it's true that we occasionally read about the athletic team composed of mediocre players who, because of excellent coaching, determination, and precision teamwork, beat a far more talented group of players. But such cases make the news precisely because they represent an aberration. As the old saying goes, "The race doesn't always go to the swiftest nor the battle to the strongest, but that's the way to bet." A group's performance is not merely the summation of its individual members' abilities. However, these abilities set parameters for what members can do and how effectively they will perform in a group.

What predictions can we make regarding ability and group perfor-mance? First, evidence indicates that individuals who hold crucial abilities for attaining the group's task tend to be more involved in group activity, generally contribute more, are more likely to emerge as the group leaders, and are more satisfied if their talents are effectively utilized by the group.[10] Second, intellectual ability and task-relevant ability have both been found to be related to overall group performance. However, the correlation is not par-ticularly high, suggesting that other factors, such as the size of the group, the type of tasks being performed, the actions of its leader, and level of con-flict within the group, also influence performance.[11]

Personality Characteristics

There has been a great deal of research on the relationship between personali-ty traits and group attitudes and behavior. The general conclusion is that attributes that tend to have a positive connotation in our culture tend to be positively related to group productivity, morale, and cohesiveness. These include traits such as sociability, self-reliance, and independence. In contrast, negatively evaluated characteristics such as authoritarianism, dominance, and unconventionality tend to be negatively related to the dependent variables.[12] These personality traits affect group performance by strongly influencing how the individual will interact with other group members.

Is any one personality characteristic a good predictor of group behavior? The answer to that question is "No." The magnitude of the effect of any *single* characteristic is small, but taking personality characteristics *together*, the consequences for group behavior are of major significance. We can conclude, therefore, that personality characteristics of group members play an important part in determining behavior in groups.

GROUP STRUCTURE

Work groups are not unorganized mobs. They have a structure that shapes the behavior of members and makes it possible to explain and predict a large portion of individual behavior within the group as well as the performance of the group itself. What are some of these structural variables? They include formal leadership, roles, norms, group status, group size, and composition of the group.

Formal Leadership

Almost every work group has a formal leader. He or she is typically identified by titles such as unit or department manager, supervisor, foreman, project leader, task force head, or committee chair. This leader can play an important part in the group's success; so much so, in fact, that we have devoted an entire chapter to the topic of leadership (see Chapter 11). As a sort of "coming attraction," let's highlight a few of the things we know about leadership and group performance.

Studies that have examined the effects of leader traits on group performance have generally provided inconclusive results. Far more promising findings have surfaced when situational variables, like the task structure in the jobs and the characteristics of followers, have been used as moderating variables. In terms of achieving high group satisfaction, participative leadership seems to be more effective than an autocratic style. But participation doesn't necessarily lead to higher performance. In some situations, the group guided by a directive, autocratic leader will outperform its participative counterpart. Most research studies in recent years have been focused on trying to identify the contingency variables associated with leader success. That is, *when* should a leader be democratic and *when* should a leader be autocratic? As previously noted, we'll provide some answers for you in Chapter 11.

Roles

Shakespeare said, "All the world's a stage, and all the men and women merely players." Using the same metaphor, all group members are actors, each playing a **role.** By this term, we mean a set of expected behavior patterns attributed to someone occupying a given position in a social unit. The understanding of role behavior would be dramatically simplified if each of us chose

Role A set of expected behavior patterns attributed to someone occupying a given position in a social unit.

one role and "played it out" regularly and consistently. Unfortunately, we are required to play a number of diverse roles, both on and off our jobs. As we shall see, one of the tasks in understanding behavior is grasping the role that a person is currently playing.

For example, Bill Patterson is a plant manager with Electrical Industries, a large electrical equipment manufacturer in Phoenix. He has a number of roles that he fulfills on that job—for instance, Electrical Industries employee, member of middle management, electrical engineer, and the primary company spokesperson in the community. Off the job, Bill Patterson finds himself in still more roles: husband, father, Catholic, Rotarian, tennis player, member of the Thunderbird Country Club, and president of his homeowners' association. Many of these roles are compatible; some create conflicts. For instance, how does his religious involvement influence his managerial decisions regarding layoffs, expense account padding, and providing accurate information to government agencies? A recent offer of promotion requires Bill to relocate, yet his family very much wants to stay in Phoenix. Can the role demands of his job be reconciled with the demands of his husband and father roles?

The issue should be clear: Like Bill Patterson, we all are required to play a number of roles, and our behavior varies with the role we are playing. Bill's behavior when he attends church on Sunday morning is different from his behavior on the golf course later that same day. So different groups impose different role requirements on individuals.

Role Identity Certain attitudes and behaviors consistent with a role.

ROLE IDENTITY   There are certain attitudes and actual behaviors consistent with a role, and they create the **role identity.** People have the ability to shift roles rapidly when they recognize that the situation and its demands clearly require major changes. For instance, when union stewards were promoted to supervisory positions, it was found that their attitudes changed from pro-union to pro-management within a few months of their promotion. When these promotions had to be rescinded later because of economic difficulties in the firm, it was found that the demoted supervisors had once again adopted their pro-union attitudes.[13]

Role Perception An individual's view of how he or she is supposed to act in a given situation.

ROLE PERCEPTION   One's view of how one is supposed to act in a given situation is a **role perception.** Based on an interpretation of how we believe we are supposed to behave, we engage in certain types of behavior.

Where do we get these perceptions? We get them from stimuli all around us—friends, books, movies, television. Undoubtedly many of today's young surgeons formed their role identities from their perception of Hawkeye on *M*A*S*H.* It also seems reasonable that many current law enforcement officers learned their roles from reading Joseph Wambaugh novels or watching Dirty Harry movies. Tomorrow's lawyers will certainly be influenced by *L.A. Law.* Of course, the primary reason that apprenticeship programs exist in many trades and professions is to allow beginners to watch an "expert," so that they can learn to act as they are supposed to.

Role Expectations How others believe a person should act in a given situation.

ROLE EXPECTATIONS   **Role expectations** are defined as how others believe you should act in a given situation. How you behave is determined to a large extent by the role defined in the context in which you are acting. The role of a United States senator is viewed as having propriety and dignity, whereas a football coach is seen as aggressive, dynamic, and inspiring to his players. In the same context, we might be surprised to learn that the neighborhood priest moonlights during the week as a bartender, because our role expectations of priests and bartenders tend to be considerably different.

When role expectations are concentrated into generalized categories, we have role stereotypes.

During the last four decades, we have seen a major change in the general population's role stereotypes of females. In the 1950s, a woman's role was to stay home, take care of the house, raise children, and generally care for her husband. Today, most of us no longer hold this stereotype. Boys *can* play with Barbie Dolls and girls *can* play with G.I. Joes. Girls can aspire to be doctors, lawyers, and astronauts as well as to the more traditional female careers of nurse, schoolteacher, secretary, and housewife. In other words, many of us have changed our role expectations of women, and, similarly, many women carry new role perceptions.

Psychological Contract An unwritten agreement that sets out what management expects from the employee, and vice versa.

In the workplace, it can be helpful to look at the topic of role expectations through the perspective of the **psychological contract.** There is an unwritten agreement that exists between employees and their employer. This psychological contract sets out mutual expectations—what management expects from workers, and vice versa.[14] In effect, this contract defines the behavioral expectations that go with every role. Management is expected to treat employees justly, provide acceptable working conditions, clearly communicate what is a fair day's work, and give feedback on how well the employee is doing. Employees are expected to respond by demonstrating a good attitude, following directions, and showing loyalty to the organization.

What happens when role expectations as implied in the psychological contract are not met? If management is derelict in keeping up its part of the bargain, we can expect negative repercussions on employee performance and satisfaction. When employees fail to live up to expectations, the result is usually some form of disciplinary action up to and including firing.

The psychological contract should be recognized as a "powerful determiner of behavior in organizations."[15] It points out the importance of accurately communicating role expectations. In Chapter 17, we shall discuss how organizations socialize employees in order to get them to play out their roles in the way management desires.

Role Conflict A situation in which an individual is confronted by divergent role expectations.

ROLE CONFLICT When an individual is confronted by divergent role expectations, the result is **role conflict.** It exists when an individual finds that compliance with one role requirement may make more difficult the compliance with another. At the extreme, it would include situations in which two or more role expectations are mutually contradictory.

Our previous discussion of the many roles Bill Patterson had to deal with included several role conflicts—for instance, Bill's attempt to reconcile the expectations placed on him as a husband and father with those placed on him as an executive with Electrical Industries. The former, as you will remember, emphasizes stability and concern for the desire of his wife and children to remain in Phoenix. Electrical Industries, on the other hand, expects its employees to be responsive to the needs and requirements of the company. Although it might be in Bill's financial and career interests to accept a relocation, the conflict comes down to choosing between family and career role expectations.

The issue of ethics in business demonstrates a well-publicized area of role conflict among corporate executives. For example, one study found that fifty-seven percent of *Harvard Business Review* readers had experienced the dilemma of having to choose between what was profitable for their firms and what was ethical.[16]

All of us have faced and will continue to face role conflicts. The critical issue, from our standpoint, is how conflicts imposed by divergent expectations within the organization impact on behavior. Certainly they increase internal tension and frustration. There are a number of behavioral responses one may engage in. For example, one can give a formalized bureaucratic response. The conflict is then resolved by relying on the rules, regulations, and procedures that govern organizational activities. For example, a worker faced with the conflicting requirements imposed by the corporate controller's office and his own plant manager decides in favor of his immediate boss—the plant manager. Other behavioral responses may include withdrawal, stalling, negotiation, or, as we found in our discussion of dissonance in Chapter 6, redefining the facts or the situation to make them appear congruent.

AN EXPERIMENT: ZIMBARDO'S SIMULATED PRISON   One of the more illuminating role experiments was done by Stanford University psychologist Philip Zimbardo and his associates.[17] They created a "prison" in the basement of the Stanford psychology building; hired at $15 a day two dozen emotionally stable, physically healthy, law-abiding students who scored "normal average" on extensive personality tests; randomly assigned them the role of either "guard" or "prisoner"; and established some basic rules. The experimenters then stood back to see what would happen.

At the start of the planned two-week simulation, there were no measurable differences between those individuals assigned to be guards and those chosen to be prisoners. Additionally, the guards received no special training in how to be prison guards. They were told only to "maintain law and order" in the prison and not to take any nonsense from the prisoners: Physical violence was forbidden. To simulate further the realities of prison life, the prisoners were allowed visits from relatives and friends. But while the mock guards worked eight-hour shifts, the mock prisoners were kept in their cells around the clock and were allowed out only for meals, exercise, toilet privileges, head-count lineups, and work details.

Students at Stanford University play roles of "guard" and "prisoner" in a simulated prison experiment.   Philip G. Zimbardo, Stanford University

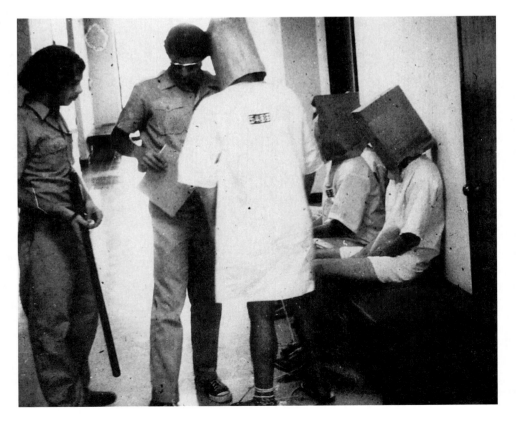

It took the "prisoners" little time to accept the authority positions of the guards, or the mock guards to adjust to their new authority roles. After the guards crushed a rebellion attempt on the second day, the prisoners became increasingly passive. Whatever the guards "dished out," the prisoners took. The prisoners actually began to believe and act as if they were, as the guards constantly reminded them, inferior and powerless. And every guard, at some time during the simulation, engaged in abusive, authoritative behavior. For example, one guard said, "I was surprised at myself...I made them call each other names and clean the toilets out with their bare hands. I practically considered the prisoners cattle, and I kept thinking: 'I have to watch out for them in case they try something.'" Another guard added, "I was tired of seeing the prisoners in their rags and smelling the strong odors of their bodies that filled the cells. I watched them tear at each other on orders given by us. They didn't see it as an experiment. It was real and they were fighting to keep their identity. But we were always there to show them who was boss."

The simulation actually proved *too* successful in demonstrating how quickly individuals learn new roles. The researchers had to stop the experiment after only six days because of the pathological reactions that the participants were demonstrating. And remember, these were individuals chosen precisely for their normalcy and emotional stability.

What should you conclude from this prison simulation? The participants in this prison simulation had, like the rest of us, learned stereotyped conceptions of guard and prisoner roles from the mass media and their own personal experiences in power and powerlessness relationships gained at home (parent–child), in school (teacher–student), and in other situations. This, then, allowed them easily and rapidly to assume roles that were very different from their inherent personalities. In this case, we saw that people with no prior personality pathology or training in their roles could execute extreme forms of behavior consistent with the roles they were playing.

Norms

Did you ever notice that golfers don't speak while their partners are putting on the green or that employees don't criticize their bosses in public? This is because of **"norms."**

All groups have established norms; that is, acceptable standards of behavior that are shared by the group's members. Norms tell members what they ought and ought not to do under certain circumstances. From an individual's standpoint, they tell what is expected of you in certain situations. When agreed to and accepted by the group, norms act as a means of influencing the behavior of group members with a minimum of external controls. Norms differ among groups, communities, and societies, but they all have them.

Formalized norms are written up in organizational manuals setting out rules and procedures for employees to follow. By far, the majority of norms in organizations are informal. You do not need someone to tell you that throwing paper airplanes or engaging in prolonged gossip sessions at the water cooler are unacceptable behaviors when the "big boss from New York" is touring the office. Similarly, we all know that when we are in an employment interview discussing what we did not like about our previous job, there are certain things we should not talk about (difficulty in getting along with co-workers or our supervisor), while it is very appropriate to talk about other things (inadequate opportunities for advancement or unimportant and meaningless work). Evidence suggests that even high

Norms Acceptable standards of behavior within a group that are shared by the group's members.

school students recognize that in such interviews certain answers are more socially desirable than others.[18]

Students quickly learn how to assimilate classroom norms. Depending upon the environment created by the instructor, the norms may support unequivocal acceptance of the material suggested by the instructor, or, at the other extreme, students may be expected to question and challenge the instructor on any point that is unclear. For example, in most classroom situations, the norms dictate that one not engage in loud, boisterous discussion that makes it impossible to hear the lecturer, or humiliate the instructor by pushing him or her "too far," even if one has obviously located a weakness in something the instructor has said. Should some in the classroom group behave in such a way as to violate these norms, we can expect pressure to be applied against the deviant members to bring their behavior into conformity with group standards.

COMMON CLASSES OF NORMS   A work group's norms are like an individual's fingerprints—each is unique. Yet there are still some common classes of norms that appear in most work groups.[19]

Probably the most widespread norms deal with *performance-related processes*. Work groups typically provide their members with explicit cues on how hard they should work, how to get the job done, their level of output, appropriate communication channels, and the like. These norms are extremely powerful in affecting an individual employee's performance—they are capable of significantly modifying a performance prediction that was based solely on the employee's ability and level of personal motivation.

A second category of norms encompasses *appearance factors*. This includes things like appropriate dress, loyalty to the work group or organization, when to look busy, and when it's acceptable to goof off. Some organizations have formal dress codes. However, even in their absence, norms frequently develop to dictate the kind of clothing that should be worn to work. Presenting the appearance of loyalty is important in many work groups and organizations. For instance, in many organizations, especially among professional employees and those in the executive ranks, it is considered inappropriate to be openly looking for another job. This concern for demonstrating loyalty, incidentally, often explains why ambitious aspirants to top-management positions in an organization willingly take work home at night, come in on weekends, and accept transfers to cities they would otherwise not prefer to live in.

Another class of norms concerns *informal social arrangements*. These norms come from informal work groups and primarily regulate social interactions within the group. With whom group members eat lunch, friendships on and off the job, social games, and the like are influenced by these norms.

A final category of norms relates to *allocation of resources*. These norms can originate in the group or in the organization and cover things like pay, assignment of difficult jobs, and allocation of new tools and equipment. In some organizations, for example, new personal computers are distributed equally to all groups. So every department might get five, regardless of the number of people in the department or their need for the computers. In another organization, equipment is allocated to those groups who can make the best use of it. So some departments might get twenty computers and some none. These resource allocation norms can have a direct impact on employee satisfaction and an indirect effect on group performance.

THE "HOW" AND "WHY" OF NORMS   *How* do norms develop? *Why* are they enforced? A review of the research allows us to answer these questions.[20]

Norms typically develop gradually as group members learn what behaviors are necessary for the group to function effectively. Of course, critical events in the group might short-circuit the process and act quickly to solidify new norms. Most norms develop in one or more of the following four ways: (1) *Explicit statements made by a group member*—often the group's supervisor or a powerful member. The group leader might, for instance, specifically say that no personal phone calls are allowed during working hours or that coffee breaks are to be kept to ten minutes. (2) *Critical events in the group's history*. These set important precedents. A bystander is injured while standing too close to a machine and, from that point on, members of the work group regularly monitor each other to ensure that no one other than the operator gets within five feet of any machine. (3) *Primacy*. The first behavior pattern that emerges in a group frequently sets group expectations. Friendship groups of students often stake out seats near each other on the first day of class and become perturbed if an outsider takes "their" seats in a later class. (4) *Carry-over behaviors from past situations*. Group members bring expectations with them from other groups of which they have been members. This can explain why work groups typically prefer to add new members who are similar to current ones in background and experience. This is likely to increase the probability that the expectations they bring are consistent with those already held by the group.

But groups do not establish or enforce norms for every conceivable situation. The norms that the group will enforce tend to be those that are important to it. But what makes a norm important? (1) *If it facilitates the group's survival*. Groups don't like to fail, so they look to enforce those norms that increase their chances for success. This means that they will try to protect themselves from interference from other groups or individuals. (2) *If it increases the predictability of group members' behaviors*. Norms that increase predictability enable group members to anticipate each other's actions and to prepare appropriate responses. (3) *If it reduces embarrassing interpersonal problems for group members*. Norms are important if they ensure the satisfaction of their members and prevent as much interpersonal discomfort as possible. (4) *If it allows members to express the central values of the group and clarify what is distinctive about the group's identity*. Norms that encourage expression of the group's values and distinctive identity help to solidify and maintain the group.

CONFORMITY   As a member of a group, you desire acceptance by the group. Because of your desire for acceptance, you are susceptible to conforming to the group's norms. There is considerable evidence that groups can place strong pressures on individual members to change their attitudes and behaviors to conform to the group's standard.[21]

Do individuals conform to the pressures of all the groups they belong to? Obviously not, because people belong to many groups and their norms vary. In some cases, they may even have contradictory norms. So what do people do? They conform to the important groups to which they belong or hope to belong. The important groups have been referred to as *reference* groups and are characterized as ones where the person is aware of the others; the person defines himself or herself as a member, or would like to be a member; and the person feels that the group members are significant to him or her.[22] The implication, then, is that *all* groups do not impose equal conformity pressures on their members.

Conformity Adjusting one's behavior to align with the norms of the group.

The impact that group pressures for **conformity** can have on an individual member's judgment and attitudes was demonstrated in the now-classic studies by Solomon Asch.[23] Asch made up groups of seven or eight people, who sat in a classroom and were asked to compare two cards held by the experimenter. One card had one line, the other had three lines of varying length. As shown in Figure 9–4, one of the lines on the three-line card was identical to the line on the one-line card. Also as shown in Figure 9–4, the difference in line length was quite obvious; under ordinary conditions, subjects made fewer than one percent errors. The object was to announce aloud which of the three lines matched the single line. But what happens if the members in the group begin to give incorrect answers? Will the pressures to conform result in an unsuspecting subject (USS) altering his or her answer to align with the others? That was what Asch wanted to know. So he arranged the group so that only the USS was unaware that the experiment was "fixed." The seating was prearranged: The USS was placed so as to be the last to announce his or her decision.

The experiment began with several sets of matching exercises. All the subjects give the right answers. On the third set, however, the first subject gives an obviously wrong answer—for example, saying "C" in Figure 9–4. The next subject gives the same wrong answer, and so do the others until it gets to the unknowing subject. He knows "B" is the same as "X," yet everyone has said "C." The decision confronting the USS is this: Do you publicly state a perception that differs from the preannounced position of the others in your group? Or do you give an answer that you strongly believe is incorrect in order to have your response agree with that of the other group members?

The results obtained by Asch demonstrated that over many experiments and many trials, subjects conformed in about thirty-five percent of the trials; that is, the subjects gave answers that they knew were wrong but that were consistent with the replies of other group members.

What can we conclude from this study? The results suggest that there are group norms that press us toward conformity. We desire to be one of the group and avoid being visibly different. We can generalize further to say that when an individual's opinion of objective data differs significantly from that of others in the group, he or she is likely to feel extensive pressure to align his or her opinions to conform with that of the others.

Status

While teaching a college course on adolescence, the instructor asked the class to list things that contributed to status when they were in high school. The list was long and included being an athlete or a cheerleader and being able to cut class without getting caught. Then the instructor asked the students to list things that didn't contribute to status. Again, it was easy for the

FIGURE 9–4   Examples of Cards Used in Asch Study

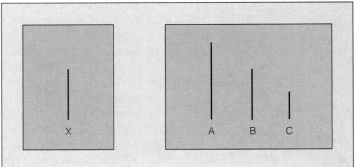

Should You Agree with Your Boss When You Don't?

The Asch conformity studies point up a related dilemma that many employees face: whether it is ethical to outwardly agree with your boss when, in actuality, you think that he or she is wrong.

There is an old adage: The boss isn't always right, but he's always the boss. The underlying message is that one doesn't argue with one's superior because the superior has authority over one. But what about when you know the boss is acting unethically? Would openly agreeing with the boss in those circumstances mean compromising your personal standards of integrity? What about merely suppressing your disagreement? That might be more politically astute, but would it mean you lack moral character?

The norms of conformity can be very strong in an organization. Individuals who openly challenge long-condoned but questionable practices may be labeled as disloyal or lacking in commitment to the organization. One perspective argues that conformance with group and organizational norms bonds people together. Such conformity facilitates cooperation and cohesiveness and contributes to standardizing behavior. These are qualities that can enhance organizational effectiveness. An opposite argument can be made that the suppression of dissent and the appearance of conformity don't improve organizational effectiveness, but rather plant the seeds for later hostilities and conflicts.

What should *you* do when you disagree with your boss about an ethical issue? If you were the boss, would you want your employees to openly disagree with you? If so, how would you want them to express their views? What can *organizations* do to avoid encouraging individuals to unethically conform but, at the same time, encourage cohesiveness and commitment?

students to create a long list: getting straight A's, having your mother drive you to school, and so forth. Finally, the students were asked to develop a third list—those things that didn't matter one way or the other. There was a long silence. At last one student in the back row volunteered, "In high school, nothing didn't matter."[24]

Status A socially defined position or rank given to groups or group members by others.

Status—that is, a socially defined position or rank given to groups or group members by others—permeates society far beyond the walls of high school. It would not be extravagant to rephrase the preceding quotation to read, "In the status hierarchy of life, nothing doesn't matter." We live in a class-structured society. Despite all attempts to make it more egalitarian, we have made little progress toward a classless society. Even the smallest group will develop roles, rights, and rituals to differentiate its members. Status is an important factor in understanding human behavior because it is a significant motivator and has major behavioral consequences when individuals perceive a disparity between what they believe their status to be and what others perceive it to be.

FORMAL AND INFORMAL STATUS   Status may be formally imposed by a group—that is, organizationally imposed through titles or amenities. This is the status that goes with being crowned "the heavyweight champion of the world" or receiving the "teacher-of-the-year" award. We are all familiar with the trappings of high organizational status—large offices with impressive views, fancy titles, high pay, preferred work schedules, and so on. (See Table 9–1.) Whether or not management acknowledges the existence of a status hierarchy, organizations are filled with amenities that are not uniformly available and, hence, carry status value. More often, we deal with status in an informal sense. Status may be informally acquired by such characteristics as education, age, sex, skill, and experience. Anything can have status value if others in the group evaluate it as status-conferring. Keep in mind that informal status is not necessarily less important than the formal variety.

In his classic restaurant study, William F. Whyte demonstrated the importance of status.[25] Whyte proposed that people work together more smoothly if high-status personnel customarily originate action for lower-status personnel. He found a number of instances in which the initiating of action by lower-status people created a conflict between formal and informal status systems. In one instance he cited, waitresses were passing their customers' orders directly on to countermen—which meant that low-status servers were initiating action for high-status cooks. By the simple addition of an aluminum spindle to which the order could be hooked, a buffer was created between the lower-status waitresses and the higher-status countermen, allowing the latter to initiate action on orders when they felt ready.

Whyte also noted that in the kitchen, supply men secured food supplies from the chefs. This was, in effect, a case of low-skilled employees initiating action to be taken by high-skilled employees. Conflict was stimulated when supply men, either explicitly or implicitly, urged the chefs to "get a move on." However, Whyte observed that one supply man had little trouble with

TABLE 9–1   Examples of What May Connote Formal Status

Titles

Director
Manager
Chief
Head
Senior

Relationships

Work for an important individual
Job requires working with high-ranking organizational members
Work in a critical group or on an important assignment

Pay and Benefits

Expense account
Liberal travel opportunities
Reserved parking space with one's name on it
Company-paid car

Work Schedule

Day work rather than evening or shift
Freedom from punching a time clock
Freedom to come and go as one pleases

Office Amenities

Large office
Large desk with high-back chair
Windows with attractive view
Private secretary to screen visitors

the chefs because he gave the order and asked that the chef call him when it was ready, thus reversing the initiating process. In his analysis, Whyte suggested several changes in procedures that aligned interactions more closely with the accepted status hierarchy and resulted in substantial improvements in worker relations and effectiveness.

STATUS EQUITY   It is important for group members to believe that the status hierarchy is equitable. When inequity is perceived, it creates disequilibrium that results in various types of corrective behavior.[26]

The concept of equity presented in Chapter 7 applies to status. People expect rewards to be proportionate to costs incurred. If Dana and Anne are the two finalists for the head nurse position in a hospital, and it is clear that Dana has more seniority and better preparation for assuming the promotion, Anne will view the selection of Dana to be equitable. However, if Anne is chosen because she is the daughter-in-law of the hospital director, Dana will believe an injustice has been committed.

The trappings that go with formal positions are also important elements in maintaining equity. When we believe there is an inequity between the perceived ranking of an individual and the status accouterments that person is given by the organization, we are experiencing *status incongruence*. Examples of this kind of incongruence are the more desirable office location being held by a lower-ranking individual and paid country club membership being provided by the company for division managers but not for vice presidents. Pay incongruence has long been a problem in the insurance industry, where top sales agents often earn two to five times more than senior corporate executives. The result is that it is very hard for insurance companies to entice agents into management positions. Our point is that employees expect the things an individual has and receives to be congruent with his or her status.

Groups generally agree within themselves on status criteria and, hence, there is usually high concurrence in group rankings of individuals. However, individuals can find themselves in a conflict situation when they move between groups whose status criteria are different or when they join groups whose members have heterogeneous backgrounds. For instance, business executives may use income, total wealth, or size of the companies they run as determinants of status. Government bureaucrats may use the size of their agencies. Academics may use the number of grants received or articles published. Blue-collar workers may use years of seniority, job assignments, or bowling scores. In groups made up of heterogeneous individuals or when heterogeneous groups are forced to be interdependent, status differences may initiate conflict as the group attempts to reconcile and align the differing hierarchies.

Size

Does the size of a group affect the group's overall behavior? The answer to this question is a definite "Yes," but the effect depends on what dependent variables you look at.[27]

The evidence indicates, for instance, that smaller groups are faster at completing tasks than are larger ones. However, if the group is engaged in problem solving, large groups consistently get better marks than their smaller counterparts. Translating these results into specific numbers is a bit more hazardous, but we can offer some parameters. Large groups—with a dozen or more members—are good for gaining diverse input. So if the goal of the group is fact-finding, larger groups should be more effective. On the other hand, smaller groups are better at doing something productive with that input. Groups of approximately seven members, therefore, tend to be more effective for taking action.

One of the most important findings related to the size of a group has been labeled **social loafing.** Social loafing is the tendency of group members to do less than they are capable of as individuals. It directly challenges the logic that the productivity of the group as a whole should at least equal the sum of the productivity of each individual in that group.

A common stereotype about groups is that the sense of team spirit spurs individual effort and enhances the group's overall productivity. In the late 1920s, a German psychologist named Ringelmann compared the results of individual and group performance on a rope-pulling task.[28] He expected that the group's effort would be equal to the sum of the efforts of individuals within the group. That is, three people pulling together should exert three times as much pull on the rope as one person, and eight people should exert eight times as much pull. Ringelmann's results, however, did not confirm his expectations. Groups of three people exerted a force only two-and-a-half times the average individual performance. Groups of eight collectively achieved less than four times the solo rate.

Replications of Ringelmann's research with similar tasks have generally supported his findings.[29] Increases in group size are inversely related to individual performance. More may be better in the sense that the total productivity of a group of four is greater than that of one or two people, but the individual productivity of each group member declines.

What causes this social loafing effect? It may be due to a belief that others in the group are not pulling their own weight. If you see others as lazy or inept, you can reestablish equity by reducing your effort. Another explanation is the dispersion of responsibility. Because the results of the group cannot be attributed to any single person, the relationship between an individual's input and the group's output is clouded. In such situations, individuals may be tempted to become "free riders" and coast on the group's efforts. In other words, there will be a reduction in efficiency where individuals think that their contribution cannot be measured.

The implications for OB of this effect on work groups are significant. Where managers utilize collective work situations to enhance morale and teamwork, they must also provide means by which individual efforts can be identified. If this is not done, management must weigh the potential losses in productivity from using groups against any possible gains in worker satisfaction.[30]

The research on group size leads us to two additional conclusions: (1) groups with an odd number of members tend to be preferable to those with an even number; and (2) groups made up of five or seven members do a pretty good job of exercising the best elements of both small and large groups.[31] Having an odd number of members eliminates the possibility of ties when votes are taken. And groups made up of five or seven members are large enough to form a majority and allow for diverse input, yet small enough to avoid the negative outcomes often associated with large groups, such as domination by a few members, development of subgroups, inhibited participation by some members, and excessive time taken to reach a decision.

Composition

Most group activities require a variety of skills and knowledge. Given this requirement, it would be reasonable to conclude that heterogeneous groups—those composed of dissimilar individuals—would be more likely to have diverse abilities and information and should be more effective. Research studies substantiate this conclusion.[32]

Social Loafing May Be a Culturally-Bound Phenomenon

Is the social-loafing phenomenon universal? Preliminary evidence suggests not.[33] Let's look at why the social-loafing effect is probably consistent with a highly individualistic society like the United States and not collectivist societies like Japan or the People's Republic of China.

An individualistic culture is dominated by self-interest. Social loafing is likely to occur in such cultures because it will maximize an individual's personal gain. But social loafing shouldn't appear in collective societies since individuals in such cultures are motivated by in-group goals rather than self-interest. Work group members in countries like Japan will work to attain their group's collective goals regardless of the identifiability of their inputs. That is, they view their actions as a component essential to the group's goal attainment.

As noted, the preliminary evidence confirms this logic. A comparison of managerial trainees from the United States and the People's Republic of China found that the social-loafing effect surfaced among the Americans but not among the Chinese. The Chinese didn't demonstrate any social-loafing effect and, in fact, appeared to actually perform better in a group than when working alone.

What this research suggests is that social loafing does not appear in all cultural settings. Predominantly studied by American researchers, it seems to be most applicable to such highly individualistic countries as the United States. As a result, the implications for OB of this effect on work groups need to be qualified to reflect cultural differences. In highly collectivistic societies, managers should feel comfortable in using groups even if individual efforts cannot be readily identified.

When a group is heterogeneous in terms of personalities, opinions, abilities, skills, and perspectives, there is an increased probability that the group will possess the needed characteristics to complete its tasks effectively.[34] The group may be more conflict-laden and less expedient as diverse positions are introduced and assimilated, but the evidence generally supports the conclusion that heterogeneous groups perform more effectively than do those that are homogeneous.

An offshoot of the composition issue has recently received a great deal of attention by group researchers. This is the degree to which members of a group share a common demographic attribute, such as age, sex, race, educational level, or length of service in the organization, and the impact of this attribute on turnover. We'll call this variable **group demography.**

We discussed individual demographic factors in Chapter 4. Here we consider the same type of factors, but in a group context. That is, it is not whether a person is male or female or has been employed with the organization a year rather than ten years that concerns us now, but rather the individual's attribute in relationship to the attributes of others with whom he or she works. Let's work through the logic of group demography, review the evidence, and then consider the implications.

Groups and organizations are composed of **cohorts,** which we define as individuals who hold a common attribute. For instance, everyone born in 1960 is of the same age. This means they also have shared common experi-

Group Demography The degree to which members of a group share a common demographic attribute, such as age, sex, race, educational level, or length of service in the organization, and the impact of this attribute on turnover.

Cohort Individuals who, as part of a group, hold a common attribute.

ences. People born in 1960 have experienced the women's movement, but not the Korean conflict. People born in 1945 shared the Vietnam War, but not the Great Depression. Women in organizations today who were born before 1945 matured prior to the women's movement and have had substantially different experiences from women born after 1960. Group demography, therefore, suggests that such attributes as age or the date that someone joins a specific work group or organization should help us to predict turnover. Essentially, the logic goes like this: Turnover will be greater among those with dissimilar experiences because communication is more difficult. Conflict and power struggles are more likely, and more severe when they occur. The increased conflict makes group membership less attractive, so employees are more likely to quit. Similarly, the losers in a power struggle are more apt to leave voluntarily or be forced out.

Several studies have sought to test this thesis, and the evidence is quite encouraging.[35] For example, in departments or separate work groups where a large portion of members entered at the same time, there is considerably more turnover among those outside this cohort. Also, where there are large gaps between cohorts, turnover is higher. People who enter a group or an organization together, or at approximately the same time, are more likely to associate with one another, have a similar perspective on the group or organization, and thus be more likely to stay. On the other hand, discontinuities or bulges in the group's date-of-entry distribution is likely to result in a higher turnover rate within that group.

The implication of this line of inquiry is that the composition of a group may be an important predictor of turnover. Differences per se may not predict turnover. But large differences within a single group will lead to turnover. If everyone is moderately dissimilar from everyone else in a group, the feelings of being an outsider are reduced. So, it's the degree of dispersion on an attribute, rather than the level, that matters most. We can speculate that variance within a group in respect to attributes other than date of entry, such as social background, sex differences, and levels of education,

The research on group demography indicates that group members who are different from the majority—because of age, sex, race, educational level, or length of service in the organization—are more likely to quit. Abe Rezny/The Image Works

might similarly create discontinuities or bulges in the distribution that will encourage some members to leave. To extend this idea further, the fact that a group member is a female may, in itself, mean little in predicting turnover. In fact, if the work group is made up of nine women and one man, we'd be more likely to predict that the lone male would leave. In the executive ranks of organizations, however, where females are in the minority, we would predict that this minority status would increase the likelihood that female managers would quit.

GROUP PROCESSES

The next component of our group behavior model considers the processes that go on within a work group—the communication patterns used by members for information exchanges, group decision processes, leader behavior, power dynamics, conflict interactions, and the like. Chapters 10 through 13 elaborate on many of these processes.

Why are processes important to understanding work group behavior? One way to answer this question is to return to the topic of social loafing. We found that one-plus-one-plus-one doesn't necessarily add up to three. In group tasks where each member's contribution is not clearly visible, there is a tendency for individuals to decrease their effort. Social loafing, in other words, illustrates a process loss as a result of using groups. But group processes can also produce positive results. That is, groups can create outputs greater than the sum of their inputs. Figure 9–5 illustrates how group processes can impact on a group's actual effectiveness.

Synergy is a term used in biology that refers to an action of two or more substances that results in an effect that is different from the individual summation of the substances. We can use the concept to better understand group processes.

Social loafing, for instance, represents negative synergy. The whole is *less* than the sum of the parts. On the other hand, research teams are often used in research laboratories because they can draw on the diverse skills of various individuals to produce more meaningful research as a group than could be generated by all of the researchers working independently. That is, they produce positive synergy. Their process gains exceed their process losses.

Synergy An action of two or more substances that results in an effect that is different from the individual summation of the substances.

GROUP TASKS

Imagine, for a moment, that there are two groups at a major oil company. The job of the first is to consider possible location sites for a new refinery. The decision is going to affect people in many areas of the company—production, engineering, marketing, distribution, personnel, purchasing, real estate development, and the like—so key people from each of these areas will need to provide input into the decision. The job of the second group is to coordinate the building of the refinery after the site has been selected, the design finalized, and the financial arrangements completed. Research on group

FIGURE 9–5   Effects of Group Processes

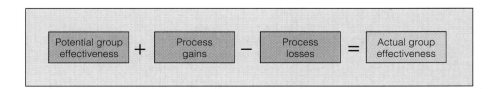

effectiveness tells us that management would be well advised to use a larger group for the first task than for the second.[36] The reason is that large groups facilitate pooling of information. The addition of a diverse perspective to a problem-solving committee typically results in a process gain. But when a group's task is coordinating and implementing a decision, the process loss created by each additional member's presence is likely to be greater than the process gain he or she makes. So the size–performance relationship is moderated by the group's task requirements.

The preceding conclusions can be extended: The impact of group processes on the group's performance and member satisfaction is also moderated by the tasks that the group is doing. The evidence indicates that the complexity and interdependence of tasks influence the group's effectiveness.[37]

Tasks can be generalized as either simple or complex. Complex tasks are ones that tend to be novel or nonroutine. Simple ones are routine and standardized. We would hypothesize that the more complex the task, the more the group will benefit from discussion among members on alternative work methods. If the task is simple, group members don't need to discuss such alternatives. They can rely on standardized operating procedures for doing the job. Similarly, if there is a high degree of interdependence among the tasks that group members must perform, they'll need to interact more. Effective communication and minimal levels of conflict, therefore, should be more relevant to group performance when tasks are interdependent.

These conclusions are consistent with what we know about information-processing capacity and uncertainty.[38] Tasks that have higher uncertainty—those that are complex and interdependent—require more information processing. This, in turn, puts more importance on group processes. So just because a group is characterized by poor communication, weak leadership, high levels of conflict, and the like, it doesn't necessarily mean that it will be low-performing. If the group's tasks are simple and require little interdependence among members, the group still may be effective.

SHOULD MANAGEMENT SEEK COHESIVE WORK GROUPS?

Cohesiveness Degree to which group members are attracted to each other and are motivated to stay in the group.

It is often implied that effective work groups are cohesive. In this section, we want to determine whether **cohesiveness,** as a group characteristic, is desirable. More specifically, should management actively seek to create work groups that are highly cohesive?

Intuitively, it would appear that groups in which there is a lot of internal disagreement and a lack of cooperative spirit would be relatively less effective at completing their tasks than would groups in which individuals generally agree and cooperate and where members like each other. Research to test this intuition has focused on the concept of group cohesiveness, defined as the degree to which members are attracted to one another and are motivated to stay in the group.[39] In the following pages, we'll review the factors that have been found to influence group cohesiveness and then look at the effect of cohesiveness on group productivity.[40]

Determinants of Cohesiveness

What factors determine whether group members will be attracted to one another? Cohesiveness can be affected by such factors as time spent together, the severity of initiation, group size, the gender make-up of the group, external threats, and previous successes.

TIME SPENT TOGETHER If you rarely get an opportunity to see or interact with other people, you're unlikely to be attracted to them. The amount of time that people spend together, therefore, influences cohesiveness. As people spend more time together, they become more friendly. They naturally begin to talk, respond, gesture, and engage in other interactions. These interactions typically lead to the discovery of common interests and increased attraction.[41]

The opportunity for group members to spend time together is dependent on their physical proximity. We would expect more close relationships among members who are located close to one another rather than far apart. People who live on the same block, ride in the same car pool, or share a common office are more likely to become a cohesive group because the physical distance between them is minimal. For instance, among clerical workers in one organization it was found that the distance between their desks was the single most important determinant of the rate of interaction between any two of the clerks.[42]

SEVERITY OF INITIATION The more difficult it is to get into a group, the more cohesive that group becomes. The hazing through which fraternities typically put their pledges is meant to screen out those who don't want to "pay the price" and to intensify the desire of those who do to become fraternity actives. But group initiation needn't be as blatant as hazing. The competition to be accepted into a good medical school results in first-year medical school classes that are highly cohesive. The common initiation rites—applications, test taking, interviews, and the long wait for a final decision—all contribute to creating this cohesiveness.

GROUP SIZE If group cohesiveness tends to increase with the time members are able to spend together, it seems logical that cohesiveness should decrease as group size increases, since it becomes more difficult for a member to interact with all the other members. This is generally what the research indicates.[43] As a group's size expands, interaction with all members becomes more difficult, as does the ability to maintain a common goal. Not surprisingly, too, as the group's size increases, the likelihood of cliques forming also increases. The creation of groups within groups tends to decrease overall cohesiveness.

GENDER OF MEMBERS A consistent finding in recent studies is that women report greater cohesion than men.[44] For example, in one study, all-female and mixed-sex six-person personal growth groups rated themselves higher on cohesion than did members of all-male groups.[45] In another study, female intercollegiate basketball players reported higher group cohesion than their male counterparts.[46] Just why this occurs is not evident. A reasonable hypothesis, however, is that women are less competitive and/or more cooperative with people they see as friends, colleagues, or teammates than men are, and this results in greater group bonding.

EXTERNAL THREATS Most of the research supports the proposition that a group's cohesiveness will increase if the group comes under attack from external sources.[47] Management threats frequently bring together an otherwise disarrayed union. Efforts by management to redesign unilaterally even one or two jobs or to discipline one or two employees occasionally grab local headlines because the entire work force walks out in support of the abused few. These examples illustrate the kind of cooperative phenomenon that can develop within a group when it is attacked from outside.

While a group generally moves toward greater cohesiveness when threatened by external agents, this does not occur under all conditions. If group members perceive that their group may not meet an attack well, then the group becomes less important as a source of security, and cohesiveness will not necessarily increase. Additionally, if members believe the attack is directed at the group merely because of its existence and that it will cease if the group is abandoned or broken up, there is likely to be a decrease in cohesiveness.[48]

PREVIOUS SUCCESSES   If a group has a history of successes, it builds an esprit de corps that attracts and unites members. Successful firms find it easier to attract and hire new employees than unsuccessful ones. The same holds true for successful research teams, well-known and prestigious universities, and winning athletic teams. In the 1950s and 1960s, General Motors was the premier manufacturing company in the world—and it never had trouble attracting the best engineering and business school graduates. Today, the recent successes of Microsoft make it easy for that company to recruit "the best and the brightest." If you harbor ambitions of attending a top-quality graduate school of business, you should recognize that the success of these schools attracts large numbers of candidates—many have twenty or more applicants for every vacancy.

Effects of Cohesiveness on Group Productivity

The previous section indicates that, generally speaking, group cohesiveness is increased when members spend time together and undergo a severe initiation, when the group size is small and predominantly female, when external threats exist, and when the group has a history of previous successes. But is increased cohesiveness always desirable from the point of view of management? That is, is it related to increased productivity?

Research has generally shown that highly cohesive groups are more effective than those with less cohesiveness,[49] but the relationship is more complex than merely allowing us to say high cohesiveness is good. First, high cohesiveness is both a cause and an outcome of high productivity. Second, the relationship is moderated by performance-related norms.

Cohesiveness influences productivity and productivity influences cohesiveness. Camaraderie reduces tension and provides a supportive environment for the successful attainment of group goals. But as already noted, the successful attainment of group goals, and the members' feelings of having been a part of a successful unit, can serve to enhance the commitment of members. Basketball coaches, for example, are famous for their devotion to teamwork. They believe that if the team is going to win games, its members have to learn to play together. Popular coaching phrases include "There are no individuals on this team" and "We win together, or we lose together." The other side of this view is that winning reinforces camaraderie and leads to increased cohesiveness; that is, successful performance leads to increased intermember attractiveness and sharing.

More important has been the recognition that the relationship of cohesiveness and productivity depends on the performance-related norms established by the group.[50] The more cohesive the group, the more its members will follow its goals. If performance-related norms are high (for example, high output, quality work, cooperation with individuals outside the group), a cohesive group will be more productive than a less cohesive group. But if cohesiveness is high and performance norms are low, productivity will be low. If cohesiveness is low and performance norms are high, productivity

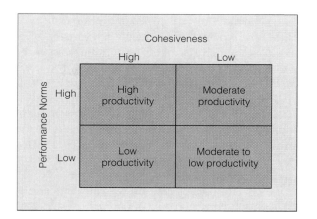

FIGURE 9–6 Relationship Between Group Cohesiveness, Performance Norms, and Productivity

increases, but less than in the high cohesiveness–high norms situation. Where cohesiveness and performance-related norms are both low, productivity will tend to fall into the low-to-moderate range. These conclusions are summarized in Figure 9–6.

IMPLICATIONS FOR PERFORMANCE AND SATISFACTION

We've covered a lot of territory in this chapter. Since we essentially organized our discussion around the group behavior model in Figure 9–3, let's use this model to draw our conclusions regarding performance and satisfaction.

Performance

Any predictions about a group's performance must begin by recognizing that work groups are part of a larger organization and that factors such as the organization's strategy, authority structure, selection procedures, and reward system can provide a favorable or unfavorable climate for the group to operate within. For example, if an organization is characterized by distrust between management and workers, it is more likely that work groups in that organization will develop norms to restrict effort and output than will work groups in an organization where trust is high. So don't look at any group in isolation. Rather, begin by assessing the degree of support external conditions provide the group. It is obviously a lot easier for any work group to be productive when the overall organization of which it is a part is growing and it has both top management's support and abundant resources. Similarly, a group is more likely to be productive when its members have the requisite skills to do the group's tasks and the personality characteristics that facilitate working well together.

A number of structural factors show a relationship to performance. Among the more prominent are role perception, norms, status inequities, the size of the group, its demographic makeup, the group's task, and cohesiveness.

There is a positive relationship between role perception and an employee's performance evaluation.[51] The degree of congruence that exists between an employee and his or her boss in the perception of the employee's job influences the degree to which that employee will be judged as an effective performer by the boss. To the extent that the employee's role perception fulfills the boss's role expectations, the employee will receive a higher performance evaluation.

Norms control group member behavior by establishing standards of right and wrong. If we know the norms of a given group, it can help us to explain the behaviors of its members. Where norms support high output, we can expect individual performance to be markedly higher than where group norms aim to restrict output. Similarly, acceptable standards of absenteeism will be dictated by the group norms.

Status inequities create frustration and can adversely influence productivity and the willingness to remain with an organization. Among those individuals who are equity sensitive, incongruence is likely to lead to reduced motivation and an increased search for ways to bring about fairness (i.e., taking another job).

The impact of size on a group's performance depends upon the type of task in which the group is engaged. Larger groups are more effective at fact-finding activities. Smaller groups are more effective at action-taking tasks. Our knowledge of social loafing suggests that if management uses larger groups, efforts should be made to provide measures of individual performance within the group.

We found the group's demographic composition to be a key determinant of individual turnover. Specifically, the evidence indicates that group members who share a common age or date of entry into the work group are less prone to resign.

The primary contingency variable moderating the relationship between group processes and performance is the group's task. The more complex and interdependent the tasks, the more that inefficient processes will lead to reduced group performance.

Finally, we found that cohesiveness can play an important function in influencing a group's level of productivity. Whether or not it does depends on the group's performance-related norms.

Satisfaction

As with the role perception–performance relationship, high congruence between a boss and employee, as to the perception of the employee's job, shows a significant association with high employee satisfaction.[52] Similarly, role conflict is associated with job-induced tension and job dissatisfaction.[53]

Most people prefer to communicate with others at their own status level or a higher one rather than with those below them.[54] As a result, we should expect satisfaction to be greater among employees whose job minimizes interaction with individuals who are lower in status than themselves.

The group size–satisfaction relationship is what one would intuitively expect: Larger groups are associated with lower satisfaction.[55] As size increases, opportunities for participation and social interaction decrease, as does the ability of members to identify with the group's accomplishments. At the same time, having more members also prompts dissension, conflict, and the formation of subgroups, which all act to make the group a less pleasant entity to be a part of.

Finally, we can make a set of predictions regarding both performance and satisfaction based on the impact of task as a moderating variable and research on the job characteristics model discussed in Chapter 7. A group can be expected to work especially hard on its tasks and members of that group are likely to be satisfied with their work when: (1) the group task requires members to use a variety of relatively high-level skills; (2) the group task is a whole and meaningful piece of work, with a visible outcome; (3) the outcomes of the group's work on the task have significant consequences for other people either inside or outside the organization; (4) the task provides group members with substantial autonomy for deciding about how they do the work; and (5) work on the task generates regular, trustworthy feedback about how well the group is performing.[56]

FOR DISCUSSION

1. Compare and contrast command, task, interest, and friendship groups.
2. What might motivate you to join a group?
3. How could you use the five-stage group development model to better understand group behavior?
4. How could you use the punctuated-equilibrium model to better understand group behavior?
5. What is the relationship between a work group and the organization of which it is a part?
6. Identify five roles you play. What behaviors do they require? Are any of these roles in conflict? If so, in what way? How do you resolve these conflicts?
7. What is the relationship between the psychological contract and role expectations?
8. How do norms develop?
9. What are the implications of Whyte's restaurant study for organizational behavior?
10. How can a group's demography help you to predict turnover?
11. What factors influence the degree to which group members will be attracted to each other?
12. "High cohesiveness in a group leads to higher group productivity." Do you agree or disagree? Explain.

P O I N T

Designing Jobs Around Groups

It's time to take small groups seriously; that is, to use groups, rather than individuals, as the basic building blocks for an organization. I propose that we can design organizations from scratch around small groups rather than the way we have always done it—around individuals.

Why would management want to do such a thing? At least seven reasons can be identified. First, small groups seem to be good for people. They can satisfy important membership needs. They can provide a moderately wide range of activities for individual members. They can provide support in times of stress and crisis. They are settings in which people can learn not only cognitively but empirically to be reasonably trusting and helpful to one another. Second, groups seem to be good problem-finding tools. They seem to be useful in promoting innovation and creativity. Third, in a wide variety of decision situations, they make better decisions than individuals do. Fourth, they are great tools for implementation. They gain commitment from their members so that group decisions are likely to be willingly carried out. Fifth, they can control and discipline individual members in ways that are often extremely difficult through impersonal quasilegal disciplinary systems. Sixth, as organizations grow large, small groups appear to be useful mechanisms for fending off many of the negative effects of large size. They help to prevent communication lines from growing too long, and

the hierarchy from growing too steep, and the individual from getting lost in the crowd. There is also a seventh, but altogether different, kind of argument for taking groups seriously. Groups are natural phenomena, and facts of organizational life. They can be created, but their spontaneous development cannot be prevented.

Operationally, how would an organization that was designed around groups function? One answer to this question is merely to take the things that organizations do with individuals and apply them to groups. The idea would be to raise the level from the atom to the molecule and *select* groups rather than individuals, *train* groups rather than individuals, *pay* groups rather than individuals, *promote* groups rather than individuals, *fire* groups rather than individuals, and so on down the list of activities that organizations have traditionally carried on in order to use human beings in their organizations.

In the past, the human group has been primarily used for patching and mending organizations that were built around the individual. The time is rapidly approaching, and it may already be here, for management to begin redesigning organizations around groups.

Based on H. J. Leavitt, "Suppose We Took Groups Seriously," in E. L. Cass and F. G. Zimmer (eds.), *Man and Work in Society* (New York: Van Nostrand Reinhold, 1975), pp. 67–77.

Jobs Should Be Designed Around Individuals

The argument that organizations can and should be designed around groups might hold in a socialistic society, but not in the United States. The following response directly relates to the United States and American workers, although it is probably generalizable to other economically advanced capitalistic countries. In fact, given the recent political changes in Eastern Europe and the increasing acceptance of profit-motivated businesses, the case for the individually oriented organization may be applicable throughout the world.

America was built on the ethic of the individual. This ethic has been pounded into Americans from birth. The result is that it is deeply embedded in the psyche of every American. They strongly value individual achievement. They praise competition. Even in team sports, they want to identify individuals for recognition. Sure, they enjoy group interaction. They like being part of a team, especially a winning team. But it is one thing to be a member of a work group while maintaining a strong individual identity and another to sublimate one's identity to that of the group. The latter is inconsistent with the values of American life.

The American worker likes a clear link between his or her individual effort and a visible outcome. It is not happenstance that the United States, as a nation, has a considerably larger proportion of high achievers than exists in socialistic countries. America breeds achievers, and achievers seek personal responsibility. They would be frustrated in job situations where their contribution is commingled and homogenized with the contributions of others.

Americans want to be hired based on their individual talents. They want to be evaluated on their individual efforts. They also want to be rewarded with pay raises and promotions based on their individual performances. Americans believe in an authority and status hierarchy. They accept a system where there are bosses and subordinates. They are not likely to accept a group's decision on such issues as their job assignments and wage increases.

One of the more interesting illustrations of America's commitment to the individualistic ethic is research that has assessed the public's views on the American tax structure. We'd expect the rich to favor low tax rates on individuals with high incomes—$80,000 a year or more. But studies consistently find that Americans below the government's defined "poverty level" also strongly favor lower tax rates for high-income earners. A reasonable interpretation of these findings is that there is a very strong belief, held across the full range of economic levels, that anyone can make it in America. And when they make it, they don't want to be saddled with a heavy tax burden! Isn't this consistent with the stereotype of the individualistic American, motivated by his or her self-interest? Yes! Is this a worker who would be satisfied, and reach his or her full productive capacity, in a group-centered organization? Not likely!

The Paper Tower Exercise

STEP 1 Organize the class into groups of five to eight people.

STEP 2 Each group will receive one twelve-inch stack of newspapers and one roll of masking tape from your instructor. The groups have twenty minutes to plan a paper tower that will be judged on the basis of three criteria: height, stability, and beauty. No physical work is allowed during this planning period.

STEP 3 Each group has thirty minutes for the actual construction of the paper tower.

STEP 4 Each tower will be identified by a number assigned by your instructor. Each student is to individually examine all the paper towers. Your group is then to come to a consensus as to which tower is the winner. A spokesperson from your group should report its decision and the criteria the group used in reaching it.

STEP 5 In your small groups, discuss the following questions:

   a. What percent of the plan did each member of your group contribute?

   b. To what degree did your group follow the five-step group development model?

   c. Did a single leader emerge from the group? If so, who? Why do you think this person became the leader?

   d. In groups, someone typically assumes a task-oriented role, concerned with "getting the job done"; while another takes a human relations role, making encouraging, friendly, and supportive comments. Did these roles emerge in your group? Did these roles aid or hinder the group's effectiveness?

   e. How did the group generally respond to the ideas that were expressed?

   f. List specific behaviors exhibited during the planning and building sessions that you felt were helpful to the group.

   g. List specific behaviors exhibited during the planning and building sessions that you felt were dysfunctional to the group.

STEP 6 Discuss the following questions with the entire class:

   a. How did the groups' behavior differ?

   b. What characterized the most effective groups?

   c. How could the behavior of the less effective groups be improved?

Source: Adapted from P. L. Hunsaker and J. S. Hunsaker, "The Paper Tower Exercise: Experiencing Leadership and Group Dynamics," unpublished manuscript. With permission of the authors.

The Term Paper Assessment Exercise

Most of us have had experience in writing a term paper. Some of these have been individual assignments. That is, the instructor expected each student to hand in a separate paper and your grade was determined solely by your own effort and contribution. But sometimes instructors assign group term papers, where students must work together on the project and share in the grade.

Think back to your most recent experience in doing a group term paper. Now envision yourself at about the halfway point in the completion of that group assignment. Using your mind-set at this halfway point, answer the following twenty questions. This questionnaire measures your feelings about that work group.*

	Agree							Disagree	
1. I want to remain a member of this group.	1	2	3	4	5	6	7	8	9
2. I like my group.	1	2	3	4	5	6	7	8	9
3. I look forward to coming to the group.	1	2	3	4	5	6	7	8	9
4. I don't care what happens in this group.	1	2	3	4	5	6	7	8	9
5. I feel involved in what is happening in my group.	1	2	3	4	5	6	7	8	9
6. If I could drop out of the group now, I would.	1	2	3	4	5	6	7	8	9
7. I dread coming to this group.	1	2	3	4	5	6	7	8	9
8. I wish it were possible for the group to end now.	1	2	3	4	5	6	7	8	9
9. I am dissatisfied with the group.	1	2	3	4	5	6	7	8	9
10. If it were possible to move to another group at this time, I would.	1	2	3	4	5	6	7	8	9
11. I feel included in the group.	1	2	3	4	5	6	7	8	9
12. In spite of individual differences, a feeling of unity exists in my group.	1	2	3	4	5	6	7	8	9
13. Compared to other groups I know of, I feel my group is better than most.	1	2	3	4	5	6	7	8	9
14. I do not feel a part of the group's activities.	1	2	3	4	5	6	7	8	9
15. I feel it would make a difference to the group if I were not here.	1	2	3	4	5	6	7	8	9
16. If I were told my group would not meet today, I would feel bad.	1	2	3	4	5	6	7	8	9
17. I feel distant from the group.	1	2	3	4	5	6	7	8	9
18. It makes a difference to me how this group turns out.	1	2	3	4	5	6	7	8	9
19. I feel my absence would not matter to the group.	1	2	3	4	5	6	7	8	9
20. I would not feel bad if I had to miss a meeting of this group.	1	2	3	4	5	6	7	8	9

*Reproduced from N. J. Evans and P. A. Jarvis, "The Group Attitude Scale: A Measure of Attraction to Group," *Small Group Behavior,* May 1986, pp. 203–16. With permission.

After completing the questionnaire, add your scores for items 4, 6, 7, 8, 9, 10, 14, 17, 19, and 20. Obtain a corrected score by subtracting the score for each of the remaining questions from 10. For example, if you marked 3 for item 1, you would obtain a corrected score of 7 (10–3). Add the corrected scores together with the total obtained on the ten items scored directly.

Now form groups of three to five members to:

1. Compare your scores. Were your group term paper experiences generally positive or negative?

2. Assess the degree to which you felt any different about your group at the end of the project than you felt at the halfway point. If your feelings changed, explain why.

3. Discuss the degree to which your feelings about the group may have influenced your group's grade.

4. Discuss to what degree you think the grade your team got on the paper influenced your subsequent feelings about the group.

CASE INCIDENT 9

Games People Play in the Shipping Department

The Science Fiction Book Club (SFBC) sells a large list of science fiction books, at discount prices, entirely by mail order. In 1992, the club shipped over 370,000 books and generated revenues of $6.4 million. Anyone familiar with the mail-order business realizes that it offers extremely high profit potential because, under careful management, inventory costs and overhead can be kept quite low. The biggest problems in mail-order businesses are filling orders, shipping the merchandise, and billing the customers. At SFBC, the Packing and Shipping (P&S) Department employs eight full-time people:

Ray, forty-four years old, has worked in P&S for seven years.

Al, forty-nine years old, has worked in P&S for nine years.

R. J., fifty-three years old, has worked in P&S for sixteen years. He had been head of the department for two years back in the late 1970s, but stepped down voluntarily because of continuing stomach problems that doctors attributed to supervisory pressures.

Pearl, fifty-nine years old, was the original employee hired by the founder. She has been at SFBC for twenty-five years and in P&S for twenty-one years.

Margaret, thirty-one years old, is the newest member of the department. She has been employed less than a year.

Steve, twenty-seven years old, has worked in P&S for three years. He goes to college at nights and makes no effort to hide that he plans on leaving P&S and probably SFBC when he gets his degree next year.

George, forty-six years old, is currently head of P&S. He has been with SFBC for ten years, and in P&S for six.

Gary, twenty-five years old, has worked in P&S for two years.

The jobs in a shipping department are uniformly dull and repetitive. Each person is responsible for wrapping, addressing, and making the bills out on anywhere from one hundred to two hundred books a day. Part of George's responsibilities are to make allocations to each worker and to ensure that no significant backlogs occur. However, George spends less than ten percent of his time in supervisory activities. The rest of the time he wraps, addresses, and makes out bills just like everyone else.

Apparently to deal with the repetitiveness of their jobs, the department members have created a number of games that they play among themselves. They seem almost childish, but it is obvious that the games mean something to these people. Importantly, each is played regularly. Some of the ones that will be described are played at least once a day. All are played a minimum of twice a week.

"The Stamp Machine Is Broken" is a game that belongs to Al. At least once a day, Al goes over to the postage meter in the office and unplugs it. He then proceeds loudly to attempt to make a stamp for a package. "The stamp machine is broken again," he yells. Either Ray or Gary, or both, will come over and spend thirty seconds or so trying to "fix" it, then "discover" that it's unplugged. The one who finds it unplugged then says "Al, you're a mechanical spastic" and others in the office join and laugh.

Gary is the initiator of the game "Steve, There's a Call for You." Usually played in the late afternoon, an hour or so before everyone goes home, Gary will pick up the phone and pretend that there is someone on the line. "Hey, Steve, it's for you," he'll yell out. "It's Mr. Big [the president of SFBC]. Says he wants you to come over to his office right away. You're going to be the new vice president!" The game is an obvious sarcastic jab at Steve's going to college and his frequent comments about someday being a big executive.

R. J., though fifty-three years old, has never married and lives with his mother. The main interests in his life are telling stories, showing pictures of last year's vacation, and planning for this year's trip. Without exception, everyone finds R. J.'s vacation talk boring. But that doesn't stop Pearl or George from "setting him up" several times a week. "Hey R. J., can we see those pictures you took last year in Oregon again?" That question always gets R. J. to drop whatever he's doing and pull seventy-five to one hundred pictures from his top drawer. "Hey, R. J., what are you planning to do on your vacation this year?" always gets R. J.'s eyes shining and invariably leads to the unfolding of maps he also keeps in his top drawer.

George's favorite game is "What's It Like to Be Rich?" which he plays with Pearl. Pearl's husband had been a successful banker and had died a half-dozen years earlier. He left her very well off financially. Pearl enjoys everyone knowing that she doesn't have to work, has a large lovely home, buys a new car every year, and includes some of the city's more prominent business people and politicians among her friends. George will mention the name of some big shot in town, and Pearl never fails to take the bait. She proceeds to tell how he is a close friend of hers. George might also bring up money in some context in order to allow Pearl to complain about high taxes, the difficulty in finding good housekeepers, the high cost of traveling to Europe, or some other concern of the affluent.

Questions

1. Analyze the group's interactions using the group behavior model.
2. How do these games affect the department's performance?
3. Are these games functional? Dysfunctional? Explain.

FOR FURTHER READING

ASHFORTH, B. E., and F. MAEL, "Social Identity Theory and the Organization," *Academy of Management Review*, January 1989, pp. 20–39. People tend to classify themselves and others into various social categories. This article reviews the implications of this finding for organizational socialization, role conflict, and intergroup relations.

CHANCE, P., "Great Experiments in Team Chemistry," *Across the Board,*" May 1989, pp. 18–25. Describes successful efforts at creating team-based organizations and labels such organizations as one of the grand business experiments of our time.

HACKMAN, J. R. (ed.), *Groups That Work (and Those That Don't)* (San Francisco: Jossey-Bass, 1990). Describes conditions necessary for effective teamwork.

LARSON, C. E., and F. M. LAFASTO, *Teamwork: What Must Go Right/What Can Go Wrong* (Newbury Park, CA: Sage Publications, 1989). A practical guide on how to make teams work more effectively.

SUNDSTROM, E., K. P. DE MEUSE, and D. FUTRELL, "Work Teams: Applications and Effectiveness," *American Psychologist*, February 1990, pp. 120–33. Reviews factors that influence the effectiveness of work teams.

WORCHEL, S., W. WOOD, and J. A. SIMPSON (eds.), *Group Process and Productivity* (Newbury Park, CA: Sage Publications, 1991). Reviews current research in the area of productivity and functioning in small groups.

NOTES

[1]Based on B. Acohido, "Boeing Workforce Tries New Direction," *Dallas Morning News*, May 5, 1991, p. H8.

[2]L. R. Sayles, "Work Group Behavior and the Larger Organization," in C. Arensburg et al. (eds.), *Research in Industrial Relations* (New York: Harper & Row, 1957), pp. 131–45.

[3]B. W. Tuckman, "Developmental Sequences in Small Groups," *Psychological Bulletin,* June 1965, pp. 384–99; B. W. Tuckman and M. C. Jensen, "Stages of Small-Group Development Revisited," *Group and Organizational Studies*, December 1977, pp. 419–27; and M. F. Maples, "Group Development: Extending Tuckman's Theory," *Journal for Specialists in Group Work,* Fall 1988, pp. 17–23.

[4]C. J. G. Gersick, "Time and Transition in Work Teams: Toward a New Model of Group Development," *Academy of Management Journal*, March 1988, pp. 9–41; and C. J. G. Gersick, "Marking Time: Predictable Transitions in Task Groups," *Academy of Management Journal*, June 1989, pp. 274–309.

[5]This model is substantially based on the work of P. S. Goodman, E. Ravlin, and M. Schminke, "Understanding Groups in Organizations," in L. L. Cummings and B. M. Staw (eds.), *Research in Organizational Behavior,* Vol. 9 (Greenwich, CT: JAI Press, 1987), pp. 124–28; J. R. Hackman, "The Design of Work Teams," in J. W. Lorsch (ed.), *Handbook of Organizational Behavior* (Englewood Cliffs, NJ: Prentice Hall, 1987), pp. 315–42; and G. R. Bushe and A. L. Johnson, "Contextual and Internal Variables Affecting Task Group Outcomes in Organizations," *Group and Organization Studies*, December 1989, pp. 462–82.

[6]F. Friedlander, "The Ecology of Work Groups," in J. W. Lorsch (ed.) *Handbook of Organizational Behavior,* pp. 301–14; and E. Sundstrom and I. Altman, "Physical Environments and Work-Group Effectiveness," in L. L. Cummings and B. M. Staw (eds.), *Research in Organizational Behavior,* Vol. 11 (Greenwich, CT: JAI Press, 1989), pp. 175–209.

[7]See, for example, J. Krantz, "Group Processes Under Conditions of Organizational Decline," *The Journal of Applied Behavioral Science,* Vol. 21, No. 1, 1985, pp. 1–17.

[8]Hackman, "The Design of Work Teams," pp. 325–26.

[9]See, for instance, G. R. Oldham and Y. Fried, "Employee Reactions to Workspace Characteristics," *Journal of Applied Psychology,* February 1987, pp. 75–80.

[10]A. D. Szilagyi, Jr., and M. J. Wallace, Jr., *Organizational Behavior and Performance,* 4th ed. (Glenview, IL: Scott, Foresman, 1987), p. 223.

[11]Ibid.

[12]M. E. Shaw, *Contemporary Topics in Social Psychology* (Morristown, NJ: General Learning Press, 1976), pp. 350–51.

[13]S. Lieberman, "The Effects of Changes in Roles on the Attitudes of Role Occupants," *Human Relations,* November 1956, pp. 385–402.

[14]H. G. Baker, "The Unwritten Contract: Job Perceptions," *Personnel Journal,* July 1985, pp. 37–41.

[15]E. H. Schein, *Organizational Psychology,* 3rd ed. (Englewood Cliffs, NJ: Prentice Hall, 1980), p. 24.

[16]S. N. Brenner and E. A. Molander, "Is the Ethics of Business Changing?" *Harvard Business Review,* January-February 1977, pp. 57–71.

[17]P. G. Zimbardo, C. Haney, W. C. Banks, and D. Jaffe, "The Mind Is a Formidable Jailer: A Pirandellian Prison," *The New York Times,* April 8, 1973, pp. 38–60.

[18]A. Harlan, J. Kerr, and S. Kerr, "Preference for Motivator and Hygiene Factors in a Hypothetical Interview Situation: Further Findings and Some Implications for the Employment Interview," *Personnel Psychology,* Winter 1977, pp. 557–66.

[19]Adapted from Goodman, Ravlin, and Schminke, "Understanding Groups in Organizations," p. 159.

[20]D. C. Feldman, "The Development and Enforcement of Group Norms," *Academy of Management Journal,* January 1984, pp. 47–53; and K. L. Bettenhausen and J. K. Murnighan, "The Development of an Intragroup Norm and the Effects of Interpersonal and Structural Challenges," *Administrative Science Quarterly,* March 1991, pp. 20–35.

[21]C. A. Kiesler and S. B. Kiesler, *Conformity* (Reading, MA: Addison-Wesley, 1969).

[22]Ibid, p. 27.

[23]S. E. Asch, "Effects of Group Pressure upon the Modification and Distortion of Judgments," in H. Guetzkow (ed.), *Groups, Leadership and Men* (Pittsburgh: Carnegie Press, 1951), pp. 177–90.

[24]R. Keyes, *Is There Life After High School?* (New York: Warner Books, 1976).

[25]W. F. Whyte, "The Social Structure of the Restaurant," *American Journal of Sociology,* January 1954, pp. 302–08.

[26]J. Greenberg, "Equity and Workplace Status: A Field Experiment," *Journal of Applied Psychology,* November 1988, pp. 606–13.

[27]E. J. Thomas and C. F. Fink, "Effects of Group Size," *Psychological Bulletin,* July 1963, pp. 371–84; A. P. Hare, *Handbook of Small Group Research* (New York: Free Press, 1976); and M. E. Shaw, *Group Dynamics: The Psychology of Small Group Behavior,* 3rd ed. (New York: McGraw-Hill, 1981).

[28]W. Moede, "Die Richtlinien der Leistungs-Psychologie," *Industrielle Psychotechnik,* Vol. 4 (1927), pp. 193–207. See also D. A. Kravitz and B. Martin, "Ringelmann Rediscovered: The Original Article," *Journal of Personality and Social Psychology,* May 1986, pp. 936–41.

[29]See, for example, G. Jones, "Task Visibility, Free Riding, and Shirking: Explaining the Effect of Structure and Technology on Employee Behavior," *Academy of Management Review,* October 1984, pp. 684–95; and R. Albanese and D. D. Van Fleet, "Rational Behavior in Groups: The Free-Riding Tendency," *Academy of Management Review,* April 1985, pp. 244–55.

[30]S. G. Harkins and K. Szymanski, "Social Loafing and Group Evaluation," *Journal of Personality and Social Psychology,* December 1989, pp. 934–41.

[31]Thomas and Fink, "Effects of Group Size"; Hare, *Handbook;* Shaw, *Group Dynamics;* and P. Yetton and P. Bottger, "The Relationships Among Group Size, Member Ability, Social Decision Schemes, and Performance," *Organizational Behavior and Human Performance,* October 1983, pp. 145–59.

[32]See P. C. Earley, "Social Loafing and Collectivism: A Comparison of the United States and the People's Republic of China," *Administrative Science Quarterly,* December 1989, pp. 565–81.

[33]See, for example, P. S. Goodman, E. C. Ravlin, and L. Argote, "Current Thinking About Groups: Setting the Stage for New Ideas," in P. S. Goodman and Associates, *Designing Effective Work Groups* (San Francisco: Jossey-Bass, 1986), pp. 15–16.

[34]Shaw, *Contemporary Topics,* p. 356.

[35]B. E. McCain, C. A. O'Reilly III, and J. Pfeffer, "The Effects of Departmental Demography on Turnover: The Case of a University," *Academy of Management Journal,* December 1983, pp. 626–41; W. G. Wagner, J. Pfeffer, and C. A. O'Reilly III, "Organizational Demography and Turnover in Top-Management Groups," *Administrative Science Quarterly,* March 1984, pp. 74–92; J. Pfeffer and C. A. O'Reilly III, "Hospital Demography and Turnover Among Nurses," *Industrial Relations,* Spring 1987, pp. 158–73; and C. A. O'Reilly III, D. F. Caldwell, and W. P. Barnett, "Work Group Demography, Social Integration, and Turnover," *Administrative Science Quarterly,* March 1989, pp. 21–37.

[36]V. F. Nieva, E. A. Fleishman, and A. Rieck, "Team Dimensions: Their Identity, Their Measurement, and Their Relationships." Final Technical Report for Contract No. DAHC 19-C-0001. Washington, DC: Advanced Research Resources Organizations, 1978.

[37]See, for example, J. R. Hackman and C. G. Morris, "Group Tasks, Group Interaction Process and Group Performance Effectiveness: A Review and Proposed Integration," in L. Berkowitz (ed.), *Advances in Experimental Social Psychology* (New York: Academic Press, 1975), pp. 45–99.

[38]J. Galbraith, *Organizational Design* (Reading, MA: Addison-Wesley, 1977).

[39]For some of the controversy surrounding the definition of cohesion, see J. Keyton and J. Springston, "Redefining Cohesiveness in Groups," *Small Group Research,* May 1990, pp. 234–54.

[40]See, for example, I. Summers, T. Coffelt, and R. E. Horton, "Work-Group Cohesion," *Psychological Reports,* October 1988, pp. 627–36.

[41]C. Insko and M. Wilson, "Interpersonal Attraction as a Function of Social Interaction," *Journal of Personality and Social Psychology,* December 1977, pp. 903–11.

[42]J. T. Gullahorn, "Distance and Friendship as Factors in the Gross Interaction Matrix," *Sociometry,* February-March 1952, pp. 123–34.

[43]E. J. Thomas and C. F. Fink, "Effects of Group Size," *Psychological Bulletin,* July 1963, pp. 371–84.

[44]Bettenhausen, "Five Years of Groups Research: What We Have Learned and What Needs to Be Addressed," p. 362.

[45]J. R. Taylor and D. S. Strassberg, "The Effects of Sex Composition on Cohesiveness and Interpersonal Learning in Short-Term Personal Growth Groups," *Psychotherapy,* Summer 1986, pp. 267–73.

[46]C. A. Wrisberg and M. V. Draper, "Sex, Sex Role Orientation, and the Cohesion of Intercollegiate Basketball Teams," *Journal of Sports Behavior,* March 1988, pp. 45–54.

[47]A. Stein, "Conflict and Cohesion: A Review of the Literature," *Journal of Conflict Resolution,* March 1976, pp. 143–72.

[48]A. Zander, "The Psychology of Group Processes," in M. R. Rosenzweig and L. W. Porter (eds.), *Annual Review of Psychology,* Vol 30 (Palo Alto, CA: Annual Reviews, 1979), p. 436.

[49]See, for example, L. Berkowitz, "Group Standards, Cohesiveness, and Productivity," *Human Relations,* November 1954, pp. 509–19; and C. N. Greene, "Cohesion and Productivity in Work Groups," *Small Group Behavior,* February 1989, pp. 70–86.

[50]Nieva, Fleishman, and Rieck, "Team Dimensions," p. 17.

[51]T. P. Verney, "Role Perception Congruence, Performance, and Satisfaction," in D. J. Vredenburgh and R. S. Schuler (eds.), *Effective Management: Research and Application,* Proceedings of the 20th Annual Eastern Academy of Management, Pittsburgh, PA, May 1983, pp. 24–27.

[52]Ibid.

[53]M. Van Sell, A. P. Brief, and R. S. Schuler, "Role Conflict and Role Ambiguity: Integration of the Literature and Directions for Future Research," *Human Relations,* January 1981, pp. 43–71; and A. G. Bedeian and A. A. Armenakis, "A Path-Analytic Study of the Consequences of Role Conflict and Ambiguity," *Academy of Management Journal,* June 1981, pp. 417–24.

[54]Shaw, *Group Dynamics.*

[55]B. Mullen, C. Symons, L. Hu, and E. Salas, "Group Size, Leadership Behavior, and Subordinate Satisfaction," *Journal of General Psychology,* April 1989, pp. 155–70.

[56]Hackman, "The Design of Work Teams," p. 324.

COMMUNICATION AND GROUP DECISION MAKING

CHAPTER OUTLINE

Functions of Communication

The Communication Process

Communication Fundamentals

Key Communication Skills

Group Decision Making

Implications for Performance and
    Satisfaction

LEARNING OBJECTIVES

After studying this chapter, you should be able to:

1. Describe the process of communication

2. Contrast the three popular small-group networks

3. Identify factors affecting the use of the grapevine

4. Describe common barriers to effective communication

5. Outline the behaviors related to effective active listening

6. Identify the behaviors associated with providing effective feedback

7. List the advantages and disadvantages of group decision making

8. Contrast the effectiveness of interacting, brainstorming, nominal, Delphi, and electronic meeting groups

Can a few words literally mean the difference between life and death? They did on January 25, 1990. On that date, a communication breakdown between the pilots on Avianca Flight 52 and the air traffic controllers at New York's Kennedy airport resulted in a crash that killed seventy-three people.[1]

At 7:40 P.M. on January 25, Flight 52 was cruising at thirty-seven thousand feet above the southern New Jersey coast. The aircraft had enough fuel to last nearly two hours—a healthy cushion since the plane was less than half an hour from touchdown. Then a series of delays began. First, at 8 P.M., the controllers at Kennedy told Flight 52 that it would have to circle in a holding pattern because of heavy traffic. At 8:45, the Avianca co-pilot advised Kennedy that they were "running low on fuel." The controller at Kennedy acknowledged the message but the plane was not cleared to land until 9:24. In the interim, the Avianca crew relayed no information to Kennedy that an emergency was imminent, yet the cockpit crew spoke worriedly among themselves about their dwindling fuel supplies.

Flight 52's first attempt to land at 9:24 was aborted. The plane had come in too low and poor visibility made a safe landing uncertain. When the Kennedy controllers gave Flight 52's pilot new instructions for a second attempt, the crew again told them they were running low on fuel. But the pilot told the controllers that the newly assigned flight path was "O.K." At 9:32, two of Flight 52's engines lost power. A minute later, the other two cut off. The plane, out of fuel, crashed on Long Island at 9:34 P.M.

When investigators reviewed cockpit tapes and talked with the controllers involved, they learned that a communication breakdown caused this tragedy. A closer look at the events of that evening help to explain why a simple message was neither clearly transmitted nor adequately received.

First, the pilots kept saying they were "running low on fuel." Traffic controllers told investigators that it is fairly common for pilots to use this phrase. In times of delay, controllers assume that everyone has a fuel problem. However, had the pilots uttered the words "fuel emergency," the controllers would have been obligated to direct the jet ahead of all others and clear it to land as soon as possible. As one controller put it, if a pilot "declares an emergency, all rules go out the window and we get the guy to the airport as quickly as possible." Unfortunately, the pilots of Flight 52 never used the word "emergency," so the people at Kennedy never understood the true nature of the pilots' problem.

Second, the vocal tone of the pilots on Flight 52 didn't convey the severity or urgency of the fuel problem to the air traffic controllers. Many of these controllers are trained to pick up subtle tones in a pilot's voice in such situations. While the crew of Flight 52 expressed considerable concern among themselves about the fuel problem, their voice tones in communicating to Kennedy were cool and professional.

Finally, the culture and traditions of pilots and airport authorities may have made the pilot of Flight 52 reluctant to declare an emergency. A pilot's expertise and pride can be at stake in such a situation. Declaration of a formal emergency requires the pilot to complete a wealth of paperwork. Moreover, if a pilot has been found to be negligent in calculating how much fuel was needed for a flight, the Federal Aviation Administration can suspend his license. These negative reinforcers strongly discourage pilots from calling an emergency. ■

*T*he Avianca Flight 52 tragedy demonstrates the importance of good communication to any group's or organization's effectiveness. In fact, research indicates that poor communication is probably the most frequently cited source of interpersonal conflict.[2] Because individuals spend nearly seventy percent of their waking hours communicating—writing, reading, speaking, listening—it seems reasonable to conclude that one of the most inhibiting forces to successful group performance is a lack of effective communication.

No group can exist without communication: the transference of meaning among its members. It is only through transmitting meaning from one person to another that information and ideas can be conveyed. Communication, however, is more than merely imparting meaning. It must also be understood. In a group where one member speaks only German and the others do not know German, the individual speaking German will not be fully understood. Therefore, **communication** must include both the *transference and the understanding of meaning*.

Communication The transference and understanding of meaning.

An idea, no matter how great, is useless until it is transmitted and understood by others. Perfect communication, if there were such a thing, would exist when a thought or an idea was transmitted so that the mental picture perceived by the receiver was exactly the same as that envisioned by the sender. Although elementary in theory, perfect communication is never achieved in practice, for reasons we shall expand upon later.

Before making too many generalizations concerning communication and problems in communicating effectively, we need to review briefly the functions that communication performs and describe the communication process.

FUNCTIONS OF COMMUNICATION

Communication serves four major functions within a group or organization: control, motivation, emotional expression, and information.[3]

Communication acts to *control* member behavior in several ways. Organizations have authority hierarchies and formal guidelines that employees are required to follow. When employees, for instance, are required to first communicate any job-related grievance to their immediate boss, to follow their job description, or to comply with company policies, communication is performing a control function. But informal communication also controls behavior. When work groups tease or harass a member who produces too much (and makes the rest of the group look bad), they are informally communicating with, and controlling, the member's behavior.

Communication fosters *motivation* by clarifying to employees what is to be done, how well they are doing, and what can be done to improve performance if it's subpar. We saw this operating in our review of goal-setting and reinforcement theories in Chapter 7. The formation of specific goals, feedback on progress toward the goals, and reinforcement of desired behavior all stimulate motivation and require communication.

For many employees, their work group is a primary source for social interaction. The communication that takes place within the group is a fundamental mechanism by which members show their frustrations and feelings of satisfaction. Communication, therefore, provides a release for the *emotional expression* of feelings and for fulfillment of social needs.

The final function that communication performs relates to its role in facilitating decision making. It provides the *information* that individuals and groups need to make decisions by transmitting the data to identify and evaluate alternative choices.

No one of these four functions should be seen as being more important than the others. For groups to perform effectively, they need to maintain some form of control over members, stimulate members to perform, provide a means for emotional expression, and make decision choices. You can assume that almost every communication interaction that takes place in a group or organization performs one or more of these four functions.

THE COMMUNICATION PROCESS

Communication can be thought of as a process or flow. Communication problems occur when there are deviations or blockages in that flow. In this section, we will describe the process in terms of a communication model, consider how distortions can disrupt the process, and introduce the concept of communication apprehension as another potential disruption.

A Communication Model

Before communication can take place, a purpose, expressed as a message to be conveyed, is needed. It passes between a source (the sender) and a receiver. The message is encoded (converted to symbolic form) and is passed by way of some medium (channel) to the receiver, who retranslates (decodes) the message initiated by the sender. The result is a transference of meaning from one person to another.[4]

Communication Process The steps between a source and a receiver that result in the transference and understanding of meaning.

Figure 10–1 depicts the **communication process.** This model is made up of seven parts: (1) the communication source, (2) encoding, (3) the message, (4) the channel, (5) decoding, (6) the receiver, and (7) feedback.

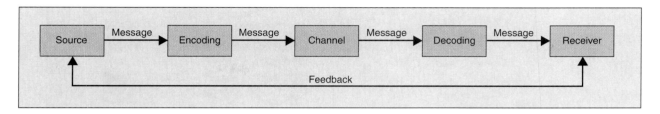

FIGURE 10–1   **The Communication Process Model**

Encoding Converting a communication message to symbolic form.

The source initiates a message by **encoding** a thought. Four conditions have been described that affect the encoded message: skill, attitudes, knowledge, and the social–cultural system.

My success in communicating to you is dependent upon my writing skills; if the authors of textbooks are without the requisite writing skills, their messages will not reach students in the form desired. One's total communicative success includes speaking, reading, listening, and reasoning skills as well. As we discussed in Chapter 6, our attitudes influence our behavior. We hold predisposed ideas on numerous topics, and our communications are affected by these attitudes. Further, we are restricted in our communicative activity by the extent of our knowledge of the particular topic. We cannot communicate what we do not know, and should our knowledge be too extensive, it is possible that our receiver will not understand our message. Clearly, the amount of knowledge the source holds about his or her subject will affect the message he or she seeks to transfer. And, finally, just as attitudes influence our behavior, so does our position in the social–cultural system in which we exist. Your beliefs and values, all part of your culture, act to influence you as a communicative source.

Message What is communicated.

The **message** is the actual physical product from the source encoding. "When we speak, the speech is the message. When we write, the writing is the message. When we paint, the picture is the message. When we gesture, the movements of our arms, the expressions on our face are the message."[5] Our message is affected by the code or group of symbols we use to transfer meaning, the content of the message itself, and the decisions that we make in selecting and arranging both codes and content.

Channel The medium through which a communication message travels.

The **channel** is the medium through which the message travels. It is selected by the source, who must determine which channel is formal and which one is informal. Formal channels are established by the organization and transmit messages that pertain to the job-related activities of members. They traditionally follow the authority network within the organization. Other forms of messages, such as personal or social, follow the informal channels in the organization.

Decoding Retranslating a sender's communication message.

The receiver is the object to whom the message is directed. But before the message can be received, the symbols in it must be translated into a form that can be understood by the receiver. This is the **decoding** of the message. Just as the encoder was limited by his or her skills, attitudes, knowledge, and social–cultural system, the receiver is equally restricted. Just as the source must be skillful in writing or speaking, the receiver must be skillful in reading or listening, and both must be able to reason. One's knowledge, attitudes, and cultural background influence one's ability to receive, just as they do the ability to send.

Feedback Loop The final link in the communication process; puts the message back into the system as a check against misunderstandings.

The final link in the communication process is a **feedback loop.** "If a communication source decodes the message that he encodes, if the message is put back into his system, we have feedback."[6] Feedback is the

Is It Wrong to Tell a Lie?

When we were children, our parents told us, "It's wrong to tell a lie." Yet we all have told lies at one time or another. If most of us agree that telling lies is wrong, how do we justify continuing to do it? We often differentiate between "real lies" and "little white lies"—the latter being an acceptable, even necessary, part of social interaction. Since lying is so closely intertwined with interpersonal communication, let's look at a specific dilemma that managers regularly confront: Does a sound purpose justify intentionally distorting information?

You have just seen your division's sales report for last month. Sales are down considerably. Your boss, who works two thousand miles away in another city, is unlikely to see last month's sales figures. You're optimistic that sales will pick up this month and next, so that your quarterly number will be acceptable. You also know that your boss is the type of person who hates to hear bad news. You're having a phone conversation today with your boss. He happens to ask, in passing, how last month's sales went. Do you tell him the truth?

A subordinate asks you about a rumor she's heard that your department and all its employees will be transferred from New York to Dallas. You know the rumor is true, but you would rather not let the information out just yet. You're fearful that it could hurt departmental morale and lead to premature resignations. What do you say to your employee?

These two incidents illustrate dilemmas that managers face regarding evasion, distortion, and outright lying to others. Is it unethical to purposely distort communications to get a favorable outcome? Is distortion acceptable, but lying not? What about "little white lies" that really don't hurt anybody? What do *you* think?

---

check on how successful we have been in transferring our messages as originally intended. It determines whether understanding has been achieved.

Sources of Distortion

Unfortunately, most of the seven components in the process model have the potential to create distortion and, therefore, impinge upon the goal of communicating perfectly. These sources of distortion explain why the message that is decoded by the receiver is rarely the exact message that the sender intended.

If the encoding is done carelessly, the message decoded by the sender will have been distorted. The message itself can also cause distortion. The poor choice of symbols and confusion in the content of the message are frequent problem areas. Of course, the channel can distort a communication if a poor one is selected or if the noise level is high. The receiver represents the final potential source for distortion. His or her prejudices, knowledge, perceptual skills, attention span, and care in decoding are all factors that can result in interpreting the message somewhat differently than envisioned by the sender.

Communication Apprehension

Communication Apprehension
Undue tension and anxiety about oral communication, written communication, or both.

Another major roadblock to effective communication is that some people—an estimated five to twenty percent of the population[7]—suffer from debilitating **communication apprehension** or anxiety. Although lots of people dread speaking in front of a group, communication apprehension is a more serious problem because it affects a whole category of communication techniques. People who suffer from it experience undue tension and anxiety in oral communication, written communication, or both.[8] For example, oral apprehensives may find it extremely difficult to talk with others face-to-face or become extremely anxious when they have to use the telephone. As a result, they may rely on memos or letters to convey messages when a phone call would not only be faster but more appropriate.

Studies demonstrate that oral-communication apprehensives avoid situations that require them to engage in oral communication.[9] We should expect to find some self-selection in jobs so that such individuals don't take positions, such as teacher, where oral communication is a dominant requirement.[10] But almost all jobs require some oral communication. And of greater concern is the evidence that high-oral-communication apprehensives distort the communication demands of their jobs in order to minimize the need for communication.[11] So we need to be aware that there is a set of people in organizations who severely limit their oral communication and rationalize this practice by telling themselves that more communication isn't necessary for them to do their job effectively.

COMMUNICATION FUNDAMENTALS

A working knowledge of communication requires a basic understanding of some fundamental concepts. In this section, we'll review those concepts. Specifically, we'll look at the flow patterns of communication, compare formal and informal communication networks, describe the importance of nonverbal communication, consider how individuals select communication channels, and summarize the major barriers to effective communication.

Direction of Communication

Communication can flow vertically or laterally. The vertical dimension can be further divided into downward and upward directions.[12]

DOWNWARD   Communication that flows from one level of a group or organization to a lower level is a downward communication.

When we think of managers communicating with subordinates, the downward pattern is the one we usually think of. It is used by group leaders and managers to assign goals, provide job instructions, inform underlings of policies and procedures, point out problems that need attention, and offer feedback about performance. But downward communication doesn't have to be oral or face-to-face contact. When management sends letters to employees' homes to advise them of the organization's new sick leave policy, it is using downward communication.

UPWARD   Upward communication flows to a higher level in the group or organization. It is used to provide feedback to higher-ups, inform them of progress toward goals, and relay current problems. Upward communication keeps managers aware of how employees feel about their jobs, co-workers, and the organization in general. Managers also rely on upward communication for ideas on how things can be improved.

Some organizational examples of upward communication are performance reports prepared by lower management for review by middle and top management, suggestion boxes, employee attitude surveys, grievance procedures, superior–subordinate discussions, and informal "gripe" sessions where employees have the opportunity to identify and discuss problems with their boss or representatives of higher management.

LATERAL   When communication takes place among members of the same work group, among members of work groups at the same level, among managers at the same level, or among any horizontally equivalent personnel, we describe it as lateral communications.

Why would there be a need for horizontal communications if a group or organization's vertical communications are effective? The answer is that horizontal communications are often necessary to save time and facilitate coordination. In some cases, these lateral relationships are formally sanctioned. Often, they are informally created to short-circuit the vertical hierarchy and expedite action. So lateral communications can, from management's viewpoint, be good or bad. Since strict adherence to the formal vertical structure for all communications can impede the efficient and accurate transfer of information, lateral communications can be beneficial. In such cases, they occur with the knowledge and support of superiors. But they can create dysfunctional conflicts when the formal vertical channels are breached, when members go above or around their superiors to get things done, or when bosses find out that actions have been taken or decisions made without their knowledge.

Formal vs. Informal Networks

Communication Networks
Channels by which information flows.

Formal Networks   Task-related communications that follow the authority chain.

Informal Network   The communication grapevine.

Communication networks define the channels by which information flows. These channels are one of two varieties—either formal or informal. **Formal networks** are typically vertical, follow the authority chain, and are limited to task-related communications. In contrast, the **informal network**—usually better known as the *grapevine*—is free to move in any direction, skip authority levels, and is as likely to satisfy group members' social needs as it is to facilitate task accomplishments.

FORMAL SMALL-GROUP NETWORKS   Figure 10–2 illustrates three common small-group networks. These are the chain, wheel, and all-channel. The chain rigidly follows the formal chain of command. The wheel relies on the leader to act as the central conduit for all the group's communication. The all-channel network permits all group members to actively communicate with each other.

As Table 10–1 demonstrates, the effectiveness of each network depends on the dependent variable you are concerned about. For instance, the structure of the wheel facilitates the emergence of a leader, the all-channel network is best if you are concerned with having high member satisfaction, and the chain is best if accuracy is most important. So Table 10–1 leads us to the conclusion that no single network will be best for all occasions.

THE INFORMAL NETWORK   The previous discussion of networks emphasized formal communication patterns, but the formal system is not the only communication system in a group or between groups. Let us, therefore, turn our attention to the informal system, where information flows along the well-known grapevine and rumors can flourish.

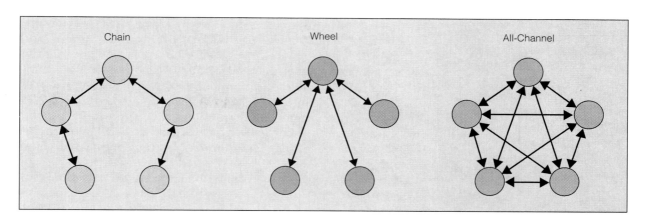

FIGURE 10–2   **Three Common Small-Group Networks**

The grapevine has three main characteristics.[13] First, it is not controlled by management. Second, it is perceived by most employees as being more believable and reliable than formal communiques issued by top management. Third, it is largely used to serve the self-interests of those people within it.

One of the most famous studies of the grapevine investigated the communication pattern among sixty-seven managerial personnel in a small manufacturing firm.[14] The basic approach used was to learn from each communication recipient how he first received a given piece of information and then trace it back to its source. It was found that, while the grapevine was an important source of information, only ten percent of the executives acted as liaison individuals; that is, passed the information on to more than one other person. For example, when one executive decided to resign to enter the insurance business, eighty-one percent of the executives knew about it, but only eleven percent transmitted this information on to others.

Two other conclusions from this study are also worth noting. Information on events of general interest tended to flow between the major functional groups (that is, production, sales) rather than within them. Also, no evidence surfaced to suggest that members of any one group consistently acted as liaisons; rather, different types of information passed through different liaison persons.

An attempt to replicate this study among employees in a small state government office also found that only a small percentage (ten percent) acted as liaison individuals.[15] This is interesting since the replication contained a wider spectrum of employees—including rank-and-file as well as managerial personnel. However, the flow of information in the government office took place within, rather than between, functional groups. It was proposed that

TABLE 10–1   **Small-Group Networks and Effectiveness Criteria**

Criteria	Networks		
	Chain	**Wheel**	**All-Channel**
Speed	Moderate	Fast	Fast
Accuracy	High	High	Moderate
Emergence of a leader	Moderate	High	None
Member satisfaction	Moderate	Low	High

this discrepancy might be due to comparing an executive-only sample against one that also included rank-and-file workers. Managers, for example, might feel greater pressure to stay informed and thus cultivate others outside their immediate functional group. Also, in contrast to the findings of the original study, the replication found that a consistent group of individuals acted as liaisons by transmitting information in the government office.

Is the information that flows along the grapevine accurate? The evidence indicates that about seventy-five percent of what is carried is accurate.[16] But what conditions foster an active grapevine? What gets the rumor mill rolling?

It is frequently assumed that rumors start because they make titillating gossip. Such is rarely the case. Rumors have at least four purposes: to structure and reduce anxiety; to make sense of limited or fragmented information; to serve as a vehicle to organize group members, and possibly outsiders, into coalitions; and to signal a sender's status ("I'm an insider and, with respect to this rumor, you're an outsider") or power ("I have the power to make you into an insider").[17] Research indicates that rumors emerge as a response to situations that are *important* to us, where there is *ambiguity,* and under conditions that arouse *anxiety.*[18] Work situations frequently contain these three elements, which explains why rumors flourish in organizations. The secrecy and competition that typically prevail in large organizations—around such issues as the appointment of new bosses, the relocation of offices, and the realignment of work assignments—create conditions that encourage and sustain rumors on the grapevine. A rumor will persist either until the wants and expectations creating the uncertainty underlying the rumor are fulfilled or until the anxiety is reduced.

What can we conclude from this discussion? Certainly the grapevine is an important part of any group or organization's communication network and well worth understanding. It identifies for managers those confusing issues that employees consider important and anxiety provoking. It acts, therefore, as both a filter and a feedback mechanism, picking up the issues that employees consider relevant. Maybe more important, again from a managerial perspective, it seems possible to analyze grapevine information and to predict its flow, given that only a small set of individuals (around ten percent) actively passes on information to more than one other person. By assessing which liaison individuals will consider a given piece of information to be relevant, we can improve our ability to explain and predict the pattern of the grapevine.

Can management entirely eliminate rumors? No! What management *can* do, however, is minimize the negative consequences of rumors by limiting their range and impact. Table 10–2 offers a few suggestions for minimizing those negative consequences.

TABLE 10–2   **Suggestions for Reducing the Negative Consequences of Rumors**

---

1. Announce timetables for making important decisions.
2. Explain decisions and behaviors that may appear inconsistent or secretive.
3. Emphasize the downside, as well as the upside, of current decisions and future plans.
4. Openly discuss worst-case possibilities—it is almost never as anxiety provoking as the unspoken fantasy.

Source: Adapted from L. Hirschhorn, "Managing Rumors," in L. Hirschhorn (ed.), *Cutting Back* (San Francisco: Jossey-Bass, 1983), pp. 54–56. With permission.

Managers Can Make Office Gossip Work for Them

Managers often view office gossip with mixed feelings. On the one hand, they see it as harmful, potentially undermining formal communication channels, especially when it conveys erroneous information. On the other hand, managers want to have access to the gossip chain. It gives them early warnings of others' plans and problems that may be brewing.

The best managers are selective in using gossip.[19] They keep their ears open to grapevine information. They recognize that gossip is a natural phenomenon whenever people get together. It helps bind people together, lets the powerless blow off steam, and conveys concerns of employees. But effective managers aren't perceived as part of the gossip chain. For instance, they may have a loyal subordinate or colleague who discreetly shares grapevine information with them. Then they only pass along news that is likely to improve relationships in the organization while, at the same time, acting quickly to stamp out gossip that might be harmful to specific individuals or to their unit's overall performance.

Nonverbal Communications

Nonverbal Communications
Messages conveyed through body movements, the intonations or emphasis we give to words, facial expressions, and the physical distance between the sender and receiver.

Kinesics   The study of body motions.

Anyone who has ever paid a visit to a singles bar or a nightclub is aware that communication need not be verbal in order to convey a message. A glance, a stare, a smile, a frown, a provocative body movement—they all convey meaning. This example illustrates that no discussion of communication would be complete without a discussion of **nonverbal communications.** This includes body movements, the intonations or emphasis we give to words, facial expressions, and the physical distance between the sender and receiver.

The academic study of body motions has been labeled **kinesics.** It refers to gestures, facial configurations, and other movements of the body. But it is a relatively new field, and it has been subject to far more conjecture and popularizing than the research findings support. Hence, while we acknowledge that body movement is an important segment of the study of communication and behavior, conclusions must be necessarily guarded. Recognizing this qualification, let us briefly consider the ways in which body motions convey meaning.

It has been argued that every *body movement* has a meaning and that no movement is accidental.[20] For example, through body language,

> We say, "Help me, I'm lonely. Take me, I'm available. Leave me alone, I'm depressed." And rarely do we send our messages consciously. We act out our state of being with nonverbal body language. We lift one eyebrow for disbelief. We rub our noses for puzzlement. We clasp our arms to isolate ourselves or to protect ourselves. We shrug our shoulders for indifference, wink one eye for intimacy, tap our fingers for impatience, slap our forehead for forgetfulness.[21]

As this photograph demonstrates, nonverbal messages can be a powerful mode for conveying meaning.
Superstock

While we may disagree with the specific meaning of these movements, body language adds to and often complicates verbal communication. A body position or movement does not by itself have a precise or universal meaning, but when it is linked with spoken language, it gives fuller meaning to a sender's message.

If you read the verbatim minutes of a meeting, you could not grasp the impact of what was said in the same way you could if you had been there or saw the meeting on video. Why? There is no record of nonverbal communication. The emphasis given to words or phrases is missing. To illustrate how *intonations* can change the meaning of a message, consider the student in class who asks the instructor a question. The instructor replies, "What do you mean by that?" The student's reaction will be different depending on the tone of the instructor's response. A soft, smooth tone creates a different meaning from an intonation that is abrasive with strong emphasis placed on the last word.

The facial expression of the instructor will also convey meaning. A snarled face says something different from a smile. Facial expressions, along with intonations, can show arrogance, aggressiveness, fear, shyness, and other characteristics that would never be communicated if you read a transcript of what had been said.

The way individuals space themselves in terms of *physical distance* also has meaning. What is considered proper spacing is largely dependent on cultural norms. For example, what is "businesslike" distance in some European countries would be viewed as "intimate" in many parts of North America. If someone stands closer to you than is considered appropriate, it may indicate aggressiveness or sexual interest. If farther away than usual, it may mean disinterest or displeasure with what is being said.

It is important for the receiver to be alert to these nonverbal aspects of communication. You should look for nonverbal cues as well as listen to the literal meaning of a sender's words. You should particularly be aware of contradictions between the messages. The boss may say that she is free to talk to you about that raise you have been seeking, but you may see nonverbal signals that suggest that this is *not* the time to discuss the subject. Regardless of what is being said, an individual who frequently glances at her wristwatch is giving the message that she would prefer to terminate the conversation. We misinform others when we express one emotion verbally, such as trust, but nonverbally communicate a contradictory message that reads, "I don't have confidence in you." These contradictions often suggest that "actions speak louder (and more accurately) than words."

Choice of Communication Channel

Why do individuals choose one channel of communication over another—for instance, a phone call instead of a face-to-face talk? One answer might be: Anxiety! As you will remember, some people are apprehensive about certain kinds of communication. What about the eighty to ninety-five percent of the population who don't suffer from this problem? Is there any general insight we might be able to provide regarding choice of communication channel? The answer is a qualified "Yes." A model of media richness has been developed to explain channel selection among managers.[22]

Recent research has found that channels differ in their capacity to convey information. Some are rich in that they have the ability to (1) handle multiple cues simultaneously, (2) facilitate rapid feedback, and (3) be very personal. Others are lean in that they score low on these three factors. As

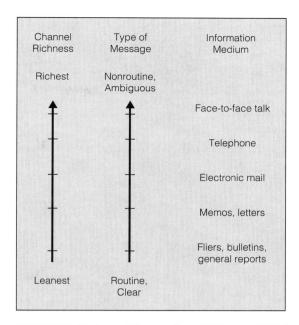

FIGURE 10–3   **Hierarchy of Channel Richness**

Channel Richness The amount of information that can be transmitted during a communication episode.

Figure 10–3 illustrates, face-to-face talk scores highest in terms of **channel richness** because it provides for the maximum amount of information to be transmitted during a communication episode. That is, it offers multiple information cues (words, posture, facial expressions, gestures, intonations), immediate feedback (both verbal and nonverbal), and the personal touch of "being there." Impersonal written media such as bulletins and general reports rate lowest in richness.

The choice of one channel over another depends on whether the message is routine or nonroutine. The former types of messages tend to be straightforward and have a minimum of ambiguity. The latter are likely to be complicated and have the potential for misunderstanding. Managers can communicate routine messages efficiently through channels that are lower in richness. However, they can communicate nonroutine messages effectively only by selecting rich channels.

The media richness model is consistent with organizational trends and practices during the past decade. It is not just coincidence that more and more senior managers have been using meetings to facilitate communication and regularly leaving the isolated sanctuary of their executive offices to manage by walking around. These executives are relying on richer channels of communication to transmit the more ambiguous messages they need to convey. The past decade has been characterized by organizations closing facilities, imposing large layoffs, restructuring, merging, consolidating, and introducing new products and services at an accelerated pace—all nonroutine messages high in ambiguity and requiring the use of channels that can convey a large amount of information. It is not surprising, therefore, to see the most effective managers expanding their use of rich channels.

Barriers to Effective Communication

We conclude our discussion of communication fundamentals by reviewing several of the more prominent barriers to effective communication of which you should be aware.

Communication Barriers Between Women and Men

Deborah Tannen's book *You Just Don't Understand: Women and Men in Conversation*[23] was on the best-seller list for nearly a year, and rightly so! For this important book lucidly explains why gender often creates oral communication barriers.

The essence of Tannen's research is that men use talk to emphasize status, while women use it to create connection. Tannen states that communication is a continual balancing act, juggling the conflicting needs for intimacy and independence. Intimacy emphasizes closeness and commonalities. Independence emphasizes separateness and differences. But here's the kick: Women speak and hear a language of connection and intimacy; men speak and hear a language of status and independence. So, for many men, conversations are primarily a means to preserve independence and maintain status in a hierarchical social order. For many women, conversations are negotiations for closeness in which people try to seek and give confirmation and support. A few examples will illustrate Tannen's thesis:

Men frequently complain that women talk on and on about their problems. Women criticize men for not listening. What's happening is that when men hear a problem, they frequently assert their desire for independence and control by providing solutions. Many women, on the other hand, view telling a problem as a means to promote closeness. The women present the problem to gain support and connection, not to get the male's advice.

Men are often more direct than women in conversation. A man might say, "I think you're wrong on that point." A woman might say, "Have you looked at the marketing department's research report on that point?" (the implication being that the report will show the error). Men frequently see female indirectness as "covert" or "sneaky," but women are not as concerned as men with the status and one-upmanship that directness often creates.

Finally, men often criticize women for seeming to apologize all the time. Men tend to see the phrase "I'm sorry" as a weakness because they interpret the phrase to mean the woman is accepting blame, when he knows she's not to blame. The woman also knows she is not to blame. The problem is that women typically use "I'm sorry" to express regret: "I know you must feel bad about this; I do, too."

Filtering A sender's manipulation of information so that it will be seen more favorably by the receiver.

FILTERING **Filtering** refers to a sender manipulating information so that it will be seen more favorably by the receiver. For example, when a manager tells his boss what he feels his boss wants to hear, he is filtering information. Does this happen much in organizations? Sure! As information is passed up to senior executives, it has to be condensed and synthesized by underlings so those on top don't become overloaded with information. The personal interests and perceptions of what is important by those doing the synthesizing are going to result in filtering. As a former group vice president of General Motors described it, the filtering of communications through levels at GM made it impossible for senior managers to get objective information because "lower-level specialists...provided information in such a way that they would get the answer they wanted. I know. I used to be down below and do it."[24]

The major determinant of filtering is the number of levels in an organization's structure. The more vertical levels in the organization's hierarchy, the more opportunities there are for filtering.

SELECTIVE PERCEPTION   We have mentioned selective perception before in this book. It appears again because the receivers in the communication process selectively see and hear based on their needs, motivations, experience, background, and other personal characteristics. Receivers also project their interests and expectations into communications as they decode them. The employment interviewer who *expects* a female job applicant to put her family ahead of her career is likely to *see* that in female applicants, regardless of whether the applicants feel that way or not. As we said in Chapter 5, we don't see reality; rather, we interpret what we see and call it reality.

EMOTIONS   How the receiver feels at the time of receipt of a communication message will influence how he or she interprets it. The same message received when you're angry or distraught is likely to be interpreted differently when you're in a neutral disposition. Extreme emotions—such as jubilation or depression—are most likely to hinder effective communication. In such instances, we are most prone to disregard our rational and objective thinking processes and substitute emotional judgments.

LANGUAGE   Words mean different things to different people. "The meanings of words are *not* in the words; they are in us."[25] Age, education, and cultural background are three of the more obvious variables that influence the language a person uses and the definitions he or she gives to words. The language of William F. Buckley, Jr., is clearly different from that of the typical high school–educated Burger King employee. The latter, in fact, would undoubtedly have trouble understanding much of Buckley's vocabulary (but then, so do a lot of people with graduate degrees!).

In an organization, employees usually come from diverse backgrounds and, therefore, have different patterns of speech. Additionally, the grouping of employees into departments creates specialists who develop their own jargon or technical language. In large organizations, members are also frequently widely dispersed geographically—even operating in different countries—and individuals in each locale will use terms and phrases that are unique to their area. Table 10–3 provides a humorous look at how jargon can hinder, as well as improve, general communication.

TABLE 10–3   The Jargon of the Politically Correct, or Terms to Ensure You Offend No One*

Jargon facilitates communication among those who are part of the in-group. The following *politically correct* terms, ironically, probably hinder general communication because their meaning is less well understood than the terms they were created to replace.

1. Physically challenged (*replaces* physically disabled or handicapped)
2. Educational equity (*replaces* quotas)
3. Undocumented workers (*replaces* illegal aliens)
4. Monocultural (*replaces* white)
5. Senior (*replaces* elderly or old)
6. Vertically challenged (*replaces* dwarfs or midgets)
7. Indigenous people (*replaces* Native Americans or American Indians)
8. Differently-sized people (*replaces* significantly overweight or obese)
9. Visually impaired (*replaces* blind)
10. Eurocentric suit (*replaces* Western clothes)

*With apologies to those who may be humor-disabled.

The existence of vertical levels can also cause language problems. For instance, differences in meaning with regard to words such as *incentives* and *quotas* have been found at different levels in management. Top managers often speak about the need for incentives and quotas, yet these terms imply manipulation and create resentment among many lower managers.

The point is that while you and I speak a common language—English—our usage of that language is far from uniform. If we knew how each of us modified the language, communication difficulties would be minimized. The problem is that members in an organization usually don't know how others with whom they interact have modified the language. Senders tend to assume that the words and terms they use mean the same to the receiver as they do to them. This, of course, is often incorrect, thus creating communication difficulties.

KEY COMMUNICATION SKILLS

Given the barriers that exist to retard effective communications, what can a person do to reduce those barriers?

Good communication skills take considerable effort to learn and years to perfect. But they *can* be learned. In this section, we'll briefly introduce two of the more critical skills related to effective communication—active listening and providing feedback—and demonstrate how you can begin to apply them immediately and develop your proficiency with them.[26]

Active Listening Skills

Too many people take their listening skills for granted. They confuse hearing with listening. What's the difference? Hearing is merely picking up sound vibrations. Listening is making sense out of what we hear. That is, listening requires paying attention, interpreting, and remembering sound stimuli.

ACTIVE VS. PASSIVE LISTENING   Effective listening is active rather than passive. In passive listening, you're much like a tape recorder. You absorb the information given. If the speaker provides you with a clear message and makes his or her delivery interesting enough to keep your attention, you'll probably get most of what the speaker is trying to communicate. But active listening requires you to get inside the speaker so that you can understand the communication from his or her point of view. As you'll see, active listening is hard work. You have to concentrate and you have to want to fully understand what a speaker is saying. Students who use active listening techniques for an entire fifty-minute lecture are as tired as their instructor when that lecture is over because they have put as much energy into listening as the instructor put into speaking.

There are four essential requirements for **active listening**. You need to listen with (1) intensity, (2) empathy, (3) acceptance, and (4) a willingness to take responsibility for completeness.[27]

Our brain is capable of handling a speaking rate of about four times the speed of the average speaker. That leaves a lot of time for idle mind-wandering while listening. The active listener concentrates intensely on what the speaker is saying and tunes out the thousands of miscellaneous thoughts (about money, sex, vacations, parties, friends, getting the car fixed,

Active Listening Listening with intensity, empathy, acceptance, and a willingness to take responsibility for completeness.

Active listening is hard work. Because our brain can handle a speaking rate of about four times the speed of the average speaker, many of us have learned bad listening habits. But practicing active listening skills can greatly improve our ability to accurately understand others' verbal messages.
Joseph Pobereskin/Tony Stone Worldwide

and the like) that create distractions. What do active listeners do with their idle brain time? Summarize and integrate what has been said! They put each new bit of information into the context of what has preceded it.

Empathy requires you to put yourself in the speaker's shoes. You try to understand what the *speaker* wants to communicate rather than what *you* want to understand. Notice that empathy demands both knowledge of the speaker and flexibility on your part. You need to suspend your own thoughts and feelings and adjust what you see and feel to your speaker's world. In that way, you increase the likelihood that you will interpret the message being spoken in the way the speaker intended.

An active listener demonstrates acceptance. He or she listens objectively without judging content. This is no easy task. It is natural to be distracted by the content of what a speaker says, especially when we disagree with it. When we hear something we disagree with, we begin formulating our mental arguments to counter what is being said. Of course, in doing so, we miss the rest of the message. The challenge for the active listener is to absorb what is being said and to withhold judgment on content until the speaker is finished.

The final ingredient of active listening is taking responsibility for completeness. That is, the listener does whatever is necessary to get the full intended meaning from the speaker's communication. Two widely used active listening techniques to achieve this end are listening for feelings as well as for content and asking questions to ensure understanding.

DEVELOPING EFFECTIVE ACTIVE LISTENING SKILLS   Based on a review of the active listening literature, we can identify eight specific behaviors that effective listeners demonstrate.[28] (See Table 10–4.) As you review these behaviors, ask yourself the degree to which they describe your listening practices. If you're not currently using these techniques, there is no better time than today to begin developing them.

1. *Make eye contact.* How do you feel when somebody doesn't look at you when you're speaking? If you're like most people, you're likely to interpret this as aloofness or disinterest. It's ironic that while "you listen with your ears, people judge whether you are listening by looking at your eyes."[29]

TABLE 10–4   Behaviors Related to Effective Active Listening

1. Make eye contact.
2. Exhibit affirmative head nods and appropriate facial expressions.
3. Avoid distracting actions or gestures.
4. Ask questions.
5. Paraphrase.
6. Avoid interrupting the speaker.
7. Don't overtalk.
8. Make smooth transitions between the roles of speaker and listener.

Paraphrasing   Restating what the speaker has said in one's own words.

2. *Exhibit affirmative head nods and appropriate facial expressions.* The effective listener shows interest in what is being said. How? Through nonverbal signals. Affirmative head nods and appropriate facial expressions, when added to good eye contact, convey to the speaker that you're listening.

3. *Avoid distracting actions or gestures.* The other side of showing interest is avoiding actions that suggest your mind is somewhere else. When listening, *don't* look at your watch, shuffle papers, play with your pencil, or engage in similar distractions. They make the speaker feel you're bored or uninterested. Maybe more importantly, they indicate that you *aren't* fully attentive and may be missing part of the message that the speaker wants to convey.

4. *Ask questions.* The critical listener analyzes what he or she hears and asks questions. This behavior provides clarification, ensures understanding, and assures the speaker that you're listening.

5. *Paraphrase.* **Paraphrasing** means restating what the speaker has said *in your own words.* The effective listener uses phrases like: "What I hear you saying is. . ." or "Do you mean. . ?" Why rephrase what's already been said? Two reasons! First, it's an excellent control device to check on whether you're listening carefully. You can't paraphrase accurately if your mind is wandering or if you're thinking about what you're going to say next. Second, it's a control for accuracy. By rephrasing what the speaker has said in your own words and feeding it back to the speaker, you verify the accuracy of your understanding.

6. *Avoid interrupting the speaker.* Let the speaker complete his or her thought before you try to respond. Don't try to second-guess where the speaker's thoughts are going. When the speaker is finished, you'll know it!

7. *Don't overtalk.* Most of us would rather speak our own ideas than listen to what someone else says. Too many of us listen only because it's the price we have to pay to get people to let us talk. While talking may be more fun and silence may be uncomfortable, you can't talk and listen at the same time. The good listener recognizes this fact and doesn't overtalk.

8. *Make smooth transitions between the roles of speaker and listener.* As a student sitting in a lecture hall, you find it relatively easy to get into an effective listening frame of mind. Why? Because communication is essentially one-way: The teacher talks and you listen. But the teacher–student dyad is atypical. In most work situations, you're continually shifting back and forth between the roles of speaker and listener. The effective listener, therefore, makes transitions smoothly from speaker to listener and back to speaker. From a listening perspective,

this means concentrating on what a speaker has to say and practicing not thinking about what you're going to say as soon as you get your chance.

Feedback Skills

Ask a manager how much feedback he or she gives subordinates and you're likely to get a qualified answer. If the feedback is positive, it's likely to be given promptly and enthusiastically. Negative feedback, however, is often treated very differently. Managers, like most of us, don't particularly enjoy being the bearers of bad news. They fear offending or having to deal with defensiveness by the recipient. The result is that negative feedback is often avoided, delayed, or substantially distorted.[30] The purposes of this section are to show you the importance of providing both positive and negative feedback and to identify specific techniques to make your feedback more effective.

POSITIVE VS. NEGATIVE FEEDBACK   We said that managers treat positive and negative feedback differently. So, too, do recipients. You need to understand this fact and adjust your style accordingly.

Positive feedback is more readily and accurately perceived than negative feedback. Further, while positive feedback is almost always accepted, the negative variety often meets resistance.[31] Why? The logical answer seems to be that people want to hear good news and block out the bad. Positive feedback fits what most people wish to hear and already believe about themselves.

Does this mean that you should avoid giving negative feedback? No! What it means is that you need to be aware of potential resistance and learn to use negative feedback in situations where it is most likely to be accepted.[32] What are those situations? Research indicates that negative feedback is most likely to be accepted when it comes from a credible source or if it is objective in form. Subjective impressions carry weight only when they come from a person with high status and credibility.[33] This suggests that negative feedback that is supported by hard data—numbers, specific examples, and the like— has a good chance of being accepted. Negative feedback that is subjective can be a meaningful tool for experienced managers, particularly those high in the organization who have earned the respect of their employees. From less experienced managers, those in the lower ranks of the organization, and those whose reputation has not yet been established, negative feedback is not likely to be well received.

DEVELOPING EFFECTIVE FEEDBACK SKILLS   There are six specific suggestions we can make to help you be more effective in providing feedback (see Table 10–5).

1. *Focus on specific behaviors.* Feedback should be specific rather than general.[34] Avoid statements like "You have a bad attitude" or "I'm really impressed with the good job you did." They're vague, and while

TABLE 10–5   Behaviors Related to Providing Effective Feedback

1. Focus on specific behaviors.
2. Keep feedback impersonal.
3. Keep feedback goal-oriented.
4. Make feedback well-timed.
5. Ensure understanding.
6. Direct negative feedback toward behavior that is controllable by the recipient.

they provide information, they don't tell the recipient enough to correct the "bad attitude" or *on what basis* you concluded that a "good job" had been done.

Suppose you said something like "Bob, I'm concerned with your attitude toward your work. You were a half hour late to yesterday's staff meeting, and then told me you hadn't read the preliminary report we were discussing. Today you tell me you're taking off three hours early for a dental appointment"; or "Jan, I was really pleased with the job you did on the Phillips account. They increased their purchases from us by twenty-two percent last month and I got a call a few days ago from Dan Phillips complimenting me on how quickly you responded to those specification changes for the MJ-7 microchip." Both of these statements focus on specific behaviors. They tell the recipient *why* you are being critical or complimentary.

2. *Keep feedback impersonal.* Feedback, particularly the negative kind, should be descriptive rather than judgmental or evaluative.[35] No matter how upset you are, keep the feedback job-related and never criticize someone personally because of an inappropriate action. Telling people they're "stupid," "incompetent," or the like is almost always counterproductive. It provokes such an emotional reaction that the performance deviation itself is apt to be overlooked. When you're criticizing, remember that you're censuring a job-related behavior, not the person. You may be tempted to tell someone he or she is "rude and insensitive" (which may well be true); however, that's hardly impersonal. Better to say something like "You interrupted me three times, with questions that were not urgent, when you knew I was talking long distance to a customer in Scotland."

3. *Keep feedback goal-oriented.* Feedback should not be given primarily to "dump" or "unload" on another.[36] If you have to say something negative, make sure it's directed toward the *recipient's* goals. Ask yourself whom the feedback is supposed to help. If the answer is essentially *you*—"I've got something I just want to get off my chest"—bite your tongue. Such feedback undermines your credibility and lessens the meaning and influence of future feedback.

4. *Make feedback well-timed.* Feedback is most meaningful to a recipient when there is a very short interval between his or her behavior and the receipt of feedback about that behavior.[37] To illustrate, a new employee who makes a mistake is more likely to respond to his manager's suggestions for improvement right after the mistake or at the end of that working day than during a performance review session several months later. If you have to spend time recreating a situation and refreshing someone's memory of it, the feedback you're providing is likely to be ineffective.[38] Moreover, if you are particularly concerned with *changing* behavior, delays providing feedback on the undesirable actions lessen the likelihood that the feedback will be effective in bringing about the desired change.[39] Of course, making feedback prompt merely for promptness' sake can backfire if you have insufficient information, if you're angry, or if you're otherwise emotionally upset. In such instances, "well-timed" may mean "somewhat delayed."

5. *Ensure understanding.* Is your feedback concise and complete enough so that the recipient clearly and fully understands your communication? Remember, every successful communication requires both transference and understanding of meaning. So if feedback is to be effective, you need to ensure that the recipient understands it.[40] Consistent with our discussion of listening techniques, you should have the recipient rephrase the content of your feedback to see whether it fully captures the meaning you intended.

Four Rules for Improving Cross-Cultural Communication

Effective communication is difficult under the best of conditions. Cross-cultural factors clearly create the potential for increased communication problems.[41]

The encoding and decoding of messages into symbols is based on an individual's cultural background and, as a result, is not the same for each person. The greater the differences in backgrounds between sender and receiver, the greater the differences in meanings attached to particular words or behaviors. People from different cultures see, interpret, and evaluate things differently, and consequently act upon them differently.

When communicating with people from a different culture, what can you do to reduce misperceptions, misinterpretations, and misevaluations? Following these four rules can be helpful:

1. *Assume differences until similarity is proven.* Most of us assume that others are more similar to us than they actually are. But people from different countries often are very different from us. So you are far less likely to make an error if you assume others are different from you rather than assuming similarity until difference is proven.

2. *Emphasize description rather than interpretation or evaluation.* Interpreting or evaluating what someone has said or done, in contrast to description, is based more on the observer's culture and background than on the observed situation. As a result, delay judgment until you've had sufficient time to observe and interpret the situation from the differing perspectives of all the cultures involved.

3. *Practice empathy.* Before sending a message, put yourself in the recipient's shoes. What are his or her values, experiences, and frames of reference? What do you know about his or her education, upbringing, and background that can give you added insight? Try to see the other person as he or she really is.

4. *Treat your interpretations as a working hypothesis.* Once you've developed an explanation for a new situation or think you empathize with someone from a foreign culture, treat your interpretation as a hypothesis that needs further testing rather than as a certainty. Carefully assess the feedback provided by recipients to see if it confirms your hypothesis. For important decisions or communiques, you can also check with other foreign and home-country colleagues to make sure that your interpretations are on target.

6. *Direct negative feedback toward behavior that is controllable by the recipient.* There's little value in reminding a person of some shortcoming over which he or she has no control. Negative feedback, therefore, should be directed toward behavior the recipient can do something about.[42] So, for example, to criticize an employee who is late because he forgot to set his wake-up alarm is valid. To criticize him for being late when the subway he takes to work every day had a power failure, trapping him underground for half an hour, is pointless. There is nothing he could have done to correct what happened.

Additionally, when negative feedback is given concerning something that is controllable by the recipient, it may be a good idea to indicate specifically *what* can be done to improve the situation. This takes some of the sting out of the criticism and offers guidance to recipients who understand the problem but don't know how to resolve it.

GROUP DECISION MAKING

Compaq Computer Corp. is a true success story. In its first year of existence, 1982, it generated sales of over $111 million. Today, its sales exceed $3 billion. Of course, Compaq has created a number of innovative and quality products. But no small part of the company's success is due to the way they make decisions.[43]

Groups of executives and employees decide on everything—from whether or not to bring out a new product to how Compaq's assembly line in Houston should be run. Initially, this group decision process was used only by the company's top executives for developing manufacturing strategies and other critical issues. But as it proved itself, it was quickly pushed all the way down to the assembly line. Assembly workers at Compaq now have a meeting every day to talk about their problems, and every participant contributes to finding the solutions to those problems.

More and more organizations are following Compaq's example and relying on groups as their primary vehicle for decision making. In the remainder of this chapter, we will review group decision making.

Why discuss group decision making here? Why didn't we present this topic in Chapter 5, when we reviewed individual decision making? Because there is an inherent and obvious link between communication concepts and the subject of group decision making. We communicate information, and information is used in the making of decisions. Moreover, group decisions require transmitting messages between members, and the effectiveness of this communication process will have a significant impact on the quality of the group's decisions.

The belief—characterized by juries—that two heads are better than one has long been accepted as a basic component of North American and many other countries' legal systems. This belief has expanded to the point that, today, many decisions in organizations are made by groups or committees. There are permanent executive committees that meet on a regular basis, special task forces created to analyze unique problems, temporary project teams used to develop new products, and "quality circles" made up of representatives from management and labor who meet to identify and solve production problems, to name a few of the more obvious examples.

Groups vs. the Individual

Decision-making groups may be widely used in organizations, but does that imply that group decisions are preferable to those made by an individual alone? The answer to this question depends on a number of factors. Let's begin by looking at the advantages and disadvantages that groups afford.[44]

ADVANTAGES OF GROUPS Individual and group decisions each have their own set of strengths. Neither is ideal for all situations. The following identifies the major advantages that groups offer over individuals in the making of decisions:

1. *More complete information and knowledge.* By aggregating the resources of several individuals, we bring more input into the decision process.

2. *Increased diversity of views.* In addition to more input, groups can bring heterogeneity to the decision process. This opens up the opportunity for more approaches and alternatives to be considered.

3. *Increased acceptance of a solution.* Many decisions fail after the final choice has been made because people do not accept the solution. However, if people who will be affected by a decision and who will be instrumental in implementing it are able to participate in the decision itself, they will be more likely to accept it and encourage others to accept it. This translates into more support for the decision and higher satisfaction among those required to implement it.

4. *Increased legitimacy.* North American and many other capitalistic societies value democratic methods. The group decision-making process is consistent with democratic ideals and, therefore, may be perceived as being more legitimate than decisions made by a single person. When an individual decision maker fails to consult with others before making a decision, the decision maker's complete power can create the perception that the decision was made autocratically and arbitrarily.

DISADVANTAGES OF GROUPS   Of course, group decisions are not without drawbacks. Their major disadvantages include:

1. *Time-consuming.* It takes time to assemble a group. The interaction that takes place once the group is in place is frequently inefficient. The result is that groups take more time to reach a solution than would be the case if an individual were making the decision. This can limit management's ability to act quickly and decisively when necessary.

2. *Pressures to conform.* As noted in the previous chapter, there are social pressures in groups. The desire by group members to be accepted and considered as an asset to the group can result in squashing any overt disagreement, thus encouraging conformity among viewpoints.

3. *Domination by the few.* Group discussion can be dominated by one or a few members. If this dominant coalition is composed of low- and medium-ability members, the group's overall effectiveness will suffer.

4. *Ambiguous responsibility.* Group members share responsibility, but who is actually accountable for the final outcome? In an individual decision, it is clear who is responsible. In a group decision, the responsibility of any single member is watered down.

EFFECTIVENESS AND EFFICIENCY   Whether groups are more effective than individuals depends on the criteria you use for defining effectiveness. In terms of *accuracy,* group decisions will tend to be more accurate. The evidence indicates that, on the average, groups make better-quality decisions than individuals.[45] This doesn't mean, of course, that all groups will outperform *every* individual. Rather, group decisions have been found to be better than those that would be reached by the average individual in the group. However, they are seldom better than the performance of the best individual.[46]

If decision effectiveness is defined in terms of *speed,* individuals are superior. If *creativity* is important, groups tend to be more effective than individuals. And if effectiveness means the degree of *acceptance* the final solution achieves, the nod again goes to the group.

But effectiveness cannot be considered without also assessing efficiency. In terms of efficiency, groups almost always stack up as a poor second to the individual decision maker. With few exceptions, group decision making consumes more work hours than if an individual were to tackle the same problem alone. The exceptions tend to be those instances where, to achieve comparable quantities of diverse input, the single decision maker must spend a great deal of time reviewing files and talking to people. Because groups can include members from diverse areas, the time spent searching for information can be reduced. However, as we noted, these advantages in efficiency tend to be the exception. Groups are generally less efficient than individuals. In deciding whether to use groups, then, consideration should be given to assessing whether increases in effectiveness are more than enough to offset the losses in efficiency.

SUMMARY   Groups offer an excellent vehicle for performing many of the steps in the decision-making process. They are a source of both breadth and depth of input for information gathering. If the group is composed of individuals with diverse backgrounds, the alternatives generated should be more extensive and the analysis more critical. When the final solution is agreed upon, there are more people in a group decision to support and implement it. These pluses, however, can be more than offset by the time consumed by group decisions, the internal conflicts they create, and the pressures they generate toward conformity. Table 10–6 briefly outlines the group's assets and liabilities. It allows you to evaluate the net advantage or disadvantage that would accrue in a given situation when you have to choose between an individual and a group decision.

Groupthink and Groupshift

Two by-products of group decision making have received a considerable amount of attention by researchers in OB. As we'll show, these two phenomena have the potential to affect the group's ability to appraise alternatives objectively and arrive at quality decision solutions.

Groupthink Phenomenon in which the norm for consensus overrides the realistic appraisal of alternative courses of action.

Groupshift A change in decision risk between the group's decision and the individual decision that members within the group would make; can be either toward conservatism or greater risk.

The first phenomenon, called **groupthink,** is related to norms. It describes situations in which group pressures for conformity deter the group from critically appraising unusual, minority, or unpopular views. Groupthink is a disease that attacks many groups and can dramatically hinder their performance. The second phenomenon we shall review is called **groupshift.** It indicates that in discussing a given set of alternatives and arriving at a solution, group members tend to exaggerate the initial positions that they hold. In some situations, caution dominates, and there is a conservative shift. More often, however, the evidence indicates that groups tend toward a risky shift. Let's look at each of these phenomena in more detail.

GROUPTHINK   A number of years ago I had a peculiar experience. During a faculty meeting, a motion was placed on the floor stipulating each faculty member's responsibilities in regard to counseling students. The motion received a second, and the floor was opened for questions. There were

TABLE 10–6   **The Group Decision: Its Assets and Liabilities**

Assets	Liabilities
Breadth of information	Time-consuming
Diversity of information	Conformity
Acceptance of solution	Domination of discussion
Legitimacy of process	Ambiguous responsibility

none. After about fifteen seconds of silence, the chairperson asked if he could "call for the question" (fancy terminology for permission to take the vote). No objections were voiced. When the chair asked for those in favor, a vast majority of the thirty-two faculty members in attendance raised their hands. The motion was passed, and the chair proceeded to the next item on the agenda.

Nothing in the process seemed unusual, but the story is not over. About twenty minutes following the end of the meeting, a professor came roaring into my office with a petition. The petition said that the motion on counseling students had been rammed through and requested the chairperson to replace the motion on the next month's agenda for discussion and a vote. When I asked this professor why he had not spoken up less than an hour earlier, he gave me a frustrated look. He then proceeded to tell me that in talking with people after the meeting, he realized there actually had been considerable opposition to the motion. He didn't speak up, he said, because he thought he was the only one opposed. Conclusion: The faculty meeting we had attended had been attacked by the deadly groupthink "disease."

Have you ever felt like speaking up in a meeting, classroom, or informal group, but decided against it? One reason may have been shyness. On the other hand, you may have been a victim of groupthink, the phenomenon that occurs when group members become so enamored of seeking concurrence that the norm for consensus overrides the realistic appraisal of alternative courses of action and the full expression of deviant, minority, or unpopular views. It describes a deterioration in an individual's mental efficiency, reality testing, and moral judgment as a result of group pressures.[47]

We have all seen the symptoms of the groupthink phenomenon:

1. Group members rationalize any resistance to the assumptions they have made. No matter how strongly the evidence may contradict their basic assumptions, members behave so as to reinforce those assumptions continually.

2. Members apply direct pressures on those who momentarily express doubts about any of the group's shared views or who question the validity of arguments supporting the alternative favored by the majority.

3. Those members who have doubts or hold differing points of view seek to avoid deviating from what appears to be group consensus by keeping silent about misgivings and even minimizing to themselves the importance of their doubts.

4. There appears to be an illusion of unanimity. If someone does not speak, it is assumed that he or she is in full accord. In other words, abstention becomes viewed as a "Yes" vote.[48]

In studies of historic American foreign policy decisions, these symptoms were found to prevail when government policy-making groups failed—unpreparedness at Pearl Harbor in 1941, the U.S. invasion of North Korea, the Bay of Pigs fiasco, and the escalation of the Vietnam War. Importantly, these four groupthink characteristics could not be found where group policy decisions were successful—the Cuban missile crisis and the formulation of the Marshall Plan.[49]

Groupthink appears to be closely aligned with the conclusions Asch drew in his experiments with a lone dissenter. Individuals who hold a position that is different from that of the dominant majority are under pressure to suppress, withhold, or modify their true feelings and beliefs. As members of a group, we find it more pleasant to be in agreement—to be a positive part of the group—than to be a disruptive force, even if disruption is necessary to improve the effectiveness of the group's decisions.

Are all groups equally vulnerable to groupthink? The evidence suggests not. Researchers have focused in on three moderating variables—the group's cohesiveness, its leader's behavior, and its insulation from outsiders—but the findings have not been consistent.[50] At this point, the most valid conclusions we can make are: (1) highly cohesive groups have more discussion and bring out more information, but it's unclear whether such groups discourage dissent; (2) groups with impartial leaders who encourage member input generate and discuss more alternative solutions; (3) leaders should avoid expressing a preferred solution early in the group's discussion because this tends to limit critical analysis and significantly increase the likelihood that the group will adopt this solution as the final choice; and (4) insulation of the group leads to fewer alternatives being generated and evaluated.

GROUPSHIFT   In comparing group decisions with the individual decisions of members within the group, evidence suggests that there are differences.[51] In some cases, the group decisions are more conservative than the individual decisions. More often, the shift is toward greater risk.[52]

What appears to happen in groups is that the discussion leads to a significant shift in the positions of members toward a more extreme position in the direction toward which they were already leaning before the discussion. So conservative types become more cautious and the more aggressive types take on more risk. The group discussion tends to *exaggerate* the initial position of the group.

The groupshift can be viewed as actually a special case of groupthink. The decision of the group reflects the dominant decision-making norm that develops during the group's discussion. Whether the shift in the group's decision is toward greater caution or more risk depends on the dominant prediscussion norm.

The greater occurrence of the shift toward risk has generated several explanations for the phenomenon.[53] It's been argued, for instance, that the discussion creates familiarization among the members. As they become more comfortable with each other, they also become more bold and daring. Another argument is that our society values risk, that we admire individuals who are willing to take risks, and that group discussion motivates members to show that they are at least as willing as their peers to take risks. The most plausible explanation of the shift toward risk, however, seems to be that the group diffuses responsibility. Group decisions free any single member from accountability for the group's final choice. Greater risk can be taken because even if the decision fails, no one member can be held wholly responsible.

So how should you use the findings on groupshift? You should recognize that group decisions exaggerate the initial position of the individual members, that the shift has been shown more often to be toward greater risk, and that whether a group will shift toward greater risk or caution is a function of the members' prediscussion inclinations.

Group Decision–Making Techniques

Interacting Groups Typical groups, where members interact with each other face-to-face.

The most common form of group decision making takes place in face-to-face **interacting groups.** But as our discussion of groupthink demonstrated, interacting groups often censor themselves and pressure individual members toward conformity of opinion. Brainstorming, nominal group and Delphi techniques, and electronic meetings have been proposed as ways to reduce many of the problems inherent in the traditional interacting group. We'll discuss each in this section.

Brainstorming An idea-generation process that specifically encourages any and all alternatives, while withholding any criticism of those alternatives.

BRAINSTORMING **Brainstorming** is meant to overcome pressures for conformity in the interacting group that retard the development of creative alternatives.[54] It does this by utilizing an idea-generation process that specifically encourages any and all alternatives, while withholding any criticism of those alternatives.

In a typical brainstorming session, a half-dozen to a dozen people sit around a table. The group leader states the problem in a clear manner so that it is understood by all participants. Members then "free-wheel" as many alternatives as they can in a given length of time. No criticism is allowed, and all the alternatives are recorded for later discussion and analysis. That one idea stimulates others and that judgments of even the most bizarre suggestions are withheld until later encourages group members to "think the unusual."

Brainstorming, however, is merely a process for generating ideas. The next three techniques go further by offering methods of actually arriving at a preferred solution.[55]

Nominal Group Technique A group decision-making method in which individual members meet face-to-face to pool their judgments in a systematic but independent fashion.

NOMINAL GROUP TECHNIQUE The **nominal group technique** restricts discussion or interpersonal communication during the decision-making process; hence, the term *nominal.* Group members are all physically present, as in a traditional committee meeting, but members operate independently. Specifically, a problem is presented and then the following steps take place:

1. Members meet as a group but, before any discussion takes place, each member independently writes down his or her ideas on the problem.

2. This silent period is followed by each member presenting one idea to the group. Each member takes his or her turn, going around the table, presenting a single idea until all ideas have been presented and recorded (typically on a flip chart or chalkboard). No discussion takes place until all ideas have been recorded.

3. The group now discusses the ideas for clarity and evaluates them.

4. Each group member silently and independently rank-orders the ideas. The final decision is determined by the idea with the highest aggregate ranking.

The chief advantage of the nominal group technique is that it permits the group to meet formally but does not restrict independent thinking, as does the interacting group.

Delphi Technique A group decision method in which individual members, acting separately, pool their judgments in a systematic and independent fashion.

DELPHI TECHNIQUE A more complex and time-consuming alternative is the **Delphi technique.** It is similar to the nominal group technique except that it does not require the physical presence of the group's members. In fact, the Delphi technique never allows the group's members to meet face-to-face. The following steps characterize the Delphi technique.

1. The problem is identified and members are asked to provide potential solutions through a series of carefully designed questionnaires.

2. Each member anonymously and independently completes the first questionnaire.

3. Results of the first questionnaire are compiled at a central location, transcribed, and reproduced.

4. Each member receives a copy of the results.

5. After viewing the results, members are again asked for their

solutions. The results typically trigger new solutions or cause changes in the original position.

6. Steps 4 and 5 are repeated as often as necessary until consensus is reached.

Like the nominal group technique, the Delphi technique insulates group members from the undue influence of others. Because it does not require the physical presence of the participants, the Delphi technique can be used for decision making among geographically scattered groups. For instance, Sony could use the technique to query its managers in Tokyo, Brussels, Paris, London, New York, Toronto, Rio de Janeiro, and Melbourne as to the best worldwide price for one of the company's products. The cost of bringing the executives together at a central location is avoided. Of course, the Delphi technique has its drawbacks. Because the method is extremely time-consuming, it is frequently not applicable where a speedy decision is necessary. Additionally, the method may not develop the rich array of alternatives that the interacting or nominal group technique does. Ideas that might surface from the heat of face-to-face interaction may never arise.

ELECTRONIC MEETINGS The most recent approach to group decision making blends the nominal group technique with sophisticated computer technology.[56] It's called the *electronic meeting*.

Once the technology is in place, the concept is simple. Up to fifty people sit around a horseshoe-shaped table, empty except for a series of computer terminals. Issues are presented to participants and they type their responses onto their computer screen. Individual comments, as well as aggregate votes, are displayed on a projection screen in the room.

The major advantages of electronic meetings are anonymity, honesty, and speed. Participants can anonymously type any message they want and it flashes on the screen for all to see at the push of a participant's board key. It also allows people to be brutally honest without penalty. And it's fast because chitchat is eliminated, discussions don't digress, and many participants can "talk" at once without stepping on one another's toes.

Experts claim that electronic meetings are as much as fifty-five percent faster than traditional face-to-face meetings. Phelps Dodge Mining, for instance, used the approach to cut its annual planning meeting from several days down to twelve hours. Yet there are drawbacks to this technique. Those who can type fast can outshine those who are verbally eloquent but lousy typists; those with the best ideas don't get credit for them; and the process lacks the information richness of face-to-face oral communication. But although this technology is currently in its infancy, the future of group decision making is very likely to include extensive use of electronic meetings.

SUMMARY: EVALUATING EFFECTIVENESS How do these various techniques stack up against the traditional interacting group? As we find so often, each technique has its own set of strengths and weaknesses. The choice of one technique over another will depend on what criteria you want to emphasize. For instance, as Table 10–7 indicates, the interacting group is good for building group cohesiveness, brainstorming keeps social pressures to a minimum, the Delphi technique minimizes interpersonal conflict, and electronic meetings process ideas fast. So the "best" technique is defined by the criteria you use to evaluate the group.

IBM uses electronic meetings to bring people from diverse backgrounds in the company together. More than 7000 IBMers have taken part in these meetings.   Katherine Lambert

TABLE 10–7   Evaluating Group Effectiveness

Effectiveness Criteria	Type of Group				
	Interacting	Brainstorming	Nominal	Delphi	Electronic
Number of ideas	Low	Moderate	High	High	High
Quality of ideas	Low	Moderate	High	High	High
Social pressure	High	Low	Moderate	Low	Low
Money costs	Low	Low	Low	Low	High
Speed	Moderate	Moderate	Moderate	Low	High
Task orientation	Low	High	High	High	High
Potential for inter-personal conflict	High	Low	Moderate	Low	Low
Feelings of accomplishment	High to low	High	High	Moderate	High
Commitment to solution	High	Not applicable	Moderate	Low	Moderate
Develops group cohesiveness	High	High	Moderate	Low	Low

Source: Based on J. K. Murnighan, "Group Decision Making: What Strategies Should You Use?", *Management Review*, February 1981, p. 61.

IMPLICATIONS FOR PERFORMANCE AND SATISFACTION

A careful review of this chapter finds a common theme regarding the relationship between communication and employee satisfaction: The less the uncertainty, the greater the satisfaction. Distortions, ambiguities, and incongruities all increase uncertainty and, hence, have a negative impact on satisfaction.[57]

The less distortion that occurs in communication, the more that goals, feedback, and other management messages to employees will be received as they were intended.[58] This, in turn, should reduce ambiguities and clarify the group's task. Extensive use of vertical, lateral, and informal channels will increase communication flow, reduce uncertainty, and improve group performance and satisfaction. We should also expect incongruities between verbal and nonverbal communiqués to increase uncertainty and reduce satisfaction.

Findings in the chapter further suggest that the goal of perfect communication is unattainable. Yet, there is evidence that demonstrates a positive relationship between effective communication (which includes factors such as perceived trust, perceived accuracy, desire for interaction, top-management receptiveness, and upward information requirements) and worker productivity.[59] Choosing the correct channel, clarifying jargon, and utilizing feedback may, therefore, make for more effective communication. But the human factor generates distortions that can never be fully eliminated. The communication process represents an exchange of messages, but the outcome is meanings that may or may not approximate those that the sender intended. Whatever the sender's expectations, the decoded message in the mind of the receiver represents his or her reality. And it is this "reality" that will determine performance, along with the individual's level of motivation and his or her degree of satisfaction. The issue of motivation is critical, so we should briefly review how communication is central in determining an individual's degree of motivation.

You will remember from expectancy theory that the degree of effort an individual exerts depends on his or her perception of the effort–performance, performance-reward, and reward–goal satisfaction linkages. If individuals are not given the data necessary to make the perceived probability of these linkages high, motivation will suffer. If rewards are not made clear, if the criteria for determining and measuring performance are ambiguous, or if individuals are not relatively certain that their effort will lead to satisfactory performance, then effort will be reduced. So communication plays a significant role in determining the level of motivation.

A final implication from the communication literature relates to predicting turnover. The use of realistic job previews acts as a communication device for clarifying role expectations (see the "Counterpoint" in Chapter 5). Employees who have been exposed to a realistic job preview have more accurate information about that job. Comparisons of turnover rates between organizations that use the realistic job preview versus either no preview or only presentation of positive job information show that those *not* using the realistic preview have, on average, almost twenty-nine percent higher turnover.[60] This makes a strong case for management conveying honest and accurate information about a job to applicants during the recruiting and selection process.

■ *FOR DISCUSSION*

1. "Communication is the transference of meaning among group members." Discuss this definition and indicate what is missing from this definition to ensure that communication is effective.

2. Describe the functions that communication provides within a group or organization. Give an example of each.

3. Describe the communication process and identify its key components. Give an example of how this process operates with both oral and written messages.

4. "Ineffective communication is the fault of the sender." Do you agree or disagree? Discuss.

5. What characterizes a communication that is rich in capacity to convey information?

6. Contrast active and passive listening.

7. When is negative feedback most likely to be accepted?

8. What can you do to improve the likelihood that your communiqués will be received and understood as you intend?

9. "Informal communication can facilitate a group's effectiveness." Do you agree or disagree? Discuss.

10. "Rumors start because something makes titillating gossip." Do you agree or disagree? Discuss.

11. What is groupthink? Is the concept applicable to the family unit as well as to organizations? Explain.

12. When are group decisions likely to be better than those made by individuals?

POINT

The Case for Improved Understanding

The major barrier to interpersonal communication is our very natural tendency to judge, to evaluate, and to approve (or disapprove) the statements of the other person or the other group. Let me illustrate this view with a couple of simple examples. Suppose that someone commenting on this discussion says, "I didn't like what that man said." What will you respond? Almost invariably your reply will be either approval or disapproval of the attitude expressed. Either you respond, "I didn't either; I thought it was terrible," or else you tend to reply, "Oh, I thought it was really good." In other words, the primary reaction is to evaluate it from *your* point of view, your own frame of reference.

Or take another example. Suppose that I say with some feeling, "I think the Republicans are showing a lot of good sound sense these days." What is the response that arises in your mind? The overwhelming likelihood is that it will be evaluative. In other words, you will find yourself agreeing, or disagreeing, or making some judgment about me, such as "He must be a conservative" or "He seems solid in his thinking."

Although the tendency to make evaluations is common in almost all interchange of language, it is greatly heightened in those situations where feelings and emotions are deeply involved. So the stronger our feelings, the more likely it is that there will be no mutual element in the communication.

There will be just two ideas, two feelings, two judgments, missing each other in psychological space.

I am sure you recognize this from your own experience. When you are not emotionally involved yourself and listen to a heated discussion, you often go away thinking, "Well, actually they weren't talking about the same thing." And they were not. Each was making a judgment, an evaluation, from his or her own frame of reference. There was really nothing that could be called communication in any genuine sense. This tendency to react to any emotionally meaningful statement by forming an evaluation of it from our own point of view is, I repeat, the major barrier to interpersonal communication.

The solution to this evaluative tendency is to see the expressed idea and attitudes from the other person's point of view, to sense how it feels to that person, to achieve his or her frame of reference in regard to the thing about which he or she is talking. When each of the different parties comes to *understand* the other from the *other's* point of view rather than *judge* that point of view, the insincerities, the lies, and the "false fronts" drop away with astonishing speed.

Based on C. R. Rogers, in C. R. Rogers and F. J. Roethlisberger, "Barriers and Gateways to Communication," *Harvard Business Review,* August 1952, pp. 46–50.

The Case for Ambiguous Communication

The major barrier to communication is the naive assumption that individuals actually want to *improve* communication. Most of us seem to overlook a very basic fact: It is often in the sender's and/or receiver's best interest to keep communication ambiguous.

"Lack of communication" seems to have replaced original sin as the explanation for the ills of the world. We're continually hearing that problems would go away if we could "just communicate better." Some of the basic assumptions underlying this view need to be looked at carefully.

One assumption is the way in which poor communication resembles original sin: Both tend to get tangled up with control of the situation. If one defines communication as mutual understanding, this does not imply control for either party, and certainly not for both. However, equating good communication with control appears in the assumption that better communication will necessarily reduce strife and conflict. Each individual's definition of better communication, like his or her definition of virtuous conduct, becomes that of having the other party accept his or her views, which would reduce conflict at that party's expense. A better understanding of the situation might serve only to underline the differences rather than to resolve them. Indeed, many of the techniques thought of as poor communication were apparently developed with the aim of bypassing or avoiding confrontation.

Another assumption that grows from this view is that when a conflict has existed for a long time and shows every sign of continuing, lack of communication must be one of the basic problems. Usually, if the situation is examined more carefully, plenty of communication will be found; the problem is, again, one of equating communication with agreement.

Still a third assumption, somewhat related but less squarely based on the equation of commu-nication with control, is that it is always in the interest of at least one of the parties to an interaction, and often of both, to attain maximum clarity as measured by some more or less objective standard. Aside from the difficulty of setting up this standard—whose standard? and doesn't this give *him* or *her* control of the situation?—there are some sequences, and perhaps many of them, in which it is in the interests of both parties to leave the situation as fuzzy and undefined as possible. This is notably true in culturally or personally sensitive and taboo areas involving prejudices, preconceptions, and so on, but it can also be true when the area is merely a new one that could be seriously distorted by using old definitions and old solutions.

Too often we forget that keeping organizational communications fuzzy cuts down on questions, permits faster decision making, minimizes objections, reduces opposition, makes it easier to deny one's earlier statements, preserves freedom to change one's mind, helps to preserve mystique and hide insecurities, allows one to say several things at the same time, permits one to say "No" diplomatically, and helps to avoid confrontation and anxiety.

If you want to see the fine art of ambiguous communication up close, all you have to do is watch a television interview with a politician who is running for office. The interviewer attempts to get specific information, while the politician tries to retain multiple possible interpretations. Such ambiguous communications allow the politician to approach his or her ideal image of being "all things to all people."

Based on C. O. Kursh, "The Benefits of Poor Communication," *The Psychoanalytic Review,* Summer–Fall 1971, pp. 189–208; and E. M. Eisenberg and M. G. Witten, "Reconsidering Openness in Organizational Communication," *Academy of Management Review,* July 1987, pp. 418–26.

An Absence of Nonverbal Communication

This exercise will help you to see the value of nonverbal communication to small-group interaction

STEP 1   The class should be organized into an even number of groups composed of five or six people each. Next, pair up each of the groups with one other. The two groups will work together; one acting as a decision-making group, and the other as observers.

STEP 2   The decision-making group should rank-order the following fifteen crimes in terms of their severity, from most severe (1) to least severe (15). Twenty minutes are allowed to complete this task. During the ranking procedure, the decision-making group may communicate only verbally. They may *not* use gestures, facial movements, body movements, or any other nonverbal communication. It may help to have members of the decision-making group sit on their hands to remind them of their restrictions.

List of crimes:

___   Person kills victim by recklessly driving a car
___   Person runs a narcotic ring
___   Parent beats young child to death with fists
___   Person plants bomb in public building; explosion kills one person
___   Wife stabs husband to death
___   Man forcibly rapes woman, who dies from injuries
___   Legislator takes $10,000 company bribe to support favoring firm
___   Man tries to entice minor into car for immoral purposes
___   Person runs prostitution ring
___   Husband stabs wife to death
___   Person smuggles marijuana into country for resale
___   Person shoots victim fatally during robbery
___   Person commits arson—$500,000 damage
___   Person breaks into home and steals $1000
___   Person kidnaps a victim

STEP 3   After watching the decision making, the observers should answer the following questions:
   a. How effective was communication?
   b. What barriers to communication existed?
   c. What purpose does nonverbal communication serve?

STEP 4   Convene the entire class and again answer the three questions posed in Step 3.

Source: Based on J. Powers, "The Blind Decision-Makers," *Exchange: The Organizational Behavior Teaching Journal,* January 1975, pp. 32–33; and C. Taylor, "Crimes, Death, and Stress: Three New Consensus Tasks," *Organizational Behavior Teaching Review,* Vol. 12, No. 2, 1987–88, pp. 115–17.

The Story Evaluation Exercise

OBJECTIVE   To contrast individual and group decision making.
TIME   Fifteen minutes.
PROCEDURE

A. You have five minutes to read the following story* and respond to each of the eleven questions as either *true, false,* or *unknown* (indicated by a question mark). Begin.

The Story   A businessman had just turned off the lights in the store when a man appeared and demanded money. The owner opened a cash register. The contents of the cash register were scooped up, and the man sped away. A member of the police force was notified promptly.

STATEMENTS ABOUT THE STORY

1. A man appeared after the owner had turned off his store lights.   T   F   ?

2. The robber was a *man.*   T   F   ?

3. The man did not demand money.   T   F   ?

4. The man who opened the cash register was the owner.   T   F   ?

5. The store owner scooped up the contents of the cash register and ran away.   T   F   ?

6. Someone opened a cash register.   T   F   ?

7. After the man who demanded the money scooped up the contents of the cash register, he ran away.   T   F   ?

8. While the cash register contained money, the story does *not* state *how much.*   T   F   ?

9. The robber demanded money of the owner.   T   F   ?

10. The story concerns a series of events in which only three persons are referred to: the owner of the store, a man who demanded money, and a member of the police force.   T   F   ?

11. The following events in the story are true: Someone demanded money, a cash register was opened, its contents were scooped up, and a man dashed out of the store.   T   F   ?

B. When your five minutes are up, form groups of four to five members each. Group members have ten minutes to discuss their answers and agree on the correct answers to each of the eleven statements.

C. Your instructor will give you the actual correct answers. How many correct answers did you get at the conclusion of Step A? How many did your group achieve at the conclusion of Step B? Did the group outperform the average individual? The best individual? Discuss the implications of these results.

*Adapted from W. V. Haney, *Communication and Interpersonal Relations,* 6th ed. (Homewood, IL: Richard D. Irwin, Inc., 1992), pp. 232-33. Reprinted by special permission.

Open-Book Management

John Davis—J.D. to his friends—is a vice president at Re:Member Data Services. His company sells data-processing systems to credit unions and J.D. runs the department known as Conversions and Training in Re:Member's Memphis office. Once a sale is made, J.D.'s group converts the customer's database to the new system and then trains the customer's employees.

Until 1989, when Re:Member bought it, J.D.'s office was owned by a large Minneapolis firm that prided itself on keeping its employees in the dark. J.D. would learn about a new job when it landed on his desk, deadline attached. He never knew which prospects were being courted or what the salesperson was promising them or how many jobs he and his colleagues would be faced with in the next month or three. Nor did he know how much money his department made or lost or, indeed, how the office itself was doing.

When Re:Member came in, J.D. was made a vice president and thereby gained access to all the information he needed. But the frustrating experience of working in the dark stuck with him. What would happen, J.D. wondered, if every employee knew as much as he knew now—about upcoming jobs, about how the department was doing, even about how much they themselves contributed to the business? J.D. decided to let this kind of information permeate his office: He introduced open-book management.

J.D. developed a detailed cost accounting system. It required each employee to keep a record of time spent on each job, materials costs, travel and entertainment, and so on. He had the computer track each employee's time, daily billing, salary costs, and expenses. Then he explained to his employees that each of them would now be responsible for his or her own profitability. Every month, J.D. would provide his twelve-person staff with printouts showing how much the company made or lost on each job. Every person would also get a printout showing how much money he or she had made or lost for the company that month.

The new system made some people nervous at first because they feared it would be found out that they weren't making any money for the firm. But gradually those fears subsided. And with their newfound information, employees began coming up with ways their group could generate revenues, cut costs, and expand their skills to improve their individual accounts. In the first year of the program, J.D. found that employee-initiated ideas saved the company $37,000. In addition, he believes he has made his office a more exciting and challenging place to work.

Questions

1. Secrecy is power. Sharing information undermines the separation of management and labor. A boss's claim to authority rests on knowing more about company affairs than subordinates do. Isn't J.D.'s approach to managing, therefore, an example of poor management?
2. J.D.'s program assumes that employees care. But not all employees want the bottom-line responsibility and pressure that come with information. What type of people do you think would prefer working for this kind of organization?
3. Would J.D.'s program work in an office where employees belonged to a labor union? Would it succeed with blue-collar workers who have assembly-line jobs? Discuss.

Source: Based on J. Case, "The Open-Book Managers," *INC.*, September 1990, pp. 104–13.

FOR FURTHER READING

ASHFORD, S. J., and A. S. TSUI, "Self-Regulation for Managerial Effectiveness: The Role of Active Feedback Seeking," *Academy of Management Journal,* June 1991, pp. 251–80. These researchers found that managers who seek negative feedback both increase their own understanding about how others evaluate their work and enhance the others' opinions of the managers' overall effectiveness.

CLAMPITT, P. G., *Communicating for Managerial Effectiveness* (Newbury Park, CA: Sage Publications, 1991). Analyzes the challenges facing managers and suggests creative action plans to resolve critical organizational dilemmas.

GOLEN, S., "A Factors Analysis of Barriers to Effective Listening," *The Journal of Business Communication,* Winter 1990, pp. 25–36. Found six barriers that limit effective listening.

PEARCE, C. G., "Doing Something About Your Listening Ability," *Supervisory Management,* March 1989, pp. 29–34. Presents four rules for improving listening by fifty to one hundred percent.

REILLY, B. J., AND J. A. DiANGELO, JR., "Communication: A Cultural System of Meaning and Value," *Human Relations,* February 1990, pp. 129–40. The embedded organizational culture presets communication among people and gives meaning to any messages that are communicated within the organization.

RICE, F., "Champions of Communication," *Fortune,* June 3, 1991, pp. 111–20. Describes how the CEOs at Union Pacific Railroad, Mattel, and other organizations are getting out of their executive offices and engaging in more face-to-face communication with employees.

NOTES

[1] Based on J. Cushman, "Avianca Flight 52: The Delays That Ended in Disaster," *The New York Times,* February 5, 1990, p. B-1; and E. Weiner, "Right Word Is Crucial in Air Control," *The New York Times,* January 29, 1990, p. B-5.

[2] See, for example, K. W. Thomas and W. H. Schmidt, "A Survey of Managerial Interests with Respect to Conflict," *Academy of Management Journal,* June 1976, p. 317.

[3] W. G. Scott and T. R. Mitchell, *Organization Theory: A Structural and Behavioral Analysis* (Homewood, IL: Richard D. Irwin, 1976).

[4] D. K. Berlo, *The Process of Communication* (New York: Holt, Rinehart & Winston, 1960), pp. 30–32.

[5] Ibid., p. 54.

[6] Ibid., p. 103.

[7] J. C. McCroskey, J. A. Daly, and G. Sorenson, "Personality Correlates of Communication Apprehension," *Human Communication Research,* Spring 1976, pp. 376–80.

[8] B. H. Spitzberg and M. L. Hecht, "A Competent Model of Relational Competence," *Human Communication Research,* Summer 1984, pp. 575–99.

[9] See, for example, L. Stafford and J. A. Daly, "Conversational Memory: The Effects of Instructional Set and Recall Mode on Memory for Natural Conversations," *Human Communication Research,* Spring 1984, pp. 379–402.

[10] J. A. Daly and J. C. McCrosky, "Occupational Choice and Desirability as a Function of Communication Apprehension," paper presented at the annual meeting of the International Communication Association, Chicago, 1975.

[11] J. A. Daly and M. D. Miller, "The Empirical Development of an Instrument of Writing Apprehension," *Research in the Teaching of English,* Winter 1975, pp. 242–49.

[12] R. L. Simpson, "Vertical and Horizontal Communication in Formal Organizations," *Administrative Science Quarterly,* September 1959, pp. 188–96; and B. Harriman, "Up and Down the Communications Ladder," *Harvard Business Review,* September–October 1974, pp. 143–51.

[13] See, for instance, J. W. Newstrom, R. E. Monczka, and W. E. Reif, "Perceptions of the Grapevine: Its Value and Influence," *Journal of Business Communication,* Spring 1974, pp. 12–20; and S. J. Modic, "Grapevine Rated Most Believable," *Industry Week,* May 15, 1989, p. 14.

[14] K. Davis, "Management Communication and the Grapevine," *Harvard Business Review,* September–October 1953, pp. 43–49.

[15] H. Sutton and L. W. Porter, "A Study of the Grapevine in a Governmental Organization," *Personnel Psychology,* Summer 1968, pp. 223–30.

[16]K. Davis, cited in R. Rowan, "Where Did *That* Rumor Come From?" *Fortune,* August 13, 1979, p. 134.

[17]L. Hirschhorn, "Managing Rumors," in L. Hirschhorn (ed.), *Cutting Back* (San Francisco: Jossey-Bass, 1983), pp. 49–52.

[18]R. L. Rosnow and G. A. Fine, *Rumor and Gossip: The Social Psychology of Hearsay* (New York: Elsevier, 1976).

[19]W. Kiechel III, "In Praise of Office Gossip," *Fortune,* August 19, 1985, pp. 253–56.

[20]R. L. Birdwhistell, *Introduction to Kinesics* (Louisville, KY: University of Louisville Press, 1952).

[21]J. Fast, *Body Language* (Philadelphia: M. Evan, 1970), p. 7.

[22]R. L. Daft and R. H. Lengel, "Information Richness: A New Approach to Managerial Behavior and Organization Design," in B. M. Staw and L. L. Cummings (eds.), *Research in Organizational Behavior,* Vol. 6 (Greenwich, CT: JAI Press, 1984), pp. 191–233; R. E. Rice and D. E. Shook, "Relationships of Job Categories and Organizational Levels to Use of Communication Channels, Including Electronic Mail: A Meta-Analysis and Extension," *Journal of Management Studies,* March 1990, pp. 195–229; G. S. Russ, R. L. Daft, and R. H. Lengel, "Media Selection and Managerial Characteristics in Organizational Communications," *Management Communication Quarterly,* November 1990, pp. 151–75; and L. K. Trevino, R. H. Lengel, W. Bodensteiner, E. Gerloff, and N. K. Muir, "The Richness Imperative and Cognitive Style: The Role of Individual Differences in Media Choice Behavior," *Management Communication Quarterly,* November 1990, pp. 176–97.

[23]D. Tannen, *You Just Don't Understand: Women and Men in Conversation* (New York: Ballentine Books, 1991).

[24]J. DeLorean, quoted in S. P. Robbins, *The Administrative Process* (Englewood Cliffs, NJ: Prentice Hall, 1976), p. 404.

[25]S. I. Hayakawa, *Language in Thought and Action* (New York: Harcourt Brace Jovanovich, 1949), p. 292.

[26]This section is based on S. P. Robbins, *Training in InterPersonal Skills: TIPS for Managing People at Work* (Englewood Cliffs, NJ: Prentice Hall, 1989), Chapters 3 and 5.

[27]C. R. Rogers and R. E. Farson, *Active Listening* (Chicago: Industrial Relations Center of the University of Chicago, 1976).

[28]Robbins, *Training in InterPersonal Skills,* pp. 31–34.

[29]P. L. Hunsaker and A. J. Alessandra, *The Art of Managing People* (Englewood Cliffs, NJ: Prentice Hall, 1980), p. 123.

[30]C. Fisher, "Transmission of Positive and Negative Feedback to Subordinates: A Laboratory Investigation," *Journal of Applied Psychology,* October 1979, pp. 533–40.

[31]D. Ilgen, C. D. Fisher, and M. S. Taylor, "Consequences of Individual Feedback on Behavior in Organizations," *Journal of Applied Psychology,* August 1979, pp. 349–71.

[32]F. Bartolome, "Teaching About Whether to Give Negative Feedback," *The Organizational Behavior Teaching Review,* Vol. XI, Issue 2, 1986–87, pp. 95–104.

[33]K. Halperin, C. R. Snyder, R. J. Shenkel, and B. K. Houston, "Effect of Source Status and Message Favorability on Acceptance of Personality Feedback," *Journal of Applied Psychology,* February 1976, pp. 85–88.

[34]C. R. Mill, "Feedback: The Art of Giving and Receiving Help," in L. Porter and C. R. Mill (eds.), *The Reading Book for Human Relations Training* (Bethel, ME: NTL Institute for Applied Behavioral Science, 1976), pp. 18–19.

[35]Ibid.

[36]Ibid.

[37]Ibid.

[38]K. S. Verderber and R. F. Verderber, *Inter-Act: Using Interpersonal Communication Skills,* 4th ed. (Belmont, CA: Wadsworth, 1986).

[39]L. E. Bourne, Jr., and C. V. Bunderson, "Effects of Delay of Information Feedback and Length of Post-Feedback Interval on Concept Identification," *Journal of Experimental Psychology,* January 1963, pp. 1–5.

[40]Verderber and Verderber, *Inter-Act.*

[41]This box is based on N. Adler, *International Dimensions of Organizational Behavior,* 2nd ed. (Boston: PWS-Kent, 1991), pp. 83–84.

[42]Mill, "Feedback," pp. 18–19.

[43]J. McCune, "Consensus Builder," *Success,* October 1990, pp. 43–45.

[44]See N. R. F. Maier, "Assets and Liabilities in Group Problem Solving: The Need for an Integrative Function," *Psychological Review,* April 1967, pp. 239–49; G. W. Hill, "Group versus Individual Performance: Are *N* + 1 Heads Better Than One?" *Psychological Bulletin,* May 1982, pp. 517–39; and A. E. Schwartz and J. Levin, "Better Group Decision Making," *Supervisory Management,* June 1990, p. 4.

[45]See, for example, R. A. Cooke and J. A. Kernaghan, "Estimating the Difference Between Group versus Individual Performance on Problem-Solving Tasks," *Group & Organization Studies,* September 1987, pp. 319–42; and L. K. Michaelsen, W. E. Watson, and R. H. Black, "A

Realistic Test of Individual versus Group Consensus Decision Making," *Journal of Applied Psychology,* October 1989, pp. 834–39.

⁴⁶See, for example, F. C. Miner, Jr., "Group versus Individual Decision Making: An Investigation of Performance Measures, Decision Strategies, and Process Losses/Gains," *Organizational Behavior and Human Performance,* February 1984, pp. 112–24.

⁴⁷I. L. Janis, *Groupthink* (Boston: Houghton Mifflin, 1982).

⁴⁸Ibid.

⁴⁹Ibid.

⁵⁰C. R. Leana, "A Partial Test of Janis' Groupthink Model: Effects of Group Cohesiveness and Leader Behavior on Defective Decision Making," *Journal of Management,* Spring 1985, pp. 5–17; and G. Moorhead and J. R. Montanari, "An Empirical Investigation of the Groupthink Phenomenon," *Human Relations,* May 1986, pp. 399–410.

⁵¹See D. J. Isenberg, "Group Polarization: A Critical Review and Meta-Analysis," *Journal of Personality and Social Psychology,* December 1986, pp. 1141–51; and J. L. Hale and F. J. Boster, "Comparing Effect Coded Models of Choice Shifts," *Communication Research Reports,* April 1988, pp. 180–86.

⁵²See, for example, N. Kogan and M. A. Wallach, "Risk Taking as a Function of the Situation, the Person, and the Group," in *New Directions in Psychology,* Vol. 3 (New York: Holt, Rinehart and Winston, 1967); and M. A. Wallach, N. Kogan, and D. J. Bem, "Group Influence on Individual Risk Taking," *Journal of Abnormal and Social Psychology,* Vol. 65 (1962), pp. 75–86.

⁵³R. D. Clark III, "Group-Induced Shift Toward Risk: A Critical Appraisal," *Psychological Bulletin,* October 1971, pp. 251–70.

⁵⁴A. F. Osborn, *Applied Imagination: Principles and Procedures of Creative Thinking* (New York: Scribner's, 1941).

⁵⁵See A. L. Delbecq, A. H. Van deVen, and D. H. Gustafson, *Group Techniques for Program Planning: A Guide to Nominal and Delphi Processes* (Glenview, IL: Scott, Foresman, 1975); and W. M. Fox, "Anonymity and Other Keys to Successful Problem-Solving Meetings," *National Productivity Review,* Spring 1989, pp. 145–56.

⁵⁶See A. R. Dennis, J. F. George, L. M. Jessup, J. F. Nunamaker, Jr., and D. R. Vogel, "Information Technology to Support Group Work," *MIS Quarterly,* December 1988, pp. 591–619; D. W. Straub and R. A. Beauclair, "Current and Future Uses of Group Decision Support System Technology: Report on a Recent Empirical Study," *Journal of Management Information Systems,* Summer 1988, pp. 101–16; J. Bartimo, "At These Shouting Matches, No One Says a Word," *Business Week,* June 11, 1990, p. 78; and M. S. Poole, M. Holmes, and G. DeSanctis, "Conflict Management in a Computer-Supported Meeting Environment," *Management Science,* August 1991, pp. 926–53.

⁵⁷See, for example, R. S. Schuler, "A Role Perception Transactional Process Model for Organizational Communication-Outcome Relationships," *Organizational Behavior and Human Performance,* April 1979, pp. 268–91.

⁵⁸J. P. Walsh, S. J. Ashford, and T. E. Hill, "Feedback Obstruction: The Influence of the Information Environment on Employee Turnover Intentions," *Human Relations,* January 1985, pp. 23–46.

⁵⁹S. A. Hellweg and S. L. Phillips, "Communication and Productivity in Organizations: A State-of-the-Art Review," in *Proceedings of the 40th Annual Academy of Management Conference,* Detroit, 1980, pp. 188–92.

⁶⁰R. R. Reilly, B. Brown, M. R. Blood, and C. Z. Malatesta, "The Effects of Realistic Previews: A Study and Discussion of the Literature," *Personnel Psychology,* Winter 1981, pp. 823–34.

LEADERSHIP

LEARNING OBJECTIVES

After studying this chapter, you should be able to:

1. Describe the nature of leadership

2. Summarize the conclusions of trait theories

3. Identify the limitations of behavioral theories

4. Describe Fiedler's contingency model

5. Summarize the path–goal theory

6. State the situational leadership theory

7. Explain leader–member exchange theory

8. Describe the leader–participation model

9. Explain why no one leadership style is ideal in all situations

10. Define the qualities that characterize charismatic leaders

If anything goes bad, I did it. If anything goes semi-good, then we did it. If anything goes real good, then you did it. That's all it takes to get people to win football games for you.

COACH P. BRYANT

*I*n December 1990, H. Norman Schwarzkopf was a competent, but unknown, four-star general in the U.S. Army. Then came Operation Desert Storm in the Persian Gulf. In a war that took only weeks to win, Schwarzkopf led Allied troops to a sweeping victory over Iraq and freed Kuwait from Iraqi occupation. By May of 1991, Stormin' Norman Schwarzkopf was a hero all over the United States. Wherever he went, the crowds screamed their approval. No major leadership position in America seemed beyond his grasp. *Time* magazine wrote that his next job might be head football coach for the Philadelphia Eagles, chancellor of Texas A&M University, chairman of Chrysler Corporation (succeeding Lee Iacocca), senator from Florida, or even candidate for President of the United States.[1]

What made Schwarzkopf an "overnight" leader? Certainly the quick and overwhelming victory of his troops was impressive. So, too, was the fact that fewer than 150 Allied soldiers lost their lives when almost every media analyst had forecast Allied losses in the many thousands. Then, of course, there was the bold and charismatic Schwarzkopf style. He was blunt, not glib; passionate, not packaged. He had a wealth of confidence in his troops and it showed; he had the courage to speak his mind; and he had the ability to mesmerize reporters with his sense of humor and willingness to give straight answers. This overweight, balding man didn't look like most people's image of a military leader. Rather, he came across more like a favorite uncle you knew you could always depend on.

But what was it that made people think that someone who could command loyalty from troops in battle could transfer that leadership to business, sports, education, or the political arena? True, General Eisenhower moved from the military to the head of Columbia University and, eventually, to the White House. But does military leadership transfer across organization types? For that matter, does successful leadership in any arena automatically transfer to other arenas? ■

This chapter will help you answer these and a number of other questions about leadership. Let's begin by clarifying what we mean by the term *leadership*.

WHAT IS LEADERSHIP?

Few terms in OB inspire less agreement on definition than *leadership*. As one expert put it, "there are almost as many definitions of leadership as there are persons who have attempted to define the concept."[2]

While almost everyone seems to agree that leadership involves an influence process, differences tend to center around whether leadership must be noncoercive (as opposed to using authority, rewards, and punishments to exert influence over followers) and whether it is distinct from management.[3] The latter issue has been a particularly heated topic of debate in recent years, with most experts arguing that leadership and management are different.

For instance, Abraham Zaleznik of the Harvard Business School argues that leaders and managers are very different kinds of people.[4] They differ in motivation, personal history, and how they think and act. Zaleznik says that managers tend to adopt impersonal, if not passive, attitudes toward goals, whereas leaders take a personal and active attitude toward goals. Managers tend to view work as an enabling process involving some combination of people and ideas interacting to establish strategies and make decisions. Leaders work from high-risk positions—indeed, they are often temperamentally disposed to seek out risk and danger, especially when opportunity and reward appear high. Managers prefer to work with people; they avoid solitary activity because it makes them anxious. They relate to people according to the role they play in a sequence of events or in a decision-making process. Leaders, who are concerned with ideas, relate to people in more intuitive and empathic ways.

John Kotter, a colleague of Zaleznik at Harvard, also argues that leadership is different from management, but for different reasons.[5] Management, he proposes, is about coping with complexity. Good management brings about order and consistency by drawing up formal plans, designing rigid organization structures, and monitoring results against the plans. Leadership, in contrast, is about coping with change. Leaders establish direction by developing a vision of the future, then they align people by communicating this vision and inspiring them to overcome hurdles. Kotter sees both strong leadership and strong management as necessary for optimum organizational effectiveness. But he believes that most organizations are underled and overmanaged. He claims we need to focus more on developing leadership in organizations because the people in charge today are too concerned with keeping things on time and on budget and with doing what was done yesterday, only doing it five percent better.

So where do we stand? We will use a broad definition of leadership—one that can encompass all the current approaches to the subject. Thus, we define **leadership** as the ability to influence a group toward the achievement of goals. The source of this influence may be formal, such as that provided by the possession of managerial rank in an organization. Since management positions come with some degree of formally designated authority, a person

Leadership The ability to influence a group toward the achievement of goals.

Ethical Standards Come from the Top Down

Regardless of how personally ethical an employee is or how much attention management pays to developing an ethical code for the organization, if the organization's top leaders act unethically, they implicitly encourage their employees to do the same. The opposite is also true: Leaders who visibly exhibit high ethical standards become role models for others in the organization and raise its overall level of ethical behavior.

It is an organization's top leadership that sets the ethical tone. Through both their words and their actions—though what they do is probably more important than what they say—an organization's leaders convey what is acceptable and unacceptable behavior. If leaders, for example, use company resources for their personal benefit, inflate their expense accounts, give favored treatment to friends, or employ similar practices, they imply that such behavior is acceptable for all employees.

The organization's top leaders also set the ethical tone by their reward and punishment practices. The choice of whom and what to reward with pay increases and promotions sends a strong message to employees. The promotion of a manager for achieving impressive results in questionable ways indicates to everyone that those questionable ways are acceptable. When they uncover wrongdoing, leaders must not only punish the wrongdoer, they must publicize the fact and make the outcome visible for all to see. This sends another message: Doing wrong has a price, and it's *not* in your best interest at this organization to act unethically!

may assume a leadership role simply because of the position he or she holds in the organization. But not all leaders are managers; nor, for that matter, are all managers leaders. Just because an organization provides its managers with certain formal rights is no assurance that they will be able to lead effectively. We find that nonsanctioned leadership—that is, the ability to influence that arises outside the formal structure of the organization—is as important or more important than formal influence. In other words, leaders can emerge from within a group as well as by formal appointment to lead a group.

TRANSITION IN LEADERSHIP THEORIES

The leadership literature is voluminous, and much of it is confusing and contradictory. In order to make our way through this "forest," we shall consider four approaches to explaining what makes an effective leader. The first sought to find universal personality traits that leaders had to some greater degree than nonleaders. The second tried to explain leadership in terms of the behavior that a person engaged in. Both approaches have been described as "false starts," based on their erroneous and oversimplified conception of leadership.[6] The third looked to contingency models to explain the inadequacies of previous leadership theories in reconciling and bringing together the diversity of research findings. Most recently, attention has returned to traits, but from a different perspective. Researchers are now attempting to identify the set of traits that people implicitly refer to when they characterize someone as a leader. This line of thinking proposes that leadership is as much style—projecting the appearance of being a leader—as it is substance. In this chapter, we shall present the contributions and limitations of each of these four approaches and conclude by attempting to ascertain the value of the leadership literature in explaining and predicting behavior.

TRAIT THEORIES

Trait Theories of Leadership
Theories that sought personality, social, physical, or intellectual traits that differentiated leaders from nonleaders.

What traits characterize leaders like Jesse Jackson? The research has identified six: ambition and energy; the desire to lead; honesty and integrity; self-confidence; intelligence; and job-relevant knowledge.   Ron Haviv/SABA

If we were to describe a leader based on the general connotations presented in today's media, we might list qualities such as intelligence, charisma, decisiveness, enthusiasm, strength, bravery, integrity, self-confidence, and so on—possibly eliciting the conclusion that effective leaders must be one part Boy Scout and two parts Jesus Christ. The search for characteristics such as those listed that would differentiate leaders from nonleaders occupied the early psychologists who studied leadership as they attempted to develop **trait theories.**

Is it possible to isolate one or more personality, social, physical, or intellectual characteristics in individuals we generally acknowledge as leaders—Mahatma Gandhi, Martin Luther King, Jr., Joan of Arc, Winston Churchill, General Douglas MacArthur, John F. Kennedy, Lee Iacocca, Ted Turner, Nelson Mandela, Margaret Thatcher—that nonleaders do not possess? We may agree that these people meet our definition of a leader, but they are individuals with utterly different characteristics. If the concept of traits is to be proved valid, there must be specific characteristics that *all* leaders possess.

Research efforts at isolating these traits resulted in a number of dead ends. For instance, a review of twenty different studies identified nearly eighty leadership traits, but only five of these traits were common to four or more of the investigations.[7] If the search was intended to identify a set of traits that would always differentiate leaders from followers and effective from ineffective leaders, the search obviously failed. Perhaps it was a bit optimistic to believe that there could be consistent and unique traits that would apply across the board to all effective leaders, no matter whether they were in charge of the Hell's Angels, the Mormon Tabernacle Choir, General Electric, the CIA, the Ku Klux Klan, or Harvard University.

If, however, the search was intended to identify traits that were consistently associated with leadership, the results can be interpreted in a more impressive light. For example, six traits on which leaders tend to differ from nonleaders are ambition and energy, the desire to lead, honesty and integrity, self-confidence, intelligence, and job-relevant knowledge.[8] Additionally, recent research provides strong evidence that people who are high self-monitors—that is, are highly flexible in adjusting their behavior in different situations—are much more likely to emerge as leaders in groups than low self-monitors.[9] But, overall, the correlations between specific traits and leadership have generally been in the range of +0.25 to +0.35[10]—interesting results, but not earth-shattering!

These results are based on more than seventy years of trait research. The modest correlations achieved, coupled with the inherent limitations of the trait approach—it overlooks the needs of followers, generally fails to clarify the relative importance of various traits, doesn't separate cause from effect (for example, are leaders self-confident or does success as a leader build self-confidence?), and ignores situational factors—naturally led researchers in other directions. Although there has been some resurgent interest in traits during the past decade,[11] a major movement away from traits began as early as the 1940s. Leadership research from the late 1940s through the mid-1960s emphasized the preferred behavioral styles that leaders demonstrated.

BEHAVIORAL THEORIES

Behavioral Theories of Leadership Theories proposing that specific behaviors differentiate leaders from nonleaders.

The inability to strike "gold" in the trait mines led researchers to look at the **behaviors** that specific leaders exhibited. They wondered if there was something unique in the way that effective leaders behave. For example, do they tend to be more democratic than autocratic?

It was hoped that not only would the behavioral approach provide more definitive answers about the nature of leadership but, if successful, would also have practical implications quite different from those of the trait approach. If trait research had been successful, it would have provided a basis for *selecting* the "right" person to assume formal positions in groups and organizations requiring leadership. In contrast, if behavioral studies were to turn up critical behavioral determinants of leadership, we could *train* people to be leaders. The difference between trait and behavioral theories, in terms of application, lies in their underlying assumptions. If trait theories were valid, then leadership is basically inborn: You either have it or you don't. On the other hand, if there were specific behaviors that identified leaders, then we could teach leadership—we could design programs that implanted these behavioral patterns in individuals who desired to be effective leaders. This was surely a more exciting avenue, for it meant that the supply of leaders could be expanded. If training worked, we could have an infinite supply of effective leaders.

There were a number of studies that looked at behavioral styles. We shall briefly review the most popular: the Ohio State group and the University of Michigan group. Then we shall see how the concepts that these studies developed could be used to create a grid for looking at and appraising leadership styles.

Ohio State Studies

The most comprehensive and replicated of the behavioral theories resulted from research that began at Ohio State University in the late 1940s.[12] These researchers sought to identify independent dimensions of leader behavior. Beginning with over a thousand dimensions, they eventually narrowed the list into two categories that substantially accounted for most of the leadership behavior described by subordinates. They called these two dimensions *initiating structure* and *consideration*.

Initiating Structure The extent to which a leader is likely to define and structure his or her role and those of subordinates in the search for goal attainment.

Initiating structure refers to the extent to which a leader is likely to define and structure his or her role and those of subordinates in the search for goal attainment. It includes behavior that attempts to organize work, work relationships, and goals. The leader characterized as high in initiating structure could be described in terms such as "assigns group members to particular tasks," "expects workers to maintain definite standards of performance," and "emphasizes the meeting of deadlines."

Army drill instructors exemplify individuals who are high in initiating structure. In boot camp, they give orders continuously and structure recruits' activities from sunrise to bedtime. Emphasis on task accomplishment takes precedence over the recruits' personal needs because much learning must be condensed into a short period and emphasis is placed on accepting authority.
Courtesy of the U.S. Army.

Consideration The extent to which a leader is likely to have job relationships characterized by mutual trust, respect for subordinates' ideas, and regard for their feelings.

Consideration is described as the extent to which a person is likely to have job relationships that are characterized by mutual trust, respect for subordinates' ideas, and regard for their feelings. He or she shows concern for followers' comfort, well-being, status, and satisfaction. A leader high in consideration could be described as one who helps subordinates with personal problems, is friendly and approachable, and treats all subordinates as equals.

Extensive research, based on these definitions, found that leaders high in initiating structure and consideration (a "high-high" leader) tended to achieve high subordinate performance and satisfaction more frequently than those who rated low on either consideration, initiating structure, or both. However, the "high-high" style did not always result in positive consequences. For example, leader behavior characterized as high on initiating structure led to greater rates of grievances, absenteeism, and turnover and lower levels of job satisfaction for workers performing routine tasks. Other studies found that high consideration was negatively related to performance ratings of the leader by his or her superior. In conclusion, the Ohio State studies suggested that the "high-high" style generally resulted in positive outcomes, but enough exceptions were found to indicate that situational factors needed to be integrated into the theory.

University of Michigan Studies

Leadership studies undertaken at the University of Michigan's Survey Research Center, at about the same time as those being done at Ohio State, had similar research objectives: to locate behavioral characteristics of leaders that appeared to be related to measures of performance effectiveness.

Employee-Oriented Leader
One who emphasizes interpersonal relations.

Production-Oriented Leader
One who emphasizes technical or task aspects of the job.

The Michigan group also came up with two dimensions of leadership behavior that they labeled **employee-oriented** and **production-oriented.**[13] Leaders who were employee-oriented were described as emphasizing interpersonal relations; they took a personal interest in the needs of their subordinates and accepted individual differences among members. The production-oriented leaders, in contrast, tended to emphasize the technical or task aspects of the job—their main concern was in accomplishing their group's tasks, and the group members were a means to that end.

The conclusions arrived at by the Michigan researchers strongly favored the leaders who were employee-oriented in their behavior. Employee-oriented leaders were associated with higher group productivity and higher job satisfaction. Production-oriented leaders tended to be associated with low group productivity and lower job satisfaction.

The Managerial Grid

Managerial Grid A nine-by-nine matrix outlining eighty-one different leadership styles.

A graphic portrayal of a two-dimensional view of leadership style was developed by Blake and Mouton.[14] They proposed a **Managerial Grid**® based on the styles of "concern for people" and "concern for production," which essentially represent the Ohio State dimensions of consideration and initiating structure or the Michigan dimensions of employee-oriented and production-oriented.

The grid, depicted in Figure 11–1, has nine possible positions along each axis, creating eighty-one different positions in which the leader's style may fall. The grid does not show results produced but, rather, the dominating factors in a leader's thinking in regard to getting results.

Based on the findings of Blake and Mouton, managers were found to perform best under a 9,9 style, as contrasted, for example, with a 9,1 (author-

FIGURE 11–1   The Managerial Grid   Source: Reprinted by permission of *Harvard Business Review*. An exhibit from "Breakthrough in Organization Development" by R.R. Blake, J.S. Mouton, L.B. Barnes, and L.E. Greiner (November-December 1964). Copyright ©1964 by the President and Fellows of Harvard College; all rights reserved.

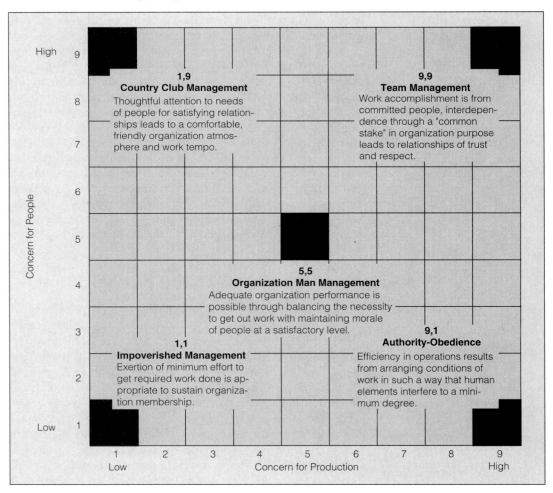

Gender: Do Males and Females Lead Differently?

Women often use a different leadership style than men and that different style can be a plus in the dynamic organizational world of the 1990s. Those are the most important conclusions we can make based on a number of recent studies focusing on gender and leadership style.[15]

Women tend to adopt a more democratic leadership style. They encourage participation, share power and information, and attempt to enhance followers' self-worth. They lead through inclusion and rely on their charisma, expertise, contacts, and interpersonal skills to influence others. Men, on the other hand, are more likely to use a directive command-and-control style. They rely on the formal authority of their position for their influence base. However, there is an interesting qualification to these findings. The tendency for female leaders to be more democratic than males declines when women are in male-dominated jobs. Apparently, group norms and masculine stereotypes of leaders override personal preferences so that women abandon their feminine styles in such jobs and act more autocratically.

Given that men have historically held the great majority of leadership positions in organizations, it is tempting to assume that the existence of differences between men and women would automatically work to favor men. It doesn't. In today's organizations, flexibility, teamwork, trust, and information sharing are replacing rigid structures, competitive individualism, control, and secrecy. The best managers listen, motivate, and provide support to their people. And many women seem to do those things better than men. As a specific example, the expanded use of cross-functional teams in organizations means that effective managers must become skillful negotiators. The leadership styles women typically use can make them better at negotiating, as they are less likely to focus on wins, losses, and competition, as do men. They tend to treat negotiations in the context of a continuing relationship—trying hard to make the other party a winner in its own and others' eyes.

ity type) or 1,9 (country club type) style.[16] Unfortunately, the grid offers a better framework for conceptualizing leadership style than for presenting any tangible new information in clarifying the leadership quandary, since there is little substantive evidence to support the conclusion that a 9,9 style is most effective in all situations.[17]

Summary of Behavioral Theories

We have described the most popular and important of the attempts to explain leadership in terms of the behavior exhibited by the leader. There were other efforts,[18] but they faced the same problem that confronted the Ohio State and Michigan findings. They had very little success in identifying consistent relationships between patterns of leadership behavior and group performance. General statements could not be made because results varied over different ranges of circumstances. What was missing was consideration of the *situational* factors that influence success or failure. For example, it seems unlikely that Jesse Jackson would have been a great leader of black causes at the turn of the century, yet he is in the 1990s. Would Ralph Nader

Judith Rogala, now CEO of Flagship Express in Ypsilanti, Michigan, climbed the ladder at former employers TWA and Federal Express by using a "feminine" management style of sharing information with employees and encouraging participation.   Kevin Horan

have risen to lead a consumer activist group had he been born in 1834 rather than 1934, or in Costa Rica rather than Connecticut? It seems quite unlikely, yet the behavioral approaches we have described could not clarify these situational factors.

CONTINGENCY THEORIES

It became increasingly clear to those who were studying the leadership phenomenon that the predicting of leadership success was more complex than isolating a few traits or preferable behaviors. The failure to obtain consistent results led to a focus on situational influences. The relationship between leadership style and effectiveness suggested that under condition a, style x would be appropriate, while style y would be more suitable for condition b, and style z for condition c. But what were the conditions a, b, c, and so forth? It was one thing to say that leadership effectiveness was dependent on the situation and another to be able to isolate those situational conditions.

There has been no shortage of studies attempting to isolate critical situational factors that affect leadership effectiveness. For instance, popular moderating variables used in the development of contingency theories include the degree of structure in the task being performed, the quality of leader–member relations, the leader's position power, subordinates' role clarity, group norms, information availability, subordinate acceptance of leader's decisions, and subordinate maturity.[19]

Several approaches to isolating key situational variables have proven more successful than others and, as a result, have gained wider recognition. We shall consider five of these: the Fiedler model, Hersey and Blanchard's situational theory, leader–member exchange theory, and the path-goal and leader–participation models.

Fiedler Model

Fiedler Contingency Model
The theory that effective groups depend upon a proper match between a leader's style of interacting with subordinates and the degree to which the situation gives control and influence to the leader.

The first comprehensive contingency model for leadership was developed by Fred Fiedler.[20] The **Fiedler contingency model** proposes that effective group performance depends upon the proper match between the leader's style of interacting with his or her subordinates and the degree to which the situation gives control and influence to the leader. Fiedler developed an instrument, which he called the least preferred co-worker (**LPC**) questionnaire, that purports to measure whether a person is task- or relationship-oriented. Further, he isolated three situational criteria—leader-member relations, task structure, and position power—that he believes can be manipulated so as to create the proper match with the behavioral orientation of the leader. In a sense, the Fiedler model is an outgrowth of trait theory, since the LPC questionnaire is a simple psychological test. However, Fiedler goes significantly beyond trait and behavioral approaches by attempting to isolate situations, relating his personality measure to his situational classification, and then predicting leadership effectiveness as a function of the two.

This description of the Fiedler model is somewhat abstract. Let us now look at the model more closely.

IDENTIFYING LEADERSHIP STYLE Fiedler believes a key factor in leadership success is the individual's basic leadership style. So he begins by trying to find out what that basic style is. Fiedler created the LPC questionnaire for this purpose. It contains sixteen contrasting adjectives (such as pleasant–unpleasant, efficient-inefficient, open-guarded, supportive-hostile). The questionnaire then asks the respondent to think of all the co-workers they have ever had and to describe the one person they *least enjoyed* working with by rating him or her on a scale of 1 to 8 for each of the sixteen sets of contrasting adjectives. Fiedler believes that based on the respondents' answers to this LPC questionnaire, he can determine their basic leadership style. If the least preferred co-worker is described in relatively positive terms (a high LPC score), then the respondent is primarily interested in good personal relations with this co-worker. That is, if you essentially describe the person you are least able to work with in favorable terms, Fiedler would label you relationship-oriented. In contrast, if the least preferred co-worker is seen in relatively unfavorable terms (a low LPC score), the respondent is primarily interested in productivity and thus would be labeled task-oriented. About sixteen percent of respondents score in the middle range.[21] Such individuals cannot be classified as either relationship- or task-oriented and thus

Bob Knight, the highly successful basketball coach at Indiana University, generally confirms Fiedler's belief that a person's leadership style is fixed. Knight's intense, task-oriented style seems unvarying. He regularly argues with referees and once threw a chair across the floor to protest a call. In one recent season he benched all his starters in a key conference game because they weren't practicing intensely enough and kicked his own son off the team for a rules infraction.   Jim Gund/Allsport

fall outside the theory's predictions. The rest of our discussion, therefore, relates to the eighty-four percent who score in either the high or low range of the LPC.

Fiedler assumes that an individual's leadership style is fixed. As we'll show in a moment, this is important because it means that if a situation requires a task-oriented leader and the person in that leadership position is relationship-oriented, either the situation has to be modified or the leader removed and replaced if optimum effectiveness is to be achieved. Fiedler argues that leadership style is innate to a person—you *can't* change your style to fit changing situations!

DEFINING THE SITUATION   After an individual's basic leadership style has been assessed through the LPC, it is necessary to match the leader with the situation. Fiedler has identified three contingency dimensions that, he argues, define the key situational factors that determine leadership effectiveness. These are **leader–member relations, task structure,** and **position power.** They are defined as follows:

1. *Leader–member relations:* The degree of confidence, trust, and respect subordinates have in their leader

2. *Task structure:* The degree to which the job assignments are procedurized (that is, structured or unstructured)

3. *Position power:* The degree of influence a leader has over power variables such as hiring, firing, discipline, promotions, and salary increases

So the next step in the Fiedler model is to evaluate the situation in terms of these three contingency variables. Leader–member relations are either good or poor, task structure is either high or low, and position power is either strong or weak.

Fiedler states the better the leader–member relations, the more highly structured the job, and the stronger the position power, the more control or influence the leader has. For example, a very favorable situation (where the leader would have a great deal of control) might involve a payroll manager who is well respected and whose subordinates have confidence in her (good leader-member relations), where the activities to be done—such as wage computation, check writing, report filing—are specific and clear (high task structure), and the job provides considerable freedom for her to reward and punish her subordinates (strong position power). On the other hand, an unfavorable situation might be the disliked chairman of a voluntary United Way fundraising team. In this job, the leader has very little control. Altogether, by mixing the three contingency variables, there are potentially eight different situations or categories in which a leader could find him or herself.

MATCHING LEADERS AND SITUATIONS   With knowledge of an individual's LPC and an assessment of the three contingency variables, the Fiedler model proposes matching them up to achieve maximum leadership effectiveness.[22] Based on Fiedler's study of over twelve hundred groups, in which he compared relationship- versus task-oriented leadership styles in each of the eight situational categories, he concluded that task-oriented leaders tend to perform better in situations that were *very favorable* to them and in situations that were *very unfavorable* (see Figure 11–2). So Fiedler would predict that when faced with a category I, II, III, VII, or VIII situation, task-oriented leaders perform better. Relationship-oriented leaders, however, perform better in moderately favorable situations—categories IV through VI.

Leader–Member Relations The degree of confidence, trust, and respect subordinates have in their leader.

Task Structure The degree to which job assignments are procedurized.

Position Power Influence derived from one's formal structural position in the organization; includes power to hire, fire, discipline, promote, and give salary increases.

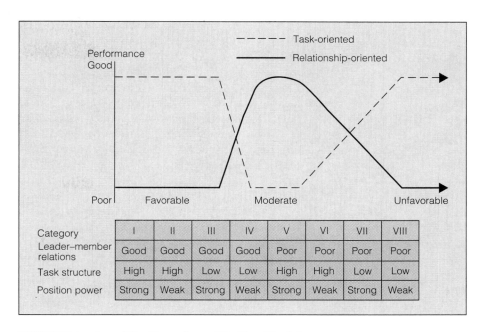

Category	I	II	III	IV	V	VI	VII	VIII
Leader–member relations	Good	Good	Good	Good	Poor	Poor	Poor	Poor
Task structure	High	High	Low	Low	High	High	Low	Low
Position power	Strong	Weak	Strong	Weak	Strong	Weak	Strong	Weak

FIGURE 11–2   Findings from Fiedler Model

Given Fiedler's findings, how would you apply them? You would seek to match leaders and situations. Individuals' LPC scores would determine the type of situation for which they were best suited. That "situation" would be defined by evaluating the three contingency factors of leader–member relations, task structure, and position power. But remember that Fiedler views an individual's leadership style as being fixed. Therefore, there are really only two ways in which to improve leader effectiveness.

First, you can change the leader to fit the situation—as in a baseball game, a manager can reach into his bullpen and put in a right-handed pitcher or a left-handed pitcher, depending on the situational characteristics of the hitter. So, for example, if a group situation rates as highly unfavorable but is currently led by a relationship-oriented manager, the group's performance could be improved by replacing that manager with one who is task-oriented. The second alternative would be to change the situation to fit the leader. That could be done by restructuring tasks or increasing or decreasing the power that the leader has to control factors such as salary increases, promotions, and disciplinary actions. To illustrate, assume a task-oriented leader is in a category IV situation. If this leader could increase his or her position power, then the leader would be operating in category III and the leader–situation match would be compatible for high group performance.

EVALUATION   One should not surmise that Fiedler has closed all the gaps and put to rest all the questions underlying leadership effectiveness. Research finds that the Fiedler model predicts all except category II when laboratory studies are reviewed; however, when field studies are analyzed, the model produces supportive evidence for only categories II, V, VII, and VIII.[23] So we have conflicting results depending on the type of studies used.

On the whole, reviews of the major studies undertaken to test the overall validity of the Fiedler model lead to a generally positive conclusion. That is, there is considerable evidence to support the model.[24] But additional variables are probably needed if an improved model is to fill in some of the remaining gaps. Moreover, there are problems with the LPC and the practical use of the model that need to be addressed. For instance, the logic underlying the LPC is not well understood and studies have shown that respondents' LPC scores are not stable.[25] Also, the contingency variables are complex and difficult for practitioners to assess. It's often difficult in practice to determine how good the leader–member relations are, how structured the task is, and how much position power the leader has.[26]

Our conclusion is that Fiedler has clearly made an important contribution toward understanding leadership effectiveness. His model has been the object of much controversy and probably will continue to be. Field studies fall short of providing full support and the model could benefit by including additional contingency variables. But Fiedler's work continues to be a dominant input in the development of a contingency explanation of leadership effectiveness.

COGNITIVE RESOURCE THEORY: AN UPDATE ON FIEDLER'S CONTINGENCY MODEL Recently, Fiedler and an associate, Joe Garcia, reconceptualized the former's original theory[27] to deal with "some serious oversights that need to be addressed."[28] Specifically, they are concerned with trying to explain the *process* by which a leader obtains effective group performance. They call this reconceptualization **cognitive resource theory.**

They begin by making two assumptions. First, intelligent and competent leaders formulate more effective plans, decisions, and action strategies than less intelligent and competent leaders. Second, leaders communicate their plans, decisions, and strategies through directive behavior. Fiedler and Garcia then show how stress and cognitive resources such as experience, tenure, and intelligence act as important influences on leadership effectiveness.

The essence of the new theory can be boiled down to three predictions: (1) directive behavior results in good performance only if linked with high intelligence in a supportive, nonstressful leadership environment; (2) in highly stressful situations, there is a positive relationship between job experience and performance; and (3) the intellectual abilities of leaders correlate with group performance in situations that the leader perceives as nonstressful.

Fiedler and Garcia admit that their data supporting cognitive resource theory are far from overwhelming. And a recent outside evaluation of the theory with Air Force enlisted personnel was not especially supportive.[29] Clearly, more research is needed. Yet, given the impact of Fiedler's original contingency model of leadership on organizational behavior, the new theory's link to this earlier model, and the new theory's introduction of the leader's cognitive abilities as an important influence on leadership effectiveness, cognitive resource theory should not be dismissed out of hand.

Hersey and Blanchard's Situational Theory

One of the most widely practiced leadership models is Paul Hersey and Ken Blanchard's **situational leadership theory.**[30] It has been used as a major training device at such Fortune 500 companies as BankAmerica, Caterpillar, IBM, Mobil Oil, and Xerox; it has also been widely accepted in all the military services.[31] Although the theory has not undergone extensive evaluation to test its validity, we include it here because of its wide acceptance and its strong intuitive appeal. Additionally, in defense of the theory, it's too early at this point in its development to dismiss it out of hand merely because researchers have not chosen to evaluate it more thoroughly.

Situational leadership is a contingency theory that focuses on the followers. Successful leadership is achieved by selecting the right leadership style, which Hersey and Blanchard argue is contingent on the level of the

Cognitive Resource Theory
A theory of leadership that proposes a leader obtains effective group performance by, first, making effective plans, decisions, and strategies, and then communicating them through directive behavior.

Situational Leadership Theory
A contingency theory that focuses on followers' maturity.

followers' maturity. Before we proceed, we should clarify two points: Why focus on the followers? What is meant by the term *maturity?*

The emphasis on the followers in leadership effectiveness reflects the reality that it is they who accept or reject the leader. Regardless of what the leader does, effectiveness depends on the actions of his or her followers. This is an important dimension that has been overlooked or underemphasized in most leadership theories.

The term **maturity,** as defined by Hersey and Blanchard, is the ability and willingness of people to take responsibility for directing their own behavior. It has two components: job maturity and psychological maturity. The first encompasses one's knowledge and skills. Individuals who are high in job maturity have the knowledge, ability, and experience to perform their job tasks without direction from others. Psychological maturity relates to the willingness or motivation to do something. Individuals high in psychological maturity don't need much external encouragement; they are already intrinsically motivated.

Situational leadership uses the same two leadership dimensions that Fiedler identified: task and relationship behaviors. However, Hersey and Blanchard go a step farther by considering each as either high or low and then combining them into four specific leadership styles: telling, selling, participating, and delegating. They are described as follows:

Telling (high task–low relationship). The leader defines roles and tells people what, how, when, and where to do various tasks. It emphasizes directive behavior.

Selling (high task–high relationship). The leader provides both directive behavior and supportive behavior.

Participating (low task–high relationship). The leader and follower share in decision making, with the main role of the leader being facilitating and communicating.

Delegating (low task–low relationship). The leader provides little direction or support.

The final component in Hersey and Blanchard's theory is defining four stages of maturity:

M1. People are both unable and unwilling to take responsibility to do something. They are neither competent nor confident.

M2. People are unable but willing to do the necessary job tasks. They are motivated but currently lack the appropriate skills.

M3. People are able but unwilling to do what the leader wants.

M4. People are both able and willing to do what is asked of them.

Figure 11–3 integrates the various components into the situational leadership model. As followers reach high levels of maturity, the leader responds by not only continuing to decrease control over activities, but also by continuing to decrease relationship behavior as well. At stage M1, followers need clear and specific directions. At stage M2, both high-task and high-relationship behavior is needed. The high-task behavior compensates for the followers' lack of ability, and the high-relationship behavior tries to get the followers psychologically to "buy into" the leader's desires. M3 creates motivational problems that are best solved by a supportive, nondirective, participative style. Finally, at stage M4, the leader doesn't have to do much because followers are both willing and able to take responsibility.

Maturity The ability and willingness of people to take responsibility for directing their own behavior.

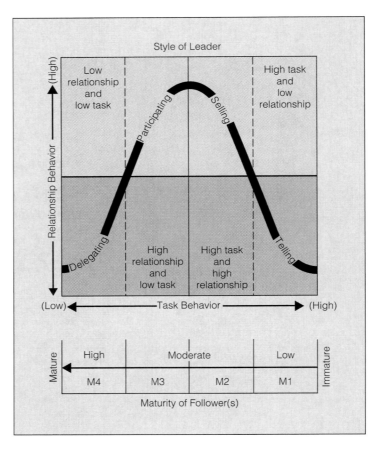

FIGURE 11–3
Situational Leadership
Model   Source: Adopted from P.
Hersey and K. Blanchard, *Management
Of Organizational Behavior: Utilizing
Human Resources,* 4th ed. ©1982, p. 152.
Reprinted by permission of Prentice-Hall,
Inc., Englewood Cliffs, N.J.

The astute reader might have noticed the high similarity between Hersey and Blanchard's four leadership styles and the four extreme "corners" in the Managerial Grid. The telling style equates to the 9,1 leader; selling equals 9,9; participating is equivalent to 1,9; and delegating is the same as the 1,1 leader. Is situational leadership, then, merely the Managerial Grid with one major difference—the replacement of the 9,9 ("one style for all occasions") contention with the recommendation that the "right" style should align with the maturity of the followers? Hersey and Blanchard say "No!"[32] They argue that the grid emphasizes *concern* for production and people, which are attitudinal dimensions. Situational leadership, in contrast, emphasizes task and relationship *behavior.* In spite of Hersey and Blanchard's claim, this is a pretty minute differentiation. Understanding of the situational leadership theory is probably enhanced by considering it as a fairly direct adaptation of the grid framework to reflect four stages of follower maturity.

Finally, we come to the critical question: Is there evidence to support situational leadership theory? As noted earlier, the theory has received little attention from researchers,[33] but on the basis of the research to date, conclusions must be guarded. Some researchers provide partial support for the theory,[34] while others find no support for its assumptions.[35] As a result, any enthusiastic endorsement should be cautioned against.

Leader–Member Exchange Theory

For the most part, the leadership theories we've covered to this point have largely assumed that leaders treat all their subordinates in the same man-

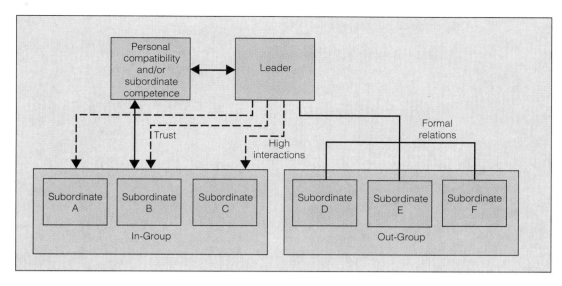

FIGURE 11–4   Leader–Member Exchange Theory

ner. But think about your experiences in groups. Did you notice that leaders often act very differently toward different subordinates? Did the leader tend to have favorites who made up his or her "in" group? If you answered "Yes" to both these questions, you're acknowledging what George Graen and his associates have observed, which creates the foundation for their leader–member exchange theory (recently renamed from the vertical dyad linkage theory).[36]

The **leader-member exchange (LMX) theory** argues that because of time pressures, leaders establish a special relationship with a small group of their subordinates. These individuals make up the in-group—they are trusted, get a disproportionate amount of the leader's attention, and are more likely to receive special privileges. Other subordinates fall into the out-group. They get less of the leader's time, fewer of the preferred rewards that the leader controls, and have superior-subordinate relations based on formal authority interactions.

The theory proposes that early in the history of the interaction between a leader and a given subordinate, the leader implicitly categorizes the subordinate as an "in" or an "out" and that relationship is relatively stable over time.[37] Just precisely how the leader chooses who falls into each category is unclear, but there is evidence that leaders tend to choose in-group members because they have personal characteristics (for example, age, sex, personality) that are compatible with the leader and/or a higher level of competence than out-group members.[38] (See Figure 11–4). LMX theory predicts that subordinates with in-group status will have higher performance ratings, less turnover, and greater satisfaction with their superior.

Research to test LMX theory has been generally supportive.[39] More specifically, the theory and research surrounding it provide substantive evidence that leaders do differentiate among subordinates, that these disparities are far from random, and that in-group and out-group status are related to employee performance and satisfaction.[40]

Path–Goal Theory

Currently, one of the most respected approaches to leadership is the path-goal theory. Developed by Robert House, path-goal theory is a contingency model of leadership that extracts key elements from the Ohio State leadership research on initiating structure and consideration and the expectancy theory of motivation.[41]

The essence of the theory is that it's the leader's job to assist his or her followers in attaining their goals and to provide the necessary direction and/or support to ensure that their goals are compatible with the overall objectives of the group or organization. The term "path-goal" is derived from the belief that effective leaders clarify the path to help their followers get from where they are to the achievement of their work goals and make the journey along the path easier by reducing roadblocks and pitfalls.

According to **path-goal theory,** a leader's behavior is *acceptable* to subordinates to the degree that it is viewed by them as an immediate source of satisfaction or as a means of future satisfaction. A leader's behavior is *motivational* to the degree that it (1) makes subordinate need satisfaction contingent on effective performance and (2) provides the coaching, guidance, support, and rewards that are necessary for effective performance. To test these statements, House identified four leadership behaviors. The *directive leader* lets subordinates know what is expected of them, schedules work to be done, and gives specific guidance as to how to accomplish tasks. This closely parallels the Ohio State dimension of initiating structure. The *supportive leader* is friendly and shows concern for the needs of subordinates. This is essentially synonymous with the Ohio State dimension of consideration. The *participative leader* consults with subordinates and uses their suggestions before making a decision. The *achievement-oriented leader* sets challenging goals and expects subordinates to perform at their highest level. In contrast to Fiedler's view of a leader's behavior, House assumes that leaders are flexible. Path-goal theory implies that the same leader can display any or all of these behaviors depending on the situation.

As Figure 11–5 illustrates, path-goal theory proposes two classes of situational or contingency variables that moderate the leadership behavior-outcome relationship—those in the *environment* that are outside the control of the subordinate (task structure, the formal authority system, and the work group) and those that are part of the personal characteristics of the *subordinate* (locus of control, experience, and perceived ability).

Path-Goal Theory The theory that a leader's behavior is acceptable to subordinates insofar as they view it as a source of either immediate or future satisfaction.

FIGURE 11–5   The Path-Goal Theory

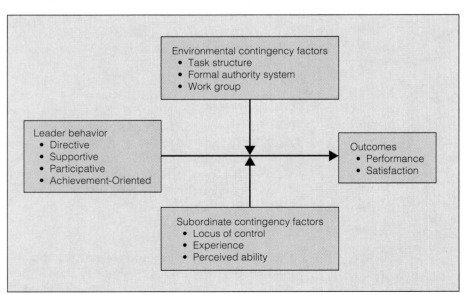

Environmental factors determine the type of leader behavior required as a complement if subordinate outcomes are to be maximized, while personal characteristics of the subordinate determine how the environment and leader behavior are interpreted. So the theory proposes that leader behavior will be ineffective when it is redundant with sources of environmental structure or incongruent with subordinate characteristics.

The following are some examples of hypotheses that have evolved out of path-goal theory:

- Directive leadership leads to greater satisfaction when tasks are ambiguous or stressful than when they are highly structured and well laid out.

- Supportive leadership results in high employee performance and satisfaction when subordinates are performing structured tasks.

- Directive leadership is likely to be perceived as redundant among subordinates with high perceived ability or with considerable experience.

- The more clear and bureaucratic the formal authority relationships, the more leaders should exhibit supportive behavior and de-emphasize directive behavior.

- Directive leadership will lead to higher employee satisfaction when there is substantive conflict within a work group.

- Subordinates with an internal locus of control (those who believe they control their own destiny) will be more satisfied with a participative style.

- Subordinates with an external locus of control will be more satisfied with a directive style.

- Achievement-oriented leadership will increase subordinates' expectancies that effort will lead to high performance when tasks are ambiguously structured.

Research to validate hypotheses such as these is generally encouraging.[42] The evidence supports the logic underlying the theory. That is, employee performance and satisfaction are likely to be positively influenced when the leader compensates for things lacking in either the employee or the work setting. However, the leader who spends time explaining tasks when those tasks are already clear or when the employee has the ability and experience to handle them without interference is likely to be ineffective because the employee will see such directive behavior as redundant or even insulting.

What does the future hold for path–goal theory? Its framework has been tested and appears to have moderate to high empirical support. We can, however, expect to see more research focused on refining and extending the theory by incorporating additional moderating variables.

Leader–Participation Model

Leader–Participation Model
A leadership theory that provides a set of rules to determine the form and amount of participative decision making in different situations.

Back in 1973, Victor Vroom and Phillip Yetton developed a **leader-participation model** that related leadership behavior and participation to decision making.[43] Recognizing that task structures have varying demands for routine and nonroutine activities, these researchers argued that leader behavior must adjust to reflect the task structure. Vroom and Yetton's model was normative—it provided a sequential set of rules that should be followed for determining the form and amount of participation desirable in decision making, as dictated by different types of situations. The model was a complex decision tree incorporating seven contingencies (whose relevance could be identified by making "Yes" or "No" choices) and five alternative leadership styles.

More recent work by Vroom and Arthur Jago has resulted in a revision of this model.[44] The new model retains the same five alternative leadership styles but expands the contingency variables to twelve, ten of which are answered along a five-point scale. Table 11–1 lists the twelve variables.

The model assumes that any of five behaviors may be feasible in a given situation—Autocratic I (AI), Autocratic II (AII), Consultative I (CI), Consultative II (CII), and Group II (GII):

- *AI*. You solve the problem or make a decision yourself using information available to you at that time.

- *AII*. You obtain the necessary information from subordinates and then decide on the solution to the problem yourself. You may or may not tell subordinates what the problem is when getting the information from them. The role played by your subordinates in making the decision is clearly one of providing the necessary information to you rather than generating or evaluating alternative solutions.

TABLE 11–1   **Contingency Variables in the Revised Leader–Participation Model**

QR: Quality Requirement
How important is the technical quality of this decision?

1	2	3	4	5
No Importance	Low Importance	Average Importance	High Importance	Critical Importance

CR: Commitment Requirement
How important is subordinate commitment to the decision?

1	2	3	4	5
No Importance	Low Importance	Average Importance	High Importance	Critical Importance

LI: Leader Information
Do you have sufficient information to make a high-quality decision?

1	2	3	4	5
No	Probably No	Maybe	Probably Yes	Yes

ST: Problem Structure
Is the problem well structured?

1	2	3	4	5
No	Probably No	Maybe	Probably Yes	Yes

CP: Commitment Probability
If you were to make the decision by yourself, is it reasonably certain that your subordinates would be committed to the decision?

1	2	3	4	5
No	Probably No	Maybe	Probably Yes	Yes

GC: Goal Congruence
Do subordinates share the organizational goals to be attained in solving this problem?

1	2	3	4	5
No	Probably No	Maybe	Probably Yes	Yes

- *CI.* You share the problem with relevant subordinates individually, getting their ideas and suggestions without bringing them together as a group. Then *you* make the decision, which may or may not reflect your subordinates' influence.

- *CII.* You share the problem with your subordinates as a group, collectively obtaining their ideas and suggestions. Then you make the decision that may or may not reflect your subordinates' influence.

- *GII.* You share the problem with your subordinates as a group. Together you generate and evaluate alternatives and attempt to reach an agreement (consensus) on a solution.

Vroom and Jago have developed a computer program that cuts through the complexity of the new model. But managers can still use decision trees to select their leader style if there are no "shades of gray" (that is, when the status of a variable is clearcut so that a "Yes" or "No" response will be accurate),

TABLE 11–1 Cont.

CO: Subordinate Conflict

Is conflict among subordinates over preferred solutions likely?

1	2	3	4	5
No	Probably No	Maybe	Probably Yes	Yes

SI: Subordinate Information

Do subordinates have sufficient information to make a high-quality decision?

1	2	3	4	5
No	Probably No	Maybe	Probably Yes	Yes

TC: Time Constraint

Does a critically severe time constraint limit your ability to involve subordinates?

1	5
No	Yes

GD: Geographical Dispersion

Are the costs involved in bringing together geographically dispersed subordinates prohibitive?

1	5
No	Yes

MT: Motivation–Time

How important is it to you to minimize the time it takes to make the decision?

1	2	3	4	5
No Importance	Low Importance	Average Importance	High Importance	Critical Importance

MD: Motivation–Development

How important is it to you to maximize the opportunities for subordinate development?

1	2	3	4	5
No Importance	Low Importance	Average Importance	High Importance	Critical Importance

Source: V. H. Vroom and A. G. Jago, *The New Leadership: Managing Participation in Organizations* (Englewood Cliffs, NJ: Prentice Hall, 1988), pp. 111–12. With permission.

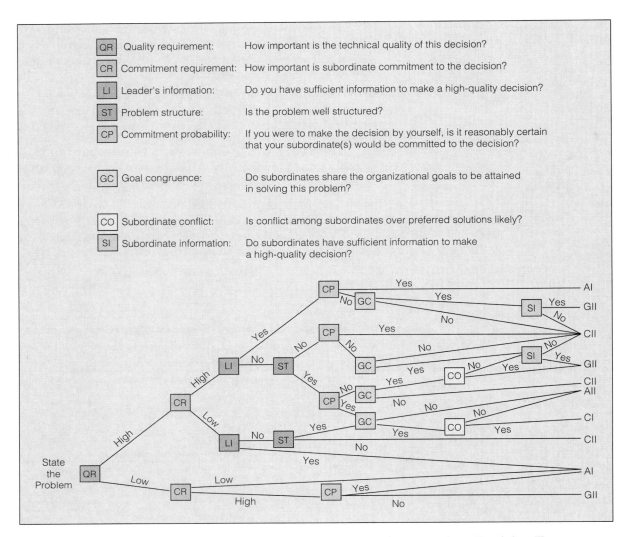

QR	Quality requirement:	How important is the technical quality of this decision?
CR	Commitment requirement:	How important is subordinate commitment to the decision?
LI	Leader's information:	Do you have sufficient information to make a high-quality decision?
ST	Problem structure:	Is the problem well structured?
CP	Commitment probability:	If you were to make the decision by yourself, is it reasonably certain that your subordinate(s) would be committed to the decision?
GC	Goal congruence:	Do subordinates share the organizational goals to be attained in solving this problem?
CO	Subordinate conflict:	Is conflict among subordinates over preferred solutions likely?
SI	Subordinate information:	Do subordinates have sufficient information to make a high-quality decision?

FIGURE 11–6   **The Revised Leader Participation Model (Time-Driven Decision Tree-Group Problems)**

there are no critically severe time constraints, and subordinates are not geographically dispersed. Figure 11–6 illustrates one of these decision trees.

Research testing of the original leader–participation model was very encouraging.[45] Because the revised model is new, its validity still needs to be assessed. But the new model is a direct extension of the 1973 version and it's also consistent with our current knowledge of the benefits and costs of participation. So, at this time, we have every reason to believe that the revised model provides an excellent guide to help managers choose the most appropriate leadership style in different situations.

Two last points before we move on. First, the revised leader–participation model is very sophisticated and complex, which makes it impossible to describe in detail in a basic OB textbook. But the variables identified in Table 11–1 provide you with some solid insights about which contingency variables you need to consider when choosing your leadership style.

Second, the leader–participation model confirms that leadership research should be directed at the situation rather than the person. It probably makes more sense to talk about autocratic and participative *situations*

FIGURE 11–7   Source: B. Parker and J. Hart, *Let There Be Reign* (Greenwich, CT: Fawcett Books, 1972).

than about autocratic and participative *leaders*. As did House in his path–goal theory, Vroom, Yetton, and Jago argue against the notion that leader behavior is inflexible. The leader–participation model assumes that the leader can adjust his or her style to different situations.

The cartoon in Figure 11–7 proposes adjusting the individual to the coat, rather than vice versa. In terms of leadership, we can think of "coat" as analogous to "situation." If an individual's leadership style range is very narrow, as Fiedler proposes, we are required to place that individual into the appropriate-size situation if he or she is to lead successfully. But there is another possibility: If House and Vroom-Yetton-Jago are right, the individual leader has to assess the situation that is available and adjust his or her style accordingly. Whether we should adjust the situation to fit the person or fix the person to fit the situation is an important issue. The answer is probably that it depends on the leader—specifically, on whether that person rates high or low on self-monitoring.[46] As we know, individuals differ in their behavioral flexibility. Some people show considerable ability to adjust their behavior to external, situational factors; they are adaptable. Others, however, exhibit high levels of consistency regardless of the situation. High self-monitors are generally able to adjust their leadership style to suit changing situations.

The leader-participation model reaffirms the logic for a contingency approach to leadership. The leadership behaviors necessary for Michele Hooper, who heads up hospital-equipment supplier Baxter International's Canadian division, should obviously be different from the behaviors required to lead members of armed guerrillas in Nicaragua. The importance of decisions, the types of problems they confront, and the need for acceptance by subordinates to ensure proper implementation are just three variables that are likely to differ in the two situations.   Left, © Alex Mayboom; right, Jose Azel/Contact Press Images

National Culture as an Important Contingency Variable

One general conclusion that surfaces from the leadership literature is that effective leaders don't use any single style. They adjust their style to the situation. While not mentioned explicitly, certainly national culture is an important situational variable determining which leadership style will be most effective.

National culture affects leadership style by way of the subordinate. Leaders cannot choose their styles at will. They are constrained by the cultural conditions that their subordinates have come to expect. For example, a manipulative or autocratic style is compatible with high power distance, and we find high power distance scores in Arab, Far Eastern, and Latin countries. Power distance rankings should also be good indicators of employee willingness to accept participative leadership. Participation is likely to be most effective in such low power distance cultures as exist in Norway, Finland, Denmark, and Sweden. Not incidentally, this may explain the fact that a number of leadership theories (the more obvious being ones like the University of Michigan behavioral studies and the leader–participation model) implicitly favor the use of a participative or people-oriented style. Remember that most of these theories were developed by North Americans, using North American subjects; countries like the United States and Canada rate below average on power distance.

Sometimes Leadership Is Irrelevant!

In keeping with the contingency spirit, we want to conclude this section by offering this notion: the belief that *some* leadership style *will always* be effective *regardless* of the situation may not be true. Leadership may not always be important. Data from numerous studies collectively demonstrate that, in many situations, whatever behaviors leaders exhibit are irrelevant. Certain individual, job, and organizational variables can act as *substitutes* for leadership or *neutralize* the leader's effect to influence his or her subordinates.[47]

Neutralizers make it impossible for leader behavior to make any difference to subordinate outcomes. They negate the leader's influence. Substitutes, on the other hand, make a leader's influence not only impossible but also unnecessary. They act as a replacement for the leader's influence. For instance, characteristics of subordinates such as their experience, training, "professional" orientation, or need for independence can neutralize the effect of leadership. These characteristics can replace the need for a leader's support or ability to create structure and reduce task ambiguity. Jobs that are inherently unambiguous and routine or that are intrinsically satisfying may place fewer demands on the leadership variable. Organizational characteristics like explicit formalized goals, rigid rules and procedures, and cohesive work groups can replace formal leadership.

This recent recognition that leaders don't always have an impact on subordinate outcomes should not be that surprising. After all, we have introduced a number of independent variables—attitudes, personality, ability, and group norms, to name but a few—that have been documented as having an impact on employee performance and satisfaction. Yet supporters of the leadership concept have tended to place an undue burden on this variable for explaining and predicting behavior. It is too simplistic to consider subordinates as guided to goal accomplishments solely by the behavior of their leader. It is important, therefore, to recognize explicitly that leadership is merely another independent variable in our overall OB model. In some situations, it may contribute a lot to explaining employee productivity, absence, turnover, and satisfaction, but in other situations, it may contribute little toward that end.

LOOKING FOR COMMON GROUND: WHAT DOES IT ALL MEAN?

The topic of leadership certainly doesn't lack for theories. But from an overview perspective, what does it all mean? Let's try to identify commonalities among the leadership theories and attempt to determine what, if any, practical value the theories hold for application to organizations.

Careful examination discloses that the concepts of "task" and "people"—often expressed in more elaborate terms that hold substantially the same meaning—permeate most of the theories.[48] The task dimension is called just that by Fiedler, but it goes by the name of "initiating structure" for the Ohio State group, "directive leadership" by path–goal supporters, "production orientation" by the Michigan researchers, and "concern for production" by Blake and Mouton. The people dimension gets similar treatment, going under such aliases as "consideration," "employee-oriented," "supportive," or "relationship-oriented" leadership. It seems clear that leadership behavior can be reduced to two dimensions—task and people—but researchers continue to differ as to whether the orientations are two ends of a single continuum (you could be high on one or the other but not both) or two independent dimensions (you could be high or low on both).

Although one well-known scholar argues that virtually every theory has also "wrestled with the question of how much a leader should share power with subordinates in decision making,"[49] there is far less support for this contention. The situational leadership theory and the leader–participation model address this issue, but the task–people dichotomy appears to be far more encompassing.

Leadership theorists don't agree on the issue of whether a leader's style is fixed or flexible. For example, Fiedler takes the former position, while Vroom, Yetton, and Jago argue for the latter. As previously noted, our position is that both are probably right—it depends on the leader's personality. High self-monitors are more likely to adjust their leadership style to changing situations than are low self-monitors.[50] So the need to adjust the situation to the leader in order to improve the leader–situation match seems to be necessary only with low self-monitoring individuals.

How should we interpret the findings presented so far in this chapter? Some traits have proved, over time, to be modest predictors of leadership effectiveness. But knowing that a manager possesses intelligence, ambition, self-confidence, or the like would by no means assure us that his or her subordinates would be productive and satisfied employees. The ability of these traits to predict leadership success is just not that strong.

The early task–people approaches (such as the Ohio State, Michigan, and Managerial Grid theories) also offer us little substance. The strongest statement one can make based on these theories is that leaders who rate high in people orientation should end up with satisfied employees. The research is too mixed to make predictions regarding employee productivity or the effect of a task orientation on productivity and satisfaction.

Controlled laboratory studies designed to test the Fiedler contingency model, in aggregate, have generally supported the theory. But field studies provide more limited support. We suggest that when category II, V, VII, and VIII situations exist, the utilization of the LPC instrument to assess whether there is a leader-situation match and the use of that information to predict employee productivity and satisfaction outcomes seem warranted.

Hersey and Blanchard's situational leadership theory is straightforward, intuitively appealing, and important for its explicit recognition that the subordinate's ability and motivation are critical to the leader's success. Yet, in spite of its wide acceptance by practitioners, the mixed empirical support renders the theory, at least at this time, more speculative than substantive.

Leader–member exchange theory looks at leadership from a different angle. It focuses on in-groups and out-groups. Given the impressive evidence that in-group employees have higher performance and satisfaction than out-group members, the theory provides valuable insight for predicting leader effect as long as we know whether an employee is an "in" or an "out."

Studies testing the original Vroom-Yetton version of the leader-participation model were supportive. Given that the revised Vroom-Jago version is a sophisticated extension of the original model, we should expect it to be even better. But the complexity of the model is a major limitation to its usage. With five styles and twelve contingency variables, it is difficult to use as a day-to-day guide for practicing managers. Still, leadership and decision making are complex issues requiring a complex process. To hope for some easy but valid model may be wishful thinking. The important conclusion here seems to be that where we find leaders who follow the model, we should expect also to find productive and satisfied employees.[51]

Finally, the path-goal model provides a framework for explaining and predicting leadership effectiveness that has developed a solid, empirical foundation. It recognizes that a leader's success depends on adjusting his or her style to the environment the leader is placed in, as well as to the individual characteristics of followers. In a limited way, path-goal theory validates contingency variables in other leadership theories. For example, its emphasis on task structure is consistent with the Fiedler contingency model and Vroom and Jago's leader-participation model (remember their question: Is the problem well structured?). Path-goal theory's recognition of individual characteristics is also consistent with Hersey and Blanchard's focus on the experience and ability of followers.

THE MOST RECENT APPROACHES TO LEADERSHIP

We conclude our review of leadership by presenting three more recent approaches to the subject. These are an attribution theory of leadership, charismatic leadership, and transactional versus transformational leadership. If there is one theme to the approaches in this section, it is that they all deemphasize theoretical complexity and look at leadership more the way the average "person on the street" views the subject.

Attribution Theory of Leadership

In Chapter 5, we discussed attribution theory in relation to perception. Attribution theory has also been used to help explain the perception of leadership.

Attribution theory, as you remember, deals with people trying to make sense out of cause–effect relationships. When something happens, they want to attribute it to something. In the context of leadership, attribution theory says that leadership is merely an attribution that people make about other individuals.[52] Using the attribution framework, researchers have found that people characterize leaders as having such traits as intelligence, outgoing personality, strong verbal skills, aggressiveness, understanding, and industriousness.[53] Similarly, the high-high leader (high on both initiating structure and consideration) has been found to be consistent with attributions of what makes a good leader.[54] That is, regardless of the situation, a high-high leadership style tends to be perceived as best. At the organizational level, the attribution framework accounts for the conditions under which people use leadership to explain organizational outcomes. Those conditions are *extremes* in organizational performance. When an organization has either extremely negative or extremely positive performance, people are prone to make leadership attributions to explain the performance.[55] This helps to account for the vulnerability of CEOs when their organizations suffer a major financial setback, regardless of whether they had much to do with it. It also accounts for why these CEOs tend to be given credit for extremely positive financial results—again, regardless of how much or how little they contributed.

One of the more interesting themes in the **attribution theory of leadership** literature is the perception that effective leaders are generally considered consistent or unwavering in their decisions. That is, one of the explanations for why Lee Iacocca and Ronald Reagan (during his first term as President) were perceived as leaders was that both were fully committed, steadfast, and consistent in the decisions they made and the goals they set. Evidence indicates that a "heroic" leader is perceived as being someone who takes up a difficult or unpopular cause and, through determination and persistence, ultimately succeeds.[56]

Charismatic Leadership Theory

Charismatic leadership theory is an extension of attribution theory. It says that followers make attributions of heroic or extraordinary leadership abilities when they observe certain behaviors.[57] Studies on charismatic leadership have, for the most part, been directed at identifying those behaviors that differentiate charismatic leaders—the Jesse Jacksons, Ted Turners, and John F. Kennedys of the world—from their noncharismatic counterparts.

Several authors have attempted to identify personal characteristics of the charismatic leader. Robert House (of path-goal fame) has identified three: extremely high confidence, dominance, and strong convictions in his or her beliefs.[58] Warren Bennis, after studying ninety of the most effective and successful leaders in the United States, found that they had four common competencies: They had a compelling vision or sense of purpose; they could communicate that vision in clear terms that their followers could readily identify with; they demonstrated consistency and focus in the pursuit of their vision; and they knew their own strengths and capitalized on them.[59] The most recent and comprehensive analysis, however, has been completed by Conger and Kanungo at McGill University.[60] Among their conclusions,

Attribution Theory of Leadership Proposes that leadership is merely an attribution that people make about other individuals.

Charismatic Leadership Followers make attributions of heroic or extraordinary leadership abilities when they observe certain behaviors.

TABLE 11–2   Key Characteristics of Charismatic Leaders

1. *Self-confidence.* They have complete confidence in their judgment and ability.
2. *A vision.* This is an idealized goal that proposes a future better than the status quo. The greater the disparity between this idealized goal and the status quo, the more likely that followers will attribute extraordinary vision to the leader.
3. *Ability to articulate the vision.* They are able to clarify and state the vision in terms that are understandable to others. This articulation demonstrates an understanding of the followers' needs and, hence, acts as a motivating force.
4. *Strong convictions about the vision.* Charismatic leaders are perceived as being strongly committed, and willing to take on high personal risk, incur high costs, and engage in self-sacrifice to achieve their vision.
5. *Behavior that is out of the ordinary.* Those with charisma engage in behavior that is perceived as being novel, unconventional, and counter to norms. When successful, these behaviors evoke surprise and admiration in followers.
6. *Perceived as being a change agent.* Charismatic leaders are perceived as agents of radical change rather than as caretakers of the status quo.
7. *Environment sensitivity.* These leaders are able to make realistic assessments of the environmental constraints and resources needed to bring about change.

Source: Based on J. A. Conger and R. N. Kanungo, "Behavioral Dimensions of Charismatic Leadership," in J. A. Conger and R. N. Kanungo, *Charismatic Leadership* (San Francisco: Jossey-Bass, 1988), p. 91.

they propose that charismatic leaders have an idealized goal that they want to achieve, a strong personal commitment to their goal, are perceived as unconventional, are assertive and self-confident, and are perceived as agents of radical change rather than managers of the status quo. Table 11–2 summarizes the key characteristics that appear to differentiate charismatic leaders from noncharismatic ones.

What can we say about the charismatic leader's effect on his or her followers? There is an increasing body of research that shows impressive correlations between charismatic leadership and high performance and satisfaction among followers.[61] People working for charismatic leaders are motivated to exert extra work effort and, because they like their leader, express greater satisfaction.

If charisma is desirable, can people learn to be charismatic leaders? Or are charismatic leaders born with their qualities? While a small minority

Herbert Kelleher is a charismatic leader. He is CEO of Southwest Airlines, the world's only short-haul, high-frequency, low-fare, point-to-point carrier. Kelleher champions nonconforming and radical change. He enthusiastically motivates his 8700 employees by combining inspiration and insanity in what he calls "management by fooling around." His style seems to work: Southwest's operating costs per revenue mile is more than one-third lower than the industry average.   T. Michael Keza/Nation's Business

still think charisma cannot be learned, most experts believe that individuals can be trained to exhibit charismatic behaviors and can thus enjoy the benefits that accrue to being labeled "a charismatic leader."[62] For example, researchers have succeeded in actually scripting undergraduate business students to "play" charismatic.[63] The students were taught to articulate an overarching goal, communicate high performance expectations, exhibit confidence in the ability of subordinates to meet these expectations, and empathize with the needs of their subordinates; they learned to project a powerful, confident, and dynamic presence; and they practiced using a captivating and engaging voice tone. To further capture the dynamics and energy of charisma, the leaders were trained to evoke charismatic nonverbal characteristics: They alternated between pacing and sitting on the edges of their desks, leaned toward the subordinate, maintained direct eye contact, and had a relaxed posture and animated facial expressions. These researchers found that these students could *learn* how to project charisma. Moreover, subordinates of these leaders had higher task performance, task adjustment, and adjustment to the leader and to the group than did subordinates who worked under groups led by noncharismatic leaders.

One last word on this topic: Charismatic leadership may not always be needed to achieve high levels of employee performance. It may be most appropriate when the follower's task has an ideological component.[64] This may explain why, when charismatic leaders surface, it is more likely to be in politics, religion, wartime, or when a business firm is introducing a radically new product or facing a life-threatening crisis. Such conditions tend to involve ideological concerns. Franklin D. Roosevelt offered a vision to get Americans out of the Great Depression. General MacArthur was unyielding in promoting his strategy for defeating the Japanese in World War II. Steve Jobs achieved unwavering loyalty and commitment from the technical staff he oversaw at Apple Computer during the late 1970s and early 1980s by articulating a vision of personal computers that would dramatically change the way people lived. Charismatic leaders, in fact, may become a liability to an organization once the crisis and need for dramatic change subside.[65] Why? Because then the charismatic leader's overwhelming self-confidence often becomes a liability. He or she is unable to listen to others, becomes uncomfortable when challenged by aggressive subordinates, and begins to hold an unjustifiable belief in his or her "rightness" on issues.

Transactional vs. Transformational Leadership

The final stream of research we'll touch on is the recent interest in differentiating transformational leaders from transactional leaders.[66] As you'll see, because transformational leaders are also charismatic, there is some overlap between this topic and our previous discussion of charismatic leadership.

Most of the leadership theories presented in this chapter—for instance, the Ohio State studies, Fiedler's model, path-goal theory, and the leader–participation model—have concerned **transactional leaders.** These kinds of leaders guide or motivate their followers in the direction of established goals by clarifying role and task requirements. But there is another type of leader who inspires followers to transcend their own self-interests for the good of the organization, and who is capable of having a profound and extraordinary effect on his or her followers. These are **transformational leaders** like Leslie Wexner of The Limited retail chain and Jack Welch at General Electric. They pay attention to the concerns and developmental needs of individual followers; they change followers' awareness of issues by helping them to look at old problems in new ways; and they are able to

Transactional Leaders
Leaders who guide or motivate their followers in the direction of established goals by clarifying role and task requirements.

Transformational Leaders
Leaders who provide individualized consideration and intellectual stimulation, and who possess charisma.

TABLE 11–3   Characteristics of Transactional and Transformational Leaders

Transactional Leader

Contingent Reward: Contracts exchange of rewards for effort, promises rewards for good performance, recognizes accomplishments.

Management by Exception (active): Watches and searches for deviations from rules and standards, takes corrective action.

Management by Exception (passive): Intervenes only if standards are not met.

Laissez-Faire: Abdicates responsibilities, avoids making decisions.

Transformational Leader

Charisma: Provides vision and sense of mission, instills pride, gains respect and trust.

Inspiration: Communicates high expectations, uses symbols to focus efforts, expresses important purposes in simple ways.

Intellectual Stimulation: Promotes intelligence, rationality, and careful problem solving.

Individualized Consideration: Gives personal attention, treats each employee individually, coaches, advises.

Source: B. M. Bass, "From Transactional to Transformational Leadership: Learning to Share the Vision," *Organizational Dynamics*, Winter 1990, p. 22. Reprinted, by permission of publisher, from ORGANIZATIONAL DYNAMICS, Winter 1990. American Management Association, New York. All rights reserved.

excite, arouse, and inspire followers to put out extra effort to achieve group goals. Table 11–3 briefly identifies and defines the four characteristics that differentiate these two types of leaders.

Transactional and transformational leadership should not, however, be viewed as opposing approaches to getting things done.[67] Transformational leadership is built *on top of* transactional leadership—it produces levels of subordinate effort and performance that go beyond what would occur with a transactional approach alone. Moreover, transformational leadership is more than charisma. "The purely charismatic [leader] may want followers to adopt the charismatic's world view and go no further; the transformational leader will attempt to instill in followers the ability to question not only established views but eventually those established by the leader."[68]

The evidence supporting the superiority of transformational leadership over the transactional variety is overwhelmingly impressive. For instance, a number of studies with U.S., Canadian, and German military officers found, at every level, that transformational leaders were evaluated as more effective than their transactional counterparts.[69] Managers at Federal Express who were rated by their followers as exhibiting more transformational leadership were evaluated by their immediate supervisors as higher performers and more promotable.[70] In summary, the overall evidence indicates that transformational leadership is more strongly correlated than transactional leadership with lower turnover rates, higher productivity, and higher employee satisfaction.[71]

IMPLICATIONS FOR PERFORMANCE AND SATISFACTION

Leadership plays a central part in understanding group behavior, for it is the leader who usually provides the direction toward goal attainment. Therefore, a more accurate predictive capability should be valuable in improving group performance.

All This Talk About Leadership . . . But What About Followership?

When someone was once asked what it took to be a great leader, he responded: Great followers! While the response may have seemed sarcastic, it has some truth. We have long known that many managers can't lead a horse to water. But many subordinates can't follow a parade.

Only recently have we begun to recognize that in addition to having leaders who can lead, successful organizations need followers who can follow.[72] In fact, it's probably fair to say that all organizations have far more followers than leaders, so ineffective followers may be more of a handicap to an organization than ineffective leaders.

What qualities do effective followers have? One writer focuses on four.[73]

1. *They manage themselves well.* They are able to think for themselves. They can work independently and without close supervision.

2. *They are committed to a purpose outside themselves.* Effective followers are commit-ted to something—a cause, a product, a work group, an organization, an idea—in addition to the care of their own lives. Most people like working with colleagues who are emotionally, as well as physically, committed to their work.

3. *They build their competence and focus their efforts for maximum impact.* Effective followers master skills that will be useful to their organizations, and they hold higher performance standards than their job or work group requires.

4. *They are courageous, honest, and credible.* Effective followers establish themselves as independent, critical thinkers whose knowledge and judgment can be trusted. They hold high ethical standards, give credit where credit is due, and aren't afraid to own up to their mistakes.

In this chapter, we described a transition in approaches to the study of leadership—from the simple trait orientation to increasingly complex and sophisticated transactional models, such as path-goal and leader-participation models. With the increase in complexity has also come an increase in our ability to explain and predict behavior.

A major breakthrough in our understanding of leadership came when we recognized the need to include situational factors. Recent efforts have moved beyond mere recognition toward specific attempts to isolate these situational variables. We can expect further progress to be made with leadership models, but in the last decade, we have taken several large steps—large enough that we now can make moderately effective predictions as to who can best lead a group and explain under what conditions a given approach (such as task-oriented or people-oriented) is likely to lead to high performance and satisfaction.

In addition, the study of leadership has expanded to include more heroic and visionary approaches to leadership. As we learn more about the personal characteristics that followers attribute to charismatic and transformational leaders, and about the conditions that facilitate their emergence, we should be better able to predict when followers will exhibit extraordinary commitment and loyalty to their leaders and to those leaders' goals.

1. Trace the development of leadership research.

2. Discuss the strengths and weaknesses in the trait approach to leadership.

3. "Behavioral theories of leadership are static." Do you agree or disagree? Discuss.

4. What is the Managerial Grid? Contrast its approach to leadership with the approaches of the Ohio State and Michigan groups.

5. Develop an example where you operationalize the Fiedler model.

6. Contrast the situational leadership theory with the Managerial Grid.

7. How do Hersey and Blanchard define *maturity?* Is this contingency variable included in any other contingency theory of leadership?

8. Develop an example where you operationalize path–goal theory.

9. Reconcile Hersey and Blanchard's situational leadership theory, path–goal theory, and substitutes for leadership.

10. Describe the leader-participation model. What are its contingency variables?

11. When might leaders be irrelevant?

12. What kind of activities could a full-time college student pursue that might lead to the perception that he or she is a charismatic leader? In pursuing those activities, what might the student do to enhance this perception of being charismatic?

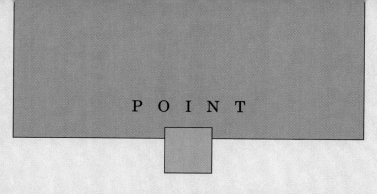

Leaders Make a Real Difference!

There can be little question that the success of an organization, or any group within an organization, depends largely on the quality of its leadership. Whether in business, government, education, medicine, or religion, the quality of an organization's leadership determines the quality of the organization itself. Successful leaders anticipate change, vigorously exploit opportunities, motivate their followers to higher levels of productivity, correct poor performance, and lead the organization toward its objectives.

The importance relegated to the leadership function is well known. Rarely does a week go by that we don't hear or read about some leadership concern: "President Fails to Provide the Leadership America Needs!" "The Democratic Party Searches for New Leadership!" "Sculley Leads Apple Turnaround!" A review of the leadership literature led two academics to conclude that the research shows "a consistent effect for leadership explaining twenty to forty-five percent of the variance on relevant organizational outcomes."*

Why is leadership so important to an organization's success? The answer lies in the need for coordination and control. Organizations exist to achieve objectives that are either impossible or extremely inefficient to achieve if done by individuals acting alone. The organization itself is a coordination and control mechanism. Rules, policies, job descriptions, and authority hierarchies are illustrations of devices created to facilitate coordination and control. But leadership, too, contributes toward integrating various job activities, coordinating communication between organizational subunits, monitoring activities, and controlling deviations from standard. No amount of rules and regulations can replace the experienced leader who can make rapid and decisive decisions.

The importance of leadership is not lost on those who staff organizations. Corporations, government agencies, school systems, and institutions of all shapes and sizes cumulatively spend billions of dollars every year to recruit, select, evaluate, and train individuals for leadership positions. The best evidence, however, of the importance organizations place on leadership roles is exhibited in salary schedules. Leaders are routinely paid ten, twenty, or more times the salary of those in nonleadership positions. The head of General Motors earns more than $1.5 million annually. The highest skilled auto worker, in contrast, earns under $50,000 a year. The president of this auto worker's union makes better than $100,000 a year. Police officers typically make around $25,000 to $35,000 a year. Their boss probably earns twenty-five percent more, and his or her boss another twenty-five percent. The pattern is well established. The more responsibility a leader has, as evidenced by his or her level in the organization, the more he or she earns. Would organizations voluntarily pay their leaders so much more than their nonleaders if they didn't strongly believe that leaders make a real difference?

*D. V. Day and R. G. Lord, "Executive Leadership and Organizational Performance: Suggestions for a New Theory and Methodology," *Journal of Management,* Fall 1988, pp. 453–64.

Leaders Don't Make a Difference!

Given the resources that have been spent on studying, selecting, and training leaders, you'd expect there to be clear evidence supporting the positive impact of leadership on a group or organization's performance. That evidence has failed to surface!

Analyses of leadership have frequently presumed that leadership style or leader behavior was an independent variable that could be selected or trained at will to conform to what research would find to be optimal. Even theorists who took a more contingent view of appropriate leadership behavior generally assumed that, with proper training, appropriate behavior could be produced. Fiedler, noting how hard it is to change behavior, suggested changing the situational characteristics rather than the person, but this was an unusual proposal in the context of prevailing literature, which suggested that leadership style was something to be strategically selected according to the variables of the particular leadership theory.

But the leader is embedded in a social system, which constrains behavior. The leader has a role set, in which members have expectations for appropriate behavior and persons make efforts to modify the leader's behavior. Pressures to conform to the expectations of peers, subordinates, and superiors are all relevant in determining actual behavior.

Leaders, even in high-level positions, have unilateral control over fewer resources and fewer policies than might be expected. Investment decisions may require approval of others, while hiring and promotion decisions may be accomplished by committees. Leader behavior is constrained both by the demands of others in the role set and by organizationally prescribed limitations on the sphere of activity and influence.

Many factors that may affect organizational performance are outside a leader's control, even if he or she were to have complete discretion over major areas of organizational decision. For example, consider the executive in a home construction firm. Costs are largely determined by the operations of commodities and labor markets, and demand is largely dependent on interest rates, availability of mortgage money, and economic conditions that are affected by governmental policies over which the executive has little control. School superintendents have little control over birth rates and community economic development, both of which profoundly affect school system budgets. While the leader may react to contingencies as they arise, or may be a better or worse forecaster in accounting for variation in organizational outcomes, he or she probably accounts for little compared to external factors.

The leader's success or failure may also be partly due to circumstances unique to the organization but still outside his or her control. Leader positions in organizations vary in terms of the strength and position of the organization. The choice of a new executive does not fundamentally alter a market and financial position that has developed over years and affects the leader's ability to make strategic changes and the likelihood that the organization will do well or poorly. Organizations have relatively enduring strengths and weaknesses. The choice of a particular leader for a particular position has limited impact on these capabilities.

There is a basic myth associated with leadership. We believe in attribution—when something happens, we believe something has *caused* it. Leaders play that role in organizations. So leaders may not matter, but the *belief* in leadership does. Although leaders take the credit for successes and the blame for failures, a more realistic conclusion would probably be that, except in times of rapid growth, change, or crisis, leaders don't make much of a difference in an organization's actual performance. But people want to believe that leadership is the cause of performance changes, particularly at the extremes.

Much of this argument is based on J. Pfeffer, "The Ambiguity of Leadership," *Academy of Management Review,* January 1977, pp. 104–11. See also A. B. Thomas, "Does Leadership Make a Difference to Organizational Performance?", *Administrative Science Quarterly,* September 1988, pp. 388–400, for a recent review of this issue.

The Pre-Post Leadership Assessment Exercise

OBJECTIVE To compare characteristics intuitively related to leadership with leadership characteristics found in research.

TIME Part I takes approximately ten minutes.
Part II takes about twenty-five minutes.

PROCEDURE Part I is to be completed *prior* to reading Chapter 11. Identify three people (i.e., friends, relatives, public figures) whom you consider to be leaders. For each one of these individuals, make a list of characteristic traits. Then compare your three lists. Which traits, if any, are common to all three lists?

Part II is to be completed *after* reading Chapter 11. Your instructor will lead the class in a discussion of leadership traits based on the lists developed in Part I. Students will call out traits they identified and your instructor will write them on the chalkboard. When all students have shared their lists, class discussion will focus on:

1. What traits consistently appear on students' lists?
2. To what degree do these traits match research evidence on leader characteristics?
3. What, if anything, does this exercise suggest about leadership attributions?

Compute Your LPC Score

Think of the person with whom you work least well. He or she may be someone you work with now, or may be someone you knew in the past. He or she does not have to be the person you like least well, but should be the person with whom you now have or have had the most difficulty in getting a job done. Describe this person as he or she appears to you by placing an "x" at that point which you believe best describes that person. Do this for each pair of adjectives.

Pleasant	8	7	6	5	4	3	2	1	Unpleasant
Friendly	8	7	6	5	4	3	2	1	Unfriendly
Rejecting	1	2	3	4	5	6	7	8	Accepting
Helpful	8	7	6	5	4	3	2	1	Frustrating
Unenthusiastic	1	2	3	4	5	6	7	8	Enthusiastic

Tense									Relaxed
	1	2	3	4	5	6	7	8	
Distant									Close
	1	2	3	4	5	6	7	8	
Cold									Warm
	1	2	3	4	5	6	7	8	
Cooperative									Uncooperative
	8	7	6	5	4	3	2	1	
Supportive									Hostile
	8	7	6	5	4	3	2	1	
Boring									Interesting
	1	2	3	4	5	6	7	8	
Quarrelsome									Harmonious
	1	2	3	4	5	6	7	8	
Self-assured									Hesitant
	8	7	6	5	4	3	2	1	
Efficient									Inefficient
	8	7	6	5	4	3	2	1	
Gloomy									Cheerful
	1	2	3	4	5	6	7	8	
Open									Guarded
	8	7	6	5	4	3	2	1	

Turn to page 715 for scoring directions and key.

Source: From *Leadership and Effective Management* by F. E. Fiedler and M. M. Chemers. Copyright ©1974 by Scott, Foresman & Co. Reprinted by permission.

CASE INCIDENT 11

Developing Leaders at the Sembawang Group

Ng Pock Too has a serious problem. He can't find enough of the right kind of managers.

Ng is chief executive of the Sembawang Group, a Singapore shipyard and construction company that he is trying to expand into a diversified multinational corporation. Like many other chief executives in Asia, he sees an abundance of business opportunities and has the financial resources to pursue them. Yet there is a shortage of managers in the region. Not just any managers, but flexible, creative professionals who are comfortable in an increasingly competitive and sophisticated market. Most managers that Ng finds have skills that are no longer appropriate for the changing competition they face. As wages have risen, the region's traditionally low-tech companies have had to move into higher-value-added products whose success depends on expertise—overseas marketing sophistication and ability to direct highly skilled professionals, for instance—that old-line managers often do not have.

To compound Ng's problem, the pool of potential managers with the educational level he needs is small. In Singapore, only six percent of workers are university educated. This compares with twenty-three percent in the

United States and sixteen percent in Japan. And the competition among Asian companies for skilled and educated managers is fierce.

Ng realizes that he must invest in developing his company's future leaders. He could offer formal classes in management and leadership, and supplement this with on-the-job training. But he's not exactly sure what such a formal leadership program might look like. Or maybe he should look to graduates of business schools outside of Asia.

Questions

1. What kind of leadership do you think is necessary to succeed in Singapore?
2. Do you think hiring non-Asians with advanced business degrees could solve Ng's problem? Discuss.
3. Should Ng hire Asians from Europe or North America? Discuss.
4. As a consultant hired by Ng, design a leadership program that would meet his needs.

Source: Based on F. S. Worthy, "You Can't Grow If You Can't Manage," *Fortune,* June 13, 1991, pp. 83–88.

FOR FURTHER READING

BASS, B. M., AND R. M. STOGDILL, *Bass and Stogdill's Handbook of Leadership: Theory, Research, and Managerial Applications,* 3rd. ed. (New York: Free Press, 1990). With over twelve hundred pages of information, this has become the definitive resource on leadership.

HOUSE, R. J., W. D. SPANGLER, AND J. WOYCKE, "Personality and Charisma in the U.S. Presidency: A Psychological Theory of Leader Effectiveness," *Administrative Science Quarterly,* September 1991, pp. 364–96. A study of U. S. Presidents found that personality and charisma contribute significantly to presidential performance.

HOWELL, J. M., AND C. A. HIGGINS, "Champions of Technological Innovation," *Administrative Science Quarterly,* June 1990, pp. 317–41. This study investigates the personality characteristics, leadership behaviors, and influence tactics used by champions of technological innovation.

HUNT, J. G., *Leadership: A New Synthesis* (Newbury Park, CA: Sage Publications, 1991). A multiple-level synthesis of leadership by one of the major contributors to the leadership field.

MEINDL, J. R., "On Leadership: An Alternative to the Conventional Wisdom," in B. M. Staw and L. L. Cummings (eds.), *Research in Organizational Behavior,* Vol. 12 (Greenwich, CT: JAI Press, 1990), pp. 159–203. Proposes a follower-centered approach to the study of transformational leadership.

ZALEZNIK, A., "The Leadership Gap," *Academy of Management Executive,* February 1990, pp. 7–22. A critical assessment of the mystique, subscribed to in business and taught in business schools, that places a premium on the team over the individual.

NOTES

[1] N. Gibbs, "Welcome the Unknown Soldier," *Time,* May 6, 1991, pp. 25–26.

[2] R. M. Stogdill, *Handbook of Leadership: A Survey of the Literature* (New York: Free Press, 1974), p. 259.

[3] For a review of the controversies, see G. Yukl, "Managerial Leadership: A Review of Theory and Research," *Journal of Management,* June 1989, pp. 252–53.

[4] A. Zaleznik, "Excerpts from 'Managers and Leaders: Are They Different?'" *Harvard Business Review,* May-June 1986, p. 54.

[5] J. P. Kotter, "What Leaders Really Do," *Harvard Business Review,* MayJune 1990, pp. 103–11; and J. P. Kotter, *A Force for Change: How Leadership Differs from Management* (New York: Free Press, 1990).

[6] V. H. Vroom, "The Search for a Theory of Leadership," in J. W. McGuire (ed.), *Contemporary Management: Issues and Viewpoints* (Englewood Cliffs, NJ: Prentice Hall, 1974), p. 396.

[7] J. G. Geier, "A Trait Approach to the Study of Leadership in Small Groups," *Journal of Communication,* December 1967, pp. 316–23.

[8] S. A. Kirkpatrick and E. A. Locke, "Leadership: Do Traits Matter?" *Academy of Management Executive,* May 1991, pp. 48–60.

[9] G. H. Dobbins, W. S. Long, E. J. Dedrick, and T. C. Clemons, "The Role of Self-Monitoring and Gender on Leader Emergence: A Laboratory and Field Study," *Journal of Management,* September 1990, pp. 609–18.

[10] Stogdill, *Handbook of Leadership.*

[11] D. A. Kenny and S. J. Zaccaro, "An Estimate of Variance Due to Traits in Leadership," *Journal of Applied Psychology,* November 1983, pp. 678–85; Dobbins, Long, Dedrick, and Clemons, "The Role of Self-Monitoring and Gender on Leader Emergence"; and Kirkpatrick and Locke, "Leadership."

[12] R. M. Stogdill and A. E. Coons (eds.), *Leader Behavior: Its Description and Measurement,* Research Monograph No. 88 (Columbus: Ohio State University, Bureau of Business Research, 1951). For an updated review of the Ohio State research, see S. Kerr, C. A. Schriesheim, C. J. Murphy, and R. M. Stogdill, "Toward a Contingency Theory of Leadership Based upon the Consideration and Initiating Structure Literature," *Organizational Behavior and Human Performance,* August 1974, pp. 62–82; and B. M. Fisher, "Consideration and Initiating Structure and Their Relationships with Leader Effectiveness: A Meta-Analysis," F. Hoy (ed.), *Proceedings of the 48th Academy of Management Conference,* Anaheim, CA, 1988, pp. 201–05.

[13]R. Kahn and D. Katz, "Leadership Practices in Relation to Productivity and Morale," D. Cartwright and A. Zander (eds.), *Group Dynamics: Research and Theory,* 2nd ed. (Elmsford, NY: Row, Paterson, 1960).

[14]R. R. Blake and J. S. Mouton, *The Managerial Grid* (Houston: Gulf, 1964).

[15]This box is based on J. Grant, "Women as Managers: What They Can Offer to Organizations," *Organizational Dynamics,* Winter 1988, pp. 56–63; S. Helgesen, *The Female Advantage: Women's Ways of Leadership* (New York: Doubleday, 1990); A. H. Eagly and B. T. Johnson, "Gender and Leadership Style: A Meta-Analysis," *Psychological Bulletin,* September 1990, pp. 233–56; A. H. Eagly and S. J. Karau, "Gender and the Emergence of Leaders: A Meta-Analysis," *Journal of Personality and Social Psychology,* May 1991, pp. 685–710. J. B. Rosener, "Ways Women Lead," *Harvard Business Review,* November-December 1990, pp. 119–25; and "Debate: Ways Men and Women Lead," *Harvard Business Review,* January-February 1991, pp. 150–60.

[16]See, for example, R. R. Blake and J. S. Mouton, "A Comparative Analysis of Situationalism and 9,9 Management by Principle," *Organizational Dynamics,* Spring 1982, pp. 20–43.

[17]See, for example, L. L. Larson, J. G. Hunt, and R. N. Osborn, "The Great Hi-Hi Leader Behavior Myth: A Lesson from Occam's Razor," *Academy of Management Journal,* December 1976, pp. 628–41; and P. C. Nystrom, "Managers and the Hi-Hi Leader Myth," *Academy of Management Journal,* June 1978, pp. 325–31.

[18]See, for example, the three styles—autocratic, participative, and laissez-faire—proposed by K. Lewin and R. Lippitt, "An Experimental Approach to the Study of Autocracy and Democracy: A Preliminary Note," *Sociometry,* no. 1 (1938), pp. 292–380; or the 3-D theory proposed by W. J. Reddin, *Managerial Effectiveness* (New York: McGraw-Hill, 1970).

[19]J. P. Howell, P. W. Dorfman, and S. Kerr, "Moderating Variables in Leadership Research," *Academy of Management Review,* January 1986, pp. 88–102.

[20]F. E. Fiedler, *A Theory of Leadership Effectiveness* (New York: McGraw-Hill, 1967).

[21]S. Shiflett, "Is There a Problem with the LPC Score in LEADER MATCH?", *Personnel Psychology,* Winter 1981, pp. 765–69.

[22]F. E. Fiedler, M. M. Chemers, and L. Mahar, *Improving Leadership Effectiveness: The Leader Match Concept* (New York: John Wiley, 1977).

[23]L. H. Peters, D. D. Hartke, and J. T. Pohlmann, "Fiedler's Contingency Theory of Leadership: An Application of the Meta-Analysis Procedures of Schmidt and Hunter," *Psychological Bulletin,* March 1985, pp. 274–85.

[24]Ibid.

[25]See, for instance, R. W. Rice, "Psychometric Properties of the Esteem for the Least Preferred Coworker (LPC) Scale," *Academy of Management Review,* January 1978, pp. 106–18; C. A. Schriesheim, B. D. Bannister, and W. H. Money, "Psychometric Properties of the LPC Scale: An Extension of Rice's Review," *Academy of Management Review,* April 1979, pp. 287–90; and J. K. Kennedy, J. M. Houston, M. A. Korgaard, and D. D. Gallo, "Construct Space of the Least Preferred Co-Worker (LPC) Scale," *Educational & Psychological Measurement,* Fall 1987, pp. 807–14.

[26]See E. H. Schein, *Organizational Psychology,* 3rd ed. (Englewood Cliffs, NJ: Prentice Hall, 1980), pp. 116–17; and B. Kabanoff, "A Critique of Leader Match and Its Implications for Leadership Research," *Personnel Psychology,* Winter 1981, pp. 749–64.

[27]F. E. Fiedler and J. E. Garcia, *New Approaches to Effective Leadership: Cognitive Resources and Organizational Performance* (New York: John Wiley & Sons, 1987).

[28]Ibid, p. 6.

[29]R. P. Vecchio, "Theoretical and Empirical Examination of Cognitive Resource Theory," *Journal of Applied Psychology,* April 1990, pp. 141–47.

[30]P. Hersey and K. H. Blanchard, "So You Want to Know Your Leadership Style?" *Training and Development Journal,* February 1974, pp. 1–15; and P. Hersey and K. H. Blanchard, *Management of Organizational Behavior: Utilizing Human Resources,* 4th ed. (Englewood Cliffs, NJ: Prentice Hall, 1982), pp. 150–61.

[31]Hersey and Blanchard, *Management of Organizational Behavior,* p. 171.

[32]P. Hersey and K. H. Blanchard, "Grid Principles and Situationalism: Both! A Response to Blake and Mouton," *Group and Organization Studies,* June 1982, pp. 207–10.

[33]R. K. Hambleton and R. Gumpert, "The Validity of Hersey and Blanchard's Theory of Leader Effectiveness," *Group & Organizational Studies,* June 1982, pp. 225–42; C. L. Graeff, "The Situational Leadership Theory: A Critical View," *Academy of Management Review,* April 1983, pp. 285–91; R. P. Vecchio, "Situational Leadership Theory: An Examination of a Prescriptive Theory," *Journal of Applied Psychology,* August 1987, pp. 444–51; J. R. Goodson, G. W. McGee, and J. F. Cashman, "Situational Leadership Theory: A Test of Leadership Prescriptions," *Group & Organization Studies,* December 1989, pp. 446–61; and W. Blank, J. R. Weitzel, and S. G. Green, "A Test of the Situational Leadership Theory," *Personnel Psychology,* Autumn 1990, pp. 579–97.

[34]Vecchio, "Situational Leadership Theory."

[35]W. Blank, J. R. Weitzel, and S. G. Green, "A Test of the Situational Leadership Theory."

³⁶F. Dansereau, J. Cashman, and G. Graen, "Instrumentality Theory and Equity Theory as Complementary Approaches in Predicting the Relationship of Leadership and Turnover Among Managers," *Organizational Behavior and Human Performance,* October 1973, pp. 184–200; and G. Graen, M. Novak, and P. Sommerkamp, "The Effects of Leader-Member Exchange and Job Design on Productivity and Satisfaction: Testing a Dual Attachment Model," *Organizational Behavior and Human Performance,* August 1982, pp. 109–31.

³⁷G. Graen and J. Cashman, "A Role-Making Model of Leadership in Formal Organizations: A Development Approach," in J. G. Hunt and L. L. Larson (eds.), *Leadership Frontiers* (Kent, OH: Kent State University Press, 1975), pp. 143–65; and R. Liden and G. Graen, "Generalizability of the Vertical Dyad Linkage Model of Leadership," *Academy of Management Journal,* September 1980, pp. 451–65.

³⁸D. Duchon, S. G. Green, and T. D. Taber, "Vertical Dyad Linkage: A Longitudinal Assessment of Antecedents, Measures, and Consequences," *Journal of Applied Psychology,* February 1986, pp. 56–60.

³⁹See, for example, G. Graen, M. Novak, and P. Sommerkamp, "The Effects of Leader-Member Exchange;" T. Scandura and G. Graen, "Moderating Effects of Initial Leader-Member Exchange Status on the Effects of a Leadership Intervention," *Journal of Applied Psychology,* August 1984, pp. 428–36; R. P. Vecchio and B. C. Gobdel, "The Vertical Dyad Linkage Model of Leadership: Problems and Prospects," *Organizational Behavior and Human Performance,* August 1984, pp. 5–20; and T. M. Dockery and D. D. Steiner, "The Role of the Initial Interaction in Leader-Member Exchange," *Group and Organization Studies,* December 1990, pp. 395–413.

⁴⁰A. Jago, "Leadership: Perspectives in Theory and Research," *Management Science,* March 1982, pp. 331.

⁴¹R. J. House, "A Path-Goal Theory of Leader Effectiveness," *Administrative Science Quarterly,* September 1971, pp. 321–38; R. J. House and T. R. Mitchell, "Path-Goal Theory of Leadership," *Journal of Contemporary Business,* Autumn 1974, p. 86; and R. J. House, "Retrospective Comment," in L. E. Boone and D. D. Bowen (eds.), *The Great Writings in Management and Organizational Behavior,* 2nd ed. (New York: Random House, 1987), pp. 354–64.

⁴²See J. Indik, "Path-Goal Theory of Leadership: A Meta-Analysis," paper presented at the National Academy of Management Conference, Chicago, August 1986; and R. T. Keller, "A Test of the Path-Goal Theory of Leadership with Need for Clarity as a Moderator in Research and Development Organizations," *Journal of Applied Psychology,* April 1989, pp. 208–12.

⁴³V. H. Vroom and P. W. Yetton, *Leadership and Decision-Making* (Pittsburgh: University of Pittsburgh Press, 1973).

⁴⁴V. H. Vroom and A. G. Jago, *The New Leadership: Managing Participation in Organizations* (Englewood Cliffs, NJ: Prentice Hall, 1988). See especially Chapter 8.

⁴⁵See, for example, R. H. G. Field, "A Test of the Vroom-Yetton Normative Model of Leadership," *Journal of Applied Psychology,* October 1982, pp. 523–32; C. R. Leana, "Power Relinquishment versus Power Sharing: Theoretical Clarification and Empirical Comparison of Delegation and Participation," *Journal of Applied Psychology,* May 1987, pp. 228–33; J. T. Ettling and A. G. Jago, "Participation Under Conditions of Conflict: More on the Validity of the Vroom-Yetton Model," *Journal of Management Studies,* January 1988, pp. 73–83; and R. H. G. Field and R. J. House, "A Test of the Vroom-Yetton Model Using Manager and Subordinate Reports," *Journal of Applied Psychology,* June 1990, pp. 362–66.

⁴⁶Dobbins, Long, Dedrick, and Clemons, "The Role of Self-Monitoring and Gender on Leader Emergence"; and S. J. Zaccaro, R. J. Foti, and D. A. Kenny, "Self-Monitoring and Trait-Based Variance in Leadership: An Investigation of Leader Flexibility Across Multiple Group Situations," *Journal of Applied Psychology,* April 1991, pp. 308–15.

⁴⁷S. Kerr and J. M. Jermier, "Substitutes for Leadership: Their Meaning and Measurement," *Organizational Behavior and Human Performance,* December 1978, pp. 375–403; J. P. Howell and P. W. Dorfman, "Substitutes for Leadership: Test of a Construct," *Academy of Management Journal,* December 1981, pp. 714–28; P. W. Howard and W. F. Joyce, "Substitutes for Leadership: A Statistical Refinement," paper presented at the 42nd Annual Academy of Management Conference, New York, August 1982; J. P. Howell, P. W. Dorfman, and S. Kerr, "Leadership and Substitutes for Leadership," *Journal of Applied Behavioral Science,* Vol. 22, No. 1, 1986, pp. 29–46; J. P. Dorfman, P. W. Dorfman, and S. Kerr, "Moderator Variables in Leadership Research," *Academy of Management Review,* January 1986, pp. 88–102; N. J. Pitner, "Leadership Substitutes: Their Factorial Validity in Educational Organizations," *Educational & Psychological Measurement,* Summer 1988, pp. 307–15; and J. P. Howell, D. E. Bowen, P. W. Dorfman, S. Kerr, and P. M. Podsakoff, "Substitutes for Leadership: Effective Alternatives to Ineffective Leadership," *Organizational Dynamics,* Summer 1990, pp. 21–38.

⁴⁸B. Karmel, "Leadership: A Challenge to Traditional Research Methods and Assumptions," *Academy of Management Review,* July 1978, pp. 477–79.

⁴⁹Schein, *Organizational Psychology,* p. 132.

⁵⁰See L. R. Anderson, "Toward a Two-Track Model of Leadership Training: Suggestions from Self-Monitoring Theory," *Small Group Research,* May 1990, pp. 147–67.

⁵¹C. Margerison and R. Glube, "Leadership Decision-Making: An Empirical Test of the Vroom and Yetton Model," *Journal of Management Studies,* February 1979, pp. 45–55.

[52]See, for instance, J. C. McElroy, "A Typology of Attribution Leadership Research," *Academy of Management Review,* July 1982, pp. 413–17; J. R. Meindl and S. B. Ehrlich, "The Romance of Leadership and the Evaluation of Organizational Performance," *Academy of Management Journal,* March 1987, pp. 91–109; and J. C. McElroy and J. D. Hunger, "Leadership Theory as Causal Attribution of Performance," in J. G. Hunt, B. R. Baliga, H. P. Dachler, and C. A. Schriesheim (eds.), *Emerging Leadership Vistas* (Lexington, MA: Lexington Books, 1988).

[53]R. G. Lord, C. L. DeVader, and G. M. Alliger, "A Meta-Analysis of the Relation Between Personality Traits and Leadership Perceptions: An Application of Validity Generalization Procedures," *Journal of Applied Psychology,* August 1986, pp. 402–10.

[54]G. N. Powell and D. A. Butterfield, "The "High-High" Leader Rides Again!", *Group and Organization Studies,* December 1984, pp. 437–50.

[55]J. R. Meindl, S. B. Ehrlich, and J. M. Dukerich, "The Romance of Leadership," *Administrative Science Quarterly,* March 1985, pp. 78–102.

[56]B. M. Staw and J. Ross, "Commitment in an Experimenting Society: A Study of the Attribution of Leadership from Administrative Scenarios," *Journal of Applied Psychology,* June 1980, pp. 249–60.

[57]J. A. Conger and R. N. Kanungo, "Behavioral Dimensions of Charismatic Leadership," in J. A. Conger, R. N. Kanungo and Associates, *Charismatic Leadership* (San Francisco: Jossey-Bass, 1988), p. 79.

[58]R. J. House, "A 1976 Theory of Charismatic Leadership," in J. G. Hunt and L. L. Larson (eds.), *Leadership: The Cutting Edge* (Carbondale: Southern Illinois University Press, 1977), pp. 189–207.

[59]W. Bennis, "The 4 Competencies of Leadership," *Training and Development Journal,* August 1984, pp. 15–19.

[60]Conger and Kanungo, "Behavioral Dimensions of Charismatic Leadership," pp. 78–97.

[61]R. J. House, J. Woycke, and E. M. Fodor, "Charismatic and Noncharismatic Leaders: Differences in Behavior and Effectiveness," in Conger and Kanungo, *Charismatic Leadership,* pp. 103–04.

[62]J. A. Conger and R. N. Kanungo, "Training Charismatic Leadership: A Risky and Critical Task," in Conger and Kanungo, *Charismatic Leadership,* pp. 309–23.

[63]J. M. Howell and P. J. Frost, "A Laboratory Study of Charismatic Leadership," *Organizational Behavior and Human Decision Processes,* April 1989, pp. 243–69.

[64]House, "A 1976 Theory of Charismatic Leadership."

[65]D. Machan, "The Charisma Merchants," *Forbes,* January 23, 1989, pp. 100–01.

[66]See J. M. Burns, *Leadership* (New York: Harper & Row, 1978); B. M. Bass, *Leadership and Performance Beyond Expectations* (New York: Free Press, 1985); and B. M. Bass, "From Transactional to Transformational Leadership: Learning to Share the Vision," *Organizational Dynamics,* Winter 1990, pp. 19–31.

[67]B. M. Bass, "Leadership: Good, Better, Best," *Organizational Dynamics,* Winter 1985, pp. 26–40; and J. Seltzer and B. M. Bass, "Transformational Leadership: Beyond Initiation and Consideration," *Journal of Management,* December 1990, pp. 693–703.

[68]B. J. Avolio and B. M. Bass, "Transformational Leadership, Charisma and Beyond," working paper, School of Management, State University of New York, Binghamton, 1985, p. 14.

[69]Cited in B. M. Bass and B. J. Avolio, "Developing Transformational Leadership: 1992 and Beyond," *Journal of European Industrial Training,* January 1990, p. 23.

[70]J. J. Hater and B. M. Bass, "Supervisors' Evaluation and Subordinates' Perceptions of Transformational and Transactional Leadership," *Journal of Applied Psychology,* November 1988, pp. 695–702.

[71]Bass and Avolio, "Developing Transformational Leadership."

[72]R. E. Kelley, "In Praise of Followers," *Harvard Business Review,* November-December 1988, pp. 142–48; and E. P. Hollander and L. R. Offermann, "Power and Leadership in Organizations," *American Psychologist,* February 1990, pp. 179–89.

[73]Kelley, "In Praise of Followers."

POWER AND POLITICS

LEARNING OBJECTIVES

After studying this chapter, you should be able to:

1. Define the four bases of power
2. Define the four sources of power
3. List seven power tactics and their contingencies
4. Clarify what creates dependency in power relationships
5. Describe the importance of a political perspective
6. List those individual and organizational factors that stimulate political behavior
7. Identify seven techniques for managing the impression one makes on others
8. Explain how defensive behaviors can protect an individual's self-interest

You can get much farther with a kind word and a gun than you can with a kind word alone.

A. CAPONE

The song lyric goes: "You don't pull on Superman's cape, you don't spit in the wind, you don't pull the mask off the old Lone Ranger, and you don't mess around with Jim."* In the movie industry, that last line could be rewritten to ". . . and you don't mess around with Steven." The Steven we're talking about here is Spielberg.[1]

Steven Spielberg is unquestionably the most powerful film maker in Hollywood. That power comes from his string of megahits. Five of his films are among the highest-grossing movies in Hollywood's history—*E. T. The Extraterrestrial, Jaws, Raiders of the Lost Ark, Back to the Future,* and *Indiana Jones and the Temple of Doom.* In all, his films have sold more than $4 billion worth of tickets worldwide. As the president of Columbia Pictures put it, "Who's going to argue with his track record?"

Spielberg's power in his industry is truly awesome. He can pick the projects he wants—and can choose from among any of the major studios to make them. According to the chairman of Walt Disney Studios, "Steven operates very uniquely in Hollywood, really as a sovereign state." Says the chairman of Warner Bros.: "I'd take anything the man does."

While Spielberg, because he is an independent producer, is free to shop his projects around, Universal Pictures tried to get on his good side in 1984 by spending $6 million to build a sprawling complex for his Amblin Entertainment operations on the Universal lot. However, it didn't do much good. Spielberg made only one film at Universal during the 1980s. Why? He didn't like Universal's presidents during that period. Universal's current president knows the importance of keeping Spielberg happy: "One of the most important things I can do in this job is make sure that Steven wants to work with us." ■

*By Jim Croce, copyright 1974, 1985 DenJac Music Co. Used by permission. All rights reserved.

*P*ower has been described as the last dirty word. It is easier for most of us to talk about money or even sex than it is to talk about power. People who have it deny it, people who want it try not to appear to be seeking it, and those who are good at getting it are secretive about how they got it.[2]

Twenty years ago, we knew little about power. That's no longer true. In recent years we've gained considerable insights into the topic.[3] We can now offer some fairly solid suggestions, for example, about what one should do if one wants to have power in a group or organization. In this chapter, we'll demonstrate that the acquisition and distribution of power is a natural process in any group or organization. Power determines the goals to be sought and how resources will be distributed. These, in turn, have important implications for member performance and satisfaction.

A DEFINITION OF POWER

Power A capacity that A has to influence the behavior of B so that B does things he or she would not otherwise do.

Dependency B's relationship to A when A possesses something that B requires.

Power refers to a capacity that A has to influence the behavior of B, so that B does something he or she would not otherwise do. This definition implies (1) a *potential* that need not be actualized to be effective, (2) a *dependency* relationship, and (3) the assumption that B has some *discretion* over his or her own behavior. Let's look at each of these points more closely.

Power may exist but not be used. It is, therefore, a capacity or potential. One can have power but not impose it.

Probably the most important aspect of power is that it is a function of **dependency.** The greater B's dependence on A, the greater is A's power in the relationship. Dependence, in turn, is based on alternatives that B perceives and the importance that B places on the alternative(s) that A controls. A person can have power over you only if he or she controls something you desire. If you want a college degree and have to pass a certain course to get it, and your current instructor is the only faculty member in the college who teaches that course, he or she has power over you. Your alternatives are highly limited and you place a high degree of importance on obtaining a passing grade. Similarly, if you're attending college on funds totally provided by your parents, you probably recognize the power that they hold over you. You are dependent on them for financial support. But once you're out of school, have a job, and are making a solid income, your parents' power is reduced significantly. Who among us, though, has not known or heard of the rich relative who is able to control a large number of family members merely through the implicit or explicit threat of "writing them out of the will"?

For A to get B to do something he or she otherwise would not do means that B must have the discretion to make choices. At the extreme, if B's job behavior is so programmed that he is allowed no room to make choices, he obviously is constrained in his ability to do something other than what he is doing. For instance, job descriptions, group norms, and organizational rules and regulations, as well as community laws and standards, constrain people's choices. As a nurse, you may be dependent on your supervisor for continued employment. But, in spite of this dependence, you're unlikely to comply with her request to perform heart surgery on a patient or steal several thousand dollars from petty cash. Your job description and laws against stealing constrain your ability to make these choices.

The toppling of a right–wing coup in what was then the Soviet Union in August of 1991 illustrated two differences between power and leadership: (1) Power is often a group phenomenon; and (2) power can be exerted upward. The Soviet people exerted their power and quickly brought down the eight conspirators who sought to take over the country.   A. Hernandez/SIPA

CONTRASTING LEADERSHIP AND POWER

A careful comparison of our description of power with our description of leadership in the previous chapter should bring the recognition that the two concepts are closely intertwined. Leaders use power as a means of attaining group goals. Leaders achieve goals, and power is a means of facilitating their achievement.

What differences are there between the two terms? One difference relates to goal compatibility. Power does not require goal compatibility, merely dependence. Leadership, on the other hand, requires some congruence between the goals of the leader and the led. A second difference relates to the direction of influence. Leadership focuses on the downward influence on one's subordinates. It minimizes the importance of lateral and upward influence patterns. Power does not. Still another difference deals with research emphasis. Leadership research, for the most part, emphasizes style. It seeks answers to such questions as: How supportive should a leader be? How much decision making should be shared with subordinates? In contrast, the research on power has tended to encompass a broader area and focus on tactics for gaining compliance. It has gone beyond the individual as exerciser because power can be used by groups as well as by individuals to control other individuals or groups.

BASES AND SOURCES OF POWER

Referent Power Influence held by A based on B's admiration and desire to model himself or herself after A.

Where does power come from? What is it that gives an individual or a group influence over others? The early answer to these questions was a five-category classification scheme identified by French and Raven.[4] They proposed that there were five bases or sources of power that they termed coercive, reward, expert, legitimate, and referent power. Coercive power depends on fear; reward power derives from the ability to distribute anything of value (typically money, favorable performance appraisals, interesting work assignments, friendly colleagues, and preferred work shifts or sales territories); expert power refers to influence that derives from special skills or knowledge; legitimate power is based on the formal rights one receives as a result of holding an authoritative position or role in an organization; and **referent**

power develops out of others' admiration for a person and their desire to model their behavior and attitudes after that person. While French and Raven's classification scheme provided an extensive repertoire of possible bases of power, their categories created ambiguity because they confused bases of power with sources of power.[5] The result was much overlapping. We can improve our understanding of the power concept by separating bases and sources so as to develop clearer and more independent categories.

Bases of power refers to what the powerholder has that gives him or her power. Assuming that you're the powerholder, your bases are what you control that enables you to manipulate the behavior of others. There are four power bases—coercive power, reward power, persuasive power, and knowledge power.[6] We'll expand on each in a moment.

How are **sources of power** different from bases of power? The answer is that sources tell us where the powerholder gets his or her power base. That is, sources refer to how you come to control your base of power. There are four sources—the position you hold, your personal characteristics, your expertise, and the opportunity you have to receive and obstruct information.[7] Each of these will also be discussed in a moment.

Let us now consider the four bases of power.

Bases of Power

COERCIVE POWER   The **coercive** base depends on fear. One reacts to this power out of fear of the negative ramifications that might result if one fails to comply. It rests on the application, or the threat of application, of physical sanctions such as infliction of pain, deformity, or death; the generation of frustration through restriction of movement; or the controlling through force of basic physiological or safety needs.

In the 1930s, when John Dillinger went into a bank, held a gun to the teller's head, and asked for the money, he was incredibly successful at getting compliance with his request. His power base? Coercive. A loaded gun gives its holder power because others are fearful that they will lose something that they hold dear—their lives.

> Of all the bases of power available to man, the power to hurt others is possibly most often used, most often condemned, and most difficult to control. . . the state relies on its military and legal resources to intimidate nations, or even its own citizens. Businesses rely upon the control of economic resources. Schools and universities rely upon their right to deny students formal education, while the church threatens individuals with loss of grace. At the personal level, individuals exercise coercive power through a reliance upon physical strength, verbal facility, or the ability to grant or withhold emotional support from others. These bases provide the individual with the means to physically harm, bully, humiliate, or deny love to others.[8]

At the organization level, A has coercive power over B if A can dismiss, suspend, or demote B, assuming that B values his or her job. Similarly, if A can assign B work activities that B finds unpleasant or treat B in a manner that B finds embarrassing, A possesses coercive power over B.

REWARD POWER   The opposite of coercive power is the power to reward. People comply with the wishes of another because it will result in positive benefits; therefore, one who can distribute rewards that others view as valuable will have power over them. Our definition of rewards is here limited to only material rewards. This would include salaries and wages, commissions, fringe benefits, and the like.

Bases of Power   What powerholders control that allow them to manipulate the behavior of others.

Sources of Power   How powerholders come to control the bases of power.

Coercive Power   Power that is based on fear.

Coercive Power and Sexual Harassment

The issue of sexual harassment got increasing attention by corporations and the media in the 1980s because of the growing ranks of female employees, especially in nontraditional work environments. But it was the congressional hearings in the fall of 1991 in which law professor Anita Hill graphically accused Supreme Court nominee Clarence Thomas of sexual harassment that challenged organizations to reassess their harassment policies and practices.[9]

Legally, sexual harassment is defined as unwelcome advances, requests for sexual favors, and other verbal or physical conduct of a sexual nature. But there is a great deal of disagreement as to what *specifically* constitutes sexual harassment. For example, a recent study found that eighty-one percent of women consider suggestive looks by a supervisor as harassment, but only sixty-eight percent of men do. Similarly, seventy-two percent of women viewed sexual remarks as harassment, compared to only fifty-eight percent of men.

Sexual harassment is illegal whether it's done by a co-worker or a supervisor, but the latter case is particularly difficult for the victim because of the boss's power to retaliate. No one should have to tolerate a threat such as "Have sex with me if you want that promotion or want to keep your job."

More and more corporations have gotten tough about eliminating sexual harassment. Honeywell, for instance, publicizes its policy against sexual harassment in a handbook given to every employee and on posters placed in conspicuous places. Corning provides intensive seminars for employees. Du Pont has a twenty-four-hour hotline and provides security for victims fearful of reprisals. AT&T warns its employees that they can be fired for repeatedly making unwelcome sexual advances, using sexually degrading words to describe someone, or displaying sexually offensive pictures or objects at work.

Persuasive Power   The ability to allocate and manipulate symbolic rewards.

PERSUASIVE POWER   **Persuasive power** rests on the allocation and manipulation of symbolic rewards. If you can decide who is hired, manipulate the mass media, control the allocation of status symbols, or influence a group's norms, you have persuasive power. For instance, when a teacher uses the class climate to control a deviant student, or when a union steward arouses the members to use their informal power to bring a deviant member into line, you are observing the use of persuasive power.

Knowledge Power   The ability to control unique and valuable information.

KNOWLEDGE POWER   **Knowledge,** or access to information, is the final base of power. We can say that when an individual in a group or organization controls unique information, and when that information is needed to make a decision, that individual has knowledge-based power.

To summarize, the bases of power refer to what the powerholder controls that enables him or her to manipulate the behavior of others. The coercive base of power is the control of punishment, the reward base is the control of material rewards, the persuasive base is the control of symbolic rewards, and the knowledge base is the control of information. Table 12–1 offers some common symbols that would suggest that a manager has developed strong power bases.

TABLE 12–1   Common Symbols of a Manager's Power

To what extent a manager can
- Intercede favorably on behalf of someone in trouble with the organization
- Get a desirable placement for a talented subordinate
- Get approval for expenditures beyond the budget
- Get above-average salary increases for subordinates
- Get items on the agenda at policy meetings
- Get fast access to top decision makers
- Get regular, frequent access to top decision makers
- Get early information about decisions and policy shifts

Source: Reprinted by permission of the *Harvard Business Review*. An exhibit from "Power Failure in Management Circuits," by Rosabeth M. Kanter (July–August 1979), p. 67. Copyright ©1979 by the President and Fellows of Harvard College; all rights reserved.

Sources of Power

POSITION POWER   In formal groups and organizations, probably the most frequent access to one or more of the power bases is one's structural position. A teacher's position includes significant control over symbols, a secretary frequently is privy to important information, and the head coach of a football team has substantial coercive resources at his disposal. All of these bases of power are achieved as a result of the formal position each holds within his or her structural hierarchy.

FIGURE 12–1

" I was just going to say ' Well, I don't make the rules.' But, of course, I do make the rules."

Source: Drawing by Leo Cullum; © 1986 The New Yorker Magazine, Inc.

Personal Power Influence attributed to one's personal characteristics.

PERSONAL POWER Personality traits were discussed in Chapter 4 and again in the previous chapter on leadership. They reappear within the topic of power when we acknowledge the fact that one's **personal** characteristics can be a source of power. If you are articulate, domineering, physically imposing, or charismatic, you hold personal characteristics that may be used to get others to do what you want.

EXPERT POWER Expertise is a means by which the powerholder comes to control specialized information (rather than the control itself, which we have discussed as the knowledge base of power). Those who have expertise in terms of specialized information can use it to manipulate others. Expertise is one of the most powerful sources of influence, especially in a technologically-oriented society. As jobs become more specialized, we become increasingly dependent on "experts" to achieve goals. So, while it is generally acknowledged that physicians have expertise and hence **expert power**—when your doctor talks, you listen—you should also recognize that computer specialists, tax accountants, solar engineers, industrial psychologists, and other specialists are able to wield power as a result of their expertise.

Expert Power Influence based on special skills or knowledge.

OPPORTUNITY POWER Finally, being in the right place at the right time can give one the **opportunity** to exert power.[10] One need not hold a formal position in a group or organization to have access to information that is important to others or to be able to exert coercive influence. An example of how one can use an opportunity to create a power base is the story of the former United States President Lyndon Johnson when he was a student at Southwestern Texas State Teachers College. He had a job as special assistant to the college president's personal secretary.

Opportunity Power Influence obtained as a result of being in the right place at the right time.

> As special assistant, Johnson's assigned job was simply to carry messages from the president to the department heads and occasionally to other faculty members. Johnson saw that the rather limited function of messenger had possibilities for expansion; for example, encouraging recipients of the messages to transmit their own communications through him. He occupied a desk in the president's outer office, where he took it upon himself to announce the arrival of visitors. These added services evolved from a helpful convenience into an aspect of the normal process of presidential business. The messenger had become an appointments secretary, and, in time, faculty members came to think of Johnson as a funnel to the president. Using a technique which was later to serve him in achieving mastery over the Congress, Johnson turned a rather insubstantial service into a process through which power was exercised.[11]

Johnson eventually broadened his informal duties to include handling the president's political correspondence, preparing his reports for state agencies, and even regularly accompanying him on his trips to the state capital—the president eventually relying on his young apprentice for political counsel. Certainly this represents an example of someone using an opportunity to redefine his job and to give himself power.

Summary

The foundation to understanding power begins by identifying where power comes from (sources) and, given that one has the means to exert influence, what it is that one manipulates (bases). Figure 12–2 visually depicts the relationship between sources and bases. Sources are the means. Individuals can use their position in the structure, rely on personal characteristics,

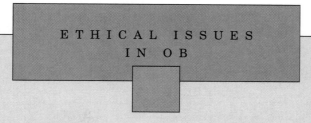

Ethics in the Use of Power

Is it true that power corrupts and absolute power corrupts absolutely? Or is it that power corrupts, but *lack* of power corrupts absolutely? These concerns beg the question: Is it unethical for organizational members to use power? Many contemporary behavioral scientists would argue that it isn't. They note that power is a natural part of human interactions—"we influence, or try to influence, other people every day under all sorts of conditions"—that carries into organizational life.[12]

Power really has two faces—one negative and the other positive.[13] The negative side is associated with abuse—when, for example, powerholders exploit others or use their power to merely accumulate status symbols. The positive side is characterized by a concern for group goals, helping the group to formulate its goals, and providing group members with the support they need to achieve those goals.

If you accept that using power is not unethical per se, then we should further inquire: Are certain *bases* of power more ethical than others? For instance, is reward power always more ethically preferable to coercive power? Is knowledge preferable to persuasion? What do *you* think?

develop expertise, or take advantage of opportunities to control information. Control of one or more of these sources allows the powerholder to manipulate the behavior of others via coercion, reward, persuasion, or knowledge bases. To reiterate, sources are *where* you get power. Bases are *what* you manipulate. Those who seek power must develop a source of power. Then, and only then, can they acquire a power base.

DEPENDENCY: THE KEY TO POWER

Earlier in this chapter it was said that probably the most important aspect of power is that it is a function of dependence. In this section, we'll show how an understanding of dependency is central to furthering your understanding of power itself.

FIGURE 12–2   Sources and Bases of Power

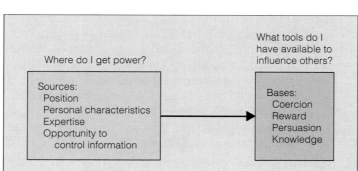

Predictions About People with a High Need for Power

David McClelland and his associates have conducted nearly one hundred studies on the power motive.[14] These studies provide convincing evidence that there is, in fact, something called *a need for power* (see Chapter 7), and that it allows for meaningful predictions of behavior. The following represent some of the more interesting findings related to individuals high in the need for power:

- They show partiality toward ingratiating followers.
- They inhibit group discussion when they are group leaders, resulting in the group considering fewer alternatives and producing lower quality decisions.
- They pursue occupations such as teaching, psychology, journalism, and business that allow them to exert significant influence over others.
- High-power males report that they have more arguments, play competitive sports more, have less stable interpersonal relations, experience more emotional problems, and are more impulsively aggressive than low-power males.

The General Dependency Postulate

Let's begin with a general postulate: *The greater B's dependency on A, the greater the power A has over B.* When you possess anything that others require but that you alone control, you make them dependent upon you and, therefore, you gain power over them.[15] Dependency, then, is inversely proportional to the alternative sources of supply. If something is plentiful, possession of it will not increase your power. If everyone is intelligent, intelligence gives no special advantage. Similarly, among the super-rich, money is no longer power. But, as the old saying goes, "In the land of the blind, the one-eyed man is king!" If you can create a monopoly by controlling information, prestige, or anything that others crave, they become dependent on you. Conversely, the more that you can expand your options, the less power you place in the hands of others. This explains, for example, why most organizations develop multiple suppliers rather than give their business to only one. It also explains why so many of us aspire to financial independence. Financial independence reduces the power that others can have over us.

Joyce Fields provides an example of the role that dependency plays in a work group or organization.[16] In 1975, she took a job with the Times Mirror Company in its Los Angeles headquarters. Fields moved quickly up the organization ladder, eventually becoming treasurer of the company. Among her many accomplishments at Times Mirror has been setting up a full-scale commercial-paper borrowing program from scratch and negotiating $1 billion of new debt to finance the company's media purchases. In 1988, Fields' husband was offered a promotion to chief financial officer at Paramount Communications in New York City. The job was too good to pass up, so the couple decided to pack up and move to Manhattan. However, Times Mirror didn't want to lose Fields to a New York company. So, in a tribute to her importance, top management at Times Mirror moved the company's entire treasury operations across the country to New York.

What Creates Dependency?

Dependency is increased when the resource you control is *important, scarce,* and *nonsubstitutable.*[17]

IMPORTANCE   If nobody wants what you've got, it's not going to create dependency. To create dependency, therefore, the thing(s) you control must be perceived as being important. It's been found, for instance, that organizations actively seek to avoid uncertainty.[18] We should, therefore, expect that those individuals or groups who can absorb an organization's uncertainty will be perceived as controlling an important resource. For instance, a study of industrial organizations found that the marketing departments in these firms were consistently rated as the most powerful.[19] It was concluded by the researcher that the most critical uncertainty facing these firms was selling their products. This might suggest that during a labor strike, the organization's negotiating representatives have increased power, or that engineers, as a group, would be more powerful at Apple Computer than at Procter & Gamble. These inferences appear to be generally valid. Labor negotiators do become more powerful within the personnel area and the organization as a whole during periods of labor strife. An organization such as Apple Computer, which is heavily technologically oriented, is highly dependent on its engineers to maintain its products' technical advantages and quality. And, at Apple, engineers are clearly a powerful group. At Procter & Gamble, marketing is the name of the game, and marketers are the most powerful occupational group. These examples support not only the view that the ability to reduce uncertainty increases a group's importance and, hence, its power but also that what's important is situational. It varies between organizations and undoubtedly also varies over time within any given organization.

If you want to talk to or see Clive Davis, head of Arista Records, you've got to go through his personal assistant, Rose Gross-Marino. Davis receives dozens of calls every day, but it's Marino who decides which ones get through to her boss. Those who might be inclined to ignore the Rose Marinos of the world should heed her advice: "Be honest," she says to those seeking access. "And don't tick me off."
Ed Quinn/New York Times Pictures

SCARCITY As noted previously, if something is plentiful, possession of it will not increase your power. A resource needs to be perceived as scarce to create dependency.

This can help to explain how low-ranking members in an organization who have important knowledge not available to high-ranking members gain power over the high-ranking members. Possession of a scarce resource—in this case, important knowledge—makes the high-ranking member dependent on the low-ranking member. This also helps to make sense out of behaviors of low-ranking members that otherwise might seem illogical, such as destroying the procedure manuals that describe how a job is done, refusing to train people in their jobs or even to show others exactly what they do, creating specialized language and terminology that inhibits others from understanding their jobs, or operating in secrecy so an activity will appear more complex and difficult than it really is.

The scarcity–dependency relationship can further be seen in the power of occupational categories. Individuals in occupations in which the supply of personnel is low relative to demand can negotiate compensation and benefit packages far more attractive than can those in occupations where there is an abundance of candidates. College administrators have no problem today finding English instructors. The market for accounting teachers, in contrast, is extremely tight, with the demand high and the supply limited. The result is that the bargaining power of accounting faculty allows them to negotiate higher salaries, lower teaching loads, and other benefits.

Elasticity of Power The relative responsiveness of power to change in available alternatives.

NONSUBSTITUTABILITY The more that a resource has no viable substitutes, the more power that control over that resource provides. This is illustrated in a concept we'll call the **elasticity of power.**

In economics, considerable attention is focused on the elasticity of demand, which is defined as the relative responsiveness of quantity demanded to change in price. This concept can be modified to explain the strength of power.

FIGURE 12–3 Elasticity of Power

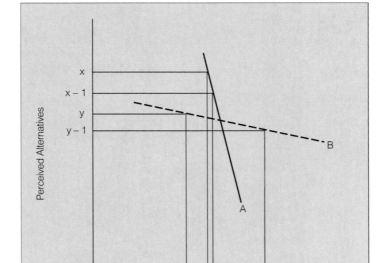

Elasticity of power is defined as the relative responsiveness of power to change in available alternatives. One's ability to influence others is viewed as being dependent on how these others perceive their alternatives.

As shown in Figure 12–3, assume that there are two individuals. Mr. A's power elasticity curve is relatively inelastic. This would describe, for example, an employee who believed that he had a large number of employment opportunities outside his current organization. Fear of being fired would have only a moderate impact on Mr. A, for he perceives that he has a number of other alternatives. Mr. A's boss finds that threatening A with termination has only a minimal impact on influencing his behavior. A reduction in alternatives (from X to $X–1$) only increases the power of A's boss slightly (A' to A''). However, Mr. B's curve is relatively elastic. He sees few other job opportunities. His age, education, present salary, or lack of contacts may severely limit his ability to find a job somewhere else. As a result, Mr. B is dependent on his present organization and boss. If B loses his job (Y to $Y–1$), he may face prolonged unemployment, and it shows itself in the increased power of B's boss. As long as B perceives his options as limited and B's boss holds the power to terminate his employment, B's boss will hold considerable power over him. In such a situation, it is obviously important for B to get his boss to believe that his options are considerably greater than they really are. If this is not achieved, B places his fate in the hands of his boss and makes himself captive to almost any demands the boss devises.

Higher education provides an excellent example of how this elasticity concept operates. In universities where there are strong pressures for the faculty to publish, we can say that a department head's power over a faculty member is inversely related to that member's publication record. The more recognition the faculty member receives through publication, the more mobile he or she is. That is, since other universities want faculty who are highly published and visible, there is an increased demand for his or her services. Although the concept of tenure can act to alter this relationship by restricting the department head's alternatives, those faculty members with little or no publications have the least mobility and are subject to the greatest influence from their superiors.

Elementary school teachers are suddenly a hot property. Enrollments are up and school districts are competing for a limited number of new teachers. As a result, the power of recent elementary education majors to select the kinds of jobs they want, with the resources they need, and in the geographic locations they prefer is much higher than 15 years ago—when there was a large over-supply of elementary education majors.

Laima Druskis

POWER TACTICS

Power Tactics Identifies how individuals manipulate the power bases.

This section is a logical extension of our previous discussions. We've reviewed *where* power comes from and *what* it is that powerholders manipulate. Now, we go the final step—to **power tactics.** Tactics tell us *how* to manipulate the bases. The following discussion will show you how employees translate their power bases into specific actions.

One of the few elements of power that has gone beyond anecdotal evidence or armchair speculation is the topic of tactics. Recent research indicates that there are standardized ways by which powerholders attempt to get what they want.[20]

When 165 managers were asked to write essays describing an incident in which they influenced their bosses, co-workers, or subordinates, a total of 370 power tactics grouped into fourteen categories were identified. These answers were condensed, rewritten into a fifty-eight-item questionnaire, and given to over 750 employees. These respondents were not only asked how they went about influencing others at work but also for the possible reasons for influencing the target person. The results, which are summarized here, give us considerable insight into power tactics—how managerial employees influence others and the conditions under which one tactic is chosen over another.[21]

The findings identified seven tactical dimensions or strategies:

- *Reason:* Use of facts and data to make a logical or rational presentation of ideas
- *Friendliness:* Use of flattery, creation of goodwill, acting humble, and being friendly prior to making a request
- *Coalition:* Getting the support of other people in the organization to back up the request
- *Bargaining:* Use of negotiation through the exchange of benefits or favors
- *Assertiveness:* Use of a direct and forceful approach such as demanding compliance with requests, repeating reminders, ordering individuals to do what is asked, and pointing out that rules require compliance
- *Higher authority:* Gaining the support of higher levels in the organization to back up requests
- *Sanctions:* Use of organizationally derived rewards and punishments such as preventing or promising a salary increase, threatening to give an unsatisfactory performance evaluation, or withholding a promotion

The researchers found that employees do not rely on the seven tactics equally. However, as shown in Table 12–2, the most popular strategy was the use of reason, regardless of whether the influence was directed upward or downward. Additionally, the researchers uncovered four contingency variables that affect the selection of a power tactic: the manager's relative power, the manager's objectives for wanting to influence, the manager's expectation of the target person's willingness to comply, and the organization's culture.

A manager's relative power impacts the selection of tactics in two ways. First, managers who control resources that are valued by others, or who are perceived to be in positions of dominance, use a greater variety of tactics than do those with less power. Second, managers with power use assertiveness with greater frequency than do those with less power. Initially, we can

TABLE 12–2   Usage of Power Tactics: From Most to Least Popular

	When Managers Influenced Superiors*	When Managers Influenced Subordinates
Most Popular	Reason	Reason
↑	Coalition	Assertiveness
│	Friendliness	Friendliness
│	Bargaining	Coalition
↓	Assertiveness	Bargaining
Least Popular	Higher authority	Higher authority
		Sanctions

*Sanctions is omitted in the scale that measures upward influence.

Source: Reprinted, by permission of the publisher, from "Patterns of Managerial Influence: Shotgun Managers, Tacticians, and Bystanders," by D. Kipnis et al. *Organizational Dynamics,* Winter 1984, p. 62. © 1984 Periodicals Division, American Management Associations, New York. All rights reserved.

expect that most managers will attempt to use simple requests and reason. Assertiveness is a backup strategy, used when the target of influence refuses or appears reluctant to comply with the request. Resistance leads to managers using more directive strategies. Typically, they shift from using simple requests to insisting that their demands be met. But the manager with relatively little power is more likely to stop trying to influence others when he or she encounters resistance, because he or she perceives the costs associated with assertiveness as unacceptable.

Managers vary their power tactics in relation to their objectives. When managers seek benefits from a superior, they tend to rely on kind words and the promotion of pleasant relationships; that is, they use friendliness. In comparison, managers attempting to persuade their superiors to accept new ideas usually rely on reason. This matching of tactics to objectives also holds true for downward influence. For example, managers use reason to sell ideas to subordinates and friendliness to obtain favors.

The manager's expectations of success guide his or her choice of tactics. When past experience indicates a high probability of success, managers use simple requests to gain compliance. Where success is less predictable, managers are more tempted to use assertiveness and sanctions to achieve their objectives.

Finally, we know that cultures within organizations differ markedly—for example, some are warm, relaxed, and supportive; others are formal and conservative. The organizational culture in which a manager works, therefore, will have a significant bearing on defining which tactics are considered appropriate. Some cultures encourage the use of friendliness, some encourage reason, and still others rely on sanctions and assertiveness. So the organization itself will influence which subset of power tactics is viewed as acceptable for use by managers.

POWER IN GROUPS: COALITIONS

Coalition Two or more individuals who combine their power to push for or support their demands.

Those "out of power" and seeking to be "in" will first try to increase their power individually. Why spread the spoils if one doesn't have to? But if this proves ineffective, the alternative is to form a **coalition.** There is strength in numbers.

The natural way to gain influence is to become a powerholder. Therefore, those who want power will attempt to build a personal power

Individuals had little success in attempting to influence local, state, and federal legislation to protect the rights of those suffering from AIDS. However, coalitions like ACTUP have successfully increased public awareness and lobbied for greater rights protections.
Laima Druskis

base. But, in many instances, this may be difficult, risky, costly, or impossible. In such cases, efforts will be made to form a coalition of two or more "outs" who, by joining together, can combine their resources to increase rewards for themselves.[22]

Historically, employees in organizations who were unsuccessful in bargaining on their own behalf with management resorted to labor unions to bargain for them. In recent years, even some managers have joined unions after finding it difficult to exert power individually to attain higher wages and greater job security.

What predictions can we make about coalition formation?[23] First, coalitions in organizations often seek to maximize their size. In political science theory, coalitions move the other way—they try to minimize their size. They tend to be just large enough to exert the power necessary to achieve their objectives. But legislatures are different from organizations. Specifically, decision making in organizations does not end just with selection from among a set of alternatives. The decision must also be implemented. In organizations, the implementation of and commitment to the decision is at least as important as the decision itself. It's necessary, therefore, for coalitions in organizations to seek a broad constituency to support the coalition's objectives. This means expanding the coalition to encompass as many interests as possible. This coalition expansion to facilitate consensus building, of course, is more likely to occur in organizational cultures where cooperation, commitment, and shared decision making are highly valued. In autocratic and hierarchically controlled organizations, this search for maximizing the coalition's size is less likely to be sought.

Another prediction about coalitions relates to the degree of interdependence within the organization. More coalitions will likely be created where there is a great deal of task and resource interdependence. In contrast, there will be less interdependence among subunits and less coalition formation activity where subunits are largely self-contained or resources are abundant.

Finally, coalition formation will be influenced by the actual tasks that workers do. The more routine the task of a group, the greater the likelihood that coalitions will form. The more that the work that people do is routine, the greater their substitutability for each other and, thus, the greater their

The Role of Power in Different Countries

The role of power in organizations is likely to vary between countries. We can make some predictions based on how a given society scores on power distance and the quantity–quality dimensions.

We know that power distance measures the extent to which a society accepts that power in organizations is distributed unequally. High-power-distance societies such as Mexico accept the use of power by superiors. Low-power-distance societies, because they're more egalitarian, tend to frown on the overt use of power. "In high power distance countries, such as the Philippines, Venezuela, and India, superiors and subordinates consider bypassing to be insubordination, whereas in low power distance countries, such as Israel and Denmark, employees expect to bypass the boss frequently in order to get work done."[24]

Assertive and dominating behavior is more acceptable in quantity-of-life cultures than in quality ones, so a broader use of power tactics can be expected in countries such as Italy and Austria.

While the research is scant, we might also speculate on how different cultures might rely more heavily on different power bases. For instance, coercion in organizations is frowned upon in North America. But in such high-power-distance countries as the Philippines or Mexico, it is likely to be a more viable alternative. Similarly, knowledge is likely to carry more weight as an influence base in high-power-distance countries, because such nations tend to have a small ruling upper class, little or no middle class, and a huge underclass. In low-power-distance countries, which are more egalitarian, access to information is more readily accessible to everyone.

dependence. To offset this dependence, they can be expected to resort to a coalition. We see, therefore, that unions appeal more to low-skill and nonprofessional workers than to skilled and professional types. Of course, where the supply of skilled and professional employees is high relative to their demand or where organizations have standardized traditionally nonroutine jobs, we would expect even these incumbents to find unionization attractive.

POLITICS: POWER IN ACTION

When people get together in groups, power will be exerted. People want to carve out a niche from which to exert influence, to earn awards, and to advance their careers.[25] When employees in organizations convert their power into action, we describe them as being engaged in politics. Those with good political skills have the ability to use their bases of power effectively.[26]

Definition

Political Behavior Those activities that are not required as part of one's formal role in the organization, but that influence, or attempt to influence, the distribution of advantages and disadvantages within the organization.

There has been no shortage of definitions for organizational politics. Essentially, however, they have focused on the use of power to affect decision making in the organization or on behaviors by members that are self-serving and organizationally nonsanctioned.[27] For our purposes, we shall define **political behavior** in organizations as *those activities that are not required as part of one's formal role in the organization, but that influence, or attempt to influence, the distribution of advantages and disadvantages within the organization.*[28]

This definition encompasses key elements from what most people mean when they talk about organizational politics. Political behavior is *outside* one's specified job requirements. The behavior requires some attempt to use one's *power* bases. Additionally, our definition encompasses efforts to influence the goals, criteria, or processes used for *decision making* when we state that politics is concerned with "the distribution of advantages and disadvantages within the organization." Our definition is broad enough to include such varied political behaviors as withholding key information from decision makers, whistleblowing, spreading rumors, leaking confidential information about organizational activities to the media, exchanging favors with others in the organization for mutual benefit, and lobbying on behalf of or against a particular individual or decision alternative.

A final comment relates to what has been referred to as the "legitimate–illegitimate" dimension in political behavior.[29] **Legitimate political behavior** refers to normal everyday politics—complaining to your supervisor, bypassing the chain of command, forming coalitions, obstructing organizational policies or decisions through inaction or excessive adherence to rules, and developing contacts outside the organization through one's professional activities. On the other hand, there are also **illegitimate** or extreme political behaviors that violate the implied "rules of the game." Those who pursue such activities are often described as individuals who "play hardball." Illegitimate activities include sabotage, whistleblowing, and symbolic protests such as wearing unorthodox dress or protest buttons, and groups of employees simultaneously calling in sick.

The vast majority of all organizational political actions are of the legitimate variety. The reasons are pragmatic: The extreme illegitimate forms of political behavior pose a very real risk of loss of organizational membership or extreme sanctions against those who use them and then fall short in having enough power to ensure that they work.

Legitimate Political Behavior
Normal everyday politics.

Illegitimate Political Behavior
Extreme political behavior that violates the implied rules of the game.

The Reality of Politics

Politics is a fact of life in organizations. People who ignore this fact of life do so at their own peril. But why, you may wonder, must politics exist? Isn't it possible for an organization to be politics-free? It's *possible,* but most unlikely.

Organizations are made up of individuals and groups with different values, goals, and interests.[30] This sets up the potential for conflict over resources. Departmental budgets, space allocations, project responsibilities, and salary adjustments are just a few examples of the resources about whose allocation organizational members will disagree.

Resources in organizations are also limited, which often turns potential conflict into real conflict. If resources were abundant, then all the various constituencies within the organization could satisfy their goals. But because they are limited, not everyone's interests can be provided for. Further, whether true or not, gains by one individual or group are often *perceived* as being at the expense of others within the organization. These forces create a competition among members for the organization's limited resources.

Maybe the most important factor leading to politics within organizations is the realization that most of the "facts" that are used to allocate the limited resources are open to interpretation. What, for instance, is *good* performance? What's an *adequate* improvement? What constitutes an *unsatisfactory* job? The manager of any major league baseball team knows a .400 hitter is a high performer and a .125 hitter a poor performer. You don't need to be a

Politics Is in the Eye of the Beholder

A behavior that one person labels as "organizational politics" is very likely to be characterized as an instance of "effective management" by another.[31] The fact is not that effective management is necessarily political, though in some cases it might be. Rather, a person's reference point determines what he or she classifies as organizational politics. Take a look at the following labels used to describe the same phenomenon. These suggest that politics, like beauty, is in the eye of the beholder.

"Political" label	"Effective management" label
1. Blaming others	1. Fixing responsibility
2. Ingratiation	2. Positive reinforcement
3. "Kissing up"	3. Developing working relationships
4. Apple-polishing	4. Demonstrating loyalty
5. Passing the buck	5. Delegating authority
6. Coopting	6. Negotiation
7. Covering your rear	7. Documenting decisions
8. Creating conflict	8. Encouraging change and innovation
9. Forming coalitions	9. Facilitating teamwork
10. Whistleblowing	10. Improving efficiency
11. Nitpicking	11. Meticulous attention to detail
12. Scheming	12. Planning ahead

baseball genius to know you should play your .400 hitter and send the .125 hitter back to the minors. But what if you have to choose between players who hit .280 and .290? Then other factors—less objective ones—come into play: fielding expertise, attitude, potential, ability to perform in the clutch, loyalty to the team, and so on. More managerial decisions resemble choosing between a .280 and a .290 hitter than deciding between a .125 hitter and a .400 hitter. It is in this large and ambiguous middle ground of organizational life—where the facts *don't* speak for themselves—that politics flourish.

Finally, because most decisions have to be made in a climate of ambiguity—where facts are rarely fully objective, and thus are open to interpretation—people within organizations will use whatever influence they can to taint the facts to support their goals and interests. That, of course, creates the activities we call *politicking*.

So, to answer the earlier question—Isn't it possible for an organization to be politics-free?—we can say: Yes, if all members of that organization hold the same goals and interests; if organizational resources are not scarce; and if performance outcomes are completely clear and objective. But that doesn't describe the organizational world that most of us live in!

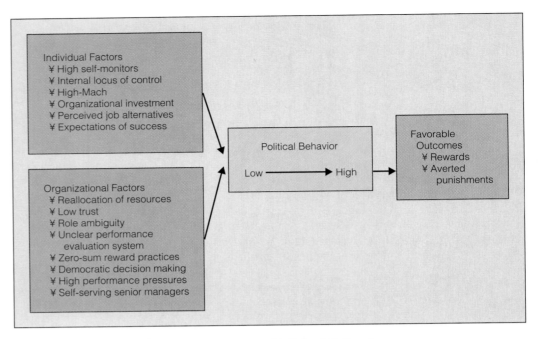

FIGURE 12–4   Factors Influencing Political Behavior

Factors Contributing to Political Behavior

Not all groups or organizations are equally political. In some organizations, for instance, politicking is overt and rampant; while in others, politics plays a small role in influencing outcomes. Why is there this variation? Recent research and observation have identified a number of factors that appear to encourage political behavior. Some are individual characteristics, derived from the unique qualities of the people the organization employs; others are a result of the organization's culture or internal environment. Figure 12–4 illustrates how both individual and organizational factors can increase political behavior and provide favorable outcomes (increased rewards and averted punishments) for both individuals and groups in the organization.

INDIVIDUAL FACTORS   At the individual level, researchers have identified certain personality traits, needs, and other factors that are likely to be related to political behavior. In terms of traits, we find that employees who are high self-monitors, possess an internal locus of control, and have a high need for power are more likely to engage in political behavior.[32]

The high self-monitor is more sensitive to social cues, exhibits higher levels of social conformity, and is more highly to be skilled in political behavior than the low self-monitor. Individuals with an internal locus of control, because they believe they can control their environment, are more prone to take a pro-active stance and attempt to manipulate situations in their favor. And, not surprisingly, the Machiavellian personality—which is characterized by the will to manipulate and the desire for power—is comfortable using politics as a means to further his or her self-interest.

Additionally, an individual's investment in the organization, perceived alternatives, and expectations of success will influence the degree to which he or she will pursue illegitimate means of political action[33] The more that a person has invested in the organization in terms of expectations of increased future benefits, the more a person has to lose if forced out and the less likely he or she is to use illegitimate means. The more alternative job opportunities an individual has—due to a favorable job market or the possession of scarce skills or knowledge, a prominent reputation, or influential contacts outside the organization—the more likely he or she is to risk illegitimate political actions. Last, if an individual has a low expectation of success in using illegitimate means, it is unlikely that he or she will attempt them. High expectations of success in the use of illegitimate means are most likely to be the province of both experienced and powerful individuals with polished political skills and inexperienced and naive employees who misjudge their chances.

ORGANIZATIONAL FACTORS   Political activity is probably more a function of the organization's characteristics than of individual difference variables. Why? Because many organizations have a large number of employees with the individual characteristics we listed, yet the extent of political behavior varies widely.

While we acknowledge the role that individual differences can play in fostering politicking, the evidence more strongly supports that certain situations and cultures promote politics. More specifically, when an organization's resources are declining or when the existing pattern of resources is changing, politics is more likely to surface.[34] In addition, cultures characterized by low trust, role ambiguity, unclear performance evaluation systems, zero-sum reward allocation practices, democratic decision making, high pressures for performance, and self-serving senior managers will create breeding grounds for politicking.[35]

When organizations cut back to improve efficiency, reductions in resources have to be made. Threatened with the loss of resources, people may engage in political actions to safeguard what they have. But any changes, especially those that imply significant reallocation of resources within the organization, are likely to stimulate conflict and increase politicking.

The less trust there is within the organization, the higher the level of political behavior and the more likely that the political behavior will be of the illegitimate kind. So high trust should suppress the level of political behavior in general and inhibit illegitimate actions in particular.

Role ambiguity means that the prescribed behaviors of the employee are not clear. There are fewer limits, therefore, to the scope and functions of the employee's political actions. Since political activities are defined as those not required as part of one's formal role, the greater the role ambiguity, the more one can engage in political activity with little chance of it being visible.

The practice of performance evaluation is far from a perfected science. The more that organizations use subjective criteria in the appraisal, emphasize a single outcome measure, or allow significant time to pass between the time of an action and its appraisal, the greater the likelihood that an employee can get away with politicking. Subjective performance criteria create ambiguity. The use of a single outcome measure encourages individuals to do whatever is necessary to "look good" on that measure, but often at the expense of performing well on other important parts of the job that are being appraised. The amount of time that elapses between an action and its appraisal is also a relevant factor. The longer the time period, the more unlikely that the employee will be held accountable for his or her political behaviors.

The more that an organization's culture emphasizes the zero-sum or win-lose approach to reward allocations, the more employees will be motivated to engage in politicking. The zero-sum approach treats the reward "pie" as fixed so that any gain one person or group achieves has to come at the expense of another person or group. If I win, you must lose! If $10,000 in annual raises is to be distributed among five employees, then any employee who gets more than $2,000 takes money away from one or more of the others. Such a practice encourages making others look bad and increasing the visibility of what you do.

In the last twenty-five years, there has been a general move in North America toward making organizations less autocratic. While much of this trend has been more in theory than in practice, it is undoubtedly true that in many organizations, managers are being asked to behave more democratically. Managers are told that they should allow subordinates to advise them on decisions and that they should rely to a greater extent on group input into the decision process. Such moves toward democracy, however, are not necessarily desired by individual managers. Many managers sought their positions in order to have legitimate power so as to be able to make unilateral decisions. They fought hard and often paid high personal costs to achieve their influential positions. Sharing their power with others runs directly against their desires. The result is that managers may use the required committees, conferences, and group meetings in a superficial way—as arenas for maneuvering and manipulating.

The more pressure that employees feel to perform well, the more likely they are to engage in politicking. When people are held strictly accountable for outcomes, this puts great pressure on them to "look good." If a person perceives that his or her entire career is riding on next quarter's sales figures or next month's plant productivity report, there is motivation to do whatever is necessary to make sure the numbers come out favorably.

Finally, when employees see the people on top engaging in political behavior, especially when they do so successfully and are rewarded for it, a climate is created that supports politicking. Politicking by top management, in a sense, gives permission to those lower in the organization to play politics by implying that such behavior is acceptable.

Impression Management

We know that people have an ongoing interest in how others perceive and evaluate them. For example, North Americans spend billions of dollars on diets, health club memberships, cosmetics, and plastic surgery—all intended to make them more attractive to others.[36] Being perceived positively by others should have benefits for people in organizations. It might, for instance, help them initially to get the jobs they want in an organization and, once hired, to get favorable evaluations, superior salary increases, and more rapid promotions. In a political context, it might help sway the distribution of advantages in their favor.

The process by which individuals attempt to control the impression others form of them is called **impression management**.[37] It's a subject that only quite recently has gained the attention of OB researchers.[38]

Is *everyone* concerned with impression management (IM)? No! Who, then, might we predict to engage in IM? No surprise here! It's our old friend, the high self-monitor.[39] Low self-monitors tend to present images of themselves that are consistent with their personalities, regardless of the beneficial or detrimental effects for them. In contrast, high self-monitors are good at reading situations and molding their appearances and behavior to fit each situation.

Given that you want to control the impression others form of you, what techniques could you use? Table 12–3 summarizes some of the more popular IM techniques and provides an example of each.

Keep in mind that IM does not imply that the impressions people convey are necessarily false (although, of course, they sometimes are).[40] Excuses and acclaiming, for instance, may be offered with sincerity. Referring to the exam-

Impression Management The process by which individuals attempt to control the impression others form of them.

TABLE 12–3   Impression Management (IM) Techniques

Conformity

Agreeing with someone else's opinion in order to gain his or her approval.

Example: A manager tells his boss, "You're absolutely right on your reorganization plan for the western regional office. I couldn't agree with you more."

Excuses

Explanations of a predicament-creating event aimed at minimizing the apparent severity of the predicament.

Example: Sales manager to boss, "We failed to get the ad in the paper on time, but no one responds to those ads anyway."

Apologies

Admitting responsibility for an undesirable event and simultaneously seeking to get a pardon for the action.

Example: Employee to boss, "I'm sorry I made a mistake on the report. Please forgive me."

Acclaiming

Explanation of favorable events to maximize the desirable implications for oneself.

Example: A salesperson informs a peer, "The sales in our division have nearly tripled since I was hired."

Flattery

Complimenting others about their virtues in an effort to make oneself appear perceptive and likable.

Example: New sales trainee to peer, "You handled that client's complaint *so* tactfully! I could never have handled that as well as you did."

Favors

Doing something nice for someone to gain that person's approval.

Example: Salesperson to prospective client, "I've got two tickets to the theater tonight that I can't use. Take them. Consider it a thank-you for taking the time to talk with me."

Association

Enhancing or protecting one's image by managing information about people and things with which one is associated.

Example: A job applicant says to an interviewer, "What a coincidence. Your boss and I were roommates in college."

Source: Based on B. R. Schlenker, *Impression Management* (Monterey, CA: Brooks/Cole, 1980); W. L. Gardner and M. J. Martinko, "Impression Management in Organizations," *Journal of Management,* June 1988, p. 332; and R. B. Cialdini, "Indirect Tactics of Image Management: Beyond Basking," in R. A. Giacalone and P. Rosenfeld (eds.), *Impression Management in the Organization* (Hillsdale, NJ: Lawrence Erlbaum Associates, 1989), pp. 45–71.

ples used in Table 12–3, you can *actually* believe that ads contribute little to sales in your region or that you *are* the key to the tripling of your division's sales. But misrepresentation can have a high cost. If the image claimed is false, you may be discredited.[41] If you "cry wolf" once too often, no one is likely to believe you when the wolf really comes. So the impression manager must be cautious not to be perceived as insincere or manipulative.[42]

Are there *situations* where individuals are more likely to misrepresent themselves or more likely to get away with it? Yes—situations that are characterized by high uncertainty or ambiguity.[43] These situations provide relatively little information for challenging a fraudulent claim and reduce the risks associated with misrepresentation.

Only a limited number of studies have been undertaken to test the effectiveness of IM techniques, and these have been essentially limited to determining whether IM behavior is related to job interview success. This makes a particularly relevant area of study since applicants are clearly attempting to present positive images of themselves and there are relatively objective outcome measures (written assessments and typically a hire–don't hire recommendation).

The evidence is that IM behavior works.[44] In one study, for instance, interviewers felt that those applicants for a position as a customer-service representative who used IM techniques performed better in the interview, and they seemed somewhat more inclined to hire these people.[45] Moreover, when the researchers considered applicants' credentials, they concluded that it was the IM techniques alone that influenced the interviewers. That is, it didn't seem to matter if applicants were well or poorly qualified. If they used IM techniques, they did better in the interview.

Another employment interview study looked at whether certain IM techniques work better than others.[46] The researchers compared applicants who used IM techniques that focused the conversation on themselves (called a *controlling style*) to applicants who used techniques that focused on the interviewer (referred to as a *submissive style*). The researchers hypothesized that applicants who used the controlling style would be more effective because of the implicit expectations inherent in employment interviews. We tend to expect job applicants to use self-enhancement, self-promotion and other active controlling techniques in an interview because they reflect self-confidence and initiative. The researchers predicted that these active controlling techniques would work better for applicants than submissive tactics like conforming their opinions to those of the interviewer and offering favors to the interviewer. The results confirmed the researchers' predictions. Those applicants who used the controlling style were rated higher by interviewers on factors such as motivation, enthusiasm, and even technical skills—and they received more job offers.

Defensive Behaviors

Organizational politics includes *protection* of self-interest as well as *promotion*. Individuals often engage in reactive and protective "defensive" behaviors to avoid action, blame, or change.[47] This section discusses common varieties of **defensive behaviors,** classified by their objective.

Defensive Behaviors Reactive and protective behaviors to avoid action, blame, or change.

AVOIDING ACTION Sometimes the best political strategy is to avoid action. That is, the best action is no action! However, role expectations typically dictate that one at least give the impression of doing something. Here are six popular ways to avoid action:

1. *Overconforming.* You strictly interpret your responsibility by saying things like, "The rules clearly state . . . " or "This is the way we've always done it." Rigid adherence to rules, policies, and precedents avoid the need to consider the nuances of a particular case.

2. *Passing the buck.* You transfer responsibility for the execution of a task or decision to someone else.

3. *Playing dumb.* This is a form of strategic helplessness. You avoid an unwanted task by falsely pleading ignorance or inability.

4. *Depersonalization.* You treat other people as objects or numbers, distancing yourself from problems and avoiding having to consider the idiosyncrasies of particular people or the impact of events on them. Hospital physicians often refer to patients by their room number or disease in order to avoid becoming too personally involved with them.

5. *Stretching and smoothing.* Stretching refers to prolonging a task so that you appear to be occupied—for example, you turn a two-week task into a four-month job. Smoothing refers to covering up fluctuations in effort or output. Both these practices are designed to make you appear continually busy and productive.

6. *Stalling.* This "foot-dragging" tactic requires you to appear more or less supportive publicly while doing little or nothing privately.

AVOIDING BLAME   What can you do to avoid blame for actual or anticipated negative outcomes? You can try one of the following six tactics:

1. *Buffing.* This is a nice way to refer to "covering your butt." It describes the practice of rigorously documenting activity to project an image of competence and thoroughness. "I can't provide that information unless I get a formal written requisition from you," is an example.

2. *Playing safe.* This encompasses tactics designed to evade situations that may reflect unfavorably on you. It includes taking on only projects with a high probability of success, having risky decisions approved by superiors, qualifying expressions of judgment, and taking neutral positions in conflicts.

3. *Justifying.* This tactic includes developing explanations that lessen your responsibility for a negative outcome and/or apologizing to demonstrate remorse.

4. *Scapegoating.* This is the classic effort to place the blame for a negative outcome on external factors that are not entirely blameworthy. "I would have had the paper in on time but my computer went down—and I lost everything—the day before the deadline."

5. *Misrepresenting.* This tactic involves the manipulation of information by distortion, embellishment, deception, selective presentation, or obfuscation.

6. *Escalation of commitment.* One way to vindicate an initially poor decision and a failing course of action is to escalate support for the decision. By further increasing the commitment of resources to a previous course of action, you indicate that the previous decision was not wrong. When you "throw good money after bad," you demonstrate confidence in past actions and consistency over time.

AVOIDING CHANGE   Finally, there are two forms of defensiveness frequently used by people who feel personally threatened by change:

1. *Resisting change.* This is a catch-all name for a variety of behaviors, including some forms of overconforming, stalling, playing safe, and misrepresenting.

2. *Protecting turf.* This is defending your territory from encroachment by others. As one purchasing executive commented, "Tell the people in production that it's *our* job to talk with vendors, not theirs."

EFFECTS OF DEFENSIVE BEHAVIOR   In the short run, extensive use of defensiveness may well promote an individual's self-interest. But in the long run, it more often than not becomes a liability. This is because defensive behavior frequently becomes chronic or even pathological over time. People who constantly rely on defensiveness find that, eventually, it is the *only* way they know how to behave. At that point, they lose the trust and support of their peers, bosses, subordinates, and clients. In moderation, however, defensive behavior can be an effective device for surviving and flourishing in an organization because it is often deliberately or unwittingly encouraged by management.

In terms of the organization, defensive behavior tends to reduce effectiveness. In the short run, defensiveness delays decisions, increases interpersonal and intergroup tensions, reduces risk-taking, makes attributions and evaluations unreliable, and restricts change efforts. In the long term, defensiveness leads to organizational rigidity and stagnation, detachment from the organization's environment, an organizational culture that is highly politicized, and low employee morale.

IMPLICATIONS FOR PERFORMANCE AND SATISFACTION

Knowledge-based power is the most strongly and consistently related to effective performance.[48] For example, in a study of five organizations, knowledge was the most effective base for getting others to perform as desired.[49] Competence appears to offer wide appeal, and its use as a power base results in high performance by group members.

In contrast, position power does *not* appear to be related to performance differences. In spite of position being the most widely given reason for complying with a superior's wishes, it does not seem to lead to higher performance, though the findings are far from conclusive. Among blue-collar workers, one researcher found significantly positive relations between position power and four to six production measures. However, position power was not related to average earnings or performance against schedule.[50] Another study could find no relationship between the use of position power and high efficiency ratings.[51] One's position is effective for exacting compliance, but there is little evidence to suggest that it leads to higher levels of performance. This may be explained by the fact that position power tends to be fairly constant within a given organization.

The use of reward and coercive power has a significant inverse relationship to performance. People hold a negative view of reward and coercion as reasons for complying with a superior's requests. This view is reflected in the finding that these bases are associated with lower performance.[52] Further, research finds the use of coercive power to be negatively related to group effectiveness.[53]

We find that knowledge power is also strongly and consistently related to satisfaction. The evidence overwhelmingly indicates that this base is most satisfying to subjects of the power.[54] Knowledge-based power obtains both public and private compliance and avoids the problem of making subjects comply merely because the powerholder has the "right" to request compliance.

The use of coercive power is inversely related to individual satisfaction.[55] Coercion not only creates resistance, it is generally disliked by individuals. Studies of college teachers and sales personnel found coercion the least preferred power base.[56] A study of insurance company employees also drew the same conclusion.[57]

We can only speculate at this time on whether organizational politics is positively related to *actual* performance. However, there seems to be ample evidence that good political skills are positively related to high performance evaluations and, hence, to salary increases and promotions. The relationship between politics and employee satisfaction is also one where lack of hard data leads to more speculation than substantive findings. On the positive side, people with polished political skills should get increased satisfaction from their job because they tend to receive a disproportionate share of organizational rewards. Yet those who are perceived as insincere or manipulative are likely to be resented by colleagues and excluded from informal group activities. So while effective politicians may be well liked and rewarded by higher-ups in the organization, their job satisfaction may suffer as a result of being shunned by those in their immediate work group. For the politically naive or inept, we propose that job satisfaction is likely to be low. These people tend to feel continually powerless to influence those decisions that most affect them. They look at actions around them and are perplexed at why they are regularly "shafted" by colleagues, bosses, and "the system."

FOR DISCUSSION

1. What is power? How is it different from leadership?

2. Contrast French and Raven's power classification to the bases and sources presented in this chapter.

3. What is the difference between a source of power and a base of power?

4. Contrast power tactics with power bases and sources. What are some of the key contingency variables that determine which tactic a powerholder is likely to use?

5. "Knowledge power and expert power are the same thing." Do you agree or disagree? Discuss.

6. What is a coalition? When is it likely to develop?

7. Based on the information presented in this chapter, what would you do as a new college graduate entering a new job to maximize your power and accelerate your career progress?

8. How are power and politics related?

9. "More powerful managers are good for an organization. It is the powerless, not the powerful, who are the ineffective managers." Do you agree or disagree with this statement? Discuss.

10. Define political behavior. Why is politics a fact of life in organizations?

11. What factors contribute to political activity?

12. You're a sales representative for an international software company. After four excellent years, sales in your territory are off thirty percent this year. Describe three defensive responses you might use to reduce the potential negative consequences of this decline in sales.

It's a Political Jungle Out There!

Politics in organizations is simply a fact of life. Those who fail to acknowledge political behavior ignore the reality that organizations are political systems.

It would be nice if all organizations or formal groups within organizations could be described in such terms as supportive, harmonious, objective, trusting, collaborative, or cooperative. A nonpolitical perspective can lead one to believe that employees will always behave in ways consistent with the interests of the organization. In contrast, a political view can explain much of what may seem to be irrational behavior in organizations. It can help to explain, for instance, why employees withhold information, restrict output, attempt to "build empires," publicize their successes, hide their failures, distort performance figures to make themselves look better, and engage in similar activities that appear to be at odds with the organization's desire for effectiveness and efficiency.

For those who want tangible evidence that "it's a political jungle out there" in the real world, let's look at two studies. The first analyzed what it takes to get promoted fast in organizations. The second addressed the performance appraisal process.

As previously described in Chapter 1, Luthans and his associates* studied more than 450 managers. They found that these managers engaged in four managerial activities: traditional management (decision making, planning, and controlling), communication (exchanging routine information and processing paperwork), human resource management (motivating, disciplining, managing conflict, staffing, and training), and networking (socializing, politicking, and interacting with outsiders). Those managers who got promoted fastest spent forty-eight percent of their time networking. The average managers spent most of their efforts on traditional management and communication activities and only nineteen percent of their time networking. We suggest that this provides strong evidence of the importance that social and political skills play in getting ahead in organizations.

Longenecker and his associates** held in-depth interviews with sixty upper-level executives to find out what went into performance ratings. What they found was that executives frankly admitted to deliberately manipulating formal appraisals for political purposes. Accuracy was *not* a primary concern of these executives. Rather, they manipulated the appraisal results in an intentional and systematic manner to get the outcomes they wanted.

*F. Luthans, R. M. Hodgetts, and S. A. Rosenkrantz, *Real Managers* (Cambridge, MA: Ballinger, 1988).

**C. O. Longenecker, D. A. Gioia, and H. P. Sims, Jr., "Behind the Mask: The Politics of Employee Appraisal," *Academy of Management Executive,* August 1987, pp. 183–94.

The Myth of the Corporate Political Jungle

Organizational behavior currently appears to be undergoing a period of fascination with workplace politics. Proponents argue that politics is inevitable in organizations—that power struggles, alliance formations, strategic maneuverings, and cutthroat actions are as endemic to organizational life as are planning, organizing, leading, and controlling.

While political behavior certainly occurs, it is not inevitable in organizations. This myth is based on the erroneous assumption that there is a universal power motive, and it is perpetuated because its acceptance works in the best interest of management.

Organizational members are not necessarily driven by a power motive. On the contrary, highly variable data gathered from personality inventories indicate that the power motive may be subordinate to such other motives as affiliation or achievement or may be absent altogether. So why the belief in the universality of the power motive? It is consistent with the philosophical belief that human beings are primarily motivated to achieve their own good. The innateness of self-interest is difficult to refute, for it can be located in any personal goal, even the goal of advancing the interests of others. However, self-interest does not necessarily require the maximization of power, but rather may be satisfied by nothing more ambitious than survival. The competitive nature of some organizations requires individuals to *appear* to seek power maximization but that is only a survival measure. Under less competitive conditions, self-interest may be satisfied without engaging in defensive measures that appear to be power-related. So the lessening of competitive pressures can make political behavior unnecessary.

There is no doubt that the political jungle myth provides important benefits to those managers who are already in power. A few examples will illustrate this point. By arguing the need for political skills to achieve managerial positions, and given that managers are already incumbents, they demonstrate that they already have proven that they possess the political skills to acquire and retain resources for the organization. The existence of workplace politics also lessens the need for managers to be concerned with objectivity, fairness, and performance criteria when they allocate rewards. If organizations are political systems—and others accept them as such—managers have a greater latitude of discretion to legitimately reward their friends and punish their enemies.

Much of this argument is based on J. I. Klein, "The Myth of the Corporate Political Jungle: Politicization as a Political Strategy," *Journal of Management Studies*, January 1988, pp. 1–11.

Power Orientation Test

Instructions: For each statement, circle the number that most closely resembles your attitude.

	Disagree			Agree	
Statement	A Lot	A Little	Neutral	A Little	A Lot
1. The best way to handle people is to tell them what they want to hear.	1	2	3	4	5
2. When you ask someone to do something for you, it is best to give the real reason for wanting it rather than giving reasons that might carry more weight.	1	2	3	4	5
3. Anyone who completely trusts anyone else is asking for trouble.	1	2	3	4	5
4. It is hard to get ahead without cutting corners here and there.	1	2	3	4	5
5. It is safest to assume that all people have a vicious streak, and it will come out when they are given a chance.	1	2	3	4	5
6. One should take action only when it is morally right.	1	2	3	4	5
7. Most people are basically good and kind.	1	2	3	4	5
8. There is no excuse for lying to someone else.	1	2	3	4	5
9. Most people more easily forget the death of their father than the loss of their property.	1	2	3	4	5
10. Generally speaking, people won't work hard unless they're forced to do so.	1	2	3	4	5

Source: R. Christie and F. L. Geis, *Studies in Machiavellianism.* © Academic Press 1970. Reprinted by permission.

Turn to page 715 for scoring directions and key.

How Political Are You?

Mark each of the following statements either mostly true or mostly false. In some instances, "mostly true" refers to "mostly agree" and "mostly false" refers to "mostly disagree." We are looking for general tendencies, so don't be concerned if you are uncertain as to the more accurate response to a given statement.

	Mostly true	Mostly false
1. I would stay late in the office just to impress my boss.	_____	_____
2. Why teach your subordinates everything you know about your job? One of them could then replace you.	_____	_____
3. I have no interest in using gossip to personal advantage.	_____	_____
4. Be extra-careful about ever making a critical comment about your firm, even if it is justified.	_____	_____
5. I would go out of my way to cultivate friendships with powerful people.	_____	_____
6. I would never raise questions about the capabilities of my competition. Let his or her record speak for itself.	_____	_____
7. I am unwilling to take credit for someone else's work.	_____	_____
8. If I discovered that a co-worker was looking for a job, I would inform my boss.	_____	_____
9. Even if I made only a minor contribution to an important project, I would get my name listed as being associated with that project.	_____	_____
10. There is nothing wrong with tooting your own horn.	_____	_____
11. My office should be cluttered with personal mementos, such as pencil holders and decorations, made by my friends and family.	_____	_____
12. One should take action only when one is sure that it is ethically correct.	_____	_____
13. Only a fool would publicly correct mistakes made by the boss.	_____	_____

14. I would purchase stock in my company even though it might not be a good financial investment.   _____   _____

15. Even if I thought it would help my career, I would refuse a hatchetman assignment.   _____   _____

16. It is better to be feared than loved by your subordinates.   _____   _____

17. If others in the office were poking fun at the boss, I would decline to join in.   _____   _____

18. In order to get ahead, it is necessary to keep self-interest above the interests of the organization.   _____   _____

19. I would be careful not to hire a subordinate who might outshine me.   _____   _____

20. A wise strategy is to keep on good terms with everybody in your office even if you don't like everyone.   _____   _____

Turn to page 716 for scoring directions and key.

Source: A. J. DuBrin, *Winning Office Politics* (Englewood Cliffs, NJ: Prentice Hall, 1990), pp. 19–27. Used by permission of the publisher, Prentice Hall/A Simon & Schuster Company, Englewood Cliffs, NJ.

C A S E   I N C I D E N T   12

Damned If You Do; Damned If You Don't

Fran Gilson has spent fifteen years with the Thompson Grocery Company.* Starting out as a part-time cashier while attending college, Fran has risen up through the ranks of this 50-store grocery store chain. Today, at the age of 34, she is a regional manager, overseeing seven stores and earning nearly $80,000 a year. Fran also thinks she's ready to take on more responsibility. About five weeks ago, she was contacted by an executive-search recruiter inquiring about her interest in the position of vice-president and regional manager for a national drug store chain. She would be responsible for more than 100 stores in five states. She agreed to meet with the recruiter. This led to two meetings with top executives at the drug store chain. The recruiter called Fran two days ago to tell her she was one of the two finalists for the job.

The only person at Thompson who knows Fran is looking at this other job is her good friend and colleague, Ken Hamilton. Ken is director of finance for the grocery chain. "It's a dream job," Fran told Ken. "It's a lot more responsibility and it's a good company to work for. The regional office is just 20 miles from here so I wouldn't have to move. And the pay is first-rate. With the performance bonus, I could make nearly $200,000 a year. But best of all, the job provides terrific visibility. I'd be their only female vice president. The job would allow me to be a more visible role model for young women and give me a bigger voice in opening up doors for women and ethnic minorities in retailing management."

Since Fran considered Ken a close friend and wanted to keep the fact that she was looking at another job secret, she asked Ken last week if she could use his name as a reference. Said Ken, "Of course. I'll give you a great recommendation. We'd hate to lose you here, but you've got a lot of talent. They'd be lucky to get someone with your experience and energy." Fran passed Ken's name on to the executive recruiter as her only reference at Thompson. She made it very clear to the recruiter that Ken was the only person at Thompson who knew she was considering another job. Thompson's top management is old fashioned and places a high value on loyalty. If they heard she was talking to another company, it might seriously jeopardize her chances for promotion. But she trusted Ken completely. It's against this backdrop that this morning's incident became more than just a question of sexual harrassment. It became a full-blown ethical and political dilemma for Fran.

Jennifer Chung has been a financial analyst in Ken's department for five months. Fran met Jennifer through Ken. The three have chatted together on a number of occasions down in the coffee room. Fran's impression of Jennifer is quite positive. In many ways, Jennifer strikes Fran as a lot like she was ten or so years ago. This morning, Fran came to work around 6:30 A.M. as she usually does. It allows her to get a lot accomplished before "the troops" roll in at 8 A.M. At about 6:45, Jennifer came into Fran's office. It was immediately evident that something was wrong. Jennifer was very nervous and uncomfortable, which was most unlike her. She asked Fran if they could talk. Fran sat her down and listened to her story.

What Fran heard was hard to believe, but she had no reason to think Jennifer was lying. Jennifer said that Ken began making off-color comments to her when they were alone within a month after Jennifer joined Thompson. From there it got progressively worse. Ken would leer at her. He put his arm over her shoulder when they were reviewing reports. He patted her rear. Every time one of these occurrences happened, Jennifer would ask him to stop and not do it again. But it fell on deaf ears. Yesterday, Ken reminded Jennifer that her six-month probationary review was coming up. "He told me that if I didn't sleep with him that I couldn't expect a very favorable evaluation." She told Fran that all she could do was go to the ladies room and cry.

Jennifer said that she had come to Fran because she didn't know what to do or whom to turn to. "I came to you, Fran, because you're a friend of Ken's and the highest ranking woman here. Will you help me?" Fran had never heard anything like this about Ken before. About all she knew regarding his personal life was that he was in his late 30s, single, and involved in a long-term relationship.

Questions

1. Analyze Fran's situation in a purely legalistic sense. You might want to talk to friends or relatives who are in management or the legal profession for advice in this analysis.

2. Analyze Fran's dilemma in political terms.

3. Analyze Fran's situation in an ethical sense. What is the *ethically* right thing for her to do? Is that also the *politically* right thing to do?

4. If you were Fran, what would *you* do?

*The identity of this organization and the people described are disguised for obvious reasons.

FOR FURTHER READING

BAUM, H. S., "Organizational Politics Against Organizational Culture: A Psychoanalytic Perspective," *Human Resource Management,* Summer 1989, pp. 191–206. Organizational politics arouses anxiety that induces workers to withdraw emotionally. This article argues that politics makes it psychologically difficult for workers to feel loyal to an organization.

GIACALONE, R. A., AND P. ROSENFELD, *Applied Impression Management: How Image-Making Affects Managerial Decisions* (Newbury Park, CA: Sage Publications, 1991). Offers a practical look at how impression management affects specific facets of work.

KRACKHARDT, D., "Assessing the Political Landscape: Structure, Cognition, and Power in Organizations," *Administrative Science Quarterly,* June 1990, pp. 342–69. Findings support that having an accurate picture of the informal network significantly correlates with power.

KUMAN, P., AND R. GHADIALLY, "Organizational Politics and Its Effects on Members of Organizations," *Human Relations,* April 1989, pp. 305–14. Finds that political behaviors have significant negative consequences for interpersonal relationships and performance in organizations.

RAGINS, B. R., AND E. SUNDSTROM, "Gender and Power in Organizations: A Longitudinal Perspective," *Psychological Bulletin,* January 1989, pp. 51–88. Presents a model of power in organizations and uses it to organize a comprehensive review of empirical research and related theory concerning differences between the genders in power. Research reveals a consistent difference favoring men in accessibility to resources for power.

SAUNDERS, C. S., "The Strategic Contingencies Theory of Power: Multiple Perspectives," *Journal of Management Studies,* January 1990, pp. 1–18. Findings suggest that departmental control of strategic contingencies is a moderating variable in the relationship between power and capacity for power.

NOTES

[1]Based on R. Grover, "Fear Not, Hollywood: Golden Boy is Still Golden," *Business Week,* May 29, 1989, pp. 64–65; and S. Andrews, "The Man Who Would Be Walt," *New York Times,* January 26, 1992, p. H1.

[2]R. M. Kanter, "Power Failure in Management Circuits," *Harvard Business Review,* July–August 1979, p. 65.

[3]See, for example, D. Kipnis, *The Powerholders* (Chicago: University of Chicago Press, 1976); S. B. Bacharach and E. J. Lawler, *Power and Politics in Organizations* (San Francisco: Jossey-Bass, 1980); J. Pfeffer, *Power in Organizations* (Marshfield, MA: Pitman, 1981); H. Mintzberg, *Power In and Around Organizations* (Englewood Cliffs, NJ: Prentice Hall, 1983); R. J. House, "Power and Personality in Complex Organizations," in B. M. Staw and L. L. Cummings (eds.), *Research in Organizational Behavior,* Vol. 10 (Greenwich, CT: JAI Press, 1988), pp. 305–57; and J. Pfeffer, *Managing with Power* (Boston: Harvard Business School Press, 1992).

[4]J. R. P. French, Jr., and B. Raven, "The Bases of Social Power," in D. Cartwright (ed.), *Studies in Social Power* (Ann Arbor: University of Michigan, Institute for Social Research, 1959), pp. 150–67. For an update on French and Raven's work, see D. E. Frost and A. J. Stahelski, "The Systematic Measurement of French and Raven's Bases of Social Power in Workgroups," *Journal of Applied Social Psychology,* April 1988, pp. 375–89; and T. R. Hinkin and C. A. Schriesheim, "Development and Application of New Scales to Measure the French and Raven (1959) Bases of Social Power," *Journal of Applied Psychology,* August 1989, pp. 561–67.

[5]Bacharach and Lawler, *Power and Politics,* pp. 34–36.

[6]Adapted from ibid., and A. Etzioni, *Comparative Analysis of Complex Organizations* (New York: Free Press, 1961).

[7]Bacharach and Lawler, *Power and Politics,* pp. 34–36.

[8]Kipnis, *Powerholders,* pp. 77–78.

[9]The facts in this box are from A. Deutschman, "Dealing with Sexual Harassment," *Fortune,* November 4, 1991, pp. 145–48.

[10]D. J. Brass, "Being in the Right Place: A Structural Analysis of Individual Influence in an Organization," *Administrative Science Quarterly,* December 1984, pp. 518–39; and R.

Lachman, "Power from What? A Reexamination of Its Relationships with Structural Conditions," *Administrative Science Quarterly,* June 1989, pp. 231–51.

[11]D. Kearns, "Lyndon Johnson and the American Dream," *The Atlantic Monthly,* May 1976, p. 41.

[12]D. C. McClelland and D. H. Burnham, "Power Is the Great Motivator," *Harvard Business Review,* March–April 1976, pp. 100–110.

[13]Ibid.

[14]D. C. McClelland, *Human Motivation* (Glenview, IL: Scott, Foresman, 1985). For a condensed version of this research, see House, "Power and Personality in Complex Organizations," pp. 319–24.

[15]R. E. Emerson, "Power-Dependence Relations," *American Sociological Review,* Vol. 27 (1962), pp. 31–41.

[16]Cited in *Business Month,* April 1989, p. 41.

[17]Mintzberg, *Power In and Around Organizations,* p. 24.

[18]R. M. Cyert and J. G. March, *A Behavioral Theory of the Firm* (Englewood Cliffs, NJ: Prentice Hall, 1963).

[19]C. Perrow, "Departmental Power and Perspective in Industrial Firms," in M. N. Zald (ed.), *Power in Organizations* (Nashville, TN: Vanderbilt University Press, 1970).

[20]See, for example, D. Kipnis, S. M. Schmidt, C. Swaffin-Smith, and I. Wilkinson, "Patterns of Managerial Influence: Shotgun Managers, Tacticians, and Bystanders," *Organizational Dynamics,* Winter 1984, pp. 58–67; T. Case, L. Dosier, G. Murkison, and B. Keys, "How Managers Influence Superiors: A Study of Upward Influence Tactics," *Leadership and Organization Development Journal,* Vol. 9, No. 4, 1988, pp. 25–31; D. Kipnis and S. M. Schmidt, "Upward-Influence Styles: Relationship with Performance Evaluations, Salary, and Stress," *Administrative Science Quarterly,* December 1988, pp. 528–42; T. R. Hinkin and C. A. Schriesheim, "Relationships Between Subordinate Perceptions of Supervisor Influence Tactics and Attributed Bases of Supervisory Power," *Human Relations,* March 1990, pp. 221–37; G. Yukl and C. M. Falbe, "Influence Tactics and Objectives in Upward, Downward, and Lateral Influence Attempts," *Journal of Applied Psychology,* April 1990, pp. 132–40; H. E. Chacko, "Methods of Upward Influence, Motivational Needs, and Administrators' Perceptions of Their Supervisors' Leadership Styles," *Group and Organization Studies,* September 1990, pp. 253–65; and B. Keys and T. Case, "How to Become an Influential Manager," *Academy of Management Executive,* November 1990, pp. 38–51.

[21]This section is adapted from Kipnis, Schmidt, Swaffin-Smith, and Wilkinson, "Patterns of Managerial Influence."

[22]P. P. Poole, "Coalitions: The Web of Power," in D. J. Vredenburgh and R. S. Schuler (eds.), *Effective Management: Research and Application,* Proceedings of the 20th Annual Eastern Academy of Management, Pittsburgh, May 1983, pp. 79–82.

[23]See Pfeffer, *Power in Organizations,* pp. 155–57.

[24]N. J. Adler, *International Dimensions of Organizational Behavior,* 2nd ed. (Boston: PWS-Kent, 1991), p. 50.

[25]S. A. Culbert and J. J. McDonough, *The Invisible War: Pursuing Self-Interest at Work* (New York: John Wiley, 1980), p. 6.

[26]Mintzberg, *Power In and Around Organizations,* p. 26.

[27]D. J. Vredenburgh and J. G. Maurer, "A Process Framework of Organizational Politics," *Human Relations,* January 1984, pp. 47–66.

[28]D. Farrell and J. C. Petersen, "Patterns of Political Behavior in Organizations," *Academy of Management Review,* July 1982, p. 405. For a thoughtful analysis of the academic controversies underlying any definition of organizational politics, see A. Drory and T. Romm, "The Definition of Organizational Politics: A Review," *Human Relations,* November 1990, pp. 1133–54.

[29]Farell and Peterson, "Patterns of Political Behavior," pp. 406–07; and A. Drory, "Politics in Organization and Its Perception Within the Organization," *Organization Studies,* Vol. 9, No. 2, 1988, pp. 165–79.

[30]Pfeffer, *Power in Organizations.*

[31]Based on T. C. Krell, M. E. Mendenhall, and J. Sendry, "Doing Research in the Conceptual Morass of Organizational Politics," paper presented at the Western Academy of Management Conference, Hollywood, CA, April 1987.

[32]See, for example, G. Biberman, "Personality and Characteristic Work Attitudes of Persons with High, Moderate, and Low Political Tendencies," *Psychological Reports,* October 1985, pp. 1303–10; and G. R. Ferris, G. S. Russ, and P. M. Fandt, "Politics in Organizations," in R. A. Giacalone and P. Rosenfeld (eds.), *Impression Management in the Organization* (Hillsdale, NJ: Lawrence Erlbaum Associates, 1989), pp. 155–56.

[33]Farrell and Petersen, "Patterns of Political Behavior," p. 408.

[34]S. C. Goh and A. R. Doucet, "Antecedent Situational Conditions of Organizational Politics: An Empirical Investigation," paper presented at the Annual Administrative Sciences Association of Canada Conference, Whistler, B. C., May 1986; and C. Hardy, "The Contribution of Political Science to Organizational Behavior," in J. W. Lorsch (ed.), *Handbook of*

Organizational Behavior (Englewood Cliffs, NJ: Prentice Hall, 1987), p. 103.

[35]See, for example, Farrell and Petersen, "Patterns of Political Behavior," p. 409; P. M. Fandt and G. R. Ferris, "The Management of Information and Impressions: When Employees Behave Opportunistically," *Organizational Behavior and Human Decision Processes,* February 1990, pp. 140–58; and Ferris, Russ, and Fandt, "Politics in Organizations," p. 147.

[36]M. R. Leary and R. M. Kowalski, "Impression Management: A Literature Review and Two-Component Model," *Psychological Bulletin,* January 1990, pp. 34–47.

[37]Ibid., p. 34.

[38]See, for instance, B. R. Schlenker, *Impression Management: The Self-Concept, Social Identity, and Interpersonal Relations* (Monterey, CA: Brooks/Cole, 1980); W. L. Gardner and M. J. Martinko, "Impression Management in Organizations," *Journal of Management,* June 1988, pp. 321–38; D. C. Gilmore and G. R. Ferris, "The Effects of Applicant Impression Management Tactics on Interviewer Judgments," *Journal of Management,* December 1989, pp. 557–64; Leary and Kowalski, "Impression Management: A Literature Review and Two-Component Model," pp. 34–47; S. J. Wayne and K. M. Kacmar, "The Effects of Impression Management on the Performance Appraisal Process," *Organizational Behavior and Human Decision Processes,* February 1991, pp. 70–88; and E. W. Morrison and R. J. Bies, "Impression Management in the Feedback-Seeking Process: A Literature Review and Research Agenda," *Academy of Management Review,* July 1991, pp. 522–41.

[39]M. Snyder and J. Copeland, "Self-Monitoring Processes in Organizational Settings," in Giacalone and Rosenfeld, *Impression Management in the Organization,* p. 11.

[40]Leary and Kowalski, "Impression Management," p. 40.

[41]Gardner and Martinko, "Impression Management in Organizations," p. 333.

[42]R. A. Baron, "Impression Management by Applicants During Employment Interviews: The 'Too Much of a Good Thing' Effect," in R. W. Eder and G. R. Ferris (eds.), *The Employment Interview: Theory, Research, and Practice* (Newbury Park, CA: Sage Publishers, 1989), pp. 204–15.

[43]Ferris, Russ, and Fandt, "Politics in Organizations."

[44]Baron, "Impression Management by Applicants During Employment Interviews"; and Gilmore and Ferris, "The Effects of Applicant Impression Management Tactics on Interviewer Judgments."

[45]Gilmore and Ferris, "The Effects of Applicant Impression Management Tactics on Interviewer Judgments."

[46]K. M. Kacmar, J. E. Kelery, and G. R. Ferris, "Effectiveness of the Use of Impression Management Tactics by Applicants on Employment Interview Outcomes," in D. F. Ray (ed.), *Proceedings of the Southern Management Association* (Orlando, FL: 1990), pp. 351–53.

[47]This section is based on B. E. Ashforth and R. T. Lee, "Defensive Behavior in Organizations: A Preliminary Model," *Human Relations,* July 1990, pp. 621–48.

[48]See, for example, M. A. Rahim, "Relationships of Leader Power to Compliance and Satisfaction with Supervision: Evidence from a National Sample of Managers," *Journal of Management,* December 1989, pp. 545–56.

[49]J. G. Bachman, D. G. Bowers, and P. M. Marcus, "Bases of Supervisory Power: A Comparative Study in Five Organizational Settings," in A. S. Tannenbaum (ed.), *Control in Organizations* (New York: McGraw-Hill, 1968), p. 236.

[50]K. Student, "Supervisory Influence and Work-Group Performance," *Journal of Applied Psychology,* June 1968, pp. 188–94.

[51]J. Ivancevich, "An Analysis of Control, Bases of Control, and Satisfaction in an Organizational Setting," *Academy of Management Journal,* December 1970, pp. 427–36.

[52]J. G. Bachman, "Faculty Satisfaction and the Dean's Influence: An Organizational Study of Twelve Liberal Arts Colleges," *Journal of Applied Psychology,* February 1968, pp. 55–61; and J. G. Bachman, C. G. Smith, and J. A. Slesinger, "Control, Performance and Satisfaction: An Analysis of Structure and Individual Effort," *Journal of Personality and Social Psychology,* August 1966, pp. 127–36.

[53]Bachman, Bowers, and Marcus, "Bases of Supervisory Power."

[54]P. Busch, "The Sales Managers' Bases of Social Power and Influence Upon the Sales Force," *Journal of Marketing,* Fall 1980, pp. 91–101; Rahim, "Relationships of Leader Power to Compliance and Satisfaction;" and Hinkin and Schriesheim, "Relationships Between Subordinate Perceptions."

[55]Busch, "The Sales Managers' Bases of Social Power."

[56]See footnote 52.

[57]Ivancevich, "An Analysis of Control."

CONFLICT, NEGOTIATION, AND INTERGROUP BEHAVIOR

LEARNING OBJECTIVES

After studying this chapter, you should be able to:

1. Differentiate between the traditional, human relations, and interactionist views of conflict

2. Outline the conflict process

3. Differentiate between functional and dysfunctional conflict

4. Summarize the sources of conflict

5. Describe the five conflict-handling intentions

6. List the benefits and disadvantages of conflict

7. Contrast distributive and integrative bargaining

8. Identify four basic third-party negotiation roles

9. Explain the factors that affect intergroup relations

10. Identify methods for managing intergroup relations

Part of my job as a coach is to keep the five guys who hate me away from the five guys who are undecided.

C. STENGEL

John Akers, chairman of IBM, is out to shake up his company.[1] Why? IBM's overall market share in the computer industry has slipped to about twenty-three percent from thirty-seven percent less than a decade ago; and between 1985 and 1991, the company's net income dropped from $6.5 billion to $4 billion.

While many people think of conflict as bad, Akers believes that IBM's problem is that it has too little of it. "The tension level is not high enough in the business—everyone is too damn comfortable at a time when the business is in crisis . . . I'm sick and tired of visiting plants to hear nothing but great things about quality and cycle time—and then to visit customers who tell me of problems. If the people in labs and plants miss deadlines . . . tell them their job is on the line."[2]

Historically, IBM prided itself on never laying off employees. But the dramatic changes in the computer industry during the late 1980s—in terms of both new technology and new competitors—forced mighty IBM to bite the bullet and cut staff. From a high of 407,000 employees in 1986, it has cut its work force to fewer than 360,000. Some analysts think the company may still be overstaffed by 100,000 or more.

Akers is talking tough and is determined to "play hardball." He is encouraging marginal employees to leave the company and striving to increase the productivity of those who remain. "Our people have to be competitive, and if they can't change fast enough, as fast as our industry . . . goodbye!"[3] His remarks have been meant to shake up the entire company, including IBM's famed research and sales personnel. In 1991, Akers was quoted as saying that only one of every two hundred people at an IBM lab was fired in the previous year and that wasn't enough. He's also stated that he is very unhappy with the performance of the company's sales force. In 1986, IBM had twenty-thousand people in sales and they generated $26 billion in revenue. After expanding the sales staff to twenty-five-thousand by 1990, sales increased to just $27 billion. "Where's my return for the extra five thousand people?" he is quoted as asking.[4] ■

*J*ohn Akers' attempt to shake up IBM demonstrates the side of conflict that rarely gets much attention—its positive or functional aspects. In this chapter, we'll discuss both the functional and dysfunctional sides of conflict and show how they affect employee behavior and organizational performance. We'll also present two topics closely related to conflict—negotiation and intergroup relations. However, let's begin by clarifying what we mean by *conflict*.

A DEFINITION OF CONFLICT

There has been no shortage of definitions of conflict.[5] But despite the divergent meanings the term has acquired, several common themes underlie most definitions. Conflict must be *perceived* by the parties to it; whether or not conflict exists is a perception issue. If no one is aware of a conflict, then it is generally agreed that no conflict exists. Additional commonalities in the definitions are opposition or incompatibility and some form of interaction.[6] These factors set the conditions that determine the beginning point of the conflict process.

Conflict A process that begins when one party perceives that another party has negatively affected, or is about to negatively affect, something that the first party cares about.

We can define **conflict,** then, as a process that begins when one party perceives that another party has negatively affected, or is about to negatively affect, something that the first party cares about.[7]

This definition is purposely broad. It describes that point in any ongoing activity when an interaction "crosses over" to become an interparty conflict. It encompasses the wide range of conflicts that people experience in organizations—incompatibility of goals, differences over interpretations of facts, disagreements based on behavioral expectations, and the like. Finally, our definition is flexible enough to cover the full range of conflict levels—from overt and violent acts to subtle forms of disagreement.

TRANSITIONS IN CONFLICT THOUGHT

It is entirely appropriate to say that there has been "conflict" over the role of conflict in groups and organizations. One school of thought has argued that conflict must be avoided—that it indicates a malfunctioning within the group. We call this the *traditional* view. Another school of thought, the *human relations* view, argues that conflict is a natural and inevitable outcome in any group and that it need not be evil, but rather has the potential to be a positive force in determining group performance. The third, and most recent, perspective proposes not only that conflict *can* be a positive force in a group but explicitly argues that some conflict is *absolutely necessary* for a group to perform effectively. We label this third school the *interactionist* approach. Let us take a closer look at each of these views.

The Traditional View

The early approach to conflict assumed that all conflict was bad. Conflict was viewed negatively, and it was used synonymously with such terms as violence, destruction, and irrationality to reinforce its negative connotation. Conflict, by definition, was harmful and was to be avoided.

The **traditional view** was consistent with the attitudes that prevailed about group behavior in the 1930s and 1940s. Conflict was seen as a dysfunctional outcome resulting from poor communication, a lack of openness and trust between people, and the failure of managers to be responsive to the needs and aspirations of their employees.

The view that all conflict is bad certainly offers a simple approach to looking at the behavior of people who create conflict. Since all conflict is to be avoided, we need merely direct our attention to the causes of conflict and correct these malfunctionings in order to improve group and organizational performance. Although research studies now provide strong evidence to dispute that this approach to conflict reduction results in high group performance, most of us still evaluate conflict situations utilizing this outmoded standard.

The Human Relations View

The **human relations** position argued that conflict was a natural occurrence in all groups and organizations. Since conflict was inevitable, the human relations school advocated acceptance of conflict. They rationalized its existence: It cannot be eliminated, and there are even times when conflict may benefit a group's performance. The human relations view dominated conflict theory from the late 1940s through the mid-1970s.

The Interactionist View

John Akers at IBM subscribes to the current view of conflict—the **interactionist** perspective. While the human relations approach *accepted* conflict, the interactionist approach *encourages* conflict on the grounds that a harmonious, peaceful, tranquil, and cooperative group is prone to becoming static, apathetic, and nonresponsive to needs for change and innovation. The major contribution of the interactionist approach, therefore, is encouraging group

The interactionist view of conflict supports disagreements and open questioning of others as is taking place in this group when it aids the group's performance. Andy Freeberg

Is Stimulating Conflict Unethical?

The research demonstrates that conflict can, at times, actually improve a group or an organization's performance. So managers may find themselves in situations where the conflict level in their unit is too low and in need of stimulation. In spite of this conclusion, North Americans tend to view conflict negatively. They prefer cooperation to conflict. As a result, they are likely to take a dim view of someone who purposely seeks to increase conflict levels, regardless of how good that person's intentions may be.

These opposing facts—the positive potential of conflict for organizational performance and the negative view of it held by most North Americans—place U.S. and Canadian managers in a difficult position. Do they try to stifle all conflicts in order to stay in step with society's preferences? Or do they ignore societal norms and do what is best for their organizations? Managers who decide in favor of the organization then face another ethical issue: Is it wrong to deceive others?

Since employees are likely to negatively interpret any efforts to overtly stimulate conflict, managers may be tempted to mask their intentions. Why? Because managers aren't likely to endear themselves to their staffs by admitting that they are "purposely trying to increase conflict levels."

Is it unethical to try to increase conflict for organizational ends? Is it wrong to do so by masking one's true intentions? What do *you* think?

---

leaders to maintain an ongoing minimum level of conflict—enough to keep the group viable, self-critical, and creative.

Given the interactionist view—and it is the one that we shall take in this chapter—it becomes evident that to say conflict is all good or bad is inappropriate and naive. Whether a conflict is good or bad depends on the type of conflict. Specifically, it's necessary to differentiate between functional and dysfunctional conflicts.

FUNCTIONAL VS. DYSFUNCTIONAL CONFLICT

Functional Conflict Conflict that supports the goals of the group and improves its performance.

Dysfunctional Conflict Conflict that hinders group performance.

The interactionist view does not propose that *all* conflicts are good. Rather, some conflicts support the goals of the group and improve its performance; these are **functional,** constructive forms of conflict. Additionally, there are conflicts that hinder group performance; these are **dysfunctional** or destructive forms of conflict.

Of course, it is one thing to argue that conflict can be valuable for the group, and another to be able to tell if a conflict is functional or dysfunctional.

The demarcation between functional and dysfunctional is neither clear nor precise. No one level of conflict can be adopted as acceptable or unacceptable under all conditions. The type and level of conflict that creates healthy and positive involvement toward one group's goals today may, in another group or in the same group at another time, be highly dysfunctional.

The criterion that differentiates functional from dysfunctional conflict is group performance. Since groups exist to attain a goal or goals, it is the impact that the conflict has on the group, rather than on any individual member, that determines functionality. Of course, the impact of conflict on the individual and its impact on the group are rarely mutually exclusive, so the ways that individuals perceive a conflict may have an important influence on its effect on the group. However, this need not be the case, and when it is not, our focus will be on the group. So whether an individual group member perceives a given conflict as being personally disturbing or positive is irrelevant. For example, a group member may perceive an action as dysfunctional, in that the outcome is personally dissatisfying to him or her. However, for our analysis, that action would be functional if it furthers the objectives of the group.

THE CONFLICT PROCESS

The conflict process can be seen as comprising five stages: potential opposition or incompatibility, cognition and personalization, intentions, behavior, and outcomes. The process is diagrammed in Figure 13–1.

Stage I: Potential Opposition or Incompatibility

The first step in the conflict process is the presence of conditions that create opportunities for conflict to arise. They *need not* lead directly to conflict, but one of these conditions is necessary if conflict is to arise. For simplicity's sake, these conditions (which also may be looked at as causes or sources of conflict) have been condensed into three general categories: communication, structure, and personal variables.[8]

COMMUNICATION   The communicative source represents those opposing forces that arise from semantic difficulties, misunderstandings, and "noise" in the communication channels. Much of this discussion can be related back to our comments on communication in Chapter 10.

One of the major myths that most of us carry around with us is that poor communication is the reason for conflicts—"if we could just communicate with each other, we could eliminate our differences." Such a conclusion is not unreasonable, given the amount of time each of us spends communicating. But, of course, poor communication is certainly not the source

FIGURE 13–1   The Conflict Process

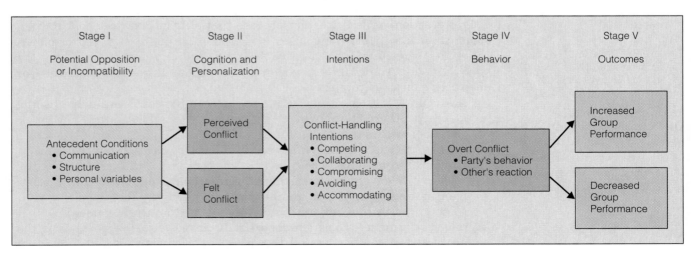

of *all* conflicts, though there is considerable evidence to suggest that problems in the communication process act to retard collaboration and stimulate misunderstanding.

A review of the research suggests that semantic difficulties, insufficient exchange of information, and noise in the communication channel are all barriers to communication and potential antecedent conditions to conflict. Specifically, evidence demonstrates that semantic difficulties arise as a result of differences in training, selective perception, and inadequate information about others. Research has further demonstrated a surprising finding: The potential for conflict increases when either too little or too much communication takes place. Apparently, an increase in communication is functional up to a point, whereupon it is possible to overcommunicate, with a resultant increase in the potential for conflict. So, too much information as well as too little can lay the foundation for conflict. Further, the channel chosen for communicating can have an influence on stimulating opposition. The filtering process that occurs as information is passed between members and the divergence of communications from formal or previously established channels offer potential opportunities for conflict to arise.

STRUCTURE   The term *structure* is used, in this context, to include variables such as size, degree of specialization in the tasks assigned to group members, jurisdictional clarity, member goal compatibility, leadership styles, reward systems, and the degree of dependence between groups.

Research indicates that size and specialization act as forces to stimulate conflict. The larger the group and the more specialized its activities, the greater the likelihood of conflict. Tenure and conflict have been found to be inversely related. The potential for conflict tends to be greatest where group members are younger and where turnover is high.

The greater the ambiguity in precisely defining where responsibility for actions lies, the greater the potential for conflict to emerge. Such jurisdictional ambiguities increase intergroup fighting for control of resources and territory.

Groups within organizations have diverse goals. For instance, purchasing is concerned with the timely acquisition of inputs at low prices, marketing's goals concentrate on disposing of outputs and increasing revenues, quality control's attention is focused on improving quality and ensuring that the organization's products meet standards, and production units seek efficiency of operations by maintaining a steady production flow. This diversity of goals among groups is a major source of conflict. Where groups within an organization seek diverse ends, some of which—like sales and credit—are inherently at odds, there are increased opportunities for conflict.

There is some indication that a close style of leadership—tight and continuous observation with general control of others' behaviors—increases conflict potential, but the evidence is not particularly strong. Too much reliance on participation may also stimulate conflict. Research tends to confirm that participation and conflict are highly correlated, apparently because participation encourages the promotion of differences. Reward systems, too, are found to create conflict when one member's gain is at another's expense. Finally, if a group is dependent on another group (in contrast to the two being mutually independent) or if interdependence allows one group to gain at another's expense, opposing forces are stimulated.

PERSONAL VARIABLES   Personal factors include the individual value systems that each person has and the personality characteristics that account for individual idiosyncrasies and differences.

The evidence indicates that certain personality types—for example, individuals who are highly authoritarian and dogmatic, and who demon-

Using Diversity to Create Functional Conflict

Groups or organizations that have become stagnant, uncreative, and apathetic often have one thing in common: a lot of people with similar values and attitudes. Research demonstrates that heterogeneity among group and organization members can increase creativity, improve the quality of decisions, and facilitate change by enhancing member flexibility.[9]

For example, researchers compared decision-making groups composed of all-Anglo individuals with groups that also contained members from Asian, Hispanic, and Black ethnic groups. What the researchers found supported the value-in-diversity perspective. The ethnically diverse groups produced more effective and more feasible ideas and the unique ideas they generated tended to be of higher quality than the unique ideas produced by the all-Anglo group.

Sears, Roebuck provides an example of what can happen when an organization's members become too homogeneous and too similar in their thinking. The people at Sears got complacent in the 1970s and 1980s. They uniformly came to believe that Sears was a permanent

institution in retailing and was invulnerable to the competition. Of course, they were wrong. Wal-Mart, Kmart, Circuit City, The Gap, The Limited, and a host of other retailers have taken large chunks of Sears' business. Sears, in fact, has become a victim of its own success. Senior managers were all long-time Sears employees—most with 25 years or more of service with the company—and had many common attributes. They were, for the most part, white Anglo-Saxon males raised in the midwestern part of the United States, with similar conservative values. As the marketplace changed and competition intensified, these managers uniformly fought to maintain the status quo. Sears illustrates an organization that could have benefited from more diversity in its top-management group.

By including people of different gender, ethnic background, national origin, and even different technical expertise (i.e., engineers and marketing people), organizations bring new and different perspectives to problem solving. They can create functional conflict by attacking conformity, common assumptions, and groupthink.

strate low esteem—lead to potential conflict. Most important, and probably the most overlooked variable in the study of social conflict, is differing value systems. Value differences, for example, are the best explanation of such diverse issues as prejudice, disagreements over one's contribution to the group and the rewards one deserves, and assessments of whether this particular book is any good. That John dislikes African Americans and Dana believes John's position indicates his ignorance, that an employee thinks he is worth $35,000 a year but his boss believes him to be worth $30,000, and that Ann thinks this book is interesting to read while Jennifer views it as "a crock of . . . " are all value judgments. And differences in value systems are important sources for creating the potential for conflict.

Stage II: Cognition and Personalization

If the conditions cited in Stage I negatively affect something that one party cares about, then the potential for opposition or incompatibility becomes actualized in the second stage. The antecedent conditions can only lead to conflict when one or more of the parties are affected by, and aware of, the conflict.

As we noted in our definition of conflict, perception is required. Therefore, one or more of the parties must be aware of the existence of the antecedent conditions. However, because a conflict is **perceived** does not mean that it is personalized. In other words, "A may be aware that B and A are in serious disagreement . . . but it may not make A tense or anxious, and it may have no effect whatsoever on A's affection towards B."[10] It is at the **felt** level, when individuals become emotionally involved, that parties experience anxiety, tenseness, frustration, or hostility.

Keep in mind two points. First, Stage II is important because it's where conflict issues tend to be defined. This is the place in the process where the parties decide what the conflict is about.[11] And, in turn, this "sense making" is critical because the way a conflict is defined goes a long way toward establishing the sort of outcomes that might settle it. For instance, if I define our salary disagreement as a zero-sum situation—that is, if you get the increase in pay you want, there will be just that amount less for me—I am going to be far less willing to compromise than if I frame the conflict as a potential win–win situation (i.e., the dollars in the salary pool might be increased so that both of us could get the added pay we want). So the definition of a conflict is important, for it typically delineates the set of possible settlements. Our second point is that emotions play a major role in shaping perceptions.[12] For example, negative emotions have been found to produce oversimplification of issues, reductions in trust, and negative interpretations of the other party's behavior.[13] In contrast, positive feelings have been found to increase the tendency to see potential relationships among the elements of a problem, to take a broader view of the situation, and to develop more innovative solutions.[14]

Stage III: Intentions

Intentions intervene between people's perceptions and emotions and their overt behavior. These intentions are decisions to act in a given way.[15]

Why are intentions separated out as a distinct stage? You have to infer the other's intent in order to know how to respond to that other's behavior. A lot of conflicts are escalated merely by one party attributing the wrong intentions to the other party. Additionally, there is typically a great deal of "slippage" between intentions and behavior, so that behavior does not always accurately reflect a person's intentions.

Figure 13–2 represents one author's effort to identify the primary conflict-handling intentions. Using two dimensions—*cooperativeness* (the degree to which one party attempts to satisfy the other party's concerns) and *assertiveness* (the degree to which one party attempts to satisfy his or her own concerns)—five conflict-handling intentions can be identified: *competing* (assertive and uncooperative), *collaborating* (assertive and cooperative), *avoiding* (unassertive and uncooperative), *accommodating* (unassertive and cooperative), and *compromising* (midrange on both assertiveness and cooperativeness).[16]

COMPETING When one person seeks to satisfy his or her own interests, regardless of the impact on the other parties to the conflict, he or she is **competing.** Examples are intending to achieve your goal at the sacrifice of the other's goal, attempting to convince another that your conclusion is correct and theirs is mistaken, and trying to make someone else accept blame for a problem.

Perceived Conflict Awareness by one or more parties of the existence of conditions that create opportunities for conflict to arise.

Felt Conflict Emotional involvement in a conflict creating anxiety, tenseness, frustration, or hostility.

Intentions Decisions to act in a given way in a conflict episode.

Competing A desire to satisfy one's interests, regardless of the impact on the other parties to the conflict.

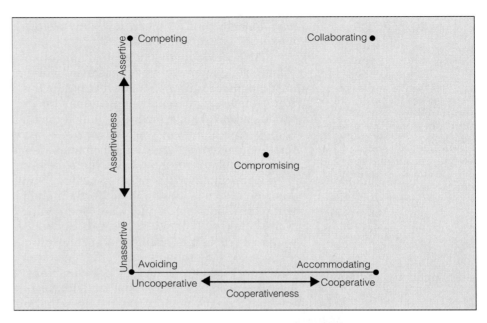

FIGURE 13–2   Dimensions of Conflict–Handling Intentions
Source: K. Thomas, "Conflict and Negotiation Processes in Organizations," in M. D. Dunnette and L.M. Hough (eds.), *Handbook of Industrial and Organizational Psychology,* 2nd ed., Vol. 3 (Palo Alto, CA: Consulting Psychologists Press, in press). With permission.

Collaborating A situation where the parties to a conflict each desire to satisfy fully the concerns of all parties.

COLLABORATING   When the parties to conflict each desire to fully satisfy the concern of all parties, we have cooperation and the search for a mutually beneficial outcome. In **collaborating,** the intention of the parties is to solve the problem by clarifying differences rather than by accommodating various points of view. Examples are attempting to find a win–win solution that allows both parties' goals to be completely achieved and seeking a conclusion that incorporates the valid insights of both parties.

Avoiding The desire to withdraw from or suppress a conflict.

AVOIDING   A person may recognize that a conflict exists and want to withdraw from it or suppress it. Examples of **avoiding** are trying to just ignore a conflict and avoiding others with whom you disagree.

Accommodating The willingness of one party in a conflict to place the opponent's interests above his or her own.

ACCOMMODATING   When one party seeks to appease an opponent, that party may be willing to place the opponent's interests above his or her own. In other words, in order for the relationship to be maintained, one party is willing to be self-sacrificing. We refer to this intention as **accommodating.** Examples are a willingness to sacrifice your goal so the other party's goal can be attained, supporting someone else's opinion despite your reservations about it, and forgiving someone for an infraction and allowing subsequent ones.

Compromising A situation in which each party to a conflict is willing to give up something.

COMPROMISING   When each party to the conflict seeks to give up something, sharing occurs, resulting in a compromised outcome. In **compromising,** there is no clear winner or loser. Rather, there is a willingness to ration the object of the conflict and accept a solution that provides incomplete satisfaction of both parties' concerns. The distinguishing characteristic of compromising, therefore, is that each party intends to give up something. Examples might be willingness to accept a raise of $1 an hour rather than $2, to acknowledge partial agreement with a specific viewpoint, and to take partial blame for an infraction.

Intentions provide general guidelines for parties in a conflict situation. They define each party's purpose. Yet, people's intentions are not fixed. During the course of a conflict, they might change because of reconceptualization or because of an emotional reaction to the behavior of the other party. However, research indicates that people have an underlying disposition to handle conflicts in certain ways.[17] Specifically, individuals have preferences among the five conflict-handling intentions just described; these preferences tend to be relied upon quite consistently; and a person's intentions can be predicted rather well from a combination of intellectual and personality characteristics. So it may be more appropriate to view the five conflict-handling intentions as relatively fixed rather than as a set of options from which individuals choose to fit an appropriate situation. That is, when confronting a conflict situation, some people want to win it all at any cost, some want to find an optimum solution, some want to run away, others want to be obliging, and still others want to "split the difference."

Stage IV: Behavior

When most people think of conflict situations, they tend to focus on Stage IV. Why? Because this is where conflicts become visible. The behavior stage includes the statements, actions, and reactions made by the conflicting parties.

These conflict behaviors are usually overt attempts to implement each party's intentions. But these behaviors have a stimulus quality that is separate from intentions. As a result of miscalculations or unskilled enactments, overt behaviors sometimes deviate from original intentions.[18]

It helps to think of Stage IV as a dynamic process of interaction. For example, you make a demand on me; I respond by arguing; you threaten me; I threaten you back; and so on. Figure 13–3 provides a way of visualizing conflict behavior. All conflicts exist somewhere along this continuum. At the lower part of the continuum, we have conflicts characterized by subtle, indirect, and highly controlled forms of tension. An illustration might be a student questioning in class a point the instructor has just made. Conflict intensities escalate as they move upward along the continuum until they become highly destructive. Strikes, riots, and wars clearly fall in this upper range. For the most part, you should assume that conflicts that reach the upper ranges of the continuum are almost always dysfunctional. Functional conflicts are typically confined to the lower range of the continuum.

FIGURE 13–3   Conflict Intensity Continuum

Source: Based on S. P. Robbins, *Managing Organizational Conflict: A Nontraditional Approach* (Englewood Cliffs, NJ: Prentice Hall, 1974), pp. 93–97; and F. Glasl, "The Process of Conflict Escalation and Roles of Third Parties," in G. B. J. Bomers and R. Peterson (eds.), *Conflict Management and Industrial Relations* (Boston: Kluwer–Nijhoff, 1982), pp. 119–40.

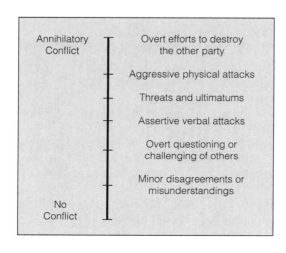

Conflict Management The use of resolution and stimulation techniques to achieve the desired level of conflict.

If a conflict is dysfunctional, what can the parties do to de-escalate it? Or, conversely, what options exist if conflict is too low and needs to be increased? This brings us to **conflict management** techniques. Table 13–1 lists the major resolution and stimulation techniques that allow managers to control conflict levels. Notice that several of the resolution techniques were earlier described as conflict-handling intentions. This, of course, shouldn't be surprising. Under ideal conditions, a person's intentions should translate into comparable behaviors.

TABLE 13–1   Conflict Management Techniques

Conflict Resolution Techniques

Problem solving.	Face-to-face meeting of the conflicting parties for the purpose of identifying the problem and resolving it through open discussion.
Superordinate goals.	Creating a shared goal that cannot be attained without the cooperation of each of the conflicting parties.
Expansion of resources.	When a conflict is caused by the scarcity of a resource—say, money, promotion opportunities, office space—expansion of the resource can create a win–win solution.
Avoidance.	Withdrawal from, or suppression of, the conflict.
Smoothing.	Playing down of differences while emphasizing common interests between the conflicting parties.
Compromise.	Each party to the conflict gives up something of value.
Authoritative command.	Management uses its formal authority to resolve the conflict and then communicates its desires to the parties involved.
Altering the human variable.	Using behavioral change techniques such as human relations training to alter attitudes and behaviors that cause conflict.
Altering the structural variables.	Changing the formal organization structure and the interaction patterns of conflicting parties through job redesign, transfers, creation of coordinating positions, and the like.

Conflict Stimulation Techniques

Communication.	Using ambiguous or threatening messages to increase conflict levels.
Bringing in outsiders.	Adding employees to a group whose backgrounds, values, attitudes, or managerial styles differ from those of present members.
Restructuring the organization.	Realigning work groups, altering rules and regulations, increasing interdependence, and making similar structural changes to disrupt the status quo.
Appointing a devil's advocate.	Designating a critic to purposely argue against the majority positions held by the group.

Source: Based on S. P. Robbins, *Managing Organizational Conflict: A Nontraditional Approach* (Englewood Cliffs, NJ: Prentice Hall, 1974), pp. 59–89.

Stage V: Outcomes

The action-reaction interplay between the conflicting parties results in consequences. As our model on page 448 demonstrates, these outcomes may be functional, in that the conflict results in an improvement in the group's performance, or dysfunctional, in that it hinders group performance.

FUNCTIONAL OUTCOMES   How might conflict act as a force to increase group performance? It is hard to visualize a situation where open or violent aggression could be functional. But there are a number of instances where it is possible to envision how low or moderate levels of conflict could improve the effectiveness of a group. Because people often find it difficult to think of instances where conflict can be constructive, let us consider some examples and then review the research evidence.

Conflict is constructive when it improves the quality of decisions, stimulates creativity and innovation, encourages interest and curiosity among group members, provides the medium through which problems can be aired and tensions released, and fosters an environment of self-evaluation and change. The evidence suggests that conflict can improve the quality of decision making by allowing all points, particularly the ones that are unusual or held by a minority, to be weighed in important decisions.[19] Conflict is an antidote for groupthink. It does not allow the group passively to "rubberstamp" decisions that may be based on weak assumptions, inadequate consideration of relevant alternatives, or other debilities. Conflict challenges the status quo and therefore furthers the creation of new ideas, promotes reassessment of group goals and activities, and increases the probability that the group will respond to change.

Research studies in diverse settings confirm the functionality of conflict. Consider the following findings:

The comparison of six major decisions made during the administration of four different United States Presidents found that conflict reduced the chance that groupthink would overpower policy decisions. The comparisons demonstrated that conformity among presidential advisors was related to poor decisions, while an atmosphere of constructive conflict and critical thinking surrounded the well-developed decisions.[20]

The bankruptcy of the Penn Central Railroad has been generally attributed to mismanagement and the failure of the company's board of directors to question actions taken by management. The board was composed of outside directors who met monthly to oversee the railroad's operations. Few questioned decisions made by the operating management, though there was evidence that several board members were uncomfortable with many decisions made by them. Apathy and a desire to *avoid* conflict allowed poor decisions to stand unquestioned.[21] This, however, should not be surprising, since a review of the relationship between bureaucracy and innovation has found that conflict encourages innovative solutions.[22] The corollary of this finding also appears true: Lack of conflict results in a passive environment with reinforcement of the status quo.

Not only do better and more innovative decisions result from situations where there is some conflict, but there is evidence indicating that conflict can be positively related to productivity. It was demonstrated that, among established groups, performance tended to improve more when there was conflict among members than when there was fairly close agreement. The investigators observed that when groups analyzed decisions that had been made by the individual members of that group, the average improvement among the high-conflict groups was seventy-three percent greater than was that of those groups characterized by low-conflict conditions.[23] Others have found similar results: Groups composed of members with different interests tend to produce higher-quality solutions to a variety of problems than do homogeneous groups.[24]

Similarly, studies of professionals—systems analysts and research and development scientists—support the constructive value of conflict. An investigation of twenty-two teams of systems analysts found that the more incompatible groups were likely to be more productive.[25] Research and development scientists have been found to be most productive where there is a certain amount of intellectual conflict.[26]

How to Create Functional Conflict

How can an organization encourage functional conflict?[27] For most organizations, it's a tough job. As one consultant put it, "A high proportion of people who get to the top are conflict avoiders. They don't like hearing negatives, they don't like saying or thinking negative things. They frequently make it up the ladder in part because they don't irritate people on the way up." Another suggests that at least seven out of ten people in American business hush up when their opinions are at odds with those of their superiors, allowing bosses to make mistakes even when they know better.

Such anticonflict cultures may have been tolerable in the past, but not in today's fiercely competitive global economy. Those organizations that don't encourage and support dissent may not survive the 1990s. Let's look at some of the approaches organizations are taking to encourage their people to challenge the system and develop fresh ideas.

Hewlett-Packard rewards dissenters by recognizing go-against-the-grain types, or people who stay with the ideas they believe in even when those ideas are rejected by management. Herman Miller Inc., an office-furniture manufacturer, has a formal system in which employees evaluate and criticize their bosses. IBM also has a formal system that encourages dissension. Employees can question their boss with impunity. If the disagreement can't be resolved, the system provides a third party for counsel.

Royal Dutch Shell Group, General Electric, and Anheuser-Busch build devil's advocates into the decision process. For instance, when the policy committee at Anheuser-Busch considers a major move, such as getting into or out of a business or making a major capital expenditure, it often assigns teams to make the case for each side of the question. This process frequently results in decisions and alternatives that previously hadn't been considered.

The governor of Maryland stimulates conflict and invigorates his organization by requiring state cabinet officials to swap jobs for one month every year, then write reports and suggestions based on their experiences.

One common ingredient in organizations that successfully creates functional conflict is that they reward dissent and punish conflict-avoiders. The president of Innovis Interactive Technologies, for instance, fired a top executive who refused to dissent. His explanation: "He was the ultimate yes-man. In this organization, I can't afford to pay someone to hear my own opinion." But the real challenge for managers is when they hear news that they don't want to hear. The news may make their blood boil or their hopes collapse, but they can't show it. They have to learn to take the bad news without flinching. No tirades, no tight-lipped sarcasm, no eyes rolling upward, no gritting of teeth. Rather, managers should ask calm, even-tempered questions: "Can you tell me more about what happened?" "What do you think we ought to do?" A sincere "Thank you for bringing this to my attention" is likely to reduce the likelihood that managers will be cut off from similar communications in the future.

Conflict can even be constructive on sports teams and in unions. Studies of sports teams indicate that moderate levels of group conflict contribute to team effectiveness and provide an additional stimulus for high achievement.[28] An examination of local unions found that conflict between members of the local was positively related to the union's power and to member loyalty and participation in union affairs.[29] These findings might suggest that conflict within a group indicates strength rather than, as in the traditional view, weakness.

DYSFUNCTIONAL OUTCOMES   The destructive consequences of conflict upon a group or organization's performance are generally well known. A reasonable summary might state: Uncontrolled opposition breeds discontent, which acts to dissolve common ties, and eventually leads to the destruction of the group. And, of course, there is a substantial body of literature to document how conflict—the dysfunctional varieties—can reduce group effectiveness.[30] Among the more undesirable consequences are a retarding of communication, reductions in group cohesiveness, and subordination of group goals to the primacy of infighting between members. At the extreme, conflict can bring group functioning to a halt and potentially threaten the group's survival.

This discussion has again returned us to the issue of what is functional and what is dysfunctional. Research on conflict has yet to identify those situations where conflict is more likely to be constructive than destructive. However, the difference between functional and dysfunctional conflict is important enough for us to go beyond the substantive evidence and propose a hypothesis. The type of group activity should be a prime factor determining functionality. We hypothesize that the more creative or unprogrammed the decision-making tasks of the group, the greater the probability that internal conflict will be constructive. Groups that are required to tackle problems demanding new and novel approaches—as in research, advertising, and other professional activities—will benefit more from conflict than will groups performing highly programmed activities—for instance, those of work teams on an automobile assembly line.

NEGOTIATION

The "lawyers" in "L.A. Law" rely on their negotiating skills in almost every weekly episode. But negotiating skills are not unique to lawyers. All of us regularly need to negotiate with colleagues, friends, lovers, and in a wide range of business transactions.

Negotiation   A process in which two or more parties exchange goods or services and attempt to agree upon the exchange rate for them.

It's a rare episode of *L.A. Law* where you won't find some negotiation going on. For instance, the following negotiations took place in recent episodes: Lawyers at McKenzie and Brackman plea-bargained a lower sentence for a client. The managing partner negotiated a lower price in renewing the firm's office lease. That same managing partner negotiated an arrangement to bring in a prized judge as a new partner. One partner persuaded another that he shouldn't leave the firm to start his own practice. An associate made a deal with one of the senior partners that she will support him in an internal power struggle in exchange for his support when she comes up for partner.

While we tend to think of lawyers as always in a negotiating stance, the reality is that negotiation permeates the interactions of almost everyone in groups and organizations. There's the obvious: Labor bargains with management. There's the not-so-obvious: Managers negotiate with subordinates, peers, and bosses; salespeople negotiate with customers; purchasing agents negotiate with suppliers. And there's the subtle: A worker agrees to answer a colleague's phone for a few minutes in exchange for some past or future benefit.

We'll define **negotiation** as a process in which two or more parties exchange goods or services and attempt to agree upon the exchange rate for them.[31] Note that we use the terms *negotiation* and *bargaining* interchangeably.

In this section, we'll contrast two bargaining strategies, offer some research insights into negotiator–opponent interactions, ascertain the role of personality traits on negotiation, and take a brief look at third-party negotiations.

Bargaining Strategies

There are two general approaches to negotiation—*distributive bargaining* and *integrative bargaining*.[32] These are compared in Table 13–2.

TABLE 13-2 Distributive vs. Integrative Bargaining

Bargaining Characteristic	Distributive Bargaining	Integrative Bargaining
Available resources	Fixed amount of resources to be divided	Variable amount of resources to be divided
Primary motivations	I win, you lose	I win, you win
Primary interests	Opposed to each other	Convergent or congruent with each other
Focus of relationships	Short-term	Long-term

Source: Based on R. J. Lewicki and J. A. Litterer, *Negotiation* (Homewood, IL: Irwin, 1985), p. 280.

Distributive Bargaining
Negotiation that seeks to divide up a fixed amount of resources; a win–lose situation.

DISTRIBUTIVE BARGAINING   You see a used car advertised for sale in the newspaper. It appears to be just what you've been looking for. You go out to see the car. It's great and you want it. The owner tells you the asking price. You don't want to pay that much. The two of you then negotiate over the price. The negotiating process you are engaging in is called **distributive bargaining.** It's most identifying feature is that it operates under zero-sum conditions. That is, any gain I make is at your expense, and vice versa. Referring back to the used car example, every dollar you can get the seller to cut from the car's price is a dollar you save. Conversely, every dollar more he can get from you comes at your expense. So the essence of distributive bargaining is negotiating over who gets what share of a fixed pie.

Probably the most widely cited example of distributive bargaining is in labor–management negotiations over wages. Typically, labor's representatives come to the bargaining table determined to get as much money as possible out of management. Since every cent more that labor negotiates increases management's costs, each party bargains aggressively and treats the other as an opponent who must be defeated.

The essence of distributive bargaining is depicted in Figure 13–4. "Party" and "Other" are the two negotiators. Each has a *target point* that defines what he or she would like to achieve. Party and Other also each have a *resistance point,* which marks the lowest outcome that is acceptable—the point below which they would break off negotiations rather than accept a less favorable settlement. The area between these two points makes up each one's aspiration range. If Party and Other's aspiration ranges overlap, there exists a settlement range where each one's aspirations can be met.

When engaged in distributive bargaining, one's tactics focus on trying to get one's opponent to agree to one's specific target point or to get as close to it as possible. Examples of such tactics are persuading your opponent of the impossibility of getting to his or her target point and the advisability of accepting a settlement near yours; arguing that your target is fair, while your opponent's isn't; and attempting to get your opponent to feel emotionally generous toward you and thus accept an outcome close to your target point.

INTEGRATIVE BARGAINING   A sales representative for a women's sportswear manufacturer has just closed a $15,000 order from a small clothing retailer. The sales rep calls in the order to her firm's credit department. She is told that the firm can't approve credit to this customer because of a past slow-pay record. The next day, the sales rep and the firm's credit manager meet to discuss the problem. The sales rep doesn't want to lose the business. Neither does the credit manager, but he also doesn't want to get stuck with an uncollectable debt. The two openly review their options. After

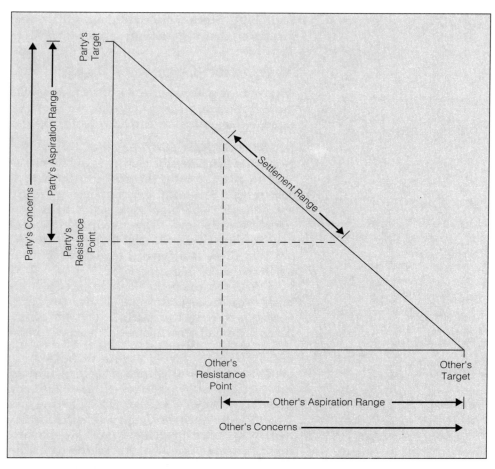

FIGURE 13–4   Defining the Settlement Range in Distributive Bargaining
Source: Adapted from K. W. Thomas, "Conflict and Negotiation Processes in Organizations," in M. D. Dunnette and L. M. Hough (eds.), *Handbook of Industrial and Organizational Psychology, 2nd ed.* Vol. 3 (Palo Alto, CA: Consulting Psychologists Press, in press).

considerable discussion, they agree on a solution that meets both their needs: The credit manager will approve the sale, but the clothing store's owner will provide a bank guarantee that will assure payment if the bill isn't paid within sixty days.

This sales–credit negotiation is an example of **integrative bargaining.** In contrast to distributive bargaining, integrative problem solving operates under the assumption that there exists one or more settlements that can create a win–win solution.

In terms of intraorganizational behavior, all things being equal, integrative bargaining is preferrable to distributive bargaining. Why? Because the former builds long-term relationships and facilitates working together in the future. It bonds negotiators and allows each to leave the bargaining table feeling that he or she has achieved a victory. Distributive bargaining, on the other hand, leaves one party a loser. It tends to build animosities and deepen divisions when people have to work together on an ongoing basis.

Why, then, don't we see more integrative bargaining in organizations? The answer lies in the conditions necessary for this type of negotiation to succeed. These include parties who are open with information and candid about their concerns; a sensitivity by both parties to the other's needs; the ability to trust one another; and a willingness by both parties to maintain

Integrative Bargaining
Negotiation that seeks one or more settlements that can create a win–win solution.

flexibility.[33] Since these conditions often do not exist in organizations, it isn't surprising that negotiations often take on a win-at-any-cost dynamic.

Negotiator–Opponent Interaction

What advice can we give negotiators that will help them better understand the negotiation process and improve their negotiating ability? Based on an extensive amount of research, we can make the following recommendations.[34]

DEMANDS AND CONCESSIONS   A substantial amount of evidence suggests that consistently high demands and low concessions by one party will lead to the same by the other. Negotiators who take a tough approach encourage a reciprocal tough stance by their opponents. Note, however, that low demands and high concessions by one party do not necessarily lead to complete reciprocity. The research indicates that the *amount* of the opponent's concessions will usually be less than those offered by the negotiator, but that there is a general tendency for the opponent to match the negotiator in *frequency* of concessions.

So expect competitiveness to beget competitiveness. And while cooperation tends to yield cooperativeness, it may be at a reduced level. Based on these tendencies, you should probably begin your bargaining with a positive overture—perhaps a small concession—and then reciprocate your opponent's concessions.

PRECEDENTS   Few negotiations in organizations are conducted on a blank slate. Typically, each of the negotiating parties brings a history of past interactions and practices to the bargaining table. So, for example, an understanding of past bargaining tactics used by General Motors and the United Auto Workers Union can help to predict both future tactics and opponent responses. Precedent can help explain the rise in hostility between unions and management in recent years. Union negotiators remember how their demands in the 1970s and early 1980s tended to be accepted by management because they could be passed on to customers through higher prices for products. However, fierce global competition and declining inflation rates

Nabisco Brands' management and the Bakery, Confectionary and Tobacco Workers International Union have been using integrative bargaining teams to settle work-force disputes for several years. It has worked so well that Nabisco and the BCT recently won the U. S. government's first annual award for Excellence in Industrial Relations.
Charlie Archambault

TABLE 13–3   Differences Between Skilled and Average Negotiators

Negotiating Behavior	Skilled Negotiators	Average Negotiators
Use of irritating phrases (i.e., "generous offer," "fair price," "reasonable arrangement") per hour of face-to-face negotiating time that reflect favorably on Party and unfavorably on Other	2.3	10.8
Frequency of counterproposals per hour	1.7	3.1
Percent of negotiator's time spent responding defensively and attacking opponent	1.9%	6.3%
Test for understanding through active listening	9.7%	4.1%
Questions as a percent of all negotiating behavior	21.3%	9.6%
Average number of reasons given to back up each argument (large number of weak arguments generally dilute strong arguments)	1.8	3.0

Source: Based on N. Rackham, *The Successful Negotiator* (Reston, VA: Huthwaite Research Group, 1976).

have made it more difficult for companies to pass on higher costs to customers today. As a result, management has become more stingy about concessions and unions have reacted negatively to management's unwillingness to match past settlements.

Precedents *do* matter. So before entering a negotiation, review previous demands, concessions, and settlements. Opponents are likely to use these precedents to define their standards of fairness in current bargaining.

EXPERIENCE   As negotiators gain experience bargaining, they become better at it. Experienced negotiators tend to be better at understanding a specific negotiation process and at reaching an integrative agreement. This can be seen in Table 13–3. Skilled negotiators are better listeners, ask more questions, focus their arguments more directly, are less defensive, and have learned to avoid words and phrases that can irritate an opponent. In other words, they are better at creating the open and trusting climate necessary for reaching an integrative settlement. This suggests that you shouldn't expect perfection from your early efforts at negotiating but that you can expect to become more effective as you gain experience.

The Role of Personality Traits in Negotiation

Can you predict an opponent's negotiating tactics if you know something about his or her personality? It's tempting to answer "Yes" to this question. For instance, you might assume that high risk-takers would be more aggressive bargainers who make fewer concessions. Surprisingly, the evidence doesn't support this intuition.[35]

Overall assessments of the personality–negotiation relationship finds that personality traits have no significant direct effect on either the bargaining process or negotiation outcomes. This conclusion is important. It suggests that you should concentrate on the issues and the situational factors in each bargaining episode and not on your opponent and his or her characteristics.

Third-Party Negotiations

To this point, we've discussed bargaining in terms of direct negotiations. Occasionally, however, individuals or group representatives reach a stalemate and are unable to resolve their differences through direct negotiations. In such cases, they may turn to a third party to help them find a solution. There are four basic third-party roles: mediator, arbitrator, conciliator, and consultant.[36]

Mediator A neutral third party who facilitates a negotiated solution by using reasoning, persuasion, and suggestions for alternatives.

MEDIATOR A **mediator** is a neutral third party who facilitates a negotiated solution by using reasoning and persuasion, suggesting alternatives, and the like. Mediators are widely used in labor–management negotiations and in civil court disputes.

The overall effectiveness of mediated negotiations is fairly impressive. The settlement rate is approximately sixty percent, with negotiator satisfaction at about seventy-five percent. But the situation is the key to whether mediation will succeed; the conflicting parties must be motivated to bargain and resolve their conflict. Additionally, conflict intensity can't be too high; mediation is most effective under moderate levels of conflict. Finally, perceptions of the mediator are important; to be effective, the mediator must be perceived as neutral and noncoercive.

Arbitrator A third party to a negotiation who has the authority to dictate an agreement.

ARBITRATOR An **arbitrator** is a third party with the authority to dictate an agreement. Arbitration can be voluntary (requested) or compulsory (forced on the parties by law or contract).

The authority of the arbitrator varies according to the rules set by the negotiators. For instance, the arbitrator might be limited to choosing one of the negotiator's last offers or to suggesting an agreement point that is non-binding, or free to choose and make any judgment he or she wishes.

The big plus of arbitration over mediation is that it always results in a settlement. Whether there is a negative side depends on how "heavy-handed" the arbitrator appears. If one party is left feeling overwhelmingly defeated, that party is certain to be dissatisfied and unlikely to graciously accept the arbitrator's decision. Hence, the conflict may resurface at a later time.

In the first Godfather film, Robert DuVal (right) was the Corleone family's conciliator in relations with other Mafioso families.   Neal Peters Collection

Cultural Differences in Negotiation

While there appears to be no significant direct relationship between an individual's personality and negotiation style, cultural background does seem to be relevant. Negotiating styles clearly vary across national cultures.[37] The cultural context of the negotiation significantly influences the amount and type of preparation for bargaining, the relative emphasis on task versus interpersonal relationships, the tactics used, and even where the negotiation should be conducted. To illustrate some of these differences, let's look at two studies comparing the influence of culture on business negotiations.

The first study compared North Americans, Arabs, and Russians.[38] Among the factors that were looked at were their negotiating style, how they responded to an opponent's arguments, their approach to making concessions, and how they handled negotiating deadlines. North Americans tried to persuade by relying on facts and appealing to logic. They countered opponents' arguments with objective facts. They made small concessions early in the negotiation to establish a relationship, and usually reciprocated opponent's concessions. North Americans treated deadlines as very important. The Arabs tried to persuade by appealing to emotion. They countered opponents' arguments with subjective feelings. They made concessions throughout the bargaining process and almost always

reciprocated opponents' concessions. Arabs approached deadlines very casually. The Russians based their arguments on asserted ideals. They made few, if any, concessions. Any concession offered by an opponent was viewed as a weakness and almost never reciprocated. Finally, the Russians tended to ignore deadlines.

The second study looked at verbal and nonverbal negotiation tactics exhibited by North Americans, Japanese, and Brazilians during half-hour bargaining sessions.[39] Some of the differences were particularly interesting. For instance, the Brazilians on average said "No" eighty-three times, compared to five times for the Japanese and nine times for the North Americans. The Japanese displayed more than five periods of silence lasting longer than ten seconds during the thirty-minute sessions. North Americans averaged 3.5 such periods; the Brazilians had none. The Japanese and North Americans interrupted their opponent about the same number of times, but the Brazilians interrupted two-and-a-half to three times more often than the North Americans and the Japanese. Finally, while the Japanese and the North Americans had no physical contact with their opponents during negotiations except for handshaking, the Brazilians touched each other almost five times every half-hour.

Conciliator A trusted third party who provides an informal communication link between the negotiator and the opponent.

CONCILIATOR   A **conciliator** is a trusted third party who provides an informal communication link between the negotiator and the opponent. This role was made famous by Robert Duval in the first *Godfather* film. As Don Corleone's adopted son and a lawyer by training, Duval acted as an intermediary between the Corleone family and the other Mafioso families.

Conciliation is used extensively in international, labor, family, and community disputes. Comparing its effectiveness to mediation has proven difficult because the two overlap a great deal. In practice, conciliators typically act as more than mere communication conduits. They also engage in fact-finding, interpreting messages, and persuading disputants to develop agreements.

Consultant as Negotiator An impartial third party skilled in conflict management who attempts to facilitate creative problem solving through communication and analysis.

CONSULTANT   A **consultant** is a skilled and impartial third party who attempts to facilitate problem solving through communication and analysis, aided by his or her knowledge of conflict management. In contrast to the previous roles, the consultant's role is not to settle the issues but, rather, to improve relations between the conflicting parties so that they can reach a settlement themselves. Instead of putting forward specific solutions, the consultant tries to help the parties learn to understand and work with each other. Therefore, this approach has a longer-term focus: to build new and positive perceptions and attitudes between the conflicting parties.

INTERGROUP RELATIONS

For the most part, the concepts we've discussed from Chapter 9 on have dealt with *intra*group activities. For instance, the previous material in this chapter emphasized interpersonal and intragroup conflict as well as interpersonal negotiations. But we need to understand relationships between groups as well as within groups. In this section, we'll focus on *inter*group relationships. These are the coordinated bridges that link two distinct organizational groups.[40] As we'll show, the efficiency and quality of these relationships can have a significant bearing on one or both of the groups' performances and their members' satisfaction.

Factors Affecting Intergroup Relations

Successful intergroup performance is a function of a number of factors. The umbrella concept that overrides these factors is *coordination*. Each of the following can affect efforts at coordination.

INTERDEPENDENCE   The first overriding question we need to ask is: Do the groups really need coordination? The answer to this question lies in determining the degree of interdependence that exists between the groups. That is, do the groups depend on each other and, if so, how much? The three most frequently identified types of interdependence are pooled, sequential, and reciprocal.[41] Each requires an increasing degree of group interaction (see Figure 13–5).

Pooled Interdependence Where two groups function with relative independence but their combined output contributes to the organization's overall goals.

When two groups function with relative independence but their combined output contributes to the organization's overall goals, **pooled interdependence** exists. At a firm such as Apple Computer, for instance, this would describe the relationship between the Product Development department and the Shipping department. Both are necessary if Apple is to develop new products and get those products into consumers' hands, but each is essentially separate and distinct from the other. All other things being equal, coordination requirements between groups linked by pooled interdependence are less than with sequential or reciprocal interdependence.

Sequential Interdependence One group depends on another for its input but the dependency is only one way.

The Purchasing and Parts Assembly departments at Apple are **sequentially interdependent.** One group—Parts Assembly—depends on another—Purchasing—for its inputs, but the dependency is only one way. Purchasing is not directly dependent on Parts Assembly for its inputs. In sequential interdependence, if the group that provides the input doesn't perform its job properly, the group that is dependent on the first will be significantly affected. In our Apple example, if Purchasing fails to order an important component that goes into the assembly process, then the Parts Assembly department may have to slow down or temporarily close its assembly operations.

Reciprocal Interdependence Where groups exchange inputs and outputs.

The most complex form of interdependence is **reciprocal.** In these instances, groups exchange inputs and outputs. For example, Sales and

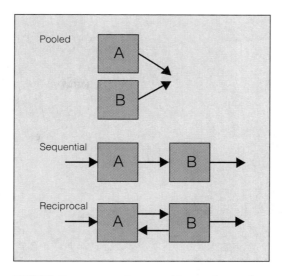

FIGURE 13–5 **Types of Interdependence**

Product Development groups at Apple are reciprocally interdependent. Salespeople, in contact with customers, acquire information about their future needs. Sales then relays this back to Product Development so they can create new computer products. The long-term implications are that if Product Development doesn't come up with new products that potential customers find desirable, Sales personnel are not going to get orders. So there is high interdependence—Product Development needs Sales for information on customer needs so it can create successful new products, and Sales depends on the Product Development group to create products that it can successfully sell. This high degree of dependency translates into greater interaction and increased coordination demands.

TASK UNCERTAINTY   The next coordination question is: What type of tasks are the groups involved in? For simplicity's sake, we can think of a group's tasks as ranging from highly routine to highly nonroutine.[42] (See Figure 13–6).

Highly routine tasks have little variation. Problems that group members face tend to contain few exceptions and are easy to analyze. Such group activities lend themselves to standardized operating procedures. For example, manufacturing tasks in a tire factory are made up of highly routine tasks. At the other extreme are nonroutine tasks. These are activities that are unstructured, with many exceptions and problems that are hard to analyze. Many of the tasks undertaken by marketing research and product

FIGURE 13–6 **Task Continuum**

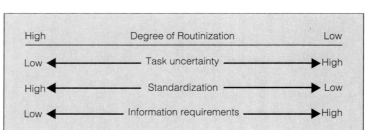

The work of designers at Chadick & Kimball, a Washington, D. C. design firm that specializes in developing corporate identity programs, requires reciprocal interdependence with the firm's marketing staff. Design and marketing people are required to exchange information in order to meet client needs.   Nation's Business

Task Uncertainty The greater the uncertainty in a task, the more custom the response. Conversely, low uncertainty encompasses routine tasks with standardized activities.

development groups are of this variety. Of course, a lot of group tasks fall somewhere in the middle or combine both routine and nonroutine tasks.

The key to **task uncertainty** is that nonroutine tasks require considerably more processing of information. Tasks with low uncertainty tend to be standardized. Further, groups that do such tasks do not have to interact much with other groups. In contrast, groups that undertake tasks that are high in uncertainty face problems that require custom responses. This, in turn, leads to a need for more and better information. We would expect the people in the marketing research department at Goodyear Tire & Rubber to interact much more with other departments and constituencies—marketing, sales, product design, tire dealers, advertising agencies, and the like—than would people in Goodyear's manufacturing group.

TIME AND GOAL ORIENTATION   How different are the groups in terms of their members' background and thinking? This is the third question relevant to the degree of coordination necessary between groups. Research demonstrates that a work group's perceptions of what is important may differ on the basis of the time frame that governs their work and their goal orientation.[43] This can make it difficult for groups with different perceptions to work together.

Why might work groups have different time and goal orientations? Top management divides work up by putting common tasks into common functional groups and assigning these groups specific goals. Then people are hired with the appropriate background and skills to complete the tasks and help the group achieve its goals. This differentiation of tasks and hiring of specialists makes it easier to coordinate intragroup activities. But it makes it increasingly difficult to coordinate interaction between groups.

To illustrate how orientations differ between work groups, manufacturing personnel have a short-term time focus. They worry about today's production schedule and this week's productivity. In contrast, people in research and development focus on the long run. They're concerned about developing new products that may not be produced for several years. Similarly, work groups often have different goal orientations. Sales, as a case in point, wants to sell anything and everything. Their goals center on sales volume, and

FIGURE 13–7 Source: Cathy Guisewite, *Cathy*. Copyright 1989 Universal Press Syndicate. Reprinted with permission. All rights reserved.

increasing revenue and market share. Their customers' ability to pay for the sales they make are not their concern. But people in the credit department want to ensure that sales are made only to creditworthy customers. These differences in goals often make it difficult for sales and credit to communicate. It also makes it harder to coordinate their interactions.

Methods for Managing Intergroup Relations

What coordination methods are available for managing intergroup relations? There are a number of options; the seven most frequently used are identified in Figure 13–8. These seven are listed on a continuum, in order of increasing cost.[44] They also are cumulative in the sense that succeeding methods higher on the continuum add to, rather than are substituted for, lower methods.

RULES AND PROCEDURES   The most simple and least costly method for managing intergroup relations is to establish, in advance, a set of formalized rules and procedures that will specify how group members are to interact with each other. In large organizations, for example, standard operating procedures are likely to specify that when additional permanent staff are needed in any department, a "request for new staff" form is to be filed with the personnel department. Upon receipt of this form, the personnel department begins a standardized process to fill the request. Notice that such rules and procedures minimize the need for interaction and information flow between the departments or work groups. The major drawback to this method is that it works well only when intergroup activities can be anticipated ahead of time and when they recur often enough to justify establishing rules and procedures for handling them.

HIERARCHY   If rules and procedures are inadequate, the use of the organization's hierarchy becomes the primary method for managing intergroup relations. What this means is that coordination is achieved by refer-

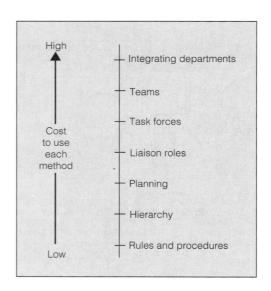

FIGURE 13–8   Methods for Managing Intergroup Relations

ring problems to a common superior higher in the organization. In a college, if the chairpersons for the English and Speech Communication departments can't agree on where the new courses in debate will be taught, they can take the issue to the college dean for a resolution. The major limitation to this method is that it increases demands on the common superior's time. If all differences were resolved by this means, the organization's chief executive would be overwhelmed with resolving intergroup problems, leaving little time for other matters.

PLANNING   The next step up the continuum is the use of planning to facilitate coordination. If each work group has specific goals for which it is responsible, then each knows what it is supposed to do. Intergroup tasks that create problems are resolved in terms of the goals and contributions of each group. In a state motor vehicle office, each of the various work groups—testing and examinations, driving permits, vehicle registration, cashiering, and the like—has a set of goals that defines its area of responsibility and

The production line at Westinghouse illustrates the application of rules and procedures to facilitate intergroup relations. Standard operating procedures define how group members are to interact with each other.   Insight Magazine/ Brig Cabe

acts to reduce intergroup conflicts. Planning tends to break down as a coordination device where work groups don't have clearly defined goals or where the volume of contacts between groups is high.

LIAISON ROLES   Liaison roles are specialized roles designed to facilitate communication between two interdependent work units. In one organization where accountants and engineers had a long history of conflict, management hired an engineer with an MBA degree and several years of experience in public accounting. This person could speak the language of both groups and understood their problems. After this new liaison role was established, conflicts that had previously made it difficult for the accounting and engineering departments to coordinate their activities were significantly reduced. The major drawback to this coordination device is that there are limits to any liaison person's ability to handle information flow between interacting groups, especially where the groups are large and interactions are frequent.

TASK FORCES   A task force is a temporary group made up of representatives from a number of departments. It exists only long enough to solve the problem it was created to handle. After a solution is reached, task force participants return to their normal duties.

Task forces are an excellent device for coordinating activities when the number of interacting groups is more than two or three. For example, when Audi began receiving numerous complaints about its cars accelerating when the transmission was put in reverse, even though drivers swore that their feet were firmly on the brakes, the company created a task force to assess the problem and develop a solution. Representatives from design, production, legal, and engineering departments were brought together. After a solution was determined, the task force was disbanded.

TEAMS   As tasks become more complex, additional problems arise during the act of execution. Previous coordination devices are no longer adequate. If the delays in decisions become long, lines of communication become extended, and top managers are forced to spend more time on day-to-day operations, the next response is to use permanent teams. They are typically formed around frequently occurring problems—with team members maintaining a responsibility to both their primary functional department and to the team. When the team has accomplished its task, each member returns full time to his or her functional assignment.

This form of coordination device is popular in aerospace firms. There are functional departments based on common functions. Teams are formed around the major problem areas or projects on which the firm is working. So, for instance, manufacturing operations might have a wing team located in one place in the plant (see Figure 13–9), with members coming from the various functional areas.

INTEGRATING DEPARTMENTS   When intergroup relations become too complex to be coordinated through plans, task forces, teams, and the like, organizations may create integrating departments. These are permanent departments with members formally assigned to the task of integration between two or more groups. While they're permanent and expensive to maintain, they tend to be used when an organization has a number of groups with conflicting goals, nonroutine problems, and intergroup decisions that have a significant impact on the organization's total operations. They are also excellent devices to manage intergroup conflicts for organizations facing long-term retrenchments. When organizations are forced to shrink in size—as has

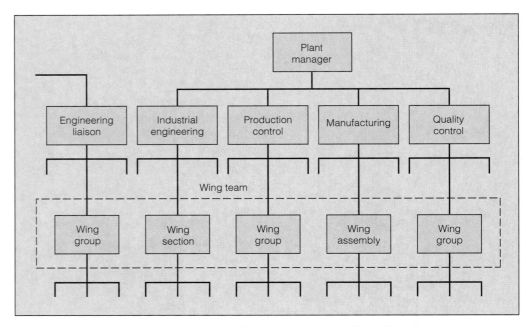

FIGURE 13-9 **Example of a Team Intergroup–Coordination Device**
Source: J. R. Galbraith, *Organization Design* (Reading, MA: Addison–Wesley, 1977), p. 117.

recently occurred in a wide range of industries—conflicts over how cuts are to be distributed and how the smaller resource pie is to be allocated become major and ongoing dilemmas. The use of integrating departments in such cases can be an effective means for managing these intergroup relations.

SUMMARY

It may help to put this discussion in perspective by considering methods for managing intergroup relations in terms of effectiveness.

Researchers state that the effectiveness of intergroup relations can be evaluated in terms of efficiency and quality.[45] Efficiency considers the costs to the organization of transforming an intergroup conflict into actions agreed to by the groups. Quality refers to the degree to which the outcome results in a well-defined and enduring exchange agreement. Using these definitions, the seven methods introduced in this section were presented, in order, from most efficient to least efficient. That is, ignoring outcomes for a moment, rules and procedures are less costly to implement than hierarchy, hierarchy is less costly than planning, and so forth. But, of course, keeping costs down is only one consideration. The other element of effectiveness is quality, or how well the coordination device works in facilitating interaction and reducing dysfunctional conflicts. As we've shown, the least costly alternative may not be adequate. So managers have a number of options at their disposal for managing intergroup relations. But since they tend to be cumulative, with costs rising as you move up the continuum in Figure 13–8, the most effective coordination device will be the one lowest on the continuum that facilitates an enduring integrative exchange.

IMPLICATIONS FOR PERFORMANCE AND SATISFACTION

Many people automatically assume that conflict is related to lower group and organizational performance. This chapter has demonstrated that this assumption is frequently fallacious. Conflict can be either constructive or destructive to the functioning of a group or unit. As shown in Figure 13–10, levels of conflict can be either too high or too low. Either extreme hinders performance. An optimal level is where there is enough conflict to prevent stagnation, stimulate creativity, allow tensions to be released, and initiate the seeds for change; yet not so much as to be disruptive or deter coordination of activities.

Inadequate or excessive levels of conflict can hinder the effectiveness of a group or an organization, resulting in reduced satisfaction of group members, increased absence and turnover rates, and, eventually, lower productivity. On the other hand, when conflict is at an optimal level, complacency and apathy should be minimized, motivation should be enhanced through the creation of a challenging and questioning environment with a vitality that makes work interesting, and there should be the amount of turnover needed to rid the organization of misfits and poor performers.

Negotiation was shown to be an ongoing activity in groups and organizations. Distributive bargaining can resolve disputes but it often negatively

Figure 13–10 Conflict and Unit Performance

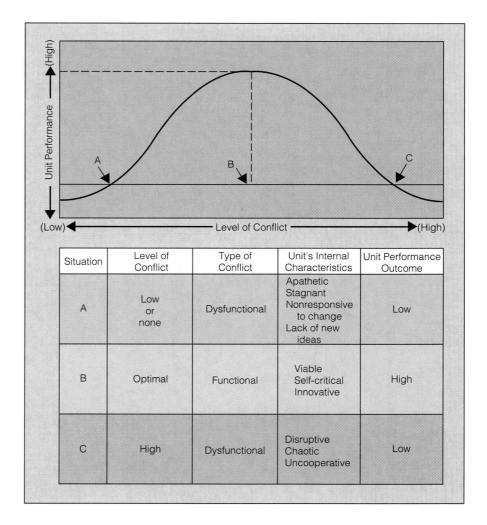

Situation	Level of Conflict	Type of Conflict	Unit's Internal Characteristics	Unit Performance Outcome
A	Low or none	Dysfunctional	Apathetic Stagnant Nonresponsive to change Lack of new ideas	Low
B	Optimal	Functional	Viable Self-critical Innovative	High
C	High	Dysfunctional	Disruptive Chaotic Uncooperative	Low

affects one or more negotiators' satisfaction because it is focused on the short term and is confrontational. Integrative bargaining, in contrast, tends to provide outcomes that satisfy all parties and to build lasting relationships.

Intergroup conflicts can also affect an organization's performance. Emphasis at this level, however, has tended to focus on dysfunctional conflicts and methods for managing them. Where organizational performance depends on effective group relations and where there is high interdependence between groups, management needs to ensure that the proper integrative device is put in place. However, consistent with the interactionist perspective on conflict, there is no reason to believe that *all* intergroup conflicts are dysfunctional. Some minimal levels of conflict can facilitate critical thinking among group members, make a group more responsive to the need for change, and provide similar benefits that can enhance group and organizational performance.

FOR DISCUSSION

1. Define conflict.
2. Name, discuss, and contrast three views on conflict.
3. What is the difference between functional and dysfunctional conflict? What determines functionality?
4. Under what conditions might conflict be beneficial to a group?
5. Identify various types of conflict.
6. What are the components in the conflict process model? From your own experiences, give an example of how a conflict proceeded through the five stages.
7. How could a manager stimulate conflict in his or her department?
8. "Participation is an excellent method for identifying differences and resolving conflicts." Do you agree or disagree? Discuss.
9. What defines the settlement range in distributive bargaining?
10. Why isn't integrative bargaining more widely practiced in organizations?
11. Identify half-a-dozen behaviors associated with effective negotiations in North America.
12. How do you assess the effectiveness of intergroup relations?

Conflict Is Good for an Organization

We've made considerable progress in the last twenty-five years toward overcoming the negative stereotype given to conflict. Most behavioral scientists and an increasing number of practitioners now accept that the goal of effective management is not to eliminate conflict. Rather, it is to create the right intensity of conflict so as to reap its functional benefits.

Since conflict can be good for an organization, it is only logical to acknowledge that there may be times when managers will purposely want to increase its intensity. Let's briefly review how stimulating conflict can provide benefits to the organization.

Conflict is a means by which to bring about radical change. It is an effective device by which management can drastically change the existing power structure, current interaction patterns, and entrenched attitudes.

Conflict facilitates group cohesiveness. While conflict increases hostility between groups, external threats tend to cause a group to pull together as a unit. Intergroup conflicts raise the extent to which members identify with their own group and increase feelings of solidarity, while, at the same time, internal differences and irritations dissolve.

Conflict improves group and organizational effectiveness. The stimulation of conflict initiates the search for new means and goals and clears the way for innovation. The successful solution of a conflict leads to greater effectiveness, to more trust and openness, to greater attraction of members for each other, and to depersonalization of future conflicts. In fact, it has been found that as the number of minor disagreements increases, the number of major clashes decreases.

Conflict brings about a slightly higher, more constructive level of tension. This enhances the chances of solving the conflicts in a way satisfactory to all parties concerned. When the level of tension is very low, the parties are not sufficiently motivated to do something about a conflict.

These points are clearly not comprehensive. As noted in the chapter, conflict provides a number of benefits to an organization. However, groups or organizations devoid of conflict are likely to suffer from apathy, stagnation, groupthink, and other debilitating diseases.

The points presented here were influenced by E. Van de Vliert, "Escalative Intervention in Small-Group Conflicts," *Journal of Applied Behavioral Science,* Winter 1985, pp. 19–36.

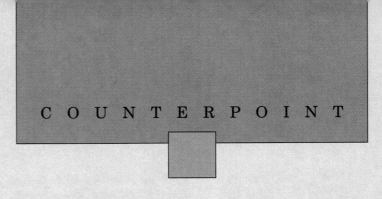

All Conflicts Are Dysfunctional!

It may be true that conflict is an inherent part of any group or organization. It may not be possible to eliminate it completely. However, just because conflicts exist is no reason to deify them. *All* conflicts are dysfunctional, and it is one of management's major responsibilities to keep conflict intensity as low as humanly possible. A few points will support this case.

The negative consequences from conflict can be devastating. The list of negatives associated with conflict are awesome. The most obvious are increased turnover, decreased employee satisfaction, inefficiencies between work units, sabotage, labor grievances and strikes, and physical aggression.

Effective managers build teamwork. A good manager builds a coordinated team. Conflict works against such an objective. A successful work group is like a successful sports team; each member knows his or her role and supports his or her teammates. When a team works well, the whole becomes greater than the sum of the parts. Management creates teamwork by minimizing internal conflicts and facilitating internal coordination.

Competition is good for an organization, but not conflict. Competition and conflict should not be confused with each other. *Conflict* is behavior directed against another party, whereas *competition* is behavior aimed at obtaining a goal without interference from another party. Competition is healthy; it is the source of organizational vitality. Conflict, on the other hand, is destructive.

Managers who accept and stimulate conflict don't survive in organizations. The whole argument on the value of conflict may be moot as long as senior executives in organizations view conflict from the traditional view. In the traditional view, *any* conflict will be seen as bad. Since the evaluation of a manager's performance is made by higher-level executives, those managers who do not succeed in eliminating conflicts are likely to be appraised negatively. This, in turn, will reduce opportunities for advancement. Any manager who aspires to move up in such an environment will be wise to follow the traditional view and eliminate any outward signs of conflict. Failure to follow this advice might result in the premature departure of the manager.

FOUNDATIONS OF ORGANIZATION STRUCTURE

LEARNING OBJECTIVES

After studying this chapter, you should be able to:

1. Define organization structure
2. Identify the advantages and disadvantages to division of labor
3. Explain the reason for maintaining unity of command
4. Differentiate line from staff authority
5. Define the span of control
6. List the ways an organization can departmentalize
7. Explain why structure may be a perceptual phenomenon

> *One man's red tape is another man's system.*
>
> D. WALDO

Michele and Tony Chen are twins. Both grew up in Seattle, attended the University of Washington, and graduated with degrees in computer science in 1991. Upon graduation, Michele joined a San Francisco consulting firm as a systems specialist. Tony went to work for a Boston firm that writes computer software programs. At a recent family Thanksgiving dinner, the two spent some time comparing their job impressions.

"Did I ever make a mistake," began Tony. "I had four job offers and I took the one I did because it was a well-known company, provided me the opportunity to specialize in writing expert systems programs, and the promotion potential looked good because there were a number of levels of management. Well, there are many opportunities to move up here, but there's also a lot of competition. Of course, I've never been afraid of competition. It's just that jobs are so specialized and top management so removed from the daily routine that no one seems to notice what I do. I'm just a cog in this wheel. I'm a number—employee number HO 297, to be exact—and except for my boss and a few people in adjoining cubicles, no one even knows my name. It couldn't be more impersonal. You wouldn't believe the umpteen-zillion rules and regulations we have to follow. The company's policy manual has over five hundred pages! I spent my first four weekends with the firm in my office reading that manual. The actual work I do is really interesting and I've learned a lot of technical aspects about programming. But I hate this feeling of alienation I have. This company, day by day, is stripping me of my identity. I've begun making a few calls to some of our old college friends to let them know I'm back in the job market and to let me know if they hear of anything interesting. But maybe it's me. Maybe all companies are like this. What's your firm like?"

"It's nothing like yours," was Michele's reply. "Managers are purposely given a large number of people to supervise. This cuts down on the number of managers and minimizes the number of levels from the top of the company to the bottom. The place is really very informal. No policy manuals, no job descriptions, no complex chain of command. If I have a question or problem, I can take it up with anyone. We're all treated as equals. I think our firm is about the same size as yours—between four hundred and five hundred people—but we operate very loosely. The office layouts don't even include walls, which encourages us to communicate regularly with people at different ranks and in different areas. I'm on a first-name basis with everyone, including the president. They ask for my ideas on projects. And my ideas are always listened to and often implemented. We're all supposed to be professionals, and we're treated as such." ■

*T*ony and Michele work in organizations with very different structures. And as their comments suggest, these structures have a bearing on each twin's attitudes and behavior. In this chapter, we'll lay the foundation for an understanding of organization structure. We'll define the key dimensions that make up structure, describe the basic structural components, and consider how they affect organizational behavior.

WHAT IS STRUCTURE?

Organizations create structure to facilitate the coordination of activities and to control the actions of their members. Structure itself is made up of three components. The first has to do with the degree to which activities within the organization are broken up or differentiated. We call this *complexity.* Second is the degree to which rules and procedures are utilized. This component is referred to as *formalization.* The third component of structure is *centralization,* which considers where decision-making authority lies. Combined, these three components make up an organization's structure.[1] Some organizations, such as General Electric or the United States Department of Defense, are rigidly structured. They have lots of differentiated units, a great number of vertical levels between top management and the workers at the bottom, numerous rules and regulations that members are required to follow, and elaborate decision-making networks. At the other extreme are organizations that are loosely structured—few differentiated units, only a couple of levels of management hierarchy, little in terms of formalized regulations to restrict employees, and a simple system for making decisions. Of course, in between these two extremes lie a number of structural combinations. But while organizations differ in the ways they are structured, our primary interest is what impact these structural differences have on employee attitudes and behavior. First, however, let's briefly elaborate on the three components we have identified to ensure we have a common understanding of what is meant when we use the term **organization structure.**

Complexity

Complexity encompasses three forms of differentiation: horizontal, vertical, and spatial. **Horizontal differentiation** considers the degree of horizontal separation between units. The larger the number of different occupations

Organization Structure The degree of complexity, formalization, and centralization in the organization.

Complexity The degree of vertical, horizontal, and spatial differentiation in an organization.

Horizontal Differentiation The degree of differentiation between units based on the orientation of members, the nature of the tasks they perform, and their education and training.

487

within an organization that require specialized knowledge and skills, the more horizontally complex that organization is, because diverse orientations make it more difficult for organizational members to communicate and more difficult for management to coordinate their activities. When organizations have coordination problems because the cost accountants can't understand the priorities of the industrial engineers or because marketing and credit personnel have conflicting goals, the source of the problems is horizontal differentiation.

Vertical differentiation refers to the depth of the organizational hierarchy. The more levels that exist between top management and the operatives, the more complex the organization is. This is because there is a greater potential for communication distortion, it's more difficult to coordinate the decisions of managerial personnel, and it's harder for top management to oversee closely the actions of operatives where there are more vertical levels. For example, it's a lot more likely that if information has to go through eight or ten levels of management hierarchy, it will become distorted or misinterpreted than if it had to move through only two or three levels.

Spatial differentiation encompasses the degree to which the location of an organization's physical facilities and personnel are geographically dispersed. As spatial differentiation increases, so does complexity, because communication, coordination, and control become more difficult. Coordinating Sheraton's hundreds of hotels located around the world is a far more complex undertaking than coordinating the dozen New York City hotels that make up the Helmsley chain.

Formalization

The second component of structure is **formalization.** This term refers to the degree to which jobs within the organization are standardized. If a job is highly formalized, then the job incumbent has a minimum amount of discretion over what is to be done, when it is to be done, and how he or she should do it. Employees can be expected always to handle the same input in exactly the same way, resulting in a consistent and uniform output. There are explicit job descriptions, lots of organizational rules, and clearly defined procedures covering work processes in organizations where there is high formalization. Where formalization is low, job behaviors are relatively nonprogrammed and employees have a great deal of freedom to exercise discretion in their work. Since an individual's discretion on the job is inversely related to the amount of behavior in that job that is preprogrammed by the organization, the greater the standardization, the less input the employee has into how his or her work is to be done. Standardization not only eliminates the possibility of employees engaging in alternative behaviors, but it even removes the need for employees to consider alternatives.

The degree of formalization can vary widely between organizations and within organizations. Certain jobs, for instance, are well known to have little formalization. College book travelers—the representatives of publishers who call on professors to inform them of their company's new publications—have a great deal of freedom in their jobs. They have no standard sales "spiel," and the extent of rules and procedures governing their behavior may be little more than the requirement that they submit a weekly sales report and some suggestions on what to emphasize for the various new titles. At the other extreme, there are clerical and editorial positions in the same publishing houses where employees are required to "clock in" at their work stations by 8:00 A.M.. or be docked a half-hour of pay and, once at that work station, to follow a set of precise procedures dictated by management.

Vertical Differentiation The number of hierarchical levels in the organization.

Spatial Differentiation The degree to which the location of an organization's offices, plants, and personnel are geographically dispersed.

Formalization The degree to which jobs within the organization are standardized.

Centralization

In some organizations, top managers make all the decisions. Lower-level managers merely carry out top management's directives. At the other extreme, there are organizations where decision making is pushed down to those managers who are closest to the action. The former organizations are highly centralized; the latter are decentralized.

The term **centralization** refers to the degree to which decision making is concentrated at a single point in the organization. The concept includes only formal authority; that is, the rights inherent in one's position. Typically, it is said that if top management makes the organization's key decisions with little or no input from lower-level personnel, then the organization is centralized. In contrast, the more that lower-level personnel provide input or are actually given the discretion to make decisions, the more decentralized the organization is.

An organization characterized by centralization is an inherently different structural animal from one that is decentralized. In a decentralized organization, action can be taken more quickly to solve problems, more people provide input into decisions, and employees are less likely to feel alienated from those who make the decisions that affect their work lives.

Centralization The degree to which decision making is concentrated at a single point in the organization.

BASIC ORGANIZATIONAL CONCEPTS

Both management practitioners and theorists have been concerned with developing organizational principles since before the turn of the century. For instance, Adam Smith wrote on the advantages of division of labor in his celebrated *The Wealth of Nations* in the late eighteenth century.[2] During the first half of this century, a group of management practitioners and academics postulated a set of principles to guide managers in making structural decisions.[3] This group has come to be known as the *classical theorists* and their recommendations as the *classical principles.*

A number of decades have passed since most of these principles were originally proposed. Given the passing of that much time and all the changes that have taken place in our society, you might think these principles would be pretty worthless today. Surprisingly, they're not! For the most part, they still provide valuable insight into understanding the structure of organizations. Of course, we've also gained a great deal of knowledge over the years as to the limitations of these principles. In this section, we'll discuss the five basic classical principles. We'll also present an updated analysis of how each has had to be modified to reflect the increasing complexity and changing nature of today's organizational activities.

Division of Labor

Division of Labor Specialization; breaking jobs down into simple and repetitive tasks.

THE CLASSICAL VIEW **Division of labor** means that, rather than an entire job being done by one individual, it is broken down into a number of steps, each step being completed by a separate individual. In essence, individuals specialize in doing part of an activity rather than the entire activity. Assembly-line production, in which each worker does the same standardized task over and over again, is an example of division of labor.

The classical theorists were strong proponents of division of labor. They saw it as a way to significantly increase the economic efficiencies of organizations.

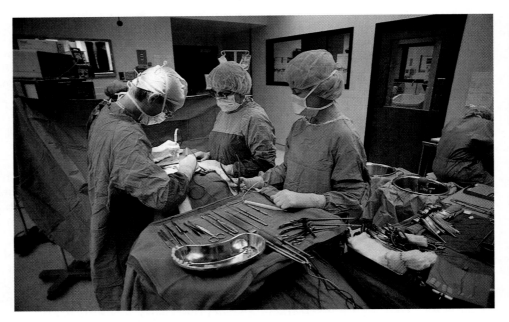

We see the results of division of labor in medical organizations. In this operating room, doctors, nurses, and other medical professionals each perform a precise and repetitive set of tasks. Much of the progress in modern medicine can be traced to increased expertise made possible by high degrees of specialization.

Richard Pasley/Stock, Boston

Division of labor makes efficient use of the diversity of skills that workers hold. In most organizations, some tasks require highly developed skills; others can be performed by the untrained. If all workers were engaged in each step of, say, an organization's manufacturing process, all would have to have the skills necessary to perform both the most demanding and the least demanding jobs. The result would be that, except when performing the most skilled or highly sophisticated tasks, employees would be working below their skill levels. And since skilled workers are paid more than unskilled workers and their wages tend to reflect their highest level of skill, it represents an inefficient usage of organizational resources to pay highly skilled workers to do easy tasks.

A number of other efficiencies are achieved through division of labor. One's skills at performing a task successfully increase through repetition. Less time is spent in changing tasks, in putting away one's tools and equipment from a prior step in the work process, and in getting ready for another. Equally important, training for specialization is more efficient from the organization's perspective. It is easier and less costly to find and train workers to do specific and repetitive tasks. This is especially true of highly sophisticated and complex operations. For example, could Lear produce one Lear jet a year if one person had to build the entire plane alone? Finally, division of labor increases efficiency and productivity by encouraging the creation of special inventions and machinery.

THE CONTEMPORARY VIEW   The classical theorists viewed division of labor as an unending source of increased productivity. At the turn of the century and earlier, this generalization was undoubtedly accurate. Because specialization was not widely practiced, its introduction almost always generated higher productivity. But a good thing can be carried too far. There is a point when the human diseconomies from division of labor—which surface as boredom, fatigue, stress, low productivity, poor quality, increased absenteeism, and high turnover—exceed the economic advantages. (See Figure 14–1.)

By the 1960s, it became clear that that point had been reached in a number of jobs. In such cases, productivity could be increased by enlarging,

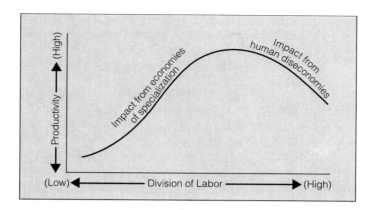

FIGURE 14–1   **Economies and Diseconomies of Division of Labor**

rather than narrowing, the scope of job activities. If you'll remember back to Chapters 7 and 8, where we discussed motivation, we dealt with job characteristics and design. We demonstrated that when employees are given a variety of activities to do, allowed to do a whole and complete piece of work, and put together into teams, they often achieve higher productivity and satisfaction. But notice that increasing skill variety, task identity, and the like runs counter to the division of labor concept.

So where are we today? In spite of all the recent attention focused on expanding and enriching jobs, it is probably accurate to conclude that the division of labor concept is still alive and well in most organizations today. But it is not seen as a panacea nor as an unending source of increased productivity. Rather, managers recognize the economies it provides in certain types of jobs and also the problems it creates when it is carried too far.

Unity of Command

Unity of Command A subordinate should have only one superior to whom he or she is directly responsible.

THE CLASSICAL VIEW   Classical theorists professing the **unity of command** principle argued that a subordinate should have one and only one superior to whom he or she is directly responsible. No person should report to two or more bosses. Otherwise, a subordinate might have to cope with conflicting demands or priorities from several superiors. In those rare instances when the unity of command principle had to be violated, the classical viewpoint always explicitly designated that there be a clear separation of activities and a supervisor responsible for each.

THE CONTEMPORARY VIEW   The unity of command concept was logical when organizations were comparatively simple in nature. Under most circumstances, it is still sound advice. Most organizations today closely adhere to this principle. Yet there are instances—and we'll introduce them in the next chapter—when strict adherence to the unity of command creates a degree of inflexibility that hinders an organization's performance.

Authority and Responsibility

Authority The rights inherent in a managerial position to give orders and expect the orders to be obeyed.

THE CLASSICAL VIEW   **Authority** refers to the rights inherent in a managerial position to give orders and expect the orders to be obeyed. It was a major tenet of the classical theorists, in that authority was viewed as the glue that held the organization together. It was to be delegated downward to subordinate managers, giving them both certain rights and certain prescribed limits within which they could operate.

Each management position has specific inherent rights that incumbents acquire from the position's rank or title. Authority relates, therefore, to one's position within an organization and ignores the personal characteristics of the individual manager. It has nothing directly to do with the individual. The expression "The king is dead; long live the king" illustrates the concept. Whoever is king acquires the rights inherent in the king's position. When a position of authority is vacated, the person who has left the position no longer has any authority. The authority remains with the position and the new incumbent.

Responsibility An obligation to perform.

When we delegate authority, the classicists argued, we must allocate commensurate **responsibility.** That is, when one is given *rights,* one also

FIGURE 14–2   Source: John Hart, *The Wizard of Id.* By permission of Johnny Hart and Creative Syndicate, Inc.

assumes a corresponding *obligation* to perform. To allocate authority without responsibility creates opportunities for abuse, and no one should be held responsible for what he or she has no authority over.

Classical theorists recognized the importance of equating authority and responsibility. Additionally, they stated that responsibility cannot be delegated. They supported this contention by noting that the delegator was held responsible for the actions of his or her delegates. But how is it possible to have equal authority and responsibility if responsibility cannot be delegated?

The classicists' answer was to recognize two forms of responsibility: *operating* responsibility and *ultimate* responsibility. Managers pass on operating responsibility, which in turn may be passed on further. But there is an aspect of responsibility—its ultimate component—that must be retained. A manager is ultimately responsible for the actions of his or her subordinates to whom the operating responsibility has been passed. Therefore, managers should delegate operating responsibility equal to the delegated authority; however, ultimate responsibility can never be delegated.

The classical theorists also distinguished between two forms of authority relations: line authority and staff authority. **Line authority** is the authority that entitles a manager to direct the work of a subordinate. It is the superior–subordinate authority relationship that extends from the top of the organization to the lowest echelon, following what is called the **chain of command.** As a link in the chain of command, a manager with line authority has the right to direct the work of subordinates and to make certain decisions without consulting others. Of course, in the chain of command, every manager is also subject to the direction of his or her superior.

Sometimes the term *line* is used to differentiate *line* managers from *staff* managers. In this context, line emphasizes those managers whose organizational function contributes directly to the achievement of the organizational objectives. In a manufacturing firm, line managers are typically in

Line Authority Authority to direct the work of a subordinate.

Chain of Command The superior–subordinate authority chain that extends from the top of the organization to the lowest echelon.

EDS Corp. a wholly-owned subsidiary of General Motors, provides supportive computer and information services to organizations. In the typical manufacturing firm, management information specialists are in a staff function. However, at EDS, such specialists are line.
Courtesy of EDS Corporation, Dallas, Texas.

the production function, whereas executives in personnel or accounting are considered staff managers. But whether a manager's function is classified as line or staff depends on the organization's objectives. At a firm like Kelly Services, which is a temporary personnel placement organization, personnel interviewers have a line function. Similarly, at the accounting firm of Price Waterhouse, accounting is a line function.

The definitions given above are not contradictory but, rather, represent two ways of looking at the term *line.* Every manager has line authority over his or her subordinates, but not every manager is in a line function or position. This latter determination depends on whether or not the function directly contributes to the organization's objectives.

Staff Authority Positions that support, assist, and advise line managers.

As organizations get larger and more complex, line managers find that they do not have the time, expertise, or resources to get their jobs done effectively. In response, they create **staff authority** functions to support, assist, advise, and in general reduce some of the informational burdens they have. The hospital administrator can't effectively handle all the purchasing of supplies that the hospital needs, so she creates a purchasing department. The purchasing department is a staff department. Of course, the head of the purchasing department has line authority over her subordinate purchasing agents. The hospital administrator may also find that she is overburdened and needs an assistant. In creating the position of assistant-to-the-hospital-administrator, she has created a staff position.

Figure 14–3 illustrates line and staff authority.

THE CONTEMPORARY VIEW   The classical theorists were enamored of authority. They naively assumed that the rights inherent in one's formal position in an organization were the sole source of influence. They believed that managers were all-powerful.

FIGURE 14–3   Line and Staff Authority

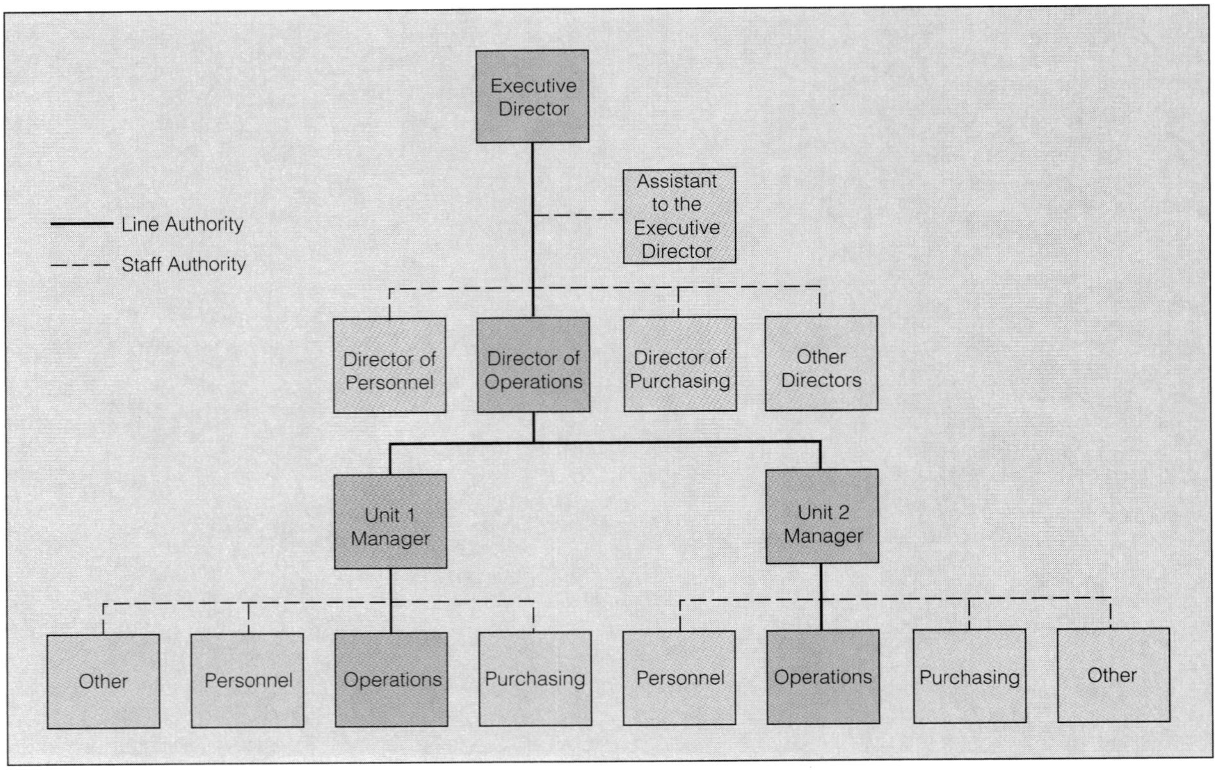

Should You Follow Orders with Which You Don't Agree?

A few years back, a study of business executives revealed that most had obeyed orders that they had found personally objectionable or unethical.[4] Far more thought-provoking was a survey taken among the general public near the end of the Vietnam War. In spite of public dismay over the actions of some military personnel during that war, about half the respondents said that they would have shot civilian men, women, and children in cold blood if they had been ordered to do so by their commanding officer![5] And remember the Milgram study described in Chapter 2. Although the majority of subjects in this study dissented from what the experimenter was telling them to do, they still followed orders and increased the shock level to the maximum.

If you were asked to follow orders that you believed were unconscionable, would you comply? For example, what if your boss asked you to destroy evidence that he or she had been stealing a great deal of money from the organization?

What if you merely disagreed with the orders? For instance, what if your boss asked you to bring him or her coffee each morning even though no such task is included in your job description and you consider coffee-getting to be demeaning? What would *you* do?

This may have been true fifty or more years ago. Organizations were simpler. Staff was less important. Managers were only minimally dependent on technical specialists. Under such conditions, influence is the same as authority; and the higher a manager's position in the organization, the more influence he or she had. But, as we described in Chapter 12, those conditions no longer hold. Researchers and practitioners of management now recognize that you don't have to be a manager to have power, nor is power perfectly correlated to one's level in the organization. Authority is an important concept in organizations, but an exclusive focus on it produces a narrow and unrealistic view of influence in organizations. Today we recognize that authority is but one element in the larger concept of power.

Moreover, as we have mentioned many times previously, organizations today have increasingly turned to participation, teams, and other devices to downplay authoritative superior–subordinate relationships. Managers are increasingly viewing their jobs as liberating and enabling their employees rather than supervising them. As one former chief executive of a large office furniture manufacturer put it: "Take a thirty-three-year-old man who assembles chairs. He's been doing it several years. He has a wife and two children. He knows what to do when the children have earaches, and how to get them through school. He probably serves on a volunteer board. And when he comes to work we give him a supervisor. He doesn't need one."[6]

Span of Control

Span of Control The number of subordinates a manager can efficiently and effectively direct.

THE CLASSICAL VIEW   How many subordinates can a manager efficiently and effectively direct? This question of **span of control** received a great deal of attention from the classicists. While there is no consensus on a specific number, the classical theorists favored small spans—typically no more than six—in order to maintain close control.[7] Several, however, did acknowledge level in the organization as a contingency variable. They argued that as a manager rises in an organization, he or she has to deal with a greater number of ill-structured problems, so top executives need a smaller span than do middle managers, and middle managers require a span smaller than do supervisors.

The span of control concept was important to the classical theorists because, to a large degree, it determines the number of levels and managers an organization has. All things being equal, the wider or larger the span, the more efficient the organization. An example can illustrate the validity of this statement.

Assume that we have two organizations, both of which have approximately forty-one hundred operative-level employees. As Figure 14–4 illustrates, if one has a uniform span of four and the other a span of eight, the wider span would have two fewer levels and approximately eight hundred fewer managers. If the average manager made $40,000 a year, the wider span would save $32 million a year in management salaries! Obviously, wider spans are more *efficient* in terms of cost. However, at some point wider spans reduce *effectiveness*.

THE CONTEMPORARY VIEW   A few years back, management guru Tom Peters correctly predicted that Wal-Mart would pass Sears, Roebuck to become the number-one retailer in the United States: "Sears doesn't have a chance!" he said. "A twelve-layer company can't compete with a three-layer company."[8] Peters may have exaggerated the point a bit, but it clearly reflects the fact that the pendulum has swung in recent years toward creating flat structures with wide spans of control.

More and more organizations today are increasing their spans of control. For example, the span for managers at companies such as General

FIGURE 14–4   Contrasting Spans of Control

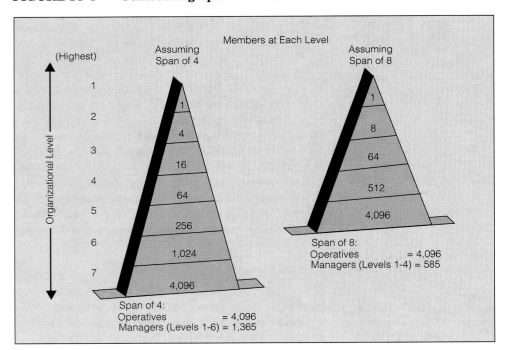

Electric and Reynolds Metals has expanded to ten or twelve subordinates—twice the number of a dozen years ago.[9] The span of control is increasingly being determined by looking at contingency variables. For instance, it's obvious that the more training and experience subordinates have, the less direct supervision they need. This is fully consistent with the research findings on the path–goal theory of leadership presented in Chapter 11. So managers who have well-trained and experienced employees can function with a wider span. Other contingency variables that will determine the appropriate span include similarity of subordinate tasks, the complexity of those tasks, the physical proximity of subordinates, the degree to which standardized procedures are in place, and the preferred style of the manager.[10]

Departmentalization

THE CLASSICAL VIEW   The classical theorists argued that activities in an organization should be specialized and grouped into departments. Division of labor creates specialists who need coordination. This coordination is facilitated by putting specialists together in departments under the direction of a manager. Creation of these departments is typically based on the work functions being performed, the product or service being offered, the target customer or client, the geographic territory being covered, or the process being used to turn inputs into outputs. No single method of departmentalization was advocated by the classical theorists. The method or methods used should reflect the grouping that would best contribute to the attainment of the organization's objectives and the goals of individual units.

Functional Departmentalization
Grouping activities by functions performed.

One of the most popular ways to group activities is by functions performed—**functional departmentalization.** A manufacturing manager might organize his or her plant by separating engineering, accounting, manufacturing, personnel, and purchasing specialists into common departments. (See Figure 14–5.) Of course, departmentalization by function can be used in all types of organizations. Only the functions change to reflect the organization's objectives and activities. A hospital might have departments devoted to research, patient care, accounting, and so forth. A professional football franchise might have departments entitled Player Personnel, Ticket Sales, and Travel and Accommodations. The major advantage to this type of grouping is obtaining efficiencies from putting like specialists together. Functional departmentalization seeks to achieve economies of scale by placing people with common skills and orientations into common units.

Product Departmentalization
Grouping activities by product line.

Figure 14–6 illustrates the **product departmentalization** method used at Sun Petroleum Products. Each major product area in the corporation

FIGURE 14–5   Departmentalization by Function

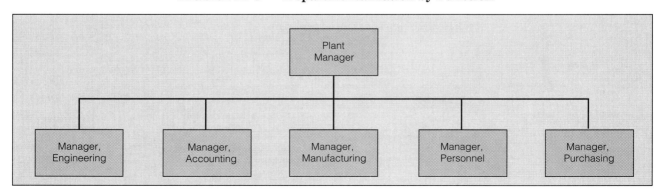

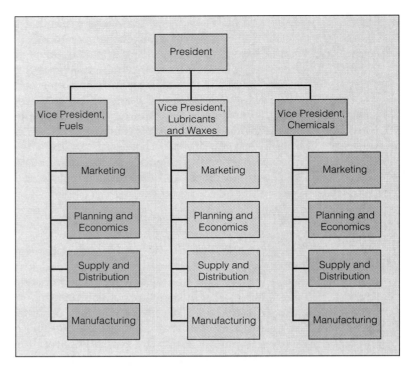

FIGURE 14–6   Departmentalization by Product

is placed under the authority of a vice president who is a specialist in, and responsible for, everything having to do with his or her product line. Notice, for example, in contrast to functional departmentalization, that manufacturing and other major activities have been divided up to give the product managers (vice presidents, in this case) considerable autonomy and control. The major advantage to this type of grouping is increased accountability for product performance.

If an organization's activities are service-rather than product-related, each service would be autonomously grouped. For instance, an accounting firm would have departments for tax, management consulting, auditing, and the like. Each would offer a common array of services under the direction of a product or service manager.

The particular type of customer the organization seeks to reach can also be used to group employees. The sales activities in an office supply firm, for instance, can be broken down into three departments to service retail, wholesale, and government customers. (See Figure 14–7.) A large law office can segment its staff on the basis of whether they service corporate or indi-

FIGURE 14–7   Departmentalization by Customer

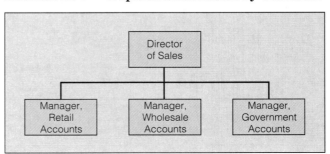

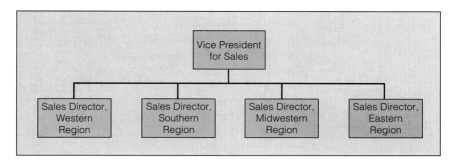

FIGURE 14–8   Departmentalization by Geography

vidual clients. The assumption underlying **customer departmentalization** is that customers in each department have a common set of problems and needs that can best be met by having specialists for each.

Another way to departmentalize is on the basis of geography or territory—**geographic departmentalization.** The sales function may have western, southern, midwestern, and eastern regions. (See Figure 14–8.) A large school district may have six high schools to provide for each of the major geographical territories within the district. If an organization's customers are scattered over a large geographic area, then this form of departmentalization can be valuable.

Figure 14–9 depicts the various production departments in an aluminum plant. Each department specializes in one specific phase in the production of aluminum tubing. The metal is cast in huge furnaces; sent to the press department, where it is extruded into aluminum pipe; transferred to the tube mill, where it is stretched into various sizes and shapes of tubing; moved to finishing, where it is cut and cleaned; and finally arrives in the inspect, pack, and ship department. Since each process requires different skills, this method offers a basis for the homogeneous categorizing of activities.

Process departmentalization can be used for processing customers as well as products. If you have ever been to a state motor vehicle office to get a driver's license, you probably went through several departments before receiving your license. In one state, applicants must go through three steps, each handled by a separate department: (1) validation, by motor vehicles division; (2) processing, by the licensing department; and (3) payment collection, by the treasury department.

THE CONTEMPORARY VIEW   Most large organizations continue to use most or all of the departmental groupings suggested by the classical theo-

FIGURE 14–9   Departmentalization by Process

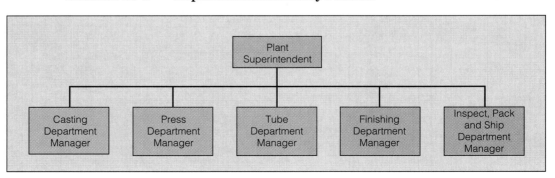

rists. A major electronics firm, for instance, organizes each of its divisions along functional lines and its manufacturing units around processes; departmentalizes sales around four geographic regions; and divides each sales region into three customer groupings. But two recent trends need to be mentioned. First, customer departmentalization has become increasingly emphasized. Second, rigid departmentalization is being complemented by the use of teams that cross over traditional departmental lines.

Today's competitive environment has refocused management's attention on its customers. In order to better monitor the needs of customers and to be able to respond to changes in those needs, many organizations have given greater emphasis to customer departmentalization. Xerox, for example, has eliminated its corporate marketing staff and placed marketing specialists out in the field.[11] This allows the company to better understand who their customers are and to respond faster to their requirements.

As discussed in a number of previous places in this book, you see a great deal more use of teams today as a device for accomplishing organizational objectives. As tasks have become more complex and more diverse skills are needed to accomplish them, management has introduced the use of teams and task forces. For example, IBM is currently working on a development project to produce a new version of OS/2 software to meet the challenge of Microsoft's Windows program.[12] It has put together teams of programmers in Boca Raton, Florida, and stripped away traditional distinctions—for instance, between designers and those who actually write the programs—to overcome historical coordination problems in large software projects.

STRUCTURAL VARIABLES AND ORGANIZATIONAL BEHAVIOR

We opened this chapter by implying that an organization's structure can have profound effects on its members. In this section, we want to directly assess just what those effects might be.[13] Let's look again at each of the five basic organizational concepts we've just reviewed, but this time consider their implications on organizational behavior.

Division of Labor

Generalizing across the population, the evidence indicates that division of labor contributes to higher employee productivity but at the price of reduced job satisfaction. However, this generalization ignores individual differences and the type of job tasks people do.

As we noted previously, division of labor is not an unending source of higher productivity. Problems start to surface, and productivity begins to suffer, when the human diseconomies of doing repetitive and narrow tasks overtake the economies of specialization. As the work force has become more highly educated and desirous of jobs that are intrinsically rewarding, the point where productivity begins to decline seems to be reached more quickly than in decades past.

While more people today are undoubtedly turned off by overly specialized jobs than were their parents or grandparents, it would be naive to ignore the reality that there is still a segment of the work force that prefers the routine and repetitiveness of highly specialized jobs. Some individuals want work that makes minimal intellectual demands and provides the security of routine. For these people, high division of labor is a source of job satisfaction. The empirical question, of course, is whether this represents two percent of the work force or fifty-two percent. Given that there is some self-selection operating in the choice of careers, we might conclude that negative behavioral outcomes from high division of labor are most likely to surface in professional jobs occupied by individuals with high needs for personal growth and diversity.

Unity of Command

There is little evidence to indicate that any significant segment of the work force actually *prefers* jobs where they must live under the rule of multiple bosses. It's hard—sometimes impossible—to serve two masters. The exception is when those bosses coordinate their actions so as not to place unrealistic or conflicting demands upon their mutual subordinates.

From the worker's perspective, organizations that closely apply the unity of command concept reduce ambiguity and hence lessen employee stress. But not without a price! The clarity and predictability that the unity of command concept provides also tends to contribute toward making organizations hierarchically obsessed. Everything has to "go through channels." Communication becomes highly formalized. The result is that employees can become frustrated from a feeling of being "boxed in."

Combine strict adherence to the unity of command with high division of labor and you have the probable explanation for some of your worst personal experiences in dealing with large corporations or government agencies. For example, have you ever been frustrated when trying to return merchandise to a big department store or in seeking clarification on a tax matter from the Internal Revenue Service? Well, the frustration works both ways. Organizations that divide jobs up into narrow tasks and require employees to closely follow the unity of command create an impersonal climate for their employees. Just as this can frustrate you as a customer or client, it can also frustrate those people who have to work in such places.

Authority and Responsibility

Authority provides employees with clarity and minimizes ambiguity because people know whose directives they are expected to follow.

While the classical theorists may have viewed authority as the glue that held organizations together, an overreliance by managers on their formal authority is likely to cause problems in organizations today. The "might makes right" thesis was effective, for the most part, when people in organizations had minimal levels of education and supervisors could do their subordinates' jobs as well or better than the subordinates could. Nowadays, as jobs have become more technical and specialized, those "in authority" often don't know exactly what their people do or how they do it. As a result, they are more dependent on their employees. An overreliance on formal authority, in such situations, is likely to alienate employees.

Competence and respect are not necessarily perfectly correlated with authority. When managers rely on authority rather than on knowledge, persuasive skills, or other bases of power, they can lose credibility among their followers. Managers who hide behind their formal rights are likely to have less productive and less satisfied employees than those who develop additional sources of power.

Close supervision at the Army's SDI battle-management center in Alabama is possible with a small span of control while the printers at Banta Corporation in Wisconsin work with less supervision. Some employees may find the close supervision at the SDI battle-management center frustrating or dehumanizing but those new to a job or with minimal experience are likely to find that small spans of control mean bosses are readily available when they need them.   Left; courtesy of U.S. Army Strategic Defense Command, Huntsville, Ala.; right, James Schnepf.

Span of Control

A review of the research indicates that it is probably safe to say there is no evidence to support a relationship between span of control and employee performance. While it is intuitively attractive to argue that large spans might lead to higher employee performance because they provide more distant supervision and more opportunity for personal initiative, the research fails to support this notion. At this point it is impossible to state that any particular span of control is best for producing high performance or high satisfaction among subordinates. The reason is probably individual differences. That is, some people like to be left alone, while others prefer the security of a boss who is quickly available at all times. Consistent with several of the contingency theories of leadership, we would expect factors such as employees' experiences and abilities and the degree of structure in their tasks to explain when wide or narrow spans of control are likely to contribute to their performance and job satisfaction. However, there is some evidence indicating that a *manager's* job satisfaction increases as the number of subordinates he or she supervises increases.

Departmentalization

Organizations departmentalize in order to increase efficiency and effectiveness. But what effect does it have on the people in the organization?

From an employee's perspective, putting together people who share similar interests, skills, concerns for a product, or the like facilitates intradepartmental communication. For instance, in functional departmentalization, marketing people get to work closely with other marketing people and design engineers get to do the same. In product departmentalization, all the members of a department can put their individual efforts into developing, making, and selling a common product and can experience the common feeling of accomplishment when the product succeeds.

National Differences and Organization Structure

The willingness to accept unquestioningly a superior's authority and the determination of what is the right size for a manager's span of control are both affected by the cultural values of the society in which an organization operates. Let's see how these two structural variables might need to be modified in different countries.

To what degree are people in a given country likely to unquestioningly accept the authority of their bosses? To what degree will managers in that country delegate authority? The concept of power distance can help us answer these questions. In high-power-distance cultures, people accept wide differences in power. As a result, they should also readily accept directives from a boss, even if they strongly disagree with those orders. So formal authority is likely to be a potent influencing device in such places as Mexico or the Philippines. In contrast, in low-power-distance countries such as Austria or Denmark, authoritative directives are likely to be rejected by employees. We might also speculate that in low-power-distance cultures people are more willing to accept or even seek delegated authority. In high-power-distance countries, employees expect to be told what to do rather than actually to make decisions themselves.

In our updated discussion on span of control, we noted the emphasis on contingency variables to help managers identify the most effective group size. To that list of contingency variables should be added *national culture*. For example, quality-of-life cultures emphasize human relationships. This is consistent with confidence in subordinates and wide spans of control. So we could expect resistance to the imposition of narrow spans in Scandinavian countries like Sweden and Norway. Additionally, research on human nature discussed in Chapter 3 indicates cultures vary on whether they view people as good or evil. Clearly, in those countries where the evil perspective dominates, tight spans of control should be more readily accepted by employees. In fact, these employees may expect tight controls and be *less* productive and satisfied when not closely supervised.

As with all the other structural variables we've discussed, there is a downside to departmentalization. It develops a narrow perspective among its department members. In some cases, especially in the functional and process varieties, jobs can become repetitious and boring. Additionally, rigid departmentalization tends to create barriers to effective interdepartmental communication and to cross-fertilization of ideas. These barriers, then, can contribute to reducing employee productivity and satisfaction.

ARE ORGANIZATIONAL STRUCTURES REAL OR IN PEOPLE'S MINDS?

Complexity, formalization, and centralization are objective structural components that can be measured by organizational researchers. Every organization can be evaluated as to the degree to which it is high or low in all three. But employees don't objectively measure these components. They observe things around them in an unscientific fashion and then form their own implicit models of what the organization's structure is like. How many different people did they have to interview with before they were offered their jobs? How many people work in their departments and buildings? How visible is the organization's policy manual, if one exists? Is everyone given a copy? If not, is one readily available? Is it referred to frequently? How is the organization and its top management described in newspapers and periodicals? Answers to questions such as these, when combined with an employee's past experiences and comments made by peers, leads members to form an overall subjective image of what their organization's structure is like. This image, though, may in no way resemble the organization's actual objective structural characteristics.

The importance of implicit models of organization structure should not be overlooked. As we noted in Chapter 5, people respond to their perceptions rather than to objective reality. The research, for instance, on the relationship between many structural variables and subsequent levels of performance or job satisfaction are inconsistent. Some of this is explained as being attributable to individual differences. Some employees, for instance, prefer narrowly defined and routine jobs; others abhor such characteristics. Additionally, however, a contributing cause to these inconsistent findings may be diverse perceptions of the objective characteristics. Researchers have focused on actual levels of the various structural components, but these may be irrelevant if people interpret similar components differently. The bottom line, therefore, is to understand how employees interpret their organization's structure. That should prove a more meaningful predictor of their behavior than the objective characteristics themselves.

IMPLICATIONS FOR PERFORMANCE AND SATISFACTION

This chapter defined organization structure, presented the classical cornerstones of organizing, and updated the discussion by reviewing contemporary theories and practices. We introduced these concepts because there is clear evidence that an organization's internal structure contributes to explaining and predicting behavior. That is, in addition to individual and group factors, the structural relationships in which people work have an important bearing on employee attitudes and behavior.

What is the basis for the argument that structure has an impact on both attitudes and behavior? To the degree that an organization's structure reduces ambiguity for employees and clarifies such concerns as "What am I supposed to do?" "How am I supposed to do it?" "Whom do I report to?" and "Whom do I go to if I have a problem?", it shapes their attitudes and facilitates and motivates them to higher levels of performance.

Of course, structure also constrains employees to the extent that it limits and controls what they do.[14] For example, organizations structured around high levels of formalization and division of labor, strict adherence to the unity of command, limited delegation of authority, and narrow spans of control give employees little autonomy. Controls in such organizations are tight and behavior will tend to vary within a narrow range. In contrast, organizations that are structured around limited division of labor, low formalization, wide spans of control, and the like provide employees greater freedom and, thus, will be characterized by greater behavioral diversity. As we pointed out previously, the effect of these structural variables on employee performance and satisfaction will be substantially a function of an employee's preferences and how he or she cognitively interprets the actual structure.

1. Describe a highly *complex* organization.

2. What characteristics would describe an organization that is high in formalization?

3. Why isn't division of labor an unending source of increased productivity?

4. Why is the unity of command concept important?

5. All things being equal, which is more efficient, a wide or narrow span of control? Why?

6. Why did the classical theorists argue that authority should equal responsibility?

7. Can the manager of a staff department have line authority? Explain.

8. In what ways can management departmentalize?

9. "Employees prefer to work in flat, decentralized organizations." Do you agree or disagree? Discuss.

10. Do you think most employees prefer high formalization? Support your position.

11. Which form of departmentalization has become increasingly popular in recent years? Why?

12. What is the importance of the statement: "Employees form implicit models of organization structure."

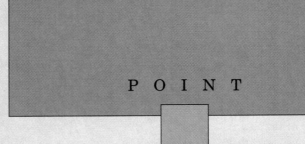

Tomorrow's Organizations Will Be Like Large Symphony Orchestras

Tomorrow's organizations are going to be flatter, less hierarchical, and more decentralized. In structural terminology, they're going to be less complex, less formalized, and more decentralized. What are they going to look like? Not like a pyramid, which has been the traditional metaphor for organization structure. No! Tomorrow's organizations will resemble a large symphony orchestra.

Why is the pyramid doomed? There are at least four reasons:

1. *Rapid and unexpected change.* The pyramid's strength is its capacity to manage efficiently the routine and predictable events that an organization confronts. The pyramid, with its nicely defined chain of command, its rules, and its rigidities, is ill adapted to the rapid changes that all organizations now face.

2. *Increasing diversity.* Today's organizational activities require people with very diverse and highly specialized levels of competence. The narrow departmental boxes of the pyramid are inappropriate for handling diversity.

3. *Change in managerial behavior.* Managers no longer rule by dictum. Managerial philosophy has changed. Managers increasingly project humanistic–democratic values. Moreover, they increasingly rely on collaboration and reason rather than coercion and threats to lead their people.

4. *Adoption of computer technology.* Computers are changing the way things are done within organizations. Information-based technology demands a higher degree of flexibility.

The first three points are rather straightforward, but we should elaborate on our fourth point.

Knowledge-based organizations are composed largely of specialists who direct and discipline their own performances through organized feedback from colleagues, customers, and headquarters. This requires a structure that looks a lot like that of a symphony orchestra. Instead of doing things sequentially—research, development, manufacturing, and marketing—they'll be done by *synchrony*. Clear, simple, common objectives will allow the chief executive directly to "conduct" hundreds of employees or musicians. The CEO will be able to have a wide span of control because each employee will be a specialist who knows his or her part. Similarly, rules and regulations will be minimal because employees will be skilled professionals who had their standards of performance and expectations "indoctrinated" into them during their professional training. Like conductors, managers won't have to explain much. They'll merely need to provide the musical score or plan, and then give subtle overall direction.

This argument is largely based on P. F. Drucker, "The Coming of the New Organization," *Harvard Business Review,* January–February 1988, pp. 45–53.

The Future Still Belongs to the Pyramid!

There is no doubt that organizations are changing. But are these changes leaving the pyramid-shaped structure behind? Nothing could be further from the truth! The pyramid is alive, well, and flourishing. We'll make our position by emphasizing four points.

1. *The future lies with large organizations.* Large size demands the efficiency that division of labor, high formalization, and other pyramid-creating devices use to maintain control. While many "experts" have predicted the demise of large organizations, the globalization of markets has turned the tide back in favor of large size. Global competition in major industries will require resources and managerial skills not available to small organizations. The pendulum, in the 1990s, is swinging back toward large organizations that will be able to compete aggressively in markets throughout the world.

2. *Employees like pyramids.* Employees like the predictability and security that pyramid-shaped organizations offer. They minimize ambiguity. Employees know what to do, whom to report to, and the like.

3. *Managers like pyramids.* Managers, too, like pyramids, because they provide tight controls. Humanistic–democratic values sound good, and many managers prefer to use collaboration and reason, but when the pressure is on and managers must perform, they often fall back on coercion and threats.

4. *The "information-technology" theme has been oversold in North America.* Some 82 million jobs in the United States do not require a four-year college education. Moreover, American business has been moving toward de-skilling jobs—that is, downgrading skills—in order to cut wages and increase productivity. A recent study found that less than ten percent of employers are creating jobs that call for workers with broad-based skills and the ability to adapt to fast-changing technology and markets. The symphony orchestra metaphor might be appropriate for managing groups of Ph.D. research scientists, but the de-skilling of jobs such as machine operator, retail clerk, assembler, and health service worker is more compatible with the tight control provided by the pyramid-shaped organization.

These facts argue for a very different scenario than that predicted in the previous argument. Tomorrow's organizations won't look like symphony orchestras. A few might, but they're likely to be quite small in size. The organization of tomorrow will look like the organization of yesterday—it will be a tightly controlled structure shaped like a pyramid.

Facts on de-skilling mentioned here are from J. Hoerr, "Business Shares the Blame for Workers' Low Skills," *Business Week,* June 25, 1990, p. 71.

Division of Labor Exercise

OBJECTIVE   To compare task performance in generalist versus specialist groups.

TIME   Approximately twenty-five minutes.

PROCEDURE

1. Select six students to participate in the exercise. Divide them into two teams of three each. Call one Team A; the other Team B. The teams will be working on a letter-counting task. The three letters that will be counted are *a, i,* and *h.*

2. All six participants are to turn to page 449 in this text. There are 39 lines on this page. Divide this page into thirds by counting down 18 and 36 lines from the top and making a mark with a pen.

3. In the first trial, Team A will be the "specialists" and Team B will be the "generalists." Your instructor will assign each member of the specialists one of the three letters (see Step 1). Your instructor will also assign each member of the generalists one of the following sets of lines on page 449: 1–18; 19–36; or 37–54.

4. When given the word by your instructor to proceed:

   a. Each member of Team A will count the number of times his or her assigned letter appears on page 449. You can use a pencil and scratch pad if you wish. Signify when you are finished with this task by raising your hand.

   b. Each member of Team B will count the number of times each of the three letters appears in the 18 lines he or she has been assigned. Keep a separate count for each letter. You can also use a pencil and scratch pad if you wish. Signify when you are finished with this task by raising your hand.

5. When all team members are finished with their task, tabulate a team score by computing the number of times each letter appeared on page 449.

6. Now do this same exercise again, only this time Team A will be the generalists and Team B will become the specialists. Repeat Steps 4 and 5.

7. Compare the task performance of the specialists and the generalists in terms of both speed and accuracy.

8. Discuss the results:

   a. Did division of labor contribute to higher performance?

   b. Why do you think you got the results you did?

   c. What are the positive and negative implications from this exercise for the design of jobs?

*I want to thank Del Hanson for his assistance in designing this exercise.

Authority Figures

PURPOSE To learn about one's experiences with, and feelings about, authority.

TIME Approximately seventy-five minutes.

PROCEDURE

1. Your instructor will separate class members into groups based on their *birth* order. Groups are formed consisting of "Only children," "Eldest," "Middle," and "Youngest," according to placement in families. Larger groups will be broken into smaller ones, with four or five members, to allow for freer conversation.

2. Each group member should talk about how he or she "typically *reacts* to the authority of others." Focus should be on specific situations that offer general information about how individuals deal with authority figures (for example, bosses, teachers, parents, or coaches). The group has twenty-five minutes to develop a written list of how the *group* generally deals with others' authority. Be sure to separate tendencies that group members share and those they do not.

3. Repeat Step 2 above, except this time discuss how group members "typically *are as* authority figures." Again make a list of shared characteristics.

4. Each group will share its general conclusions with the entire class.

5. Class discussion will focus on questions such as:

   a. What patterned differences have surfaced between the groups?

   b. What may account for these differences?

   c. What hypotheses might explain the connection between how individuals react to the authority of others and how they are as authority figures?

Source: This exercise is adapted from W. A. Kahn, "An Exercise of Authority," *Organizational Behavior Teaching Review*, Vol. XIV, Issue 2, 1989–90, pp. 28–42.

CASE INCIDENT 14

Celestial Seasonings

If you walk into your local supermarket and find the aisle where coffee and tea products are displayed, odds are you'll see boxes of herbal teas with animated pictures of bears frolicking under waterfalls, chipmunks blowing gold trumpets, and buffalo charging out of the sunset. The teas will have names like Mo's 24, Sleepytime, Red Zinger, Emperor's Choice, Cinnamon Rose, Almond Sunset, and Morning Thunder. The company that brings these teas to your supermarket is Celestial Seasonings, Inc. In 1991, the company had sales in excess of $50 million. It has made its founders—Mo Siegel and John Hay—millionaires. But Celestial Seasonings wasn't always a multimillion-dollar organization. In fact, it has grown from the most humble of beginnings.

In the summer of 1971, Mo Siegel and John Hay were in their early twenties and lived in Boulder, Colorado. Both were "free spirits"—more interested in religion, music, and health than the security of an eight-to-five job. But even free spirits have to eat, so Mo and John decided to make and sell herb teas.

Mo and John spent their summer days picking herbs in the canyons surrounding Boulder. Meanwhile, their wives—Peggy Siegel and Beth Hay—sewed bulk tea bags: ten thousand bulk tea bags that first summer! The two couples screened the hundreds of pounds of herbs that the men had collected and mixed them into a concoction that would eventually be called Mo's 24. The mixture would then be crammed into the bulk tea bags and marked. The completed products—which they sold under the brand name of Celestial Seasonings—were sold to natural food stores in the Boulder area.

During the first few years, the people who made up Celestial Seasonings were nothing more than a group of friends and relatives. There were no job descriptions, no production lines, and little specialization of labor. The way the group made decisions was fully in keeping with the values of the founders. Informal meetings were held once a week. It was not unusual for these meetings to last eight hours, while participants dwelled on such topics as the philosophical attributes of tea bags. There were volleyball games during every lunch hour.

But something began to happen in the mid-1970s that changed Celestial Seasonings' structure dramatically. Demand for their herbal teas was exploding. They were moving out of health food stores and into Safeways and A&Ps. More people had to be hired to meet the increased demand. When Celestial Seasonings had been merely two friends and their wives, it could adjust rapidly to new conditions because everyone knew everyone else's job. Communication was easy—they all worked in the same small room. But with more people came the need to develop a more formal structure within which to make and sell their herbal teas. Today Celestial Seasonings employs more than three hundred people who work out of five buildings in the Boulder area. There are departments, production lines, and written job descriptions. The simple days of four people doing everything are gone. Herbs are received in one warehouse and then taken to a highly automated factory for cleaning, milling, and blending. Blending, for instance, is carefully done by specialists to ensure consistency of flavor. On a good day workers will blend eight tons or more of tea into fifteen varieties.

Not surprisingly, Celestial Seasonings has lost a large degree of its "one big happy family" atmosphere. With specialization and departmentalization came the separation of management from workers. Professionals now abound. Executives—many specializing in production, advertising, and distribution—were hired away from PepsiCo, General Foods, Quaker Oats, and Procter & Gamble. The company has expanded into laundry products, garbage bags, and other environmentally related products.

Source: Based on E. Morgenthaler, "Herb Tea's Pioneer: From Hippie Origins to $16 Million a Year," *The Wall Street Journal,* May 7, 1981, p. 1; and S. D. Atchison, "Putting the Red Zinger Back into Celestial," *Business Week,* November 4, 1991, pp. 74–78.

Questions

1. How would you describe Celestial Seasonings' structural dimensions in 1971? In 1991?

2. Why couldn't Celestial Seasonings keep its original structure and still be effective?

3. After being away for a number of years, Mo Siegel is back as chairman and CEO of Celestial Seasonings. How do you think his job changed between 1971 and 1991?

4. How would the typical employee's job at Celestial Seasonings have changed between 1971 and 1991?

FOR FURTHER READING

DAFT, R. L., *Organization Theory and Design,* 4th ed. (St. Paul, MN: West Publishing, 1992). Offers a comprehensive review of organization theory concepts.

JAQUES, E., "In Praise of Hierarchy," *Harvard Business Review,* January–February 1990, pp. 127–33. Argues that hierarchy is more efficient and provides greater accountability than flat organizations.

ORTON, J. D., and K. E. WEICK, "Loosely Coupled Systems: A Reconceptualization," *Academy of Management Review,* April 1990, pp. 203–23. Loosely coupled organizations have low levels of interdependence. This article reviews the literature on this concept.

PETERS, T., *Thriving on Chaos,* (New York: Alfred Knopf, 1988). Argues that organizations of tomorrow will thrive on chaos and appear to be similar to focused anarchy.

ROBBINS, S. P., *Organization Theory: Structure, Design, and Applications,* 3rd ed. (Englewood Cliffs, NJ: Prentice Hall, 1990). Provides a comprehensive overview of the organization theory literature and its practical applications.

ROBEY, D., *Designing Organizations,* 3rd ed. (Homewood, IL: Richard D. Irwin, 1991). Overviews organization theory, with particular emphasis on innovation and information processing.

NOTES

[1] S. P. Robbins, *Organization Theory: Structure, Design, and Applications,* 3rd ed. (Englewood Cliffs, NJ: Prentice Hall, 1990), Chapter 4.

[2] A. Smith, *An Inquiry into the Nature and Causes of the Wealth of Nations* (New York: Modern Library 1937). Originally published in 1776.

[3] See, for example, H. Fayol, *Administration Industrielle et Générale* (Paris: Dunod, 1916); M. Weber, *The Theory of Social and Economic Organizations,* ed., T. Parsons, trans. A. M. Henderson and T. Parsons (New York: Free Press, 1947); and R. C. Davis, *The Fundamentals of Top Management* (New York: Harper & Row, 1951).

[4] S. N. Brenner and E. A. Molander, "Is the Ethics of Business Changing?", *Harvard Business Review,* January-February 1977, pp. 57–71.

[5] H. C. Kelman and L. H. Lawrence, "American Response to the Trial of Lt. William L. Calley," *Psychology Today,* June 1972, pp. 41–45, 78–81.

[6] "Max DePree: It's Not What You Preach But How You Behave," *Fortune,* March 26, 1990, p. 36.

[7] L. Urwick, *The Elements of Administration* (New York: Harper & Row, 1944), pp. 52–53.

[8] Quoted in J. Braham, "Money Talks," *Industry Week,* April 17, 1989, p. 23.

[9] J. S. McClenahen, "Managing More People in the '90s," *Industry Week,* March 20, 1989, p. 30.

[10] D. Van Fleet, "Span of Management Research and Issues," *Academy of Management Journal,* September 1983, pp. 546–52.

[11] J. H. Sheridan, "Sizing Up Corporate Staffs," *Industry Week,* November 21, 1988, p. 47.

[12] J. Markoff, "When I.B.M.'s Big Guns Won't Do," *The New York Times,* July 18, 1991, p. C1.

[13] A number of the conclusions presented in this section are drawn from L. W. Porter and E. E. Lawler III, "Properties of Organization Structure in Relation to Job Attitudes and Job Behavior," *Psychological Bulletin,* July 1965, pp. 23–51; L. R. James and A. P. Jones, "Organization Structure: A Review of Structural Dimensions and Their Conceptual Relationships with Individual Attitudes and Behavior," *Organizational Behavior and Human Performance,* June 1976, pp. 74–113; D. R. Dalton, W. D. Todor, M. J. Spendolini, G. J. Fielding, and L. W. Porter, "Organization Structure and Performance: A Critical Review," *Academy of Management Review,* January 1980, pp. 49–64; and W. Snizek and J. H. Bullard, "Perception of Bureaucracy and Changing Job Satisfaction: A Longitudinal Analysis," *Organizational Behavior and Human Performance,* October 1983, pp. 275–87.

[14] D. A. Nadler, J. R. Hackman, and E. E. Lawler III, *Managing Organizational Behavior* (Boston: Little, Brown, 1979), pp. 182–84.

ORGANIZATION DESIGN

LEARNING OBJECTIVES

After studying this chapter, you should be able to:

1. Differentiate between mechanistic and organic structures

2. List the factors that favor different organization structures

3. Identify the five basic parts to any organization

4. Describe Mintzberg's five design configurations

5. Explain the behavioral implications of each design configuration

6. Summarize the strengths and weaknesses of the matrix structure

7. Explain why there is a growth bias in organizations

8. Describe how organizational decline affects employees

The problem with a bureaucracy is that it can't respond rapidly to change. Its motto is: "Ready, aim, aim, aim, aim..." It just can't pull the trigger!

ANONYMOUS

W. L. Gore & Associates is a company with sales in excess of $700 million a year. The firm is best known for producing the highly successful Gore-Tex fabric. Impervious to sunlight, heat, cold, or water, the fiber is used in high-quality tents, sleeping bags, gloves, ski clothes, boots, and other outdoor products. But the fascinating fact about this company is that it employs more than five thousand people in forty-one plants around the world, yet has *no formal hierarchy or structure.*[1] There are no job titles, no bosses, no chains of command.

Everyone at Gore is an "associate," with equal authority. Plants and staff departments are headed by "leaders." However, these are *not* bosses with less autocratic names! Leaders must share key personnel decisions—such as hiring, pay determination, disciplining, and firing—with peer committees, personnel staffers, and each associate's mentor, who functions in the organization as a counselor and advocate. Take pay, for example. Groups of associates meet every six months to rank peers by subjective assessment of their contributions. Committees merge the lists and set raises, ranking pay from the highest contributor on down. The result is that Gore has created a free-form structure with a large number of units that are purposely kept at under two hundred people each to maintain flexibility. The company claims that this unusual form of organization generates double the productivity of an average manufacturing work force and triple the creativity. And Gore's structure certainly hasn't constrained its growth: Sales tripled between 1984 and 1991. ■

Contrast W. L. Gore & Associates with the typical firm that employs five thousand people. As described in the previous chapter, its workers probably perform specialized activities in departments. Its departments have supervisors who report to middle managers who, in turn, report to top-level managers. And this pyramid-shaped hierarchy is justified as necessary to achieve efficiency, to establish clear lines of responsibility, and to maintain control. Yet, as the Gore company illustrates, there is more than one way to structure a successful organization. Moreover, the different structural designs that organizations use do not emerge at random. They are chosen by management for certain reasons. In this chapter, we'll build on concepts introduced in Chapter 14. More specifically, we'll review the factors that influence management's choice of an organization design, present a framework for categorizing design options, and consider the effect of various organization designs on the employees in those organizations.

MECHANISTIC VS. ORGANIC STRUCTURES

Mechanistic Structure A structure characterized by high complexity, high formalization, and centralization.

Organic Structure A structure characterized by low complexity, low formalization, and decentralization.

Before we begin reviewing the factors that influence management's choice of an organization design, we need to introduce a simple designation device for generalizing about organization structures.

There are many ways that management can mix and match the three structural components of complexity, formalization, and centralization. However, an organization's overall structure generally falls into one of two designs.[2] One is the **mechanistic structure,** which is characterized by high complexity (especially a great deal of horizontal differentiation), high formalization, a limited information network (mostly downward communication), and little participation by low-level members in decision making. The mechanistic structure is synonymous with the rigid pyramid-shaped organization. At the other extreme is the **organic structure.** It is low in complexity and formalization, it possesses a comprehensive information network (utilizing lateral and upward communication as well as downward), and it involves high participation in decision making. W. L. Gore & Associates has many of the characteristics associated with the organic structure.

As Figure 15–1 depicts, mechanistic structures are rigid, relying on authority and a well-defined hierarchy to facilitate coordination. The organic structure, on the other hand, is flexible and adaptive. Coordination is achieved through constant communication and adjustment.

In the next section, you'll find that we regularly refer back to these two generic structural designs.

WHY DO STRUCTURES DIFFER?

Why are some organizations structured along more mechanistic lines while others follow organic characteristics? What are the forces that influence the form that is chosen? In the following pages, we'll present the major forces that have been identified as causes or determinants of an organization's structure.

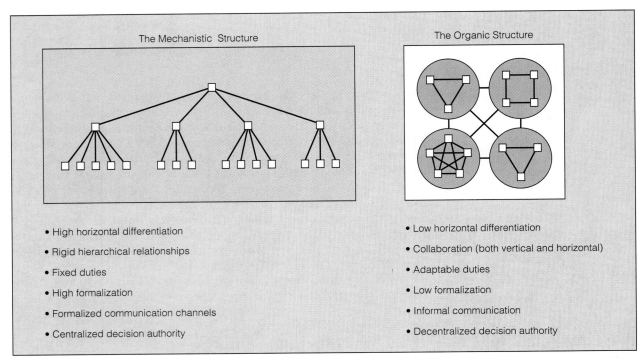

Figure 15–1   Mechanistic vs. Organic Structures

Strategy

An organization's structure is a means to help management achieve its objectives. Since objectives are derived from the organization's overall strategy, it is only logical that strategy and structure should be closely linked. More specifically, structure should follow strategy. If management makes a significant change in its organization's strategy, the structure will need to be modified to accommodate and support this change.

CHANDLER'S STRATEGY–STRUCTURE THESIS   The classic research supporting this strategy–structure relationship was a study of close to one hundred large United States companies conducted by Alfred Chandler and published in the early 1960s.[3] Tracing the development of these organizations over a period of fifty years, and compiling extensive case histories of companies such as DuPont, General Motors, Standard Oil of New Jersey, and Sears, Roebuck, Chandler concluded that changes in corporate strategy precede and lead to changes in an organization's structure. Chandler found that organizations usually begin with a single product or line. They do only one thing, like manufacturing, sales, or warehousing. The simplicity of the strategy requires only a simple, or loose, form of structure to execute it. Decisions can be centralized in the hands of a single senior manager, while complexity and formalization will be low.

As organizations grow, their strategies become more ambitious and elaborated. From the single product line, companies often expand their activities within their industry. This vertical integration strategy makes for increased interdependence between organizational units and creates the need for a more complex coordination device. This is achieved by redesigning the structure to form specialized units based on functions performed.

Finally, if growth proceeds further into product diversification, structure needs to be adjusted again to gain efficiency. A product diversification strategy demands a structural form that allows for the efficient allocation of resources, accountability for performance, and coordination between units. This can be achieved best by creating many independent divisions, each responsible for a specified product line.

In summary, Chandler's thesis argued that as strategies move from single product through vertical integration to product diversification, management will need to develop more elaborate structures to maintain effectiveness. That is, they will begin with an organic structure and, over time, move to a more mechanistic structure.

CONTEMPORARY RESEARCH ON THE STRATEGY–STRUCTURE THESIS More recent research confirms the strategy–structure thesis, but the notion of strategy has been rethought from Chandler's original framework.[4] Most strategy frameworks now focus on three strategy dimensions—innovation, cost minimization, and imitation—and the structural design that works best with each.

Innovation Strategy A strategy that emphasizes the introduction of major new products or services.

To what degree does an organization introduce major new products or services? An **innovation strategy** does not mean a strategy merely for simple or cosmetic changes from previous offerings but rather one for meaningful and unique innovations. Obviously, not all firms pursue innovation. This strategy may appropriately characterize 3M Co., but it certainly is not a strategy pursued by Reader's Digest.

Cost-Minimization Strategy A strategy that emphasizes tight cost controls, avoidance of unnecessary innovation or marketing expenses, and price-cutting.

An organization that is pursuing a **cost-minimization strategy** tightly controls costs, refrains from incurring unnecessary innovation or marketing expenses, and cuts prices in selling a basic product. This would describe the strategy pursued by Wal-Mart or the sellers of generic grocery products.

Imitation Strategy A strategy that seeks to move into new products or new markets only after their viability has been already proven.

Organizations following an **imitation strategy** try to capitalize on the best of both of the previous strategies. They seek to minimize risk and maximize opportunity for profit. Their strategy is to move into new products or new markets only after viability has been proven by innovators. They take the successful ideas of innovators and copy them. Manufacturers of mass-marketed fashion goods that are rip-offs of designer styles follow the imitation strategy. This label also probably characterizes such well-known firms as IBM and Caterpillar. They essentially follow their smaller and more innovative competitors with superior products, but only after their competitors have demonstrated that the market is there.

Table 15–1 describes the structural option that best matches each strategy. Innovators need the flexibility of the organic structure, while cost minimizers seek the efficiency and stability of the mechanistic structure. Imitators combine the two structures. They use a mechanistic structure in order to maintain tight controls and low costs in their current activities, while at the same time they create organic subunits in which to pursue new undertakings.

TABLE 15–1   Contemporary Strategy-Structure Thesis

Strategy	Structural Option
Innovation	**Organic:** A loose structure; low division of labor, low formalization, decentralized
Cost minimization	**Mechanistic:** Tight control; extensive division of labor, high formalization, high centralization
Imitation	**Mechanistic and organic:** Mix of loose with tight properties; tight controls over current activities and looser controls for new undertakings

Organization Size

A quick glance at the organizations we deal with regularly in our lives would lead most of us to conclude that **size** would have some bearing on an organization's structure. The more than 800,000 employees of the United States Postal Service, for example, do not neatly fit into one building, or into several departments supervised by a couple of managers. It's pretty hard to envision 800,000 people being organized in any manner other than one that contains a great deal of horizontal, vertical, and spatial differentiation, uses a large number of procedures and regulations to ensure uniform practices, and follows a high degree of decentralized decision making. On the other hand, a local messenger service that employs ten people and generates less than $300,000 a year in service fees is not likely to need decentralized decision making or formalized procedures and regulations.

A little more thought suggests that the same conclusion—size influences structure—can be arrived at through a more sophisticated reasoning process. As an organization hires more operative employees, it will attempt to take advantage of the economic benefits of specialization. The result will be increased horizontal differentiation. Grouping like functions together will facilitate intragroup efficiencies, but will cause intergroup relations to suffer as each performs its different activities. Management, therefore, will need to increase vertical differentiation to coordinate the horizontally differentiated units. This expansion in size is also likely to result in spatial differentiation. All of this increase in complexity will reduce top management's ability to directly supervise the activities within the organization. The control achieved through direct surveillance, therefore, will be replaced by the implementation of formal rules and regulations. This increase in formalization may also be accompanied by still greater vertical differentiation as management creates new units to coordinate the expanding and diverse activities of organizational members. Finally, with top management further removed from the operating level, it becomes difficult for senior executives to make rapid and informative decisions. The solution is to substitute decentralized decision making for centralization. Following this reasoning, we see changes in size leading to major structural changes.

But does it actually happen this way? Does structure change directly as a result of a change in the total number of employees? A review of the evidence indicates that size has a significant influence on some, but certainly not all, elements of structure.

Size appears to have a decreasing rate of impact on complexity.[5] That is, increases in organization size are accompanied by initially rapid and subsequently more gradual increases in differentiation. The biggest effect, however, is on vertical differentiation.[6] As organizations increase their number of employees, more levels are added, but at a decreasing rate.

The evidence linking size and formalization is quite strong.[7] There is a logical connection between the two. Management seeks to control the behavior of its employees. This can be achieved by direct surveillance or by the use of formalized regulations. While not perfect substitutes for each other, as one increases, the need for the other should decrease. Because surveillance costs should increase very rapidly as an organization expands in size, it seems reasonable to expect that it would be less expensive for management to substitute formalization for direct surveillance as size increases.

There is also a strong inverse relationship between size and centralization.[8] In small organizations, it's possible for management to exercise control by keeping decisions centralized. As size increases, management is physically unable to maintain control in this manner and, therefore, is forced to decentralize.

Technology

The term **technology** refers to how an organization transfers its inputs into outputs. Every organization has at least one technology for converting financial, human, and physical resources into products or services. The Ford Motor Co., for instance, predominantly uses an assembly-line process to make its products. On the other hand, colleges may use a number of instruction technologies—the ever-popular formal lecture method, the case analysis method, the experiential exercise method, the programmed learning method, and so forth.

The central theme in this section is that organization structures adapt to their technology. That is, technology is a major determinant of an organization's structure.

JOAN WOODWARD   The initial interest in technology as a determinant of structure can be traced to the work of Joan Woodward.[9] She studied nearly one hundred small manufacturing firms in the south of England to determine the extent to which classical principles such as unity of command and span of control were related to firm success. She was unable to derive any consistent pattern from her data until she segmented her firms into three categories based on the size of their production runs. The three categories, representing three distinct technologies, had increasing levels of complexity and sophistication. The first category, **unit production,** comprised unit or small-batch producers that manufactured such custom products as tailor-made suits and turbines for hydroelectric dams. The second category, **mass production,** included large-batch or mass-production manufacturers that made items like refrigerators and automobiles. The third and most complex group, **process production,** included continuous-process producers like oil and chemical refiners.

Woodward found that: (1) distinct relationships existed between these technology classifications and the subsequent structure of the firms and (2) the effectiveness of the organizations was related to the "fit" between technology and structure.

For example, the degree of vertical differentiation increased with technical complexity. The median levels for firms in the unit, mass, and process categories were three, four, and six, respectively. More important, from an effectiveness standpoint, the more successful firms in each category clustered around the median for their production group. But not all the relationships were linear. As a case in point, the mass-production firms scored high in terms of overall complexity and formalization, whereas the unit and process firms rated low on these structural dimensions. Imposing rules and regulations, for instance, was impossible with the nonroutine technology of unit production and unnecessary in the highly standardized process technology.

After carefully analyzing her findings, Woodward concluded that specific structures were associated with each of the three categories and that successful firms met the requirements of their technology by adopting the proper structural arrangements. Within each category, the firms that most nearly conformed to the median figure for each structural component were the most effective. She found that there was no one best way to organize a manufacturing firm. Unit and process production are most effective when matched with an organic structure; mass production is most effective when matched with a mechanistic structure. A summary of Woodward's findings is shown in Table 15–2.

TABLE 15–2 Woodward's Findings on Technology, Structure, and Effectiveness

	Unit Production	Mass Production	Process Production
Structural characteristics	Low vertical differentiation	Moderate vertical differentiation	High vertical differentiation
	Low horizontal differentiation	High horizontal differentiation	Low horizontal differentiation
	Low formalization	High formalization	Low formalization
Most effective structure	Organic	Mechanistic	Organic

CHARLES PERROW   One of the major limitations of Woodward's technological classification scheme was that it applied only to manufacturing organizations. Since manufacturing firms represent less than half of all organizations, technology needed to be operational in a more generic way if the concept was to have meaning across all organizations. Charles Perrow suggested such an alternative.[10]

Perrow directed his attention to knowledge technology rather than production technology. He proposed that technology be viewed in terms of two dimensions: (1) the number of exceptions individuals encountered in their work and (2) the type of search procedures followed to find successful methods for responding adequately to these exceptions. The first dimension he termed **task variability;** the second he called **problem analyzability.**

The exceptions in task variability are few when the job is high in routineness. Examples of jobs that normally have few exceptions in their day-to-day practice are a worker on a manufacturing assembly line and a fry cook at McDonald's. At the other end of the spectrum, if a job has a great deal of variety, it will have a large number of exceptions. This would characterize top-management positions, consulting jobs, and jobs such as putting out fires on offshore oil platforms.

The second dimension, problem analyzability, assesses search procedures. The search can, at one extreme, be described as well defined. An individual can use logical and analytical reasoning in the search for a solution. If you're basically a high B student and you suddenly fail the first exam in a course, you logically analyze the problem and find a solution. Did you spend enough time studying for the exam? Did you study the right material? Was the exam fair? How did other good students do? Using this kind of logic, you can find the source of the problem and rectify it. At the other extreme are ill-defined problems. If you're an architect given an assignment to design a building to conform to standards and constraints that you've never encountered or read about before, you won't have any formal search technique to use. You will have to rely on your prior experience, judgment, and intuition to find a solution. Through guesswork and trial and error you might find an acceptable choice.

Perrow used these two dimensions, task variability and problem analyzability, to construct a two-by-two matrix, shown in Figure 15–2. The four cells in this matrix represent four types of technology: routine, engineering, craft, and nonroutine.

Routine technologies (cell 1) have few exceptions and have easy-to-analyze problems. The mass-production processes used to make steel and automobiles or to refine petroleum belong in this category. Engineering technologies (cell 2) have a large number of exceptions, but they can be handled in a rational and systemized manner. The construction of bridges falls in this cat-

Task Variability The number of exceptions individuals encounter in their work.

Problem Analyzability The type of search procedures employees follow in responding to exceptions.

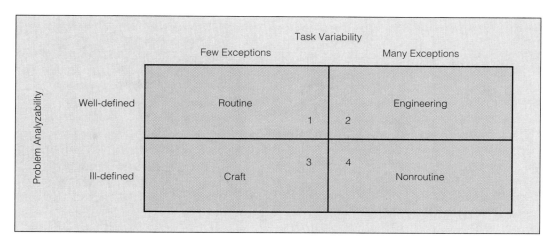

Task Variability

Few Exceptions | Many Exceptions

Problem Analyzability

Well-defined | Routine (1) | (2) Engineering

Ill-defined | (3) Craft | (4) Nonroutine

FIGURE 15–2   Perrow's Technology Classification

egory. Craft technologies (cell 3) deal with relatively difficult problems, but with a limited set of exceptions. Shoemaking and furniture restoring fit in this category. Finally, nonroutine technologies (cell 4) are characterized by many exceptions and by difficult-to-analyze problems. This technology describes many aerospace operations, such as NASA's development of the Hubble Space Telescope.

In summary, Perrow argued that if problems can be systematically analyzed, cells 1 and 2 are appropriate. Problems that can be handled only by intuition, guesswork, or unanalyzed experience require the technology of cells 3 or 4. Similarly, if new, unusual, or unfamiliar problems appear regularly, they would be in either cells 2 or 4. If problems are familiar, then cells 1 or 3 are appropriate. Using our mechanistic–organic classification, Perrow would suggest that cells 1 and 2 fit with mechanistic structures and cells 3 and 4 align with organic structures.

JAMES THOMPSON   Another approach to technology was proposed by James D. Thompson.[11] His technology categories, which he argued could be used to classify all organizations, are long-linked, mediating, and intensive.

If tasks or operations are sequentially interdependent, Thompson called them long-linked. This technology is characterized by a fixed sequence of repetitive steps, as shown in Figure 15–3A. That is, activity A must be performed before activity B, activity B before activity C, and so forth. Examples of **long-linked technology** are mass-production assembly lines and most school cafeterias.

Thompson identified **mediating technology** as one that links clients on both the input and output side of the organization. Banks, telephone utilities, most large retail stores, computer dating services, employment and welfare agencies, and post offices are examples. As shown in Figure 15–3B, mediators perform an interchange function, linking units that are otherwise independent. The linking unit responds by standardizing the organization's transactions and establishing conformity in clients' behavior. Banks, for instance, bring together those who want to save (depositors) with those who want to borrow. They don't know each other, but the bank's success depends on attracting both.

Thompson's third category—**intensive technology**—represents a customized response to a diverse set of contingencies. The exact response depends on the nature of the problem and the variety of problems, which cannot be predicted accurately. This includes technologies dominant in hos-

Long-Linked Technology
Tasks or operations that are sequentially interdependent.

Mediating Technology
Linking of independent units.

Intensive Technology   A customized response to a diverse set of contingencies.

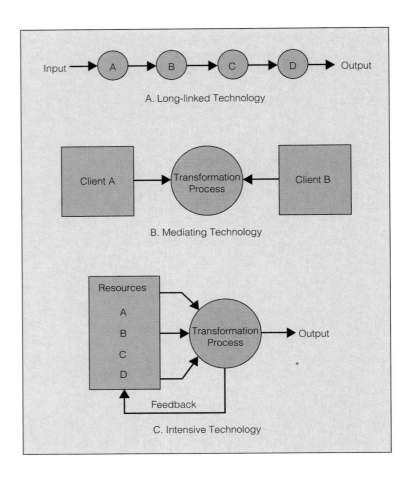

FIGURE 15–3
Thompson's Technology Classification

pitals, universities, research labs, full-service management-consulting firms, and military combat teams.

> The intensive technology is most dramatically illustrated by the general hospital. At any moment an emergency admission may require some combination of dietary, X-ray, laboratory, and housekeeping or hotel services, together with the various medical specialties, pharmaceutical services, occupational therapies, social work services, and spiritual or religious services. Which of these, and when, can be determined only from evidence about the state of the patient.[12]

Thompson was not directly concerned with demonstrating a link between his technology categories and structural options. Rather, he is most recognized for suggesting that organizations arrange themselves to protect their technology from uncertainty. He proposed that technology determines the selection of a strategy for reducing uncertainty and that specific structural arrangements can facilitate uncertainty reduction. So, for example, organizations using long-linked technology might vertically integrate to ensure the availability of inputs and the ability to dispose of its outputs.

While Thompson didn't directly address structural options, it is not difficult to make the connection. It seems logical that long-linked and mediating technologies tend to fit best with mechanistic structures, while intensive technology is best matched to the organic form.

SYNTHESIS   If there is a common denominator among the various classification schemes it is the *degree of routineness*. By this we mean that technologies tend toward either routine or nonroutine activities. The former are characterized by automated and standardized operations. This essentially encompasses mass, process, engineering, long-linked, and mediating technologies. Nonroutine activities are customized. They include such varied operations as furniture restoring, custom shoemaking, and genetic research. Nonroutine technologies include unit, craft, and intensive.

What relationships have been found between technology and the three components in our definition of structure? Although the relationship is not overwhelmingly strong, we do find that routine tasks are associated with high complexity. Repetition essentially encourages increased horizontal and vertical differentiation, which leads to taller and more complex structures.[13]

The technology–formalization relationship is stronger. Studies consistently show routineness to be associated with the presence of rule manuals, job descriptions, and other formalized documentation.[14]

Finally, the technology–centralization relationship is less straightforward. It seems logical that routine technologies would be associated with a centralized structure, whereas nonroutine technologies, which rely more heavily on the knowledge of specialists, would be characterized by delegated decision authority. This position has met with some support.[15] However, a more generalizable conclusion is that the technology–centralization relationship is moderated by the degree of formalization.[16] Formal regulations and centralized decision making are both control mechanisms and management can substitute one for the other. Routine technologies should be associated with centralized control if there is a minimum of rules and regulations. However, if formalization is high, routine technology can be accompanied by decentralization. So, we would predict that routine technology would lead to centralization, but only if formalization is low.

Environment

An organization's environment represents anything outside the organization itself. The problem of defining an organization's environment, however, is often quite difficult. "Nature has neatly packaged people into skins, animals into hides, and allowed trees to enclose themselves with bark. It is easy to see where the unit is and where the environment is. Not so for social organizations."[17] We'll define the **environment** as composed of those institutions or forces that are outside the organization and potentially affect the organization's performance. These typically include suppliers, customers, government regulatory agencies, and the like. But keep in mind that it is not always clear who or what is included in any specific organization's relevant environment.

Why should an organization's structure be affected by its environment? Because of environmental uncertainty. Some organizations face relatively static environments—few forces in their environment are changing. There are, for example, no new competitors, no new technological breakthroughs by current competitors, or little activity by public pressure groups to influence the organization. Other organizations face very dynamic environments—rapidly changing government regulations affecting their business, new competitors, difficulties in acquiring raw materials, continually changing product preferences by customers, and so on. Static environments create significantly less uncertainty for managers than do dynamic ones. And since uncertainty is a threat to an organization's effectiveness,

Environment Those institutions or forces outside the organization that potentially affect the organization's performance.

management will try to minimize it. One way to reduce environmental uncertainty is through adjustments in the organization's structure.

EMERY AND TRIST Fred Emery and Eric Trist identified four kinds of environments that an organization might confront: (1) placid–randomized, (2) placid–clustered, (3) disturbed–reactive, and (4) turbulent field.[18] Emery and Trist described each as increasingly more complex than the previous one.

Placid–Randomized Environment An environment in which demands are randomly distributed and change occurs slowly.

1. The **placid–randomized environment** is relatively unchanging and therefore poses the least threat to an organization. Demands are randomly distributed, and changes take place slowly over time. Environmental uncertainty is low. Although not many organizations are fortunate enough to find themselves in a placid–randomized environment, many state workers' compensation agencies enjoy this type of environment. Their environment is relatively stable, and no single client can have a significant impact on their operation.

Placid–Clustered Environment An environment in which change occurs slowly, but threats occur in clusters.

2. The **placid–clustered environment** also changes slowly, but presents clusters of threats to the organization. Thus an organization must be more aware of such an environment than it would of one in which threats occurred at random. For instance, suppliers or customers may join forces to form a powerful coalition. This would describe a public utility like Consolidated Edison. If Con Ed seeks a large rate hike, it faces a potential unified action by a mass of consumers. So organizations in a placid–clustered environment are motivated to engage in long-range, strategic planning, and to centralize their decision making.

Disturbed–Reactive Environment An environment dominated by one or more large organizations.

3. The **disturbed–reactive environment** is more complex than the previous two. Here many competitors seek similar ends. One or more organizations may be large enough to exert influence over their own environment and over other organizations. Two or three large companies in an industry can dominate it. A couple of large firms, for instance, can exert price leadership in such industries as business computers, automobiles, and tobacco. Compaq and Hewlett-Packard cannot afford to ignore the future plans or current actions of IBM. Organizations facing a disturbed–reactive environment need to be able to develop a series of tactical maneuvers, calculate reactions by others to their tactics, and evolve counteractions. In other words, they need to maintain a relative degree of flexibility.

Turbulent–Field Environment An environment that changes constantly and that contains interrelated elements.

4. The **turbulent-field environment** is the most dynamic and has the highest degree of uncertainty. Change is ever present, and elements in the environment are increasingly interrelated. In a turbulent-field environment, the organization may be required to consistently develop new products or services in order to survive. Also, it may have to reevaluate continually its relationship to government agencies, customers, and suppliers. Two obvious examples of organizations currently facing this type of environment are producers of microchips and business software programming.

Although Emery and Trist offered no specific suggestions concerning which type of structure best suited each environment, the first two environments will be responded to with more mechanistic structures, whereas the dynamic environments will require a structure that offers the advantages of the organic form.

LAWRENCE AND LORSCH Paul Lawrence and Jay Lorsch, both of the Harvard Business School, went beyond Emery and Trist. They undertook a study of ten firms in three industries to test empirically the relationship between environmental differences and effective organization structures.[19]

Lawrence and Lorsch chose to do their research on firms in the plastics, food, and container industries. (These were selected because they operated in what the researchers believed to be diverse environments.) The plastics industry was highly competitive. The life cycle of any product was historically short, and firms were characterized by considerable new-product and process development. The container industry, on the other hand, was quite different. There had been no significant new products in two decades. Sales growth had kept pace with population growth, but nothing more. Lawrence and Lorsch described the container firms as operating in a relatively certain environment, with no real threats to consider. The food industry was midway between the two. There was heavy innovation, but new-product generation and sales growth were less than in the plastics industry and more than in the container industry.

Lawrence and Lorsch measured two dimensions of structure: what they called *differentiation* and *integration*. **Differentiation** refers to the degree to which individuals in different functional departments vary in their goal and value orientations. **Integration** refers to the degree to which members of various departments achieve unity of effort.

First, they proposed that different departments within a firm face different environments. Therefore, they expected to find that the more successful firms in each industry would structure their departments to align with their specific subenvironments. That is, the same organization might have different structures across its departments. The research and development department, because it faces a turbulent environment, might use an organic structure, whereas production, if it has a stable environment, would be organized along mechanistic lines. Second, they hypothesized that the degree of differentiation within firms in the three industries was related to the environments they face, and that the more diverse the environments, the more differentiated the organization's structure. They expected the plastics firms to be the most differentiated, followed by food and container firms, in that order. Third, Lawrence and Lorsch proposed that, inside the organization, the more successful firms have achieved a higher degree of integration than the less successful firms. By that they meant that the successful firms would have devised more effective mechanisms for coordinating the various departments toward achieving the organization's overall goals.

Lawrence and Lorsch's research confirmed their expectations. Their firms did not all have uniform internal structures. It depended on whether or not the organizations faced a homogeneous environment. When they divided the firms within each industry into high, moderate, and low performers, they found that the high-performing firms had a structure that best fit their environmental demands. In the turbulent plastics industry, this meant high differentiation. In the stable container industry, this meant low differentiation. Firms in the food industry were midway in terms of differentiation. In addition, the most successful firms in all three industries had a higher degree of integration than their low-performing counterparts.

What are the implications of Lawrence and Lorsch's research? First, environments are not uniformly stable or turbulent. Organizations face multiple specific environments with different degrees of uncertainty. Second, successful organizations' departments or subunits meet the demands of their subenvironments. Because differentiation and integration represent opposing forces, the key is to appropriately match the two. An organization needs to differentiate enough to deal with the specific problems and tasks it faces; but the more differentiation, the more difficult it is to get people to integrate

Differentiation The degree to which individuals in different functional departments vary in their goal and value orientations.

Integration The degree to which members of various departments achieve unity of effort.

and work as a cohesive team toward the organization's goals. Successful organizations have more nearly solved the dilemma of providing both differentiation and integration by matching their internal subunits to the demands of the subenvironments. Finally, Lawrence and Lorsch presented evidence confirming that environment is critically important in determining the structure of successful organizations.

SYNTHESIS Recent research has synthesized much of the discussion on environmental uncertainty. It has been found that there are three key dimensions to any organization's environment. They are labeled capacity, volatility, and complexity.[20]

The capacity of an environment refers to the degree to which it can support growth. Rich and growing environments generate excess resources, which can buffer the organization in times of relative scarcity. Abundant capacity, for example, leaves room for an organization to make mistakes, while scarce capacity does not. In 1992, firms operating in the cellular-telephone business had relatively abundant environments, whereas those in the U.S. savings and loan industry faced relative scarcity.

The degree of instability in an environment is captured in the volatility dimension. Where there is a high degree of unpredictable change, the environment is dynamic. This makes it difficult for management to predict accurately the probabilities associated with various decision alternatives. At the other extreme is a stable environment. The accelerated changes in Eastern Europe and the demise of the Cold War had dramatic effects on the defense industry in the early 1990s. This moved the environment of major defense contractors like McDonnell-Douglas, General Dynamics, and Northrop from relatively stable to dynamic.

Finally, the environment needs to be assessed in terms of complexity; that is, the degree of heterogeneity and concentration among environmental elements. Simple environments are homogeneous and concentrated. This might describe the tobacco industry, since there are relatively few players. Its easy for firms in this industry to keep a close eye on the competition. In contrast, environments characterized by heterogeneity and dispersion are called complex. This is essentially the current environment in the computer

The end of the Cold War—characterized by the democratization of Eastern Europe and the dismantling of the Soviet Union's states—is a severe threat to Northrop's contract with the Air Force to build the B–2 bomber. The U.S. Senate may decide that the military no longer needs this plane's capabilities and cancel the contract.   UPI/Bettmann Newsphotos

National Culture Is Part of the Environment

Strategy, size, technology, and environment have been shown to be major factors influencing the structural design an organization has. Environment, of course, would include differences across national cultures.

In a country with a high-power-distance rating, people prefer that decisions be centralized. Similarly, uncertainty avoidance characteristics relate to formalization. That is, high uncertainty avoidance relates to high formalization. Based on these relationships, we should expect to find certain patterns. The French and Italians tend to create rigid mechanistic structures, high in both centralization and formalization. In India, preference is given to centralization and low formalization. Germans prefer formalization with decentralization.[21]

This suggests that multinational organizations face a real challenge. They have to balance the dual objectives of adjusting the structure of their units to the unique characteristics of each country in which they operate while, at the same time, developing uniform practices to facilitate interunit coordination. This may explain why many multinationals have had trouble in countries that differ significantly from their home country. In management's effort to achieve common standards of coordination and control, it has imposed standardized structures on its units. When those structures fit poorly with a country's culture, it results in lower organizational performance.

software business. Every day there is another "new kid on the block" with whom established software firms have to deal.

Figure 15–4 summarizes our definition of the environment along its three dimensions. The arrows in this figure are meant to indicate movement toward higher uncertainty. So organizations that operate in environments characterized as scarce, dynamic, and complex face the greatest degree of uncertainty. Why? Because they have little room for error, high unpredictability, and a diverse set of elements in the environment to constantly monitor.

Given this three-dimensional definition of environment, we can offer some general conclusions. There is evidence that relates the degrees of envi-

FIGURE 15–4
Three–Dimensional Model of the Environment

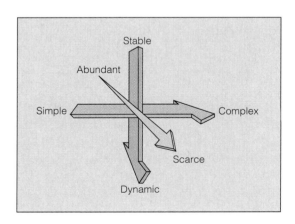

ronmental uncertainty to different structural arrangements. Specifically, the more scarce, dynamic, and complex the environment, the more organic a structure should be. The more abundant, stable, and simple the environment, the more the mechanistic structure will be preferred.

Power-Control

An increasingly popular and insightful approach to the question of what causes structure is to look to a political explanation. Strategy, size, technology, and environment—even when combined—can at best explain only fifty to sixty percent of the variability in structure.[22] There is a growing body of evidence that suggests that power and control can explain a good portion of the residual variance. More specifically, the **power-control** explanation states that an organization's structure is the result of a power struggle by internal constituencies who are seeking to further their interests.[23] Like all decisions in an organization, the structural decision is not fully rational. Managers do not necessarily choose those alternatives that will maximize the organization's interest. They choose criteria and weight them so that the "best choice" will meet the minimal demands of the organization, and also satisfy or enhance the interests of the decision maker. Strategy, size, technology, and environmental uncertainty act as constraints by establishing parameters and defining how much discretion is available. Almost always, within the parameters, there is a great deal of room for the decision maker to maneuver. The power-control position, therefore, argues that those in power will choose a structure that will maintain or enhance their control. Consistent with this perspective, we should expect structures to change very slowly, if at all. Significant changes would occur only as a result of a political struggle in which new power relations evolve. But this rarely occurs. Transitions in the executive suite are usually peaceful. They are evolutionary rather than revolutionary. However, major shake-ups in top management occasionally do occur. Not surprisingly, they are typically followed by major structural changes.

Predictions based on the power-control viewpoint differ from those based on the four previous approaches in that those approaches were basically contingency models: Structures change to reflect changes in strategy, size, technology, or environmental uncertainty. The power-control approach, however, is essentially noncontingent. It assumes little change within the organization's power coalition. Hence, it would propose that structures are relatively stable over time. More important, power-control advocates would predict that after taking into consideration strategy, size, technology, and environmental factors, those in power would choose a structure that would best serve their personal interests. What type of structure would that be? Obviously one that would be low in complexity, high in formalization, and centralized. These structural dimensions will most likely maximize control in the hands of senior management. A structure with these properties becomes the single "one best way" to organize. Of course, *best* in this context refers to "maintenance of control" rather than enhancement of organizational performance.

Is the power-control position an accurate description? The evidence suggests that it explains a great deal of why organizations are structured the way they are.[24] The dominant structural forms in organizations today are essentially mechanistic. Organic structures have received a great deal of attention by academicians, but the vast majority of real organizations, especially those of moderate and large size, are mechanistic.

Power-control View of Structure An organization's structure is the result of a power struggle by internal constituencies who are seeking to further their interests.

Applying the Contingency Factors

Under what conditions would each of the contingency factors we've introduced—strategy, organization size, technology, and environment—be the dominant determinant of an organization's structure? More specifically, when should we expect to find mechanistic structures and when should organic structures be most prevalent?

STRATEGY   The strategy-determines-structure thesis argues that managers change their organization's structure to align with changes in strategy. Organizations that seek innovation demand a flexible structure. Organizations that attempt to be low-cost operators must maximize efficiency, and the mechanistic structure helps achieve that. Those organizations that pursue an imitation strategy need structures that contain elements of both the mechanistic and the organic forms.

Studies generally support that strategy influences structure at the top levels of business firms.[25] But strategy undoubtedly has less impact on the structure of subunits within the overall organization. Additionally, it is not clear how the strategy–structure relationship operates in service businesses or among not-for-profit organizations such as hospitals, educational institutions, and government agencies.

ORGANIZATION SIZE   The larger an organization's size, in terms of the number of members it employs, the more likely it is to use the mechanistic structure. The creation of extensive rules and regulations only makes sense when there is a large number of people to be coordinated. Similarly, given the fact that a manager's ability to supervise a set of subordinates directly has some outside limit, as more people are hired to do the work, more managers will be needed to oversee these people. This creates increased complexity.

We should not, however, expect the size–structure relationship to be linear over a wide range. This is because once an organization becomes relatively large—with fifteen hundred to two thousand employees or more—it will tend to have already acquired most of the properties of a mechanistic structure. So the addition of five hundred employees to an organization that has only one hundred employees is likely to lead to significantly increased levels of complexity and formalization. Yet adding five hundred employees to an organization that already employs ten thousand is likely to have little or no impact on that organization's structure.

TECHNOLOGY   The evidence demonstrates that routine technologies are associated with mechanistic structures, whereas organic structures are best for dealing with the uncertainties inherent with nonroutine technologies. But we shouldn't expect technology to affect all parts of the organization equally.

The closer a department or unit within the organization is to the operating core, the more it will be affected by technology and, hence, the more technology will act to define structure. The primary activities of the organization take place at the operating core. State motor vehicle divisions, for example, process driver's license applications, distribute vehicle license plates, and monitor the ownership of vehicles within their state. Those departments within the motor vehicle division that are at the operating core—giving out driver's tests, collecting fees for plates, and so on—will be significantly affected by technology. But as units become removed from this core, technology will play a less important role. The structure of the executive offices at the motor vehicle division, for instance, are not likely to be affected much by technology. So, to continue with the motor

Computers and Organization Design

When organizations introduce sophisticated, computer-based management information systems, they are changing technology. For instance, a computer-based MIS lessens the need to depend on direct supervision and staff reports as control mechanisms. A senior executive can monitor what's going on on the operating floor or in the accounts payable department by simply pushing a few keys on his or her desktop terminal. And such changes in technology have a very real effect on the organization's structure.[26] The most obvious result: Organizations become flatter and more organic.

Computer-based information systems allow managers to handle more subordinates because computer control substitutes for personal supervision. As a result, managers can effectively oversee more people and the organization will require fewer managers and, hence, there will be fewer levels in the hierarchy. The need for staff support is also reduced with a computer-based information system. Managers can tap information directly, which makes large staff support groups redundant. Both forces—wider spans of supervision and reduced staff—lead to flatter organizations.

One of the more interesting phenomena created by sophisticated information systems is that they have allowed management to make organizations more organic without any loss in control.[27] Management can lessen formalization and become more decentralized—thus making their organizations more organic—without giving up control. Why? An MIS substitutes computer control for rules and decision discretion. Computer technology rapidly apprises top managers of the consequences of any decision and allows them to take corrective action if the decision is not to their liking. Thus there's the appearance of decentralization without any commensurate loss of control.

---

vehicle example, the use of routine technology at the operating core should result in the units at the core being high in both complexity and formalization. As units within the division move farther away from activities at the operating core, technology will become less of a constraint on structural choices.

ENVIRONMENT   Will a dynamic and uncertain environment always lead to an organic structure? Not necessarily. Whether environment is a major determinant of an organization's structure depends on the degree of dependence of the organization on its environment.

IBM operates in a highly dynamic environment—the result of a continual stream of new competitors introducing products to compete against theirs. But IBM's size, reputation for quality and service, and marketing expertise act as potent forces to lessen the impact of this uncertain environment on IBM's performance. IBM's ability to lessen its dependence on its environment results in a structure that is much more mechanistic in design than would be expected given the uncertain environment within which it exists. In contrast, firms like Apple Computer and Digital Equipment Corporation have been far less successful in managing their dependence on their environment. Environment, therefore, is a much stronger influence on Apple and DEC's structure than at IBM.

Now it's time to move from the general to the specific. While up to this point we've used the terms *mechanistic* and *organic* to classify organizations, these labels are too generic and abstract to be of much practical value. They really don't capture much of the details in actual organization designs. In this section, we'll present Henry Mintzberg's work, which develops a richer classification scheme that allows us to discuss organization designs and their impact on employee behavior.

Common Elements in Organizations

Mintzberg proposes that there are five basic parts to any organization.[28] They are shown in Figure 15–5 and defined as follows:

Operating Core Employees who perform the basic work related to the production of products and services.

Strategic Apex Top-level managers.

Middle Line Managers who connect the operating core to the strategic apex.

Technostructure Analysts in the organization.

Support Staff People in an organization who fill the staff units.

1. **The operating core.** Employees who perform the basic work related to the production of products and services.
2. **The strategic apex.** Top-level managers, who are charged with the overall responsibility for the organization.
3. **The middle line.** Managers who connect the operating core to the strategic apex.
4. **The technostructure.** Analysts, who have the responsibility for effecting certain forms of standardization in the organization.
5. **The support staff.** People who fill the staff units, who provide indirect support services for the organization.

Any one of these five parts can dominate an organization. Moreover, depending on which part is in control, a given structural configuration is likely to be used. So, according to Mintzberg, there are five distinct design configurations, and each one is associated with the domination by one of the five basic parts. If control lies with the operating core, decisions are decentralized. This creates the *professional bureaucracy*. When the strategic apex is dominant, control is centralized and the organization is a *simple structure*. If middle management is in control, you'll find groups of essentially autonomous units operating in a *divisional structure*. Where the analysts in

FIGURE 15–5   Five Basic Elements of an Organization
Source: H. Mintzberg, *Structure in Fives: Designing Effective Organizations,* © 1983, p. 194. Reprinted by permission of Prentice Hall, Englewood Cliffs, NJ.

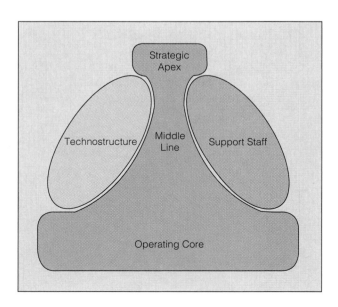

the technostructure are dominant, control will be through standardization, and the resultant structure will be a *machine bureaucracy*. Finally, in those situations where the support staff rules, control will be via mutual adjustment and the *adhocracy* arises.

Let's look at these five designs, present each one's strengths and weaknesses, and consider what effect each might have on its members.

The Simple Structure

What do a small retail store, an electronics firm run by a hard-driving entrepreneur, a new Planned Parenthood office, and an airline in the midst of a companywide pilot's strike have in common? They probably all utilize the simple structure.

The simple structure is said to be characterized most by what it is not rather than what it is. The simple structure is not elaborated.[29] It is low in complexity, has little formalization, and has authority centralized in a single person. As shown in Figure 15–6, the **simple structure** is depicted best as a flat organization, with an organic operating core and almost everyone reporting to a one-person strategic apex where the decision-making power is centralized.

Simple Structure A structure characterized by low complexity, low formalization, and authority centralized in a single person.

STRENGTHS AND WEAKNESSES   The strength of the simple structure lies in its simplicity. It's fast and flexible and requires little cost to maintain. There are no layers of cumbersome structure. Accountability is clear. There is a minimum amount of goal ambiguity because members are able to identify readily with the organization's mission, and it is fairly easy to see how one's actions contribute to the organization's goals.

The simple structure's predominant weakness is its limited applicability. When confronted with increased size, this structure generally proves inadequate. Additionally, the simple structure concentrates power in one person. Rarely does the structure provide countervailing forces to balance the chief executive's power. Therefore, the simple structure can easily succumb to the abuse of authority by the person in power. This concentration of power, of course, can work against the organization's effectiveness and survival. The simple structure, in fact, has been described as the "riskiest of structures hinging on the health and whims of one individual."[30] One heart attack can literally destroy the organization's decision-making center.

BEHAVIORAL IMPLICATIONS   Many people enjoy working in a small, intimate organization under a strong leader. It's easy for employees to feel involved in a simple structure. Because they tend to be small, these organizations also provide high task identity. Employees can readily relate to the organization's goals and see how their work contributes to those goals.

FIGURE 15–6   The Simple Structure
Source: H. Mintzberg, *Structure in Fives: Designing Effective Organizations,* © 1983, p. 159. Reprinted by permission of Prentice Hall, Englewood Cliffs, NJ

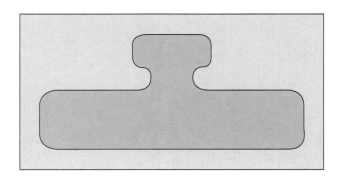

Decision making in the simple structure is basically informal. All important decisions are centralized in the senior executive, who, because of the organization's low complexity, can obtain key information readily and act rapidly when required. In addition, since complexity is low and decision making is centralized, the owner–manager of this clothing store can manage effectively with a wide span of control.
Peter Menzel/Stock, Boston

Simple structures can be especially exciting for employees when an organization is new and entrepreneurial. Apple Computer and Microsoft, for instance, began as simple structures. Reports by those who were part of these organizations' early years indicate they experienced a kind of psychological "rush" by being part of something new and innovative.

How individuals respond to the simple structure largely depends on their relationship to the central authority figure. Since one boss "calls the shots," the interpersonal relations between the boss and employees becomes critical in determining employee satisfaction. At its worst, the simple structure becomes highly restrictive and paternalistic. "Big brother" is constantly watching over you and all important decisions will be made, or at least approved, by the person in power.

The Machine Bureaucracy

Standardization! That's the key concept that underlies all machine bureaucracies. Take a look at the bank where you keep your checking account; the department store where you buy your clothes; or the government offices that collect your taxes, enforce health regulations, or provide local fire protection. They all rely on standardized work processes for coordination and control.

Machine Bureaucracy A structure that rates high in complexity, formalization, and centralization.

The **machine bureaucracy** has highly routine operating tasks, very formalized rules and regulations, tasks that are grouped into functional departments, centralized authority, decision making that follows the chain of command, and an elaborate administrative structure with a sharp distinction between line and staff activities. It is Mintzberg's operationalizing of what we've been calling the mechanistic structure.

Figure 15–7 depicts the machine bureaucracy. Rules and regulations permeate the entire structure. While not explicitly evident from Figure 15–7, the key part of this design is the technostructure. That's because this is where the staff analysts who do the standardizing—time-and-motion engineers, job-description designers, planners, budgeters, accountants, auditors, systems-and-procedures analysts—are housed.

STRENGTHS AND WEAKNESSES The primary strength of the machine bureaucracy lies in its ability to perform standardized activities in a highly

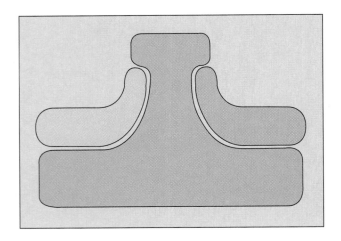

FIGURE 15–7   The Machine Beureaucrac
Source: H. Mintzberg, *Structure in Fives: Designing Effective Organizations,* © 1983, p. 170. Reprinted by permission of Prentice Hall, Englewood Cliffs, NJ.

efficient manner. Putting like specialties together results in economies of scale, minimization of duplication of personnel and equipment, and comfortable and satisfied employees who have the opportunity to talk "the same language" among their peers. Further, machine bureaucracies can get by nicely with less talented—and, hence, less costly—middle- and lower-level managers. The pervasiveness of rules and regulations substitute for managerial discretion. Standardized operations, coupled with high formalization, allow decision making to be centralized. There is little need, therefore, for innovative and experienced decision makers below the level of senior executives.

One of the major weaknesses of the machine bureaucracy is illustrated in the following dialogue between four executives in one company: "Ya know, nothing happens in this place until we *produce* something," said the production executive. "Wrong," commented the research-and-development manager, "nothing happens until we *design* something!" "What are you talking about?" asked the marketing executive. "Nothing happens here until we *sell*

Government agencies, like this Internal Revenue Service office, are typically machine bureaucracies. They rate high in complexity, have numerous rules and procedures that employees must follow, and concentrate decision authority in high–ranking officials.
Andrew Popper/Picture Group

something!" Finally, the exasperated accounting manager responded, "It doesn't matter what you produce, design or sell. No one knows what happens until we *tally up the results!"*

This conversation points up the fact that specialization creates subunit conflicts. Functional unit goals can override the overall goals of the organization.

The other major weakness of the machine bureaucracy is something we've all experienced at one time or another when having to deal with people who work in these organizations: obsessive concern with following the rules. When cases arise that don't precisely fit the rules, there is no room for modification. The machine bureaucracy is efficient only as long as employees confront problems that they have previously encountered and for which programmed decision rules have already been established.

BEHAVIORAL IMPLICATIONS   The machine bureaucracy is obsessed with control. But, in contrast to the simple structure where control is exercised through direct supervision, the machine bureaucracy achieves its control over people through rules and regulations. Consistent with our discussion of power-control, we should expect that top management will like this design.

Whether or not employees like the machine bureaucracy and perform well under its restrictions depends on their bureaucratic orientation. (See Exercise 15–A at the end of this chapter.) For people who enjoy routine work, this structure provides security and regularity. High division of labor, high formalization, narrow spans of control, and limited decision discretion make jobs seem menial. For the most part, jobs in this structure will score low on skill variety, task identity, task significance, and autonomy. So employee alienation often surfaces in response to unchallenging job tasks and management's obsession with ensuring that everyone follow the rules, with a feeling that they are treated as machines rather than human beings with individual needs and concerns.

The Professional Bureaucracy

Professional Bureaucracy A structure that rates high in complexity and formalization, and low in centralization.

The last quarter of a century has seen the birth of a new structural animal. It has been created to allow organizations to hire highly trained specialists for the operating core, while still achieving the efficiencies from standardization. The configuration is called the **professional bureaucracy,** and it combines standardization with *decentralization.*

The jobs that people do today increasingly require a high level of specialized expertise. An undergraduate college degree is required for more and more jobs. So, too, are graduate degrees. The knowledge explosion has created a whole class of organizations that require professionals to produce their goods and services. Obvious examples are hospitals, school districts, universities, museums, libraries, engineering design firms, social service agencies, and public accounting firms. This has created the need for an organizational design that substitutes *individuals* who are specialized for *work* that is specialized. By hiring professionals, who through years of schooling and training have mastered specific skills, the organization can free them up to perform their activities relatively autonomously.

Figure 15–8 illustrates the configuration for professional bureaucracies. The power in this design rests with the operating core because they have the critical skills that the organization needs, and they have the autonomy—provided through decentralization—to apply their expertise. The only other part of the professional bureaucracy that is fully elaborated is the support staff, but their activities are focused on serving the operating core.[31]

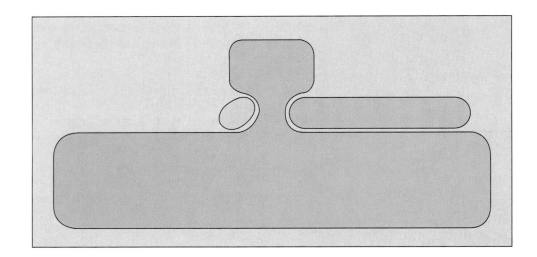

FIGURE 15–8   The Professional Bureaucracy
Source: H. Mintzberg, *Structure in Fives: Designing Effective Organizations*, © 1983, p. 194. Reprinted by permission of Prentice Hall, Englewood Cliffs, NJ.

STRENGTHS AND WEAKNESSES   The strength of the professional bureaucracy is that it can perform specialized tasks—ones that require the skills of highly trained professionals—with the same relative efficiency as the machine bureaucracy can. Why, then, you may ask, didn't management just choose the latter? It's not because management wouldn't *prefer* the machine form! In power-control terms, the professional bureaucracy requires top management to give up a considerable degree of control. But what's their alternative? The professionals need the autonomy to do their jobs effectively.

The weaknesses of the professional bureaucracy are the same as for the machine form. First, there is the tendency for subunit conflicts to develop. The various professional functions seek to pursue their own narrow objectives, often sublimating the interests of other functions and the organization as a whole. Second, the specialists in the professional bureaucracy, like their counterparts in the machine form, are compulsive in their determination to follow the rules. Only the rules in professional bureaucracies are the making of the professionals themselves. Standards of professional conduct and codes

The New York City Public Library, like most libraries, is a professional bureaucracy. Decision making is decentralized to free up professional librarians so they can perform their activities relatively autonomously.   Naoki Okamoto/Black Star

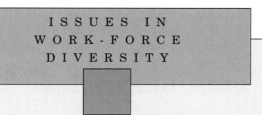

The Feminine Model of Organization

Organizational sociologist Joyce Rothschild argues that gender differences in values and moral principles often lead women to prefer an organizational form that is very different from the traditional bureaucratic structure. She calls this structure "the feminine model of organization."[32]

Rothschild has identified six characteristics for her feminine model:

1. *Values members as individual human beings.* People are treated as individuals, with individual values and needs, rather than as occupants of roles or offices.
2. *Nonopportunistic.* Relationships are seen as possessing value in themselves, not just as formal means to the achievement of organizational goals.
3. *Careers are defined in terms of service to others.* While organization members in the bureaucratic model define career success in terms of promotions, acquisition of power, and pay increases, organization members in the feminine model measure success in terms of service to others.
4. *Commitment to employee growth.* Feminine organizations create extensive personal growth opportunities for their members. Rather than emphasizing specialization and the development of narrow expertise, these organizations expand member skills and broaden employee competencies by offering new learning experiences.
5. *Creation of a caring community.* Members become closely bound in a community sense, much as in small towns where people have learned to trust and care for their neighbors.
6. *Power sharing.* In the traditional bureaucracy, information and decision-making authority are coveted and hierarchically allocated. In the feminine organization, information is generously shared. All members who will be affected by a decision are given the opportunity to participate in that decision.

According to Rothschild, the feminine model may be more effective and the model of choice in organizations that are essentially managed by and for women. This would include, but certainly not be limited to, rape crisis centers, battered women's shelters, and entrepreneurial firms that sell products directed to the female market such as Mary Kay Cosmetics. For instance, Rothschild studied several "new wave" clerical trade unions that were led by women and had mostly female members. She found that (1) their organizational structure more closely resembled the feminine model than a hierarchical bureaucratic one and (2) they succeeded in organizing female clerical and service-sector employees where the bureaucratically designed AFL-CIO unions had failed.

for ethical practices have been socialized into the employees during their training. So, for example, while lawyers or nurses have autonomy on their jobs, their professional standards of how their work is to be done can be a hindrance to an organization's effectiveness when the standards are rigid and unable to adjust to unique or changing conditions.

BEHAVIORAL IMPLICATIONS   This design provides employees with the best of both worlds: the benefits of being attached to a large organization, yet the freedom to serve clients as they see fit, constrained only by the standards of their profession. The professional bureaucracy, then, allows people with professional skills, high levels of education, and strong needs for autonomy to survive—even thrive—in a large organization.

In contrast to the machine bureaucracy, this design empowers its employees and creates enriched jobs. For professionals who are competent and conscientious, this structure should produce high job performance.

The Divisional Structure

General Motors, Hershey Foods, Du Pont, Burlington Industries, and Xerox are examples of organizations that use the divisional structure.

Divisional Structure   A set of autonomous units coordinated by a central headquarters.

As Figure 15–9 illustrates, the power in the divisional structure lies with middle management. The reason is that the **divisional structure** is actually a set of autonomous units, each typically a machine bureaucracy unto itself, coordinated by a central headquarters. Since the divisions are autonomous, it allows middle management—the division managers—a great deal of control.[33]

STRENGTHS AND WEAKNESSES   One of the problems associated with the machine bureaucracy is that the goals of the functional units tend to override the organization's overall goals. One of the strengths of the divisional structure is that it seeks to remedy this problem by placing full responsibility for a product or service in the hands of the divisional manager. So one of the advantages to the divisional structure is that it provides more accountability and focus on outcomes than does the machine bureaucracy alone.

Another strength of the divisional structure is that it frees up the headquarters staff from being concerned with the day-to-day operating details so they can pay attention to the long term. Big-picture, strategic decision making is done at headquarters. At General Motors, for instance, senior executives in Detroit can wrestle with the world's future transportation needs while the division managers can go about the business of producing Chevrolets and Buicks as efficiently as possible.

It should be obvious that the autonomy and self-containment characteristics of the divisional form make it an excellent vehicle for training and developing general managers. This is a distinct advantage over the machine bureaucracy and its emphasis on specialization. That is, the divisional structure gives managers a broad range of experience with the autonomous units.

It's evident that the real strengths of the divisional form come from its creation of self-contained "businesses within a business." The divisions have

FIGURE 15–9   The Divisional Structure
Source: H. Mintzberg, *Structure in Fives: Designing Effective Organizations,* © 1983, p. 225. Reprinted by permission of Prentice Hall, Englewood Cliffs, NJ.

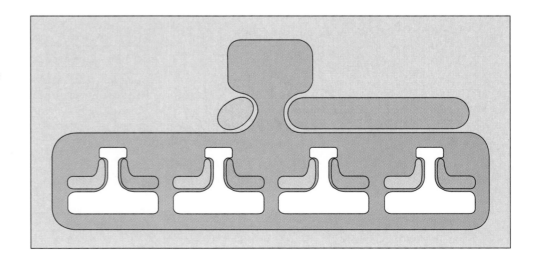

the responsiveness, the accountability, and the benefits of specialization and are able to process information as if they were organizations unto themselves. Yet they also have the benefits of large size that allow economies of scale in planning, acquisition of capital, and spreading of risk. Returning to our example of General Motors, when its Saturn Corporation needs $500 million to build a new plant, GM is able to borrow that money at a rate several percentage points below what Saturn could negotiate if it were not part of General Motors. Similarly, that division can be provided with legal expertise that could never be available "in house" if Saturn were a separate corporation independent of GM.

Let us turn now to the weaknesses of the divisional structure, of which there are no shortage. First is the duplication of activities and resources. Each division, for instance, may have a marketing research department. In the absence of autonomous divisions, all the organization's marketing research might be centralized and done for a fraction of the cost that divisionalization requires. So the divisional form's duplication of functions increases the organization's costs and reduces efficiency.

Another disadvantage is the propensity of the divisional form to stimulate conflict. There is little incentive in this structural design for cooperation among divisions. Further conflicts are created as divisions and headquarters argue about where to locate support services. The more the divisions succeed in having these services decentralized to their level, the less dependent they are on headquarters and, hence, the less power headquarter's personnel can wield over them.

The autonomy of the divisions, to the degree that it is more theory than practice, can breed resentment in the division managers. While the structure gives general autonomy to the divisions, the autonomy is exercised within constraints. The division manager is being held fully accountable for results in his or her unit, but because he or she must operate within the uniform policies imposed from headquarters, the manager is likely to be resentful and argue that his or her authority is less than the responsibility.

Finally, the divisional form creates coordination problems. Personnel are frequently unable to transfer between divisions, especially when the divisions operate in highly diverse product or service markets. Du Pont employees in the Remington Arms Division, for instance, have little transferability to the Textile Fibers or Petro-Chemicals divisions. This reduces the flexibility of headquarters' executives to allocate and coordinate personnel.

BEHAVIORAL IMPLICATIONS   In giant corporations, where you're most likely to find this design, the divisional structure concentrates enormous amounts of power in very few hands. In this sense, it is not unlike the machine bureaucracy. In fact, the behavioral implications of the divisional structure are the same as those of the machine bureaucracy since the former is nothing more than a grouping of machine bureaucracies under a common umbrella.

The Adhocracy

When Steven Spielberg or Woody Allen goes about making a film, he brings together a diverse group of professionals. This team—composed of producers, scriptwriters, film editors, set designers, and hundreds of other specialists—exists for the singular purpose of making a single movie. They may be called back by Spielberg or Allen when they begin another film, but that is irrelevant when the current project begins. These professionals frequently find themselves with overlapping activities because no formal rules or regulations are provided to guide them. While there is a production schedule, it often must be modified to take into consideration unforeseen contingencies. The film's production team may be together for a few months, or, in some unusual cases, for several years. But the organization is temporary. In contrast to bureaucracies or divisional structures, the filmmaking organizations have no entrenched hierarchy, no permanent departments, no formalized rules, and no standardized procedures for dealing with routine problems. Welcome to our last design configuration: the **adhocracy.** It's characterized by high horizontal differentiation, low vertical differentiation, low formalization, decentralization, and great flexibility and responsiveness. As such, it is synonymous with the organic structure.

Horizontal differentiation is great because adhocracies are staffed predominantly by professionals with a high level of expertise. Vertical differentiation is low because the many levels of administration would restrict the organization's ability to adapt. Also, the need for supervision is minimal because professionals have internalized the behaviors that management wants.

There are few rules and regulations in adhocracies. Those that exist tend to be loose and unwritten. The reason is that flexibility demands an absence of formalization. Rules and regulations are effective only where standardization of behavior is sought. In this context, it may be valuable to compare the professional bureaucracy with adhocracy. Both employ professionals. The key difference is that the professional bureaucracy, when faced with a problem, immediately classifies it into some standardized program so that the professionals can treat it in a uniform manner. In an adhocracy, a novel solution is needed, so standardization and formalization are inappropriate.

Decision making in adhocracies is decentralized. This is necessary for speed and flexibility and because senior management cannot be expected to possess the expertise necessary to make all decisions. So the adhocracy depends on decentralized teams of professionals for decision making.

The adhocracy is a very different design from those we've encountered earlier. This can be seen in Figure 15–10. Because the adhocracy has little standardization or formalization, the technostructure is almost nonexistent. Because middle managers, the support staff, and operatives are typically all professionals, the traditional distinctions between supervisor and employee and line and staff become blurred. The result is a central pool of expert tal-

Adhocracy A structure characterized as low in complexity, formalization, and centralization.

The crew that Steven Spielberg brings together for filming the "Indiana Jones" series is organized as an adhocracy.   SIPA Press

FIGURE 15–10   The Adhocracy   Source: H. Mintzberg, *Structure in Fives: Designing Effective Organizations,* © 1983, p. 262. Reprinted by permission of Prentice Hall, Englewood Cliffs, NJ.

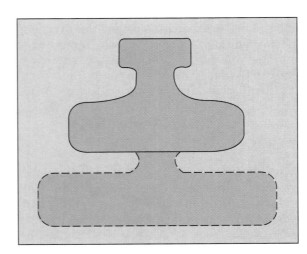

ent that can be drawn from to innovate, solve unique problems, and perform flexible activities. Power flows to anyone in the adhocracy with expertise, regardless of his or her position.[34]

Adhocracies are best conceptualized as groups of teams. Specialists are grouped together into flexible teams that have few rules, regulations, or standardized routines. Coordination between team members is through mutual adjustment. As conditions change, so do the activities of the members. But adhocracies don't have to be devoid of horizontally differentiated departments. Frequently, departments are used for clarity, but then department members are deployed into small teams, which cut across functional units, to do their tasks.

STRENGTHS AND WEAKNESSES The history of adhocracy can be traced to the development of task forces during World War II, when the military created ad hoc teams that were disbanded after completion of their missions. There was no rigid time span for their existence—teams could last a day, a month, or a year. Roles performed in the teams were interchangeable, and, depending upon the nature and complexity of the mission, the group could be divided into subunits, each responsible for different facets of the job to be performed. The advantages of these ad hoc teams included their ability to respond rapidly to change and innovation and to facilitate the coordination of diverse specialists. Fifty years have passed since World War II, but the advantage of ad hoc teams, or what we call adhocracy, continues today. When it is important that the organization be adaptable and creative, when individual specialists from diverse disciplines are required to collaborate to achieve a common goal, and when tasks are technical, nonprogrammed, and too complex for any one person to handle, the adhocracy represents a viable alternative.

On the negative side, conflict is a natural part of adhocracy. There are no clear boss–subordinate relationships. Ambiguities exist over authority and responsibilities. Activities cannot be compartmentalized. In short, adhocracy lacks the advantages of standardized work.

In contrast to bureaucracy, adhocracy is clearly an inefficient configuration. It is also a vulnerable design. As one author noted, "Many of them either die early or else shift to bureaucratic configurations to escape the uncertainty."[35] So why, you might ask, would it ever be used? Because its inefficiencies, in certain circumstances, are more than offset by the need for flexibility and innovation.

BEHAVIORAL IMPLICATIONS The adhocracy is the antithesis of the machine bureaucracy. Nothing is standardized. There are no rules or procedures. It's exhilarating for members because every day brings new and unexpected challenges. But with this exhilaration comes ambiguity and confusion.

Adhocracy can create social stress and psychological tension for its members. It is not easy to quickly set up and dismantle work relationships on a continuing basis. Some employees find it difficult to cope with rapid change, living in temporary work systems, and having to share responsibilities with other team members.

Adhocracy also creates highly competitive and, at times, ruthless work climates. Because there are no well-defined ground rules, politics can often run rampant. This can add further to employee stress and reduce job satisfaction.

THE MATRIX STRUCTURE

Matrix Structure A structure that creates dual lines of authority; combines functional and product departmentalization

Still another organizational design option is the **matrix structure.** You'll find it being used in advertising agencies, aerospace firms, research and development laboratories, construction companies, hospitals, government agencies, universities, management consulting firms, and entertainment companies.[36] Essentially, the matrix combines two forms of departmentalization—functional and product.

Combining Functions and Products

Referring back to our discussion in the previous chapter, the strength of functional departmentalization lies in putting like specialists together, which minimizes the number necessary, while it allows the pooling and sharing of specialized resources across products. Its major disadvantage is the difficulty of coordinating the tasks of diverse functional specialists so that their activities are completed on time and within budget. Product departmentalization, on the other hand, has exactly the opposite benefits and disadvantages. It facilitates coordination among specialties to achieve on-time completion and meet budget targets. Further, it provides clear responsibility for all activities related to a product, but with duplication of activities and costs. The matrix attempts to gain the strengths of each, while avoiding their weaknesses.

The most obvious structural characteristic of the matrix is that it breaks the unity-of-command concept. Employees in the matrix have two bosses—their functional department managers and their product managers. Therefore, the matrix has a dual chain of command.

Figure 15–11 shows the matrix form as used in a college of business administration. The academic departments of accounting, economics, marketing, and so forth are functional units. Additionally, specific programs (that is, products) are overlaid on the functions. In this way, members in a matrix structure have a dual assignment—to their functional department,

FIGURE 15–11   Matrix Structure for a College of Business Administration

Programs / Academic Departments	Undergraduate	Master's	Ph. D.	Research	Executive Programs	Community-Service Programs
Accounting						
Administrative Studies						
Economics						
Finance						
Marketing						
Organizational Behavior						
Quantitative Methods						

and to their product groups. For instance, a professor of accounting teaching an undergraduate course reports to the director of undergraduate programs as well as to the chairperson of the accounting department.

Strengths and Weaknesses

The strength of the matrix lies in its ability to facilitate coordination when the organization has a multiplicity of complex and interdependent activities. As an organization gets larger, its information-processing capacity can become overloaded. In a bureaucracy, complexity results in increased formalization. The direct and frequent contact between different specialties in the matrix can make for better communication and more flexibility. Information permeates the organization and more quickly reaches those people who need to take account of it. Further, the matrix reduces bureaupathologies. The dual lines of authority reduce tendencies of departmental members to become so busy protecting their little worlds that the organization's overall goals become secondary.

There are other advantages to the matrix. It facilitates the efficient allocation of specialists. When individuals with highly specialized skills are lodged in one functional department or product group, their talents are monopolized and underutilized. The matrix achieves the advantages of economies of scale by providing the organization with both the best resources and an effective way of ensuring their efficient deployment. Further advantages of the matrix are that it creates (1) increased ability to respond rapidly to changes in the environment, (2) an effective means for balancing the customer's or client's requirements for product performance with the organization's need for economic efficiency and development of technical capability for the future, and (3) increased motivation by providing an environment more in line with the democratic norms preferred by scientific and professional employees.[37]

The major disadvantages of the matrix lie in the confusion it creates, its propensity to foster power struggles, and the stress it places on individuals.[38] When you dispense with the unity-of-command concept, ambiguity is significantly increased and ambiguity often leads to conflict. For example, it's frequently unclear who reports to whom, and it is not unusual for product managers to fight over getting the best specialists assigned to their products. Confusion and ambiguity also create the seeds of power struggles. Bureaucracy reduces the potential for power grabs by defining the rules of the game. When those rules are "up for grabs," power struggles between functional and product managers result. For individuals who desire security and absence from ambiguity, this work climate can produce stress. Reporting to more than one boss introduces role conflict, and unclear expectations introduce role ambiguity. The comfort of bureaucracy's predictability is absent, replaced by insecurity and stress.

ORGANIZATIONS IN MOTION: GROWTH VS. DECLINE

To this point, we've treated organizations as static entities. In reality, of course, they're not. Organizations are fluid—in a constant state of change. Some are growing and expanding. Others are shrinking. In recent years, we've seen a definite trend toward the latter in North America. Terms such as *retrenchment, downsizing,* and *lean and mean* have become increasingly used to describe the direction in which management has been taking organizations in the last decade.

In this section, we'll briefly discuss the historical growth bias in organizations, what has precipitated the recent emphasis on making organizations smaller, and the differing effects that decline and growth have on employees in organizations.

The Growth Bias

There has been an historical bias, especially in the United States, toward growth.[39] It reflects an inherent optimism about the future that permeates American values. Let's look at a few ways in which this bias has infiltrated managerial thinking.

BIGGER IS BETTER One of the strong forces for growth has been the "bigger is better" notion in America. Although under attack in recent years, this view still has its advocates. For instance, many Americans still covet large incomes and large homes. This bias, when applied to organizations, was often couched in economic terms. Growth was desirable because with increases in size came economies of scale. Bigger, in fact, was frequently more efficient.

GROWTH INCREASES THE LIKELIHOOD OF SURVIVAL Large organizations are not permitted to go out of existence the way small organizations are. In 1980, for instance, the United States government came to the rescue of Chrysler Corporation by guaranteeing $1.5 billion in loans. Chrysler's large size alone assured it of strong constituencies who would fight for its survival. Wherever Chrysler had assembly plants, suppliers, bankers it owed money to, and dealers—which included just about every state in the Union—the company had supporters fighting for government assistance. Your community drugstore or laundromat, should it face financial difficulties, certainly would not attract that kind of support.

In addition to providing a large constituency, growth facilitates survival by providing more resources with which the organization can buffer itself against uncertainty. Larger organizations can make errors and live to talk about them. Similarly, more resources provide a buffer in times of setbacks. Growing organizations have slack resources that can be cut more easily than those of small or stable organizations.

GROWTH BECOMES SYNONYMOUS WITH EFFECTIVENESS Growth is often used by managers to imply success. Business executives flaunt that "sales are up significantly." Hospital administrators produce charts showing that they are handling more patients than ever. College deans brag about having record enrollments. If those in the environment on whom the organization depends for continued support—suppliers, customers, lenders, and the like—also equate growth with effectiveness, managers will obviously be predisposed to the values of growth.

GROWTH IS POWER Growth is almost always consistent with the self-interest of the top management in the organization. It increases prestige, power, and job security for this group. It should certainly be of more than passing interest to know that growth is linked to executive compensation. Size, in fact, is a better predictor of executive salaries than is profit margin.[40] Growth also provides an organization more power relative to other organizations and groups in its environment. Larger organizations have more influence with suppliers, unions, large customers, government, and the like.

Pressures Toward Retrenchment

The twenty-five-year period following World War II was generally a time of growth and prosperity for organizations in North America. The last two decades, however, have been a different story. It is the unusual Fortune 500 company that has *not* cut back the size of its operations in recent years. Instead of expanding markets and adding new divisions, companies have been selling off assets and cutting jobs. A recent survey of nine hundred-ten companies, for instance, found that fifty-six percent had eliminated jobs in the prior year.[41] Every week, business periodicals report corporate layoffs: Colgate-Palmolive lays off two thousand people world-wide; First Interstate Bancorp cuts thirty-five hundred; Digital Equipment Corp. eliminates thousands of jobs. Banks, savings and loans, airlines, advertising agencies, retailers, the Big Three television networks, and all the major automobile manufacturers have recently joined the downsizing trend. What, you may wonder, has brought this all about?

The initial impetus came from the dramatic increase in energy costs in the early 1970s. Oil and gas were no longer available in unlimited supplies at low costs. This jolted many industries and forced cutbacks.

The globalization of markets shocked many companies that had gotten fat by competing within protected borders. General Motors, as a case in point, found that Honda, Toyota, and a host of other foreign competitors could build higher-quality and more innovative products at extremely competitive prices. GM saw its United States market share drop by more than twenty-five percent, requiring the closing of inefficient plants and the layoff of tens of thousands of employees. The same also occurred in such other industries as steel, rubber, textiles, and consumer electronics.

Three other forces in the 1980s ganged up to further increase the pressures on management to shrink their organizations—reduction of inflation, aggressive corporate raiders, and expanded merger and acquisition activities. The stabilizing of inflation made it harder for companies to pass on higher costs to consumers, so management had to prune excessive costs. Corporate raiders aggressively sought out firms that were overstaffed and inefficient, then cut costs in order to improve profitability. Mergers and acquisitions (including leveraged buyouts) typically result in significant cutbacks to eliminate waste and redundant operations.

Effect on Employees

Growth creates opportunities to work on new projects, more promotion possibilities, and higher salary increases. It's not surprising that Apple Computer's management had no problem finding and keeping highly talented computer engineers in its early years. These employees, in the early 1980s, worked sixty or more hours a week, yet expressed very high levels of job satisfaction. Employee turnover was negligible. The reason, of course, was that Apple's rapid growth created exciting opportunities and enough excess resources to enable them to reward high performers generously.

Organizational retrenchment, unfortunately, creates a very different work climate. Let's look at what retrenchment does to organizations and their employees.[42]

CONFLICT   Growth creates slack that acts as a grease to smooth over conflict-creating forces. Management uses this slack as a currency for buying off potentially conflicting interest groups within the organization. Conflicts can be

Firing People During Retrenchment

There are few actions that managers find harder to take than firing an employee. Many managers confide that this task is especially hard when the reason is cost cutting. It's typically easier to justify firing someone who hasn't performed well—you can attribute the action to the employee: "If they had done a good job, I wouldn't have to let them go." But when an organization is downsizing and laying off large numbers of people, the task is tougher. It's often not the employee's fault. "I had eight years of excellent performance reviews," said a recently terminated graphic arts specialist. "They showed them to me. What have I done wrong? What have I done wrong?"[43]

Managers may argue that they have no alternatives. If the organization is to be competitive, costs have to be trimmed. Those organizations that "have a heart" and don't make the tough decisions will eventually fail in the marketplace to organizations that are "lean and mean." But do organizations have a moral obligation to repay their employees' long-term loyalty by providing job security?

Being fired can be devastating. Losing a job is not unlike suffering a divorce or the death of a close family member. It undermines people's self-esteem. It forces many to question their identity. It can cause mental illness, family breakups, and even suicides. And finding a new job can be a long and dehumanizing experience. For instance, one forty-four-year-old computer executive who was laid off reported that he sent out one hundred letters, answered two hundred ads, made twenty-five hundred phone calls, and exhausted $25,000 of savings during his job hunt.[44] And this guy was lucky; he found a job. One recent study found that among laid-off workers over fifty-five years of age, one in three is forced to leave the work force altogether.[45]

It's not as if there are no alternatives to firing people. For example, a few organizations are spreading the cutbacks among all their employees. Instead of firing twenty percent of their staff, they are having all employees cut their hours by twenty percent and take a commensurate pay cut.

Does an organization have an ethical obligation to keep its employees on the job? Or are employees no different from a machine or a piece of clothing—disposable when no longer needed?

resolved readily by expanding everyone's resources. However, in retrenchment, conflict over resources increases because there is less slack to divvy up.

POLITICKING Less slack also translates into more politicking. Many organized and vocal groups will emerge, each actively pursuing its own self-interest. Politically naive managers will find their jobs difficult, if not impossible, as they are unable to adjust to the changing decision-making criteria. Remember, in retrenchment, the pie of resources shrinks. If one department can successfully resist a cut, typically the result will be that other departments have to cut deeper. Weak units not only will take a disproportional part of the cut but may be most vulnerable to elimination. In a "fight-for-life" situation, the standard rules are disregarded. Critical data for decisions are twisted and interpreted by various coalitions so as to further their groups' interests. Such a climate encourages "no holds barred" politicking.

DECLINE IN WORK-FORCE DIVERSITY Retrenchment requires personnel cuts. The most popular criterion for determining who gets laid off is seniority; that is, the most recent hires are the first to go. Laying off personnel on the basis of seniority, however, tends to reshape the composition of the organization's work force. It makes that work force more homogeneous in terms of age, gender, and racial mix.

Since newer employees tend to be younger, seniority-based layoffs typically create an older work force. When organizations operating in mature industries are required to make substantial cuts, the average age of employees may increase ten years or more.

One of the most disheartening results of seniority-based layoffs is that it undermines much of the progress made in the past twenty-five years toward opening up job opportunities for women and minorities. Members of these groups tend to be among the most recently hired and therefore are the first to be let go. The organization's labor force will become more homogeneous as a result of retrenchment, looking more white and male.

VOLUNTARY TURNOVER   The other side of employee departures are voluntary quits. This becomes a major potential problem in retrenchment because the organization will want to retain its most valuable employees. Yet some of the first people to voluntarily leave a shrinking organization are the most mobile individuals, such as skilled technicians, professionals, and talented managerial personnel. These, of course, are the individuals whom the organization can least afford to lose.

MOTIVATION   Employee motivation is different when an organization is contracting than when it is enjoying growth. On the growth side, motivation can be provided by promotional opportunities and the excitement of being associated with a dynamic organization. During decline, there are layoffs, reassignments of duties that frequently require absorbing the tasks that were previously done by others, and similar stress-inducing changes. It's usually hard for employees to stay motivated when there is high uncertainty as to whether they will still have a job next month or next year. Retrenchment, in other words, directly attacks an employee's basic lower-order needs.

IMPLICATIONS FOR PERFORMANCE AND SATISFACTION

Figure 15–12 visually depicts what we have discussed in this chapter. Strategy, size, technology, environment, and power-control determine the type of structure an organization will have. Complexity, formalization, and centralization represent the structural components that can be mixed and matched to form various structural designs. For simplicity's sake, we can classify structural designs as mechanistic or organic. The former rates high on complexity, formalization, and centralization; the latter rates low on the same three components. Mintzberg's machine and professional bureaucracies plus his divisional form fall into the mechanistic category. His simple structure and adhocracy are examples of organic forms. Common structural components, however, do not necessarily have a uniform impact on every employee's level of performance and satisfaction. The impact of objective structural characteristics on members of the organization is moderated by the employees' individual preferences and their subjective interpretation of the objective characteristics. Let us now offer some general thoughts.

For a large proportion of the population, high structure—that is, high complexity, high formalization, and centralization—leads to reduced job

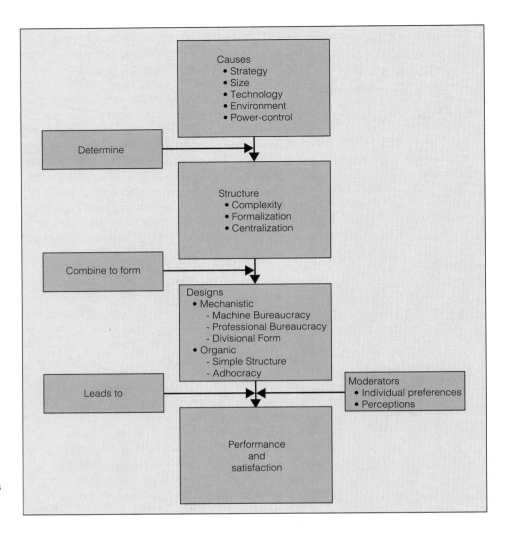

FIGURE 15–12
Organization Structure: Its Determinants and Outcomes

satisfaction. High vertical differentiation tends to alienate lower-level employees because vertical communication becomes more difficult and one can feel like "low man on the totem pole." On the other hand, upper management undoubtedly finds that the rewards that go with *their* positions enhance job satisfaction.

Specialization would also tend to be inversely related to satisfaction, especially where jobs have been divided into extremely minute tasks. This conclusion would have to be moderated to reflect individual differences among employees. While most prefer variety in their work, not *all* do.

For individuals who value autonomy and self-actualization, large size, when accompanied by high centralization, results in lower satisfaction. As we have noted, there are fewer opportunities to participate in decision making, less proximity and identification with organizational goals, and less feeling that individual effort is linked to an identifiable outcome. In other words, the larger the organization, the more difficult it is for the individual to see the impact of his or her contribution to the final goods or service produced.

Organic structures increase cohesiveness among unit members and more closely align their authority with the responsibility for completion of a particular assignment. For certain types of activities, these structures are undoubtedly superior from management's standpoint. For instance, if tasks are nonroutine and there exists a great deal of environmental uncertainty, the organization can be more responsive when structured along organic rather than mechanistic lines. But these more responsive structures provide both advantages and disadvantages to employees. They rarely have restrictive job descriptions or excessive rules and regulations, and they do not require workers to obey commands that are issued by distant executives. But they usually have overlapping layers of responsibility and play havoc with individuals who need the security of doing standardized tasks. To maximize employee performance and satisfaction, individual differences should be taken into account. Individuals with a high degree of bureaucratic orientation tend to place a heavy reliance on higher authority, prefer formalized and specific rules, and prefer formal relationships with others on the job. These people are better suited to mechanistic structures. Those individuals with a low degree of bureaucratic orientation would be better suited to organic structures.

FOR DISCUSSION

1. Explain Chandler's strategy–structure thesis.
2. What type of structure works best with an innovation strategy? A cost-minimization strategy? An imitation strategy?
3. Summarize the size–structure relationship.
4. Define and give an example of what is meant by the term *technology*.
5. Summarize the technology–structure relationship.
6. Summarize the environment–structure relationship.
7. Describe the power-control thesis.
8. How do coordination and control change in each of Mintzberg's five configurations?
9. Contrast the machine and the professional bureaucracy.
10. Does management ever blend designs; for example, combining the machine bureaucracy with adhocracy? Discuss.
11. What is a matrix structure? When would management use it?
12. Why is organizational retrenchment currently so widespread?

Management Can Control Its Environment

The external environment has received a great deal of attention in the organization literature because it is one of the most important contingency factors that managers must take into consideration when making organization design decisions. The flaw in this analysis is that it ignores the fact that the environment can be controlled by management, and, for that reason, is relatively unimportant in influencing the structural decision.

Almost all large and powerful organizations, and many small ones as well, clearly have the means to shape major elements of their environment. In so doing, they reduce environmental uncertainty and minimize the impact of the environment on the organization. The following provides a quick overview of some of the techniques managers use to reduce environmental uncertainty.

DOMAIN CHOICE   The most comprehensive action management can take when faced with an unfavorable environment is to change to a domain with less environmental uncertainty. Management could consider, for instance, staking out a niche that has fewer or less powerful competitors; barriers that keep other competitors out as a result of high entry costs, economies of scale, or regulatory approval; little regulation; numerous suppliers; no unions; less powerful public pressure groups, and the like.

RECRUITMENT   The practice of selective hiring to reduce environmental uncertainty is widespread. For example, corporations hire executives from competing firms to acquire information about their competitors' future plans.

ENVIRONMENTAL SCANNING   This entails scrutinizing the environment to identify actions by competitors, government, unions, and the like that might impinge on the organization's operations. To the extent that this scanning can lead to accurate forecasts of environmental fluctuations, it can reduce uncertainty.

BUFFERING   Organizations can protect their operating core by ensuring supplies or absorption of outputs. When organizations stockpile materials, use multiple suppliers, engage in preventive maintenance, or create finished-goods inventories, they are buffering their operations from environmental uncertainties.

GEOGRAPHIC DISPERSION   Environmental uncertainty sometimes varies with location. To lessen location-induced uncertainty, organizations can move to a different community or lessen risk by operating in multiple locations.

CONTRACTING   Contracting protects the organization from changes in quantity or price on either the input or output side. For instance, management may agree to a long-term fixed contract to purchase materials and supplies or to sell a certain part of the organization's output.

COOPTING   Organizations can absorb those individuals or organizations in the environment that threaten their stability. This is most frequently accomplished in business firms through selective appointments to the organization's board of directors.

COALESCING   Mergers, joint ventures, and cooperative (though illegal) agreements to fix prices or split markets are examples of how organizations can combine with one or more other organizations for joint action. Many mergers, for instance, reduce environmental uncertainty by lessening interorganizational competition and dependency.

LOBBYING   Using influence—for example, through trade associations and political action committees—to achieve favorable outcomes is a widespread practice used by organizations to control their environments.

This argument is based on S. Robbins, *Organization Theory: Structure, Design, and Applications,* 3rd ed. (Englewood Cliffs, NJ: Prentice Hall, 1990), pp. 362–77.

The Environment Controls Management

Organizations are not merely *influenced* by their environment, they are *totally captive* to it. Management is impotent in determining an organization's success or failure. The environment selects certain types of organizations to survive and others to perish based on the fit between their structural characteristics and the characteristics of their environment.

Look at any population of organizations—for example, fast-food restaurants, chemical firms, general hospitals, or private colleges—and you will find variations in organizational forms; that is, there will be diversity in organization structures. But some of these variations are better suited to their environments than others. They may, for example, have lower costs, superior service, higher quality, or more convenient locations. Those that are well suited survive, while others either fail or change to match their environmental requirements. As long as the carrying capacity of an environment is limited, there will be a competitive arena where some organizations will succeed and others will fail. For instance, there are only so many hospitals that a given community's size can absorb. Regardless of how good management is, survival of the fittest argues that the strongest and most adaptable organizations will survive over time.

Management, at least in the short or intermediate term, has little impact on an organization's survival. Managers are merely observers. If there is a shift in the environmental niche that an organization occupies, there is little that management can do. Survival is determined solely by how well the environment supports the organization. Success, therefore, is a result of luck or chance. Organizations that survive are merely in the right place at the right time, and positioning has nothing to do with managerial choice.

For a vivid illustration of this argument, consider the fate of afternoon daily newspapers. In most major cities they have gone the way of the horse and buggy. Their failure had little to do with the quality of their management or any actions that their management did or didn't take. Rather, the environment changed—the evening news on television could provide the same information in a more timely manner; and fewer people, in general, are reading newspapers. Those newspapers that have survived in metropolitan areas have tended to be the large morning papers. For the management of afternoon dailies, their problem was merely being in the wrong place at the wrong time.

This argument is based on D. Ulrich, "The Population Perspective: Review, Critique, and Relevance," *Human Relations*, March 1987, pp. 137–52.

Bureaucratic Orientation Test

Instructions: For each statement, check the response (either mostly agree or mostly disagree) that best represents your feelings.

	Mostly Agree	Mostly Disagree
1. I value stability in my job.	___	___
2. I like a predictable organization.	___	___
3. The best job for me would be one in which the future is uncertain.	___	___
4. The federal government would be a nice place to work.	___	___
5. Rules, policies, and procedures tend to frustrate me.	___	___
6. I would enjoy working for a company that employed 85,000 people worldwide.	___	___
7. Being self-employed would involve more risk than I'm willing to take.	___	___
8. Before accepting a job, I would like to see an exact job description.	___	___
9. I would prefer a job as a freelance house painter to one as a clerk for the Department of Motor Vehicles.	___	___
10. Seniority should be as important as performance in determining pay increases and promotion.	___	___
11. It would give me a feeling of pride to work for the largest and most successful company in its field.	___	___
12. Given a choice, I would prefer to make $40,000 per year as a vice-president in a small company to $45,000 as a staff specialist in a large company.	___	___
13. I would regard wearing an employee badge with a number on it as a degrading experience.	___	___
14. Parking spaces in a company lot should be assigned on the basis of job level.	___	___
15. If an accountant works for a large organization, he or she cannot be a true professional.	___	___
16. Before accepting a job (given a choice), I would want to make sure that the company had a very fine program of employee benefits.	___	___

	Mostly Agree	Mostly Disagree
17. A company will probably not be successful unless it establishes a clear set of rules and procedures.	___	___
18. Regular working hours and vacations are more important to me than finding thrills on the job.	___	___
19. You should respect people according to their rank.	___	___
20. Rules are meant to be broken.	___	___

Turn to page 717 for scoring directions and key.

Source: A. J. DuBrin, *Human Relations: A Job Oriented Approach* © 1978, pp. 687–88. Reprinted with permission of Reston Publishing Co., a Prentice Hall Co., 11480 Sunset Hills Road, Reston, VA 22090.

E X E R C I S E   1 5 – B

Analyzing North American Football

Observe a game of American or Canadian football. Then answer the following questions:

1. In what ways are the basic organizational concepts presented in Chapter 14 evident in the team's organization?

2. Analyze football teams' strategy, size, technology, and environment.

3. Based on the analysis you did for Question 2, what type of structure should a football team have? Do football teams have the predicted structure? Discuss.

4. Do you think member satisfaction would be higher or lower in an organically structured football team? Explain.

Source: Based on G. Morgan, *Creative Organization Theory: A Resourcebook* (Newbury Park, CA: Sage Publications, 1989), p. 267.

CHAPTER 15   ORGANIZATION DESIGN   553

Honda Goes Against the Trend

Most of the world's large corporations have spent a good part of the past decade emulating highly successful Japanese firms like Honda Motor Co. in organizational design. The result: Corporations have become more decentralized and now put more emphasis on group decision making. It certainly must have come as a shock, then, for these corporations to learn in 1991 that Honda was moving back toward centralization and individual responsibility for decisions.

In 1974, Honda created what was at the time a unique collegial organization structure. Its president was merely first among equals, and decision making was spread among the approximately thirty senior executives, who spent most of their day gathered around conference tables at headquarters in Tokyo. Private offices were replaced with a communal executive suite. Product design and development decisions were made by groups composed of people from research, sales, and production. The structure worked. Honda became the world's most spectacularly successful automobile maker.

But by the late 1980s, Honda found that its structure was not as effective as it once was. Its cars had become too conservative and were losing market share to Toyota, Nissan, and Mitsubishi. Honda's decision making had become too sluggish. Product design teams would get together and talk a lot, but fail to come to agreement. Honda's president, Nobuhiko Kawamoto, concluded that his company had simply grown too big for democracy. With 87,000 employees and manufacturing operations in thirty-eight countries, Kawamoto became convinced that Honda had contracted "big company disease" and had lost touch with its customers. Among the company's Japan-based thirty-two board members (equivalent to vice president and above), only twelve had specific responsibilities. Specific issues tended to gravitate to executives with experience in those areas, but there were no formal reporting relationships. As a result, when a problem arose, the board members tended to thrash it out among themselves until they reached agreement. In addition, middle managers had become complacent and were no longer taking much initiative. So Kawamoto is moving his company back to increased centralization and more top management control. We did "too many things in groups" says Kawamoto. And, as a result, people "lost a sense of responsibility, the feeling that every individual has his own specific duties."

In the new structure, the company's top three executives will make more decisions and every board member will have a specific responsibility, such as quality or purchasing. Individual product designers will also get more responsibility. Moreover, according to Kawamoto, if senior executives think that they need private offices to fulfill their new obligations, "they can have them." Kawamoto's goal is not to abandon Honda's democratic structure. Rather, it's to pull in its democratic reins abit so it can be a flexible and responsive big company, just as it had been a flexible and responsive small company twenty years ago.

Questions

1. How have strategy, size, technology, and environment influenced Honda's organization design?

2. What role might power-control play in Honda's structure?

3. Since other companies in the same industry—for instance, General Motors and Ford—are aggressively moving to decentralize their organizations and empower their employees, how can *increasing* centralization at Honda be consistent with improved organizational effectiveness?

4. Can you reconcile Honda's move to centralization with the historical importance of teamwork at Honda and the collectivist tradition in Japan?

5. Besides centralizing and placing more emphasis on individual decision making, how else might Kawamoto have achieved his goal of increased flexibility and responsiveness?

Source: Based on C. Chandler and P. Ingrassia, "Just as U.S. Firms Try Japanese Management, Honda Is Centralizing," *The Wall Street Journal,* April 11, 1991, p. A1; and A. Taylor III, "A U.S.-Style Shakeup at Honda," *Fortune,* December 30, 1991, pp. 115–20.

FOR FURTHER READING

BOSCHKEN, H. L., "Strategy and Structure: Reconceiving the Relationship," *Journal of Management,* March 1990, pp. 135–50. Presents a framework that looks at subunit strategies and microstructures within an overall organization.

BURKHART, M. E., AND D. J. BRASS, "Changing Patterns or Patterns of Change: The Effects of a Change in Technology on Social Network Structure and Power," *Administrative Science Quarterly,* March 1990, pp. 104–27. Reviews the effects of a change in technology on organizational structure and power in a longitudinal study of the introduction and diffusion of a computerized information system.

CAMERON, K. S., S. J. FREEMAN, AND A. K. MISHRA, "Best Practices in White-Collar Downsizing: Managing Contradictions," *Academy of Management Executive,* August 1991, pp. 57–73. Identifies the processes used in effective downsizing and the consequences that result.

CAPPELLI, P., AND P. D. SHERER, "The Missing Role of Context in OB: The Need for a Meso-Level Analysis," in L. L. Cummings and B. M. Staw (eds.), *Research in Organizational Behavior,* Vol. 13 (Greenwich, CT: JAI Press, 1991), pp. 55–110. Reviews the influence of the external environment on the responses of individuals.

COURTRIGHT, J. A., G. T. FAIRHURST, AND L. E. ROGERS, "Interaction Patterns in Organic and Mechanistic Systems," *Academy of Management Journal,* December 1989, pp. 773–802. Provides empirical support for hypotheses suggesting that communicative forms are consultative in organic systems and command-like in mechanistic systems.

MILLER, D., "Organizational Configurations: Cohesion, Change, and Prediction," *Human Relations,* August 1990, pp. 771–89. Argues that four configurations explain a large percentage of firms' structures; then analyzes the cohesion, dynamics, and predictive implications of this limited set of configurations.

NOTES

[1]See S. W. Angrist, "Classless Capitalists," *Forbes,* May 9, 1983, pp. 122–24; and J. Weber, "No Bosses. And Even "Leaders" Can't Give Orders,' *Business Week,* December 10, 1990, pp. 196–97.

[2]See T. Burns and G. M. Stalker, *The Management of Innovation* (London: Tavistock, 1961); and J. A. Courtright, G. T. Fairhurst, and L. E. Rogers, "Interaction Patterns in Organic and Mechanistic Systems," *Academy of Management Journal,* December 1989, pp. 773–802.

[3]A. D. Chandler, Jr., *Strategy and Structure: Chapters in the History of the Industrial Enterprise* (Cambridge, MA: MIT Press, 1962).

[4]See R. E. Miles and C. C. Snow, *Organizational Strategy, Structure, and Process* (New York: McGraw-Hill, 1978); and D. Miller, "The Structural and Environmental Correlates of Business Strategy,: *Strategic Management Journal,* January–February 1987, pp. 55–76.

[5]P. M. Blau, "A Formal Theory of Differentiation in Organizations," *American Sociological Review,* April 1970, pp. 201–18.

[6]D. S. Mileti, D. F. Gillespie, and J. E. Haas, "Size and Structure in Complex Organizations," *Social Forces,* September 1977, pp. 208–17.

[7]W. A. Rushing, "Organizational Size, Rules, and Surveillance," in J. A. Litterer (ed.), *Organizations: Structure and Behavior,* 3rd ed. (New York: John Wiley, 1980), pp. 396–405; and Y. Samuel and B. F. Mannheim, "A Multidimensional Approach Toward a Typology of Bureaucracy," *Administrative Science Quarterly,* June 1970, pp. 216–28.

[8]See, for example, P. M. Blau and R. A. Schoenherr, *The Structure of Organizations* (New York: Basic Books, 1971); and J. Child and R. Mansfield, "Technology, Size, and Organization Structure," *Sociology,* September 1972, pp. 369–93.

[9]J. Woodward, *Industrial Organization: Theory and Practice* (London: Oxford University Press, 1965).

[10]C. Perrow, "A Framework for the Comparative Analysis of Organizations," *American Sociological Review,* April 1967, pp. 194–208.

[11]J. D. Thompson, *Organizations in Action* (New York: McGraw-Hill, 1967).

[12]*Ibid.,* p. 17.

[13]J. Hage and M. Aiken, "Routine Technology, Social Structure, and Organizational Goals," *Administrative Science Quarterly,* September 1969, pp. 366–77.

[14]C. C. Miller, W. H. Glick, Y. Wang, and G. P. Huber, "Understanding Technology–Structure Relationships: Theory Development and Meta-Analytic Theory Testing," *Academy of Management Journal,* June 1991, pp. 370–99.

[15]A. Van De Ven, A. Delbecq, and R. Koenig, Jr., "Determinants of Coordination Modes Within Organizations," *American Sociological Review,* April 1976, pp. 322–38.

[16]J. Hage and M. Aiken, "Relationship of Centralization to Other Structural Properties," *Administrative Science Quarterly,* June 1967, pp. 72–92.

[17]J. Pfeffer and G. R. Salancik, *The External Control of Organizations: A Resource Dependence Perspective* (New York: Harper & Row, 1978), p. 29.

[18]F. E. Emery and E. Trist, "The Causal Texture of Organizational Environments," *Human Relations,* February 1965, pp. 21–32.

[19]P. Lawrence and J. W. Lorsch, *Organization and Environment: Managing Differentiation and Integration* (Boston: Harvard Business School, Division of Research, 1967).

[20]G. G. Dess and D. W. Beard, "Dimensions of Organizational Task Environments," *Administrative Science Quarterly,* March 1984, pp. 52–73.

[21]G. Hofstede, "Motivation, Leadership, and Organization: Do American Theories Apply Abroad?" *Organizational Dynamics,* Summer 1980, p. 60.

[22]J. Child, "Organization Structure, Environment and Performance: The Role of Strategic Choice," *Sociology,* January 1972, pp. 1–22; and D. S. Pugh, "The Management of Organization Structures: Does Context Determine Form?" *Organizational Dynamics,* Spring 1973, pp. 19–34.

[23]J. Pfeffer, *Organizational Design* (Arlington Heights, IL: AHM, 1978).

[24]Ibid.

[25]For a review of this research, see S. P. Robbins, *Organization Theory: Structure, Design, and Applications,* 3rd ed. (Englewood Cliffs, N.J.: Prentice Hall, 1990), pp. 123–24.

[26]See S. Zuboff, *In the Age of the Smart Machine: The Future of Work and Power* (New York: Basic Books, 1988); and J. Chalykoff and T. A. Kochan, "Computer-Aided Monitoring: Its Influence on Employee Job Satisfaction and Turnover," *Personnel Psychology,* Winter 1989, pp. 807–29.

[27]Robbins, *Organization Theory,* p. 107.

[28]H. Mintzberg, *Structure in Fives: Designing Effective Organizations* (Englewood Cliffs, NJ: Prentice Hall, 1983).

[29]*Ibid.,* p. 157.

[30]H. Mintzberg, *The Structuring of Organizations* (Englewood Cliffs, NJ: Prentice Hall, 1979), p. 312.

[31]Mintzberg, *Structure in Fives,* p. 194.

[32]J. Rothschild, "Towards a Feminine Model of Organization," working paper, Department of Sociology, Virginia Polytechnic Institute and State University, 1991.

[33]Mintzberg, *Structure in Fives*, p. 217.

[34]Ibid., p. 261.

[35]D. Miller and P. H. Friesen, *Organizations: A Quantum View* (Englewood Cliffs, NJ: Prentice Hall, 1984), p. 85.

[36]S. M. Davis and P. R. Lawrence, "The Matrix Diamond," *Wharton Magazine,* Winter 1978, pp. 19–27.

[37]K. Knight, "Matrix Organization: A Review," *Journal of Management Studies,* May 1976, pp. 111–30.

[38]Ibid.; and S. M. Davis and P. R. Lawrence, "Problems of Matrix Organizations," *Harvard Business Review,* May–June 1978, pp. 131–42.

[39]For a review of this bias, see J. Case and E. Conlin, "Second Thoughts on Growth," *INC.,* March 1991, pp. 46–57.

[40]Pfeffer and Salancik, *The External Control of Organizations.*

[41]"Downsizing Record Set by Firms in Year: 56% Report Job Cuts," *The Wall Street Journal,* August 12, 1991, p. A2.

[42]This section is based on Robbins, *Organization Theory: Structure, Design, and Applications,* pp. 481–85.

[43]A. Bennett, *The Death of the Organization Man* (New York: William Morrow, 1990), p. 19.

[44]Ibid., p. 196.

[45]Ibid., p. 184.

HUMAN RESOURCE POLICIES AND PRACTICES

CHAPTER OUTLINE

Selection Practices

Training and Development Programs

Performance Evaluation

Reward Systems

The Union–Management Interface

Implications for Performance and
Satisfaction

LEARNING OBJECTIVES

After studying this chapter, you should be
able to:

1. Define the purposes of job analysis
2. Explain when to use interviews in selection
3. List the advantages of performance simulation tests over written tests
4. Define three skill categories
5. Summarize the four stages in a career
6. Describe five specific career anchors
7. Outline the best procedure for making an individual career choice
8. Explain the purposes of performance evaluation
9. Identify the advantages of using behaviors rather than traits in evaluating performance
10. Describe the potential problems in performance evaluation and actions that can correct these problems
11. Outline the various types of rewards
12. Clarify how the existence of a union affects employee behavior

You've got a job vacancy to fill. What can you do to increase the probability that the person you pick for this job will stay with your organization and be a productive performer? Well, you could have applicants complete a battery of personality, interest, and aptitude tests. And you might also consider putting candidates through a set of interviews.

But if you did some reading on the subject of employee selection, you'd find that paper-and-pencil tests and interviews don't get very high marks for validity. That is, they're not strong predictors of later job performance. The reason seems to be that they're too removed from actual job behaviors. It's like trying to choose a basketball team by having prospective players take a multiple-choice test on their knowledge of basketball and then spending half an hour discussing basketball theory with the coach. This may be why companies like Colgate-Palmolive are taking a different tack in selection. Just as basketball coaches use "tryouts" to determine who makes the team, Colgate uses simulated job situations, where candidates demonstrate their actual skills, to choose people to fill its management slots.

When Colgate-Palmolive's Cambridge, Ohio, plant opened in 1987, management simulations were used to fill all key positions.[1] For example, Cathy Waybright (see photo above) got her management job after successfully acting out real on-the-job problems. Executives and human resource experts familiar with each job independently evaluated every candidate's performance, and their evaluations were used in making the final choice. Four years after this management simulation approach was introduced at the Cambridge plant, Colgate reported that turnover was averaging only five to ten percent, compared with twenty to twenty-five percent for the rest of the company. Moreover, two-thirds of the managers hired in 1987 had been promoted by the spring of 1991—more than three times the estimated promotion rate at the company's other plants. ∎

*T*he lower turnover and higher promotion rates at Colgate-Palmolive's Cambridge plant illustrate how human resource policies and practices—in this case, the company's use of simulated job situations for employee selection—can affect important organizational behavior outcomes. In this chapter, we'll discuss a number of human resource concerns that add important pieces to our puzzle as we attempt to explain and predict employee behavior. Specifically, we'll look at selection practices, training and career development programs, performance evaluation, reward systems, and union–management relations.

SELECTION PRACTICES

The objective of effective selection is to match individual characteristics (ability, experience, and so on) with the requirements of the job.[2] When management fails to get a proper match, both employee performance and satisfaction suffer. In this search to achieve the right individual–job fit, where does management begin? The answer is to assess the demands and requirements of the job. The process of assessing the activities within a job is called *job analysis.*

Job Analysis Developing a detailed description of the tasks involved in a job, determining the relationship of a given job to other jobs, and ascertaining the knowledge, skills, and abilities necessary for an employee to perform the job successfully.

Job Description A written statement of what a jobholder does, how it is done, and why it is done.

Job Specification States the minimum acceptable qualifications that an employee must possess to perform a given job successfully.

Job Analysis

Job analysis involves developing a detailed description of the tasks involved in a job, determining the relationship of a given job to other jobs, and ascertaining the knowledge, skills, and abilities necessary for an employee to successfully perform the job.[3]

How is this information attained? Table 16–1 describes the more popular job analysis methods.

Information gathered by using one or more of the job analysis methods results in the organization being able to create a **job description** and **job specification.** The former is a written statement of what a jobholder does, how it is done, and why it is done. It should accurately portray job content, environment, and conditions of employment. The job specification states the minimum acceptable qualifications that an employee must possess to perform

TABLE 16-1   Popular Job Analysis Methods

1. **Observation Method.** An analyst watches employees directly or reviews films of workers on the job.
2. **Individual Interview Method.** Selected job incumbents are extensively interviewed, and the results of a number of these interviews are combined into a single job analysis.
3. **Group Interview Method.** Same as individual except that a number of job incumbents are interviewed simultaneously.
4. **Structured Questionnaire Method.** Workers check or rate the items they perform in their jobs from a long list of possible task items.
5. **Technical Conference Method.** Specific characteristics of a job are obtained from "experts," who typically are supervisors with extensive knowledge of the job.
6. **Diary Method.** Job incumbents record their daily activities in a diary.

a given job successfully. It identifies the knowledge, skills, and abilities needed to do the job effectively. So job descriptions identify characteristics of the job, while job specifications identify characteristics of the successful job incumbent.

The job description and specification are important documents for guiding the selection process. The job description can be used to describe the job to potential candidates. The job specification keeps the attention of those doing the selection on the list of qualifications necessary for an incumbent to perform a job and assists in determining whether or not candidates are qualified.

Selection Devices

What do application forms, interviews, employment tests, background checks, and personal letters of recommendation have in common? Each is a device for obtaining information about a job applicant that can help the organization determine whether the applicant's skills, knowledge, and abilities are appropriate for the job in question. In this section, we review the more important of these selection devices—interviews, written tests, and performance simulation tests.

INTERVIEWS   Do you know anyone who has gotten a job without at least one interview? You may have an acquaintance who got a part-time or summer job through a close friend or relative without having to go through an interview, but such instances are rare. There is little doubt that the interview is the most widely used selection device that organizations rely upon to differentiate candidates. It plays a part in over ninety percent of selection decisions.[4]

With a bit less certainty, we can also say that the interview seems to carry a great deal of weight. That is, not only is it widely used, but its results tend to have a disproportionate amount of influence on the selection decision. The candidate who performs poorly in the employment interview is likely to be cut from the applicant pool, regardless of his or her experience, test scores, or letters of recommendation. Conversely, "all too often, the person most polished in job-seeking techniques, particularly those used in the interview process, is the one hired, even though he or she may not be the best candidate for the position."[5]

These findings are important because, to many people's surprise, the typical loosely structured interview is a poor selection device for most jobs.[6] Why? Because the data gathered from such interviews are often biased and unrelated to future job performance. Research indicates that prior knowledge about an applicant biases the interviewer's evaluation, that interviewers tend to favor applicants who share their attitudes, that the order in which applicants are interviewed influences evaluations, that negative information is given unduly high weight, and that an applicant's ability to do well in an interview is irrelevant in most jobs.[7] On this last point: What relevance do "good interviewing skills" have for successful performance as a bricklayer, drillpress operator, data-entry operator, or laboratory technician? The answer is: "Little or none!" These jobs don't require this skill. Yet employers typically use the interview as a selection device for such jobs.

The evidence suggests that interviews are good for assessing an applicant's intelligence, level of motivation, and interpersonal skills. Where these qualities are related to job performance, the interview should be a valuable tool. For example, these qualities have demonstrated relevance for performance in upper managerial positions. So the use of the interview in selecting senior executives makes sense. But its use in identifying "good performers" for most lower-level jobs appears questionable.

One factor that can improve the validity of any interview is structuring the content.[8] Unstructured interviews—those without a predetermined set of questions—have too much variability to be effective decision guides. The most valid interviews use a consistent structure and ask applicants questions that require answers giving detailed accounts of actual behaviors they have displayed on the job.

WRITTEN TESTS   Typical written tests are tests of intelligence, aptitude, ability, and interest. Long popular as selection devices, they have markedly declined in use since the late 1960s. The reason is that such tests have frequently been characterized as discriminating, and many organizations have not validated, or cannot validate, such tests as being job related.

Tests in intellectual ability, spatial and mechanical ability, perceptual accuracy, and motor ability have shown to be moderately valid predictors for many semiskilled and unskilled operative jobs in industrial organizations.[9] Intelligence tests are reasonably good predictors for supervisory positions.[10] But the burden is on management to demonstrate that any test used is job related. Since the characteristics that many of these tests tap are considerably removed from the actual performance of the job itself, getting high validity coefficients has often been difficult. The result has been a decreased use of traditional written tests and increased interest in performance simulation tests.

PERFORMANCE SIMULATION TESTS   What better way is there to find out if an applicant can do a job successfully than by having him or her do it? That is precisely the logic of the simulation tests described at the opening of this chapter as used by Colgate-Palmolive.

Performance simulation tests have increased significantly in popularity during the past two decades. Undoubtedly, the enthusiasm for these tests comes from the fact that they are based on job analysis data and, therefore, should more easily meet the requirement of job relatedness than do written tests. Performance simulation tests are made up of actual job behaviors rather than surrogates, as are written tests.

The two best-known performance simulation tests are work sampling and assessment centers. The former is suited to routine jobs, whereas the latter is relevant for the selection of managerial personnel.

Work Sampling Creating a miniature replica of a job to evaluate the performance abilities of job candidates.

Work sampling is an effort to create a miniature replica of a job. Applicants demonstrate that they possess the necessary talents by actually doing the tasks. By carefully devising work samples based on job analysis data, the knowledge, skills, and abilities needed for each job are determined. Then each work sample element is matched with a corresponding job performance element. For instance, a work sample for a job where the employee has to use computer spreadsheet software would require the applicant to actually solve a problem using a spreadsheet.

The results from work sample experiments are impressive. Studies almost consistently demonstrate that work samples yield validities superior to written aptitude and personality tests.[11]

Assessment Centers A set of performance simulation tests designed to evaluate a candidate's managerial potential.

A more elaborate set of performance simulation tests, specifically designed to evaluate a candidate's managerial potential, is administered in **assessment centers.** In assessment centers, line executives, supervisors, and/or trained psychologists evaluate candidates as they go through two to four days of exercises that simulate real problems that they would confront on the job. Based on a list of descriptive dimensions that the actual job incumbent has to meet, activities might include interviews, in-basket problem-solving exercises, group discussions, and business decision games.

The evidence on the effectiveness of assessment centers is extremely impressive. They have consistently demonstrated results that predict later job performance in managerial positions.[12] Although they are not cheap—AT&T, which has assessed more than 200,000 employees, computes its assessment costs at $800 to $1500 per employee—the selection of an ineffective manager is unquestionably far more costly.

TRAINING AND DEVELOPMENT PROGRAMS

Competent employees will not remain competent forever. Their skills can deteriorate; technology may make their skills obsolete; the organization may move into new areas, changing the types of jobs it has and the skills necessary to do them. Moreover, given the reality that seventy-five percent of the people who will be working in the year 2000 are already on the job,[13] an ongoing commitment by organizations to continually train and upgrade their employees' skills seems absolutely necessary if these organizations are to remain competitive.

These facts have not been lost on management. It has been estimated, for instance, that United States business firms spend an astounding $30 *billion* a year on formal courses and training programs to build their workers' skills.[14] Managers, too, participate in skill development programs. For instance, a survey of U.S. firms found that, in a typical year, approximately 10 million managers receive an average of about thirty-five hours of skill training.[15]

In this section, we'll look at the type of skills that training can improve; then we'll review various skill training methods, as well as the career development programs that can prepare employees for a future that's different from today.

Skill Categories

We can dissect skills into three categories: technical, interpersonal, and problem solving. Most training activities seek to modify one or more of these skills.

TECHNICAL   Most training is directed at upgrading and improving an employee's technical skills. This applies as much to white-collar as to blue-collar jobs. Jobs change as a result of new technologies and improved methods. Postal sorters have had to undergo technical training in order to learn to operate automatic sorting machines. Many auto repair personnel have had to undergo extensive training to fix and maintain recent models with front-wheel-drive trains, electronic ignitions, fuel injection, and other innovations. Not many clerical personnel during the past decade have been unaffected by the computer. Literally millions of such employees have had to be trained to operate and interface with a computer terminal.

INTERPERSONAL   Almost all employees belong to a work unit. To some degree, their work performance depends on their ability to effectively interact with their co-workers and their boss. Some employees have excellent interpersonal skills, but others require training to improve theirs. This includes learning how to be a better listener, how to communicate ideas more clearly, and how to reduce conflict.

One employee who had had a history of being difficult to work with found that a three-hour group session in which she and co-workers openly discussed how each perceived the others significantly changed the way she interacted with her peers. Her co-workers were unanimous in describing her as arrogant. They all interpreted her requests as sounding like orders. Once she was made aware of this tendency, she began to make conscious efforts to change the tone and content of her requests, and these changes had very positive results on her relationships with her colleagues.

PROBLEM SOLVING Managers, as well as many employees who perform nonroutine tasks, have to solve problems on their job. When people require these skills, but are deficient, they can participate in problem-solving training. This would include activities to sharpen their logic, reasoning, and problem-defining skills, as well as their abilities to assess causation, develop alternatives, analyze alternatives, and select solutions.

Training Methods

Most training takes place on the job. This preference can be attributed to the simplicity and, usually, lower cost of on-the-job training methods. However, on-the-job training can disrupt the workplace and result in an increase in errors as learning proceeds. Also, some skill training is too complex to learn on the job. In such cases, it should take place outside the work setting.[16]

ON-THE-JOB TRAINING Popular on-the-job training methods include job rotation and understudy assignments. *Job rotation* involves lateral transfers that enable employees to work at different jobs. Employees get to learn a wide variety of jobs and gain increased insight into the interdependency between jobs and a wider perspective on organizational activities. New employees frequently learn their jobs by understudying a seasoned veteran. In the trades, this is usually called an *apprenticeship*. In white-collar jobs, it is called a *coaching,* or *mentor,* relationship. In each, the understudy works under the observation of an experienced worker, who acts as a model whom the understudy attempts to emulate.

Both job rotation and understudy assignments apply to the learning of technical skills. Interpersonal and problem-solving skills are acquired more effectively by training that takes place off the job.

Philadelphia Newspapers, Inc., Employee Relations Manager Chris Bonanducci, left, works through a customer service role-playing exercise with Circulation Training Manager Ed Delfin. Courtesy Knight–Ridder.

OFF-THE-JOB TRAINING There are a number of off-the-job training methods that managers may want to make available to employees. The more popular are classroom lectures, films, and simulation exercises. *Classroom lectures* are well suited for conveying specific information. They can be used effectively for developing technical and problem-solving skills. *Films* can also be used to explicitly demonstrate technical skills that are not easily presented by other methods. Interpersonal and problem-solving skills may be best learned through *simulation exercises* such as case analyses, experiential exercises, role playing, and group interaction sessions. Complex computer models, such as those used by airlines in the training of pilots, are another kind of simulation exercise, which in this case is used to teach technical skills. So, too, is *vestibule training,* in which employees learn their jobs on the same equipment they will be using, only the training is conducted away from the actual work floor.

Career Development

Career development is a means by which an organization can sustain or increase its employees' current productivity, while at the same time preparing them for a changing world. Effective career development programs can

Ethics Training: Smoke or Substance?

Approximately eighty percent of the largest U.S. corporations have formal ethics programs, and forty-four percent of these firms provide ethics training.[17] Forty-five out of forty-six of America's largest defense contractors report that they conduct employee ethics training programs. In addition, most college and university programs in business now require courses in ethics or have added an ethics component to their courses in marketing, finance, and management.

What do proponents of ethics training expect to achieve with these programs? Ethics educators include among their goals: stimulating moral thought, recognizing ethical dilemmas, creating a sense of moral obligation, developing problem-solving skills, and tolerating or reducing ambiguity. But can you *teach* ethics in college? The evidence is mixed. Let's briefly review the evidence presented by both sides.

Critics argue that ethics are based on values, and value systems are fixed at an early age.

By the time people reach college, their ethical values are already established. The critics also claim that ethics cannot be formally "taught," but must be learned by example. Leaders set ethical examples by what they say and do. If this is true, then ethics training is relevant only as part of leadership training.

Supporters of ethics training argue that values *can* be learned and changed after early childhood. And even if they couldn't, ethics training would be effective because it gets employees to think about ethical dilemmas and become more aware of the ethical issues underlying their actions. Supporters of ethics training point to the research evidence on the last point: A meta-analysis of the effectiveness of ethics training programs found that they improved students' ethical awareness and reasoning skills.

Can colleges and universities teach ethics? Should business firms be spending money on ethics training programs? What do *you* think?

---

reduce employee turnover and increase productivity.[18] For example, a formal career counseling program in a bank saved $1.95 million in one year, an estimate based on a sixty-five percent reduction in turnover, a twenty-five-percent increase in productivity, and a seventy-five percent increase in promotability.[19]

To help you personalize the value of career development, consider the fact that the average corporation loses fifty percent of its college recruits within five years.[20] Apparently, employees' goals, satisfaction, and needs have been incongruent with their company's operating styles and policies, which led to dissatisfaction and eventually the decision to leave. Research tells us that the implementation of career development programs by companies can help to lessen this high turnover rate.

Career A sequence of positions occupied by a person during the course of a lifetime.

CAREER STAGES   A **career** is a "sequence of positions occupied by a person during the course of a lifetime."[21] This definition does not imply advancement or success or failure. Any work, paid or unpaid, pursued over an extended period of time, can constitute a career. In addition to formal job work, it may include schoolwork, homemaking, or volunteer work.[22]

Career Stages The four steps most people go through in their careers: exploration, establishment, midcareer, and late career.

Careers can be more easily understood if we think of them as proceeding through **stages.**[23] Most of us have gone or will go through four stages: exploration, establishment, midcareer, and late career.

Exploration begins prior to even entering the work force on a paid basis and ends for most of us in our mid-twenties as we make the transition from school to our primary work interest. It's a time of self-exploration and an assessment of alternatives. The *establishment* stage includes being accepted by our peers, learning the job, and gaining tangible evidence of successes or failures in the "real world." Most people don't face their first severe career dilemmas until they reach the *midcareer* stage, a stage that is typically reached between the ages of thirty-five and fifty. This is a time where one may continue to improve one's performance, level off, or begin to deteriorate. At this stage, the first dilemma is accepting the fact that you're no longer seen as a "learner." Mistakes carry greater penalties. At this point in a career, you are expected to have moved beyond apprenticeship to journeyman status. For those who continue to grow through the midcareer stage, the *late career* usually is a pleasant time when you are allowed the luxury to relax a bit and enjoy playing the part of the elder statesman. For those who have stagnated or deteriorated during the previous stage, the late career brings the reality that they will not have a lasting impact or change the world as they once thought. It is a time when individuals recognize that they have decreased work mobility and may be locked into their current jobs. They begin to look forward to retirement and the opportunities of doing something different.

If employees are to remain productive, career development and training programs need to be available that can support an employee's task and emotional needs at each stage. Table 16–2 identifies the more important of these needs.

CAREER ANCHORS   In addition to stages, another concept that can help to understand people in their jobs is that of career anchors.[24]

Just as boats put down anchors to keep them from drifting too far, people put down anchors to stabilize their career decisions and keep them within constraints. **Career anchors,** then, are distinct patterns of self-perceived talents and abilities, motives and needs, and attitudes and values that guide and stabilize a person's career after several years of real-world experience and feedback.

As people reach their late twenties and early thirties, they have to begin making decisions about which jobs to pursue and how to balance personal and work life. To avoid erratic or random decisions, they develop these career anchors. If they sense that a job or job situation will not be consistent

Career Anchors Distinct patterns of self-perceived talents and abilities, motives and needs, and attitudes and values that guide and stabilize a person's career after several years of real-world experience and feedback.

Tim Baldwin experienced career plateauing at age 38. As a senior product manager at Borden Consumer Products Division, he saw his long-term plans stalled. So he left Borden to become director of marketing at a manufacturing firm. Now, at age 44, Baldwin is a vice president for sales, marketing, and engineering applications for Freund Precision.
Jack Van Antwerp

TABLE 16–2   Training Needs Within Career Stages

Stage	Task Needs	Emotional Needs
Exploration	1. Varied job activities 2. Self-exploration	1. Make preliminary job choices 2. Settling down
Establishment	1. Job challenge 2. Develop competence in a specialty area 3. Develop creativity and innovation 4. Rotate into new area after three to five years	1. Deal with rivalry and competition; face failures 2. Deal with work/family conflicts 3. Support 4. Autonomy
Midcareer	1. Technical updating 2. Develop skills in training and coaching others (younger employees) 3. Rotation into new job requiring new skills 4. Develop broader view of work and own role in organization	1. Express feelings about midlife 2. Reorganize thinking about self in relation to work, family, community 3. Reduce self-indulgence and competitiveness
Late career	1. Plan for retirement 2. Shift from power role to one of consultation and guidance 3. Identify and develop successors 4. Begin activities outside the organization	1. Support and counseling to see one's work as a platform for others 2. Develop sense of identity in extraorganizational activities

Source: Adapted from D. T. Hall and M. Morgan, "Career Development and Planning," in K. Perlman, F. L. Schmidt, and W. C. Hamner, *Contemporary Problems in Personnel* (3rd ed.). Copyright © 1983 by John Wiley & Sons. Reprinted by permission of John Wiley & Sons.

with their talents, needs, and values, their anchor pulls them back into situations that are more congruent with their self-image.

Research has identified five specific patterns:

TECHNICAL/FUNCTIONAL COMPETENCE   This anchor focuses on the actual content of a person's work. Someone with an accounting degree and a C.P.A. certificate might find jobs outside of accounting as a challenge to her feelings of competence yet inconsistent with her basic occupational self-concept.

MANAGERIAL COMPETENCE   This anchor emphasizes holding and exercising managerial responsibility. These people seek situations where they can be analytical, utilize their interpersonal skills, and exercise power.

SECURITY   For some people, a key factor in career decision making is work stability. A new position with great opportunities and challenges, but little job security, would be incongruent with these people's needs. They prefer job and organizational stability, employment contracts, good employment benefits, attractive pension plans, and the like.

AUTONOMY   The overriding factor for some people in career decisions is to maintain their independence and freedom. They seek to minimize organizational constraints. These people, not surprisingly, prefer small, organic types of organizations in which to work.

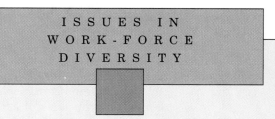

Diversity Training

Ten years ago, few organizations had diversity training programs. Today, the list of those that have such programs includes some of the world's most prestigious companies: Avon, Corning, Digital Equipment, Hewlett-Packard, Lotus Development, McDonnell-Douglas, Monsanto, Motorola, Procter & Gamble, U.S. West, Xerox.[25] The two most popular types of training focus on increasing awareness and building skills.

Awareness training tries to create an understanding of the need for, and meaning of, managing and valuing diversity. Skill-building training educates employees about specific cultural differences and how to respond to these differences in the workplace. The most sophisticated diversity training programs combine both these goals. A few examples will illustrate what some organizations are currently doing in this area.

Xerox has worked with Cornell University's theater department to create a set of short plays that increase awareness of work-related racial and gender conflicts. The show has been presented to more than thirteen hundred Xerox managers. U.S. West runs day-long gender workshops in which executives of both sexes participate in role-playing exercises and discussion groups designed to search and destroy stereotypical assumptions. At a manufacturing plant in San Diego, Hewlett-Packard conducts training on cultural differences between American Anglos and Mexicans, Indochinese, and Filipinos; much of the content focuses on cultural differences in communication styles. As part of Monsanto's two-day diversity program, small groups of employees anonymously write down the characteristics they believe are associated with different racial, ethnic, and gender groups. Those stereotypes are then displayed, and each employee publicly places a mark next to those he or she agrees with. This acts as a catalyst for discussion about racial and sexual roles in the workplace.

CREATIVITY   These people are driven by an overarching desire to create something that is entirely of their own making. For creativity-anchored people, starting a new business, working in a research laboratory, being a major player on a new project's team, and similar activities are important to their self-worth.

The career-anchor perspective has both selection and motivational implications. For example, it can help to explain why dramatic changes in career focus are so difficult for people to make. They require great effort and are not likely to occur very frequently. The perspective also helps to explain why individuals may have very different reactions to similar jobs. Any understanding of how job characteristics will affect an individual has to take into consideration the dynamics between the job's task attributes and the career anchors of the person in that job.

EFFECTIVE CAREER DEVELOPMENT PRACTICES   What kind of practices would characterize an organization that understood the value of career development? The following summarizes a few of the more effective practices.

There is an increasing body of evidence indicating that employees who receive especially *challenging job assignments* early in their careers do better on later jobs.[26] More specifically, the degree of stimulation and challenge in a person's initial job assignment tends to be significantly related to later career success and retention in the organization.[27] Apparently, initial challenges, particularly if they are successfully met, stimulate a person to perform well in subsequent years.

To provide information to all employees about job openings, job opportunities should be posted. *Job postings* list key job specification data—abilities, experience, and seniority requirements to qualify for vacancies—and are typically communicated through bulletin board displays or organizational publications.

One of the most logical parts of career development is *career counseling*. An effective program will cover the following issues with employees:

1. The employee's career goals, aspirations, and expectations for five years or longer

2. Opportunities available within the organization and the degree to which the employee's aspirations are realistic and match the opportunities available

3. Identification of what the employee would have to do in the way of further self-development to qualify for new opportunities

4. Identification of the actual next steps in the form of plans for new development activities or new job assignments that would prepare the employee for further career growth[28]

Organizations can offer group *workshops* to facilitate career development. By bringing together groups of employees with their supervisors and managers, problems and misperceptions can be identified and, it is hoped, resolved. These workshops can be general, or they can be designed to deal with problems common to certain groups of employees—new members, minorities, older workers, and so forth.

Periodic job changes can prevent obsolescence and stimulate career growth.[29] The changes can be lateral transfers, vertical promotions, or temporary assignments. The important element in periodic job changes is that they give the employee a variety of experiences that offer diversity and new challenges.

A PERSONAL NOTE: INDIVIDUAL CAREER DEVELOPMENT   Career development is a two-way street. While students of organizational behavior are concerned with the issue in the interests of improving organizational performance, individuals should be concerned about it for their own self-interest. This personal note from your author presents a framework for helping you make your occupational and career choices.

Most young people go at the problem of choosing an occupation backwards. They start by identifying a market or job opportunity and then attempt to assess whether they like it or not. I can't count the number of students I've had who tell me, for instance, that they're majoring in accounting because of the job opportunities in that area. When I ask them if they like accounting work, a number tell me, "Not really, but the starting salaries are great!" My experience leads me to conclude that the market-driven job choice often leads to frustration and establishment-stage career changes for people.

You should begin by assessing your basic strengths. Figure out what you do best. What skill or skills do you excel at? Writing, speaking, concentrating, interacting with people, organizing things, logical reasoning? (See Table 16–3.) Everyone does some things better than other things. The idea is to play off your strengths.

Next, determine what it is you like to do. Forget, for a moment, what you're good at and think about what "turns you on." Do you like to talk to people? Be left alone? Participate in sports? Read? Explain things to others? Research subjects? Do something risky?

TABLE 16–3   Where Does Your Strength Lie?

Analytical skills:	Comparing, evaluating, and understanding complex problems or situations
Interpersonal communication skills:	Speaking with clarity, clarifying misunderstandings, and listening effectively
Making presentations:	Presenting ideas to groups of people with a clear and logical presentation
Writing skills:	Writing with clarity and conciseness
Manipulating data and numbers:	Processing information and numbers skillfully; handling budgets and statistical reports
Entrepreneurial skills and innovation:	Recognizing and seizing opportunities for new ideas or products, creating new services or processes or products
Leading and managing others:	Inspiring others, assessing others' abilities, delegating effectively, motivating others to achieve a set of goals
Learning skills:	Grasping new information quickly, using common sense to deal with new situations, using feedback effectively
Team membership skills:	Working well on committees, incorporating a variety of perspectives toward a common goal
Conflict resolution skills:	Dealing with differences, confronting others effectively
Developing, helping, teaching, training others:	Encouraging, guiding, and evaluating others; explaining and/or demonstrating new ideas or skills, creating an environment for learning and growth

Source: This list is based on an exercise developed by F. Bartolome and D. McKinney Kellogg and published in D. Marcic Hai, *Organizational Behavior: Experiences and Cases* (St. Paul, MN: West Publishing, 1986), pp. 251–52.

Now, you should merge what you do *best* with what you *like* to do. If you're a good writer and like to be left alone, maybe your life's work should be as a novelist or researcher. If your strength is writing, but you like to interact with people, maybe you should consider journalism. Think about linking jobs with both your strengths and preferences. Strong interpersonal skills are needed in management, sales, and a host of other jobs. If you're good at organizing things, management may be right for you—or a career as a library cataloger. If you like sports, coaching is a possibility. If you like to explain things, you'd probably find a great deal of satisfaction in teaching. Keep in mind that the *Dictionary of Occupational Titles,* published by the U.S. federal government, lists over thirty thousand job titles!

Once you've got a set of jobs that you think you'd like and also do well at, ask yourself: Do I want to work in a large organization? A small firm? For myself? In a major urban center or a rural community?

The final step in a personal career assessment is to evaluate market conditions. Where are the opportunities? It does little good to identify the perfect job if it doesn't exist or if the probability of your getting it is extremely remote. For example, regardless of their predilections, Americans should think hard nowadays before deciding on a career in the United States military. Not that the military can't be challenging and rewarding. It's just that in the 1990s and maybe well into the twenty-first century—with the demise of the Cold War and the reduction in United States military operations worldwide—factors don't favor the military as an occupation. So don't ignore the market. It's a critical variable in your choice of an occupation. However, consider it only as a constraint that you impose on yourself after you've considered your strengths and preferences.

One last point: No matter how thorough your career plans, there can be no guarantees. Market demand and your personal preferences will change. Just as you might have wanted to be a fire fighter or flight attendant at age six but not today, your current choice may not be appealing twenty years from now.

PERFORMANCE EVALUATION

Would you study differently or exert a different level of effort for a college course graded on a pass–fail basis than for one where letter grades from A to F are used? When I ask that question of students, I usually get an affirmative answer. Students typically tell me that they study harder when letter grades are at stake. Additionally, they tell me that when they take a course on a pass–fail basis, they tend to do just enough to ensure a passing grade.

This finding illustrates how performance evaluation systems influence behavior. Major determinants of your in-class behavior and out-of-class studying effort in college are the criteria and techniques your instructor uses to evaluate your performance. Of course, what applies in the college context also applies to employees at work. In this section, we'll show how the choice of a performance evaluation system and the way it's administered can be an important force influencing employee behavior.

Purposes of Performance Evaluation

Performance evaluation serves a number of purposes in organizations (see Table 16–4 for survey results on primary uses of evaluations).[30] Management uses evaluations for general *personnel decisions*. Evaluations provide input into such important decisions as promotions, transfers, and terminations. Evaluations *identify training and development needs*. They pinpoint employee skills and competencies that are currently inadequate but for which programs can be developed to remedy. Performance evaluations can be used as a *criterion against which selection and development programs are validated*. Newly hired employees who perform poorly can be identified through performance evaluation. Similarly, the effectiveness of training and development programs can be determined by assessing how well those employees who have participated do on their performance evaluation. Evaluations also fulfill the purpose of *providing feedback to employees* on how the organization views their performance. Further, performance evaluations are used as the *basis for reward allocations*. Decisions as to who gets merit pay increases and other rewards are frequently determined by performance evaluations.

Each of these functions of performance evaluation is important. Yet their importance to us depends on the perspective we're taking. Several are clearly relevant to personnel management decisions. But our interest is in organizational behavior. As a result, we shall be emphasizing performance

TABLE 16–4   Primary Uses of Performance Evaluations

Use	Percent[a]
Compensation	85.6
Performance feedback	65.1
Training	64.3
Promotion	45.3
Personnel planning	43.1
Retention/discharge	30.3
Research	17.2

[a]Based on responses from 600 organizations.

Source: Based on "Performance Appraisal: Current Practices and Techniques," *Personnel*, May–June 1984, p. 57.

evaluation in its role as a mechanism for providing feedback and as a determinant of reward allocations.

Performance Evaluation and Motivation

In Chapter 7, considerable attention was given to the expectancy model of motivation. We argued that this model currently offers one of the best explanations of what conditions the amount of effort an individual will exert on his or her job. A vital component of this model is performance, specifically the effort–performance and performance–reward linkages. Do people see effort leading to satisfactory performance and satisfactory performance to the rewards that they value? Clearly, they have to know what is expected of them. They need to know how their performance will be measured. Further, they must feel confident that if they exert an effort within their capabilities, it will result in a satisfactory performance as defined by the criteria by which they are being measured. Finally, they must feel confident that if they perform as they are being asked, they will achieve the rewards they value.

In brief, if the objectives that employees are expected to achieve are unclear, if the criteria for measuring those objectives are vague, and if the employees lack confidence that their efforts will lead to a satisfactory appraisal of their performance or believe that there will be an unsatisfactory payoff by the organization when their performance objectives are achieved, we can expect individuals to work considerably below their potential.

What Do We Evaluate?

The criteria or criterion that management chooses to evaluate, when appraising employee performance, will have a major influence on what employees do. Two examples illustrate this:

In a public employment agency, which served workers seeking employment and employers seeking workers, employment interviewers were appraised by the number of interviews they conducted. Consistent with the thesis that the evaluating criteria influence behavior, interviewers emphasized the *number* of interviews conducted rather than the *placements* of clients in jobs.[31]

A management consultant specializing in police research noticed that, in one community, officers would come on duty for their shift, proceed to get into their police cars, drive to the highway that cut through the town, and speed back and forth along this highway for their entire shift. Clearly this fast cruising had little to do with good police work, but this behavior made considerably more sense once the consultant learned that the community's City Council used mileage on police vehicles as an evaluative measure of police effectiveness.[32]

These examples demonstrate the importance of criteria in performance evaluation. This, of course, begs the question: What should management evaluate? The three most popular sets of criteria are individual task outcomes, behaviors, and traits.

INDIVIDUAL TASK OUTCOMES   If ends count, rather than means, then management should evaluate an employee's task outcomes. Using task outcomes, a plant manager could be judged on criteria such as quantity produced, scrap generated, and cost per unit of production. Similarly, a salesperson could be assessed on overall sales volume in his or her territory, dollar increase in sales, and number of new accounts established.

BEHAVIORS   In many cases, it's difficult to identify specific outcomes that can be directly attributable to an employee's actions. This is particularly true of personnel in staff positions and individuals whose work assignments are intrinsically part of a group effort. In the latter case, the group's performance may be readily evaluated, but the contribution of each group member may be difficult or impossible to identify clearly. In such instances, it is not unusual for management to evaluate the employee's behavior. Using the previous examples, behaviors of a plant manager that could be used for performance evaluation purposes might include promptness in submitting his or her monthly reports or the leadership style that the manager exhibits. Pertinent salesperson behaviors could be average number of contact calls made per day or sick days used per year.

TRAITS   The weakest set of criteria, yet one that is still widely used by organizations, is individual traits. We say they are weaker than either task outcomes or behaviors because they are farthest removed from the actual performance of the job itself. Traits such as having "a good attitude," showing "confidence," being "intelligent" or "friendly," "looking busy," or possessing "a wealth of experience" may or may not be highly correlated with positive task outcomes, but only the naive would ignore the reality that such traits are frequently used in organizations as criteria for assessing an employee's level of performance.

Who Should Do the Evaluating?

Who should evaluate an employee's performance? The obvious answer would seem to be: his or her immediate boss! By tradition, a manager's authority typically has included appraising subordinates' performance. The logic behind this tradition seems to be that since managers are held responsible for their subordinates' performance, it only makes sense that these managers do the evaluating of that performance. But that logic may be flawed. Others may actually be able to do the job better.

IMMEDIATE SUPERIOR   As we implied, about ninety-five percent of all performance evaluations at the lower and middle levels of the organization are conducted by the employee's immediate boss.[33] Yet a number of organizations are recognizing the drawbacks to using this source of evaluation. For instance, many bosses feel unqualified to evaluate the unique contributions of each of their subordinates. Others resent being asked to "play God" with their employees' careers. Additionally, in the 1990s, when many organizations are using matrix structures, telecommuting, and other organizing devices that distance bosses from their employees, an employee's immediate superior may not be a reliable judge of that employee's performance.

PEERS   While not widely used in practice, peer evaluations are one of the most reliable sources of appraisal data. Why? First, peers are close to the action. Daily interactions provide them with a comprehensive view of an employee's job performance. Second, using peers as raters results in a number of independent judgments. A boss can offer only a single evaluation, but peers can provide multiple appraisals. And the average of several ratings is often more reliable than a single evaluation. On the downside, peer evaluations can suffer from co-workers' unwillingness to evaluate one another and from friendship-based biases.

SELF-EVALUATION   After ratings by the immediate superior, the most widespread appraisal method is having employees evaluate their own performance.[34] Self-evaluations get high marks from employees themselves; they tend to lessen employees' defensiveness about the appraisal process; and they make excellent vehicles for stimulating job performance discussions between employees and their superiors. However, as you might guess, they suffer from overinflated assessment and self-serving bias. Moreover, self-evaluations are often low in agreement with superiors' ratings.[35] Because of these serious drawbacks, organizations typically use self-evaluations more for developmental than for evaluative purposes.

IMMEDIATE SUBORDINATES A fourth judgment source is an employee's immediate subordinates. Although not widely used, immediate subordinates' evaluations can provide accurate and detailed information about a manager's behavior because the evaluators typically have frequent contact with the evaluatee. The obvious problem with this form of rating is fear of reprisal from bosses given unfavorable evaluations. Therefore, respondent anonymity is crucial if these evaluations are to be accurate.

Methods of Performance Evaluation

The previous sections explained *what* we evaluate and *who* should do the evaluating. Now we ask: *How* do we evaluate an employee's performance? That is, what are the specific techniques for evaluation? This section reviews the major performance evaluation methods.

WRITTEN ESSAYS Probably the simplest method of evaluation is to write a narrative describing an employee's strengths, weaknesses, past performance, potential, and suggestions for improvement. The written essay requires no complex forms or extensive training to complete. But the results often reflect the ability of the writer. A good or bad appraisal may be determined as much by the evaluator's writing skill as by the employee's actual level of performance.

Critical Incidents Evaluating those behaviors that are key in making the difference between executing a job effectively and executing it ineffectively.

CRITICAL INCIDENTS **Critical incidents** focus the evaluator's attention on those behaviors that are key in making the difference between executing a job effectively and executing it ineffectively. That is, the appraiser writes down anecdotes that describe what the employee did that was especially effective or ineffective. The key here is that only specific behaviors, not vaguely defined personality traits, are cited. A list of critical incidents provides a rich set of examples from which the employee can be shown those behaviors that are desirable and those that call for improvement.

Graphic Rating Scales An evaluation method where the evaluator rates performance factors on an incremental scale.

GRAPHIC RATING SCALES One of the oldest and most popular methods of evaluation is the use of **graphic rating scales.** In this method, a set of performance factors, such as quantity and quality of work, depth of knowledge, cooperation, loyalty, attendance, honesty, and initiative, are listed. The evaluator then goes down the list and rates each on incremental scales. The scales typically specify five points, so a factor like *job knowledge* might be rated 1 ("poorly informed about work duties") to 5 ("has complete mastery of all phases of the job").

Why are graphic ratings scales so popular? Though they don't provide the depth of information that essays or critical incidents do, they are less time-consuming to develop and administer. They also allow for quantitative analysis and comparison.

Behaviorally Anchored Rating Scales An evaluation method where actual job-related behaviors are rated along a continuum.

BEHAVIORALLY ANCHORED RATING SCALES **Behaviorally anchored rating scales** have received a great deal of attention in recent years.[36]

These scales combine major elements from the critical incident and graphic rating scale approaches: The appraiser rates the employees based on items along a continuum, but the points are examples of actual behavior on the given job rather than general descriptions or traits.

Behaviorally anchored rating scales specify definite, observable, and measurable job behavior. Examples of job-related behavior and performance dimensions are found by asking participants to give specific illustrations of effective and ineffective behavior regarding each performance dimension. These behavioral examples are then translated into a set of performance dimensions, each dimension having varying levels of performance. The results of this process are behavioral descriptions, such as *anticipates, plans, executes, solves immediate problems, carries out orders,* and *handles emergency situations.*

MULTIPERSON COMPARISONS   Multiperson comparisons evaluate one individual's performance against the performance of one or more others. It is a relative rather than an absolute measuring device. The three most popular comparisons are group order ranking, individual ranking, and paired comparisons.

Group Order Ranking An evaluation method that places employees into particular classifications such as quartiles.

The **group order ranking** requires the evaluator to place employees into a particular classification, such as top one-fifth or second one-fifth. This method is often used in recommending students to graduate schools. Evaluators are asked whether the student ranks in the top five percent of the class, the next five percent, the next fifteen percent, and so forth. But when used by managers to appraise employees, managers deal with all their subordinates. Therefore, if a rater has twenty subordinates, only four can be in the top fifth and, of course, four must also be relegated to the bottom fifth.

Individual Ranking An evaluation method that rank-orders employees from best to worst.

The **individual ranking** approach rank-orders employees from best to worst. If the manager is required to appraise thirty subordinates, this approach assumes that the difference between the first and second employee is the same as that between the twenty-first and twenty-second. Even though some of the employees may be closely grouped, this approach allows for no ties. The result is a clean ordering of employees, from the highest performer down to the lowest.

IBM set new guidelines in 1992 which more strictly enforced its system of ranking employees on a numerical scale. Using a scale of 1 (highest) to 4, few employees were previously rated below three. But the new guidelines force managers to rank people as fours. Industry executives expect about 10 percent of IBM's U.S. work-force, or about 20,000 people, to get this low rating and face pressure to resign.   Courtesy IBM

Paired Comparison An evaluation method that compares each employee with every other employee and assigns a summary ranking based on the number of superior scores that the employee achieves.

The **paired comparison** approach compares each employee with every other employee and rates each as either the superior or the weaker member of the pair. After all paired comparisons are made, each employee is assigned a summary ranking based on the number of superior scores he or she achieved. This approach ensures that each employee is compared against every other, but it can obviously become unwieldy when many employees are being compared.

Multiperson comparisons can be combined with one of the other methods to blend the best from both absolute and relative standards. For example, a college might use the graphic rating scale and the individual ranking method to provide more accurate information about its students' performance. The student's relative rank in the class could be noted next to an absolute grade of A, B, C, D, or F. A prospective employer or graduate school could then look at two students who each got a B in their different financial accounting courses and draw considerably different conclusions about each because next to one grade it says "ranked fourth out of twenty-six," while next to the other it says "ranked seventeenth out of thirty." Obviously, the latter instructor gives out a lot more high grades!

Potential Problems

While organizations may seek to make the performance evaluation process free from personal biases, prejudices, and idiosyncrasies, a number of potential problems can creep into the process. To the degree that the following factors are prevalent, an employee's evaluation is likely to be distorted.

SINGLE CRITERION The typical employee's job is made up of a number of tasks. An airline flight attendant's job, for example, includes welcoming passengers, seeing to their comfort, serving meals, and offering safety advice. If performance on this job were assessed by a single criterion measure—say, the time it took to provide food and beverages to a hundred passengers—the result would be a limited evaluation of that job. More important, flight attendants whose performance evaluation included assessment on only this single criterion would be motivated to ignore those other tasks in their job. Similarly, if a football quarterback were appraised only on his percentage of completed passes, he would be likely to throw short passes and only in situations where he felt assured that they would be caught. Our point is that where employees are evaluated on a single job criterion, and where successful performance on that job requires good performance on a number of criteria, employees will emphasize the single criterion to the exclusion of other job-relevant factors.

Leniency Error The tendency to evaluate a set of employees too high (positive) or too low (negative).

LENIENCY ERROR Every evaluator has his or her own value system that acts as a standard against which appraisals are made. Relative to the true or actual performance an individual exhibits, some evaluators mark high and others low. The former is referred to as positive **leniency error,** and the latter as negative leniency error. When evaluators are positively lenient in their appraisal, an individual's performance becomes overstated; that is, rated higher than it actually should be. Similarly, a negative leniency error understates performance, giving the individual a lower appraisal than deserved.

If all individuals in an organization were appraised by the same person, there would be no problem. Although there would be an error factor, it would be applied equally to everyone. The difficulty arises when we have different raters with different leniency errors making judgments. For example, assume that Jones and Smith are performing the same job for different supervisors, but they have absolutely identical job performance. If Jones' supervisor tends to err toward positive leniency, while Smith's supervisor errs toward negative leniency, we might be confronted with two dramatically different evaluations.

HALO ERROR   The halo effect or error, as we noted in Chapter 5, is the tendency for an evaluator to let the assessment of an individual on one trait influence his or her evaluation of that person on other traits. For example, if an employee tends to be dependable, we might become biased toward that individual to the extent that we will rate him or her high on many desirable attributes.

People who design teaching appraisal forms for college students to fill out to evaluate the effectiveness of their instructors each semester must confront the halo error. Students tend to rate a faculty member as outstanding on all criteria when they are particularly appreciative of a few things he or she does in the classroom. Similarly, a few bad habits—like showing up late for lectures, for example, or being slow in returning papers, or assigning an extremely demanding reading requirement—might result in students' evaluating the instructor as "lousy" across the board.

SIMILARITY ERROR   When evaluators rate other people giving special consideration to those qualities that they perceive in themselves, they are making a **similarity error.** For example, the evaluator who perceives himself as aggressive may evaluate others by looking for aggressiveness. Those who demonstrate this characteristic tend to benefit, while others are penalized.

Again, this error would tend to wash out if the same evaluator appraised all the people in the organization. However, interrater reliability obviously suffers when various evaluators are utilizing their own similarity criteria.

LOW DIFFERENTIATION   It is possible that, regardless of whom the appraiser evaluates and what traits are used, the pattern of evaluation remains the same. It is possible that the evaluator's ability to appraise objectively and accurately has been impeded by social differentiation—that is, the evaluator's style of rating behavior.

It has been suggested that evaluators may be classified as (1) high differentiators, who use all or most of the scale; or (2) low differentiators, who use a limited range of the scale.[37]

Low differentiators tend to ignore or suppress differences, perceiving the universe as being more uniform than it really is. High differentiators, on the other hand, tend to utilize all available information to the utmost extent and thus are better able to perceptually define anomalies and contradictions than are low differentiators.[38]

This finding tells us that evaluations made by low differentiators need to be carefully inspected and that the people working for a low differentiator have a high probability of being appraised as being significantly more homogeneous than they really are.

FORCING INFORMATION TO MATCH NONPERFORMANCE CRITERIA
While rarely advocated, it is not an infrequent practice to find the formal evaluation taking place *following* the decision as to how the individual has been performing. This may sound illogical, but it merely recognizes that subjective, yet formal, decisions are often arrived at prior to the gathering of objective information to support those decisions. For example, if the evaluator believes that the evaluation should not be based on performance, but

rather on seniority, he or she may be unknowingly adjusting each "performance" evaluation so as to bring it into line with the employee's seniority rank. In this and other similar cases, the evaluator is increasing or decreasing performance appraisals to align with the nonperformance criteria actually being utilized.

Overcoming the Problems

Just because organizations can encounter problems with performance evaluations should not lead managers to give up on the process. Some things can be done to overcome most of the problems we have identified.[39]

USE MULTIPLE CRITERIA   Since successful performance on most jobs requires doing a number of things well, all those "things" should be identified and evaluated. The more complex the job, the more criteria that will need to be identified and evaluated. But everything need not be assessed. The critical activities that lead to high or low performance are the ones that need to be evaluated.

DEEMPHASIZE TRAITS   Many traits often considered to be related to good performance may, in fact, have little or no performance relationship. For example, traits like loyalty, initiative, courage, reliability, and self-expression are intuitively appealing as desirable characteristics in employees. But the relevant question is: Are individuals who are evaluated as high on those traits higher performers than those who rate low? We can't answer this question easily. We know that there are employees who rate high on these characteristics and are poor performers. We can find others who are excellent performers but do not score well on traits such as these. Our conclusion is that traits like loyalty and initiative may be prized by managers, but there is no evidence to support that certain traits will be adequate synonyms for performance in a large cross section of jobs.

Another weakness of trait evaluation is the judgment itself. What is "loyalty"? When is an employee "reliable"? What you consider "loyalty," I may not. So traits suffer from weak interrater agreement.

USE MULTIPLE EVALUATORS   As the number of evaluators increases, the probability of attaining more accurate information increases. If rater error tends to follow a normal curve, an increase in the number of appraisers will tend to find the majority congregating about the middle. You see this approach being used in athletic competitions in such sports as diving and gymnastics. A set of evaluators judges a performance, the highest and lowest scores are dropped, and the final performance evaluation is made up from the cumulative scores of those remaining. The logic of multiple evaluators applies to organizations as well.

If an employee has had ten supervisors, nine having rated her excellent and one poor, we can discount the value of the one poor evaluation. Therefore, by moving employees about within the organization so as to gain a number of evaluations, or by using multiple peers and/or subordinates, we increase the probability of achieving more valid and reliable evaluations.

EVALUATE SELECTIVELY   It has been suggested that appraisers should evaluate in only those areas in which they have some expertise.[40] If raters make evaluations on *only* those dimensions on which they are in a good position to rate, we increase the interrater agreement and make the evaluation a more valid process. This approach also recognizes that different organizational levels often have different orientations toward ratees and observe them in different settings. In general, therefore, we would recommend that appraisers should be as close as possible, in terms of organizational level, to the individual being evaluated. Conversely, the more levels that separate the evaluator and evaluatee, the less opportunity the evaluator has to observe the individual's behavior and, not surprisingly, the greater the possibility for inaccuracies.

The specific application of these concepts would result in having immediate supervisors, co-workers, subordinates, or some combination of these people provide the major input into the appraisal and having them evaluate those factors they are best qualified to judge. For example, it has been suggested that when professors are evaluating secretaries within a university, they use such criteria as judgment, technical competence, and conscientiousness, whereas peers (other secretaries) use such criteria as job knowledge, organization, cooperation with co-workers, and responsibility.[41] Using both professors and peers as appraisers is a logical and reliable approach, since it results in having people appraise only those dimensions on which they are in a good position to make judgments.

TRAIN EVALUATORS   If you can't *find* good evaluators, the alternative is to *make* good evaluators. There is evidence that training evaluators can make them more accurate raters.[42]

Common errors such as halo and leniency have been minimized or eliminated in workshops where managers practice observing and rating behaviors. These workshops typically run from one to three days, but allocating many hours to training may not always be necessary. One case has been cited where both halo and leniency errors were decreased immediately after exposing evaluators to explanatory training sessions lasting only five minutes.[43] But the effects of training do appear to diminish over time.[44] This suggests the need for regular refresher sessions.

Providing Performance Feedback

For many managers, few activities are more unpleasant than providing performance feedback to employees. In fact, unless pressured by organizational policies and controls, managers are likely to ignore this responsibility.[45]

Why the reluctance to give performance feedback? There seem to be at least three reasons. First, managers are often uncomfortable discussing performance weaknesses with employees. Given that almost every employee could stand to improve in some areas, managers fear a confrontation when presenting negative feedback. Second, many employees tend to become defensive when their weaknesses are pointed out. Instead of accepting the feedback as constructive and a basis for improving performance, some employees challenge the evaluation by criticizing the manager or redirecting blame to someone else. Finally, employees tend to have an inflated assessment of their own performance. Statistically speaking, half of all employees must be below-average performers. But the evidence indicates that the average employee's estimate of his or her own performance level generally falls around the seventy-fifth percentile.[46] So even when managers are providing good news, employees are likely to perceive it as not good enough!

The solution to the performance-feedback problem is not to ignore it, but to train managers in how to conduct constructive feedback sessions. (See our previous discussion of feedback skills in Chapter 10). An effective review— one in which the employee perceives the appraisal as fair, the manager as sincere, and the climate as constructive—can result in the employee leaving the interview in an upbeat mood, informed about the performance areas in which he or she needs to improve and determined to correct the deficiencies. Additionally, the performance review should be designed more as a counseling activity than a judgment process. This can best be accomplished by allowing the review to evolve out of the employee's own self-evaluation.

REWARD SYSTEMS

Our knowledge of motivation tells us that people do what they do to satisfy needs. Before they do anything, they look for the payoff or reward. Many of these rewards—salary increases, employee benefits, preferred job assignments—are organizationally controlled. While we previously discussed some organizational reward programs in Chapter 8, we should spend a moment to describe rewards that are under managerial discretion and the important role they can play in influencing employee behavior.

The types of rewards that an organization can allocate are more complex than is generally thought. Obviously, there is direct compensation. But there are also indirect compensation and nonfinancial rewards. Each of these types of rewards can be distributed on an individual, group, or organization-wide basis. Figure 16–1 presents a structure for looking at rewards.

Intrinsic Rewards The pleasure or value one receives from the content of a work task.

Intrinsic rewards are those that individuals receive for themselves. They are largely a result of the worker's satisfaction with his or her job. As we noted in Chapter 8, techniques like job enrichment and efforts to redesign or restructure work to increase its personal worth to the employee may make the work more intrinsically rewarding.

Extrinsic Rewards Rewards received from the environment surrounding the context of the work.

Extrinsic rewards include direct compensation, indirect compensation, and nonfinancial rewards. Of course, an employee expects some form of direct compensation: a basic wage or salary, overtime and holiday premium pay, bonuses based on performance, profit sharing, and/or opportunities to purchase stock options. Employees will expect their direct compensation generally to align with their assessment of their contribution to the organization and, additionally, will expect it to be comparable to the direct compensation given to other employees with similar abilities and performance.

The organization will provide employees with indirect compensation: insurance, pay for holidays and vacations, services, and perquisites. Inasmuch as these are generally made uniformly available to all employees at a given job level, regardless of performance, they are really not motivating rewards. However, where indirect compensation is controllable by management and is used to reward performance, then it clearly needs to be considered as a motivating reward. To illustrate, if a company-paid membership in a country club is not available to all middle- and upper-level executives, but only to those who have shown particular performance ratings, then it is a motivating reward. Similarly, if company-owned automobiles and aircraft are made available to certain employees based on their performance rather than their "entitlement," we should view these indirect compensations as motivating rewards for those who might deem these forms of compensation attractive.

As with direct compensation, indirect compensation may be viewed in an individual, group, or organizational context. However, if rewards are to be linked closely with performance, we should expect individual rewards to be emphasized. On the other hand, if a certain group of managers within the organization has made a significant contribution to the effective performance of the organization, a blanket reward such as a membership in a social club might be appropriate. Again, it is important to note that since rewards achieve the greatest return when they are specifically designed to meet the needs of each individual, and since group and organizational

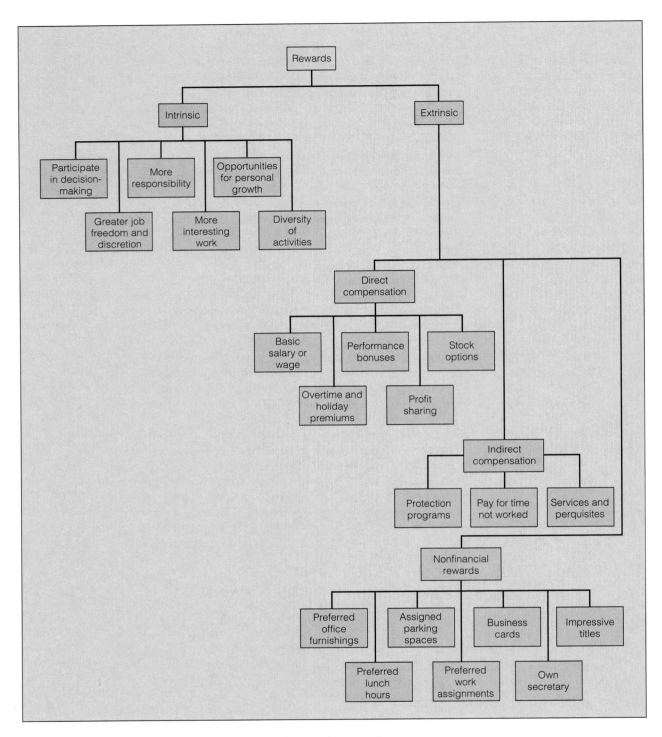

FIGURE 16–1   Types of Rewards

rewards tend to deal in homogeneity—that is, they tend to treat all people alike—these types of rewards must, by definition, be somewhat less effective than individual rewards. The only exceptions to that statement are those instances where there is a high need for cohesiveness and group congeniality. In such instances, individuals may find group rewards more personally satisfying than individual rewards.

The classification of nonfinancial rewards tends to be a smorgasbord of desirable "things" that are potentially at the disposal of the organization. The creation of nonfinancial rewards is limited only by managers' ingenuity and ability to assess "payoffs" that individuals with the organization find desirable and that are within the managers' discretion.

The old saying "One man's food is another man's poison" certainly applies to rewards. What one employee views as highly desirable, another finds superfluous. Therefore *any* reward may not get the desired result; however, where selection has been done assiduously, the benefits to the organization by way of higher worker performance should be impressive.

Some workers are very status conscious. A paneled office, a carpeted floor, a large walnut desk, or a private bathroom may be just the office furnishing that stimulates them toward top performance. Status-oriented employees may also value an impressive job title, their own business cards, their own secretary, or a well-located parking space with their name clearly painted underneath the "Reserved" sign.

Some employees value having their lunch at, say 1 P.M. to 2 P.M. If lunch is normally from 11 A.M. to 12 noon, the benefit of being able to take their lunch at another, more desirable time can be viewed as a reward. Having a chance to work with congenial colleagues, achieving a desired work assignment, and getting an assignment where the worker can operate without close supervision are all rewards that are within the discretion of management and, when carefully aligned to individual needs, can provide stimulus for improved performance.

THE UNION–MANAGEMENT INTERFACE

Labor Union An organization, made up of employees, that acts collectively to protect and promote employee interests.

Labor unions are a vehicle by which employees act collectively to protect and promote their interests. Currently, in the United States, approximately sixteen percent of the work force belongs to and is represented by a union. For this segment of the labor force, wage levels and conditions of employment are explicitly articulated in a contract that is negotiated, through collective bargaining, between representatives of the union and the organiza-

National Medical Enterprises paid its CEO, Richard Eamer (pictured), an average of $13,585,000 a year between 1987 and 1989. That was 625 times the average U.S. factory worker's annual pay. Contrast that with Ben & Jerry's Homemade Inc., which has a company rule that restricts the highest paid executive to only five times that paid the lowest Ben & Jerry's employee.
Alan Levenson

A Look at Selected International Human Resource Issues

Most of the human resource policies and practices discussed in this chapter have to be modified to reflect societal differences. To illustrate this point, let's briefly look at the problem of selecting managers for foreign assignments and the importance of performance evaluation in different cultures.

The global corporation increasingly needs managers who have experience in diverse cultures and who are sensitive to the challenges of international operations.[47] At Ford Motor Co., for instance, an international assignment is a requirement for a rising executive's career. But many domestic managers don't have the attitudes or characteristics associated with successful international executives. One selection technique that an increasing number of companies are using is the Overseas Assignment Inventory (OAI). This eighty-five-item questionnaire assesses fifteen predictors: motivations, expectations, open-mindedness, respect for others' beliefs, trust in people, flexibility, tolerance, personal control, patience, adaptability, self-confidence/initiative, sense of humor, interpersonal interest, interpersonal harmony, and spouse/family communication. Results are compared against a database of more than ten thousand previous test takers. Research indicates that using the OAI as a prescreening device eliminates about forty percent of traditional overseas assignment problems.

Earlier in the chapter, we examined the role that performance evaluation plays in motivation and in affecting behavior. Caution must be used, however, in generalizing across cultures. Why? Because many cultures are not particularly concerned with performance appraisal or, if they are, they don't look at it the same way as we do in the United States and Canada.

Let's look at three cultural dimensions discussed in Chapter 3: a person's relationship to the environment, time orientation, and focus of responsibility.

United States and Canadian organizations hold people responsible for their actions because people in these countries believe that they can dominate their environment. In Middle Eastern countries, on the other hand, performance evaluations aren't likely to be widely used since managers in these countries tend to see people as subjugated to their environment.

Some countries, such as the United States, have a short-term time orientation. Performance evaluations are likely to be frequent in such a culture—at least once a year. In Japan, however, where people hold a long-term time frame, performance appraisals may occur only every five or ten years.

Israel's culture values group activities much more than does the United States or Canada. So, while North American managers focus on the individual in performance evaluations, their counterparts in Israel are much more likely to emphasize group contributions and performance.

tion's management. But the impact of unions on employees is broader than their sixteen percent representation figure might imply. This is because nonunionized employees benefit from the gains that unions make. There is a spillover effect so that the wages, benefits, and working conditions provided nonunionized employees tend to mirror—with some time lag—those negotiated for union members.

Labor unions influence a number of organizational activities.[48] Recruitment sources, hiring criteria, work schedules, job design, redress procedures, safety rules, and eligibility for training programs are examples of

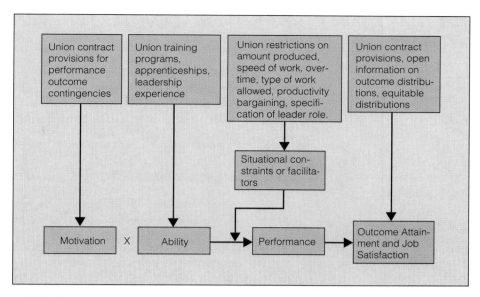

FIGURE 16–2 **The Union's Impact on Employee Performance and Job Satisfaction** Source: T. H. Hammer, Relationships Between Local Union Characteristics and Worker Behavior and Attitudes," *Academy of Management Journal,* December 1978, p. 573.

activities that are influenced by unions. The most obvious and pervasive area of influence, of course, is wage rates and working conditions. Where unions exist, performance evaluation systems tend to be less complex because they play a relatively small part in reward decisions. Wage rates, when determined through collective bargaining, emphasize seniority and downplay performance differences.

Figure 16–2 shows what impact a union has on an employee's performance and job satisfaction. The union contract affects motivation through determination of wage rates, seniority rules, layoff procedures, promotion criteria, and security provisions. Unions can influence the competence with which employees perform their jobs by offering special training programs to their members, by requiring apprenticeships, and by allowing members to gain leadership experience through union organizational activities. The actual level of employee performance will be further influenced by collective bargaining restrictions placed on the amount of work produced, the speed with which work can be done, overtime allowances per worker, and the kind of tasks a given employee is allowed to perform.

The research evaluating the specific effect of unions on productivity is mixed.[49] Some studies found that unions had a positive effect on productivity as a result of improvements in labor-management relations as well as improvements in the quality of the labor force. In contrast, other studies have shown that unions negatively impact on productivity by reducing the effectiveness of some productivity-enhancing managerial practices and by contributing to a poorer labor–management climate. The evidence, then, is too inconsistent to draw any meaningful conclusions.

Are union members more satisfied with their jobs than their nonunion counterparts? The answer to this question is more complicated than a simple "Yes" or "No." The evidence consistently demonstrates that unions have only indirect effects on job satisfaction.[50] They increase pay satisfaction, but negatively affect satisfaction with the work itself (by decreasing job scope perceptions), satisfaction with co-workers and supervision (through less favorable perceptions of supervisory behavior), and satisfaction with promotions (through the lower importance placed on promotions).

IMPLICATIONS FOR PERFORMANCE
AND SATISFACTION

An organization's human resource policies and practices represent important forces for shaping employee behavior and attitudes. In this chapter, we specifically discussed the influence of selection practices, training and development programs, performance evaluation systems, reward systems, and the existence of a union.

Selection Practices

An organization's selection practices will determine who gets hired. If properly designed, they will identify competent candidates and accurately match them to the job. The use of the proper selection devices will increase the probability that the right person will be chosen to fill a slot.

While employee selection is far from a science, some organizations fail to design their selection systems so as to maximize the likelihood that the right person–job fit will be achieved. When errors are made, the chosen candidate's performance may be less than satisfactory. Training may be necessary to improve the candidate's skills. At the worst, the candidate will prove unacceptable and a replacement will need to be found. Similarly, where the selection process results in the hiring of less qualified candidates or individuals who don't fit into the organization, those chosen are likely to feel anxious, tense, and uncomfortable. This, in turn, is likely to increase dissatisfaction with the job.

Training and Development Programs

Training programs can affect work behavior in two ways. The most obvious is by directly improving the skills necessary for the employee to successfully complete his or her job. An increase in ability improves the employee's potential to perform at a higher level. Of course, whether that potential becomes realized is largely an issue of motivation.

A second benefit from training is that it increases an employee's self-efficacy. As you'll remember from Chapter 7, self-efficacy is a person's expectation that he or she can successfully execute the behaviors required to produce an outcome.[51] For employees, those behaviors are work tasks and the outcome is effective job performance. Employees with high self-efficacy have strong expectations about their abilities to perform successfully in new situations. They're confident and expect to be successful. Training, then, is a means to positively affect self-efficacy. In so doing, employees may be more willing to undertake job tasks and exert a high level of effort. Or in expectancy terms (see Chapter 7), individuals are more likely to perceive their effort as leading to performance.

We also discussed career development programs in this chapter. Organizations that provide formal career development activities and match them to needs that employees experience at various stages in their careers reduce the likelihood that productivity will decrease as a result of obsolescence or that job frustrations will create reduced satisfaction.[52]

In today's job environment—with cutbacks, increasingly wider spans of control, and reduced promotion opportunities—employees will increasingly confront the reality of career plateauing. Out of frustration, employees may look for other jobs. Organizations that have well-designed career programs will have employees with more realistic expectations and career tracking systems that will lessen the chance that good employees will leave because of inadequate opportunities.

Performance Evaluation

A major goal of performance evaluation is to assess accurately an individual's performance contribution as a basis for making reward allocation decisions. If the performance evaluation process emphasizes the wrong criteria or inaccurately appraises actual job performance, employees will be over- or underrewarded. As equity theory demonstrated in Chapter 7, this can lead to negative consequences such as reduced effort, increases in absenteeism, or search for alternative job opportunities. In addition, the content of the performance evaluation has been found to influence employee performance and satisfaction.[53] Specifically, performance and satisfaction are increased when the evaluation is based on behavioral, results-oriented criteria; when career issues as well as performance issues are discussed; and when the subordinate has an opportunity to participate in the evaluation.

Reward Systems

If employees perceive that their efforts will be accurately appraised, and if they further perceive that the rewards they value are closely linked to their evaluations, the organization will have optimized the motivational properties from its evaluation and reward procedures and policies. More specifically, based on the contents of this chapter and our discussion of motivation in Chapters 7 and 8, we can conclude that rewards are likely to lead to high employee performance and satisfaction when they are (1) perceived as being equitable by the employee, (2) tied to performance, and (3) tailored to the needs of the individual. These conditions should foster a minimum of dissatisfaction among employees, reduce withdrawal patterns, and increase organizational commitment. If these conditions do not exist, the probability of withdrawal behavior increases, and the prevalence of marginal or barely adequate performance increases. If workers perceive that their efforts are not recognized or rewarded, and if they view their alternatives as limited, they may continue working, but will perform at a level considerably below their capability.

Employee benefits like flexible work hours, paternity leaves, and day-care centers may be most relevant for the impact they have on reducing absenteeism and improving job satisfaction. These rewards reduce barriers that many employees—particularly those with significant responsibilities outside the job—find get in the way of being at work on time or even making it to work at all. To the degree that these benefits lessen an employee's worries over outside responsibilities, they may increase satisfaction with the job and the organization.

Union–Management Interface

The existence of a union in an organization adds another variable in our search to explain and predict employee behavior. The union has been found to be an important contributor to employees' perceptions, attitudes, and behavior.

The power of the union surfaces in the collective bargaining agreement that it negotiates with the organization's management. Much of what an employee can and cannot do on the job is formally stipulated in this agreement. In addition, the informal norms that union cohesiveness fosters can encourage or discourage high productivity, organizational commitment, and morale.

FOR DISCUSSION

1. What is job analysis? How is it related to those the organization hires?

2. If you were the dean of a college of business, how would you determine which job candidates would be effective teachers?

3. Describe several *on-the-job* training methods and several *off-the-job* methods.

4. What would an effective career development program look like?

5. What effect do career anchors have on employee behavior?

6. If you were the dean of a college of business, how would you evaluate the performance of your faculty members?

7. What relationship, if any, is there between job analysis and performance evaluation?

8. Why do organizations evaluate employees?

9. What are the advantages and disadvantages of the following performance evaluation methods: (1) written essays, (b) graphic rating scales, and (c) behaviorally anchored rating scales?

10. How can an organization's performance evaluation system affect employee behavior?

11. Some organizations have a personnel policy that pay information be kept secret. Not only is pay information not given out by management, but employees are also discouraged from talking about their pay with co-workers. How do you think this practice affects employee behavior?

12. What impact do unions have on an organization's reward system?

Capitalism, Control, and the De-Skilling of Labor

There is a pervasive tendency in contemporary capitalistic countries to reorganize jobs at increasingly lower skill levels. Managers systematically destroy all-around skills where they exist and replace them with skills and occupations that fit management's needs. This de-skilling of work allows management to cut costs, increase profits, and impose control over labor.

These statements constitute the central thesis proposed in the mid-1970s by Harry Braverman.* His controversial views, clearly Marxist in origin, have gained little attention from OB scholars in business schools. But they have been enthusiastically adopted by many organizational sociologists. The basic elements of Braverman's thesis can be briefly summarized as follows.

Control is the central concept of all management systems. Therefore, it is not surprising that management seeks to control labor. It does this by de-skilling jobs. And managers in twentieth-century capitalistic countries have been able to impose de-skilling on the labor force without significant resistance.

De-skilling minimizes management's dependence on its workers. Division of labor, for instance, leads to the eradication of craft or skilled work. So, too, does mechanization. Additionally, de-skilling creates a two-class system—an informed management cadre and an uninformed labor force. By hoarding knowledge (through centralized decision making) and imposing secrecy requirements, management ensures that labor will be powerless. By de-skilling jobs, management has "appropriated" the intellectual skills once held by craft labor.

Interestingly, Braverman understands that division of labor is prevalent in all social groups. Citing Marx, he notes that the social division of labor allows species to capitalize on their inherent strengths—"the spider weaves, the bear fishes, the beaver builds dams and houses" (p. 72). But while the social division of labor merely subdivides *society,* Braverman believes that the extreme division of labor enforced in modern organizations subdivides *human beings.* Although "the subdivision of society may enhance the individual and the species, the subdivision of the individual, when carried on without regard to human capabilities and needs, is a crime against the person and against humanity" (p. 73).

Braverman doesn't ignore contemporary trends toward worker participation and the humanization of work, but he dismisses them as superficial—"allowing the worker to adjust a machine, replace a light bulb, move from one fractional job to another, and to have the illusion of making decisions by choosing among fixed and limited alternatives designed by a management which deliberately leaves insignificant matters open to choice" (p. 39).

Proponents of Braverman's thesis might add another dimension to his argument that he, understandably, overlooked at the time he was writing. That's the widespread introduction by management of computer controls. Management is increasingly monitoring the work of employees who use computers through the use of sophisticated software that, for instance, can calculate the average number of keystrokes made per minute, the average number of forms processed per hour, the number of "nonprocessing" minutes per day, and the like for each worker.

*H. Braverman, *Labor and Monopoly Capital: The Degradation of Work in the Twentieth Century* (New York: Monthly Review Press, 1974).

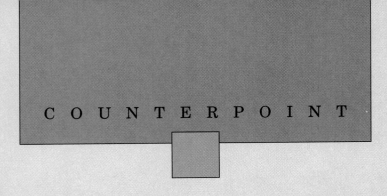

The Myth of De-Skilling in Capitalistic Societies

There are a number of flaws in Braverman's analysis. The following paragraphs highlight some of them.

The assumption that de-skilling is pervasive in capitalistic societies is false. There is ample evidence that the profit motive sometimes dictates a higher-skilled (and higher-paid) work force. High-skilled employees are, in some jobs, more productive and cost-effective than those with lower skills. A good example of this is the rapid growth of high-skilled professional jobs in the areas of health, education, high-technology industries, and government. Braverman has minimized the importance of the new high-skilled intellectual jobs.

He has also overlooked the fact that specialization through division of labor does not necessarily imply a lessening of skill. Dermatologists, neurosurgeons, endocrinologists, and other medical specialists are clearly not less skilled than general practitioners.

Braverman underrates the knowledge needed by "unskilled" workers. Even routinized machine-paced work demands a considerable amount of conceptual and practical knowledge. He understates the extent of mental work in modern jobs. Moreover, he ignores the common practice in organizations of transferring the simplest tasks of highly paid craft workers to lower-paid noncraft workers. What this practice does is to moderately upgrade the work of the noncraft worker and reserve the more complex tasks for the craft worker. So rather than de-skilling jobs, this practice actually upgrades the jobs of both the high-skilled and the low-skilled.

Braverman further errs in ignoring the evidence that some people prefer routine, de-skilled jobs. He assumes that all individuals want jobs composed of complex and sophisticated tasks, and this is clearly untrue. Some portion of the labor force prefers and seeks work that makes minimal demands on their intellectual capabilities.

Braverman argues that managers impose their will on the work force without significant resistance. This claim ignores the role and influence of labor unions. Unions have actively fought management's efforts to dominate the labor force.

While automation and mechanization have certainly replaced a significant number of workers during this century, this does not necessarily result in de-skilling, for automation typically only replaces already de-skilled, repetitious labor. So, in fact, automation has decreased the number of de-skilled jobs and improved the overall quality of the remaining jobs.

Finally, Braverman's thesis runs counter to recent trends by management to enrich jobs, create self-managed work teams, decentralize work units, and implement other improvements to give control of jobs back to workers.

This argument is substantially based on P. Attewell, "The Deskilling Controversy," *Work and Occupations,* August 1987, pp. 323–46.

Career Assessment Test

Complete the following questionnaire by circling the answer that best describes your feelings about each statement. For each item, circle your response according to the following:

SA = Strongly Agree, A = Agree, D = Disagree, SD = Strongly Disagree.

1. I would leave my company rather than be promoted out of my area of expertise.   SA   A   D   SD

2. Becoming highly specialized and highly competent in some specific functional or technical area is important to me.   SA   A   D   SD

3. A career that is free from organization restriction is important to me.   SA   A   D   SD

4. I have always sought a career in which I could be of service to others.   SA   A   D   SD

5. A career that provides a maximum variety of types of assignments and work projects is important to me.   SA   A   D   SD

6. To rise to a position in general management is important to me.   SA   A   D   SD

7. I like to be identified with a particular organization and the prestige that accompanies that organization.   SA   A   D   SD

8. Remaining in my present geographical location rather than moving because of a promotion is important to me.   SA   A   D   SD

9. The use of my skills in building a new business enterprise is important to me.   SA   A   D   SD

10. I would like to reach a level of responsibility in an organization where my decisions really make a difference.   SA   A   D   SD

11. I see myself more as a generalist as opposed to being committed to one specific area of expertise.   SA   A   D   SD

12. An endless variety of challenges in my career is important to me.   SA   A   D   SD

13. Being identified with a powerful or prestigious employer is important to me.   SA   A   D   SD

14. The excitement of participating in many areas of work has been the underlying motivation behind my career.   SA   A   D   SD

15. The process of supervising, influencing, leading, and controlling people at all levels is important to me.   SA   A   D   SD

16. I am willing to sacrifice some of my autonomy to stabilize my total life situation.   SA   A   D   SD

17. An organization that will provide security through guaranteed work, benefits, a good retirement, and so forth, is important to me.   SA   A   D   SD

18. During my career I will be mainly concerned with my own sense of freedom and autonomy.   SA   A   D   SD

19. I will be motivated throughout my career by the number of products that I have been directly involved in creating.   SA   A   D   SD

20. I want others to identify me by my organization and job.   SA   A   D   SD

21. Being able to use my skills and talents in the service of an important cause is important to me.   SA   A   D   SD

22. To be recognized by my title and status is important to me.   SA   A   D   SD

23. A career that permits a maximum of freedom and autonomy to choose my own work, hours, and so forth, is important to me.   SA   A   D   SD

24. A career that gives me a great deal of flexibility is important to me.   SA   A   D   SD

25. To be in a position in general management is important to me.   SA   A   D   SD

26. It is important for me to be identified by my occupation.   SA   A   D   SD

27. I will accept a management position only if it is in my area of expertise.   SA   A   D   SD

28. It is important for me to remain in my present geographical location rather than move because of a promotion or new job assignment.   SA   A   D   SD

29. I would like to accumulate a personal fortune to prove to myself and others that I am competent.   SA   A   D   SD

30. I want to achieve a position that gives me the opportunity to combine analytical competence with supervision of people.   SA   A   D   SD

31. I have been motivated throughout my career by using my talents in a variety of different areas of work.   SA   A   D   SD

32. An endless variety of challenges is what I really want from my career.   SA   A   D   SD

33. An organization that will give me long-run stability is important to me.   SA   A   D   SD

34. To be able to create or build something that is entirely my own product or idea is important to me.   SA   A   D   SD

35. Remaining in my specialized area, as opposed to being promoted out of my area of expertise, is important to me.   SA   A   D   SD

36. I do not want to be constrained by either an organization or the business world.   SA   A   D   SD

37. Seeing others change because of my efforts is important to me.   SA   A   D   SD

38. My main concern in life is to be competent in my area of expertise.   SA   A   D   SD

39. The chance to pursue my own lifestyle and not be constrained by the rules of an organization is important to me.   SA   A   D   SD

40. I find most organizations to be restrictive and intrusive.   SA   A   D   SD

41. Remaining in my area of expertise, rather than being promoted into general management, is important to me.   SA   A   D   SD

42. I want a career that allows me to meet my basic needs through helping others.   SA   A   D   SD

43. The use of my interpersonal and helping skills in the service of others is important to me.   SA   A   D   SD

44. I like to see others change because of my efforts.   SA   A   D   SD

Turn to page 717 for scoring direction and key.

Source: Adapted, by permission of the publisher, from "Reexamining the Career Anchor Model," by T. J. Delong, *PERSONNEL,* May-June 1982, pp. 56–57. © 1982 AMACOM, a division of American Management Associations, New York. All rights reserved.

Evaluating Performance and Providing Feedback

OBJECTIVE To experience the assessment of performance and observe the providing of performance feedback.

TIME Approximately thirty minutes.

PROCEDURE A class leader is to be selected. He or she may be either a volunteer or some-one chosen by your instructor. The class leader will preside over class discussion and perform the role of manager in the evaluation review.

Your instructor will leave the room. The class leader is then to spend up to fifteen minutes evaluating your instructor. Your instructor understands that this is only a class exercise and is prepared to accept criticism (and, of course, any praise you may want to convey). Your instructor also recognizes that the leader's evaluation is actually a composite of many students' input. So be open and honest in your evaluation and have confidence that your instructor will not be vindictive.

Research has identified seven performance dimensions to the college instructor's job: (1) instructor knowledge, (2) testing procedures, (3) student–teacher relations, (4) organizational skills, (5) communication skills, (6) subject relevance, and (7) utility of assignments. The discussion of your instructor's performance should focus on these seven dimensions. The leader may want to take notes for personal use, but will not be required to give your instructor any written documentation.

When the fifteen-minute class discussion is complete, the leader will invite the instructor back into the room. The performance review will begin as soon as the instructor walks through the door, with the class leader becoming the manager and the instructor playing him or herself.

When completed, class discussion will focus on performance evaluation criteria and how well your class leader did in providing performance feedback.

Is the Honeymoon Over at Flat Rock?

It began in 1986 with such great promise: Mazda Motor Corp. was going to build an assembly plant in Flat Rock, Michigan—just outside Detroit—that would eventually provide thousands of high-paying and secure jobs. By 1990, however, conditions had seriously deteriorated and Mazda's honeymoon with Flat Rock seemed to have come to an end. Four top U.S. managers had quit the company since 1988, and now Japanese executives had taken the senior posts that Americans once held. The company was on its fourth director of labor relations since hiring began in 1986. Unionized workers were boycotting Mazda's suggestion box, a cornerstone of Japanese-style management. Workers complained of job stress and increased injuries and absenteeism was running approximately ten percent, which was higher than other Japanese plants in the U.S. But let's start at the beginning, when Mazda began the task of staffing its new plant.

All job candidates applying at Flat Rock for assembly jobs went through a five-step screening process that was specifically designed to assess interpersonal skills, aptitude for teamwork, planning skills, and flexibility. This screening process encompassed a lot more than taking a paper-and-pencil test, enduring a few interviews, and providing some references. At Mazda, applicants also had to perform tasks that simulated jobs that they might do on the actual factory floor. For example, applicants might bolt fenders onto a car or attach hoses in a simulated engine compartment. This helped Mazda's management to match workers' abilities with specific job requirements, and it also provided applicants with a realistic preview of what they were getting into.

For the initial work force, 10,000 out of 100,000 candidates passed the five-step screening process. Of these, only 1,300 were hired. The cost of screening each one of these new employees was about $13,000 per worker.

But new hires didn't just report to the factory floor and join a work team. First, they had to undergo detailed training. That started with a three-week hodgepodge of sessions in which they learned about interpersonal relations, charting quality, stimulating creativity, and the like. This was followed by three days devoted to learning Mazda's philosophy of increasing efficiency through continual improvement. After this basic training came job-specific training. Line workers, for example, spent five to seven more weeks picking up specific technical skills, then spent another three or four weeks being supervised on the assembly line.

Why did Mazda go to all this expense and effort? The company wanted literate, versatile employees who would accept the company's emphasis on teamwork, loyalty, efficiency, and quality. Moreover, it wanted to weed out any troublemakers. What Mazda got was a work force more educated and nearly a generation younger than the old line auto workers at most Big Three plants. Mazda also wanted smooth relations with its workers. So it invited the United Auto Workers to organize the plant's employees before operations began. What went wrong? How could all this preparatory work have resulted in a disgruntled work force? The following highlights a few of the causes.

The high turnover among U.S. managers created instability. U.S. managers complained about being left out of the information network. Major decisions were controlled by Mazda executives in Japan or local Japanese superiors. Each morning, for instance, U.S. managers get a "laundry list" from their Japanese "adviser" telling them just what they were supposed to do that day.

Workers' complaints were numerous. They said that the Japanese managers didn't listen to them. They criticized the company's policy for continuous improvement, claiming that this translates into a never-ending push to cut the number of worker-hours spent building each car. To support their argument, they pointed out that American plants use fifteen to twenty percent more workers to produce a similar number of cars. Workers said that even Mazda's team system, which is supposed to give employees more authority and flexibility, is a gimmick. Power is gradually taken away from team leaders; flexibility is a one-way street that management uses to control workers; and the team system encouraged workers to pressure each other to keep up the rapid pace.

Japanese executives at Flat Rock responded by publicly lambasting workers for lacking dedication. As to the high turnover in the management ranks, Japanese executives admit that Mazda's practice of making decisions by consensus often gives the appearance of keeping authority away from its U.S. executives. But Japanese executives can also claim that the American workers just have not adapted to Mazda's way of doing business. In spite of worker complaints, management can proudly point to the fact that independent experts give Flat Rock's cars high marks for quality; every bit, in fact, as good as those built in Japan.

Questions

1. Contrast Mazda's selection and training process with those more typically used for manufacturing workers.

2. "Mazda's management doesn't understand the American worker." Do you agree or disagree with this statement? Discuss.

3. What suggestions, if any, would you make to Flat Rock's top management regarding its employee practices that might reduce absenteeism, turnover, and improve employee job satisfaction?

Source: Based on W. J. Hampton, "How Does Japan Inc. Pick Its American Workers?," *Business Week,* October 3, 1988, pp. 84–88; G. A. Patterson, "Mazda-UAW's Michigan Honeymoon Is Over," *The Wall Street Journal,* April 17, 1990, p. B1; and J. J. Fucini and S. Fucini, *Working For the Japanese* (New York: Free Press, 1990).

FOR FURTHER READING

DESHPANDE, S. P., and J. FIORITO, "Specific and General Beliefs in Union Voting Models," *Academy of Management Journal,* December 1989, pp. 883–97. Survey data revealed that roughly three-fourths of nonunion employees view unions as effective in improving wages and working conditions, yet only about one-third would vote for unionization of their workplace. This article explains why.

FERRIS, G. R., and K. M. ROWLAND (eds.), *Career and Human Resources Development* (Greenwich, CT: JAI Press, 1990). A collection of seven monographs on career and development issues.

FERRIS, G. R., and K. M. ROWLAND (eds.), *Performance Evaluation, Goal Setting, and Feedback* (Greenwich, CT: JAI Press, 1990). A collection of seven monographs focusing on performance evaluation and feedback issues.

NEVELS, P., "Why Employees Are Being Asked to Rate Their Supervisors," *Supervisory Management,* December 1989, pp. 5–11. Traditional top-down evaluations are being supplemented by new bottom-up evaluations. This article reviews why this is being done and the problems it might create.

SCOTT, W. R., and J. W. MEYER, "The Rise of Training Programs in Firms and Agencies: An Institutional Perspective," in L. L. Cummings and B. M. Staw (eds.), *Research in Organizational Behavior,* Vol. 13 (Greenwich, CT: JAI Press, 1991), pp. 297–326. Provides varied explanations for the growth and changing content of organizational training programs.

SHERIDAN, J. E., J. W. SLOCUM, JR., R. BUDA, and R. C. THOMPSON, "Effects of Corporate Sponsorship and Departmental Power on Career Tournaments," *Academy of Management Journal,* September 1990, pp. 578–602. A ten-year study of over three hundred managers found that how they started their careers in their company and the power of the department in which they started strongly influenced rates of job promotion, transfer, and salary progression.

NOTES

[1]A. Saltzman, "To Get Ahead, You May Have to Put on an Act," *U.S. News & World Report,* May 13, 1991, p. 90.

[2]See, for instance, C. T. Dortch, "Job-Person Match," *Personnel Journal,* June 1989, pp. 49–57; and S. Rynes and B. Gerhart, "Interviewer Assessments of Applicant 'Fit': An Exploratory Investigation," *Personnel Psychology,* Spring 1990, pp. 13–34.

[3]See, for example, J. V. Ghorpade, *Job Analysis: A Handbook for the Human Resource Director* (Englewood Cliffs, NJ: Prentice Hall, 1988).

[4]G. Johns, *Organizational Behavior: Understanding Life at Work,* 2nd ed. (Glenview, IL: Scott, Foresman, 1988), p. 19.

[5]T. J. Hanson and J. C. Balestreri-Spero, "An Alternative to Interviews," *Personnel Journal,* June 1985, p. 114.

[6]See R. D. Arvey and J. E. Campion, "The Employment Interview: A Summary and Review of Recent Research," *Personnel Psychology,* Summer 1982, pp. 281–322; and M. M. Harris, "Reconsidering the Employment Interview: A Review of Recent Literature and Suggestions for Future Research," *Personnel Psychology,* Winter 1989, pp. 691–726.

[7]See, for example, A. P. Phillips and R. L. Dipboye, "Correlational Tests of Predictions from a Process Model of the Interview," *Journal of Applied Psychology,* February 1989, pp. 41–52.

[8]See, for example, Harris, "Reconsidering the Employment Interview"; and J. Solomon, "The New Job Interview: Show Thyself," *The Wall Street Journal,* December 4, 1989, p. B1.

[9]E. E. Ghiselli, "The Validity of Aptitude Tests in Personnel Selection," *Personnel Psychology,* Winter 1973, p. 475.

[10]G. Grimsley and H. F. Jarrett, "The Relation of Managerial Achievement to Test Measures Obtained in the Employment Situation: Methodology and Results," *Personnel Psychology,* Spring 1973, pp. 31–48; and A. K. Korman, "The Prediction of Managerial Performance: A Review," *Personnel Psychology,* Summer 1968, pp. 295–322.

[11]J. J. Asher and J. A. Sciarrino, "Realistic Work Sample Tests: A Review," *Personnel Psychology,* Winter 1974, pp. 519–33; and I. T. Robertson and R. S. Kandola, "Work Sample Tests: Validity, Adverse Impact and Applicant Reaction," *Journal of Occupational Psychology,* 1982, pp. 171–82.

[12]See, for example, B. B. Gaugher, D. B. Rosenthal, G. C. Thornton III, and C. Bentson, "Meta-Analysis of Assessment Center Validity," *Journal of Applied Psychology,* August 1987,

pp. 493–511; G. M. McEvoy and R. W. Beatty, "Assessment Centers and Subordinate Appraisals of Managers: A Seven-Year Examination of Predictive Validity," *Personnel Psychology,* Spring 1989, pp. 37–52; and M. J. Papa, "A Comparison of Two Methods of Managerial Selection," *Management Communication Quarterly,* November 1989, pp. 191–218.

[13]Cited in N. J. Perry, "The Workers of the Future," *Fortune,* 1991 Special Issue: The New American Century, p. 68.

[14]"Corporate Training Has Itself Become Big Business," *The Wall Street Journal,* August 5, 1986, p. 1.

[15]C. Lee, "Where the Training Dollars Go," *Training,* Vol. 24, No. 10, 1987, pp. 51–65.

[16]For an extended discussion of on-the-job and off-the-job training methods, see D. DeCenzo and S. P. Robbins, *Personnel/Human Resource Management,* 3rd ed. (Englewood Cliffs, NJ: Prentice Hall, 1988), pp. 248–51, 255–61.

[17]This box is based on G. L. Pamental, "The Course in Business Ethics: Can It Work?", *Journal of Business Ethics,* July 1989, pp. 547–51; P. F. Miller and W. T. Coady, "Teaching Work Ethics," *Education Digest,* February 1990, pp. 54–55; D. Rice and C. Dreilinger, "Rights and Wrongs of Ethics Training," *Training and Development Journal,* May 1990, pp. 103–08; and J. Weber, "Measuring the Impact of Teaching Ethics to Future Managers: A Review, Assessment, and Recommendations," *Journal of Business Ethics,* March 1990, pp. 183–90.

[18]R. Wowk, D. Williams, and G. Halstead, "Do Formal Career Development Programs Really Increase Employee Participation?", *Training and Development Journal,* September 1983, pp. 82–83.

[19]M. Moravec, "A Cost-Effective Career Planning Program Requires a Strategy," *Personnel Administrator,* January 1982, pp. 28–32.

[20]From a study conducted by the Sterling Institute and reported in J. Keller and C. Piotrowski, "Career Development Programs in *Fortune* 500 Firms," *Psychological Reports,* December 1987, p. 921.

[21]D. E. Super and D. T. Hall, "Career Development Exploration and Planning," in M. R. Rosenzweig and L. W. Porter (eds.), *Annual Review of Psychology,* Vol. 29 (Palo Alto, CA: Annual Reviews, 1978), p. 334.

[22]D. T. Hall, *Careers in Organizations* (Santa Monica, CA: Goodyear, 1976), pp. 3–4.

[23]See, for example, D. E. Super, *The Psychology of Careers* (New York: Harper & Row, 1957); and E. H. Schein, "The Individual, the Organization, and the Career: A Conceptual Scheme," *Journal of Applied Behavioral Science,* August 1971, pp. 401–26.

[24]E. H. Schein, "How Career Anchors Hold Executives to Their Career Paths," *Personnel,* May 1975, pp. 11–24; and E. H. Schein, *Career Dynamics: Matching Individual and Organizational Needs* (Reading, MA: Addison-Wesley, 1978).

[25]This box is based on L. E. Wynter, "Theatre Program Tackles Issues of Diversity," *The Wall Street Journal,* April 18, 1991, p. B1; T. Cox, Jr., "The Multicultural Organization," *Academy of Management Executive,* May 1991, pp. 40–41; J. E. Ellis, "Monsanto's New Challenge: Keeping Minority Workers," *Business Week,* July 8, 1991, p. 61; and T. Cox, Jr., and S. Blake, "Managing Cultural Diversity: Implications for Organizational Competitiveness," *Academy of Management Executive,* August 1991, p. 53.

[26]D. E. Berlew and D. T. Hall, "The Socialization of Managers: Effects of Expectations on Performance," *Administrative Science Quarterly,* September 1966, pp. 207–23; and D. W. Bray, R. J. Campbell, and D. L. Grant, *Formulative Years in Business: A Long-Term AT&T Study of Managerial Lives* (New York: John Wiley, 1974).

[27]See Super and Hall, "Career Development: Exploration and Planning," p. 362.

[28]J. Van Maanen and E. H. Schein, "Career Development," in J. R. Hackman and J. L. Suttle (eds.), *Improving Life at Work* (Santa Monica: CA: Goodyear, 1977), p. 87.

[29]H. G. Kaufman, *Obsolescence and Professional Career Development* (New York: AMA-COM, 1974).

[30]See J. N. Cleveland, K. R. Murphy, and R. E. Williams, "Multiple Uses of Performance Appraisal: Prevalence and Correlates," *Journal of Applied Psychology,* February 1989, pp. 130–35.

[31]P. M. Blau, *The Dynamics of Bureaucracy,* rev. ed. (Chicago: University of Chicago Press, 1963).

[32]"The Cop-Out Cops," *National Observer,* August 3, 1974.

[33]G. P. Latham and K. N. Wexley, *Increasing Productivity Through Performance Appraisal* (Reading, MA: Addison-Wesley, 1981), p. 80.

[34]Ibid., p. 81.

[35]D. J. Campbell and C. Lee, "Self-Appraisal in Performance Evaluation: Developmental versus Evaluation," *Academy of Management Review,* April 1988, pp. 302–14.

[36]For two diverse conclusions on behaviorally anchored rating scales, see A. Tziner, "Effects of Rating Format on Goal-Setting Dimensions: A Field Experiment," *Journal of Applied Psychology,* May 1988, pp. 323–26; and L. R. Gomez-Mejia, "Evaluating Employee Performance: Does the Appraisal Instrument Make a Difference?", *Journal of Occupational Behavior Management,* Vol. 9, No. 2, 1988, pp. 155–72.

[37]A. Pizam, "Social Differentiation—A New Psychological Barrier to Performance Appraisal," *Public Personnel Management,* July-August 1975, pp. 244–47.

[38]Ibid., pp. 245–46.

[39]See, for example, W. M. Fox, "Improving Performance Appraisal Systems," *National Productivity Review,* Winter 1987–88, pp. 20–27.

[40]W. C. Borman, "The Rating of Individuals in Organizations: An Alternate Approach," *Organizational Behavior and Human Performance,* August 1974, pp. 105–24.

[41]Ibid.

[42]G. P. Latham, K. N. Wexley, and E. D. Pursell, "Training Managers to Minimize Rating Errors in the Observation of Behavior," *Journal of Applied Psychology,* October 1975, pp. 550–55.

[43]H. J. Bernardin, "The Effects of Rater Training on Leniency and Halo Errors in Student Rating of Instructors," *Journal of Applied Psychology,* June 1978, pp. 301–08.

[44]Ibid.; and J. M. Ivancevich, "Longitudinal Study of the Effects of Rater Training on Psychometric Error in Ratings, *Journal of Applied Psychology,* October 1979, pp. 502–08.

[45]Much of this section is based on H. H. Meyer, "A Solution to the Performance Appraisal Feedback Enigma," *Academy of Management Executive,* February 1991, pp. 68–76.

[46]R. J. Burke, "Why Performance Appraisal Systems Fail," *Personnel Administration,* June 1972, pp. 32–40.

[47]This section is based on W. Lobdell, "Who's Right for an Overseas Position?" *World Trade,* April-May 1990, pp. 20–26.

[48]This material was adapted from T. H. Hammer, "Relationship Between Local Union Characteristics and Worker Behavior and Attitudes," *Academy of Management Journal,* December 1978, pp. 560–77.

[49]See J. B. Arthur and J. B. Dworkin, "Current Topics in Industrial and Labor Relations Research and Practice," *Journal of Management,* September 1991, pp. 530–32.

[50]See, for example, C. J. Berger, C. A. Olson, and J. W. Boudreau, "Effects of Unions on Job Satisfaction: The Role of Work-Related Values and Perceived Rewards," *Organizational Behavior and Human Performance,* December 1983, pp. 289–324; and M. G. Evans and D. A. Ondrack, "The Role of Job Outcomes and Values in Understanding the Union's Impact on Job Satisfaction: A Replication," *Human Relations,* May 1990, pp. 401–18.

[51]A. Bandura, "Self-Efficacy: Towards a Unifying Theory of Behavioral Change," *Psychological Review,* March 1977, pp. 191–215.

[52]M. K. Mount, "Managerial Career Stage and Facets of Job Satisfaction," *Journal of Vocational Behavior,* June 1984, pp. 340–54; and C. S. Granrose and J. D. Portwood, "Matching Individual Career Plans and Organizational Career Management," *Academy of Management Journal,* December 1987, pp. 699–720.

[53]B. R. Nathan, A. M. Mohrman, Jr., and J. Milliman, "Interpersonal Relations as a Context for the Effects of Appraisal Interviews on Performance and Satisfaction: A Longitudinal Study," *Academy of Management Journal,* June 1991, pp. 352–69.

ORGANIZATIONAL CULTURE

LEARNING OBJECTIVES

After studying this chapter, you should be able to:

1. Describe institutionalization and its relationship to organizational culture

2. Define the common characteristics making up organizational culture

3. Contrast strong and weak cultures

4. Identify the functional and dysfunctional effects of organizational culture on people

5. Explain the factors determining an organization's culture

6. List the factors that maintain an organization's culture

7. Clarify how culture is transmitted to employees

8. Outline the various socialization alternatives available to management

*In any organization, there are the ropes to skip
and the ropes to know.*

R. RITTI AND G. FUNKHOUSER

Wal-Mart is one of the most remarkable success stories in the history of modern business.[1] It was founded in 1962. As recently as 1980, its annual sales of $2.4 billion were less than twelve percent of Sears' sales. But during the 1980s, Wal-Mart's annual revenues grew at a compounded rate of twenty-five percent per year! With sales now approaching $40 billion a year, it has overtaken Sears and Kmart to become the largest retailer in America.

How did Wal-Mart do it? After all, it sells the same merchandise as hundreds of other retailers. Part of the answer lies in founder Sam Walton's original growth strategy: Locate in small towns, where there is little major competition, and build stores close enough to one another so that they can be supplied from huge central distribution centers. But that's only a small part of the explanation. The real secret of Wal-Mart's success lies in the strong culture that the late Sam Walton (pictured above) created and his 350,000 employees' commitment to it. This culture stresses quality, low cost, and customer service. From an OB perspective, what makes Wal-Mart special are practices such as treating its employees like true partners, encouraging them to take risks and innovate, and including those working at all levels in the decision-making process. A brief story will illustrate Wal-Mart's culture.

In 1985, John Love, an assistant store manager in Oneonta, Alabama, made a mistake—he ordered four to five times more of a marshmallow confection called Moon Pies than the store needed. It was the kind of stupid mistake that could have gotten him fired at another company. But not at Wal-Mart. Love's store manager told him, "John, use your imagination; be creative and figure out a way to sell them." John's solution: The first World Championship Moon Pie Eating Contest, held in his store's parking lot. The promotion proved so successful at selling Moon Pies that the contest has now become an annual rite at the Oneonta store. ■

A strong organizational culture like that found at Wal-Mart provides employees with a clear understanding of "the way things are done around here." In this chapter, we'll show that every organization has a culture and, depending on its strength, culture can have a significant influence on the attitudes and behaviors of organization members.

INSTITUTIONALIZATION: A FORERUNNER OF CULTURE

Institutionalization When an organization takes on a life of its own, apart from any of its members, and acquires immortality.

The idea of viewing organizations as cultures—where there is a system of shared meaning among members—is a relatively recent phenomenon. Fifteen years ago, organizations were, for the most part, simply thought of as rational means by which to coordinate and control a group of people. They had vertical levels, departments, authority relationships, and so forth. But organizations are more. They have personalities too, just like individuals. They can be rigid or flexible, unfriendly or supportive, innovative or conservative. General Electric offices and people *are* different from the offices and people at General Mills. Harvard and MIT are in the same business—education—and separated only by the width of the Charles River, but each has a unique feeling and character beyond its structural characteristics. Organizational theorists, in recent years, have begun to acknowledge this by recognizing the important role that culture plays in the lives of organization members. Interestingly, though, the origin of culture as an independent variable affecting an employee's attitudes and behavior can be traced back forty-five years ago to the notion of **institutionalization.**[2]

When an organization becomes institutionalized, it takes on a life of its own, apart from any of its members. The Internal Revenue Service, Eastman Kodak, and Timex Corporation are examples of organizations that have existed beyond the life of any one member. Additionally, when an organization becomes institutionalized, it becomes valued for itself, not merely for the goods or services it produces. It acquires immortality. If its original goals are no longer relevant, it doesn't go out of business. Rather, it redefines itself. When the demand for Timex's watches declined, the company merely redirected itself into the consumer electronics business—making, in addition to watches, clocks, computers, and health-care products such as digital thermometers and blood pressure testing devices. Timex took on an existence that went beyond its original mission to manufacture low-cost mechanical watches.

Institutionalization operates to produce common understandings among members about what is appropriate and, fundamentally, meaningful behavior.[3] So when an organization takes on institutional permanence, acceptable modes of behavior become largely self-evident to its members. As we'll see, this is essentially the same thing that organizational culture does. So an understanding of what makes up an organization's culture, and how it is created, sustained, and learned will enhance our ability to explain and predict the behavior of people at work.

WHAT IS ORGANIZATIONAL CULTURE?

A few years back, I asked an executive to tell me what he thought *organizational culture* meant and he gave me essentially the same answer that a Supreme Court Justice once gave in attempting to define pornography: "I can't define it, but I know it when I see it." This executive's approach to defining organizational culture isn't acceptable for our purposes. We need a basic definition to provide a point of departure for our quest to better understand the phenomenon. In this section, we'll propose a specific definition and review several peripheral issues that revolve around this definition.

A Definition

Organizational Culture A common perception held by the organization's members; a system of shared meaning.

There seems to be wide agreement that **organizational culture** refers to a system of shared meaning held by members that distinguishes the organization from other organizations.[4] This system of shared meaning is, on closer examination, a set of key characteristics that the organization values. Recent research suggests that there are ten primary characteristics that, in aggregate, capture the essence of an organization's culture.[5]

1. *Member identity:* The degree to which employees identify with the organization as a whole rather than with their type of job or field of professional expertise.
2. *Group emphasis:* The degree to which work activities are organized around groups rather than individuals.
3. *People focus:* The degree to which management decisions take into consideration the effect of outcomes on people within the organization.
4. *Unit integration:* The degree to which units within the organization are encouraged to operate in a coordinated or interdependent manner.
5. *Control:* The degree to which rules, regulations, and direct supervision are used to oversee and control employee behavior.
6. *Risk tolerance:* The degree to which employees are encouraged to be aggressive, innovative, and risk-seeking.
7. *Reward criteria:* The degree to which rewards such as salary increases and promotions are allocated according to employee performance rather than seniority, favoritism, or other nonperformance factors.
8. *Conflict tolerance:* The degree to which employees are encouraged to air conflicts and criticisms openly.
9. *Means-ends orientation:* The degree to which management focuses on results or outcomes rather than on the techniques and processes used to achieve those outcomes.
10. *Open-system focus:* The degree to which the organization monitors and responds to changes in the external environment.

As shown in Figure 17–1, each of these characteristics exists on a continuum. Appraising the organization on these ten characteristics, then, gives a composite picture of the organization's culture. This picture becomes the basis for feelings of shared understanding that members have about the organization, how things are done in it, and the way members are supposed to behave. Table 17–1 demonstrates how these characteristics can be mixed to create highly diverse organizations.

Cultural Typologies

Jeffrey Sonnenfeld of Emory University has developed a labeling schema that can help us see differences between organizational cultures and the importance of properly matching people to cultures. From his study of organizations, he has identified four cultural "types": *academy, club, baseball team,* and *fortress.*[6]

FIGURE 17–1   The Key Characteristics Defining an Organization's Culture

Job	1. Member identity	Organization
Individual	2. Group emphasis	Group
Task	3. People focus	People
Independent	4. Unit integration	Interdependent
Loose	5. Control	Tight
Low	6. Risk tolerance	High
Performance	7. Reward criteria	Other
Low	8. Conflict tolerance	High
Means	9. Means-ends orientation	Ends
Internal	10. Open-system focus	External

ACADEMY   An academy is the place for steady climbers who want to thoroughly master each new job they hold. These companies like to recruit young college graduates, provide them with much special training, and then carefully steer them through a myriad of specialized jobs within a particular function. IBM is a classic academy. So, too, are Coca-Cola, Procter & Gamble, and General Motors.

CLUB   Clubs place a high value on "fitting in," on loyalty, and on commitment. Seniority is the key at clubs. Age and experience count. In contrast to an academy, the club grooms managers as generalists. Examples of clubs are United Parcel Service, Delta Airlines, the Bell operating companies, government agencies, and the military.

Les Wexner, founder of The Limited, seeks to create a culture that encourages risk taking. Buyers, for example, are graded not only on their successes, but also on their failures. Too many hits means buyers aren't taking enough chances.   Lynn Johnson/Black Star

TABLE 17-1   Contrasting Organizational Cultures

Organization A

This organization is a manufacturing firm. Employees' loyalty is to the organization. There are extensive rules and regulations that employees are required to follow. Managers supervise employees closely to ensure there are no deviations. Management is concerned with high productivity, regardless of the impact on employee morale or turnover.

Work activities are designed around individuals. There are distinct departments and lines of authority, and employees are expected to minimize formal contact with other employees outside their functional area or line of command. Effort, loyalty, cooperation, and avoidance of errors are highly valued and rewarded. The company promotes only from within and believes the best products are those developed inside the firm.

Organization B

This organization is also a manufacturing firm. Here, however, employees pride themselves on their technical skills, current expertise, and professional contacts outside the company. There are few rules and regulations, and supervision is loose because management believes that its employees are hardworking and trustworthy. Management is concerned with high productivity, but believes that this comes through treating its people right. The company is proud of its reputation as being a good place to work.

Job activities are designed around work teams and team members are encouraged to interact with people across functions and authority levels. Managers are evaluated not only on their department's performance but also on how well their department coordinates its activities with other departments in the organization. Promotions and other valuable rewards go to employees who make the greatest contributions to the organization, even when those employees have strange ideas, unusual personal mannerisms, or unconventional work habits. The company fills upper-level positions with the best people available, which sometimes means hiring people away from competitors. The company prides itself on being market-driven and rapidly responsive to the changing needs of its customers.

BASEBALL TEAM   These organizations are entrepreneurially oriented havens for risk-takers and innovators. Baseball teams seek out talented people of all ages and experiences, then reward them for what they produce. Because they offer huge financial incentives and great freedom to their star performers, job hopping among these organizations is commonplace. Organizations that fit the baseball team description are common in accounting, law, investment banking, and consulting firms; advertising agencies; software developers; and bio-research concerns.

FORTRESS   While baseball teams prize inventiveness, fortresses are preoccupied with survival. Many were once academies, clubs, or baseball teams, but fell on hard times and are now seeking to reverse their sagging fortunes. Fortresses offer little job security, yet they can be exciting places to work for those who like the challenge of a turnaround. Fortress organizations include large retailers, hotels, forest products companies, and oil and natural gas exploration firms.

Sonnenfeld found that many organizations can't be neatly categorized into one of the four categories either because they have a blend of cultures or because they are in transition. General Electric, for instance, was found to have distinctly different cultures within its different units, and Apple Computer started out as a baseball team but is maturing into an academy.

Sonnenfeld found that each of the four cultural types tends to attract certain personalities and the personality–organizational culture match affects how far and how easily a person will move up the management ranks. For instance, a risk-taker will thrive at a baseball team, but fall flat on his or her face at an academy.

Using Sonnenfeld's cultural typologies, we would predict that a stock brokerage firm like Dean Witter Reynolds would be a baseball team. Employee satisfaction would be highest and turnover lowest when brokers are high risk takers, achievement oriented, and possessing an internal locus of control.   Courtesy Sears Roebuck & Company

Culture Is a Descriptive Term

Organizational culture is concerned with how employees perceive the characteristics of an organization's culture, not with whether or not they like them. That is, it is a descriptive term. This is important because it differentiates this concept from that of job satisfaction.

Research on organizational culture has sought to measure how employees see their organization: Does it encourage teamwork? Does it reward innovation? Does it stifle conflict?

In contrast, job satisfaction seeks to measure affective responses to the work environment. It is concerned with how employees feel about the organization's expectations, reward practices, methods for handling conflict, and the like. Although the two terms undoubtedly have overlapping characteristics, keep in mind that the term *organizational culture* is descriptive, while *job satisfaction* is evaluative.

Do Organizations Have Uniform Cultures?

Organizational culture represents a common perception held by the organization's members. This was made explicit when we defined culture as a system of *shared* meaning. We should expect, therefore, that individuals with different backgrounds or at different levels in the organization will tend to describe the organization's culture in similar terms.[7]

Acknowledgement that organizational culture has common properties does not mean, however, that there cannot be subcultures within any given culture. Most large organizations have a dominant culture and numerous sets of subcultures.[8]

Dominant Culture Expresses the core values that are shared by a majority of the organization's members.

Subcultures Minicultures within an organization, typically defined by department designations and geographical separation.

A **dominant culture** expresses the core values that are shared by a majority of the organization's members. When we talk about an *organization's* culture, we are referring to its dominant culture. It is this macro view of culture that gives an organization its distinct personality. **Subcultures** tend to develop in large organizations to reflect common problems, situations, or experiences that members face. These subcultures are likely to be defined by department designations and geographical separation. The pur-

Core Values The primary or dominant values that are accepted throughout the organization.

chasing department, for example, can have a subculture that is uniquely shared by members of that department. It will include the **core values** of the dominant culture plus additional values unique to members of the purchasing department. Similarly, an office or unit of the organization that is physically separated from the organization's main operations may take on a different personality. Again, the core values are essentially retained but modified to reflect the separated unit's distinct situation.

If organizations had no dominant culture and were composed only of numerous subcultures, the value of organizational culture as an independent variable would be significantly lessened because there would be no uniform interpretation of what represented appropriate and inappropriate behavior. It is the "shared meaning" aspect of culture that makes it such a potent device for guiding and shaping behavior. But we cannot ignore the reality that many organizations also have subcultures that can influence the behavior of members.

Strong vs. Weak Cultures

It has become increasingly popular to differentiate between strong and weak cultures.[9] The argument here is that strong cultures have a greater impact on employee behavior and are more directly related to reduced turnover.

Strong Cultures Cultures where the core values are intensely held and widely shared.

In a **strong culture,** the organization's core values are both intensely held and widely shared.[10] The more members who accept the core values and the greater their commitment to those values, the stronger the culture is. Consistent with this definition, a strong culture will have a great influence on the behavior of its members because the high degree of sharedness and intensity creates an internal climate of high behavioral control. For example, Seattle-based Nordstrom has developed one of the strongest service cultures in the retailing industry. Nordstrom employees know in no uncertain terms what is expected of them and these expectations go a long way in shaping their behavior.

One specific result of a strong culture should be lower employee turnover. A strong culture demonstrates high agreement among members

Nordstrom, the Seattle-based retailer, has a strong culture. It distinguishes itself from its competition by its service. Employees understand that they are to do whatever is necessary to please the customer. That often means employees will call other company stores to find the right item for a customer or even personally deliver an item to the customer's home.   Susan Steinkamp/SABA

Cultural Factors That Breed Unethical Behavior

An organization's culture socializes people. It subtly conveys to members that certain actions are acceptable, even though they are illegal. For instance, when executives at General Electric, Westinghouse, and other manufacturers of heavy electrical equipment illegally conspired to set prices in the early 1960s, the defendants invariably testified that they came new to their jobs, found price-fixing to be an established way of life, and simply entered into it as they did into other aspects of their job. One GE manager noted that every one of his bosses had directed him to meet with the competition: "It had become so common and gone on for so many years that I think we lost sight of the fact that it was illegal."[11]

Both the content and the strength of an organization's culture have an influence on the ethical behavior of its managers.[12] A culture that is likely to shape high ethical standards is one that is high in both risk and conflict tolerance and whose members identify with their job's pro-fessional standards. Managers in such a culture will be encouraged to be aggressive and innovative, will feel free to openly challenge demands or expectations they consider unrealistic or personally distasteful, and will have professional standards to guide them. A strong culture will exert more influence on managers than a weak one. If the culture is strong and supports high ethical standards, it should have a very powerful positive influence on a manager's ethical behavior. However, in a weak culture, managers are more likely to rely on subculture norms to guide their behavior. So work groups and departmental standards will more strongly influence ethical behavior in organizations that have weak overall cultures.

Given this evidence, is it possible for a manager with high ethical standards to uphold those standards in an organizational culture that tolerates, or even encourages, unethical practices? What do *you* think?

about what the organization stands for. Such unanimity of purpose builds cohesiveness, loyalty, and organizational commitment. These qualities, in turn, lessen employees' propensity to leave the organization.[13]

Culture vs. Formalization

A strong organizational culture increases behavioral consistency. In this sense, we should recognize that a strong culture can act as a substitute for formalization.

In Chapter 14, we discussed how formalization's rules and regulations act to regulate employee behavior. High formalization in an organization creates predictability, orderliness, and consistency. Our point is that a strong culture achieves the same end without the need for written documentation. Therefore, we should view formalization and culture as two different roads to a common destination. The stronger an organization's culture, the less management need be concerned with developing formal rules and regulations to guide employee behavior. Those guides will be internalized in employees when they accept the organization's culture.

WHAT DOES CULTURE DO?

We've alluded to organizational culture's impact on behavior. We've also explicitly argued that a strong culture should be associated with reduced turnover. In this section, we will more carefully review the functions that culture performs and assess whether culture can be a liability for an organization.

Culture's Functions

Culture performs a number of functions within an organization. First, it has a boundary-defining role; that is, it creates distinctions between one organization and others. Second, it conveys a sense of identity for organization members. Third, culture facilitates the generation of commitment to something larger than one's individual self-interest. Fourth, it enhances social system stability. Culture is the social glue that helps hold the organization together by providing appropriate standards for what employees should say and do. Finally, culture serves as a sense-making and control mechanism that guides and shapes the attitudes and behavior of employees. It is this last function that is of particular interest to us. As the following quote makes clear, culture defines the rules of the game:

> Culture by definition is elusive, intangible, implicit, and taken for granted. But every organization develops a core set of assumptions, understandings, and implicit rules that govern day-to-day behavior in the workplace . . . .Until newcomers learn the rules, they are not accepted as full-fledged members of the organization. Transgressions of the rules on the part of high-level executives or front-line employees result in universal disapproval and powerful penalties. Conformity to the rules becomes the primary basis for reward and upward mobility.[14]

As we'll show later in this chapter, who receives a job offer to join the organization, who is appraised as a high performer, and who gets the promotion are strongly influenced by the individual–organization "fit"—that is, whether the applicant or employee's attitudes and behavior are compatible with the culture. It is not a coincidence that employees at Disneyland and Disney World appear to be almost universally attractive, clean, and wholesome-looking, with bright smiles. That's the image Disney seeks. The company selects employees who will maintain that image. And once on the job, both the informal norms and formal rules and regulations ensure that Disney employees will act in a relatively uniform and predictable way.

Culture as a Liability

We are treating culture in a nonjudgmental manner. We haven't said that it's good or bad, only that it exists. Many of its functions, as outlined, are valuable for both the organization and the employee. Culture enhances organizational commitment and increases the consistency of employee behavior. These are clearly benefits to an organization. From an employee's standpoint, culture is valuable because it reduces ambiguity. It tells employees how things are done and what's important. But we shouldn't ignore the potentially dysfunctional aspects of culture, especially a strong one, on an organization's effectiveness.

Culture is a liability where the shared values are not in agreement with those that will further the organization's effectiveness. This is most likely to occur when the organization's environment is dynamic. When the environment is undergoing rapid change, the organization's entrenched culture may no longer be appropriate. So consistency of behavior is an asset to an organization when it faces a stable environment. It may, however, burden the organization and make it difficult to respond to changes in the environment. This helps to explain the challenges AT&T has had adapting to a deregulated environment.[15] Its strong service- and technology-oriented culture, which originated in the nineteenth century, was amazingly effective as long as the company remained in the telephone business and held a monopoly there. But after deregulation, AT&T chose to compete in the telecommunications and computer industries against the likes of IBM, Xerox, and the Japanese. AT&T has had a difficult time adjusting to its new environment, largely because it has had to try to create a new, more market-driven culture to supersede a preregulation culture that was very strong.

CREATING AND SUSTAINING CULTURE

An organization's culture doesn't pop out of thin air. Once established, it rarely fades away. What forces influence the creation of a culture? What reinforces and sustains these forces once they are in place? We'll answer both of these questions in this section.

How a Culture Begins

An organization's current customs, traditions, and general way of doing things are largely due to what it has done before and the degree of success it has had with those endeavors. This leads us to the ultimate source of an organization's culture: its founders.[16]

The founders of an organization traditionally have a major impact on that organization's early culture. They have a vision of what the organization should be. They are unconstrained by previous customs or ideologies. The

McDonald's founder, Ray Kroc, died in 1984. But his philosophy is preserved on tape at company headquarters and continues to guide McDonald's current management.   Kevin Horan

small size that typically characterizes new organizations further facilitates the founders' imposition of their vision on all organizational members.

Wal-Mart's culture, discussed at the opening of this chapter, is largely a reflection of Sam Walton. Even though he was worth more than $8 billion, Walton lived in an unpretentious ranch home in Bentonville, Arkansas, drove a Ford pickup truck, and worked in a modest office with plywood paneling. Wal-Mart's culture reflects its founder's belief in frugality, simplicity, and value. Other contemporary examples of founders who have had an immeasurable impact on their organization's culture are Fred Smith at Federal Express, Steve Jobs at Apple Computer, and Bill Gates at Microsoft. For instance, Bill Gates is personally aggressive, competitive, and highly disciplined. Those are the same characteristics often used to describe Microsoft, the software giant he founded and currently heads.

Keeping a Culture Alive

Once a culture is in place, there are practices within the organization that act to maintain it by giving employees a set of similar experiences. For example, many of the human resource practices discussed in the previous chapter reinforce the organization's culture. The selection process, performance evaluation criteria, reward practices, training and career development activities, and promotion procedures ensure that those hired fit in with the culture, reward those who support it, and penalize (and even expel) those who challenge it. Three forces play a particularly important part in sustaining a culture—selection practices, the actions of top management, and socialization methods. Let's take a closer look at each.

SELECTION   The explicit goal of the selection process is to identify and hire individuals who have the knowledge, skills, and abilities to perform the jobs within the organization successfully. But, typically, more than one candidate will be identified who meets any given job's requirements. When that point is reached, it would be naive to ignore that the final decision as to who is hired will be significantly influenced by the decision maker's judgment of how well the candidates will fit into the organization. This attempt to ensure a proper match, whether purposely or inadvertently, results in the hiring of people who have values essentially consistent with those of the organization, or at least a good portion of those values.[17] Additionally, the selection process provides information to applicants about the organization. Candidates learn about the organization, and, if they perceive a conflict between their values and those of the organization, they can self-select themselves out of the applicant pool. Selection, therefore, becomes a two-way street, allowing either employer or applicant to abrogate a marriage if there appears to be a mismatch. In this way, the selection process sustains an organization's culture by selecting out those individuals who might attack or undermine its core values.

Applicants for entry-level positions in brand management at Procter & Gamble experience an exhaustive application and screening process. Their interviewers are part of an elite cadre who have been selected and trained extensively via lectures, videotapes, films, practice interviews, and role plays to identify applicants who will successfully fit in at P&G. Applicants are interviewed in-depth for such qualities as their ability to "turn out high volumes of excellent work," "identify and understand problems," and "reach thoroughly substantiated and well-reasoned conclusions that lead to action." P&G values rationality and seeks applicants who think that way. College applicants receive two interviews and a general knowledge test on campus, before being flown back to Cincinnati for three more one-on-one interviews and a group interview at lunch. Each encounter seeks corroborating evidence of the traits that the firm believes correlate highly with "what counts" for success at P&G.[18] Applicants for positions at Compaq Computer are carefully chosen for their ability to fit into the company's teamwork-oriented culture. As one executive put it, "We can find lots of people who are competent . . . .The No. 1 issue is whether they fit into the way we do business."[19] At Compaq, that means job candidates who are easy to get along with and who feel comfortable with the company's consensus management style. To increase the likelihood that loners and those with big egos get screened out, it's not unusual for an applicant to be interviewed by fifteen people, who represent all departments of the company and a variety of seniority levels.[20]

TOP MANAGEMENT   The actions of top management also have a major impact on the organization's culture.[21] Through what they say and how they behave, senior executives establish norms that filter down through the organization as to whether risk-taking is desirable; how much freedom managers should give their subordinates; what is appropriate dress; what actions will pay off in terms of pay raises, promotions, and other rewards; and the like.

For example, look at Xerox Corp.[22] Its chief executive from 1961 to 1968 was Joseph C. Wilson. An aggressive, entrepreneurial type, he oversaw Xerox's staggering growth on the basis of its 914 copier, one of the most successful products in American history. Under Wilson, Xerox had an entrepreneurial environment, with an informal, high-camaraderie, innovative, bold, risk-taking culture. Wilson's replacement as CEO was C. Peter McColough, a Harvard MBA with a formal management style. He instituted bureaucratic controls and a major change in Xerox's culture. When McColough stepped down in 1982, Xerox had become stodgy and formal, with lots of politics and turf battles and layers of watchdog managers. His replacement was David T. Kearns. He believed the culture he inherited hindered Xerox's ability to compete. To increase the company's competitiveness, Kearns trimmed Xerox down by cutting fifteen thousand jobs, delegated decision making downward, and refocused the organization's culture around a simple theme: boosting the quality of Xerox products and services. By his actions and those of his senior managerial cadre, Kearns conveyed to everyone at Xerox that the company valued and rewarded quality and efficiency. When Kearns retired in 1990, Xerox still had its problems. The copier business was mature and Xerox had fared badly in developing computerized office systems. The new CEO, Paul Allaire, has again sought to reshape Xerox's culture. Specifically, he has reorganized the corporation around a world-wide marketing department, has unified product development and manufacturing divisions, and has replaced half of the company's top-management team with outsiders. Allaire seeks to reshape Xerox's culture to focus on innovative thinking and outhustling the competition.

SOCIALIZATION   No matter how good a job the organization does in recruiting and selection, new employees are not fully indoctrinated in the organization's culture. Maybe most important, because they are unfamiliar with the organization's culture, new employees are potentially likely to disturb the beliefs and customs that are in place. The organization will, therefore, want to help new employees adapt to its culture. This adaptation process is called **socialization.**[23]

All Marines must go through boot camp, where they "prove" their commitment. Of course, at the same time, the Marine trainers are indoctrinating new recruits in the "Marine way." New Morgan Guaranty bank employees go

Socialization The process that adapts employees to the organization's culture.

through a one-year training program that tests their intellect and endurance, and that requires teamwork as an essential factor for survival. The reason is that Morgan Guaranty wants to mold new members into the firm's collegial style.

As we discuss socialization, keep in mind that the most critical socialization stage is at the time of entry into the organization. This is when the organization seeks to mold the outsider into an employee "in good standing." Those employees who fail to learn the essential or pivotal role behaviors risk being labeled "nonconformists" or "rebels," which often leads to expulsion. But the organization will be socializing every employee, though maybe not as explicitly, throughout his or her entire career in the organization. This further contributes to sustaining the culture.

Socialization can be conceptualized as a process made up of three stages: prearrival, encounter, and metamorphosis.[24] The first stage encompasses all the learning that occurs before a new member joins the organization. In the second stage, the new employee sees what the organization is really like and confronts the possibility that expectations and reality may diverge. In the third stage, the relatively long-lasting changes take place. The new employee masters the skills required for his or her job, successfully performs his or her new roles, and makes the adjustments to his or her work group's values and norms.[25] This three-stage process impacts on the new employee's work productivity, commitment to the organization's objectives, and eventual decision to stay with the organization. Figure 17–2 depicts this process.

Prearrival Stage The period of learning in the socialization process that occurs before a new employee joins the organization.

The **prearrival stage** explicitly recognizes that each individual arrives with a set of values, attitudes, and expectations. These cover both the work to be done and the organization. For instance, in many jobs, particularly professional work, new members will have undergone a considerable degree of prior socialization in training and in school. One major purpose of a business school, for example, is to socialize business students to the attitudes and behaviors that business firms want. If business executives believe that successful employees value the profit ethic, are loyal, will work hard, desire to achieve, and willingly accept directions from their superiors, they can hire individuals out of business schools who have been premolded in this pattern. But prearrival socialization goes beyond the specific job. The selection process is used in most organizations to inform prospective employees about the organization as a whole. In addition, as noted previously, the selection process also acts to ensure the inclusion of the "right type"—those who will fit in. "Indeed, the ability of the individual to present the appropriate face during the selection process determines his ability to move into the organization in the first place. Thus, success depends on the degree to which the aspiring member has correctly anticipated the expectations and desires of those in the organization in charge of selection."[26]

Figure 17–2   A Socialization Model

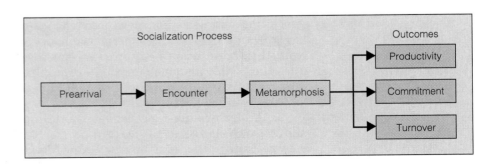

As part of Toshiba's efforts to indoctrinate new employees in its organization's culture, recruits are even required to learn the company song.
R. Wallis/SIPA–PRESS

Encounter Stage The stage in the socialization process in which a new employee sees what the organization is really like and confronts the possibility that expectations and reality may diverge.

Metamorphosis Stage The stage in the socialization process in which a new employee adjusts to his or her work group's values and norms.

Upon entry into the organization, the new member enters the **encounter stage.** Here the individual confronts the possible dichotomy between her expectations—about her job, her co-workers, her boss, and the organization in general—and reality. If expectations prove to have been more or less accurate, the encounter stage merely provides for a reaffirmation of the perceptions gained earlier. However, this is often not the case. Where expectations and reality differ, the new employee must undergo socialization that will detach her from her previous assumptions and replace them with another set that the organization deems desirable. At the extreme, a new member may become totally disillusioned with the actualities of her job and resign. Proper selection should significantly reduce the probability of the latter occurrence.

Finally, the new member must work out any problems discovered during the encounter stage. This may mean going through changes—hence, we call this the **metamorphosis stage.** The options presented in Table 17–2 are alternatives designed to bring about the desired metamorphosis. Note, for example, that the more management relies on socialization programs that are formal, collective, fixed, serial, and emphasize divestiture, the greater the likelihood that newcomers' differences and perspectives will be stripped away and replaced by standardized and predictable behaviors. Careful selection by management of newcomers' socialization experiences can—at the extreme—create conformists who maintain traditions and customs, or inventive and creative individualists who consider no organizational practice sacred.

We can say that metamorphosis and the entry socialization process is complete when the new member has become comfortable with the organization and his or her job. She has internalized the norms of the organization and her work group, and understands and accepts these norms. The new member feels accepted by her peers as a trusted and valued individual, is self-confident that she has the competence to complete the job successfully, and understands the system—not only her own tasks, but the rules, procedures, and informally accepted practices as well. Finally, she knows how she

TABLE 17–2   Entry Socialization Options

Formal vs. Informal   The more a new employee is segregated from the ongoing work setting and differentiated in some way to make explicit his or her newcomer's role, the more formal socialization is. Specific orientation and training programs are examples. Informal socialization puts the new employee directly into his or her job, with little or no special attention.

Individual or Collective   New members can be socialized individually. This describes how it's done in many professional offices. They can also be grouped together and processed through an identical set of experiences, as in military boot camp.

Fixed vs. Variable   This refers to the time schedule in which newcomers make the transition from outsider to insider. A fixed schedule establishes standardized stages of transition. This characterizes rotational training programs. It also includes probationary periods, such as the six-year "tenure or out" procedure commonly used with new assistant professors in colleges. Variable schedules give no advanced notice of their transition timetable. This describes the typical promotion system, where one is not advanced to the next stage until he or she is "ready."

Serial vs. Random   Serial socialization is characterized by the use of role models who train and encourage the newcomer. Apprenticeship and mentoring programs are examples. In random socialization, role models are deliberately withheld. The new employee is left on his or her own to figure things out.

Investiture vs. Divestiture   Investiture socialization assumes that the newcomer's qualities and qualifications are the necessary ingredients for job success, so these qualities and qualifications are confirmed and supported. Divestiture socialization tries to strip away certain characteristics of the recruit. Fraternity and sorority "pledges" go through divestiture socialization to shape them into the proper role.

Source: Based on J. Van Maanen, "People Processing: Strategies of Organizational Socialization," *Organizational Dynamics,* Summer 1978, pp. 19–36; and E. H. Schein, "Organizational Culture," *American Psychologist,* February 1990, p. 116.

will be evaluated, that is, what criteria will be used to measure and appraise her work. She knows what is expected, and what constitutes a job "well done." As Figure 17–2 shows, successful metamorphosis should have a positive impact on the new employee's productivity and her commitment to the organization, and reduce her propensity to leave the organization.

Summary: How Cultures Form

Figure 17–3 summarizes how an organization's culture is established and sustained. The original culture is derived from the founder's philosophy. This, in turn, strongly influences the criteria used in hiring. The actions of the current top management set the general climate of what is acceptable behavior and what is not. How employees are to be socialized will depend both on the degree of success achieved in matching new employees' values to those of the organization's in the selection process and on top management's preference for socialization methods.

FIGURE 17–3   How Organization Cultures Form

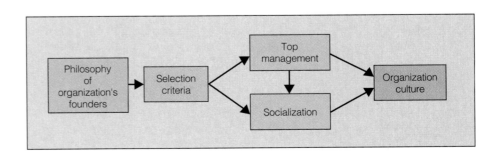

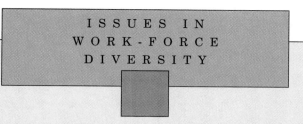

The Paradox of Diversity

Socializing new employees who, because of race, gender, ethnic, or other differences, are not like the majority of the organization's members creates a paradox.[27] Management wants new employees to accept the organization's core cultural values. Otherwise, these employees are unlikely to fit in or be accepted. But at the same time, management wants to openly acknowledge and demonstrate support for the differences that these employees bring to the workplace.

Strong cultures put considerable pressure on employees to conform. They limit the range of values and styles that are acceptable. Obviously, this creates a dilemma. Organizations hire diverse individuals because of the alternative strengths these people bring to the workplace. Yet these diverse behaviors and strengths are likely to diminish in strong cultures as people attempt to fit in.

Management's challenge in this paradox of diversity is to balance two conflicting goals: get employees to accept the organization's dominant values and encourage the acceptance of differences. Too much attention to investiture rites is likely to create employees who are misfits. On the other hand, too much emphasis on divestiture rites may eliminate those unique strengths that people of different backgrounds bring to the organization.

HOW EMPLOYEES LEARN CULTURE

Culture is transmitted to employees in a number of forms, the most potent being stories, rituals, material symbols, and language.

Stories

During the days when Henry Ford II was chairman of the Ford Motor Co., one would have been hard pressed to find a manager who hadn't heard the story about Mr. Ford reminding his executives, when they got too arrogant, that "it's *my* name that's on the building." The message was clear: Henry Ford II ran the company!

IBM employees tell the story of a plant security supervisor who challenged Thomas Watson, Jr., who, at the time of the story, was the all-powerful chairman of IBM's board. The supervisor, a twenty-two-year-old woman, was required to make certain that people entering security areas wore the correct clearance identification. One day, surrounded by his usual entourage, Watson approached the doorway to an area where the supervisor was on guard. He wore an orange badge acceptable elsewhere in the plant, but not a green badge, which alone permitted entrance at her door. Although she knew who Watson was, she told him what she had been instructed to say to anyone without proper clearance: "You cannot enter. Your admittance is not recognized." The group accompanying Watson were taken aback. Would this young security guard be fired on the spot? "Don't you know who he is?" someone asked. Watson raised his hand for silence while one of the party strode off and returned with the appropriate badge. The message to IBM employees: No matter who you are, you obey the rules.[28]

No, it's not a royal coronation or presidential ball. This photo depicts part of the pageantry of a Mary Kay Cosmetics annual award meeting. Here, Mary Kay makes her grand entrance   Nin Berman/SIPA

Stories such as these circulate through many organizations. They typically contain a narrative of events about the organization's founders, rule-breaking, rags-to-riches successes, reductions in the work-force, relocation of employees, reactions to past mistakes, and organizational coping.[29] These stories anchor the present in the past and provide explanations and legitimacy for current practices.[30]

Rituals

Rituals   Repetitive sequences of activities that express and reinforce the key values of the organization, what goals are most important, which people are important and which are expendable.

Rituals are repetitive sequences of activities that express and reinforce the key values of the organization, what goals are most important, which people are important and which are expendable.[31]

College faculty members undergo a lengthy ritual in their quest for permanent employment—tenure. Typically, the faculty member is on probation for six years. At the end of that period, the member's colleagues must make one of two choices: extend a tenured appointment or issue a one-year terminal contract. What does it take to obtain tenure? It usually requires satisfactory teaching performance, service to the department and university, and scholarly activity. But, of course, what satisfies the requirements for tenure in one department at one university may be appraised as inadequate in another. The key is that the tenure decision, in essence, asks those who are tenured to assess whether the candidate has demonstrated, based on six years of performance, whether he or she fits in. Colleagues who have been socialized properly will have proved themselves worthy of being granted tenure. Every year, hundreds of faculty members at colleges and universities are denied tenure. In some cases, this action is a result of poor performance across the board. More often, however, the decision can be traced to the faculty member's not doing well in those areas that the tenured faculty believe are important. The instructor who spends dozens of hours each week preparing for class and achieves outstanding evaluations by students, but neglects his or her research and publication activities, may be passed over for tenure. What has happened, simply, is that the instructor has failed to adapt to the norms set by the department. The astute faculty member will assess early on in the probationary period what attitudes and behaviors his or her colleagues want and will then proceed to give them what they want. And, of course, by demanding certain attitudes and behaviors, the tenured faculty have made significant strides toward standardizing tenure candidates.

One of the best-known corporate rituals is Mary Kay Cosmetics' annual award meeting.[32] Looking like a cross between a circus and a Miss America pageant, the meeting takes place over a couple of days in a large auditorium, on a stage in front of a large, cheering audience, with all the participants dressed in glamorous evening clothes. Saleswomen are rewarded with an array of flashy gifts—gold and diamond pins, fur stoles, pink Cadillacs—based on success in achieving sales quota. This "show" acts as a motivator by publicly recognizing outstanding sales performance. In addition, the ritual aspect reinforces Mary Kay's personal determination and optimism, which enabled her to overcome personal hardships, found her own company, and achieve material success. It conveys to her salespeople that reaching their sales quota is important and that through hard work and encouragement they too can achieve success.

Material Symbols

Tandem Computers' headquarters in Cupertino, California, doesn't look like your typical head office operation. It has jogging trails, a basketball court, space for dance and yoga classes, and a large swimming pool—all for its employees' enjoyment. Every Friday afternoon at 4:30, employees partake in the weekly beer bust, courtesy of the company. This informal corporate headquarters conveys to employees that Tandem values openness and equality.

Some corporations provide their top executives with chauffeur-driven limousines and, when they travel by air, unlimited use of the corporate jet. Others may not get to ride in limousines or private jets but they might still get a car and air transportation paid for by the company. Only the car is a Chevrolet (with no driver) and the jet seat is in the economy section of a commercial airliner.

The layout of corporate headquarters, the types of automobiles top executives are given, and the presence or absence of corporate aircraft are a few examples of material symbols. Others include the size and layout of offices, the elegance of furnishings, executive perks, and dress attire. These material symbols convey to employees who is important, the degree of egalitarianism desired by top management, and the kinds of behavior (for example, risk-taking, conservative, authoritarian, participative, individualistic, social) that are appropriate.

Language

Many organizations and units within organizations use language as a way to identify members of a culture or subculture. By learning this language, members attest to their acceptance of the culture and, in so doing, help to preserve it.

The following are examples of terminology used by employees at Dialog, a California-based data redistributor: *accession number* (a number assigned each individual record in a database); *KWIC* (a set of key-words-in-context); and *relational operator* (searching a database for names or key

Organizational Culture vs. National Culture

This chapter has taken the anthropologist's concept of societal cultures and applied it at the organizational level. Our main thesis has been that members of an organization develop common perceptions that, in turn, affect their attitudes and behavior. The strength of that effect, however, depends on the strength of the organization's culture.

Throughout this book we've argued that national differences—that is, national cultures—must be taken into account if accurate predictions are to be made about organizational behavior in different countries.

In this box, we want to address an integrated question: Does national culture override an organization's culture? Is an IBM facility in Germany, for example, more likely to reflect German ethnic culture or IBM's corporate culture?

The research indicates that national culture has a greater impact on employees than does their organization's culture.[33] German employees

at an IBM facility in Munich, therefore, will be influenced more by German culture than by IBM's culture. This means that as influential as organizational culture is to understanding the behavior of people at work, national culture is even more so.

The above conclusion has to be qualified to reflect the self-selection that goes on at the hiring stage. IBM, for example, may be less concerned with hiring the "typical Italian" for its Italian operations than in hiring an Italian who fits within the IBM way of doing things.[34] Italians who have a high need for autonomy are more likely to go to Olivetti than IBM. Why? Because Olivetti's organizational culture is informal and nonstructured. It allows employees considerably more freedom than IBM does.[35] In fact, Olivetti seeks to hire individuals who are impatient, risk-taking, and innovative—qualities in job candidates that IBM's Italian operations would purposely seek to exclude in new hires.

terms in some order). Librarians are a rich source of terminology foreign to people outside their profession. They sprinkle their conversations liberally with acronyms like *ARL* (Association for Research Libraries), *OCLC* (a center in Ohio that does cooperative cataloging), and *OPAC* (for on-line patron accessing catalog).

Organizations, over time, often develop unique terms to describe equipment, offices, key personnel, suppliers, customers, or products that relate to its business. New employees are frequently overwhelmed with acronyms and jargon that, after six months on the job, have become fully part of their language. Once assimilated, this terminology acts as a common denominator that unites members of a given culture or subculture.

ORGANIZATIONAL CULTURE IN ACTION

We now turn our attention to three specific organizations and their cultures—the Walt Disney Co., MCI, and Time Warner. They are of interest for different reasons. Disney is fascinating because of its culture's strength; MCI because it is so untraditional; and Time Warner as an illustration of what happens when diverse cultures merge.

This photo of Disney World employees depicts the Disney "look." Both the young man and woman are clean cut, slim, and healthy-looking. They are selected to reinforce the wholesome Disney image.   Stephen R. Swinburne/Stock, Boston

The Walt Disney Co.

The Walt Disney Co. is made up of three main divisions: filmed entertainment, consumer products, and theme parks and resorts. Currently, the company's theme parks in California, Florida, Tokyo and Paris account for fifty-six percent of Disney's revenues and sixty-four percent of its operating profits. Since these theme parks are the part of the Disney operation that most of us know best—and where the Disney culture is strongest—let's take a look at how management creates and sustains that "Disney look."[36]

Suppose you wanted a summer job at Disneyland. You'd increase your chance of getting that job if you knew someone already working in the organization. Disney has found that personal links reduce social variability in the hiring pool. All final hirees will get at least two personal interviews with park representatives. Emphasis will be placed on identifying people who conform to Disney's highly specific standards of appearance—complexion, height and weight, straightness and color of teeth, and the like. It's not by chance that most Disneyland employees are single white males and females in their early twenties, of healthy appearance, without facial blemishes, of above-average height and below-average weight, with conservative grooming standards. The lengthy hiring process reduces the likelihood that "misfits" will be selected.

Once hired, new employees undergo entry socialization that is formal, collective, and serial. Incoming identities are not so much dismantled as they are set aside as employees are schooled in their new identities. They'll receive eight hours of orientation, followed by forty hours or so of apprenticeship training on park grounds.

One of the essential parts of the Disney orientation is learning the language. There are no employees, only "cast members." People don't have jobs, they're cast in roles. In fact, the company has a whole language of its own. Customers are "guests," rides are called "attractions," law enforcement personnel are "security hosts," uniforms are "costumes," accidents are "incidents," people aren't working but are "onstage"—the list goes on and on.

Of course, new hires also learn the company's history, Walt Disney's philosophy, and the standards of guest service. Values such as "everyone is a child at heart when at Disneyland" are emphasized.

To further ensure consistency of behavior, the company encourages employees to spend their off-work hours together. Disneyland's softball and volleyball leagues, its official picnics, employee nights at the park, and beach parties provide a busy social scene for those interested and, at the same time, limit exposure to non-Disney values.

Once trained, Disneyland employees come to believe that they are really "onstage" while working. The ease with which they glide into their user-friendly roles and the everyday acting skill they display in bringing off these roles—whether as a ride operator at Space Mountain, a candy merchant on "Main Street" or Donald Duck himself—are, in large measure, feats of social engineering.

MCI

The late Bill McGowan founded MCI in 1968. In 1991, it had revenues of $8.4 billion and earned $551 million in profits. In contrast to most successful executives, who create organization out of chaos, McGowan shaped MCI's culture to create chaos out of organization.[37]

MCI reflects McGowan's belief that both seniority and corporate loyalty are unimportant. Five-year pins and ten-year pins are nonexistent. Why? They imply that people who have been with the company longer are somehow better. McGowan said "the opposite is almost always the truth. It's the newcomers, the young people, who bring the fresh ideas and the energy." Consistent with these values, the company has an official goal of filling at least half of all job openings from outside. Moreover, people who quit MCI aren't treated as traitors, as they are at most large companies. Instead, they're given parties and reminded that MCI will hire them back.

The same amount of effort that Disney exerts to standardize the behavior of its employees at Disneyland is exerted at MCI to encourage individuals to be unique. MCI wants its employees to be free and flexible. McGowan cringed at the thought of rewarding employees for adhering to standardized rules and procedures. At annual companywide meetings, he was fond of saying, "I know that somewhere, someone out there is trying to write up a manual on procedures. Well, one of these days I'm going to find out who you are, and when I do, I'm going to fire you."

Time Warner

When an acquisition succeeds or fails, cultural compatibility has increasingly been looked to for an explanation. While a favorable financial statement or product synergy may be the initial attraction of an acquisition candidate, whether the acquisition actually works may have more to do with how well the two organizations' cultures match up. The case of Time Warner illustrates this point.[38]

Time Warner is one of the world's largest media companies, with annual revenues of nearly $12 billion. It was created by Time Inc.'s acquisition of Warner Communications in 1989. Time brought an impressive list of publication properties—such as *Sports Illustrated, People, Time,* and *Fortune* magazines—to the marriage. Warner contributed movie, cable television, and record businesses. The underlying logic behind the merger of these two giants was the creation of an integrated media conglomerate.

In its first two years, Time's acquisition of Warner has not proved to be the success that management and stockholders had hoped for. In 1990, Time Warner lost $227 million. In 1991, it lost another $99 million. Certainly a number of factors contributed to these losses—including heavy interest expenses from debt incurred in the buyout and a prolonged economic recession—but the merger of two very different organizational cultures has clearly been a major problem.

From its founding by Henry Luce, Time prospered by isolating editorial concerns from those of business. Time's culture was conservative and paternalistic. Consistent with journalistic values, the company fostered a strong belief in integrity. Time provided its employees with a stable work environment, a feeling of family, and as close to lifetime employment as one could find in an American corporation.

Warner, on the other hand, was a firm that lived in a world of deal making. Its products—music, TV series, recordings—re-create themselves constantly as a new deal to be made. Hollywood and entertainment industry values blurred Warner's corporate morality. Warner experienced considerable turnover, as one might expect in a "high-risk, high-reward" climate. Time veterans regularly use the word *sleazy* when speaking of Warner's Hollywood deal makers. While Time's people grew up in a company that encouraged and rewarded caution, Warner's people survived by moving fast and taking risks.

Can two such diverse cultures live happily ever after? Excuse the pun, but Time will tell!

IMPLICATIONS FOR PERFORMANCE AND SATISFACTION

Figure 17–4 depicts organizational culture as an intervening variable. Employees form an overall subjective perception of the organization based on such factors as degree of group emphasis, support of people, risk tolerance, and management's willingness to tolerate conflict. This overall perception becomes, in effect, the organization's culture or personality. These favorable or unfavorable perceptions then affect employee performance and satisfaction, with the impact being greater for stronger cultures.

Does culture have an equal impact on both employee performance and satisfaction? The evidence says "No." There is a relatively strong relationship between culture and satisfaction, but this is moderated by individual differences.[39] In general, we propose that satisfaction will be highest when

FIGURE 17–4 How Organizational Culture Impacts Performance and Satisfaction

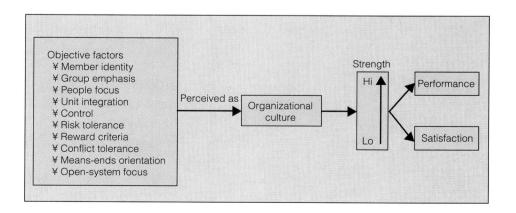

there is congruence between individual needs and the culture. For instance, an organization whose culture would be described as emphasizing individual tasks, having loose supervision, and rewarding people for high achievement is likely to have more satisfied employees if those employees have a high achievement need and prefer autonomy. Our conclusion, therefore, is that job satisfaction often varies according to the employee's perception of the organization's culture.

The relationship between culture and performance is less clear, although a number of studies find the two related.[40] But the relationship is moderated by the organization's technology.[41] Performance will be higher when the culture suits the technology. If the culture is informal, creative, and supports risk taking and conflict, performance will be higher if the technology is nonroutine. The more formally structured organizations that are risk aversive, that seek to eliminate conflict, and that are prone to more task-oriented leadership will achieve higher performance when routine technology is utilized.

It has been noted that organizations have "absence cultures" that represent shared understandings about absence legitimacy and that define appropriate absence behavior.[42] Once a new employee has been socialized into an organization, he or she learns whether, for example, it's acceptable to take three-day weekends in the summer, use up sick leave days at the end of the year, or take a day off from work because relatives are in from out of town.

We should also not overlook the influence socialization has on employee performance. An employee's performance depends to a considerable degree on knowing what he should or should not do. Understanding the right way to do a job indicates proper socialization. Further, the appraisal of an individual's performance includes how well the person fits into the organization. Can he or she get along with co-workers? Does he or she have acceptable work habits, and demonstrate the right attitude? These qualities differ between jobs and organizations. For instance, on some jobs, employees will be evaluated more favorably if they are aggressive and outwardly indicate that they are ambitious. On another job, or on the same job in another organization, such an approach may be evaluated negatively. As a result, proper socialization becomes a significant factor in influencing both actual job performance and how it's perceived by others.

■ FOR DISCUSSION

1. Contrast individual personality and organizational culture. How are they similar? How are they different?
2. What is the relationship between institutionalization, formalization, and organizational culture?
3. What's the difference between job satisfaction and organizational culture?
4. Can an employee survive in an organization if he or she rejects its core values? Explain.
5. What forces might contribute toward making a culture strong or weak?
6. How is an organization's culture maintained?
7. Is socialization brainwashing? Explain.
8. What benefits can socialization provide for the organization? For the new employee?
9. If management sought a culture characterized as innovative and autonomous, what might its socialization program look like?

10. If management sought a culture characterized as formalized and conflict-free, what might its socialization program look like?

11. Can you identify a set of characteristics that describe your college's culture? Compare them with several of your peers. How closely do they agree?

12. "We should be opposed to the manipulation of individuals for organizational purposes, but a degree of social uniformity enables organizations to work better." Do you agree or disagree with this statement? Discuss.

The Case Against Cultural Change

That an organization's culture is made up of relatively stable characteristics would imply that culture is very difficult for management to change. Such a conclusion would be correct.

An organization's culture develops over many years and is rooted in deeply held values to which employees are strongly committed. In addition, there are several forces continually operating to maintain a given culture. These would include written statements about the organization's mission and philosophy, the design of physical spaces and buildings, the dominant leadership style, hiring criteria, past promotion practices, entrenched rituals, popular stories about key people and events, the organization's historic performance evaluation criteria, and the organization's formal structure.

Selection and promotion policies are particularly important devices that work against cultural change. Employees chose the organization because they perceived their values to be a "good fit" with the organization. They become comfortable with that fit and will strongly resist efforts to disturb the equilibrium. Those in control will also select senior managers who will continue the current culture. Even attempts to change a culture by going outside the organization to hire a new chief executive are unlikely to be effective. The evidence indicates that the culture is more likely to change the executive than the other way around. Why? It's too entrenched, and change becomes a potential threat to member self-interest. In fact, a more pragmatic view of the relationship between an organization's culture and its chief executive would be to note that the practice of filling senior-level management positions from current managerial employees ensures that those who run the organization have been fully indoctrinated in the organization's culture. Promoting from within provides stability and lessens uncertainty. When Exxon's board of directors selects as a new chief executive officer an individual who has spent thirty years in the company, it virtually guarantees that the culture will continue unchanged.

Our argument, however, should not be viewed as saying that culture can never be changed. In the unusual case when an organization confronts a survival-threatening crisis—a crisis that is universally acknowledged as a true life-or-death situation—all members of the organization will be responsive to efforts at cultural change. But anything less is unlikely to be effective.

How to Change an Organization's Culture

Changing an organization's culture is extremely difficult, but cultures *can* be changed. For example, Lee Iacocca came to Chrysler Corp. in 1978, when the company appeared to be only weeks away from bankruptcy. It took him about five years but, in what is now a well-worn story, he took Chrysler's conservative, inward-looking, and engineering-oriented culture and changed it into an action-oriented, market-responsive culture.

The evidence suggests that cultural change is most likely to take place when most or all of the following conditions exist:

A dramatic crisis. This is the shock that undermines the status quo and calls into question the relevance of the current culture. Examples of these crises might be a surprising financial setback, the loss of a major customer, or a dramatic technological breakthrough by a competitor.

Turnover in leadership. New top leadership, which can provide an alternative set of key values, may be perceived as more capable of responding to the crisis. This would definitely be the organization's chief executive but also might need to include all senior management positions.

Young and small organization. The younger the organization is, the less entrenched its culture will be. Similarly, it's easier for management to communicate its new values when the organization is small.

Weak culture. The more widely held a culture is and the higher the agreement among members on its values, the more difficult it will be to change. Conversely, weak cultures are more amenable to change than strong ones.

If conditions support cultural change, you should consider the following suggestions:

1. Have top-management people become positive role models, setting the tone through their behavior.
2. Create new stories, symbols, and rituals to replace those currently in vogue.
3. Select, promote, and support employees who espouse the new values that are sought.
4. Redesign socialization processes to align with the new values.
5. Change the reward system to encourage acceptance of a new set of values.
6. Replace unwritten norms with formal rules and regulations that are tightly enforced.
7. Shake up current subcultures through extensive use of job rotation.
8. Work to get peer group consensus through utilization of employee participation and creation of a climate with a high level of trust.

Implementing most or all of these suggestions will not result in an immediate or dramatic shift in the organization's culture. Cultural change is a lengthy process—measured in years rather than months. But if the question is, "*Can* culture be changed?" the answer is "Yes!"

What Kind of Organizational Culture Fits You Best?

For each of the following statements, circle the level of agreement or disagreement that you personally feel:

SA = Strongly Agree
 A = Agree
 U = Uncertain
 D = Disagree
SD = Strongly disagree

1. I like being part of a team and having my performance assessed in terms of my contribution to the team.   SA   A   U   D   SD

2. No person's needs should be compromised in order for a department to achieve its goals.   SA   A   U   D   SD

3. I prefer a job where my boss leaves me alone.   SA   A   U   D   SD

4. I like the thrill and excitement from taking risks.   SA   A   U   D   SD

5. People shouldn't break rules.   SA   A   U   D   SD

6. Seniority in an organization should be highly rewarded.   SA   A   U   D   SD

7. I respect authority.   SA   A   U   D   SD

8. If a person's job performance is inadequate, it's irrelevant how much effort he or she made.   SA   A   U   D   SD

9. I like things to be predictable.   SA   A   U   D   SD

10. I'd prefer my identity and status to come from my professional expertise than from the organization that employs me.   SA   A   U   D   SD

Turn to page 718 for scoring direction and key.

Rate Your Classroom Culture

Listed here are ten statements. Score each statement by indicating the degree to which you agree with it. If you strongly agree, give it a five. If you strongly disagree, give it a one.

1. My classmates are friendly and supportive. _____
2. My instructor is friendly and supportive. _____
3. My instructor encourages me to question and challenge him or her as well as other students. _____
4. My instructor clearly expresses his or her expectations to the class. _____
5. I think the grading system used by my instructor is based on clear standards of performance. _____
6. My instructor's behavior during examinations demonstrates his or her belief that students are honest and trustworthy. _____
7. My instructor provides regular and rapid feedback on my performance. _____
8. My instructor uses a strict bell curve to allocate grades. _____
9. My instructor is open to suggestions on how the course might be improved. _____
10. My instructor makes me want to learn. _____

Turn to page 718 for scoring directions and key.

C A S E   I N C I D E N T   1 7

The Nordstrom Culture

Nordstrom employees are fond of this story: When this specialty retail chain was in its infancy, a customer came in and wanted to return a set of automobile tires. The sales clerk was a bit uncertain how to handle the problem. As the customer and sales clerk spoke, Mr. Nordstrom walked by and overheard the conversation. He immediately interceded, asking the customer how much he had paid for the tires. Mr. Nordstrom then instructed the clerk to take the tires back and provide a full cash refund. After the customer had received his refund and left, the perplexed clerk looked at the boss. "But, Mr. Nordstrom, we don't sell tires!" "I know," replied the boss, "but we do whatever we need to do to make the customer happy. I mean it when I say we have a no-questions-asked return policy." Nordstrom then picked up the telephone and called a friend in the auto parts business to see how much he could get for the tires.

Without sacrificing style, variety, or value, Nordstrom distinguishes itself from its competition by its service. Each store employs a concierge stationed near the entrance to help customers with special requests. Cheerful Nordstrom employees are readily available to assist customers and they will go to incredible lengths to make a sale. It is not unusual, for example, for a salesperson to call a Nordstrom store hundreds of miles away to see if it has the item a customer wants. If it does, the salesperson has it shipped. Upon its arrival, the salesperson may personally deliver the item to the customer's home. And how many salespeople have you encountered who take time to write thank-you notes to customers? They do at Nordstrom!

In contrast to the practice at many retailers, almost every Nordstrom executive started on the selling floor. Nordstrom rewards its salespeople with a salary, commission, and profit-sharing package that is among the highest in its industry. College graduates start at $20,000 a year and top-performing sales people can make more than $80,000. But the Nordstrom culture isn't for everyone. Its intense competitive atmosphere generates high job turnover, especially during the first year of employment.

The firm's rapid growth has meant quick promotion for those who produce. The company, which began in Seattle, has been expanding rapidly in recent years. It entered California in 1978 and within ten years had grabbed almost a third of the market. By 1988, it opened its first store on the East Coast—just outside Washington, D.C. It was an immediate success, and almost singlehandedly put Garfinckel's, the once-dominant Washington retailer, into bankruptcy. With stores now open or planned in New Jersey, Chicago, Minneapolis, Denver, and Boston, Nordstrom is on its way to achieving its goal of eighty stores and sales of more than $5 billion by 1995. Most specialty stores shiver at the thought of competing against Nordstrom. They know it has a service culture that works. It also makes plenty of money. The company has the highest sales per square foot of any department store—nearly twice the industry average. And Nordstrom's profit growth ranks in retailing's top tier.

One big question outsiders continually ask about Nordstrom is: Can it clone its culture in all its new stores? Management is certain it can. Its secret? Bring in transplants from other Nordstrom stores. For instance, in Paramus, New Jersey, two hundred of the eight hundred employees who opened the store were permanent transfers from other Nordstrom branches. They acted as role models for conveying to new recruits what the Nordstrom service culture is all about.

Questions

1. Have you been in a Sears store recently? If so, compare Sears' culture with Nordstrom's. If not, compare Nordstrom's culture with the culture of any large department store you're familiar with.

2. What is the effect of the Nordstrom culture on its employees?

3. If the Nordstrom culture has proved so successful, why don't competitors copy it?

Source: This case is partially based on T. Peters, "The Store Where the Action Is," *U.S. News & World Report,* May 12, 1986; and "Why Rivals Are Quaking as Nordstrom Heads East," *Business Week,* June 15, 1987, pp. 99–100. For an update on this case, see "Nordstrom's Push East Will Test Its Renown for the Best in Service," *The Wall Street Journal,* August 1, 1989, p. 1; and "Will 'The Nordstrom Way' Travel Well?" *Business Week,* September 3, 1990, pp. 82–83.

FOR FURTHER READING

BUONO, A. F., and J. L. BOWDITCH, *The Human Side of Mergers and Acquisitions* (San Francisco: Jossey-Bass, 1989). Describes strategies that managers can use to handle the collisions between people, culture, and organizations that occur when mergers and acquisitions take place.

GORDON, G. G., "Industry Determinants of Organizational Culture," *Academy of Management Review,* April 1991, pp. 396–415. Argues that organizational culture is strongly influenced by the characteristics of the industry in which the organization operates and that organizations within an industry share certain cultural elements.

GREY, R. J., and T. J. F. THÖNE, "Differences Between North American and European Corporate Cultures," *Canadian Business Review,* Autumn 1990, pp. 26–30. Research reveals that European corporate cultures embody greater vision, responsiveness, innovation, and employee involvement than North American cultures.

ISHIZUNA, Y., "The Transformation of Nissan—The Reform of Corporate Culture," *Long Range Planning,* June 1990, pp. 9–15. Describes how a change in corporate culture affected corporate strategy and led to the turnaround of Nissan Motors.

SCHEIN, E. H., "Organizational Culture," *American Psychologist,* February 1990, pp. 109–19. A concise review of the "state" of organizational culture.

SCHNEIDER, B., *Organizational Climate and Culture* (San Francisco: Jossey-Bass, 1991). Provides insight into how an organization's activities are perceived and interpreted by its members and how these collective interpretations affect organizational behavior and effectiveness.

NOTES

[1]Based on J. H. Boyett and H. P. Conn, *Workplace 2000* (New York: Dutton, 1991), pp. 338–43; J. Castro, "Mr. Sam Stuns Goliath," *Time,* February 25, 1991, pp. 62–63; and J. Huey, "America's Most Successful Merchant," *Fortune,* September 23, 1991, pp. 46–59.

[2]P. Selznick, "Foundations of the Theory of Organizations," *American Sociological Review,* February 1948, pp. 25–35.

[3]L. G. Zucker, "Organizations as Institutions," in S. B. Bacharach (ed.), *Research in the Sociology of Organizations* (Greenwich, CT: JAI Press, 1983), pp. 1–47; and A. J. Richardson, "The Production of Institutional Behaviour: A Constructive Comment on the Use of Institutionalization Theory in Organizational Analysis," *Canadian Journal of Administrative Sciences,* December 1986, pp. 304–16.

[4]See, for example, H. S. Becker, "Culture: A Sociological View," *Yale Review,* Summer 1982, pp. 513–27; and E. H. Schein, *Organizational Culture and Leadership* (San Francisco: Jossey-Bass, 1985), p. 168.

[5]Based on G. Hofstede, B. Neuijen, D. D. Ohayv, and G. Sanders, "Measuring Organizational Culture: A Qualitative and Quantitative Study Across Twenty Cases," *Administrative Science Quarterly,* June 1990, pp. 286–316; and C. A. O'Reilly III, J. Chatman, and D. F. Caldwell, "People and Organizational Culture: A Profile Comparison Approach to Assessing Person-Organization Fit," *Academy of Management Journal,* September 1991, pp. 487–516.

[6]C. Hymowitz, "Which Culture Fits You?", *The Wall Street Journal,* July 17, 1989, p. B1.

[7]The view that there will be consistency among perceptions of organizational culture has been called the "integration" perspective. For a review of this perspective and conflicting approaches, see D. Meyerson and J. Martin, "Cultural Change: An Integration of Three Different Views," *Journal of Management Studies,* November 1987, pp. 623–47; and P. J. Frost, L. F. Moore, M. R. Louis, C. C. Lundberg, and J. Martin (eds.), *Reframing Organizational Culture* (Newbury Park, CA: Sage Publications, 1991).

[8]See K. L. Gregory, "Native-View Paradigms: Multiple Cultures and Culture Conflicts in Organizations," *Administrative Science Quarterly,* September 1983, pp. 359–76; and J. M. Jermier, J. W. Slocum, Jr., L. W. Fry, and J. Gaines, "Organizational Subcultures in a Soft Bureaucracy: Resistance Behind the Myth and Facade of an Official Culture," *Organization Science,* May 1991, pp. 170–94.

[9]See, for example, T. E. Deal and A. A. Kennedy, *Corporate Cultures* (Reading, MA: Addison-Wesley, 1982); and T. J. Peters and R. H. Waterman, Jr., *In Search of Excellence* (New York: Harper & Row, 1982). For a counterargument, see G. S. Saffold III, "Culture Traits, Strength, and Organizational Performance: Moving Beyond 'Strong' Culture," *Academy of Management Review,* October 1988, pp. 546–58.

[10]Y. Wiener, "Forms of Value Systems: A Focus on Organizational Effectiveness and Cultural Change and Maintenance," *Academy of Management Review,* October 1988, p. 536.

[11]As described in P. C. Yeager, "Analyzing Corporate Offenses: Progress and Prospects," in W. C. Frederick and L. E. Preston (eds.), *Business Ethics: Research Issues and Empirical Studies* (Greenwich, CT: JAI Press, 1990, p. 174.

[12]B. Victor and J. B. Cullen, "The Organizational Bases of Ethical Work Climates," *Administrative Science Quarterly,* March 1988, pp. 101–25.

[13]R. T. Mowday, L. W. Porter, and R. M. Steers, *Employee-Organization Linkages: The Psychology of Commitment, Absenteeism, and Turnover* (New York: Academic Press, 1982).

[14]T. E. Deal and A. A. Kennedy, "Culture: A New Look Through Old Lenses," *Journal of Applied Behavioral Science,* November 1983, p. 501.

[15]M. Langley, "AT&T Has Call for a New Corporate Culture," *The Wall Street Journal,* February 28, 1984, p. 24; S. P. Feldman, "Culture and Conformity: An Essay on Individual Adaptation in Centralized Bureaucracy," *Human Relations,* April 1985, pp. 341–56; and J. J. Keller, "Bob Allen Is Turning AT&T into a Live Wire," *Business Week,* November 6, 1989, pp. 140–52.

[16]E. H. Schein, "The Role of the Founder in Creating Organizational Culture," *Organizational Dynamics,* Summer 1983, pp. 13–28.

[17]G. Salaman, "The Sociology of Assessment: The Regular Commissions Board Assessment Procedure," in *People and Organizations: Media Booklet II* (Milton Keynes, England: Open University Press, 1974). See also J. A. Chatman, "Matching People and Organizations: Selection and Socialization in Public Accounting Firms," *Administrative Science Quarterly,* September 1991, pp. 459–84.

[18]R. Pascale, "The Paradox of 'Corporate Culture': Reconciling Ourselves to Socialization," *California Management Review,* Winter 1985, pp. 26–27.

[19]"Who's Afraid of IBM?" *Business Week,* June 29, 1987, p. 72.

[20]Ibid.

[21]D. C. Hambrick and P. A. Mason, "Upper Echelons: The Organization as a Reflection of Its Top Managers," *Academy of Management Review,* April 1984, pp. 193–206; B. P. Niehoff, C. A. Enz, and R. A. Grover, "The Impact of Top-Management Actions on Employee Attitudes and Perceptions," *Group and Organization Studies,* September 1990, pp. 337–52; and H. M. Trice and J. M. Beyer, "Cultural Leadership in Organizations," *Organization Science,* May 1991, pp. 149–69.

[22]"Culture Shock at Xerox," *Business Week,* June 22, 1987, pp. 1, 6–10; and T. Vogel, "At Xerox, They're Shouting 'Once More into the Breach,'" *Business Week,* July 23, 1990, pp. 62–63.

[23]See, for instance, R. L. Falcione and C. E. Wilson, "Socialization Processes in Organizations," in G. M. Goldhar and G. A. Barnett (eds.), *Handbook of Organizational Communication* (Norwood, NJ: Ablex Publishing, 1988), pp. 151–70; N. J. Allen and J. P. Meyer, "Organizational Socialization Tactics: A Longitudinal Analysis of Links to Newcomers' Commitment and Role Orientation," *Academy of Management Journal,* December 1990, pp. 847–58; V. D. Miller and F. M. Jablin, "Information Seeking During Organizational Entry: Influences, Tactics, and a Model of the Process," *Academy of Management Review,* January 1991, pp. 92–120; and Chatman, "Matching People and Organizations: Selection and Socialization in Public Accounting Firms."

[24]J. Van Maanen and E. H. Schein, "Career Development," in J. R. Hackman and J. L. Suttle (eds.), *Improving Life at Work* (Santa Monica, CA: Goodyear, 1977), pp. 58–62.

[25]D. C. Feldman, "The Multiple Socialization of Organization Members," *Academy of Management Review,* April 1981, p. 310.

[26]Van Maanen and Schein, "Career Development," p. 59.

[27]See C. Lindsay, "Paradoxes of Organizational Diversity: Living Within the Paradoxes," in L. R. Jauch and J. L. Wall (eds.), *Proceedings of the 50th Academy of Management Conference* (San Francisco, 1990), pp. 374–78.

[28]W. Rodgers, *Think* (New York: Stein & Day, 1969), pp. 153–54.

[29]D. M. Boje, "The Storytelling Organization: A Study of Story Performance in an Office-Supply Firm," *Administrative Science Quarterly,* March 1991, pp. 106–26; and C. H. Deutsch, "The Parables of Corporate Culture," *The New York Times,* October 13, 1991, p. F25.

[30]A. M. Pettigrew, "On Studying Organizational Cultures," *Administrative Science Quarterly,* December 1979, p. 576.

[31]Ibid.

[32]Cited in J. M. Beyer and H. M. Trice, "How an Organization's Rites Reveal Its Culture," *Organizational Dynamics,* Spring 1987, p. 15.

[33]See N. J. Adler, *International Dimensions of Organizational Behavior* (Boston: Kent Publishing, 1986), pp. 46–48.

[34]S. C. Schneider, "National vs. Corporate Culture: Implications for Human Resource Management," *Human Resource Management,* Summer 1988, p. 239.

[35]Ibid.

[36]This section is based on C. Knowlton, "How Disney Keeps the Magic Going," *Fortune,*

December 4, 1989, pp. 111–32; C. M. Solomon, "How Does Disney Do It?", *Personnel Journal,* December 1989, pp. 50–57; J. Van Maanen and G. Kunda, " 'Real Feelings': Emotional Expression and Organizational Culture," in L. L. Cummings and B. M. Staw (eds.), *Research in Organizational Behavior,* Vol. 11 (Greenwich, CT: JAI Press, 1989), pp. 58–70; and J. Van Maanen, "The Smile Factory: Work at Disneyland," in P. J. Frost, L. F. Moore, M. R. Louis, C. C. Lundberg, and J. Martin (eds.), *Reframing Organizational Culture* (Newbury Park, CA: Sage Publications, 1991), pp. 58–75.

[37]E. L. Andrews, "Out of Chaos," *Business Month,* December 1989, p. 33.

[38]J. Marchese, "Time Warp," *Business Month,* September 1990, pp. 32–40; P. M. Reilly, "Time Warner Posts a Narrowed Loss of $62 Million for the Third Quarter," *The Wall Street Journal,* October 22, 1991, p. A8; and M. Lander, "Time and Warner May Now Become Time Warner," *Business Week,* March 9, 1992, pp. 31–32.

[39]Chatman, "Matching People and Organizations: Selection and Socialization in Public Accounting Firms," pp. 459–84; and O'Reilly, Chatman, and Caldwell, "People and Organizational Culture: A Profile Comparison Approach to Assessing Person-Organization Fit."

[40]See D. Hellriegel and J. W. Slocum, Jr., "Organizational Climate: Measures, Research, and Contingencies," *Academy of Management Journal,* June 1974, pp. 255–80; and B. M. Meglino, E. C. Ravlin, and C. L. Adkins, "Work Values Approach to Corporate Culture: A Field Test of the Value Congruence Process and Its Relationship to Individual Outcomes," *Journal of Applied Psychology,* June 1989, pp. 424–32.

[41]J. W. Lorsch and J. J. Morse, *Organizations and Their Members* (New York: Harper & Row, 1974).

[42]N. Nicholson and G. Johns, "The Absence Culture and the Psychological Contract— Who's in Control of Absence?" *Academy of Management Review,* July 1985, pp. 397–407.

WORK STRESS

LEARNING OBJECTIVES

After studying this chapter, you should be able to:

1. Define stress
2. Describe potential sources of stress
3. Explain individual difference variables that moderate the stress-outcome relationship
4. Identify stress consequences
5. Outline individual stress management strategies
6. List organizational stress management strategies

Ulcers? I give 'em, I don't get 'em.

ANONYMOUS CEO

Pan American World Airways was once the premier global airline. It was the first airline to fly to Latin America and the first to circle the globe. In its heyday, job applicants would wait all day in a crowded room just to get an interview. A job at Pan Am meant security, great benefits, and the opportunity to work with a dedicated and loyal group of people. But that's history.[1] Management mistakes, a turbulent world economy, and U. S. airline deregulation favoring carriers with strong domestic route systems forced the company into bankruptcy. In December 1991, after selling much of its assets and laying off tens of thousands of people, the company threw in the towel and went out of business.

During the last year of its life, the declining fortunes of Pan Am wreaked havoc on its ten thousand or so employees. Many workers reported suffering severe emotional distress. A number complained of constant headaches, insomnia, and digestive problems. The company experienced a significant increase in employees seeking counseling for marital and financial problems. Absences went way up. And the stress surfaced even in the cockpit of Pan Am planes. For instance, Dallas Butler, a Pan Am captain with twenty-six years of company flying experience, admitted to making a dangerously high and fast approach to Guatemala City's airport. He attributed his poor judgment to the fear of losing his job and other distractions at the airline. He told the company's medical director that "stress is off the scale" among flight personnel. ■

The work stress experienced by Pan Am employees during its last months is not unique. Employees everywhere seem to be feeling more stressed nowadays. A recent sample of six hundred U.S. workers found that forty-six percent said their jobs were highly stressful and thirty-four percent reported that the stress was so bad they were thinking of quitting.[2] What's going on? Why are so many people complaining about work stress? And what can individuals and organizations do to reduce it? You'll find the answers to these questions in this chapter.

One point of clarification is necessary before we proceed. The topic of stress has individual and group-level relevance as well as organization system implications. As we will show, an individual's stress level can be increased by such varied factors as his or her personality, role conflicts, and the job's design. So work stress, while presented in Part IV of this book, The Organization System, is a multilevel concept.

WHAT IS STRESS?

Stress A dynamic condition in which an individual is confronted with an opportunity, constraint, or demand related to what he or she desires and for which the outcome is perceived to be both uncertain and important.

Stress is a dynamic condition in which an individual is confronted with an opportunity, constraint, or demand related to what he or she desires and for which the outcome is perceived to be both uncertain and important.[3] This is a complicated definition. Let's look at its components more closely.

Stress is not necessarily bad in and of itself. While stress is typically discussed in a negative context, it also has positive value. It is an opportunity when it offers potential gain. Consider, for example, the superior performance that an athlete or stage performer gives in "clutch" situations. Such individuals often use stress positively to rise to the occasion and perform at or near their maximum.

Constraints Forces that prevent individuals from doing what they desire.

Demands The loss of something desired.

More typically, stress is associated with **constraints** and **demands.** The former prevent you from doing what you desire. The latter refers to the loss of something desired. So when you take a test at school or you undergo your annual performance review at work, you feel stress because you confront opportunities, constraints, and demands. A good performance review may lead to a promotion, greater responsibilities, and a higher salary. But a poor review may prevent you from getting the promotion. An extremely poor review might even result in your being fired.

Two conditions are necessary for potential stress to become actual stress.[4] There must be uncertainty over the outcome and the outcome must be important. Regardless of the conditions, it is only when there is doubt or uncertainty regarding whether the opportunity will be seized, the constraint removed, or the loss avoided that there is stress. That is, stress is highest for those individuals who perceive that they are uncertain as to whether they will win or lose and lowest for those individuals who think that winning or losing is a certainty. But importance is also critical. If winning or losing is an unimportant outcome, there is no stress. If keeping your job or earning a promotion doesn't hold any importance to you, you have no reason to feel stress over having to undergo a performance review.

As we noted earlier, a large portion of the work force report that their jobs are highly stressful. Some argue, however, that it's now "hip to be stressed."[5] Who would admit, even if it were true, that he feels *less* stressed than he did a year ago? Job cutbacks, increased demands by employers to speed up work, the pressures of balancing dual careers and children, longer work commutes, and pay increases that fail to keep up with inflation are some of the reasons people cite to explain why they're feeling stressed out.

Whether work stress is actually a widespread problem depends on your definition of "widespread." There are no reliable statistics on stress intensity at work or the percentage of the working population suffering serious stress symptoms. However, we can approach the question from several other directions.

First, a lot of people seem to be suffering from stress symptoms. For instance, the American Academy of Family Physicians estimates that two-thirds of office visits to its members are attributable to stress-related symptoms.[6]

Second, a recent Gallup survey of personnel and medical directors at over two hundred big and small companies showed that, on average, twenty-five percent of their companies' employees suffered from anxiety or stress-related disorders.[7]

Third, stress-related health problems cost business and society a ton of money. The cost to business of stress-related problems and mental illness has been estimated as high as $150 billion a year, including health insurance and disability claims plus lost productivity.[8] In California, for instance, mental stress claims are the mostly rapidly increasing type of workers' compensation cases, having risen seven hundred percent in a decade.[9]

Fourth, some stress seems to come with every job. Can you name three or four jobs that are completely stress-free? It's not as easy as it seems. Most of us can identify jobs that are high in stress—air traffic controllers, police officers, fire fighters, emergency room physicians. But low-stress or, better yet, no-stress jobs are harder to identify.

Fifth, the dramatic changes that have taken place in the economy—mergers and acquisitions, increased global competition, new technological innovations, and the like—have resulted in large layoffs in many organizations and the restructuring of jobs. Few jobs are totally secure anymore. When co-workers or friends are losing their jobs and you fear for your own, your stress level is naturally going to increase.

Sixth, restructuring is not only undermining employee security, it is also putting pressure on employees—especially managers—to work longer hours. Twelve-hour days and six-day weeks have become the norm for many up-and-coming managers. A recent survey of CEOs found that they expect their middle managers to average forty-nine hours a week and their high-level executives to put in fifty-four hours. The CEOs themselves devote more than sixty hours a week to their jobs.[10]

Returning to our question—Is work stress widespread?—the answer would seem to be "Yes." We're not saying that this stress level is necessarily high or even that it is seriously hindering most people in their work. A national survey of managers found that sixty-five percent believed that their jobs were more stressful than the average job.[11] But as Table 18–1 illustrates, the stressors that created above-average stress were factors such as

Certain jobs can be extremely stress–creating. An air-traffic controller's job, for instance, requires tremendous vigilance and errors carry a very high cost in life and dollars.
Matthew Borkoski/Stock, Boston

Rating Occupations by Stress

Recent research divides occupations into four categories: active jobs, low-strain jobs, passive jobs, and high-strain jobs.[12]

Active jobs have heavy pressure to perform but allow leeway for problem solving. The hours tend to be long, but are partly at the worker's discretion. Doctors, engineers, farmers, executives, and other professionals, for example, hold active jobs.

Low-strain jobs put low demands on people and give them a high degree of decision-making latitude. Tenured professors, carpenters, repair people, and successful artists, among others, hold low-strain jobs.

Passive jobs combine low demands on skills and mental processes with little leeway for learning or decision making. These jobs offer almost no latitude for innovation. Examples are the jobs held by billing clerks, night watchmen, janitors, dispatchers, and keypunchers.

High-strain jobs have heavy pressure to perform and little leeway in decision making. These jobs tend to have long hours, require following rigid procedures, and allow little latitude for taking breaks or time off for personal needs. Assembly-line workers, waiters and waitresses, nurse's aides, and telephone operators are good examples of people who hold high-strain jobs.

There is strong evidence indicating that people in high-strain jobs have the highest rates for many diseases. In fact, the risk of illness for such people is two to four times what it is for others, independent of all other risk factors.

---

interruptions, role conflicts, and workload demands. And the ratings on these factors indicate that they were nowhere near the "always stressful" point (4 on a scale of 1 to 4).

UNDERSTANDING STRESS AND ITS CONSEQUENCES

What causes stress? What are its consequences for individual employees? Why is it that the same set of conditions that creates stress for one person seems to have little or no effect on another person? Figure 18–1 provides a model that can help to answer questions such as these.[13]

The model identifies three sets of factors—environmental, organizational, and individual—that act as *potential* sources of stress. Whether they become *actual* stress depends on individual differences such as job experience and personality. When stress is experienced by an individual, its symptoms can surface as physiological, psychological, and behavioral outcomes.

In the remainder of this chapter, we'll consider this model in more detail by reviewing the potential sources of stress, key individual difference variables, and stress consequences. Then we'll focus on stress management strategies that individuals themselves and organizations can utilize to help people cope with dysfunctional stress levels.

TABLE 18–1   The Impact of Workplace Stressors on Managerial Respondents (n = 315)

Stressor	Average Rating of All Respondents*
Interruptions	2.8
Role conflict (conflicting demands on time by others)	2.7
Work load	2.6
Managing time on the job	2.4
Organizational politics	2.3
Finding time for outside activities	2.3
Responsibility for subordinates	2.3
Firing someone	2.3
Reprimanding or disciplining	2.3
Balancing personal life with worklife	2.2
Dealing with upper management	2.1
Reviewing performance	2.0
Role ambiguity (uncertainty of what others expect)	2.0
Pay/compensation	1.8
Interviewing and hiring	1.8
Overtime	1.7
Working with budgets	1.7
Working with computers	1.5
Travel	1.4

*On a scale of 1 to 4, where 1 means never or rarely stressful and 4 means always stressful.

Source: Reprinted from *Management World,* June–August 1987, with permission from AMS, Trevose, PA 19047. Copyright (1987) AMS.

POTENTIAL SOURCES OF STRESS

As the model in Figure 18–1 shows, there are three categories of potential stressors: environmental, organizational, and individual. Let's take a look at each.[14]

Environmental Factors

Just as environmental uncertainty influences the design of an organization's structure, it also influences stress levels among employees in that organization.

Changes in the business cycle create *economic uncertainties.* When the economy is contracting, people become increasingly anxious about their security. It was not a chance occurrence that suicide rates skyrocketed during the Great Depression of the 1930s. Minor recessions, too, increase stress levels. Downward swings in the economy are often accompanied by permanent reductions in the work force, temporary layoffs, reduced pay, shorter workweeks, and the like.

Political uncertainties don't tend to create stress among North Americans as they do for employees in countries like Nicaragua or Iraq. The obvious reason is that the United States and Canada have stable political systems where change is typically implemented in an orderly manner. Yet political threats and changes, even in countries like the United States and Canada, can be stress-inducing. Efforts by Quebec officials to negotiate an agreement with the rest of Canada that would recognize and preserve Quebec's unique French culture have increased political uncertainty in Canada. Failure to arrive at a mutually acceptable arrangement might pre-

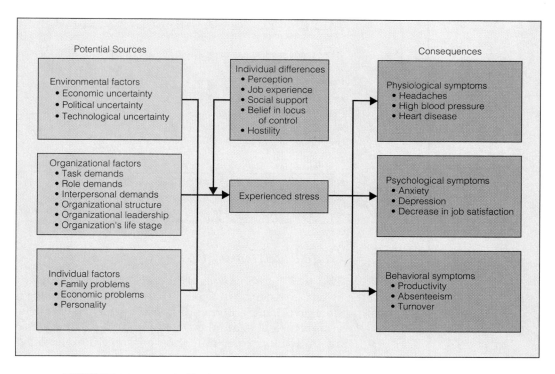

Potential Sources

Environmental factors
• Economic uncertainty
• Political uncertainty
• Technological uncertainty

Organizational factors
• Task demands
• Role demands
• Interpersonal demands
• Organizational structure
• Organizational leadership
• Organization's life stage

Individual factors
• Family problems
• Economic problems
• Personality

Individual differences
• Perception
• Job experience
• Social support
• Belief in locus of control
• Hostility

Experienced stress

Consequences

Physiological symptoms
• Headaches
• High blood pressure
• Heart disease

Psychological symptoms
• Anxiety
• Depression
• Decrease in job satisfaction

Behavioral symptoms
• Productivity
• Absenteeism
• Turnover

FIGURE 18–1   A Model of Stress

cipitate Quebec's separation from the rest of Canada. Until fully resolved, this difficult problem increases stress among many Canadians, especially among Quebecers with little or no skills in the French language.

New innovations can make an employee's skills and experience obsolete in a very short period of time. *Technological uncertainty,* therefore, is a third type of environmental factor that can cause stress. Computers, robotics, automation, and other forms of technological innovation are a threat to many people and cause them stress.

An example of the dramatic changes that have recently taken place in the economy is the shake-out in the American airline industry. The demise of Eastern Airlines, as a specific case, put thousands of Eastern employees on the street.
Michael A. Schwarz

TABLE 18–2   Primary Causes of Stress at Work

What factors cause the most stress on the job? A *Wall Street Journal* survey reported:

Factor	Percentage Response*
Not doing the kind of work I want to	34
Coping with current job	30
Working too hard	28
Colleagues at work	21
A difficult boss	18

*Percentages exceed 100 as a result of some multiple responses.

Source: "Worries at Work," *Wall Street Journal*, April 7, 1988, p. 27. Reprinted by permission of *Wall Street Journal*, © 1988 Dow Jones & Company, Inc. All rights reserved worldwide.

Organizational Factors

There is no shortages of factors within the organization that can cause stress. Pressures to avoid errors or complete tasks in a limited time period, work overload, a demanding and insensitive boss, and unpleasant co-workers are a few examples. (See Table 18–2.) We've categorized these factors around task, role, and interpersonal demands; organization structure; organizational leadership; and the organization's life stage.[15]

Task demands are factors related to a person's job. They include the design of the individual's job (autonomy, task variety, degree of automation), working conditions, and the physical work layout. Assembly lines can put pressure on people when their speed is perceived as excessive. The more interdependence between a person's tasks and the tasks of others, the more potential stress there is. Autonomy, on the other hand, tends to lessen stress. Jobs where temperatures, noise, or other working conditions are dangerous or undesirable can increase anxiety. So, too, can working in an overcrowded room or in a visible location where interruptions are constant.

Role demands relate to pressures placed on a person as a function of the particular role he or she plays in the organization. Role conflicts create expectations that may be hard to reconcile or satisfy. Role overload is experienced when the employee is expected to do more than time permits. Role ambiguity is created when role expectations are not clearly understood and the employee is not sure what he or she is to do.

Interpersonal demands are pressures created by other employees. Lack of social support from colleagues and poor interpersonal relationships can cause considerable stress, especially among employees with a high social need.

Organization structure defines the level of differentiation in the organization, the degree of rules and regulations, and where decisions are made. Excessive rules and lack of participation in decisions that affect an employee are examples of structural variables that might be potential sources of stress.

Organizational leadership represents the managerial style of the organization's senior executives. Some chief executive officers create a culture characterized by tension, fear, and anxiety. They establish unrealistic pressures to perform in the short run, impose excessively tight controls, and routinely fire employees who don't "measure up." For instance, when Harold Geneen was chairman and CEO at ITT, division executives had to formally present their annual business plan to Geneen and his senior staff group. Each division executive would then be interrogated about every number in every graph, exhibit, and analysis in the plan. The exercise was known to put fear into the hearts of all the division executives and to occasionally bring tears to some of their eyes.

So much mail; so little time. The pressure is high for many of these postal workers who have about one second to read an address and punch in the first three digits of the zip code, which is then translated into a bar code symbol for sorting mail by carrier route
Jodi Buren/Time magazine

Monitoring Employee Performance by Telephone or Computer

If you worked at General Electric's Answering Center handling telephone inquiries from customers all day long, how would you feel if you knew all your phone conversations were being recorded and possibly reviewed later by management? Or how would you feel if you were a data-entry clerk at the Southern California Gas Co. and knew managers were using computerized devices to count your keystrokes and calculate your daily productivity? Technology makes spying on employees possible. The question is: When does such silent monitoring become unethical?[16]

Just how many workers are being electronically monitored on their jobs is not clear. One U.S. government office put the number at 6 million. Interestingly, the practice is not confined to low-paid workers doing repetitive tasks. At the Charles Schwab discount brokerage, for instance, experienced stockbrokers earning as much as $70,000 a year are routinely listened in on through computerized voice-recording systems.

Knowing that somebody may be listening in on your phone calls makes stress-related complaints more common. For example, a study of telephone operators found that monitored employees experienced significantly more headaches, severe fatigue or exhaustion, and extreme anxiety than unmonitored employees.

Are employers overstepping the bounds of decency and privacy in the workplace by scrutinizing computer entries and eavesdropping on telephone calls? It can be argued that this type of surveillance helps people do their jobs better. It enables managers to review employee performance and provide feedback that can improve the quality of the employees' work. But when does management's need for more information about employee performance cross over the line and interfere with a worker's right to privacy?

Organizations go through a cycle. They're established, they grow, become mature, and eventually decline. An *organization's life stage*—that is, where it is in this four-stage cycle—creates different problems and pressures for employees. The establishment and decline stages are particularly stressful. The former is characterized by a great deal of excitement and uncertainty, while the latter typically requires cutbacks, layoffs, and a different set of uncertainties. Stress tends to be least in maturity where uncertainties are at their lowest ebb.

Individual Factors

The typical individual only works about forty hours a week. The experiences and problems that people encounter in those other 128 nonwork hours each week can spill over to the job. Our final category, then, encompasses factors in the employee's personal life. Primarily, these factors are family issues, personal economic problems, and inherent personality characteristics.

National surveys consistently show that people hold *family* and personal relationships dear. Marital difficulties, the breaking off of a relationship, and discipline troubles with children are examples of relationship problems that create stress for employees and that aren't left at the front door when they arrive at work.

Economic problems created by individuals overextending their financial resources is another set of personal troubles that can create stress for employees and distract their attention from their work. Regardless of income level—people who make $80,000 a year seem to have as much trouble handling their finances as those who earn $18,000—some people are poor money managers or have wants that always seem to exceed their earning capacity.

Recent research in three diverse organizations found that stress symptoms reported prior to beginning a job accounted for most of the variance in stress symptoms reported nine months later.[17] This led the researchers to conclude that some people may have an inherent tendency to accentuate negative aspects of the world in general. If true, then a significant individual factor influencing stress is a person's basic dispositional nature. That is, stress symptoms expressed on the job may actually originate in the person's *personality*.

Stressors Are Additive

A fact that tends to be overlooked when stressors are reviewed individually is that stress is an additive phenomenon.[18] Stress builds up. Each new and persistent stressor adds to an individual's stress level. A single stressor may seem relatively unimportant in and of itself, but if it is added to an already high level of stress, it can be "the straw that breaks the camel's back." If we want to appraise the total amount of stress an individual is under, we have to sum up his or her opportunity stresses, constraint stresses, and demand stresses.

INDIVIDUAL DIFFERENCES

Some people thrive on stressful situations, while others are overwhelmed by them. What is it that differentiates people in terms of their ability to handle stress? What individual difference variables moderate the relationship between *potential* stressors and *experienced* stress? At least five variables—perception, job experience, social support, belief in locus of control, and hostility—have been found to be relevant moderators.

Perception

In Chapter 5, we demonstrated that employees react in response to their perception of reality rather than to reality itself. Perception, therefore, will moderate the relationship between a potential stress condition and an employee's reaction to it. One person's fear that he'll lose his job because his company is laying off personnel may be perceived by another as an opportunity to get a large severance allowance and start his own business. Similarly, what one employee perceives as an efficient and challenging work environment may be viewed as threatening and demanding by others. So the stress potential in environmental, organizational, and individual factors doesn't lie in their objective condition. Rather, it lies in an employee's interpretation of those factors.

Job Experience

Experience is said to be a great teacher. It can also be a great stress-reducer. Think back to your first date or your first few days in college. For most of us, the uncertainty and newness of these situations created stress. But as we gained experience, that stress disappeared or at least significantly decreased. The same phenomenon seems to apply to work situations. That is, experience on the job tends to be negatively related to work stress. Two explanations have been offered.[19] First is the idea of selective withdrawal. Voluntary turnover is more probable among people who experience more stress. Therefore, people who remain with the organization longer are those with more stress-resistant traits, or those who are more resistant to the stress characteristics of their organization. Second, people eventually develop coping mechanisms to deal with stress. Because this takes time, senior members of the organization are more likely to be fully adapted and should experience less stress.

Social Support

There is increasing evidence that social support—that is, collegial relationships with co-workers or supervisors—can buffer the impact of stress.[20] The logic underlying this moderating variable is that social support acts as a palliative, mitigating the negative effects of even high-strain jobs.

For individuals whose work associates are unhelpful or even actively hostile, social support may be found outside the job. Involvement with family, friends, and community can provide the support—especially for those with a high social need—that is missing at work and this can make job stressors more tolerable.

Belief in Locus of Control

Locus of control was introduced in Chapter 4 as a personality attribute. Those with an internal locus of control believe they control their own destiny. Those with an external locus believe their lives are controlled by outside forces. Evidence indicates that internals perceive their jobs to be less stressful than do externals.[21]

When internals and externals confront a similar stressful situation, the internals are likely to believe that they can have a significant effect on the results. They, therefore, act to take control of events. Externals are more

One of the most potent buffers against stress is membership in a stable, close-knit group. The U.S. Army discovered in World War II that the small, primary work group lessens stress because the soldier feels his squad is listening to him and he can talk to other members about his fears and anxieties.
Eric Bouvet/Gamma–Liaison

likely to be passive and defensive. Rather than do something to reduce the stress, they acquiesce. So externals, who are more likely to feel helpless in stressful situations, are also more likely to experience stress.

Hostility

Type A Behavior Aggressive involvement in a chronic, incessant struggle to achieve more and more in less and less time and, if necessary, against the opposing efforts of other things or other people.

For much of the 1970s and 1980s, a great deal of attention was directed at what became known as **Type A behavior.**[22] In fact, throughout the 1980s, it was undoubtedly the most frequently used moderating variable related to stress.

Type A behavior is characterized by feeling a chronic sense of time urgency and by an *excessive* competitive drive. A Type A individual is "*aggressively* involved in a *chronic, incessant* struggle to achieve more and more in less and less time, and if required to do so, against the opposing efforts of other things or other persons."[23] In the North American culture, such characteristics tend to be highly prized and positively correlated with ambition and the successful acquisition of material goods. Type A's

1. are always moving, walking, and eating rapidly;
2. feel impatient with the rate at which most events take place;
3. strive to think or do two or more things simultaneously;
4. cannot cope with leisure time; and
5. are obsessed with numbers, measuring their success in terms of how much of everything they acquire.

Type B Behavior Rarely harried by the desire to obtain a wildly increasing number of things or to participate in an endlessly growing series of events in an ever-decreasing amount of time.

The opposite of Type A is **Type B behavior.** Type B's are "rarely harried by the desire to obtain a wildly increasing number of things or participate in an endless growing series of events in an ever-decreasing amount of time."[24] Type B's

1. never suffer from a sense of time urgency, with its accompanying impatience;
2. feel no need to display or discuss their achievements or accomplishments unless such exposure is demanded by the situation;
3. play for fun and relaxation, rather than to exhibit their superiority at any cost; and
4. can relax without guilt.

Until quite recently, researchers believed that Type A's were more likely to experience stress on and off the job. More specifically, Type A's were widely believed to be at higher risk for heart disease. A closer analysis of the evidence, however, has produced new conclusions.[25] By looking at various components of Type A behavior, it's been found that only the hostility and anger associated with Type A behavior is actually related to heart disease. The chronically angry, suspicious, and mistrustful person is the one at risk.

So just because a person is a workaholic, rushes around a lot, and is impatient or competitive does not mean that he or she is unduly susceptible to heart disease or the other negative effects of stress. Rather, it's the quickness to anger, the persistently hostile outlook, and the cynical mistrust of others that are harmful.

STRESS CONSEQUENCES

Stress shows itself in a number of ways. For instance, an individual who is experiencing a high level of stress may develop high blood pressure, ulcers, irritability, difficulty in making routine decisions, loss of appetite, accident proneness, and the like. These can be subsumed under three general categories: physiological, psychological, and behavioral symptoms.[26]

Physiological Symptoms

Most of the early concern with stress was directed at **physiological symptoms.** This was predominately due to the fact that the topic was researched by specialists in the health and medical sciences. This research led to the conclusion that stress could create changes in metabolism, increase heart and breathing rates, increase blood pressure, bring on headaches, and induce heart attacks.

The link between stress and particular physiological symptoms is not clear. There are few, if any, consistent relationships.[27] This is attributed to the complexity of the symptoms and the difficulty of objectively measuring them. But of greater relevance is the fact that physiological symptoms have the least direct relevance to students of OB. Our concern is with behaviors and attitudes. Therefore, the two other categories of symptoms are more important to us.

Psychological Symptoms

Stress can cause dissatisfaction. Job-related stress can cause job-related dissatisfaction. Job dissatisfaction, in fact, is "the simplest and most obvious psychological effect" of stress.[28] But stress shows itself in other **psychological** states—for instance, tension, anxiety, irritability, boredom, and procrastination.

The evidence indicates that when people are placed in jobs that make multiple and conflicting demands or in which there is a lack of clarity as to the incumbent's duties, authority, and responsibilities, both stress and dissatisfaction are increased.[29] Similarly, the less control people have over the pace of their work, the greater the stress and dissatisfaction. While more research is needed to clarify the relationship, the evidence suggests that jobs that provide a low level of variety, significance, autonomy, feedback, and identity to incumbents create stress and reduce satisfaction and involvement in the job.[30]

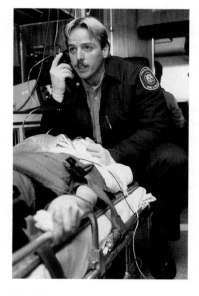

Fire Department emergency medical personnel frequently experience all three types of stress symptoms—physiological, psychological, and behavioral—as a result of the stress from their jobs.
Jon A. Rembold/Insight Magazine

Behavioral Symptoms

Behaviorally related stress symptoms include changes in productivity, absence, and turnover, as well as changes in eating habits, increased smoking or consumption of alcohol, rapid speech, fidgeting, and sleep disorders.

There has been a significant amount of research investigating the stress-performance relationship. The most thoroughly documented pattern in the stress-performance literature is the inverted-U relationship.[31] This is shown in Figure 18–2.

The logic underlying the inverted U is that low to moderate levels of stress stimulate the body and increase its ability to react. Individuals then often perform their tasks better, more intensely, or more rapidly. But too much stress places unattainable demands or constraints on a person, which results in lower performance. This inverted-U pattern may also describe the reaction to stress over time, as well as to changes in stress intensity. That is, even moderate levels of stress can have a negative influence on performance over the long term as the continued intensity of the stress wears down the individual and saps his or her energy resources. An athlete may be able to

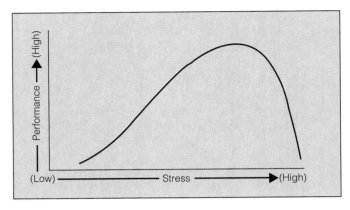

FIGURE 18–2   Relationship Between Stress and Job Performance

use the positive effects of stress to obtain a higher performance during every Saturday's game in the fall season, or a sales executive may be able to psych herself up for her presentation at the annual national meeting. But moderate levels of stress experienced continually over long periods of time—as typified by the emergency room staff in a large urban hospital—can result in lower performance. This may explain why emergency room staffs at such hospitals are frequently rotated and why it is unusual to find individuals who have spent the bulk of their career in such an environment. In effect, to do so would expose the individual to the risk of "career burnout."

Considerable attention has also been focused on how the Type A-Type B dichotomy affects job performance. Research findings, unfortunately, are inconclusive.[32] For instance, some indicate that Type A's emphasize quantity of output while Type B's focus on quality. Other studies, however, fail to replicate these findings. The most confident statement we can make is that Type A's outperform Type B's in those jobs calling for persistence or endurance. This is because Type A's set higher performance goals and are not easily derailed by setbacks.

STRESS MANAGEMENT STRATEGIES

From the organization's standpoint, management may not be concerned when employees experience low-to-moderate levels of stress. The reason, as we showed earlier, is that such levels of stress can be functional and lead to higher employee performance. But high levels of stress, or even low levels sustained over long periods of time, can lead to reduced employee performance and, thus, require action by management.

While a limited amount of stress may benefit an employee's performance, don't expect employees to see it that way. From the individual's standpoint, even low levels of stress are likely to be perceived as undesirable. It's not unlikely, therefore, for employees and management to have different notions of what constitutes an acceptable level of stress on the job. What management may consider as "a positive stimulus that keeps the adrenaline running" is very likely to be seen as "excessive pressure" by the employee. Keep this in mind as we discuss individual and organizational approaches toward managing stress.[33]

Job Burnout: The Malady of Our Age?

Many people have undoubtedly suffered from job burnout for decades but it didn't become a primary concern of health specialists and behavioral scientists until the 1980s. Now, some are calling it "the malady of our age."[34]

What *is* job burnout? Burnout is defined as a three-dimensional concept characterized by: (1) depersonalization or a negative shift in responses to others; (2) a decreased sense of personal accomplishment; and (3) physical, mental, and emotional exhaustion.[35] It is this last characteristic that most of us associate with burnout—sufferers appear to have become worn out from their jobs. They are low in energy, fatigued, feel helpless and trapped, and exhibit negative attitudes about themselves, work, and life in general.

Is job burnout synonymous with stress? No, but it's closely related. Work-related stressors can culminate in burnout, but do not always do so. What conditions, then, lead to job burnout? First, there is the existence of such organizational or individual stressors as role ambiguity, performance pressures, work overload, and interpersonal conflicts. Second, the burnout candidate tends to hold unrealistic expectations or ambitions. These combine to create stress, fatigue, frustration, and feelings of helplessness

and guilt.[36] When burnout sets in, the person finds that he or she has difficulty coping with the demands of the job. The eventual result is reduced organizational commitment and job satisfaction, increased absenteeism, and impairment of interpersonal relationships with work colleagues, friends, and family.

Who is vulnerable to job burnout? Maybe somewhat surprisingly, it tends to attack the best, the brightest, and the most highly motivated—those who had once been among the most idealistic and enthusiastic.[37] It seems particularly to strike middle managers and helping professionals such as nurses, physicians, social workers, lawyers, schoolteachers, and police officers.[38]

The combination of stress and acceptance of the fact that many job problems have no clear-cut solutions may explain why some professionals drop out of the careers that they've spent years in and for which they underwent extensive training. The decision by many nurses and secondary school teachers, for instance, to switch to other careers after only ten or fifteen years in these professions is probably at least in part a response to job burnout. Some of the strategies for managing stress that we discuss in the next section can also help reduce the causes and symptoms of burnout.

Individual Approaches

An employee can take personal responsibility for reducing his or her stress level. Individual strategies that have proven effective include implementing time management techniques, increasing physical exercise, relaxation training, and expanding the social support network.

TIME MANAGEMENT   Many people manage their time poorly. The things they have to accomplish in any given day or week are not necessarily beyond completion if they manage their time properly. The well-organized employee, like the well-organized student, can often accomplish twice as much as the person who is poorly organized. So an understanding and utilization of basic time management principles can help individuals better cope with job demands. A few of the more well-known time management principles are: (1) making daily lists of activities to be accomplished; (2) prioritizing activities by importance and urgency; (3) scheduling activities according to the priorities set; and (4) knowing your daily cycle and handling the most demanding parts of your job during the high part of your cycle when you are most alert and productive.[39]

PHYSICAL EXERCISE   Noncompetitive physical exercise such as aerobics, race walking, jogging, swimming, and riding a bicycle have long been recommended by physicians as a way to deal with excessive stress levels. These forms of exercise increase heart capacity, lower at-rest heart rate, provide a mental diversion from work pressures, and offer a means to "let off steam."[40]

RELAXATION TRAINING   Individuals can teach themselves to relax through techniques such as meditation, hypnosis, and biofeedback. The objective is to reach a state of **deep relaxation,** where one feels physically relaxed, somewhat detached from the immediate environment, and detached from body sensations.[41] Fifteen or twenty minutes a day of deep relaxation releases tension and provides a person with a pronounced sense of peacefulness. Importantly, significant changes in heart rate, blood pressure, and other physiological factors result from achieving the deep relaxation condition.

Deep Relaxation A state of physical relaxation, where the individual is somewhat detached from both the immediate environment and body sensations.

SOCIAL SUPPORT   As we noted earlier in this chapter, having friends, family, or work colleagues to talk to provides an outlet when stress levels become excessive. Expanding your social support network, therefore, can be a means for tension reduction. It provides you with someone to hear your problems and a more objective perspective on the situation. Research also demonstrates that social support moderates the stress-burnout relationship.[42] That is, high support reduces the likelihood that heavy work stress will result in job burnout.

Organizational Approaches

Several of the factors that cause stress—particularly task and role demands, and organization structure—are controlled by management. As such, they can be modified or changed. Strategies that management might want to consider include improved personnel selection and job placement, use of realistic goal setting, redesigning of jobs, use of participative decision making, improved organizational communication, and establishment of corporate wellness programs.

SELECTION AND PLACEMENT   While certain jobs are more stressful than others, we learned earlier in this chapter that individuals differ in their response to stress situations. We know, for example, that individuals with little experience or an external locus of control tend to be more stress-prone. Selection and placement decisions should take these facts into consideration. Obviously, while management shouldn't restrict hiring to only experienced individuals with an internal locus, such individuals may adapt better to high-stress jobs and perform those jobs more effectively.

GOAL SETTING   We discussed goal setting in Chapter 7. Based on an extensive amount of research, we concluded that individuals perform better when they have specific and challenging goals and receive feedback on how well they are progressing toward these goals. The use of goals can reduce stress as well as provide motivation. Specific goals that are perceived as attainable clarify performance expectations. Additionally, goal feedback reduces uncertainties as to actual job performance. The result is less employee frustration, role ambiguity, and stress.

JOB REDESIGN   Redesigning jobs to give employees more responsibility, more meaningful work, more autonomy, and increased feedback can reduce stress, because these factors give the employee greater control over work activities and lessen dependence on others. But as we noted in our discussion of job design in Chapter 8, not all employees want enriched jobs. The right job redesign, then, for employees with a low need for growth might be less responsibility and increased division of labor. If individuals prefer structure and routine, reducing skill variety should also reduce uncertainties and stress levels.

PARTICIPATIVE DECISION MAKING   Role stress is detrimental to a large extent because employees feel uncertain about goals, expectations, how they'll be evaluated, and the like. By giving these employees a voice in those decisions that directly affect their job performances, management can increase employee control and reduce this role stress. So managers should consider increasing employee participation in decision making.[43]

ORGANIZATIONAL COMMUNICATION   Increasing formal communication with employees reduces uncertainty by lessening role ambiguity and role conflict. Given the importance that perceptions play in moderating the stress-response relationship, management can also use effective communications as a means to shape employee perceptions. Remember that what employees categorize as demands, threats, or opportunities are merely an interpretation, and that interpretation can be affected by the symbols and actions communicated by management.

Wellness Programs
Organizationally supported programs that focus on the employee's total physical and mental condition.

WELLNESS PROGRAMS   Our final suggestion is to offer organizationally supported **wellness programs.** These programs focus on the employee's total physical and mental condition.[44] For example, they typically provide workshops to help people quit smoking, control alcohol use, lose weight, eat

Quaker Oats has installed a fitness center at its headquarters to encourage employees to stay healthy. To further encourage employees, the company offers financial incentives for employees who stay well.
David Walberg

Work Stress Is a World-Wide Phenomenon

The prevalence of work stress doesn't usually surprise North Americans. They see it as a side effect of cultures that emphasize individualism, competitiveness, achievement, and material acquisitions. But North Americans have no monopoly on work stress. Quite to the contrary, the fact that the United States and Canada score well below average on uncertainty avoidance seems to suggest societies relatively free from the threat of uncertainty and the stress that goes with it. Other countries undoubtedly induce higher levels of environmental stress on their organizational members. As an illustration, take the case of Japan.[45]

If you'll remember from Chapter 3, Japan scores high on uncertainty avoidance. This may contribute to explaining a sad statistic: The chief executives of at least twelve major Japanese companies, including Seiko Epson, Kawasaki Steel, and All Nippon Airways, all died suddenly during a recent seven-month period. Most were in their fifties and sixties, quite young to die in a country where the average male lives to age seventy-five. Many experts think that stress may be a prime contributor to the deaths of these executives.

During a prior two-year period, the value of the Japanese yen had risen forty percent. This made Japanese products more expensive and reduced exports. The result was that many Japanese companies suffered slipping sales and profits.

Business executives in every country face downturns now and then. But in Japan, such downturns put extraordinary stress on top executives. Japanese managers are very competitive. Moreover, because they tend to spend their entire careers with a single company, they personally identify very closely with their firm's performance. Their company's success is their success. Their company's setbacks are also their setbacks. Additionally, the typical Japanese executive doesn't leave the office behind at the end of the day. Top executives have to attend a party or two after work almost every day, where they eat high-calorie food, drink a lot, and continue to talk business. Combine these cultural characteristics with the added stress in economic hard times, and you have the ingredients for physiological disaster.

Interestingly, research indicates that there may be a pattern to the relationship between downturns in the Japanese economy and increased stress levels (as evidenced by sudden deaths among corporate executives) that goes beyond the previous data. Evidence demonstrates that the incidence of heart attacks among Japanese managers was nearly four times as high during the oil crises of 1974 and 1979 as in the high-growth period of 1966–68.

better, and develop a regular exercise program. The assumption underlying most wellness programs is that employees need to take personal responsibility for their physical and mental health. The organization is merely a vehicle to facilitate this end.

Organizations, of course, aren't altruistic. They expect a payoff from their investment in wellness programs. And most of those firms that have introduced wellness programs have found the benefits to exceed the costs. For instance, General Electric's aircraft engines headquarters in Cincinnati estimates it saves up to $1 million a year in health insurance costs alone from its wellness program.[46] Johnson & Johnson computes the cost of its program at $200 per employee, yet claims that it saves $370 per employee by lowering absenteeism and slowing the rise in the company's health-care expenses.[47]

IMPLICATIONS FOR PERFORMANCE AND SATISFACTION

A number of factors (environmental, organizational, and individual), moderated by individual differences, cause employees to feel stressed. The more frequently these factors occur and the more intensely stressful they are for the employee, the greater the stress that he or she experiences. How intensely stressful the work situation is for a particular employee depends in part on his or her perceptions, job experience, social support, belief in locus of control, and the extent to which he or she expresses hostility.

The existence of work stress, in and of itself, does not imply lower performance. The evidence indicates that stress can be either a positive or negative influence on employee performance. For many people, low-to-moderate amounts of stress enable them to perform their jobs better, by increasing their work intensity, alertness, and ability to react. However, a high level of stress, or even a moderate level sustained over a long period of time, eventually takes its toll and performance declines.

As stress increases, so typically does absenteeism.[48] Alcohol and drug abuse, for example, cost employers billions of dollars each year in lost work time. A substantial part of this loss is undoubtedly a reaction to personal and work-related stress. It's interesting to note that studies demonstrate that women suffer more stress than men and have higher absentee rates.[49] But this is certainly largely due to role conflicts created by being career woman, homemaker, and parent. As we noted in Chapter 4, as traditional male and female roles at home are redefined toward greater sharing of home and parenting responsibilities, these differences between the sexes on absentee rates should disappear.

The impact of stress on satisfaction is pretty straightforward. Job-related tension tends to decrease general job satisfaction.[50] Even though low-to-moderate levels of stress may improve job performance, employees find stress dissatisfying.

■ FOR DISCUSSION

1. How are opportunities, constraints, and demands related to stress? Give an example of each.

2. How prevalent is work-related stress?

3. Describe the three sources of potential stress. Which of these are controllable by management?

4. What turns potential stress into actual stress?

5. Contrast Type A and Type B behavior. Are Type B individuals less effective employees than Type A's?

6. Do you think the proportion of Type A's in a society differs from country to country? Explain.

7. What are the symptoms of stress?

8. What is the relationship between stress and performance?

9. What can individuals do to reduce their stress levels?

10. What can organizations do to reduce employee stress?

11. Some people say living in Los Angeles, New York, or other large, urban centers creates stresses on employees that don't exist in rural or small-town communities. Is this a potential source of work stress? If so, where would it go in Figure 18–1?

12. With very few exceptions, labor unions have not been receptive to stress management programs. Why do you suppose this is true? What can management do that might gain a union's support for an organizationally sponsored stress management program?

Employee Stress Isn't a Management Problem!

The recent attention given employee stress by behavioral scientists has been blown totally out of proportion. There is undoubtedly a small proportion of the working population that suffers from stress. These people have ongoing headaches, ulcers, high blood pressure, and the like. They may even turn to alcohol and drugs as an outlet to deal with their stress. But if there is a problem, it's a medical one. It is *not* a management problem. In support of this position, I'll argue that (1) stress is not that important because human beings are highly adaptive; (2) most stress that employees experience is of the positive type; and (3) even if the first two points weren't relevant, a good portion of what causes excessive work stress tends to be uncontrollable by management anyway.

Those who seem to be so concerned about employee stress forget that people are more adaptable than we traditionally give them credit for. They are amazingly resilient. Most successfully adjust to illnesses, misfortune, and other changes in their lives. All through their school years, they adapted to the demands that dozens of teachers put on them. They survived the trials of puberty, dating, beginning and ending relationships, and leaving home—to name a few of the more potentially stressful times we have all gone through. By the time individuals enter the work force, they have experienced many difficult situations and, for the most part, they have adjusted to each. There is no reason to believe that this ability to adapt to changing or uncomfortable conditions breaks down once people begin their working careers.

Stress, like conflict, has a positive as well as a negative side. But that positive side tends to be overshadowed by concern with the negative. A life without stress is a life without challenge, stimula-tion, or change. As the table in Exercise 18–A so clearly illustrates, many positive and exciting life events—marriage, the birth of a child, inheriting a large sum of money, buying a new home, a job promotion, vacations—create stress. Does that mean that these positive events should be avoided? The answer is obviously "No." Unfortunately, when most people talk about stress and the need to reduce it, they tend to overlook its positive side.

Finally, there is the reality that many sources of employee stress are outside the control of management. Management can't control environmental factors. If stress is due to an inherent personality characteristic, here again, the source lies outside management's control. Most other individual factors, too, are outside management's influence. Even if stresses created by such individual factors as family and economic problems can be influenced by managerial actions, there remains the ethical question: Does management have the right to interfere in an employee's personal life? Undoubtedly, a good portion of any employee's total stress level is created by factors that are uncontrollable by management—marital problems; divorce; children who get into trouble; poor personal financial management; uncertainty over the economy; societal norms to achieve and acquire material symbols of success; pressures of living in a fast-paced, urban world; and the like. The actions of management didn't create these stressors. Most are just part of modern living. More importantly, there is little that employers can do to lessen these stressors without extending their influence beyond the organization and into the employee's personal life. That's something that most of us would agree is outside the province of the employer-employee relationship.

Stress Creates Real Costs to Organizations

Those who think management should ignore the problem of employee stress need to take a look at what stress is costing organizations.*

The total cost of work-related accidents in the United States is approximately $32 billion per year. It is estimated that at least three-quarters of all industrial accidents are caused by the inability of employees to cope with emotional distress.

Stress-related absenteeism, organizational medical expenses, and lost productivity are estimated to cost between $50 billion and $75 billion per year, or an average of about $750 per worker. Stress-related headaches are the leading cause of lost work time in United States industry.

Coronary heart disease is a leading killer of Americans. Over one million Americans suffer heart attacks each year, and half of them are fatal. One out of every five average, healthy male Americans will suffer a heart attack before he reaches the age of sixty-five. Heart disease causes an annual loss of more than 135 million workdays. The premature loss of valued employees means the loss of experienced personnel and the additional cost of replacing these people. These facts are important because there now exists a wealth of research that links stress to heart disease.

More than sixty percent of long-term disability is related to psychological or psychosomatic problems often brought on or made worse by stress.

State workers' compensation boards are increasingly awarding compensation for physical- and mental-stress claims. A single claim for permanent total disability can cost in excess of $250,000. Since each employer's workers' compensation costs are based on claims against that employer, any increase in awards is an added cost of doing business.

Two facts about stress cannot be ignored. First, people get sick from stress at work. Second, the costs associated with stress are significant to every employer. They include lost time, increased accidents, higher insurance premiums and health-care costs, and lower productivity. The only natural conclusion one can draw is that managers cannot ignore the stress issue and must actively seek to do something about it. It is in management's self-interest to take an active stance because, if for no other reason, it provides a basis for defending the organization against claims that its jobs and working conditions are stress-creating and the primary cause for compensable emotional problems.

*These figures come from K. Albrecht, *Stress and the Manager* (Englewood Cliffs, NJ: Prentice Hall, 1979), pp. 33–34; "Stress: Can We Cope?", *Time,* June 6, 1983, pp. 48–54; J. W. Jones, "A Cost Evaluation for Stress Management," *EAP Digest,* November-December 1984, p. 34; "Stress Claims Are Making Business Jumpy," *Business Week,* October 14, 1985, pp. 152–54; and M. J. McCarthy, "Stressed Employees Look for Relief in Workers' Compensation Claims," *The Wall Street Journal,* April 7, 1988, p. 27.

The Social Readjustment Rating Scale

DIRECTIONS   Read the following list of life events and enter the score for each event that has occurred in your life in the *past year*. If any event has occurred *more than once*, multiply the point value by the number of times it occurred. When you finish, total your score.

Rank	Life Event	Mean Value
1.	Death of spouse	100
2.	Divorce	73
3.	Marital separation	65
4.	Detention in jail or other institution	63
5.	Death of a close family member	63
6.	Major personal injury or illness	53
7.	Marriage	50
8.	Fired at work	47
9.	Marital reconciliation	45
10.	Retirement	45
11.	Major change in the health or behavior of a family member	44
12.	Pregnancy	40
13.	Sexual difficulties	39
14.	Gaining a new family member (through birth, adoption, relative moving in, etc.)	39
15.	Major business readjustment (merger, reorganization, bankruptcy, etc.)	39
16.	Major change in financial status (a lot worse off or a lot better off than usual)	38
17.	Death of a close friend or family member (other than spouse)	37
18.	Change to a different line of work	36
19.	Major change in the number of arguments with spouse (either a lot more or a lot less than usual regarding child-rearing, personal habits, etc.)	35
20.	Taking out a mortgage or loan for a major purchase (for a home, business, etc.)	31
21.	Foreclosure on a mortgage or loan	30
22.	Major change in responsibilities at work (promotion, demotion, lateral transfer)	29
23.	Son or daughter leaving home (marriage, attending college, etc.)	29
24.	Trouble with in-laws	29
25.	Outstanding personal achievement	28
26.	Spouse beginning or ceasing work outside the home	26
27.	Beginning or ceasing formal schooling	26
28.	Major change in living conditions (building a new home, remodeling, deterioration of home or neighborhood, etc.)	25
29.	Revision of personal habits (dress, manners, associations, etc.)	24
30.	Trouble with your boss	23
31.	Major change in working hours or conditions	20
32.	Change in residence	20
33.	Change in schools	20
34.	Major change in usual type and/or amount of recreation	19
35.	Major change in church activities (a lot more or a lot less than usual)	19
36.	Major change in social activities (clubs, dancing, movies, visiting, etc.)	18
37.	Taking out a mortgage or loan for a lesser purchase (for a car, TV, VCR, etc.)	17
38.	Major change in sleeping habits (a lot more or a lot less sleep, or change in part of day when asleep)	16
39.	Major change in number of family get-togethers (a lot more or a lot less than usual, etc.)	15
40.	Major change in eating habits (a lot more or a lot less food intake, or very different meal hours or surroundings)	15
41.	Vacation	13
42.	Christmas/holiday season	12
43.	Minor violations of the law (traffic tickets, jaywalking, disturbing the peace, etc.)	11

Source: Adapted from T. H. Holmes and R. H. Rahe, "The Social Readjustment Scale," *Journal of Psychosomatic Research,* 11 (1967), p. 216. With permission from Pergamon Press, Ltd.

Turn to page 719 for scoring directions and key.

The Type A—Type B Group Exercise

This exercise takes approximately forty-five minutes to complete.

1. Each student should independently complete the following questionnaire.* Circle the number on the scale below that best characterizes your behavior for each trait.

1. Casual about appointments	1 2 3 4 5 6 7 8	Never late
2. Not competitive	1 2 3 4 5 6 7 8	Very competitive
3. Never feel rushed even under pressure	1 2 3 4 5 6 7 8	Always rushed
4. Take things one at a time	1 2 3 4 5 6 7 8	Try to do many things at once, think about what I am going to do next
5. Slow doing things	1 2 3 4 5 6 7 8	Fast (eating, walking, etc.)
6. Express feelings	1 2 3 4 5 6 7 8	"Sit" on feelings
7. Many interests	1 2 3 4 5 6 7 8	Few interests outside work

2. Turn to page 719 for scoring directions. Calculate your Type A-Type B score.

3. Your instructor will use a show of hands to calculate the distribution of your class into categories A+, A, A-, B+, and B.

4. Break into groups of five to seven and discuss the accuracy of the following statements:

   a. "Most college students are Type A's."

   b. "Type A's achieve more material success and are happier than Type B's."

   c. "If a person doesn't like his or her Type A-Type B rating, he or she can do things to change it."

5. Return to a full class discussion. What conclusions did the groups arrive at?

*This questionnaire is adapted from R. W. Bortner, "Short Rating Scale as a Potential Measure of Pattern A Behavior," *Journal of Chronic Diseases*, June 1969, pp. 87–91. With permission.

Stress and Long Work Hours in Japan

The Japanese work some of the longest hours in the industrialized world. They average sixty-five days a year more than the Germans and twenty-five more than Americans. Fifteen-hour days and seven-day workweeks are not that unusual! The dark side of Japan's economic success story is that its employers are working their employees to death.

Japan is a nation of workaholics. Many employees leave for work at daybreak and don't return home until midnight. Two out of three workers fear death from overwork. But do stress and long working hours *cause* death? When critics point out the high number of worker deaths and attribute it to the stress of long hours, companies respond that those people died from obesity and heart trouble.

In terms of world competitiveness, Japan's strong work culture gives it a major advantage. Officially, workers only put in eight-hour days, but actually it's more like twelve to fourteen hours. Because Japanese employees believe they have to put in extra hours without extra compensation, Japanese firms have an edge in competitive world markets. For instance, assume both Japanese and Canadian workers earn $17 an hour for doing the same job. If the Japanese worker puts in a sixty-hour week but gets paid for only forty, while his Canadian counterpart gets time-and-a-half for his extra twenty hours, the total weekly labor costs are seventy-five percent higher for the Canadian's employer.

Questions

1. What factors in Japanese society do you think make Japanese employees work so hard?

2. Should the Japanese government intervene to stop employers from overworking people? If so, do you think such intervention would be successful?

3. "The long hours that Japanese workers put in only *appear* to make them more productive. The downside from these long hours is actually lower overall productivity." Do you agree or disagree? Support your position.

Source: The facts in this case are based on a story from *20/20*, August 16, 1991.

FOR FURTHER READING

CAVANAGH, M. E., "What You Don't Know About Stress," *Personnel Journal*, July 1988, pp. 53–59. Discusses the positive as well as the negative aspects of stress and reviews five misconceptions about burnout.

COOPER, C. L., and R. PAYNE (eds.), *Causes, Coping and Consequences of Stress at Work* (New York: John Wiley, 1990). Reviews recent research findings, theories, methodological issues, and actions for coping with stress at work.

GANSTER, D. C., and J. SCHAUBROECK, "Work Stress and Employee Health," *Journal of Management,* June 1991, pp. 235–71. Excellent review and summary of the literature on work stress, with particular emphasis on those studies that examine the effects of work characteristics on employee health.

LEE, C., S. J. ASHFORD, and P. BOBKO, "Interactive Effects of "Type A" Behavior and Perceived Control on Worker Performance, Job Satisfaction, and Somatic Complaints," *Academy of Management Journal,* December 1990, pp. 870–81. Found that people with high levels of Type A behavior who also have high perceived control perform better and have greater job satisfaction than those low in perceived control.

NELSON, D. L., J. C. QUICK, and J. D. QUICK, "Corporate Warfare: Preventing Stress and Battle Fatigue," *Organizational Dynamics,* Summer 1989, pp. 65–79. Offers prevention strategies from stress and fatigue of corporate warfare.

SLOAN, R. P., and J. C. GRUMAN, "Does Wellness in the Workplace Work?", *Personnel Administrator,* July 1988, pp. 42–48. Argues that the main benefits from wellness programs is not direct reductions in health-care costs. It is in making employees feel better about themselves and their organization.

NOTES

[1] B. Pulley, "A Grand Tradition Can Make a Fall That Much Harder," *The Wall Street Journal,* September 26, 1991, p. A1.

[2] Cited in A. Farnham, "Who Beats Stress Best—And How," *Fortune,* October 7, 1991, p. 71.

[3] Adapted from R. S. Schuler, "Definition and Conceptualization of Stress in Organizations," *Organizational Behavior and Human Performance,* April 1980, p. 189.

[4] Ibid., p. 191.

[5] Farnham, "Who Beats Stress Best," p. 71.

[6] C. Wallis, "Stress: Can We Cope?", *Time,* June 6, 1983.

[7] Cited in T. A. Stewart, "Do You Push Your People Too Hard?", *Fortune,* October 22, 1990, p. 121.

[8] Cited in "Stress: The Test Americans Are Failing," *Business Week,* April 18, 1988, p. 74.

[9] T. F. O'Boyle, "Fear and Stress in the Office Take Toll," *The Wall Street Journal,* November 6, 1990, p. B1.

[10] S. Solo, "Stop Whining and Get Back to Work," *Fortune,* March 12, 1990, pp. 49–50.

[11] M. A. Tipgos, "The Things That Stress Us," *Management World,* June-August 1987, pp. 17–18.

[12] R. Karasek and T. Theorell, *Healthy Work* (New York: Basic Books, 1990).

[13] This model is based on D. F. Parker and T. A. DeCotiis, "Organizational Determinants of Job Stress," *Organizational Behavior and Human Performance,* October 1983, p. 166; S. Parasuraman and J. A. Alutto, "Sources and Outcomes of Stress in Organizational Settings: Toward the Development of a Structural Model," *Academy of Management Journal,* June 1984, p. 333; and C. L. Cooper, "The Stress of Work: An Overview," *Aviation, Space, and Environmental Medicine,* July 1985, p. 628.

[14] This section is adapted from C.L. Cooper and R. Payne, *Stress at Work* (London: John Wiley, 1978); and Parasuraman and Alutto, "Sources and Outcomes of Stress in Organizational Settings," pp. 330–50.

[15] See, for example, D. R. Frew and N. S. Bruning, "Perceived Organizational Characteristics and Personality Measures as Predictors of Stress/Strain in the Work Place," *Journal of Management,* Winter 1987, pp. 633–46.

[16] This box is based on G. Bylinksy, "How Companies Spy on Employees," *Fortune,* November 4, 1991, pp. 131–40.

[17] D. L. Nelson and C. Sutton, "Chronic Work Stress and Coping: A Longitudinal Study

and Suggested New Directions," *Academy of Management Journal,* December 1990, pp. 859–69.

[18]H. Selye, *The Stress of Life,* rev. ed. (New York: McGraw-Hill, 1956).

[19]S. J. Motowidlo, J. S. Packard, and M. R. Manning, "Occupational Stress: Its Causes and Consequences for Job Performance," *Journal of Applied Psychology,* November 1987, pp. 619–20.

[20]See, for instance, J. J. House, *Work Stress and Social Support* (Reading, MA: Addison Wesley, 1981); S. Jayaratne, D. Himle, and W. A. Chess, "Dealing with Work Stress and Strain: Is the Perception of Support More Important Than Its Use?", *The Journal of Applied Behavioral Science,* Vol. 24, No. 2, 1988, pp. 191–202; and R. C. Cummings, "Job Stress and the Buffering Effect of Supervisory Support," *Group & Organization Studies,* March 1990, pp. 92–104.

[21]See, for instance, G. R. Gemmill and W. J. Heisler, "Fatalism as a Factor in Managerial Job Satisfaction, Job Strain, and Mobility," *Personnel Psychology,* Summer 1972, pp. 241–50; and C. R. Anderson, D. Hellriegel, and J. W. Slocum, Jr., "Managerial Response to Environmentally Induced Stress," *Academy of Management Journal,* June 1977, pp. 260–72.

[22]M. Friedman and R. H. Rosenman, *Type A Behavior and Your Heart* (New York: Alfred A. Knopf, 1974).

[23]Ibid., pp. 84.

[24]Ibid., pp. 84–85.

[25]R. Williams, *The Trusting Heart: Great News About Type A Behavior* (New York: Times Books, 1989).

[26]Schuler, "Definition and Conceptualization of Stress," pp. 200–205.

[27]See T. A. Beehr and J. E. Newman, "Job Stress, Employee Health, and Organizational Effectiveness: A Facet Analysis, Model, and Literature Review," *Personnel Psychology,* Winter 1978, pp. 665–99; and B. D. Steffy and J. W. Jones, "Workplace Stress and Indicators of Coronary-Disease Risk," *Academy of Management Journal,* September 1988, pp. 686–98.

[28]Ibid., p. 687.

[29]C. L. Cooper and J. Marshall, "Occupational Sources of Stress: A Review of the Literature Relating to Coronary Heart Disease and Mental Ill Health," *Journal of Occupational Psychology,* Vol. 49, No. 1 (1976), pp. 11–28.

[30]J. R. Hackman and G. R. Oldham, "Development of the Job Diagnostic Survey," *Journal of Applied Psychology,* April 1975, pp. 159–70.

[31]See, for instance, J. E. McGrath, "Stress and Behavior in Organizations," in M. D. Dunnette (ed.), *Handbook of Industrial and Organizational Psychology* (Chicago: Rand McNally, 1976); J. M. Ivancevich and M. T. Matteson, *Stress and Work* (Glenview, IL: Scott, Foresman, 1981); and R. D. Allen, M. A. Hitt, and C. R. Greer, "Occupational Stress and Perceived Organizational Effectiveness in Formal Groups: An Examination of Stress Level and Stress Type," *Personnel Psychology,* Summer 1982, pp. 359–70.

[32]See, for instance, K. A. Matthews, "Psychological Perspectives on the Type A Behavior Pattern," *Psychological Bulletin,* March 1982, pp. 293–323; M. Jamal, "Type A Behavior and Job Performance: Some Suggestive Findings," *Journal of Human Stress,* Summer 1985, pp. 60–68; and C. Lee, P. C. Earley, and L. A. Hanson, "Are Type A's Better Performers?" *Journal of Organizational Behavior,* July 1988, pp. 263–69.

[33]The following discussion has been strongly influenced by J. E. Newman and T. A. Beehr, "Personal and Organizational Strategies for Handling Job Stress," *Personnel Psychology,* Spring 1979, pp. 1–38; A. P. Brief, R. S. Schuler, and M. Van Sell, *Managing Job Stress;* R. L. Rose and J. F. Veiga, "Assessing the Sustained Effects of a Stress Management Intervention on Anxiety and Locus of Control," *Academy of Management Journal,* March 1984, pp. 190–98; E. R. Kemery, A. G. Bedeian, K. W. Mossholder, and J. Touliatos, "Outcomes of Role Stress: A Multisample Constructive Replication," *Academy of Management Journal,* June 1985, pp. 363–75; N. S. Bruning and D. R. Frew, "Effects of Exercise, Relaxation, and Management Skills Training on Physiological Stress Indicators: A Field Experiment," *Journal of Applied Psychology,* November 1987, pp. 515–21; J. M. Ivancevich and M. T. Matteson, "Organizational Level Stress Management Interventions: A Review and Recommendations," *Journal of Organizational Behavior Management,* Fall-Winter 1986, pp. 229–48; M. T. Matteson and J. M. Ivancevich, "Individual Stress Management Interventions: Evaluation of Techniques," *Journal of Management Psychology,* January 1987, pp. 24–30; and J. M. Ivancevich, M. T. Matteson, S. M. Freedman, and J. S. Phillips, "Worksite Stress Management Interventions," *American Psychologist,* February 1990, pp. 252–61.

[34]S. J. Modic, "Surviving Burnout: The Malady of Our Age," *Industry Week,* February 20, 1989, pp. 29–34.

[35]R. T. Lee and B. E. Ashforth, "On the Meaning of Maslach's Three Dimensions of Burnout," *Journal of Applied Psychology,* December 1990, pp. 743–47.

[36]D. P. Rogers, "Helping Employees Cope with Burnout," *Business,* October-December 1984, pp. 3–7.

[37]Modic, "Surviving Burnout," p. 29.

[38]A. Shirom, "Burnout in Work Organizations," in C. L. Cooper and I. Robertson (eds.), *International Review of Industrial and Organizational Psychology 1989,* Vol. 4 (Chichester,

England: John Wiley, 1989), pp. 25–48.

[39]See, for example, M. E. Haynes, *Practical Time Management: How to Make the Most of Your Most Perishable Resource* (Tulsa, OK: PennWell Books, 1985).

[40]J. Kiely and G. Hodgson, "Stress in the Prison Service: The Benefits of Exercise Programs," *Human Relations,* June 1990, pp. 551–72.

[41]H. Benson, *The Relaxation Response* (New York: William Morrow, 1975).

[42]D. Etzion, "Moderating Effects of Social Support on the Stress-Burnout Relationship," *Journal of Applied Psychology,* November 1984, pp. 615–22; and Jackson, Schwab, and Schuler, "Toward an Understanding of the Burnout Phenomenon."

[43]S. E. Jackson, "Participation in Decision Making as a Strategy for Reducing Job-Related Strain," *Journal of Applied Psychology,* February 1983, pp. 3–19.

[44]See, for instance, R. A. Wolfe, D. O. Ulrich, and D. F. Parker, "Employee Health Management Programs: Review, Critique, and Research Agenda," *Journal of Management,* Winter 1987, pp. 603–15; and D. L. Gebhardt and C. E. Crump, "Employee Fitness and Wellness Programs in the Workplace," *American Psychologist,* February 1990, pp. 262–72.

[45]This box is based on J. M. Horowitz, "A Puzzling Toll at the Top," *Time,* August 3, 1987, p. 46; and K. Makihara, "Attention: Hurry Up and Relax," *Time,* September 9, 1991, p. 63.

[46]"Fitness Center Gets Couch Potatoes Moving," *The Wall Street Journal,* April 12, 1991, p. B1.

[47]"Health: More in the Middle Class Forgo Care," *Los Angeles Times,* July 21, 1991, p. A7.

[48]V. V. Baba and M. J. Harris, "Stress and Absence: A Cross-Cultural Perspective," in G. R. Ferris and K. M. Rowland (eds.), *Research in Personnel and Human Resources Management,* Supplement 1 (Greenwich, CT: JAI Press, 1989), pp. 317–37.

[49]T. D. Jick and L. F. Mitz, "Sex Differences in Work Stress," *Academy of Management Review,* July 1985, pp. 408–20; and R. D. Hackett, "A Multiple Case Study of Employee Absenteeism," paper presented at the 1986 ASAC Conference, Whisler, British Columbia.

[50]M. Jamal, "Relationship of Job Stress and Type-A Behavior to Employees' Job Satisfaction, Organizational Commitment, Psychosomatic Health Problems, and Turnover Motivation," *Human Relations,* August 1990, pp. 727–38; and J. Wolpin, R. J. Burke, and E. R. Greenglass, "Is Job Satisfaction an Antecedent or a Consequence of Psychological Burnout?", *Human Relations,* February 1991, pp. 193–209.

ORGANIZATIONAL CHANGE AND DEVELOPMENT

LEARNING OBJECTIVES

After studying this chapter, you should be able to:

1. Describe forces that act as stimulants to change
2. Define *planned change*
3. Summarize sources of individual resistance to change
4. Explain sources of organizational resistance to change
5. List techniques for overcoming resistance to change
6. Summarize Lewin's three-step change model
7. Contrast change and innovation
8. Describe specific actions that will facilitate empowering employees
9. Define organizational development (OD)
10. Describe five specific OD interventions

Most people hate any change that doesn't jingle in their pockets.

ANONYMOUS

*T*hings are changing at AT&T.[1] As a regulated monopoly, the old Bell System was the picture of stability. It had no serious competition. New managerial slots were always filled from the inside. And managing itself was easy because thick manuals spelled out precise procedures for every eventuality. But in 1984, the U.S. government broke up Bell. No longer a monopoly, American Telephone and Telegraph would have to change or die.

As noted in Chapter 17, AT&T has had trouble adjusting to its new environment. It has not been easy for the company to change its strong service- and technology-oriented culture to one that is market-driven. What the company badly needed was new leadership—executives who could teach AT&T's 270,000 troops lessons in marketing and entrepreneurship. Pursuing a direction never taken before at AT&T, chairman Robert E. Allen has gone outside the company to tap new talent.

In 1990, Allen hired Richard S. Bodman, who was president of Washington National Investment, to become AT&T's senior vice president in charge of corporate strategy and development. In early 1991, Alex J. Mandl, the former chairman of Sea-Land Service, joined AT&T as its chief financial officer. Recently, Allen hired Jerre L. Stead (pictured above), chairman of Square D Co., to become president of AT&T's Business Communications Systems unit.

Like the other newcomers at AT&T, Stead's primary role will be as a change agent. At Square D, Stead built a reputation for raising productivity and profits. Allen recruited him to shake up the company's office phone systems group, which had been losing more than $200 million a year. Stead's job will be to cut costs, stimulate teamwork, and teach AT&T people how to respond rapidly to customers. At Square D, he preached customers first and bureaucracy last. He plans to do the same at AT&T. To turn the company's office phone system business around, he'll have two major hurdles to jump. First, as an outsider in a company that has historically filled key slots with insiders, Stead's got to be careful not to alienate AT&T veterans. Second, he'll need to energize employees whose morale has been badly hurt by endless layoffs and budget cuts in recent years. ■

*T*his chapter is about the kind of challenges Jerre Stead faces at AT&T. It's about organizational change. We'll present environmental forces that are requiring managers like Stead to implement comprehensive change programs. We'll also consider why people and organizations often resist change and how this resistance can be overcome. We'll review various processes for managing organizational change. We'll discuss two change themes for the 1990s: stimulating innovation and empowering people. Finally, we'll present the concept of organizational development as a means to empowerment.

FORCES FOR CHANGE

More and more organizations today face a dynamic and changing environment that, in turn, requires these organizations to adapt. In this section, we'll look at six specific forces that are acting as stimulants for change—the changing nature of the work force, technology, economic shocks, changing social trends, the "new" world politics, and the changing nature of competition.

Nature of the Work Force

In a number of places in this book, we've discussed the changing nature of the work force. This is as good a time as any to summarize these changes.

We pointed out the different work values expressed by different generations. Workers over fifty tend to value loyalty to their employer. Workers in their forties are generally loyal to themselves. The later-born Baby Boomers tend to be pragmatists who value loyalty to their careers. Recent entrants to the work force place a higher value on flexibility, job satisfaction, and relationships. They generally want to spend more time cultivating relationships with friends, relatives, and children. One of the more interesting observations about these new labor-force entrants is their preference for short-term tasks with observable results. This was a generation raised on the importance of grades, class rank, and SAT scores. They want a quantification of their achievements. Unlike the pragmatists, who were driven from within, today's younger people seek external reinforcement.

We described the 1990s as a decade in which organizations will have to learn to manage diversity. The work force is changing, with a rapid increase in the percentage of women and minorities. Human resource policies and practices will have to change in order to attract and keep this more diverse work force.

The increase in the participation rate of women in the work force also means more dual-career couples. Organizations are having to modify transfer and promotion policies, as well as make child care and elder care available, in order to respond to the needs of two-career couples.

It's easy to focus on the increasing educational levels of the work force. Yet there is a dark side that has important implications for organizations. A significant portion of new work-force entrants do not have marketable skills. Many are high school dropouts. But a good number—and this is the really alarming part—have high school and college degrees but can't adequately perform the basic reading, writing, and computational skills that organizations require. This is forcing organizations to introduce training programs to upgrade skills and, in some cases, de-skill jobs so that they can be adequately performed by employees.

Technology

Changes in technology change the nature of work. The adoption of new technologies such as computers, telecommunication systems, robotics, and flexible manufacturing operations have a profound impact on the organizations that adopt them.

For instance, IBM has built a system of modular work stations at a plant in Austin, Texas, that uses flexible manufacturing concepts to build personal computers.[2] From receiving dock to exit dock, computers are assembled, tested, packed, and shipped without a human being so much as turning a screw. The entire operation is handled by thirteen robots. Moreover, the entire manufacturing system was built with flexibility in mind. The plant is designed to be able to build *any* electronic product that is no bigger than two feet by two feet by fourteen inches. So IBM's management can build printers, other types of computers, or even toasters in this plant.

Computers and sophisticated information systems, while only the tip of the technology iceberg, are having an enormous impact on organizations. They are stimulating widespread changes in the required skill levels of employees, the daily activities of managers, and the organization's ability to respond to the changing needs of customers. For instance, as many routine tasks are being automated, people are being freed up to take on more varied and challenging tasks. Of course, employee skills are also becoming obsolete more quickly, so organizations are having to increase their investment in employee training and education. The substitution of computer control for direct supervision is resulting in wider spans of control for managers and flatter organizations. Sophisticated information technology is also making organizations more responsive. Companies such as Motorola, General

Motorola used to turn out electronic pagers three weeks after the factory got the order. Now this process takes two hours.
Courtesy Motorola

Electric, and Chrysler can now develop, make, and distribute their products in a fraction of the time it took them a decade ago. And, as organizations have had to become more adaptable, so too have their employees. As we noted in our discussion of groups and organization design, many jobs are being reshaped. Individuals doing narrow, specialized, and routine jobs are being replaced by work teams whose members can perform multiple tasks and actively participate in team decisions.

Economic Shocks

We live in an "age of discontinuity." In the 1950s and 1960s, the past was a pretty good prologue to the future. Tomorrow was essentially an extended trend line from yesterday. That is no longer true. Beginning in the early 1970s, with the overnight quadrupling of world oil prices, economic shocks have continued to impose changes on organizations. In an indirect way, the changes we'll mention have affected all organizations. However, economic shocks typically hit some industries and firms much harder than others.

In the last twenty years, we can pinpoint at least five major economic shocks experienced in the United States, beginning with the explosion in oil prices.

When OPEC raised the price of oil from under $3.00 to nearly $12.00 a barrel, automobile, recreational vehicle, and building-insulation manufacturers, for example, felt an immediate effect. General Motors and Winnebago, for instance, saw the demand for their "gas-guzzling" vehicles collapse. Toyota, Honda, and other manufacturers of small, fuel-efficient cars, on the other hand, experienced a sales bonanza. Firms such as Johns-Mansville, which manufactured building insulation, found that, in spite of running multiple shifts, they were unable to meet the increased market demand for their product.

In the mid-1970s, the United States and Canada underwent a two-year-or-so period of accelerated inflation and interest rates never before experienced in this century. Inflation reached an annual peak of over thirteen percent, and interest rates exceeded sixteen percent. Potential home buyers found it difficult to qualify for loans and many homebuilders went bankrupt. Almost all well-managed companies changed their bill-paying and inventory policies. It made good sense, for instance, to use suppliers' money and delay paying bills for as long as possible. It also made good sense to reduce inventories to absolute minimum levels to reduce the high carrying costs. In terms of organizational behavior, employees' expectations for wage increases rose sharply. Many firms found it impossible even to provide merit increases because cost-of-living adjustments were consuming all of the pool of money they had set aside for wage increases. Morale in many organizations fell during this period and turnover increased.

The stock market crash of October 1987 is another example of an economic shock. While this had an impact upon the financing plans and market value of almost all publicly held businesses, the crash proved devastating to the financial services industry. Large layoffs on Wall Street immediately followed. Several of the major brokerage firms were forced to restructure or merge in order to survive.

Another shock to the financial services industry hit in late 1989 with the collapse of the so-called junk-bond market. This almost single-handedly ended the corporate takeover and leveraged buyout frenzy of the 1980s. It also significantly reduced the assets of many insurance companies and pension funds.

One of the latest shocks to the economy has been the massive defaults of savings and loans. This, in turn, has depressed real estate prices and resulted in large losses for real estate developers and others closely connected with the real estate industry.

During the remainder of the 1990s, we can forecast with almost one-hundred-percent certainty that there will be one or more economic shocks of similar magnitude to those of the past two decades. The only problem is that it is impossible to predict what those shocks will be and where they will come from. That is the irony of change in the age of discontinuity: We know almost for sure that tomorrow won't be like today but we don't know how it will be different.

Social Trends

Take a look at social trends during the 1970s and 1980s. They suggest changes for the 1990s that organizations will need to adjust for. Consider, as examples, shifts in the value placed on higher education, views on marriage, and shopping preferences.

In the early 1960s, less than twenty-five percent of all United States high school graduates enrolled in college. By 1978, it was forty-nine percent. In 1992, the figure reached sixty percent. The higher-education industry now provides a mass-market product. The makeup of the typical student body has also changed a great deal in the past decade or two. Women have gone from a small minority to the majority, part-time students now outnumber full-timers, and an increasing proportion of students are over thirty years of age. Those colleges and universities that fail to respond to these changes in the student population may not be around at the end of the decade.

There has been a clear trend in marriage and divorce during the past two decades. Young people are delaying marriage, and half of all marriages are ending in divorce. One obvious result of this social trend is an increasing number of single households and demand for housing by singles.

Another social trend of interest, particularly to those organizations in the retail industry, has been the shift in consumer preferences for specialty stores. Large chains such as Sears, which try to be all things to all people, have suffered at the hands of discount and niche stores. Wal-Mart, K mart, Circuit City, Toys 'R' Us, Waldenbooks, Victoria's Secret, and Blockbuster Video are examples of firms that have responded positively to this trend.

World Politics

In Chapter 3, we argued strongly for the importance of seeing OB in a global context. We reinforced this argument with boxes in each of the following chapters. While business schools have been preaching a global perspective for over a decade, no one—not even the strongest proponents of globalization—could have imagined how world politics would change in the late 1980s and early 1990s. A few examples make the point: the fall of the Berlin Wall; the reunification of Germany; Iraq's invasion of Kuwait; the declaration of sovereignty by a number of the Soviet Union's republics; and Israeli and Palestinian representatives negotiating in Middle East peace talks.

What do the new world politics mean to students of management and organizational behavior? It's too soon to predict the full impact of these changes, yet some predictions seem relatively safe.

One certainty is that companies that have survived on U.S. defense contracts will be undergoing changes. General Dynamics and McDonnell Douglas—the two largest defense companies in the United States—are currently going through wrenching changes in an effort to adjust to a shrinking

Pentagon budget.[3] General Dynamics is planning on eliminating thirty-five thousand jobs, cutting capital spending by sixty percent, and reducing research and development expenses by half. McDonnell Douglas is making similar cuts, including the layoff of fifteen thousand employees. Employees in the United States and former Soviet Union armed services and intelligence agencies should also be preparing themselves for new assignments as these organizations rethink their role in the post–Cold War world.

Managers of most firms and a good portion of their employees will need to become attuned to cultural differences. They will increasingly be interacting with people in other countries and working alongside people raised in different cultures. So don't be surprised to find yourself working for a boss who was raised in a different land. It also may not be a bad idea to brush up or begin developing your foreign language skills—especially in Japanese and Spanish.

Ownership of companies and property by people and organizations from other countries is likely to continue worldwide. As long as currencies fluctuate and some economies outperform others, assets will flow across borders. In the 1980s, Japanese money flowed into the United States. In the 1990s, it may well be United States, Canadian, and Japanese funds that flow into Eastern Europe. Where investment goes will fluctuate at different times, but in a true global economy, resources will constantly seek out their best return, wherever in the world that might be. What this means, of course, is the realization that some businesses in some countries will fail because their products or services can be more efficiently produced in another country. Along these lines, it is no longer preposterous to conceive of a General Motors Corp., headquartered in Detroit, that builds every one of its automobiles in plants outside the United States.

Is this supermarket in Hong Kong? No! It's in suburban Los Angeles. This picture illustrates the changing makeup of many American communities and the need for managers to become attuned to cultural differences.
Lynn Johnson/Black Star.

Competition

The last area we want to discuss is the changes that derive from increased competition. The global economy means that competitors are as likely to come from Japan, Mexico, or Germany as from the other side of town. But heightened competition also means that established organizations need to defend themselves against both traditional competitors who develop new products and services and small, entrepreneurial firms with innovative offerings.

Successful organizations will be the ones that can change in response to the competition. They'll be fast on their feet, capable of developing new products rapidly and getting them to market quickly. They'll rely on short production runs, short product cycles, and an ongoing stream of new products. In other words, they'll be flexible. They will require an equally flexible and responsive work force that can adapt to rapidly and even radically changing conditions.

MANAGING PLANNED CHANGE

A group of employees who work in a small retail women's clothing store confronted the owner: "The air pollution in this store from cigarette smoking has gotten awful," said their spokeswoman. "We won't continue to work here if you allow smoking in the store. We want you to post no smoking signs on the entrance doors and not allow any employee to smoke on the floor. If people have to smoke, they can go into the mall." The owner listened thoughtfully to the group's ultimatum and agreed to their request. The next day the owner posted the no smoking signs and advised all of her employees of the new rule.

A major automobile manufacturer spent several billion dollars to install state-of-the-art robotics. One area that would receive the new equipment was quality control. Sophisticated computer-controlled equipment would be put in place to significantly improve the company's ability to find and correct defects. Since the new equipment would dramatically change the jobs of the people working in the quality control area, and since management anticipated considerable employee resistance to the new equipment, executives were developing a program to help people become familiar with the equipment and to deal with any anxieties they might be feeling.

Change Making things different.

Both of the previous scenarios are examples of **change.** That is, both were concerned with making things different. However, only the second scenario described a planned change. In this section, we want to clarify what we mean by planned change, describe its goals, and consider who is responsible for bringing about **planned change** in an organization.

Planned Change Change activities that are intentional and goal-oriented.

Many changes in organizations are like the one that occurred in the retail clothing store—they just happen. Some organizations treat all change as an accidental occurrence. However, we're concerned with change activities that are proactive and purposeful. In this chapter, we'll address change as an intentional, goal-oriented activity.

What are the goals of planned change? Essentially there are two. First, it seeks to improve the ability of the organization to adapt to changes in its environment. Second, it seeks to change employee behavior.

If an organization is to survive, it must respond to changes in its environment. When competitors introduce new products or services, government agencies enact new laws, important sources of supply go out of business, or similar environmental changes take place, the organization needs to adapt. As you'll see in the rest of this chapter, efforts to stimulate innovation, empower employees, and introduce work teams are examples of planned-change activities directed at responding to changes in the environment.

Since an organization's success or failure is essentially due to the things that its employees do or fail to do, planned change also is concerned with changing the behavior of individuals and groups within the organization. In this chapter, we'll review a number of techniques that organizations can use to get people to behave differently in the tasks they perform and in their interactions with others.

Change Agents Persons who act as catalysts and assume the responsibility for managing change activities.

Who in organizations is responsible for managing change activities? The answer is **change agents.** Change agents can be managers or nonmanagers, employees of the organization or outside consultants.

As we noted at the opening of this chapter, AT&T recently went outside to hire executives for key positions precisely because it wanted change agents. More and more companies seem to be doing the same.[4] And the reason most often cited for going outside is the need to find people who will challenge the conventional wisdom.[5] Outsiders are more likely to throw out the traditional rules of the game and institute radical, rather than incremental, change.

For major change efforts, top management may also contract with outside consultants on a temporary basis. Consultant change agents can offer a more objective perspective than insiders can. However, they are disadvantaged in that they often have an inadequate understanding of the organization's history, culture, operating procedures, and personnel. Outside consultants are also prone to initiate drastic changes—which can be a benefit or a disadvantage—because they do not have to live with the repercussions. In contrast, internal staff specialists or managers, especially those who've spent many years with the organization, are often more cautious because they fear offending long-term friends and associates.

What can a change agent change? The options essentially fall into three categories: structure, technology, and people.[6] (See Figure 19–1.) Changing *structure* involves making an alteration in authority relations, coordination mechanisms, job redesign, or similar structural variables. Changing *technology* encompasses modifications in the way work is processed and in the methods and equipment used. Changing *people* refers to changes in employee attitudes, skills, expectations, perceptions, and/or behavior.

Changing Structure

In Chapters 14 and 15, we discussed structural issues such as division of labor, span of control, allocation of authority, and various organizational designs. But organizational structures are not set in concrete. Changing conditions demand structural changes. As a result, the change agent might need to modify the organization's structure.

An organization's structure is defined in terms of its degree of complexity, formalization, and centralization. Change agents can alter one or more of these structural components. For instance, departmental responsibilities can be combined, vertical layers removed, and spans of control widened to make the organization flatter and less bureaucratic. More rules and procedures can be implemented to increase standardization. An increase in decentralization can be made to speed up the decision-making process.

Change agents can also introduce major modifications in the actual structural design. This might include a shift from a simple structure to a divisional structure or the creation of a matrix design. Change agents might consider redesigning jobs or work schedules. Job descriptions can be redefined, jobs enriched, or flexible work hours introduced. Still another option is to modify the organization's compensation system. Motivation could be increased by, for example, introducing performance bonuses or profit sharing.

Changing Technology

Most of the early studies in management and organizational behavior dealt with efforts aimed at technological change. At the turn of the century, for example, scientific management sought to implement changes based on time-and-motion studies that would increase production efficiency. Today, major technological changes usually involve the introduction of new equipment, tools, or methods; automation; or computerization.

FIGURE 19–1   Change Options

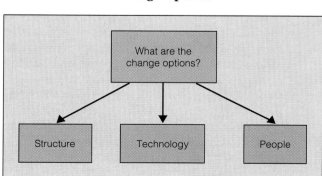

Competitive factors or innovations within an industry often require change agents to introduce new equipment, tools, or operating methods. For example, many aluminum companies have significantly modernized their plants in recent years to compete more effectively. More efficient handling equipment, furnaces, and presses have been installed to reduce the cost of manufacturing a ton of aluminum.

Automation is a technological change that replaces people with machines. It began in the Industrial Revolution and continues as a change option today. Examples of automation are the introduction of automatic mail sorters by the U.S. Postal Service and robots on automobile assembly lines.

Probably the most visible technological change in recent years has been expanding computerization. Many organizations now have sophisticated management information systems. Large supermarkets have converted their cash registers into input terminals and linked them to computers to provide instant inventory data. The office of 1993 is dramatically different from its counterpart of 1973, predominantly because of computerization. This is typified by desktop microcomputers that can run hundreds of business software packages and network systems that allow these computers to communicate with one another.

Changing People

The final area in which change agents operate is in helping individuals and groups within the organization to work more effectively together. This category typically involves changing the attitudes and behaviors of organizational members through processes of communication, decision making, and problem solving. As you'll see near the end of this chapter, the concept of *organizational development* has come to encompass an array of interventions that are designed to change people and the nature and quality of their work relationships. We'll review these people-changing interventions in our discussion of organizational development.

RESISTANCE TO CHANGE

One of the most well-documented findings from studies of individual and organizational behavior is that organizations and their members resist change. In a sense, this is positive. It provides a degree of stability and predictability to behavior. If there weren't some resistance, organizational behavior would take on characteristics of chaotic randomness. Resistance to change can also be a source of functional conflict. For example, resistance to a reorganization plan or a change in a product line can stimulate a healthy debate over the merits of the idea and result in a better decision. But there is a definite downside to resistance to change. It hinders adaptation and progress.

Resistance to change doesn't necessarily surface in standardized ways. Resistance can be overt, implicit, immediate, or deferred. It is easiest for management to deal with resistance when it is overt and immediate. For instance, a change is proposed and employees quickly respond by voicing complaints, engaging in a work slowdown, threatening to go on strike, or the like. The greater challenge is managing resistance that is implicit or deferred. Implicit resistance efforts are more subtle—loss of loyalty to the organization, loss of motivation to work, increased errors or mistakes, increased absenteeism due to "sickness"—and hence more difficult to recognize. Similarly, deferred actions cloud the link between the source of the

Changing Attitudes Through Persuasive Messages

You hear through the grapevine that one of your employees thinks you're insensitive to the needs of racial minorities. You know that not to be the case. Is there anything you can do to change this employee's attitude?

In Chapter 6, we introduced the concept of cognitive dissonance and evidence demonstrating that people dislike inconsistency. Based on that research, we know that one way for employees to reduce dissonance is to change their attitudes to bring them into line with other attitudes or behavior. So if you can arouse dissonance with your employee—possibly through making her aware of specific actions you've taken that clearly demonstrate your concern for racial minorities—you might be able to change her attitude about you.

Another technique for inducing attitude change involves the use of persuasive messages. That is, we can induce others to change their attitudes by consciously manipulating what we say to them. The following summarizes the research on persuasive skills.[7] It emphasizes oral persuasion but can be easily adapted for written communications.

1. *Establish your credibility.* Nothing undermines persuasive efforts more than lack of credibility. People don't want to listen to a person they don't trust or believe. Credibility is developed through demonstrating competence, objectivity, and high ethical standards.
2. *Use a positive, tactful tone.* Assume the person you're trying to persuade is intelligent and mature. Don't talk down to that person. Be respectful, direct, sincere, and tactful.

3. *Make your presentation clear.* Before you can convincingly articulate your view to someone else, you need to be clear about what it is you want to say. Once your objective is clear, you should present your argument one idea at a time. Don't jump from issue to issue, and avoid unrelated topics. Focus on your end objective, and then present your ideas in a straight path that will lead the person to the conclusion you want and the objective you set.
4. *Present strong evidence to support your position.* You need to explain why what you want is important. Merely saying your viewpoint is important is not enough.
5. *Tailor your argument to the listener.* Effective persuasion demands flexibility. You have to select your argument for your specific target. Whom are you talking to? What are his or her goals, needs, interests, fears, and aspirations? How much does the target know about the subject you're discussing? What are his or her preconceived attitudes on this subject? How entrenched are those attitudes?
6. *Use logic.* While a logical, reasoned argument is not guaranteed to change another's attitudes, if you lack facts and reasons to support your argument, your persuasiveness will almost certainly be undermined.
7. *Use emotional appeals.* Presenting clear, rational, and objective evidence in support of your view is often not enough. You should also appeal to a person's emotions. Try to reach inside the subject and understand his or her loves, hates, fears, and frustrations. Then use that information to mold what you say and how you say it.

resistance and the reaction to it. A change may produce what appears to be only a minimal reaction at the time it is initiated, but then resistance surfaces weeks, months, or even years later. Or a single change that in and of itself might have little impact becomes the straw that breaks the camel's back. Reactions to change can build up and then explode in some response that seems totally out of proportion to the change action it follows. The resistance, of course, has merely been deferred and stockpiled. What surfaces is a response to an accumulation of previous changes.

Let's look at the sources of resistance. For analytical purposes, we've categorized them by individual and organizational sources. In the real world, the sources often overlap.

Individual Resistance

Individual sources of resistance to change reside in basic human characteristics such as perceptions, personalities, and needs. The following summarizes five reasons why individuals may resist change. (See Figure 19–2.)

HABIT   Every time you go out to eat, do you try a different restaurant? Probably not. If you're like most people, you find a couple of places you like and return to them on a somewhat regular basis.

As human beings, we're creatures of habit. Life is complex enough; we don't need to consider the full range of options for the hundreds of decisions we have to make every day. To cope with this complexity, we all rely on habits or programmed responses. But when confronted with change, this tendency to respond in our accustomed ways becomes a source of resistance. So when your department is moved to a new office building across town, it means you're likely to have to change many habits: waking up ten minutes earlier, taking a new set of streets to work, finding a new parking place, adjusting to the new office layout, developing a new lunchtime routine, and so on.

SECURITY   People with a high need for security are likely to resist change because it threatens their feeling of safety. When General Dynamics announces personnel cutbacks or Ford introduces new robotic equipment, many employees at these firms may fear that their jobs are in jeopardy.

ECONOMIC FACTORS   Another source of individual resistance is concern that changes will lower one's income. Changes in job tasks or established work routines also can arouse economic fears if people are concerned that they won't be able to perform the new tasks or routines to their previous standards, especially when pay is closely tied to productivity.

FIGURE 19–2   Sources of Individual Resistance to Change

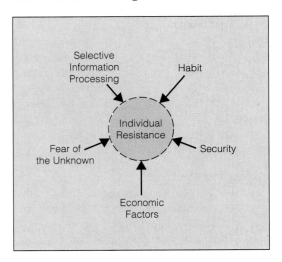

FEAR OF THE UNKNOWN   Changes substitute ambiguity and uncertainty for the known. Regardless of how much you may dislike attending college, at least you know what is expected of you. But when you leave college and venture out into the world of full-time employment, regardless of how much you want to get out of college, you have to trade the known for the unknown.

Employees in organizations hold the same dislike for uncertainty. If, for example, the introduction of word processors means that departmental secretaries will have to learn to operate these new pieces of equipment, some of the secretaries may fear that they will be unable to do so. They may, therefore, develop a negative attitude toward working with word processors or behave dysfunctionally if required to use them.

SELECTIVE INFORMATION PROCESSING   As we learned in Chapter 5, individuals shape their world through their perceptions. Once they have created this world, it resists change. So individuals are guilty of selectively processing information in order to keep their perceptions intact. They hear what they want to hear. They ignore information that challenges the world that they've created. To return to the secretaries who are faced with the introduction of word processors, they may ignore the arguments that their bosses make in explaining why the new equipment has been purchased or the potential benefits that the change will provide them.

Organizational Resistance

Organizations, by their very nature, are conservative.[8] They actively resist change. You don't have to look far to see evidence of this phenomenon. Government agencies want to continue doing what they have been doing for years, whether the need for their service changes or remains the same. Organized religions are deeply entrenched in their history. Attempts to change church doctrine require great persistence and patience. Educational institutions, which exist to open minds and challenge established doctrine, are themselves extremely resistant to change. Most school systems are using essentially the same teaching technologies today as they were fifty years ago. The majority of business firms, too, appear highly resistant to change.

Six major sources of organizational resistance have been identified.[9] They are shown in Figure 19–3.

FIGURE 19–3   Sources of Organizational Resistance to Change

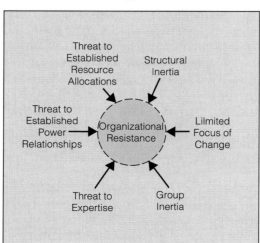

STRUCTURAL INERTIA   Organizations have built-in mechanisms to produce stability. For example, the selection process systematically selects certain people in and certain people out. Training and other socialization techniques reinforce specific role requirements and skills. Formalization provides job descriptions, rules, and procedures for employees to follow.

The people who are hired into an organization are chosen for fit; they are then shaped and directed to behave in certain ways. When an organization is confronted with change, this structural inertia acts as a counterbalance to sustain stability.

LIMITED FOCUS OF CHANGE   Organizations are made up of a number of interdependent subsystems. You can't change one without affecting the others. For example, if management changes the technological processes without simultaneously modifying the organization's structure to match, the change in technology is not likely to be accepted. So limited changes in subsystems tend to get nullified by the larger system.

GROUP INERTIA   Even if individuals want to change their behavior, group norms may act as a constraint. An individual union member, for instance, may be willing to accept changes in his job suggested by management. But if union norms dictate resisting any unilateral change made by management, he's likely to resist.

THREAT TO EXPERTISE   Changes in organizational patterns may threaten the expertise of specialized groups. The introduction of decentralized personal computers, which allow managers to gain access to information directly from a company's mainframe, is an example of a change that was strongly resisted by many information systems departments in the early 1980s. Why? Because decentralized end-user computing was a threat to the specialized skills held by those in the centralized information systems departments.

THREAT TO ESTABLISHED POWER RELATIONSHIPS   Any redistribution of decision-making authority can threaten long-established power relationships within the organization. The introduction of participative decision making or self-managed work teams is the kind of change that is often seen as threatening by supervisors and middle managers.

THREAT TO ESTABLISHED RESOURCE ALLOCATIONS   Those groups in the organization that control sizable resources often see change as a threat. They tend to be content with the way things are. Will the change, for instance, mean a reduction in their budgets or a cut in their staff size? Those that most benefit from the current allocation of resources often feel threatened by changes that may affect future allocations.

Overcoming Resistance to Change

Six tactics have been suggested for use by change agents in dealing with resistance to change.[10] Let's review them briefly.

EDUCATION AND COMMUNICATION   Resistance can be reduced through communicating with employees to help them see the logic of a change. This tactic basically assumes that the source of resistance lies in misinformation or poor communication: If employees receive the full facts and get any misunderstandings cleared up, resistance will subside. Communication can be achieved through one-on-one discussions, memos, group presentations, or reports. Does it work? It does, provided that the source of resistance is inadequate communication and that management–employee relations are characterized by mutual trust and credibility. If these conditions do not exist, the change is unlikely to succeed.

PARTICIPATION It's difficult for individuals to resist a change decision in which they participated. Prior to making a change, those opposed can be brought into the decision process. Assuming that the participants have the expertise to make a meaningful contribution, their involvement can reduce resistance, obtain commitment, and increase the quality of the change decision. However, against these advantages are the negatives: potential for a poor solution and great time consumption.

FACILITATION AND SUPPORT Change agents can offer a range of supportive efforts to reduce resistance. When employee fear and anxiety are high, employee counseling and therapy, new-skills training, or a short paid leave of absence may facilitate adjustment. The drawback of this tactic is that, as with the others, it is time-consuming. Additionally, it is expensive, and its implementation offers no assurance of success.

NEGOTIATION Another way for the change agent to deal with potential resistance to change is to exchange something of value for a lessening of the resistance. For instance, if the resistance is centered in a few powerful individuals, a specific reward package can be negotiated that will meet their individual needs. Negotiation as a tactic may be necessary when resistance comes from a powerful source. Yet one cannot ignore its potentially high costs. Additionally, there is the risk that, once a change agent negotiates with one party to avoid resistance, he or she is open to the possibility of being blackmailed by other individuals in positions of power.

MANIPULATION AND COOPTATION Manipulation refers to covert influence attempts. Twisting and distorting facts to make them appear more attractive, withholding undesirable information, and creating false rumors to get employees to accept a change are all examples of manipulation. If corporate management threatens to close down a particular manufacturing plant if that plant's employees fail to accept an across-the-board pay cut, and if the threat is actually untrue, management is using manipulation. Cooptation, on the other hand, is a form of both manipulation and participation. It seeks to "buy off" the leaders of a resistance group by giving them a key role in the change decision. The leaders' advice is sought, not to seek a better decision, but to get their endorsement. Both manipulation and cooptation are relatively inexpensive and easy ways to gain the support of adversaries, but the tactics can backfire if the targets become aware that they are being tricked or used. Once discovered, the change agent's credibility may drop to zero.

COERCION Last on the list of tactics is coercion; that is, the application of direct threats or force upon the resisters. If the corporate management mentioned in the previous discussion really is determined to close a manufacturing plant if employees don't acquiesce to a pay cut, then coercion would be the label attached to its change tactic. Other examples of coercion are threats of transfer, loss of promotions, negative performance evaluations, and a poor letter of recommendation. The advantages and drawbacks of coercion are approximately the same as those mentioned for manipulation and cooptation.

An International Look at Organizational Change

A number of the issues addressed in this chapter are culture-bound. To illustrate, let's briefly look at four questions: (1) Do people believe change is possible? (2) If it is possible, how long will it take to bring it about? (3) Is resistance to change greater in some cultures than in others? (4) Does culture influence how change efforts will be implemented?

Do people believe change is possible? Remember that cultures vary in terms of beliefs about their ability to control their environment. In cultures where people believe that they can dominate their environment, individuals will take a proactive view of change. This would describe the United States and Canada. In other countries, such as Iran and Saudi Arabia, people see themselves as subjugated to their environment and thus will tend to take a passive approach toward change.

If change is possible, how long will it take to bring it about? A culture's time orientation can help us answer this question. Societies that focus on the long term, such as Japan, will

demonstrate considerable patience while waiting for positive outcomes from change efforts. In societies with a short-term focus, such as the United States and Canada, people expect quick improvements and will seek change programs that promise fast results.

Is resistance to change greater in some cultures than in others? Resistance to change will be influenced by a society's reliance on tradition. Italians, as an example, focus on the past, while Americans emphasize the present. Italians, therefore, should generally be more resistant to change efforts than their American counterparts.

Does culture influence how change efforts will be implemented? Power distance can help with this issue. In high-power-distance cultures, such as the Philippines or Venezuela, change efforts will tend to be autocratically implemented by top management. In contrast, low-power-distance cultures value democratic methods. We'd predict, therefore, a greater use of participation in countries such as Denmark and Israel.

APPROACHES TO MANAGING ORGANIZATIONAL CHANGE

Now we turn to several popular approaches to managing change. Specifically, we'll discuss Lewin's classic three-step model of the change process and present the action research model.

Lewin's Three-Step Model

Unfreezing Change efforts to overcome the pressures of both individual resistance and group conformity.

Kurt Lewin argued that successful change in organizations should follow three steps: **unfreezing** the status quo, *movement* to a new state, and **refreezing** the new change to make it permanent.[11] (See Figure 19–4.) The value of this model can be seen in the following example when the management of a large oil company decided to reorganize its marketing function in the western United States.

Refreezing Stabilizing a change intervention by balancing driving and restraining forces.

The oil company had three divisional offices in the West, located in Seattle, San Francisco, and Los Angeles. The decision was made to consolidate the divisions into a single regional office to be located in San Francisco.

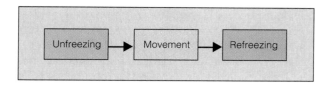

FIGURE 19–4   Lewin's Three–Step Change Model

The reorganization meant transferring over 150 employees, eliminating some duplicate managerial positions, and instituting a new hierarchy of command. As you might guess, a move of this magnitude was difficult to keep secret. The rumor of its occurrence preceded the announcement by several months. The decision itself was made unilaterally. It came from the executive offices in New York. Those people affected had no say whatsoever in the choice. For those in Seattle or Los Angeles, who may have disliked the decision and its consequences—the problems inherent in transferring to another city, pulling youngsters out of school, making new friends, having new co-workers, undergoing the reassignment of responsibilities—their only recourse was to quit. In actuality, less than ten percent did.

The status quo can be considered to be an equilibrium state. To move from this equilibrium—to overcome the pressures of both individual resistance and group conformity—unfreezing is necessary. It can be achieved in one of three ways. (See Figure 19–5.) The **driving forces,** which direct behavior away from the status quo, can be increased. The **restraining forces,** which hinder movement from the existing equilibrium, can be decreased. A third alternative is to *combine the first two approaches.*

The oil company's management could expect employee resistance to the consolidation. To deal with that resistance, management could use positive incentives to encourage employees to accept the change. For instance, increases in pay can be offered to those who accept the transfer. Very liberal moving expenses can be paid by the company. Management might offer low-cost mortgage funds to allow employees to buy new homes in San Francisco.

Driving Forces Forces that direct behavior away from the status quo.

Restraining Forces Forces that hinder movement away from the status quo.

**FIGURE 19–5
Unfreezing the Status Quo**

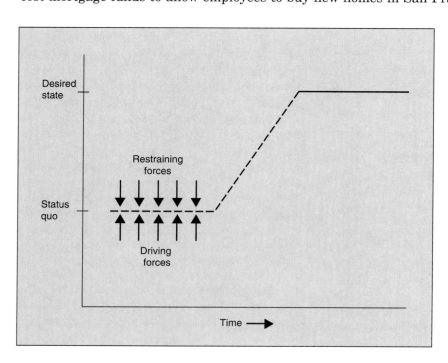

Of course, management might also consider unfreezing acceptance of the status quo by removing restraining forces. Employees could be counseled individually. Each employee's concerns and apprehensions could be heard and specifically clarified. Assuming that most of the fears are unjustified, the counselor could assure the employees that there was nothing to fear and then demonstrate, through tangible evidence, that restraining forces are unwarranted. If resistance is extremely high, management may have to resort to both reducing resistance and increasing the attractiveness of the alternative if the unfreezing is to be successful.

Once the consolidation change has been implemented, if it is to be successful, the new situation needs to be refrozen so that it can be sustained over time. Unless this last step is taken, there is a very high chance that the change will be short-lived and that employees will attempt to revert to the previous equilibrium state. The objective of refreezing, then, is to stabilize the new situation by balancing the driving and restraining forces.

How could the oil company's management refreeze their consolidation change? By systematically replacing temporary forces with permanent ones. For instance, they might impose a permanent upward adjustment of salaries or permanently remove time clocks to reinforce a climate of trust and confidence in employees. The formal rules and regulations governing behavior of those affected by the change should also be revised to reinforce the new situation. Over time, of course, the work group's own norms will evolve to sustain the new equilibrium. But until that point is reached, management will have to rely on more formal mechanisms.

Action Research

Action Research A change process based on systematic collection of data and then selection of a change action based on what the analyzed data indicate.

Action research refers to a change process based on systematic collection of data and then selection of a change action based on what the analyzed data indicates.[12] Its importance lies in providing a scientific methodology for managing planned change.

The process of action research consists of five steps: diagnosis, analysis, feedback, action, and evaluation. You'll note that these steps closely parallel the scientific method.

DIAGNOSIS   The change agent, often an outside consultant in action research, begins by gathering information about problems, concerns, and needed changes from members of the organization. This diagnosis is analogous to the physician's search to find what specifically ails a patient. In action research, the change agent asks questions, interviews employees, reviews records, and listens to the concerns of employees.

ANALYSIS   The information gathered during the diagnostic stage is then analyzed. What problems do people key in on? What patterns do these problems seem to take? The change agent synthesizes this information into primary concerns, problem areas, and possible actions.

FEEDBACK   Action research includes extensive involvement of the change targets. That is, the people who will be involved in any change program must be actively involved in determining what the problem is and participating in creating the solution. So the third step is sharing with employees what has been found from steps one and two. The employees, with the help of the change agent, develop action plans for bringing about any needed change.

ACTION   Now the "action" part of action research is set in motion. The employees and the change agent carry out the specific actions to correct the problems that have been identified.

EVALUATION   Finally, consistent with the scientific underpinnings of action research, the change agent evaluates the effectiveness of the action plans. Using the initial data gathered as points of reference, any subsequent changes can be compared and evaluated.

Action research provides at least two specific benefits for an organization. First, it's problem-focused. The change agent objectively looks for problems and the type of problem determines the type of change action. While this may seem intuitively obvious, a lot of change activities aren't done this way. Rather, they're solution-centered. The change agent has a favorite solution—for example, implementing flextime or a management-by-objectives program—and then seeks out problems that his or her solution fits. Second, because action research so heavily involves employees in the process, resistance to change is reduced. In fact, once employees have actively participated in the feedback stage, the change process typically takes on a momentum of its own. The employees and groups that have been involved become an internal source of sustained pressure to bring about the change.

FOCUS FOR CHANGE IN THE 1990s

Talk to managers. Read the popular business periodicals. What you'll find is that two issues have risen above the rest as change topics for the 1990s. They are organizational *innovation* and the *empowerment* of people. Why these two specific issues have gained so much attention is fairly obvious. In the dynamic world of global competition, the innovative organization is more adaptive and more likely to thrive. Similarly, as organizations seek to become more efficient and responsive, management is finding that it can cut costs, improve employee motivation, and increase productivity by empowering its work force. In the following pages, we'll take a closer look at each of these topics.

Innovation

The relevant question is: How can an organization become more innovative? The standard toward which many organizations strive is that achieved by the 3M Co.[13] It has developed a reputation for being able to stimulate innovation over a long period of time. 3M has a stated objective that twenty-five percent of each division's profits are to come from products developed in the prior five years. In 1990 alone, 3M launched more than two hundred new products and better than thirty percent of its $13 billion in revenues came from products introduced since 1986.

What's the secret of 3M's success? What can other organizations do to clone 3M's track record for innovation? While there is no guaranteed formula, certain characteristics surface again and again when researchers study innovative organizations. We've grouped them into structural, cultural, and human resource categories. Our message to change agents is that they should consider introducing these characteristics into their organization if they want to create an innovative climate. Before we look at these characteristics, however, let's clarify what we mean by *innovation*.

Innovation A new idea applied to initiating or improving a product, process, or service.

DEFINITION We said *change* refers to making things different. Innovation is a more specialized kind of change. **Innovation** is a new idea applied to initiating or improving a product, process, or service.[14] So all innovations involve change, but not all changes necessarily involve new ideas or lead to significant improvements. Innovations in organizations can range from small incremental improvements, such as RJR Nabisco's extension of the Oreo product line to include double stuffs and chocolate-covered Oreos, up to radical breakthroughs, such as McGraw-Hill's recent creation of customized textbooks that utilize computer networks to link bookstore laser printers to McGraw's central database of text material. Keep in mind that while our examples are mostly of product innovations, the concept of innovation also encompasses new production process technologies, new structures or administrative systems, and new plans or programs pertaining to organizational members.

SOURCES OF INNOVATION *Structural variables* have been the most-studied potential source of innovation.[15] A meta-analysis of the structure–innovation relationship leads to the following conclusions.[16] First, organic structures positively influence innovation. Because they're lower in vertical differentiation, formalization, and centralization, organic organizations facilitate the flexibility, adaptation, and cross-fertilization that make the adoption of innovations easier. Second, long tenure in management is associated with innovation. Managerial tenure apparently provides legitimacy and knowledge of how to accomplish tasks and obtain desired outcomes. Third,

America West does many of the right things to encourage and support innovation. Among them is employee cross-utilization. The company doesn't have flight attendants—it has multitalented customer service representatives. These individuals can handle in-flight duties and can work at the ticket counter, on the ramp, or in the reservation center.
Courtesy America West Airlines

innovation is nurtured where there are slack resources. Having an abundance of resources allows an organization to afford to purchase innovations, bear the cost of instituting innovations, and absorb failures. Finally, interunit communication is high in innovative organizations. These organizations are high users of committees, task forces, and other mechanisms that facilitate interaction across departmental lines.

Innovative organizations tend to have similar *cultures*. They encourage experimentation. They reward both successes and failures. They celebrate mistakes. Unfortunately, in too many organizations, people are rewarded for the *absence* of failures rather than for the *presence* of successes. Such cultures extinguish risk-taking and innovation. People will suggest and try new ideas only where they feel such behaviors exact no penalties.

Within the *human resources* category, we find that innovative organizations actively promote the training and development of their members so that they keep current, offer high job security so employees don't fear getting fired for making mistakes, and encourage individuals to become champions of change. Once a new idea is developed, champions of change actively and enthusiastically promote the idea, build support, overcome resistance, and ensure that the innovation is implemented.[17] Recent research finds that champions have common personality characteristics: extremely high self-confidence, persistence, energy, and a tendency to risk-taking. Champions also display characteristics associated with transformational leadership. They inspire and energize others with their vision of the potential of an innovation and through their strong personal conviction in their mission. They are also good at gaining the commitment of others to support their mission. Additionally, champions have jobs that provide considerable decision-making discretion. This autonomy helps them introduce and implement innovations in organizations.[18]

Given the status of 3M as a premier product innovator, we would expect it to have most or all of the properties we've identified. And it does. The company is so highly decentralized that it has many of the characteristics of small, organic organizations. All of 3M's scientists and managers are challenged to "keep current." Idea champions are created and encouraged by allowing scientists and engineers to spend up to fifteen percent of their time on projects of their own choosing. The company encourages its employees to take risks—and rewards the failures as well as the successes. And very importantly, 3M doesn't hire and fire with the business cycle. During the 1991–92 recession, while almost all major companies cut costs by firing employees, 3M initiated no layoffs.

Empowerment

Chrysler Corp. has been empowering its people and achieving some spectacular results.[19] Catherine Diethorn of Chrysler Financial designed a self-calculating branch cash system on her personal computer at home that saves the company $525,000 annually. John Rousseau and James Groves, who work at a Chrysler stamping plant in Michigan, created a sound deadener used on car and truck doors that saves the company $2 million a year. A twelve-person cross-functional paint analysis team came up with ideas to improve vehicle paint quality that are saving Chrysler a staggering $115 million a year.

Johnsonville Foods, a family-owned sausage company in Wisconsin, is proving that empowerment can work in small organizations, too.[20] Johnsonville workers hire and fire one another, buy the company's equipment, and act as their own bosses. Volunteers from the shop floor write the manufacturing budget. Another group of workers designs the manufacturing line. And empowering employees has positively affected the company's performance. In one recent six-year period, Johnsonville doubled its return on assets, experienced a fifteen-percent annual rise in sales, and kept its payroll increase to only about half the growth in sales.

Even the public sector is jumping on the empowerment bandwagon. The state of Kentucky, for example, is putting into place an innovative incentive-pay system keyed to how well each school's students perform.[21] The program involves a dramatic shift of power to teachers. School boards and principals become merely advisors as teacher-dominated governing councils in each school are given the authority to override a wide range of state and union rules. Disappointed with the traditional way schools have been run, reformers hope that empowering teachers will produce better ideas in every area of education, from curriculum to teaching methods. The Kentucky plan provides bonuses of up to fifteen percent to the entire staff if its school improves—and to no one if it doesn't.

Organizations like Chrysler, Johnsonville Foods, and the state of Kentucky have joined other prominent companies—AT&T, Colgate-Palmolive, PPG Industries, General Dynamics, Delta Airlines, Federal Express, Hewlett-Packard, IBM, Motorola, Wal-Mart—in recently moving to empower their employees. The impetus for this movement is clearly illustrated by AT&T's experience. Downsizing has meant that the people who are left often have to take over the tasks of others. One AT&T manager had to assume managerial responsibilities for three areas that had previously been handled by three people. This manager had to empower her people "because you can't know every data system and every policy. It's been a letting-go process and a stretching."[22] Empowerment allows organizations like AT&T to become more efficient and more effective—to do more with less.

In the following pages, we'll provide a detailed definition of empowerment, show the kind of changes management needs to make if it wants to successfully empower its people, and consider some of the barriers to the effective introduction of empowerment.

Empowerment A process that increases employees' intrinsic task motivation.

DEFINITION   We empower people by involving them in their work through a process of inclusion. **Empowerment,** then, is a process that increases employees' intrinsic task motivation.[23] What does management need to do to increase intrinsic motivation? Take actions that positively affect *impact, competence, meaningfulness,* and *choice.*[24] Let's briefly define what's meant by these terms:

Impact.   An employee's task has impact if it is perceived as "making a difference" in terms of accomplishing the purposes of the task.

Competence.   If a person can perform task activities skillfully when he or she tries, then the task positively affects competence.

Meaningfulness.   If you view the task you're doing as worthwhile—if you care about what you do—it provides meaningfulness.

Choice.   A task provides choice if it allows the employee self-determination in performing task activities.

These four dimensions might remind you of our discussion of task characteristics theories in Chapters 7 and 8, specifically the job characteristics model. If they did, you're on the right track. Impact is analogous to knowledge of results. In the JCM, feedback creates this psychological state. In the JCM, skill variety, task identity, and task significance lead to the psychological state of meaningfulness. Finally, choice is analogous to autonomy in the

"A lot of us thought it'd be a waste of time at first," says Noah Zimmerly, a metal cutter for the Will-Burt Co., about the firm's intensive education effort to facilitate Will-Burt's empowerment program. When the program began, the overall education level in the company was around the 10th grade level. Says Zimmmerly, "If you quit and go someplace else to work, the education is a plus for you." Roger Mastroianni

JCM. So the only real difference between the concept of empowering people and designing jobs that score high on the JCM's core dimensions is that empowerment requires that people believe they are able to perform activities competently. As you'll see, empowerment is an excellent concept for integrating many of the contemporary practices introduced in this book.

APPLICATION How does management specifically empower its employees? Table 19–1 provides a partial answer. It offers a list of actions that management can take that, in the aggregate, lead to empowerment. The table also postulates some tentative linkages between the action and the four empowerment dimensions.

A few comments will elaborate on some of the actions specified in Table 19–1. Since delegation involves the distributing of power while participation implies only the sharing of power, delegation should be more effective at truly empowering others.[25] Because job enrichment is based on the JCM, it obviously should be a major part of any empowerment program. Self-managed work teams—which allow members to select and train new members, allocate activities and schedule work, set production levels, solve operating problems, and the like—enrich jobs at the group level and should be encouraged. Companies like Amoco, Cigna, and DuPont have begun using subordinates' ratings of how well their bosses manage to help make their operations less hierarchical and lessen the power of supervisors.[26] Creating a supportive culture is a long and demanding process. Building trust takes time. Training and reeducating managers to become facilitators rather than controllers is typically a major undertaking. And the commitment to educate and train workers who may be badly lacking in basic skills like reading blueprints and calculating with fractions—never mind much more challenging tasks such as negotiating with suppliers and writing up purchasing specifications for new equipment—requires a revolution in thinking.

TABLE 19–1   Actions That Empower Employees

	Empowerment Dimensions			
Actions	**Impact**	**Competence**	**Meaningfulness**	**Choice**
Delegate authority				x
Use participative decision making				x
Encourage self-management		x		x
Enrich jobs	x		x	x
Create self-managed work teams	x		x	x
Create tasks that provide intrinsic feedback	x			
Install upward performance appraisals			x	
Lessen formalization				x
Create a supportive culture	x		x	x
Encourage goal setting	x			
Educate and train employees		x		

Empowering Minorities at Avon

Avon Products has found that empowering minority employees improves their work environment and bolsters the company's bottom line. Two examples illustrate these points.[27]

Most diversity programs are top-down projects. But Avon's management uses a bottom-up approach by encouraging minorities to develop their own in-house networks. The Black Professionals Association, the Avon Hispanic Network, and the Avon Asian Network developed independently of one another in the mid-1980s. They began as social groups but eventually evolved into self-help organizations, devoted to encouraging minority recruiting and career development, and into vehicles for providing direct feedback to management on their unique problems. Each network head meets regularly with top management to discuss the network's

needs. Currently, Avon's 1525-person headquarters staff is thirteen percent black, six percent Hispanic, and four percent Asian. Maybe somewhat surprisingly, there is no women's network at Avon. There was a number of years ago, but with women holding seventy-nine percent of the management positions at Avon, the group came to realize that its existence was unnecessary.

Avon also found that empowering minority managers was an excellent means for turning around its dismal performance in inner-city markets. Avon made changes to give black and Hispanic managers substantial authority over these markets. Formerly unprofitable, the inner city is now among Avon's most productive U.S. markets. Top management has concluded that its minority managers better understand the culture and needs of inner-city customers.

Avon encourages employees to organize into Black, Hispanic, and Asian networks by granting them official recognition and providing a senior manager to act as a mentor. Steve Hill

BARRIERS TO EMPOWERMENT Despite the recent popularity of empowerment, some notes of caution need to be sounded. There are potential barriers to empowerment that can doom any program.[28] Some of these barriers are fairly easily removed, while others present long-term, or even impossible, obstacles to empowerment's success.

There are organizations where empowerment's goal of inclusion is incongruent with the culture. These are cultures in which employees lack commitment, members fail to share the organization's goals, or employees are fearful of retribution if they take the initiative. A recent survey, for example, found that workers are often reluctant to take the initiative unless they have a union to protect them.[29] Management, of course, can change its organizational culture to be more supportive of empowerment, but this is typically a long-term proposition.

Fear of retribution can be a problem for management, too. It is unreasonable to expect managers to distribute power to others if they can expect to be punished when those others make mistakes. Managers will not delegate authority if they must retain full responsibility for decisions made in their units. The practice of firing the coach when the team loses can be changed, but where it exists and has an entrenched history, managers will fight the process of empowering their people.

Some organizations have, intentionally or otherwise, hired employees with a low need for autonomy. They then reinforce this need by providing directive or autocratic leadership. Employees who want the security of having someone tell them what to do and when to do it will resist empowerment. Training and education can often be effective in overcoming this obstacle, however.

Certain managerial personalities can be a handicap to implementing an empowerment program. For example, managers with a high power need are likely to be reluctant to give up the control they have worked hard to earn. While some of these managers may "get the empowerment message," others may not. Managers in the latter group will probably need to be replaced if empowerment is to work.

Finally, we suggest that some national cultures are incompatible with the empowerment philosophy. We might hypothesize that national cultures that are high in power distance, that view people as evil, or hold hierarchy in high regard are unlikely to readily embrace empowerment.

ORGANIZATIONAL DEVELOPMENT: THE ROAD TO EMPOWERMENT

Organizational Development (OD) A collection of planned-change interventions, built on humanistic–democratic values, that seek to improve organizational effectiveness and employee well-being.

Organizational development (OD) is not an easily definable single concept. Rather, it is a term used to encompass a collection of planned-change interventions, built on humanistic–democratic values, that seek to improve organizational effectiveness and employee well-being.

OD Values

The OD paradigm values human and organizational growth, collaborative and participative processes, and a spirit of inquiry.[30] The change agent may be directive in OD; however, there is a strong emphasis on collaboration. Concepts such as power, authority, control, conflict, and coercion are held in relatively low esteem among OD change agents. The following briefly identifies the underlying values in most OD efforts:

1. *Respect for people.* Individuals are perceived as being responsible, conscientious, and caring. They should be treated with dignity and respect.
2. *Trust and support.* The effective and healthy organization is characterized by trust, authenticity, openness, and a supportive climate.
3. *Power equalization.* Effective organizations de-emphasize hierarchical authority and control.
4. *Confrontation.* Problems shouldn't be swept under the rug. They should be openly confronted.
5. *Participation.* The more that people who will be affected by a change are involved in the decisions surrounding that change, the more they will be committed to implementing those decisions.

OD Interventions

OD can be thought of as a road to empowerment. By that we mean that OD interventions can provide the change vehicle for making people more accepting and comfortable with empowerment. In the following pages, we'll present five interventions that change agents might consider using to help create the climate of trust, openness, and support needed to make empowerment work.

Sensitivity Training Training groups that seek to change behavior through unstructured group interaction.

SENSITIVITY TRAINING It can go by a variety of names—laboratory training, **sensitivity training,** encounter groups, or T-groups (training groups)—but all refer to a method of changing behavior through unstructured group interaction. Members are brought together in a free and open environment in which participants discuss themselves and their interactive processes, loosely directed by a professional behavioral scientist. The group is process-oriented, which means that individuals learn through observing and participating rather than being told. The professional creates the opportunity for participants to express their ideas, beliefs, and attitudes. He or she does not accept—in fact, overtly rejects—any leadership role.

The objectives of the T-groups are to provide the subjects with increased awareness of their own behavior and how others perceive them, greater sensitivity to the behavior of others, and increased understanding of group processes. Specific results sought include increased ability to empathize with others, improved listening skills, greater openness, increased tolerance of individual differences, and improved conflict resolution skills.

If individuals lack awareness of how others perceive them, then the successful T-group can effect more realistic self-perceptions, greater group cohesiveness, and a reduction in dysfunctional interpersonal conflicts. Further, it will ideally result in a better integration between the individual and the organization.

Survey Feedback The use of questionnaires to identify discrepancies among member perceptions; discussion follows and remedies are suggested.

SURVEY FEEDBACK   One tool for assessing attitudes held by organizational members, identifying discrepancies among member perceptions, and solving these differences is the **survey feedback** approach.

Everyone in an organization can participate in survey feedback, but of key importance is the organizational family—the manager of any given unit and those employees who report directly to him or her. A questionnaire is usually completed by all members in the organization or unit. Organization members may be asked to suggest questions or may be interviewed to determine what issues are relevant. The questionnaire typically asks members for their perceptions and attitudes on a broad range of topics, including decision-making practices; communication effectiveness; coordination between units; and satisfaction with the organization, job, peers, and their immediate supervisor.

The data from this questionnaire are tabulated with data pertaining to an individual's specific "family" and to the entire organization and distributed to employees. These data then become the springboard for identifying problems and clarifying issues that may be creating difficulties for people. In some cases, the manager may be counseled by an external change agent about the meaning of the responses to the questionnaire and may even be given suggested guidelines for leading the organizational family in group discussion of the results. Particular attention is given to the importance of encouraging discussion and ensuring that discussions focus on issues and ideas and not on attacking individuals.

Finally, group discussion in the survey feedback approach should result in members identifying possible implications of the questionnaire's findings. Are people listening? Are new ideas being generated? Can decision making, interpersonal relations, or job assignments be improved? Answers to questions like these, it is hoped, will result in the group agreeing upon commitments to various actions that will remedy the problems that are identified.

Process Consultation Consultant gives a client insight into what is going on around the client, within the client, and between the client and other people; identifies processes that need improvement.

PROCESS CONSULTATION   No organization operates perfectly. Managers often sense that their unit's performance can be improved, but they are unable to identify what can be improved and how it can be improved. The purpose of **process consultation** is for an outside consultant to assist a client, usually a manager, "to perceive, understand, and act upon process events" with which he or she must deal.[31] These might include work flow, informal relationships among unit members, and formal communication channels.

Process consultation (PC) is similar to sensitivity training in its assumption that organizational effectiveness can be improved by dealing with interpersonal problems and in its emphasis on involvement. But PC is more task directed than sensitivity training.

Consultants in PC are there to "give the client 'insight' into what is going on around him, within him, and between him and other people."[32] They do not solve the organization's problems. Rather, the consultant is a guide or coach who advises on the process to help the client solve his or her own problems.

The consultant works with the client in *jointly* diagnosing what processes need improvement. The emphasis is on "jointly," because the client develops a skill at analyzing processes within his or her unit that can be continually called on long after the consultant is gone. Additionally, by having the client actively participate in both the diagnosis and the development of alternatives, there will be greater understanding of the process and the remedy and less resistance to the action plan chosen.

Importantly, the process consultant need not be an expert in solving the particular problem that is identified. The consultant's expertise lies in diagnosis and developing a helping relationship. If the specific problem uncovered requires technical knowledge outside the client and consultant's expertise, the consultant helps the client to locate such an expert and then instructs the client in how to get the most out of this expert resource.

TEAM BUILDING   Organizations are made up of people working together to achieve some common end. Since people are frequently required to work in groups, considerable attention has been focused in OD on **team building.**[33]

Team Building High interaction among group members to increase trust and openness.

Team building can be applied within groups or at the intergroup level where activities are interdependent. For our discussion, we shall emphasize the intragroup level and leave intergroup development to the next section. As a result, our interest concerns applications to organizational families (command groups), as well as to communities, project teams, and task groups.

Not all group activity has interdependence of functions. To illustrate, consider a football team and a track team:

> Although members on both teams are concerned with the team's total output they function differently. The football team's output depends synergistically on how well each player does his particular job in concert with his teammates. The quarterback's performance depends on the performance of his linemen and receivers, and ends on how well the quarterback throws the ball, and so on. On the other hand, a track team's performance is determined largely by the mere addition of the performances of the individual members.[34]

Team building is applicable to the case of interdependence, such as in football. The objective is to improve coordinative efforts of team members which will result in increasing the group's performance.

The activities considered in team building typically include goal setting, development of interpersonal relations among team members, role analysis to clarify each member's role and responsibilities, and team process analysis. Of course, team building may emphasize or exclude certain activities depending on the purpose of the development effort and the specific problems with which the team is confronted. Basically, however, team building attempts to use high interaction among group members to increase trust and openness.

It may be beneficial to begin by having members attempt to define the goals and priorities of the group. This will bring to the surface different per-

Chrysler Corp. has used team building to reduce historical conflicts with unionized employees. This group of employees from Chrysler's Newark assembly plant in Delaware implemented the first modern operating agreement negotiated between Chrysler and the United Auto Workers. It allows more flexibility and communication in the workplace and helps labor and management function as a team. Courtesy Chrysler

ceptions of what the group's purpose may be. Following this, members can evaluate the group's performance—how effective are they in structuring priorities and achieving their goals? This should identify potential problem areas. This self-critique discussion of means and ends can be done with members of the total group present or, where large size impinges on a free interchange of views, may initially take place in smaller groups followed up by the sharing of their findings with the total group.

Team building can also address itself to clarifying each member's role in the group. Each role can be identified and clarified. Previous ambiguities can be brought to the surface. For some individuals, it may offer one of the few opportunities they have had to think through thoroughly what their job is all about and what specific tasks they are expected to carry out if the group is to optimize its effectiveness.

Still another team-building activity can be similar to that performed by the process consultant; that is, to analyze key processes that go on within the team to identify the way work is performed and how these processes might be improved to make the team more effective.

INTERGROUP DEVELOPMENT   A major area of concern in OD is the dysfunctional conflict that exists between groups. As a result, this has been a subject to which change efforts have been directed.

Intergroup Development
OD efforts to improve interactions between groups.

Intergroup development seeks to change the attitudes, stereotypes, and perceptions that groups have of each other. For example, in one company, the engineers saw the accounting department as composed of shy and conservative types, and the personnel department as having a bunch of "smiley types who sit around and plan company picnics." Such stereotypes can have an obvious negative impact on the coordinative efforts between the departments.

Although there are several approaches for improving intergroup relations,[35] a popular method emphasizes problem solving.[36] In this method, each group meets independently to develop lists of its perception of itself, the other group, and how it believes the other group perceives it. The groups then share their lists, after which similarities and differences are discussed. Differences are clearly articulated, and the groups look for the causes of the disparities.

Are the groups' goals at odds? Were perceptions distorted? On what basis were stereotypes formulated? Have some differences been caused by misunderstandings of intentions? Have words and concepts been defined dif-

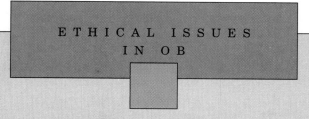

The Ethics of Control

OD interventions typically are based on humanistic–democratic values. They rely heavily on processes such as participation, collaboration, and confrontation. OD interventions are viewed as effective to the degree to which they increase openness, trust, risk-taking, autonomy, and respect for people, and how far they go to equalize power within the organization. The assumption by OD proponents is that these outcomes are desirable and lead to more effective organizational performance.

Some writers have noted, however, that when OD change agents use humanistic processes to achieve democratic outcomes, they are imposing their values on organizational participants.[37] For example, if employees in a given department have had trouble working with one another over a fairly long period of time, an OD change agent might recommend that the department members get together in an informal ses-

sion and openly discuss their perceptions of one another, the sources of their disagreements, and similar issues. But some people don't feel comfortable participating in a process that requires them to be open about their feelings and attitudes. OD interventions that demand openness reduce the privacy and freedom of such individuals. Even if participation is voluntary, the decision not to participate might carry negative connotations, result in lower performance appraisals, and have adverse career effects. Moreover, what if an employee does participate, is authentically open, reveals to the group some very personal fears and concerns, and then someone in the group uses this information vindictively against that employee at some later date? And doesn't even voluntary participation in an OD intervention imply control by the change agent over participants? What do *you* think?

ferently by each group? Answers to questions like these clarify the exact nature of the conflict. Once the causes of the difficulty have been identified, the groups can move to the integration phase—working to develop solutions that will improve relations between the groups.

Subgroups, with members from each of the conflicting groups, can now be created for further diagnosis and to begin to formulate possible alternative actions that will improve relations.

IMPLICATIONS FOR PERFORMANCE AND SATISFACTION

The need for change has been implied throughout this text. "A casual reflection on change should indicate that it encompasses almost all our concepts in the organizational behavior literature. Think about leadership, motivation, organizational environment, and roles. It is impossible to think about these and other concepts without inquiring about change."[38]

If environments were perfectly static, if employees' skills and abilities were always up-to-date and incapable of deteriorating, and if tomorrow was always exactly the same as today, organizational change would have little or no relevance to employee performance and satisfaction. But the real world is turbulent, requiring organizations and their members to undergo dynamic change if they are to perform at competitive levels.

The trend in the 1990s is toward making organizations more adaptive. This translates into less hierarchy, wider spans of control, enriched jobs, increased use of work teams, more delegation, and a commitment to educating and training workers to assume greater decision-making responsibility. It's premature, however, to conclude that these empowerment tactics will automatically lead to improved employee performance and satisfaction. There are barriers to empowerment that can impede success. But the effectiveness of change interventions, in general, is encouraging. While the strength of effects varies by type of program, change interventions appear to have a positive impact on employee behavior and attitudes.[39]

■ *FOR DISCUSSION*

1. How might changes in the makeup of an organization's work force require implementation of organizational change programs?

2. What is meant by the phrase "we live in an age of discontinuity"?

3. "Managing today is easier than at the turn of the century because the years of real change took place between the Civil War and World War I." Do you agree or disagree? Discuss.

4. Are all managers change agents? Discuss.

5. "Resistance to change is an irrational response." Do you agree or disagree? Discuss.

6. How does Lewin's three-step model of change deal with resistance to change?

7. Describe the action research process.

8. Discuss the link between learning theories discussed in Chapter 4 and the issue of organizational change.

9. What changes can an organization that has a history of "following the leader" make to foster innovation?

10. What actions does management need to take to introduce empowerment in its organization?

11. What obstacles are likely to reduce the effectiveness of an empowerment program?

12. What characteristics distinguish organizational development?

Change Is an Episodic Activity

The study of planned organizational change has, with very few exceptions, viewed it as an episodic activity. That is, it starts at some point, proceeds through a series of steps, and culminates in some outcome that those involved hope is an improvement over the starting point. When change is seen as an episodic activity, it has a beginning, a middle, and an end.

Both Lewin's three-step model and action research follow this perspective. In the former, change is seen as a break in the organization's equilibrium. The status quo has been disturbed, and change is necessary to establish a new equilibrium state. The objective of refreezing is to stabilize the new situation by balancing the driving and restraining forces. Action research begins with a diagnostic assessment in which problems are identified. These problems are then analyzed, and shared with those who are affected, solutions are developed, and action plans are initiated. The process is brought to closure by an evaluation of the action plan's effectiveness. Even though supporters of action research recognize that the cycle may need to go through numerous iterations, the process is still seen as a cycle with a beginning and an end.

Some experts have argued that organizational change should be thought of as balancing a system made up of five interacting variables within the organization—people, tasks, technology, structure, and strategy. A change in any one variable has repercussions on one or more of the others. Again, this perspective is episodic in that it treats organizational change as essentially an effort to sustain an equilibrium. A change in one variable begins a chain of events that, if properly managed, requires adjustments in the other variables to achieve a new state of equilibrium.

Another way to conceptualize the episodic way of looking at change is to think of managing change as analogous to captaining a ship. The organization is like a large ship traveling across the calm Mediterranean Sea to a specific port. The ship's captain has made this exact trip hundreds of times before with the same crew. Every once in a while, however, a storm will appear, and the crew has to respond. The captain will make the appropriate adjustments—that is, implement changes—and, having maneuvered through the storm, will return to calm waters. Managing an organization should therefore be seen as a journey with a beginning and an end, and implementing change as a response to a break in the status quo and needed only in occasional situations.

Change Is an Ongoing Activity

The episodic approach may be the dominant paradigm for handling planned organizational change, but it has become obsolete. It applies to a world of certainty and predictability. The episodic approach was developed in the 1950s and 1960s, and it reflects the environment of those times. It treats change as the occasional disturbance in an otherwise peaceful world. However, this paradigm has little resemblance to the 1990s environment of constant and chaotic change.

If you want to understand what it's like to manage change in today's organizations, think of it as equivalent to permanent white-water rafting.* The organization is not a large ship, but more akin to a forty-foot raft. Rather than sailing a calm sea, this raft must traverse a raging river made up of an uninterrupted flow of permanent white-water rapids. To make things worse, the raft is manned by ten people who have never worked together or traveled the river before, much of the trip is in the dark, the river is dotted by unexpected turns and obstacles, the exact destination of the raft is not clear, and at irregular intervals the raft needs to pull to shore, where some new crew members are added and others leave. Change is a natural state and managing change is a continual process. That is, managers never get the luxury of escaping the white-water rapids.

To get a feeling for what managers are facing, think of what it would be like to attend a college that had the following structure: Courses vary in length. When you sign up for a course, however, you don't know how long it will last. It might go for two weeks or thirty weeks. Furthermore, the instructor can end a course any time he or she wants, with no prior warning. If that isn't frustrating enough, the length of the class changes each time it meets—sometimes it lasts twenty minutes, while other times it runs for three hours—and determination of when the next class meeting will take place is set by the instructor during the previous class. And one more thing: The exams are all unannounced, so you have to be ready for a test at any time.

A growing number of managers are coming to accept that their jobs are much like what a student would face in such a college. The stability and predictability of the episodic perspective don't exist. Nor are disruptions in the status quo only occasional, temporary, and followed by a return to an equilibrium state. Managers today face constant change, bordering on chaos. They are being forced to play a game they've never played before, governed by rules that are created as the game progresses.

---

*This perspective is based on P. B. Vaill, *Managing as a Performing Art: New Ideas for a World of Chaotic Change* (San Francisco: Jossey-Bass, 1989).

Managing-in-a-Turbulent-World Tolerance Test

INSTRUCTIONS   Listed below are some statements a thirty-seven-year-old manager made about his job at a large, successful corporation. If your job had these characteristics, how would you react to them? After each statement are five letters, A to E. Circle the letter that best describes how you think you would react according to the following scale:

A   *I would enjoy this very much: it's completely acceptable.*
B   *This would be enjoyable and acceptable most of the time.*
C   *I'd have no reaction to this feature one way or another, or it would be about equally enjoyable and unpleasant.*
D   *This feature would be somewhat unpleasant for me.*
E   *This feature would be very unpleasant for me.*

1. I regularly spend 30 to 40 percent of my time in meetings.
   A   B   C   D   E

2. A year and a half ago, my job did not exist, and I have been essentially inventing it as I go along.   A   B   C   D   E

3. The responsibilities I either assume or am assigned consistently exceed the authority I have for discharging them.   A   B   C   D   E

4. At any given moment in my job, I have on the average about a dozen phone calls to be returned.   A   B   C   D   E

5. There seems to be very little relation in my job between the quality of my performance and my actual pay and fringe benefits.   A   B   C   D   E

6. About two weeks a year of formal management training is needed in my job just to stay current.   A   B   C   D   E

7. Because we have very effective equal employment opportunity in my company and because it is thoroughly multinational, my job consistently brings me into close working contact at a professional level with people of many races, ethnic groups, and nationalities and of both sexes. A   B   C   D   E

8. There is no objective way to measure my effectiveness.   A   B   C   D   E

9. I report to three different bosses for different aspects of my job, and each has an equal say in my performance appraisal.   A   B   C   D   E

10. On average, about a third of my time is spent dealing with unexpected emergencies that force all scheduled work to be postponed.
    A   B   C   D   E

11. When I have to have a meeting of the people who report to me, it takes my secretary most of a day to find a time when we are all available, and even then, I have yet to have a meeting where everyone is present for the entire meeting.   A   B   C   D   E

12. The college degree I earned in preparation for this type of work is now obsolete, and I probably should go back for another degree.
    A   B   C   D   E

13. My job requires that I absorb 100–200 pages per week of technical materials.   A   B   C   D   E

14. I am out of town overnight at least one night per week.   A B   C D E

15. My department is so interdependent with several other departments in the company that all distinctions about which departments are responsible for which tasks are quite arbitrary.   A B   C D E

16. I will probably get a promotion in about a year to a job in another division that has most of these same characteristics.   A B   C D E

17. During the period of my employment here, either the entire company or the division I worked in has been reorganized every year or so.

A B   C D E

18. While there are several possible promotions I can see ahead of me, I have no real career path in an objective sense.   A   B   C   D   E

19. While there are several possible promotions I can see ahead of me, I think I have no realistic chance of getting to the top levels of the company.

A B   C D E

20. While I have many ideas about how to make things work better, I have no direct influence on either the business policies or the personnel policies that govern my division.   A B   C D E

21. My company has recently put in an "assessment center" where I and all other managers will be required to go through an extensive battery of psychological tests to assess our potential.   A   B   C   D   E

22. My company is a defendant in an antitrust suit, and if the case comes to trial, I will probably have to testify about some decisions that were made a few years ago.   A   B   C   D   E

23. Advanced computer and other electronic office technology is continually being introduced into my division, necessitating constant learning on my part.   A   B   C   D   E

24. The computer terminal and screen I have in my office can be monitored in my bosses' offices without my knowledge.   A   B   C   D   E

Turn to page 719 for scoring directions and key.

Source: From P. B. Vaill, *Managing as a Performing Art: New Ideas for a World of Chaotic Change* (San Francisco: Jossey-Bass, 1989), pp. 8–9. Reproduced with permission of publisher. All rights reserved.

E X E R C I S E   19-B

The Beacon Aircraft Co.

OBJECTIVES

1. To illustrate how forces for change and stability must be managed in organizational development programs.

2. To illustrate the effects of alternative change techniques on the relative strength of forces for change and forces for stability.

THE SITUATION The marketing division of the Beacon Aircraft Co. has gone through two reorganizations in the past two years. Initially, its structure changed from a functional to a matrix form. But the matrix structure did not satisfy some functional managers. They complained that the structure confused the authority and responsibility relationships.

In reaction to these complaints, the marketing manager revised the structure back to the functional form. This new structure maintained market and project groups, which were managed by project managers with a few general staff personnel. But no functional specialists were assigned to these groups.

After the change, some problems began to surface. Project managers complained that they could not obtain adequate assistance from functional staffs. It not only took more time to obtain necessary assistance, but it also created problems in establishing stable relationships with functional staff members. Since these problems affected their services to customers, project managers demanded a change in the organizational structure—probably again toward a matrix structure. Faced with these complaints and demands from project managers, the vice president is pondering another reorganization. He has requested an outside consultant to help him in the reorganization plan.

THE PROCEDURE
1. Divide yourselves into groups of five to seven and take the role of consultants.
2. Each group identifies the driving and resisting forces found in the firm. List these forces below.

The Driving Forces	The Resisting Forces
_____	_____
_____	_____
_____	_____
_____	_____
_____	_____
_____	_____

3. Each group develops a set of strategies for increasing the driving forces and another set for reducing the resisting forces.
4. Each group prepares a list of changes it wants to introduce.
5. The class reassembles and hears each group's recommendations.

Source: Adapted from K. H. Chung and L. C. Megginson, *Organizational Behavior* (New York: Harper & Row, 1981), pp. 498–99. With permission.

C A S E   I N C I D E N T   1 9

Leadership Development at Pacific Bell

Following its divestiture from AT&T in 1983, Pacific Bell's management decided its company needed to transform its traditional, risk-aversive culture into a less hierarchical, more entrepreneurial one. To help change the culture and give employees a common purpose and common approach to their work, management implemented a leadership development program. The program, which involved more than twenty-three thousand of Pac Bell's sixty-seven thousand employees, consisted of a series of ten two-day work sessions during which participants learned about running effective meetings, resolving conflicts, cutting costs, evaluating current situations, and implementing new ideas. The emphasis, however, was on communication—to provide employees with common "frameworks" and vocabulary for communicating with each other.

Almost from the beginning, the program was controversial. It used unusual training methods and introduced a language that employees were expected to use that was full of buzz phrases. For instance, employees were taught to be attentive to the needs of "multiple stakeholders" and that the organization and its members were "a nested set of open, living systems and subsystems dependent on the larger environment for survival." A number of participants described the program with terms like "brainwashing," "mind control," "Eastern mysticism," and "coercion."

An evaluation of the program by the California Public Utilities Commission identified several positive results of the program, including better and more productive meetings, more participation by union members in problem solving, and a feeling that the company was trying something new. But the PUC couldn't ignore the negative comments. A large proportion of the participants disliked the nonoptional aspect of the program and the way it intimidated dissenters, and believed that it was damaging productivity and morale.

In 1987, Pac Bell decided to put the program—which had already cost the company in excess of $39 million—on hold. Management said it would actively solicit employee opinions of the program and make improvements based on those responses.

Questions

1. What type of intervention does this Pac Bell program use?

2. Relate employee response to this program to the discussion of the ethics of control in the chapter.

3. How might Pac Bell's management have improved its evaluation of this program's effectiveness?

Source: Based on "Pacific Bell's Management Plan Draws PUC Fire," *Telephony,* June 22, 1987, pp. 14–15; and P. Waldman, "Motivate or Alienate? Firms Hire Gurus to Change Their 'Cultures,' " *The Wall Street Journal,* July 24, 1987, p. 19.

FOR FURTHER READING

GERSICK, C. J. G., "Revolutionary Change Theories: A Multilevel Exploration of the Punctuated Equilibrium Paradigm," *Academy of Management Review,* January 1991, pp. 10–36. Compares models of change, clarifies the punctuated-equilibrium paradigm, and shows the broad applicability of this paradigm for organizational studies.

GOODSTEIN, L. D., and W. W. BURKE, "Creating Successful Organization Change," *Organizational Dynamics,* Spring 1991, pp. 5–17. Explains why organizational change is a difficult task, then outlines how it can be accomplished, with specific reference to a change successfully made by British Airways.

ISABELLA, L. A., "Evolving Interpretations as a Change Unfolds: How Managers Construe Key Organizational Events," *Academy of Management Journal,* March 1990, pp. 7–41. Develops a model of how managers construe organizational events as a change unfolds. The model suggests that interpretations of key events unfold in four stages: anticipation, confirmation, culmination, and aftermath, linked to the process of change.

KANTER, R. M., "Transcending Business Boundaries: 12,000 World Managers View Change," *Harvard Business Review,* May-June 1991, pp. 151–64. Provides results from a comprehensive review of change practices in organizations in twenty-five countries.

WELLINS, R. S., W. C. BYHAM, and J. M. WILSON, *Empowered Teams* (San Francisco: Jossey-Bass, 1991). Describes how to create self-directed work groups that improve quality, productivity, and participation.

WOODMAN, R. W., and W. A. PASMORE (eds.), *Research in Organizational Change and Development,* Vol. 6 (Greenwich, CT: JAI Press, 1992). An annual volume of theories, models, ideas, and empirical data on organizational change.

NOTES

[1] P. Coy, "AT&T Reaches Out and Taps Some New Talent," *Business Week,* September 2, 1991, p. 80; and J. J. Keller, "Some AT&T Clients Gripe That Cost Cuts Are Hurting Service," *The Wall Street Journal,* January 24, 1992, p. A1.

[2] B. Saporito, "IBM's No-Hands Assembly Line," *Fortune,* September 15, 1986, pp. 105–09.

[3] J. E. Ellis, "Flight Plans for a Much Altered Future," *Business Week,* May 27, 1991, pp. 74–75.

[4] B. Hager, "CEO Wanted. No Insiders, Please," *Business Week,* August 12, 1991, pp. 44–45.

[5] J. Huey, "Nothing Is Impossible," *Fortune,* September 23, 1991, pp. 134–40.

[6] H. J. Leavitt, "Applied Organization Change in Industry," in W. Cooper, H. Leavitt, and M. Shelly (eds.), *New Perspectives on Organization Research* (New York: John Wiley, 1964).

[7] See S. P. Robbins, *Training in InterPersonal Skills: TIPS for Managing People at Work* (Englewood Cliffs, NJ: Prentice Hall, 1989), pp. 149–56.

[8] R. H. Hall, *Organizations: Structures, Processes, and Outcomes,* 4th ed. (Englewood Cliffs, NJ: Prentice Hall, 1987), p. 29.

[9] D. Katz and R. L. Kahn, *The Social Psychology of Organizations,* 2nd ed. (New York: John Wiley & Sons, 1978), pp. 714–15.

[10] J. P. Kotter and L. A. Schlesinger, "Choosing Strategies for Change," *Harvard Business Review,* March-April 1979, pp. 106–14.

[11] K. Lewin, *Field Theory in Social Science* (New York: Harper & Row, 1951).

[12] See, for example, A. B. Shani and W. A. Pasmore, "Organization Inquiry: Towards a New Model of the Action Research Process," in D. D. Warrick (ed.), *Contemporary Organization Development: Current Thinking and Applications* (Glenview, IL: Scott, Foresman, 1985), pp. 438–48.

[13] Discussions of the 3M Co. in this chapter are based on K. Labich, "The Innovators," *Fortune,* June 6, 1988, p. 49; R. Mitchell, "Masters of Innovation," *Business Week,* April 10, 1989, p. 58; and K. Kelly, "3M Run Scared? Forget About It," *Business Week,* September 16, 1991, pp. 59–62.

[14] R. M. Kanter, *The Change Masters* (New York: Simon & Schuster, 1983), p. 20.

[15] F. Damanpour, "Organizational Innovation: A Meta-Analysis of Effects of Determinants and Moderators," *Academy of Management Journal,* September 1991, p. 557.

[16]Ibid., pp. 555–90.

[17]J. M. Howell and C. A. Higgins, "Champions of Change," *Business Quarterly,* Spring 1990, pp. 31–32.

[18]Ibid.

[19]"Empowered People Get Results at Chrysler," *Fortune,* September 23, 1991, p. 121.

[20]T. A. Stewart, "New Ways to Exercise Power," *Fortune,* November 6, 1989, pp. 53–54; and S. Cohen, " 'The New Workplace' Begins to Pay Dividends," *San Diego Union,* December 2, 1990, p. I–1.

[21]A. Bernstein, "Letting Teachers Call the Shots," *Business Week,* January 28, 1991, pp. 54–56.

[22]A. Bennett, *The Death of the Organization Man* (New York: William Morrow, 1990), p. 205.

[23]K. W. Thomas and B. A. Velthouse, "Cognitive Elements of Empowerment: An 'Interpretive' Model of Intrinsic Task Motivation," *Academy of Management Review,* October 1990, pp. 666–81.

[24]Ibid.

[25]E. P. Hollander and L. R. Offermann, "Power and Leadership in Organizations," *American Psychologist,* February 1990, p. 184.

[26]A. J. Michels, "More Employees Evaluate the Boss," *Fortune,* July 29, 1991, p. 13.

[27]This box is based on J. Dreyfuss, "Get Ready for the New Work Force," *Fortune,* April 23, 1990, p. 176; H. Keets, "Avon Calling—On Its Troops," *Business Week,* July 8, 1991, p. 53; and T. H. Cox and S. Blake, "Managing Cultural Diversity: Implications for Organizational Competitiveness," *Academy of Management Executive,* August 1991, p. 49.

[28]See, for example, Hollander and Offermann, "Power and Leadership in Organizations," pp. 184–85.

[29]"Empowering Workers: Is It Real or Overplayed?", *The Wall Street Journal,* June 18, 1991, p. A1.

[30]L. D. Brown and J. G. Covey, "Development Organizations and Organization Development: Toward an Expanded Paradigm for Organization Development," in R. W. Woodman and W. A. Pasmore (eds.), *Research in Organizational Change and Development,* Vol. 1 (Greenwich, CT: JAI Press, 1987), p. 63.

[31]E. H. Schein, *Process Consultation: Its Role in Organizational Development* (Reading, MA: Addison-Wesley, 1969), p. 9.

[32]Ibid.

[33]See, for instance, P. F. Buller, "The Team Building-Task Performance Relation: Some Conceptual and Methodological Refinements," *Group and Organization Studies,* September 1986, pp. 147–68; and D. Eden, "Team Development: Quasi-Experimental Confirmation Among Combat Companies," *Group and Organization Studies,* September 1986, pp. 133–46.

[34]N. Margulies and J. Wallace, *Organizational Change: Techniques and Applications* (Glenview, IL: Scott, Foresman, 1973), pp. 99–100.

[35]See, for example, E. H. Neilsen, "Understanding and Managing Intergroup Conflict," in J. W. Lorsch and P. R. Lawrence (eds.), *Managing Group and Intergroup Relations* (Homewood, IL: Irwin-Dorsey, 1972), pp. 329–43.

[36]R. R. Blake, J. S. Mouton, and R. L. Sloma, "The Union-Management Intergroup Laboratory: Strategy for Resolving Intergroup Conflict," *Journal of Applied Behavioral Science,* No. 1 (1965), pp. 25–57.

[37]See, for example, G. A. Walter, "Organizational Development and Individual Rights," *Journal of Applied Behavioral Science,* November 1984, pp. 423–39.

[38]P. S. Goodman and L. B. Kurke, "Studies of Change in Organizations: A Status Report," in P. S. Goodman (ed.), *Change in Organizations* (San Francisco: Jossey-Bass, 1982), pp. 1–2.

[39]See, for instance, R. A. Katzell and R. A. Guzzo, "Psychological Approaches to Productivity Improvement," *American Psychologist,* April 1983, pp. 468–72; R. A. Guzzo, R. D. Jette, and R. A. Katzell, "The Effects of Psychologically Based Intervention Programs on Worker Productivity: A Meta-Analysis," *Personnel Psychology,* Summer 1985, pp. 275–92, and B. A. Macy, P. D. Bliese, and J. J. Norton, "Organizational Change and Work Innovation: A Meta-Analysis of 131 North American Field Experiments—1961–1990." Paper presented at the National Academy of Management Conference; Miami, Florida; August 1991.

APPENDIX A:
THE HISTORICAL
EVOLUTION OF
ORGANIZATIONAL BEHAVIOR

Why study history? Oliver Wendell Holmes answered that question succinctly when he said, "When I want to understand what is happening today or try to decide what will happen tomorrow, I look back." By *looking back* at the history of organizational behavior, you gain a great deal of insight into how the field got to where it is today. It'll help you understand, for instance, how management came to impose rules and regulations on employees, why many workers in organizations do standardized and repetitive tasks on assembly lines, and why a number of organizations in recent years have replaced their assembly lines with team-based work units. In this appendix, you'll find a brief description of how the theory and practice of organizational behavior has evolved.

So where do we start? Human beings and organized activities have been around for thousands of years, but we needn't go back beyond the eighteenth or nineteenth century to find OB's roots.

EARLY PRACTICES

There is no question that hundreds of people helped to plant the "seeds" from which the OB "garden" has grown.[1] Three individuals, however, were particularly important in promoting ideas that would eventually have a major influence in shaping the direction and boundaries of OB. These were Adam Smith, Charles Babbage, and Robert Owen.

Adam Smith

Adam Smith is more typically cited by economists for his contributions to classical economic doctrine, but his discussion in *The Wealth of Nations,*[2] published in 1776, included a brilliant argument on the economic advantages that organizations and society would reap from the division of labor. Smith used the pin-manufacturing industry for his examples. He noted that ten individuals, each doing a specialized task, could produce about forty-eight thousand pins a day among them. He proposed, however, that if each were working separately and independently, the ten workers together would be lucky to make ten pins in one day. If each had to draw the wire, straighten it, cut it, pound heads for each pin, sharpen the point, and solder the head and pin shaft, it would be quite a feat to produce ten pins a day!

Smith concluded that division of labor raised productivity by increasing each worker's skill and dexterity, by saving time that is commonly lost in changing tasks, and by encouraging the creation of laborsaving inventions and machinery. The extensive development of assembly-line production processes during this century has undoubtedly been stimulated by the economic advantages of job specialization cited over two hundred years ago by Adam Smith.

Charles Babbage

Charles Babbage was a British mathematics professor who expanded on the virtues of division of labor first articulated by Adam Smith. In his book *On the Economy of Machinery and Manufactures,*[3] published in 1832, Babbage added to Smith's list of the advantages that accrue from division of labor the following:

1. It reduces the time needed for learning a job.
2. It reduces the waste of material during the learning stage.
3. It allows for the attainment of high skill levels.
4. It allows a more careful matching of people's skills and physical abilities with specific tasks.

Moreover, Babbage proposed that the economies from specialization should be as relevant to doing mental work as physical labor. Today, for example, we take specialization for granted among professionals. When we have a skin rash, we go to a dermatologist. When we buy a home, we consult a lawyer who specializes in real estate. The professors you encounter in your business school classes specialize in areas such as tax accounting, entrepreneurship, consumer behavior, and organizational behavior. These applications of division of labor were unheard of in eighteenth-century England. But contemporary organizations around the world—in both manufacturing and service industries—make wide use of division of labor.

Robert Owen

Robert Owen was a Welsh entrepreneur who bought his first factory in 1789, at the age of eighteen. He is important in the history of OB because he was one of the first industrialists to recognize how the growing factory system was demeaning to workers.

Repulsed by the harsh practices he saw in factories—such as the employment of young children (many under the age of ten), thirteen-hour workdays, and miserable working conditions—Owen became a reformer. He chided factory owners for treating their equipment better than their employees. He said that they would buy the best machines, but then buy the cheapest labor to run them. Owen argued that money spent on improving labor was one of the best investments that business executives could make. He claimed that showing concern for employees both was profitable for management and would relieve human misery.

For his time, Owen was an idealist. What he proposed was a utopian workplace that would reduce the suffering of the working class. He was more than a hundred years ahead of his time when he argued, in 1825, for regulated hours of work for all, child labor laws, public education, company-furnished meals at work, and business involvement in community projects.[4]

THE CLASSICAL ERA

The classical era covered the period from about 1900 to the mid-1930s. It was during this period that the first general theories of management began to evolve. The classical contributors—who include Frederick Taylor, Henri Fayol, Max Weber, Mary Parker Follett, and Chester Barnard—laid the foundation for contemporary management practices.

Scientific Management

The typical United Parcel Service driver today makes 120 stops during his or her work shift. Every step on that driver's daily route has been carefully studied by UPS industrial engineers to maximize efficiency. Every second taken up by stoplights, traffic, detours, doorbells, walkways, stairways, and coffee breaks has been documented by their engineers so as to cut wasted time. It's no accident, for instance, that all UPS drivers tap their horns when they approach a stop in hopes that the customer will hurry to the door seconds sooner. It's also no accident that all UPS drivers walk to a customer's door at the brisk pace of three feet per second and knock first lest seconds be lost searching for the doorbell.

Today's UPS drivers are following principles that were laid down more than eighty years ago by Frederick W. Taylor in his *Principles of Scientific Management.*[5] In this book, Taylor described how the scientific method could be used to define the "one best way" for a job to be done. In this section, we'll review his work.

As a mechanical engineer at the Midvale and Bethlehem Steel companies in Pennsylvania, Taylor was consistently appalled at the inefficiency of workers. Employees used vastly different techniques to do the same job. They were prone to "taking it easy" on the job. Taylor believed that worker output was only about one-third of what was possible. Therefore, he set out to correct the situation by applying the scientific method to jobs on the shop floor. He spent more than two decades pursuing with a passion the "one best way" for each job to be done.

It's important to understand what Taylor saw at Midvale Steel that aroused his determination to improve the way things were done in the plant. At the time, there were no clear concepts of worker and management responsibilities. Virtually no effective work standards existed. Workers purposely worked at a slow pace. Management decisions were of the "seat-of-the-pants" nature, based on hunch and intuition. Workers were placed on jobs with little or no concern for matching their abilities and aptitudes with the tasks they were required to do. Most important, management and workers considered themselves to be in continual conflict. Rather than cooperating to their mutual benefit, they perceived their relationship as a zero-sum game—any gain by one would be at the expense of the other.

Taylor sought to create a mental revolution among both the workers and management by defining clear guidelines for improving production efficiency. He defined four principles of management, listed in Table A–1; he argued that following these principles would result in the prosperity of both management and workers. Workers would earn more pay, and management more profits.

TABLE A–1   Taylor's Four Principles of Management

1. Develop a science for each element of an individual's work. (Previously, workers used the "rule-of-thumb" method.)
2. Scientifically select and then train, teach, and develop the worker. (Previously, workers chose their own work and trained themselves as best they could.)
3. Heartily cooperate with the workers so as to ensure that all work is done in accordance with the principles of the science that has been developed. (Previously, management and workers were in continual conflict.)
4. Divide work and responsibility almost equally between management and workers. Management takes over all work for which it is better fitted than the workers. (Previously, almost all the work and the greater part of the responsibility were thrown upon the workers.)

Probably the most widely cited example of scientific management has been Taylor's pig iron experiment. The average daily output of 92-pound pigs loaded onto rail cars was 12.5 tons per worker. Taylor believed that by scientifically analyzing the job to determine the one best way to load pig iron, the output could be increased to between 47 and 48 tons per day.

Taylor began his experiment by looking for a physically strong subject who placed a high value on the dollar. The individual Taylor chose was a big, strong Dutch immigrant, whom he called Schmidt. Schmidt, like the other loaders, earned $1.15 a day, which even at the turn of the century, was barely enough for a person to survive on. As the following quotation from Taylor's book demonstrates, Taylor used money—the opportunity to make $1.85 a day—as the primary means to get workers like Schmidt to do exactly as they were told:

> "Schmidt, are you a high-priced man?" "Vell, I don't know vat you mean." "Oh, yes you do. What I want to know is whether you are a high-priced man or not." "Vell, I don't know vat you mean." "Oh, come now, you answer my questions. What I want to find out is whether you are a high-priced man or one of these cheap fellows here. What I want to know is whether you want to earn $1.85 a day or whether you are satisfied with $1.15, just the same as all those cheap fellows are getting." "Did I vant $1.85 a day? Vas dot a high-priced man? Vell, yes. I vas a high-priced man."[6]

Using money to motivate Schmidt, Taylor went about having him load the pig irons, alternating various job factors to see what impact the changes had on Schmidt's daily output. For instance, on some days Schmidt would lift the pig irons by bending his knees, whereas on other days he would keep his legs straight and use his back. He experimented with rest periods, walking speed, carrying positions, and other variables. After a long period of scientifically trying various combinations of procedures, techniques, and tools, Taylor succeeded in obtaining the level of productivity he thought possible. By putting the right person on the job with the correct tools and equipment, by having the worker follow his instructions exactly, and by motivating the worker through the economic incentive of a significantly higher daily wage, Taylor was able to reach his forty-eight-ton objective.

Another Taylor experiment dealt with shovel sizes. Taylor noticed that every worker in the plant used the same-size shovel, regardless of the material he was moving. This made no sense to Taylor. If there was an optimum weight that would maximize a worker's shoveling output over an entire day, then Taylor thought the size of the shovel should vary depending on the weight of the material being moved. After extensive experimentation, Taylor found that twenty-one pounds was the optimum shovel capacity. To achieve this optimum weight, heavy material like iron ore would be moved with a small-faced shovel and light material like coke with a large-faced shovel. Based on Taylor's findings, supervisors would no longer merely tell a worker to "shovel that pile over there." Depending on the material to be moved, the supervisor would now have to determine the appropriate shovel size and assign that size to the worker. The result, of course, was again significant increases in worker output.

Using similar approaches in other jobs, Taylor was able to define the one best way for doing each job. He could then, after selecting the right people for the job, train them to do it precisely in this one best way. To motivate workers, he favored incentive wage plans. Overall, Taylor achieved consistent improvements in productivity in the range of two hundred percent or more. He reaffirmed the role of managers to plan and control and that of workers to perform as they were instructed. The *Principles of Scientific Management,* as well as papers that Taylor wrote and presented, spread his ideas not only in the United States, but also in France, Germany, Russia, and Japan. One of the biggest boosts in interest in scientific management in the United States came during a 1910 hearing on railroad rates before the Interstate Commerce Commission. Appearing before the commission, an efficiency expert claimed that railroads could save a million dollars a day (equivalent to about $14 million a day in 1993 dollars) through the application of scientific management! The early acceptance of scientific management techniques by U.S. manufacturing companies, in fact, gave them a comparative advantage over foreign firms that made U.S. manufacturing efficiency the envy of the world—at least for fifty years or so!

Administrative Theory

Administrative theory describes efforts to define the universal functions that managers perform and principles that constitute good management practice. The major contributor to administrative theory was a French industrialist named Henri Fayol.

Writing at about the same time as Taylor, Fayol proposed that all managers perform five management functions: They plan, organize, command, coordinate, and control.[7] The importance of this simple insight is underlined when we acknowledge that almost every introductory management textbook today uses these same five functions, or a very close variant of them, as a basic framework for describing what managers do.

In addition, Fayol described the practice of management as something distinct from accounting, finance, production, distribution, and other typical business functions. He argued that management was an activity common to all human undertakings in business, in government, and even in the home. He then proceeded to state fourteen principles of management that could be taught in schools and universities. These principles are shown in Table A–2.

Structural Theory

While Taylor was concerned with management at the shop level (or what we today would describe as the job of a supervisor) and Fayol focused on general management functions, the German sociologist Max Weber (pronounced *Vayber*) was developing a theory of authority structures and describing organizational activity as based on authority relations.[8] He was one of the first to look at management and organizational behavior from a structural perspective.

TABLE A-2   Fayol's Fourteen Principles of Management

1. *Division of Work.* This principle is the same as Adam Smith's "division of labor." Specialization increases output by making employees more efficient.
2. *Authority.* Managers must be able to give orders. Authority gives them this right. Along with authority, however, goes responsibility. Wherever authority is exercised, responsibility arises.
3. *Discipline.* Employees must obey and respect the rules that govern the organization. Good discipline is the result of effective leadership, a clear understanding between management and workers regarding the organization's rules, and the judicious use of penalties for infractions of the rules.
4. *Unity of Command.* Every employee should receive orders from only *one* superior.
5. *Unity of Direction.* Each group of organizational activities that have the same objective should be directed by one manager using one plan.
6. *Subordination of Individual Interests to the General Interests.* The interests of any one employee or group of employees should not take precedence over the interests of the organization as a whole.
7. *Remuneration.* Workers must be paid a fair wage for their services. 8. *Centralization.* Centralization refers to the degree to which subordinates are involved in decision making. Whether decision making is centralized (to management) or decentralized (to subordinates) is a question of proper proportion. The problem is to find the optimum degree of centralization for each situation.
9. *Scalar Chain.* The line of authority from top management to the lowest ranks represents the scalar chain. Communications should follow this chain. However, if following the chain creates delays, cross-communications can be allowed if agreed to by all parties and superiors are kept informed.
10. *Order.* People and materials should be in the right place at the right time.
11. *Equity.* Managers should be kind and fair to their subordinates.
12. *Stability of Tenure of Personnel.* High employee turnover is inefficient. Management should provide orderly personnel planning and ensure that replacements are available to fill vacancies.
13. *Initiative.* Employees who are allowed to originate and carry out plans will exert high levels of effort.
14. *Esprit de Corps.* Promoting team spirit will build harmony and unity within the organization.

Weber described an ideal type of organization that he called a *bureaucracy*. Bureaucracy was a system characterized by division of labor, a clearly defined hierarchy, detailed rules and regulations, and impersonal relationships. Weber recognized that this "ideal bureaucracy" didn't exist in reality but, rather, represented a selective reconstruction of the real world. He meant it to be taken as a basis for theorizing about work and how work could be done in large groups. His theory became the design prototype for almost all of today's large organizations. The detailed features of Weber's ideal bureaucratic structure are outlined in Table A–3.

"Social Man" Theory

People like Taylor, Fayol, and Weber could be faulted for forgetting that human beings are the central core of every organization and that human

TABLE A-3   Weber's Ideal Bureaucracy

1. *Division of Labor.* Jobs are broken down into simple, routine, and well-defined tasks.
2. *Authority Hierarchy.* Offices or positions are organized in a hierarchy, each lower one being controlled and supervised by a higher one.
3. *Formal Selection.* All organizational members are to be selected on the basis of technical qualifications demonstrated by training, education, or formal examination.
4. *Formal Rules and Regulations.* To ensure uniformity and to regulate the actions of employees, managers must depend heavily on formal organizational rules.
5. *Impersonality.* Rules and controls are applied uniformly, avoiding involvement with personalities and personal preferences of employees.
6. *Career Orientation.* Managers are professional officials rather than owners of the units they manage. They work for fixed salaries and pursue their careers within the organization.

beings are social animals. Mary Parker Follett and Chester Barnard were two theorists who saw the importance of the social aspects of organizations. Their ideas were born late in the scientific management period but didn't achieve any large degree of recognition until the 1930s.[9]

MARY PARKER FOLLETT　　Mary Parker Follett was one of the earliest writers to recognize that organizations could be viewed from the perspective of individual and group behavior.[10] A transitionalist writing during the time when scientific management dominated, Follett was a social philosopher who proposed more people-oriented ideas. Her ideas had clear implications for organizational behavior. Follett thought that organizations should be based on a group ethic rather than individualism. Individual potential, she argued, remained only potential until released through group association. The manager's job was to harmonize and coordinate group efforts. Managers and workers should view themselves as partners—as part of a common group. Therefore, managers should rely more on their expertise and knowledge than on the formal authority of their position to lead subordinates.

Follett's humanistic ideas have influenced the way we look at motivation, leadership, power, and authority today. In fact, Japanese organization and management styles, which have been in vogue in North America for the past decade, are indebted to Follett. They place a heavy emphasis on group togetherness and team effort.

CHESTER BARNARD　　Like Henri Fayol, Chester Barnard was a practitioner. He joined the American Telephone and Telegraph system in 1909 and became president of New Jersey Bell in 1927. Barnard had read Weber and was influenced by his writings. But unlike Weber, who had a mechanistic and impersonal view of organizations, Barnard saw organizations as social systems that require human cooperation. He expressed his views in *The Functions of the Executive*,[11] published in 1938.

Barnard viewed organizations as made up of people who have interacting social relationships. Managers' major roles were to communicate and to stimulate subordinates to high levels of effort. A major part of an organization's success, as Barnard saw it, depended on obtaining cooperation from its personnel. Barnard also argued that success depended on maintaining good relations with people and institutions outside the organization with whom the organization regularly interacted. By recognizing the organization's dependence on investors, suppliers, customers, and other external constituencies, Barnard introduced the idea that managers had to examine the environment and then adjust the organization to maintain a state of equilibrium. So, for instance, regardless of how efficient an organization's production might be, if management failed to ensure a continuous input of materials and supplies or to find markets for its outputs, then the organization's survival would be threatened. Much of the current interest in how the environment affects organizations and their employees can be traced to ideas initially suggested by Barnard.

THE BEHAVIORAL ERA

The "people side" of organizations came into its own during the period we'll call the behavioral era. As we'll show, this era was marked by the human relations movement and the widespread application in organizations of behavioral science research. While this behavioral era really didn't begin to roll until the 1930s, two earlier events deserve brief mention because they played an important part in the application and development of organizational behavior. These are the birth of the "personnel office" around the turn of the century and the creation of the field of industrial psychology with the publication of Hugo Münsterberg's textbook in 1913.

The Birth of the "Personnel Office"

In response to the growth of trade unionism at the turn of the century, a few firms—for example, H. J. Heinz, Colorado Fuel & Iron, and International Harvester—created the position of "welfare secretary." Welfare secretaries were supposed to assist workers by suggesting improvements in working conditions, housing, medical care, educational facilities, and recreation. These people, who were the forerunners of today's personnel or human resource management directors, acted as a buffer between the organization and its employees. The B. F. Goodrich Co. developed the first employment department in 1900, but its responsibilities consisted only of hiring. In 1902, the National Cash Register Company established the first comprehensive labor department responsible for wage administration, grievances, employment and working conditions, health conditions, record-keeping, and worker improvement.

The Birth of Industrial Psychology

Hugo Münsterberg created the field of industrial psychology with the publication of his text *Psychology and Industrial Efficiency*[12] in 1913. In it, he argued for the scientific study of human behavior to identify general patterns and to explain individual differences. Interestingly, Münsterberg saw a link between scientific management and industrial psychology. Both sought increased efficiency through scientific work analyses and through better alignment of individual skills and abilities with the demands of various jobs.

Münsterberg suggested the use of psychological tests to improve employee selection, the value of learning theory in the development of training methods, and the study of human behavior in order to understand what techniques are most effective for motivating workers. Much of our current knowledge of selection techniques, employee training, job design, and motivation is built on Münsterberg's work.

The Magna Carta of Labor

Following the stock market crash of 1929, the United States and much of the world's economy entered the Great Depression. To help relieve the effects of the Depression on the U.S. labor force, President Franklin Roosevelt supported the Wagner Act, which was passed in 1935. This act recognized unions as the authorized representatives of workers, able to bargain collectively with employers in the interests of their members. The Wagner Act would prove to be the Magna Carta of labor. It legitimized the role of trade unions and encouraged rapid growth in union membership. In response to this legislation, managers in industry became much more open to finding new ways to handle their employees. Having lost the battle to keep unions out of their factories, management began to try to improve working conditions and seek better relations with their work force. A set of studies done at Western Electric's Hawthorne plant would be the prime stimulus for the human relations movement that swept American industry from the late 1930s through the 1950s.

Human Relations

The essence of the human relations movement was the belief that the key to higher productivity in organizations was increasing employee satisfaction. In addition to the Hawthorne studies, three people played important roles in conveying the message of human relations. These were Dale Carnegie, Abraham Maslow, and Douglas McGregor. In this section, we'll briefly review each man's contribution. But first, we'll briefly describe the very influential Hawthorne studies.

THE HAWTHORNE STUDIES   Without question, the most important contribution to the human relations movement within organizational behavior came out of the Hawthorne studies undertaken at the Western Electric Company's Hawthorne Works in Cicero, Illinois. These studies, originally begun in 1924 but eventually expanded and carried on through the early 1930s, were initially devised by Western Electric industrial engineers to examine the effect of various illumination levels on worker productivity. Control and experimental groups were established. The experimental group was presented with varying illumination intensities, while the control group worked under a constant intensity. The engineers had expected individual output to be directly related to the intensity of light. However, they found that as the light level was increased in the experimental group, output for both groups rose. To the surprise of the engineers, as the light level was dropped in the experimental group, productivity continued to increase in both groups. In fact, a productivity decrease was observed in the experimental group only when the light intensity had been reduced to that of moonlight. The engineers concluded that illumination intensity was not directly related to group productivity, but they could not explain the behavior they had witnessed.

The Western Electric engineers asked Harvard professor Elton Mayo and his associates in 1927 to join the study as consultants. Thus began a relationship that would last through 1932 and encompass numerous experiments covering the redesign of jobs, changes in the length of the workday and workweek, introduction of rest periods, and individual versus group wage plans.[13] For example, one experiment was designed to evaluate the effect of a group piecework incentive pay system on group productivity. The results indicated that the incentive plan had less effect on a worker's output than did group pressure and acceptance and the concomitant security. Social norms or standards of the group, therefore, were concluded to be the key determinants of individual work behavior.

Scholars generally agree that the Hawthorne studies had a large and dramatic impact on the direction of organizational behavior and management practice. Mayo's conclusions were that behavior and sentiments were closely related, that group influences significantly affected individual behavior, that group standards established individual worker output, and that money was less a factor in determining output than were group standards, group sentiments, and security. These conclusions led to a new emphasis on the human factor in the functioning of organizations and the attainment of their goals. They also led to increased paternalism by management.

The Hawthorne studies have not been without critics. Attacks have been made on their procedures, analyses of findings, and the conclusions they drew.[14] However, from a historical standpoint, it is of little importance whether the studies were academically sound or their conclusions justified. What is important is that they stimulated an interest in human factors.

DALE CARNEGIE   Dale Carnegie's book *How to Win Friends and Influence People*[15] was read by millions during the 1930s, 1940s, and 1950s. During this same period, tens of thousands of managers and aspiring managers attended his management speeches and seminars. So Carnegie's ideas deserve attention because of the wide audience they commanded.

Carnegie's essential theme was that the way to success was through winning the cooperation of others. He advised his audience to: (1) make others feel important through a sincere appreciation of their efforts; (2) strive to make a good first impression; (3) win people to your way of thinking by letting others do the talking, being sympathetic, and "never telling a man he is wrong"; and (4) change people by praising their good traits and giving the offender the opportunity to save face.[16]

ABRAHAM MASLOW   Few students of college age have not been exposed to the ideas of Abraham Maslow. A humanistic psychologist, Maslow proposed a theoretical hierarchy of five needs: physiological, safety, social, esteem, and self-actualization.[17] From a motivation standpoint, Maslow argued that each step in the hierarchy must be satisfied before the next can be activated, and that once a need was substantially satisfied, it no longer motivated behavior. Moreover, he believed that self-actualization—that is, achieving one's full potential—was the summit of a human being's existence. Managers who accepted Maslow's hierarchy attempted to alter their organizations and management practices to reduce barriers to employees' self-actualization.

DOUGLAS MCGREGOR   Douglas McGregor is best known for his formulation of two sets of assumptions—Theory X and Theory Y—about human nature.[18] Briefly, Theory X rests on an essentially negative view of people. It assumes that they have little ambition, dislike work, want to avoid responsibility, and need to be closely directed to work effectively. Theory Y, on the other hand, rests on a positive view of people. It assumes they can exercise self-direction, accept responsibility, and consider work to be as natural as rest or play. McGregor personally believed that Theory Y assumptions best captured the true nature of workers and should guide management practice. As a result, he argued that managers should free up their employees to unleash their full creative and productive potential.

Behavioral Science Theorists

The final category within the behavioral era encompasses a group of researchers who, as Taylor did in scientific management, relied on the scientific method for the study of organizational behavior. Unlike members of the human relations movement, the behavioral science theorists engaged in *objective* research of human behavior in organizations. They carefully attempted to keep their personal beliefs out of their work. They sought to develop rigorous research designs that could be replicated by other behavioral scientists in the hope that a science of organizational behavior could be built.

A full review of the contributions made by behavioral science theorists would cover hundreds of pages, since their work makes up a large part of today's foundations of organizational behavior. But to give you the flavor of their work, we'll briefly summarize the contributions of a few of the major theorists.

JACOB MORENO   Jacob Moreno created an analytical technique called *sociometry* for studying group interactions.[19] Members of a group were asked whom they liked or disliked, and whom they wished to work with or not work with. From these data, collected in interviews, Moreno was able to construct sociograms that identified attraction, repulsion, and indifference patterns among group members. Moreno's sociometric analysis has been used in organizations to create cohesive and high-performing work groups.

B. F. SKINNER Few behavioral scientists' names are more familiar to the general public than that of B. F. Skinner. His research on operant conditioning and behavior modification had a significant effect on the design of organizational training programs and reward systems.[20]

Essentially, Skinner demonstrated that behavior is a function of its consequences. He found that people will most likely engage in desired behavior if they are rewarded for doing so; these rewards are most effective if they immediately follow the desired response; and behavior that is not rewarded, or is punished, is less likely to be repeated.

DAVID McCLELLAND Harvard psychologist David McClelland tested the strength of individual achievement motivation by asking subjects to look at a set of somewhat ambiguous pictures and to write their own story about each picture. Based on these projective tests, McClelland found he was able to differentiate people with a high need to achieve—individuals who had a strong desire to succeed or achieve in relation to a set of standards—from people with a low need to achieve.[21] His research has been instrumental in helping organizations better match people with jobs and in redesigning jobs for high achievers so as to maximize their motivation potential. In addition, McClelland and his associates have successfully trained individuals to increase their achievement drive. For instance, in India, people who underwent achievement training worked longer hours, initiated more new business ventures, made greater investments in productive assets, employed a larger number of employees, and saw a greater increase in their gross incomes than did a similar group who did not undergo achievement training.

FRED FIEDLER Leadership is one of the most important and extensively researched topics in organizational behavior. The work of Fred Fiedler on the subject is significant for its emphasis on the situational aspects of leadership as well as for its attempt to develop a comprehensive theory of leadership behavior.[22]

From the mid-1960s through the late-1970s, Fiedler's contingency model dominated leadership research. He developed a questionnaire to measure an individual's inherent leadership orientation and identified three contingency variables that, he argued, determined what type of leader behavior is most effective. In testing his model, Fiedler and his associates studied hundreds of groups. Dozens of researchers have attempted to replicate his results. Although some of the predictions from the model have not stood up well under closer analysis, Fielder's model has been a major influence on current thinking and research on leadership.

FREDERICK HERZBERG With the possible exception of the Hawthorne Studies, no single stream of research has had a greater impact on undermining the recommendations of scientific management than the work of Frederick Herzberg.[23]

Herzberg sought an answer to the question: What do individuals want from their jobs? He asked hundreds of people that question in the late 1950s, and then carefully analyzed their responses. He concluded that people preferred jobs that offered opportunities for recognition, achievement, responsibility, and growth. Managers who concerned themselves with things like company policies, employee pay, creating narrow and repetitive jobs, and developing favorable working conditions might placate their workers, but they wouldn't motivate them. According to Herzberg, if managers want to motivate their people, they should redesign jobs to allow workers to perform more and varied tasks. Much of the current interest in enriching jobs and improving the quality of work life can be traced to Herzberg's research.

J. RICHARD HACKMAN AND GREG OLDHAM   While Herzberg's conclusions were greeted with enthusiasm, the methodology he used for arriving at those conclusions was far less enthusiastically embraced. It would be the work of J. Richard Hackman and Greg Oldham in the 1970s that would provide an explanation of how job factors influence employee motivation and satisfaction, and would offer a valid framework for analyzing jobs.[24] Hackman and Oldham's research also uncovered the core job dimensions— skill variety, task identity, task significance, autonomy, and feedback—that have stood up well as guides in the design of jobs. More specifically, Hackman and Oldham found that among individuals with strong growth needs, jobs that score high on these five core dimensions lead to high employee performance and satisfaction.

OB TODAY: A CONTINGENCY PERSPECTIVE

We've attempted to demonstrate in this appendix that the present state of organizational behavior encompasses ideas introduced dozens, and sometimes hundreds, of years ago. So don't think of one era's concepts as *replacing* an earlier era's; rather, view them as *extensions* and *modifications* of earlier ideas. As United Parcel Service demonstrates, many of Taylor's scientific management principles can be applied today with impressive results. Of course, that doesn't mean that those principles will work as well in other organizations. If there is anything we've learned over the last quarter of a century, it's that few ideas—no matter how attractive—are applicable to *all* organizations or to *all* jobs or to *all* types of employees. In the 1990s, organizational behavior must be studied and applied in a contingency framework.

Baseball fans know that a batter doesn't *always* try for a home run. It depends on the score, the inning, whether runners are on base, and similar *contingency* variables. Similarly, you can't say that students always learn more in small classes than in large ones. An extensive body of research tells us that *contingency* factors such as course content and teaching style of the instructor influence the relationship between class size and learning effectiveness. Applied to organizational behavior, contingency theory recognizes that there is no "one best way" to manage people in organizations and no single set of simple principles that can be applied universally.[25]

A contingency approach to the study of OB is intuitively logical. Why? Because organizations obviously differ in size, objectives, and environmental uncertainty. Similarly, employees differ in values, attitudes, needs, and experiences. So it would be surprising to find that there are universally applicable principles that work in *all* situations. But, of course, it is one thing to say "it all depends" and another to say *what* it all depends upon.

The most popular OB topics for research investigation in recent years have been theories of motivation, leadership, job design, and job satisfaction.[26] But while the 1960s and 1970s saw the development of new theories, the emphasis since has been on refining existing theories, clarifying previous assumptions, and identifying relevant contingency variables.[27]

That is, researchers have been trying to identify the "what" variables and which ones are relevant for understanding various behavioral phenomena. This essentially reflects the maturing of OB as a scientific discipline. The near-term future of OB research is likely to continue to focus on fine-tuning current theories so as to better help us understand those situations where they are most likely to be useful.

SUMMARY

While the seeds of organizational behavior were planted more than two hundred years ago, current OB theory and practice are essentially products of the twentieth century.

Frederick Taylor's principles of scientific management were instrumental in engineering precision and standardization into people's jobs. Henri Fayol defined the universal functions that all managers perform and the principles that constitute good management practice. Max Weber developed a theory of authority structures and described organizational activity based on authority relations.

The "people side" of organizations came into its own in the 1930s, predominately as a result of the Hawthorne studies. These studies led to a new emphasis on the human factor in organizations and increased paternalism by management. In the late 1950s, managers' attention was caught by the ideas of people like Abraham Maslow and Douglas McGregor, who proposed that organization structures and management practices had to be altered so as to bring out the full productive potential of employees. Motivation and leadership theories offered by David McClelland, Fred Fiedler, Frederick Herzberg, and other behavioral scientists during the 1960s and 1970s provided managers with still greater insights into employee behavior.

Almost all contemporary management and organizational behavior concepts are contingency based. That is, they provide various recommendations dependent upon situational factors. As a maturing discipline, current OB research is emphasizing the refinement of existing theories.

NOTES

[1]See, for instance, D. A. Wren, *The Evolution of Management Thought,* 3rd ed. (New York: John Wiley & Sons, 1987), especially Chapters 4, 9, 13–15, 17, and 20.

[2]A. Smith, *An Inquiry into the Nature and Causes of the Wealth of Nations* (New York: Modern Library, 1937; orig. pub. 1776).

[3]C. Babbage, *On the Economy of Machinery and Manufactures* (London: Charles Knight, 1832).

[4]R. A. Owen, *A New View of Society* (New York: E. Bliss & White, 1825).

[5]F. W. Taylor, *Principles of Scientific Management* (New York: Harper & Brothers, 1911).

[6]Ibid., p. 44.

[7]H. Fayol, *Industrial and General Administration* (Paris: Dunod, 1916).

[8]M. Weber, *The Theory of Social and Economic Organizations,* ed. T. Parsons, trans. A. M. Henderson and T. Parsons (New York: Free Press, 1947).

[9]Wren, *The Evolution of Management Thought,* p. 234.

[10]See, for example, M. P. Follett, *The New State: Group Organization the Solution of Popular Government* (London: Longmans, Green & Co., 1918).

[11]C. I. Barnard, *The Functions of the Executive* (Cambridge, MA: Harvard University Press, 1938).

[12]H. Münsterberg, *Psychology and Industrial Efficiency* (Boston: Houghton Mifflin, 1913).

[13]E. Mayo, *The Human Problems of an Industrial Civilization* (New York: Macmillan, 1933); and F. J. Roethlisberger and W. J. Dickson, *Management and the Worker* (Cambridge, MA: Harvard University Press, 1939).

[14]See, for example, A. Carey, "The Hawthorne Studies: A Radical Criticism," *American Sociological Review,* June 1967, pp. 403–16; R. H. Franke and J. Kaul, "The Hawthorne Experiments: First Statistical Interpretations," *American Sociological Review,* October 1978, pp. 623–43; B. Rice, "The Hawthorne Defect: Persistence of a Flawed Theory," *Psychology Today,* February 1982, pp. 70–74; and J. A. Sonnenfeld, "Shedding Light on the Hawthorne Studies," *Journal of Occupational Behavior,* April 1985, pp. 111–30.

[15]D. Carnegie, *How to Win Friends and Influence People* (New York: Simon & Schuster, 1936).

[16]Wren, *The Evolution of Management Thought,* p. 422.

[17]A. Maslow, *Motivation and Personality* (New York: Harper & Row, 1954).

[18]D. McGregor, *The Human Side of Enterprise* (New York: McGraw-Hill, 1960).

[19]J. L. Moreno, "Contributions of Sociometry to Research Methodology in Sociology," *American Sociological Review,* June 1947, pp. 287–92.

[20]See, for instance, B. F. Skinner, *Science and Human Behavior* (New York: Free Press, 1953); and B. F. Skinner, *Beyond Freedom and Dignity* (New York: Knopf, 1972).

[21]D. C. McClelland, *The Achieving Society* (New York: Van Nostrand Reinhold, 1961); and D. C. McClelland and D. G. Winter, *Motivating Economic Achievement* (New York: Free Press, 1969).

[22]F. E. Fiedler, *A Theory of Leadership Effectiveness* (New York: McGraw-Hill, 1967).

[23]F. Herzberg, B. Mausner, and B. Snyderman, *The Motivation to Work* (New York, John Wiley, 1959); and F. Herzberg, *The Managerial Choice: To Be Efficient or to Be Human,* rev. ed (Salt Lake City: Olympus, 1982).

[24]J. R. Hackman and G. R. Oldham, "Development of the Job Diagnostic Survey," *Journal of Applied Psychology,* April 1975, pp. 159–70.

[25]See, for instance, J. M. Shepard and J. G. Hougland, Jr., "Contingency Theory: 'Complex Man' or 'Complex Organization'?", *Academy of Management Review,* July 1978, pp. 413–27; and H. L. Tosi, Jr., and J. W. Slocum, Jr., "Contingency Theory: Some Suggested Directions," *Journal of Management,* Spring 1984, pp. 9–26.

[26]C. A. O'Reilly III, "Organizational Behavior: Where We've Been, Where We're Going," in M. R. Rosenzweig and L. W. Porter (eds.), *Annual Review of Psychology,* Vol. 42 (Palo Alto, CA: Annual Reviews, Inc., 1991), pp. 429–30.

[27]Ibid., pp. 427–58.

APPENDIX B: SCORING KEYS FOR EXERCISES

Exercise 1–A. What Do You Know About Human Behavior?

The correct answers to this exercise are as follows:

1. T	**6.** F	**11.** F	**16.** T
2. F	**7.** T	**12.** T	**17.** T
3. F	**8.** F	**13.** F	**18.** F
4. F	**9.** F	**14.** F	**19.** F
5. F.	**10.** T	**15.** F	**20.** F

How well did you do? Most people get between twelve and sixteen right. Did you beat the average?

The value of this exercise is to dramatize that some of what you "know" about human behavior is erroneous. The systematic study of OB will help you to sort out fact from fiction regarding the behavior of people at work.

Exercise 4–A. Who Controls Your Life?

This exercise is designed to measure your locus of control. Give yourself 1 point for each of the following selections: 1B, 2A, 3A, 4B, 5B, 6A, 7A, 8A, 9B, and 10A. Scores can be interpreted as follows:

8–10 = High internal locus of control

6–7 = Moderate internal locus of control

5 = Mixed

3–4 = Moderate external locus of control

1–2 = High external locus of control

The higher your internal score, the more you believe that you control your own destiny. The higher your external score, the more you believe that what happens to you in your life is due to luck or chance.

Exercise 4–B. How Self-Monitoring Are You?

To obtain your total score, add up the numbers circled, except reverse scores for questions 9 and 12. On those, a circled 5 becomes a 0, 4 becomes 1, and so forth.

This test is designed to tap your self-monitoring score. High self-monitors (these are scores of approximately 53 or higher) are particularly sensitive to other people and alter their responses to others' cues. In other words, high self-monitors are more flexibile and responsive to their environment than low self-monitors are. The lower your score, the greater your rigidity. High self-monitors can be expected to demonstrate greater flexibility in adapting their leadership style to changing situations, using a variety of conflict-resolution techniques and the like.

Exercise 5–B. Decision-Making Style Questionnaire

Mark each of your responses on the following scales. Then use the point value column to arrive at your score. For example, if you answered *a* to the first question, you would check *1a* in the feeling column.

This response receives zero points when you add up the point value column. Instructions for classifying your scores are indicated below the scales.

Sensation	Point Value	Intuition	Point Value	Thinking	Point Value	Feeling	Point Value
2 b ___	1	2 a ___	2	1 b ___	1	1 a ___	0
4 a ___	1	4 b ___	1	3 b ___	2	3 a ___	1
5 a ___	1	5 b ___	1	7 b ___	1	7 a ___	1
6 b ___	1	6 a ___	0	8 a ___	0	8 b ___	1
9 b ___	2	9 a ___	2	10 b ___	2	10 a ___	1
12 a ___	1	12 b ___	0	11 a ___	2	11 b ___	1
15 a ___	1	15 b ___	1	13 b ___	1	13 a ___	1
16 b ___	2	16 a ___	0	14 b ___	0	14 a ___	1
Maximum Point Value	(10)		(7)		(9)		(7)

Write *intuition* if your intuition score is equal to or greater than your sensation score. Write *sensation* if your sensation score is greater than your intuition score. Write *feeling* if your feeling score is greater than your thinking score. Write *thinking* if your thinking score is greater than your feeling score.

A high score on *intuition* indicates you see the world in holistic terms. You tend to be creative. A high score on *sensation* indicates that you are realistic and see the world in terms of facts. A high score on *feeling* means you make decisions based on gut feeling. A high score on *thinking* indicates a highly logical and analytical approach to decision making.

Exercise 7–A. What Motivates You?

To determine your dominant needs—and what motivates you—place the number 1 through 5 that represents your score for each statement next to the number for that statement.

	Achievement	Power	Affiliation
	1. ___	2. ___	3. ___
	4. ___	5. ___	6. ___
	7. ___	8. ___	9. ___
	10. ___	11. ___	12. ___
	13. ___	14. ___	15. ___
Totals:	___	___	___

Add up the total of each column. The sum of the numbers in each column will be between 5 and 25 points. The column with the highest score tells you your dominant need.

Exercise 7–B. How Equity-Sensitive Are You?

Sum up the points you allocated to the following items: 1B; 2A; 3B; 4A; and 5B. Your total will be between zero and fifty.

Researchers have identified three equity sensitivity groups. They are labeled and defined as follows:

- Benevolents—Individuals who prefer that their outcome/input ratios be less than the comparison others.
- Equity Sensitives—Individuals who prefer outcome/input ratios to be equal.
- Entitleds—Individuals who prefer that their outcome/input ratios exceed those of the comparison others.

Based on data from more than 3500 respondents, the researchers have found that scores less than twenty-nine are classified as Entitleds; those between twenty-nine and thirty-two are Equity Sensitives; and those with scores above thirty-two are Benevolents.

What does all this mean? First, not all individuals are equity sensitive. Second, equity theory predictions are most accurate with individuals in the Equity Sensitive group. And third, Benevolents actually prefer lower outcome/input ratios and tend to provide higher levels of inputs than either Equity Sensitives or Entitleds.

Exercise 11–B. Compute Your LPC Score

Your score on the LPC scale is a measure of your leadership style. More specifically, it indicates your primary motivation or goal in a work setting.

To determine your LPC score, add up the points (1 through 8) for each of the sixteen items. If your score is sixty-four or above, you're a *high* LPC person or *relationship*-oriented. If your score is fifty-seven or below, you're a *low* LPC person or *task*-oriented. If your score falls between fifty-eight and sixty-three, you'll need to determine for yourself in which category you belong.

According to Fiedler, knowing your LPC score can allow you to find a situational match and, therefore, help you to be a more effective leader.

Exercise 12–A. Power Orientation Test

This test is designed to compute your Machiavellianism (Mach) score. To obtain your score, add the number you have checked on questions 1, 3, 4, 5, 9, and 10. For the other four questions, reverse the numbers you have checked: 5 becomes 1, 4 is 2, 2 is 4, 1 is 5. Total your ten numbers to find your score. The National Opinion Research Center, which used this short form of the scale in a random sample of American adults, found that the national average was 25.

The results of research using the Mach test have found that (1) men are generally more Machiavellian than women; (2) older adults tend to have lower Mach scores than younger adults; (3) there is no significant difference between high-Machs and low-Machs on measures of intelligence or ability; (4) Machiavellianism is not significantly related to demographic characteristics such as educational level or marital status; and (5) high-Machs tend to be in professions that emphasize the control and manipulation of individuals—for example, managers, lawyers, psychiatrists, and behavioral scientists.

Exercise 12–B. How Political Are You?

Give yourself a +1 for each answer you gave in agreement with the keyed answer. Note that we did not use the term *correct* answer. Whether an answer is correct is a question of personal values and ethics. Each question that receives a score of +1 shows a tendency toward playing office politics or grabbing power. The scoring key is as follows:

1	Mostly true	**11**	Mostly false
2	Mostly true	**12**	Mostly false
3	Mostly false	**13**	Mostly true
4	Mostly true	**14**	Mostly true
5	Mostly true	**15**	Mostly false
6	Mostly false	**16**	Mostly true
7	Mostly false	**17**	Mostly true
8	Mostly true	**18**	Mostly true
9	Mostly true	**19**	Mostly true
10	Mostly true	**20**	Mostly true

Your score provides a rough index of your overall tendencies toward craving for power and being an office politician. The higher your score, the more political you are likely to be in your dealings at work. The lower your score, the less you are inclined toward politicking.

According to the author of this questionnaire, scores of 14 or above indicate that you are a pretty shrewd politician. Scores of 10 to 13 indicate that you probably practice enough politics to keep you out of trouble with your boss and other people of higher rank. Scores of 6 to 9 indicate that you believe most people are honest, hardworking, and trustworthy. You may overlook some important career advancement tactics. Scores of 5 or less indicate you're politically naive. Unless you have extraordinary talents, you will find it hard to move up in the organization.

Exercise 13–A. What Is Your Primary Conflict-Handling Intention?

To determine your primary conflict-handling intention, place the number 1 through 5 that represents your score for each statement next to the number for that statement. Then total up the columns.

	Competing	Collaborating	Avoiding	Accommodating	Compromising
	1. ___	4. ___	6. ___	3. ___	2. ___
	5. ___	9. ___	10. ___	11. ___	8. ___
	7. ___	12. ___	15. ___	14. ___	13. ___
Totals:	___	___	___	___	___

Your primary conflict-handling intention is the category with the highest total. Your fall-back intention is the category with the second-highest total.

Exercise 15–A. Bureaucratic Orientation Test

Give yourself one point for each statement for which you responded in the bureaucratic direction:

1. Mostly agree	**11.** Mostly agree
2. Mostly agree	**12.** Mostly disagree
3. Mostly disagree	**13.** Mostly disagree
4. Mostly agree	**14.** Mostly agree
5. Mostly disagree	**15.** Mostly disagree
6. Mostly disagree	**16.** Mostly agree
7. Mostly agree	**17.** Mostly disagree
8. Mostly agree	**18.** Mostly agree
9. Mostly disagree	**19.** Mostly agree
10. Mostly agree	**20.** Mostly disagree

A very high score (15 or over) suggests that you would enjoy working in a bureaucracy. A very low score (5 or lower) suggests that you would be frustrated by working in a bureaucracy, especially a large one.

Do you think your score is representative of most college students in your major? Discuss.

Exercise 16–A. Career Assessment Test

This instrument is an expanded version of Schein's five career anchors. It adds service, identity, and variety anchors. Score your responses by writing the number that corresponds to your response (SA = 4, A = 3, D = 2, SD = 1) to each question in the space next to the item number.

1 ___	2 ___	3 ___	4 ___	5 ___	6 ___
7 ___	8 ___	9 ___	10 ___	11 ___	12 ___
13 ___	14 ___	15 ___	16 ___	17 ___	18 ___
19 ___	20 ___	21 ___	22 ___	23 ___	24 ___
25 ___	26 ___	27 ___	28 ___	29 ___	30 ___
31 ___	32 ___	33 ___	34 ___	35 ___	36 ___
37 ___	38 ___	39 ___	40 ___	41 ___	42 ___
43 ___	44 ___				

Now obtain subscale scores by adding your scores on the items indicated and then divide by the number of items in the scale, as shown:

Technical Competence	_____	÷ 6 = _____
	#1, 2, 27, 35, 38, 41	
Autonomy	_____	÷ 6 = _____
	#3, 18, 23, 36, 39, 40	
Service	_____	÷ 6 = _____
	#4, 21, 37, 42, 43, 44	
Identity	_____	÷ 5 = _____
	#7, 13, 20, 22, 26	
Variety	_____	÷ 6 = _____
	#5, 12, 14, 24, 31, 32	
Managerial Competence	_____	÷ 6 = _____
	#6, 10, 11, 15, 25, 30	
Security	_____	÷ 5 = _____
	#8, 16, 17, 28, 33	
Creativity	_____	÷ 4 = _____
	#9, 19, 29, 34	

Briefly, the eight career anchors mean the following:

- *Technical competence.* You organize your career around the challenge of the actual work you're doing.
- *Autonomy.* You value freedom and independence.
- *Service.* You're concerned with helping others or working on an important cause.
- *Identity.* You're concerned with status, prestige, and titles in your work.
- *Variety.* You seek an endless variety of new and different challenges.
- *Managerial competence.* You like to solve problems and want to lead and control others.
- *Security.* You want stability and career security.
- *Creativity.* You have a strong need to create something of your own.

The higher your score on a given anchor, the stronger your emphasis. You'll function best when your job fits with your career anchor. Lack of fit between anchor and a job can cause you to leave the organization or suffer excessive stress.

Ask yourself now: On which anchor did I receive the highest score? What jobs fit best with this anchor? You can use your analysis to help you select the right job and career for you.

Exercise 17–A. What Kind of Organizational Culture Fits You Best?

For items 5, 6, 7, 8, and 9, score as follows:

$$
\begin{aligned}
\text{Strongly agree} &= +2 \\
\text{Agree} &= +1 \\
\text{Uncertain} &= 0 \\
\text{Disagree} &= -1 \\
\text{Strongly disagree} &= -2
\end{aligned}
$$

For items 1, 2, 3, 4, and 10, reverse the score (Strongly agree = −2, and so on). Add up your total. Your score will fall somewhere between +20 and -20.

What does your score mean? The higher your score (positive), the more comfortable you'll be in a formal, mechanistic, rule-oriented, and structured culture. This is synonymous with large corporations and government agencies. Negative scores indicate a preference for informal, humanistic, flexible, and innovative cultures, which are more likely to be found in research units, advertising firms, high-tech companies, and small businesses.

Exercise 17–B. Rate Your Classroom Culture

Add up your score for all the statements except number eight. For number eight, reverse the score (strongly agree = 1; strongly disagree = 5) and add it to your total. Your score will fall between ten and fifty.

A high score (thirty-seven or above) describes an open, warm, human, trusting, and supportive culture. A low score (twenty-five or below) describes a closed, cold, task-oriented, autocratic, and tense culture.

Compare your score against the ones tabulated by your classmates. How close do they align? Discuss perceived discrepancies.

Exercise 18–A. The Social Readjustment Rating Scale

According to the research, the higher your score (the more changes in your life in the past year), the more likely you are to experience a significant illness sometime soon.

If your score is below 150 points, statistically you have a thirty percent chance of experiencing a significant health problem in the near future. If your score is between 150 and 300 points, you have a fifty percent chance of getting sick, and if you totaled more than 300 points, you have an eighty percent chance of coming down with something "significant" soon.

Exercise 18–B. The Type A–Type B Group Exercise

To calculate your Type A—Type B rating, total your score on the seven questions. Now multiply it by 3. A total of 120 or more indicates you're a hard-core Type A. Scores below 90 indicate you're a hard-core Type B. The following gives you more specifics:

Points	Personality Type
120 or more	A+
106—-119	A
100—-105	A–
90—-99	B+
Less than 90	B

Exercise 19–A. Managing-in-a-Turbulent-World Tolerance Test

Score 4 points for each A, 3 for each B, 2 for each C, 1 for each D, and 0 for each E. Compute the total, divide by 24, and round to one decimal place.

While the results are not intended to be more than suggestive, the higher your score, the more comfortable you seem to be with change. The test's author suggests analyzing scores as if they were grade-point averages. In this way, a 4.0 average is an A, a 2.0 is a C, and scores below 1.0 flunk.

Using replies from nearly 500 M.B.A. students and young managers, the range of scores was found to be narrow—between 1.0 and 2.2. The average score was between 1.5 and 1.6—equivalent to a D+/C- grade! If these scores are generalizable to the work population, clearly people are not very tolerant of the kind of changes that come with a turbulent environment.

GLOSSARY

The number in parentheses following each term indicates the chapter in which the term was defined.

Ability (4)   An individual's capacity to perform the various tasks in a job.

Absenteeism (2)   Failure to report to work.

Accommodating (13)   The willingness of one party in a conflict to place the opponent's interests above his or her own.

Achievement need (7)   The drive to excel, to achieve in relation to a set of standards, to strive to succeed.

Action research (19)   A change process based on systematic collection of data and then selection of a change action based on what the analyzed data indicate.

Active listening (10)   Listening with intensity, empathy, acceptance, and a willingness to take responsibility for completeness.

Adhocracy (15)   A structure characterized as low in complexity, formalization, and centralization.

Adjourning (9)   The final stage in group development for temporary groups, characterized by concern with wrapping up activities rather than task performance.

Affective component of an attitude (6)   The emotional or feeling segment of an attitude.

Affiliation need (7)   The desire for friendly and close interpersonal relationships.

Arbitrator (13)   A third party to a negotiation who has the authority to dictate an agreement.

Assessment centers (16)   A set of performance simulation tests designed to evaluate a candidate's managerial potential.

Attitudes (6)   Evaluative statements or judgments concerning objects, people, or events.

Attitude surveys (6)   Eliciting responses from employees through questionnaires about how they feel about their jobs, work groups, supervisors, and/or the organization.

Attribution theory (5)   When individuals observe behavior, they attempt to determine whether it is internally or externally caused.

Attribution theory of leadership (11)   Proposes that leadership is merely an attribution that people make about other individuals.

Authoritarianism (4)   The belief that there should be status and power differences among people in organizations.

Authority (14)   The rights inherent in a managerial position to give orders and expect the orders to be obeyed.

Autonomy (7)   The degree to which the job provides substantial freedom and discretion to the individual in scheduling the work and in determining the procedures to be used in carrying it out.

Avoiding (13)   The desire to withdraw from or suppress a conflict.

Bases of power (12)   What powerholders control that allows them to manipulate the behavior of others.

Behavioral component of an attitude (6)   An intention to behave in a certain way toward someone or something.

Behavioral symptoms of stress (18)   Changes in an individuals' behavior—including productivity, absence, and turnover—as a result of stress.

Behavioral theories of leadership (11)   Theories proposing that specific behaviors differentiate leaders from nonleaders.

Behaviorally anchored rating scales (16)   An evaluation method where actual job-related behaviors are rated along a continuum.

Biographical characteristics (4)   Personal characteristics—such as age, sex, and marital status—that are objective and easily obtained from personnel records.

Bounded rationality (5)   Individuals make decisions by constructing simplified models that extract the essential features from problems without capturing all their complexity.

Brainstorming (10)   An idea-generation process that specifically encourages any and all alternatives, while withholding any criticism of those alternatives.

Career (16)   A sequence of positions occupied by a person during the course of a lifetime.

Career anchors (16)   Distinct patterns of self-perceived talents and abilities, motives and needs, and attitudes and values that guide and stabilize a person's career after several years of real-world experience and feedback.

Career stages (16)   The four steps most people go through in their careers: exploration, establishment, midcareer, and late career.

Case study (2)   An in-depth analysis of one setting.

Causality (2)   The implication that the independent variable causes the dependent variable.

Centralization (14)   The degree to which decision making is concentrated at a single point in the organization.

Chain of command (14)   The superior-subordinate authority chain that extends from the top of the organization to the lowest echelon.

Change (19)   Making things different.

Change agents (19)   Persons who act as catalysts and assume the responsibility for managing change activities.

Channel (10)   The medium through which a communication message travels.

Channel richness (10)   The amount of information that can be transmitted during a communication episode.

Charismatic leadership (11) Followers make attributions of heroic or extraordinary leadership abilities when they observe certain behaviors.

Classical conditioning (4)   A type of conditioning where an individual responds to some stimulus that would not invariably produce such a response.

Coalition (12)   Two or more individuals who combine their power to push for or support their demands.

Coercive power (12)   Power that is based on fear.

Cognitive component of an attitude (6)   The opinion or belief segment of an attitude.

Cognitive dissonance (6)   Any incompatibility between two or more attitudes or between behavior and attitudes.

Cognitive evaluation theory (7) Allocating extrinsic rewards for behavior that had been previously intrinsically rewarded tends to decrease the overall level of motivation.

Cognitive resource theory (11)   A theory of leadership that states that a leader obtains effective group performance by, first, making effective plans, decisions, and strategies, and then communicating them through directive behavior.

Cohesiveness (9)   Degree to which group members are attracted to each other and are motivated to stay in the group.

Cohorts (9)   Individuals who, as part of a group, hold a common attribute.

Collaborating (13)   A situation where the parties to a conflict each desire to satisfy fully the concerns of all parties.

Collectivism (3)   A national culture attribute that describes a tight social framework in which people expect others in groups of which they are a part to look after them and protect them.

Command group (9)   A manager and his or her immediate subordinates.

Communication (10)   The transference and understanding of meaning.

Communication apprehension (10)   Undue tension and anxiety about oral communication, written communication, or both.

Communication networks (10) Channels by which information flows.

Communication process (10)   The steps between a source and a receiver that result in the transference and understanding of meaning.

Comparable worth (8)   A doctrine that holds that jobs equal in value to an organization should be equally compensated, whether or not the work content of those jobs is similar.

Competing (13)   A desire to satisfy one's interests, regardless of the impact on the other party to the conflict.

Complexity (14)   The degree of vertical, horizontal, and spatial differentiation in an organization.

Compressed workweek (8)   A four-day week, with employees working ten hours a day.

Compromising (13)   A situation in which each party to a conflict is willing to give up something.

Conceptual skills (1)   The mental ability to analyze and diagnose complex situations.

Conciliator (13)   A trusted third party who provides an informal communication link between the negotiator and the opponent.

Conflict (13)   A process that begins when one party perceives that another party has negatively affected, or is about to negatively affect, something that the first party cares about.

Conflict management (13)   The use of resolution and stimulation techniques to achieve the desired level of conflict.

Conformity (9)   Adjusting one's behavior to align with the norms of the group.

Consideration (11)   The extent to which a leader is likely to have job relationships characterized by mutual trust, respect for subordinates' ideas, and regard for their feelings.

Constraints (18)   Forces that prevent individuals from doing what they desire.

Consultant as negotiator (13) An impartial third party, skilled in conflict management, who attempts to facilitate creative problem solving through communication and analysis.

Contingency variables (1)   Those variables that moderate the relationship between the independent and dependent variables and improve the correlation.

Continuous reinforcement (4)   A desired behavior is reinforced each and every time it is demonstrated.

Contrast effects (5)   Evaluations of a person's characteristics that are affected by comparisons with other people recently encountered who rank higher or lower on the same characteristics.

Controlling (1)   Monitoring activities to ensure they are being accomplished as planned and correcting any significant deviations.

Core values (17)   The primary or dominant values that are accepted throughout the organization.

Correlation coefficient (2)   Indicates the strength of a relationship between two or more variables.

Cost-minimization strategy (15) A strategy that emphasizes tight cost controls, avoidance of unnecessary innovation or marketing expenses, and price-cutting.

Critical incidents (16)   Evaluating those behaviors that are key in making the difference between executing a job effectively and executing it ineffectively.

Culture shock (3)   Confusion, disorientation, and emotional upheaval caused by being immersed in a new culture.

Customer departmentalization (14) Grouping activities on the basis of common customers.

Decisional roles (1) Roles that include those of entrepreneur, disturbance handler, resource allocator, and negotiator.

Decoding (10) Retranslating a sender's communication message.

Deep relaxation (18) A state of physical relaxation, where the individual is somewhat detached from both the immediate environment and body sensations.

Defensive behaviors (12) Reactive and protective behaviors to avoid action, blame, or change.

Delphi technique (10) A group decision method in which individual members, acting separately, pool their judgments in a systematic and independent fashion.

Demands (18) The loss of something desired.

Democratic leader (11) One who shares decision making with subordinates.

Dependency (12) B's relationship to A when A possesses something that B requires.

Dependent variable (2) A response that is affected by an independent variable.

Differentiation (15) The degree to which individuals in different functional departments vary in their goal and value orientations.

Distributive bargaining (13) Negotiation that seeks to divide up a fixed amount of resources; a win-lose situation.

Disturbed-reactive environment (15) An environment dominated by one or more large organizations.

Division of labor (14) Specialization; breaking jobs down into simple and repetitive tasks.

Divisional structure (15) A set of autonomous units coordinated by a central headquarters.

Dominant culture (17) Expresses the core values that are shared by a majority of the organization's members.

Driving forces (19) Forces that direct behavior away from the status quo.

Dysfunctional conflict (13) Conflict that hinders group performance.

Effectiveness (2) Achievement of goals.

Efficiency (2) The ratio of effective output to the input required to achieve it.

Elasticity of power (12) The relative responsiveness of power to changes in available alternatives.

Employee-oriented leader (11) One who emphasizes interpersonal relations.

Empowerment (19) A process that increases employees' intrinsic task motivation.

Encoding (10) Converting a communication message to symbolic form.

Encounter stage (17) The stage in the socialization process in which a new employee sees what the organization is really like and confronts the possibility that expectations and reality may diverge.

Environment (15) Those institutions or forces outside the organization that potentially affect the organization's performance.

Equity theory (7) Individuals compare their job inputs and outcomes with those of others and then respond so as to eliminate any inequities.

ERG theory (7) There are three groups of core needs: existence, relatedness, and growth.

Ethnocentric views (3) The belief that one's cultural values and customs are superior to all others.

Exit (6) Dissatisfaction expressed through behavior directed toward leaving the organization.

Expectancy theory (7) The strength of a tendency to act in a certain way depends on the strength of an expectation that the act will be followed by a given outcome and on the attractiveness of that outcome to the individual.

Expert power (12) Influence based on special skills or knowledge.

Externals (4) Individuals who believe that what happens to them is controlled by outside forces such as luck or chance.

Extrinsic rewards (16) Rewards received from the environment surrounding the context of the work.

Feedback (7) The degree to which carrying out the work activities required by a job results in the individual obtaining direct and clear information about the effectiveness of his or her performance.

Feedback loop (10) The final link in the communication process; puts the message back into the system as a check against misunderstandings.

Felt conflict (13) Emotional involvement in a conflict creating anxiety, tenseness, frustration, or hostility.

Fiedler contingency model (11) The theory that effective groups depend upon a proper match between a leader's style of interacting with subordinates and the degree to which the situation gives control and influence to the leader.

Field experiment (2) A controlled experiment conducted in a real organization.

Field survey (2) Questionnaire or interview responses are collected from a sample, analyzed, and then inferences are made from the representative sample about the larger population.

Filtering (10) A sender's manipulation of information so that it will be seen more favorably by the receiver.

Fixed-interval schedule (4) Rewards are spaced at uniform time intervals.

Fixed-ratio schedule (4) Rewards are initiated after a fixed or constant number of responses.

Flexible benefits (8) Employees tailor their benefit program to meet their personal needs by picking and choosing from a menu of benefit options.

Flextime (8) Employees work during a common core time period each day but have discretion in forming their total workday from a flexible set of hours outside the core.

Formal group (9) A designated work group defined by the organization's structure.

Formal networks (10) Task-related communications that follow the authority chain.

Formalization (14) The degree to which jobs within the organization are standardized.

Forming (9) The first stage in group development, characterized by much uncertainty.

Friendship group (9) Those brought together because they share one or more common characteristics.

Functional conflict (13) Conflict that supports the goals of the group and improves its performance.

Functional departmentalization (14) Grouping activities by functions performed.

Fundamental attribution error (5) The tendency to underestimate the influence of external factors and overestimate the influence of internal factors when making judgments about the behavior of others.

Generalizability (2) The degree to which results of a research study are applicable to groups of individuals other than those who participate in the original study.

Geographic departmentalization (14) Grouping activities on the basis of territory.

Goal-setting theory (7) The theory that specific and difficult goals lead to higher performance.

Graphic rating scales (16) An evaluation method where the evaluator rates performance factors on an incremental scale.

Group (9) Two or more individuals, interacting and interdependent, who have come together to achieve particular objectives.

Group demography (9) The degree to which members of a group share a common demographic attribute, such as age, sex, race, educational level, or length of service in the organization, and the impact of this attribute on turnover.

Group order ranking (16) An evaluation method that places employees into a particular classification such as quartiles.

Groupshift (10) A change in decision risk between the group's decision and the individual decision that members within the group would make; can be either toward conservatism or greater risk.

Groupthink (10) Phenomenon in which the norm for consensus overrides the realistic appraisal of alternative courses of action.

Halo effect (5) Drawing a general impression about an individual based on a single characteristic.

Hierarchy of needs theory (7) There is a hierarchy of five needs—physiological, safety, social, esteem, and self-actualization—and as each need is sequentially satisfied, the

next need becomes dominant.

Higher-order needs (7) Needs that are satisfied internally; social, esteem, and self-actualization needs.

Horizontal differentiation (14) The degree of differentiation between units based on the orientation of members, the nature of the tasks they perform, and their education and training.

Human relations view of conflict (13) The belief that conflict is a natural and inevitable outcome in any group.

Human skills (1) The ability to work with, understand, and motivate other people, both individually and in groups.

Hygiene factors (7) Those factors—such as company policy and administration, supervision, and salary—that, when adequate in a job, placate workers. When these factors are adequate, people will not be dissatisfied.

Hypothesis (2) A tentative explanation of the relationship between two or more variables.

Illegitimate political behavior (12) Extreme political behavior that violates the implied rules of the game.

Imitation strategy (15) A strategy that seeks to move into new products or new markets only after their viability has already been proven.

Implicit favorite model (5) A decision-making model where the decision maker implicitly selects a preferred alternative early in the decision process and biases the evaluation of all other choices.

Impression management (12) The process by which individuals attempt to control the impression others form of them.

Independent variable (2) The presumed cause of some change in the dependent variable.

Individual ranking (16) An evaluation method that rank-orders employees from best to worst.

Individualism (3) A national culture attribute describing a loosely knit social framework in which people emphasize only the care of themselves and their immediate family.

Informal group (9) A group that is neither formally structured nor organizationally determined; appears in response to the need for social contact.

Informal network (10) The communication grapevine.

Informational roles (1) Roles that include monitoring, disseminating, and spokesperson activities.

Initiating structure (11) The extent to which a leader is likely to define and structure his or her role and those of subordinates in the search for goal attainment.

Innovation (19) A new idea applied to initiating or improving a product, process, or service.

Innovation strategy (15) A strategy that emphasizes the introduction of major new products and services.

Institutionalization (17) When an organization takes on a life of its own, apart from any of its members, and acquires immortality.

Instrumental values (6) Preferable modes of behavior or means of achieving one's terminal values.

Integration (15) The degree to which members of various departments achieve unity of effort.

Integrative bargaining (13) Negotiation that seeks one or more settlements that can create a win-win solution.

Intellectual ability (4) That required to do mental activities.

Intensive technology (15) A customized response to a diverse set of contingencies.

Intentions (13) Decisions to act in a given way in a conflict episode.

Interacting groups (10) Typical groups, where members interact with each other face-to-face.

Interactionist view of conflict (13) The belief that conflict is not only a positive force in a group but that it is absolutely necessary for a group to perform effectively.

Interest group (9) Those working together to attain a specific objective with which each is concerned.

Intergroup development (19) OD efforts to improve interactions between groups.

Interpersonal roles (1) Roles that include figurehead, leadership, and liaison activities.

Intermittent reinforcement (4) A desired behavior is reinforced often enough to make the behavior worth repeating, but not every time it is demonstrated.

Internals (4) Individuals who believe that they control what happens to them.

Intrinsic rewards (16) The pleasure or value one receives from the content of a work task.

Intuition (1) A feeling not necessarily supported by research.

Intuitive decision making (5) An unconscious process created out of distilled experience.

Job analysis (16) Developing a detailed description of the tasks involved in a job, determining the relationship of a given job to other jobs, and ascertaining the knowledge, skills, and abilities necessary for an employee to perform the job successfully.

Job characteristics model (7) Identifies five job characteristics and their relationship to personal and work outcomes.

Job description (16) A written statement of what a jobholder does, how it is done, and why it is done.

Job design (8) The way that tasks are combined to form complete jobs.

Job enlargement (8) The horizontal expansion of jobs.

Job enrichment (8) The vertical expansion of jobs.

Job involvement (6) The degree to which a person identifies with his or her job, actively participates in it, and considers his or her performance important to self-worth.

Job rotation (8) The periodic shifting of a worker from one task to another.

Job satisfaction (2) A general attitude toward one's job; the difference between the amount of rewards workers receive and the amount they believe they should receive.

Job sharing (8) The practice of having two or more people split a forty-hour-a-week job.

Job specification (16) States the minimum acceptable qualifications that an employee must possess to perform a given job successfully.

Justice view of ethics (1) Requires individuals to improve and enforce rules fairly and impartially so there is an equitable distribution of benefits and costs.

Kinesics (10) The study of body motions.

Knowledge power (12) The ability to control unique and valuable information.

Labor union (16) An organization, made up of employees, that acts collectively to protect and promote employee interests.

Laboratory experiment (2) In an artificial environment, the researcher manipulates an independent variable under controlled conditions, and then concludes that any change in the dependent variable is due to the manipulation or change imposed on the independent variable.

Leader-member-exchange theory (11) Leaders create in-groups and out-groups, and subordinates with in-group status will have higher performance ratings, less turnover, and greater satisfaction with their superior.

Leader-member relations (11) The degree of confidence, trust, and respect subordinates have in their leader.

Leader-participation model (11) A leadership theory that provides a set of rules to determine the form and amount of participative decision making in different situations.

Leadership (11) The ability to influence a group toward the achievement of goals.

Leading (1) Includes motivating subordinates, directing others, selecting the most effective communication channels, and resolving conflicts.

Learning (4) Any relatively permanent change in behavior that occurs as a result of experience.

Legitimate political behavior (12) Normal everyday politics.

Leniency error (16) The tendency to evaluate a set of employees too high (positive) or too low (negative).

Line authority (14) Authority to direct the work of a subordinate.

Locus of control (4) The degree to which people believe they are masters of their own fate.

Long-linked technology (15) Tasks or operations that are sequentially interdependent.

Lower-order needs (7) Needs that are satisfied externally; physiological and safety needs.

Loyalty (6) Dissatisfaction expressed by passively waiting for conditions to improve.

LPC (11) Least preferred co-worker questionnaire that measures task or relationship-oriented leadership style.

Machiavellianism (4) Degree to which an individual is pragmatic, maintains emotional distance, and believes that ends can justify means.

Machine bureaucracy (15) A structure that rates high in complexity, formalization, and centralization.

McClelland's theory of needs (7) Achievement, power, and affiliation are three important needs that help to understand motivation.

Management by objectives (MBO) (8) A program that encompasses specific goals, participatively set, for an explicit time period, with feedback on goal progress.

Managerial Grid (11) A nine-by-nine matrix outlining eighty-one different leadership styles.

Managers (1) Individuals who achieve goals through other people.

Maquiladoras (3) Domestic Mexican firms that manufacture or assemble products for a company of another nation, which are then sent back to the foreign company for sale and distribution.

Mass production (15) Large-batch manufacturing.

Matrix structure (15) A structure that creates dual lines of authority; combines functional and product departmentalization.

Maturity (11) The ability and willingness of people to take responsibility for directing their own behavior.

Mechanistic structure (15) A structure characterized by high complexity, high formalization, and centralization.

Mediating technology (15) Linking of independent units.

Mediator (13) A neutral third party who facilitates a negotiated solution by using reasoning, persuasion, and suggestions for alternatives.

Message (10) What is communicated.

Meta-analysis (2) A statistical technique that quantitatively integrates and synthesizes a number of independent studies to determine if they consistently produced similar results.

Metamorphosis stage (17) The stage in the socialization process in which a new employee adjusts to his or her work group's values and norms.

Middle line (15) Managers who connect the operating core to the strategic apex.

Model (2) **Abstraction of reality;** simplified representation of some real-world phenomenon.

Moderating variable (2) Abates the effect of the independent variable on the dependent variable; also known as *contingency variable*.

Motivating potential score (7) A predictive index suggesting the motivation potential in a job.

Motivation (7) The willingness to exert high levels of effort toward organizational goals, conditioned by the effort's ability to satisfy some individual need.

Motivation-hygiene theory (7) Intrinsic factors are related to job satisfaction, while extrinsic factors are associated with dissatisfaction.

nAch (4) Need to achieve or strive continually to do things better.

National culture (3) The primary values and practices that characterize a particular country.

Need (7) Some internal state that makes certain outcomes appear attractive.

Neglect (6) Dissatisfaction expressed through allowing conditions to worsen.

Negotiation (13) A process in which two or more parties exchange goods or services and attempt to agree upon the exchange rate for them.

Nominal group technique (10) A group decision-making method in which individual members meet face-to-face to pool their judgments in a systematic but independent fashion.

Nonverbal communications (10) Messages conveyed through body movements, the intonations or emphasis we give to words, facial expressions, and the physical distance between the sender and receiver.

Norming (9) The third stage in group development, characterized by close relationships and cohesiveness.

Norms (9) Acceptable standards of behavior within a group that are shared by the group's members.

OB Mod (8) A program where managers identify performance-related employee behaviors and then implement an intervention strategy to strengthen desirable performance behaviors and weaken undeirable behaviors.

Operant conditioning (4) A type of conditioning in which desired voluntary behavior leads to a reward or prevents a punishment.

Operating core (15) Employees who perform the basic work related to the production of products and services.

Opportunity power (12) Influence obtained as a result of being in the right place at the right time.

Opportunity to perform (7) High levels of performance are partially a function of an absence of obstacles that constrain the employee.

Optimizing model (5) A decision-making model that describes how individuals should behave in order to maximize some outcome.

Organic structure (15) A structure characterized by low complexity, low formalization, and decentralization.

Organization (1) A consciously coordinated social unit, composed of two or more people, that functions on a relatively continuous basis to achieve a common goal or set of goals.

Organization size (14) The number of people employed in an organization.

Organization structure (14) The degree of complexity, formalization, and centralization in the organization.

Organizational behavior (OB) (1) A field of study that investigates the impact that individuals, groups, and structure have on behavior within organizations, for the purpose of applying such knowledge toward improving an organization's effectiveness.

Organizational commitment (6) An individual's orientation toward the organization in terms of loyalty, identification, and involvement.

Organizational culture (17) A common perception held by the organization's members; a system of shared meaning.

Organizational development (19) A collection of planned-change interventions, built on humanistic-democratic values, that seek to improve organizational effectiveness and employee well-being.

Organizing (1) Determining what tasks are to be done, who is to do them, how the tasks are to be grouped, who reports to whom, and where decisions are to be made.

Paired comparison (16) An evaluation method that compares each employee with every other employee and assigns a summary ranking based on the number of superior scores that the employee achieves.

Paraphrasing (10) Restating what the speaker has said in one's own words.

Parochialism (3) A narrow view of the world; an inability to recognize differences between people.

Participative management (8) A process where subordinates share a significant degree of decision-making power with their immediate superiors.

Path-goal theory (11) The theory that a leader's behavior is acceptable to subordinates insofar as they view it as a source of either immediate or future satisfaction.

Perceived conflict (13) Awareness by one or more parties of the existence of conditions that create opportunities for conflict to arise.

Perception (5) A process by which individuals organize and interpret their sensory impressions in order to give meaning to their environment.

Performance-based compensation (8) Paying employees on the basis of some performance measure.

Performing (9) The fourth stage in group development, when the group is fully functional.

Personal power (12) Influence attributed to one's personal characteristics.

Personality (4) The sum total of ways in which an individual reacts and interacts with others.

Personality traits (4) Enduring characteristics that describe an individual's behavior.

Persuasive power (12) The ability to allocate and manipulate symbolic rewards.

Physical ability (4) That required to do tasks demanding stamina, dexterity, strength, and similar skills.

Physiological symptoms of stress (18) Changes in an individual's health as a result of stress.

Piece-rate pay plans (8) Workers are paid a fixed sum for each unit of production completed.

Placid-clustered environment (15) An environment in which change occurs slowly, but threats occur in clusters.

Placid-randomized environment (15) An environment in which demands are randomly distributed and change occurs slowly.

Planned change (19) Change activities that are intentional and goal-oriented.

Planning (1) Includes defining goals, establishing strategy, and developing plans to coordinate activities.

Political behavior (12) Those activities that are not required as part of one's formal role in the organization, but that influence, or attempt to influence, the distribution of advantages and disadvantages within the organization.

Pooled interdependence (13) Where two groups function with relative independence but their combined output contributes to the organization's overall goals.

Position power (11) Influence derived from one's formal structural position in the organization; includes power to hire, fire, discipline, promote, and give salary increases.

Power (12) A capacity that A has to influence the behavior of B so that B does things he or she would not otherwise do.

Power-control view of structure (15) An organization's structure is the result of a power struggle by internal constituencies who are seeking to further their interests.

Power distance (3) A national culture attribute describing the extent to which a society accepts that power in institutions and organizations is distributed unequally.

Power need (7) The desire to make others behave in a way that they would not otherwise have behaved in.

Power tactics (12) Identifies how individuals manipulate the power bases.

Prearrival stage (17) The period of learning in the socialization process that occurs before a new employee joins the organization.

Problem analyzability (15) The type of search procedure employees follow in responding to exceptions.

Process consultation (19) Consultant gives a client insights into what is going on around the client, within the client, and between the client and other people; identifies processes that need improvement.

Process departmentalization (14) Grouping activities on the basis of product or customer flow.

Process production (15) Continuous-process production.

Product departmentalization (14) Grouping activities by product line.

Production-oriented leader (11) One who emphasizes technical or task aspects of the job.

Productivity (2) A performance measure including effectiveness and efficiency.

Professional bureaucracy (15) A structure that rates high in complexity and formalization, and low in centralization.

Projection (5) Attributing one's own characteristics to other people.

Psychological contract (9) An unwritten agreement that sets out what management expects from the employee, and vice versa.

Psychological symptoms of stress (18) Changes in an individual's attitudes and disposition due to stress.

Quality circle (8) A work group of employees who meet regularly to discuss their quality problems, investigate causes, recommend solutions, and take corrective actions.

Quality of life (3) A national culture attribute that emphasizes relationships and concern for others.

Quantity of life (3) A national culture attribute describing the extent to which societal values are characterized by assertiveness and materialism.

Rationality (5) Choices that are consistent and value-maximizing.

Reciprocal interdependence (13) Where groups exchange inputs and outputs.

Referent power (12) Influence held by A based on B's admiration and desire to model himself or herself after A.

Refreezing (19) Stabilizing a change intervention by balancing driving and restraining forces.

Reinforcement theory (7) Behavior is a function of its consequences.

Reliability (2) Consistency of measurement.

Research (2) The systematic gathering of information.

Responsibility (14) An obligation to perform.

Restraining forces (19) Forces that hinder movement away from the status quo.

Rights view of ethics (1) Decisions are concerned with respecting and protecting the basic rights of individuals.

Rituals (17) Repetitive sequences of activities that express and reinforce the key values of the organization, what goals are most important, which people are important and which are expendable.

Role (9) A set of expected behavior patterns attributed to someone occupying a given position in a social unit.

Role conflict (9) A situation in which an individual is confronted by divergent role expectations.

Role expectations (9) How others believe a person should act in a given situation.

Role identity (9) Certain attitudes and behaviors consistent with a role.

Role perception (9) An individual's view of how he or she is supposed to act in a given situation.

Satisficing model (5) A decision-making model where a decision maker chooses the first solution that is "good enough"; that is, satisfactory and sufficient.

Selective perception (5) People selectively interpret what they see based on their interests, background, experience, and attitudes.

Self-actualization (7) The drive to become what one is capable of becoming.

Self-efficacy (7) The individual's belief that he or she is capable of performing a task.

Self-esteem (4) Individuals' degree of liking or disliking for themselves.

Self-managed work teams (8) Groups that are free to determine how the goals assigned to them are to be accomplished and how tasks are to be allocated.

Self-management (4) Learning techniques that allow individuals to manage their own behavior so that less external management control is necessary.

Self-monitoring (4) A personality trait that measures an individual's ability to adjust his or her behavior to external, situational factors.

Self-perception theory (6) Attitudes are used after the fact to make sense out of an action that has already occurred.

Self-serving bias (5) The tendency for individuals to attribute their own successes to internal factors while putting the blame for failures on external factors.

Sensitivity training (19) Training groups that seek to change behavior through unstructured group interaction.

Sequential interdependence (13) One group depends on another for its input but the dependency is only one way.

Shaping behavior (4) Systematically reinforcing each successive step that moves an individual closer to the desired response.

Similarity error (16) Giving special consideration when rating others to those qualities that the evaluator perceives in himself or herself.

Simple structure (15) A structure characterized by low complexity, low formalization, and authority centralized in a single person.

Situational leadership theory (11) A contingency theory that focuses on followers' maturity.

Skill variety (7) The degree to which the job requires a variety of different activities.

Socialization (17) The process that adapts employees to the organization's culture.

Social information-processing model (7) Employees adopt attitudes and behaviors in response to the social cues provided by others with whom they have contact.

Social-learning theory (4) People can learn through observation and direct experience.

Social loafing (9) The tendency of group members to do less than they are capable of individually, resulting in an inverse relationship between group size and individual performance.

Sources of power (12) How power-holders come to control the bases of power.

Span of control (14) The number of subordinates a manager can efficiently and effectively direct.

Spatial differentiation (14) The degree to which the location of an organization's offices, plants, and personnel are geographically dispersed.

Staff authority (14) Positions that support, assist, and advise line managers.

Status (9) A socially defined position or rank given to groups or group members by others.

Stereotyping (5) Judging someone on the basis of one's perception of the group to which that person belongs.

Storming (9) The second stage in group development, characterized by intragroup conflict.

Strategic apex (15) Top-level managers.

Stress (18) A dynamic condition in which an individual is confronted with an opportunity, constraint, or demand related to what he or she desires and for which the outcome is perceived to be both uncertain and important.

Strong cultures (17) Cultures where the core values are intensely held and widely shared.

Subcultures (17) Minicultures within an organization, typically defined by department designations and geographical separation.

Support staff (15) People in an organization who fill the staff units.

Survey feedback (19) The use of questionnaires to identify discrepancies among member perceptions; discussion follows and remedies are suggested.

Synergy (9) An action of two or more substances that results in an effect that is different from the individual summation of the substances.

Systematic study (1) Looking at relationships, attempting to attribute causes and effects, and drawing conclusions based on scientific evidence.

Task characteristic theories (7) Seek to identify task characteristics of jobs, how these characteristics are combined to form different jobs, and their relationship to employee motivation, satisfaction, and performance.

Task group (9) Those working together to complete a job task.

Task identity (7) The degree to which the job requires completion of a whole and identifiable piece of work.

Task significance (7) The degree to which the job has a substantial impact on the lives or work of other people.

Task structure (11) The degree to which job assignments are procedurized.

Task uncertainty (13) The greater the uncertainty in a task, the more custom the response. Conversely, low uncertainty encompasses routine tasks with standardized activities.

Task variability (15) The number of exceptions individuals encounter in their work.

Team building (19) High interaction among group members to increase trust and openness.

Technical skills (1) The ability to apply specialized knowledge or expertise.

Technology (15) How an organization transfers its inputs into outputs.

Technostructure (15) Analysts in the organization.

Telecommuting (8) Employees do their work at home on a computer that is linked to their office.

Terminal values ( ) Desirable end-states of existence; the goals that a person would like to achieve during his or her lifetime.

Theory (2) A set of systematically interrelated concepts or hypotheses that purport to explain and predict phenomena.

Theory X (7) The assumption that employees dislike work, are lazy, dislike responsibility, and must be coerced to perform.

Theory Y (7) The assumption that employees like work, are creative, seek responsibility, and can exercise self-direction.

Traditional view of conflict (13) The belief that all conflict is harmful and must be avoided.

Trait theories of leadership (11) Theories that sought personality, social, physical, or intellectual traits that differentiated leaders from nonleaders.

Transactional leader (11) Leaders who guide or motivate their followers in the direction of established goals by clarifying role and task requirements.

Transformational leaders (11) Leaders who provide individualized consideration and intellectual stimulation, and who possess charisma.

Turbulent-field environment (15) An environment that changes constantly and that contains interrelated elements.

Turnover (2) Voluntary and involuntary permanent withdrawal from the organization.

Type A behavior (18) Aggressive involvement in a chronic, incessant struggle to achieve more and more in less and less time and, if necessary, against the opposing efforts of other things or other people.

Type B behavior (18) Rarely harried by the desire to obtain a wildly increasing number of things or to participate in an endlessly growing series of events in an ever-decreasing amount of time.

Uncertainty avoidance (3)   A national culture attribute describing the extent to which a society feels threatened by uncertain and ambiguous situations and tries to avoid them.

Unfreezing (19)   Change efforts to overcome the pressures of both individual resistance and group conformity.

Unit production (15)   The production of items in units or small batches.

Unity of command (14)   A subordinate should have only one superior to whom he or she is directly responsible.

Utilitarian view of ethics (1)   Decisions are made solely on the basis of their outcomes or consequences.

Validity (2)   The degree to which a research study is actually measuring what it claims to be measuring.

Values (6)   Basic convictions that a specific mode of conduct or end-state of existence is personally or socially preferable to an opposite or converse mode of conduct or end-state of existence.

Variable (2)   Any general characteristic that can be measured and that changes in either amplitude, intensity, or both.

Variable-interval schedule (4)   Rewards are distributed in time so that reinforcements are unpredictable.

Variable-ratio schedule (4)   The reward varies relative to the behavior of the individual.

Vertical differentiation (14)   The number of hierarchical levels in the organization.

Voice (6)   Dissatisfaction expressed through active and constructive attempts to improve conditions.

Wellness programs (18)   Organizationally supported programs that focus on the employee's total physical and mental condition.

Work-force diversity (1)   The increasing heterogeneity of organizations with the inclusion of different groups.

Work sampling (16)   Creating a miniature replica of a job to evaluate the performance abilities of job candidates.

NAME INDEX

NAME INDEX

ORGANIZATION INDEX

ORGANIZATION INDEX

SUBJECT INDEX

SUBJECT INDEX